British Drama
1533–1642

British Drama
1533–1642

A Catalogue

Volume IX
1632–1636

MARTIN WIGGINS

in association with

CATHERINE RICHARDSON

OXFORD
UNIVERSITY PRESS

Great Clarendon Street, Oxford, OX2 6DP,
United Kingdom

Oxford University Press is a department of the University of Oxford.
It furthers the University's objective of excellence in research, scholarship,
and education by publishing worldwide. Oxford is a registered trade mark of
Oxford University Press in the UK and in certain other countries

© Martin Wiggins 2018

The moral rights of the author have been asserted

First Edition published in 2018

Impression: 1

All rights reserved. No part of this publication may be reproduced, stored in
a retrieval system, or transmitted, in any form or by any means, without the
prior permission in writing of Oxford University Press, or as expressly permitted
by law, by licence or under terms agreed with the appropriate reprographics
rights organization. Enquiries concerning reproduction outside the scope of the
above should be sent to the Rights Department, Oxford University Press, at the
address above

You must not circulate this work in any other form
and you must impose this same condition on any acquirer

Published in the United States of America by Oxford University Press
198 Madison Avenue, New York, NY 10016, United States of America

British Library Cataloguing in Publication Data

Data available

Library of Congress Control Number: 2012462315

ISBN 978-0-19-877772-4

Printed and bound by
CPI Group (UK) Ltd, Croydon, CR0 4YY

Links to third party websites are provided by Oxford in good faith and
for information only. Oxford disclaims any responsibility for the materials
contained in any third party website referenced in this work.

CONTENTS

ABBREVIATIONS	vii
LIST OF ENTRIES	xi
BRITISH DRAMA, 1632–1636	1
INDEX OF PERSONS	509
INDEX OF PLACES	529
INDEX OF PLAYS	533

ABBREVIATIONS

Adams	Joseph Quincy Adams (ed.), *The Dramatic Records of Sir Henry Herbert, Master of the Revels, 1623–1673*, Cornell Studies in English 3 (New Haven, London, and Oxford, 1917)
Annals	Alfred Harbage and S. Schoenbaum, *Annals of English Drama, 975–1700*, 2nd edn (London, 1964)
Annals 3	Alfred Harbage and S. Schoenbaum, *Annals of English Drama, 975–1700*, 3rd edn, rev. Sylvia Stoler Wagonheim (London, 1989)
ant.	antimasque
Arber	Edward Arber (ed.), *A Transcript of the Register of the Company of Stationers of London, 1554–1640 A.D.* (London, 1875–94)
arg.	argument
Ashbee	Andrew Ashbee, *Records of English Court Music*, 9 vols. (Aldershot, 1986–96)
B	Broadsheet
Bawcutt	N. W. Bawcutt, *The Control and Censorship of Caroline Drama: The Records of Sir Henry Herbert, Master of the Revels, 1623–73* (Oxford, 1996)
Beal	Peter Beal, *Index of English Literary Manuscripts*, vol. 1: 1450–1625 (London, 1980)
Beal 2	Peter Beal, *Index of English Literary Manuscripts*, vol. 2: 1625–1700 (London, 1987–93)
Beal Online	Peter Beal, *Catalogue of English Literary Manuscripts 1450–1700* (internet, 2013)
Bentley	Gerald Eades Bentley, *The Jacobean and Caroline Stage*, 7 vols. (Oxford, 1941–68)
Bergeron	David M. Bergeron, *English Civic Pageantry, 1558–1642* (London, 1971)
Butler	Martin Butler, *The Stuart Court Masque and Political Culture* (Cambridge, 2008)
Cal. Dom.	*Calendar of State Papers (Domestic)*
Cal. Ven.	*Calendar of State Papers (Venetian)*
Chambers	E. K. Chambers, *The Elizabethan Stage*, 4 vols. (Oxford, 1923)
Cho.	chorus
Churchill-Keller	George B. Churchill and Wolfgang Keller, 'Die lateinischen Universitäts-Dramen Englands in der Zeit der Königen Elisabeth', *Shakespeare Jahrbuch* 34 (1898), 220–323

D	Duodecimo
ded.	dedication
desc.	description
DNB	*Dictionary of National Biography*
d.p.	dramatis personae
DS	dumb show
ELH	*English Literary History*
ELR	*English Literary Renaissance*
EMS	*English Manuscript Studies*
ep.	epilogue
Eyre & Rivington	G. E. Briscoe Eyre and Charles Robert Rivington (eds.), *A Transcript of the Registers of the Worshipful Company of Stationers; from 1640–1708 A.D.* (London, 1913–14)
F	Folio
Fletcher	Alan J. Fletcher, *Drama and the Performing Arts in Pre-Cromwellian Ireland* (Cambridge, 2001)
Greg	W. W. Greg, *A Bibliography of the English Printed Drama to the Restoration*, 4 vols. (London, 1939–59)
Hazlitt	W. Carew Hazlitt, *A Manual for the Collector and Amateur of Old English Plays* (London, 1892)
Heawood	Edward Heawood, *Watermarks, Mainly of the 17th and 18th Centuries* (Hilversum, 1950)
Herz	E. Herz, *Englische Schauspieler und englisches Schauspiel zur Zeit Shakespeares in Deutschland* (Hamburg and Leipzig, 1903)
HLQ	*Huntington Library Quarterly*
HMC	Historical Manuscripts Commission
ind.	induction
JEGP	*Journal of English and Germanic Philology*
JWCI	*Journal of the Warburg and Courtauld Institutes*
Lancashire	Ian Lancashire, *Dramatic Texts and Records of Britain: A Chronological Topography to 1558* (Toronto and Cambridge, 1984)
Loomie	Albert J. Loomie (ed.), *Ceremonies of Charles I: The Note Books of John Finet, Master of Ceremonies, 1628–41* (New York, 1987)
Materialien	Materialien zur Kunde des älteren Englischen Dramas
McCabe	William H. McCabe SJ, *An Introduction to the Jesuit Theater* (St Louis, 1983)
McGee-Meagher:	C. E. McGee and John C. Meagher, 'Preliminary Checklist of Tudor and Stuart Entertainments':
1625–34	*RORD* 36 (1997), 23–95
1634–42	*RORD* 38 (1999), 23–85
Mill	Anna Jean Mill, *Mediaeval Plays in Scotland*, St Andrews University Publications 24 (St Andrews, 1924)
MLN	*Modern Language Notes*

MLQ	*Modern Language Quarterly*
MLR	*Modern Language Review*
MP	*Modern Philology*
MRDE	*Medieval and Renaissance Drama in England*
MSC	Malone Society *Collections*
N&Q	*Notes and Queries*
O	Octavo
OED	*Oxford English Dictionary*
Orgel and Strong	Stephen Orgel and Roy Strong, *Inigo Jones: The Theatre of the Stuart Court*, 2 vols. (London, Berkeley, and Los Angeles, 1973)
PBSA	*Papers of the Bibliographical Society of America*
PMLA	*Proceedings of the Modern Language Association*
prol.	prologue
Q	Quarto
REED	Records of Early English Drama
RenD	*Renaissance Drama*
RenQ	*Renaissance Quarterly*
repr.	reprinted
RES	*Review of English Studies*
Reyher	Paul Reyher, *Les Masques Anglaises* (Paris, 1909)
RORD	*Research Opportunities in Renaissance Drama*
Sabol	Andrew J. Sabol, *Four Hundred Songs and Dances from the Stuart Masque* (Hanover and London, 1978)
SB	*Studies in Bibliography*
sc.	scene
SEL	*Studies in English Literature*
ShS	*Shakespeare Survey*
Sibley	Gertrude Marian Sibley, *The Lost Plays and Masques, 1500–1642*, Cornell Studies in English 19 (Ithaca and London, 1933)
Smith	G. C. Moore Smith, *College Plays performed in the University of Cambridge* (Cambridge, 1923)
SP	*Studies in Philology*
S.R.	Stationers' Register
STC	A. W. Pollard and G. R. Redgrave, *A Short-Title Catalogue of Books Printed in England, Scotland, and Ireland, and English Books Printed Abroad, 1475–1640*, 2nd edn, 3 vols. (London, 1976–91)
Steele	Mary Susan Steele, *Plays and Masques at Court during the Reigns of Elizabeth, James, and Charles*, Cornell Studies in English (New Haven and London, 1926)
Stratman	Carl Joseph Stratman, 'Dramatic Performances at Oxford and Cambridge, 1603–1642', unpublished Ph.D. thesis (University of Illinois, 1947)
Sullivan	Mary Sullivan, *Court Masques of James I* (New York and London, 1913)

Tilley	Morris Palmer Tilley, *A Dictionary of the Proverbs in England in the Sixteenth and Seventeenth Centuries* (Ann Arbor, 1950)
TLN	Through Line Number
TLS	*Times Literary Supplement*
t.p.	title page
tr.	translator/translation
Wing	Donald Goddard Wing, *Short-Title Catalogue of Books Printed in England, Scotland, Ireland, Wales, and British America, and of English Books Printed in Other Countries, 1641–1700*, 3 vols. (New York, 1945–51)
Withington	Robert Withington, *English Pageantry: An Historical Outline*, 2 vols. (Cambridge, Mass., 1918)

LIST OF ENTRIES

1632
2353: Albion's Triumph
2354: Masque for the Earl of Cumberland
2355: The Changes
2356: Masque at Goring House
2357: The Corporal
2358: Antimasque at Gray's Inn
2359: Tempe restauratum
2360: Love's Sacrifice
2361: Money is an Ass
2362: Versipellis
2363: Hogshead
2364: The Rival Friends
2365: The Jealous Lovers
2366: Tarquinius Superbus
2367: Hyde Park
2368: Love Yields to Honour
2369: Queen's Court Masque
2370: Hannibal and Scipio
2371: The Sad One
2372: Masque for the Earl of Cumberland
2373: The City Madam
2374: Love Crowns the End
2375: Antipelargesis
2376: The Obstinate Lady
2377: Love's Masterpiece
2378: A Fine Companion
2379: Puppet Play of Queen Elizabeth
2380: The Eunuch
2381: The Country Girl
2382: Tragedy of the Imperial Favourite Crispinus
2383: The Novella
2384: Queen's Court Masque
2385: The Magnetic Lady
2386: The Countryman
2387: Londini artium et scientiarum scaturigo
2388: Nothing Impossible to Love
2389: The Ball
2390: The Country Gentleman
2391: Necromantes
2392: Play
2393: Masque of Soldiers

1633
2394: Masque at West Harting
2395: The Shepherds' Paradise
2396: The Beauties
2397: The New Moon
2398: Pastoral Court Masque
2399: Perkin Warbeck
2400: The Coursing of a Hare
2401: The Weeding of the Covent Garden
2402: The Shepherds' Holiday
2403: A Tale of a Tub
2404: Royal Entertainment at Welbeck Abbey
2405: Tottenham Court
2406: The City Shuffler
2407: Trappolin Supposed a Prince
2408: Royal Entry of King Charles I into Edinburgh
2409: The Seaman's Honest Wife
2410: The Young Admiral
2411: The Cunning Lovers
2412: The Fatal Contract
2413: The Rebellion
2414: The Amazon
2415: 2 The City Shuffler
2416: Londini emporia
2417: The Guardian
2418: The Gamester
2419: The City Wit
2420: Aristocratic Entertainment: Hospitality and Delight

1634
2421: The Wits
2422: The Pastoral
2423: The Triumph of Peace
2424: Covent Garden
2425: Play with a Flamen
2426: The City Honest Man
2427: The London Merchant
2428: Coelum Britannicum
2429: Cornelianum dolium
2430: Confessor utinam feliciter nata
2431: The Spartan Ladies
2432: The Seven Champions of Christendom
2433: Arcades
2434: A Challenge for Beauty
2435: The Triumph of Beauty
2436: Christianetta
2437: The Example
2438: A Dialogue between Policy and Piety
2439: Royal Entertainment at Bolsover Castle
2440: Entertainment at Chirk Castle
2441: The Witches of Lancashire
2442: Masque at Holdenby House

2443:	Possible Play of the Battle of Lepanto	2499:	Mercury and Maia
2444:	Comedy of an Eccentric Magistrate	2500:	Vulcan and Jupiter
2445:	Masque of Lost Children and Comus	2501:	Neptune and Mercury
2446:	Truth's Triumph	2502:	Diogenes and Mausolus
2447:	Charles, Duke of Bourbon	2503:	Crates and Diogenes
2448:	The Triumphs of Fame and Honour	2504:	Charon, Menippus, Mercury
2449:	The Queen's Exchange	2505:	Menippus, Aeacus, Pythagoras, Empedocles, and Socrates
2450:	A Projector Lately Dead		
2451:	Love's Mistress	2506:	Nireus, Thersites, Menippus
2452:	Love's Riddle	2507:	Deorum iudicium
2453:	Love and Honour	2508:	Jupiter and Io
2454:	The Proxy	2509:	Apollo and Daphne
2455:	The Opportunity	2510:	Amphrisa, the Forsaken Shepherdess
2456:	The City Find . . .	2511:	Byrsa basilica
2457:	Christmas Masque	2512:	The Strange Discovery
		2513:	The Partial Law
1635		2514:	Unused London Lord Mayor's Pageant
2458:	The Antiquary	2515:	The Lady of Pleasure
2459:	The Conspiracy	2516:	The Lady Mother
2460:	The Orator	2517:	Londini sinus salutis
2461:	Tragedy of Prince Alexander and Lorenzo	2518:	The Queen and Concubine
2462:	The Apprentice's Prize	2519:	The Platonic Lovers
2463:	Eumorphus	2520:	Philenzo and Hippolyta
2464:	The Coronation	2521:	Wit's Triumvirate
2465:	Tragedy of Pedro the Cruel	2522:	Pastoral Court Masque
2466:	Tragedy of Alfonso of Castile	2523:	The Christmas Ordinary
2467:	Comedy of Geometry		
2468:	The Ordinary	**1636**	
2469:	Templum amoris	2524:	Masque of Ladies
2470:	The Royal Combat	2525:	The Wasp
2471:	The Italian Night Masque	2526:	The Duke's Mistress
2472:	Messalina, the Roman Empress	2527:	Masque at Skipton Castle
2473:	Sir Martin Schenck	2528:	The Fancies
2474:	Senilis amor	2529:	Claracilla
2475:	The Converted Robber	2530:	1 Arviragus and Philicia
2476:	Floral Play	2531:	2 Arviragus and Philicia
2477:	Freewill	2532:	Les Triomphes du Prince D'Amour
2478:	The Witches of Lancashire	2533:	Corona Minervae
2479:	The Sparagus Garden	2534:	Play of a Jealous Lover
2480:	Hannibal and Scipio	2535:	One or Two Masques
2481:	The Arcadia	2536:	Love's Trial
2482:	Icon ecclesiastici	2537:	Masque of Mariners
2483:	Love's Changelings' Change	2538:	The Princess
2484:	News of Plymouth	2539:	Entertainment for the Elector Palatine
2485:	Pastoral	2540:	A Fiddler and a Poet
2486:	Court Masque at Oatlands Palace	2541:	The Governor
2487:	The Prisoners	2542:	The Faithless Relict
2488:	Adrasta	2543:	Microcosmus
2489:	Puppet Play of Susanna and the Elders	2544:	The New Academy
2490:	Naiagaion	2545:	The Bashful Lover
2491:	Procus et puella	2546:	The Merchant of Dublin
2492:	The Dialogue betwixt Earth and Age	2547:	Andronicus Comnenus
2493:	Misanthropos	2548:	A Dialogue betwixt a Citizen and a Poor Countryman and his Wife
2494:	Jupiter and Ganymede		
2495:	Jupiter and Juno	2549:	Royal Entertainment at Enstone
2496:	Jupiter and Cupid	2550:	Passions Calmed
2497:	Vulcan and Apollo	2551:	The Hospital of Lovers
2498:	Mercury and Apollo	2552:	The Royal Slave

2553: *The City Match*
2554: Comedy
2555: Royal Entertainment at Richmond Palace
2556: *Love in Its Ecstasy*
2557: Masque of Moors
2558: Masque for the Dowager Countess of Devonshire
2559: Play with Cutpurses
2560: Masque for the Earl of Newcastle

1632

2353. Albion's Triumph

TEXT
Printed in 1632 (STC 24155). Additional information derives from Inigo Jones's design drawings (cited as J).

GENRE
masque
Contemporary: masque (t.p.)

TITLE
Performed/Printed: Albion's Triumph

AUTHOR
Aurelian Townshend

DATE
8 January 1632

ORIGINAL PRODUCTION
English Court at the Banqueting House, Whitehall

PLOT
Mercury descends to inform the goddess Alba that Jove has decreed a triumph in Albipolis. When he attempts to return to heaven, he has difficulty flying because his wings have been singed by proximity to the sun (implying the shining beauty of Alba).

The triumph takes place, and is discussed by two citizens. Platonicus insists that he has seen the true triumph even though he missed the physical event, for he is able to understand the allegorical meaning. They go to see sports in the amphitheatre.

Cupid and Diana join forces to shoot at Albanactus: he is conquered by the beauty of Alba and presented to her as love's sacrifice. Dancing ensues, after which Albanactus joins Alba in the audience. The happy couple are given presents by allegorical figures wishing them happiness and fruitful issue; they are further blessed by the arrival of Peace. The gods seem disgruntled, but Peace enlists them in the support of Albion: Neptune will defend the navy, Bellona vanquish the nation's enemies, Cybele ensure prosperity, and Plutus bring in wealth from overseas. A final song identifies King Charles and Queen Henrietta Maria (no longer shadowed as Albanactus and Alba) as Hymen's twins, and wishes them long life.

SCENE DESIGNATION
sc.1–5 (Q undivided), defined by the changes of scenery. The triumphal procession takes place during sc.2, seven numbered antimasque entries (ant.1–7) during sc.3, and the main masque during sc.4–5.

ROLES
MERCURY, a god, Jove's messenger
Six old (or ancient) POETS AND MUSICIANS, the chorus, including Orpheus, Amphion, and Arion
ALBA, goddess of Albion (*non-speaking*)
ALBANACTUS Caesar, Emperor of Albion, the principal masquer (*non-speaking*)
ATTENDANTS on Albanactus, possibly including captive kings, ladies, wild beasts, giants, dwarfs (or pygmies), lictors, pictors, priests, and princes (*non-speaking*)
PLATONICUS, a patrician
PUBLIUS, a plebeian
Six FOOLS (ant.1, *non-speaking*)
Seven TUMBLERS (ant.2, *non-speaking*)
Three PUGILISTS (ant.3, *non-speaking*)
Two SATYRS (ant.4, *non-speaking*)
A GIANT (ant.5, *non-speaking*)
Four or five PYGMIES (ant.5, *non-speaking*)
Four GLADIATORS (ant.6, *non-speaking*)
Seven MIMICS (ant.7, *non-speaking*)
CUPID, a god; also called Love
DIANA, chaste goddess of the moon
Fourteen CONSULS, the masquers (*non-speaking*)
SACRIFICERS, a chorus (sing collectively)
The HIGH PRIESTS of Jove (sing collectively; called Flamens on the design drawing)
INNOCENCY, a goddess; also called Innocence
JUSTICE, a goddess
RELIGION, a goddess
AFFECTION TO THE COUNTRY, a young god
CONCORD, a god
PEACE, a female figure
NEPTUNE, god of the sea
PLUTUS, god of wealth; also called Pluto
BELLONA, god of war
CYBELE, god of prosperity

It is unclear whether, in the antimasque, the number '5' after the Giant and Pygmies refers to the total number of figures or the number of Pygmies alone; thus it is uncertain whether there are four or five Pygmies. (J seems to assume there will only be one.)

Inigo Jones also designed a costume for a Vestal Virgin, who may also have appeared (singly or in a group), perhaps with the Sacrificers and High Priests; but no such figure is mentioned in the text, so the character may have been an abandoned early idea.

Speaking Parts: 21
Allegorical Roles: 6

Stage Directions and Speech Prefixes
MERCURY: *Mercury, the Messenger of Jove* (s.d.s); *Mercury* (s.d.s and s.p.s)

POETS AND MUSICIANS: *Orpheus, Amphion, Arion, and three old Poets and Musicians more* | *Orpheus and his Poetic Choir* (s.d.s); *Chorus* (s.p.s)
ALBA: *the Goddess Alba* (s.d.s)
ALBANACTUS: *Albanactus* | *the Emperor Albanactus* | [one of] *the Masquers* (s.d.s)
PLATONICUS: *a Patrician* | *Platonicus* (s.d.s); *Pla<tonicus>* (s.p.s)
PUBLIUS: *a Plebeian* | *Publius* (s.d.s); *Pub<lius>* (s.p.s)
FOOLS: *Fools* (s.d.s)
TUMBLERS: *Saltators or Tumblers* (s.d.s)
PUGILISTS: *Pugili or Buffeters* (s.d.s)
SATYRS: *Satyrs like Dancers* (s.d.s)
GIANT: *One Giant* (s.d.s)
PYGMIES: *Pigmies* (s.d.s)
GLADIATORS: *Gladiators or Fencers* (s.d.s)
MIMICS: *Mimics or Moriscoes* (s.d.s)
CUPID: *Cupid* (s.d.s and s.p.s)
DIANA: *Diana* (s.d.s and s.p.s)
CONSULS: *fourteen Consuls* | *the Masquers* (s.d.s)
SACRIFICERS: *the Chorus of Sacrificers* | *Sacrificers* (s.d.s)
HIGH PRIESTS: *the High Priests* (s.d.s)
INNOCENCY: *Innocency* | *Innocence* | [one of] *the five Deities* (s.d.s); [one of] *The 5 in the lower Cloud* (s.p.s)
JUSTICE: *Justice* | [one of] *the five Deities* (s.d.s); [one of] *The 5 in the lower Cloud* (s.p.s)
RELIGION: *Religion* | [one of] *the five Deities* (s.d.s); [one of] *The 5 in the lower Cloud* (s.p.s)
AFFECTION TO THE COUNTRY: *Affection to the Country* | [one of] *the five Deities* (s.d.s); [one of] *The 5 in the lower Cloud* (s.p.s)
CONCORD: *Concord* | [one of] *the five Deities* (s.d.s); [one of] *The 5 in the lower Cloud* (s.p.s)
PEACE: *Peace* (s.d.s and s.p.s)
NEPTUNE: [one of] *4 Gods* | *Neptune* (s.d.s); [one of] *The four Gods* (s.p.s)
PLUTUS: [one of] *4 Gods* | *Plutus* (s.d.s); [one of] *The four Gods* (s.p.s)
BELLONA: [one of] *4 Gods* | *Bellona* (s.d.s); [one of] *The four Gods* (s.p.s)
CYBELE: [one of] *4 Gods* | *Cebele* (s.d.s); [one of] *The four Gods* (s.p.s)

OTHER CHARACTERS
Jove, who sent Mercury (sc.1)
Aurora, a dewy morning goddess (sc.1)
Tethys, a watery goddess (sc.1)
Iris, a rainy goddess (sc.1)
The crowds at the triumph (sc.3)

SETTING
Place: Albipolis, chief city of Albion (in effect, England)

Geography
London: Whitehall Palace
[Greece]: Mount Olympus

The West Indies
The East Indies
[Hades]: River Lethe

SOURCES
Narrative: Andrea Mantegna, *The Triumphs of Caesar* (1484-92)
Verbal: Bible: Isaiah 11.6, amended (sc.5)
Design: the Arundel Marbles (atrium); Marcantonio Raimondi, *Trajan Crowned by Victory* (before 1534; Albanactus), Engraving of a Sarcophagus showing a Lion Hunt (before 1534; Albanactus); Francesco Primaticcio, *Jupiter Sending the Three Goddesses to the Judgement of Paris* (1543; Jones used an engraving by Antonio Fantuzzi; proscenium); Cornelius Scribonius, *Le triumphe d'Anvers* (1550; atrium); Léonard Thiry, *Livre de la conqueste de la toison de l'or* (1563; proscenium); Onuphrio Panvinio, *De ludis circensibus* (1581; amphitheatre; antimasque costumes), *De triumpho Romanorum commentarius* (1600; Captive King); Giovanni Battista Cavalieri, *Antiquarum statuarum urbis Romae* (1585-93; atrium); Cesare Vecellio, *Habiti antichi e moderni di tutto il mondo* (1590; Jones used the 1598 edn; Captives); Cesare Ripa, *Iconologia* (1593, repr. 1611; Concord); Bernardo Buontalenti, designs for Giulio Caccini, *Il rapimento di Cefalo* (1600; proscenium); Hans Vredeman de Vries, *Perspective* (1604-5; atrium); Giulio Parigi, *Il giudizio di Paride* (1608; atrium); Octavius de Strada, *De vitis Imperatorum et Caesarum Romanorum*: Medal of Alexander Severus (1615; Albanactus' head-dress); Vincenzo Scamozzi, *L'idea della architectura universale* (1615; proscenium); Jacques Callot, *Capricci di varie figure* (1617; Mimics); Sebastiano Serlio, *Architettura* (1618 Vicenza edn; proscenium)

LANGUAGE
English

FORM
Metre: tetrameter and prose
Rhyme: couplets
Lines (Spoken): 275 (164 verse, 111 prose)
Lines (Written): 537

STAGING
Stage: there are steps leading down from the stage to the dance floor (sc.4, desc.)
Above: Mercury descends in a cloud (sc.1, desc.); Cupid descends in a cloud, and Diana in a chariot (sc.4, desc.; the cloud and chariot go back up afterwards); five characters descend in a cloud (sc.5, desc.); Peace descends in a cloud (sc.5, desc.)
Other Openings: four characters enter from 'the four corners of the scene' (sc.5, desc.)
Audience: The Queen in the audience is identified as a character in the action, Alba (sc.1, 4), and is directly addressed (sc.4). Albanactus (the King) takes a seat beside her after the main dance, effectively becoming

part of the audience (sc.4), and they are given gifts by characters who are still part of the action (sc.5). The masquers dance with ladies from the audience (sc.5, desc.).

MUSIC
Music: soft, sweet music (sc.1, desc.; accompanying Song 2)
On-Stage Music: music by the Sacrificers, accompanying the masquers' stately descent from the temple (sc.4, desc.)
Songs:
1: 'Behold! I come not from above', sc.1, Mercury and Poets, in parts, 22 lines;
2: 'Olympian Jove to the bright Alba sends', sc.1, Mercury and Poets, in parts, 22 lines, with musical accompaniment; sung in recitative;
3: 'What makes me so unnimbly rise', sc.1, Mercury and Poets, in parts, 18 lines;
4: 'Ye worthies of this isle', sc.4, Sacrificers, 18 lines;
5: 'Great Alba, though each grandee here', sc.4, High Priests and Sacrificers, 14 lines;
6: 'Blessed pair, whose prayers like incense rise', sc.5, Innocency, Justice, Religion, Affection to the Country, and Concord, 16 lines;
7: 'Frighted by day, and in the night diseased', sc.5, Peace, Innocency, Justice, Religion, Affection to the Country, and Concord, in parts, 14 lines;
8: 'Arms are laid by, early and late', sc.5, Neptune, Plutus, Bellona, Cybele, Peace, Innocency, Justice, Religion, Affection to the Country, and Concord, in parts, 14 lines;
9: 'Loaden with wealth and honour may', sc.5, Neptune, Plutus, Bellona, Cybele, Innocency, Justice, Religion, Affection to the Country, Concord, Poets, Priests, 6 lines.
Other Singing: Poets sing 4 lines (sc.4, desc.)
Dance: High Priests and Sacrificers tread 'a grave measure' (sc.4, desc.); main masque dance by Albanactus and masquers (sc.4, desc.); masquers dance with ladies from the audience (sc.5, desc.)

PROPS
Weapons: seven spears (sc.3/ant.2, J); seven daggers (sc.3/ant.2, J); seven shields (sc.3/ant.2, J); four swords (sc.3/ant.2, J); two bows and arrows (sc.4, dialogue; the arrows are shot at characters, and therefore need to be harmless); a quiver (sc.4, J); a sword (sc.5, desc.; given to the King and Queen in the audience); a bunch of arrows tied with a white band (sc.5, desc.; probably represents a hand; given to the King and Queen in the audience)
Musical Instruments: possibly pipes (J; design marked 'Tibicen'); possibly harps (J; design marked 'Cytharoedus'); see also COSTUMES: MIMICS
Clothing: a robe (sc.5, dialogue; given to the King and Queen in the audience); an imperial crown (sc.5, desc.)
Small Portable Objects: a caduceus (sc.1, desc.); a stone (sc.3, s.d.); an open book (sc.5, desc.; given to the King and Queen in the audience); a garland of long grass (sc.5, desc.; probably represents a heart, given to the King and Queen in the audience); a palm branch (sc.5, desc.)
Large Portable Objects: High Priests' wands (sc.4–5, J)
Scenery: a proscenium with the royal arms and elaborate decoration, including figures (desc.; *design drawing survives*); a curtain (desc.; raised to show the action); a Roman atrium with columns and gold statues on pedestals, with sky above (sc.1, desc.; *design drawing survives*); a cloud (sc.1, desc.; descends with Mercury seated on board; he is discovered during the descent); the forum of a city (sc.2, desc.); a golden chariot (sc.2, desc.); an amphitheatre (sc.3, desc.; *design drawing survives*); a cloud (sc.4, desc.; descends with Cupid on board, and rises again empty); a chariot (sc.4, desc.; descends with Diana on board, and rises again empty; *design drawing survives*); a grove of trees with a temple (sc.4, desc.; *preliminary design sketch survives*); seating for one character (sc.4, implicit); a prospect of Whitehall Palace and the city of London (sc.5, desc.); a bright cloud (sc.5, desc.; descends; seats five characters; *design drawing survives*); a cloud (sc.5, desc.; seats one); a gilt throne (sc.5, desc./J)

COSTUMES
MERCURY: a petasus (sc.1, desc); wings on his feet (sc.1, dialogue)
ALBANACTUS: a yellow satin cuirass embroidered with silver; a silver gorget; a silver girdle; a gold angel's head on his breast; sleeves with watchet labels and short watchet bases embroidered with gold; white puffed under-sleeves; long white bases; white close sleeves (initially planned to be light carnation); white long stockings (also initially planned to be light carnation); a yellow burgonet enchased with silver on his head, with white feathers; an artificial green-and-gold laurel wreath with golden coronal rays (sc.2, implicit; sc.4, desc./J); at some stage the costume was also planned to include carnation round hose embroidered with silver at the bottom, a white tiffany ruff, and silver and yellow buskins (J); *five design drawings survive*.
ATTENDANTS: the captive kings have their hands bound and the priests are in their shirts (sc.2, dialogue)
TUMBLERS: plumed helmets; long robes; girdles (sc.3, J); *design drawing survives*
PUGILISTS: a single sleeve on their right arms; bare chests; faces on their knees (sc.3, J); *design drawing survives*
SATYRS: leafy headgear; cloven hoofs (sc.3, J); *design drawing survives*
GLADIATORS: short, loose gowns (sc.3, J); *design drawing survives*
MIMICS: bells on their shoulders, waists, and ankles; hats (sc.3, J); *design drawing survives*
DIANA: a head-dress; a sleeved robe (sc.4, J); *design drawing survives* (for her chariot, with her in it)

CONSULS: yellow satin cuirasses embroidered with silver; metal gorgets; gold angel's heads on their breasts; sleeves with labels and short watchet bases embroidered with gold; white under-sleeves; long white stockings; burgonets enchased with silver on their heads; artificial laurel wreaths (sc.4, desc.)

HIGH PRIESTS: round headgear; robes (sc.4–5, J); *design drawing survives*

INNOCENCY: a long, pure white robe; a garland of flowers on her head (sc.5, desc.); *design drawing survives* (for the cloud, with figures)

JUSTICE: a richly adorned yellow garment; a white mantle; golden rays on her head (sc.5, desc.); *design drawing survives* (for the cloud)

RELIGION: a short surplice of lawn, over a watchet garment; a silver veil; golden solar beams on her head (sc.5, desc.); *design drawing survives* (for the cloud)

AFFECTION TO THE COUNTRY: yellow coat armour; a purple mantle; decorated buskins; a silver plumed helm (sc.5, desc.); *design drawing survives* (for the cloud)

CONCORD: a sky-coloured robe; a yellow mantle; a garland of wheat (sc.5, desc.); *design drawing survives* (for the cloud)

PEACE: a decorated carnation robe; a silver veil; a garland of olive (sc.5, desc.)

Miscellaneous: Design drawings also survive for two musicians' costumes, marked Tibicen and Cytharoedus. (Orgel and Strong identify the design captioned 'Tibicen' as representing one of the Sacrificers, but their reasoning is unclear.) The design for a Vestal Virgin may or may not have been used. Five rejected designs also survive, for four female captives and a captive king.

EARLY STAGE HISTORY

Inception: Rehearsals had begun by Monday 12 December. Initially the masque was planned for performance on Friday 6 January 1632 (Twelfth Night), but was delayed owing to the Queen's indisposition; the decision to defer took place at some time after Monday 2 January.

Costumes: Inigo Jones instructed the tailor making Innocency's costume to ensure that her robe was long enough not only to cover her feet but also to hide her gilt throne; presumably the intention was that initially she should seem to be sitting directly on the cloud.

Preparation of Venue: The Works Office erected a stage and scenery in the Banqueting House. Lighting was ordered on Saturday 31 December 1631, for delivery by 6 p.m. on Monday 2 January: 48 torches, 192 wax lights, 36 ordinary torches, and 200 sizes (i.e. small candles).

Performance: in the Banqueting House, Whitehall, on Sunday 8 January 1632. The cast included: King Charles I (Albanactus); Queen Henrietta Maria (Alba); Henry Rich, 1st Earl of Holland; Mountjoy Blount, 1st Earl of Newport; James Hay, 2nd Viscount Doncaster; Randall MacDonnell, Viscount Dunluce; Philip, 4th Baron Wharton; William, 5th Baron Paget; Thomas, 3rd Lord Bruce of Kinloss; Sir Robert Stanley; George Goring; Sir William Brooke; Sir John Maynard; Mr Dimmock [or Dymoke?]; Mr [Abraham?] Abercrombie; Mr [Henry?] Murray (Masquers). The scenery and costumes were designed by Inigo Jones. The audience included: Queen Henrietta Maria (who was still unwell); Katherine Villiers, Dowager Duchess of Buckingham; Michael Zon (Secretary to the Venetian Ambassador); possibly John Pory. No ambassadors were invited, but those of Savoy (Alessandro-Cesare di Scaglia) and France (François du Val, Marquis of Fontenay-Mareuil) came anyway; the Venetian Ambassador himself (Giovanni Soranzo) did not attend.

Aftermath: The King reportedly decided after the performance that there would be no more masques performed on a Sunday.

Production Finance and Expenses

Edmund Taverner was paid £1,000 towards production expenses by an order dated Monday 2 January (warrant dated Thursday 29 or Saturday 31 December 1631); the payment was made in two instalments, £700 on Monday 2 January and the balance of £300 on Friday 3 February. It was commented at the time that this masque and *Tempe Restored* (**2359**) were exceptionally costly.

Works: The carpenters Ralph Brice and John Davenport were paid £10 for supervising preparations for the two masques. The preparation of the Banqueting House for both masques cost the Works Office a total of £455.12s.9½d.

Costumes: By a warrant dated Saturday 24 December 1631, George Kirke was paid £450 towards the provision of costumes for the King and such others as the King chose to provide outfits for; the payment was made in two instalments, £300 on Monday 2 January 1632, and the balance of £150 on Monday 6 February. Kirke later failed to send in an account of his expenses, and in March 1632 the responsible clerk, William George, formally complained to Richard, Lord Weston (Lord Treasurer) and Francis, Lord Cottington.

The petition against Kirke over the unpaid account is identified by Herford and Simpson (*Ben Jonson*, x. 681) as relating to *Love's Triumph through Callipolis* (**2328**) and *Chloridia* (**2332**); however, the petition itself refers to the two masques concerned as having been performed at Christmas 1631 and 'Christmas last' (i.e. 1632); in effect, it relates to the King's masques for two years running, not the King's and Queen's masques for Christmas and Shrovetide in a single year.

EARLY TEXTUAL HISTORY

1632: **Q** printed (probably in January, certainly before Saturday 24 March) by Augustine Matthews for Robert Allot; collation A–C⁴, 12 leaves. Parts of the book were reset during printing, the most important alteration being the insertion of the author's name at the foot of the text.

1632: Aurelian Townshend sent a copy of Q (now at the Huntington Library, shelfmark 69679) to John Egerton, 1st Earl of Bridgewater, with handwritten corrections to the text.

1632 (?): John Newdigate bought a copy of 'a book of the masque', probably this one; the purchase is recorded in his accounts for December 1631 and January 1632 (and, if it was in December, then the masque was presumably either **2328** or **2332**).

1684: Nicholas Cox (Manciple of St Edmund Hall, Oxford) had a copy of Q in his bookshop. It had probably been previously owned by Gerard Langbaine, and appears on a list compiled by Anthony Wood on Saturday 13 December.

EDITIONS
E. K. Chambers, *Aurelian Townshend's Poems and Masks* (Oxford, 1912), 55–78.
Orgel and Strong, ii. 452–77.
Cedric C. Brown in Aurelian Townshend, *The Poems and Masques* (Reading, 1983), 75–91.

REFERENCES
Annals 1632; *Art Bulletin* 64 (1982), 207–8; Ashbee, iii. 64; Beal Online ToA 89; Bentley, v. 1227–8; Thomas Birch (ed.), *The Court and Times of Charles I* (London, 1848), ii. 158–9; Bodleian, MS Wood E. 4, art. 1, p. 107; *Burlington Magazine* 115 (1973), 561; Butler, 294–8, 372; *Cal. Dom. 1631–3*, 207, 270, 299–300; Greg 453; Hazlitt, 6; David Howarth, *Lord Arundel and his Circle* (New Haven and London, 1985), 82–3; *John Donne Journal* 5 (1986), 221–4; *Journal of Medieval and Renaissance Studies* 16 (1986), 75–90; Vivienne Larminie, *Wealth, Kinship and Culture* (Woodbridge, 1995), 201; David Lindley (ed.), *The Court Masque* (Manchester, 1984), 160–1; Loomie, 119; McGee-Meagher 1625–34, 58–62; MSC 2.3, 356; MSC 10, 42–3; *N&Q* 207 (1962), 146–7; John Peacock, *The Stage Designs of Inigo Jones* (Cambridge, 1995), 92, 94–5, 128–9, 132–3, 308–15; REED: Lincolnshire, 352; Reyher, 530; Steele, 240; *Theatre Survey* 20 (1979), 16.

2354. Masque for the Earl of Cumberland

EVIDENCE
Clifford accounts (Chatsworth: Bolton MSS, book 168).

GENRE
masque

DATE
10 January 1632

ORIGINAL PRODUCTION
Earl of Cumberland's household

EARLY STAGE HISTORY
1632: performed on Tuesday 10 January in the household of Francis Clifford, 4th Earl of Cumberland, presumably either at Londesborough House or Skipton Castle, Yorkshire. The design may have been by either Hendrik de Keyser or John Vester.

REFERENCES
Lynn Mary Hulse, 'The Musical Patronage of the English Aristocracy, c. 1590–1640', unpublished Ph.D. thesis (London, 1992), 346.

2355. The Changes

TEXT
Printed in 1632 (STC 22437).

GENRE
comedy
Contemporary: play (ep.); comedy (S.R., t.p.)

TITLE
Performed: *The Changes*
Printed: *Changes, or Love in a Maze*
Contemporary: *The Changes, or Love in a Maze*; *Love in a Maze*
Later Assigned: *Love Changes, or Love in a Maze*; possibly *Amor in labyrintho*

AUTHOR
James Shirley

DATE
January 1632

ORIGINAL PRODUCTION
King's Revels Company at the Fortune (?; or Prince Charles's Men at Salisbury Court)

Q's title page states that the King's Revels performance took place at Salisbury Court, but by the time the play was licensed for performance, the King's Revels had already been replaced as the tenants of that playhouse by Prince Charles's Men, who performed *Holland's Leaguer* (**2351**) there in December 1631, with a prologue stating explicitly that the theatre had been 'forsook of late' by its previous occupants. There are three substantive pieces of incompatible information: the date of the licence, the acting company, and the playhouse. The issue is which of them we should discount.

Gifford silently assumes that the licence must date from a year earlier, January 1631 rather than January 1631/2. This is superficially attractive in that it would mean that the play was released for publication, in February 1632, thirteen months after it was licensed rather than just one month. However, Malone's record of the licence not only contains an explicit indication of the year but also places it in a chronological sequence of licences; both would have to be wrong to support antedating this particular licence.

Bentley proposes that the play was written for Salisbury Court in the autumn of 1631, but that the theatre's occupancy had changed by the time it was licensed; thus he would assign it to Prince Charles's Men rather than the King's Revels Company, whose name appears on the title page, he proposes, because Shirley's manuscript still carried the name of the intended company rather than the eventual one. As printed fourteen years later in Shirley's *Poems &c.* (1646), the prologue again carries the ascription to Salisbury Court but—like every other prologue in the collection—names no acting company.

The third possibility is that the title page assigns the play (and acting company) to the wrong playhouse, perhaps as an innocent mistake or false assumption abetted by the uncommon brevity of the interval between licensing and publication, or the recency of the move. Since it was a move down-market to the Fortune, the publisher might have had some incentive for mendacity, and Shirley for wishful thinking.

The prologue can be interpreted in two possible ways. It expresses the hope that the play will not be let down by 'this place | And weak performances', which might imply some dissatisfaction on the part of the company with the playhouse in which they are performing, and that would make sense in the context of a recent move to the Fortune. However, it also seems to indicate that it is a new company: they 'have no name' and the audience is asked to 'Encourage our beginning'. That might indicate Prince Charles's Men, but such modesty might be disingenuous after the great success of *Holland's Leaguer*; it also seems odd to describe the newest playhouse in London as 'this barren mountain'. Perhaps, after all, the company was only beginning its tenure of a new house.

PLOT

Goldsworth's twin daughters, Chrysolina and Aurelia, are daily courted by numerous suitors, including the foolish knight Simple, whom Mistress Goldsworth favours for his title, and the would-be poet Caperwit. Both girls favour the same suitor, Gerard, but with selfless sisterly affection, each wants the other to have him. Gerard comes under pressure to choose between them, not only from Goldsworth but also from his friend Thornay, who wants to woo whichever one he leaves; but, loving them equally, he cannot decide. Thornay decides to seize the initiative and woos Chrysolina (who consequently thinks him disloyal to Gerard), then misleads Gerard into thinking that she has reciprocated and that he should concentrate on Aurelia. But Chrysolina is offended by Gerard's sudden neglect, and Aurelia takes it as a sign of his fickleness, and refuses him. She also rejects Simple's suit, but her attempts to be polite about it to her mother are misconstrued, and Mistress Goldsworth sets about making wedding plans.

Sir John Woodhamore keeps his niece Eugenia inside, away from the world and its temptations, while he seeks a husband worthy of her; he has decided on Youngrave. When Youngrave is left alone to woo her, however, she asks him to carry a letter to Thornay, the man she loves. Thornay protests that he isn't interested: he loves Chrysolina. To get her own back on Gerard, Chrysolina pretends to return Thornay's love; but she is upset to hear that he has rejected Eugenia, and sends him to make amends. He does so, feeling guilty at the way he has treated her, and her uncle catches them kissing. They pretend that he was only delivering a message from Youngrave, who then arrives to find Woodhamore planning their wedding. The miserly uncle decides it will be a secret marriage: he prefers the scandal of a supposed elopement to the expense of a public celebration; consequently he will not be present. This will enable an appropriate substitution of bridegroom.

Admiring Youngrave's self-sacrificing willingness to put Eugenia's choice of suitor above his own wishes, Chrysolina falls for him. Despite her hints, Youngrave decides on a life of celibacy. The twins worry that they may end up unmarried. Chrysolina asks Eugenia to use her influence to win Youngrave for her. Thornay explains to Chrysolina why Gerard neglected her; Aurelia visits the melancholy Gerard and apologises for her behaviour.

In a separate strand of action, Caperwit is pursued to the Goldsworths' house by Lady Bird, a rich widow who mistook his poetical compliments for love; her advances discredit Caperwit in the eyes of the twins, but Simple decides that, since Caperwit isn't interested, he will have the lady himself. She accepts him, and he invites everyone to their wedding.

So, there are now to be four weddings: Aurelia to Gerard; Chrysolina to Youngrave; Eugenia to Thornay; and Lady Bird to Simple. Caperwit arranges a wedding masque for Simple, intending to use it to promote his own wooing of the twins, but is disconcerted to find the plan pre-empted: all four pairs of masquers are married. Woodhamore is even more disconcerted to find that Eugenia has married Thornay. Simple is the most disconcerted of all: Lady Bird is actually Caperwit's page.

SCENE DESIGNATION

prol., 1.1–2, 2.1–3, 3.1–3, 4.1–3, 5.1–5, ep. (Q has act-division only)

ROLES

PROLOGUE
Sir John WOODHAMORE [or Wouldha'more], Eugenia's avaricious uncle and guardian
Master GOLDSWORTH, Mistress Goldsworth's husband, father of Chrysolina and Aurelia
Master Frank GERARD, a gentleman, suitor to the Goldsworth twins; later Aurelia's husband
Master Jack YOUNGRAVE, a gentleman, suitor to Eugenia; later Chrysolina's husband
Goldsworth's SERVANT (1.1–2, 3.1, 5.5; may be a different character in each of the scenes)
Sir Gervase SIMPLE, a foolish country knight and landowner, suitor to the Goldsworth twins
THUMP, Simple's man
MISTRESS GOLDSWORTH, Goldsworth's wife, mother of Chrysolina and Aurelia
Master CAPERWIT, a poet, suitor to the Goldsworth twins

Caperwit's PAGE, possibly named Bird; poses as Lady Bird, a rich city widow
Mistress CHRYSOLINA, the Goldsworths' daughter, Aurelia's twin sister (and the elder by one minute); later Youngrave's wife
AURELIA, a gentlewoman, the Goldsworths' daughter, Chrysolina's twin sister; later Gerard's wife
EUGENIA, a gentlewoman, Woodhamore's niece; later Thornay's wife
Master Thomas THORNAY, a gentleman, Gerard's friend; later Eugenia's husband
A FOOTMAN, servant of 'Lady Bird'; possibly named Trot (3.1)
Eugenia's MAID (4.1)
A DANCER hired by Caperwit (4.2)
A SERVANT, who brings Chrysolina's letter (5.1, *non-speaking*)
Gerard's SERVANT (5.3)
Four TORCHBEARERS (5.5, *non-speaking*)
EPILOGUE (but the speaker may be Gerard)

Speaking Parts: 19–23

Stage Directions and Speech Prefixes
PROLOGUE: *Prologus* (heading)
WOODHAMORE: *Sir John Wood-hamore* (s.d.s); *Woodhamore* (s.d.s and s.p.s); *Master Woodhamore, Uncle to Eugenia* (d.p.)
GOLDSWORTH: *Master Goldsworth | Goldsworth* (s.d.s); *Golds<worth>* (s.p.s); *Master Goldsworth, father to Chrysolina and Aurelia* (d.p.)
GERARD: *Master Gerard | Gerard* (s.d.s); *Ger<ard>* (s.p.s); *Master Gerard [Gentleman Lover] of ... Aurelia* (d.p.)
YOUNGRAVE: *Master Yongrave | Yongrave* (s.d.s); *Yon<grave>* (s.p.s); *Master Yongrave [Gentleman Lover] of ... Eugenia* (d.p.)
SERVANT: *Servant* (s.d.s and s.p.s); [one of the] *Servants* (d.p.)
SIMPLE: *Sir Gervase Simple | Simple* (s.d.s); *Sim<ple>* (s.p.s); *Sir Gervace Simple* (d.p.)
THUMP: [Simple's] *man Thumpe | Thumpe* (s.d.s); *Thump* (s.d.s and s.p.s); *Thumpe, Sir Gervace's Man* (d.p.)
MISTRESS GOLDSWORTH: *Mistress Goldsworth* (s.d.s and d.p.); *Mistress* (s.p.s)
CAPERWIT: *Caperwit* (s.d.s); *Cap<erwit>* (s.p.s); *Master Caperwit, a Poetaster* (d.p.)
PAGE: [Caperwit's] *Page | Lady Bird | Bird* (s.d.s); *Bir<d> | Page* (s.p.s); *Bird, Caperwit's Page* (d.p.)
CHRYSOLINA: *Chrisolina | Chrisalina* (s.d.s); *Chrysolina* (s.d.s and d.p.); *Chrys<olina>* (s.p.s)
AURELIA: *Aurelia* (s.d.s and d.p.); *Aur<elia>* (s.p.s)
EUGENIA: *Eugenia* (s.d.s and d.p.); *Eug<enia>* (s.p.s)
THORNAY: *Master Thornay | Thornay* (s.d.s); *Thor<nay>* (s.p.s); *Master Thornay [Gentleman Lover] of Chrysolina* (d.p.)
FOOTMAN: *Servant* (s.p.s); [one of the] *Servants* (d.p.)
MAID: [Eugenia's] *Maid* (s.d.s); *Maid* (s.p.s)
DANCER: *Dancer* (s.d.s, s.p.s, and d.p.)
SERVANT: *Servant* (s.d.s); [one of the] *Servants* (d.p.)
SERVANT: *Servant* (s.d.s and s.p.s); [one of the] *Servants* (d.p.)
EPILOGUE: *Epilogus* (heading)

OTHER CHARACTERS
Simple's chaplain (1.2)
Simple's tenants (1.2)
The midwife who delivered Caperwit (1.2)
Caperwit's nurse, said to be a descendant of Geoffrey Chaucer (1.2)
A lord who has travelled 99 miles to hear one of Caperwit's poems (1.2; possibly imaginary)
Eugenia's dead father, Woodhamore's brother (2.1, 5.1)
Eugenia's dead mother (2.1)
People at Gerard's lodgings who directed Thornay to Goldsworth's house (2.2)
Caperwit's footman (2.2)
Attendants on 'Lady Bird' (3.1)
Thornay's father (3.2, 4.2)
Simple's mother, whom some supposed a witch (4.3)

A number of personages associated with 'Lady Bird' are mentioned in 3.1: Bird, a rich alderman, her dead husband; the Raven family, Bird's kinsfolk; Sir Walter Cormorant, her uncle; Bullfinch, her kinsman and steward; Hawk and Buzzard, residents of Fleet Street; and Master Kite, to whom she lent £1,000. Presumably all of these are imaginary figures, since all are named by either Caperwit, who set up the deception, or the lady 'herself'. It is possible that there really is supposed to have been an Alderman Bird and his widow: there are only 26 aldermen of London, so it might not be easy to invent one; but Caperwit takes care to say that Bird died out of town, a point perhaps designed to ensure that Goldsworth and the others don't wonder why they haven't heard of an important, recently deceased civic worthy. (Bird may in reality have been an allusion to Alderman Sir Heneage Finch, whose name is doubly avine and who died in Buckinghamshire on 5 December 1631.)

SETTING
Period: contemporary (?)
Time-Scheme: 5.1 takes place in the morning, and 5.5 later the same day
Place: London

Geography
London: Cheapside; Charing Cross; the Exchange; Fleet Street; the Poultry; Bedlam; Gresham College
[*Europe*]: Spain; Switzerland; Flanders; Italy; France
Persia
The West Indies

SOURCES
Verbal: Virgil, *Georgics* 3 (t.p. motto); Sir Philip Sidney, *Defence of Poetry* (*c.* 1580; adapting Ovid, *Tristia* 4.10; 1.2, cited); Thomas Kyd, *The Spanish Tragedy* (**783**; 4.3)

8 | 2355. The Changes

Works Mentioned: Aristotle, *De caelo* (4.2); Franciscus Titelmannus, unspecified work (sixteenth century; 4.2); Statute of Bigamy (1603; 1 James I c. 11; 1.1); Thomas Tomkis, *Lingua* (**1524**; 4.2)

LANGUAGE
English
Latin: 6 words (1.2; Caperwit)
Greek: 1 word (2.2; Caperwit)
French: 2 words (1.2; Simple)

FORM
Metre: pentameter and prose
Rhyme: blank verse
Prologue: 20 lines, in couplets
Act-Division: 5 acts
Epilogue: 18 lines, in couplets, probably spoken by Gerard
Lines (Spoken): 2,430 (1,813 verse, 617 prose)
Lines (Written): 2,544

STAGING
Doors: characters enter at two doors (1.1, 2.2, s.d.)
Stage: mentioned (5.5, s.d.)
Audience: addressed as 'gentlemen' (prol.) and referred to as 'these gentlemen' (5.5)

MUSIC
Music: recorders (5.5, s.d.); unspecified music (5.5, dialogue)
Songs:
    1: 'Melancholy, hence!', 4.1, Maid, 8 lines;
    2: 'If Love his arrows shoot so fast', 5.3, Gerard's Servant, 14 lines.
Dance: masquers dance (5.5, s.d.)

PROPS
Lighting: four torches (5.5, s.d.)
Weapons: Simple's rapier (1.2, dialogue); possibly Gerard's sword (2.3, implicit); Youngrave's sword (4.2, dialogue); Thornay's sword (4.2, implicit)
Clothing: a ring (3.1, dialogue)
Small Portable Objects: a letter (2.1, 3.2, s.d.); a document (2.2, implicit); another letter (5.1, s.d.); a document (5.3, implicit)
Large Portable Objects: a chair (5.3, dialogue)

COSTUMES
GERARD: possibly hangers (2.3, implicit); a gown and cap (5.3, s.d.); a mask (5.5, s.d.; removed on stage)
YOUNGRAVE: hangers (4.2, implicit); a cloak (4.2, dialogue); a mask (5.5, s.d.; removed on stage)
SIMPLE: a dark complexion and a black beard (dialogue); spurs (1.2, dialogue); a cloak (1.2, dialogue; removed on stage); hangers (1.2, implicit); an orange-tawny satin doublet with rich lace; blue trunk hose; an elbow-length Italian cloak; a Spanish ruff; long French stockings (2.2, dialogue); a mask (5.5, s.d.; removed on stage)
CAPERWIT: a slashed doublet with buttons (3.1, dialogue); disguised as a conjuror (5.5, s.d.)
PAGE: cross-dressed as Lady Bird (3.1, 4.2–3, 5.5, implicit), including a wig (implicit; removed on stage); jewels (4.3, dialogue); a diamond ring (4.3, dialogue; put on and removed on stage); a mask and head-dress (5.5, s.d.; removed on stage)
CHRYSOLINA: a veil (5.5, s.d.; removed on stage)
AURELIA: probably golden hair (implicit); a gown (2.2, s.d.); a veil (5.5, s.d.; removed on stage)
EUGENIA: a veil (5.5, s.d.; removed on stage)
THORNAY: hangers (4.2, implicit); a mask (5.5, s.d.; removed on stage)

EARLY STAGE HISTORY
1632: said to have been performed by the King's Revels Company at Salisbury Court (but more probably either by one or at the other, not both).

EARLY TEXTUAL HISTORY
1632: On Tuesday 10 January, Sir Henry Herbert licensed the text for performance.
1632: entered to William Cooke in the Stationers' Register on Thursday 9 February; entry names author. Sir Henry Herbert had licensed the book for publication.
1632: Q printed by George Purslowe for William Cooke; collation A^4 (–A1) B–I^4 K^2 L1, 38 leaves; title page names author, acting company, and playhouse; Latin title-page motto; authorial verse dedication to Lady Dorothy Shirley; list of roles.
Before 1640: a copy of Q was owned by Robert Burton.
c. 1630s–40s: a copy of Q was in the possession of John Horne (Vicar of Headington, Oxfordshire). After his death, his entire collection of play-books passed into the possession of John Houghton of Brasenose College, Oxford (c. 1608–77), then to James Herne (died 1685), and then to the library of Ralph Sheldon (1623–84) at Weston, where it was catalogued by Anthony Wood, probably in the late 1670s. By then the copy had been bound into a single volume with 21 other plays by Shirley (and, presumably in error, with Henry Shirley's *The Martyred Soldier*, **2030**).
c. 1640: Abraham Wright transcribed extracts into a MS miscellany (London: British Library, Add. MS 22608, fos. 78^v–79^v). The MS later passed to Wright's son, the antiquarian James Wright (c. 1644–c. 1717).
c. 1642: songs transcribed in a MS collection of verse (Oxford: Bodleian, MS Rawlinson poet. 88, pp. 12–13, 33–4); Song 2 is headed 'One that loved two mistresses at once'.
1645: Song 2 included in the fourth edition of 'Philomusus', *The Academy of Compliments*, sigs. I5^v–I6^r; printed by Thomas Badger for Humphrey Moseley.
1646: *The Academy of Compliments* reprinted by Moses Bell for Humphrey Moseley; the song now appears on sig. K8^{r-v}.

1646: rights to James Shirley's *Poems &c.* transferred in the Stationers' Register from Francis Constable to Humphrey Moseley on Saturday 31 October.

1646: prologue, epilogue, songs, and verse dedication included in Shirley's *Poems &c.*, sigs. C1^v, C2^r, D4^{r-v}, ²D3^{r-v}; printed by Ruth Raworth for Humphrey Moseley; Song 1 is headed 'Upon his Mistress Sad', and Song 2, 'A Gentleman in Love with Two Ladies'.

c. 1647–8: extracts included in a MS notebook (Oxford: Bodleian, MS Ashmole 420, fos. 5^r–7^r) compiled by the astrologer William Lilly. Later, probably after his death in 1681 (and certainly before 1692), in the MS passed into the possession of Elias Ashmole; after Ashmole died in turn, in 1692, the MS passed to the Ashmolean Museum, Oxford.

1650: *The Academy of Compliments* reprinted for Humphrey Moseley; the song now appears on sig. K4^v.

1655: *The English Treasury of Wit and Language* entered in the Stationers' Register to Humphrey Moseley on Tuesday 16 January.

1655: two extracts (from 1.2, 4.2) included in John Cotgrave's *The English Treasury of Wit and Language*, sigs. K6^{r-v}, M8^v; printed for Humphrey Moseley.

1655: *Wit's Interpreter* entered to Nathaniel Brooke in the Stationers' Register on Wednesday 14 March.

1655: extract (from 3.1) included in John Cotgrave's *Wit's Interpreter*, sig. G2^{r-v}; printed for Nathaniel Brooke.

c. 1655: extracts transcribed by John Evans in a miscellany, *Hesperides*, intended for publication and entered to Humphrey Moseley in the Stationers' Register on Thursday 16 August 1655. The book remained unpublished in 1660, and Evans continued to add to the collection until at least 1666. Two MS exemplars are known; one was cut up by J. O. Halliwell-Phillipps in the nineteenth century; the other survives (Washington: Folger, MS V. b. 93).

c. 1656: extract (from 3.1) included in *Cupid's Masterpiece*, sigs. B4^r; printed for John Andrews.

1658: *The Academy of Compliments* reprinted for Humphrey Moseley.

1662: *Wit's Interpreter* reprinted (before Thursday 8 June) for Nathaniel Brooke; the extract now appears on sigs. E6^v–E7^r, and is titled 'Kindness Contemned'.

1663: *The Academy of Compliments* reprinted by Thomas Leach and Thomas Child.

1671: *Wit's Interpreter* reprinted for Nathaniel Brooke and Obadiah Blagrave.

1673: possibly translated into Latin (as *Amor in labyrintho*); the play was performed at the King's School, Canterbury, on Friday 12 December, and the translation may have been specifically made for that purpose.

1684: Nicholas Cox (Manciple of St Edmund Hall, Oxford) had a copy of Q in his bookshop. It had probably been previously owned by Gerard Langbaine, and appears on a list compiled by Anthony Wood on Saturday 13 December.

The record of the Canterbury performance refers to the play as having been 'composita' rather than translated, but leaves a blank for the name of the author, implying a lack of information that would be consistent with the hypothesis that it was a translation rather than an original composition. All other notes of performances in the same document use English or Latin to match the language of the performance.

EDITIONS

William Gifford, in *The Dramatic Works and Poems of James Shirley* (London, 1833), ii. 269–364.

Eva Griffith, in James Shirley, *The Complete Works*, gen. eds. Eugene Giddens, Teresa Grant, and Barbara Ravelhofer (Oxford, forthcoming).

REFERENCES

Annals 1632; Bawcutt 228, C42; Beal 2 ShJ 136–7; Bentley, v. 1091–4; Bodleian, MS Wood E. 4, art. 1, p. 9; Canterbury Cathedral Archives, CCA-LitMS/E/41, fo. 229^v; Eyre & Rivington, i. 250, 463, 467, ii. 8; Robert Stanley Forsythe, *The Relations of Shirley's Plays to the Elizabethan Drama* (New York, 1914), 342–9; Greg 462; Hazlitt, 38; Nicolas K. Kiessling, *The Library of Robert Burton* (Oxford, 1988) 1472; *The Library*, 5th ser., 28 (1973), 294–308; *The Library*, 7th ser., 10 (2009), 372–404; *MLR* 13 (1918), 401–11; *MP* 66 (1968–9), 256–61; *RES* NS 54 (2003), 601–14; *SP* 40 (1943), 186–203.

2356. Masque at Goring House

EVIDENCE

Letter from John Pory to John, 1st Viscount Scudamore, dated 14 January 1632; William Davenant, 'In the Person of a Spy, at the Queen's Entertainment by the Lord Goring' (printed 1673; Wing D320).

GENRE

masque

Contemporary: masque (Pory); entertainment (Davenant)

TITLE

Later Assigned: *Lord Goring's Masque for the Queen*

DATE

12 January 1632

ORIGINAL PRODUCTION

Goring House, London

The house stood on the modern site of Buckingham Palace.

ROLES

The MASQUERS, six lords and six ladies

2357. The Corporal

EARLY STAGE HISTORY
1632: performed on Thursday 12 January at Goring House, London. The cast included Robert Rich, 2nd Earl of Warwick. The audience included: Queen Henrietta Maria; Lord George Goring (host); possibly William Davenant. The Queen may have found the show crude and dull; Davenant, if present, certainly did.

REFERENCES
Butler, 372; Sir William Davenant, *The Shorter Poems*, ed. A. M. Gibbs (Oxford, 1972), 171; McGee-Meagher 1625–34, 62–3; *ShS* 11 (1958), 108.

2357. The Corporal

TEXT
Three MSS, none of them complete:
- **D**: Oxford: Bodleian, MS Douce C. 2; a late transcript;
- **R**: Oxford: Bodleian, MS Rawlinson poet. 9, fo. 45^v; title and list of roles only; authorial holograph at the end of the holograph presentation copy of *The Inconstant Lady* (**2293**);
- **V**: London: Victoria and Albert Museum, Forster Collection MS 638; holograph fragment of two non-cognate leaves (parts of 1.1–2 and 1.3), with corrections.

The least incomplete of the three is D; the other two, though of earlier date and authorial provenance, supply no part of the play which is not also present there.

GENRE
comedy

TITLE
Performed/MS: *The Corporal*

AUTHOR
Arthur Wilson

DATE
Limits: 1631–3
Best Guess: 1632

The allusion in 1.2 to the successful Swedish invasion of Germany establishes that the play was written no earlier than mid-1631. Whether it can be dated exactly or only roughly turns on the interpretation of a record in Sir Henry Herbert's office-book which is now known only through two contradictory reports. F. G. Fleay claimed that Herbert licensed the play on 14 January 1633, which would fix its date definitively. However, Hazlitt says, in respect of the same date, that Herbert was noting a payment to the King's Men for allowing a performance by the Earl of Essex's servants. This is not information that one would expect to have arisen from a misreading, whereas a cursory glance at the records, or inadequate note-taking, might have led Fleay to suggest something more commonplace.

If Hazlitt is correct, this would seem to indicate that the play was already in the King's Men's repertory by the second week of January 1633, and that it was an attractive option for performance by others, so much so that they were willing to pay for the privilege. Such a transaction may not have been unique; this might explain how Sir Edward Dering's household was able to mount an amateur performance of *The Spanish Curate* (**2025**) a quarter of a century before it was published. Herbert may have been involved in the deal because he seems to have thought of his licences as pertaining to particular companies or theatres, and so might have been informed, though there is no indication that this was more than a courtesy.

ORIGINAL PRODUCTION
King's Men at the Blackfriars (and perhaps also the Globe)

PLOT
With war at an end, Lord Theodore becomes interested in amorous matters: in particular, he shows an interest in his friend Erfort's new wife. Erfort becomes jealous and tries to prevent her from coming to the city. Theodore also chats up the heiress Felicia, but only arouses her interest in saving him from his own lust.

Theodore's behaviour so disgusts his soldiers that they all turn moral. Corporal Jogalon refuses to act as his bawd, and joins Eurick in a plot to discover the city ladies' sexual secrets: Eurick will pose as a Lapland conjurer and Jogalon as a lord. Jogalon is unhappy to have to give up his plebeian recreations, but falls in love with Cladia. Cladia in turn has recently been jilted by Halladin in favour of her mother, Callida. [*The rest of the play is lost.*]

The central issue in establishing a hypothesis about the likely resolution of the plot is the link between the two disguises in Eurick's plot. One possibility is that the 'Lapland conjurer' matches the ambitious Callida with Jogalon, who turns out to be a corporal rather than the lord she expected.

SCENE DESIGNATION
1.1–3, 2.1 (MS)

ROLES
RODERICK, a gentleman
CLODIAN, a gentleman
Lord THEODORE, a military commander
Captain EURICK, a soldier; poses as a Lapland conjurer
Corporal JOGALON, a soldier; he may be small of stature; poses as a lord
Lady CALLIDA, an old woman; Cladia's mother, Felicia's aunt and guardian
HALLADIN, a young man, Cladia's former lover
Colonel ERFORT, Theodore's friend, Thamira's husband
Erfort's SERVANTS (1.2, *non-speaking*)
FELICIA, an heiress, Callida's niece, Cladia's cousin
CLADIA, Callida's daughter, Felicia's cousin
POPIER, Callida's gentleman usher (*has no lines in the surviving fragment*)

THAMIRA, Erfort's wife (*has no lines in the surviving fragment*)
A NURSE (*has no lines in the surviving fragment*)

Speaking Parts: 10 in fragment (at least 12–13 in complete text)

Stage Directions and Speech Prefixes
RODERICK: *Roderick | Rodorick* (s.d.s); *Rod<erick>* (s.p.s); *Roderick,* [one of] *Two Gentlemen relating to Theodore* (d.p.)
CLODIAN: *Clodian* (s.d.s); *Clod<ian>* (s.p.s); *Clodian,* [one of] *Two Gentlemen relating to Theodore* (d.p.)
THEODORE: *Theodore* (s.d.s); *Theod<ore>* (s.p.s); *Theodore, A Commander in the Wars* (d.p.)
EURICK: *Eurick* (s.d.s and s.p.s); *Eurick, A Captain* (d.p.)
JOGALON: *Jogalon* (s.d.s); *Jog<alon>* (s.p.s); *Jogalon, A Corporal* (d.p.)
CALLIDA: *Callida* (s.d.s); *Call<ida>* (s.p.s); *Callida, An old painted Lady* (d.p.)
HALLADIN: *Halladin* (s.d.s); *Hall<adin>* (s.p.s); *Halladin, A young man in love with Callida* (d.p.)
ERFORT: *Erfort* (s.d.s and s.p.s); *Erfort, Friend to Theodore* (d.p.)
SERVANTS: *Servants* (s.d.s and d.p.)
FELICIA: *Felicia* (s.d.s); *Fel<icia>* (s.p.s); *Feli<cia>* (V s.p.s); *Felicia, niece to Callida, a great heir* (d.p.)
CLADIA: *Cladia* (s.d.s); *Clad<ia>* (s.p.s); *Cladia, daughter to Callida, A lover of Halladin* (d.p.)
POPIER: *Popier* (s.d.s); *Popier, Gentleman Usher to Callida* (d.p.)
THAMIRA: *Thamira, wife to Erfort* (d.p.)
NURSE: *Nurse* (d.p.)

Based mainly on D.

OTHER CHARACTERS
A sutler's wife kissed by Jogalon (1.1)
Renati, Halladin's father (1.1)
The Swedes, who have invaded Germany (1.2)
A Lapland conjurer and fortune-teller, whom Eurick impersonates (1.2)
Felicia's dead father (1.3)
Suitors, including a stupid young lord, whom Callida introduced as potential husbands for Felicia, but whom Felicia refused (1.3)
The tailor who made Eurick's fur disguise (2.1)
Eurick's customers in his Laplander disguise, including chambermaids and plebeian women (2.1)
An old knight whom Eurick matched with one of his customers (2.1)
Jogalon's new servants, including a groom, a French cook, a coachman, and a boy (2.1)

SETTING
Place: Nancy, Lorraine

Geography
France

[*Italy*]: Rome; Naples
Germany: Styria
Sweden
Lapland

SOURCES
Works Mentioned: Jacobus de Voragine, *Legenda aurea* (c. 1275; 2.1)

LANGUAGE
English
Latin: 2 words (1.2; Eurick)

FORM
Metre: pentameter and prose; some alexandrines
Rhyme: blank verse
Act-Division: first two acts marked in fragment
Lines (Spoken): 596 (546 verse, 50 prose)
Lines (Written): 720

COSTUMES AND MAKE-UP
EURICK: disguised as a Laplander, in furs (2.1, s.d.)
JOGALON: disguised as a lord (2.1, s.d.), including stockings (dialogue)
CALLIDA: wrinkles (dialogue); a painted face (1.1, 2.1, dialogue)

EARLY STAGE HISTORY
c. 1632 (?): performed at the Blackfriars by the King's Men.

1633: Sir Henry Herbert recorded a payment of £2 to the King's Men on Monday 14 January, for allowing the play to be performed by the Earl of Essex's 'servants'.

1641: The play was still in the repertory of the King's Men.

Who were Essex's 'servants'? The term might have meant a minor company of professional players under his patronage, but such a troupe is not otherwise known. Alternatively, they might have been literally his household servants looking to mount an amateur performance at Chartley, possibly for the Earl himself. The play would have been of interest not least because its author was a former colleague, in Essex's service until 1631.

EARLY TEXTUAL HISTORY
c. 1632: transcribed by Arthur Wilson in MS (**V**); only a 2-leaf fragment now survives.

c. 1632–52: transcribed by Wilson as a MS presentation copy (**R**), apparently as part of a collection of his plays which also included *The Inconstant Lady* (**2293**); only the title and list of roles now survives.

1641: On Saturday 7 August, Robert Devereux, 3rd Earl of Essex (Lord Chamberlain) issued a warrant prohibiting the printing of this and sixty other plays without the consent of the King's Men. On Saturday 14 August, the order was read to the Stationers' Company and instructions issued for its observance.

1646: entered to Humphrey Robinson and Humphrey Moseley in the Stationers' Register between Friday 4 and Tuesday 15 September; group entry, play and author individually named. John Langley had licensed the book for publication.

1673: Robinson's rights transferred in the Stationers' Register by his executor (also named Humphrey Robinson) to John Martin and Henry Herringman on Thursday 30 January, as part of a list of 105 titles, by assignment of Saturday 13 May 1671.

1683: Martin's rights transferred in the Stationers' Register from his widow, Sarah, to Robert Scott, on Tuesday 21 August, by assignment of Tuesday 14 June 1681 and order of a court of Monday 7 November 1681; individually named as part of a group transfer of 360 titles.

Late seventeenth century (or early eighteenth?): transcribed in MS (**D**); list of roles; only a 13-leaf fragment survives.

REFERENCES
Annals 1633; Bawcutt 247; Bentley, v. 1270–1; Greg Θ56; Hazlitt, 50; MSC 1.4–5, 364–9; Sibley, 31.

2358. Antimasque at Gray's Inn

EVIDENCE
Gray's Inn Pension Book.

GENRE
antimasque
Contemporary: antimasque

DATE
February (?) 1632

ORIGINAL PRODUCTION
Gray's Inn

EARLY STAGE HISTORY
1632: performed at Gray's Inn, possibly in February and perhaps on Thursday 2 (Candlemas).

Production Expenses
On Friday 3 February, the Gray's Inn authorities gave orders that the expenses of the antimasque should be paid from common funds.

REFERENCES
Reginald J. Fletcher (ed.), *The Pension Book of Gray's Inn* (London, 1901), i. 310; REED: Inns of Court, 229.

2359. *Tempe restauratum* [Tempe Restored]

TEXT
Printed in 1632 (STC 24156). Additional information derives from:

D: tradesmen's bills in Queen Henrietta Maria's debenture accounts (Kew: National Archives, LR 5/64–5);
F: a warrant for the Fugitive Favourite's costume (Kew: National Archives, LR 5/132);
J: Inigo Jones's design drawings;
S: the Earl of Salisbury's 1631–2 household accounts (Hatfield: Cecil Papers, CFEP, Box H/7, pp. 10, 30).

GENRE
masque
Contemporary: masque (t.p.)

TITLE
Performed: *Tempe restauratum*
Printed: *Tempe Restored*

AUTHOR
Aurelian Townshend, *from a concept by* Inigo Jones

DATE
14 February 1632

ORIGINAL PRODUCTION
English Court at Whitehall Palace, probably in the Banqueting House

PLOT
Circe's favourite, formerly transformed by her into a lion, takes advantage of his return to human form, and flees. Circe angrily pursues him, but is persuaded by her nymphs to watch a show of her remaining bestial subjects, the present occupiers of the Vale of Tempe. Divine Beauty appears, as do the gods. Cupid claims sovereignty over Circe's victims, and Jupiter over the land. Circe anticipates Jupiter's intentions by ceding her dominion to the King and Queen. Tempe is restored to the followers of the Muses.

SCENE DESIGNATION
sc.1–5 (Q undivided) The division reflects the changes of scenery; for sc.3, the scenery reverts to its state during sc.1. The seven antimasques (ant.1–7) occur during sc.2, the main masque during sc.4, and the revels during sc.5.

ROLES
The FUGITIVE FAVOURITE, a young gentleman
CIRCE, an enchantress
Four NYMPHS attending Circe, dryads of woods and naiads of waters (sing collectively)
A CHORUS of twelve musicians attending Circe (sing collectively)
Seven INDIANS (ant.1, *non-speaking*; two reappear in ant.7)
A PAGODA or idol, worshipped by the Indians (ant.1, *non-speaking*)
A HARE (ant.2, *non-speaking*)

Two HOUNDS (ant.2, 7, *non-speaking*)
Four LIONS (ant.3, *non-speaking*; two reappear in ant.7)
Three APES (ant.4, *non-speaking?*; two reappear in ant.7)
An ASS, represented as a pedant (ant.4, 7, *non-speaking?*)
Six BARBARIANS (ant.5, *non-speaking*; two reappear in ant.7)
Five HOGS (ant.6, *non-speaking*; two reappear in ant.7)
HARMONY, a female figure
A CHORUS of eight singers attending Harmony (sing collectively)
The fourteen INFLUENCES of the stars, seven male and seven female (*non-speaking*)
HEROIC VIRTUE, highest of the eight spheres
The other seven SPHERES (only speak collectively)
Fourteen STARS attending Divine Beauty, the masquers, female figures (*non-speaking*)
DIVINE BEAUTY, the principal masquer, a female figure (*non-speaking*)
JUPITER, a god, father of Pallas; also called Jove
CUPID, a god
PALLAS, a goddess, Jupiter's daughter
A CHORUS of 35 musicians (possibly includes the twenty singers in the other choruses)

The ass is said to be teaching the apes to sing; all four may, therefore, be speaking parts, but no words are scripted for them.
It's not made explicit that the highest sphere is indeed Heroic Virtue, but there seems to be no other character it could be.

Speaking Parts: 53–77 (only 7 speak individually)
Allegorical Roles: 3 (interact with non-allegorical figures)

Stage Directions and Speech Prefixes
FUGITIVE FAVOURITE: *a young Gentleman* | [*Circe's*] *Lover* | *the Gentleman* | *the young Gentleman*, [*Circe's*] *Lover* (s.d.s); *The Fugitive Favourite* (s.p.s)
CIRCE: *Circe* (s.d.s and s.p.s)
NYMPHS: *the Nayades and Dryades* | [*Circe's*] *Nymphs* (s.d.s); [*Circe's*] *four Nymphs* (s.d.s and s.p.s)
CHORUS: *Chorus* (s.p.s)
INDIANS: *7 Indians* | *2 Indians* (s.d.s)
PAGODA: *1 Pagoda* (s.d.s)
HARE: *1 Hare* (s.d.s)
HOUNDS: *2 Hounds* (s.d.s)
LIONS: *4 Lions* | *2 Lions* (s.d.s)
APES: *3 Apes* | *2 Apes* (s.d.s)
ASS: *An Ass* | *1 Ass* (s.d.s)
BARBARIANS: *6 Barbarians* | *2 Barbarians* (s.d.s)
HOGS: *5 Hogs* | *2 Hogs* (s.d.s)
HARMONY: *Harmony* (s.d.s and s.p.s)
CHORUS: *the Chorus* (s.d.s); *Chorus* | [*Harmony's*] *Choir* (s.p.s)
INFLUENCES: *the fourteen Influences* (s.d.s)
HEROIC VIRTUE: *heroic virtue* | [*one of*] *the eight Spheres* (s.d.s); *The Highest Sphere* | *Highest Sphere* | *The eighth Sphere* (s.p.s)

SPHERES: [*seven of*] *the eight Spheres* (s.d.s); *The rest of the Spheres* (s.p.s)
STARS: *eight Stars* | *other glistering Stars* | *the eight Stars* [*Divine Beauty's*] *attendants* | *The Masquers* (s.d.s)
DIVINE BEAUTY: *divine Beauty* | [*one of*] *The Masquers* (s.d.s)
JUPITER: *Jove* (s.d.s); *Jupiter* (s.p.s)
CUPID: *Cupid* (s.d.s and s.p.s)
PALLAS: *Minerva* | *Palas* (s.d.s); *Pallas* (s.d.s and s.p.s)
CHORUS: *the great Chorus* (s.d.s)

OTHER CHARACTERS
Io, whom Jove turned into a cow (sc.5)

SETTING
Place: the Vale of Tempe

SOURCES
Narrative: Baltazar de Beaujoyeulx, *Balet comique de la Reine* (1581)
Design: Léonard Thiry, *Livre de la conqueste de la toison de l'or* (1563; proscenium); *Balet comique de la Reine* (1581; Divine Beauty); Cesare Ripa, *Iconologia* (1593, repr. 1611; Harmony); Giulio Parigi, *Il giudizio di Paride* (1608; Vale of Tempe; Jupiter in Heaven); Matthias Greuter, *Il giuoco del ponte* (1608; Indians, Lions); Jacques Callot, *Seascape* (early seventeenth century; haven and citadel)

LANGUAGE
English

FORM
Metre: pentameter
Rhyme: couplets; some blank verse
Lines (Spoken): 141
Lines (Written): 470

STAGING
Stage: mentioned (sc.2, desc.)
Above: characters descend on clouds, which go back up empty (sc.4, desc.); Jupiter hovers and ascends on an eagle (sc.5, desc.); Cupid flies (sc.5, desc.)
Audience: characters approach the King's state (sc.1, 3, desc.); the King (and Queen) are mentioned (sc.4–5); the masquers probably dance with members of the audience in the revels (sc.5, implicit). A number of characters are placed with the audience once their parts are finished and effectively join them in watching the rest of the masque: the Fugitive Favourite lies at the foot of the lords' seats (sc.1, desc.); the Influences are seated beside the lords and ladies (sc.3, desc.); Divine Beauty is seated under the King's state (sc.4, desc.).

The use of the audience to accommodate actors who are no longer needed, developing the dramaturgy of *Albion's Triumph* (**2353**), was probably adopted as a technique of space management in a masque with an unusually large cast.

MUSIC
Music: music of the spheres (sc.4, desc.)
On-Stage Music: lutes (sc.2, desc.; accompanying Song 1)
Songs:
1: 'Dissembling traitor, now I see the cause', sc.2, Circe and Nymphs, in parts, 21 lines, with lute accompaniment;
2: 'Not as myself, but as the brightest star', sc.3, Harmony and Chorus, in parts, 23 lines;
3: 'How rich is earth and poor the skies', sc.4, Harmony, Heroic Virtue, and the other Spheres, in parts, 18 lines.

Other Singing: the Ass teaches the Apes prick-song (sc.2, desc.)
Dance: Harmony and the Chorus dance a saraband (sc.3, desc.); the Influences dance (sc.3, desc.); masquers' entry dance (sc.4, desc.); masquers' main dance (sc.4, desc.); revels (sc.5, desc.)

Q seems to imply that Circe accompanies herself on the lute; the designs, however, equip the Chorus of Musicians with lutes, whereas Circe is carrying a magic wand and so does not have her hands free to play an instrument.

PROPS
Weapons: probably four swords (sc.2, J; lion design)
Musical Instruments: lutes (sc.2–3, desc., J)
Small Portable Objects: a handkerchief (sc.1, desc.); Circe's magic wand (sc.2, J); Jupiter's thunderbolt (sc.5, J)
Large Portable Objects: seating for one character (sc.2, desc.); seating in degrees for fourteen characters (sc.3, desc.); possibly a shield with a gorgon's head (sc.5, implicit); possibly a golden rod (sc.5, argument)
Scenery: a decorated border with large allegorical figures, and the Latin title displayed centrally (desc.); a curtain (desc.; raised to reveal the first scene); a valley with a prospect of arbours, marble pilasters, niches, statues, terms with women's faces, treetops with moving leaves (sc.1, 3, desc.; the far part opens to reveal the next scene); a hill and marble-walled palace with an open terrace, stair, and cypress trees (sc.2, desc.); an eastern sky with a landscape and sea in the distance, haven and citadel on one side and rocky crags on the other (sc.4, desc.; *design drawing survives*); a cloud, descending on a chain (sc.4, desc.; carries eight characters); two other clouds (sc.4, desc.; carry eight and six characters respectively); a large cloud (sc.4, desc.; descends slowly; carries at least three characters in a chariot); a golden chariot (sc.4, desc.); a shady wood with heavens, which close (sc.5, desc.; *design drawing survives*); an eagle (sc.5, desc.; big enough to carry an actor; *design drawing survives*)
Miscellaneous: water (sc.1, 3, desc.)

COSTUMES AND MAKE-UP
FUGITIVE FAVOURITE: a white satin doublet; carnation satin breeches; a carnation satin cloak lined with carnation plush and trimmed with silver lace; silk stockings of pearl colour; white shoes with carnation roses; carnation garters; a hat with a feather; a falling band with lace 'of the newest fashion'; gloves; a girdle; points (sc.1, F)
CIRCE: headgear with tinsel puffs (sc.2, J); *three design drawings survive*
CHORUS (MUSICIANS): head-dresses and skirted garments (sc.2–3, J); *two design drawings survive, including an alternative head-dress*
INDIANS: olive flesh-coloured skin-coats; feathers; scalloped gold tinsel collars (sc.2, J); *two design drawings survive*
PAGODA: a head-dress; black wings; long fingernails; white and blue leggings; gold shoes (sc.2, J); *design drawing survives*
LIONS: head masks with manes; bases (sc.2, J); *design drawing survives*
APES: masks and hairy skin-coats (sc.2, J); *design drawing survives*
ASS: a mask, ruff, and cape (sc.2, J); *design drawing survives*
BARBARIANS: turbans (sc.2, J); *two design drawings survive*
HOGS: masks, black and yellow breeches (sc.2, J); *design drawing survives*
HARMONY: a gown with tight bodice, sleeves, and tiered skirt; a head-dress (sc.3–4, J); *three design drawings survive*
CHORUS (SINGERS): head-dresses; shoes (sc.3–4, J); *two design drawings survive*
MALE INFLUENCES: plumed head-dresses; ruffs (sc.3–4, J); *three design drawings survive*
FEMALE INFLUENCES: white satin garments with embroidered, scalloped decoration in white taffeta; bands decorated with lace; plumed head-dresses; petticoats; carnation silk stockings; embroidered satin shoes with silk roses (sc.3, S); *four design drawings survive*
SPHERES: rich habits (sc.4, desc.)
STARS: watchet satin gowns embroidered and embossed with silver stars; crowns of stars with small sleeves embroidered with Os; falls of white feathers (sc.4, desc./D); at least two of the performers wore plain silk stockings (D); *three design drawings survive*
DIVINE BEAUTY: a watchet satin gown embroidered and embossed with silver stars; a crown of stars with small falls of white feathers (sc.4, desc.); a mask; watchet sleeves lined with pink, and two other pairs of large linen cambric sleeves; a gorget embroidered with silver (D); *three design drawings survive, including one for an alternate head-dress*
JUPITER: a head-dress (sc.5, J); *design drawing survives*
PALLAS: possibly armour (sc.5, implicit)
Miscellaneous: An unknown character, perhaps Divine Beauty, wore a silver lace girdle, with pink lace around it and a deep, buttoned lace at the ends. Three characters (other than Divine Beauty) wore gorgets

embroidered with silver. Jeffery Hudson's character wore garters and roses, upper gloves, and white gloves underneath them. Cloth used in making some costumes included cambric and lawn. At least five characters wore farthingales. (D) A rejected design drawing for a wolf survives.

EARLY STAGE HISTORY
Scheduling: At some stage it was apparently intended that the masque should be performed soon after the King's (*Albion's Triumph*, 2353), but it was decided to delay it because the Queen had an eye infection; by Tuesday 20 December 1631, it was being planned for Shrovetide. The Queen reportedly wanted the performance to be rescheduled for Shrove Sunday (12 February), but the King had taken against Sunday masquing and insisted that it should be the Tuesday.

Rehearsals: Rehearsals had begun by Monday 12 December 1631. The Queen and her ladies were said on Thursday 2 February to be rehearsing twice a week, and on Friday 3 February to be doing so daily.

Costume Making: On Thursday 26 January, George Gellin made two calico patterns for gowns, which were delivered to the Queen by Inigo Jones. On Saturday 4 February, Peter le Huc prepared two sets of calico patterns for the Influences' costumes; this work was commissioned by Susan Feilding, Countess of Denbigh. The Great Wardrobe was ordered to provide Thomas Killigrew's costume by a warrant dated Wednesday 8 February. On Thursday 9 February, Anna Henshawe delivered silks for three gowns. On Monday 13 February, Charles Gentile embroidered costumes for Divine Beauty and two of the Stars.

Preparation of Venue: The carpenters Ralph Brice and John Davenport were paid £10 for supervising preparations for this masque and *Albion's Triumph* (2353). Scaffolds had been erected in the Banqueting House by Sunday 29 January.

Performance: on Tuesday 14 February 1632 (Shrove Tuesday) at Whitehall Palace, probably in the Banqueting House (but records are contradictory). The performance began in the evening and lasted all night. The cast was said to be larger than that of any previous masque, and included: Thomas Killigrew (Fugitive Favourite); Madam Coniack [possibly Elizabeth Coignet] (Circe); Mrs Shepherd [possibly Anne Sheppard] (Harmony); Nicholas Lanier (Highest Sphere); Queen Henrietta Maria (Divine Beauty); Charles Cavendish; Lady Diana Cecil; Lady Elizabeth Cecil; Lady Alice Egerton; John Egerton, Lord Ellesmere; Lady Elizabeth Feilding; Lady Elizabeth Grey of Stamford; Thomas, Lord Grey of Groby; Lord Charles Herbert; Philip Herbert; Lady Frances Howard of Berkshire; Henry Howard of Berkshire; Robert, Lord Rich of Holland; Lady Mary Villiers (Influences); Lucy Hay, Countess of Carlisle; Anne Sophia Dormer, Countess of Carnarvon; Ann Blount, Countess of Newport; Beatrice de Vere, Countess of Oxford; Lady Anne Cavendish; Lady Katherine Egerton; Lady Anne Feilding; Lady [Frances?] Howard; Lady Anne Russell; Lady Mary Russell; Mrs Sophia Carew; Mrs Victoria Cary; Mrs Paget; Mrs Anne Weston (Stars); Jeffery Hudson. The masque was conceived and designed by Inigo Jones; the music may have been composed by Nicholas Lanier. The audience included: King Charles I; Sir John Finet; probably Giovanni Soranzo (outgoing Venetian Ambassador); François du Val, Marquis of Fontenay-Mareuil (French Ambassador); Alessandro-Cesare di Scaglia (Savoy Agent). No ambassadors were formally invited, but they came privately; Vicenzo Gussoni (the new Venetian Ambassador) made arrangements for himself and his secretary to be present, but excused himself on the morning before the performance; Juan de Necolalde (Spanish Agent) also excused himself on grounds of protocol.

Production Finance and Expenses
Edmund Taverner was paid £800 towards the expenses by a warrant dated either Monday 23 or Monday 30 January; a further £800 was made available by a warrant dated Tuesday 7 February, and was paid in two instalments of £400 each on Tuesday 7 and Friday 10 February. It was commented at the time that the season's two masques—the other being *Albion's Triumph* (2353)—were exceptionally costly.

Works: The preparation of the Banqueting House for both masques cost a total of £455.12s.9½d.

Costumes (Queen): The Queen paid for her own gown and those worn by Sophia Carew and Victoria Cary, and for some other costumes. The payments were mainly made in May 1633, and totalled £283.15s.10d; a saving of £79.14s.7d was made by unilaterally reducing the tradesmen's bills. The milliner Humphrey Bradborne supplied a girdle, and was paid £1.10s (16s less than billed) on Saturday 4 May. The hosier John Buckner supplied two pairs of stockings for the Stars and was paid £3 (6s less than billed) on Tuesday 7 May. On the same day, the feather-maker Peter Lermitt was paid £5.10s (half the sum billed) for eleven falls of white feathers. The tailor George Gellin made gown patterns and was paid £2.4s (10s less than billed) on Thursday 9 May. Anna Henshawe supplied silks and was paid £4.14s.10d (7s.4d less than billed) on Saturday 11 May. On the same day, the linen-draper Gilbert Ward was paid for the following: watchet (£1.9s.4d); fine cambric (£4, 16s less than billed); lawn (£2, 15s less than billed); cambric (£3.18s; 17s.3d less than billed). On Sunday 12 May, the brusher Hugh Pope was paid for the following: sticking silver stars on costumes (£5); making garters and gloves for Jeffery Hudson (£1); other services (£12). John Ager supplied five farthingales, and was paid £7.10s (£2 less than billed) on Monday 13 May 1633. On Wednesday 15 May, the mercer Richard Miller was paid for materials used for the following performers' costumes: the Queen (£21.5s.6d, 16s less than billed); Sophia Carew (£17.15s.6d, 6s less than billed); Victoria Cary (£17.15s.6d, 6s less than billed); and a bag to carry the

Queen's mask (12s.6d). On Friday 24 May, Charles Gentile was paid for embroidering the following costumes: Divine Beauty's gown (£50, £20 less than billed); Stars' gowns (£100, £40 less than billed); four gorgets (£5.10s, £2.10s less than billed); also for gluing and cutting bases and jackets (£4, £3.1s less than billed). Peter le Huc was not paid until Monday 20 March 1637, when he received the following sums for the patterns he had made: male Influences (£6.13s.4d); female Influences (£6.7s.4d).

See also **2369** for a further payment which might have been for this masque.

Costumes (Private): William Cecil, 2nd Earl of Salisbury, paid a total of £46.19s.9d for the costumes worn by his daughters, Diana and Elizabeth Cecil, comprising the following materials and services: white satin (£11.1s.6d); white calico to line petticoats (13s); white taffeta for scallops (19s.6d); two rolls for petticoats (£1.10s); broad and narrow bone-lace for bands (£3); two feathers for head-dresses (£1.4s); two chains (10s); two pairs of carnation silk stockings (£1.15s); two pairs of embroidered satin shoes (5s.6d); two whalebone busks (2s); fine holland set with Os to make sleeves (16s.7d); two pairs of silk roses (14s.6d); Richard Hubbard the embroiderer, for embroidering the garments all over with Os (£19) and drawing and cutting scallops (£2.19s); Paul Parre the tailor, for making the garments (£1.18s.2d); Mrs [Blanche?] Brown, for two head-dressings (£1).

Miscellaneous (Private): William Cecil, 2nd Earl of Salisbury, paid a gratuity of 2s.6d to the Countess of Carnarvon's coachman.

McGee-Meagher identify Salisbury's payment to the coachman as pertaining to **2384**, but that was not a 'masque at Whitehall' as specified. The payment is recorded in the Salisbury accounts four entries after one dated 26 September 1632; but there was no Whitehall masque in late September, right at the end of the period covered by the accounts, and in any event the dated entries do not appear in strict chronological order.

EARLY TEXTUAL HISTORY

1632: **Q** printed (before Saturday 24 March) by Augustine Matthews for Robert Allot and George Baker; collation A–C⁴, 12 leaves. Parts of the book were reset (in some cases up to six times) during printing; some of the changes must have been made at the behest of Inigo Jones, Aurelian Townshend, or some other person responsible for the masque.

1632: In February, John Newdigate bought a copy.

1632: On Friday 20 July, Townshend was paid £50 for writing the masque, by a warrant dated Monday 9 July.

1684: Nicholas Cox (Manciple of St Edmund Hall, Oxford) had a copy of Q in his bookshop. It had probably been previously owned by Gerard Langbaine, and appears on a list compiled by Anthony Wood on Saturday 13 December.

EDITIONS
E. K. Chambers, *Aurelian Townshend's Poems and Masks* (Oxford, 1912), 79–100.
Orgel and Strong, ii. 478–503.
Cedric Brown, in Aurelian Townshend, *The Poems and Masques* (Reading, 1983), 93–108.
David Lindley, in *Court Masques* (Oxford, 1995), 155–65.

REFERENCES
Annals 1632; Ashbee, iii. 64; Bentley, v. 1229–30; Thomas Birch (ed.), *The Court and Times of Charles I* (London, 1848), ii. 158; Bodleian, MS Wood E. 4, art. 1, p. 105; Karen Britland, *Drama at the Courts of Queen Henrietta Maria* (Cambridge, 2006), 90–110; Butler, 156–60, 372; *Cal. Dom. 1631-3*, 207, 270; *Cal. Ven. 1629-32*, 592–3; Greg 454; Hazlitt, 224; HMC Salisbury, xxii. 267; Vivienne Larminie, *Wealth, Kinship and Culture* (Woodbridge, 1995), 201; David Lindley (ed.), *The Court Masque* (Manchester, 1984), 158–9, 161; Loomie, 120–2; McGee-Meagher 1625–34, 63–7; MSC 2.3, 356–8; MSC 10, 42–3; *N&Q* 207 (1962), 146–7; *N&Q* 242 (1997), 533; John Peacock, *The Stage Designs of Inigo Jones* (Cambridge, 1995), 247–9; REED: Lincolnshire, 352; Reyher, 511–12, 530; Steele, 241; *Theatre Survey* 20 (1979), 16–17.

2360. Love's Sacrifice

TEXT
Printed in 1633 (STC 11164), from an authorial fair copy; there are lacunae in 1.1 and 5.1, the former possibly the result of censorship.

GENRE
tragedy
Contemporary: tragedy (t.p.); work (ded.)

TITLE
Performed/Printed: *Love's Sacrifice*

AUTHOR
John Ford

DATE
Limits: 1626–33
Best Guess: 1632

As with many of Ford's plays, the dating depends on biographical imponderables concerning his relationship with theatre companies and other calls on his time. The play is imaginatively and lexically close to *'Tis Pity She's a Whore* (**2329**), which seems to have been the 'first fruits' of the cessation of his association with the King's Men, and so the first he wrote for his new clients, Queen Henrietta's Men. *Love's Sacrifice* may therefore have been the second, in which case it was written in either 1631 or 1632. Deciding between the two depends on two chicken-and-egg cases of possible indebtedness.

Moore, who demonstrates the flimsiness of the positive evidence in favour of 1632, believes that a passage in 5.1 was echoed by Shirley in *Love's Cruelty* (**2349**), which was licensed in November 1631. The lines do not seem very similar to me, with only the word 'sacrifice' in common, and even if there is intertextual traffic, I do not know how the direction might be determined. But the possibility needs to be taken seriously in view of the other evidence of Ford's influence on Shirley in 1631, in both *Love's Cruelty* and *The Duke* (**2339**). If *Love's Sacrifice* was another source of that influence, it would need to have been completed and staged (or otherwise encountered by Shirley) by no later than the early autumn of 1631. It is also worth noting the shared form of the two titles, one of which might accordingly be taken as a comment on the other; but again, it is hard to say which is on which side of the relationship.

The phrase 'love's sacrifice' also appears in Aurelian Townshend's 1632 court masque, *Albion's Triumph* (**2353**). This and Ford's play are its two earliest traceable appearances in English literature; in all likelihood, one borrowed from the other. In this case there is some basis on which to hypothesize the direction of the influence. In *Albion's Triumph*, the masquers, among them the King, are shot with Cupid's arrows and presented to the Queen, summoned in Song 4 with the refrain 'Come down, Love's sacrifice' at the end of each of the three stanzas. Cupid is also known as Love, so the usage is specific to the fictive context of the masque, whereas it is only generalized as a title of the play. Moreover, it is unlikely that Townshend would have applied the phrase to the King and his marriage if there was a risk that it might have carried a recognizable echo from the play. Conversely, the phrase's long-term currency in the title of the play would quickly supersede any memory of its use in a one-off elite performance. This means that, in all likelihood, *Love's Sacrifice* was not completed until 1632, but not necessarily very far into the year: *Albion's Triumph* became available, for those who had not seen the court performance on 8 January, in a printed edition with a title page dated 1631 (i.e. by 24 March 1632).

This conclusion brings with it a corollary: no more than a year passed between the play's theatrical premiere and its appearance in print. This is not necessarily a problem. Queen Henrietta's Men were careful about the publication of their plays—this was one of the restrictions imposed in their 1635 contract with Richard Brome—but in early 1633 there seems to have been a temporary relaxation of this policy. On the same day that *Love's Sacrifice* was entered in the Stationers' Register, *The Beauties* (**2396**) was licensed for the stage; it was released to the printer just under two months later.

ORIGINAL PRODUCTION
Queen Henrietta's Men at the Cockpit

PLOT
D'Avolos induces Roseilli to leave court by inventing a ducal order of banishment, then intervenes in a developing love-quadrangle: the Duke has recently married Bianca, who is loved by Fernando, who in turn is loved by Fiormonda. Bianca repeatedly refuses to hear Fernando's protestations, but later visits him in bed while the Duke is away hunting, and admits that she reciprocates his love. However, he will not take dishonourable advantage of the situation, and adultery does not occur. D'Avolos learns of their mutual attraction, and tells Fiormonda. With Fernando's connivance, Roseilli returns to court disguised as a fool, and is placed in Fiormonda's household.

Ferentes woos three women—Colona, Julia, and old Morona—and under promise of marriage gets each of them pregnant; he then refuses to honour his word to any of them. Fernando proposes to welcome Bianca's uncle to court with a masque, but the jilted women use it as a front for revenge, and kill Ferentes during the performance. They are bailed into male custody and eventually pardoned, but old Mauruccio, the only other masquer deemed criminally responsible, is imprisoned. Bianca and Fernando plead for his release, which is granted after Morona agrees to marry him, but the couple are then banished.

D'Avolos casually draws the Duke's attention to Bianca's solicitude towards Fernando, and works with Fiormonda to foster his jealousy: they insinuate that Ferentes was killed to silence him, but the Duke asks for ocular proof of adultery. Fiormonda gives Fernando a chance to accept her love in preference to Bianca's, but his refusal confirms her vindictiveness; Roseilli hears her plotting against the favourite. The Duke pretends to leave court, then returns to find Fernando and Bianca together. Fernando is arrested, and the Duke kills Bianca. Fernando affirms Bianca's chastity, and the penitent Duke visits her tomb. Inside he finds Fernando in a winding sheet, who rebukes the Duke and poisons himself; the Duke stabs himself in remorse. Having learned Roseilli's true identity, Fiormonda bestows the dukedom on him by choosing him as her husband. After accepting, he demands that she live out the rest of her life in repentance and married celibacy. D'Avolos is imprisoned and starved to death.

SCENE DESIGNATION
1.1–2, 2.1–4, 3.1–4, 4.1–2, 5.1–3 (act-division Q, scene-division Revels)

ROLES
Lord ROSEILLI, a young nobleman of the house of Lesui, Petruccio and Fernando's kinsman; later poses as a 'natural' (mentally handicapped) fool; ultimately Duke of Pavia and Fiormonda's husband
Roderico D'AVOLOS, secretary to the Duke and state
Lord FERNANDO, the Duke's favourite, Petruccio's nephew, Colona's cousin, Roseilli's kinsman; a young man
Lord PETRUCCIO, a counsellor of state, Fernando's uncle, Colona's father, Roseilli's kinsman
Philippo Caraffa, DUKE of Pavia; Bianca's husband, Fiormonda's brother
BIANCA, Duchess of Pavia; the Duke's wife, the Abbot's niece; a young woman
Lady FIORMONDA, a marquess, the Duke's sister, a widow; ultimately Duchess of Pavia and Roseilli's wife
Lord NIBRASSA, a counsellor of state, Julia's father; also (ignorantly) called Lord Narbassa

Lord FERENTES, a young man; later a father of bastards
JULIA, Nibrassa's daughter, Fiormonda's servant; a young woman; later the mother of one of Ferentes's bastards
COLONA, Petruccio's daughter, Fernando's cousin; a young woman; later the mother of one of Ferentes's bastards
Lord MAURUCCIO, an old man, 60 years old; later Morona's husband
GIACOPO, Mauruccio's servant
LORDS of the court (2.1, *non-speaking*, but they laugh)
LADIES of the court (2.1, *non-speaking*, but they laugh)
TORCHBEARERS attending Bianca (2.3, *non-speaking*)
Madam MORONA, an old lady and widow; 46 years old; later the mother of one of Ferentes's bastards; later still Mauruccio's wife
Three or four TORCHBEARERS attending the Duke (3.3–4, *non-speaking*)
Two FRIARS attending the Abbot (3.3, 5.3; speak collectively)
Paulo Baglione, ABBOT of Monaco, Bianca's uncle; later probably a cardinal; also called Paul
ATTENDANTS on the Abbot (3.3, *non-speaking*)
A CHOIR of singers (3.3)
A VOICE (3.4, *within*)
The Duke's GUARD (5.1, 5.3; speak collectively)
A SERVANT (5.3)
Four TORCHBEARERS (5.3; speak collectively)

Speaking Parts: 22

Stage Directions and Speech Prefixes
ROSEILLI: *Roseilli* | [one of] *the men* (s.d.s); *Ros<eilli>* (s.p.s); *Roseilli, A young Nobleman* (d.p.)
D'AVOLOS: *Roderico D'avolos* | *D'avolos* (s.d.s); *R<oderico> D<'avolos>* (s.p.s); *D'avolos, Secretary to the Duke* (d.p.)
FERNANDO: *Fernando* | [one of the] *Lords* (s.d.s); *Fer<nando>* (s.p.s); *Fernando, Favourite to the Duke* (d.p.)
PETRUCCIO: *Petruchio* (s.d.s); *Petr<uchio>* (s.p.s); *Petruchio,* [one of] *Two Counsellors of State* (d.p.)
DUKE: *Duke* (s.d.s and s.p.s); *the Duke | Caraffa* (s.d.s); *Phillippo Caraffa, Duke of Pavy* (d.p.)
BIANCA: *Biancha* | [one of the] *Ladies | Duchess* (s.d.s); *Bian<cha>* (s.p.s); *Biancha, The Duchess* (d.p.)
FIORMONDA: *Fiormonda* | [one of the] *Ladies* (s.d.s); *Fior<monda>* (s.p.s); *Fiormonda, The Duke's Sister* (d.p.)
NIBRASSA: *Nibrassa* (s.d.s); *Nibr<assa>* (s.p.s); *Nibrassa,* [one of] *Two Counsellors of State* (d.p.)
FERENTES: *Ferentes* | [one of] *the men* (s.d.s); *Feren<tes>* (s.p.s); *Ferentes, A wanton Courtier* (d.p.)
JULIA: *Julia* | [one of] *the women* (s.d.s); *Jul<ia>* (s.p.s); *Julia, Daughter to Nibrassa* (d.p.)
COLONA: *Colona* (s.d.s and s.p.s); [one of] *the women* (s.d.s); *Colona, Daughter to Petruchio* (d.p.)
MAURUCCIO: *Maurucio* | [one of] *the men* (s.d.s); *Mau<rucio>* (s.p.s); *Maurucio, An old Antic* (d.p.)

GIACOPO: *Giacopo* (s.d.s); *Gia<copo>* (s.p.s); *Giacopo, servant to Maurucio* (d.p.)
LORDS: *Lords* (s.d.s)
LADIES: *Ladies* (s.d.s)
TORCHBEARERS: *Attendants* (d.p.)
MORONA: *Morona* | [one of] *the women* (s.d.s); *Mor<ona>* (s.p.s); *Morona, an old Lady* (s.d.s and d.p.)
TORCHBEARERS: *3 or 4* | *some* (s.d.s); *Attendants* (d.p.)
FRIARS: *two Friars* (s.d.s)
ABBOT: *the Abbot* (s.d.s); *Abbot* (s.d.s and s.p.s); *Paulo Baglione, Uncle to the Duchess* (d.p.)
ATTENDANTS: *Attendants* (s.d.s and d.p.)
CHOIR: *the Choir* (s.d.s)
VOICE: *Within* (s.p.s)
GUARD: *a Guard* | *guard* (s.d.s)
SERVANT: *Servant* (s.d.s and s.p.s)
TORCHBEARERS: *four* (s.d.s); *Attendants* (d.p.)

OTHER CHARACTERS
Bianca's father, a Milanese gentleman (1.1, 4.1)
The Duke of Milan (1.1)
Fiormonda's dead husband, a prince (1.1–2)
Don Pedro de Toledo, Roseilli's kinsman (1.2)
Alphonso Trinultio, a painter (2.2)
Fiormonda's gentlemen (2.2)
Julia's dead mother (3.1)
The Pope (3.2, 3.4)
The conclave of cardinals (3.2)
The Duke of Brabant (3.2)
The Archbishop of Mainz (3.2)
Knights and ladies of the court of Brabant, who performed an antic (3.2)
Colona's new-born bastard child (3.4; represented on stage by a prop)
Julia's new-born bastard child (3.4, 4.2; represented on stage by a prop)
Morona's new-born bastard child (3.4, 4.1; represented on stage by a prop)
The Duke's ancestors, dukes of Pavia (4.1)
Lorenzo, Duke of Pavia, dead father of the Duke and Fiormonda (4.1)

SETTING
Period: sixteenth or seventeenth century, during or after the professional ascendancy of Michelangelo (died 1564)
Time-Scheme: 2.3–4 take place on the same night; at least two days pass between 2.1 and 3.2; 3.3 takes place the day after 3.2; the Abbot journeys from Pavia to Rome and back between 3.4 and 5.2; 5.1–2 take place at night
Place: Pavia

Geography
Pavia: the castle; the college church
Italy: Milan; Benevento; Rome; Naples; Lucca

Monaco
Spain: Seville; Toledo
[*The Low Countries*]: Flanders; Brussels; Brabant
England
Europe: France; Mainz
Turkey
[*Africa*]: Barbary; Tangier (?)
India

SOURCES
Narrative: William Shakespeare, *The Moor of Venice* (**1437**; jealousy plot); Sir Philip Sidney, *Arcadia* (written c. 1580, printed 1590, repr. 1629; Ferentes plot); John Marston, *Antonio and Mellida* (**1218**; 2.1); John Webster, *The Duchess of Malfi* (**1726**; 1.2); John Fletcher, *Father's Own Son* (**1788**; 2.4); John Ford, *The Queen* (**2224**; 5.3); Ford may also have drawn aspects of the plot from a MS account of a murder committed by Carlo Gesualdo in Naples in 1590.
Verbal: Bible: Jeremiah 32.19 (1.1); *The Squire of Low Degree* (fifteenth century; 4.1); Christopher Marlowe, *Tamburlaine* (**784**; 2.1); Robert Greene, *Orlando* (**876**; 2.1); William Shakespeare, *2 Henry IV* (**1083**; 4.1); John Webster, *The White Devil* (**1689**; 3.4); John Ford, *The Queen* (**2224**; 5.1); probably Aurelian Townshend, *Albion's Triumph* (**2353**; title)

LANGUAGE
English
Latin: 3 words (1.2, 3.1; Ferentes, Nibrassa)
Italian: 1 word (2.3; D'Avolos)
Gibberish: When posing as the fool, Roseilli talks semi-intelligible nonsense (2.2, 3.2, 4.2).

In 3.2, it is explicitly pointed out that the characters understand themselves to be speaking in Italian.

FORM
Metre: pentameter and prose
Rhyme: blank verse; some couplets and ABAB
Act-Division: 5 acts
Dumb Show: 3.3 (compresses action)
Lines (Spoken): 2,511 (1,650 verse, 861 prose)
Lines (Written): 2,861

STAGING
Doors: two characters exit 'sundry ways' (2.3, s.d.); groups enter at two doors (3.3, s.d.), and enter and exit at several doors (3.4, s.d.).
Discovery Space: curtained (2.4, 5.1, s.d.); Fernando is discovered in bed (2.4, s.d.); Fernando and Bianca are discovered at a table (5.1, s.d.); set with a tomb (5.3, s.d.).
Stage: characters stand at different ends of the stage (3.4, s.d.).
Within: music (3.3, implicit); speech (3.4, s.d.; 5.1, implicit)
Above: characters appear above (2.1, 5.1, s.d.; at least five simultaneously)

Miscellaneous: No provision is made to remove Bianca's dead body at the end of 5.1 (so she probably dies in the discovery space).

MUSIC
Music: music within (3.3, s.d.); loud music (3.3, s.d.); unspecified music (3.4, implicit; accompanying the masque); 'a sad sound of soft music' (5.3, s.d.)
Singing: a choir sings (3.3, s.d.)
Dance: the masquers dance (3.4, s.d.)

PROPS
Lighting: lights (2.3, 3.4, s.d.); a candle (2.4, s.d.); three or four torches (3.3, s.d.); four torches (5.3, s.d.)
Weapons: three blade weapons (3.4, implicit); the Duke's sword (4.2, dialogue; 5.1–2, s.d.); Fernando's sword (4.2, dialogue); D'Avolos's sword (5.1, implicit); the Duke's poniard (5.1–2, s.d.; 5.3, implicit); Nibrassa's old sword (5.2, s.d.)
Money: gold (4.1, dialogue)
Food and Drink: a phial of poison (5.3, s.d.; drunk on stage)
Small Portable Objects: a looking-glass (2.1, s.d.); scissors or a razor (2.1, implicit); possibly a brush (2.1, implicit); a letter (2.2, dialogue); two pictures (2.2, s.d.); a toothpick (2.2, dialogue); a chessboard (2.3, s.d.) and pieces (implicit); a handkerchief (3.2, dialogue); napkins (3.4, s.d.)
Large Portable Objects: a table (2.3, 5.1, s.d.); probably seating for two characters (2.3, implicit); three babies (3.4, s.d.); a cushion (5.1, s.d.)
Scenery: curtains (2.4, 5.1, s.d.); a bed (2.4, s.d.); a tomb (5.3, s.d.)
Miscellaneous: blood (1.2, 5.1, dialogue; 5.2, s.d.)

COSTUMES AND MAKE-UP
ROSEILLI: dressed as a fool (2.2, 3.2, s.d.; 4.2, implicit); a mask (3.4, implicit)
FERNANDO: a winding sheet (5.3, s.d.; covers him completely except for his face)
DUKE: an untrimmed beard (dialogue); a scabbard (4.2, 5.1, implicit); 'dressed like a hangman' (5.1, dialogue; i.e. perhaps hooded); a dagger sheath (5.1, implicit); mourning clothes (5.3, s.d.)
BIANCA: a pale complexion (implicit); her hair about her ears (2.4, s.d.); a night-mantle (2.4, s.d.); night attire (5.1, s.d.)
FIORMONDA: a ring (1.2, dialogue; removed on stage)
FERENTES: a mask (3.4, s.d.; removed on stage)
JULIA and COLONA: 'odd shapes' (3.4, s.d.), including masks (implicit)
MAURUCCIO: a beard (s.d.); silver hair (dialogue); a mask (3.4, implicit); poor rags (4.1, s.d.)
MORONA: an 'odd shape' (3.4, s.d.), including a mask (implicit)

EARLY STAGE HISTORY
Performed by Queen Henrietta's Men at the Cockpit by 1633, and 'received generally well'.

1639: The play was in the repertory of the King's and Queen's Young Company (Beeston's Boys) at the Cockpit. On Saturday 10 August, Philip Herbert, 4th Earl of Pembroke (Lord Chamberlain) issued an order restraining performances by other companies of this and 44 other plays.

EARLY TEXTUAL HISTORY
1633: entered in the Stationers' Register to Hugh Beeston on Monday 21 January; entry names author. Sir Henry Herbert had licensed the book for publication.

1633: **Q** printed by John Beale for Hugh Beeston; collation π1 A² B–K⁴ L⁴ (–L4), 42 leaves; title page names acting company and playhouse; authorial dedication to John Ford of Gray's Inn; commendatory verses by James Shirley; list of roles.

Mid-seventeenth century (before 1677): a copy of Q was owned by Frances Wolfreston, who wrote a detailed plot summary on her copy.

1652: a copy of Q was bound with six other Ford quartos, with a specially printed title page: *Comedies, tragi-comedies, & tragaedies*; the book was owned by Walter Chetwynd of Ingestre, Staffordshire. The other plays were *The Lover's Melancholy* (**2259**), *The Broken Heart* (**2281**), *'Tis Pity She's a Whore* (**2329**), *Perkin Warbeck* (**2399**), *The Fancies* (**2528**), and *The Lady's Trial* (**2617**).

1655: *The English Treasury of Wit and Language* entered in the Stationers' Register to Humphrey Moseley on Tuesday 16 January.

1655: four extracts (from 1.2, 2.3, 4.1–2) included in John Cotgrave's *The English Treasury of Wit and Language*, sigs. C3ʳ, E8ᵛ, F8ʳ, L8ʳ; printed for Humphrey Moseley.

1656: *The English Parnassus* entered to Evan Tyler, Thomas Johnson, and Thomas Davies in the Stationers' Register on Wednesday 24 December.

1657: seven extracts (from 1.1–2, 2.1, 4.1, 5.1) included in Joshua Poole's *The English Parnassus*, sigs. Q7ʳ, R4ᵛ, 2D2ᵛ, 2I6ʳ, 2M6ʳ, 2S5ʳ; printed for Thomas Johnson.

1677: *The English Parnassus* reprinted by Henry Brome for Thomas Bassett and John Wright; the extracts now appear on sigs. Q3ʳ, Q8ᵛ, 2C6ᵛ, 2I2ʳ, 2M2ʳ, 2S1ʳ.

Mid- to late seventeenth century (before 1686): a copy was owned by William Cartwright.

Mid- to late seventeenth century (before 1689): a copy of Q was owned by Elizabeth Puckering.

1684: Nicholas Cox (Manciple of St Edmund Hall, Oxford) had a copy of Q in his bookshop. It had probably been previously owned by Gerard Langbaine, and appears on a list compiled by Anthony Wood on Saturday 13 December.

1690: a copy of Q was in the library at Petworth House.

EDITIONS
A. T. Moore, Revels Plays (Manchester, 2002).

Curtis Perry, in *Eros and Power in English Renaissance Drama* (Jefferson and London, 2008), 437–537.
Nigel Bawcutt, in *The Collected Works of John Ford*, gen. ed. Brian Vickers (Oxford, 2012–), vol. v.

REFERENCES
Annals 1632; Bawcutt C64; Bentley, iii. 451–3; Bodleian, MS Wood E. 4, art. 1, p. 13; Eyre & Rivington, i. 463, ii. 103; Charles R. Forker, *Skull Beneath the Skin* (Carbondale and Edwardsville, 1986), 494–5; Greg 478; Hazlitt, 143; E. A. J. Honigmann and Susan Brock (eds.), *Playhouse Wills, 1558–1642* (Manchester and New York, 1993), 241; *The Library*, 6th ser., 11 (1989), 204, 214; *The Library*, 6th ser., 14 (1992), 299–336; *The Library*, 7th ser., 1 (2000), 376; MSC 2.3, 389–90; *N&Q* 233 (1988), 66–7; *National Trust Year Book 1975–6* (London, [1976]), 62–4; *SP* 40 (1943), 186–203.

2361. Money is an Ass

TEXT
Printed in 1668 (Wing J1047), from prompt copy, possibly of an incompletely abbreviated or augmented version.

The prologue claims that the play is tailored for the eight available actors, presumably those named in the cast list printed in 1668. However, the Silver and Hammerhead sequence in 4.3 brings on four more characters, to no apparent purpose, when the eight actors are all already on stage; these four characters then seem to disappear in mid-scene. If the prologue is correct, then the Silver and Hammershin material must be an incomplete insertion; if not, the extant text may have been cut down from a longer version, and this scene incompletely deleted.

GENRE
comedy
Contemporary: play (prol.); comedy (t.p.)

TITLE
Printed: *Money is an Ass*
Contemporary: *Money's an Ass*; *Wealth Outwitted, or Money's an Ass*

AUTHOR
Thomas Jordan

DATE
Limits: 1628–35
Best Guess: 1632

The dating of the play rests squarely on Jordan's claim in the 1668 dedication that it was written and staged before he was 15 years old. The problem is that we do not know for sure when he was born. A Thomas Jordan was baptised in Clerkenwell on Monday 9 November 1614, but this would put the play no later than November 1629, producing an uncomfortably tight chronology, given that its likely original company, the King's

Revels, was formed in about October 1629 and did not then have a London playhouse to perform in. (They moved into Salisbury Court when it opened.) Conversely, Bentley supposes that Jordan must have been born in c. 1620, because in the mid-1630s he was cast as the title character's mother in *Messalina the Roman Empress* (**2472**), which would push the play to the other end of the limits. But it would not be impossible for a relatively older actor to play an older woman, and a younger Jordan would have been a prodigy indeed to have been entrusted with a literary contribution to a royal entertainment as early as 1636 (**2549**). David Kathman (in *ShS*) presents evidence that he claimed to be 48 years old in 1665, which would date his birth to c. 1617 and the play to 1631–2.

ORIGINAL PRODUCTION
King's Revels Company at the Fortune (or, if earlier or later, Salisbury Court)

PLOT
Featherbrain has gambled his way into penury, and is offended to learn that now Money and Credit don't want to know him. He plans to make fools of them as they pursue their love-lives. Clutch the usurer hopes to marry them to his daughters, and thereby cheat them out of their estates; he asks for the help of his servant Calumny, promising him marriage to the elder girl by way of reward. Money and Credit come wooing and secure the girls' agreement to the match, then leave on business.
   Featherbrain and his friend Penniless pose as servants, and come to Clutch's house bringing letters from their masters Money and Credit. Each contrives to be left alone with one of the daughters, who are successfully seduced away from their earlier marriage plans. Using funds arranged for them by the girls, the young men buy new clothes and lie their way into the company and confidence of Money and Credit, posing as the cavaliers Gold and Jewel. Clutch sees them all together and intervenes, assuming the newcomers are going to disrupt his scheme; but when he learns who they (supposedly) are, he thinks up a new stratagem. Money and Credit are persuaded to sign over their estates to him in return for his consent to marry the daughters, in the expectation that the property will revert to them on Clutch's death; the daughters will then withhold their consents and marry 'Gold and Jewel' instead.
   Calumny sees Featherbrain wooing Felixina, the elder daughter whom he covets for himself, and tells Money and Credit that their positions have been compromised. He induces them to claim that they have anticipated the marriage by already having sex with the girls; but when Featherbrain confronts Felixina with the accusation, she faints and thereby establishes her innocence. The girls tell their father that the slander has caused 'Gold and Jewel' to jilt them, throwing his plans off course. He accepts Felixina's proposal that he should settle on them, as marriage portions, half of the estates he has cozened from Money and Credit, and so attract back 'Gold and Jewel'. After confronting Money and Credit with their slanders, Featherstone and Penniless are confirmed as fiancés, whereupon they reveal their true penurious identities.

SCENE DESIGNATION
prol., 1.1–2, 2.1–3, 3.1–2, 4.1–3, 5.1–5 (Q is divided into acts and partially into scenes)

The stage is not clear at 4.2–3.

ROLES
NIGHT, the prologue
Master Frank FEATHERBRAIN, a prodigal young gentleman; poses as Money's servant, then adopts the alias Master Gold, a cavalier, Money's kinsman
Master MONEY, said to be old
Master CREDIT, Money's associate
Master CLUTCH, an old usurer, father of Felixina and Feminia, Hammerhead's kinsman
FELIXINA, Clutch's elder daughter, Feminia's sister; a young woman
FEMINIA, Clutch's younger daughter, Felixina's sister; also called Mistress Simper
Master CALUMNY, Clutch's servant; a bastard
Captain Ben PENNILESS, a prodigal soldier, Featherbrain's friend; also called Master Penniless; poses as Credit's servant, then adopts the alias Master Precious Jewel, a cavalier, Gold's brother
Master SILVER, a moneyer
Master HAMMERHEAD, a goldsmith, Clutch's kinsman; a married man
Silver's FIANCÉE
MISTRESS HAMMERHEAD, Hammerhead's wife

Speaking Parts: 13
Allegorical Roles: 4 (3 of them integrated with the non-allegorical characters)

Doubling
According to the prologue, the play was designed for a cast of eight actors; therefore the prologue itself must have been doubled with some other role. (All parts but Featherbrain are available for the purpose.) However, see TEXT.

Stage Directions and Speech Prefixes
NIGHT: *The Prologue* (heading); *Night* (s.d.s)
FEATHERBRAIN: *Mr Featherbrain* (s.d.s and d.p.); *Featherbrain* | *Frank Featherbrain* (s.d.s); *Feath<erbrain>* (s.p.s)
MONEY: *Money* (s.d.s and d.p.); *Mony* (s.d.s); *Mo<ney>* (s.p.s)
CREDIT: *Credit* (s.d.s and d.p.); *Cred<it>* (s.p.s)
CLUTCH: *Clutch* (s.d.s, s.p.s, and d.p.)
FELIXINA: *Felixina* (s.d.s and d.p.); [one of] *the Daughters* | [one of Clutch's] *two daughters* (s.d.s); *Felix<ina>* (s.p.s)

FEMINIA: *Feminia* (s.d.s and d.p.); [one of] the Daughters | [one of Clutch's] *two daughters* (s.d.s); *Fem<inia>* (s.p.s)
CALUMNY: *Callumney* (s.d.s and d.p.); *Calumny* | *Calumney* | *Callumny* (s.d.s); *Calum<ny>* | *Callum<ny>* (s.p.s)
PENNILESS: *Captain Penniless* (s.d.s and d.p.); *Captain Pennyless* | *Penniless* | *the Captain* (s.d.s); *Captain* (s.d.s and s.p.s)
SILVER: *Silver* (s.d.s and s.p.s); [one of] the men (s.d.s)
HAMMERHEAD: *Hammer-head* | [one of] the men (s.d.s); *Ham<mer-head>* (s.p.s)
FIANCÉE: [Silver's] *Wife* | [one of] the Women (s.d.s); *1 Woman* (s.p.s)
MISTRESS HAMMERHEAD: [Hammerhead's] *Wife* | [one of] the Women (s.d.s); *2 Woman* (s.p.s)

OTHER CHARACTERS
Featherbrain's former associates in his time of prosperity (1.1)
A young heir and a usurer, who have recently had dealings with Money (1.1)
Credit's mercer (1.1, 3.1)
Clutch's cooks (1.2)
Credit's creditors (2.1)
Master Vein (or Vain?), a young gentleman who caught Felixina's eye when he brought a mortgage to Clutch (2.2)
A gentleman, reputedly Calumny's father (2.3)
Calumny's mother (2.3)
City merchants, Credit's friends (3.1)
Penniless's father, said to be of the Malice family (3.1)
Penniless's mother, said to be of the Mischief family (3.1)
Suburban justices, Money's acquaintances (4.1)
Money's mother, of the Pecunia family (4.2)
Argent, Money's father (4.2)
Featherbrain's parents (4.2)
Lady Portion, Money's niece (4.2)
Beauty, Lady Portion's younger sister (4.2)
Money's younger brother, Lady Portion's father (4.2)
Calumny's kinsman, a bone-setter (4.2; possibly imaginary)

SETTING
Time-Scheme: 1.2 and 4.3 both end at dinner-time on different days
Place: London

Geography
London: Gray's Inn; St John's Street; the Exchange; Cheapside; the city walls; Bedlam
[*Middlesex*]: Islington
[*Iberia*]: River Tagus
Barbary
Arabia
New England

SOURCES
Verbal: Ovid, *Tristia* 1.6 (t.p. motto on the reissued Q; wrongly identified as Martial, *Epigrams*); William Shakespeare, *The Moor of Venice* (**1437**; 3.2); Thomas Heywood, *The Fair Maid of the West* (**1607**; 3.2); Ben Jonson, *The Devil is an Ass* (**1810**; title)
Works Mentioned: John Seton, *Dialectica* (1545; 5.3); Diego Ortúñez de Calahorra, Pedro de la Sierra, and Marcos Martínez, *Espejo de príncipes y caballeros* (1555–87; English tr., *The Mirror of Princely Deeds and Knighthood*, by Margaret Tyler, R. P., and L. A., 1578–99; 4.3); Christopher Marlowe, *Doctor Faustus* (**810**; 2.3); Christopher Marlowe and George Chapman, *Hero and Leander* (1593–8; 3.2); *De arte venerea* (5.3; imaginary work?)

LANGUAGE
English
Latin: 18 words (1.1, 2.1–2, 3.1, 4.2, 5.1, 5.3, 5.5; Featherbrain, Penniless, Feminia, Money)

FORM
Metre: prose; a little pentameter
Rhyme: couplets; a little blank verse
Prologue: 26 lines, in couplets, spoken by Night
Act-Division: 5 acts
Lines (Spoken): 1,742 (59 verse, 1,683 prose)
Lines (Written): 1,794

STAGING
Doors: characters enter two ways (2.1, s.d.)
Discovery Space: Calumny hides behind the arras (4.3, dialogue)
Within: speech (2.3, implicit)
Above: Calumny appears above 'in the music room' (4.2, s.d.); Clutch appears above (4.2, s.d.)
Miscellaneous: The prologue assumes that the performance takes place at night. Q includes a prompt warning for Calumny to appear above, ten lines before his entrance.

MUSIC
Singing: Penniless sings (2.1, 3.2, s.d.); Felixina sings (3.2, s.d.)

PROPS
Weapons: Featherbrain's sword (5.5, dialogue); probably Penniless's sword (5.5, implicit)
Money: gold (1.2, 3.2, dialogue)
Small Portable Objects: a letter (1.2, dialogue); a key (4.2, dialogue)
Scenery: arras hangings (4.3, dialogue)

COSTUMES
FEATHERBRAIN: mean clothes (2.1, 3.1, dialogue; 3.2, implicit); fine new clothes (4.2–3, 5.1, 5.3, 5.5, implicit); a false beard (4.2–3, 5.1, 5.3, implicit; 5.5, dialogue; removed on stage); hangers (5.5, implicit)

CALUMNY: possibly spectacles (3.2, dialogue; may be just a figure of speech); black clothes (4.2, dialogue)

PENNILESS: mean clothes (2.1, 3.2, implicit; 3.1, dialogue); a doublet (3.2, dialogue); fine new clothes (4.2–3, 5.3, 5.5, implicit); a false beard (4.2–3, 5.3, implicit; 5.5, dialogue; removed on stage); hangers (5.5, implicit)

EARLY STAGE HISTORY
said (in 1668) to have been 'acted with good applause'. The prologue implies a cast entirely of children. The cast list printed in the 1668 edition includes: William Cherrington (Feminia); Thomas Jordan (Penniless); Thomas Loveday (Clutch); Thomas Lovel (Money); Nicholas Lowe (Credit); Ambrose Matchit (Felixina); Thomas Sandes (Calumny); Walter Williams (Featherbrain). This may relate to a pre–1636 performance by the King's Revels Company.

EARLY TEXTUAL HISTORY
c. 1631–2 (?): Thomas Jordan later claimed that he wrote the play before he had reached the age of fifteen.

1667: On Saturday 16 November, Roger L'Estrange licensed the text for the press.

1668: Q printed by Peter Lillicrap for Francis Kirkman; collation A² B–G⁴ H², 28 leaves; title page names author and refers to performance in general terms; list of roles and actors.

1668: Q reissued, in copies for the author's own use, with cancel leaves A1–2; retitled *Wealth Outwitted, or Money's an Ass*; omits prologue and list of roles; adds Latin title-page motto and verse dedication, apparently with a blank for a dedicatee's name. (The only surviving copy has the name John Philips stamped in.)

1669–75: advertised as for sale by Francis Kirkman; the price was quoted in 1673 as 1s stitched.

1684: Nicholas Cox (Manciple of St Edmund Hall, Oxford) had a copy of Q in his bookshop. It had probably been previously owned by Gerard Langbaine, and appears on a list compiled by Anthony Wood on Saturday 13 December.

REFERENCES
Annals 1635; Bentley, iv. 685–7; Bodleian, MS Wood E. 4, art. 1, p. 34; Greg 830; Hazlitt, 160; *ShS* 58 (2005), 238–9.

2362. *Versipellis* [The Shape-Changer *or* The Werewolf *or* The Apostate]

EVIDENCE
A MS was seen by John Nichols in the late eighteenth or early nineteenth century, and reported by him in *The History and Antiquities of the County of Leicester* (1804); if it is still extant, its whereabouts are unknown.

GENRE
comedy
Contemporary: comedy (Cambridge records)

TITLE
MS: *Versipellis*

AUTHOR
Thomas Pestell

DATE
Limits: 1631–2
Best Guess: 1632

ORIGINAL PRODUCTION
Queens' College, Cambridge

PLOT
Speculation about the play's contents must necessarily turn on the precise meaning of the ambiguous title, translated three ways in this entry's heading; the literal sense is 'skin-changer'. Two of these senses are standard; the third, 'apostate', derives from usage in *Ignoramus* (**1768**; 2.3); the word is also an attribute of the trickster god Mercury. Perhaps the play was a comedy centring on a metaphorical chameleon who constantly changes allegiance. Versipellis is also the name of a character in *Alopichos* (**2042**), but not one important enough to be the title role; it is also another name for the shape-changing god Proteus in *Porta pietatis* (**2658**).

ROLES
Speaking Parts: 23 or more

SETTING
Place: Antwerp

LANGUAGE
Latin

EARLY STAGE HISTORY
1632: planned for performance by Queens' College, Cambridge, probably at Trinity College on the afternoon of Wednesday 7 March as the first comedy to be presented during the visit of King Charles I and Queen Henrietta Maria. The cast included: Robert (or Thomas) Allen; Edward Beale; Peter Bradley; [Richard or Oliver] Bryan; Thomas Cantrell; Thomas Carlisle; William Crofts; John Flout; Michael Frear; Charles Harflet; Hemson; Simon Jocelin; William Johnson; Edward Kemp; Richard Overton; John Pearson; Thomas Pestell, the author; Thomas Ramsbottom; Richards (Joseph or Lambert Richardson?); John Rogers; Samuel Rogers; William Wells; Woodhall (Horatio Woodhouse?). The performance was cancelled owing to the indisposition of the University's Chancellor, Henry Rich, 1st Earl of Holland (who had injured himself falling off a horse). When the royal visit took place, the King and Queen saw *The Rival Friends* (**2364**) instead. Nine to twelve of the actors

who had been cast in this play appeared in *The Rival Friends*, and eleven to fourteen did not.

EARLY TEXTUAL HISTORY
Included in a MS collection of Thomas Pestell's poems, possibly belonging to Pestell himself.

REFERENCES
Annals 1632; Bentley, iv. 954–5; Hazlitt, 245–6; REED: Cambridge, 638–9, 934, 959–60; Sibley, 171; Smith, 85–6, 109–10; Stratman, 184–6.

2363. Hogshead

EVIDENCE
Sir Henry Herbert's licence.

GENRE
Contemporary: play

TITLE
Performed: *Hogshead*
Alternative Modernization: [*The*] *Hog's Head*

DATE
Limits: 1631–9

The unanswerable question is how old this 'old play' was in 1639 when it was adapted and the new scene licensed. The limits are assigned on the assumption that it was not only owned by but written for Prince Charles's Men, but there is no knowing for sure.

ORIGINAL PRODUCTION
Prince Charles's Men (?)

PLOT
The plot may have dealt in some way with a cask (containing either liquor or, perhaps, an ascetic ancient philosopher) or with the literal head of a hog; but the title may instead (or even also) operate in the same way as *The Coxcomb* (**1598**), implying that the principal character is pig-headed. It is also remotely possible that Hogshead was a proper name, or the name of a tavern.

PROPS
Animals: possibly a hog's head
Food and Drink: possibly a hogshead of liquor

EARLY STAGE HISTORY
1639: revised version presumably performed by Prince Charles's Men, as licensed; at the time their usual playhouse was the Red Bull.

EARLY TEXTUAL HISTORY
1639: a new scene was added, and was licensed by Sir Henry Herbert for performance by Prince Charles's Men.

REFERENCES
Bawcutt 392.

2364. The Rival Friends

TEXT
Printed in 1632 (STC 12935). In his preface, the author Peter Hausted says that the play is printed exactly as performed; George Jeffreys's MS songbook (London: British Library, Add. MS 10338, fo. 46) includes an additional song (here designated α), which he says was 'made for the comedy but I think not sung'. Further possibly relevant information derives from a list of costumes in the possession of Queens' College, Cambridge, in January 1637.

GENRE
comedy
Contemporary: comedy (ind., S.R., t.p.); play (William Whiteway's diary); 'an idle play' (Simonds D'Ewes)

TITLE
Printed: *The Rival Friends*

AUTHOR
Peter Hausted

DATE
March 1632

ORIGINAL PRODUCTION
Queens' College, at Trinity College, Cambridge

PLOT
With Placenta's help, Constantina disguises herself as a boy and leaves her father's house in search of her missing love, Cleopes; she leaves a former boy-actor in her place. The friends Neander and Lucius both love Pandora, but she cannot decide between them. Each asks old Lively to help him win her love, not for himself but for his friend. Favouring Lucius, Lively plans to arrange a bogus wedding that will remove Neander from the rivalry, leaving Pandora for Lucius, without being subsequently binding. The 'boy' whom Lively selects to pose as Neander's bride is actually Constantina; but he allows the wedding to go ahead even after discovering her identity. Meanwhile Placenta advises Pandora to make her lovers jealous by pretending interest in someone else, so she woos the page Endymion. When she learns that Neander is married, and when Lucius claims to be a eunuch, she transfers her affections to Endymion in earnest.

It emerges that Lucius has jilted Endymion's sister Isabella, who subsequently disappeared. Constantina is brought in apparently dead, killed by Neander, and her brother Love-All recognizes her. In fact, she is only injured, and revives, calling for Cleopes. Neander admits that he is Cleopes: he had wooed her, but became more interested in Pandora, and feigned a voyage overseas; he then returned with a new identity to pursue Pandora. Love-All wants to know who was pretending to be his sister while Constantina has been out of the house; the 'boy' is brought in, and is recognized as the absent Isabella. Lucius agrees to marry her, waiving a dowry, and Pandora is allowed to marry Endymion.

In one sub-plot, Lively's house, a parsonage, will revert to the church upon his death. Pandora's father, Justice Hook, has the living in his gift, and has promised it to whoever marries his other daughter, the deformed Ursely. Suitors flock to Hook's house, but Lively intends to outlive them. While Hook is interviewing the candidates, Lively feigns death and names Hook his heir, but comes back to life when Hook rushes off to take possession of the property. Ursely herself wants to marry the misogynistic Anteros, and Anteros overhears Hook acceding to her wishes. To win the compliance of Anteros' father Terpander, Hook surrenders a mortgage on his lands, which Anteros destroys. Placenta then reveals that the marriage cannot take place: Ursely is Anteros' sister, given up at birth by her mother to simulate the results of a phantom pregnancy in Hook's wife. Though the mortgage has been destroyed, Terpander agrees to repay Hook half the money.

In another sub-plot, Anteros and Love-All pit two pairs of gulls against one another. They induce a fight, and the scholar Hammershin gets the best of it, even though his only weapon is a key. The gulls are then persuaded that one of them was killed in the fight and that an arrest is imminent. They are hidden in undignified places, including a pigsty, and left there until the end of the play. Anteros arranges for Hammershin to marry Ursely—and get the parsonage.

In a third sub-plot, Anteros gets Placenta's husband, Stipes the shepherd, to hire a servant on his recommendation—but the servant Jeoffrey is Anteros himself in disguise. Stipes thinks 'Jeoffrey' a possible husband for his daughter Merda, but is disconcerted to hear Merda talking in her sleep about a sexual encounter with the new servant. He ties 'Jeoffrey' to a tree, but while he is away fetching a cudgel, Anteros is released by Love-All, changes back to his own clothes, and persuades Stipes that anyone tied to the tree will be transformed by Oberon into a gentleman. Stipes has himself and Merda tied up; Anteros covers them with a cloak (to protect them, he says, from bird droppings) and has a mad beggar impersonate Oberon's voice. Stipes and Merda are left there for the rest of the play, until they are finally released and beaten by Placenta.

SCENE DESIGNATION
ind., prol., 1.1–8, 2.1–7, 3.1–8, 4.1–15, 5.1–11, ep. (Q), with entr'acte songs

The stage is not clear at the following scene-divisions: 1.2–6, 2.1–7, 3.1–8, 4.1–13, 4.14–15, 5.1–11. Verse lines are split across the following scene-divisions: 1.4–5, 1.5–6.

ROLES
Induction
VENUS, the morning star and goddess of love; also called Phosphorus and Vesper
THETIS, a sea-goddess, Phoebus' lover
PHOEBUS, the sun, god of light; also called Sol
A CHORUS of singers
A BOY

Main Action
PROLOGUE, an old man
PLACENTA, a midwife, Stipes's wife, Merda's mother
A BOY said to be a former actor with a London company; in reality, Isabella, Laurentio's daughter, Endymion's sister
CONSTANTINA, Hook's niece, Love-All's sister, Pandora's cousin; poses as a boy; later Neander's wife
ANTEROS, a misogynist, Terpander's son; turns out to be Ursely's brother; assumes the identity of Jeoffrey, a servant (and later called Master Jeoffrey, a gentleman)
LUCIUS, Neander's friend
ENDYMION, Laurentio's son, Isabella's brother, Lucius' page
LUSCINIO, Lucius' boy
PANDORA, a gentlewoman, Hook's daughter, cousin of Love-All and Constantina
NEANDER, Lucius' friend; later Constantina's husband; in reality Cleopes
Bully LIVELY, a householder, Hammershin's uncle, 80 years old; also called Master Lively and Master Lickthumb
Lively's BOY
GANYMEDE Filpot, a former butler, Ursely's suitor
TEMPEST Allmouth, a decayed Puritan clothworker, Ursely's suitor
ARTHUR Armstrong, a young scholar and football player, Ursely's suitor
ZEALOUS Knowlittle, a Puritan box-maker, Ursely's suitor
STUTCHELL Legg, a young scholar and football player, large of stature; Ursely's suitor
HUGO Obligation, a Puritan scrivener, Ursely's suitor
Master Jack LOVE-ALL, a court page, Hook's nephew, Constantina's brother, Pandora's cousin
SINGERS, who sing in the entr'actes, including two trebles
STIPES, a shepherd, Placenta's husband, Merda's father, Hook's tenant
Mistress URSELY, a crook-backed, incontinent young woman, 17 years old; supposed Hook's daughter and Pandora's sister, but in reality Terpander's daughter and Anteros' sister

MERDA, daughter of Stipes and Placenta, 18 years old; also called Madam Gillian

Justice Sacrilege HOOK, a widower, Pandora's father (and, supposedly, Ursely's), uncle of Love-All and Constantina; also called Master Hook

Master MONGREL, a gentleman, elder brother, and heir, Hammershin's kinsman

Sir HAMMERSHIN, a scholar, Lively's nephew, Mongrel's kinsman

Master NODDLE-EMPTY, an Inns of Court man, Wiseacres's kinsman; also called Master Noddle and Master Empty

Master William WISEACRES, formerly an attorney's clerk, Noddle-Empty's kinsman

Two RUSTIC SERVANTS in Lively's household, named Edward and Robin

Two MAIDS in Lively's household, one of them named Kate

Three FIDDLERS (*non-speaking*)

LAURENTIO, an old man, father of Endymion and Isabella

A MAD BEGGAR, addressed as Tom; impersonates Oberon, King of the Fairies

TERPANDER, an old gentleman widower, Anteros' father (and, it turns out, Ursely's)

Speaking Parts: 38

Doubling
The cast list for the original performance indicates that the following roles were doubled:
  1: Boy, Love-All;
  2: Ganymede, Terpander;
  3: Arthur, Hammershin.

Hammershin is shut in the chest in 3.8 and remains there, presumably with the chest continuously on stage, until 5.11. However, Arthur appears in 5.9, so it must be possible to exit the chest from beneath.

Stage Directions and Speech Prefixes
VENUS: *Venus* (s.d.s and s.p.s)
THETIS: *Thetis* (s.d.s and s.p.s)
PHOEBUS: *Phoebus* (s.d.s and s.p.s); *Sol* (s.d.s)
CHORUS: *the Chorus* (s.d.s)
BOY: *a Boy* | *Boy* (s.d.s)
PROLOGUE: *Prologue* (s.d.s)
PLACENTA: *Placenta* (s.d.s); *Plac<enta>* (s.p.s); *Placenta,* [Stipes's] *Wife, a Midwife* (d.p.)
BOY: *Isabella* (s.d.s); *Isab<ella>* (s.p.s); *Isabella, Laurentio's Daughter, in love with Lucius* (d.p.)
CONSTANTINA: *Constantina* (s.d.s); *Constan<tina>* (s.p.s); *Constantina, Jack Love-All's sister* (d.p.)
ANTEROS: *Anteros* (s.d.s); *Anter<os>* (s.p.s); *Anteros,* [Terpander's] *son, a humorous mad fellow, that could not endure women* (d.p.)
LUCIUS: *Lucius* (s.d.s); *Luc<ius>* (s.p.s); *Lucius,* [one of] *the two Friends, and Rivals in Pandora's love* (d.p.)

ENDYMION: *Endymion* (s.d.s); *Endym<ion>* (s.p.s); *Endymion,* [Laurentio's] *son, and Page to Lucius* (d.p.)
LUSCINIO: *Lusc<inio>* (s.d.s and s.p.s); *Lucscino, Lucius' boy* (d.p.)
PANDORA: *Pandora* (s.d.s); *Pand<ora>* (s.p.s); *Pandora,* [Hook's] *fair Daughter* (d.p.)
NEANDER: *Neander* (s.d.s); *Nean<der>* | *Cleo<pes>* (s.p.s); *Neander, or Cleopes* [one of] *the two Friends, and Rivals in Pandora's love* (d.p.)
LIVELY: *Lively* (s.d.s); *Live<ly>* (s.p.s); *Bully Lively, an old merry fellow, that lives in the impropriate Parsonage* (d.p.)
BOY: [Lively's] *boy* | *The Boy* (s.d.s); *Boy* (s.d.s and s.p.s)
GANYMEDE: [one of] *6 Suitors to Mistress Ursely* | *Gan<imed> Filpot* | [one of] *the six Suitors* | [one of] *The 6 Scholars* | [one of the] *Suitors* (s.d.s); *Gan<imed>* (s.p.s); *Ganimed Filpot, a pretender to a Scholar, who had once been a Gentleman's Butler,* [one of] *Suitors to Mistress Ursely for the Parsonage sake* (d.p.)
TEMPEST: [one of] *6 Suitors to Mistress Ursely* | *Tem<pest> All<mouth>* | [one of] *the six Suitors* | [one of] *The 6 Scholars* | [one of the] *Suitors* (s.d.s); *Temp<est>* (s.p.s); *Tempest All-mouth, a decayed Cloth-worker,* [one of the] *Suitors to Mistress Ursely for the Parsonage sake* (d.p.)
ARTHUR: [one of] *6 Suitors to Mistress Ursely* | *Arth<ur> Armst<rong>* | [one of] *the six Suitors* | [one of] *The 6 Scholars* | [one of the] *Suitors* (s.d.s); *Arth<ur> Arm* | *Arthur* | *Arm* (s.p.s); *Arthur Armstrong,* [one of] *2 young scholars, robustious football-players* [among the] *Suitors to Mistress Ursely for the Parsonage sake* (d.p.)
ZEALOUS: [one of] *6 Suitors to Mistress Ursely* | *Zeal<ous> Know<little>* | [one of] *the six Suitors* | *This fellow* | [one of] *The 6 Scholars* | [one of the] *Suitors* (s.d.s); *Zealous Kn<owlittle>* | *Zeal<ous>* (s.p.s); *Zealous Knowlittle, a Box-maker,* [one of the] *Suitors to Mistress Ursely for the Parsonage sake* (d.p.)
STUTCHELL: [one of] *6 Suitors to Mistress Ursely* | [one of] *the six Suitors* | *Stuc<hell>* | [one of] *The 6 Scholars* | [one of the] *Suitors* (s.d.s); *Stutch<ell>* (s.d.s and s.p.s); *Stuch<ell>* (s.p.s); *Stutchell Legg,* [one of] *2 young scholars, robustious football-players* [among the] *Suitors to Mistress Ursely for the Parsonage sake* (d.p.)
HUGO: [one of] *6 Suitors to Mistress Ursely* | *Hugo Obligation* | [one of] *the six Suitors* | [one of] *The 6 Scholars* | [one of the] *Suitors* (s.d.s); *Hugo* (s.p.s); *Hugo Obligation, a precise Scrivener,* [one of the] *Suitors to Mistress Ursely for the Parsonage sake* (d.p.)
LOVE-ALL: *Loveall* | *Lovell* (s.d.s); *Love<all>* (s.p.s); *Jack Loveall, a Court Page, Nephew to Mr Hooke* (d.p.)
SINGERS: *two Trebles* (s.d.s); *1 Treble* | *2 Treble* (s.p.s)
STIPES: *Stipes* (s.d.s and s.p.s); *Stipes, Hooke's Shepherd* (d.p.)

URSELY: *Mistress Ursely* | *Mrs Ursly* (s.d.s); *Urse<ly>* | *Mrs Urse<ly>* (s.p.s); *Mistress Ursely*, [Hook's] supposed Daughter, deformed and foolish (d.p.)
MERDA: *Merda* (s.d.s and s.p.s); *Merda*, [Stipes's and Placenta's] *Daughter* (d.p.)
HOOK: *Justice Hooke* | [Love-All's] *Uncle* (s.d.s); *Hooke* (s.d.s and s.p.s); *Hook* (s.p.s); *Sacriledge Hooke, a Simoniacal Patron* (d.p.)
MONGREL: *Master Mungrell* | *Mun<grell>* (s.d.s); *Mung<rell>* (s.p.s); *Mr Mungrell, an elder brother* (d.p.)
HAMMERSHIN: *Hammershin* | *The Scholar* | *Hamershin* | *Sir Hammer<shin>* (s.d.s); *Hamm<ershin>* (s.p.s); *Hammershin, a Bachelor of Arts* (d.p.)
NODDLE-EMPTY: *Noddle-Empty* | *Noddle Empty* (s.d.s); *Noddle* (s.p.s); *Nodle Emptie, an Inns of the Court man* (d.p.)
WISEACRES: *Will Wiseacres* | *William* (s.d.s); *Wise<acres>* (s.d.s and s.p.s); *Will* (s.p.s); *William Wiseacres, a quondam Attorney's Clerk* (d.p.)
RUSTIC SERVANTS: *2 Rustical Servants* | *two of Lively's servants* (s.d.s); *1 Rustic* | *2 Rustic* | *Rustic 1* (s.p.s); *Two Men . . . of Lively's* (d.p.)
MAIDS: *two Maids* | *2 Ancillae* (s.d.s); *1 Maid* | *2 Maid* | *1 Ancilla* | *2 Ancilla* (s.p.s); *Two Maids of Lively's* (d.p.)
FIDDLERS: *Fiddlers* (s.d.s and d.p.); *three Fiddlers* (s.d.s)
LAURENTIO: *Laurentio* (s.d.s); *Laur<entio>* (s.p.s); *Laurentio, an ancient Citizen* (d.p.)
MAD BEGGAR: *A Bedlam* (s.d.s and d.p.); *Bedlam* (s.p.s)
TERPANDER: *Terpander* (s.d.s); *Ter<pander>* (s.p.s); *Terpander, an old Gentleman* (d.p.)

The Rustic Servants' speech prefixes are inconsistently assigned: in 4.10, Robin is 2 *Rustic*, but in 5.10 he is 1 *Rustic*, while 2 *Rustic* is Edward. (Mills silently alters the earlier scene in his edition.)

OTHER CHARACTERS
Adonis, a beautiful huntsman (ind.)
The Muses (ind.)
Daphne, Phoebus' lover (ind.)
The London players (1.1)
Knowlittle's father (1.7)
Lively's brother, from whom Hook acquired the parsonage (1.7)
Stutchell's father (2.3)
An audience of women, who heard Knowlittle preach (2.3)
Seventeen honest men, who have written Knowlittle testimonials (2.3)
Robert and Oliver, Hook's servants (2.3)
Madam Puss, a kitchen maid said to be Merda's true mother (2.6; possibly imaginary)
Mongrel's father, a gentleman (3.1, 3.8)
Mongrel's uncle, a Justice of the Peace (3.1)
A bachelor of Hammershin's college, from whom he borrowed a cloak and boots (3.2)
A barber, to whom Hammershin pawned his own cloak and boots for tobacco (3.2)
The local constable (3.6, 3.8)
A vicar, Lively's acquaintance, who married Neander and Constantina (4.1)
Anteros' dead mother (4.6, 5.6, 5.8)
Endymion's dead uncle (4.13)
Neander's father (4.14)
Neander's dead mother (4.14)
Stipes's mother, who taught him a charm (5.4)
Dorothea, Hook's dead wife (5.8)
A gentleman, Ganymede's former employer (5.9)

SETTING
Period: contemporary (England has both a king and a queen); the action takes place on 14 February (St Valentine's Day)
Time-Scheme: The action apparently takes place during a single day: 1.3 takes place at dawn, 1.8 at 8 a.m., 3.1 at 9.30; at least an hour passes between 4.13 and 5.3.
Place: a country village in England

Geography
London: Bedlam; St Paul's Cathedral; the [Inner or Middle] Temple; Drury Lane; Bloomsbury
England: Stamford; [Oxford]; [Cambridge]
[Europe]: France; Tempe; Belgia; Germany; Italy
[Asia]: Turkey; Persia
Africa: Egypt
New England
St Kitts

SOURCES
Narrative: Ben Jonson, *The Silent Woman* (**1603**; 3.2)
Verbal: Bible: Matthew 5.37 (5.6); Martial, *Epigrams* 8.69 (t.p. motto); William Shakespeare, *The Moor of Venice* (**1437**; 4.14)
Works Mentioned: Plautus, *Captivi* (ind.), *Persa* (preface); Albertus Magnus, *De secretis mulierum* (thirteenth century; 3.2, 3.6); Sir Thomas Littleton, *Les Tenures* (1481; 1.8); Sir Philip Sidney, *Arcadia* (c. 1580; preface, 3.2); Marcantonio Zimara, *The Problems of Aristotle* (1595; 3.2); Johannes Magirus, *Physiologiae peripateticae* (written before 1596, printed 1597; 3.8); Sir Thomas Overbury, *Characters* (1611–15; 3.2)

LANGUAGE
English
Latin: 14 words (1.8, 2.5, 3.2, 3.8, 5.9; Love-All, Anteros, Stipes, Wiseacres)
Italian: 56 words (1.8, 3.1–2, 3.8, 5.9; Anteros, Love-All)
French: 22 words (3.2, 3.6; Noddle-Empty, Hammershin, Anteros)
Spanish: 1 word (5.8; Anteros)

FORM
Metre: pentameter and prose; some trimeter and alexandrines

2364. The Rival Friends

Rhyme: blank verse
Prologue: 10 lines
Induction: Venus, Thetis, Phoebus, Boy
Act-Division: 5 acts, separated by songs
Epilogue: 24 lines, spoken by Anteros
Lines (Spoken): 3,722 (2,683 verse, 1,039 prose)
Lines (Written): 3,900

STAGING

Doors: one represents Justice Hook's house (1.7, s.d.); one represents Stipes's house (4.5, 5.3, dialogue)
Stage: mentioned (ind., s.d.); the four gulls 'come out at the four corners of the stage' (5.11, s.d.)
Above: characters appear at a window above (ind., 1.1, s.d.); it takes 21 lines for a character to get from the window down to the main stage
Beneath: there must be a trapdoor exit at one corner of the stage (see ROLES: *Doubling*)
Other Openings: a curtained area on the east side of the stage, in which Thetis and Phoebus are discovered (ind., s.d.)
Audience: the King and Queen in the audience are directly addressed (ind., prol.), the Queen as 'most sacred goddess' and the King as 'great monarch' (ep.); addressed as 'gentlemen' (ind.); ladies in the audience are mentioned (ind., ep., dialogue)
Miscellaneous: Two characters are left on stage, tied up and covered by a cloak, between 5.5 and 5.10.

MUSIC

Music: tolling bell (2.3, dialogue)
On-Stage Music: lute played by Luscinio (1.3, dialogue; accompanying Song 2); Anteros whistles (4.7, s.d.); fiddles (4.10, implicit)
Songs:
  1: 'Drowsy Phoebus, come away', ind., Venus, Thetis, Phoebus, Chorus, in parts, 43 lines interspersed with spoken lines; *musical setting survives*;
  2: 'Have pity, grief, I cannot pay', 1.3, Lucius, 14 lines, with lute accompaniment; *two musical settings survive*;
  3: 'Cupid, if a god thou art', entr'acte 1, 8 lines;
  4: 'To the ladies, joy, delight', entr'acte 2, 8 lines;
  5: 'But why | Do the winged minutes fly', entr'acte 3, two trebles in parts, 23 lines;
  6: 'Have you a desire to see', entr'acte 4, 14 lines;
  7: 'Newly from a poached toad', 5.5, Mad Beggar, 4 lines; *musical setting survives*;
  8: 'Beest thou ruder than was e'er', 5.5, Mad Beggar, 6 lines;
  α: 'Cruel! But once again', 8 lines; omitted from the final version of the play; *two musical settings survive*.
Other Singing: Ursely sings (2.1, dialogue; 2.2, implicit)
Dance: Anteros dances (4.7, s.d.); Rustic Servants, Maids, Merda, and Anteros dance (4.10, s.d.)

PROPS

Weapons: Mongrel's sword (3.2, implicit; 3.8, dialogue); Lucius' sword (4.2–5, s.d.; 4.15, dialogue); Neander's sword (4.3–5, 4.13, 5.10–11, s.d.; 4.14–15, dialogue); a rod (4.6–11, dialogue; affixed to Merda's back on stage); Love-All's sword (5.3–8, s.d.); a cudgel (5.4, 5.11, s.d.); Anteros' sword (5.9, s.d.)
Musical Instruments: a lute (1.3, s.d.); three fiddles (4.9–10, 5.10–11, s.d.); a horn (5.5, dialogue)
Clothing: a long grey cloak (5.5–11, s.d.)
Money: a teston (1.7, dialogue)
Animals: two dead lambs (4.11, s.d.)
Food and Drink: two glasses of sack (1.7, s.d.; drunk on stage); a box of conserves (2.3, s.d.; eaten on stage)
Small Portable Objects: a document (1.3, implicit); Anteros' watch (1.8, s.d.); two stones (2.2, dialogue; 5.6, s.d.); a pin (2.7, dialogue); Love-All's watch (3.1–2, s.d.); probably a handkerchief (3.6, dialogue); a document (5.6, s.d.; torn up on stage); another document (5.6, dialogue); a black box (5.9, s.d.)
Large Portable Objects: a sheep-hook (2.1, 4.8, 4.11, s.d.); seating for two characters (2.3, implicit); a staff (2.3, s.d.); baby's clouts (2.5, s.d.; probably a bundle representing a doll); a chair (2.5–6, s.d.); a chest or rabbit-hutch (3.7–8, dialogue; large enough for a character to hide in it; placed at a front corner of the stage and apparently on stage thereafter until the end of the play); a long binding cord (5.2–11, s.d.)
Scenery: an azure curtain (ind., s.d.); a tree (3.3, 5.2–11, ep., s.d.; 4.10, dialogue; Anteros climbs it and stays up there for most of two scenes); two dog-kennels (3.5–6, dialogue/s.d.; placed at two corners of the main stage, at the rear, and on either side of Hook's house; apparently on stage thereafter until the end of the play); a pigsty (3.7–8, s.d.; placed at a front corner of the stage and apparently on stage thereafter until the end of the play)

There is an inconsistency concerning swords in Act 5. Anteros is continuously on stage from 5.2 until 5.11. In 5.3, he borrows Love-All's sword, and returns it in 5.8; but in 5.9 he draws his own sword, which he must therefore have been wearing all the time. Why then did he need to borrow Love-All's in the first place?

COSTUMES AND MAKE-UP

THETIS: long hair (dialogue)
PHOEBUS: possibly a mantle or robes (Queens' costume list)
PROLOGUE: a wig and false beard (s.d.; removed on stage)
BOY/ISABELLA: Constantina's clothes (1.1, s.d.), including a scarf worn as a veil (dialogue)
CONSTANTINA: cross-dressed as a boy (1.1, s.d.; 2.5, dialogue; the style emphasizes her spindly legs); a veil (4.3, s.d.); a fair gown (4.3, dialogue)
ANTEROS: clean-shaven (dialogue); a hat (1.8, dialogue; appears to have a favour in it); possibly golden breeches (dialogue; no specific scene);

disguised in a shepherd's clothes (4.7–11, 5.2–3, s.d.; worn over his own clothes, and removed on stage); fine clothes, including a green scarlet suit (5.3–11, dialogue), and a garment with a pocket (s.d.); garters, pumps, shoe-roses, and a band (5.3–11, s.d.; put on on stage); Love-All's hat (5.3–8, s.d.; put on and removed on stage); hangers (5.9, implicit)
LUCIUS: fine clothes (4.2–5, dialogue); hangers (4.2–5, implicit)
NEANDER: disguised (1.5–6, 4.3–5, 4.13–15, implicit; 5.10–11, dialogue; removed on stage); hangers (4.3–5, 4.13, implicit)
LIVELY: grey hair (dialogue)
ZEALOUS: a girdle (5.9, s.d.)
HUGO: a short beard (dialogue); a hat (5.9, dialogue)
SUITORS: two have short hair (dialogue; it is not made explicit which two, but the likeliest candidates are Knowlittle, Tempest, and Hugo)
LOVE-ALL: a garment with a pocket (3.1, dialogue); a hat (5.3, s.d.; removed on stage)
STIPES: enters 'making of himself ready' (2.1, s.d.)
URSELY: is crook-backed (dialogue); bracelets and gloves (2.1–2, dialogue; removed on stage); a garment with a pocket (5.6, s.d.)
MERDA: possibly golden hair (dialogue); Ursely's bracelets and gloves (2.2, dialogue; put on on stage); a shoe (4.8–11, s.d.); a gown and neckerchief (5.5–11, dialogue); a garter (5.5, dialogue; removed on stage)
HOOK: silver hair and a long beard (dialogue); velvet hose (5.6, dialogue)
MONGREL: hangers (3.2, 3.8, implicit)
HAMMERSHIN: a black suit with a pocket, hose, a cloak, and boots (3.2, dialogue); a hat (5.11, dialogue)
NODDLE-EMPTY: boots (3.2, dialogue); a band-string with a ring in it (3.2, dialogue); a bloody head and face (3.6, s.d.)
MAD BEGGAR: mean clothes (5.5, dialogue)
TERPANDER: grey hair (dialogue)

EARLY STAGE HISTORY
Preparation: Plays were planned for performance during the royal visit to Cambridge in March 1632. The plays were in rehearsal by the start of March. The original plan was to perform a Latin comedy (probably *Versipellis*, **2362**) on the afternoon the King arrived and an English comedy the following morning, Thursday 8 March; this may have been *The Rival Friends*, but was more probably *The Jealous Lovers* (**2365**; since *Versipellis* and *The Rival Friends* were both Queens' College plays). Subsequently plans changed, and there was some dispute about whether *The Rival Friends* or *The Jealous Lovers* should be given first; this was settled by Dr Henry Butts, the Vice-Chancellor, who chose *The Rival Friends*. However, the royal visit was postponed owing to the indisposition of the University's Chancellor, Henry Rich, 1st Earl of Holland (who had injured himself falling off a horse).

Performance: by members of Queens' College at Trinity College, Cambridge, on Monday 19 March 1632. The performance lasted seven hours. The cast included: Richard Bryan (Hook); Thomas Cantrell (Laurentio); Thomas Carlisle (Stutchell); Daniel Chandler (Prologue); Charles Cotterel (Endymion); Michael Frear (Isabella); Peter Hards (Wiseacres); Charles Harflet (Noddle-Empty); Peter Hausted, the author (Anteros); William Hausted (Hammershin, Arthur); [Heigham, John, or Ralph] Hills (Terpander, Ganymede); Thomas Holmes (Mad Beggar); Edward Kemp (Lucius); John Kidby (Zealous); Lin (Constantina); Mannering (Pandora); John Pearson (Placenta); Thomas Ramsbottom (Ursely); [Joseph or Lambert] Richardson (Tempest); John Rogers (Stipes); Samuel Rogers (Love-All, Boy); [Edward?] Slater (Hugo); James Stanino (Lively); Benjamin Tiffin (Merda); Horatio Woodhouse (Mongrel). Music was composed by George Jeffreys and Thomas Holmes. The audience included: King Charles I; Queen Henrietta Maria; probably Robert Dormer, 1st Earl of Carnarvon (who four years later opined that a play he had seen at Cambridge, probably this one, was even worse than *Passions Calmed*, **2550**). Some members of the audience were reportedly Jesuits and Catholic priests in disguise. Burnt wine was served at the college's expense (which amounted to £1.1s for both this performance and that of *The Jealous Lovers*, **2365**). At one or other performance, Theodore Kelly was pushed by the press of the crowd into Sir Arthur Gorges, who was with a lady; Sir Arthur responded by threatening to cudgel Kelly. Sir Simonds D'Ewes pointedly avoided seeing the 'idle play' and instead spent the duration of the performance looking at manuscripts in Trinity College Library.

The play gave offence to many members of the audience. Particular criticisms included: the low status of the characters; the presentation of Anteros, a misogynistic character, to an audience which included ladies; the irrelevance of the sequence with the gulls in Act 3; and the satire on scholars and puritans. The King's displeasure was expressed to the Vice-Chancellor by the Chancellor; the Vice-Chancellor subsequently hanged himself on Sunday 1 April (Easter Sunday).

Production Finance
The cost of this and the performance of *The Jealous Lovers* (**2365**) was defrayed by a levy on the colleges. Individual colleges contributed as follows: Clare (£19.17s.6d); Emmanuel (£13.5s); King's (£79.10s); St Catharine's (£2.9s.6d); Trinity Hall (£19.17s.6d, paid by the Master, Thomas Eden, to Francis Hughes, the esquire bedell, on Saturday 19 January 1633).

EARLY TEXTUAL HISTORY
1632: entered in the Stationers' Register to Humphrey Robinson on Wednesday 13 June; entry names author. Sir Henry Herbert had licensed the book for publication.

1632: **Q** printed by Augustine Matthews for Humphrey Robinson; collation A–O⁴, 56 leaves; title page refers to performance, and to the fact that it had been 'cried down by boys, faction, envy, and confident ignorance', and names author; Latin title-page motto; authorial verse dedication to a generic patron, and preface to the reader; Latin commendatory verses by Edward Kemp; English commendatory verses by John Rogers; list of roles.

Before 1640: a copy of Q was owned by Robert Burton.

c. 1632–40s: a copy of Q was in the possession of John Horne (Vicar of Headington, Oxfordshire). After his death, his entire collection of play-books passed into the possession of John Houghton of Brasenose College, Oxford (c. 1608–77), then to James Herne (died 1685), and then to the library of Ralph Sheldon (1623–84) at Weston, where it was catalogued by Anthony Wood, probably in the late 1670s.

c. 1630s–62: Songs 1, 2, and α included, with musical settings by George Jeffreys, in a MS songbook (London: British Library, Add. MS 10338, fos. 43–51).

Mid-seventeenth century (c. 1637–62): Songs 2 and α included, with musical settings by Henry Lawes, in his autograph MS songbook (London: British Library, Add. MS 53723, fos. 43ᵛ–44ʳ); the two stanzas of Song 2 are treated as separate songs.

1646: Song 6 included in the fifth edition of 'Philomusus', *The Academy of Compliments*, sigs. L1ᵛ–L2ʳ; printed by Moses Bell for Humphrey Moseley.

Mid-seventeenth century: extracts included in a MS commonplace book (Washington: Folger, MS V. a. 87, fos. 24ᵛ–26ʳ) partly compiled by William How.

1650: *The Academy of Compliments* reprinted for Humphrey Moseley; the song now appears on sig. K8ʳ⁻ᵛ.

c. 1656–7: a longer version of Song 7 (headed 'Oberon, or The Madman's Song') included, with a musical setting by Thomas Holmes, in a MS songbook (London: British Library, Add. MS 11608, fo. 18ʳ) compiled by T. C. for John Hilton; an addendum to the heading mentions the performance occasion and identifies Holmes as the singer.

1658: *The Academy of Compliments* reprinted for Humphrey Moseley.

1663: *The Academy of Compliments* reprinted by Thomas Leach and Thomas Child.

1673: Robinson's rights transferred in the Stationers' Register by his executor (also named Humphrey Robinson) to John Martin and Henry Herringman on Thursday 30 January, as part of a list of 105 titles, by assignment of Saturday 13 May 1671.

1683: Martin's rights transferred in the Stationers' Register from his widow, Sarah, to Robert Scott, on Tuesday 21 August, by assignment of Tuesday 14 June 1681 and order of a court of Monday 7 November 1681; play and author individually named as part of a group transfer of 360 titles.

1684: Nicholas Cox (Manciple of St Edmund Hall, Oxford) had a copy, presumably of Q, in his bookshop. It had probably been previously owned by Gerard Langbaine, and appears on a list compiled by Anthony Wood on Saturday 13 December.

EDITIONS

Laurens J. Mills, University of Indiana Publications, Humanities Series 23 (Bloomington, 1951).

Ian Spink, *English Songs, 1625–1660*, 2nd edn (London, 1977), nos. 96–8 (Songs 1–2 and α, with music, only).

REFERENCES

Annals 1632; Bawcutt C46; Bentley, iv. 534–6; Bodleian, MS Wood E. 4, art. 1, p. 29; Greg 465; Hazlitt, 196; Nicolas K. Kiessling, *The Library of Robert Burton* (Oxford, 1988) 758; *MLR* 13 (1918), 401–11; *N&Q* 200 (1955), 106–9; *N&Q* 233 (1988), 495; REED: Cambridge, 630–2, 637–45, 651, 672–3, 685, 857, 881–3, 920, 960–1, 1024–5; REED: Oxford, 533; REED: Lincolnshire, 354–5; *REED Newsletter* 14.2 (1989), 13–15; *ShS* 11 (1958), 108; Smith, 86–7, 91–2; Steele, 241; Stratman, 113–21, 362–3; *Theatre Survey* 20 (1979), 17.

2365. The Jealous Lovers

TEXT
Printed in 1632 (STC 20692), from revised authorial copy.

GENRE
comedy
Contemporary: comedy (ep., S.R., t.p.)

TITLE
Printed: *The Jealous Lovers*

AUTHOR
Thomas Randolph

DATE
March 1632

ORIGINAL PRODUCTION
Trinity College, Cambridge

PLOT
Simo lives an ascetic life so that his son Asotus will inherit a large fortune. Asotus asks for money now, and is given some. His tutor Ballio persuades him that it is vulgar to carry his own purse, and undertakes to do so for him.

Tyndarus and Techmessa are both prone to jealousy of their respective lovers, Evadne and Pamphilus; Tyndarus even doubts Evadne's chastity when she kisses him over-enthusiastically. Asotus tries to chat up

Evadne, but she refuses him. He manages to purloin one of her ear-rings and, to avenge himself for the rebuff, shows it to Tyndarus, who reacts predictably. Ballio makes a play for Techmessa by encouraging her to think Pamphilus unwilling to defend her honour, and she charges him to take Pamphilus' sword from him. He steals it from Pamphilus' page while he is delivering letters to Techmessa, then tells her that he was given it by Pamphilus rather than rise to the provocation to fight. The page summons officers to arrest Ballio, and he confesses the ruse. Asotus also admits his slander of Evadne, and both are allowed to choose their own punishment; they elect to cudgel one another.

Techmessa and Tyndarus decide to test their lovers: Tyndarus asks Pamphilus to woo Evadne, and Techmessa asks Evadne to respond to Tyndarus' advances; the result confirms them in their jealousy, until the situation is explained. Techmessa's mother Dipsas is keen to cross Evadne's love, partly because she resents the fact that Evadne was brought up in her household despite being another man's child, and partly because she fancies Tyndarus herself. When the pair are due to meet at Ballio's house, Dipsas persuades Ballio to fill it with debauchees. This is easy enough, because Asotus keeps company there with poets, soldiers, and a courtesan, Phryne, whom he intends to marry. Eavesdropping on the revelry, Simo falls in love with Phryne himself, until Asotus forcefully persuades him to back off and contribute half his estate to Phryne's marriage settlement. Tyndarus and Evadne are disconcerted by the roistering going on at the house, and Tyndarus rescues her from unwelcome advances. He asks her for sex by way of reward, and is rebuffed—then explains that this was another test. Pamphilus also arrives at the house, to meet Techmessa, but his presence triggers Tyndarus' jealousy, while Evadne's does the same for Techmessa when she arrives.

Tyndarus and Techmessa agree on a ruse, and solicit the help of Ballio and Asotus: they will feign suicide and see how their lovers take their death. They are taken to the temple in coffins for burial—but, because they are suicides, a ceremony of atonement must be performed first. The sexton and his wife attempt to steal the corpses' clothes, and get a shock when they turn out to be alive: both faint, and the jealous lovers exchange clothes with them. Pamphilus, Evadne, and Dipsas all come grieving to the temple; their demeanour convinces the lovers that their jealousy is misplaced, and they reveal their identities.

Posing as an astrologer, Demetrius arrives in Thebes and meets Asotus, who is becoming anxious about his marriage. Demetrius answers his questions: Phryne is neither unchaste nor sterile, and Simo has not long to live. At the wedding ceremony, Hymen's statue turns his head away from two of the couples: Tyndarus may not marry Evadne, nor Pamphilus Techmessa. Asotus offers to bring his newly appointed household astrologer to solve the mystery. Demetrius does so, but not by astrology. Twenty years ago, he fled the city with his infant son to escape an enforced tribute of young boys to feed the Minotaur; he took Chremylus' son with him, leaving his own daughter Evadne in the care of Chremylus and Dipsas. Tyndarus is his son, and Evadne's brother; Pamphilus is likewise Techmessa's brother. The lovers' jealousy was an instinctive recoil from incest. They swap partners, and Hymen assents to the marriages. Asotus marries Phryne, and Simo marries a chambermaid, who indicates that she requires him to adopt a more extravagant lifestyle.

SCENE DESIGNATION

1.1–10, 2.1–13, 3.1–14, 4.1–9, 5.1–9, ep. (Q, corrected)

Q misprints the headings of 3.5 (as 3.3), 3.11 (as 3.2), and 5.7 (as 5.8).

The stage is clear only between the acts. Verse lines are split across the following scene-divisions: 2.5–6, 2.6–7, 3.2–3, 3.8–9, 3.11–12, 4.2–3, 4.7–8, 5.1–2, 5.2–3.

ROLES

SIMO, Asotus' father, an old, rich man
ASOTUS, Simo's son, 21 years old
BALLIO, Asotus' tutor
TYNDARUS, Evadne's boyfriend; a young man, over 20 years old; supposed Pamphilus' brother; in reality Clinias, Demetrius' son, Evadne's brother
CHREMYLUS, an old man, Dipsas' husband, father of Techmessa and Pamphilus
DIPSAS, Chremylus' wife, mother of Techmessa and Pamphilus
EVADNE, Tyndarus' girlfriend (and in reality his sister), Demetrius' daughter, foster-daughter of Chremylus and Dipsas; over 20 years old
Lady TECHMESSA, Pamphilus' girlfriend (and in reality his sister), daughter of Chremylus and Dipsas
PAEGNIUM, Pamphilus' page; said to be little
PAMPHILUS, Techmessa's boyfriend; supposed Tyndarus' brother; over 20 years old; in reality Timarchus, son of Chremylus and Dipsas, Techmessa's brother
PHRONESIUM, a chambermaid
Two OFFICERS engaged by Paegnium to arrest Ballio (2.8)
BOMOLOCHUS, a poet
CHAERYLUS, a poet
THRASYMACHUS, a soldier
HYPERBOLUS, a soldier
PHRYNE, a courtesan; later Asotus' fiancée
A SERVANT at the funerals, who is sent with letters (4.1, non-speaking)
A SEXTON, Staphyla's husband of 36 years' standing
STAPHYLA, the Sexton's wife
DEMETRIUS, an Athenian, father of Tyndarus and Evadne; poses as an astrologer
PRIESTS officiating at the wedding (5.6–9; one speaks, and the rest may sing)

A statue of HYMEN, god of marriage (5.6-9, non-speaking)

Speaking Parts: 22

Stage Directions and Speech Prefixes
SIMO: *Simo* (s.d.s and s.p.s); *Simo, an old doting father* (d.p.)
ASOTUS: *Asotus* (s.d.s); *Asot<us>* (s.p.s); *Asotus,* [Simo's] *prodigal son* (d.p.)
BALLIO: *Ballio* (s.d.s and s.p.s); *Ballio, a Pander, and Tutor to Asotus* (d.p.)
TYNDARUS: *Tyndarus* (s.d.s); *Tyn<darus>* (s.p.s); *Tyndarus, son of Demetrius, and supposed brother to Pamphilus, enamoured of Evadne* (d.p.)
CHREMYLUS: *Chremylus* (s.d.s); *Chrem<ylus>* (s.p.s); *Chremylus, an old man* (d.p.)
DIPSAS: *Dypsas* (s.d.s); *Dyps<as>* (s.p.s); *Dypsas,* [Chremylus'] *wife* (d.p.)
EVADNE: *Evadne* (s.d.s); *Evad<ne>* (s.p.s); *Evadne, supposed daughter of Chremylus* (d.p.)
TECHMESSA: *Techmessa* (s.d.s); *Tech<messa>* (s.p.s); *Techmessa, daughter to Chremylus* (d.p.)
PAEGNIUM: *Paegnium* (s.d.s); *Paeg<nium>* (s.p.s); *Paegnium, a Page* (d.p.)
PAMPHILUS: *Pamphilus* (s.d.s); *Pamp<hilus>* (s.p.s); *Pamphilus, supposed son to Demetrius, but son indeed to Chremylus* (d.p.)
PHRONESIUM: *Phronesium* (s.d.s); *Phron<esium>* (s.p.s); *Phronesium, a merry chambermaid* (d.p.)
OFFICERS: *Officers* (s.d.s and d.p.); *1 Officer | 2 Officer* (s.p.s)
BOMOLOCHUS: *Bomolochus* (s.d.s); *Bom<olochus>* (s.p.s); *Bomolochus,* [one of] *two Poets* (d.p.)
CHAERYLUS: *Chaerilus* (s.d.s); *Chaer<ilus>* (s.p.s); *Chaerilus,* [one of] *two Poets* (d.p.)
THRASYMACHUS: *Thrasymachus | Thrasimachus* (s.d.s); *Thrasim<achus>* (s.p.s); *Thrasimachus,* [one of] *two soldiers* (d.p.)
HYPERBOLUS: *Hyperbolus* (s.d.s; also misprinted *Hyperocus*); *Hyper<bolus>* (s.p.s); *Hyperbolus,* [one of] *two soldiers* (d.p.)
PHRYNE: *Phrine | Phryne* (s.d.s); *Phryn<e>* (s.p.s); *Phryne, a Courtesan, and Mistress to Asotus* (d.p.)
SERVANT: *a servant* (s.d.s); *Servants* (d.p.)
SEXTON: *Sexton* (s.d.s and s.p.s); *the Sexton* (s.d.s); *A Sexton* (d.p.)
STAPHYLA: [the Sexton's] *wife Staphyla* | [the Sexton's] *wife* (s.d.s); *Staph<yla>* (s.p.s); *Staphyla,* [the Sexton's] *wife* (d.p.)
DEMETRIUS: *Demetrius* (s.d.s); *Dem<etrius>* (s.p.s); *Astrologer* (s.d.s and s.p.s); *Demetrius, an Athenian in the disguise of an Astrologer* (d.p.)
PRIESTS: *Priests* (s.d.s); *Priest* (s.p.s); *A Priest* (d.p.)
HYMEN: *Hymen's statue* (s.d.s)

OTHER CHARACTERS
Asotus' 25 bastard children (1.1)
Evadne's many suitors (1.4)
Gentlemen ushers and chambermaids employed by Asotus' lovers (1.6)
Asotus' lovers, including ladies and countesses (1.6)
Asotus' dead mother (2.2, 5.2, 5.4)
Evadne's page (2.2)
Evadne's doctor (2.2)
Lalage, Tyndarus' dead mother (2.9, 2.12)
A dead captain (4.3)
A poet who died seven years ago (4.3)
The poet's mistress, whose dog died recently (4.3)
A woman, once beautiful, now dead (4.3)
The woman's chambermaid (4.3)
A dead lawyer (4.4)
Attendants on Pamphilus and Evadne (4.8)
Minos, who demanded a tribute of Theban boys to feed the Minotaur (5.1)

SETTING
Period: antiquity
Time-Scheme: 3.7, 3.14, and 4.8 all take place during the same night, and 5.1–9 the next day
Place: Thebes

Geography
Thebes: the Pegasus; the city walls; the seven gates
[*Greece*]: Athens; Corinth; Mount Helicon; Mount Parnassus; Mount Olympus
[*Aegean Sea*]: Lesbos; Paros
Cyprus: Paphos
[*Spain*]: Bilbao
Ireland
[*Africa*]: Egypt
[*Asia*]: Caucasus; Chaldea

SOURCES
Narrative: Macropedius, *Asotus* (1537)
Verbal: Horace, *Epistles* 2.1 (t.p. motto), *Satires* 1.4 (epistle); Bible: 1 Peter 3.7 (2.2); William Shakespeare, *Hamlet* (**1259**; 4.3–4); Ben Jonson, *The Alchemist* (**1621**; 3.6–7); Thomas Randolph, *The Fairy Knight* (**2078**; 4.4; but the debt may be vice versa), *The Drinking Academy* (**2285**; 3.4, 3.6, 5.4), Induction to *The Hungry Courtier* (**2319**; 3.5), *Amyntas* (**2321**; 2.9)
Works Mentioned: François Rabelais, *Gargantua* (1534; 2.5)

LANGUAGE
English
Latin: 20 words (2.1, 2.5, 4.1, 4.4, 5.3; Asotus, Phronesium, Thrasymachus, Sexton)
Italian: 5 words (2.2, 2.5, 3.9; Asotus, Thrasymachus)
French: 6 words (3.4, 4.1; Asotus, Thrasymachus)

FORM
Metre: pentameter and prose
Rhyme: blank verse and couplets
Act-Division: 5 acts
Epilogue: 13 lines (6 verse couplets, 7 prose), spoken in dialogue by Asotus and Demetrius

Lines (Spoken): 2,824 (2,665 verse, 159 prose)
Lines (Written): 2,876

STAGING
Discovery Space: Hymen's statue discovered (5.6, s.d.)
Within: speech (4.3, dialogue)
Miscellaneous: Simo hides 'in angulis' (in a corner; 3.4–5, s.d.)

MUSIC
Song: 5.6, Priests (?)
Other Singing: characters exit singing (5.9, s.d.)

PROPS
Weapons: Ballio's blade weapon (1.1–10, dialogue); Tyndarus' sword (1.7, 2.2, 2.12–13, 3.8–14, dialogue); Pamphilus' sword (1.10, s.d.; 2.1–13, 3.11–12, dialogue; 4.8, implicit; it has a favour tied around the hilt); Asotus' sword (2.4–8, 5.8–ep., dialogue); a sword (2.6, s.d.); two cudgels (2.8, dialogue); Hyperbolus' blade weapon (3.5–9, dialogue); Thrasymachus' blade weapon (3.5–9, dialogue); a stiletto (3.10, s.d.); an unspecified weapon (4.8, implicit); a halter (5.9, s.d.)
Musical Instruments: possibly a lyre (3.6, dialogue); a drum (5.8, s.d.); a trumpet (5.8, s.d.)
Clothing: Evadne's ear-ring (2.1–2, 2.4–8, dialogue; see also COSTUMES)
Money: gold (1.1–2, 3.6, dialogue); a purse of gold (3.1–9, dialogue); unspecified sums (3.3, 4.3, 4.6, implicit); possibly twenty drachmas (3.4, dialogue)
Animals: a sacrifice (5.6, s.d.)
Food and Drink: wine (3.4–8, dialogue; drunk on stage), with a bowl (3.5, dialogue) and cup (3.6, dialogue); perhaps a poisonous potion (4.9, dialogue; but perhaps just a figure of speech)
Small Portable Objects: dice (1.1, implicit); letters (1.10, s.d.); two letters (4.1, dialogue); four skulls (4.3–4, dialogue)
Large Portable Objects: seating for at least two characters (3.5–6, implicit); two coffins (4.1–9, 5.8, s.d.; they probably remain on stage in the intervening scenes)
Scenery: an altar (5.6–9, dialogue)

COSTUMES AND MAKE-UP
SIMO: wrinkles and silver hair (dialogue); ragged clothes (5.4, dialogue)
ASOTUS: a beard (dialogue); breeches with pockets (1.1–8, dialogue); a scabbard (2.4–8, dialogue); armour (3.4–5, 5.8–ep., s.d.; put on on stage); garments fastened with buttons and bandstrings (4.1–3, dialogue); a black cloak (5.3–6, dialogue; put on and removed on stage); a gay cloak (5.3–6, dialogue; put on and removed on stage)
BALLIO: a beard (dialogue); a scabbard (1.1–10, implicit)
TYNDARUS: a scabbard (2.12–13, implicit); a garment with a pocket (3.8–14, s.d.); a winding sheet (4.4–5, dialogue; removed on stage); the Sexton's clothes and a false beard (4.5–9, dialogue; put on on stage)
CHREMYLUS: a ring (5.6–7, dialogue)
EVADNE: a diamond ear-ring (1.7–8, s.d.; removed on stage; see also PROPS)
TECHMESSA: a winding sheet (4.4–5, dialogue; removed on stage); Staphyla's robes (4.5–9, dialogue; put on on stage)
PAMPHILUS: has no beard (dialogue); a scabbard (2.12–13, implicit)
BOMOLOCHUS and CHAERYLUS: both dressed as Mercury (3.5–8, s.d.); a laurel wreath each (3.5–8, dialogue; put on on stage)
PHRYNE: golden hair (dialogue); an antique robe and coronet (3.5–8, s.d.); lace-up shoes (3.5–8, dialogue)
SEXTON: his clothes are removed on stage (4.5, dialogue); Tyndarus' winding sheet (4.5, implicit; 5.8, dialogue; put on on stage)
STAPHYLA: robes (4.4–5, dialogue; removed on stage); Techmessa's winding sheet (4.5, implicit; 5.8, dialogue; put on on stage)
DEMETRIUS: a disguise (5.1–2, implicit; 5.7, s.d.; removed on stage); a ring (5.7, implicit)

EARLY STAGE HISTORY
Preparation: The play was one of several prepared for the King's visit to Cambridge in 1632. There was some dispute about whether *The Jealous Lovers* or Peter Hausted's *The Rival Friends* (**2364**) should be performed first during the royal visit; this was settled in Hausted's favour by Henry Butts, the Vice-Chancellor.

Postponement: The royal visit was postponed after the University's Chancellor, Henry Rich, 1st Earl of Holland, fell off his horse. The original plan was to perform a Latin comedy (probably *Versipellis*, **2362**) on the afternoon the King arrived and an English comedy (probably *The Jealous Lovers*) the following morning, Thursday 8 March.

Performance: at Trinity College, Cambridge, by members of the College on Tuesday 20 March 1632. The cast included Thomas Ryley (probably Tyndarus or Pamphilus). The audience included: King Charles I; Queen Henrietta Maria. The performance took place in the afternoon, and was over by 5 p.m. (when the royal party left Cambridge). Burnt wine was served at the college's expense (which amounted to £1.1s for both this performance and that of *The Rival Friends*, **2364**). At one or other performance, Theodore Kelly was pushed by the press of the crowd into Sir Arthur Gorges, who was with a lady; Sir Arthur responded by threatening to cudgel Kelly.

See **2364** for general information about the financing of the comedies performed at the royal visit.

EARLY TEXTUAL HISTORY
1632: Thomas Randolph was said to have written the play on the orders of Thomas Comber (Master of Trinity College), and to have revised it before publication.

1632: ¹Q₁ printed (after Sunday 1 April) at Cambridge by the University printers, Thomas and John Buck, to be sold by Richard Ireland; collation ¶⁴ 2¶⁴ A–L⁴, 52 leaves; title page names author and refers to performance; Latin title-page motto; authorial dedication to Thomas Comber (now Vice-Chancellor); authorial address to the reader; authorial verses to Sir Kenelm Digby, Sir Christopher Hatton, Anthony Stafford, Richard Lane, Lambert Osbaldeston (in Latin), and Thomas Ryley; English commendatory verses by Edward Hyde, Edward Francis, Richard Benfield, James Duport; Latin commendatory verses by Edward Hyde, Thomas Ryley, Charles Fotherbie, Francis Meres, Robert Randolph, and Thomas Vincent; list of roles. The book retailed at 6d.

1634: ²Q₂ printed at Cambridge by the University printers, Thomas Buck, John Buck, and Roger Daniel, to be sold by Richard Ireland.

c. 1630s–40s: a copy of Q₁ was in the possession of John Horne (Vicar of Headington, Oxfordshire). After his death, his entire collection of play-books passed into the possession of John Houghton of Brasenose College, Oxford (c. 1608–77), then to James Herne (died 1685), and then to the library of Ralph Sheldon (1623–84) at Weston, where it was catalogued by the antiquarian Anthony Wood, probably in the late 1670s.

1640: ³O₁ printed at Cambridge by Roger Daniel, to be sold by Richard Ireland; collation A–F⁸ G⁴, 52 leaves.

1645: entered in the Stationers' Register to Richard Royston on Tuesday 3 June, with the consent of the previous owners, Richard Ireland and Roger Daniel; entry names author. (This was a new entry effecting a transfer of rights which had not been established by prior entry because the title had hitherto been published outside London.)

1646: included as a bibliographically independent item appended to the second issue of Thomas Randolph's *Poems* (⁴O₂); printed at London for Richard Royston. The copy was O₁.

Mid-seventeenth century: extracts included in a MS miscellany (York Minster, Add. MS 122, fos. 310ʳ–313ᵛ) compiled by members of the Rawdon family.

1652: included in Randolph's *Poems* (⁵O₃), sigs. ²P8ʳ–³G4ᵛ, 53 leaves; printed surreptitiously at London.

1652: O₃ reissued at Oxford in or before June, with a cancel title page naming Francis Bowman and William Roybould as the booksellers.

1655: *The English Treasury of Wit and Language* entered in the Stationers' Register to Humphrey Moseley on Tuesday 16 January.

1655: four extracts (from 1.1, 2.2, 4.5, 5.6) included in John Cotgrave's *The English Treasury of Wit and Language*, sigs. K6ᵛ, N6ʳ, Q7ʳ; printed for Humphrey Moseley.

c. 1655: extracts transcribed by John Evans in a miscellany, *Hesperides*, intended for publication and entered to Humphrey Moseley in the Stationers' Register on Thursday 16 August 1655. The book remained unpublished in 1660, and Evans continued to add to the collection until at least 1666. Two MS exemplars are known; one was cut up by J. O. Halliwell-Phillipps in the nineteenth century; the other survives (Washington: Folger, MS V. b. 93).

1656: *The English Parnassus* entered to Evan Tyler, Thomas Johnson, and Thomas Davies in the Stationers' Register on Wednesday 24 December.

1657: 41 extracts (from Hatton, Ryley, and Hyde verses, 1.1–3, 1.5–6, 1.8–10, 2.2, 2.5–6, 2.9, 2.12, 3.1, 3.3, 3.5, 3.10–12, 3.14, 4.1, 4.3, 4.5, 4.8, 5.2, 5.4, 5.6) included in Joshua Poole's *The English Parnassus*, sigs. R1ᵛ, S3ᵛ, S4ᵛ, T3ᵛ, T8ʳ, V1ʳ⁻ᵛ, V2ᵛ, X1ʳ, Y2ᵛ, 2B3ᵛ, 2C1ᵛ, 2C2ᵛ, 2C8ʳ, 2D5ᵛ, 2E3ʳ, 2E7ᵛ, 2F3ʳ, 2F5ʳ, 2H1ʳ, 2K6ʳ, 2L8ʳ, 2N7ᵛ, 2N8ᵛ, 2O3ʳ, 2P8ᵛ, 2Q4ᵛ, 2R2ᵛ, 2R3ᵛ, 2S4ᵛ; printed for Thomas Johnson.

1662: printed at London by Thomas Newcomb for inclusion in Randolph's *Poems* (⁶O₄), sigs. Z7ʳ–2F8ᵛ, 50 leaves. The copy was O₃. The volume was eventually issued at Oxford in 1664 by Francis Bowman, and to be sold by Thomas Bowman.

1668: included in Randolph's *Poems* (⁷O₅); printed at Oxford by Henry Hall for Francis Bowman, and to be sold by John Crosley. The copy was O₄.

1677: *The English Parnassus* reprinted by Henry Brome for Thomas Bassett and John Wright; the extracts now appear on sigs. Q5ᵛ, R7ᵛ, R8ᵛ, S7ᵛ, T4ʳ, T5ʳ⁻ᵛ, T6ᵛ, V5ʳ, X6ᵛ, 2A7ᵛ, 2B5ᵛ, 2B6ᵛ, 2C4ʳ, 2C8ᵛ, 2D7ʳ, 2E3ᵛ, 2E7ʳ, 2F1ʳ, 2G5ʳ, 2K2ʳ, 2L4ʳ, 2N3ᵛ, 2N4ᵛ, 2N7ʳ, 2P4ᵛ, 2P8ᵛ, 2Q6ᵛ, 2Q7ᵛ, 2R8ᵛ.

Late seventeenth century: included in Randolph's *Poems* (⁸O₆); this was a pirated edition printed from O₅, and with a title page falsely bearing the copy edition's date, place of publication, and booksellers.

Late seventeenth century (before 1695): a copy of O₃ was owned by Anthony Wood.

EDITION
W. Carew Hazlitt, in *Poetical and Dramatic Works of Thomas Randolph* (London, 1875), i. 51–172.

REFERENCES
Annals 1632; Beal Online RnT 427.8; Bentley, v. 982–6; Eyre & Rivington, i. 463, ii. 8, 103; Greg 469; Hazlitt, 119; Nicolas K. Kiessling, *The Library of Anthony Wood* (Oxford, 2002) 5524; *The Library*, 5th ser., 28 (1973), 294–308; *The Library*, 7th ser., 10 (2009), 372–404; *MLR* 13 (1918), 401–11; *PBSA* 107 (2013), 22; REED: Cambridge, 637–45, 881–3, 903–4; *RES* 16 (1940), 435–6; *ShS* 11 (1958), 108–9; *SP* 40 (1943), 186–203; Smith, 94; Steele, 241; Stratman, 121–4, 326–30.

2366. *Tarquinius Superbus* [Tarquin the Proud]

EVIDENCE
Douai Diaries.

GENRE
tragicomedy
Contemporary: *tragico-comoedia*

TITLE
Performed: *Tragico-comoedia de Tarquinio Superbo*

AUTHOR
Richard Todkill (*also known as* Richard Tempest)

DATE
April 1632

ORIGINAL PRODUCTION
English College, Douai

PLOT
Tarquin and his brother Arruns marry the two daughters of King Servius Tullius. The younger daughter grows to despise her mild-mannered husband Arruns. She and Tarquin murder one another's siblings and then marry each other. Tarquin then seizes the throne. Tullius is murdered in the street; Tullia finds her father's dead body and drives a chariot over it. Tarquin has his political opponents killed and begins a reign of terror.

Tarquin's son, Sextus, rapes the chaste Lucretia while her husband is away at war. The public scandal results in the expulsion of Tarquin and his family and the establishment of the Roman republic.

ROLES
TARQUIN the Proud, brother of Arruns, husband of the Elder Tullia, later second husband of the Younger Tullia and father of Sextus; later still, King of Rome
ARRUNS, Tarquin's brother, first husband of the Younger Tullia
The ELDER TULLIA, Tullius' daughter, sister of the Younger Tullia, Tarquin's first wife
The YOUNGER TULLIA, Tullius' daughter, sister of the Elder Tullia, Arruns's wife; later Tarquin's second wife, and later still, Sextus' mother
Servius TULLIUS, king of Rome, father of the two Tullias
SEXTUS Tarquin, son of Tarquin and the Younger Tullia
LUCRETIA, Collatine's wife
COLLATINE, Lucretia's husband
Lucius Junius BRUTUS

SETTING
Period: sixth (and perhaps fifth) century BC; the play dramatizes events from the life and reign of Tarquin the Proud (reigned 535–509, died 496)
Place: Rome

SOURCES
Narrative: Livy, *Roman History*

EARLY STAGE HISTORY
1632: performed in the English College, Douai, on Tuesday 20 April (Gregorian). The performance took place after lunch.

REFERENCES
Annals Supp. I (t); *The Douai College Diaries: Third, Fourth, and Fifth*, ed. Edwin H. Burton (London, 1911), i. 303.

2367. *Hyde Park*

TEXT
Printed in 1637 (STC 22446).

GENRE
comedy
Contemporary: comedy (S.R.); play (Middle Temple records, Abraham Wright, *c.* 1640; *Poems &c.*, 1646)

TITLE
Performed/Printed: *Hyde Park*

AUTHOR
James Shirley

DATE
April 1632

ORIGINAL PRODUCTION
Queen Henrietta's Men at the Cockpit

PLOT
In one plot, Carol has three suitors, and, claiming to be averse to marriage, torments them all. Venture gives her a chain of pearl, and she gives it to his rival, Richer. Richer gives her a diamond ring, and she gives that to Venture. She agrees to grant a request from the third suitor, Fairfield, on condition that he is not asking her to love him, marry him, or have sex with him. In fact, he asks her *not* to love him, and not to desire his company. They try to avoid one another on a visit to Hyde Park, but she becomes jealous on seeing him with his sister, sends for him, and sparks fly. Venture writes her a letter threatening suicide on account of unrequited love. She forges Fairfield's signature on it, confronts him with it, and offers marriage to save his life. He denies the letter, refuses marriage, and proposes to castrate himself instead. Finally they admit that they love one another, and become engaged.

In a second plot, Trier is courting Fairfield's sister Julietta, but leaves her alone with the roué Lord Bonvile, who promptly tries to court her. His advances continue in Hyde Park, and she continues to resist them, hoping to convert him from loose living. Her admonitions begin to take effect, and Bonvile reflects critically on his way of life. Trier admits that he used Bonvile as a way of testing her chastity. Disgusted, she discomfits him by demanding corresponding proofs of his fitness to be her husband. She is more willing to entertain a newly modest proposal from Bonvile.

In a third plot, Bonavent the merchant has not returned from a sea voyage, and now is presumed dead: he asked his wife to wait seven years for him, and his time is up. She agrees to marry Lacy, her suitor. After the wedding, her husband arrives in disguise and witnesses the celebrations. In Hyde Park, he picks a fight with Lacy, then privately tells his wife who he really is and what happened to him: his return was delayed by pirates, and he has only now been rescued from captivity. Later, he hands out willow garlands to the four disappointed lovers, Venture, Richer, Trier, and Lacy, and reveals his identity, thereby invalidating Lacy's marriage.

SCENE DESIGNATION
1.1–2, 2.1–4, 3.1–2, 4.1–3, 5.1–2 (Q has act-division only)

ROLES
Master Frank TRIER, Julietta's suitor
Master LACY, a gentleman; later (and temporarily) Mistress Bonavent's second husband; possibly named John
Master Jack VENTURE, a gentleman; also called John
JARVIS, Mistress Bonavent's servant
Lord BONVILE, a young rake
Bonvile's PAGE; 15 years old
Master RIDER, a gentleman
MISTRESS BONAVENT, supposed Bonavent's widow, but in fact his wife; Carol's kinswoman; later (and temporarily) Lacy's wife; possibly named Cicely
Mistress CAROL, a gentlewoman, Mistress Bonavent's kinswoman
Master FAIRFIELD, a gentleman, Julietta's brother
Master BONAVENT, a merchant, Mistress Bonavent's husband; disguised as a captain
Mistress Bonavent's SERVANT (2.1; may be Jarvis)
Mistress JULIETTA Fairfield, a gentlewoman, Fairfield's sister
Julietta's WAITING-WOMAN (2.3)
ATTENDANTS (3.1, non-speaking)
Two RUNNERS, an English and an Irish footman, the latter possibly named Teague (3.1, non-speaking)
GENTLEMEN following the foot-race (3.1; only speak collectively)
A MILKMAID (4.3)
A JOCKEY; he may actually be named Jockey (4.3)
Three GENTLEMEN watching the horse-race (4.3)
A BAGPIPER (4.3, non-speaking)
A MESSENGER, who brings Carol a letter (4.3, non-speaking)
Two KEEPERS of Hyde Park (4.3)

Speaking Parts: 20–1

Stage Directions and Speech Prefixes
TRIER: *Tryer* (s.d.s and s.p.s); *Mr Tryer* [amorous servant] *To Mrs Julietta* (d.p.)
LACY: *Lacy* (s.d.s); *Lac<y>* (s.p.s); *Mr Lacy* [amorous servant] *To Mrs Bonavent* (d.p.)
VENTURE: *Venture* (s.d.s); *Ven<ture>* (s.p.s); *Mr Venture* [one of the] *amorous servants to Mrs Caroll* (d.p.)
JARVIS: *Servant* (s.d.s and s.p.s); *the servant* (s.d.s); *Servants* (d.p.)
BONVILE: *Lord Bonvile | Bonvile* (s.d.s); *Lord | my Lord* (s.d.s and s.p.s); *The Lord Bonvile* (d.p.)
PAGE: *Page* (s.d.s and s.p.s); *Lord's Page* (d.p.)
RIDER: *Master Rider | Rider* (s.d.s); *Rid<er>* (s.p.s); *Mr Rider* [one of the] *amorous servants to Mrs Caroll* (d.p.)
MISTRESS BONAVENT: *Mistress Bonavent* | [*Lacy's*] *Bride* (s.d.s); *Bon<avent> | Mistress B<onavent>* (s.p.s); *Mrs Bonavent* (d.p.)
CAROL: *Mistress Caroll | Carell | Caroll* (s.d.s); *Car<oll>* (s.p.s); *Mrs Caroll* (d.p.)
FAIRFIELD: *Mr Fairefeild | Master Fairefeild | Fairefeild | Fairefield* (s.d.s); *Fa<irefield>* (s.p.s); *Mr Fairefield* [one of the] *amorous servants to Mrs Caroll* (d.p.)
BONAVENT: *Bonavent | Master Bonavent* (s.d.s); *Bon<avent> | Master B<onavent>* (s.p.s); *Mr Bonavent* (d.p.)
SERVANT: *a Servant* (s.d.s); *Servant* (s.p.s); *Servants* (d.p.)
JULIETTA: [*Fairfield's*] *Sister Julietta | Mistress Julietta* | [*Fairfield's*] *Sister | Mistress Fairefield | Mistress Fairefield* (s.d.s); *Ju<lietta>* (s.p.s); *Mrs Julietta sister to Fairefield* (d.p.)
WAITING-WOMAN: *Servant* (s.d.s); *Waiting <Woman>* (s.p.s); *Waiting Woman* (d.p.)
ATTENDANTS: [*Bonvile's, Julietta's, and Fairfield's*] *Attendants* (s.d.s); *Servants* (d.p.)
RUNNERS: *The Runners* (s.d.s); *Runners* (s.d.s and d.p.s)
GENTLEMEN: *the Gentlemen | Gentlemen* (s.d.s)
MILKMAID: *Milkmaid* (s.d.s, s.p.s, and d.p.)
JOCKEY: *Jockey* (s.d.s); *Jo<ckey>* (s.p.s); *Jocky* (d.p.)
GENTLEMEN: *Gentlemen* (s.d.s); *1 | 2 | 3* (s.p.s)
BAGPIPER: *A Bagpipe | the bagpiper* (s.d.s)
MESSENGER: *one* (s.d.s)
KEEPERS: *Keeper | 2 | 1* (s.p.s)

OTHER CHARACTERS
Carol's mother (1.2)
Mistress Bonavent's servants (1.2; some appear on stage, but there may be more)
Mistress Bonavent's tailor (1.2)
Mistress Bonavent's doctor (1.2)
Mistress Bonavent's chaplain (1.2)
Anthony at the Rose, perhaps a drawer (3.1)
Fairfield's footman (4.1)
The priest who married Lacy and Mistress Bonavent (4.3)
A Turkish pirate, who captured Bonavent (4.3)

A merchant, who rescued Bonavent (4.3)
Ladies who were attracted to Lord Bonvile, he says, but who perhaps didn't get a proper look at him in the dark (5.1)
The King (5.1)
The barber who shaved off Bonavent's beard (5.2)

SETTING

Period: contemporary; the action takes place in the spring
Time-Scheme: the action takes place during a single day; 1.2 takes place during the morning
Place: London

Geography
London: Bedlam; the Exchange; Hyde Park; Spring Garden; the Asparagus Garden; Westminster Abbey; the Rose tavern; the Maurice; Knightsbridge
England: Coventry; Newmarket
Ireland
[Europe]: the Alps; Rome; Austria; Bavaria; Spain
The Canary Islands
Turkey
India
The North Pole

SOURCES

Narrative: William Shakespeare, *Much Ado About Nothing* (**1148**; Carol/Fairfield plot)
Verbal: *The Book of Common Prayer*: Marriage service (1549, rev. 1552; 1.2, 5.1); possibly *Titus and Vespasian* (**923**; 4.3)
Works Mentioned: Raphael Holinshed, *Chronicles of England, Scotland, and Ireland* (1577, 2nd edn 1587; 1.2); Robert Greene, *Friar Bacon and Friar Bungay* (**822**; 2.4); Edward Sharpham, *Cupid's Whirligig* (**1527**; 1.2); *The Devil and the Baker* (unidentified ballad; 2.4)

LANGUAGE

English
Latin: 2 words (1.1; Trier)
French: 6 words (2.2, 2.4, 4.3; Lacy, Carol, 3 Gentleman)

FORM

Metre: pentameter and prose
Rhyme: blank verse
Act-Division: 5 acts
Lines (Spoken): 2,043 (1,757 verse, 286 prose)
Lines (Written): 2,444

STAGING

Within: voices (2.1, 3.1, implicit); music (2.1, implicit); speech (3.1, implicit; 4.3, s.d.); sound effects (4.3, s.d.); shout (4.3, s.d.)
Miscellaneous: Bonavent exits at the end of 2.1 and immediately re-enters at the start of 2.2. The action is organized to avoid bringing horses on stage (4.3).

MUSIC AND SOUND

Sound Effects: cuckoo (4.1, 4.3, implicit); nightingale (4.2, dialogue); 'confused noise of betting within' (4.3, s.d.)
Music: music (2.1, dialogue); recorders (5.2, s.d.)
On-Stage Music: the Bagpiper plays a galliard (4.3, s.d./dialogue)
Song: 'Come, Muses all that dwell nigh the fountain', 4.3, Venture, 32 lines
Other Singing: Venture sings (4.3, implicit)
Dance: Lacy, Mistress Bonavent, Rider, Carol, and Venture enter and exit dancing (2.2, s.d.); Bonavent dances (2.2, s.d.); Lacy dances (4.3, s.d.)

PROPS

Weapons: Rider's sword (1.1, dialogue); Venture's sword (1.1, 3.1, implicit); Bonavent's sword (2.2, 4.3, dialogue; 3.1, implicit); Lacy's rapier (4.3, dialogue)
Musical Instruments: bagpipes (4.3, s.d.)
Clothing: a diamond ring (1.1, s.d.); a chain of pearl (1.1, s.d.)
Money: an unspecified sum (4.3, implicit); another unspecified sum (4.3, implicit)
Food and Drink: a bowl of milk or cream (4.3, dialogue); wine (4.3, dialogue); a syllabub (4.3, dialogue)
Small Portable Objects: a letter (4.3, implicit); another letter (4.3, s.d.; 5.1, dialogue)
Large Portable Objects: a milk-pail (4.3, dialogue)

COSTUMES AND MAKE-UP

TRIER: a willow garland (5.2, implicit; put on on stage)
LACY: hangers (4.3, implicit); a willow garland (5.2, implicit; put on on stage)
VENTURE: hangers (1.1, 3.1, implicit); breeches with a pocket (4.3, dialogue); covered in mud (4.3, dialogue); a willow garland (5.2, implicit; put on on stage)
RIDER: hangers (1.1, implicit); a willow garland (5.2, implicit; put on on stage)
CAROL: brown complexion (dialogue); a ruff (2.4, dialogue); possibly a veil (3.2, dialogue; may be a figure of speech)
FAIRFIELD: has no beard (dialogue); 'well-trussed' (3.1, dialogue)
BONAVENT: disguised (2.1–2, 3.1, 4.2–3, implicit), including a beard (dialogue); a cloak (2.2, dialogue; probably removed on stage); hangers (2.2, 3.1, 4.3, implicit); no beard (5.2, dialogue)
MILKMAID: a plain petticoat (4.3, dialogue)

EARLY STAGE HISTORY

1632: presumably performed as licensed.
1632: performed by Queen Henrietta's Men at the Middle Temple on Thursday 1 November. Anthony Turner was later paid £10 for the performance.
1639: The play was in the repertory of the King's and Queen's Young Company (Beeston's Boys) at the Cockpit. On Saturday 10 August, Philip Herbert, 4th Earl of Pembroke (Lord Chamberlain) issued an order

restraining performances by other companies of this and 44 other plays.

EARLY TEXTUAL HISTORY

1632: On Friday 20 April, Sir Henry Herbert licensed the text for performance.

1637: entered in the Stationers' Register to Andrew Crooke and William Cooke on Thursday 13 April; entry names author. Thomas Herbert, Sir Henry Herbert's deputy, had licensed the book for publication.

1637: Q printed by Thomas Cotes for Andrew Crooke and William Cooke; collation A² B–I⁴ K², 36 leaves; title page names author, acting company, and playhouse; authorial dedication to Henry Rich, 1st Earl of Holland; list of roles.

c. 1630s–40s: a copy of Q was in the possession of John Horne (Vicar of Headington, Oxfordshire). After his death, his entire collection of play-books passed into the possession of John Houghton of Brasenose College, Oxford (c. 1608–77), then to James Herne (died 1685), and then to the library of Ralph Sheldon (1623–84) at Weston, where it was catalogued by Anthony Wood, probably in the late 1670s. By then the copy had been bound into a single volume with 21 other plays by Shirley (and, presumably in error, with Henry Shirley's *The Martyred Soldier*, **2030**).

c. 1640: Abraham Wright transcribed extracts into a MS miscellany (London: British Library, Add. MS 22608, fos. 86ᵛ–87ʳ). The MS later passed to Wright's son, the antiquarian James Wright (c. 1644–c. 1717).

1640–1: Humphrey Moseley was selling copies of Q for 6d each.

1645: extract (from 5.2) included in the fourth edition of 'Philomusus', *The Academy of Compliments*, sig. I6ʳ; printed by Thomas Badger for Humphrey Moseley.

1646: *The Academy of Compliments* reprinted by Moses Bell for Humphrey Moseley; the extract now appears on sig. K8ᵛ.

1646: rights to James Shirley's *Poems &c.* transferred in the Stationers' Register from Francis Constable to Humphrey Moseley on Saturday 31 October.

1646: Song included in James Shirley's *Poems &c.*, sigs. D7ᵛ–D8ʳ; printed by Ruth Raworth for Humphrey Moseley.

1650: *The Academy of Compliments* reprinted for Humphrey Moseley; the extract now appears on sig. K5ʳ.

Mid-seventeenth century: extracts included in a MS miscellany (Washington: Folger, MS V. a. 87, fos. 12ᵛ–13ᵛ, bis) possibly compiled by William How.

1655: *The English Treasury of Wit and Language* entered in the Stationers' Register to Humphrey Moseley on Tuesday 16 January.

1655: five extracts (from 1.2, 2.4, 4.3, 5.1) included in John Cotgrave's *The English Treasury of Wit and Language*, sigs. E5ʳ, N1ᵛ–N2ʳ, T7ᵛ, V5ʳ; printed for Humphrey Moseley.

1657: *The Mysteries of Love and Eloquence* entered in the Stationers' Register to Nathaniel Brooke on Monday 7 December.

1658: Song (headed 'On an Excellent Race-Horse') included in Edward Phillips's *The Mysteries of Love and Eloquence*, sig. H2ʳ⁻ᵛ; printed for Nathaniel Brooke.

1658: *The Academy of Compliments* reprinted for Humphrey Moseley.

1663: *The Academy of Compliments* reprinted by Thomas Leach and Thomas Child.

c. 1670s: four extracts (from 1.1–2, 5.1) included in MS annotations in an interleaved copy of John Cotgrave's *The English Treasury of Wit and Language*, p. 174aʳ, 204aᵛ, 284aᵛ, 300aᵛ. (The copy is now at the British Library, pressmark G.16385.)

1684: *The Mysteries of Love and Eloquence* entered in the Stationers' Register to Obadiah Blagrave on Monday 1 December.

1684: Nicholas Cox (Manciple of St Edmund Hall, Oxford) had a copy of Q in his bookshop. It had probably been previously owned by Gerard Langbaine, and appears on a list compiled by Anthony Wood on Saturday 13 December.

1685: *The Mysteries of Love and Eloquence* reprinted by James Rawlins for Obadiah Blagrave.

1699: *The Mysteries of Love and Eloquence* reprinted as *The Beau's Academy*; printed for Obadiah Blagrave and for sale by John Sprint.

EDITIONS

William Gifford, in *The Dramatic Works and Poems of James Shirley* (London, 1833), ii. 457–541.
Eugene Giddens, Revels Plays (Manchester, forthcoming).
Brett Greatley-Hirsch and Mark Houlahan, in James Shirley, *The Complete Works*, gen. eds. Eugene Giddens, Teresa Grant, and Barbara Ravelhofer (Oxford, forthcoming).

REFERENCES

Annals 1632; Bawcutt 230, C96; Beal 2 ShJ 180–1; Bentley, v. 1121–3; Bodleian, MS Wood E. 4, art. 1, p. 17; Eyre & Rivington, i. 250, 463, ii. 157, iii. 263; Robert Stanley Forsythe, *The Relations of Shirley's Plays to the Elizabethan Drama* (New York, 1914), 349–56; Greg 517; Hazlitt, 112; *MLR* 13 (1918), 401–11; *MP* 66 (1968–9), 256–61; MSC 2.3, 389–90; *Oxford Bibliographical Society Proceedings and Papers* 2.2 (1929), 132–3; REED: Inns of Court, 233–4, 748; *SP* 40 (1943), 186–203.

2368. *Love Yields to Honour*

EVIDENCE

Sir Henry Herbert's office-book; list of plays written in a mid-seventeenth-century hand on a blank leaf of a copy of the 1634 edition of *Albumazar* (**1769**; Q₃; the copy is now in the Bodleian Library, pressmark Mal. 207 (5)).

TITLE
Performed: *Love Yields to Honour*

DATE
Limits: 1610–32
Best Guess: April 1632

The upper limit is conjecturally assigned on the basis of the other known and datable plays in the *Albumazar* list. The best guess embodies an assumption that the Queen saw one of the first performances, as was also the case two years later with *Love's Mistress* (**2451**) and probably *The Spartan Ladies* (**2431**).

ORIGINAL PRODUCTION
King's Men at the Blackfriars and/or the Globe

SOURCES
Verbal: Torquato Tasso, *Il Re Torrismondo* (1587, repr. 1588; title).

EARLY STAGE HISTORY
1632: performed at the Globe on Wednesday 25 April (or possibly at the Blackfriars, with Queen Henrietta Maria in the audience).

REFERENCES
Annals Supp. II (f); Bawcutt 231; Bentley, v. 1369; *N&Q* 20 (1973), 465–6; William Shakespeare, *The Plays and Poems*, ed. Edmond Malone (London, 1821), ii. 439; Sibley, 96.

2369. Queen's Court Masque (?)

EVIDENCE
Tirewoman's bill in Queen Henrietta Maria's debenture accounts (Kew: National Archives, LR 5/65).

This may be only a misdated bill for work on *Tempe Restored* (**2359**); it is too early to pertain to **2384**, which was apparently a swiftly arranged diplomatic courtesy in response to an event that happened overseas in September. It is striking that the Queen's warrant, dated 9 July 1632, to pay Aurelian Townshend for writing the *Tempe Restored* libretto refers to it as 'our last masque', which would seem on the face of it to preclude the existence of any other masque in the interim. Even so, the bill explicitly assigns the work to the April to June quarter. This, along with the similarly exiguous evidence for **2328**, raises the possibility that the Queen may have flirted for a few years with private spring masquing, perhaps on May Day. (The month then slipped to August in 1634–5; see **2442** and **2486**.)

GENRE
masque

Contemporary: masque

DATE
Spring 1632

ORIGINAL PRODUCTION
Queen Henrietta Maria's Court

EARLY STAGE HISTORY
1632: presumably performed on an unknown date between April and June. The cast included: Queen Henrietta Maria; Lady Elizabeth Grey of Stamford (who was about 10 years old).

Production Expenses
The tirewoman Blanche Brown submitted a bill for dressing the Queen (£3) and Elizabeth Grey (10s) for the performance. The amount for Elizabeth Grey was disallowed, but the amount in respect of the Queen was paid to William Brown on Wednesday 8 May 1633.

REFERENCES
ELR 29 (1999), 79.

2370. Hannibal and Scipio

EVIDENCE
Sir Henry Herbert's office-book; Thomas Nabbes, *Hannibal and Scipio* (**2480**).

The Herbert record, which survives only in a note taken by Malone, is problematic in the first instance because its three fundamental elements are incompatible: if *Hannibal and Scipio* was performed for the second time at Salisbury Court on 12 May 1636, then the company was not the Prince's Men but the King's Revels; if it was performed by the Prince's Men on 12 May 1636, then it was not at Salisbury Court because they were on a provincial tour at the time; and if it was performed by the Prince's Men at Salisbury Court, then it was not in 1636 but some time between December 1631 and July 1634. The problem is compounded by the existence of a play by Thomas Nabbes on the same subject and of the same title, whose title page ascribes it to a different company, Queen Henrietta's Men, and a different year, 1635, an ascription made even more secure by the inclusion of a cast list.

Which element of the evidence should we disbelieve? It would obviously be easier for Malone to misread a single digit in the year rather than the name of the company or the playhouse, and several other factors support the hypothesis. Herbert accepted the takings of the 12 May performance in settlement of a debt due by Salisbury Court's manager, Richard Gunnell, who died in early October 1634; this confirms the ascription to the theatre and tends not to support the date of 1636. There is one further reason to doubt the date: a plague closure came into effect on 12 May 1636.

Malone (and subsequent scholars) might nevertheless have been inclined to prefer that date because it allows the play's identification with the extant Nabbes play. This is circumstantially implausible in any event: it would mean that the extant play was performed once in 1635 (or, at a pinch, by 24 March 1636), then waited until mid-May for its second London performance, and was then released to the printer while the theatres were closed. (It was entered in the Stationers' Register in August 1636.) But Nabbes's prologue in fact contains a reference indicating that there had already been a play on the same subject: 'some would task | His borrowing from a former play'. This is usually understood to be an allusion to *The Wonder of Women* (**1485**), or possibly the lost Admiral's Men *Hannibal and Scipio* (**1274**), but both candidates were by then decades old; the anticipated charge of borrowing would be likelier if the source was a play of more recent memory, though it is true that *The Wonder of Women* was reprinted in 1633. The avoidance of confusion about the play's identity might explain the Q title page's uncommon specificity about the year it was performed.

TITLE
Performed: *Hannibal and Scipio*

DATE
Limits: 1632 or 1634
Best Guess: May 1632

1633 is ruled out because the date of the performance, 12 May, was a Sunday in that year. The choice between the two options is finely balanced; the Nabbes prologue reference might support the later year, but the digit 2 seems marginally easier to misread as 6 than one of Sir Henry Herbert's angular 4s.

ORIGINAL PRODUCTION
Prince Charles's Men at Salisbury Court

PLOT
Hannibal has invaded Italy and routed the Romans at Cannae. Scipio dissuades the Senate from suing for peace, and leads an expedition to Spain which conquers New Carthage. He then leads an army into Africa and routs the Carthaginians at Zama.

ROLES
HANNIBAL, a Carthaginian general
SCIPIO, a Roman general

SETTING
Period: third century BC; the play dramatizes events which took place during the Second Punic War (*c.* 216–201 BC)
Place: Italy, Spain, and Africa

Geography
Italy: Rome; Cannae
The Alps
Spain: New Carthage
Africa: Carthage; Zama

SOURCES
Narrative: Livy, *Roman History*, or analogue or derivate

EARLY STAGE HISTORY
1632 or 1634: performed by Prince Charles's Men at Salisbury Court on 12 May (which was a Saturday in 1632 and a Monday in 1634). This was the second day of the play's run, and was designated a benefit performance for Sir Henry Herbert, in satisfaction of a debt owed by the theatre's manager, Richard Gunnell; Herbert received £2.14s.

REFERENCES
Bawcutt 350.

2371. The Sad One

TEXT
Printed in 1659 (Wing S6130), from an incomplete authorial rough draft; the text lacks at least the end of the first and last acts (as marked), probably more.

GENRE
tragedy
Contemporary: tragedy (t.p.); dramatic piece (epistle)

TITLE
Printed: *The Sad One*

AUTHOR
Sir John Suckling

DATE
Limits: 1625–37
Best Guess: 1632

Suckling's other plays date from 1637–40, but *The Sad One* is unlike them in one obvious respect: it is unfinished. Beaurline argues cogently that it expresses attitudes attributable to Suckling immediately after his return from the Continent in April 1632. The main argument in support of the traditional date of 1637 is the assumption that Suckling would not have caricatured Jonson as Multecarni during his lifetime. That is a weak case in any event; but perhaps it is worth bearing in mind that the bedridden Jonson was thought to be dead before he produced *The Magnetic Lady* (**2385**) in September 1632. Arguably satire on Jonson as a court poet would be more timely sooner rather than later after his court commissions were discontinued in 1631. A date in the 1630s would also be supported by apparent verbal borrowings from *'Tis Pity She's a Whore* (**2329**) in two scenes; if so, Suckling probably saw Ford's play before leaving England in early October 1631.

PLOT
The Clarimonts helped to put King Aldebrand on the throne of Sicily, but are now out of favour: Old Clarimont is in prison, his elder son banished, and his younger son disgraced. But the family fortunes seem to be on the upturn thanks to the King's adulterous passion for Francelia, Clarimont's married daughter. Anticipating that the old man is about to be released, the corrupt courtier Lorenzo goes to the prison pretending to have an order for his immediate execution, and carries it out himself. He then plots to murder the King and seize power himself.

Young Clarimont wants revenge, and arranges for Lorenzo's plots to be leaked to the King. Aldebrand is persuaded not to have Lorenzo arrested at once, but instead arrange for his father, Lord Cleonax, to be present to witness the assassination attempt. The upshot is that Lorenzo kills his own father by mistake; his accomplice Parmenio then kills him.

Aldebrand asks Clarimont to help in the wooing of Francelia. Meanwhile the court favourite Bellamino is wooing her on his own account, and is caught kissing her by her husband, Florelio. Although Florelio's immediate impulse is to fight a duel and kill Bellamino, he cannot bring himself to go through with it. Clarimont unwillingly presents the King's suit to his sister, and she refuses, convincing him of her chastity. However, Florelio refuses to accept Clarimont's assurances on the issue, and, putting her to the test, Clarimont learns that his brother-in-law's jealousy is well-founded.

Florelio will not countenance a violent revenge, but Clarimont plans one anyway. It is to be a night of court festivity, with a masque, after which the King plans to sleep with Francelia; to that end he has arranged to swap bedrooms with Florelio. Disguised as a servant, Clarimont conveys to Francelia her husband's wish that she should stay in and not go to the masque, and, when summoned by the King, she sends word that she is ill. Clarimont persuades Bellamino to kill the King not in public but when he is in bed with Francelia. [*The rest of the play is lost, or unwritten.*]

The intended resolution presumably included a masque scene and then another in which Bellamino attempts to kill the King in bed. The two curious arrangements made in 5.2 may also have a bearing: Francelia is to stay away from the masque, and she is to sleep with the King in her husband's bed. Since Clarimont's objective is presumably the destruction of Bellamino, perhaps as well as the King, the proposed bedroom murder may incorporate a trap.

SCENE DESIGNATION

1.1–2, [*lacuna*], 2.1–5, 3.1–4, 4.1–6, 5.1–2, [*lacuna*] (Beaurline, based on O)

O is incompletely divided into acts and scenes, but Beaurline argues that the division seems not to be authorial, but rather to have been imposed by the printer, since it appears to treat the play as if it were complete. The O iteration omits necessary scene-divisions at 1.2 and 4.4 (supplied by Beaurline), and so numbers 4.5–6 as 4.4–5; it also includes a heading for 3.5 when the stage is not clear (in that Cleonax's dead body remains on stage). The stage is clear at a different point in 3.4, and also in 1.2 and 4.2.

The lacunae are as noted in O's list of errata.

ROLES

OLD CLARIMONT, a lord, father of Clarimont and Francelia; may have been originally named Floretti (as the family is named in the argument)
A SERVANT, formerly Old Clarimont's man (1.1)
FIDELIO, Old Clarimont's friend
LORENZO, a courtier, Cleonax's son
Lord CLEONAX, the Treasurer, Lorenzo's father, Bellamino's kinsman (*non-speaking*)
Cleonax's SERVANTS (1.2, *non-speaking*)
The KEEPER of the prison (1.2)
PARMENIO, Lorenzo's accomplice
CLARIMONT, a young man, Old Clarimont's younger son, Francelia's brother
ALDEBRAND, King of Sicily, Amasia's husband
FRANCELIA, Florelio's wife, Old Clarimont's daughter, Clarimont's sister
BELLAMINO, a court favourite, a young man, Cleonax's kinsman
LORDS attending the King (2.4, 3.4, 4.2; only speak collectively)
SILEO, the King's attendant (may or may not be a lord)
YOUNG FLORELIO, Florelio's younger brother
Queen AMASIA of Sicily, Aldebrand's wife
DROLLIO, a courtier
ATTENDANTS on Amasia (3.3, *non-speaking*)
ATTENDANTS on Aldebrand (3.4, *non-speaking*)
FLORELIO, a lord, Francelia's husband, Young Florelio's elder brother, Clarimont's brother-in-law
DOCODISAPIO, a would-be statesman
An AMBASSADOR from Spain (4.2, *non-speaking*)
A BOY, who sings (4.4)
Signor MULTECARNI, the Poet Laureate
Two ACTORS in Multecarni's play
PETRUCCIO, Florelio's servant
LEPIDO, a courtier
A SERVANT in Florelio's household (5.2)

Speaking Parts: 23

Stage Directions and Speech Prefixes

OLD CLARIMONT: *old Clarimont* (s.d.s); *Clar<imont>* (s.p.s); *Clarimont An old Lord* (d.p.)
SERVANT: [old Clarimont's] *Servant* (s.d.s); *Servant* (s.d.s and s.p.s)
FIDELIO: *Fidelio* (s.d.s); *Fidel<io>* (s.p.s); *Fidelio Friend to Clarimont* (d.p.)
LORENZO: *Lorenzo* | [old Cleonax's] *son* (s.d.s); *Lor<enzo>* (s.p.s); *Cleonax junior* [Cleonax senior's] *Son* | *Lorenzo – An ambitious Courtier* (d.p.)
CLEONAX: [Lorenzo's] *Father* | *Cleonax* | *Old Cleonax* (s.d.s); *Cleonax senior Treasurer* (d.p.)
SERVANTS: *servants* (s.d.s)
KEEPER: *the Keeper* (s.d.s); *Keeper* (s.p.s and d.p.)
PARMENIO: *Parmenio* (s.d.s); *Par<menio>* (s.p.s); *Parmenio* [Lorenzo's] *supposed Creature* (d.p.)
CLARIMONT: *Clarimont* (s.d.s); *Clar<imont>* (s.p.s); *Clarimont junior* [Clarimont's] *Son* (d.p.)
ALDEBRAND: *the King* (s.d.s); *King* (s.d.s and s.p.s); *Aldebrand King of Sicily* (d.p.)
FRANCELIA: *Francelia* (s.d.s); *Franc<elia>* (s.p.s); *Francelia Daughter to Clarimont* (d.p.)
BELLAMINO: *Bellamino* | *Bellamino* [the Queen Amasia's] *Favourite* | *Bellamino the Favourite* (s.d.s); *Bell<amino>* (s.p.s); *Belamino Favourite of Pleasure, and Cousin to Cleonax* (d.p.)

LORDS: *Lords* (s.d.s and s.p.s)
SILEO: [possibly one of the] *Lords* (s.d.s); *Sil<eo>* (s.p.s)
YOUNG FLORELIO: *Young Florelio* | [one of] *the Florellies* (s.d.s); *Flor<elio>* | *Fl<orelio> junior* (s.p.s); *Florelio junior* [Florelio senior's] *Brother* (d.p.)
AMASIA: *the Queen Amasia* (s.d.s); *Queen* (s.d.s and s.p.s); *Amasia Queen to Aldebrand* (d.p.)
DROLLIO: *Drollio* (s.d.s); *Droll<io>* (s.p.s); *Drollio* [one of] *Two Courtiers* (d.p.)
ATTENDANTS: *Attendants* (s.d.s)
ATTENDANTS: *Attendants* (s.d.s)
FLORELIO: *Florelio senior* | [one of] *the Florellies* | *the elder* | *Florelio* (s.d.s); *Flor<elio>* | *Fl<orelio> senior* (s.p.s); *Florelio A Lord married to Francelia* (d.p.)
DOCODISAPIO: *Docodisapio* (s.d.s); *Doc<odisapio>* (s.p.s); *Doco Discopio One that pretends to be a great Statesman* (d.p.)
AMBASSADOR: *an Ambassador from Spain* (s.d.s); *Ambassador from Spain* (d.p.)
BOY: *a Boy* | *Boy* (s.d.s)
MULTECARNI: *Signor Multecarni the Poet* (s.d.s); *Mul<tecarni>* (s.p.s); *Signor Multecarni the Poet* (d.p.)
ACTORS: *two of the Actors* (s.d.s); *1 Actor* | *2 Actor* (s.p.s); *Actors* (d.p.)
PETRUCCIO: *Petruccio* (s.d.s); *Petr<uchio>* (s.p.s); *Petruchio Servant to Florelio* (d.p.)
LEPIDO: *Lepido* (s.d.s); *Lep<ido>* (s.p.s); *Lepido* [one of] *Two Courtiers* (d.p.)
SERVANT: *Servant* (s.d.s and s.p.s)

OTHER CHARACTERS
Old Clarimont's former followers, who have left him now that his fortunes are no longer in the ascendant (1.1)
The people of Sicily (1.2, 3.2)
The executioner (1.2)
Parmenio's father (2.1)
Old Clarimont's elder son, a banished man (2.1)
The King's guards (3.1)
The Captain of the Guard (3.1)
Statesmen at court (3.3)
Pisaro, a lord whose promotion is resented by Docodisapio (4.2)
Lords of the court whom Docodisapio considers incompetent, including: Dinao, a prattling plodder; Falorio, who cannot read his own handwriting; Vasques, who needs two days' warning to talk sense; and three blockheads named Sillio (perhaps the Sileo who appears on stage), Vecchio, and Caronnio (4.2)
Francelia's mother (4.3)
Actors, including Rosselio and Tisso (4.5)
Little Robin, once a debtor, now a successful lawyer (4.5)
Borachio, a nobody who has made a success with noisy advocacy (4.5)
Bellamino's brother (5.2; possibly just a figure of speech)

SETTING
Time-Scheme: 1.2 takes place at midnight; four or six hours pass between 2.1 and 3.2; 3.1–4 take place at night; 4.6–5.2 take place on the same day, 5.2 in the evening
Place: Sicily

Geography
Sicily: the Mermaid tavern (actually in London)
Spain
Arabia

SOURCES
Narrative: William Shakespeare, *Hamlet* (**1259**; 2.5, 3.4); Thomas Middleton, *The Revenger's Tragedy* (**1520**; 4.3); possibly Francis Beaumont and John Fletcher, *The Maid's Tragedy* (**1650**; unwritten ending)
Verbal: John Donne, 'The Storm' (1597; quoted from the 1635 or 1639 edition of the *Poems*; epistle); Thomas Middleton, *The Revenger's Tragedy* (**1520**; 1.2); John Webster, *The White Devil* (**1689**; 4.4); Ben Jonson, *The Devil is an Ass* (**1810**; 4.4); John Suckling, 'A Dream' (c. 1626; 4.4); John Ford, *'Tis Pity She's a Whore* (**2329**; 3.4, 4.1)
Works Mentioned: Ben Jonson, *Mortimer's Fall* (**2569**; epistle), *The Sad Shepherd* (**2570**; epistle)

The opening moment of the play—assuming 1.1 was indeed intended to be the first scene—seems modelled on the start of *The White Devil* (**1689**), though there is no precise verbal resemblance sufficient to call Webster a verbal source. Ford opens *Love's Sacrifice* (**2360**) with a similar exclamation from a condemned man.

LANGUAGE
English

FORM
Metre: pentameter, prose, and irregular verse
Rhyme: blank verse; some couplets
Act-Division: 5 acts (but the division may not be authoritative)
Dumb Show: 1.2 (compresses action)
Lines (Spoken): 826 (744 verse, 82 prose)
Lines (Written): 1,031

STAGING
Doors: one represents the prison door (1.2, s.d.); mentioned (3.4, 4.1, s.d.); Florelio 'goes out at another door' (4.2, s.d.)
Stage: characters pass over the stage (1.2, s.d.)
Within: groan (1.2, implicit); speech (3.4, implicit)
Miscellaneous: the Keeper is left alone on stage with nothing to say or do while Lorenzo murders Old Clarimont within (1.2)

MUSIC
Music: lute, accompanying Song 1 (4.4, s.d.)

Songs:
1: 'Hast thou seen the down i' th' air', 4.4, Boy, 10 lines, with lute accompaniment;
2: 'Come away to the tavern, I say', 4.5, Actors, 4 lines; *musical setting survives.*

PROPS
Lighting: lights (3.4, dialogue)
Weapons: two swords (3.4, dialogue); Bellamino's sword (4.1, implicit); Florelio's sword (4.1, implicit); Clarimont's sword (4.4, implicit)
Small Portable Objects: a jewel (3.4, s.d.)

COSTUMES
OLD CLARIMONT: a nightgown (1.1, s.d.)
FIDELIO: disguised as a friar (1.1, s.d.)
CLARIMONT: hangers (4.4, implicit); Petruccio's clothes (5.2, s.d.)
ALDEBRAND: a nightgown (3.4, s.d.)
BELLAMINO and FLORELIO: hangers (4.1, implicit)

EARLY TEXTUAL HISTORY
1651: Song 2 included, with a musical setting by John Hilton, in *A Musical Banquet*, sig. I1^v; printed by Thomas Harper for John Benson and John Playford.

1652: Song 2 included, with Hilton's musical setting, in his *Catch that Catch Can*, sig. C2^r; printed for John Benson and John Playford.

1653: *Catch that Catch Can* entered in the Stationers' Register to John Benson and John Playford on Tuesday 3 May.

1658: *Catch that Catch Can* reprinted by William Godbid for John Benson and John Playford. The song now appears on sig. C1^v.

1659: included in *The Last Remains of Sir John Suckling* (^{1}O$_1$), sigs. E1^r–G8^r, 47 pages on 24 leaves; printed (in or before June) by Thomas Newman for Humphrey Moseley; bookseller's address to the reader; argument; list of roles. The volume also includes a variant version of Song 1 (sigs. B4^v–B5^r).

Mid to late seventeenth century: Song 2 included in a MS songbook (Washington: Folger, MS V. a. 409, fo. 5). This version includes two additional lines.

1660: Suckling's *Last Remains* entered to Humphrey Moseley in the Stationers' Register on Friday 29 June.

1661: Song 2 included in N. D.'s *An Antidote against Melancholy*, sig. K2^r; printed (before Friday 19 April) by 'Mercurius Melancholicus'.

1663: *Catch that Catch Can* reprinted by William Godbid for John Playford and Zachariah Watkins.

1667: *Catch that Catch Can* reprinted by William Godbid for John Playford. The song now appears on sig F1^r.

1667: Moseley's rights in the *Last Remains* transferred from his widow, Ann, to Henry Herringman in the Stationers' Register on Monday 19 August; group entry of nine titles, the *Last Remains* being one.

1668–86: Suckling's *Last Remains* advertised as for sale by Henry Herringman.

1669: *An Antidote against Melancholy* entered to John Playford in the Stationers' Register on Friday 1 January.

1669: *An Antidote against Melancholy* reprinted for John Playford; the song now appears on sig. M2^r.

c. 1670s: two extracts (from 1.1) included in MS annotations in an interleaved copy of John Cotgrave's *The English Treasury of Wit and Language*, pp. 130a^r, 276a^r. (The copy is now at the British Library, pressmark G.16385.)

1671: Song 2 (headed 'Two Parliament Troopers that Lay Sick in Scotland') included in William Hickes's *Oxford Drollery*, sig. B3^{r-v}; printed in Oxford for John Crosley, and for sale by Thomas Palmer.

1671: *The Musical Companion* entered to John Playford in the Stationers' Register on Saturday 23 September.

1672 (?): included in Suckling's *Last Remains* (^{2}O$_2$), sigs. E1^r–G7^v, 23 leaves; the edition has a false imprint dated 1659 and naming Humphrey Moseley as the bookseller.

1673: Song 2 included, with Hilton's musical setting, in John Playford's *The Musical Companion*, sig. E1^r; printed by William Godbid for John Playford.

1673: *The Musical Companion* reissued three times.

1674: *Oxford Drollery* reprinted.

1676: O$_2$ reissued (in the autumn) by Henry Herringman as part of Suckling's *Works*.

1676–9: Suckling's *Works* advertised as for sale by Henry Herringman.

c. 1670s–80s: Song 2 included, with a musical setting, in a MS commonplace book (Stafford: Staffordshire Record Office, D641/4, no. 48) compiled by Hugh Davis. The page containing the song is now missing.

1679: *Oxford Drollery* reprinted in Oxford by B. G. for sale in London by Daniel Major and Thomas Orrel.

1680: Song 2 included, with Hilton's musical setting, in A. B.'s *Synopsis of Vocal Music*, sig. I3^v; printed for Dorman Newman.

1686: Suckling's *Works* advertised as for sale by Henry Herringman, Joseph Knight, and Francis Saunders.

1694–6: included in Suckling's *Works* (^{3}O$_3$), sigs. 2B1^r–2D2^v, 18 leaves; printed for Henry Herringman and to be sold by Richard Bentley, Jacob Tonson, Thomas Bennett, and Francis Saunders. The play's individual title page gives the date 1694, the volume's general title page 1696. The variant version of Song 1 now appears on sig. F1^{r-v}.

EDITION
L. A. Beaurline, in *The Works of Sir John Suckling: The Plays*, Oxford English Texts (Oxford, 1971), 1–32.

REFERENCES
Annals 1637; Beal 2 SuJ 172; Bentley, v. 1213–14; Eyre & Rivington, i. 417, 463, ii. 394, 430; Charles R. Forker,

Skull Beneath the Skin (Carbondale and Edwardsville, 1986), 503; Greg 811; Hazlitt, 201; *The Library*, 5th ser, 1 (1946–7), 85; *PBSA* 107 (2013), 37–8; *RMA Research Chronicle* 32 (1999), 82.

2372. Masque for the Earl of Cumberland

EVIDENCE
Clifford accounts (Chatsworth: Bolton MSS, book 169).

GENRE
masque

DATE
24 May 1632

ORIGINAL PRODUCTION
Earl of Cumberland's household

EARLY STAGE HISTORY
1632: performed on Thursday 24 May in the household of Francis Clifford, 4th Earl of Cumberland, presumably either at Londesborough House or Skipton Castle, Yorkshire.

REFERENCES
Chelys: The Journal of the Viol de Gamba Society 12 (1983), 28.

2373. The City Madam

TEXT
Printed in 1658 (Wing M1046), from a prompt-book.

GENRE
comedy
Contemporary: comedy (t.p.); poem (ded.)

TITLE
Performed/Printed: *The City Madam*
Alternative Modernization: *The City-Madam*

AUTHOR
Philip Massinger

DATE
May 1632

ORIGINAL PRODUCTION
King's Men at the Blackfriars (and perhaps also the Globe)

PLOT
After spending all his patrimony, Luke Frugal was imprisoned for debt, but released through the intervention of his elder brother, Sir John. Now he has been taken into Sir John's household, but is treated as a servant; Lady Frugal and her daughters are especially arrogant towards him, and Sir John's habit of indulging their every material whim means that they are getting above themselves in general. Luke encourages Sir John to deal compassionately with his debtors, who will reward him with personal loyalty. He also encourages Sir John's apprentices to cheat him, which induces one of them, Goldwire, to boast about the tricks he already practises.

Lacy and Plenty are bitter rivals in wooing Sir John's daughters. Lady Frugal insists that the terms of the marriage contracts be set in accordance with her astrologer's prediction that the girls will marry submissive, obedient men: both demand lives of unbridled luxury from their future husbands. Offended, the two suitors withdraw their courtship and go into voluntary exile; moreover, Sir John also retires to an overseas monastery, appalled at his womenfolk. The estate is left to Luke, who promises to maintain Lady Frugal and her daughters in a fashion even better than they have been accustomed to. He is less keen on the proviso that he take into the household three pagan North American Indians and arrange their conversion to Christianity.

Debtors and hangers-on flock to the newly enriched Luke in hope of advantage, but he deals harshly with them in order to protect and augment the estate which is now his. He arranges a visit to Goldwire's prostitute, to find that her establishment has been furnished by theft from Sir John; it turns out that the purpose of his visit is to have everyone there arrested by officers of the law. Goldwire and his fellow apprentice Tradewell are among those taken to prison; when their fathers try to buy them out, Luke demands an exorbitant ransom. Lady Frugal and her daughters are forced to dress less fashionably; the debtors are also arrested, and Luke is deaf to their pleas for mercy. The Indians refuse religious conversion, preferring to remain devil-worshippers, and tell Luke that the devil will grant riches in return for a human sacrifice of two virgins and a married woman. Realizing that his nieces and sister-in-law fit the bill, Luke seizes the opportunity and persuades them to go to Virginia, telling them they will be treated like royalty there. They ask to take their leave of the statues of their former suitors, and show genuine penitence. The principal Indian makes the statues come to life: it turns out that the three Indians were really Sir John, Lacy, and Plenty, out to expose Luke's hypocrisy and rein in the excesses of their womenfolk. Sir John forgives his debtors, and the suitors accept the chastened girls.

SCENE DESIGNATION
1.1–3, 2.1–3, 3.1–3, 4.1–4, 5.1–3 (Q, completed)

ROLES

Master Tom GOLDWIRE, Sir John's apprentice, Old Goldwire's son; a gentleman born; poses as a Justice of the Peace
TRADEWELL, Sir John's apprentice, Old Tradewell's son; a gentleman born
Master STARGAZE, an astrologer; also called Monsieur Almanac
LADY FRUGAL, Sir John's wife, mother of Anne and Mary; 50 years old
Mistress ANNE, daughter of Sir John and Lady Frugal, Mary's sister, Luke's niece; also called Nan
MARY, daughter of Sir John and Lady Frugal, Anne's sister, Luke's niece; also called Mall
MILLICENT, Lady Frugal's servingwoman
Master LUKE Frugal, a scholar; Sir John's younger brother, uncle of Mary and Anne
SIR JOHN Frugal, a citizen merchant, recently knighted; Luke's elder brother, Lady Frugal's husband, father of Anne and Mary; poses as an American Indian priest of the devil; also called Master Frugal, and nicknamed Sir John Prodigal; called Sir John Rich in the list of roles
HOLDFAST, Sir John's steward
PORTERS (1.1, *non-speaking*)
Sir Maurice LACY, Lord Lacy's only son and heir; poses as an American Indian
LACY's PAGE (1.2)
Master Jeffrey PLENTY, a gentleman and country landowner; poses as an American Indian
Three SERVINGMEN attending Plenty (1.2, *non-speaking*)
Master HOIST, a gentleman and gamester, Sir John's debtor
PENURY, Sir John's debtor, a married man and a father
FORTUNE, a merchant, speculator, and usurer, Sir John's debtor; a married man
LORD LACY, Lacy's father
Mistress SHAVEM, a prostitute; addressed by Secret as 'daughter'
Mistress SECRET, a bawd; addressed by Shavem as 'mother' and 'dame'
Sir RAMBLE, a ruffian
Squire SCUFFLE, a ruffian
DINGEM, a pimp; poses as a constable
MUSICIANS, Goldwire's associates; pose as watchmen (3.1, *non-speaking*)
Master GETALL, an ordinary-keeper
The SHERIFF (4.2)
The city MARSHAL (4.2)
OFFICERS (4.2, *non-speaking*)
Three SERGEANTS (4.3, 5.3)
A YEOMAN, the sergeants' associate (4.3, *non-speaking*)
OLD Master GOLDWIRE, a gentleman, Goldwire's father
OLD Master TRADEWELL, a gentleman, Tradewell's father
Sir John's SERVANTS (5.3, *non-speaking*)
CERBERUS, guard-dog of the underworld, in the show (5.3, *non-speaking?*)
CHARON, ferryman of the underworld, in the show (5.3, *non-speaking?*)
ORPHEUS, a musician, in the show (5.3, *non-speaking?*)
CHORUS, in the show (5.3)

Speaking Parts: 30 (excluding parts in the show)

Since no text is given for the show of Orpheus, it is unclear what it entails. Self-evidently the chorus must speak or sing, but the named roles may only have to mime.

Doubling
The theatre musicians play the feigned watchmen in 3.1 and the roles in the Orpheus show in 5.3.

Stage Directions and Speech Prefixes
GOLDWIRE: *Goldwire* (s.d.s and s.p.s); *Young Goldwire* [Old Goldwire's] *son,* [one of the] *prentices to Sir John Rich* (d.p.)
TRADEWELL: *Tradewell* (s.d.s and s.p.s); *Tradewel* (s.p.s); *Young Tradewell* [Old Tradewell's] *son,* [one of the] *prentices to Sir John Rich* (d.p.)
STARGAZE: *Star-gaze* (s.d.s); *Stargaze* (s.d.s and s.p.s); *Stargaze, an Astrologer* (d.p.)
LADY FRUGAL: *Lady* (s.d.s and s.p.s); *Lady Rich* (d.p.)
ANNE: *Anne | Ann* (s.d.s and s.p.s); *Anne* [one of Lady Rich's] *daughters* (d.p.)
MARY: *Mary* (s.d.s and s.p.s); *Mary* [one of Lady Rich's] *daughters* (d.p.)
MILLICENT: *Millescent | Milliscent* (s.d.s and s.p.s); *Milliscent* [Lady Rich's] *woman* (d.p.)
LUKE: *Luke* (s.d.s and s.p.s); *Luke Brother to Sir John Rich* (d.p.)
SIR JOHN: *Sir John* (s.d.s and s.p.s); *Sir John Rich a Merchant* (d.p.)
HOLDFAST: *Holdfast* (s.d.s and s.p.s); *Holdfast a Steward* (d.p.)
PORTERS: *Porters* (s.d.s)
LACY: *Lacie* (s.d.s and s.p.s); *Sir John Lacie Son to Lord Lacy* (d.p.)
PAGE: *Page* (s.d.s and s.p.s)
PLENTY: *Plenty* (s.d.s and s.p.s); *Plentie* (s.p.s); *Mr Plenty a Country Gentleman* (d.p.)
SERVINGMEN: *three Serving-men* (s.d.s)
HOIST: *Hoyst* (s.d.s and s.p.s); *Hoyst a decayed gentleman* (d.p.)
PENURY: *Penury* (s.d.s and s.p.s); *Penurie* (s.d.s, s.p.s, and d.p.)
FORTUNE: *Fortune* (s.d.s and s.p.s); *Fortune a decayed Merchant* (d.p.)
LORD LACY: *Lord Lacie* (s.d.s and d.p.); *the Lord Lacie* (s.d.s); *Lord* (s.d.s and s.p.s)
SHAVEM: *Shaveem | Shavem* (s.d.s and s.p.s); *Shave'm* (s.p.s; also misprinted *Shaven*); *Shavem a Wench* (d.p.)
SECRET: *Secret* (s.d.s and s.p.s); *Secret a Bawd* (d.p.)

RAMBLE: *Ramble* (s.d.s and s.p.s); *Ramble* [one of] *two Hectors* (d.p.)
SCUFFLE: *Scuffle* (s.d.s and s.p.s); *Scuffle* [one of] *two Hectors* (d.p.)
DINGEM: *Dingem | Dinge'm* (s.d.s and s.p.s); *Dingem, a Pimp* (d.p.)
MUSICIANS: *the Musicians* (s.d.s)
GETALL: *Gettall | Gettal* (s.d.s and s.p.s); *Gettall a Box-keeper* (d.p.)
SHERIFF: *Sheriff* (s.d.s and s.p.s)
MARSHAL: *Marshal* (s.d.s and s.p.s)
OFFICERS: *Officers* (s.d.s)
SERGEANTS: *Sergeants* (s.d.s); *1 Sergeant | 2 Sergeant | 3 Sergeant* (s.p.s)
OLD GOLDWIRE: *Old Goldwire* (s.d.s and s.p.s); *Old Goldwire* [one of] *Two Gentlemen* (d.p.)
OLD TRADEWELL: *Old Tradewell* (s.d.s and s.p.s); *Old Tradewel* (s.d.s); *Old Tradewell* [one of] *Two Gentlemen* (d.p.)
SERVANTS: *Servants* (s.d.s)
CERBERUS: *Cerberus* (s.d.s)
CHARON: *Charon* (s.d.s)
ORPHEUS: *Orpheus* (s.d.s)
CHORUS: *Chorus* (s.d.s)

OTHER CHARACTERS
A tenant of Lady Frugal's, who got his lease renewed for calling her young (1.1)
A lady to whom Luke delivered cloth (1.1)
Cooks hired by Holdfast to prepare a meal for Lady Frugal, reputedly the best in the city (1.1, 2.1)
The Lord Mayor of London (1.1)
Plenty's tailor (1.2)
Plenty's neighbours in the country (1.2)
Plenty's mercer and his wife (1.2)
Plenty's great-grandfather, a butcher (1.2)
Plenty's grandfather, a grazier (1.2)
Plenty's father, a constable (1.2)
Luke's former creditors, paid off by Sir John (1.2)
Hoist's punks (1.3)
Penury's wife and family (1.3, 4.3)
Fortune's wife (1.3, 4.3)
The dead father of Sir John and Luke (1.3)
Fiddlers who provided musical accompaniment while Goldwire had sex with Shavem (2.1)
Goldwire's fellow cashiers, who often make one another unauthorized loans (2.1, 4.2)
The new French ambassador (3.1)
The new Venetian ambassador, one of the *clarissimi* (3.1)
The diplomatic staff of the two new ambassadors (3.1)
The neighbours of Shavem and Secret (3.1)
The constable (3.1)
A poor market-woman who was robbed of her bacon by either Ramble or Scuffle (3.1)
Shavem's rejected suitors, including an Irish lord, a cashiered captain, and a new-made courtier (3.1)
Hoist's dying uncle (4.1)
A sailor with whom Penury hopes to do business, only to be pre-empted by Luke (4.1, 4.3)
Shavem's doctor (4.2)
Shavem's mercer (4.2)
Shavem's silkman (4.2)
The Lord Chief Justice (4.2)
Hoist's other creditors (4.3)
Goodman Humble, Lady Frugal's father, a country farmer (4.4)
Humble's neighbours (4.4)
The city senate (5.1)

SETTING
Period: contemporary
Time-Scheme: 3.2 takes place the late afternoon or evening after 2.3, and 4.4 the day after that; two hours pass between 4.1 and 4.2, and three hours between 4.1 and 4.3
Place: London

Geography
London: the Pool; the Counter prisons; the Old Exchange; the Tower; Westminster; Fleet Lane; Pie Corner; Moorfields; Smithfield; Ludgate; Barbican; the Burse; the Neat Houses; the Asparagus Garden; St Paul's Cathedral; Bridewell; the conduits; the city walls; Cheapside; St Martin's Lane; Fleet prison
[*Middlesex*]: Brentford; Staines; Islington; Pimlico
[*Surrey*]: Lambeth Marsh
[*Kent*]: Dover; Gravesend
England: Barnet; Romford
Britain: Scotland; Ireland; Wales
France: Calais
The Low Countries: Flanders; Louvain
Spain: Toledo
Italy: Venice; Genoa; Tuscany
Europe: Hungary; the Alps
[*Africa*]: Barbary
[*Asia*]: Tyre; Persia
America: Virginia
The North-West Passage
The [*East*] *Indies*

SOURCES
Narrative: William Shakespeare, *Measure for Measure* (**1413**), *2 Henry IV* (**1083**; 3.1), *The Winter's Tale* (**1631**; 5.3); Ben Jonson, George Chapman, and John Marston, *Eastward Ho!* (**1473**); possibly John Fletcher, *The Mad Lover* (**1809**; the show of Orpheus in 5.3); Philip Massinger, *A New Way to Pay Old Debts* (**2180**; Luke)
Verbal: Bible: Judges 14.18 (2.3); Psalms 58.4 (4.3); 1 Corinthians 13.1 (4.3); 1 Timothy 5.8 (1.3); 1 John 3.17 (1.3); Juvenal, *Satires* 10 (3.3, 4.2); Christopher Marlowe, *Tamburlaine* (**784**) or *Doctor Faustus* (**810**; 4.4); William Shakespeare, *Richard III* (**950**; 4.3), *King Lear* (**1486**; 2.2); Ben Jonson, *Sejanus' Fall* (**1412**; 3.3), *Volpone* (**1493**; 3.3), *The Silent Woman* (**1603**; 3.3), *The Alchemist* (**1621**; 3.1–2, 4.2); John Fletcher and

Philip Massinger, *Rollo* (**1841**; 2.2); John Smith, *General History of Virginia, New England, and the Summer Isles* (1624; 5.1); Philip Massinger, *A New Way to Pay Old Debts* (**2180**; 3.2); possibly Henry Reynolds, *Mythomystes* (1632; 2.2)
Works Mentioned: Bible: Matthew 6.9–13 (Lord's Prayer; 3.2); 'Erra Pater', *The Prognostication for Ever* (1536?; 2.2); Edmund Spenser, *The Faerie Queene* 1 (1590; 2.2); Statute of Bankruptcy (21 James I c. 19; 1624; 1.3)

LANGUAGE
English
Latin: 20 words (1.1, 2.2, 3.2, 4.1, 4.3, 5.2; Goldwire, Sir John, Stargaze, Plenty, Lacy, Mary, Getall, Luke)
French: 3 words (2.1; Luke)
Italian: 1 word (3.1; Secret)
Spanish: 1 word (4.4; Luke)
Gibberish: 10 words (3.3; Sir John, Plenty, Lacy); supposedly a North American Indian language

FORM
Metre: pentameter; a little prose
Rhyme: blank verse
Act-Division: 5 acts
Lines (Spoken): 2,192 (2,163 verse, 29 prose)
Lines (Written): 2,925

STAGING
Doors: characters exit at two doors (4.4, s.d.), and enter likewise (5.3, s.d.); a character is directed to be 'at the door' (5.3, s.d.); probably used as porticos in which Lacy and Plenty pose as statues (5.3, implicit; if so, the doors must open outwards)
Discovery Space: probably set with a banquet (5.3, implicit)
Within: speech (1.1, 3.1–2, 4.4, 5.3, s.d.); sound effects (3.1, s.d.; 4.1, implicit)
Above: the theatre musicians are directed to come 'down' when required on stage (3.1, 5.1, s.d.)
Miscellaneous: The prompt markings in Q indicate some cue intervals. The theatre musicians are given 50 lines to come down and prepare for their on-stage appearance in 3.1, and 270 lines prior to their appearance in 5.3; the latter probably entails a major costume change. Lacy and Plenty are given 35 lines to prepare for their appearance as statues. The table, chair, and stools required in 1.3 are called for only shortly before the end of 1.2, but 150 lines are allowed to set up the banquet in 5.3.

The staging of 5.3 is a complex issue. The most obvious indication is the cue calling for Lacy and Plenty to be 'ready behind' for their appearance as statues; there is no direction for them to enter until after the statues have been viewed. Ordinarily one might assume that they would be placed in the discovery space, but the space must be already occupied by the banquet, which is cued for set-up from 5.1 but does not appear until the start of 5.3. The likeliest alternative is that the two actors stood in the flanking doorways.

MUSIC AND SOUND
Sound Effects: knocking within (3.1, 4.1, s.d.)
Music: flourish of cornetts (4.2, s.d.); unspecified music (4.2, 5.3, s.d.); entr'acte music (4.4, s.d.); sad music (5.3, s.d.)
On-Stage Music: Musicians play a lavolta (3.1, implicit) and wanton music (3.1, s.d.)
Songs: The show of Orpheus in 5.3 is described as a 'song' (s.d.), but there is no text; it may have been sung in recitative.
Dance: Goldwire and Shavem dance a lavolta (3.1, s.d.)

PROPS
Weapons: Plenty's sword (1.2, dialogue); Lacy's sword (1.2, dialogue); the Page's little rapier (1.2, dialogue); three Servingmen's blade weapons (1.2, dialogue); a knife (3.1, s.d.); Ramble's sword (3.1, s.d.); Dingem's sword (4.1, implicit)
Musical Instruments: unspecified instruments (3.1, implicit)
Clothing: shoes (1.1, s.d.); garters (1.1, s.d.); shoe-roses (1.1, s.d.)
Money: an unspecified amount (3.1, implicit)
Food and Drink: unspecified victuals (1.1, implicit); a banquet (5.3, s.d.); wine (5.3, s.d.)
Small Portable Objects: three looking-glasses (1.1, s.d.; attached to the ladies' girdles); a fan (1.1, dialogue); an account-book (1.3, s.d.); a standish (1.3, s.d.); two documents (2.2, s.d.); a will (3.2, s.d.); a key (3.2, 5.3, dialogue; 3.3, s.d.); a paper (4.1, s.d.)
Large Portable Objects: a table (1.3, s.d.); a chair (1.3, 2.2, 5.3, s.d.); stools (1.3, s.d.); a footstep (5.3, s.d.); a little table (5.3, s.d.); a pack of almanacs (5.3, s.d.)
Scenery: an arras (5.1–3, s.d.)

COSTUMES AND MAKE-UP
GOLDWIRE: disguised as a Justice of the Peace (3.1, s.d.)
TRADEWELL: fine clothes (4.2, dialogue)
LADY FRUGAL: a girdle (1.1, s.d.); courtly clothes (1.1, 3.2, dialogue); a glove (1.2, dialogue); a coarse habit (4.4, s.d.)
ANNE and MARY: a girdle each (1.1, s.d.); courtly clothes (1.1, 3.2, dialogue); coarse habits (4.4, s.d.), including buffin gowns, green aprons, and possibly French hoods (dialogue)
LUKE: fine clothes (5.2, dialogue)
SIR JOHN: disguised as an American Indian (3.3, s.d.; 5.1, 5.3, implicit), including dark facial make-up (implicit)
LACY: a beaver hat (1.2, dialogue); hangers (1.2, implicit); disguised as an American Indian (3.3, s.d.; 5.1, implicit), including dark facial make-up (implicit)
PAGE and SERVINGMEN: hangers (1.2, implicit)
PLENTY: a beaver hat (1.2, dialogue); fine clothes (1.2, implicit); hangers (1.2, implicit); disguised as an

American Indian (3.3, s.d.; 5.1, implicit), including dark facial make-up (implicit)
SHAVEM: a shoe (3.1, dialogue); thick ceruse make-up on her face, including her lips (4.2, dialogue); a blue gown (5.3, s.d.)
RAMBLE: a cloak (3.1, dialogue); hangers (3.1, implicit)
SCUFFLE: a cloak (3.1, dialogue)
DINGEM: disguised as a constable (3.1, s.d.); hangers (4.1, implicit)
MUSICIANS: disguised as watchmen (3.1, s.d.)

EARLY STAGE HISTORY
1632: presumably performed, as licensed, by the King's Men; in 1658, the Blackfriars performance was said to have received 'great applause'. The theatre musicians played Goldwire's watchmen, Cerberus, Charon, Orpheus, and the chorus.
1641: The play was in the repertory of the King's Men.

EARLY TEXTUAL HISTORY
1632: On Friday 25 May, Sir Henry Herbert licensed the text for performance by the King's Men.
1641: On Saturday 7 August, Robert Devereux, 3rd Earl of Essex (Lord Chamberlain) issued a warrant prohibiting the printing of this and sixty other plays without the consent of the King's Men. On Saturday 14 August, the order was read to the Stationers' Company and instructions issued for its observance.
1658: Q printed by Jane Bell for Andrew Pennycuicke; collation A², B–L⁴, 42 leaves; title page names author and playhouse; list of roles; publisher's dedication. The dedication was addressed to different patrons in different copies, including John Wrath, Thomas Freake, Richard Steadwell, Mr Lee (William Lee, Warden of the Stationers' Company?), and Anne de Vere, Countess of Oxford (whose dedication was the last to be printed).
1659: Q reissued.
1670: Q advertised as for sale by William Cademan.
1684: Nicholas Cox (Manciple of St Edmund Hall, Oxford) had a copy of the reissued state of Q in his bookshop. It had probably been previously owned by Gerard Langbaine, and appears on a list compiled by Anthony Wood on Saturday 13 December.

EDITIONS
T. W. Craik, New Mermaids (London, 1964).
Cyrus Hoy, Regents Renaissance Drama (Lincoln, Neb., 1964).
Colin Gibson, in *The Plays and Poems of Philip Massinger*, ed. Philip Edwards and Colin Gibson (Oxford, 1976), iv. 1–99, v. 226–42.
Cathy Shrank, Globe Quartos (London, 2005).

REFERENCES
Annals 1632; Bawcutt 232; Bentley, iv. 771–4; Bodleian, MS Wood E. 4, art. 1, p. 11; Greg 788; Hazlitt, 42; L. C. Knights, *Drama and Society in the Age of Jonson* (London, 1962), 270–2; MSC 1.4–5, 364–9.

2374. *Love Crowns the End*

TEXT
Printed in 1640 (STC 23704), from hard-to-read authorial papers. Song 3 may have been expurgated (unless the rude word is omitted for comic effect).

GENRE
pastoral
Contemporary: pastoral (t.p.)

TITLE
Printed: *Love Crowns the End*

AUTHOR
John Tatham

DATE
1632

ORIGINAL PRODUCTION
Bingham School, Nottinghamshire

PLOT
Three days before the start of the action, Cliton became suspicious that his girlfriend Florida was interested in Lysander, and attacked her, leaving her for dead. Since then he has repeatedly returned to the place he left her body, but it has vanished. Looking for a lost lamb, Alexis finds Cliton asleep, hears his story, and decides that he must spend the rest of his life expiating the murder in contrition and penitence.

A lustful shepherd, who is so ugly that he cannot get a date, threatens to rape Chloe, but she is rescued by Lysander. She falls in love with him, but he is only interested in Gloriana: having been loved by many, Chloe is now rejected by the man she loves. She goes mad, but the wood-nymphs find her and take her to Claudia, who cures her.

Francisco, Lysander's rival for Gloriana's love, ambushes the couple with the assistance of two villains; they stab Lysander and carry off Gloriana. Lysander is found groaning by Claudia and Florida, who was not killed as Cliton supposed; Claudia cures him. Meanwhile Gloriana, thinking him dead, goes mad. She meets Cliton, now a hermit, who promises to restore her to Lysander.

The characters gravitate towards Cliton's cell, where Gloriana and Lysander are reunited, as are Cliton and Florida. Gloriana's father Leon turns out to be a banished courtier; Lysander and Francisco both followed him into exile for the love of Gloriana. The servant Scrub brings news that the Duke who banished

Leon has died, and that his lands are to be restored. Francisco concedes Lysander's victory.

SCENE DESIGNATION
prol., sc.1–15 (O undivided)

There are no entrance directions at the head of sc.3, 10, and 15.

ROLES
PROLOGUE
CLITON, a shepherd, implied to be young; later a hermit, and said to be old
ALEXIS, a shepherd, Leon's son, Gloriana's brother
CHLOE, a shepherdess
A LUSTFUL SHEPHERD; later disguised as a Satyr
LYSANDER, a young shepherd; in reality, Pisander, a courtier in exile
DAPHNIS, a shepherd, one of Chloe's suitors
LEON, an old man, father of Alexis and Gloriana; in reality, a banished courtier
GLORIANA, Leon's only daughter, Alexis's sister
FRANCISCO, a shepherd; in reality, a courtier in exile
SCRUB, a servant, probably Pisander's
WOOD-NYMPHS (sc.8; sing collectively)
The DESTINIES, presumably three in number (sc.9; sing collectively)
A HEAVENLY MESSENGER (sc.9)
Two VILLAINS, Francisco's accomplices (sc.9)
CLAUDIA, a holy matron
FLORIDA, a shepherdess

Speaking Parts: 19 (assuming three Destinies; excluding Wood-Nymphs)

Stage Directions and Speech Prefixes
PROLOGUE: *The Prologue* (heading)
CLITON: *Cliton* (s.d.s and s.p.s)
ALEXIS: *Alexis* (s.d.s and s.p.s)
CHLOE: *Cloe* (s.d.s and s.p.s)
LUSTFUL SHEPHERD: *a lustful shepherd | The lustful shepherd* (s.d.s); *Lustful Shepherd* (s.d.s and s.p.s)
LYSANDER: *Lysander* (s.d.s and s.p.s)
DAPHNIS: *Daphnes* (s.d.s and s.p.s; also misprinted *Daphne*)
LEON: *Leon* (s.d.s and s.p.s)
GLORIANA: *Gloriana* (s.d.s and s.p.s)
FRANCISCO: *Francisco* (s.d.s and s.p.s)
SCRUB: *Scrub* (s.d.s and s.p.s)
WOOD-NYMPHS: *Nymphs* (s.d.s)
DESTINIES: *The Destinies* (s.d.s)
HEAVENLY MESSENGER: *A heavenly messenger* (s.d.s)
VILLAINS: *others* (s.d.s); *1 Villain | 2 Villain* (s.p.s)
CLAUDIA: *Claudia* (s.d.s and s.p.s)
FLORIDA: *Florida* (s.d.s and s.p.s)

OTHER CHARACTERS
Wenches who will not play with the Lustful Shepherd (sc.5)
Scrub's mother (sc.5)

Six bastards born to Scrub's mother before she conceived him (sc.5)
A sow-gelder who fathered the six children on Scrub's mother (sc.5)
Shepherds, Chloe's suitors (sc.6)
The pinner, who has a fold by the heath (sc.6)
The Duke who banished Leon, and who is now dead (sc.15)

SETTING
Time-Scheme: sc.1 takes place early in the morning; sc.9 takes place the day after sc.7

LANGUAGE
English
Latin: 2 words (sc.7, 10; Francisco, Scrub)

FORM
Metre: iambic pentameter, trochaic tetrameter (some of it catalectic), and prose
Rhyme: couplets, blank verse, and ABAB; occasional triplets
Prologue: 14 lines, in couplets
Lines (Spoken): 644 (499 verse, 145 prose)
Lines (Written): 879

STAGING
Discovery Space: a grove is discovered (sc.1, s.d.); scenery is discovered (sc.7, s.d.)
Within: noise (sc.4, s.d.); shouts (sc.4, 6, implicit); speech (sc.5, s.d.)
Audience: addressed as 'you stars of honour' and 'you judges' (prol.); said to be seated (prol.)

MUSIC AND SOUND
Sound Effects: noise within (sc.4, s.d.)
Songs:
  1: 'I will follow through yon grove', sc.6, Chloe, 8 lines;
  2: 'Hey down a down derry', sc.8, Chloe, 5 lines;
  3: 'When love did act a woman's part', sc.8, Chloe, 4 lines;
  4: 'Love cannot choose but pity yield', sc.8, Wood-Nymphs, 12 lines;
  5: 'Sit while I do gather flowers', sc.9, Gloriana and Lysander, in parts, 35 lines;
  6: 'Sleep on, sleep on', sc.9, Destinies, 7 lines;
  7: 'Rise, rise, Lysander, to prevent', sc.9, Heavenly Messenger, 14 lines;
  8: 'I know Lysander's dead', sc.12, Gloriana, 6 lines;
  9: 'Do you see where he doth stand', sc.12, Gloriana, 4 lines.

PROPS
Weapons: a sword (sc.1, dialogue); three swords (sc.9, dialogue)
Small Portable Objects: flowers, including a violet, a pink, and a rose (sc.9, dialogue)

Scenery: a grove (sc.1, s.d.; large enough for part of it to be 'an obscure corner'); a place of green myrtles, adorned with roses, with the title 'Lovers' Valley' written above it (sc.7, s.d.)

COSTUMES
CLITON: dressed as a hermit (sc.12, s.d.), with a large or long beard (dialogue)
CHLOE: golden hair (dialogue)
LUSTFUL SHEPHERD: disguised as a Satyr (sc.5, s.d.), with a hairy hide (dialogue)
LYSANDER: a garland on his head and scarfs on his arms (sc.6, s.d.)
FRANCISCO: disguised (sc.9, s.d.)
SCRUB: shoes (sc.10, dialogue)
HEAVENLY MESSENGER: white clothes (sc.9, s.d.)

EARLY STAGE HISTORY
1632: performed at Bingham, Nottinghamshire, by scholars (or 'scholees'). (Presumably this means schoolboys; the prologue refers to their 'not yet ripened wit'.) It may have been the third element of some school celebration.

EARLY TEXTUAL HISTORY
1640: on Tuesday 21 April, John Hansley licensed *The Fancies' Theatre* for publication.
 1640: *The Fancies' Theatre* entered in the Stationers' Register to Richard Best on Thursday 15 October.
 1640: included in John Tatham's *The Fancies' Theatre* (O), sigs. I4ʳ–L2ᵛ, 15 leaves; printed by John Norton for Richard Best; the play's individual title page refers to the original performance, specifying actors, place, and date; Latin mottos on the title page and at the foot of the text. A concluding note apologises for misprints owing to 'obscure copy' and the absence of the author.
 1656: *The English Parnassus* entered to Evan Tyler, Thomas Johnson, and Thomas Davies in the Stationers' Register on Wednesday 24 December.
 1657: three extracts (from sc.1, 7) included in Joshua Poole's *The English Parnassus*, sigs. Z2ʳ, 2F3ᵛ, 2G3ᵛ; printed for Thomas Johnson.
 1657: *The Fancies' Theatre* reissued as *The Mirror of Fancies*, with a cancel title page naming William Burden as the bookseller.
 1677: *The English Parnassus* reprinted by Henry Brome for Thomas Bassett and John Wright; the extracts now appear on sigs. Y6ʳ, 2E7ᵛ, 2F7ᵛ.
 1684: Nicholas Cox (Manciple of St Edmund Hall, Oxford) had a copy of *The Mirror of Fancies* in his bookshop. It had probably been previously owned by Gerard Langbaine, and appears on a list compiled by Anthony Wood on Saturday 13 December.

EDITION
James Maidment and W. H. Logan, in *The Dramatic Works of John Tatham*, Dramatists of the Restoration (Edinburgh and London, 1879), 1–32.

A comparison of O with the Maidment and Logan edition reveals just how far the editors took to heart the 1640 printer's request, 'with thy pen courteously correct such defects as thou shalt find': at points, the text is substantially rewritten. In their version, the metre is radically altered, with O's prose sometimes metamorphosed into verse, complete with a rhyme of the editors' devising. They also insert an entirely new (and entirely unnecessary) role, Leon Junior, having misunderstood two misprinted speech prefixes in sc.13.

REFERENCES
Annals 1632; Bentley, v. 1221–2; Bodleian, MS Wood E. 4, art. 1, p. 59; Eyre & Rivington, ii. 103; Greg 600; Hazlitt, 139.

2375. *Antipelargesis* [Filial Love]

TEXT
MS (Stonyhurst, MS B. vii. 23 (i), fos. 105ʳ–114ᵛ).

GENRE
comedy

TITLE
MS: *Antipelargesis, sive Felix liberorum in parentam pietas*

DATE
Limits: 1629–34, 1637–43, 1645–57
Best Guess: 1632

If the play was written for performance by a single class, it can only date from the period 1629–34: only then were there enough boys at St Omers for one class to meet the casting requirements. If it was written for more than one class, it probably dates from the late 1640s or 1650s. (See **2163** for further discussion of the procedure.) One reason to prefer the earlier period is the note at the foot of the text, which refers to the play's events (1604), or more probably its source (1629), as recent.

ORIGINAL PRODUCTION
English Jesuit College, St Omers (presumably)

PLOT
Prince Cuba's kingdom has just vanquished its enemies, but it is being despoiled by outlaws. His soldiers advocate a policy of severity, but his counsellors support clemency. Cuba decides to offer a pardon, but prepare an army to crush those who do not accept it. A reward is also offered for the head of the chief outlaw. The outlaws disbelieve the promise of clemency, slaughter those who want to make peace with Cuba, and swear their resolution.
 Once a powerful man in another country but now fallen on hard times, Harmonius wishes he had never been born, but his sons dissuade him from suicide. An oracle predicts that his good fortune will

return when his son Philopater is hanged for a crime committed by his brothers. Philopater has devised a scheme to help his father: he poses as the wanted outlaw leader, and has his brothers hand him over to Cuba and collect the reward. They do so, but plead for mercy. Harmonius goes to Cuba and asks him to release Philopater, and the brothers admit that he is innocent. Cuba is impressed by the sons' filial piety, and gives Harmonius a share of the kingdom. The true outlaw chief, Diomedes, offers his own head in exchange for clemency; Cuba accepts and receives Diomedes into favour with his head still attached.

SCENE DESIGNATION
prol., sc.1–8 (MS)

ROLES
RODOCHROUS, the Genius of the Orient, who speaks the prologue
JAPONIA, representing Japan; a female figure (prol., *non-speaking*)
HARMONIUS, father of Philopater, Philaretes, and Eugenius
PHILOPATER, son of Harmonius, brother of Eugenius and Philaretes
PHILARETES, a young man, son of Harmonius, brother of Philopater and Eugenius
EUGENIUS, a young man, son of Harmonius, brother of Philopater and Philaretes
CUBA, the Prince
POLEMIUS, a leader of Cuba's army
EUBULUS, Cuba's counsellor
MARTIUS, a leader of Cuba's army
IRENAEUS, Cuba's counsellor
CRANGONOR, a leader of Cuba's army
EUPREPIUS, Cuba's counsellor
DIOMEDES, leader of the outlaws
BARGULUS, an outlaw
VIRIATHUS, an outlaw
MEZENTIUS, an outlaw
PROCRUSTES, an outlaw
SCINIS, an outlaw
BUSIRIS, an outlaw
MOSIBUS, an oracle
Cuba's SOLDIERS (sc.8, *non-speaking*)

Speaking Parts: 20
Allegorical Roles: 1

Stage Directions and Speech Prefixes
RODOCHROUS: *Rodochrous* (s.d.s); *Rodochrous Genius Orientalis* (d.p.)
JAPONIA: *Japonia* (d.p.)
HARMONIUS: *Harmonius* (s.d.s); *Harm<onius>* (s.p.s); *Harmonius* (d.p.)
PHILOPATER: *Philopater* | [one of the] *filii* (s.d.s); *Philop<ater>* (s.p.s); *Philopater* [one of the] *filii Harmonii* (d.p.)

PHILARETES: *Philaretes* (s.d.s and s.p.s); [one of the] *filii* (s.d.s); *Philaretes* [one of the] *filii Harmonii* (d.p.)
EUGENIUS: *Eugenius* (s.d.s and s.p.s); [one of the] *filii* (s.d.s); *Eugenius* [one of the] *filii Harmonii* (d.p.)
CUBA: *Cuba* (s.d.s and s.p.s); *Cuba Princeps* (d.p.)
POLEMIUS: *Polemius* (s.p.s); *Polemius* [one of the] *Militiae Duces* (d.p.)
EUBULUS: *Eubulus* (s.p.s); *Eubulus* [one of the] *Consiliarii regis* (d.p.)
MARTIUS: *Martius* (s.p.s); *Martius* [one of the] *Militiae Duces* (d.p.)
IRENAEUS: *Irenaeus* (s.p.s); *Irenaeus* [one of the] *Consiliarii regis* (d.p.)
CRANGONOR: *Crangonor* (s.p.s); *Crangonor* [one of the] *Militiae Duces* (d.p.)
EUPREPIUS: *Euprepius* (s.p.s); *Euprepius* [one of the] *Consiliarii regis* (d.p.)
DIOMEDES: *Diomedes* (s.d.s and s.p.s); *Diomedes Exlegum dux* (d.p.)
BARGULUS: *Bargulus* (s.d.s); *Bargulus* [one of the] *Exleges* (d.p.)
VIRIATHUS: *Viriathus* (s.p.s); *Viriathus* [one of the] *Exleges* (d.p.)
MEZENTIUS: *Mezentius* (s.p.s); *Mezentius* [one of the] *Exleges* (d.p.)
PROCRUSTES: *Procrustes* (s.p.s); *Procrustes* [one of the] *Exleges* (d.p.)
SCINIS: *Scinis* (s.p.s); *Scinis* [one of the] *Exleges* (d.p.)
BUSIRIS: *Busiris* (s.p.s); *Busiris* [one of the] *Exleges* (d.p.)
MOSIBUS: *Mosibus* (s.p.s); *Mosibus Oraculum* (d.p.)
SOLDIERS: *Milites* (d.p.)

OTHER CHARACTERS
Harmonius' mother (sc.1)
People whom Harmonius ruled (sc.1)
Jonta, Cuba's vanquished and dead enemy (sc.2)
Cuba's subjects (sc.2)
Outlaws who rebelled against Diomedes and were killed (sc.4)

SETTING
Period: seventeenth century; the play dramatizes events which took place in 1604
Place: Japan

Geography
The [Pacific?] Ocean

SOURCES
Narrative: François Solier, *Histoire ecclesiastique des isles et royaumes du Japon* (1629)
Verbal: Ovid, *Metamorphoses* 7 (sc.3, 5)

LANGUAGE
Latin

FORM
Metre: prose

2376. The Obstinate Lady

Prologue: 30 lines of prose, spoken by Rodochrous
Dumb Shows: tableaux presented by the prologue, representing the main action to follow
Lines (Spoken): 446
Lines (Written): 469

STAGING

Discovery Space: there is a curtained section at the back large enough to contain three distinct tableaux positioned left to right (prol., dialogue; these may be three separate alcoves);
Stage: mentioned (sc.4, s.d.)
Within: sound effects (sc.4, s.d.); characters speak behind the curtain (sc.4, s.d.)

SOUND

Sound Effects: sound of fighting within (sc.4, s.d.)

PROPS

Weapons: a pointed weapon (prol., implicit; sc.1, dialogue); seven swords (prol., dialogue; sc.4, s.d.).
Large Portable Objects: chains (prol., sc.6, 8, dialogue)
Scenery: a curtain (prol., dialogue; sc.4, s.d.); a throne (sc.8, s.d.)

COSTUMES

PHILOPATER: inappropriately gay clothes (sc.3, implicit; but it is said in a later scene that the brothers have only the clothes they wear)
DIOMEDES: a coat of mail (sc.8, s.d.); headgear (sc.8, implicit; covers enough of the face to conceal his identity; removed on stage)

EARLY TEXTUAL HISTORY

c. 1657–60: included in a **MS** collection of plays and other literary writings; 10 leaves; argument; list of roles. The other plays in the collection are *Innocentia purpurata* (1650s), *Homo duplex* (1655), *Basilindus* (**2600**), *Morus* (**2680**), and *Artaxerxes* (**2866**).

EDITION

Charles Burnett, in Masahiro Takenaka, *Jesuit Plays on Japan and English Recusancy*, Renaissance Monographs 21 (Tokyo, 1995), 34–67.

REFERENCES

Annals Supp. I; McCabe, 102; *Revue de littérature comparée* 17 (1937), 374.

2376. The Obstinate Lady

TEXT

Two substantive early witnesses:

o: printed in 1658 (Wing C4898); authorized edition; the British Library copy (pressmark Kings 238.b.32) contains handwritten corrections by the author;

Q: printed in 1657 (Wing C4896); unauthorized edition; sets much of the verse as prose, omits epilogue, substitutes a brief alternative ending by another hand; some minor variants and dropped lines.

GENRE

comedy
Contemporary: play (prol., ep.); comedy (ep.)

TITLE

Performed/Printed: *The Obstinate Lady*

AUTHOR

Aston Cokayne

DATE

Limits: 1628–32
Best Guess: 1632

PLOT

A year before the start of the action, Polydacre's wife Rosinda faked her own death and introduced herself into the household as a page, 'Tandorix', aiming to find out if her husband would break his vow not to remarry. Polydacre's long-lost daughter, Cleanthe, has also adopted a male alias: coming to London upon learning her true parentage, she has fallen in love with Carionil, and become a boy to be with him. But Carionil loves her sister Lucora, who does not return his affections and claims to profess chastity. Her waiting-maid Nentis cannot understand her obstinacy, and her disguised mother secretly favours Carionil as a prospective son-in-law. But Polydacre objects to Carionil because of a family quarrel two generations ago, and is trying to persuade Lucora to marry Carionil's friend Falorus. Carionil is initially suspicious, but learns to trust Falorus' good faith in his difficult position.

Carionil sends Lucora a love-letter, but she replies with a decisive rejection. He tries to stab himself, but botches it and survives. With the help of Falorus, Cleanthe, and a sleeping drug, he has his 'dead' body shown to Lucora, who shows no remorse. She gives in to her father's entreaties: she will marry Falorus, but only after a month has passed. Carionil disguises himself as Tucapelo, a Spanish-speaking Negro who has come to England seeking vengeance on Carionil, and gets himself invited to stay at the Hispanophile Polydacre's house. Lucora falls for this black visitor and agrees to elope with him, even though it will mean living in Ethiopia; but on the night Carionil has second thoughts, realizes he cannot marry a woman who loves a blackamoor more than she does him, and breaks off the arrangement. Cleanthe tells Carionil that there is another lady in town who loves him, and arranges a meeting: the lady is, of course, herself, and she explains how she was stolen by her nurse in infancy and has only recently learned her true parentage. Meanwhile

Falorus is torn between his growing love for Lucora and his reluctance to betray a friend. The transfer of Carionil's affections to Cleanthe resolves that difficulty.

Other subsidiary amours take place around the central action. Lorece woos the widow Vandona, who secretly approves of his liking for plays and books, and eventually accepts him. Phygionis, who told Cleanthe who she really is, has fallen for Nentis, but needs to acquire himself a good suit of clothes before he can woo her; he is successful, but she is eventually discomfited to learn that he is of lower birth than he seemed. Both Polydacre and his son Phylander are courting Antiphila. Antiphila refuses Phylander, and, to get rid of him, claims that she is already contracted to Tandorix. Phylander's attempt at a violent remonstrance is forestalled when 'Tandorix' reveals that 'he' is really his mother. Antiphila accepts Polydacre's marriage proposal and writes to put off Phylander, promising that she would take him as a second choice were his father unavailable. He holds her to that promise when Rosinda reveals herself. Polydacre gives his blessing to the proposed marriages of his two daughters. Lucora at first asks to be allowed to remain single, but Cleanthe persuades her to change her mind and accept Falorus.

SCENE DESIGNATION

prol., 1.1–3, 2.1–3, 3.1–3, 4.1–5, 5.1–6, ep. (O, completed; Q includes a scene-division missing from O, but omits the epilogue)

ROLES
PROLOGUE
Lord CARIONIL, a young nobleman, kinsman of Vandona and Nentis; formerly an ambassador to Spain; also called Don Carionil; poses as Lord Tucapelo, an Ethiopian nobleman
Lord FALORUS, Carionil's friend, Lorece's brother
Lady LUCORA, elder daughter of Polydacre and Rosinda, sister of Cleanthe and Phylander
Mistress NENTIS, Lucora's waiting-woman, Vandona's sister, Carionil's kinswoman
JAQUES, Vandona's old servant
Lady CLEANTHE, younger daughter of Polydacre and Rosinda, sister of Lucora and Phylander; poses as a page, Anclethe; said to be little
TANDORIX, Polydacre's page; in reality, Rosinda, Polydacre's wife, mother of Phylander, Cleanthe, and Lucora; called Madam Rosinda in the Q ending
Master LORECE, a gentleman gallant, Falorus' brother
PHYGIONIS, a poor man; poses as Draculemion, a poet
Lord POLYDACRE, Rosinda's husband, father of Phylander, Cleanthe, and Lucora
ANTIPHILA, a fine young lady
PHYLANDER, son of Polydacre and Rosinda, brother of Lucora and Cleanthe; a young man
VANDONA, a rich young widow, Carionil's kinswoman, Nentis's sister
Carionil's SERVANTS (3.1, *non-speaking*)

Clownish (i.e. rustic?) MASQUERS (4.3, *non-speaking*)
HYMEN, god of marriage; also called Goodman Wedlock and Master Marriage; a character in the masque
A BOY in the masque (4.3)
Polydacre's SERVANTS (5.1, *non-speaking*)
MUSICIANS (5.1; one sings)
Antiphila's SERVANT (5.2)

Speaking Parts: 18

Stage Directions and Speech Prefixes
PROLOGUE: *The Prologue* (heading)
CARIONIL: *Carionil* (s.d.s); *Cario<nil>* (s.p.s); *Carionil A young Lord. The counterfeit Negro, and called Tucapelo* (d.p.)
FALORUS: *Falorus* (s.d.s); *Falor<us>* (s.p.s); *Falorus* [*Carionil's*] *friend* (d.p.)
LUCORA: *Lucora* (s.d.s and s.p.s); *Lucora The obstinate Lady* [*Rosinda's*] *daughter* (d.p.)
NENTIS: *Nentis* (s.d.s); *Nent<is>* (s.p.s); *Nentis Lucora's Woman, Vandone's sister* (d.p.)
JAQUES: *Jaques* (s.d.s and s.p.s); *Jaques An old simple daughter of Vandonae's* (d.p.; sic)
CLEANTHE: *Cleanthe* (s.d.s); *Cleanth<e>* (s.p.s); *Cleanthe* [*Lucora's*] *sister called Anclethe* (d.p.)
TANDORIX: *a Page | Rosinda | Tandorix* (s.d.s); *Page* (s.d.s and s.p.s); *Rosin<da>* (s.p.s); *Rosinda Polidare's wife, called Tandorix* (d.p.; sic)
LORECE: *Lorece* (s.d.s); *Lore<ce>* (s.p.s); *Lorece A fantastic gallant.* [*Falorus'*] *brother* (d.p.)
PHYGIONIS: *Phyginois | Phyginois* (s.d.s); *Phyg<ionis>* (s.p.s); *Phyginois. Called Draculemion* (d.p.)
POLYDACRE: *Polidacre* (s.d.s); *Polid<acre>* (s.p.s); *Polidacre An old Lord* (d.p.)
ANTIPHILA: *Antiphila* (s.d.s); *Anti<phila>* (s.p.s); *Antiphila A fine young Lady* (d.p.)
PHYLANDER: *Philander | Phylander* (s.d.s); *Phil<ander> | Phy<lander>* (s.p.s); *Philander* [*Polydacre's*] *son* (d.p.)
VANDONA: *Vandona* (s.d.s); *Vandon<a>* (s.p.s); *Vandona A young rich widow* (d.p.)
SERVANTS: *Servants* (s.d.s and d.p.s); *Servi* (s.d.s)
MASQUERS: *Clownish Masquers* (s.d.s); *Masquers* (d.p.s)
HYMEN: [*one of the*] *Clownish Masquers* (s.d.s); *Hymen* (s.p.s); *Masquers* (d.p.)
BOY: [*one of the*] *Clownish Masquers* (s.d.s); *Boy* (s.p.s); *Masquers* (d.p.)
SERVANTS: *Servants* (s.d.s and d.p.s)
MUSICIANS: *Musicians* (s.d.s)
SERVANT: *a servant* (s.d.s); *Servant* (s.p.s); [*one of the*] *Servants* (d.p.)

Based on O.

OTHER CHARACTERS
Carionil's grandfather (1.2)
Lucora's grandfather, killed in a duel by Carionil's grandfather (1.2)

Jaques's grandmother, who taught him songs (3.2)
A thief who stole Jaques's cow (3.2)
Vandona's dead husband (3.2)
Cleanthe's nurse, Phygionis's mother, who stole her as a baby (5.4, 5.6)
The vintner, who took £20 from Jaques for supplying the wedding of Lorece and Vandona (5.5)
A company of musicians bespoke for the wedding (5.5)
Phygionis's brother, the nurse's son, to whom she tried to marry Cleanthe (5.6)
Falorus' father (5.6)
A group of ladies with whom Lucora planned to go to Lisbon to avoid having to marry Falorus (5.6; probably prospective nuns)

SETTING
Period: contemporary
Time-Scheme: 1.1 and 3.3 both end around dinner-time, presumably on different days; 4.4 takes place at night, 4.5 the next morning, and 5.4 at 10 a.m. the day after 4.5
Place: London

Geography
London: the Blackfriars theatre; the Cockpit theatre; the Exchange
Great Britain: England; Ireland; Wales
The Low Countries: Holland; Brussels
Spain: Madrid; the Pyrenees; Castile
Italy: Naples; Crema; Mantua; Venice; Mount Etna
Greece: Helicon; the Isthmus; Corinth; Calydon; Aganippe; Mount Olympus; Mount Parnassus; Tempe; Boeotia; Nemea
[Europe]: the Alps; Savoy; Frankfurt; Lisbon; Russia; Norway; France; Thrace
The Mediterranean Sea
Egypt: Alexandria; Memphis; River Nile; the Nile cataracts
Africa: Ethiopia; Xoa; Caffares; Fatigar; Angola; Baru; Balignoza; Adea; Vangne; Goyame; Gamara
Asia Minor: Mount Ida; River Scamander; River Simois
Asia: Arabia; Persia; Arabia Felix; Armenia; Tyre; Scythia
India
China
The East Indies
The West Indies
Virginia: Jamestown
Mexico: Tlaxcalla
Peru
The Arctic
The Antipodes
[The Antarctic]

SOURCES
Verbal: Christopher Marlowe, *Tamburlaine* (**784**; 4.2); Alonzo de Ercilla y Zúñiga, *La Araucana* (1597 edition; 3.3); Richard Knolles, *The General History of the Turks* (1603, repr. 1631; 3.2); Thomas Coryate, *Coryate's Crudities* (1611; 2.2); Peter Heylyn, *Microcosmus* (1625; 3.3)
Works Mentioned: Cornelius Gallus, *Amores* (3.2); *Amadis de Gaul* (fourteenth century; 2.1); Francisco Vazquez, *Palmerin d'Oliva* (1511; English tr. by Anthony Munday, 1588; 2.1); Francesco Guicciardini, *History of Italy* (1537–40; 4.2); Francisco de Moraes, *Palmerin of England* (1547–8, English tr. by Anthony Munday, 1581; 2.1); Diego Ortúñez de Calahorra, Pedro de la Sierra, and Marcos Martínez, *Espejo de principes y caballeros* (1555–87; English tr., *The Mirror of Princely Deeds and Knighthood*, by Margaret Tyler, R. P., and L. A., 1578–99; 2.1); Raphael Holinshed, *Chronicles of England, Scotland, and Ireland* (1577; 2.1); Sir Philip Sidney, *Arcadia* (c. 1580; 2.1); Ben Jonson, plays (general reference; prol.); Emanuel Forde, *Parismus* (1598–9; 2.1), *Montelion* (early seventeenth century; first extant edn 1633; 2.1); Miguel de Cervantes, *Don Quixote* (1605–15; 2.1, 3.2); there is also a general reference to Homer (3.2)

LANGUAGE
English
Latin: 6 words (2.1, 2.3, 4.3; Lorece, Phygionis)
Spanish: 67 words (3.3; Carionil, Polydacre)

FORM
Metre: pentameter and prose; a few skeltonics
Rhyme: blank verse and couplets
Prologue: 38 lines, in couplets
Act-Division: 5 acts
Epilogue: 24 lines, in couplets; spoken by Lucora and Cleanthe
Lines (Spoken): 3,177 (2,009 verse, 1,168 prose)

Based on O, incorporating Cokayne's handwritten additions in the British Library copy.

Lines (Written): 2,695 (Q); 3,381 (O)

STAGING
Doors: mentioned (4.4, dialogue)
Discovery Space: a bed thrust forth (3.1, s.d.)
Above: characters appear above (1.1, 4.4, s.d.; the space accommodates at least two; it takes no more than seven lines to get down to the main stage)
Audience: addressed as 'gallants' (prol.), 'gentlemen', 'ladies' (prol., ep.), and 'gentle spectators' (ep.); the price of admission is implied to be 1s.6d (prol.); the prologue raises the possibility that the theatre may be used for prostitution and other assignations, but discourages the practice; Jaques asks the ladies in the audience if one of them will be his girlfriend (5.6, s.d.; *not in Q*); the men are directly addressed by Carionil (5.6, implicit; *not in Q*)
Miscellaneous: the stage area has 'a private place' where Lorece sits (3.2, s.d.)

MUSIC
Music: fiddles (4.3, dialogue)

On-Stage Music: Lucora plays the lute (1.1, implicit; accompanying Song 1); musicians play (5.1, dialogue)
Songs:
- 1: 'Sweet Diana, virtuous Queen', 1.1, Lucora, 12 lines, with musical accompaniment;
- 2: 'Of six shillings beer I care not to hear', 1.1, Lorece, 20 lines;
- 3: 'All that about me sit', 3.2, Jaques, 24 lines;
- 4: 'Say, boy, who are fit to be', 4.3, Hymen and Boy, in parts, 14 lines;
- 5: 'The spheres are dull, and do not make', 5.1, Musician, 16 lines.

Dance: Masquers and Jaques dance (4.3, s.d.)

PROPS
Weapons: Falorus' sword (1.2, dialogue; 5.4, s.d.); Carionil's sword (1.2, dialogue); a stiletto (2.2, dialogue); Phylander's sword (4.1, dialogue); Tucapelo's sword (4.4, dialogue)
Musical Instruments: a lute (1.1, dialogue); unspecified instruments (5.1, implicit)
Clothing: a ring (5.6, dialogue)
Money: an unspecified amount (1.1, implicit); one or more silver coins (2.3, dialogue)
Food and Drink: a banquet (5.1, s.d.)
Small Portable Objects: a paper (1.3, implicit); a letter (2.2, s.d.); another letter (5.2, s.d.); a licence (5.5, dialogue)
Large Portable Objects: a seat (3.2, implicit)
Scenery: a bed (3.1, s.d.)

COSTUMES AND MAKE-UP
CARIONIL: a sheath (1.2, implicit); disguised as a Negro, in 'strange apparel' (3.3, s.d.; 4.2, 4.4–5, implicit), and with black skin (implicit); his own clothes (5.4, s.d.)
FALORUS: a sheath (1.2, dialogue)
LUCORA: a pantofle (3.3, dialogue)
JAQUES: a doublet (5.5, dialogue)
CLEANTHE: cross-dressed as a page (1.1, 2.2, 3.1–2, 4.2, 4.5, implicit); women's apparel (5.4, s.d.; 5.6, implicit)
TANDORIX/ROSINDA: cross-dressed as a page (1.1, 1.3, 2.2–3, 4.1–2, implicit); a periwig (4.1, dialogue; removed on stage); women's apparel (5.2, s.d.; 5.6, implicit); a mask (5.2, 5.6, dialogue; removed on stage)
PHYGIONIS: mean garments (2.3, implicit); brave apparel (3.2, s.d.)
PHYLANDER: a sheath (4.1, implicit)
VANDONA: yellow hair (dialogue); black mourning clothes (3.2, dialogue); a white apron (4.3, dialogue)
HYMEN: a saffron frock (4.3, dialogue)

EARLY TEXTUAL HISTORY
On a departure from London (perhaps in July 1632, perhaps later), Aston Cokayne left the text with a friend, who subsequently died and whose papers were dispersed. A damaged copy of the text (which Cokayne either knew or presumed to be the same one) later came into the possession of the printer William Godbid; this lacked the final leaf, so Godbid engaged another author to write a brief conclusion.

1656: entered to William Godbid in the Stationers' Register on Monday 29 September; entry gives author's initials.

1657: ¹Q printed by William Godbid for Isaac Pridmore; collation A² B–I⁴ K², 36 leaves; title page names author; list of roles. Two long passages are printed in markedly smaller type.

1658: included in Cokayne's *Small Poems of Divers Sorts* (²O), sigs. V1ʳ–2D5ᵛ; 61 leaves; printed by William Godbid.

1659: O reissued in or before May as *A Chain of Golden Poems*, with the title page naming Isaac Pridmore as the bookseller.

1660: advertised as for sale by Simon Miller.

1661: O advertised as for sale by Francis Kirkman, naming this play.

1662: O reissued as *Poems &c.*, with title page naming Philip Stephens, jun., as the bookseller. A variant imprint names Francis Kirkman as the bookseller, and the volume (under the title *Poems Enriched with Wit, Mirth, and Eloquence*) was advertised as for sale by Henry Marsh.

1662 or later: Cokayne made handwritten corrections in a copy of the 1662 issue of O (now in the British Library).

1669: O reissued as *Choice Poems of Several Sorts*, with title page naming Francis Kirkman as the bookseller.

1669–75: O advertised as for sale by Francis Kirkman, naming this play.

c. 1678: advertised as for sale by Obadiah Blagrave.

1684: Nicholas Cox (Manciple of St Edmund Hall, Oxford) had a copy of O in his bookshop. It had probably been previously owned by Gerard Langbaine, and appears on a list compiled by Anthony Wood on Saturday 13 December.

EDITION
Catherine M. Shaw, The Renaissance Imagination 17 (New York and London, 1986).

REFERENCES
Annals 1639; Bentley, iii. 168–70; Bodleian, MS Wood E. 4, art. 1, p. 49; Greg 771; Hazlitt, 169; *MLN* 57 (1942), 57–8; *PBSA* 107 (2013), 36–7.

2377. Love's Masterpiece

EVIDENCE
Stationers' Register.

GENRE
comedy

Contemporary: comedy

TITLE
Contemporary: *Love's Masterpiece*

AUTHOR
Thomas Heywood

DATE
Limits: 1596–1640

The large majority of the plays which passed through the hands of John Okes in 1640 were of recent date, though it is also true that he and his father Nicholas had a long-standing association with Heywood, and seem to have had some access to his back catalogue: in 1637, they printed the first edition of *The Royal King and the Loyal Subject* (**1504**), three decades after it was written.

PLOT
The title probably uses the word *masterpiece* in the sense OED 1b, a person's greatest achievement; 'Love' could have been a person, probably Cupid; Heywood used 'Love' in this sense in the title of *Love's Mistress* (**2451**). If both those hypotheses are correct, then Cupid's masterpiece would presumably have been to induce love between people who are, or appear, completely incompatible.

ROLES
CUPID, god of love; also known as Love (?)
Some unlikely LOVERS

Allegorical Roles: 1 or more (?)

EARLY TEXTUAL HISTORY
1640: entered to John Okes in the Stationers' Register on Friday 22 May; entry names author. Thomas Wykes had licensed the book for publication.

REFERENCES
Annals 1640; Bentley, iv. 579; Greg Θ47; Hazlitt, 142; Sibley, 97.

2378. *A Fine Companion*

TEXT
Printed in 1633 (STC 17442), from an authorial manuscript.

GENRE
comedy
Contemporary: play (ind., S.R.); piece (ded.)

TITLE
Printed: *A Fine Companion*
Contemporary: *The Fine Companion*

AUTHOR
Shackerley Marmion

DATE
Limits: 1632–3
Best Guess: 1632

The play must be later than *Holland's Leaguer* (**2351**), whose success may have impelled the company to order a follow-up from Marmion sooner rather than later; it must be earlier than June 1633, when it was entered for publication. Marmion also needed time in 1632 to write *The Country Gentleman* (**2390**), which is more likely to date from after the June proclamation ordering the gentry back to their country estates. Another consideration is the play's relationship with *The Weeding of the Covent Garden* (**2401**): Captain Whibble and his boozy brotherhood either imitate or are imitated by Brome's Captain Driblow and the Philoblathici. The other dating indicators for Brome's play place it in late 1632 or, more probably, early 1633. The name Driblow more probably derives from Whibble than vice versa, especially since Whibble has its own direct source in *The Witty Fair One* (**2251**).

ORIGINAL PRODUCTION
Prince Charles's Men at Salisbury Court

PLOT
Aurelio was disinherited after his father perceived him as a rival in love, so the estate passed to his younger brother, Careless. As a result, Littlegood the usurer no longer considers Aurelio an eligible son-in-law; but Valeria, Aurelio's girlfriend, is determined to stick with him despite the material disadvantages. Careless has capitalized his inheritance by mortgaging the lands to Littlegood; intending to use his wealth to acquire the reputation of being a fine companion, he has taken up with Captain Whibble and his crew of drinkers.

Littlegood favours Spruce as a husband for Valeria. Spruce is really only interested in sex, and intends to jilt her afterwards; but her refusal only increases his interest. Aurelio sends Valeria his ring, but she drops it; Spruce finds it and uses it to make Aurelio jealous. Aurelio had planned a ruse whereby Valeria would feign madness, but now he intends to drive her truly mad. Reports of her distress bring him back to his senses: he confronts Spruce and makes him admit that the accusation against her was malicious and mendacious.

Dotario, appalled at his nephew Careless's prodigality, plans to marry and beget an heir so that the young wastrel will not get his hands on a second estate. He woos Littlegood's younger daughter, Aemilia, who puts him off by describing what a shrewish spendthrift of a wife she would be. She is more interested in Careless, who pays her a drunken visit, but is pressured by her father into giving Dotario a more respectful answer. She tells him she has vowed only to marry a man who will steal her, and makes a date to elope with him.

Importuned by his wife, Littlegood allows his son Lackwit to go out to dinner in his best hat and cloak, and gives him money. He seeks to join Captain Whibble's drinking brotherhood; but Whibble tricks him into swapping clothes and paying the bill. He explains to his parents that he lost his hat and cloak in a fight. Whibble proves to be a coward, and avoids fighting a duel when provoked by Fido; instead, he invites Fido and Aurelio to supper. Aurelio is too upset over Valeria to go, so instead Fido takes Careless in disguise. The impecunious Whibble cannot pay for the meal and postpones it; but Fido tricks him into insulting Careless, not knowing him to be present.

Careless next disguises himself as Dotario and tricks Lackwit into believing that Dotario, eloping as arranged, is the impostor; Lackwit ensures that Careless and Aemilia are married, hoping to win back his father's favour. A doctor arrives to cure Valeria, and takes her away for treatment. He is really Aurelio in disguise, and when they return, they too are married. Dotario makes Aurelio his heir, and Littlegood returns Careless's mortgaged lands. Whibble marries his landlady and becomes a tavern-keeper.

SCENE DESIGNATION
ind., 1.1–7, 2.1–6, 3.1–6, 4.1–6. 5.1–2 (Q)

The stage is not clear at the following scene-divisions: 1.1–2, 1.3–5, 1.6–7, 2.2–5, 3.1–2, 3.3–4, 4.2–3.

ROLES
Induction
A CRITIC
The AUTHOR of the play

Main Action
AURELIO, a disinherited gentleman, Careless's elder brother, Dotario's nephew; betrothed to Valeria, and later her husband; poses as a doctor
VALERIA, elder daughter of Littlegood and Fondling, sister of Aemilia and Lackwit; betrothed to Aurelio, and later his wife
Master LITTLEGOOD, an old usurer; Fondling's husband, father of Valeria, Aemilia, and Lackwit; also said to be a Jew, but this may not be meant literally
Master CARELESS, a prodigal gentleman, Aurelio's younger brother, Dotario's nephew; later Aemilia's husband
FIDO, a friend of Aurelio and Careless
A TAILOR, possibly named Master Snip
A SEMPSTER
A HABERDASHER
A BOY, who announces Spruce (1.4)
Master SPRUCE, a young gallant and landed gentleman
Master DOTARIO, an old, unmarried gentleman and citizen, rich uncle of Aurelio and Careless; Littlegood's neighbour
Captain WHIBBLE, a parasite and braggart soldier; later the Hostess's husband
STERN, a lieutenant, Whibble's drinking companion
CROTCHET, Littlegood's servant

AEMILIA, younger daughter of Littlegood and Fondling, sister of Valeria and Lackwit; later Careless's wife
Mistress FONDLING, Littlegood's wife, mother of Lackwit, Valeria, and Aemilia
Master LACKWIT, son of Littlegood and Fondling, brother of Valeria and Aemilia
Four WENCHES (4.1, *non-speaking*)
TONY, a drawer at the Horseshoe tavern (4.1)
The HOSTESS, a widow; Whibble's landlady, later his wife

Speaking Parts: 21

Stage Directions and Speech Prefixes
CRITIC: *Critic* (s.d.s and s.p.s)
AUTHOR: *Author* (s.d.s and s.p.s)
AURELIO: *Aurelio* (s.d.s); *Aur<elio>* (s.p.s); *Aurelio, An elder Brother disinherited* (d.p.)
VALERIA: *Valeria* (s.d.s); *Val<eria>* (s.p.s); *Valeria,* [one of Littlegood's and Fondling's] *Daughters* (d.p.)
LITTLEGOOD: *Littlegood* (s.d.s); *Lit<tlegood>* (s.p.s); *Littlegood, A Usurer* (d.p.)
CARELESS: *Carelesse* (s.d.s); *Care<lesse>* (s.p.s); *Carelesse,* [Aurelio's] *Brother, the Fine Companion* (d.p.)
FIDO: *Fido* (s.d.s and s.p.s); *Fido,* [Aurelio's and Careless's] *Friend* (d.p.)
TAILOR: *Tailor* (s.d.s, s.p.s, and d.p.)
SEMPSTER: *Sempster* (s.d.s, s.p.s, and d.p.)
HABERDASHER: *Haberdasher* (s.d.s, s.p.s, and d.p.)
BOY: *Boy* (s.d.s, s.p.s, and d.p.)
SPRUCE: *Spruce* (s.d.s); *Spru<se>* (s.p.s); *Spruce, A young Gallant* (d.p.)
DOTARIO: *Dotario* (s.d.s); *Dot<ario>* (s.p.s); *Dotario, An old Gentleman,* [Aurelio's and Careless's] *Uncle* (d.p.)
WHIBBLE: *Captain Whibble* (s.d.s); *Captain* (s.d.s and s.p.s); *Whibble, A Captain* (d.p.)
STERN: *Lieutenant* (s.d.s and s.p.s); *Sterne, A Lieutenant* (d.p.)
CROTCHET: *Crochet | Crotchet* (s.d.s); *Crot<chet>* (s.p.s); *Crotchet, A Clown* (d.p.)
AEMILIA: *Aemillia | Aemilia* (s.d.s); *Aemi<lia>* (s.p.s); *Aemilia,* [one of Littlegood's and Fondling's] *Daughters* (d.p.)
FONDLING: *Mistress Fondling | Fondling* (s.d.s); *Fond<ling>* (s.p.s); *Fondling,* [Littlegood's] *wife* (d.p.)
LACKWIT: *Lackwit | Lackewit* (s.d.s); *Lack<wit>* (s.p.s); *Lackwit,* [Littlegood's and Fondling's] *Son* (d.p.)
WENCHES: *four Wenches* (s.d.s); *4 Wenches* (d.p.)
TONY: *Drawer* (s.d.s and s.p.s)
HOSTESS: *Hostess* (s.d.s, s.p.s, and d.p.)
D.p. also lists: *Fiddlers; Attendants*

OTHER CHARACTERS
The dead father of Aurelio and Careless, Dotario's brother (1.1, 1.6–7)

People who have sought acquaintance with the newly wealthy Careless, including magnificos and advocates (1.3)
A new servant hired by Careless, who robbed him (1.3, 1.5)
Spruce's boy (1.5; may be the boy who appears on stage in 1.4)
Littlegood's neighbours, who enjoyed listening to the infant Lackwit (2.6)
A knight, the Littlegoods' former lodger (2.6)
Fondling's relatives, gentry (2.6)
A waterman, the Hostess's dead husband (3.4)
Lackwit's tailor (4.1)
The musicians of the Horseshoe tavern (4.1)
The host of the Horseshoe tavern (4.1)
A cobbler who mended Whibble's boots at his Hostess's expense (4.5)
The Hostess's neighbours (4.5)
Tapsters and ostlers assaulted by Whibble (4.5)
Careless's sister, whom he offers to Spruce (5.2)

SETTING
Period: contemporary (?)
Time-Scheme: 4.1 takes place at dinner-time on the same day as 1.3; 4.5 takes place the evening following 3.4
Place: London

Geography
[*London*]: the Horseshoe tavern; the Red Lattice, Southwark; Fleet Street; Temple Bar; Aldgate
Europe: Spain; Holland; Thessaly
The Bosphorus
[*Asia*]: Parthia; the Dead Sea
[*Africa*]: Syrtes
The West Indies

SOURCES
Narrative: Barnaby Rich, *Rich's Farewell to Military Profession* 8 (1581; possibly reprinted in or after 1591); Francis Beaumont, *The Knight of the Burning Pestle* (**1562**; 5.2); Francis Beaumont and John Fletcher, *The Scornful Lady* (**1626**; 4.1)
Verbal: Horace, *Epistles* 2.1 (t.p. motto; probably quoted via the title page of Ben Jonson's *The New Inn*, **2263**), *Odes* 4.2 (prol.); Seneca, *Hippolytus* (2.1); James Shirley, *The Witty Fair One* (**2251**; the name Whibble)
Music: 'The Fine Companion' (traditional tune; 4.1)
Works Mentioned: Plato, *Republic* (5.2); Giovanni Pico della Mirandola, *Disputationes adversus astrologiam divinatricem* (before 1494; 5.2); Henry Cornelius Agrippa, *De incertitudine et vanitate scientarum* (1530; 5.2); Ben Jonson, *The Silent Woman* (**1603**; 2.6), *The Alchemist* (**1621**; 3.6)

The tune 'The Fine Companion' was later printed in John Playford's *The English Dancing-Master* (1651).

LANGUAGE
English

Latin: 7 words (ind., 1.3, 2.6, 4.1; Critic, Careless, Lackwit, Crotchet)

FORM
Metre: prose and pentameter
Rhyme: blank verse
Induction: 71 lines, marked as a prologue; dialogue between the author and a critic
Act-Division: 5 acts
Lines (Spoken): 2,615 (1,101 verse, 1,514 prose)
Lines (Written): 2,809

STAGING
Within: music (4.1, implicit)
Audience: called a 'noble auditory' and said to be seated (ind.)

MUSIC
Music: 'The Fine Companion' played by off-stage musicians to accompany the dance (4.1, dialogue)
Dance: Careless, Whibble, Lieutenant, Lackwit, and Wenches dance (4.1, s.d.)

PROPS
Weapons: Fido's sword (3.3–4, implicit); Aurelio's sword (4.6, dialogue); a long sword (5.1, s.d.)
Clothing: a ring (3.1–2, 4.2, s.d.)
Money: an unspecified sum (1.3, dialogue); twenty gold pieces (2.6, dialogue); twenty pounds (4.4, dialogue)
Food and Drink: wine (4.1, dialogue); a jug of liquor (5.2, s.d.)
Small Portable Objects: a black box (1.5, s.d.; hanging from Spruce's girdle); letters (1.5, dialogue); an amethyst (2.5, dialogue); a book (2.6, dialogue); a paper (3.2, s.d.); a pearl (3.5, dialogue); a document (3.5, dialogue); drinking vessels (4.1, implicit); a little glass (4.1, dialogue); three or four napkins (5.1, s.d.); a glass (5.2, s.d.)
Large Portable Objects: three joint-stools (4.1, dialogue)

COSTUMES
AURELIO: disguised as a doctor (5.2, s.d.; removed on stage)
VALERIA: golden hair (dialogue)
CARELESS: disguised (4.5, s.d.; removed on stage); disguised as Dotario (5.1, s.d.; 5.2, implicit; removed on stage)
SPRUCE: a new suit (1.5, dialogue), with tasselled garters, one of them untied, and a girdle (s.d.)
DOTARIO: bald-headed, with a grey or white beard (dialogue); new clothes (1.4, dialogue)
WHIBBLE: a cloak (3.4, dialogue; 4.1, s.d.; removed on stage); a hat (4.1, dialogue; removed on stage); Lackwit's hat and cloak (4.1, implicit; 4.5, dialogue; put on and removed on stage); dressed as a host (5.2, s.d.)

LACKWIT: a hat (4.1, dialogue; removed on stage); a cloak (4.1, s.d.; removed on stage); Whibble's hat and cloak (4.1, implicit; put on on stage); a headpiece (5.1, s.d.)

EARLY STAGE HISTORY

1632-3: performed by Prince Charles's Men at Salisbury Court.

1632-3: performed at court by Prince Charles's Men, possibly during the period November 1632 to April 1633. (If so, the performance took place at the Cockpit in Court, and rehearsals in the Great Hall, Whitehall Palace.) The audience included: King Charles I; Queen Henrietta Maria. This may have been one of the three performances for which Joseph Moore was later paid £30 by a warrant dated Tuesday 1 October 1633.

The Chamber Account's apparelling records show that 29 performances were given at court during the November to April period, of which fourteen (between November and February) were by Queen Henrietta's Men. Many of the remaining fifteen would have been by the King's Men (who performed 21 times at Whitehall Palace and Denmark House between May 1632 and March 1633). Since the warrant to pay Queen Henrietta's Men was issued on Saturday 12 October 1633, eleven days after the warrant to pay Moore, the three Prince's Men performances in the latter warrant may also belong to the winter or early spring of 1632-3.

EARLY TEXTUAL HISTORY

1633: entered (as *The Fine Companion*) in the Stationers' Register to Richard Meighen on Saturday 15 June; entry names author. Sir Henry Herbert had licensed the book for publication.

1633: Q printed by Augustine Matthews for Richard Meighen; collation A-K⁴, 40 leaves; title page names author, acting company, and playhouse; Latin titlepage motto; list of roles; authorial dedication to Sir Ralph Dutton.

c. 1630s-40s: a copy of Q was in the possession of John Horne (Vicar of Headington, Oxfordshire). After his death, his entire collection of play-books passed into the possession of John Houghton of Brasenose College, Oxford (c. 1608-77), then to James Herne (died 1685), and then to the library of Ralph Sheldon (1623-84) at Weston, where it was catalogued by Anthony Wood, probably in the late 1670s.

1646: Meighen's rights to *The Fine Companion* transferred in the Stationers' Register from his widow, Mercy Meighen, to herself and Gabriel Bedell on Saturday 7 November, by order of a court held on Wednesday 21 October; individually named as part of a group transfer of nineteen titles.

1653-6: advertised as for sale by Mercy Meighen, Gabriel Bedell, and Thomas Collins.

1655: *The English Treasury of Wit and Language* entered in the Stationers' Register to Humphrey Moseley on Tuesday 16 January.

1655: four extracts (from 2.2, 3.3, 4.1, 5.2) included in John Cotgrave's *The English Treasury of Wit and Language*, sigs. E5ʳ, N3ʳ, N4ᵛ, X4ʳ; printed for Humphrey Moseley.

1657: advertised as for sale by the Newcastle-upon-Tyne bookseller William London.

1684: Nicholas Cox (Manciple of St Edmund Hall, Oxford) had a copy of Q in his bookshop. It had probably been previously owned by Gerard Langbaine, and appears on a list compiled by Anthony Wood on Saturday 13 December.

EDITION

Richard Sonnenshein, Garland Renaissance Drama (London and New York, 1979).

REFERENCES

Annals 1633; Bawcutt, C67; Bentley, iv. 742-5; Bodleian, MS Wood E. 4, art. 1, p. 67; Eyre & Rivington, i. 463; Greg 481; Hazlitt, 85; William London, *A Catalogue of the Most Vendible Books in England* (London, 1657), sig. 2F1ʳ; *MLR* 13 (1918), 401-11; MSC 6, 83, 123; *SP* 40 (1943), 186-203.

2379. Puppet Play of Queen Elizabeth

EVIDENCE

William Strode, Floral Play (**2476**); William Davenant, 'The Long Vacation in London' (published in his *Works*, 1673; Wing D320).

Davenant's poem refers to various amusements available in the city during the summer vacation. It was written in 1635, but the reference to a puppet play about 'our old Queen Bess' does not appear in the early version printed in 1656 (*Wit and Drollery*; Wing W3131).

GENRE

puppet show

DATE

Limits: 1604-35

PLOT

Under the reign of her Catholic sister Mary, the Protestant Princess Elizabeth is suspected of complicity in rebellion, but nothing is ever proven against her. She survives imprisonment and assassination attempts sponsored by the Roman Catholic church, and succeeds Mary as Queen of England.

The play may go on to portray the triumphs of her reign, such as the defeat of the Spanish Armada.

Strode says that the play dealt with 'Queen Bess's troubles', which indicates that at least some of the action concerned the period before she became Queen.

2380. The Eunuch

ROLES
Princess ELIZABETH, a Protestant; later Queen of England; perhaps also called Bess

Possibly also
MARY, Queen of England, Philip's wife; a Catholic
PHILIP, King of Spain, Mary's husband

SETTING
Period: sixteenth (and perhaps seventeenth) century; the play dramatizes events from the life and reign of Queen Elizabeth I (born 1533, reigned 1558–1603), perhaps concentrating in part on the period 1553–8
Place: England

Geography
Spain
Rome

SOURCES
Narrative: possibly Thomas Heywood, *The Troubles of Queen Elizabeth* (**1427**)

LANGUAGE
English

Strode and Davenant both specifically say that the play includes spoken dialogue; strictly speaking, the language is only inferential, but it could hardly have been anything but English.

PROPS
Small Portable Objects: puppets

EARLY STAGE HISTORY
1632–5: probably performed in Norwich, apparently without arousing any objection from the local antitheatricalists.

REFERENCES
Sir William Davenant, *The Shorter Poems and Songs from the Plays and Masques*, ed. A. M. Gibbs (Oxford, 1972), 129; George Speaight, *The History of the English Puppet Theatre*, 2nd edn (London, 1990), 328.

2380. The Eunuch

EVIDENCE
Stationers' Register.

A bookseller with the initials J. M., who was probably John Marriott, had *The Fatal Contract* (**2412**) printed in 1653, and that play features a supposed eunuch. Towards the end of the same year, Richard Marriott, son of John, entered this tragedy entitled *The Eunuch*; but to identify the two plays with one another entails two problems. One is that a book published in the final weeks of a year would be more likely to have a title page bearing the following year's date. The other is an antedating of more than two decades, which is even harder to set aside. *The Fatal Contract* was retitled *The Eunuch* when it was adapted, probably after 1674, and was printed with that title in 1687, but there is no reason to suppose that the title was attached to the play as early as 1653; otherwise why would J. M.'s edition bear the other title? Presumably other tragic eunuchs were conceivable; so *The Eunuch* is more likely to have been a separate play.

GENRE
tragedy
Contemporary: play; tragedy

TITLE
Contemporary: *The Eunuch*

DATE
Limits: 1610–53

The limits are defined by the datable plays among those entered in the same group; see **2294** for general discussion of their possible origins.

ROLES
A EUNUCH

EARLY TEXTUAL HISTORY
1653: entered to Richard Marriott in the Stationers' Register on Thursday 29 December (?; recorded as Tuesday 29 November); group entry of 21 plays; play individually named.

REFERENCES
Annals Supp. II (b); Greg Θ105.

2381. The Country Girl

TEXT
Printed in 1647 (Wing B4425), possibly from theatrical copy.

GENRE
comedy
Contemporary: play (prol., S.R.); comedy (t.p.)

TITLE
Performed/Printed: *The Country Girl*

AUTHOR
T. B.

DATE
Limits: 1629–33
Best Guess: 1632

ORIGINAL PRODUCTION
Prince Charles's Men at Salisbury Court (?)

The play (or at least the prologue) was probably not written before the c. 1630 revival of *The Fair Maid of the West* (**1607**), and certainly not before the first production of *The Northern Lass* (**2277**). The prologue also speculates that the title character might have come to London to 'set up some new Leaguer'. Bentley believed this to be an allusion to Nicholas Goodman's 1632 prose tract *Holland's Leaguer*; it seems to me more likely to refer, if not merely to the brothel itself, to the success of *Holland's Leaguer* (**2351**), completing a trinity of allusions to recent popular plays.

This has a bearing on the play's repertory context as well as its date. The other two plays, with which the prologue contrasts its country girl, belonged to the King's Men (*The Northern Lass*) and Queen Henrietta's Men (*The Fair Maid of the West*). These references were obviously not in-house advertising but might be read in terms of commercial competition (not necessarily of an unfriendly kind), indicating that the play belonged to a third company. There is a similar manoeuvre in the prologue to *Holland's Leaguer*. This prologue's 'Leaguer' reference is tonally different from the allusions to the other plays and might be read as entertaining the possibility of repertory continuity.

There is one other possible clue to the company provenance. In the opening scene, four exit directions for William read 'Exit Shut'. Perhaps it is just a direction for the handling of the door, pointedly shutting out the prospective suitors, rather than a trace of a proper name (either the actor's or the character's), but it is striking that the word is only associated with William. No known actor of the time had a name which could abbreviate to 'Shut', though a speculative long-shot might be a misprint for 'Stut.', referring to George Stutfield, who was a member of Prince Charles's Men from 1632–4, and of Queen Henrietta's Men in 1635.

PLOT

The widowed Lady Mosely is uninterested in remarrying, despite pressure from her sister, Lady Malory, and despite the attentions of a number of suitors, several of them fools. Lady Mosely is impressed by Sir Oliver, and promises to marry him if she does anyone. Captain Molyneux, who wooed her before but lost out to her husband, returns from sea, boisterously ejects the unworthy suitors, and challenges Sir Oliver to a duel. Sir Oliver accepts, but fights reluctantly; when Molyneux is wounded, he refuses to finish him off. Impressed by his honourable behaviour, Molyneux helps him to go into hiding and persuades Lady Mosely that Sir Oliver would have been the right man for her. She falls into a melancholy at having lost him, so Molyneux brings a doctor to attend her—but the doctor is Sir Oliver in disguise, and their marriage can go ahead.

In the second plot, Sir Robert Malory has taken an interest in the education and welfare of Margaret, his tenant's daughter, since she was a child; but that interest has become sexual now that she is old enough. Conscious of their dependence on their landlord's good will, her father Thrashard suggests that he is only testing her chastity. In fact, he is in earnest, but when he comes to woo in person, her sister Gillian interrupts his courtship with a display of morris dancing. Lady Malory hears of her husband's activities and visits Margaret in disguise. Margaret chastely refuses a bribe for her virginity, thereby confirming her good faith. Lady Malory sets the family up with apparent riches and gets them to pretend not to know Sir Robert; she herself poses as Thrashard's wife. The ruse shocks Sir Robert out of his adulterous ways, and he later bestows Margaret on Molyneux, with a handsome dowry.

In the third plot, Lady Malory gets rid of Lady Mosely's foolish suitors by having the chambermaid Barbara receive them posing as her mistress. The servant William, who has got Barbara pregnant but doesn't wish to marry her, sees an opportunity to find the child a father. He persuades each of the suitors that he alone is the one favoured by 'Lady Mosely', and arranges that each of them shall meet her. Three different meetings are procured at different places on the same street, but only one marriage takes place, and afterwards Rash the mercer is discomfited to find that he has married the maid, not the mistress. (Worse, she turns out to be a Puritan.) The other suitors take heart and rush to claim the real Lady Mosely, but they too get substitutes: one an old gentlewoman, the other the scolding Gillian.

SCENE DESIGNATION

prol., 1.1–2, 2.1–2, 3.1–2, 4.1–3, 5.1–2, ep. (Q has act-division only)

ROLES

PROLOGUE

SIR OLIVER Bellingham, a young knight

Master WILLIAM, Lady Mosely's servant; also called Will

Master RASH, a mercer; later Barbara's husband

Master Timothy PLUSH, a gallant; later Gillian's husband; also (mockingly) called Lining

SIR ROBERT Malory, an old city knight and country landowner, Lady Malory's husband, Lady Mosely's brother-in-law

Master ABRAM Thrashard, Thrashard's son, brother of Margaret and Gillian; also called Abraham

Madonna BARBARA, Lady Mosely's chambermaid, secretly a Puritan; later Rash's wife; also called Mistress Barbary and Madam Bab

LADY MOSELY, a young, rich widow, Lady Malory's sister; also called Lady Littleworth

LADY MALORY, Sir Robert's wife, Lady Mosely's sister; also addressed as Peg (but perhaps only in error)

An OLD GENTLEWOMAN, a widow, Lady Malory's companion; later Gregory's wife

Master GREGORY Dwindle, a country gentleman and heir; later the Old Gentlewoman's husband

Oliver THRASHARD, Sir Robert's tenant, father of Margaret, Gillian, and Abram; also called Master Oliver Thrashard Esquire (when he is pretending gentility)

Mistress MARGARET, the country girl; Thrashard's pretty daughter, sister of Abram and Gillian; also called Peggy and Peg

Mistress GILLIAN, Thrashard's scolding daughter, sister of Abram and Margaret; later Plush's wife; some speech prefixes name her Peg (in error?)

A FIDDLER (2.1, *non-speaking*)
Six COUNTRY WENCHES (2.1; speak collectively)
Captain George MOLYNEUX, a sailor
UNSPECIFIED PERSONS in the Mosely household (2.2, *non-speaking*)
Master CUTHBERT, Sir Robert's servant; also called Cut Hockman
HUGH, Sir Oliver's servant; also called Hughkin
The CONSTABLE at Edmonton (3.1)
A PRIEST (4.3)
A DOCTOR (5.1)
The Doctor's SERVANTS (5.1; one speaks)
A SERVANT in Sir Robert's household (5.2)

Speaking Parts: 28

Stage Directions and Speech Prefixes
PROLOGUE: *Prologue* (heading)
SIR OLIVER: *Sir Oliver Bellingham* (s.d.s and d.p.); [one of] *the two Knights | Bellingham* (s.d.s); *Sir Oliver* (s.d.s and s.p.s); *Sir Oly<ver>* (s.p.s)
WILLIAM: *Master William* (s.d.s and s.p.s); *Master Wy<lliam>* (s.p.s)
RASH: *Master Rash* (s.d.s and d.p.); *Rash* (s.d.s and s.p.s); [one of] *The 3* (s.d.s)
PLUSH: *Plush, a Gallant* | [one of] *The 3* (s.d.s); *Plush* (s.d.s and s.p.s); *Master Timothy Plush* (d.p.)
SIR ROBERT: *Sir Robert Malory* (s.d.s and d.p.); *Sir Robert | Sir Robert Malorie* | [one of] *the two Knights | Sir Robert Mallory* (s.d.s); *Sir Rob<ert>* (s.p.s)
ABRAM: *Abram | Abr'am | Brother* (s.d.s); *Abra<m>* (s.p.s); *Abraham Thrash-hard* [Old Thrashard's] *Son* (d.p.)
BARBARA: *Barbara | Barbary* | [one of the] *wenches* (s.d.s); *Bab* (s.d.s and s.p.s); *Bar<bara>* (s.p.s)
LADY MOSELY: *the Lady Mosely | Lady Mosely* (s.d.s); *Lady Mos<ely> | Lady* (s.p.s); *Lady Mosely* (d.p.)
LADY MALORY: *the Lady Malory | the Lady Malorie* | [Sir Robert Malory's] *Lady* | [Cut's] *Lady | the Lady Mallory | Lady Mallory* (s.d.s); *Lady* (s.d.s and s.p.s); *Lady Mal<ory>* (s.p.s); *Lady Malory* (d.p.)
OLD GENTLEWOMAN: *an old Gentlewoman* (s.d.s and d.p.); *the old Gentlewoman* | [one of the] *wenches* (s.d.s); *Old Gentlewoman* (s.p.s)
GREGORY: *Gregory* | [one of] *The 3 | Gregorie | Greg<ory> Dwindle* (s.d.s); *Greg<ory>* (s.p.s); *Master Gregory Dwindle* (d.p.)
THRASHARD: *old Thrashard | Thrashard | Father* (s.d.s); *Thra<shard>* (s.p.s); *Old Thrash-hard* (d.p.)
MARGARET: *Margaret* [Old Thrashard's] *daughter | Margarett* (s.d.s); *Margaret* (s.d.s and s.p.s); *Margaret, the Country Girl* (d.p.)
GILLIAN: *Gillian | Sister* | [one of the] *wenches* (s.d.s and s.p.s); *Gill* (s.d.s and s.p.s); *Peg* (s.p.s); *Gillian,* [Margaret's] *scolding Sister* (d.p.)
FIDDLER: *the Fiddler | Fiddler* (s.d.s)
COUNTRY WENCHES: *six Country Wenches | the Maids* (s.d.s); *Maids* (s.p.s)

MOLYNEUX: *Captain Mullyneux | the Captain | Mullynex* (s.d.s); *Captain* (s.d.s and s.p.s); *Captain George Mullynax* (d.p.)
UNSPECIFIED PERSONS: *others* (s.d.s)
CUTHBERT: *Cutbert* (s.d.s); *Cutt | Cut* (s.d.s and s.p.s); *Cutbert* [one of the] *Servingmen* (d.p.)
HUGH: *Hugh* (s.d.s and s.p.s); *Hugh* [one of the] *Servingmen* (d.p.)
CONSTABLE: *Constable* (s.d.s and s.p.s)
PRIEST: *a Priest* (s.d.s); *Parson* (s.p.s)
DOCTOR: *Doctor* (s.d.s and s.p.s)
SERVANTS: *Servants* (s.d.s); *Servant* (s.d.s and s.p.s)
SERVANT: *a Servant | the Servant* (s.d.s); *Servant* (s.d.s and s.p.s)

OTHER CHARACTERS
Sir James Mosely, Lady Mosely's dead husband (1.1–2, 2.2, 5.2)
Plush's tailor (1.1)
Barbara's two illegitimate children (1.2)
The Old Gentlewoman's four dead husbands (1.2)
Gregory's father, over 60 years old and inconveniently alive (1.2, 2.2, 3.2, 4.3, 5.2)
Go-betweens who wooed Margaret on Sir Robert's behalf (2.1)
The barber who lent Gillian a basin (3.1)
The barber's allegedly promiscuous wife (3.1)
Margaret's mother (5.2)

SETTING
Period: contemporary (?)
Time-Scheme: 1.1 takes place in the morning; 4.1 takes place the day after 2.2
Place: Edmonton and London

Geography
London: the Exchange; the Phoenix, Fleet Street; Cheapside; Paternoster Row; Bedlam; Lime Street; Aldgate; the Tower; Long Lane; Paris Garden
[*England*]: Waltham; Brentford

SOURCES
Verbal: Bible: Matthew 19.5 (5.2); Persius, *Satires* 3 (3.2); possibly John Ford, *'Tis Pity She's a Whore* (**2329**; 2.2)
Works Mentioned: Bible: Matthew 6.9–13 (Lord's Prayer; 2.2); Apostle's Creed (2.2); William Shakespeare, *The Merry Wives of Windsor* (**1079**; 4.2); *The Merry Devil of Edmonton* (**1392**; 4.2); Nathan Field, *A Woman is a Weathercock* (**1599**; 4.2); Thomas Heywood, *The Fair Maid of the West* (**1607**; prol.); Richard Brome, *The Northern Lass* (**2277**; prol.); Shackerley Marmion, *Holland's Leaguer* (**2351**; prol.)

The reference to Gillian of Brentford in 4.2 could, in theory, be to any work containing the character, not necessarily *The Merry Wives of Windsor*. However, it is coupled with an allusion to Sir Abraham Ninny of *A Woman is a Weathercock*, and comes shortly before a reference to *The Merry Devil of Edmonton*; so it seems likely that the dramatist was thinking specifically of a play.

LANGUAGE
English
Latin: 23 words (1.1-2, 2.2, 3.1-2, 5.1-2; Sir Robert, Abram, William, Cuthbert, Molyneux)
Greek: 1 word (4.1; Sir Oliver)

FORM
Metre: prose and pentameter
Rhyme: blank verse and couplets
Prologue: 26 lines, in couplets
Act-Division: 5 acts
Epilogue: dialogue between William, Gregory, Rash, Plush, Old Gentlewoman, Barbara, Gillian; 34 lines (14 verse, 20 prose), the verse in couplets
Lines (Spoken): 2,708 (1,352 verse, 1,356 prose)
Lines (Written): 3,012

STAGING
Doors: mentioned (1.1, s.d.); William is directed to exit the same way as he entered (4.3, s.d.)
Discovery Space: covered with an arras (5.1, s.d.)
Within: music (2.1, 4.2, s.d.); sound effect (5.1, s.d.)
Other Openings: characters exit at 'one end' and 'the other end' (4.3, s.d.)
Audience: addressed as 'gentlemen' (ep.)
Miscellaneous: music and song come from 'the music room' (5.2, s.d.)

MUSIC AND SOUND
Sound Effects: knock within (5.1, s.d.)
Music: treble plays within (2.1, s.d.); humming within (4.2, s.d.); music from 'the music room' (5.2, s.d.; accompanying the song); flourish (5.2, s.d.)
On-Stage Music: fiddle (2.1, implicit); Gillian plays the basin like a drum (3.1, implicit)
Song: 5.2, from 'the music room'; with musical accompaniment
Other Singing: Gillian sings (2.1, s.d.)
Dance: Gillian dances (2.1, s.d.); country wenches dance a morris (2.1, s.d.)

PROPS
Weapons: Gregory's rapier (1.2, s.d.; 3.2, implicit; 4.3, dialogue); Molyneux's sword (2.2, dialogue; 4.1, s.d.); a whip (3.1, s.d.); Plush's sword (3.2, implicit; 4.3, dialogue); Cuthbert's sword (3.2, implicit); Hugh's sword (3.2, implicit); Sir Oliver's sword (4.1, dialogue)
Musical Instruments: a fiddle (2.1, implicit) and bow (dialogue)
Clothing: a ring (1.1, s.d.); a diamond ring (5.2, s.d.; also worn by Molyneux)
Money: gold angels (3.1, dialogue)
Small Portable Objects: needlework (2.1, implicit); a letter (3.1, s.d.); a casknet of gold and jewels (3.1, s.d.)

Large Portable Objects: a chair (2.1, dialogue; 5.1, s.d.); a cushion (2.1, dialogue); a basin (3.1, s.d.); a painted staff (3.1, dialogue); stools (5.1, s.d.)
Scenery: an arras (5.1, s.d.)
Miscellaneous: blood (4.1, dialogue)

In 4.3, five characters are said to have 'stands'; but this probably refers to their position on stage rather than a physical prop (or 'standing').

COSTUMES AND MAKE-UP
SIR OLIVER: a scabbard (4.1, dialogue); disguised as a doctor (5.2, s.d.)
WILLIAM: bare-headed (3.2, s.d.)
PLUSH: a new suit (1.1, dialogue); a cloak lined with plush (3.2, dialogue); a scabbard (3.2, 4.3, implicit)
ABRAM: satin clothes (4.2, dialogue)
BARBARA: Lady Mosely's black mourning clothes and veil (1.2, 3.2, 4.3, s.d.; the dress is said to be loose-bodied); dressed as a Puritan (5.2, s.d.)
LADY MOSELY: black mourning clothes and a veil (1.2, s.d./dialogue; 2.2, 5.1, implicit)
LADY MALORY: disguised as a poor woman (3.1, s.d.), in tattered clothes (implicit)
OLD GENTLEWOMAN: a wrinkled face (dialogue); disguised as Lady Mosely (5.2, s.d.)
GREGORY: a scabbard (1.2, 3.2, 4.3, implicit)
THRASHARD: bravely dressed (4.2, s.d.), including a chain (dialogue)
MARGARET: neatly dressed (2.1, s.d.); very bravely dressed (4.2, 5.2, s.d.)
GILLIAN: her tippet up (2.1, s.d.); bravely dressed (4.2, s.d.); disguised as Lady Mosely (5.2, s.d.)
COUNTRY WENCHES: red petticoats, white stitched bodices, and smock-sleeves (2.1, s.d.)
MOLYNEUX: a nightgown (5.1, s.d.); a diamond ring (5.1, s.d.; removed on stage; see also PROPS)
CUTHBERT: bloody (3.2, s.d.); a scabbard (3.2, implicit)
HUGH: a scabbard (3.2, implicit)

EARLY STAGE HISTORY
'often acted with much applause' by 1647 (and presumably before 1642).

EARLY TEXTUAL HISTORY
1640: entered to Abel Roper in the Stationers' Register on Wednesday 18 November. Thomas Wykes had licensed the book for publication.
1647: **Q** printed for Abel Roper; collation A² B–L⁴ M², 44 leaves; title page gives author's initials and refers to performance in general terms; list of roles.
1684: Nicholas Cox (Manciple of St Edmund Hall, Oxford) had a copy, presumably of Q, in his bookshop. It had probably been previously owned by Gerard Langbaine, and appears on a list compiled by Anthony Wood on Saturday 13 December.

REFERENCES
Annals 1632; Bentley, iii. 5–8; Bodleian, MS Wood E. 4, art. 1, p. 29; Greg 632; Hazlitt, 51.

2382. Tragedy of the Imperial Favourite Crispinus

TEXT
MS (Arbury Hall, Warwickshire, MS A.414, fos. 145ʳ–194ʳ); authorial working MS with amendments. Most of these were made at the time of composition; but a cut in 4.2 appears to be a later intervention.

GENRE
tragedy
Contemporary: play (prol.)

TITLE
Later Assigned: *The Emperor's Favourite*; *Nero*

AUTHOR
John Newdigate

DATE
Limits: 1627–32
Best Guess: 1632

The play is a thinly veiled satire on George Villiers, 1st Duke of Buckingham. The action includes elements, notably the masque, which clearly have more to do with the seventeenth century than the first, and Buckingham is specifically identified in that, like Crispinus, he was the Master of the Horse. (On the other hand, the emphasis on Crispinus' lowly origins arguably draws more on the jibes at James's previous favourite, Somerset.) The forced marriage of Aurelia to Hilarius alludes to that of Sir Edward Coke's daughter Frances to Sir John Villiers, Buckingham's brother. There may also be a glance at the rumours that King James I was poisoned at Buckingham's instigation (4.2), and Crispinus' dealings with the King of Parthia could refer to Buckingham's entanglement with Richelieu.

T. H. Howard-Hill (in *Renaissance Papers*) proposes that the play must have been written during Buckingham's lifetime, which would argue for a date of 1628 or earlier. However, political animosities often do not disappear when they cease to be directly relevant to current affairs; hatred of Margaret Thatcher long outlasted her years in power, for example. This was demonstrably the case with Buckingham: his assassination did not cause libels against him to dry up, and Keenan shows that the end of the play may draw upon a knowledge of the circumstances of the murder.

The allusion to *The Dumb Bawd of Venice* (**2215**) establishes a firm upper limit. A possible reference to Salisbury Court ('the new playhouse', 3.2) supports a date after 1629, and Datus' mention of his seven years of assiduous flattery of the Emperor (5.1) might indicate composition some time after March 1632, if Nero can be identified, however loosely, with Charles I.

PLOT
Nero appoints Corbulus to govern Syria, and meets his demurral by insisting on obedience. At the same time, Tigranes is confirmed as King of Armenia, with the proviso that he will rule only during the Emperor's pleasure. Both men worry about what will happen to Rome while they are in the east, especially now that Nero has promoted his low-born favourite, Crispinus. The appointment of Tigranes has entailed displacing the other claimant to the Armenian throne, Tiridates. He appeals for help to his brother, the King of Parthia, who sends troops, and plans to bribe Crispinus to stop the Roman reinforcements from reaching Tigranes.

Crispinus uses his place at court to advance his friends and family. His access to Nero enables him to force a marriage between his idiot brother Hilarius and the unwilling Aurelia, in which he has an ulterior motive: he wants to sleep with her himself. When he broaches the subject, however, she refuses him, and is not moved when he threatens her with defamation. He orders a litter for himself from the chief designer of masque scenery, and is given one that has been already made—for Nero. He attempts to seduce Lucia, wife of the virtuous Rabellius, by inviting her to a masque at his house, but she refuses.

Crispinus' mother and sister arrange a diversion for Nero from the cares of state: a servant complains that Crispinus' brother-in-law Caesonius has fathered a bastard child on her, and asks Nero to order him to pay maintenance; but the child turns out to be a pig. Nero promises to compensate Caesonius for his embarrassment by giving him some office. Crispinus encourages Nero not to trust Rabellius, claiming he is seen as a possible successor, and advises that he should not be chosen to lead the troops going to Armenia; Caesonius gets the job instead. It proves a disastrous appointment: the army is routed and Nero is forced to make peace and accept Tiridates as King of Armenia. Crispinus changes his tune and recommends that Rabellius be sent to effect the arrangements, hoping that his absence from Rome will help in the seduction of Lucia. Lucia comes to plead with Crispinus that Rabellius be excused this duty, but he has already left Rome.

Despite the spread of slanderous tales about her, Aurelia continues to resist Crispinus' advances, so he decides to prosecute her for sexual misconduct, with suborned witnesses against her. Rabellius, Corbulus, and Tigranes consider the ethics of assassination. Tigranes appeals to Nero against the favourite's misconduct, but the Emperor makes excuses to defer considering the case. Though Armenia is his by right of conquest, Tiridates diplomatically accepts the throne as a gift from Nero, and is crowned in Rome. Still unable to get a hearing, Tigranes murders Crispinus; he is arrested by the favourite's family, but exults in the crime.

SCENE DESIGNATION
prol., 1.1, 2.1, 3.1–6, 4.1–2, 5.1–3 (act-division MS, scene-division Malone)

ROLES
PROLOGUE
RABELLIUS Plautus, a virtuous citizen, Lucia's husband
CORBULUS, Proconsul of Syria
NERO Claudius Caesar, Emperor of Rome; also called the King
CRISPINUS, Nero's favourite, later his Master of the Horse and a privy councillor; Locusta's younger son, brother of Hilarius and Theodora; formerly a cock-master and a seller of fish; also called Lord Crispinus
TIGRANES, King of Armenia; about the same height as Tiridates
DATUS, an actor
LOCUSTA, a widow, mother of Crispinus, Hilarius, and Theodora; said to be 80 years old (by Crispinus; she herself gives her age as 37)
CAESONIUS Paetus, Theodora's husband; later a senator and appointed the general of the army
THEODORA, Locusta's daughter, sister of Hilarius and Crispinus, Caesonius' wife
HILARIUS, Locusta's elder son, brother of Crispinus and Theodora; later Aurelia's husband, a senator, and a privy councillor; 24 years old
AURELIA, a young woman; later Hilarius' wife
VOLOGESUS, King of Parthia, Tiridates' brother
TIRIDATES, Vologesus' brother; later crowned King of Armenia; poses as a messenger; about the same height as Tigranes
Six MUSKETEERS, dragoons attending Tiridates (3.1, non-speaking)
Master PRONUS, a bawd and astrologer, Crispinus' creature; said to be little; also called Doctor Pronus
COMMODUS, a cheater, Crispinus' creature; perhaps a married man; later appointed Crispinus' Gentleman of the Horse; also called Jocky
Lady LUCIA, Rabellius' wife
A WOMAN, said to be Theodora's servant
Two BEARERS carrying Crispinus' litter (4.1, 5.2, non-speaking)
Two PAGES attending Crispinus (4.1, 5.2, non-speaking)
A MESSENGER, who brings a letter from Tiridates (4.2)
An ATTENDANT (4.2, non-speaking and deleted)
An ANTIQUARY (4.2)
A GOLDSMITH, a would-be monopolist (4.2)
A MAT MAN, Warden of the Mat-Makers' Company, a would-be monopolist (4.2)
A HERALD at the coronation (5.2–3)
SOLDIERS of the Praetorian Guard (5.3, non-speaking)

Speaking Parts: 23

Stage Directions and Speech Prefixes
PROLOGUE: *Prologue* (heading)
RABELLIUS: *Rabellius* (s.d.s); *Rab<ellius>* (s.p.s); *Rabellius a noble Roman* (d.p.)
CORBULUS: *Corbulus* (s.d.s); *Corb<ulus>* (s.p.s); *Corbulus Proconsul of Syria* (d.p.)

NERO: *Nero* (s.d.s and s.p.s); *Nero, Emperor of Rome* (d.p.)
CRISPINUS: *Crispinus* (s.d.s); *Crisp<inus>* (s.p.s); *Crispinus [Nero's] favourite* (d.p.)
TIGRANES: *Tigranes* (s.d.s); *Tig<ranes>* (s.p.s); *Tigranes Nero's deputy in Armenia* (d.p.)
DATUS: *Datus* (s.d.s and s.p.s); *Datus A player* (d.p.)
LOCUSTA: *Locusta* (s.d.s); *Loc<usta>* (s.p.s); *Locusta mother to Crispinus* (d.p.)
CAESONIUS: *Cesonius Petus* | *Cesonius* (s.d.s); *Ceso<nius>* (s.p.s); *Cesonius Petus a weak Commander* (d.p.)
THEODORA: *Theodora* | *Theodara* (s.d.s); *The<odora>* (s.p.s); *Theodora wife to Cesonius and sister to Crispinus* (d.p.)
HILARIUS: *Hillarius* (s.d.s); *Hilla<rius>* (s.p.s); *Hillarius Crispinus's elder brother a foolish Lord* (d.p.)
AURELIA: *Aurelia* (s.d.s); *Aure<lia>* (s.p.s); *Aurelia wife to Hillarius* (d.p.)
VOLOGESUS: *Vologesus King of Parthia* (s.d.s and d.p.); *Vol<ogesus>* (s.p.s)
TIRIDATES: *Tiridates [Vologesus']* *brother* (s.d.s); *Tirid<ates>* (s.p.s); *Tiridates brother to Vologesus* (d.p.)
MUSKETEERS: *6 musketeers* (s.d.s)
PRONUS: *Pronus* (s.d.s); *Pro<nus>* (s.p.s); *Pronus [one of the] servants to Crispinus* (d.p.)
COMMODUS: *Commodus* | *Comodus* (s.d.s); *Com<modus>* (s.p.s); *Commodus [one of the] servants to Crispinus* (d.p.)
LUCIA: *Lucia* (s.d.s); *Luc<ia>* (s.p.s); *Lucia wife to Rabellius* (d.p.)
WOMAN: *a woman* (s.d.s); *Woman* (s.d.s and s.p.s)
BEARERS: *bearers* (s.d.s)
PAGES: *two pages* | *the boys* | *boy* | *boys* (s.d.s)
MESSENGER: *a post* (s.d.s); *Messenger* (s.d.s and s.p.s)
ATTENDANT: *one* (s.d.s)
ANTIQUARY: *Antiquary* (s.d.s and s.p.s); [one of] *the suitors* (s.d.s); *An antiquary* (d.p.)
GOLDSMITH: *Goldsmith* (s.d.s and s.p.s); [one of] *the suitors* (s.d.s); *A Goldsmith* (d.p.)
MAT MAN: *a mat man* (s.d.s and d.p.); [one of] *the suitors* (s.d.s); *Mat <man>* (s.p.s)
HERALD: *A Herald* (s.d.s and d.p.); *Herald* (s.d.s and s.p.s)
SOLDIERS: *Soldiers* | *soldiers supposed the praetorian cohorts* (s.d.s)

OTHER CHARACTERS
The former Emperor, Nero's forefather (1.1; i.e. Claudius)
The former Emperor's minions, who ruled him (1.1)
The Syrians (1.1)
Locusta's dead second husband, a judge, father of Hilarius and Crispinus (2.1, 4.2)
The other daughters of Locusta's second husband (2.1)
Crispinus' kinsmen (2.1)

Seventeen wenches, members of Crispinus' family, whom Locusta sent to court on a wagon (2.1)
Crispinus' dry-nurse (2.1)
Driana, a chicken-breeder (2.1)
Locusta's midwife (2.1)
The midwife's youngest daughter, who used to play at stool-ball with Crispinus (2.1)
Crispinus' footman (2.1)
A crook-legged kitchen servant in Locusta's household (2.1)
Locusta's first husband, who died soon after their marriage (2.1)
The posthumous child of Locusta's first husband (2.1; but this may be Hilarius)
A pedlar (or a milliner) whose dog Hilarius played with (2.1)
Locusta's dairy-maid, who dropped little Hilarius into a kettle of hot whey and scalded his chin (2.1)
Aurelia's old father (2.1, 3.4)
The manservant of Aurelia's father (2.1)
Vologesus' soldiers (3.1)
Crispinus' creatures, who run Rome (3.1)
Vologesus' general (3.1)
One of Locusta's husbands, a drunken fool, Pronus' drinking companion (3.2, 3.4)
The engineer who makes the moveable scenery for masques, and whom Crispinus commissions to make a litter (3.2; alluding to Inigo Jones)
The common people of Armenia (3.3)
Lascivia, Lucia's young maidservant (3.3–4)
Rabellius' servants (3.3, 4.1)
A vestal nun deflowered by Crispinus, and then executed for unchastity (3.3)
Aurelia's sister (3.4)
Hilarius' uncle (3.5)
A poet who wrote a satire for Datus to perform (3.6, 4.2)
The common people of Rome (3.6, 4.2, 5.2–3)
Caesonius' mother, who told him he would father a fool if he was still a virgin when he married (3.6)
The chambermaid serving Caesonius' mother, with whom he had sex (3.6)
The footboy in Locusta's household (3.6)
The Roman army in the east, comprising two legions (3.6, 4.2; initially written as five thousand men)
An anatomist who inferred the measurements of Crispinus' whole body from his glove and spur (4.1)
Nero's professor of physic (4.1)
A woman servant who saw Crispinus naked through a keyhole (4.1)
The senators of Rome, satirized in the poet's play (4.2)
Philosophers satirized in the poet's play (4.2)
The Chatti (4.2)
The Sicambrians (4.2)
The singing boys in Datus' acting company (5.1)
Courtiers who fawn on Crispinus (5.1)
Crispinus' secretary (5.1)
The high commissioners (5.1)
Commodus' wife (5.1; possibly hypothetical)

SETTING
Period: first century AD; the action takes place during the reign of Nero (54–68), and includes a dramatization of events which took place in 61–3
Time-Scheme: an hour (or ninety minutes) passes between 3.3 and 3.6; at least a day passes between 3.3 and 4.1; 5.1–3 take place on the same day
Place: Rome; one scene (3.1) takes place in Parthia

Geography
Rome: the Emperor's Head (tavern or ordinary); the Forum; the seven hills; the city gates; River Tiber
Italy: Falernum; Venice; Naples
Spain (deleted): the Pillars of Hercules
[*Africa*]: Egypt; Barbary
[*Asia*]: Syria; River Euphrates; Arabia; Cilicia; Armenia; Babylon; Turkey; Taurus mountains

SOURCES
Narrative: Juvenal, *Satires* 1, 4 (Newdigate owned a copy of the collection of Horace, Juvenal, and Persius first published in 1574; Crispinus; cited in prol.); Suetonius, *Twelve Caesars*: Nero (Newdigate may have owned a copy of either the Isaac Casaubon or the Philemon Holland tr.; Tiridates plot; cited in prol.); Ben Jonson, *Sejanus' Fall* (**1412**; 4.2); John Newdigate, *The Twice-Changed Friar* (**2317**; 4.2)
Verbal: Virgil, *Aeneid* 3 (5.1); Horace, *Satires* 1.3 (3.4, cited); Ovid, *Ex Ponto* 3.6 (2.1, cited); John Webster, *The Duchess of Malfi* (**1726**; 5.1); Sir Francis Bacon, *Novum organum* (1620; 5.1); 'Come hear, lady Muses, and help me to sing' (ballad, 1627; 5.1)
Works Mentioned: Seneca, unspecified philosophical work (summary incorporates ideas from both *De vita beata* and *Epistulae morales* 71; 3.4); Tacitus, unspecified work (1.1); Statute of Vagabonds (1572; 14 Elizabeth I c. 5; 4.2); Henry Shirley, *The Dumb Bawd of Venice* (**2215**; 3.2)

LANGUAGE
English
Latin: 37 words (4.1–2, 5.1–2; Crispinus, Nero, Pronus, Commodus, Hilarius, Datus)

FORM
Metre: pentameter and prose
Rhyme: blank verse
Prologue: 16 lines, in couplets
Act-Division: 5 acts
Lines (Spoken): 3,437 (2,563 verse, 874 prose)

This includes the deleted 23-line prose passage in 4.2.

Lines (Written): 3,886

STAGING
Doors: a second door, different from the one used for an immediately precedent exit, is specified for entrance (3.2, 5.3, s.d.); mentioned (4.2, s.d.); characters are

directed to enter at 'the other door' (4.2, 5.1, s.d.), and at two doors (5.2, s.d.)
Stage: characters pass over the stage (5.1, s.d.); said to be 'thronged at one corner' (5.3, s.d.)
Within: music (4.2, s.d.)

MUSIC
Music: horn within (4.2, s.d.)
Singing: Locusta sings (3.6, s.d.)

PROPS
Weapons: six muskets (3.1, s.d.; with strings to hang them round the Musketeers' necks); a halter (4.2, s.d.); a knife (5.3, dialogue)
Clothing: a jewelled ring (4.2, dialogue)
Animals: a live pig wrapped in baby clothes (3.6, s.d.)
Small Portable Objects: a commission with a wax seal (1.1, s.d.); a letter (2.1, s.d.); a letter (4.2, s.d.); a pen (4.2, s.d.); ink (4.2, dialogue); paper (4.2, s.d.; written on on stage); a watch (4.2, s.d.); a letter (4.2, s.d.); a miniature portrait with a sapphire set in gold-enamelled purple (4.2, dialogue); a book (4.2, dialogue); a box of jewels (4.2, s.d.)
Large Portable Objects: a chair of state (1.1, 5.3, s.d.; 4.2, implicit; seats two)
Scenery: a litter (4.1, 5.2, s.d.); hangings (4.2, dialogue)

COSTUMES AND MAKE-UP
CRISPINUS: thin hair (dialogue); meanly clothed (1.1, s.d.); presumably more sprucely clad in his later scenes
DATUS: dark skin (dialogue)
LOCUSTA: wrinkles (dialogue)
HILARIUS: has no beard (dialogue)
AURELIA: visibly pregnant (5.1, s.d.)
TIRIDATES: disguised (4.2, s.d.), including a false beard (s.d.; removed on stage); a hat (4.2, implicit; doffed on stage); a crown (5.3, s.d.; put on on stage)
PRONUS: bare-headed (4.1, s.d.)
COMMODUS: bare-headed (4.1, s.d.); probably a taffeta suit, boots, and spurs (5.1, dialogue)
PAGES: suits with long skirts (4.1, dialogue)

EARLY TEXTUAL HISTORY
c. 1632 (?): transcribed in **MS**; 99 pages on 50 leaves; list of roles. The MS was subsequently in the possession of the Newdigate family of Arbury Hall, Warwickshire.

EDITION
Siobhan Keenan, Malone Society Reprints 174 (Manchester, 2010).

REFERENCES
Annals, Supp. I; *Early Theatre* 14.2 (2011), 63–103; Vivienne Larminie, *Wealth, Kinship and Culture* (Woodbridge, 1995), 195–6, 198; *Renaissance Papers* (1989), 51–62.

2383. The Novella

TEXT
Printed in 1653 (Wing B4870), probably from theatrical copy.

GENRE
comedy
Contemporary: play (prol., ep.); comedy (t.p.)

TITLE
Performed/Printed: *The Novella*

AUTHOR
Richard Brome

DATE
Autumn 1632

ORIGINAL PRODUCTION
King's Men at the Blackfriars (and perhaps also the Globe)

PLOT
Although Fabritio and Flavia are respectively betrothed to Victoria and Francisco, their fathers are forcing them to marry one another. While absconding at night to evade the wedding, Fabritio sees numerous men, including his father Pantaloni, flocking to the lodgings of a newly arrived courtesan, or *novella*, who has, according to Venetian custom, set a high price for her virginity and a month of her company. Fabritio aborts his escape when his friend Piso has a better idea. Flavia, meanwhile, is being kept under lock and key until the wedding.

The *novella* accepts Pantaloni's offer, even though he underbids her asking price; but when he calls for a light during sex, he finds himself in bed not with her but the blackamoor servant Jacconetta. He plans to avenge himself by arranging for the *novella* to be caught in bed with the public hangman; but his servant Nicolo, who has a grudge against him, divulges the plan to Fabritio and Piso, who decide to frustrate it. Nicolo himself takes the place of the hangman, so the intended dishonour is never conferred.

Four potential buyers visit the *novella*, but none of them seem willing to meet her price: the Italian, who is really Piso in disguise, merely moralizes at her; the Frenchman, who is really Horatio in disguise, sings and dances; the Spaniard tries to rape her; but the German, Schwarzenberg, rescues her. She admits that she priced herself highly not in order to sell but to discourage buyers: she is chaste, and has an ulterior motive. Later, Schwarzenberg calls her bluff: he returns in disguise with the money, which means that she is legally obliged to give him her virginity. She explains that she has come to Venice in search of her missing fiancé, and to that end took advantage of local custom to give her easy access to the city's menfolk: she is really Fabritio's betrothed, Victoria. Meanwhile Fabritio poses as Schwarzenberg to visit the *novella* and test her chastity. He is caught out because he speaks no German, but Victoria is delighted to have found her Fabritio at last.

Francisco disguises himself as a pedlar-woman sent by Pantaloni to sell the imprisoned Flavia trimmings for her wedding dress. He tests her constancy, then elopes with her in a gondola. They take refuge in the *novella*'s house, and are married by Victoria's bravo, Borgio. The marriage turns out to be lawful, because Borgio is a friar in disguise: Victoria's brother Paulo, who followed her from Rome to ensure her safety and chastity in Venice. The fathers are frustrated, Pantaloni especially so when he learns that his blackamoor bed-partner was not even a woman but a boy in disguise.

SCENE DESIGNATION
prol., 1.1–2, 2.1–2, 3.1, 4.1–2, 5.1, ep. (O)

ROLES
PROLOGUE
Signor PISO, Fabritio's friend
Signor FABRITIO, Pantaloni's son and heir, Victoria's fiancé, a young man; poses as Schwarzenberg
GENTLEMEN, night-walkers (1.1, *non-speaking*)
Signor PANTALONI, a rich old magnifico and tradesman, Fabritio's father
NICOLO, Pantaloni's servant, a youth; also called Nic; poses as a *Saffi*
FRANCISCO, a young man of noble birth, Flavia's fiancé, later her husband; poses as a pedlar-woman
HORATIO, Francisco's friend; poses as a French cavalier
Signor GUADAGNI, an old senator, Flavia's father
NANULO, a dwarf, Guadagni's servant; also called Go-by-Ground
ASTUTTA, Guadagni's chambermaid
Madonna FLAVIA, Guadagni's daughter; 16 years old; Francisco's fiancée, later his wife
The NOVELLA, a new courtesan; in reality, Victoria, a young Roman lady, Paulo's sister, Fabritio's fiancée
JACCONETTA, the *novella*'s blackamoor chambermaid; also called Jacconet; in reality, Jacomo, a Moorish eunuch, Fabritio's boy servant
BORGIO, the *novella*'s bravo; in reality, Paulo, an Augustinian friar, Victoria's brother
GALLANTS, would-be clients of the *novella* (2.2, *non-speaking*)
PEDRO, a Spaniard
SCHWARZENBERG, a German; poses as an English merchant; also called Hans Snortanfart
A SAFFI or officer (4.1, 5.1)
CHEQUINO, a lawyer
PROSPERO, a lawyer
A PEDLAR-WOMAN (4.1, 5.1)
EPILOGUE

O's list of roles is evidently not authorial; for example, it misunderstands '*Saffi*' to be a proper name. Accordingly, its evidence is suspect when it describes Pantaloni as a senator, whereas the text of the play treats him as a jumped-up tradesman.

Technically, '*Saffi*' is the plural form of '*Saffo*', but Brome consistently uses it as if it were singular.

Speaking Parts: 21

Stage Directions and Speech Prefixes
PROLOGUE: *Prologue* (heading)
PISO: *Piso* (s.d.s); *Pis<o>* (s.p.s); *Piso* [Fabritio's] *Friend* (d.p.)
FABRITIO: *Fabritio* (s.d.s); *Fab<ritio>* (s.p.s); *Fabritio, Son to Pantaloni* (d.p.)
GENTLEMEN: *divers Gentlemen* (s.d.s)
PANTALONI: *Pantaloni* | *Pantoloni* (s.d.s); *Pant<aloni>* (s.p.s); *Pantaloni* [one of] *Two Senators* (d.p.)
NICOLO: *Nicolo* (s.d.s); *Nic<olo>* (s.p.s); *Nicolo, Servant to Pantaloni* (d.p.)
FRANCISCO: *Francisco* (s.d.s); *Fran<cisco>* (s.p.s); *Francisco, Lover of Flavia* (d.p.)
HORATIO: *Horatio* | *a French Cavalier* (s.d.s); *Hor<atio>* (s.p.s); *Horatio* [Francisco's] *Friend* (d.p.)
GUADAGNI: *Guadagni* (s.d.s); *Gua<dagni>* (s.p.s); *Guadagni* [one of] *Two Senators* (d.p.)
NANULO: *Nanulo* (s.d.s); *Nan<ulo>* (s.p.s); *Nanulo,* [one of the] *Servants to Guadagni* (d.p.)
ASTUTTA: *Astutta* (s.d.s); *Ast<utta>* (s.p.s); *Astutta,* [one of the] *Servants to Guadagni* (d.p.)
FLAVIA: *Flavia* (s.d.s); *Fla<via>* (s.p.s)
NOVELLA: *Victoria* (s.d.s); *Vict<oria>* (s.p.s); *Victoria The Novella* (d.p.)
JACCONETTA: *Jacomo* | *Jacconetta* (s.d.s); *Jac<conetta>* (s.p.s); *Jacconetta, Servant to Victoria* (d.p.)
BORGIO: *Paulo, by-named Burgio* (s.d.s and d.p.); *Paulo* (s.d.s); *Pau<lo>* (s.p.s; also misprinted *Pan.*)
GALLANTS: *Many Gallants* (s.d.s)
PEDRO: *a brave Spaniard* | *Pedro* (s.d.s); *Ped<ro>* (s.p.s)
SCHWARZENBERG: *Swatzenburgh* (s.d.s and d.p.); *a glorious German* | *Swatzenburg* | *the glorious Dutchman* (s.d.s); *Swat<zenburgh>* (s.p.s)
SAFFI: *a Saffi* (s.d.s); *Saffi* (s.p.s); *Saffi, an Officer* (d.p.)
CHEQUINO: *Checquino* (s.d.s); *Chec<quino>* (s.p.s); *Chequino,* [one of] *Two Lawyers* (d.p.)
PROSPERO: *Prospero* (s.d.s); *Pros<pero>* (s.p.s); *Prospero,* [one of] *Two Lawyers* (d.p.)
PEDLAR-WOMAN: *Pedlar Woman* | *Pedlar-woman* (s.d.s); *Pedlar* (s.p.s); *Pedlar, Woman* (d.p.)
EPILOGUE: *Epilogue* (heading)

OTHER CHARACTERS
The Duke of Venice (1.1, 5.1)
Francisco's ancestors (1.2)
Nicolo's father, a former galley-slave manumitted by Pantaloni (2.1)
The priest who is to marry Fabritio and Flavia (2.1)

Signor Rastrofico, the city hangman (2.1, 4.1, 5.1)
Jacconetta's former master, who gave her to the *Novella* (2.2)
Twenty thousand courtesans in and around Venice (2.2)
Six famous courtesans, Borgio's former employers, including Margarita Emiliana, who founded an Augustinian monastery (2.2; perhaps imaginary)
A friend of the *Novella*'s, who procured Borgio's position as her bravo (2.2)
The *Novella*'s suitors, including a Pole, a Slavonian, a Persian, and a Greek (2.2)
The neighbours opposite Guadagni's house (4.1)
Witnesses present at the marriage of Flavia and Francisco (4.2)
The dead father of Victoria and Paulo, a Roman nobleman of the Candiani (5.1)
The mother of Victoria and Paulo (5.1)

SETTING
Time-Scheme: the action takes place during a single day; 1.1 takes place before dawn, and 1.2 at dawn
Place: Venice

Geography
Venice: the Rialto; the Grand Canal; the Merceria; the Augustinian monastery; the Arsenal; the Piazza; St Mark's Cathedral
Italy: Rome
England: London
The Low Countries: the United Provinces
[*Europe*]: France; Spain; Germany; Poland; Slavonia; Greece
Egypt
Persia
The West Indies
The East Indies

SOURCES
Narrative: Thomas Coryate, *Coryate's Crudities* (1611)
Verbal: Aesop, *Fables* (4.1); Bible: Matthew 7.24-7 (1.2); Martial, *Epigrams* 11.15 (t.p. motto); William Shakespeare, *The Merchant of Venice* (**1047**; 1.2); Richard Knolles, *The General History of the Turks* (1603, repr. 1631; the name Schwarzenberg)
Works Mentioned: Ben Jonson, *The Alchemist* (**1621**; 3.1, oblique allusion)

LANGUAGE
English
Latin: 5 words (4.1; Astutta, Nicolo, Nanulo)
Italian: 40 words (1.1-2, 2.1-2, 3.1, 4.1-2, 5.1; Piso, Francisco, Nanulo, Astutta, Nicolo, Fabritio, Horatio, *Novella*, Borgio, Pedro, *Saffi*, Pantaloni)
French: 3 words (3.1; Horatio, Borgio)
German: 33 words (2.2, 3.1, 5.1; Borgio, Schwarzenberg)

FORM
Metre: pentameter and prose
Rhyme: blank verse; some couplets
Prologue: 26 lines, in couplets
Act-Division: 5 acts
Epilogue: 6 lines, in couplets
Lines (Spoken): 2,247 (2,082 verse, 165 prose)
Lines (Written): 2,530

STAGING
Doors: knocked at (4.1, s.d.)
Discovery Space: set as Guadagni's study (1.2, s.d.); three characters are discovered at a table (2.1, implicit)
Stage: characters pass over the stage (2.2, s.d.)
Within: music (3.1, implicit); speech (4.1, s.d.)
Above: characters appear above (2.2, 4.1, 5.1, s.d.; a maximum of three); a prop is dropped from the above space to the main stage (4.1, s.d.)
Audience: addressed as 'sirs' (ep.)

MUSIC
Music: unspecified music (1.1, s.d.); bell (1.2, 4.1, 5.1, s.d.); dance music within (3.1, implicit)
On-Stage Music: Victoria plays the lute (2.2, s.d.; accompanying Song 2)
Songs:
  1: 1.1, Francisco and Horatio;
  2: 2.2, Victoria, with lute accompaniment;
  3: 'Let not the corrupted steam', 3.1, Jacconetta, 24 lines.
Dance: Horatio dances (3.1, s.d.)

PROPS
Lighting: lights (1.1, s.d.); two dark lanterns (1.1, s.d.); a taper (1.2, s.d.)
Weapons: Fabritio's blade weapon (1.1, dialogue); Piso's sword (1.1, implicit); three stilettos (2.1, s.d.); a pistol (3.1, s.d.); a halter (4.1, s.d.); a knife (4.1, s.d.); pistols (5.1, s.d.); a knife (5.1, s.d.)
Musical Instruments: a lute (2.2, dialogue)
Clothing: a *saffi*'s habit (2.1, s.d.; also worn by Nicolo)
Money: bags of money (1.2, s.d.); a thousand chequeens (1.2, dialogue); twenty gold chequeens (2.1, dialogue); four unspecified sums (2.2, s.d.); a ducatoon (3.1, dialogue); a four-gazet piece (3.1, dialogue); forty ducats (4.1, dialogue); a full bag of money (5.1, s.d.)
Food and Drink: wine (2.1, s.d.; drunk on stage); a vial of poison (4.1, s.d.)
Small Portable Objects: books (1.2, s.d.); keys (1.2, dialogue); documents (2.1, dialogue); a looking-glass (2.2, s.d.); a document (3.1, implicit); a letter (4.1, s.d.); pen and ink (4.1, implicit); a picture of Francisco (4.1, s.d.); a cabinet (4.1, s.d.)
Large Portable Objects: a seat (1.2, implicit); a table (2.1, s.d.); a box (4.1, s.d.; large enough to contain the halter, knife, and vial)

COSTUMES AND MAKE-UP
PROLOGUE: apologises for not wearing a cloak or 'starched, formal beard' (prol., dialogue)
PISO: hangers (1.1, implicit)
FABRITIO: disguised as Schwarzenberg (4.2, 5.1, s.d.), including slops (dialogue); a false beard (4.2, s.d.; 5.1, implicit; put on and removed on stage)
NICOLO: a *saffi*'s habit (4.1, 5.1, s.d.; see also PROPS)
FRANCISCO: cross-dressed as a pedlar-woman (4.1, s.d.; removed on stage)
HORATIO: disguised as a French cavalier (3.1, s.d.)
NOVELLA: tires, chains, and gauds (2.2, dialogue); painted face (2.2, 3.1, dialogue)
JACCONETTA/JACOMO: cross-dressed as a female blackamoor (2.2, 3.1, 5.1, implicit)
BORGIO/PAULO a garment with a pocket (3.1, dialogue); a peruke and a false beard (2.2, 3.1, 4.2, implicit; 5.1, s.d.; removed on stage); a friar's habit (5.1, s.d.)
PEDRO: rich clothing (2.2, dialogue)
SCHWARZENBERG: a beard (3.1, dialogue); a beard of a different, smaller cut (5.1, dialogue); disguised as an English merchant (5.1, s.d.)
SAFFI: a coat (4.1, dialogue)

EARLY STAGE HISTORY
1632: performed by the King's Men at the Blackfriars.
1641: The play was in the repertory of the King's Men.

EARLY TEXTUAL HISTORY
1641: On Saturday 7 August, Robert Devereux, 3rd Earl of Essex (Lord Chamberlain) issued a warrant prohibiting the printing of this and sixty other plays without the consent of the King's Men. On Saturday 14 August, the order was read to the Stationers' Company and instructions issued for its observance.
1653: included as the second of Richard Brome's *Five New Plays* (O), sigs. H3^r–N2^r, 79 pages on 40 leaves; printed for Richard Marriott and Thomas Dring; the play's title page names author, acting company, and playhouse; Latin title-page motto; list of roles. At a late stage, Humphrey Moseley also became involved in the project; his name is included as a bookseller on the volume's overall title page, but not on the play's individual title page.
1653: George Thomason acquired a copy of O on Friday 20 May. In *c*. 1678, some years after his death, his entire collection of books and tracts was acquired by the bookbinder Samuel Mearne, acting as agent for King Charles II; the King never paid him, and the books remained in Mearne's family until 1761.
1654: O reissued, probably in January (but possibly as early as November 1653), with a cancel title page giving the initials of James Fletcher as the printer and naming John Sweeting as the bookseller. On Wednesday 4 January, Sweeting advertised copies for sale.
1655: *Wit's Interpreter* entered to Nathaniel Brooke in the Stationers' Register on Wednesday 14 March.
1655: extract (from 3.1) included in John Cotgrave's *Wit's Interpreter*, sig. F7^{r-v}; printed for Nathaniel Brooke.
1657: O advertised as for sale by the Newcastle-upon-Tyne bookseller William London.
1659: rights in *Five New Plays* transferred in the Stationers' Register from Richard Marriott to Humphrey Moseley on Saturday 11 June; part of a group transfer of 21 titles, with the plays in the collection individually named.
1662: *Wit's Interpreter* reprinted (before Thursday 8 June) for Nathaniel Brooke; the extract now appears on sigs. E3^v–E4^r, and is entitled 'Virginity Overvalued'.
1671: *Wit's Interpreter* reprinted for Nathaniel Brooke and Obadiah Blagrave.
1684: Nicholas Cox (Manciple of St Edmund Hall, Oxford) had a copy of O in his bookshop. It had probably been previously owned by Gerard Langbaine, and appears on a list compiled by Anthony Wood on Saturday 13 December.

EDITION
Richard Cave, Richard Brome Online (internet, 2010).

REFERENCES
Annals 1632; Bentley, iii. 84–5; Bodleian, MS Wood E. 4, art. 1, p. 48; Eyre & Rivington, i. 467; Greg 719; Hazlitt, 168; William London, *A Catalogue of the Most Vendible Books in England* (London, 1657), sig. 2F2^r; MSC 1.4–5, 364–9; *PBSA* 107 (2013), 25–7; *RES* 54 (2003), 601–14; *SP* 30 (1933), 69–85.

2384. Queen's Court Masque

EVIDENCE
Venetian diplomatic correspondence (Vicenzo Gussoni to the Doge Francesco Erizzo and the Senate; Friday 15 October 1632 Gregorian).

GENRE
masque
Contemporary: masque

TITLE
Later Assigned: *The Queen's Country Village Masque*

DATE
September–October 1632

ORIGINAL PRODUCTION
Queen Henrietta Maria's Court, possibly at Nonsuch Palace, Surrey

The other obvious candidate for a royal 'pleasure resort' near London would be Oatlands Palace. Both palaces were in Surrey and both belonged to the Queen. The reason for favouring

Nonsuch is that there are positive signs of theatrical activity there in the 1632 Works Account.

STAGING
Stage: possibly a stage with ascent steps on each side

EARLY STAGE HISTORY
Preparations: Rehearsals took place in an unidentified country village, perhaps Nonsuch. This may be the event for which the Works Office equipped the Queen's Privy Chamber at Nonsuch with partitions and a stage with ascent steps on either side.
Performance: in late September or early October 1632 (before Friday 5 October), perhaps at a village near London (described as a 'pleasure resort'), in celebration of the birth of Prince Francis Hyacinth of Savoy (which took place in Turin on Tuesday 14 September Gregorian). The cast included: Queen Henrietta Maria. The audience probably included Bouvier de Bonport (Savoy Ambassador).

REFERENCES
Butler, 372; *Cal. Ven.* 1632-6, 15-16; McGee-Meagher 1625-34, 68; MSC 10, 42-3; Steele, 250.

2385. The Magnetic Lady

TEXT
Printed in 1640-1 (STC 14754a) from an authorial MS, in which an epilogue for a court performance is apparently substituted for the final chorus.

GENRE
comedy
Contemporary: play (ind.); comedy (Cho.2-4, t.p.)

TITLE
Performed/Printed: *The Magnetic Lady, or Humours Reconciled*
Contemporary: *Humours Reconciled, or The Magnetic Lady*

AUTHOR
Ben Jonson

DATE
October 1632

ORIGINAL PRODUCTION
King's Men at the Blackfriars

PLOT
Probee and Damn-Play are sent on stage by the audience to bargain for a good play; what they get is *The Magnetic Lady*. They watch the play and comment on it between the acts.

Visitors flock to Lady Loadstone's house, some brought by her lodger, Compass, others to pay court to her sickly but wealthy niece, Placentia Steel, on her birthday. By the terms of her parents' will, Placentia's marriage portion of £16,000 is to be paid when she marries, but until then is held by her uncle, Interest. There are several suitors, including Practice the lawyer and Silkworm the courtier. Lady Loadstone initially prefers Practice, but the prospect of being made a countess through a friend at court converts her to Silkworm's suit. Palate also promotes Silkworm, pointing out that Practice is already engaged to the servant Pleasance. Interest is trying to arrange a marriage between Placentia and Bias, who is a younger brother and will be content to accept less than the full dowry.

Ironside, Compass's brother, wounds Silkworm in a violent altercation at dinner, and Compass persuades the courtier to seek redress in a duel rather than at law; Bias hopes that Silkworm will be killed and the court rid of a nuisance, but in the event he merely talks to Ironside about valour.

Placentia turns out to be pregnant, and the suitors back off; Practice asks Compass to help him marry Pleasance instead. Compass learns that Pleasance and Placentia were swapped for one another in their cradles, and uses the blank licence obtained by Practice to get himself married to 'Pleasance'. His bride then disappears, and turns out to have been abducted by Polish, her supposed mother, who is trying to conceal the baby swap.

The steward Needle pretends to suffer from walking and talking in his sleep, and persuades Interest that a ghost, in love with him, has hidden treasure in the garden. Interest goes looking for it and falls into a well.

The false Placentia gives birth. Convinced that the pregnancy was only malicious gossip, Bias agrees to marry her, and Interest promises to pay him the dowry. Compass makes his peace with Practice with the gift of a court office and has Interest arrested. Polish confesses the exchange of infants, which leaves Interest obliged to pay the money twice over, to Compass in respect of the true Placentia and to Bias in respect of the false one. Fortunately for him, Polish also admits that the pregnancy was genuine, so Bias backs out of the marriage. Lady Loadstone and Ironside get engaged.

SCENE DESIGNATION
ind., 1.1-7, Cho.1, 2.1-7, Cho.2, 3.1-7, Cho.3, 4.1-8, Cho.4, 5.1-10 (F, corrected and regularized Herford and Simpson)

The fictional on-stage audience is present throughout. The stage is not clear of other characters at the following scene-divisions: 1.1-2, 1.3-7, 2.1-7, 3.1-2, 3.3-4, 3.5-7, 4.1-6, 4.7-8, 5.1-2, 5.4-6, 5.7-8, 5.9-10. Verse lines are split across the following scene-divisions: 4.3-4, 4.5-6.

2385. The Magnetic Lady

ROLES

Induction and Chorus

Master PROBEE, a London gentleman

Master DAMN-PLAY, a London gentleman; Probee calls him 'brother', but this probably indicates friendship rather than consanguinity

John TRYGUST, a Cornish boy of the house, the poet's servant; formerly a pupil at Westminster School

Main Action

Master COMPASS, a scholar and soldier, Ironside's brother, at least 20 years old; later the true Placentia's husband

Captain Rudhudibras de IRONSIDE, a soldier, formerly of Oxford, at least 20 years old; Compass's brother; also called Rud Ironside

Parson PALATE, an old clergyman

Lady LOADSTONE, a noble lady, Placentia's aunt, Interest's sister

Doctor RUT, a young physician and voluptuary; said to be little; also called Doctor Do-All

Mistress POLISH, a widow, Lady Loadstone's gossip, Pleasance's mother; also called Dame Polish and Goody Polish; Palate addresses her as 'sister'

Sir Diaphanous SILKWORM, a knight, courtier, and heir

Master PRACTICE, a young lawyer, a bencher and reader of his Inn of Court; also called Dominus Practice and Squire Practice

Sir Moth INTEREST, a knight and usurer, Lady Loadstone's brother, Placentia's uncle; possibly an alderman

Master BIAS, a lord's secretary; a younger brother; also called Don Bias

Mistress KEEP, Placentia's nurse, an old woman of St Katherine's; a sailor's wife; also called Dame Keep, Nurse Keep, Grannam Keep, and Goody Keep

Mistress PLACENTIA Steel, 14 years old; thought to be the niece of Interest and Lady Loadstone, but in reality Polish's daughter Pleasance

Mistress PLEASANCE, 14 years old, thought to be Lady Loadstone's waiting-woman and Polish's daughter; in reality, Placentia Steel; later Compass's wife and addressed as Mademoiselle Compass; also called Dame Placentia

Master NEEDLE, Lady Loadstone's steward and tailor, the father of the false Placentia's child; also called Squire Needle and Monsieur Needle

Master Tim ITEM, an apothecary

Mother CHAIR, a midwife; also called Mistress Chair and Mother Midnight

Interest's FOOTBOY (4.8, *non-speaking*)

VARLET, an officer

Speaking Parts: 20

Stage Directions and Speech Prefixes

PROBEE: [one of] *two Gentlemen* | *Mr Probee* (s.d.s); *Pro<bee>* (s.p.s); [one of the] *Chorus* (d.p.)

DAMN-PLAY: [one of] *two Gentlemen* | *Mr Damplay* (s.d.s); *Dam<play>* (s.p.s); [one of the] *Chorus* (d.p.)

TRYGUST: *A Boy of the house* (s.d.s); *Boy* (s.p.s); [one of the] *Chorus* (d.p.)

COMPASS: *Compasse* (s.d.s); *Com<passe>* (s.p.s); *Mr Compasse, A Scholar, Mathematic* (d.p.)

IRONSIDE: *Ironside* (s.d.s); *Iro<nside>* (s.p.s); *Captain Ironside, A Soldier* (d.p.)

PALATE: *Palate* (s.d.s); *Pal<ate>* (s.p.s); *Parson Palate, Prelate of the Parish* (d.p.)

LOADSTONE: *Lady* (s.d.s and s.p.s); *the Lady* (s.d.); *Lady Loadstone, The Magnetic Lady* (d.p.)

RUT: *Rut* (s.d.s and s.p.s); *Doctor* (s.d.s); *Doctor Rut, Physician to the house* (d.p.)

POLISH: *Polish* (s.d.s); *Pol<ish>* (s.p.s); *Mrs Polish* [Lady Loadstone's] *Gossip, and she-Parasite* (d.p.)

SILKWORM: *Sir Diaphanous* | *Diaphanous* | *Silkworme* | *Silkeworme* (s.d.s); *Dia<phanous>* | *Silk<worme>* | *Silke<worme>* (s.p.s); *Sir Diaph<anous> Silkworm, A Courtier* (d.p.)

PRACTICE: *Practise* (s.d.s); *Pra<ctise>* (s.p.s); *Mr Practise, A Lawyer* (d.p.)

INTEREST: *Interest* (s.d.s); *Int<erest>* (s.p.s); *Sir Moath Interest, A Usurer or Money-bawd* (d.p.)

BIAS: *Bias* (s.d.s and s.p.s); *Mr Bias, a Vi-politic, or Sub-secretary* (d.p.)

KEEP: *Keepe* | *Nurse* (s.d.s); *Keepe* (s.p.s); *Mrs Keepe, The Niece's Nurse* (d.p.)

PLACENTIA: *Placentia* (s.d.s); *Pla<centia>* (s.p.s); *Mrs Placentia,* [Lady Loadstone's] *Niece* (d.p.)

PLEASANCE: *Pleasance* | [Polish's] *daughter* (s.d.s); *Ple<asance>* (s.p.s); *Pleasance,* [Lady Loadstone's] *Waiting-Woman* (d.p.)

NEEDLE: *Needle* (s.d.s); *Nee<dle>* (s.p.s); *Mr Needle, The Lady's Steward, and Tailor* (d.p.)

ITEM: *Item* (s.d.s and s.p.s); *Tim* (s.d.s); *Tim Item,* [Doctor Rut's] *Apothecary* (d.p.)

CHAIR: *Chaire* (s.d.s); *Cha<ire>* (s.p.s); *Mother Chaire, The Midwife* (d.p.)

FOOTBOY: [Interest's] *Foot-boy* (s.d.s)

VARLET: *Varlet* (s.d.s); *Var<let>* (s.p.s)

OTHER CHARACTERS

Ben Jonson, the author of the play, who wrote epigrams about Parson Palate and Doctor Rut (ind. and Cho.1–4; 1.2, 3.6; named in the main action, but referred to only as 'the poet' in the framing material)

The audience (ind.)

A knight, Probee's brother (ind.)

A knight, Damn-Play's brother (ind.)

Knights, friends of Probee and Damn-Play (ind.)

Great statesmen who have employed Compass (1.1)

Master Silkworm, an old man, father of Sir Diaphanous (1.3)

Mistress Steel, Placentia's mother, who died giving birth to her; sister of Interest and Lady Loadstone (1.4–5, 2.2, 4.4)

Master Steel, Placentia's father, who died soon after her mother (1.4–5, 2.2, 4.4)

Polish's pastor (1.4)
The Steels' neighbours (1.5)
Master Polish, presumably Polish's dead husband and Prudence's father (1.5, 4.4)
Lord Whatchem, Bias's employer (1.7, 2.6, 3.6, 4.3)
The King, the poet's (i.e. Jonson's) master (Cho.1)
Keep's husband, a sailor (2.2)
Sir John Loadstone, the Governor of the East India Company; Lady Loadstone's husband, with whom Compass went to sea (2.4–5)
A rabbi, who diagnosed ailments by reading wine dregs (3.5)
The false Placentia's baby son (4.2, 4.5, 4.7–8, 5.4–5, 5.9–10)
The lords of the court (4.3)
The clerk who drew up the marriage licence (4.6)
Thin-Wit, Surveyor of the Projects General, who died on the morning of the action (4.6)
A person who told Practice of Thin-Wit's demise (4.6)
A coachman sent to wait at the church (4.6)
Pol, Alderman Parrot's rich widow, now dead (5.5, 5.7)
Alderman Parrot, a married man, now dead (5.5)
Sir Chime Squirrel of Do-Little Lane (5.5; but probably just a fantastical reference to a squirrel)

The recently deceased Alderman Parrot probably alludes to Alderman Sir Heneage Finch, who died in December 1631, and whc also seems to have been the subject of similar jokes in *The Changes* (**2355**) earlier the same year. (Finch's first wife, Lady Frarces, predeceased him, but he married again and, unlike the unfortunate Mistress Parrot, his widow, Lady Elizabeth Finch, was still alive; she lived on until 1661.)

SETTING
Period: roughly contemporary (after 1625), in an Ember Week
Time-Scheme: the action takes place in a single day: 1.1–2.7 in the morning, and 3.1 at dinner-time; it is afternoon by 4.6, and after 6 p.m. in 5.10
Place: London

Geography
London: the Spital; St Katherine's; Shadwell; Westminster Hall; the King's Head; the Old Exchange; Do-Little Lane; Bedlam; Merchant Taylors' Hall; Threadneedle Street
England: Oxford; St John's Wood; Waltham Forest
Great Britain
France
[*Spain*]: Cordoba
[*Asia*]: Armenia; Media; Persia; India
The East Indies
The Arctic Pole
The Antarctic Pole

Chorus Geography
London: Westminster School
England: Cornwall
The Holy Land

SOURCES
Narrative: William Stevenson, *Gammer Gurton's Needle* (**253**); possibly John Ford, *'Tis Pity She's a Whore* (**2329**; Placentia's pregnancy); Philip Massinger, *The Roman Actor* (**2190**; 3.4)
Verbal: Bible: Daniel 6.12 (1.5); Matthew 5.9 (4.7), 12.25 (5.1); 1 Timothy 6.10 (2.6); Aristotle, *Metaphysics* (1.1); Terence, *Andria* (ind., 1.3); Cicero, *De natura deorum* (3.5); Virgil, *Aeneid* 7 (1.2); Horace, *Epistles* 1.19 (1.3), *Ars poetica* (Cho.2); Valerius Maximus, *Factorum dictorumque memorabilium* (5.7; Jonson owned a copy of the 1574 edn by Stephanus Pighius); Juvenal, *Satires* 4 (2.6); Claudian, *Magnes* (t.p. motto); Lanfranc of Milan, *Chirurgia parva* (1296, English tr. by John Halle, 1565; 2.3); Geoffrey Chaucer, *Canterbury Tales*: General Prologue (*c.* 1387; printed 1478, repr. 1602; 1.2, 3.5, cited; Jonson owned a copy of the 1602 edn by Thomas Speght); Ben Jonson, *The Arraignment* (**1296**; Cho.2); Henry Parrott, *The Mastiff* (1615; 4.3)
Works Mentioned: Bible (general reference; 1.5); Homer, *Iliad* (3.4); Plautus, *Aulularia* (Cho.2), *Miles gloriosus* (Cho.2), *Pseudolus* (Cho.2); Terence, *Andria* (Cho.2), *Eunuchus* (Cho.2), *Heautontimorumenos* (Cho.2); Vitruvius, *De architectura* (ind.); Martial, *Epigrams* (Cho.2); the 'Massora' (Hebrew Bible, sixth to tenth centuries; first printed 1524–5; 1.5); *Magna Carta* (1215; Cho.3); *Guy of Warwick* (fourteenth century; Cho.2); William Barlow, *The Navigator's Supply* (1597; 1.4), *Magnetical Advertisements* (1616; 1.4); Ben Jonson, *Every Man in His Humour* (**1143**; ind.), *Every Man out of His Humour* (**1216**; ind.), *The Silent Woman* (**1603**; Cho.2) *The New Inn* (**2263**; ind., 3.6); Lewis Bayly, *The Practice of Piety* (1612; 4.4); Mark Ridley, *A Short Treatise of Magnetical Bodies and Motions* (1613; 1.4), *Magnetical Animadversions* (1617; 1.4); Richard Allestree, *Almanac* (annually from 1617; 4.2); Henry Burton, *The Baiting of the Pope's Bull* (1627; 1.5)

LANGUAGE
English
Latin: 61 words (ind., 1.3, 1.7, 2.3–4, 3.3, 3.5–6, Cho.3, 4.2–3, 4.6, 5.1, 5.10; Probee, Damn-Play, Trygust, Palate, Practice, Rut, Compass, Bias, Needle, Interest)
Greek: 10 words (1.1, 1.7, Cho.1–2, 3.4, Cho.4; Ironside, Bias, Trygust, Probee, Rut)
Italian: 1 word (2.6; Ironside)
French: 1 word (3.6; Compass)

FORM
Metre: pentameter (main play) and prose (chorus)
Rhyme: blank verse
Induction: three characters (Probee, Damn-Play, Trygust) who then become the Chorus
Chorus: entr'acte chorus, in prose, of the three characters from the induction; they do not interact with the rest of the action
Act-Division: 5 acts, separated by chorus

Epilogue: 8 lines, in couplets; court performance only
Lines (Spoken): 2,584 (2,272 verse, 312 prose)
Lines (Written): 2,701

STAGING
Stage: mentioned (ind., 3.3, s.d); characters are grouped on two different stage areas (2.4, implicit)
Within: sound effect (3.1, s.d.)
Audience: mentioned (ind., Cho.1), and called 'spectators' (Cho.4); assumed to have different areas in the auditorium according to social standing and price of admission, with 6d as the lowest price (ind.), while Damn-Play says he has paid 1s.6d or 2s for his seat (Cho.2); Probee and Damn-Play, conceived as members of the audience, sit on stage throughout; the King is directly addressed in the court epilogue.
Miscellaneous: Placentia is carried across the stage by Keep (3.3, s.d.; this may indicate their relative size or the strength of the actor playing Keep, perhaps an adult rather than a boy)

SOUND
Sound Effects: noise within (3.1, s.d.)

PROPS
Weapons: Ironside's sword (2.6, 3.6–7, dialogue; 3.2, implicit); Silkworm's sword (3.6–7, dialogue)
Clothing: a wedding ring (4.6, dialogue)
Money: five hundred pounds (2.4, dialogue); 'a piece' (4.6, dialogue)
Food and Drink: a glass of water (3.5, dialogue; thrown in Interest's face)
Small Portable Objects: a diamond (2.4, dialogue); an emerald (2.4, dialogue); a letter (3.6, implicit); a marriage licence, with a seal (4.6, dialogue)
Large Portable Objects: two seats (entire play, dialogue; seating for Probee and Damn-Play); a chair (3.5, s.d.); a stool (4.1, dialogue)
Scenery: a title-board (ind., implicit)

COSTUMES AND MAKE-UP
IRONSIDE: possibly a feathered hat (1.1–2, 3.2, dialogue); a sword-belt (2.6, dialogue; 3.2, 3.6–7, implicit); a doublet (3.6, dialogue); a buckled belt (5.10, dialogue)
PALATE: is not wearing a cope (1.2, dialogue)
POLISH: puffed sleeves (4.4, dialogue)
SILKWORM: may be fat (dialogue); a bloodstained white satin doublet (3.4, 3.6, dialogue; removed on stage); hose and silk stockings (3.4, dialogue; spattered with blood); possibly a wound on the face (3.4, dialogue); a shirt (3.6, dialogue); hangers (3.6–7, implicit)
PRACTICE: a lawyer's cap and gown, with a broad guard on the back (1.6–7, dialogue)
INTEREST: a wet hood and coat (5.10, dialogue; removed on stage)
PLACENTIA: a swollen belly (2.1–3, dialogue; 3.3, implicit)

NEEDLE: 'half naked', with linen breeks (5.5, dialogue)

In 3.4, Silkworm is contrasted with Ironside, who is said to be 'a fat, corpulent, | Unwieldy fellow', whereas Silkworm is 'a dieted spark'. The point of the joke is probably that the descriptions should be the other way around.

EARLY STAGE HISTORY
1632: performed by the King's Men at the Blackfriars, probably in October. There were probably at least three performances, and the cast probably included Joseph Taylor and John Lowin. Audiences may have included Inigo Jones (who reportedly laughed with delight that the play was considered so unfunny), Nathaniel Butter, and Alexander Gil (who wrote a satirical poem about the play, to which Jonson later replied). There are some indications in contemporary allusions that the production was not successful.

The King's Men were summoned to appear before the ecclesiastical Court of High Commission and on Thursday 15 November they were bound over to answer charges about 'profane speeches in abuse of scripture and holy things' in the play. (This may have been the discussion of Arminianism in 1.5.) The actors apparently said that the material appeared in the licensed script, thus shifting the blame onto Jonson and Sir Henry Herbert. They appeared again before the Court on Thursday 24 October 1633, and made a second submission accepting that Herbert had not acted negligently; William Laud (Archbishop of Canterbury) spoke in Herbert's favour and blamed the actors.

1632–3: prepared for performance at court, with a specially written epilogue assuming the presence of King Charles I. There is no evidence that such a performance actually took place: it may have been aborted when the play ran into controversy before Christmas. However, this is only a matter of inference, and there is also no evidence that a court performance did *not* take place. The King's Men performed at court 23 times between Thursday 3 May 1632 and Sunday 3 March 1633—twice at Hampton Court and 21 times at either Whitehall Palace or Denmark House—and *The Magnetic Lady* could have been one of the later ones. John Lowin, Joseph Taylor, and Eliard Swanston were later paid £270 for these performances (and for an afternoon rehearsal at the Cockpit in Court), by a warrant dated Saturday 16 March 1633.

The socially diverse profile of the audience described in the induction, and the admission prices, suggest that Jonson may have been anticipating a performance at the Globe rather than the Blackfriars.

EARLY TEXTUAL HISTORY
1632: The play was in existence by Thursday 20 September, when it is mentioned in a letter from John Pory to Sir Thomas Puckering; at this stage the title was *The Magnetic Lady*.

1632: on Friday 12 October, Sir Henry Herbert licensed the play for performance; the licensing fee was £2, paid by Edward Knight; the title was now *Humours Reconciled, or The Magnetic Lady*.

c. 1637–40: Not long before his death, Ben Jonson placed some of his unpublished works in the hands of Sir Kenelm Digby, with a view to their publication. This play may have been one of the texts in question. After Jonson's death in August 1637, Digby took the texts he had received to Thomas Walkley, who paid Digby £40 and procured a licence to publish them, but did not enter them in the Stationers' Register.

1640: While Walkley's volume was at the printer's, John Benson and Andrew Crooke had some of the masques therein (but not this play) entered to them in the Stationers' Register; the Stationers' Company authorities had no knowledge of Walkley's interest in the matter. Fearful that they were planning to issue their own edition, Walkley complained to a secretary of state, who issued a warrant prohibiting Benson and Crooke from doing so.

1640–1: included in the third volume of Jonson's *Works* (^{1}F$_1$), sigs ^{2}A1^r–^{2}H4^v, 32 leaves; printed by John Dawson for Thomas Walkley; Latin title-page motto; list of roles.

1640–1: The Stationers' Register entry of *The Gypsies Metamorphosed* (**1987**) in Benson's favour misled John Parker, a London stationer, into supposing that the printed copies of Walkley's volume were Benson's property. Benson allegedly owed Parker money, so Parker had the book seized from the printer's. Walkley, who valued the copies at £300 or more, suspected that this was a dishonest move planned by Benson and Crooke in preparation to issuing their own edition, and complained to the Court of Chancery on Wednesday 20 January 1641.

1648: Changes in press licensing arrangements since 1640 meant that Walkley's original licence to print his Jonson works had become void. He attempted to have the texts perused by the new licensers in preparation for having them entered in the Stationers' Register, but one of them, Sir Nathaniel Brent, was out of town and the other, John Langley, claimed to be too busy. He then approached the Stationers' Company, who in turn petitioned the House of Lords on Wednesday 20 December, asking for additional licensers to be appointed.

c. 1655: extracts transcribed from F$_1$ by John Evans in a miscellany, *Hesperides*, intended for publication and entered to Humphrey Moseley in the Stationers' Register on Thursday 16 August 1655. The book remained unpublished in 1660, and Evans continued adding to the collection until at least 1666. Two MS exemplars are known; one was cut up by J. O. Halliwell-Phillipps in the nineteenth century; the other survives (Washington: Folger, MS V. b. 93).

1658: rights to the third volume of Jonson's *Works* entered in the Stationers' Register to Thomas Walkley on Friday 17 September; the play is individually named.

1658: Walkley's rights transferred to Humphrey Moseley in the Stationers' Register on Saturday 20 November; the play is individually named.

1660: F$_1$ advertised for sale by Humphrey Moseley.

1667: Moseley's rights to the third volume of Jonson's *Works* transferred by his widow, Ann, to Henry Herringman in the Stationers' Register on Monday 19 August; group transfer of nine titles, the *Works* being one, with the play individually named.

1692: included in Jonson's *Works* (^{2}F$_2$), sigs. 3Q3^r–3T2^r, 23 pages on 12 leaves; printed by Thomas Hodgkin for Henry Herringman, Edward Brewster, Thomas Bassett, Richard Chiswell, Matthew Wotton, and George Conyers.

The books here designated F$_1$ and F$_2$ are respectively the second and third Jonson Folios.

EDITIONS
C. H. Herford, Percy Simpson, and Evelyn Simpson, in *Ben Jonson* (Oxford, 1925–52), vi. 499–597, x. 341–60.
Peter Happé, Revels Plays (Manchester & New York, 2000).
Helen Ostovitch, in *The Cambridge Edition of the Works of Ben Jonson*, gen. eds. David Bevington, Ian Donaldson, and Martin Butler (Cambridge, 2012), vi. 391–540.

REFERENCES
Annals 1632; Bawcutt 240, 266; *Ben Jonson*, ed. Herford & Simpson, ix. 253; Bentley, iv. 618–20; J. Payne Collier, *The History of English Dramatic Poetry to the Time of Shakespeare* (London, 1831), ii. 44; Eyre & Rivington, ii. 8; Greg 616; Hazlitt, 147; HMC 7, 67; *The Library*, 4th ser., 11 (1930–1), 225–9, 461–5; *The Library*, 5th ser., 28 (1973), 294–308; *The Library*, 7th ser., 10 (2009), 372–404; *MP* 89 (1991–2), 469–81; MSC 2.3, 360; *SB* 25 (1972), 177–8; *ShS* 11 (1958), 109; Steele, 242.

2386. *The Countryman*

EVIDENCE
Stationers' Register; Inner Temple accounts for 1657–8; Middle Temple accounts for 1657–60.

The Inns of Court accounts record various payments to musicians for, among other things, 'acting *The Countryman*'; the performances all fall outside the period of the play's early stage history as recorded in the Catalogue.

GENRE
Contemporary: play

TITLE
Contemporary: *The Countryman*; *The Countryman or Clown*; *The Clown*
Alternative Modernization: *The Country Man*

AUTHOR
Annals ascribes the play to William Davenant and suggests that it might have been 'from *The Wits*', i.e. presumably a cut-down droll based on Sir Morglay Thwack's scenes from **2421**. Thwack is indeed a countryman, but 'clown' seems an unlikely epithet for him; it suggests a rather desperate effort to find a character in an extant Davenant play who might fit the title, however remotely. But the attribution to Davenant is itself insecure; it presumably arose from the title's placement in the Stationers' Register list before *The Siege* (**2771**), a play which is there ascribed to him. However, *The Countryman* itself has no author assigned to it, and the two plays immediately preceding it, *The Fool would be a Favourite* (**2657**) and *Osman the Great Turk* (**2022**) are bracketed together and said to be 'both by' Lodowick Carlell. One might expect a similar formula to be used if *The Countryman* and *The Siege* were both by Davenant.

DATE
Limits: 1600–42

The limits are defined by the datable plays among those entered by Humphrey Moseley in the same group.

ROLES
A COUNTRYMAN or rustic

MUSIC
The fact that the Inns of Court performances in 1657–60 seem to have been given by musicians might be taken to indicate that the play had some significant musical content. On the other hand, musicians might simply have been the only type of performer to be available and licit during the Interregnum.

EARLY TEXTUAL HISTORY
1653: entered to Humphrey Moseley in the Stationers' Register on Friday 9 September; individually named as part of a group entry of 41 (or 55) plays.

REFERENCES
Annals 1657, Supp. II (a); Bentley, v. 1314; Greg Θ61; Hazlitt, 51; Charles Henry Hopwood (ed.), *A Calendar of the Middle Temple Records* (London, 1903), 166–8; F. A. Inderwick (ed.), *A Calendar of the Inner Temple Records* (London, 1896–1901), ii. 328; William van Lennep, *The London Stage, 1660–1800*, Part 1: 1660–1700 (Carbondale, 1965), 9; Sibley, 31; *SP* 20 (1923), 63.

2387. *Londini artium et scientiarum scaturigo* [London's Fountain of Arts and Sciences]

TEXT
Printed in 1632 (STC 13347); contains no description of 4.

GENRE
civic pageant
Contemporary: triumphs, pageants, and shows (t.p.)

TITLE
Printed: *Londini artium et scientiarum scaturigo, or London's Fountain of Arts and Sciences*
Contemporary: *London's Scaturigo*; *Scaturigo*
Later Assigned: *Device for Sir Nicholas Rainton, Haberdasher*; *Londini scaturigo*

AUTHOR
Thomas Heywood

DATE
29 October 1632

ORIGINAL PRODUCTION
London Haberdashers' Company in the city streets. The route included: River Thames; St Paul's Churchyard.

PLOT
Arion admires the Thames above all the rivers of the world, and praises the magnificent barges assembled for the new Lord Mayor's triumph.

Once the mayoral party is ashore, St Catherine explains her presence riding on a lion: she is the patroness of the Lord Mayor's livery company, and her mount signifies her royal status. She encourages the crowd to be loyal and obedient to their new Mayor. Perseus rescues Andromeda from a sea-monster, and explains that this represents a magistrate's duty to protect chastity and innocence. An Indian leads an elephant, symbolizing the far-flung trade of the Lord Mayor's mercantile career, and also his responsibility to support the city as the elephant bears the castle on its back. London is represented as the fountain of arts and sciences, founded on the secure financial basis of trade.

That evening, Arion recapitulates the lessons of the show.

SCENE DESIGNATION
The event is here divided as follows:
1: Arion, on the Thames;
2: St Catherine, at St Paul's Churchyard;
3: Perseus and Andromeda;
4: show for the vulgar (not described by Heywood);
5: Indian;
6: The Fountain of Virtue;
7: Arion's final speech at night.
Q numbers the shows as the first by water and the first to fifth by land (i.e. 2–6 here); 7 is unnumbered.

ROLES
ARION, a musician
OCEANUS, an old sea-god (1, *non-speaking*)
AMPHITRITE, an old sea-goddess (1, *non-speaking*)

PERSEUS, a hero, representing the chief virtues of a magistrate
ANDROMEDA, a princess, representing chastity and innocence (1, 3, *non-speaking*)
ST CATHERINE, a queen, martyr, and patron saint of the Haberdashers' Company
HUMILITY, a virgin (2, *non-speaking*)
TRUTH, a virgin (2, *non-speaking*)
ZEAL, a virgin (2, *non-speaking*)
CONSTANCY, a virgin (2, *non-speaking*)
An INDIAN (5)
Twelve PERSONS, representing London's twelve livery companies, i.e. the Mercers, Grocers, Drapers, Fishmongers, Goldsmiths, Skinners, Merchant Taylors, Haberdashers, Salters, Ironmongers, Vintners, and Clothworkers (6; only one speaks, probably the representative of the Haberdashers)

Speaking Parts: 5
Allegorical Roles: 4 (or 16)

Stage Directions
ARION: *Arion* (s.d.s)
OCEANUS: *Oceanus* (s.d.s)
AMPHITRITE: *Amphetrite* (s.d.s)
PERSEUS: *Perseus* (s.d.s)
ANDROMEDA: *Andromeda* (s.d.s)
ST CATHERINE: *St Katherine* (s.d.s)
HUMILITY: [one of] *four Virgins | Humility* (s.d.s)
TRUTH: [one of] *four Virgins | Truth* (s.d.s)
ZEAL: [one of] *four Virgins | Zeal* (s.d.s)
CONSTANCY: [one of] *four Virgins | Constancy* (s.d.s)
INDIAN: *an Indian | The Indian* (s.d.s)
PERSONS: *twelve sundry persons* (s.d.s)

OTHER CHARACTERS
Jove, Perseus' father (3)

SETTING
Geography
River Thames
[*France*]: Paris; River Seine
[*Italy*]: River Po; River Rubicon; Rome; River Tiber
[*Europe*]: River Tagus; River Rhine; River Ister (i.e. Danube)
[*Turkey*]: River Caister; River Meander; River Simois; River Thermodon
Palestine: River Jordan
Persia: River Choaspis; River Euphrates
India: River Ganges
[*Asia*]: River Issa; River Volga
[*Africa*]: River Nile

SOURCES
Verbal: Socrates, untraced maxim (ded.2; possibly from Nicholas Ling, *Politeuphuia: Wit's Commonwealth*, 1597); Terence, *Phormio* (ded.1); Virgil, 'Caesar et Jupiter' (t.p. motto); Seneca, *Thyestes* (desc., cited), *Octavia* (ded.2, cited); Lucan, *Pharsalia* (desc., cited); Suetonius, *Twelve Caesars*: Augustus (desc.)
Works Mentioned: Herodotus, *Histories* (desc.); *Liber de certaminibus Dionysiacis* (side-note); Ovid, *Metamorphoses* (desc.); Pliny, *Natural History* (desc.); Aulus Gellius, *Attic Nights* (desc.); Conrad Gessner, *Historiae animalium* (1585; desc.); John Minsheu, *A Dictionary in Spanish and English* (1599; desc.); Sebastián de Covarrubias, *Il tesoro della lengua Castellana o Española* (1611; desc.)

LANGUAGE
English
Latin: 2 words (1, 6; Arion, Livery Company)

FORM
Metre: pentameter
Rhyme: couplets
Lines (Spoken): 226
Lines (Written): 435

STAGING
Stage: three or four pageant stages (2, desc.; 3, 5–6, implicit)
Audience: the Lord Mayor is directly addressed (1, 3, 5–7); the crowd is directly addressed (2)

PROPS
Weapons: a wheel of blades (2, desc.); a crooked sword (3, desc.); a shield with a Gorgon's head (3, desc.); twelve shields with armorial devices (6, desc.)
Musical Instruments: a harp (1, desc.)
Animals: a dolphin (1, desc.; carries a performer on its back); two sea-horses (1, desc.; each carries a performer on its back); a lion (2, desc.; carries a performer on its back); a sea-monster (3, desc.); a winged horse (3, desc.); an elephant with a castle on its back (5, desc.)
Large Portable Objects: two staffs with banners bearing the arms of the Haberdashers' Company (1, desc.); a banner with the Haberdashers' arms (2, desc.); unspecified rich merchandise (5, desc.; in the elephant's castle)
Scenery: a platform of sea-waves (2, desc.; carries the lion and seats four besides); a rock (3, desc.; presented on both water and land); a fountain (6, desc.)

COSTUMES
ST CATHERINE: a crown (2, desc.)

EARLY STAGE HISTORY
Preparation: On Friday 22 June, an organizing committee was appointed by the authorities of the Haberdashers' Company. On Tuesday 2 October, the committee was instructed to make the arrangements, and to appoint thirty or forty of the company's yeomanry to serve in the procession as gentlemen ushers.

Performance: in London on Monday 29 October 1632 as part of the celebration of Nicholas Rainton's inauguration as Lord Mayor. The design was by Gerard Christmas. The performance took place at intervals during the day, from morning to evening. The procession was watched by: Vincente Gussoni (Venetian Ambassador); Adriaen Pawe and Arnaut van Randwyck (Dutch Ambassadors); lords and Privy Councillors (including some or all of: Edward, Lord Barrett of Newburgh; Robert Bertie, 1st Earl of Lindsay; Henry Cary, 1st Viscount Falkland; Edward Cecil, Viscount Wimbledon; William Cecil, 2nd Earl of Exeter; William Cecil, 2nd Earl of Salisbury; Sir John Coke; Francis, Lord Cottington; Thomas, 1st Baron Coventry; Henry Danvers, Earl of Danby; Sir Thomas Edmondes; John Egerton, 1st Earl of Bridgewater; Thomas Erskine, 1st Earl of Kellie; William Graham, 7th Earl of Menteith and 1st Earl of Strathearn; James Hay, 1st Earl of Carlisle; Philip Herbert, 4th Earl of Pembroke; Theophilus Howard, 2nd Earl of Suffolk; Thomas Howard, 14th Earl of Arundel; Sir Thomas Jermyn; William Laud, Bishop of London; Henry Montagu, 1st Earl of Manchester; Sir Robert Naunton; Richard Neile, Archbishop of York; Henry Rich, 1st Earl of Holland; Edward Sackville, 4th Earl of Dorset; Sir Henry Vane; Thomas, Viscount Wentworth; Richard, Lord Weston). The French Ambassador (François du Val, Marquis of Fontenay-Mareuil) was invited, but was unable to attend because he was in mourning for his mother. Two other diplomats who conspicuously failed to attend, despite being invited, were Juan de Necolalde (Spanish Agent) and Henry Taylor (Flemish Agent).

Production Finance and Expenses
On Tuesday 2 October, a levy on the members of the Haberdashers' Company processing was decreed, variously amounting to £5 per head for those in foins and £3.6s.8d per head for those in budge.
    Gerard Christmas was paid £190 for supplying the pageants.

EARLY TEXTUAL HISTORY
1632: **Q** printed by Nicholas Okes; collation A–B⁴ C², 10 leaves; title page names author and refers to performance; Latin title-page motto; title-page woodcut (the arms of the Haberdashers' Company); authorial dedications to Nicholas Rainton (Lord Mayor) and to Hugh Perry and Henry Andrews (Sheriffs). During printing, A2ᵛ–A3ʳ were partly reset to transfer, with minor amendments, a passage from the Sheriffs' dedication to that addressed to the Lord Mayor. The Haberdashers' Company ordered 300 copies, and paid £2 for them to be printed.

EDITIONS
A. M. Clark, in *Theatre Miscellany: Six Pieces Connected with the Seventeenth-Century Stage*, Luttrell Society Publications 14 (Oxford, 1953), 1–47.

David M. Bergeron, in *Thomas Heywood's Pageants*, The Renaissance Imagination 16 (New York, 1986), 33–52.

REFERENCES
Annals 1632; Bentley, iv. 575–6; Bergeron, 222–5; *Cal. Ven. 1632–6*, 28; Greg 466; Hazlitt, 132; Loomie, 131; McGee-Meagher 1625–34, 68–70; MSC 3, 121–2; *PBSA* 108 (2014), 325–41; *RenQ* 23 (1970), 46.

2388. *Nothing Impossible to Love*

EVIDENCE
Stationers' Register; list of MS plays said to have been in the possession of John Warburton (1682–1759), and destroyed by his cook (London: British Library, MS Lansdowne 807, fo. 1).

GENRE
tragicomedy
Contemporary: tragicomedy

TITLE
Contemporary: *Nothing Impossible to Love*

AUTHOR
Sir Robert Le Grys

DATE
Limits: 1585–1635
Best Guess: 1632

Sir Robert Le Grys (1571?–1635) translated Barclay's *Argenis* in 1628, and Velleius Paterculus in 1632; he moved to Cornwall in 1633, having been appointed Governor of St Mawes Castle, but was recalled to London after about nine months to answer charges of mismanagement. The wide limits are defined by his matriculation from Emmanuel College, Cambridge, and his death.
    The Stationers' Register entry for the play and Warburton's list both style him 'Sir Robert'; this probably reflects the form of his name as it appeared on the MS, which must therefore have been written or transcribed later than 1626, when he was knighted on 16 August. The options for dating the play thus fall into three possible periods: before 1626, in which case the MS registered in 1660 must have been a later transcript; 1626–33, in which case the play may have been written in London; or 1633–5, in which case the play might have been written in either Cornwall or London.
    In practice, composition in or soon before the 1630s seems consistent with the tone of the title and the fashion for courtier play-writing which seems to have begun in 1629 with *The Deserving Favourite* (**2262**). Le Grys was at a loose end between finishing his Velleius Paterculus (registered for publication on 9 May 1632) and the spring of 1633, when he offered his services as a Latin tutor to Prince Charles.

PLOT
The usual meaning of the title phrase is that, for one who loves, no feat is impossible however difficult. However, the play could

have spun it differently, suggesting that there is nothing in existence that cannot be loved.

SOURCES
Verbal: Thomas a Kempis, *Imitatio Christi* (c. 1418–27; title)

EARLY TEXTUAL HISTORY
1660: entered in the Stationers' Register to Humphrey Moseley on Friday 29 June; play and author individually named as part of a group entry of 37 plays.

REFERENCES
Annals 1634; Bentley, iv. 720; Greg Θ182; Hazlitt, 168; *The Library*, 3rd ser., 2 (1911), 225–59; Sibley, 113.

2389. The Ball

TEXT
Printed in 1639 (STC 4995), probably from authorial papers. However, changes to three characters' names may indicate (non-authorial?) revisions in response to censorship.

The original names of Lord Rainbow, Sir Marmaduke, and Sir Ambrose are inferred from the survival of traces of the names, the Lord's in the signature on his letter in 4.3 and the knights' in the s.d.s and s.p.s at their final brief appearance in 5.1. Presumably the MS was worked over to change the original names, but these minor instances were overlooked, the Lord's because it appears in dialogue when the character is not on stage, and the knights' simply because they are right at the end of the play. The likely motive for this would be censorship, in response to the complaints recorded by Sir Henry Herbert: thus more fantastical names were substituted for relatively commonplace originals. The original names might therefore be clues to the identity of some of the complainants: Love-All (an apt name for the character, which might perhaps have been misheard as Lovel), Sir Stephen, and Sir Lionel. There is no explicit indication which knight is which, but in metrical terms Marmaduke is an easier substitution for Lionel, and Ambrose for Stephen.

GENRE
comedy
Contemporary: play (Herbert); comedy (t.p.)

TITLE
Performed/Printed: *The Ball*
Contemporary: *The Ball, or The French Dancing-Master*
Later Assigned: *The French Dancing-Master*

AUTHOR
James Shirley

DATE
November 1632

ORIGINAL PRODUCTION
Queen Henrietta's Men at the Cockpit

PLOT
Lord Rainbow is to hold a ball. Ladies practise their dancing, coached by Monsieur La Frisk, and engage in amours. Lucina has four suitors whom she teases with the prospect of marriage. She plans to see each of them in turn, but unknown to her, her servant Scutilla conceals one of them, Colonel Winfield, in her room, and he witnesses her scornful treatment of his rivals: Sir Marmaduke is mocked for his money-making schemes, Sir Ambrose for his baldness, and Bostock, who habitually boasts of his imagined kinship with noblemen, is told she will only marry a commoner—which induces him to suggest that he may be illegitimate, and therefore eligible after all. The Colonel takes a more masterful line with her at his meeting. He then suggests to the other insulted suitors that they go back and treat her with contempt. Bostock nominates himself the spokesman, and is duly rude to her, whereupon the Colonel steps in to defend her honour. She agrees to marry him, on condition that he proves himself to be a virgin; he infers another jeer on her part, and takes offence. She is in earnest, however. She tests the Colonel's fidelity by telling him that he will be taking on her debts and children (both imaginary) and that he will have to live in the country; when he is undaunted, she accepts him.

In another plot, before leaving on a journey to Venice, Freshwater sold his land and laid out money to be paid back fivefold on his safe return. When he gets back, the men who took his money seem reluctant to pay him. At the ball, he is asked to describe his travels, but does so with a suspicious lack of geographical knowledge. It turns out that he spent the summer in Gravesend awaiting a favourable wind. His debtors insist that he undertake the voyage before getting anything back.

In the third plot, Lord Rainbow loves both Honoria and Rosamund, but cannot choose between them, so he asks them to decide between themselves which is worthier of him. They are annoyed to learn from the satirical Barker that this arrangement is common knowledge, and decide to get their own back by turning their affections to unlikely rivals. Barker is the first recipient of Honoria's attention, and she encourages him to learn to dance. Sir Marmaduke and Sir Ambrose also pursue the ladies on the rebound from Lucina; they have some fun by repeatedly directing each knight to woo the other lady, back and forth.

Honoria and Rosamund ask Rainbow to draw lots for them. He decides on a threesome and takes both lots, but they are blank: neither lady will have him. La Frisk presents a masque, and Barker makes an unscheduled appearance as a satyr, having fulfilled Honoria's request and learned to dance.

SCENE DESIGNATION
1.1–2, 2.1–2, 3.1–4, 4.1–3, 5.1 (Q has act-division only)

2389. The Ball

ROLES

SIR MARMADUKE Travers, a knight and projector, Lucina's suitor; originally written as Sir Lionel

Master BOSTOCK, Lucina's suitor; Lord Rainbow calls him 'cousin', but seems merely to be humouring him

SIR AMBROSE Lamont, a recently-made knight and gentleman, Lucina's suitor; also called Sir Ambrose Coxcomb; originally written as Sir Stephen

SOLOMON, Lucina's servant

Colonel WINFIELD, a gentleman soldier, Lucina's suitor; appears to be about 30 years old

Master Jack FRESHWATER, a gentleman; also called Signor Freshwater

Monsieur LA FRISK, a French dancing-master; in the masque, he plays Cupid, boy god of love, Venus' son

GUDGEON, Freshwater's man

Lord RAINBOW, a young nobleman; originally written as Lord Love-All

Master Frank BARKER, a railer

Lady ROSAMUND

Lady HONORIA

Mistress SCUTILLA, Lucina's unmarried waiting-woman

Lady LUCINA, a rich widow

SERVANTS (5.1, *non-speaking*)

VENUS, goddess of love, Cupid's mother; a character in the masque

DIANA, chaste goddess of the moon, a huntress; a character in the masque

Speaking Parts: 16

Stage Directions and Speech Prefixes

SIR MARMADUKE: *Sir Marmaduke Travers* (s.d.s and d.p.); *Sir Marmaduke | Travers | Sir Lionell* (s.d.s); *Mar<maduke>* (s.p.s)

BOSTOCK: *Mr Bostocke* (s.d.s and d.p.); *Bostocke | Bostoke* (s.d.s); *Bos<tocke>* (s.p.s)

SIR AMBROSE: *Sir Ambrose Lamount* (s.d.s and d.p.); *Sir Ambrose | Lamount | Sir Stephen* (s.d.s); *Am<brose> | Ste<phen>* (s.p.s)

SOLOMON: *a servant Solomon* (s.d.s); *Solomon* (s.d.s and d.p.); *Sol<omon>* (s.p.s)

WINFIELD: *the Colonel* (s.d.s); *Colonel* (s.d.s and s.p.s); *Colonel Winfield* (d.p.)

FRESHWATER: *Freshwater* (s.d.s); *Fre<shwater>* (s.p.s); *Mr Freshwater* (d.p.)

LA FRISK: *Monsieur Le Friske* (s.d.s and d.p.); *the Dancer | Monsieur La Friske | Cupid* (s.d.s); *Monsieur* (s.d.s and s.p.s); *Dancer | Cu<pid>* (s.p.s)

GUDGEON: *Gudgine* (s.d.s); *Gudgin* (s.d.s and d.p.); *Gud<gin>* (s.p.s)

RAINBOW: *Lord Rainebow* (s.d.s and d.p.); *my Lord | Rainebow* (s.d.s); *Lord* (s.d.s and s.p.s)

BARKER: *Barker* (s.d.s); *Bar<ker>* (s.p.s); *Mr Barker* (d.p.)

ROSAMUND: *Lady Rosomond* (s.d.s); *Rosomond* (s.d.s); *Ros<omond>* (s.p.s); *Lady Rosamond* (d.p.)

HONORIA: *Lady Honoria* (s.d.s and d.p.); *Honoria* (s.d.s); *Hon<oria>* (s.p.s)

SCUTILLA: *Scutilla* (s.d.s); *Scu<tilla>* (s.p.s); *Mistress Scutilla* (d.p.)

LUCINA: *Lady Lucina* (s.d.s and d.p.); *Luc<ina>* (s.p.s)

SERVANTS: *Servants* (s.d.s and d.p.)

VENUS: *Venus* (s.d.s and d.p.); *Ven<us>* (s.p.s)

DIANA: *Dia<na>* (s.p.s); *Diana* (d.p.)

D.p. also lists: *Confectioner*

OTHER CHARACTERS

Rosamund's dead father and living mother (1.2)

Scutilla's kinsman, whose life was saved by Winfield (2.2)

The general whom Scutilla's kinsman angered (2.2)

Lady Lucina's first husband (2.2, 4.3)

La Frisk's brother (3.1)

An English painter for whom Rosamund sits (3.3)

Gudgeon's aunt (3.3)

A foreign painter whom Freshwater recommends to Rosamund (3.3)

Bostock's father and mother (3.3)

Colonel Winfield's dry-nurse (4.3)

A city merchant from whom Rainbow rented the house for the ball (5.1)

The various unnamed aristocrats, including an earl, with whom Bostock pretends kindred are treated as imaginary; one might argue that, for the boasts to be meaningful, the individuals concerned would have to be real, but their anonymity might just as well make them generic.

SETTING

Period: contemporary; the action takes place in the autumn or winter

Time-Scheme: The action takes place during a single day, 1.1 in the morning, 2.1 in the afternoon, and 5.1 in the evening.

Place: London

Geography

London: the Magpie in the Strand; Cheapside; Bankside; St Paul's Cathedral; the Exchange; Fish Street; the Stillyard; Hyde Park; Spring Garden; the Bear Garden; the Trumpet tavern; Covent Garden; Queenhithe

[*Middlesex*]: Paddington

[*Kent*]: Dover; Greenwich; Gravesend

England: Odcombe; the Fens; Yarmouth; Newcastle; Dunstable

France: Paris; the Valtoline; the Louvre

The Low Countries: Ostend; Antwerp; Saint-Omer; Wallonia; the United Provinces; Holland; Flushing; Middleborough; Rotterdam

Spain: Alcantara; Seville; Madrid

Venice: the Rialto; the Piazza

Rome: Pompey's Theatre

Italy: Parma; Bologna; Lombardy; Naples; Florence; Milan; Piedmont; Padua; Mantua; Genoa

Europe: Greece; Lapland; Germany; the Alps
Turkey: Constantinople
[*The Holy Land*]: Jerusalem
Scythia
The Canary Islands
The Indies

SOURCES
Narrative: Ben Jonson, *Every Man Out of His Humour* (**1216**; Jack Freshwater); John Webster, *The Duchess of Malfi* (**1726**; 4.3); James Shirley, *The Changes* (**2355**; Honoria and Rosamund)
Verbal: Diego Ortúñez de Calahorra, Pedro de la Sierra, and Marcos Martínez, *Espejo de principes y caballeros* (1555–87; English tr., *The Mirror of Princely Deeds and Knighthood*, by Margaret Tyler, R. P., and L. A., 1578–99; 1.1); Francis Beaumont and John Fletcher, *The Maid's Tragedy* (**1650**; 3.4)
Works Mentioned: Ovid, *Amores* (4.3; referred to as *Elegies*, implying the Christopher Marlowe translation); *Bevis of Hampton* (c. 1300; 4.3); *Guy of Warwick* (fourteenth century; 4.3); William Shakespeare, *Venus and Adonis* (1593; 4.3); Marcantonio Zimara, *The Problems of Aristotle* (1595; 4.3); William Rowley, *A New Wonder, A Woman Never Vexed* (**2084**; 5.1)

LANGUAGE
English
Latin: 4 words (2.1, 4.3; Freshwater, Lucina)
French: 91 words (1.1, 2.1–2, 3.1, 4.2–3, 5.1; La Frisk, Winfield, Freshwater; La Frisk also speaks in 'franglais')
Italian: 6 words (1.1; Freshwater)

FORM
Metre: pentameter and prose; the masque is in tetrameter
Rhyme: blank verse; the masque is in couplets
Act-Division: 5 acts
Lines (Spoken): 2,346 (1,466 verse, 880 prose)
Lines (Written): 2,618

STAGING
Above: a golden ball descends (5.1, s.d.)

MUSIC
Music: probably accompanying the masque (5.1, dialogue)
On-Stage Music: La Frisk plays the pipe (2.2, implicit) and the fiddle (2.2, dialogue; 3.1, implicit)
Dance: ladies dance (2.2, s.d.); ladies dance 'a new country dance' (2.2, s.d.); Rainbow and Bostock dance (3.1, implicit); knights, Honoria, and Rosamund dance a country dance (4.2, s.d.); masque dance (5.1, s.d.); Barker dances (5.1, s.d.); dance at the ball (5.1, s.d.)

PROPS
Weapons: Winfield's sword (3.4, dialogue); Bostock's sword (4.1, implicit); Rainbow's sword (4.1, implicit); Cupid's bow and quiver of arrows (5.1, dialogue)

Musical Instruments: a pipe (2.2, dialogue); a fiddle (2.2, 3.1, dialogue)
Clothing: two jewels (5.1, dialogue; one is specified as a diamond)
Money: an unspecified sum (1.1, implicit); a purse (3.3, dialogue)
Small Portable Objects: a toothpick (1.1, dialogue); a scroll (2.1, dialogue); a letter (4.3, implicit); diamonds (4.3, dialogue); two lots (5.1, dialogue)
Scenery: hangings (2.2, dialogue); a golden ball (5.1, s.d.; descends from above)
Miscellaneous: perfume (5.1, s.d.)

COSTUMES
BOSTOCK: hangers (4.1, implicit)
SIR AMBROSE: is bald (implicit); muffled (2.2, dialogue)
WINFIELD: a buttoned garment (2.2, dialogue)
LA FRISK: black hair and beard (dialogue)
RAINBOW: a thin, wispy beard, if any (dialogue); satin clothes (4.1, dialogue); a hat (5.1, dialogue; removed on stage)
BARKER: a moustache (dialogue); taffeta clothes (4.1, dialogue); dressed as a satyr (5.1, s.d.)
ROSAMUND: hair overhanging her forehead in a 'penthouse' (dialogue; perhaps a fringe or widow's peak)

EARLY STAGE HISTORY
1632: performed in November by Queen Henrietta's Men at the Cockpit. (Sir Henry Herbert gives the date as Sunday 18 November, perhaps in error.) Several courtiers of both sexes later complained to Herbert that they had been impersonated in the play.

EARLY TEXTUAL HISTORY
1632: on Friday 16 November, Sir Henry Herbert licensed the text for performance.
  1632: Christopher Beeston promised Herbert, possibly on Sunday 18 November, that objectionable material would be omitted from future performances, and that the revision of the script would be done by someone other than the author.
  1638: entered in the Stationers' Register to Andrew Crooke and William Cooke on Wednesday 24 October; entry names author; double entry with *Chabot, Admiral of France* (**1676**). Thomas Wykes had licensed the book for publication.
  1639: Q printed by Thomas Cotes for Andrew Crooke and William Cooke; collation A–I⁴, 36 leaves; title page refers to playhouse and acting company, and names George Chapman and James Shirley as co-authors; list of roles. (The false ascription to Chapman arose from the re-use of type from the title page of *Chabot, Admiral of France*, **1676**.)
  c. 1630s–40s: a copy of Q was in the possession of John Horne (Vicar of Headington, Oxfordshire). After his death, his entire collection of play-books passed into the possession of John Houghton of Brasenose

College, Oxford (c. 1608–77), then to James Herne (died 1685), and then to the library of Ralph Sheldon (1623–84) at Weston, where it was catalogued by Anthony Wood, probably in the late 1670s.

1640–1: Humphrey Moseley was selling copies of Q for 6d each.

1655: *Wit's Interpreter* entered to Nathaniel Brooke in the Stationers' Register on Wednesday 14 March.

1655: four extracts (from 2.2, 3.1, 3.4, 5.1; headed 'The Lying Traveller', 'A Bastard for Love', 'At the Dancing School', and 'A Dialogue of Love') included in John Cotgrave's *Wit's Interpreter*, sigs. C5^v–C7^r, D4^v–D5^v, F3^v–F4^r, F5^v–F6^r; printed for Nathaniel Brooke.

1657: advertised as for sale by the Newcastle-upon-Tyne bookseller William London.

1657–60: advertised as for sale by Simon Miller.

1662: *Wit's Interpreter* reprinted (before Thursday 8 June) for Nathaniel Brooke; the extracts now appear on sigs. C1^r–C2^v, C8^{r-v}, D8^{r-v}, E2^{r-v}; the second, third, and fourth are respectively retitled 'The Discovery of False Love', 'The French Dancing-Master', and 'The Discreet Lover'.

1667–8: Q was being sold by Thomas Dring.

1671: *Wit's Interpreter* reprinted for Nathaniel Brooke and Obadiah Blagrave.

1684: Nicholas Cox (Manciple of St Edmund Hall, Oxford) had a copy of Q in his bookshop. It had probably been previously owned by Gerard Langbaine, and appears on a list compiled by Anthony Wood on Saturday 13 December.

EDITIONS
William Gifford, in *The Dramatic Works and Poems of James Shirley* (London, 1833), iii. 1–91.
Helen Ostovitch, in James Shirley, *The Complete Works*, gen. eds. Eugene Giddens, Teresa Grant, and Barbara Ravelhofer (Oxford, forthcoming).

REFERENCES
Annals 1632; Bawcutt 245–6; Bentley, v. 1076–9; Bodleian, MS Wood E. 4, art. 1, p. 69; Eyre & Rivington, i. 467; Robert Stanley Forsythe, *The Relations of Shirley's Plays to the Elizabethan Drama* (New York, 1914), 407–14; Greg 549; Hazlitt, 21; William London, *A Catalogue of the Most Vendible Books in England* (London, 1657), sig. 2F1^v; *MLR* 13 (1918), 401–11; *Oxford Bibliographical Society Proceedings and Papers* 2.2 (1929), 132–3; *RES* NS 54 (2003), 601–14.

2390. The Country Gentleman

EVIDENCE
Sir Henry Herbert's licence.

TITLE
Performed: [*The* or *A*] *Country Gentleman*

AUTHOR
Shackerley Marmion

DATE
1632

PLOT
The play probably responds to the proclamation of 20 June 1632 intended to discourage absentee landlords, which ordered the gentry to reside on their country estates, and forbidding them to live in and around London.

ROLES
A COUNTRY GENTLEMAN

EARLY TEXTUAL HISTORY
1632: Sir Henry Herbert licensed the text for performance.

REFERENCES
Bawcutt 227.

2391. Necromantes

TEXT
Two MSS, both late authorial transcripts:
   A: Alnwick Castle, MS 509, fos. 158^r–197^r: working interim manuscript with minor revisions;
   H: San Marino: Huntington, MS 4, fos. 152–91; final state of the text.
Both MSS also contain a note of amendments and substitutions for an alternative version of the final Act.

GENRE
comedy
Contemporary: comical invention, comedy (MSS)

TITLE
Performed: *Necromantes*
MS: *Necromantes, or The Two Supposed Heads*
Contemporary: *The Comedy of Heads*

AUTHOR
William Percy

DATE
1632

PLOT
Thirty years ago, the necromancer Busyrane sent his sons Pelorus and Opheltes to travel the world in search of their lost sister and cousin. They return home without success, but make a piratical attack on Laches and his sons Navarchus and Velinus, who are en route to the oracle of Apollo. They are captured and apparently beheaded; but actually Busyrane uses his magical powers to rescue them. He is delighted to learn

that, when they were brought ashore, they saw and fell in love with two well-born local girls, because their fathers may support his ambition to depose the local Praetor, Cannius, and make himself King; so he agrees to find the two young women.

The girls in question are the sisters Galanthis and Melanthis. They have fallen in love with the executed men, and summon the witch Herophile to reunite the heads with their bodies and bring them back to life; this must be done furtively because even to consult a witch has just been made a capital offence. Herophile reluctantly begins the magical rite, but the heads speak, asking for it to be discontinued. The sisters decide to try conventional religion instead, and meet Busyrane on their way to make an offering to Neptune. He learns that they are Cannius' daughters, but his discomfiture is short-lived, since they are concerned that their father, who has been warned by an oracle that he will lose them to unknown men, will seek to cross their marriage. Busyrane offers his help: their loves are alive after all, and he arranges for them to meet at Neptune's altar; afterwards he will take them to the security of his enchanted castle in the country.

Navarchus and Velinus are surprised to find themselves addressed as Pelorus and Opheltes, whom they resemble in every particular. After a scuffle over their suspected piracy, Laches decides it would be a good idea to leave town, and procures a ship. Each son meets his brother's lookalike on the way to the harbour, and tells him to hurry up and join their father aboard ship. In consequence, Pelorus and Opheltes fail to keep their appointment with the sisters, though Opheltes leaves a goodbye note at the altar. The sisters believe they have been jilted, and swear vengeance. At Melanthis' procurement, Herophile uses her magic to prevent the two men from leaving town and ensure their arrest by the authorities. In the event, however, it is Navarchus and Velinus who are arrested. Laches arrives just in time to see them being led away for trial, but then meets Pelorus and Opheltes, who deny knowing him and insist that Busyrane is their father. Laches lays an accusation of witchcraft, and takes him to court.

At the trial, it emerges that both Laches and Busyrane are seeking a lost daughter and niece. Once both pairs of brothers are in court, the misunderstandings start to be resolved. Busyrane insists that neither pair can possibly be the pirates, whose severed heads are still on the altar. The two families' histories emerge, and are remarkably similar: the two missing girls disappeared from their cradles at the feast of Lupercal thirty years before, along with their distinctive mantles. On the same night, two babies were delivered by a goddess into the care of Cannius, and he renamed them Galanthis and Melanthis. The mantles are produced and identified, establishing that Busyrane and Laches are long-lost brothers. But there is still the little matter of piracy and necromancy to resolve. Cannius sentences Pelorus and Opheltes to be sacrificed to Neptune, and Busyrane to crucifixion, but is persuaded merely to banish the entire family, on condition that Busyrane renounces magic hereafter.

In the sub-plot, Lavender is struck dumb. Her husband Indifferent summons a surgeon, who cures her by making an incision under her tongue. Now, however, she speaks too much for Indifferent's liking, all of it scolding. It is medically impossible to reverse the treatment, and the best Doctor Jornol can offer is a drug which induces deafness. Indifferent takes it, and Lavender is so frustrated by the effects that she threatens violence. Jornol has difficulty getting his fees from the family, but takes his revenge by administering a medicine, ostensibly to cure Indifferent's deafness; in fact it turns him into a fool. The characters take their case to law, but the play ends before it can be heard.

SCENE DESIGNATION

prol., 1.1–4, 2.1–5, 3.1–8, 4.1–8, 5.1–10, ep. (MSS; but the note of variants suggest that Percy intended to subdivide 5.5 into three scenes, 5.5–7)

The stage is clear during 5.2, but is not clear at the following scene-divisions: 2.3–4, 3.2–3, 3.5–6, 3.7–8, 4.1–3, 4.7–8, 5.2–3, 5.7–10. Props remain on stage at 2.4–5 and 3.6–7.

ROLES

ARCTURUS, who speaks the prologue
A MARSHAL (1.1, *non-speaking*)
SAILORS (1.1; sing collectively)
PELORUS, a sea-captain; Busyrane's son, brother of Opheltes and Melissa; his real name is Aristaeus; probably in his late 40s or older
OPHELTES, a sea-captain; Busyrane's son, brother of Pelorus and Melissa; his real name is Alexander; probably in his late 40s or older
Lady GALANTHIS, supposed Cannius' elder daughter and Melanthis's sister; in reality, Melissa, Busyrane's daughter, sister of Pelorus and Opheltes; around 30 years old
Lady MELANTHIS, supposed Cannius' younger daughter and Galanthis's sister; in reality, Erotium, daughter of Mylio and sister of Navarchus and Velinus; around 30 years old
THESPIA, a waiting-woman
MEROE, a waiting-woman
Two severed HEADS resembling Pelorus and Opheltes
LACHES, an old citizen of Byzantium, father of Erotium, Navarchus, and Velinus; his real name is Father Mylio, Lycophron's brother
NAVARCHUS, son of Laches, brother of Velinus and Erotium; his real name is Smerdes
VELINUS, son of Laches, brother of Navarchus and Erotium; his real name is Gnemon
Goodwife LAVENDER, Hive's daughter, Indifferent's wife of thirty years, Ignorance's mother; also called Mistress Lavender
Doctor JORNOL, a physician

Master HIVE, Lavender's father, Ignorance's grandfather; originally written as Goodman Hive
Goodman INDIFFERENT, a husbandman, Lavender's husband, Ignorance's father; also called Master Indifferent
IGNORANCE, daughter of Indifferent and Lavender, Hive's granddaughter
A SURGEON from Epidaurus
A HINE (1.3, *non-speaking*)
Lord BUSYRANE, Grand Admiral of the Locrians, a necromancer; father of Pelorus, Opheltes, and Melissa; his real name is Lycophron, Mylio's brother
Mistress HEROPHILE, a witch
PAMPHILE, a maid (2.1, *non-speaking*)
FOTIS, a maid (2.1, *non-speaking*)
HIPPARIS, a maid or wench (2.1, 4.7–8, *non-speaking*)
An APOTHECARY
NEREIDS (3.6; sing collectively)
A Sailor's BOY (3.8)
DANCERS (4.1, *non-speaking*)
Lord CANNIUS, a Roman, Praetor of Larymna, supposed father of Galanthis and Melanthis
ANTICS of the sea (4.4, *non-speaking*)
Six WITCHES (4.8; one speaks individually, the rest collectively)
Master RUGSBEY, the Constable; also called Constable Rugsbey
Goodman DIDGEON, a watchman
Two WATCHMEN, one of them in his 60s
Goodman GAUNT, a watchman and glover
Cannius' SERVANTS (5.7–8; two speak)
Two PRAETORIANS (5.7, *non-speaking*)
The TRIBUNE of the Plebs, or Recorder (5.9–ep.)

The two heads are speaking parts, but they are also evidently props, at least for some of the time: they cannot be represented by actors' heads sticking out from underneath the set, because they are flown off in the final scene.

Speaking Parts: 37

Doubling
MS A's d.p. notation in respect of the heads reads 'Either of the couple like to either of the couple of young men'. This suggests that the heads may be played by the actors playing either Pelorus and Opheltes or Navarchus and Velinus, whichever pair happens to be free at the time.

Stage Directions and Speech Prefixes
ARCTURUS: *Arcturus The Prologue* (s.d.s and d.p.)
MARSHAL: *A Marshal* (s.d.s)
SAILORS: *certain Sailors* (s.d.s)
PELORUS: [one of] *Two Prisoners* | *Pelorus* | [one of] *The Two couples of young men* (s.d.s); *Pel<orus>* | *Ar<istaeus>* (s.p.s); *Pelorus* [one of the] *Sons to Busyrane, Brothers to Galanthis* (d.p.)
OPHELTES: [one of] *Two Prisoners* | *Opheltes* | [one of] *The Two couples of young men* (s.d.s); *Oph<eltes>* | *Alex<ander>* (s.p.s); *Opheltes* [one of the] *Sons to Busyrane, Brothers to Galanthis* (d.p.)

GALANTHIS: *Galanthis* | [one of] *The Ladies* (s.d.s); *Gal<anthis>* | *Mel<issa>* (s.p.s); *Galanthis* [one of Cannius'] *supposed daughters* (d.p.)
MELANTHIS: *Melanthis* | [one of] *The Ladies* | [Meroe's] *Lady* (s.d.s); *Mel<anthis>* | *Ero<tium>* (s.p.s); *Melanthis* [one of Cannius'] *supposed daughters* (d.p.)
THESPIA: *Thespia* (s.d.s); *Thes<pia>* (s.p.s); *Thespia* [one of Galanthis' and Melanthis'] *waiting women* (d.p.)
MEROE: *Meroe* (s.d.s); *Mer<oe>* (s.p.s); *Meroe* [one of Galanthis' and Melanthis'] *waiting women* (d.p.)
HEADS: *The Heads* (s.d.s); *Heads* (s.d.s and s.p.s); *Head 1* | *Head 2* (s.p.s); *The Two Heads* (d.p.)
LACHES: *Laches* (s.d.s); *Lach<es>* (s.p.s); *Laches An old citizen, Father to Melanthis, Navarchus and Velinus* (d.p.)
NAVARCHUS: *Navarchus* | [one of] *The Two couples of young men* (s.d.s); *Nav<archus>* | *Sm<erdes>* (s.p.s); *Navarchus* [one of the] *Sons to Laches, brothers to Galanthis* (d.p.)
VELINUS: *Velinus* | [one of] *The Two couples of young men* (s.d.s); *Vel<inus>* | *Gn<emon>* (s.p.s); *velinus* [one of the] *Sons to Laches, brothers to Galanthis* (d.p.)
LAVENDER: *Lavender* (s.d.s); [one of the] *Appellants* (s.d.s and s.p.s); *Lav<ender>* (s.p.s); *Goodwife Lavender wife to Indifferent* (d.p.)
JORNOL: *Jornol* (s.d.s and d.p.); [one of the] *Defendants* (s.d.s and s.p.s); *Jor<nol>* (s.p.s); *Dr Jornol A Physician* (d.p.)
HIVE: *Hive* (s.d.s and d.p.); [one of the] *Appellants* (s.d.s and s.p.s); *Hiv<e>* (s.p.s); *Hive Father in Law to Indifferent and Father to Lavender* (d.p.)
INDIFFERENT: *Indifferent* (s.d.s and d.p.); [one of the] *Appellants* (s.d.s and s.p.s); *Ind<ifferent>* (s.p.s); *Goodman Indifferent A Husbandman a Plain fellow* (d.p.)
IGNORANCE: *Ignoraunce* (s.d.s); [one of the] *Appellants* (s.d.s and s.p.s); *Ign<oraunce>* (s.p.s); *Ignoraunce* [Indifferent's and Lavender's] *daughter* (d.p.)
SURGEON: *Chirurgeon* | [one of the] *Defendants* (s.d.s and s.p.s); *A Chirurgeon* (d.p.)
HINE: *A Hine* (s.d.s)
BUSYRANE: *Busyrane* (s.d.s); *Busy<rane>* | *Lyc<ophron>* (s.p.s); *Busyrane A Necromancer Father to Galanthis, Pelorus and Opheltes* (d.p.)
HEROPHILE: *Herophile* (s.d.s); *Her<ophile>* (s.p.s); *Mrs Herophile A witch some say woman of the Parish or A Gentlewoman of fit Property* (d.p.)
PAMPHILE: [one of] *Three bare-foot Maids* (s.d.s)
FOTIS: [one of] *Three bare-foot Maids* (s.d.s)
HIPPARIS: [one of] *Three bare-foot Maids* | *a wench* | *the Maid* (s.d.s)
APOTHECARY: *Apothecary* | [one of the] *Defendants* (s.d.s and s.p.s); *An Apothecary* (d.p.)
NEREIDS: *Nereides* (s.d.s)
BOY: *the Boy* (s.d.s)

CANNIUS: *Cannius* | *the Praetor* (s.d.s); *Cann<ius>* (s.p.s); *Cannius Praetor of Larymna* (d.p.)
ANTICS: *some Matachins or Antics of the Sea* (s.d.s)
WITCHES: *six other witches* | *Witches* | *the witches* | *chorus of witches* (s.d.s); *Witch* (s.p.s); *Witches 6* (d.p.)
RUGSBEY: *Rugsbey* (s.d.s); *Rugs<bey>* (s.p.s); *Mr Constable Rugsbeye* (d.p.)
DIDGEON: [one of] *watchmen Four* (s.d.s); *Watch 1* (s.p.s); [one of] *Watchmen 4* (d.p.)
WATCHMEN: [two of] *watchmen Four* (s.d.s); *Watch 2* | *Watch 3* (s.p.s); [two of] *Watchmen 4* (d.p.)
GAUNT: [one of] *watchmen Four* (s.d.s); *Watch 4* (s.p.s); [one of] *Watchmen 4* (d.p.)
SERVANTS: *Servants* (s.d.s and d.p.); *Servant* (s.p.s)
PRAETORIANS: *Praetorians, Two in number* (s.d.s)
TRIBUNE: *Tribunus Plebis* (s.d.s and d.p.); *Tribunus Plebis or Recorder* (s.d.s); *Tribunus* (s.p.s)

OTHER CHARACTERS
The King of Larymna (1.1; possibly imaginary)
The Roman overlords of Larymna (1.1)
Citizens of Larymna who met Navarchus and Velinus in the street, but greeted them as Pelorus and Opheltes (1.2)
A crew of mariners who, mistaking Velinus' identity, invited him to join them on a voyage to Ophir (1.2)
A recently dead magnifico of Larymna, who left a rich legacy to widows, travellers, and the needy (1.2, 3.1)
The Surgeon's mother, or grandmother (1.3)
The peoples of Argos and of Sardinia, whom the Surgeon cured of the sullens (1.3)
The Jews, Thracians, Arcadians, Goths, and Sybarites, all treated by the Surgeon (1.3)
Democritus, whom the Surgeon cured of scurvy (1.3)
Heraclitus, whom the Surgeon cured of mumps (1.3)
The citizens of Larymna (2.3, 3.8)
A crowd of people trying to claim their share of the dead magnifico's legacy, including cobblers, shoemakers, tinkers, locksmiths, coppersmiths, ironsmiths, cutlers, pewterers, braziers, carriers, curriers, carters, caters, fishmongers, butchers, brewers, bakers, cooks, sow-gelders, dung-farmers, and bricklayers (3.1)
A man who brawled with Laches in an effort to deny him a share of the legacy (3.1)
Officers who arrested Laches as a suspected pirate (3.1)
The host of the inn where Laches was staying, who vouched for him (3.1)
Mariners hired to crew a ship for Laches and his sons (3.6)
An oyster-wife who told Navarchus he was a wanted man (3.8)
A linen-draper who tried to call in a debt from Navarchus (3.8)
A lawyer who asked Navarchus to name his accomplices in the robbery (3.8)
The parson of Indifferent's parish (4.6)
A lady whose big train delayed Laches (5.2)
Pelorus' mother, Busyrane's wife (5.3)
Lavender's dead great-grandmother (5.5)
A lord who gave Meroe a pair of gloves (5.6)

SETTING
Period: antiquity. The precise indications are contradictory: Larymna is under Roman law (suggesting some time after 146 BC); the Surgeon claims to have treated both Heraclitus and Democritus (who respectively died in the 5th and 4th centuries BC); and the low-life characters' dialogue is full of Christian references. The action probably takes place in January (six months before the Feast of Neptune in July).
Time-Scheme: The action takes place during a single day, with 1.1 in the morning.
Place: Larymna

Geography
Greece: Locris; Delphos (i.e. Delphi); Epidaurus; Arcadia; Messene; Phocis; Mantinea; Malea
Rome: Santa Maria Rotunda
Italy: Sybaris
Thrace: Byzantium; Abdera
[*Europe*]: Gotland; Spain; France; Almain
Britain: Walsingham; the Counter prison
[*Mediterranean*]: Sardinia; Rhodes; Paros
Asia Minor: Ephesus; Chalcedon; Troy; Tenedos; Lystra; Iconium
Asia Major: Persia; the Isles of Ophir; Jewry; Babylon; Damascus; Antioch; Seleucia
Africa: Numidia; Libya
The Indies

SOURCES
Narrative: Plautus, *Menaechmi* or William Shakespeare, *The Comedy of Errors* (**944**), and possibly *Much Ado About Nothing* (**1148**; 5.1)
Verbal: Publilius Syrus, *Sententiae* (5.6, cited); Virgil, *Eclogues* 1 (4.2), 3 (4.5, 5.1, 5.10), 8 (epigraph), 10 (2.1), *Aeneid* 4 (1.2, 3.8, 4.3, 5.8), 10 (3.4); Horace, *Epistles* 1.6 (2.3), 1.10 (5.6); Ovid, *Heroides* 1 (2.5), 15 (5.6), *Metamorphoses* 1 (1.3, 4.5), 2 (4.5), 8 (4.5); Bible: Matthew 19.24 (4.6); Suetonius, *Twelve Caesars*: Claudius (4.1); Juvenal, *Satires* 15 (2.4, cited); *Disticha Catonis* (3.4); Ausonius, *Idylls* 20 (4.5); Edmund Spenser, *The Faerie Queene* 3 (1590, repr. 1617; the name Busyrane)
Music: John Dowland, *The Second Book of Songs or Airs* 2: Lachrymae (1600; 2.1)
Works Mentioned: *Anastisis moron*, a.k.a. *The Resurrection of Fools* (4.1)

LANGUAGE
English
Latin: 274 words (1.1–4, 2.1–3, 2.5, 3.1–5, 3.7, 4.2–3, 4.5–6, 5.1–2, 5.5–7, 5.9–10, ep.); Galanthis, Navarchus, Hive, Jornol, Surgeon, Busyrane, Lavender, Meroe,

Laches, Indifferent, Pelorus, Melanthis, Rugsbey, Thespia, Tribune, 1 Servant, Cannius)
Greek: 2 words (4.1; Thespia)
Italian: 6 words (5.2; Laches)
Spanish: 3 words (ep.; Indifferent)
Gibberish: 36 magic words (5.10; Busyrane)
Dialect: Hive and Indifferent speak intermittently in a 'rustic' accent, and Laches quotes a sample of the same in 3.1.

Indifferent's closing line, including his Spanish phrase, is present in MS A but omitted in H; both MSS, however, direct its inclusion in the variant version.

FORM
Metre: prose; a little pentameter and trochaic tetrameter
Rhyme: couplets and blank verse
Prologue: 24 lines of prose, spoken by Arcturus
Act-Division: 5 acts, with musical interludes
Epilogue: 26 lines of prose, spoken by the Tribune, Jornol, Hive, and Indifferent
Lines (Spoken):
  ORIGINAL VERSION: 3,131 (233 verse, 2,898 prose)
  VARIANT VERSION: 3,052 (233 verse, 2,819 prose)
Lines (Written): 3,534 (A); 3,645 (H)

STAGING
Doors: at least three doors (5.2, s.d. mentions the middle door)
Discovery Space: The play requires two separate discovery areas. One is covered with a 'veil' and set with two rocks above the altar of Neptune, which are visible at the start of the action and covered during the first scene (1.1, s.d.); it later opens and closes again in some scenes (2.1, 4.5, 4.7, 5.10, s.d.). The other is covered with an arras (1.3, s.d.): Lavender is discovered asleep in a chair (1.3, s.d.; an option is offered to have her simply brought on stage)
Stage: mentioned (2.1, 4.2, 5.2, s.d.)
Within: sound effects (2.1, 4.2, s.d.)
Above: Lavender pours water from above onto Hive (2.2, s.d.); Galanthis and Melanthis ascend 'within', each at a different end of the stage (4.2, s.d.; i.e. there are two backstage routes of ascent)
Audience: addressed as 'gentlemen' (prol., 3.1, 4.5, ep.), 'honest gentlemen' (1.4, ep.), and 'sirs' (4.5); said to be seated (prol.)
Miscellaneous: the heads are directed to vanish by being 'flown off' (5.10, s.d.)

MUSIC AND SOUND
Sound Effects: a long sea-fight and a 'boisterous hurricane' (1.1, s.d.); sound of dog within (2.1, 4.2, s.d.)
Music: consort of music 'knocked up' at the end of each act (1.4, 2.5, 3.8, 4.8, s.d.)
On-Stage Music: Maids play percussion on the kettles to accompany their dance (2.1, s.d.)

Songs:
1: 'Triumph, triumph sing', 1.1, Sailors, 32 lines;
2: 'Heave we our garlands to his shrine', Pelorus and Opheltes, 1.4, 18 lines;
3: 'Come along, you devilish wights', 2.1, Herophile, 18 lines, to the tune of 'Dowland's Cock' (i.e. Lachrymae); *tune extant*;
4: 'Whither now will my mistress be flying', 2.5, Meroe, 12 lines;
5: 'Will solemn pace and solemn hurrying', 3.6, Nereids, 17 lines;
6: 'Farewell, my love, my love, farewell', 3.8, Sailor's Boy, 25 lines;
7: 'See, now see, the married couple', 4.1, Thespia, 21 lines;
8: 'Hold halberds and Welsh hooks the trial', 5.1, Watchmen, 16 lines;
9: 'A wedding, a wedding, my sister dear', 5.6, Thespia, 16 lines.
Dance: Maids dance (2.1, s.d.); a dance on the shore, with Meroe, Thespia, and others (4.1, s.d.); witches dance (4.8, s.d.)

PROPS
Pyrotechnics: fire (1.3, implicit; presumably used to heat a knife for cauterizing); a pan of burning coals (4.7–8, s.d.)
Weapons: Marshal's two-handed sword (1.1, s.d.); a knife (1.3, implicit); a holly wand (2.2, dialogue); Laches' arming sword (3.1, 5.2–3, 5.7–8, s.d.); possibly a cudgel (3.1, dialogue; but it may refer to Laches' sword); possibly antics' swords (4.4, implicit); four halberds (5.1, dialogue); arrows (5.7–10, s.d.)
Musical Instruments: two silver sailors' whistles (1.1, 1.4, 3.5–6, 5.2–3, 5.7, s.d.); a silver whistle (3.8, s.d.)
Clothing: linen garments (2.4–5, dialogue); two mantles, one of crimson velvet with gold lace and purl, the other cloth of tissue with gold oak leaves (5.10, s.d.; initially packed up as trusses; each is embroidered with a different mythological scene); two large seal-rings (5.10, s.d.)
Money: a purse of gold (2.1, s.d.)
Animals: a cur or small white 'shag-whippet' (2.1, 4.2, s.d.); possibly a toad (4.7–8, dialogue; squeezed on stage)
Food and Drink: a medicine (3.3, dialogue; drunk on stage); a banquet (3.6–8, 4.3–4, s.d.; partly eaten on stage); standing bowls of wine (3.6–8, 4.3–4, dialogue; drunk on stage)
Small Portable Objects: a cushion (1.3, dialogue); a pallet (1.3, dialogue; i.e. a surgeon's cupping-glass); three copper kettles (2.1, s.d.); three iron knockers or pestles (2.1, s.d.); a dish of water (2.2, s.d.); two baskets (2.4–5, dialogue); an engraving tool (3.8, s.d.); a white staff of office (4.4, 5.7, s.d.); a book (4.5, s.d.; 5.3, implicit); a magic wand or painted staff (4.5, 5.7–10 s.d.; 5.3, dialogue); the shaft of a distaff (4.6, s.d.); trinkets, including a blue seed, a lock of hair, poisoned venom (possibly squeezed out of a toad on stage), and

a hempen double-lace (4.7–8, dialogue; all burned on stage); possibly two bills (5.4, dialogue); a box (5.5, s.d.)

Large Portable Objects: ropes (1.1, s.d.); two severed heads resembling Pelorus and Opheltes (1.1, 2.1, 4.5, 4.7, 5.10, s.d.; perhaps alternatively played by actors until 5.10; in 2.1 they have garlands of cypress and yew, in 4.7 they are blindfolded, and in 5.10 they are 'baffled and banded'); a wooden chair (1.3, s.d.); a large, square, black bag hung on a golden chain (1.4, s.d.; hung around Busyrane's neck); a long iron chain (4.8, s.d.; linking Meroe and the six witches about the waists); six broomsticks (4.8, s.d.); a stool (5.1, dialogue); a cushion (5.1, dialogue); a tribunal chair with a canopy of state over it (5.7–10, s.d.)

Scenery: a title-board (d.p.); sundry hollow rocks (1.1, s.d.); two rocks with 'chiefs of men' atop them (1.1, s.d.); an altar of Neptune, made of red marble with a black marble scutcheon, and 'Ara Neptuni' written above (1.1, 3.6, 3.8, s.d.; 1.4, 4.3–4, dialogue; in 1.4 it is decorated with Pelorus' and Opheltes' sea-garlands, which are then removed in 3.6 and 3.8; silver words are inscribed on the scutcheon in 3.8; a deleted specification is a grey stone horse painted on the altar); a 'veil' (1.1, 2.1, 4.4, 4.7, s.d.); an arras (1.3, 2.1, 4.8, s.d.)

Miscellaneous: a handful of powder or turds (4.7, s.d.; thrown in a character's face)

Oddly, two stage directions seem to contradict the action: in 2.2, Hive refers directly to the holly wand he is carrying, yet the s.d. at the head of the scene reads 'No holly wand here'. Likewise in 3.3, Indifferent must drink the medicine in order to be made deaf, but the s.d. reads 'He drank not here'. Perhaps these notations should be understood as records of things that went wrong in a particular performance, rather like a modern stage manager's report.

COSTUMES
MARSHAL: sailor's weeds (1.1, s.d.)
SAILORS: sea-garlands (1.1, s.d.)
PELORUS: black hair (dialogue); crowned with cypress and yew (1.1, s.d.); a canvas sailor's suit (1.4, 5.2–3, 5.7–10, s.d.); crowned with a sea-garland (1.4, 5.2–3, 5.7–10, s.d.; removed on stage); a red cap (1.4, 3.5–6, 5.2–3, 5.7–10, s.d.); a vizard (5.10, s.d.)
OPHELTES: fair hair (dialogue); crowned with cypress and yew (1.1, s.d.); a canvas sailor's suit (1.4, 5.2–3, 5.7–10, s.d.); crowned with a sea-garland (1.4, 5.2–3, 5.7–10, s.d.; removed on stage); a blue cap (1.4, 3.6, 5.2–3, 5.7–10, s.d.); a vizard (5.10, s.d.)
GALANTHIS: golden hair (dialogue); a mask and a scarf (1.1, s.d); 'costly' garments (1.1, dialogue); white garments (2.4, dialogue)
MELANTHIS: black hair (dialogue); a mask and a scarf (1.1, s.d); 'costly' garments (1.1, dialogue); white garments (2.4, dialogue); black clothes, with dishevelled hair (4.7–8, s.d.)
MEROE: dressed as either a horned goat or devil or a black-bearded doctor (4.8, s.d.); a vizard (4.8, s.d.; removed on stage)

HEADS: see under PROPS: **Large Portable Objects**
LACHES: a black sea-suit (5.2–3, s.d.); a hat pinned up at one side (d.p.); a red 'swashing' scarf (3.1, 5.2–3, s.d.; used to hang his sword); a garland (5.2–3, s.d.); possibly a bonnet (5.2–3, dialogue; may be just a figure of speech)
NAVARCHUS: black hair (implicit); a canvas sailor's suit (3.7–8, 5.1, 5.7–10, s.d.); a red cap (3.7–8, 5.1, 5.7–10, s.d.); a vizard (5.10, s.d.)
VELINUS: fair hair (implicit); a canvas sailor's suit (3.6, dialogue; 5.1, 5.7–10, s.d.); a blue cap (3.8, 5.1, 5.7–10, s.d.); a vizard (5.10, s.d.)
JORNOL: a beard (s.d.)
INDIFFERENT: grey hair (dialogue); pockets (2.2, 4.6, s.d.); breeches (4.6, dialogue); spectacles (4.6, dialogue; put on on stage); a biggin on his head (5.4–5, implicit); a vizard (5.10, s.d.)
BUSYRANE: a black velvet gown (d.p.); apparelled like a Turk (1.4, s.d.); a round velvet cap (1.4, s.d.); a garment with a collar (5.3, dialogue)
HEROPHILE: black clothes, with dishevelled hair (4.7–8, s.d.); a blue surplice (4.7–8, s.d.; put on on stage)
PAMPHILE and FOTIS: bare feet, red petticoats, loose hair dangling over their shoulders (2.1, s.d.)
HIPPARIS: a red petticoat, bare feet, and loose hair dangling over her shoulders (2.1, 4.7–8, s.d.)
CANNIUS: a black velvet gown, with gold lace on the sleeves (4.4, 5.7–10, s.d.)
WITCHES: black clothes, dishevelled hair (4.7–8, s.d.)
PRAETORIANS: light armour (5.7–10, s.d.)

As with the props, there is a curious notation at the head of 2.5 in MS A: Meroe is 'not an Ethiop'.

EARLY TEXTUAL HISTORY
1646: transcribed by William Percy as part of a MS collection of his plays (A); 79 pages on 40 leaves; list of roles; Latin epigraph.
1647: transcribed by Percy as part of a MS collection of his plays (H); 40 leaves. The copy was A.

EDITION
John Boyle, unpublished transcription made in c. 1978; copy in the Shakespeare Institute Library, Stratford-upon-Avon.

REFERENCES
Annals 1632; Chambers, iii. 464–5; Hazlitt, 164; HLQ 1 (1938), 412–16; REED: Ecclesiastical London, 291.

2392. Play

EVIDENCE
Henry More, *Historia missionis Anglicanae* (1660).

88 | 2393. Masque of Soldiers

GENRE
Contemporary: *drama*

AUTHOR
Thomas Strange

He was educated at Oxford and Gray's Inn, and was a friend of Ben Jonson.

DATE
Limits: 1612–39

LANGUAGE
English

EARLY STAGE HISTORY
More says that Strange 'arranged a drama which he had composed in his native tongue' ('in dramata nativo idiomate composita digerendis') at some time during his retirement in the Spanish Netherlands; this might be taken to mean that he supervised a production, perhaps in Ghent (where he died in 1639).

REFERENCES
Henry More, *Historia missionis Anglicanae* (Saint-Omer, 1660), sig. 3B4ᵛ.

2393. Masque of Soldiers

TEXT
MS (Trowbridge: Wiltshire Record Office, MS 865/502, pp. 13–15); authorial holograph.

GENRE
masque

TITLE
MS: *An Introduction to the Sword Dance*

AUTHOR
John Clavell

DATE
Christmas 1632–3

ORIGINAL PRODUCTION
Earl of Barrymore's household, at either at Castlelyons, County Cork, or the Castle of Shandon, near Cork

PLOT
Peace has sapped the vigour of some soldiers, who now pursue her in order to take reprisals; she takes refuge with the principal member of the audience. The soldiers threaten the other ladies present, but are reprimanded by Mars: the gods have renounced war and the soldiers should do likewise. He rescues Peace, then leads the soldiers in a sword dance. After further dancing, the soldiers' leader acknowledges his wrongdoing and proclaims the power of love and beauty.

ROLES
PEACE, a female character
SOLDIERS, possibly Irish kerns, the masquers (only speak *within*)
The Soldiers' LEADER
MARS, a god
A PAGE attending on Mars (*non-speaking*)

Speaking Parts: 3
Allegorical Roles: 1 (Peace, fully integrated with the others)

Stage Directions and Speech Prefixes
PEACE: *Peace* (s.d.s and s.p.s)
SOLDIERS: *the masquers* | *the soldiers* (s.d.s)
LEADER: *the Leader* (s.d.s); *Leader* (s.p.s)
MARS: *Mars* (s.d.s and s.p.s)
PAGE: *a Page* (s.d.s)

OTHER CHARACTERS
Mars's fellow gods, including Jove

LANGUAGE
English

FORM
Metre: pentameter
Rhyme: couplets and blank verse
Lines (Spoken): 52 (50 verse, 2 prose)
Lines (Written): 85

STAGING
Within: noise and speech (s.d.)
Audience: Peace appeals directly to a member of the audience, and the masquers also interact with the ladies at two points (s.d.)

Only female audience members are mentioned. This might be because the audience is all of the same gender (perhaps because the male members of the household are all in the cast), or because the ladies are sitting in a distinct, possibly segregated area of the room.

MUSIC AND SOUND
Sound Effects: noise within (s.d.)
Dance: a sword dance (s.d.); a 'few dances' by the masquers and ladies from the audience (s.d.); a 'warlike masque done with many pretty changes' by the masquers alone (s.d.)

PROPS
Weapons: masquers' swords (s.d.); Mars's sword and target (s.d.)
Clothing: a coat of mail (s.d.)

COSTUMES
PEACE: a white habit (s.d.)
MASQUERS and LEADER: cassocks, bases, and helmets (s.d.); scabbards (implicit)

EARLY STAGE HISTORY
1632–3: performed at Christmas (Tuesday 25 December 1632 to Sunday 6 January 1633) in the household of David Barry, 1st Earl of Barrymore. The audience included Alice Barry, Countess of Barrymore, and other ladies.

EARLY TEXTUAL HISTORY
1632–40: transcribed by John Clavell into a **MS** commonplace book; 3 pages on 2 leaves.

EDITION
Alan Fletcher, in *Drama, Performance, and Polity in Pre-Cromwellian Ireland* (Cork, 2000), 310–13.

REFERENCES
Fletcher, 214; Alan Fletcher, *Drama, Performance, and Polity in Pre-Cromwellian Ireland* (Cork, 2000), 234–8.

1633

2394. Masque at West Harting

EVIDENCE
Sir John Caryll's household accounts (London: British Library, Add. MS 28242, fo. 23ᵛ).

GENRE
masque
Contemporary: masque

DATE
January 1633

ORIGINAL PRODUCTION
Sir John Caryll's household at West Harting, Sussex

EARLY STAGE HISTORY
1633: performed in January at Sir John Caryll's household at West Harting, Sussex. A man was sent for by the steward, Mr Henslowe, in connection with the masque, and he was paid 5s on Friday 4 January.

REFERENCES
REED: Sussex, 197.

2395. The Shepherds' Paradise

TEXT
Six substantive witnesses:
- **C:** MS (Washington: Folger, MS V. b. 204); late scribal transcript of an early state of the text; arranges a substantial part of the dialogue as blank verse;
- **O:** printed in 1659 (Wing M2475); cut text;
- **P:** MS (London: British Library, Add. MS 41617); the 'Petworth' MS; scribal transcript of a cut text;
- **Sl:** MS (London: British Library, MS Sloane 3649); careless scribal transcript of an incompletely abbreviated text; includes induction and entr'acte songs;
- **St:** MS (London: British Library, MS Stowe 976); scribal transcript of a cut text; the MS is damaged, resulting in a lacuna in Act 4;
- **Tx:** MS (Washington: Folger, MS V. b. 203); the 'Tixall' MS; scribal transcript of a heavily abbreviated text; includes induction and entr'acte songs.

This represents at least two substantive states of the text:
- **A:** original, prolix version, represented in MS C, the fullest exemplar of the long state;
- **B:** final, heavily cut but still very long version, perhaps as performed in January 1633, represented in MS Tx.

Other exemplars probably reflect intermediate states of abbreviation. No single exemplar includes every element, but the complexity of the textual problem is incommensurate with the prospective rewards of a solution.

Additional information derives from Inigo Jones's design drawings (cited as J), and from bills presented by two haberdashers (Ha), the tailor (T), and the hosier (Ho) for work and services supplied in connection with the production (Kew: National Archives, LR 5/63–5).

GENRE
pastoral
Contemporary: pastoral (Lord Chamberlain's warrants, Works Account, Scudamore papers); comedy (hosier's bill, William Whiteway's diary, O t.p.); masque (Revels Accounts); piece (O epistle)

TITLE
Performed/Printed: *The Shepherds' Paradise*
Contemporary: *Bellessa the Shepherds' Queen*
Alternative Modernization: *The Shepherd's Paradise*

AUTHOR
Walter Montagu

DATE
January 1633

ORIGINAL PRODUCTION
Queen Henrietta Maria's Court at Denmark House

PLOT
Prince Basilino is betrothed to Saphira, the Princess of Navarre, whom he has never met; but he has fallen in love with Fidamira, not knowing that she in turn is in love with Agenor. The King cannot approve the Prince's marriage to Fidamira, since it is an affair of state rather than simply of the heart. Basilino is granted permission to leave the kingdom, in order that he may forget her; he asks that Agenor be his sole companion, and that the King act as Fidamira's protector in his absence. Fidamira asks Agenor to serve the Prince loyally as a mark of his love for her.

Basilino decides to visit the Shepherds' Paradise of Galicia, established two generations ago as a haven of chastity: it is on the way to Navarre, and there is an interesting local custom, soon to take place, of annually electing a queen, chosen for her superior beauty. He and Agenor set off incognito, and arrive in time to see

Bellessa become the new Queen, which arouses the jealousy of her predecessor, Pantamora. Meanwhile, the King has Fidamira brought to court from her father's house, but she asks permission to return home for a few days to perform some obligations. The King agrees, granting her his daughter for company, but has fallen in love with her and attempts to call on her in disguise at home. She decides to flee to Galicia, disguising herself as a Moor.

Using the name Moramante, Basilino supplicates to join the order of shepherds, and is accepted. Agenor leaves in accordance with the law which limits foreigners to a stay of only three days. Fidamira, posing as 'Gemella', tells a story of being amorously pursued by both father and son, and she too is admitted to the order. Agenor meets the penitent King and returns to Galicia, telling Basilino that Saphira is dead, which frees him to leave and marry Fidamira; but Agenor suspects he is now more interested in Bellessa, and is granted admission to the order. Both he and 'Moramante' fall in love with Bellessa, while Pantamora falls for 'Moramante'; Agenor maintains a pretence that he loves Fidamira. Basilino writes to his father that he is no longer interested in Fidamira, except as a possible stepmother.

'Moramante' finds Bellessa sleeping, and kisses her. Though unchastity is a capital offence in Galicia, Bellessa sentences him only to hope for consummation of his love. Recognizing their mutual attraction, Pantamora hopes they will take the opportunity to leave the paradise at the upcoming election, allowing her to reclaim the throne. Fidamira sheds her disguise and poses as her own ghost haunting Agenor, but then unexpectedly meets the King, who has come to Galicia incognito to see the election; he promises to keep her secret. Bellessa goes to consult an echo in the woods, and is followed by 'Moramante'; the echo establishes the truth of their love for each other.

Another visitor arrives in Galicia: Romero, charged with the custody of the King of Navarre's children. He lost two of them in their infancy at the Siege of Pamplona twenty years ago; the disappearance of Saphira makes it a hat-trick and leaves the kingdom without an heir. He is surprised to see Agenor wearing a jewel which belonged to the missing Prince, and, in view of his youth, assumes he bought it from a soldier who took it as booty at the siege. At the election ceremony, he identifies Bellessa as the missing Saphira, and she recounts how she absconded because she was unwilling to be married to Basilino, a man she has never met, purely as a diplomatic convenience. 'Moramante' confirms that he is really Basilino. It also emerges that Agenor is really the lost heir of Navarre, captured at the siege but saved by the importunacy of young Basilino. 'Gemella' is elected Queen, but Pantamora complains that this is unconstitutional because she is black (and therefore ugly). She is revealed to be Fidamira, who in turn is revealed to be the third missing child of Navarre, and therefore Agenor's sister.

A double royal wedding is arranged for the two princes, but Fidamira stays on in Galicia as Queen.

> B-Text
> In this version, the King does not attempt to visit Fidamira in her own home.

SCENE DESIGNATION

1.1–7, 2.1–5, 3.1–10, 4.1–9, 5.1–13 (C has act-division and incomplete scene-division)

A prop remains on stage between 3.6 and 3.7. The stage is not clear at 4.9–5.1.

> B-Text
> ind., 1.1–7, int.1, 2.1–4, int.2, 3.1–9, int.3, 4.1–6, int.4, 5.1–8 (MS has act-division and some inconsistent scene-division)
>
> This corresponds with the A-text division as follows: A.1.1–7 = B.1.1–7; A.2.1–2 = B.2.1–2; A.2.4–5 = B.2.3–4; A.3.1–3 = B.3.1–3; A.3.5–10 = B.3.4–9; A.4.1 = B.4.1; A.4.3–4 = B.4.2–3; A.4.5 = B.4.5; A.4.6 = B.4.4; A.4.8 = B.4.6; A.4.9 = B.5.1a; A.5.1 = B.5.1.b; A.5.3–5 = B.5.2–4; A.5.6–7 = B.5.5; A.5.8–9 = B.5.6–7; A.5.13 = B.5.8. (Note the reordering of two scenes in Act 4.) The induction and interludes are B-text additions, and the following A-text scenes are omitted: 2.3, 3.4, 4.2, 4.7, 5.2, 5.10–12. (A small amount of text from A.5.11 is used in B.5.7.)
> The scene changes in 5.5 without the stage being cleared.

ROLES

OSORIO, a Castilian courtier

TIMANTE, a Castilian courtier

Prince BASILINO of Castile, the King's son, a young man; assumes the alias Moramante

FIDAMIRA, a lady of the Castilian court, supposed Bonorio's daughter; in her early 20s; assumes the alias Gemella, a Moor; poses as her own ghost; turns out to be Princess Miranda of Navarre, sister of Pallante and Saphira

AGENOR, a Castilian courtier, Basilino's friend and companion; in his early 20s; assumes the alias Genorio; turns out to be Prince Pallante of Navarre, brother of Saphira and Miranda

The KING of Castile, Basilino's father; an old man

BELLESSA, Queen of the Galician shepherds; less than 30 years old; said to be of French birth, but in reality Princess Saphira of Navarre, sister of Pallante and Miranda

CAMENA, a shepherdess of Galicia

PANTAMORA, the previous Queen of the shepherds

MELIDORO, a shepherd of Galicia

MARTIRO, a shepherd, Romero's son

VOTORIO, a Galician priest

BONORIO, a gentleman of Castile, supposed Fidamira's father

Two SOLDIERS (3.9; one may be *non-speaking*)

An ECHO (5.7, *within*)

ROMERO, an old courtier of Navarre, Martiro's father

1633

Speaking Parts: 16–17

B-Text
Induction
DIANA, a goddess: *new role*
APOLLO, god of harmony and wit: *new role*
Two MEN attending Apollo (*non-speaking*): *new roles*

Main Action
PANTAMORA: now also called Pantamor

Speaking Parts: 18–19

Doubling
The roles of Osorio and Romero were doubled in 1633.

Stage Directions and Speech Prefixes
OSORIO: *Osorio* (s.d.s); *Oso<rio>* (s.p.s); [one of] *The King's Servants Osorio* (d.p.)
TIMANTE: *Timante* (s.d.s); *Tim<ante>* (s.p.s); [one of] *The King's Servants Timante* (d.p.)
BASILINO: *The Prince* | *Basilino* (s.d.s); *Moramante* (s.d.s and s.p.s); *Prince* | *Bas<ilino>* (s.p.s); *The Prince, Basilino, in his disguise, Moramante* (d.p.)
FIDAMIRA: *Fidamira* | *Fidamira called Gemella* | [one of] *the Ladies* (s.d.s); *Gemella* (s.d.s and s.p.s); *Fida<mira>* | *Ghost* (s.p.s); *The Prince's Mistress Fidamira, in her disguise Gemella* (d.p.)
AGENOR: *Agenor* (s.d.s); *Genorio* (s.d.s and s.p.s); *Agen<or>* (s.p.s); *The Prince's friend Agenor, in his disguise Genorio* (d.p.)
KING: *the King* (s.d.s); *King* (s.p.s); *The King of Castile* (d.p.)
BELLESSA: [one of] *the Shepherdesses* | *Bellessa* | *the Queen* | [one of] *the Ladies* (s.d.s); *Bellessa* | *Bellesa* (s.d.s and s.p.s); *Queen* (s.p.s); *The Shepherds' Queen Bellessa* (d.p.)
CAMENA: [one of] *the Shepherdesses* | [one of Bellessa's] *train* | [one of] *the Queen's Company* | [one of the Queen's] *train* | [one of] *the Ladies* *Camena* | *Camina* (s.d.s); *Camaena* (s.d.s and s.p.s); [one of the] *Shepherdesses Camaena* (d.p.)
PANTAMORA: [one of] *the Shepherdesses* | [one of Bellessa's] *train* | [one of] *the Queen's Company* | [one of the Queen's] *train* | [one of] *the Ladies* (s.d.s); *Pantamora* (s.d.s and s.p.s); [one of the] *Shepherdesses Pantamora* (d.p.)
MELIDORO: *Melidoro* (s.d.s and s.p.s); [one of Bellessa's] *train* | [one of] *the Queen's Company* | [one of the Queen's] *train* (s.d.s; also mistranscribed as *Melidora*); [one of the] *Shepherds Melidoro* (d.p.)
MARTIRO: *Martiro* (s.d.s and s.p.s); [one of Bellessa's] *train* | [one of] *the Queen's Company* | [one of the Queen's] *train* (s.d.s); [one of the] *Shepherds Martiro* (d.p.)
VOTORIO: *Votorio* (s.d.s); *Voto<rio>* (s.p.s); *The High Priest Votorio* (d.p.)
BONORIO: *Bonorio, Fidamira's Father* | [Fidamira's] *Father* (s.d.s); *Bon<orio>* (s.p.s)
SOLDIERS: *two Soldiers* (s.d.s); *Soldier* (s.p.s)
ECHO: *Echo* (s.p.s)
ROMERO: *Romero* (s.d.s); *Rom<ero>* (s.p.s)

B-Text
DIANA: *Diana* (s.p.s)
APOLLO: *Apollo* (s.p.s)
OSORIO: *Osorio* (s.d.s); *Osor<io>* (s.p.s); *Osorio* [one of] *Two Courtiers* (d.p.)
TIMANTE: *Timante* (s.d.s); *Timant<e>* (s.p.s); *Timante* [one of] *Two Courtiers* (d.p.)
BASILINO: *Basilino* | *The Prince* | *Moromante* | *Moramante* | [one of the] *Society* | [one of] *the Society* (s.d.s); *Basil<ino>* | *Moram<ante>* | *Morom<ante>* (s.p.s); *Basilino, the Prince, called in his disguise Moramante* (d.p.)
FIDAMIRA: *Fidamira* | *Gemella* | *Gamella* (s.d.s); *Fidam<ira>* | *Gemell<a>* | *Ghost* (s.p.s); *Fidamira* [Basilino's] *Mistress called in her disguise Gemella* (d.p.)
AGENOR: *Agenor* | [one of] *the Society* (s.d.s); *Genorio* | *Pallante* (s.d.s and s.p.s); *Agen<or>* (s.p.s); *Agenor* [Basilino's] *friend called in his disguise Genorio* (d.p.)
KING: *The King* (s.d.s); *King* (s.d.s and s.p.s); *King of Castile* (d.p.)
BELLESSA: *Bellessa* (s.d.s and s.p.s); *the Queen* (s.d.s); *Queen* (s.d.s and s.p.s); *Belessa the Shepherds' Queen* (d.p.)
CAMENA: *Camaena* | [part of the Queen's] *Train* | [one of the] *Society* | [one of] *the Society* (s.d.s); *Came<na>* (s.p.s); *Camaena* [one of] *Two Shepherdesses* (d.p.)
PANTAMORA: *Pantamora* | [part of the Queen's] *Train* | [one of the] *Society* | [one of] *the Society* (s.d.s); *Pant<amora>* (s.p.s); *Pantamora* [one of] *Two Shepherdesses* (d.p.)
VOTORIO: *Vortorio* | *Votorio* | [one of the] *Society* | [one of] *the Society* (s.d.s); *Voto<rio>* (s.p.s); *Votorio A Priest* (d.p.)
MELIDORO: *Melidoro* | [part of the Queen's] *Train* | [one of the] *Society* | [one of] *the Society* (s.d.s); *Melid<oro>* (s.p.s); *Melidoro* [one of] *Two Shepherds* (d.p.)
MARTIRO: *Mastiro* (s.d.s and s.p.s); [part of the Queen's] *Train* | *Martiro* | [one of the] *Society* | [one of] *the Society* (s.d.s); *Martiro* [one of] *Two Shepherds* (d.p.)
SOLDIERS: *two Soldiers* (s.d.s); *Soldier* (s.p.s)
ECHO: *Echo* (s.p.s)
ROMERO: *Romero* (s.d.s); *Romer<o>* (s.p.s); *Romero a Lord of Navarr, father to Martiro* (d.p.)
BONORIO: *Bonoso* | *Bonoso* [Fidamira's] *father* (s.d.s); *Bon<oso>* (s.p.s); *Bonoso a Lord of Castile supposed father to Fidamira* (d.p.)

OTHER CHARACTERS
The people of Castile (1.4)
The King's guard (1.4, 1.6–7)
Princess Arabella, the King's daughter (1.7, 2.2, 5.13)
The King's grandfather (2.1)
Sabina, daughter of the King's grandfather, who founded the Shepherds' Paradise (2.1, 4.4, 4.7, 4.9, 5.13)
The Dauphin of France, a suitor to Sabina (2.1)
The Prince of Navarre, a suitor to Sabina (2.1, 4.4, 4.7, 4.9)
Nobles of both sexes who accompanied Sabina to the Shepherds' Paradise (2.1)
The King of Navarre, father of Saphira, Pallante, and Miranda (2.1, 5.8, 5.13)
The King of Albion (2.9)
The mother of Pallante and Saphira (5.13)
The soldiers of Castile who sacked Pamplona (5.13)

B-Text
Jove, King of the gods (ind.)
The god of love (ind.)
Juno (ind.)

Omits: Saphira's mother; soldiers at Pamplona

SETTING
Period: the action includes scenes (2.1 and 5.9–13) which take place on 1 May in two consecutive years
Time-Scheme: three days pass between 1.6 and 2.1; 2.5 takes place on the afternoon of the same day as 2.4; 3.2–3 take place on the same day; nearly a year passes between 2.1 and 4.3; 5.9–13 take place on the same day (5.9 and 5.11 in the morning), which is four or five days after 4.8, two days after 5.1, and the day after 5.4–5; less than three hours pass between 5.7 and 5.11
Place: Castile and Galicia

Geography
Spain
Navarre: Pamplona
France
Albion
The Antipodes

B-Text
Omits Antipodes

SOURCES
Narrative: François Rabelais, *Gargantua* (1534); William Shakespeare, *Hamlet* (**1259**; 1.4), *Cymbeline* (**1623**; 1.1, 5.13).
Verbal: William Shakespeare, *Romeo and Juliet* (**987**; 5.1), *Hamlet* (**1259**; 1.4)
Design: Girolamo Rainaldi, Engraving of St Peter's, Rome (early seventeenth century; Tomb); Aegidius Sadeler (after Paul Bril), *The Twelve Months*: Maius, Junius (1615; Love's Cabinet); Jacques Callot, *Le grand parterre de Nancy* (1625; Garden); Spanish School portrait of the Infanta Maria Anna of Habsburg (*c.*

1623–9; Fidamira's costume); Alfonso Parigi, *La Flora* (1628; proscenium; Palace in Trees)

The Prince's request for permission to travel, and his father's engagement of Agenor to report on his behaviour while he is away, both draw on different aspects of *Hamlet*. The scene also includes a verbal echo: the clouds hang on Basilino (Malone TLN 337–8) just as they do on Hamlet.

LANGUAGE
English

FORM
Metre: prose; a little tetrameter

Much of the text is set out in C as if it were blank verse, whereas all the other witnesses treat it as mainly prose. I have accepted their 'majority decision' on the point and recorded the bulk of the dialogue as prose; it certainly has no metrical rhythm suggestive of verse, however loose. Even so, C's lineation might still be worth taking seriously as something other than a scribal aberration, for two reasons. First, some passages are transcribed as prose, so the scribe evidently thought in terms of some distinction between prose and verse, albeit not the same distinction as observed in the other MSS and the printed edition. Secondly, it is clear that some courtier playwrights of the 1630s, such as Thomas Killigrew, Lodowick Carlell, and William Davenant, divided up their dialogue, sausage-machine fashion, into lines (often of roughly ten syllables), apparently in the belief that this was enough to constitute dramatic verse; Montagu may well have done likewise.

Rhyme: couplets
Act-Division: 5 acts
Lines (Spoken): 7,258 (230 verse, 7,028 prose)

The figure includes the repeated lines of Martiro's poem in 4.4, which are spoken but not transcribed.

Lines (Written): 7,454 (C); 6,197 (O)

B-Text
Induction: 36 lines, in couplets
Lines (Spoken): 3,654 (293 verse, 3,361 prose)
Lines (Written): 3,844

STAGING
Doors: a character enters at 'the other door' from the one used for an exit (5.5, s.d.)
Within: speech (5.7, implicit; the echo)

B-Text
Doors: *omits* reference to 'the other door'
Above: Apollo and Diana fly (ind., J)

MUSIC
Song: 'Press me no more, kind love, I will confess', 5.1, Bellessa, 20 lines

---

B-Text
Songs:
B1: 'Victorious love, though it hath got the day', int.1, 18 lines;

> B2: 'Here meritorious humbleness doth rise', int.2, 16 lines;
> B3: 'Here frighted innocence for succour flies', int.3, 16 lines;
> B4: 'Here love hath met with such a tempered heart', int.4, 16 lines.
>
> *Varies*: the A-text song is now only 18 lines.

PROPS

Small Portable Objects: a gilt book with blue ribbon strings (2.1, implicit/Ha); a paper (3.6–7, s.d.); a paper (4.1, s.d.); a picture of Fidamira (4.1, 4.4, s.d.); a document (4.4, implicit); a letter (4.8, s.d.); a watch (5.7, 5.11, dialogue); another watch (5.11, dialogue); a paper (5.13, implicit/O s.d.)

Large Portable Objects: a short rattan staff (Ha/J; for the King); a long rattan staff (Ha/J; for Romero); a crook with ribbons (Ha; for Basilino); four crooks silvered at both ends (Ha); five scrips (Ha)

Scenery: a proscenium (J); a palace seen through trees (1.1–7, s.d.); a throne (2.1, s.d.; 2.5, 3.3, 3.10, implicit); a tomb (4.9, s.d.); a wood, called 'love's cabinet' (5.7, s.d.); *design drawings survive for all items in this section*

> B-Text
> **Small Portable Objects:** *omits* paper (from 5.13)

COSTUMES AND MAKE-UP

OSORIO and TIMANTE: soldier's suits with whalebone busks (T)

BASILINO: disguised (1.6, s.d.; 2.1, 2.5, 3.6, 3.9, 4.1–2, 4.4, 4.9, 5.1, 5.4, 5.6–7, 5.11, implicit; 5.13, implicit/B s.d.; removed on stage), presumably in a shepherd's suit of white and blue calico, silver tinsel, embroidered silver grogram sleeves, and a carnation girdle with silver roses and a breast-band (T); a belt (Ha); a hat lined with watchet taffeta and edged with silver lace, with a band of silk flowers (Ha); possibly (before 1.6?) a white and blue calico soldier's suit with tinsel and a whalebone busk (T); *two design drawings survive*

FIDAMIRA: a birthmark on her arm (s.d.); black clothes (1.7, s.d.; *three design drawings survive*); disguised as a Moor, with a black face (3.1, s.d.; 3.3, 3.7, 3.9, 4.1, 4.4–5, 4.7, 5.1, 5.3, 5.11, 5.13, implicit; 5.9, dialogue); disguised as a ghost (5.5, s.d.); a scarf or veil (5.13, s.d.; removed on stage); a jewel (5.13, s.d.); *a probable design drawing survives for one or other of her disguises*

AGENOR: disguised as a pilgrim (3.5, dialogue/B s.d.; *a design may survive*); black clothes (3.9, dialogue); a cross of diamonds (5.13, dialogue); a belt (Ha); a soldier's suit with a whalebone busk (T); a shepherd's suit (T)

KING: a crown (J); *two design drawings survive*

BELLESSA: a coronet of pearl (J); a glove (5.4, s.d.; removed on stage); *two design drawings survive*

MELIDORO and MARTIRO: belts (Ha); shepherd's suits (T)

VOTORIO: probably a laurel wreath (J); *a probable design drawing survives*

BONORIO: scarlet silk stockings (Ho); a soldier's suit with a whalebone busk (T)

ROMERO: white hair (implicit); a large hat (J); a belt (Ha); *design drawing survives*

Miscellaneous: Two attendants, possibly the two soldiers, wore white worsted stockings (Ho); also supplied were two hats covered with watchet taffeta, with ruff tinsel bands and bays (Ha). Four of the five characters wearing soldiers' suits (Osorio, Timante, Basilino, Agenor, and Bonorio) wear mantles, and one wears a black silk and taffeta cloak (T).

Although easily removable make-up had been available since 1621 (when it was a novelty and the basis of the final unmasking in *The Gypsies Metamorphosed*, **1987**), it seems curious that Fidamira has to remove her black face make-up for 5.9, where she appears as herself, but then resumes her Moorish disguise in 5.11 and 5.13. This may be the reason why she has a veil or scarf covering her face in 5.13: her intervening appearance in 5.11 is omitted from the B-text, so the scarf saves the performer from having to black up again.

Orgel and Strong were unable to identify one design for a woman's costume (no. 260). I take this to be for Fidamira when disguised. Just as the other design for Fidamira is marked 'This with the King', so this one is endorsed 'This with the Pilgrim'. Fidamira is the female character most associated with 'the pilgrim' (i.e. Agenor); she is also the only female character who certainly has a costume change. There seems to be nothing to determine whether the design is for her Moorish alter-ego as Gemella or for the sequence in 5.5 where she poses as her own ghost.

> B-Text
> APOLLO: a tinsel suit decorated with carnation, yellow, and white silk, hose with pockets, bases, a mantle, tinsel buskins, a ruff, and cuffs (ind., T); incarnadine *bas d'attache* [stockings] (ind., Ho); a long wig and a coronet of golden rays (ind., Ha)
> APOLLO'S MEN: tinsel gowns, tied at the collar, with silver lace sleeves, shoes, a ruff, and cuffs (ind., T); wigs and vizards (ind., Ha)
> AGENOR: a hat (4.1, s.d.)

EARLY STAGE HISTORY

Inception: The play was selected for the Queen to perform partly because it would enable her to practise her spoken English.

Rehearsals: The cast had begun rehearsing by Thursday 20 September 1632. A performance was planned for Monday 19 November (the King's birthday). The Queen and her ladies began rehearsing in September. The rehearsals were supervised by Joseph Taylor, who was rumoured to have been rewarded with 'the making of a knight' (which did not necessarily mean a knighthood for himself). By late October, it was reported, the Queen's performance was of especial gracefulness.

Preparation: Inigo Jones designed costumes and scenery for the production. Robert Ramsey began work making costumes on Saturday 6 October 1632. In November, the wiredrawer William Hurt, with four assistants, supplied pulleys, cords, and wires, and brought lighting branches from Whitehall to Denmark House. Thread and buttons for costumes were delivered on Friday 16 November.

Preparation of Venue: On Saturday 3 November 1632, Inigo Jones was ordered to prepare the room at Denmark House for the performance, and have the scenery, stage, and degrees made. The carpenter who built the theatre was Richard Ryder. Another carpenter, John Davenport, supervised some of the work, and was paid £2 by way of reward.

Postponement: By Thursday 25 October, it had become clear that the play was excessively long; in particular, the part of Basilino alone was rumoured to be the length of an entire play. By Friday 9 November, the Queen was rehearsing daily, but it was recognized that the projected birthday performance was not achievable: neither the performers nor the scenery were ready. Initially the performance was postponed until Saturday 1 December, but the performers were still not ready on Friday 23 November, and by Friday 7 December the performance was put off until after Christmas; the reason given was mourning for the King's brother-in-law, Frederick V, the Elector Palatine. By Thursday 3 January 1633, the date of the performance had been set as the following Wednesday, and Philip Herbert, 4th Earl of Pembroke (Lord Chamberlain) issued orders that chambermaids were only to be admitted if they were willing to sit cross-legged on bulks, that great ladies were to be admitted no matter how ill-dressed, and that meaner ladies would only be admitted if well-dressed and made up.

Preparation (II): The upholsterer Ralph Grinder came to Denmark House on Saturday 5 December and covered the Queen's throne, two forms, and a large tun for use in connection with the play. Also on two occasions in December (one of them Wednesday 19), the perfumer Jean Baptiste Ferin delivered perfumed skins to the Office of Robes. In January, the wiredrawer William Hurt, with four assistants, supplied scenery items and trimmed the lighting branches with ivy. The haberdasher John King sent costumes and props on Sunday 6 January. On the day of the performance, Wednesday 9 January, four close stools were ordered from the Great Wardrobe for the production. Richard Scutt, Groom of the Queen's Chamber, brought props and other items (including chamber pots, candlesticks, and jacks) from Whitehall to Denmark House for the production. Branches and hangings were borrowed from Whitehall and York House, and were brought to Denmark House by another Groom of the Queen's Chamber, Toby Baylie. Anthony Duvall delivered one costume (Fidamira's mourning dress) to the Office of the Robes on the same day.

Performance: on Wednesday 9 January 1633, in a specially built theatre in the paved court at Denmark House. The text had probably been abbreviated, and an induction had certainly been added. The predominantly female cast included: Queen Henrietta Maria (Bellessa); Goditha Arden (King); Mrs [Elizabeth?] Beaumont (Bonorio); Ursula Beaumont (Votorio); Sophia Carew (Fidamira); Victoria Cary (Martiro); Cecilia Crofts (Agenor); Lady Anne Feilding (Timante); Mary Hamilton, Marchioness of Hamilton (Basilino); Elizabeth Howard (Melidoro); Anne Kirke (Camena); Dorothy Seymour (Osorio, Romero); Ellenor Villiers (Pantamora). The performance reportedly lasted seven to eight hours and was poorly attended; it was rumoured that some people stayed away in the expectation that they would be unable to get in (perhaps because of the relatively small size of the theatre, 76 feet by 36). The audience included: King Charles I; Sir Lucius Cary (who found it difficult to hear the dialogue); Amerigo Salvetti. The Queen's spoken English was commended, and Cary wrote that 'her action was worthy of it, and it was worthy of her action', but some felt that acting ought to be beneath her dignity. It was also rumoured that the King disliked the play and ordered that the script should be burnt to ensure that it could never be performed again. (The text, even so, survives in abundance.)

Repeat Performance: A repeat performance was planned for Saturday 2 February (Candlemas) to allow those who had not turned up a second opportunity to see the play. However, the performance seems in the end to have taken place on Sunday 3 February.

Aftermath: Richard Scutt and Toby Baylie returned the items borrowed from Whitehall Palace and York House. Joseph Taylor was given the costumes. (They were re-used the following year in the King's Men revival of *The Faithful Shepherdess*, **1582**.)

A design for the temporary theatre survives (London: British Library, MS Lansdowne 1171, fos. 9ᵛ–10ʳ).

Production Expenses

Exchequer: The total cost of the temporary theatre erected by the Works Office was £310.16s.2d (though some of this pertained to its conversion for the Shrovetide masque, **2398**). Five men worked day and night on the two performance days, Wednesday 9 January and Sunday 3 February, and were paid a total of 16s.8d on each occasion.

Queen's Household: The total recorded cost of the production was at least £474.17s.6d (but see below for problems, anomalies, and superfluities in the surviving documents); costs totalling at least £43.10d were saved by unilaterally reducing the tradesmen's bills. Two initial payments were made on Thursday 4 April and Tuesday 7 May; the remaining bills (the bulk of them) were paid on various dates between Tuesday 18 and Monday 24 March 1634. In the following breakdown, some minor costume items cannot be disentangled from props, and are listed under *Props*.

Costumes: Payments totalled £451.18s.8d, reduced by at least £39.6s.8d. They were made on the following dates. On Tuesday 18 March 1634, to the mercers Richard Miller and Rhys Williams, for cloth (£345.10s, £13.6s less than billed), and the linen draper Margaret Ward (£24.2s, £7.19s less than billed). On Wednesday 19 March 1634, to the haberdasher Arthur Knight, for two hats (12s, 8s less than billed) and bands, ribbon, and bays (8s, 7s less than billed), and to the tailor Robert Ramsey, for the patterns for Basilino's shepherd's suit (£7.12s.6d, 18s.8d less than billed) and a soldier's suit (£4.15s.8d, £1 less than billed), and for four shepherds' suits, including Basilino's (£14.16s, £3.17s less than billed), Basilino's soldier's suit (£3.6s.8d, 17s.4d less than billed), soldiers' suits for Osorio, Timante, Agenor, and Bonorio (£15.2s.8d, £4.8s.4d less than billed), whalebone busks for the five soldiers' suits (5s), mantles and a cloak for the soldiers' suits (£1.6s, 5s less than billed), Apollo's costume (£7.15s.6d, at least 10s less than billed, one original amount illegible), and costumes for Apollo's attendants (£9.12s.10d, 14s.2d less than billed). On Thursday 20 March 1634, to the hosier John Buckner, for Bonorio's stockings (£1.10s, 6s less than billed), Apollo's *bas d'attache* (£2.3s.4d, 16s.8d less than billed), and attendants' stockings (£1, 4s less than billed); and to the haberdasher John King, for Basilino's hat (£1.4s, £1 less than billed), Apollo's wig (10s, half what was billed), Apollo's coronet (10s, half what was billed), two wigs for Apollo's men (8s; less than billed, original amount illegible), two vizards for Apollo's men (3s, 1s less than billed), and a laurel wreath (2s, 6d less than billed). On Friday 21 March 1634, to the perfumer Jean Baptiste Ferin, for perfumed skins (£4, £1 less than billed); William Geeres and Anna Henshawe, for sewing silk, loop-lace, and buttons (£1.15s.6d; 8s less than billed). On Monday 24 March 1634, to the tirewoman Mrs [Clement?] Duvall for cloth for Fidamira's mourning dress (£3.12s, paid to Clement Duvall and Antoinette Dumelle).

Props: Payments totalled £2.4s, reduced by at least 12s.6d. They were made on Thursday 20 March 1634 to the haberdasher John King, for: Basilino's crook, belt, and scrip (6s); four belts and scrips for Agenor, Romero, Melidoro, and Martiro (16s, 4s less than billed); four crooks (12s, 8s less than billed); Romero's staff (2s, 6d less than billed); King's staff (2s); a gilt book (6s; less than billed, original amount illegible).

Sundry: Payments totalled £20.14s.10d, reduced by £2.1s.8d. They were made on the following dates. On Thursday 4 April 1633, to Richard Scutt (£1, reimbursing boat-hire expenses connected with his work on this and the Shrovetide masque, **2398**). On Tuesday 7 May 1633, to Toby Baylie (£1, reimbursing expenses connected with his work on this and two weddings). On Tuesday 18 March 1634, to the upholsterer Ralph Grinder (£6.14s.10d, £2.1s.8d less than billed). On Wednesday 19 March 1634, to the wiredrawer William Hurt, for work in both November and January (£12).

Although John King's original billed amounts are illegible for Apollo's men's wigs and the gilt book, the sum of the two reductions was £1.

The bills from Henrietta Maria's debenture accounts contain a number of puzzling anomalies. There is a surviving bill (LR 5/65) by the Queen's tailor George Gellin for his work during the period 31 December 1632 to 31 March 1633, which purports to contain charges for costumes supplied on 12 January for 'the Queen's play' (also specified as her 'pastoral', which at that time could only refer to *The Shepherds' Paradise*) and in March for the Shrovetide masque (**2398**). The section relating to the pastoral was deleted and appears not to have been paid; Gellin was required to issue a separate bill for specific costs associated with the pastoral, but none survives. The items charged to this play are as follows: a white satin gown with a train, for the Queen (£5), a sky-coloured satin gown, matching the Queen's but without the train, for Cecilia Crofts (£1.10s); a carnation satin gown for Ellenor Villiers, again like the Queen's but trainless (£1.10s); two gowns for Victoria Cary, matching those for Mrs Crofts and Mrs Villiers (£2.18s); a white satin gown and a green satin kirtle, for Mrs Ogle (£1.12s); a yellow satin gown for Mrs Harding (£1); a long cloak for Mrs Harding (£1); a crimson satin gown and a white satin waistcoat for Ursula Beaumont (£1); fourteen cloaks, eight in black sarcenet, five ash-coloured, and one white (£4.17s.6d); five perfumed leather cloaks (10s); and silk (£1.10s).

This is problematic in a number of ways. First, costumes are supplied for two ladies who did not appear in the performance, Mrs Ogle and Mrs Harding. (They can hardly have played Apollo and Diana, who do not appear in the cast lists: these were probably parts for professionals, since they apparently have to fly and perhaps also sing.) Moreover, the fact that two roles (Osorio and Romero) were doubled strongly suggests that the performance used the maximum available number of ladies-in-waiting: if Ogle and Harding were also available, there would have been no need for Dorothy Seymour to have played both parts. Secondly, the costumes for performers who do appear in *The Shepherds' Paradise* do not match up with the roles they played. Cecilia Crofts cannot have worn a gown in the same style as worn by the Queen and Ellenor Villiers, because they were playing women and she was Agenor. It is also hard to understand why Victoria Cary might have needed two different woman's gowns to play a shepherd. (Jones's costume designs show the male characters wore somewhat feminized, full-skirted outfits, but there remains a modicum of gender distinction.) See also **2398** for a further mismatch. The anomalies are hard to explain, and it seems safest not to treat the bill as evidence of what was worn in the 1633 production.

A related problem is a payment totalling £561 to the embroiderer Charles Gentile, made in two instalments, one of £200 on Wednesday 29 May 1633 (by a warrant dated Wednesday 22 May) and the balance on Monday 10 March 1634. This was included in the summary of charges for *The Shepherds' Paradise*; the bill itself refers variously to 'the Queen's Majesty's masque' and 'the pastoral'. The work involved was embroidering seventeen gowns, of different colours, all with white and yellow copper stuff, for the Queen and her ladies and maids of honour; the gowns were delivered on Friday 4 January, five days before the performance. But seventeen gowns is too many, even factoring in Fidamira's costume change, for the four female characters (or five with Diana); and the use of identical materials for the embroidery suggests costumes which were identical save for their colour.

There are yet more superfluities in the records. John King's bill is for the most part closely linked to the demands of the script or the costume designs: for example, it charges for two rattans for the two characters who are shown carrying staffs in the surviving designs (King even billed more for Romero's, which is longer in the design, though the sum was reduced); and it establishes that in 2.1 Votorio reads the laws from a gilt book. But two items refer to five pilgrims, characters who cannot be traced in any version of the text: five staves (7s.6d, 5s less than billed) and five cords (10s, 5s less than billed).

The tailor Robert Ramsey's bill includes charges for making a calico suit for Jeffery Hudson with bases and a band of roses about his neck, breast, and girdle (£1.1s.6d, 6s less than billed). This fits no identifiable role in the play.

One possibility, covering both the Gellin and Gentile bills, and perhaps others, might be that there were plans to follow the pastoral with a masque on the same evening. This had happened with *Artenice* in 1626 (**2177**), and would happen again with *Florimène* in 1635 (**2522**), though the length of *The Shepherds' Paradise* could have forestalled any such plans in 1633. If there was such a masque, perhaps it drew a contrast with the pastoral by showing the performers (and others not considered competent for speaking parts?) all now dressed as women (after throwing off cloaks?). Perhaps there were five pilgrims, too. This would account for the apparently superfluous costumes, but it is as well to stress that there is not a shred of direct evidence that such a work was contemplated, let alone performed; accordingly, it is not catalogued in the main sequence here, but in Appendix 1 (**H38**).

One other oddity in Ramsey's bill is the charges for 'a soldier's suit' and for 'my Lady Marquess's soldier's suit', apparently representing different stages of work on the same costume. Lady Hamilton cannot possibly have played either of the soldiers, since her main role, Basilino, is on stage at the same time as them in the only scene in which they appear. It is most likely that the 'soldier's suit' is the one Basilino wears in his early scenes before he adopts his shepherd's disguise; it is striking that the two costumes seem to have had the same colour scheme. This is supported by the fact that four similar suits were supplied, all apparently for characters who also appear in the Castilian court scenes (Agenor, Timante, Bonorio, and presumably Osorio).

EARLY TEXTUAL HISTORY

1632: The play had been written by September when rehearsals began. That month, Walter Montagu was rewarded with gifts of £2,000 from the King and £500 from the Queen (though the money was not paid straight away).

1633: In about February, Sir Lucius Cary borrowed a MS containing part of the play from a 'noble cousin'. Returning it, he asked to borrow the rest of the text, and for permission to take a copy for himself. He also reported that the recently widowed Lady Dorothy Shirley was eager to read the play.

1633: On Wednesday 3 July, the Queen signed a warrant to pay Montagu his £500, and he received it on Saturday 6 July.

After 1633: transcribed in MS (reported by Hazlitt; now unlocated), with the title *Bellessa the Shepherds' Queen*; this MS was incomplete in the nineteenth century.

After 1633: transcribed in MS (**St**); 68 leaves; list of roles and performers.

After 1633: transcribed in MS (**Sl**); 87 leaves; list of roles.

After 1633: transcribed in MS (**P**); 112 leaves; list of roles and performers.

After 1633: transcribed in MS (**C**) by four different scribes, apparently working concurrently; 136 leaves; list of roles. Some possible cuts were later marked.

c. 1633–53: transcribed in MS (**Tx**); 63 leaves; list of roles. At some point before 1653 the MS was owned by Lady Frances Persall.

1653: MS Tx was borrowed from Lady Persall on Thursday 1 September.

1658: entered in the Stationers' Register to Thomas Dring on Monday 27 September; entry refers to the author as 'a person of honour' and mentions the private performance by the Queen and 'ladies of honour'.

1659: **O** printed (in or before June) for Thomas Dring; collation A⁴ B–M⁸, 92 leaves; publisher's epistle; anonymous commendatory verses addressed to the publisher; list of roles and performers. Some copies bear the erroneous date 1629 on the title page. A variant title page names John Starkey as the bookseller; the book was advertised for sale by him from 1660 to 1675.

1659: George Thomason acquired a copy of O in June. In *c.* 1678, some years after his death, his entire collection of books and tracts was acquired by the bookbinder Samuel Mearne, acting as agent for King Charles II; the King never paid him, and the books remained in Mearne's family until 1761.

1660: O advertised for sale by Simon Stafford on Thursday 2 February.

1662: O advertised as for sale by Henry Marsh.

1684: Nicholas Cox (Manciple of St Edmund Hall, Oxford) had a copy, presumably of O, in his bookshop. It had probably been previously owned by Gerard Langbaine, and appears on a list compiled by Anthony Wood on Saturday 13 December.

EDITION

Sarah Poynting, unpublished D.Phil. thesis (Oxford, 1999); Acts 1–3 only.

B-Text
Sarah Poynting, Malone Society Reprints 159 (Oxford, 1998 for 1997).

REFERENCES

Annals 1633; Bawcutt 280; Bentley, iv. 917–21; Bodleian, MS Wood E. 4, art. 1, p. 54; *British Library Journal* 3 (1977), 13–19; Butler, 373; *Cal. Dom. 1625–49 Add.*, 473; *Cal. Ven. 1632–6*, 28, 63; *ELR* 29 (1999), 79–87; Greg 797; Hazlitt, 25, 207–8; HMC 3, 282; David Lindley (ed.), *The Court Masque* (Manchester, 1984), 156–7, 164; MSC 2.3, 359; MSC 6, 151; MSC 10, 44–5; MSC 13, 121–2; *N&Q* 221 (1976), 223–5; *N&Q* 211 (1966), 303–4; Orgel and Strong, i. 388, ii. 504–35; John Orrell, *The Theatres of Inigo Jones and John Webb* (Cambridge, 1985), 204 n. 19; *PBSA* 107 (2013), 37; John Peacock, *The Stage*

Designs of Inigo Jones (Cambridge, 1995), 193–9; *PMLA* 51 (1936), 128; Michael C. Questier (ed.), *Newsletters from the Caroline Court, 1631–1638* (Cambridge, 2005), 145; Reyher, 530; *ShS* 11 (1958), 109–10; Steele, 243–4, 246; *Theatre Survey* 20 (1979), 17–18.

2396. The Beauties

TEXT
Printed in 1633 (STC 22436), from authorial copy.

GENRE
comedy
Contemporary: comedy (S.R., t.p.); poem (ded.); play (Abraham Wright, *c.* 1640)

TITLE
Performed: *The Beauties*
Printed: *The Bird in a Cage*
Contemporary: *The Bird in the Cage*

AUTHOR
James Shirley

DATE
January 1633

ORIGINAL PRODUCTION
Queen Henrietta's Men at the Cockpit

PLOT
After rumours of Philenzo's interest in Eugenia, her father the Duke banishes him and shuts her up in a newly-built palace, attended only by ladies, until he can find her a husband of suitable rank. Orpiano is sent to Florence with her picture to negotiate a marriage treaty; her fiancé will be the Great Duke's son. Rolliardo, an unemployed wit, comes to court looking for work. The Duke gives him the task of gaining access to Eugenia in her new quarters within a month, with the proviso that he will be executed if he fails; he agrees, subject to the condition that the Duke gives him enough money to do the job—meaning, in effect, unlimited access to the exchequer.

Pursued by creditors, the artist Bonamico sets up business disguised as a mountebank, Altomaro, offering to teach people the secret of invisibility. Rolliardo sceptically rejects this as a method of penetrating Eugenia's palace, preferring to trust in the corruptibility of the captain of the guard—who refuses to help, but keeps the bribe anyway. 'Altomaro' tries to encourage prospective clients by dressing up as a series of customers entering his shop; they are not seen leaving because, he says, they have become invisible. Dondolo and Grutti decide this would be a good way to get to see their girlfriends, two of Eugenia's attendants, and pay 'Altomaro' for a demonstration: he will be invisible, save only for his hand. And so he is—the 'hand' being a handwritten letter from him. The courtiers realize they have been cheated; Bonamico's assistant Carlo tells them his true identity and helps them to find and imprison him pending the repayment of their demonstration fee.

Morello attempts to get into the palace prison posing as a woman, but one of the guards wants a sexual fee and discovers his true gender. He is taken to the Duke and sentenced to wear his women's clothes for a month. An ambassador arrives from Florence to finalize the marriage contract; Fulvio tells him about Philenzo's love for Eugenia. Rolliardo uses his access to the exchequer to buy all debtors out of prison; one of the beneficiaries is Bonamico, who again offers his help. He brings the Duke a large cage of birds, which the Duke sends as a present to Eugenia. It arrives while the ladies are putting on a play, *The New Prison*, about Jupiter and Danaë, imprisoned by her tyrannous father. Eugenia feels sorry for the birds and opens the cage. Rolliardo is hidden inside. He woos her, but she refuses him: her heart belongs to Philenzo. He then takes off his disguise, revealing that he *is* Philenzo.

The month is up. The Duke expects Rolliardo to plead for his life, but instead he produces a handwritten paper from Eugenia proving that the task has been accomplished; fetched out, Eugenia confirms this and declares her love for 'Rolliardo'. The Duke criticizes her for fickleness to Philenzo, so he reveals his true identity—which gives the Duke the excuse to execute him for breaking his banishment. It emerges that Florence has broken off the marriage treaty in Philenzo's favour, so the Duke tries to countermand the execution, only to learn that Philenzo is already dead, having taken poison. When he shows remorse, Eugenia admits that it was only a sleeping potion. Philenzo wakes to find the Duke willing to approve his marriage to Eugenia.

SCENE DESIGNATION
1.1, 2.1, 3.1–4, 4.1–2, 5.1 (Q)

ROLES
FULVIO, a lord, Philenzo's kinsman; formerly a student at Pisa
Signor ORPIANO, a lord, Donella's fiancé
Signor MORELLO, a fashionable, foolish courtier; said to be little; poses as a lady, Madam Thorn
GENTLEMEN USHERS at court (1.1; one speaks)
Signor DONDOLO, a courtier, Mardona's boyfriend
Signor GRUTTI, a courtier, Katherina's boyfriend
The DUKE of Mantua, Eugenia's father
EUGENIA, the Princess, the Duke's daughter; plays Danaë in the inset play
Signor PERENOTTO, Captain of the Guard
ATTENDANTS on the Duke (1.1, 2.1, 5.1, *non-speaking*)

Madam DONELLA, a lady attending Eugenia, Orpiano's fiancée; plays the prologue and Jupiter in the inset play

Madam KATHERINA, a lady attending Eugenia; plays a lady attendant in the inset play

MARDONA, a lady attending Eugenia; plays King Acrisius in the inset play

FIDELIA, a lady attending Eugenia; plays a lady attendant in the inset play

ROLLIARDO, a wit of humble birth; pretends to be the Prince of Florence in disguise; in reality, Signor Philenzo, a young man, Fulvio's kinsman; also called Lord Philenzo

BONAMICO, an insolvent artist and property-maker; a married man and a debtor; poses as Signor Altomaro, a mountebank

CARLO, Bonamico's servant

The GUARD (2.1, 3.1; three or five speak)

An AMBASSADOR from Florence (originally written as Ferrara); formerly a student at Pisa, where he was Fulvio's friend

COURTIERS attending the Duke (2.1, 4.1; two speak)

CASSIANA, a lady attending Eugenia; plays a lady attendant in the inset play

SERVANTS at court (4.1, *non-speaking*)

OFFICERS of the court who bring in Philenzo's body (5.1, *non-speaking*)

Speaking Parts: 23–5

Stage Directions and Speech Prefixes

FULVIO: *Fulvio* (s.d.s); *Fulv<io>* (s.p.s); *Fulvio* [one of two] *Noblemen* (d.p.)

ORPIANO: *Orpiano* (s.d.s and s.p.s); *Orpiano* [one of two] *Noblemen* (d.p.)

MORELLO: *Morello* (s.d.s); *Mor<ello>* (s.p.s); *Morello* [one of three] *Courtiers* (d.p.)

GENTLEMEN USHERS: *Gentlemen Ushers* (s.d.s); *Gentleman* (s.p.s)

DONDOLO: *Dondolo* (s.d.s); *Dond<olo>* (s.p.s); *Dondolo* [one of three] *Courtiers* (d.p.)

GRUTTI: *Grutti* (s.d.s); *Grut<ti>* (s.p.s); *Grutti* [one of three] *Courtiers* (d.p.)

DUKE: *the Duke* (s.d.s); *Duke* (s.d.s and s.p.s); *Duke of Mantua* (d.p.)

EUGENIA: *Eugenia* (s.d.s); *Eugen<ia>* (s.p.s); *Eugenia the Duke's daughter* (d.p.)

PERENOTTO: *Perenotto* (s.d.s); *Peren<otto>* (s.p.s); *Perenotto Captain of* [the Duke's] *Guard* (d.p.)

ATTENDANTS: *Attendants* (s.d.s and d.p.)

DONELLA: *Donella* | [one of] *the Ladies* | *Jupiter* | [one of the] *Ladies* (s.d.s); *Donel<la>* | *Jupit<er>* (s.p.s); *Donella* [one of the] *Ladies attendant on the Princess* (d.p.)

KATHERINA: *Katherina* | [one of] *the Ladies* | *Katerina* | [one of the] *Ladies* (s.d.s); *Kath<erina>* (s.p.s); *Catherina* [one of the] *Ladies attendant on the Princess* (d.p.)

MARDONA: *Mardona* | [one of] *the Ladies* | [one of the] *Ladies* (s.d.s); *Mard<ona>* (s.p.s); *Mardona* [one of the] *Ladies attendant on the Princess* (d.p.)

FIDELIA: *Fidelia* | [one of] *the Ladies* | [one of the] *Ladies* (s.d.s); *Fidel<ia>* (s.p.s); *Fidelia* [one of the] *Ladies attendant on the Princess* (d.p.)

ROLLIARDO: *Rolliardo* | *Rollyardo* | *Philenzo* (s.d.s); *Roll<iardo>* (s.p.s); *Philenzo Lover of Eugenia, under the Disguise and Name of Rollyardo* (d.p.)

BONAMICO: *Bonamico* | *Bonamico* (s.d.s); *Bon<amico>* (s.p.s); *Bonamico a Mountebank, or decayed Artist* (d.p.)

CARLO: *a Servant* | *Servant to Bon<amico>* (s.d.s); *Servant* (s.d.s, s.p.s, and d.p.)

GUARD: *3 or 4 of the Guard* (s.d.s); *1* | *2* | *3* (s.p.s); *Guard* (s.d.s and d.p.)

AMBASSADOR: *Ambassador* (s.d.s and s.p.s); *Ambassador of Florence* (d.p.)

COURTIERS: *Courtiers* (s.d.s); *Courtier 1* | *1* | *2* (s.p.s)

CASSIANA: *Cassiava* (s.d.s); *Cass<iana>* (s.p.s); *Cassiana* [one of the] *Ladies attendant on the Princess* (d.p.)

OTHER CHARACTERS
Morello's barber (1.1)
Morello's tailor (1.1)
A cardinal, Philenzo's uncle (1.1)
Bonamico's creditors (2.1, 3.2, 3.4)
Gallants and ladies who flatter and court Rolliardo now that he is in favour (2.1)
The Great Duke of Florence (2.1, 3.2, 4.1–2, 5.1)
The Prince of Florence, the Great Duke's son, Eugenia's prospective fiancé (2.1, 4.2, 5.1)
The Emperor (3.1)
The keeper of the prison where Bonamico is incarcerated (3.4)
Bonamico's wife (4.1)
The pages of the court (4.1)
The Duke of Venice (4.1)
The Duke of Mantua's physicians (5.1)

SETTING
Period: seventeenth century: the death of Gondomar (1626) and the siege of Bergen (1622) are mentioned as events in the recent past
Time-Scheme: One month passes between 1.1 and 5.1, and one day between 4.2 and 5.1.
Place: Mantua

Geography
Italy: Florence (originally written as Ferrara); Tuscany; Pisa; Rome; Venice
France
[*The Low Countries*]: Bergen; Amsterdam; Dunkirk
England
Europe: Spain
[*Asia*]: Persia; Arabia; Turkey
Peru

SOURCES
Narrative: John Fletcher, *Women Pleased* (**1965**); John Ford, *Love's Sacrifice* (**2360**; Rolliardo)
Verbal: Juvenal, *Satires 7* (t.p. motto), 14 (3.2); Thomas Kyd, *The Spanish Tragedy* (**783**; 3.4); 'With a Fading' (song, before 1607; 4.1); Thomas Heywood, *The Escapes of Jupiter* (redaction of **1637** and **1645**; 3.1, 5.1); Ben Jonson, *The New Inn* (**2263**; 4.1)
Works Mentioned: Diego Ortúñez de Calahorra, Pedro de la Sierra, and Marcos Martínez, *Espejo de principes y caballeros* (1555–87; English tr., *The Mirror of Princely Deeds and Knighthood*, by Margaret Tyler, R. P., and L. A., 1578–99; 3.2); William Shakespeare, *The Merchant of Venice* (**1047**; 2.1); William Prynne, *Health's Sickness* (1628; ded.), *The Unloveliness of Love-Locks* (1628; ded.), *Histriomastix* (1633; ded.); *The Devil and the Baker* (3.2; unidentified ballad)

There are also references (in 2.1) to two unidentified and probably imaginary plays, The Invisible Knight and The Ring (discussed in Appendix 2).

LANGUAGE
English
Latin: 11 words (1.1, 2.1, 3.2; Rolliardo, Grutti)
Italian: 2 words (2.1; Rolliardo)

FORM
Metre: prose and pentameter; the inset play is partly in tetrameter
Rhyme: blank verse; the inset play is in couplets
Act-Division: 5 acts
Lines (Spoken): 2,406 (970 verse, 1,436 prose)
Lines (Written): 2,491

STAGING
Within: music (3.3, implicit; 4.2, s.d.)

MUSIC
Music: bell within (3.3, 4.2, s.d.)
On-Stage Music: lutes played by Ladies, accompanying Song 1 (3.3, dialogue)
Songs:
 1: 3.3, Ladies, with lute accompaniment;
 2: 'What other is the world than a ball', 4.1, Morello, 9 lines; *musical setting may survive*;
 3: 'There was an invisible fox by chance', 4.1, Morello, 12 lines; *musical setting survives*;
 4: 'Among all sorts of people', 5.1, Morello, 20 lines.
Dance: Ladies dance a nimble dance (3.3, s.d.)

Music which may belong to Song 2 appears in the 1719–20 edition of Pills to Purge Melancholy (iv. 99); it is there printed with 'A Ballad of the Courtier and the Country Clown', which has the same refrain as Song 2 but is otherwise entirely different. The refrain, and so perhaps the tune, appears to have been traditional.

PROPS
Weapons: a double-hatched rapier (3.4, dialogue); swords (5.1, s.d.)

Musical Instruments: two to five lutes (3.3, dialogue)
Money: gold (2.1, dialogue); gold crowns (3.1, s.d.); an unspecified sum (3.2, s.d.); another unspecified sum (3.2, implicit)
Animals: at least nine live birds in the cage (4.1–2, dialogue; said to include a woodcock, a bullfinch, a blackbird, a thrush, a pigeon, a wagtail, a rail, a nightingale, and a turtle dove; they are released on stage and fly out)
Small Portable Objects: a diamond (2.1, dialogue); other jewels (2.1, dialogue); a fan (3.1, dialogue); a letter (3.2, dialogue); a letter (3.3, s.d.); jewels (3.3, dialogue); a letter (3.4, dialogue); a watch (3.4, dialogue); a paper (5.1, dialogue); a letter (5.1, dialogue)
Large Portable Objects: a carpet (5.1, s.d.)
Scenery: a large birdcage on wheels, with a central pillar sizeable enough to conceal a man inside (4.1, dialogue; 4.2, s.d.); an arras (4.2, dialogue); a throne (5.1, implicit)

COSTUMES AND MAKE-UP
MORELLO: clean-shaven (implicit); breeches (2.1, dialogue); cross-dressed as a woman (3.1, 4.1, s.d.; 3.2, 5.1, dialogue), including a petticoat (dialogue; he also refers to his 'linen-breeches'—presumably women's drawers—but evidently isn't wearing them); a man's silk breeches (3.1, s.d.; worn under his petticoat); a glove (3.1, s.d.; removed on stage); a diamond ring (3.1, dialogue; removed on stage)
DONDOLO: breeches (3.2, dialogue); he or Grutti wears a cloak (3.4, dialogue) and scabbard (3.4, implicit)
GRUTTI: breeches (3.2, dialogue); see also DONDOLO
DUKE: wrinkled face and grey hair (dialogue)
KATHERINA: gloves (1.1, dialogue)
ROLLIARDO/PHILENZO: disguised (1.1, 2.1, 3.2, 3.4, 4.2, 5.1, implicit; removed on stage); a hat (5.1, implicit; doffed on stage)
BONAMICO: disguised as a mountebank (2.1, dialogue), including mean clothes, a wig, and a false beard (dialogue); another disguise (2.1, s.d.); 'brave' clothes (3.4, s.d.)
CARLO: two or three different costumes (2.1, s.d.)
Miscellaneous: some unspecified characters wear scabbards (5.1, implicit)

EARLY STAGE HISTORY
1633: performed by Queen Henrietta's Men at the Cockpit.

EARLY TEXTUAL HISTORY
1633: On Monday 21 January, Sir Henry Herbert licensed the play for performance.
 1633: entered (as *The Bird in the Cage*) to William Cooke in the Stationers' Register on Tuesday 19 March; entry names author. Sir Henry Herbert had licensed the book for publication.
 1633: Q printed by Bernard Alsop and Thomas Fawcet for William Cooke; collation A² B-K⁴, 38

leaves; title page names playhouse and author; Latin title-page motto; list of roles; ironical authorial dedication to William Prynne; printer's errata list.

Before 1640: a copy of Q was owned by Robert Burton.

c. 1630s–40s: a copy of Q was in the possession of John Horne (Vicar of Headington, Oxfordshire). After his death, his entire collection of play-books passed into the possession of John Houghton of Brasenose College, Oxford (c. 1608–77), then to James Herne (died 1685), and then to the library of Ralph Sheldon (1623–84) at Weston, where it was catalogued by Anthony Wood, probably in the late 1670s. By then the copy had been bound into a single volume with 21 other plays by Shirley (and, presumably in error, with Henry Shirley's *The Martyred Soldier*, **2030**).

c. 1640: Abraham Wright transcribed extracts into a MS miscellany (London: British Library, Add. MS 22608, fos. 82^r–83^r). The MS later passed to Wright's son, the antiquarian James Wright (c. 1644–c. 1717).

1645: Song 3 included in the fourth edition of 'Philomusus', *The Academy of Compliments*, sig. I5^v; printed by Thomas Badger for Humphrey Moseley.

1646: *The Academy of Compliments* reprinted by Moses Bell for Humphrey Moseley; the song now appears on sig. K8^r.

1650: *The Academy of Compliments* reprinted for Humphrey Moseley; the song now appears on sig. K4^v.

1655: *The English Treasury of Wit and Language* entered in the Stationers' Register to Humphrey Moseley on Tuesday 16 January.

1655: five extracts (from 2.1, 3.4, 4.1) included in John Cotgrave's *The English Treasury of Wit and Language*, sigs. D1^r, H6^r, H8^r, O3^r, X2^{r-v}; printed for Humphrey Moseley.

c. 1655: extracts transcribed by John Evans in a miscellany, *Hesperides*, intended for publication and entered to Humphrey Moseley in the Stationers' Register on Thursday 16 August 1655. The book remained unpublished in 1660, and Evans continued adding to the collection until at least 1666. Two MS exemplars are known; one was cut up by J. O. Halliwell-Phillipps in the nineteenth century; the other survives (Washington: Folger, MS V. b. 93).

1658: *The Academy of Compliments* reprinted for Humphrey Moseley.

1663: *The Academy of Compliments* reprinted by Thomas Leach and Thomas Child.

1667: Song 3 included, with a musical setting by John Hilton, in the fourth edition of Hilton's *Catch that Catch Can*, sig. K1^v; printed by William Godbid for John Playford.

1671: Song 3 included in *Windsor Drollery*, sig. M10^v; printed for John Macock in or before November.

1672: *Windsor Drollery* reprinted for John Macock; the song now appears on sig. E12^r.

1684: Nicholas Cox (Manciple of St Edmund Hall, Oxford) had a copy, presumably of Q, in his bookshop. It had probably been previously owned by Gerard Langbaine, and appears on a list compiled by Anthony Wood on Saturday 13 December.

Late seventeenth century: Song 3 included, with Hilton's setting, in a MS songbook (London: British Library, Add. MS 29291, fo. 14^v).

EDITIONS

Frances Frazier Senescu, Garland Renaissance Drama (New York and London, 1980).

Julie Sanders, in Hero Chalmers, Julie Sanders, and Sophie Tomlinson (eds.), *Three Seventeenth-Century Plays on Women and Performance*, Revels Plays Companion Library (Manchester and New York, 2006), 177–266.

Barbara Ravelhofer, in James Shirley, *The Complete Works*, gen. eds. Eugene Giddens, Teresa Grant, and Barbara Ravelhofer (Oxford, forthcoming).

REFERENCES

Annals 1633; Bawcutt 248, C65; Beal 2 ShJ 135; Bentley, v. 1080–1; Bodleian, MS Wood E. 4, art. 1, p. 17; Eyre & Rivington, i. 463, ii. 8; Robert Stanley Forsythe, *The Relations of Shirley's Plays to the Elizabethan Drama* (New York, 1914), 286–97; Greg 479; Hazlitt, 26; Nicolas K. Kiessling, *The Library of Robert Burton* (Oxford, 1988) 1471; *The Library*, 5th ser., 28 (1973), 294–308; *The Library*, 7th ser., 10 (2009), 372–404; *MLR* 13 (1918), 401–11; *MP* 66 (1968–9), 256–61; Claude M. Simpson, *The British Broadside Ballad and its Music* (New Brunswick, 1966), 792–4; *SP* 40 (1943), 186–203.

2397. The New Moon

TEXT

MS (Rome: English College, MS Z.142); includes one extra pasted-in leaf, apparently from an actor's part for Vertumnus. Additional information derives from the accounts of the English College, Rome.

GENRE

pastoral

Contemporary: *comedia* (accounts)

TITLE

MS: *The New Moon*

DATE

February 1633 (Gregorian)

ORIGINAL PRODUCTION

English College, Rome

PLOT

By the terms of their father's will, Phoebus must each month give Cynthia a portion of his light; but he has decided to discontinue her supply, and called a senate of the gods to ratify his decision. Cynthia is to be charged with abusing the light she has received: it has abetted thieves and nocturnal revellers, and she is further accused of spying on sleeping people through windows, helping sorceresses, and creating disorder in the realms of Neptune. Not all the gods are opposed to her, however: Saturn sends Mercury to her with a copy of the charges, so that she can prepare her answer, but insists that his help remain secret for fear of incurring censure from his fellow gods.

Cynthia gathers her allies, including Basilisco, a Moor who is angry with Phoebus for burning his nation black. However, although the hunter Meleager is inclined to support her, he will not do so out of loyalty to his studious friend Sylvanus, who detests all light, even moonlight, as a distraction from his contemplation. Vertumnus rectifies matters with a trick: he gets Meleager to play dead, and tells Sylvanus that he was killed by Basilisco in reprisal for his failure to support Cynthia. Sylvanus duly feels responsible and attempts suicide, but is forestalled when Meleager comes back to life; both friends throw in their lot with Cynthia.

The gods hold their senate: Mercury and Saturn argue in Cynthia's favour, and Vulcan is neutral, but Phoebus bullies them into endorsing his point of view. Cynthia asks permission to address the senate, but Phoebus refuses. Basilisco challenges Mars to settle the matter in single combat. Mars is keen to accept, but cannot break Jupiter's decree that the gods may not fight with mortals, so Mercury proposes a stratagem. When Basilisco arrives for the fight, he meets not Mars but Vulcan, and infers that Mars has adopted a disguise to save himself; he mocks Vulcan, and is beaten up by the Cyclopes.

Saturn is sent to talk Silenus and Argus round to Phoebus' cause, but actually encourages them to continue their support for Cynthia. They send their servants Crepusculum and Pygmalion with youthful sports and jokes in the hope of pleasing Phoebus into a better disposition; Pan also sends his satyrs to dance. Phoebus is unmoved, and, in order not to return home empty-handed, Crepusculum steals Mercury's wings and caduceus. Mercury catches him, but decides that it would be a good idea to have someone impersonate him at the hearing, so that afterwards he can disclaim anything that was said; Vertumnus takes on the role. Cynthia and her allies plead her case before the gods. Silenus asks Phoebus what he will do with the light which he once gave to Cynthia: if he keeps it for himself he will be too hot. Argus points out that, never having seen night, Phoebus cannot understand the benefits of moonlight, but Phoebus retorts that the other planets will take over Cynthia's nocturnal illumination. Cynthia rebuts the charges against her. Phoebus is initially adamant, but finally Cynthia's tears change his mind.

SCENE DESIGNATION
1.1–8, 2.1–7, 3.1–8, ep. (MS)

The stage is clear only between the acts.

ROLES
Master MERCURY, a trickster god; also called Hermes
VULCAN, a lame god
STEROPES, a Cyclops, Vulcan's apprentice
PYRAGMON, a Cyclops, Vulcan's apprentice
VERTUMNUS, Cynthia's page
CREPUSCULUM, Silenus' servant; also called Don Crepusculum and Pusculum
SILENUS, a choleric old man
MELEAGER, a hunter, Sylvanus' friend
SYLVANUS, a student of the arts, Meleager's friend; also called Sylvan
Lady CYNTHIA, the young moon goddess, Empress of the watery regions; Phoebus' twin sister; also called Mistress Cynthia, Madam Cynthia, Dame Cynthia, and Lady Moon
Don BASILISCO, a Moorish captain; also called Signor Basilisco
PAN, a woodland god
PYGMALION, Argus' fool; also called Pyg
Sir PHOEBUS, the young sun god, Cynthia's twin brother; also called Apollo and Sir Sun
SATURN, an old god and planet
MARS, god of war, a planet
ARGUS, an old man, Silenus' neighbour
Three SATYRS, Pan's followers, possibly named Hipple, Sipple, and Tripple (2.7, *non-speaking*)

Speaking Parts: 17

Stage Directions and Speech Prefixes
MERCURY: *Mercurius* | *Mercurie* | *Mercury* (s.d.s); *Me<rcury>* (s.p.s)
VULCAN: *Vulcanus* | *Vulcan* (s.d.s); *Vul<can>* (s.p.s)
STEROPES: *Steropes* (s.d.s); *Ste<ropes>* (s.p.s)
PYRAGMON: *Pyragmon* (s.d.s); *Pyr<agmon>* (s.p.s)
VERTUMNUS: *Vertumnus* (s.d.s); *Ve<rtumnus>* (s.p.s)
CREPUSCULUM: *Crepusculum* | [one of the] *servi* (s.d.s); *Cr<epusculum>* (s.p.s)
SILENUS: *Silenus* | [one of the] *senes* (s.d.s); *Si<lenus>* (s.p.s)
MELEAGER: *Meleager* (s.d.s); *Me<leager>* (s.p.s)
SYLVANUS: *Sylvanus* (s.d.s); *Sy<lvanus>* (s.p.s)
CYNTHIA: *Cynthia* (s.d.s); *Cy<nthia>* (s.p.s)
BASILISCO: *Basilisco* (s.d.s); *B<asilisco>* (s.p.s)
PAN: *Pan* (s.d.s); *Pa<n>* (s.p.s)
PYGMALION: *Pygmalion* | [one of the] *servi* (s.d.s); *Py<ragmon>* (s.p.s)
PHOEBUS: *Phebus* (s.d.s); *Ph<ebus>* (s.p.s)
SATURN: *Saturne* (s.d.s); *Sa<turne>* (s.p.s)
MARS: *Mars* (s.d.s); *Ma<rs>* (s.p.s)
ARGUS: *Argus* | [one of the] *senes* (s.d.s); *Ar<gus>* (s.p.s)
SATYRS: *tres Satyri* | *Satyri* (s.d.s)

OTHER CHARACTERS
Jupiter, ruler of the gods, also called Jove (1.1–7, 2.1–4, 2.7, 3.2, 3.4–5)
Juno, a goddess (1.2, 1.7, 2.1, 2.3)

The drinkers at the sign of Ursa Minor (1.2)
Hebe, Jove's former cupbearer (1.2, 2.7)
Mistress Aurora, the dawn, whom Phoebus visits every morning (1.3–5, 1.7, 3.6)
Thetis, whom Phoebus visits every night (1.3, 1.5, 2.1, 3.7)
Dame Tellus, one of Cynthia's accusers; also called Lady Tellus (1.4–5, 1.7, 2.5, 3.6)
The Sylvan gods, Cynthia's accusers (1.4, 3.6)
Neptune, god of the sea, one of Cynthia's accusers (1.4, 1.7, 2.5, 3.6)
Maia, Mercury's mother; also called May (1.4, 3.4)
Dromas, a hunter (1.5)
Althaea, Meleager's mother (1.6)
Planicles, Mercury's fellow (1.7)
Hyperion, dead father of Phoebus and Cynthia (1.7, 3.6)
The mother of Phoebus and Cynthia (1.7)
Pan's father, a woman's tailor (1.7)
Bruma (1.7; representing the shortest day of the year)
Boreas, Bruma's champion (1.7)
Scylla, who dislikes moonlight for allowing mariners to escape her jaws (1.7)
Flora, [goddess of flowers] (1.7)
Venus, goddess of love (1.7)
Echo, a nymph (1.8)
Daphne, a virgin whom Phoebus wishes to have burned on his altar (2.1; it is unclear whether or not she has already been transformed into a laurel)
Latona, Saturn's daughter, mother of Phoebus and Cynthia (2.1)
Mars's minions (2.1)
Io, whom Jupiter transformed into a cow, and who was committed in that form to Argus' keeping (2.1–2)
Aeolus, god of the winds (2.2)
The giants who made war on the gods; also called the Titans (2.2, 3.6)
The Muses, including Melpomene (2.2, 3.6)
Prometheus, who was chained to a rock three thousand years ago (2.3–4)
Brontes, a Cyclops, who broke Prometheus' teeth with his hammer (2.3, 2.6)
Saturn's father and mother (2.3)
The men of Arcadia, whom Saturn finds tasty (2.3)
A man recently eaten by Saturn, who escaped from his mouth and ran away (2.3)
A blind man whom Argus saw walking with a staff in Calabria (2.3)
Pluto, god of the underworld (2.5, 3.6)
Pan's fauns (2.7)
Ganymede, Hebe's successor as Jupiter's cupbearer (2.7)
Prometheus, an astronomer (3.3)
Atlas, a tall man, Mercury's grandfather (3.4)
The Dryads and Orcades (3.5)
Admetus, who once employed Mercury as a shepherd (3.5)
Phaethon, to whom Phoebus disastrously lent his chariot (3.5)
Rhadamanthus and the other judges of the underworld (3.6)
The Eumenides, tormentors of the damned (3.6)
Thetis' nymphs (3.7)

SETTING
Period: the action takes place in February
Time-Scheme: Act 1 takes place in the morning
Place: Arcadia

Geography
[*Greece*]: Mount Parnassus; Mount Olympus; Lake Lerna; Delphos (i.e. Delphi); Thessaly
The Aegean Sea: Lemnos; Delos
Italy: Mount Etna (also called Mongibell); Calabria
England
Ireland
[*Europe*]: The Low Countries; Spain; Switzerland; Poland
[*Africa*]: River Nile
[*Asia Minor*]: Maeonia; Turkey; Troy
[*Asia*]: Saba; Caucasus; River Ganges
The East Indies
The West Indies
America: River Orinoco
The Arctic Pole
The Torrid Zone
The Antarctic Pole
The Antipodes

LANGUAGE
English
Latin: 11 words (1.2, 1.4, 1.7, 2.3, 3.4, 3.6; Mercury, Crepusculum, Vertumnus, Cynthia, Pygmalion)

FORM
Metre: prose and pentameter; some trochaic trimeter; some stichomythia
Rhyme: blank verse and couplets; some ABAB
Act-Division: 3 acts
Epilogue: 12 lines of prose, spoken by Vertumnus
Lines (Spoken): 2,466 (637 verse, 1,829 prose)
Lines (Written): 2,562

The length recorded for the epilogue is that of the main MS text; the pasted-in sheet has a narrower measure which makes the same text run to 15 lines of prose. (The sheet is not included in the written length.)

STAGING
Doors: characters enter from and exit to three stage houses: that of the gods (1.1, 1.3, 2.2–7, 3.1–2, 3.5–6, 3.8, s.d.), of Cynthia (1.3, 1.6–7, 2.2, 2.4–5, 2.7, 3.3–8, s.d.), and of Silenus (1.4, 2.3, s.d.)
Discovery Space: possibly represents a cave (1.2, s.d.)
Stage: mentioned (1.2, s.d.)
Within: sound effects (1.1–2, s.d.); music (1.2, s.d.); song (1.2, s.d.); speech (1.4, s.d.)

Other Openings: a character enters from the forum (1.5, s.d.; i.e. the auditorium?)
Audience: directly addressed (1.4, 2.4–5, 3.3–4, 3.6, s.d.); a character calls into the forum when looking for another (2.3, s.d.); addressed as 'gentle spectators' (ep.)

MUSIC AND SOUND
Sound Effects: noise of hammers within (1.1–2, s.d.)
Music: lute within (1.2, s.d.)
On-Stage Music: Argus plays the pipe (2.3, s.d.); Pygmalion plays the pipe (3.6, s.d.)
Songs:
  1: 'Amongst the gods great Vulcan swayeth', 1.2, Vulcan, Steropes, Pyragmon, 12 lines, sung twice; performed to an unspecified tune by Thomas Morley;
  2: 'The nightingale that sits', 3.6, Crepusculum, 16 lines; *musical setting survives.*
Dance: Saturn and Silenus dance (2.3, s.d.); Satyrs dance (2.7, s.d.)

PROPS
Weapons: two hammers (1.2, 2.6, s.d.); a sword (1.6, s.d.)
Musical Instruments: a pipe (2.3, 3.6, s.d.)
Clothing: a gauntlet (1.7, dialogue)
Small Portable Objects: Mercury's caduceus (1.1–3, 3.1–8, s.d.); a document (1.3–4, s.d.); a little box (2.3, s.d.; hangs on Vulcan's girdle); a document (3.6, s.d.)
Large Portable Objects: a basin (1.4, s.d.); seats (3.4–6, s.d.)
Scenery: a backcloth with the sun, moon, and clouds painted on seven sheets (accounts)
Miscellaneous: a small dish of water (1.8, s.d./ accounts; splashed on a character)

COSTUMES AND MAKE-UP
MERCURY: wings on his head (1.1–3, dialogue)
VULCAN: a girdle (2.1–3, s.d.)
VERTUMNUS: a hat (1.3, implicit; doffed on stage); Mercury's wings on his head (3.4–8, s.d.; put on on stage)
CREPUSCULUM: hose (2.3, dialogue); a garment with a pocket (3.1–4, dialogue); Mercury's wings (3.1–4, s.d.; put on and removed on stage)
BASILISCO: black skin (dialogue)
PAN: half-goat, with horns and hooves (dialogue)
PYGMALION: a cap (1.8, s.d.; 2.3, 3.1–4, 3.6, dialogue; removed on stage); possibly a doublet, breeches, band, jerkin, stockings, garters, and shoes (2.3, dialogue)
ARGUS: a hundred eyes (dialogue)

EARLY STAGE HISTORY
1633: performed at the English College, Rome, probably in February. (In the Gregorian calendar, Shrove Tuesday fell on 8 February.) Some props (including the anvil and hammers) were borrowed. The cast were given a meal of pastries.

Production Expenses
The College paid for the following between Tuesday 25 January and Monday 14 February (Gregorian): paper (85); 24 cartons (84); pack-thread (10); painter's fee for painting a backcloth (6.10 scudi); sulphur (5); gunpowder (25); fee to porters (1.10 scudi); four wax torches (3.50 scudi); white lead (5); 300 pins (35); pastries (50); a harp (10); whitewash and a brush (30); painted clubs (20); two silver booklets (10); colour (15); eight 'pizzetti di bianco magneare' [lace? goatee beards?] (20). The following specific expenses related to the erection of the stage: nails (three payments totalling 1.61 scudi); pulleys or metal rings (10); Mr Bartholameo's fee for three days' work (1.5 scudi)

The currency denominations are not entirely clear from the records; the smaller amounts may be reckoned in baiocchi (1 scudo = 10 giuli = 100 baiocchi).

EARLY TEXTUAL HISTORY
c. 1633: transcribed in MS; 46 leaves; includes music for Song 2. The epilogue was transcribed again on a separate sheet, apparently as an actor's part with a cue, and pasted into the MS at some unknown date.

REFERENCES
Annals Supp. I; *ELR* 3 (1973), 60–93.

2398. Pastoral Court Masque

EVIDENCE
Florentine diplomatic correspondence (Amerigo Salvetti to Ferdinand de Medici, Grand Duke of Tuscany, 25 February, 4, 11, 18 March 1633, Gregorian); Venetian diplomatic correspondence (Vincenzo Gussoni to the Doge Francesco Erizzo and the Senate, 18 March 1633, Gregorian); letter from John Flower to John, 1st Viscount Scudamore, dated 2 March 1633; Revels Accounts; Works Accounts; Queen Henrietta Maria's debenture accounts (Kew: National Archives, LR 5/63, 5/65–6).

GENRE
masque
Contemporary: *balletto* (Salvetti); *ballet* (endorsement on mercers' bill); masque (Revels Accounts, Works Accounts)

TITLE
Later Assigned: *The Shrovetide Masque*; *The Queen's Masque at Shrovetide*; *Masque of Vices, Furies, and Witches*

DATE
5 March 1633

2398. Pastoral Court Masque — 1633

ORIGINAL PRODUCTION
Queen Henrietta Maria's Court at Denmark House

ROLES
Eight WOMEN in the antimasque (may include the Witches, Spirit, and Queen of Vices)
Four WANTON WOMEN in the antimasque, roaring girls
Four FURIES
The QUEEN OF VICES
Two WITCHES
A SPIRIT
MERCURY, a god
DIANA, goddess of chastity
CUPID, god of love
A PRIEST
Five SHEPHERDS in grey
Four SHEPHERDS in green
Three SHEPHERDS in white
Three SHEPHERDS in watchet
Six SHEPHERDESSES
MASQUERS, warriors, at least five in number

The number of gloves ordered establishes that there were twelve antimasquers, which tallies with the number of masks supplied for women (though the roles were played by men, which might be one reason why masks were required, especially if any of the performers had facial hair). These were presumably the twelve men whose names are scattered through the records: Abercrombie, Bowy, Boyce, Crofts, Guillan, Jay, la Pierre, Maynard, Murray, Prevost, Seymour, and Tartareau.

Doubling
Eight or nine actors doubled:
1–2: two Women Antimasquers, two Witches;
3: Woman Antimasquer, Queen of Vices;
4: Woman Antimasquer, Spirit, White Shepherd;
5: Woman Antimasquer, Fury;
6–7: two Wanton Women, two Furies;
8: Wanton Woman, Fury, White Shepherd;
9: Woman Antimasquer (?), Grey Shepherd.

SOURCES
Works Mentioned: possibly Bible: Genesis 30

The prop lambs might have been white and spotted purely for arbitrary reasons of verisimilitude, but there is also the chance that an allusion to Jacob and Laban was intended.

MUSIC
Dance: dancing (Gussoni)

PROPS
Weapons: a silver gilt dart, feathered like an arrow; a silver bow; a quiver of silver arrows hung on a tinsel scarf; five swords
Animals: eight bunches of artificial snakes (see also COSTUMES: FURIES); six artificial lambs, four white and two spotted

Small Portable Objects: a silver caduceus; a palm branch; a gilt book with carnation strings; five carnation scrips; four green scrips; four pink scrips; three watchet scrips; three white scrips; two silver wands; a gilt book; a kerchief
Large Portable Objects: twelve silver shepherds' hooks
Scenery: ivy; green cotton, fixed with black and yellow nails (perhaps representing grass)

COSTUMES AND MAKE-UP
WOMEN: smooth face masks; long bright hair; white gloves
WANTON WOMEN: one wears a green silk camlet gown and a hat with carnation and green ribbon, one a white taffeta waistcoat and petticoat, one a carnation taffeta waistcoat, petticoat, and a lawn '*bavolet*' head-dressing, and one a black taffeta waistcoat, petticoat, and a French hood and periwig; masks; whalebone sleeves; breeches; carnation and green ribbon about the waist instead of points; buskins with knotted carnation and green ribbon; carnation and green ribbons in their hair; tinsel night-rails (i.e. dressing gowns) edged with copper lace; taffeta garters and roses with silver lace
FURIES: masks and wigs; caps and girdles of snakes; taffeta doublets and hose and long black tiffany coats embroidered with flowers; buskins with ribbons; serpents around their legs, girdles, and necks; garters and roses
WITCHES: taffeta gowns and breeches, one black, one watchet; one wears a girdle about her head and neck and a large buckram doublet simulating a crooked back
SPIRIT: a liver-coloured taffeta suit; a scarf-girdle tied about the waist, armpits, and neck; buskins decorated with silver ribbon
QUEEN OF VICES: lemon-coloured taffeta gown and white taffeta breeches, with scalloped edging; garters and roses edged with silver lace
MERCURY: a carnation taffeta hat, with laces, a buttoned hatband, and silver wings; silver wings at his heels; white shoes
DIANA: long hair; a silver band with gold studs and a silver half-moon; robes with sleeves; stays
CUPID: yellow curly hair; a garland of roses; wings of several coloured feathers; a suit with silver bases and bays
PRIEST: black curly hair; a laurel wreath tipped with gold; white shoes
GREY SHEPHERDS: ash-coloured taffeta caps, with two flaps buttoned on the crown of the head, decorated with silver balls; ash-coloured buskins puffed with tinsel; calico hose
GREEN SHEPHERDS: green taffeta caps with a peak in front; garlands of oak leaves tipped with gold; pink belts; green leather buskins puffed with tinsel; calico hose

WHITE SHEPHERDS: white taffeta caps with flaps in front and at the neck, and a silver ball; watchet belts; white leather buskins puffed with tinsel and decorated with ribbon; white taffeta gowns and breeches decorated with carnation and green ribbon, and broad ribbon at the knees of the breeches; garters and roses with silver lace; calico hose

WATCHET SHEPHERDS: taffeta hats with tinsel puffed bands and watchet ribbon; white belts; watchet leather buskins puffed with tinsel; calico hose

SHEPHERDESSES: long hair; garlands of flowers; white shoes; suits with sleeves; stays

MASQUERS: gowns in watchet and incarnadine (or carnation?) satin embroidered with yellow and white copper; gilt helmets set with Os; white plumes tipped with incarnadine; incarnadine belts and scabbards; plain silk hose; probably white satin petticoats

Miscellaneous: A character played by Guillaume la Pierre wore a black taffeta gown and girdle. The 24 musicians wore taffeta suits and taffeta sarcenet scarves of various colours. Ten antimasquers wore taffeta suits. Unknown characters wore: a tinsel ruff; a large pair of spectacles; a cap of budge fur; and a golden crown.

The bill submitted by the Queen's tailor, George Gellin, contains some anomalies with that submitted by the mercers Richard Miller and Rhys Williams: they supplied watchet and incarnadine satin for the masquers' gowns, but the gowns Gellin billed for were of carnation colour. The simplest explanation is that the mercers' incarnadine was the tailor's carnation; however, it is also notable that Gellin's same bill also has significant unresolvable anomalies in respect of The Shepherds' Paradise (**2395**), though admittedly the masque charges seem to have been paid, whereas those for the pastoral apparently were not. This casts a little doubt over not only the colour of the masquers' gowns but also, by association, the petticoats listed in the same bill.

Since Orgel and Strong were unaware of the existence of this masque, it might be worth considering the possibility that some of the surviving Inigo Jones designs may be ascribed to it. In particular, there are two drawings of Furies. One of them (Orgel and Strong no. 416) is labelled 'Discord' and therefore was certainly executed for Salmacida spolia (**2724**). The other (no. 417) accompanies a head-dress design for a costume also sketched in no. 418, which Orgel and Strong accordingly catalogue as a rejected design for Salmacida spolia; but perhaps it belongs to this masque instead.

EARLY STAGE HISTORY

Rehearsals: Rehearsals had begun by Friday 15 February 1633. One rehearsal took place on Saturday 2 March; five men worked day and night in connection with the rehearsal and were paid 16s.8d.

Preparation: The tailor George Gellin made patterns for the masquers' gowns. The mercers Richard Miller and Rhys Williams delivered cloth for the costumes on Saturday 16 and Friday 22 February. Richard Alworth delivered green frieze on Wednesday 27 February. Charles Gentile finished making the masquers' costumes on Monday 4 March, and the day of the performance, Tuesday 5 March, saw deliveries from Joseph Atkinson (antimasquers' gloves), John Fausse (footwear), Arthur Knight (costumes and props), Peter Lermitt (plumes)

Preparation of Venue: The temporary theatre at Denmark House was joisted and boarded for the masque and the degrees at the lower end were modified; this work took place during the four weeks between Sunday 3 February and Saturday 2 March. Richard Scutt (Groom of the Queen's Chamber) brought props and other items (including chamber pots) from Whitehall to Denmark House for the production. The lighting branches at Denmark House were garnished with ivy on Monday 4 March; five men did the work, commissioned by William Hurt, and were paid 8s. The ivy was collected at Greenwich and Hyde Park, at a cost of £1.10s. Ralph Grinder laid down green cotton, presumably on the stage.

Performance: at Denmark House on Tuesday 5 March 1633 (Shrove Tuesday). The cast included: Queen Henrietta Maria; Sophia Carew; Victoria Cary; Bridget Feilding, Countess of Desmond; Mary Hamilton, Marchioness of Hamilton; Sophia Neville; Ellenor Villiers (Masquers); Mr Boyce, Mr Guillan (Women Antimasquers?); [James?] Bowy, William Crofts (Women Antimasquers, Witches); Guillaume la Pierre (Woman Antimasquer, the Queen of Vices); [Henry?] Seymour (Woman Antimasquer, Spirit, White Shepherd); [Abraham?] Abercrombie (Woman Antimasquer, Fury); Sir John Maynard (Wanton Woman); [Charles or Henry?] Murray (Wanton Woman, Fury); [Henry?] Jay (Wanton Woman, Fury); Raphael Tartareau (Wanton Woman, Fury, White Shepherd); Mr Prevost (Woman Antimasquer?/Grey Shepherd). The audience included: King Charles I; Henry Oxenstierna; Gustavus Horne and five other gentlemen of Oxenstierna's retinue; Ipolito Agostini. The performance took place at night and ended not long before dawn.

Aftermath: Richard Scutt returned the items borrowed from Whitehall Palace. The lighting branches were removed on Wednesday 6 March; five men did the work and were paid 8s.

It is conceivable that the antimasquer referred to in one bill as 'Mr Guillan' might have been Guillaume la Pierre rather than a distinct individual; this would mean that there are only eleven identifiable antimasque performers.

Production Expenses

Exchequer: The cost of converting the temporary theatre for the masque was £7. Six men worked day and night on the day of the performance, and were paid a total of 19s.

Queen's Purse: The total cost of the masque borne by the Queen amounted to £561.6s.11d; further costs totalling at least £145.14s.7d were saved by unilaterally reducing the tradesmen's bills. Payments were made over the ensuing three years, initially on Thursday 4 April 1633 and then on Monday 17, Tuesday 18, and Thursday 20 March 1634. These early payments were mainly for the costumes worn by the Queen and other masquers. On Thursday 12 March 1635, there were still bills of £442.1s.4d outstanding, and the Queen issued a warrant to pay them, but only one bill was settled that year, on Thursday 9 July. The remaining bills were paid on Friday 4 and Saturday 5 March 1636. In the following breakdown, some minor costume items cannot be disentangled from props, and are listed under *Props*.

Masquers' Costumes: Payments totalled £202.19s, reduced by £52.8s. They were made on the following dates. On Monday 17 March 1634, to the embroiderer Charles Gentile, for three masquing suits (£120, £36 less than billed), and for gluing and cutting them (£6, half what was billed). On Tuesday 18 March 1634, to the mercers Richard Miller and Rhys Williams, for materials used in masquing gowns worn by the Queen, Sophia Neville, and Victoria Cary (£44.11s), and for lining them (£10.10s, £2.2s less than billed). On Thursday 20 March 1634, to the hosier John Buckner, for the Queen's silk hose (two pairs, £3.10s). On Thursday 9 July 1635, to the feather-dresser Peter Lermitt for three plumes (£7.4s, £3.6s less than billed). On Friday 4 March 1636, to John Walker, for gilt helmets for the Queen, Sophia Neville, and Victoria Cary (£3, £1 less than billed), and for Lady Desmond and the Marchioness of Hamilton (£2, £1 less than billed). On an unknown date, the tailor George Gellin was paid for making two patterns for masquers' gowns (£1.5s, 15s less than billed), three carnation satin gowns and white satin petticoats for the Queen, 'Mrs Cary' (probably Victoria Cary, but possibly Sophia Carew), and Ellenor Villiers (£4.19s, £2.5s less than billed).

Antimasque Costumes: Payments totalled £54.5s.4d, reduced by at least £11.19s.2d. They were all made on Friday 4 March 1636, to: the milliner Joseph Atkinson, for gloves (£2, 8s less than billed); John Houseman, for a Woman's wig and Fury's mask and wig for Tartareau (£1, 12s less than billed), Fury's mask and wig and Woman's wig, headpiece, and mask for Jay (£1, 12s less than billed), wigs and masks for Bowy, Crofts, Seymour, and Murray (£2, 8s less than billed), wig for la Pierre (13s.4d, 6s.8d less than billed), Wanton Women's masks (13s.4d, 6s.8d less than billed), Fury's wig and mask for Abercrombie (10s, 2s less than billed), and masks for Jay and Tartareau (6s.8d, 3s.4d less than billed); the tailor James Masson (received on his behalf by Rhys Williams), for Tartareau's Wanton Woman costume (£5.15s.6d, at least 9s less than billed, but one original amount illegible), Tartareau's Fury costume (£3.1s.11d, 17s.4d less than billed), Jay's Fury costume (£4.2s.11d, £1.6s.1d less than billed), Jay's Wanton Woman costume (£5.10s, 15s less than billed), Murray's Wanton Woman costume (£3.2s.6d, 2s less than billed), Murray's Fury costume (£3.2s.11d, 16s.4d less than billed), Abercrombie's Fury costume (£3.2s.11d, £1.18s.7d less than billed), Seymour's Spirit costume (£2.15s, 5s less than billed), Maynard's Wanton Woman costume (£3.9s.10d, 10s.2d less than billed), Crofts's Witch costume (£1.9s.3d), Bowy's Witch costume (£2.18s.9d, 2s less than billed), and la Pierre's Queen of Vices costume (£4.14s.6d, 15s less than billed); John Walker, for caps of snakes (£1.6s.8d, 13s.4d less than billed), girdles of snakes (13s.4d, 6s.8d less than billed), and braces of snakes for the Furies' legs (16s, 4s less than billed).

Gods' and Priest's Costumes: Payments totalled £7.7s.6d, reduced by £4.15s. They were made on the following dates. On Friday 4 March 1636, to: the shoemaker John Fausse, for Mercury's and Priest's shoes (6s, 1s less than billed); the tailor Gilbert Morette, for Mercury's suit (£1.5s, £1 less than billed) and its lining (6s, half what was billed), Diana's robes (10s, 4s less than billed) and stays and lining (2s.6d, 2s less than billed), Priest's robe (5s, 2s less than billed) and stays, stiffening, and lining (2s.6d), and Cupid's costume (6s, 2s.6d less than billed), its lining and bays (4s, 3s less than billed), and silver stuff (15s, 9s less than billed). On Saturday 5 March 1636, to the haberdasher Arthur Knight, for Mercury's hat (6s, 4s less than billed), hatband (2s, 6d less than billed), hat wings (2s, 6d less than billed), and heel-wings (2s), Diana's wig (15s, half what was billed) and band (2s, 1s.6d less than billed), Cupid's wig (15s, 5s less than billed), garland (3s, 2s less than billed), and wings (10s, half what was billed), and the Priest's wig (6s, 4s less than billed) and laurel wreath (2s.6d, 3s less than billed).

Pastoral Costumes: Payments totalled £54.4s.6d, reduced by £16.17s.6d. They were made on the following dates. On Friday 4 March 1636, to: John Fausse, for ash-coloured buskins (£2, 10s less than billed), green buskins (£1.12s, 8s less than billed), watchet buskins (£1.12s, 8s less than billed), white buskins (£1.4s, 6s less than billed), shepherdesses' shoes (15s, 2s.6d less than billed), tinsel (£1.10s, £1.4s less than billed) and laces (2s.6d); James Masson (received on his behalf by Rhys Williams), for Tartareau's White Shepherd costume (£3.12s, 11s less than billed), Seymour's White Shepherd costume (£4.9s.6d, 8s.6d less than billed); Gilbert Morette for shepherds' suits (£15, £7.10s less than billed), shepherds' hose (£3.15s), calico lining (£2.7s.6d), shepherdess's suits (£6, £1.10s less than billed), and stays and sleeve lining (12s). On Saturday 5 March 1636, to Arthur Knight, for Grey Shepherds' caps (10s, 5s less than billed) and silver balls (5s, 2s.6d less than billed), Green Shepherds' caps (8s, 4s less than billed) and oak garlands (12s, 8s less than billed), White Shepherds' caps (6s, 3s less than billed) and silver balls (1s, 6d less than billed), Watchet Shepherds' hats (18s, 12s less than billed) and hatbands (10s, 5s less than billed), and the Shepherdesses' wigs (£5.10s,

£2 less than billed) and garlands (£1.4s, 16s less than billed).

Costumes (Miscellaneous and Sundry): Payments totalled £216.17s.1d, reduced by £52.14s.6d. They were made on the following dates. On Friday 4 March 1636, to: James Masson (received on his behalf by Rhys Williams), for la Pierre's black gown (11s); Richard Miller and Rhys Williams for taffeta, grogram, and satin (£188.11s, £27.12s.6d less than billed); Gilbert Morette, for fine Flanders thread (16s), nightrails (£1, half what was billed), a tinsel ruff (6s, half what was billed), bone-lace (£3.15s.7d, £3.16s less than billed), coin-lace (£5.12s.11d, £5.12s.10d less than billed), fringe (£10.4s.1d, £9.14s.6d less than billed), tinsel (£3, half what was billed), buttons (6s), lawn bands (£1.2s.6d), tinsel ribbon (12s, 12s.8d less than billed), and tiffany (£1, half what was billed).

Props: Payments totalled £16.5s.6d, reduced by £5.11s.3d. They were made on the following dates. On Friday 4 March 1636, to John Walker, for three gilt swords (£1, 10s less than billed), bunches of snakes (16s, 4s less than billed), spectacles, wand, and book (6s.8d, 3s.4d less than billed), a cap and a kerchief (13s.4d, 6s.8d less than billed), crown and wand (13s.4d, 6s.8d less than billed), shepherds' hooks (13s.4d, 6s.8d less than billed), four green scrips and belts (£2), and two gilt swords (13s.4d, 6s.8d less than billed). On Saturday 5 March 1636, to Arthur Knight, for Mercury's caduceus (2s.6d, 3s less than billed), Diana's dart (2s, 1s.6d less than billed), Cupid's bow (4s), quiver and arrows (4s, 2s less than billed), and tinsel scarf (3s, 2s less than billed), a palm branch (2s), a gilt book (2s, 1s less than billed), five carnation scrips (£1, 5s less than billed), four pink scrips and belts (16s, 4s less than billed), three watchet scrips and belts (12s, 3s less than billed), three white scrips and belts (12s, 3s less than billed), eight shepherds' hooks (£1.4s, 16s less than billed), six lambs (6s, 3s less than billed), spangled lace and fringe (£4, £1.1s.3d less than billed), and taffeta (£1, 2s.6d less than billed).

General: Other payments totalled £9.8s, reduced by £1.9s.2d. They were made on the following dates. On Thursday 4 April 1633, to Richard Scutt (£1 for his work on this and *The Shepherds' Paradise*, **2395**). On Friday 4 March 1636, to: the woollen-draper Richard Aldworth, for green frieze (£7.8s, £1.17s less than billed); the upholsterer Ralph Grinder (£1, 2s.2d less than billed), including for sewing and laying down green cotton (18s billed), nails (3s.8d billed), and carriage of the cotton (6d billed).

REFERENCES
Butler, 373; *Cal. Ven. 1632–6*, 86; *ELR* 29 (1999), 79–94; Loomie, 138–9; McGee-Meagher 1625–34, 70–1; MSC 10, 45; MSC 13, 122; *N&Q* 221 (1976), 223–5; *ShS* 11 (1958), 110; Steele, 244; *Theatre Survey* 20 (1979), 18–19.

2399. Perkin Warbeck

TEXT
Printed in 1634 (STC 11157), probably from an authorial fair copy annotated for use as a promptbook.

GENRE
history
Contemporary: history, play (prologue); chronicle history (t.p.); poem (Donne's commendatory verses); tragedy (S.R.)

TITLE
Printed: *The Chronicle History of Perkin Warbeck: A Strange Truth*
Contemporary: *Perkin Warbeck*

AUTHOR
John Ford

DATE
Limits: 1625–34
Best Guess: 1633

Ure takes the title-page reference to the play's being 'sometimes' (i.e. formerly) performed by Queen Henrietta's Men to indicate a significantly earlier date; this is possible, but the sense could just as well be that the play had been dropped from the company's repertory by the time it was published. One shred of evidence that might support that hypothesis is that *Perkin Warbeck* was not among the former Queen Henrietta's Men plays which became part of the Cockpit repertory that was protected in 1639.

ORIGINAL PRODUCTION
Queen Henrietta's Men at the Cockpit

PLOT
The Wars of the Roses are at an end, but civil war still threatens King Henry VII's throne, stirred up by Margaret of Burgundy's support for pretenders: Lambert Simnel's rebellion has been defeated, but Perkin Warbeck is coming to Scotland, claiming to be the younger of the murdered Princes in the Tower; moreover, insurrection is brewing in Cornwall. The informer Clifford also tells Henry of traitors in his court, among them his former friend, the Lord Chamberlain Stanley. Stanley is executed, and Henry takes order to deal with the Cornish rebels and to strengthen the frontier with Scotland: he anticipates that King James IV will be active in his support of Warbeck's claim. The Cornish rebels march on London, but are routed and their ringleaders executed.

In Scotland, King James receives Warbeck with honour, and has him married to his kinswoman, Catherine Gordon, despite her father's opposition. She insists on accompanying her new husband to war, and with King James they invade England. Warbeck expresses concern for the English people, even though none of them turn out in his support. The Scottish army lays siege to Norham Castle, but it is relieved by English forces under the Earl of Surrey, who then marches into Scotland. King James offers to fight Surrey in single combat, but instead the Bishop of Durham goes to the Scottish court to negotiate a diplomatic solution. He and the Spanish envoy Ayala succeed: in return for Warbeck's expulsion from Scotland, King James is to marry King Henry's daughter and be exempted from paying restitution for the war. Catherine leaves the kingdom with her husband.

Warbeck lands in Cornwall and is proclaimed King Richard IV, but takes flight when it becomes clear that a battle is imminent. King Henry's forces rout Warbeck's followers; Catherine is taken and treated honourably, and Warbeck gives himself up from sanctuary. He is sent to the Tower and, after several escape attempts, is condemned to death. The former pretender Lambert Simnel encourages him to confess in hope of mercy, but Warbeck will not admit imposture and continues to behave as if he really is the rightful Plantagenet King. He takes his leave of Catherine and goes to the gallows with his followers.

SCENE DESIGNATION
prol., 1.1–3, 2.1–3, 3.1–4, 4.1–5, 5.1–3, ep. (act-division Q, scene-division Revels)

ROLES
PROLOGUE
King HENRY VII of England, of the House of Tudor; a married man and a father; formerly Duke of Richmond; also called Harry Richmond
Bishop FOXE of Durham
Vere, Earl of OXFORD, an English courtier
Howard, Earl of SURREY, an English courtier and soldier; later general of the English army in the north
Sir William STANLEY, Henry VII's Lord Chamberlain
Lord DAUBENEY, an English courtier; later appointed Lord Chamberlain
A GUARD attending Henry VII (1.1, *non-speaking*)
URSWICK, Henry VII's chaplain
Alexander Gordon, Earl of HUNTLY, an old Scottish courtier, Catherine's father; later appointed ambassador to England
Lord DALYELL, a young Scottish nobleman
Lady CATHERINE Gordon, a young woman; Huntly's daughter, James IV's kinswoman, a princess of the blood royal; later Warbeck's wife; also called Kate
JANE Douglas, a gentlewoman, Lady Catherine's maid
The Earl of CRAWFORD, a Scottish courtier, the Countess's husband
Sir Robert CLIFFORD, an English traitor turned informer
The COUNTESS of Crawford, the Earl's wife
LADIES accompanying the Countess (2.1, *non-speaking*)

King JAMES IV of Scotland, a young, unmarried man
Perkin WARBECK, a young royal pretender, son of a Tournai Jew; later Catherine's husband; claims to be Richard, Duke of York, a Plantagenet and rightfully King Richard IV of England; also called Duke Perkin, King Perkin, and Dick IV
Stephen FRION, Warbeck's tutor and secretary; formerly Henry VII's French secretary; also called Master Secretary Frion
HERON, a bankrupt mercer, Warbeck's follower; formerly an apprentice
SKELTON, a tailor, Warbeck's follower
ASTLEY, a scrivener, Warbeck's follower
JOHN A-WATER, formerly Mayor of Cork, Warbeck's follower
An EXECUTIONER attending Stanley to his death (2.2, *non-speaking*)
Stanley's CONFESSOR (2.2, *non-speaking*)
ATTENDANTS on Daubeney and Oxford (3.1, *non-speaking*)
Four Scots ANTICS, masquers (3.2, *non-speaking*)
Four IRISHMEN, masquers (3.2, *non-speaking*)
Pedro AYALA, a Castilian, the King of Spain's ambassador to Scotland
SOLDIERS in the Scottish army (3.4, *non-speaking*)
SOLDIERS in the garrison of Norham Castle (3.4, *non-speaking*)
DRUMMERS in the English army (4.1, *non-speaking*)
MARCHMOUNT, James IV's herald
A Scottish HERALD (4.1, *non-speaking*)
A POST, who delivers a packet to Henry VII (4.4)
Catherine's SERVANT, a groom (5.1)
Oxford's MEN (5.1, *non-speaking*)
A GUARD of soldiers attending Henry VII (5.2, *non-speaking*)
ATTENDANTS on Catherine (5.2, *non-speaking*)
A CONSTABLE supervising the stocking of Warbeck
OFFICERS attending the Constable (5.3, *non-speaking*)
Lambert SIMNEL, formerly a rebel and pretender, now Henry VII's falconer
ONLOOKERS when Warbeck is stocked (5.3, *non-speaking*)
A SHERIFF supervising the execution (5.3, *non-speaking*)
OFFICERS attending the Sheriff (5.3, *non-speaking*)
EPILOGUE

Speaking Parts: 29

Stage Directions and Speech Prefixes
PROLOGUE: *Prologue* (heading)
HENRY VII: *King Henry | King Henrie* (s.d.s); *King | King H<enry>* (s.p.s); *Henry the seventh* (d.p.)
FOXE: *Durham | Darham* (s.d.s); *Durh<am>* (s.p.s); *Bishop of Durham* (d.p.)
OXFORD: *Oxford* (s.d.s and d.p.); *Ox<ford>* (s.p.s)
SURREY: *Surrey* (s.d.s, s.p.s, and d.p.)
STANLEY: *sir William Stanly, Lord Chamberlain | Stanly* (s.d.s); *Stan<ly>* (s.p.s); *Sir William Stanly* (d.p.)

DAUBENEY: *Lord Dawbney* (s.d.s); *Dawb<ney>* (s.p.s); *Dawbney* (s.d.s and d.p.)
GUARD: *A Guard* (s.d.s)
URSWICK: *Urswick | Urswicke* (s.d.s); *Ursw<ick>* (s.p.s); *Urswicke Chaplain to King Henry* (d.p.)
HUNTLY: *Huntley | [one of] the Noblemen* (s.d.s); *Hunt<ley>* (s.p.s); *Earl of Huntley* (d.p.)
DALYELL: *Daliell* (s.d.s and s.p.s); [one of] *the Noblemen* (s.d.s); *Lord Daliell* (d.p.)
CATHERINE: *Katherine* | [one of the] *Ladies* (s.d.s); *Kate | Kath<erine>* (s.p.s); *Lady Katherine Gourdon, wife to Perkin* (d.p.)
JANE: *Jane* (s.d.s and s.p.s); [one of the] *Ladies* (s.d.s); *Jane Douglas Lady Kath<erine's> maid* (d.p.)
CRAWFORD: *Crawford* | [one of] *the Noblemen* (s.d.s); *Crawf<ord>* (s.p.s); *Earl of Crawford* (d.p.)
CLIFFORD: *Sir Robert Clifford* (s.d.s and d.p.); *Clifford* (s.d.s); *Cliff<ord>* (s.p.s)
COUNTESS: *Countess of Crawford* (s.d.s and d.p.); [one of the] *Ladies* (s.d.s); *Countess* (s.d.s and s.p.s)
LADIES: *other Ladies | Ladies* (s.d.s)
JAMES IV: *King James* (s.d.s and s.p.s); *the King | King* (s.d.s); *James the 4th King of Scotl<and>* (d.p.)
WARBECK: *Perkin | Warbeck | Warbecke* (s.d.s); *Warb<eck>* (s.p.s); *Perkin Warbeck* (d.p.)
FRION: *Fryon* | [one of] *Perkin's followers* (s.d.s); *Frion* (s.d.s and s.p.s); *Frion [Perkin Warbeck's] Secretary* (d.p.)
HERON: *Heron a Mercer* (s.d.s and d.p.); [one of] *Perkin's followers* | [one of the] *Counsellors* | [one of the] *Prisoners* (s.d.s); *Heron* (s.d.s and s.p.s)
SKELTON: *Sketon a Tailor* (s.d.s and d.p.); [one of] *Perkin's followers | Sketon* | [one of the] *Counsellors* | [one of the] *Prisoners* (s.d.s); *Sket<on>* (s.p.s)
ASTLEY: *Astley a Scrivener* | [one of] *Perkin's followers* | [one of the] *Counsellors* | [one of the] *Prisoners* (s.d.s); *Astley* (s.d.s and s.p.s); *Astly a Scrivener* (d.p.)
JOHN A-WATER: *John a Watring* | [one of] *Perkin's followers* | [one of the] *Counsellors* | *John a Water* | [one of the] *Prisoners* (s.d.s); *Mayor* (s.d.s and s.p.s); *Mayor of Cork* (s.d.s and d.p.)
EXECUTIONER: *Executioner* (s.d.s)
ATTENDANTS: *attendants* (s.d.s); *Servingmen* (d.p.)
ANTICS: *four Scotch Antics* | [four of] *The Masquers* (s.d.s)
IRISHMEN: *four wild Irish* | [four of] *The Masquers* (s.d.s)
AYALA: *Hialas* (s.d.s and s.p.s); *Hialas a Spanish Agent* (d.p.)
SOLDIERS: *Soldiers* (s.d.s)
SOLDIERS: *Soldiers* (s.d.s and d.p.)
DRUMMERS: *Drums* (s.d.s)
MARCHMOUNT: *March-mount* (s.d.s); *March<mount>* (s.p.s); *Marchmount a Herald* (d.p.)
HERALD: *another Herald* (s.d.s)
POST: *a Post* (s.d.s); *Post* (s.p.s)
SERVANT: *one servant* (s.d.s); *Servant* (s.p.s); [one of the] *Servingmen* (d.p.)
MEN: *followers* (s.d.s)

GUARD: *a guard of Soldiers* (s.d.s)
ATTENDANTS: *attendants* (s.d.s)
CONSTABLE: *Constable* (s.d.s, s.p.s, and d.p.)
OFFICERS: *Officers* (s.d.s and d.p.)
SIMNEL: *Lambert Simnell* (s.d.s and d.p.); *Simnell* (s.d.s); *Lamb<ert>* (s.p.s)
SHERIFF: *Sheriff* (s.d.s)
OFFICERS: *Officers* (s.d.s and d.p.)
EPILOGUE: *Epilogue* (heading)

OTHER CHARACTERS
The people of England (1.1, 2.2, 3.1, 3.4, 4.4, 5.2)
The casualties of the Wars of the Roses, including ten English kings and princes, sixty dukes and earls, 1,000 lords and knights, and 250,000 English subjects (1.1)
King Edward IV (1.1–3, 3.3, 4.2–3, 5.3)
King Edward V, son of Edward IV (1.1, 2.1, 4.2, 5.3)
Richard, Duke of York, son of Edward IV, whom Perkin Warbeck claims to be (1.1)
King Richard III, Duke of Gloucester, a tyrant, brother of Edward IV, and uncle of Edward V and Richard, Duke of York (1.1, 1.3, 2.1, 5.2–3)
Henry VII's Queen, Edward IV's daughter (1.1, 3.3, 5.2)
Margaret, Duchess of Burgundy, sister of Edward IV and Richard III, aunt of Edward V and Richard, Duke of York (1.1, 1.3, 2.1, 4.2–3, 5.2)
The Duke of York, Margaret of Burgundy's dead father (1.1)
Simnel's supporters, including: the Earl of Lincoln; the Earl of Kildare; Lord Geraldine; Francis, Lord Lovell; Martin Schwarz, a German baron; Broughton (1.1)
De la Pole, Earl of Suffolk, Lincoln's father, appointed joint commander against the Cornish rebels (1.1, 2.2, 3.1)
Warbeck's supporters in Ireland, the Geraldines and the Butlers (1.1)
Charles, King of France, Warbeck's supporter (1.1, 1.3, 2.1)
Warbeck's followers in France, including: the bastard Neville; Sir Taylor; and 100 English rebels (1.1)
Maximilian of Bohemia, Archduke of Burgundy and Holy Roman Emperor, Warbeck's supporter (1.1, 2.1, 4.3)
Barley, a supporter of Warbeck (1.1)
Adam Muir, a Scottish knight, Dalyell's ancestor (1.2)
Adam Muir's daughter (1.2)
King James I of Scotland, son of Adam Muir's daughter (1.2)
Plotters against Henry VII, including: John Ratcliffe, Lord Fitzwater; Sir Simon Mountford; Sir Thomas Thwaites; William Daubeney; Cressoner; Astwood; Worsley, the Dean of St Paul's; two friars; Robert Ratcliffe (1.3)
The Cornish rebels, 10,000 in number (1.3, 2.2, 3.1, 4.2–3, 4.5)

Joseph, a blacksmith, ringleader of the Cornish rebellion (1.3, 3.1)
Flamank, a lawyer, ringleader of the Cornish rebellion (1.3, 3.1)
Lord Audley, supporter of the Cornish rebellion (1.3, 2.2, 3.1)
Robert Bruce, James IV's ancestor (2.1)
The Earl of Derby, Stanley's brother, Henry VII's stepfather (2.2)
Henry VII's mother, Derby's wife (2.2)
Henry VII's army of 26,000 men, including cavalry and infantry (2.2, 3.1, 4.4, 5.1)
The Earl of Essex, appointed joint commander against the Cornish rebels (2.2, 3.1)
The people of Scotland (2.3, 4.3)
The people of London (3.1)
Kentish men who resisted the Cornish rebels, including: the Earl of Kent; George Abergavenny; Cobham; Poynings; Guildford (3.1)
Dinham, High Treasurer of England (3.1)
James IV's army of 12,000 men (3.2, 3.4, 4.1)
King Ferdinand of Spain (3.3, 4.3)
Queen Isabel, Ferdinand's consort (3.3)
The Moors, expelled from Spain by Ferdinand (3.3)
Prince Arthur, Prince of Wales, Henry VII's son (3.3, 4.3)
Lady Catherine [of Aragon], Ferdinand's daughter, Arthur's fiancée (3.3, 4.3)
Edward, Earl of Warwick, Clarence's son (3.3, 5.3)
The Duke of Clarence, younger brother of Edward IV (3.3, 5.3)
The English army in the north, including twelve earls and barons, 100 knights and gentlemen, and 20,000 soldiers (3.4)
Lord Brooke, Henry VII's steward, the English admiral (3.4, 5.2)
English troops following Daubeney (3.4)
The mother of Richard, Duke of York (4.2)
English merchants who have been admitted to trade in Antwerp (4.3)
Princess Margaret, Henry VII's daughter (4.3)
Morton, the English Archbishop (4.4)
The Mayor of Exeter (4.4)
4,000 Cornish yeomen, who swear fealty to Warbeck (4.5, 5.1)
The Earl of Devonshire, wounded in the battle with Warbeck (5.1–2)
Gentlemen of Devon who repulsed Warbeck (5.1–2)
Oxford's ancestors (5.1)
Rhys ap Thomas (5.2)
The Duke of Buckingham, a young man (5.2)
Buckingham's father (5.2)
100 knights and squires attending Buckingham (5.2)
The Duke of Brittany, who sheltered Henry VII when he was Duke of Richmond (5.2)
Digby, Lieutenant of the Tower of London (5.2)
The jury who condemned Warbeck (5.3)
Osbeck, Warbeck's father, a Jew of Tournai (5.3)
The priest who married Warbeck and Catherine (5.3)

SETTING
Period: fifteenth century: the play dramatizes events which took place between 1495 and 1499; 3.1 takes place on a Saturday, and 4.5 on 10 September
Time-Scheme: 1.3 takes place at night; 3.1 takes place in the morning between 10 a.m. and dinner-time; 3.2 takes place in the evening
Place: England and Scotland

Geography
London: the Tower; Westminster; St Paul's Cathedral; St George's Fields; Newgate prison; Tower Hill; Bedlam
Kent: Cobham; Blackheath; Deptford Strand Bridge
Surrey: Richmond
[*Hampshire*]: Winchester; Beaulieu; Southampton
[*Wiltshire*]: Salisbury; Salisbury Plain
Devonshire: Exeter
Cornwall: Bodmin
[*Northumberland*]: Norham; Norham Castle; River Tweed; Berwick
England: Durham; Oxford; York; Lancaster; Gloucester; Lincoln; Bosworth; Derby; Essex; Suffolk; Warwick; Taunton; Buckingham
Scotland: Huntly; Crawford; Heydonhall; Cundrestine; Edington; Foulden; Ayton Castle
Wales: Abergavenny; Milford Haven
Ireland: Kildare; Cork
France: Burgundy; Brittany
Flanders: Tournai; Antwerp
Spain: Castile
Europe: Germany; Portugal; Bohemia
China

SOURCES
Narrative: Thomas Gainsford, *Perkin Warbeck* (1618); Sir Francis Bacon, *Henry VII* (1622); Raphael Holinshed, *Chronicles of England, Scotland, and Ireland* (1577, 2nd edn, 1587); possibly William Warner, *Albion's England* 7 (1589, repr. 1612)
Verbal: Reginald Scot, *The Discovery of Witchcraft* (1584; 5.3)

LANGUAGE
English
Latin: 13 words (4.5; Astley)

FORM
Metre: pentameter and prose
Rhyme: blank verse
Prologue: 26 lines, in couplets
Act-Division: 5 acts
Epilogue: 10 lines, in couplets
Lines (Spoken): 2,471 (2,368 verse, 103 prose)
Lines (Written): 2,662

STAGING
Doors: mentioned (2.1, s.d.); characters enter at two doors (3.2, s.d.)

Within: speech (1.3, implicit); shout (4.5, s.d.)
Above: characters appear above (2.1, 3.4, s.d.; at least five are there together at one point; there is interaction with the main stage)
Miscellaneous: Stanley scratches a cross on Clifford's face with his finger (2.2, s.d.; the context requires a wound that will scar)

MUSIC
Music: flourish (1.1, 2.2, 3.1–2, s.d.); hautboys (2.1, s.d.; 'sprightly music' has been called for); masque music (3.2, s.d.); a parley (3.4, s.d.); trumpet (4.1, s.d.)
Dance: the masquers dance (3.2, s.d.)

PROPS
Lighting: lights (1.3, s.d.; 3.2, dialogue)
Weapons: an axe (2.2, dialogue); Henry VII's sword (3.1, s.d.); a truncheon (3.4, s.d.); Dalyell's sword (5.1, dialogue); four halters (5.3, s.d.)
Musical Instruments: drums (4.1, s.d.)
Clothing: a chain (4.1, dialogue)
Money: a little purse (3.2, dialogue); crowns (4.1, dialogue)
Small Portable Objects: a paper (1.1, s.d.; 1.3, dialogue); a packet (4.4, dialogue); a padlock (5.3, dialogue); a key (5.3, dialogue)
Large Portable Objects: a white staff of office (2.2, s.d.); a leading staff (3.1, s.d.); seating for eight characters (3.2, implicit); military colours (4.1, s.d.)
Scenery: a throne (1.1, s.d.); stocks (5.3, s.d.)

COSTUMES
HENRY VII: a gorget and a plume of feathers (3.1, s.d.)
FOXE: a grey beard (dialogue); armed (3.4, s.d.)
CATHERINE: a riding suit (5.1, s.d.); her richest attire (5.2, s.d.)
JANE: a riding suit (5.1, s.d.)
SCOTS MASQUERS: 'accordingly habited' (3.2, s.d.; i.e. as Scotsmen)
IRISH MASQUERS: long hair, trousers, and 'accordingly habited' (3.2, s.d.; i.e. as Irishmen)
MARCHMOUNT: a herald's coat (4.1, s.d.)
HERALD: a coat (4.1, s.d.)
SIMNEL: dressed like a falconer (5.3, s.d.)

EARLY STAGE HISTORY
Performed by Queen Henrietta's Men at the Cockpit by 1634.

EARLY TEXTUAL HISTORY
1634: entered to Hugh Beeston in the Stationers' Register on Monday 24 February; entry names author. Sir Henry Herbert had licensed the book for publication, but evidently not unconditionally: Beeston was required to observe 'the caution in the licence'.
1634: **Q** printed by Thomas Purfoot for Hugh Beeston; collation A–K⁴ L1, 41 leaves; title page names acting company and theatre; Latin title-page motto which is also an anagram of the author's name (he is not otherwise named on the t.p.); list of roles; authorial dedication to William Cavendish, Earl of Newcastle; commendatory verses by George Donne, Ralph Eure, Sir George Grimes, John Brograve, and John Ford (the author's cousin).
c. 1630s–40s: a copy of Q was in the possession of John Horne (Vicar of Headington, Oxfordshire). After his death, his entire collection of play-books passed into the possession of John Houghton of Brasenose College, Oxford (c. 1608–77), then to James Herne (died 1685), and then to the library of Ralph Sheldon (1623–84) at Weston, where it was catalogued by Anthony Wood, probably in the late 1670s.
1652: a copy of Q was bound with six other Ford quartos, with a specially printed title page: *Comedies, tragi-comedies; & tragaedies*; the book was owned by Walter Chetwynd of Ingestre, Staffordshire. The other plays were *The Lover's Melancholy* (**2259**), *The Broken Heart* (**2281**), *'Tis Pity She's a Whore* (**2329**), *Love's Sacrifice* (**2360**), *The Fancies* (**2528**), and *The Lady's Trial* (**2617**).
1655: *The English Treasury of Wit and Language* entered in the Stationers' Register to Humphrey Moseley on Tuesday 16 January.
1655: ten extracts (from 1.1–2, 2.1, 3.1–2, 3.4, 4.3–4, 5.3) included in John Cotgrave's *The English Treasury of Wit and Language*, sigs. G8ᵛ, L1ᵛ, L8ʳ, R1ʳ, S7ᵛ, T4ᵛ, T6ᵛ, V5ᵛ; printed for Humphrey Moseley.
1657: advertised as for sale by the Newcastle-upon-Tyne bookseller William London.
1684: Nicholas Cox (Manciple of St Edmund Hall, Oxford) had a copy of Q in his bookshop. It had probably been previously owned by Gerard Langbaine, and appears on a list compiled by Anthony Wood on Saturday 13 December.
1690: a copy of Q was in the library at Petworth House.

The abbreviated MS version (Oxford: Bodleian, Rawlinson poet. 122), listed in some previous reference works as dating from c. 1700, is in fact of eighteenth-century origin.

EDITIONS
D. K. Anderson, Regents Renaissance Drama (Lincoln, Neb., 1965).
Peter Ure, Revels Plays (London, 1968).
Michael Neill and Colin Gibson, in *The Selected Plays of John Ford* (Cambridge, 1986), 221–335.
Marion Lomax, in *'Tis Pity She's a Whore and Other Plays*, Oxford English Drama (Oxford, 1995), 241–323.
Gilles Monsarrat, in *The Collected Works of John Ford*, gen. ed. Brian Vickers (Oxford, 2012–), vol. v.

REFERENCES
Annals 1633; Bawcutt C70; Bentley, iii. 454–6; Bodleian, MS Wood E. 4, art. 1, p. 13; Eyre & Rivington, i. 463; Greg 491; Hazlitt, 178; William London, *A*

Catalogue of the Most Vendible Books in England (London, 1657), sig. 2F1ᵛ; *MLR* 13 (1918), 401–11; *N&Q* 200 (1955), 223–5; *National Trust Year Book 1975–6* (London, [1976]), 62–4; *SP* 40 (1943), 186–203.

2400. The Coursing of a Hare

EVIDENCE
Sir Henry Herbert's office-book.

GENRE
comedy

TITLE
Performed: *The Coursing of a Hare, or The Madcap*

AUTHOR
William Heminges

DATE
March 1633

ORIGINAL PRODUCTION
King's Revels Company (presumably) at the Fortune

PLOT
The title refers to hunting: the chasing of game by hounds. This might have been literally represented, but might alternatively (or indeed also) have been a metaphor for the pursuit of human quarry.

ROLES
A MADCAP

EARLY STAGE HISTORY
1633: performed in March at the Fortune.

REFERENCES
Annals 1633; Bawcutt 252; Bentley, iv. 542–3; Hazlitt, 52; Sibley, 31–2.

2401. The Weeding of the Covent Garden

TEXT
Printed in 1658–9 (Wing B4872), in a version possibly with interpolations made for the revival of c. 1641.

GENRE
comedy
Contemporary: play (prol., S.R.); 'facetious comedy' (t.p.)

TITLE
Printed: *The Weeding of the Covent Garden, or The Middlesex Justice of Peace*
Contemporary: *The Covent Garden*; *Covent Garden Weeded*; *The Covent Garden Weeded*
Later Assigned: *The Weeding of Covent Garden*

AUTHOR
Richard Brome

DATE
Limits: 1632–3
Best Guess: Early 1633

The play dates from after the June 1632 proclamation requiring the gentry to remain on their country estates, and before the beginning, in May 1633, of official action against monopolists in 'the new soap-business' from which Mihil expects to make money. It may have been still in production, or at least was a recent memory, when *Covent Garden* (**2424**) premiered, probably in the early months of 1634.

PLOT
Rooksbill is building a new housing estate in Covent Garden; but such places tend to attract unworthy residents, so Cockbrain undertakes to ensure that the place will be clear of vice and enormity. He introduces Rooksbill to a potential tenant, the country gentleman Crosswill, a man of perverse temperament who always finds fault with whatever his offspring do. Two years ago, his niece Dorcas left the house after being seduced by a city gallant, and this so shocked his wild elder son Gabriel that he became a Puritan. The daughter, Katherine, has been unable to marry the man she wants, Cockbrain's son Anthony, and so refuses to marry at all. The younger son, Mihil, has been sent to town to study at the Inns of Court. Now Crosswill intends to move to London himself, and comes to inspect the new estate.

Mihil has run out of money, and cannot pay for his new boots and suit. He hears that his father is coming to pay him a surprise visit to see how he really spends his time, so he puts on a student's gown and arranges to be found poring over law-books; but he cannot get rid of the shoemaker and tailor, so they have to be disguised as law students too. Crosswill is characteristically displeased with what he finds, insists that Mihil spend his time more idly, as a gentleman should, and gives him money to that end—which Mihil uses to pay his debts.

A group of Mihil's friends tell him about Damaris, a new courtesan they heard singing on a Covent Garden balcony, but who seems unwilling to entertain clients. They invite him to join them at an assignation at the Goat tavern. Cockbrain spies on the meeting, disguised as an old soldier. Damaris fails to turn up, and the gallants sneak away, leaving Cockbrain and the gull Clotpoll to settle the bill. Rooksbill and Crosswill also dine at the Goat to discuss terms, and their respective daughters, Lucy and Katherine, become friends. Rooksbill invites the family to stay in his house until their lodgings are ready. Lucy confides to Katherine that she and Mihil, introduced to one another by her brother, are in love.

Mihil takes Gabriel to another tavern and gets him drunk. They are visited by Damaris, who turns out to be their absconded cousin Dorcas. Crosswill arrives unexpectedly, and Gabriel is put hastily to bed. Now the old man is annoyed that Mihil is wasting his time when he should be at his studies. Mihil affects a conversion to Gabriel's puritanical opinions and comes to his father asking his pardon and his permission to marry a widow—who is actually an old bawd. His father tells him to fetch a parson, but then changes his mind and insists that Mihil marry Lucy instead—which was the intention all along. After the exasperated Crosswill tells Katherine to marry *anyone*, so long as she does marry, she marries Anthony. Dorcas's seducer turns out to be Rooksbill's son, Nicholas, and he agrees to marry her. Nicholas also restores Gabriel to his original personality by putting him in soldier's clothes as he sleeps; when he wakes, he is a convinced martialist and no Puritan. Cockbrain arrives to arrest everyone, only to find that all the enormities have been committed by his friends, not least his own son. He sends them all away, and expresses the hope that Covent Garden will become a place for nobility rather than vice.

SCENE DESIGNATION
prol., 1.1–2, 2.1–2, 3.1–2, 4.1–2, 5.1–3, ep. (O, corrected)

ROLES
PROLOGUE
Master COCKBRAIN, a justice of the peace, Anthony's father; poses as an old soldier
Master ROOKSBILL, a builder, father of Nicholas and Lucy
Master Will CROSSWILL, a wealthy old country gentleman, father of Gabriel, Katherine, and Mihil, Dorcas's uncle
Master GABRIEL Crosswill, a Puritan, Crosswill's elder son, brother of Katherine and Mihil, Dorcas's cousin
Mistress KATHERINE, Crosswill's daughter, sister of Gabriel and Mihil, Dorcas's cousin; later Anthony's wife; also called Kate
BELT, Crosswill's servant, perhaps an old man
Madama DAMARIS, a courtesan; also called Dammy; in reality Dorcas, Crosswill's niece, cousin of Gabriel, Katherine, and Mihil
FRANCISCA, Damaris's woman, a whore; said to be little; also called Frank
Master NICHOLAS Rooksbill, Rooksbill's son, Lucy's brother; considered a debauched reprobate; also called Nick
ANTHONY, Cockbrain's son; also called Tony; later Katherine's husband

Mun CLOTPOLL, a gull; said to be little; also called Clot
MADGE Howlet, an old bawd; claims to be a childless widow; also called Mistress Margery Howlet
RAFE, Damaris's servant
Master MIHIL Crosswill, a law student and gentleman, Crosswill's younger son, brother of Katherine and Gabriel, Dorcas's cousin; also called Mich; later Lucy's husband
A TAILOR, Mihil's creditor
A SHOEMAKER, Mihil's creditor
A LAUNDRESS, Mihil's servant
LUCY, Rooksbill's daughter, Nicholas's sister, Dorcas's cousin; later Mihil's wife
HARRY, a drawer at the Goat (2.2)
The VINTNER at the Goat
Captain DRIBLOW, captain of the Philoblathici
A DRAWER at the Goat (3.1; may be Harry)
PIG, Damaris's young servant, a merchant's son
A DRAWER (4.1)
BETTY, a whore
A CITIZEN, possibly named Master Cuffless (4.1, 5.3)
A BOY at the Paris tavern (4.2)
A DRAWER at the Paris tavern (4.2; possibly the same as the boy)
A PARSON, who performs the marriages; possibly named Sir John (5.2–3)
The VINTNER of the Paris tavern (5.3)
The WATCH (5.3, *non-speaking*)
EPILOGUE

Speaking Parts: 29–32

Stage Directions and Speech Prefixes
PROLOGUE: *A Prologue* (heading)
COCKBRAIN: *Cockbrayne* | *Cockbrain* | *Cockbraine* (s.d.s); *Cock<brain>* (s.p.s); *Cockbrain, a Justice of Peace, the Weeder of the Garden* (d.p.)
ROOKSBILL: *Rookes-bill* | *Rooksbill* | *Rooksbill* (s.d.s); *Rookes<bill>* | *Rooks<bill>* (s.p.s); *Rooksbill, a great Builder in Covent-Garden* (d.p.)
CROSSWILL: *Croswill* | *Crossewill* (s.d.s); *Cross<ewill>* (s.p.s); *Crossewill, a Country Gentleman, Lodger in* [Rooksbill's] *Buildings* (d.p.)
GABRIEL: *Gabriel* (s.d.s); *Gab<riel>* (s.p.s); *Gabriel* [one of the] *Young Gentlemen Crossewill's elder son* (d.p.)
KATHERINE: *Katherine* | *Katharine* (s.d.s); *Kat<herine>* (s.p.s); *Katharine, Crossewill's Daughter* (d.p.)
BELT: *Belt* (s.d.s and s.p.s); *Belt, Crossewill's Servant* (d.p.)
DAMARIS: *Dorcas* | *Dorcas, alias Damaris* (s.d.s); *Dam<aris>* | *Dorc<as>* (s.p.s); *Dorcas, alias Damaris, Croswill's Niece* (d.p.)
FRANCISCA: *Frank* (s.d.s); *Fran<k>* (s.p.s); *Francisca* [one of] *Two Punks* (d.p.)
NICHOLAS: *Nich<olas> Rookesbill* | *Nick Rookesbill* (s.d.s); *Nick* (s.d.s and s.p.s); *Nich<olas>* (s.p.s); *Nicholas* [one of the] *Young Gentlemen Rookesbill's son* (d.p.)

ANTHONY: *Anthony* | *Anthonie* (s.d.s); *Ant<hony>* (s.p.s); *Anthony* [one of the] *Young Gentlemen Cockbraine's son* (d.p.)
CLOTPOLL: *Clotpoll* (s.d.s); *Clot<poll>* (s.p.s); *Mun Clotpoll, a foolish Gull* (d.p.)
MADGE: *Madge* (s.d.s and s.p.s); *Bawd* (s.d.s); *Margerie Howlet, a Bawd* (d.p.)
RAFE: *Rafe* (s.d.s); *Ra<fe>* (s.p.s); *Ralph, Dorcas' Servant* (d.p.)
MIHIL: *Mihill* | *Mihil* (s.d.s); *Mih<il>* (s.p.s); *Mihil* [one of the] *Young Gentlemen Cross<will's> younger son* (d.p.)
TAILOR: *Tailor* (s.d.s and s.p.s); *A Tailor* (d.p.)
SHOEMAKER: *Shoemaker* (s.d.s and s.p.s); *A Shoemaker* (d.p.)
LAUNDRESS: *Laundress* (s.d.s and s.p.s); *A Laundress* (d.p.)
LUCY: *Lucy* | *Lucie* (s.d.s); *Luc<y>* (s.p.s); *Lucie, Rooksbill's Daughter* (d.p.)
HARRY: *Drawer* (s.d.s and s.p.s); *A Drawer* (d.p.)
VINTNER: *Vintner* (s.p.s); *A Vintner* (d.p.)
DRIBLOW: *Captain Driblow* (s.d.s); *Captain* (s.d.s and s.p.s); *Driblow, Captain of the Philoblathici* (d.p.)
DRAWER: *Drawer* (s.d.s and s.p.s)
PIG: *Pig* (s.d.s and s.p.s); *Pig, Damaris' Servant* (d.p.)
DRAWER: *Drawer* (s.d.s and s.p.s)
BETTY: *Bettie* (s.d.s); *Bett<ie>* (s.p.s); *Bettie* [one of] *Two Punks* (d.p.)
CITIZEN: *Citizen* (s.d.s and s.p.s); *A Citizen* (d.p.)
BOY: *Boy* (s.d.s and s.p.s)
DRAWER: *Drawer* (s.d.s and s.p.s)
PARSON: *Parson* (s.d.s and s.p.s); *A Parson* (d.p.)
VINTNER: *Vintner* (s.d.s and s.p.s)
WATCH: *Watch* (s.d.s)
EPILOGUE: *Epilogue* (heading)

OTHER CHARACTERS
Justice Adam Overdo, Cockbrain's ancestor (1.1)
Katherine's dead mother (1.1)
A mountebank's wife (1.1)
A disreputable mountebank, Covent Garden's first tenant (1.1)
Idle people who gave up attending the theatre in order to see the mountebank instead (1.1)
The players, who cursed the mountebank (1.1)
Bess Bufflehead, a prostitute once employed by Madge (1.2)
The cook at the Goat (2.2)
Will and Zachary, drawers at the Goat (2.2; may appear on stage)
Tavern fiddlers (2.2, 4.2)
Fennor, a rhyming soldier (3.1; a real person)
A cobbler poet of Drury Lane (3.1)
A tapster poet of Drury Lane (3.1)
Hog, Pig's father, a merchant (3.1)
Gabriel's youthful companions, from twenty parishes (3.2)
Country maids who fancied Gabriel (3.2)
A bishop, Gabriel's master (3.2)
Madge's customers, whom Dorcas refused to see (4.2)
Madge's four dead husbands (5.1; possibly imaginary)

SETTING
Period: contemporary
Time-Scheme: The action takes place during a single day, beginning in the morning; 2.2 takes place at dinner-time and 4.2 at dusk. Two hours pass between 4.2 and 5.3.
Place: London

Geography
Covent Garden: the Piazza; [St Paul's Church]; the Goat tavern
London: the Paris tavern; Bankside; Whitefriars Dock; Duck Lane; St Paul's Churchyard; Drury Lane; the Dutch Church; St Helen's Church; Bridewell; Codpiece Row; Bedlam
[*Middlesex*]: Hammersmith; Knightsbridge Spital; Bloomsbury
England: Halifax
Ireland
France: Paris
The Low Countries: Amsterdam
Venice: the Piazza
Italy: Rome
Cyprus
Turkey
The Equator
The Torrid Zone

SOURCES
Narrative: Ben Jonson, *Bartholomew Fair* (**1757**; Cockbrain); Shackerley Marmion, *A Fine Companion* (**2378**; Driblow and the Philoblathici); Richard Brome, *The Novella* (**2383**; Dorcas)
Verbal: Virgil, *Eclogues* 1 (3.1); Horace, *Ars poetica* (t.p. motto); *The Book of Common Prayer*: Marriage service (1549, rev. 1552; 5.2); William Shakespeare, *1 Henry IV* (**1059**; 3.1); Ben Jonson, *Bartholomew Fair* (**1757**; 1.1; cited)
Works Mentioned: Bible: Bel and the Dragon (2.1); Ovid, *Tristia* 1.5 (4.1); *Amadis de Gaul* (fourteenth century; 2.1); Sir Thomas Littleton, *Les Tenures* (1481; 2.2, 4.2); Sir Anthony Fitzherbert, *The Book of Justices of Peace* (1505; 2.1); John Perkins, *The Laws of England* (1528; 2.1); Lord Berners (tr.), *Arthur of Britain* (written before 1533; printed 1560; 2.1); Sir James Dyer, *Reports* (1535-82; 2.1); *Adam Bell, Clim of the Clough, William of Cloudesly* (1536; 2.1); Anthony Munday, *Primaleon of Greece* (1595-6; 2.1); George Chapman, *Bussy D'Amboise* (**1428**; 4.2); there is a general reference to the demotic poet William Fennor (3.1)

LANGUAGE
English
Latin: 24 words (1.1, 2.1, 3.1, 5.2-3; Cockbrain, Clotpoll, Mihil, Lucy)

Italian: 1 word (1.2; Nicholas)
French: 10 words (4.2, 5.3; Mihil, Gabriel)

FORM
Metre: prose and pentameter
Rhyme: blank verse; some couplets
Prologue: 30 lines, in couplets (an alternative 12-line prologue was written for a revival)
Act-Division: 5 acts
Epilogue: 8 lines, in couplets (an alternative 4-line epilogue was written for a revival)
Lines (Spoken): 3,291 (128 verse, 3,163 prose)
Lines (Written): 3,409

STAGING
Doors: Mihil tries to hold the door shut (2.1, s.d.); characters 'make fast the doors', which are then forced open (4.1, s.d.)
Discovery Space: a bed put forth (5.3, s.d.)
Within: speech (1.2, 3.1, 4.1, s.d.; 2.1, implicit); music (4.2, implicit)
Above: Damaris appears on a balcony (1.1, s.d.); speech from above (2.2, s.d.)
Beneath: speech and music from below (2.2, s.d.)
Miscellaneous: The prologue assumes a performance at night.

MUSIC AND SOUND
Sound Effects: clink of pots being thrown (2.2, s.d.)
Music: a bell (2.2, s.d.); fiddlers tuning below (2.2, s.d.); rude tunes played on fiddles (2.2, s.d.); fiddles (4.2, dialogue)
On-Stage Music: Damaris plays the lute (1.1, implicit; accompanying Song 1); Gabriel hums a psalm tune (2.2, s.d.)
Songs:
  1: 1.1, Damaris, with lute accompaniment;
  2: 'Away with all grief and give us more sack', 3.1, Cockbrain, 8 lines;
  3: 'To prove the battoon the most noble to me', 3.1, Cockbrain, 14 lines.
Dance: Nick, Francisca, Betty, and Mihil dance (4.2, s.d.)

PROPS
Lighting: a light (1.2, s.d.)
Weapons: Nicholas's sword (1.2, 4.2, implicit); a knife (1.2, implicit); Mihil's sword (2.1, dialogue); batons (3.1, s.d.); Clotpoll's sword (3.1, 5.3, dialogue; 4.2, implicit); two swords (4.1, s.d.); Clotpoll's baton (5.3, dialogue)
Musical Instruments: a lute (1.1, s.d.)
Money: an unspecified sum (1.1, dialogue); money totalling at least £8, including two shilling coins (2.1, dialogue); two shillings (2.2, dialogue); an unspecified sum (3.1, s.d.); an unspecified sum (3.2, implicit); an unspecified sum (4.2, dialogue); two unspecified sums (5.2, implicit)
Food and Drink: a bottle of wine (1.2, s.d.; drunk on stage); cups (1.2, dialogue); tobacco stales (1.2, dialogue; a pot of wine (3.1, s.d.; drunk on stage); wine-glasses (3.1, s.d.); glasses of wine (4.2, dialogue; drunk on stage); sack (5.3, dialogue; drunk on stage)
Small Portable Objects: a writing-table (1.1, s.d.; 1.2, implicit); a pen (1.1–2, implicit); books (2.1, dialogue); two bills (2.1, dialogue); a book (3.1, dialogue); a bill (3.1, dialogue); a letter (3.2, dialogue); probably a key (4.2, dialogue); a letter (5.1, implicit)
Large Portable Objects: a table (1.2, s.d.); seating for four characters (1.2, implicit); three stools (2.1, dialogue); a table (3.1, s.d.); a chair (4.1, dialogue)
Scenery: a bed (2.1, dialogue; 5.3, s.d.)

COSTUMES AND MAKE-UP
COCKBRAIN: disguised (3.1, implicit)
GABRIEL: short hair (dialogue); a garment with a pocket (1.1, dialogue); martial clothes (5.3, dialogue)
DAMARIS: dressed like a Venetian courtesan (1.1, s.d.); gaudy clothes (4.2, dialogue)
NICHOLAS: a scabbard (1.2, 4.2, implicit)
ANTHONY: a false beard (1.1, s.d.)
CLOTPOLL: a coat (3.1, dialogue); a garment with a pocket (3.1, s.d.); a scabbard (4.2, dialogue)
MADGE: grey hair (dialogue); possibly black clothes (4.2, dialogue)
MIHIL: long, curly hair (2.1–2, 3.1, 4.2, dialogue; needs to be a wig); a new suit (2.1, dialogue); new boots with spurs (2.1, dialogue); a gown and cap (2.1, dialogue; put on on stage); short hair (5.1, 5.3, dialogue)
TAILOR: a sleeved garment (2.1, dialogue); a gown and cap (2.1, dialogue; put on on stage)
SHOEMAKER: a dirty face (2.1, dialogue); a gown and cap (2.1, dialogue; put on on stage)
CITIZEN: a beard (dialogue); a cloak (4.1, s.d.; removed on stage); breeches (4.1, dialogue)

EARLY STAGE HISTORY
c. 1641: The play was revived about a decade after its first performance, probably in May or June, perhaps at the Cockpit; a new prologue and epilogue were written for the production.

EARLY TEXTUAL HISTORY
1640: entered (as *The Covent Garden*) in the Stationers' Register to Andrew Crooke on Tuesday 4 August; play and author individually named as part of a group entry of six Brome plays. Thomas Wykes had licensed the book for publication.
1658–9: included as the third of Richard Brome's *Five New Plays* (O), sigs. 2A1^r–2H1^r, 105 pages on 53 leaves; printed for Andrew Crooke, and to be sold by Henry Brome; the play's individual title page names author; Latin title-page motto; list of roles. The volume also includes miscellaneous poems by Brome.
1659: George Thomason acquired a copy of O in January. In *c.* 1678, some years after his death, his entire collection of books and tracts was acquired by the bookbinder Samuel Mearne, acting as agent for

King Charles II; the King never paid him, and the books remained in Mearne's family until 1761.

1659: O reissued.

1664: O advertised (with the title mistakenly given as *Four New Plays*) as for sale by Henry Brome.

c. 1670s: extract (from 1.1) included in MS annotations in an interleaved copy of John Cotgrave's *The English Treasury of Wit and Language*, p. 290a^v. (The copy is now at the British Library, pressmark G.16385.)

1684: Nicholas Cox (Manciple of St Edmund Hall, Oxford) had a copy of O in his bookshop. It had probably been previously owned by Gerard Langbaine, and appears on a list compiled by Anthony Wood on Saturday 13 December.

EDITIONS
Donald S. McClure, Garland Renaissance Drama (New York, 1980).
Michael Leslie, Richard Brome Online (internet, 2010).

REFERENCES
Annals 1632; Bentley, iii. 89–92; Bodleian, MS Wood E. 4, art. 1, p. 55; Greg 808; Hazlitt, 250; *Renaissance Forum* 5.2 (2001, online), Steggle.

2402. The Shepherds' Holiday

TEXT
Printed in 1635 (STC 21470).

GENRE
pastoral
Contemporary: play (prol.); piece (ep.); tragicomedy (S.R.); pastoral tragicomedy (t.p.); poem (ded.); pastoral (May comm. verses)

TITLE
Performed/Printed: *The Shepherds' Holiday*

AUTHOR
Joseph Rutter

DATE
Limits: 1629–35
Best Guess: 1633

In 3.1, Sylvia mentions a theatre built by the present King solely to house entertainments brought to court by shepherds; this seems to allude either to the Cockpit in Court, which sets the upper limit, or to the 'paved court theatre' set up at Denmark House for the performance of the Queen's own pastoral, *The Shepherds' Paradise* (**2395**).

The dedication seems to imply that the play was written before Sir Kenelm Digby went into mourning, whereas the Oxford *DNB* article on Rutter infers that this is the context for the melancholy characterization of Thyrsis. The argument seems rather strained, but a best guess of 1633 leaves open both interpretations. Moreover, it seems likely that the court performance would have followed, rather than pre-empted, *The Shepherds' Paradise*.

ORIGINAL PRODUCTION
Queen Henrietta's Men, presumably at the Cockpit

PLOT
Thyrsis, who was found by Montanus as a baby with a mysterious inscribed circlet around his neck, is distraught. He left his girlfriend Sylvia in a grove, and she has disappeared; he self-reproachfully worries that she has been raped by a passing satyr, and neglects his flocks. The oracle of Apollo reassures him that he will get her back, but only when they cease to be Thyrsis and Sylvia.

Sylvia is really the Princess, Calligone. She fell in love with Thyrsis when the shepherds last came to court with some musical entertainment, and went into the country in pastoral disguise to be with him; she was also hoping to escape the amorous attentions of Cleander, but he found her in the grove and took her home. Her father, Euarchus, suspects the reason she absconded, and summons the shepherds to perform at court again, in the hope of identifying one of them as her lover. They prepare a masque.

Cleander is warned off Calligone by his father, Eubulus. Before she was born, the oracle foretold that King Euarchus would see his only son after having a child who is not really his own, that he would twice condemn that son to death, and that the son would marry Euarchus' daughter. The King took this to mean that, should the pregnant Queen produce a baby boy, it would be a bastard, so he ordered Eubulus to have the infant killed if male. When the child was indeed a boy, Eubulus plotted with the Queen to swap it for his own new-born daughter, who grew up to be Calligone. He then left the baby boy in the forest with money for his education and an identifying necklet inscribed in a diplomatic code known only to him and the King. Calligone is therefore Cleander's sister.

'Sylvia' sends for Thyrsis, but Cleander sees her with him and reports the fact to the King, who orders their execution: Calligone dishonours herself in romantic entanglement with a mere shepherd. The shepherds arrive at court, but are sent away with their masque unseen. When Thyrsis removes his doublet to be strangled, however, Cleander sees the necklet, realizes that this is the long-lost Prince, and arranges for him to marry Calligone instead. The oracle is fulfilled, and King Euarchus gives his blessing to his son and daughter-in-law.

In the sub-plot, Dorinda loves the wealthy Daphnis, but he only has eyes for Nerina and, moreover, has her father's favour. Nerina loves only Hylas, but finds herself caught between love and duty. She tells both Hylas and her father that she prefers not to marry at all, but will marry Daphnis against her will if her father insists. Daphnis procures a magic mirror which will make the gazer fall in love with him, and gives it to Nerina. She looks into it, falls sick, and makes a last request of her father: that he give his blessing to her love for Hylas. She is interred, and Daphnis confronts the vendor of the mirror, Alcon, who insists that it was made of a sleep-inducing substance: Nerina is not dead, and Alcon has the antidote. They remove her from her tomb, but Daphnis is disappointed when she wakes: she still loves Hylas, and now has her father's permission to marry him. Daphnis threatens to rape her, but Hylas, coming to pay respect at her grave, rescues her. Dorinda forgives Daphnis and he accepts her love.

SCENE DESIGNATION
prol., 1.1–4, 2.1–5, 3.1–4, 4.1–5, 5.1–4 (O)

The stage is not clear at the following scene-divisions: 2.1–3, 2.4–5.

ROLES
PROLOGUE
THYRSIS, a young piper shepherd, supposed Montanus' son; in reality, Archigenes, son of Euarchus; later Calligone's husband
MONTANUS, an old shepherd, Thyrsis' foster-father
A SHEPHERD BOY, who sings (1.1)
HYLAS, a shepherd
MYRTILLUS, a shepherd
NERINA, a young nymph, huntress, and shepherdess, Charinus' daughter
DORINDA, a nymph and shepherdess
CHARINUS, Nerina's father, more than 50 years old
DAPHNIS, a rich young shepherd
SYLVIA, a shepherdess of Smyrna; in reality, Calligone, the Princess, supposed Euarchus' daughter and heir, but actually Eubulus' daughter and Cleander's sister; later Archigenes' wife
DELIA, a court lady, Sylvia's confidante
CLEANDER, Eubulus' son, Calligone's brother
EUBULUS, Euarchus' counsellor, father of Cleander and Calligone
A CHORUS of shepherds and shepherdesses in the masque; some play Paris (*non-speaking*), Oenone (*non-speaking*), Helena (*non-speaking*), Venus, and the Graces, who are presumably three in number (two others speak)
A MESSENGER, who brings news of Nerina's collapse (3.3)
Prince EUARCHUS, King of Arcadia, an old widower; supposed Calligone's father, and actually Archigenes' father
ATTENDANTS at court (4.2, *non-speaking*)
ALCON, an old shepherd

Speaking Parts: 23 (counting the chorus as six individual speakers)

Stage Directions and Speech Prefixes
PROLOGUE: *The Prologue* (heading)
THYRSIS: *Thyrsis* (s.d.s); *Thyr<sis>* (s.p.s); *Thyrsis the Lover of Sylvia* (d.p.)
MONTANUS: *Montanus* (s.d.s); *Mon<tanus>* (s.p.s); *Montanus, an ancient Shepherd* (d.p.)
SHEPHERD BOY: *Boy* (s.p.s)
HYLAS: *Hylas* (s.d.s); *Hy<las>* (s.p.s); *Hylas, the Lover of Nerina* (d.p.)
MYRTILLUS: *Mirtillus* (s.d.s); *Mi<rtillus>* (s.p.s); *Mirtillus, the common Lover* (d.p.)
NERINA: *Nerina* (s.d.s; also misprinted *Merina*); *Ne<rina>* (s.p.s; also misprinted *Me.*); *Nerina, a huntress, beloved of Hylas & of Daphnis* (d.p.)
DORINDA: *Dorinda* (s.d.s); *Do<rinda>* (s.p.s); *Dorinda, enamoured of Daphnis* (d.p.)
CHARINUS: *Charinus | Carinus* (s.d.s); *Cha<rinus>* (s.p.s); *Charinus, Father to Nerina* (d.p.)
DAPHNIS: *Daphnis* (s.d.s); *Da<phnis>* (s.p.s); *Daphnis, the rich Shepherd* (d.p.)
SYLVIA: *Sylvia* (s.d.s); *Syl<via>* (s.p.s); *Sylvia, beloved of Thyrsis* (d.p.)
DELIA: *Delia* (s.d.s); *Del<ia>* (s.p.s); *Delia, a Court Lady* (d.p.)
CLEANDER: *Cleander* (s.d.s); *Cle<ander>* (s.p.s); *Cleander, Son to Eubulus* (d.p.)
EUBULUS: *Eubulus* (s.d.s); *Eub<ulus>* (s.p.s); *Eubulus, [Euarchus'] Counsellor* (d.p.)
CHORUS: *Chorus of Shepherds and Shepherdesses, representing Paris, Oenone, Venus, and the Graces | Venus, and the Graces* (s.d.s and d.p.); *Chorus of Shepherds* (s.d.s and d.p.); *1 shepherd | 2 shepherd* (s.p.s)
MESSENGER: *a Messenger* (s.d.s); *Nuntius* (s.d.s, s.p.s, and d.p.)
EUARCHUS: *Euarchus* (s.d.s); *Eu<archus>* (s.p.s); *Euarchus, King of Arcady* (d.p.)
ATTENDANTS: *Attendants* (s.d.s and d.p.)
ALCON: *Alcon* (s.d.s); *Al<con>* (s.p.s); *Alcon, an ancient Shepherd* (d.p.)

OTHER CHARACTERS
Cloris, one of many women whom Myrtillus loves, and who looks nothing like Nerina (1.2, 1.4)
Amaryllis, one of many women whom Myrtillus loves (1.2)
The ranger of the forest deer (1.3)
Acrisius, a wise, virtuous man, who advised against trying to foretell the future (2.1)
Corisca, Nerina's maid, who was stung on the face by a bee (2.2)
Nerina's mother, who taught her a charm for bee-stings (2.2)
Old, avaricious shepherds, who tried to cheat Sylvia (3.1)
Eudora, Queen of Arcadia, Euarchus' dead wife, Archigenes' mother (3.2)
Eubulus' wife, mother of Cleander and Calligone (3.2)
Thieves who attacked Eubulus as he sought a home for the infant Archigenes (3.2)

The princes of the states neighbouring Arcadia (4.2)
The man who gave Alcon the magic mirror (5.2)
Stella, a nymph falsely rumoured to have been impregnated by Myrtillus (5.2)
A servant whom Cleander ordered to kill Thyrsis (5.4)

SETTING
Period: antiquity (?)
Place: Arcadia

Geography
Sicily
[*Thrace*]: River Hebrus
[*Asia Minor*]: Smyrna; Mount Ida
Cyprus
[*Egypt*]: Memphis
Persia

SOURCES
Narrative: Torquato Tasso, *Aminta* (1573; English translations by Abraham Fraunce, **877**, and Henry Reynolds, **2223**; 2.2); Samuel Daniel, *Hymen's Triumph* (**1742**)
Verbal: Virgil, *Eclogues* 6 (t.p. motto); Ovid, *Ars amatoria* (4.5); Statius, *Silvae* (ded.); Sir Philip Sidney, *Arcadia* (c. 1580, printed 1590, repr. 1633; the name Euarchus); Honoré D'Urfé, *L'Astrée*, Part 2 (1610; the name Hylas)

LANGUAGE
English

FORM
Metre: pentameter
Rhyme: blank verse and couplets
Prologue: 32 lines, in couplets
Act-Division: 5 acts
Epilogue: 8 lines, in couplets; court performance only
Lines (Spoken): 2,299 (2,297 verse, 2 prose)
Lines (Written): 2,592

STAGING
Beneath: possibly representing Nerina's grave, with the trapdoor as the slab on top (5.2, implicit; alternatively, a scenic tomb may be used)
Audience: called a 'fair company' (prol.); the King and Queen are directly addressed as 'most royal pair' (ep.)

MUSIC
Songs:
   1: 'Shall I, because my love is gone', 1.1, Boy, 15 lines;
   2: 'He that mourns for a mistress', 2.1, Myrtillus, 8 lines;
   3: 'Tell me what you think on earth', 3.1, Sylvia and Delia, in parts, 18 lines;
   4: 'Come, lovely boy, unto my court', 3.3, Venus and Graces, 28 lines;
   5: 'Hymen, god of marriage bed', 5.4, Myrtillus, 20 lines.
Dance: shepherds dance (3.3, s.d.)

PROPS
Clothing: a signet ring (4.2, dialogue)
Food and Drink: a cordial (5.2, dialogue; drunk on stage)
Small Portable Objects: a looking-glass (2.4–5, 4.5, 5.2, dialogue); a paper (3.3, dialogue); flowers (5.2, dialogue); a document (5.4, implicit)
Scenery: a tomb (5.2, dialogue; alternatively represented by the stage trapdoor)
Miscellaneous: water (3.4, dialogue)

COSTUMES AND MAKE-UP
THYRSIS: a golden circlet around his neck (1.1, 4.1, 4.3, implicit; 2.1, 5.4, dialogue; it may not be visible in all scenes); a doublet (4.3, dialogue)
MONTANUS: grey hair (dialogue)
MYRTILLUS: a ribbon (1.2, dialogue); hair (1.2, dialogue; probably a bracelet of hair)
CHARINUS: white hair (dialogue); a wrinkled face (implicit)
DELIA: courtly clothes (4.1, dialogue)

EARLY STAGE HISTORY
Performed by Queen Henrietta's Men at Whitehall Palace by 1635. The audience included: King Charles I; Queen Henrietta Maria. This may have been one of the seven court performances in the year 1633–4 for which Christopher Beeston was paid £70 by a warrant dated either Monday 22 or Wednesday 31 December 1634, or one of the seven in 1634–5 for which he was paid £70 (plus a further £20 for a performance at Hampton Court) by a warrant dated either Wednesday 10 February or Thursday 24 March 1636.
The play was also publicly performed by Queen Henrietta's Men, presumably at the Cockpit, by 1635.

EARLY TEXTUAL HISTORY
1633 or earlier: Joseph Rutter's dedication says that he wrote the play in Sir Kenelm Digby's house, perhaps at around the time the death of Lady Venetia Digby on Wednesday 1 May 1633.
   1635 or earlier: Ben Jonson read the play before it was published.
   1635: entered to John Benson in the Stationers' Register on Monday 19 January; entry names author. Sir Henry Herbert had licensed the book for publication.
   1635: O printed by Nicholas Okes and John Okes for John Benson; collation A⁴ B–G⁸ H⁴, 56 leaves; title page gives author's initials, names acting company, and refers to court performance; Latin title-page motto; authorial dedication to Sir Kenelm Digby; commendatory verses by Ben Jonson and Thomas May; list of roles; the volume also contains an English

elegy and a Latin epigram on Lady Venetia Digby (on sigs. H1ʳ–H3ᵛ; the main play text ends on sig. G8ᵛ).

1635: In February, John Newdigate bought a copy.

c. 1630s–40s: a copy of O was in the possession of John Horne (Vicar of Headington, Oxfordshire). After his death, his entire collection of play-books passed into the possession of John Houghton of Brasenose College, Oxford (c. 1608–77), then to James Herne (died 1685), and then to the library of Ralph Sheldon (1623–84) at Weston, where it was catalogued by Anthony Wood, probably in the late 1670s.

1640–1: Humphrey Moseley was selling copies of O for 6d each.

1655: *Wit's Interpreter* entered to Nathaniel Brooke in the Stationers' Register on Wednesday 14 March.

1655: three extracts (from 1.3, 2.2, 5.3) included in John Cotgrave's *Wit's Interpreter*, sigs. E3ʳ⁻ᵛ, F2ʳ–F3ʳ; printed for Nathaniel Brooke.

c. 1656: extract (from 2.2) included in *Cupid's Masterpiece*, sigs. B3ᵛ–B4ʳ; printed for John Andrews.

1662: *Wit's Interpreter* reprinted (before Thursday 8 June) for Nathaniel Brooke; two of the extracts now appear on sigs. D6ᵛ–D7ᵛ (that from 1.3 is omitted) and are entitled 'The Penitent Shepherd' and 'An Importunate Love'.

1671: *Wit's Interpreter* reprinted for Nathaniel Brooke and Obadiah Blagrave.

1684: Nicholas Cox (Manciple of St Edmund Hall, Oxford) had a copy of O in his bookshop. It had probably been previously owned by Gerard Langbaine, and appears on a list compiled by Anthony Wood on Saturday 13 December.

EDITION
W. Carew Hazlitt, in *A Select Collection of Old English Plays*, 4th edn (London, 1875), xii. 361–444.

REFERENCES
Annals 1634; Bawcutt C75; Bentley, v. 1032–4; Bodleian, MS Wood E. 4, art. 1, p. 106; Eyre & Rivington, i. 467; Greg 499; W. W. Greg, *Pastoral Poetry and Pastoral Drama* (London, 1906), 358–61; Alfred Harbage, *Cavalier Drama* (New York, 1936), 118; Hazlitt, 207; Vivienne Larminie, *Wealth, Kinship and Culture* (Woodbridge, 1995), 203; *MLR* 13 (1918), 401–11; *Oxford Bibliographical Society Proceedings and Papers* 2.2 (1929), 132–3; *RES* NS 54 (2003), 601–14; Steele, 278.

2403. *A Tale of a Tub*

TEXT
Printed in 1640–1 (STC 14754a), from an authorial MS or a copy thereof. The text has been censored, but some material (including 4.int. and 5.10) may have been restored (or perhaps newly written) for the printed version.

GENRE
comedy
Contemporary: play (prol., ep.); comedy (t.p.)

TITLE
Performed/Printed: *A Tale of a Tub*
Contemporary: *The Tale of the Tub*
Later Assigned: *The Tale of a Tub*

AUTHOR
Ben Jonson

DATE
May 1633

ORIGINAL PRODUCTION
Queen Henrietta's Men at the Cockpit

PLOT
Audrey Turf is to be married to John Clay, even though her father has promised her to Squire Tub: she drew Clay in a Valentine's Eve lottery and her parents are determined that she should marry him on Valentine's Day. The vicar, Sir Hugh, alerts Tub, and lays a plot to stop the wedding; but also abets Justice Preamble's scheming to get the girl for himself.

Tub's governor Hilts poses as a servant whose master, Captain Thumbs, was attacked nearby; he has brought Constable Turf orders from the Queen to raise a hue and cry to catch the criminals; moreover, his description of one of them fits Clay, the bridegroom. Turf is obliged to postpone the wedding, and leaves his daughter with Hilts, who hands her over to Tub. Audrey at first thinks herself too low-born to be the Squire's wife, but is won over by the prospect of social advancement. But before Tub can get her to church, he is arrested by Preamble. The judge leaves Tub with a pursuivant, saying he must return Audrey to her father; but the pursuivant turns out to be Preamble's clerk, Metaphor, in disguise, and he explains that Preamble is actually taking her to church to marry her himself.

Clay goes into hiding. Tub tells Turf that the robbery was a ruse by Preamble to enable him to take Audrey. Turf breaks off the hue and cry and intervenes in time to prevent the marriage, and takes Audrey home. Sir Hugh poses as the robbed man, Captain Thumbs, and complains of Turf's negligence. Turf is summoned before Preamble to answer for abandoning the chase; he must produce the thief, presumed to be Clay, or pay back the stolen money himself. He sends Metaphor to fetch the cash, but Sir Hugh tells Metaphor to bring Audrey too.

Tub and Hilts bully the plot out of Metaphor, and arrange to intercept him as he returns with Audrey. Tub takes the girl and lets Hilts and Metaphor have the money; but his mother, who has been out looking for him, catches up with him just as he is about to take Audrey to church. He claims he was taking her home, but Lady Tub will not be put off, and sends Audrey home with her gentleman usher, Pol-Marten—who woos her for himself. Tub roots out a supposed devil in Turf's barn; it turns out to be Clay, hiding in the straw.

Pol-Marten disguises Audrey in Lady Tub's clothes, and Sir Hugh marries them, not realizing who they are. Tub invites the company home to supper, where he has arranged a masque whose central feature is a tub, representing his family; it has been devised by the cooper Medley, who will brook no collaborator, and it dramatizes the day's events.

SCENE DESIGNATION

prol., 1.1–7, 2.1–6, 3.1–9, 4.1, 4.int, 4.2–6, 5.1–10, ep. (F; 4.int is specified as 'the scene interloping')

The stage is not clear at the following scene-divisions: 1.2–4, 1.6–7, 2.1–6, 3.1–3, 3.4–5, 3.8–9, 4.2–3, 4.4–5, 5.2–5, 5.6–7, 5.9–10. A verse line is split across a scene-division at 1.6–7.

ROLES

PROLOGUE

SIR HUGH, the vicar of St Pancras; also called Canon Hugh and Vicar Hugh; poses as Captain Thumbs, a soldier

Squire Tripoli TUB, a young man, Lady Tub's son

Master Basket HILTS, Tub's governor; poses as a servingman

Goodman Rhazes CLENCH, a farrier, horse-leech, and petty constable; also called Rasi'

Master In-and-in MEDLEY, a cooper, joiner, and headborough; originally written as Vitruvius (or Vitru) Hoop

Diogenes SCRIBEN, a writer; also called D'oge

TO-PAN, a tinker and thirdborough; also called Pan

Hannibal PUPPY, Turf's servant, a young man; also called Master 'Bal, Master Hannibal, and Ball-Hanny

Master Tobias TURF, an old man, High Constable of Kentish Town; Sibyl's husband, Audrey's father; also called Toby and Constable Turf; taller than Clay

John CLAY, a tile-maker, the bridegroom; shorter than Turf

MADGE, a maid of the bridal

Five MAIDS of the bridal, named Joan, Joyce, Parnell, Grissell, and Kate (either Joan or Joyce speaks individually, the rest collectively)

Father ROSIN, an old minstrel (1.4, 5.9, *non-speaking*)

Justice Richard PREAMBLE, a young judge; also called Justice Bramble

Miles METAPHOR, Preamble's clerk; poses as a pursuivant; also called Sir Metaphor and Master Metaphor

LADY TUB, Tub's mother, a widow

POL-MARTEN, Lady Tub's gentleman usher; formerly a basket-carrier; his real name is Martin Polecat; later Audrey's husband

Mistress Dido WISP, Lady Tub's waiting-woman

Dame SIBYL Turf, Turf's wife of 30 years, Audrey's mother; also called Mistress Turf

Mistress AUDREY Turf, a young woman, daughter of Turf and Sibyl; later Pol-Marten's wife, and styled Mistress Pol-Marten

Black JACK, Lady Tub's butler

Two GROOMS, who prepare the masque (5.9)

Two BOYS employed by Rosin (5.9, *non-speaking*)

Speaking Parts: 27

Stage Directions and Speech Prefixes

PROLOGUE: *Prologue* (heading)

SIR HUGH: *Sir Hugh | Canon Hugh* (s.d.s); *Hugh* (s.d.s and s.p.s); *Canon Hugh, Vicar of Pancrace, and Captain Thums* (d.p.)

TUB: *Tub* (s.d.s and s.p.s); *The Squire | Squire Tub* (s.d.s); *Squire Tub, Of Totten-Court, or Squire Tripoly* (d.p.)

HILTS: *Hilts* (s.d.s); *Hilt<s>* (s.p.s); *Basket Hilts, [Tub's] man, and Governor* (d.p.)

CLENCH: *Clench* | [one of Dame Turf's] *neighbours* | [one of] *the neighbours* (s.d.s); *Cle<nch>* (s.p.s); *Rasi<s> Clench, Of Hamsted, Farrier, and petty Constable* (d.p.)

MEDLEY: *Medlay* | [one of Dame Turf's] *neighbours* | *Med-lay* | [one of] *the neighbours* (s.d.s); *Med<lay>* (s.p.s); *In-and-In Medlay Of Islington, Cooper and Headborough* (d.p.)

SCRIBEN: *Scriben* | [one of Dame Turf's] *neighbours* | [one of] *the neighbours* (s.d.s); *Scri<ben>* (s.p.s); *D'oge Scriben, of Chalcot the great Writer* (d.p.)

TO-PAN: *Pan | To-Pan* | [one of Dame Turf's] *neighbours* | [one of] *the neighbours* (s.d.s and s.p.s); *To-Pan, Tinker, or Metal-man of Belsise. Thirdborough* (d.p.)

PUPPY: *Puppy* (s.d.s); *Pup<py>* (s.p.s); *Ball Puppy, The high Constable's man* (d.p.)

TURF: *Turfe* | [Dame Turf's] *husband* (s.d.s); *Tur<fe>* (s.p.s); *Tobie Turfe, High Constable of Kentish Town* (d.p.)

CLAY: *Clay* (s.d.s and s.p.s); [one of Dame Turf's] *neighbours* (s.d.s); *John Claw, Of Kilborne Tile-maker, the appointed Bridegroom* (d.p.)

MADGE: [one of the] *Maids* (s.d.s); *Mad<ge>* (s.p.s); *Madge* [one of the] *Maids of the Bridal* (d.p.)

MAIDS: *Maids* (s.d.s); *Jo<ne>* or *Jo<yce>* (s.p.s); *Jone, Joyce, ... Parnel, Grisell, Kate Maids of the Bridal* (d.p.)

ROSIN: *Father Rosin* (s.d.s); *Father Rosin, The Minstrel* (d.p.)

PREAMBLE: *Preamble* (s.d.s); *Pre<amble>* (s.p.s); *Justice Preamble, Of Maribone, alias Bramble* (d.p.)

METAPHOR: *Metaphor | Metaphore* (s.d.s); *Met<aphor>* (s.p.s); *Miles Metaphor, [Preamble's] Clerk* (d.p.)

TUB: *Lady Tub* (s.d.s); *Lady* (s.d.s and s.p.s); *Lady Tub, Of Totten, the Squire's Mother* (d.p.)

POL-MARTEN: *Pol-Marten* (s.d.s); *Pol<-Marten>* (s.p.s); *Pol-Marten* [Lady Tub's] *Usher* (d.p.)
WISP: *Wispe | Dido* (s.d.s); *Wis<pe> | Did<o>* (s.p.s); *Dido Wispe* [Lady Tub's] *woman* (d.p.)
SIBYL: *Dame Turfe* (s.d.s and s.p.s); *Dame Sibil Turfe* [Turf's] *Wife* (d.p.)
AUDREY: *Awdrey* (s.d.s); *Awd<rey>* (s.p.s); *Mrs Awdrey Turfe*, [the Turfs'] *Daughter the Bride* (d.p.)
JACK: *Jack* (s.d.s); *Jac<k>* (s.p.s); *Black Jack, The Lady Tub's Butler* (d.p.)
GROOMS: 2 *Grooms* (s.d.s and d.p.); *Groom 1 | Groom 2* (s.p.s)
BOYS: [Rosin's] 2 *Boys* (s.d.s)

OTHER CHARACTERS
Sir Peter Tub, Tub's dead father, Lady Tub's husband who made his fortune from saltpetre (1.1, 1.6, 4.int., 5.3, 5.7, 5.10)
A messenger sent by the Turfs to summon Clay (1.1)
The Queen (1.4, 1.7, 2.1–2, 2.5–6, 4.1, 5.2)
A messenger of the chamber living in Marylebone, who lends Metaphor his coat (1.5)
Lady Tub's porter (1.6)
Bess Mole and Margery Turnup, Audrey's acquaintances (2.4)
Dick Toter [or Tooter], also called Vadian, a drunken city wait (3.6)
Tom Long, a carrier, Metaphor's friend (4.1)
In-and-In Shuttle, a weaver, Medley's godfather (4.int.)
An alewife whom Clench cured of the staggers (4.int.)
Doctor Rasi, King Henry VIII's doctor, a Jew, Clench's godfather (4.int.)
To-Pan's godfather, a tinker, also named To-Pan (4.int.)
Scriben's godfather, also named Diogenes (4.int.)
Vitruvius, a London cooper (5.2)
John Heywood, an old man (5.2; i.e. the dramatist)

SETTING
Period: sixteenth century; the action takes place on 14 February [1558]
Time-Scheme: the action takes place during a single day: 1.1–3.9 take place in the morning; at least an hour passes between 1.1 and 1.6; 4.1 takes place at noon and 5.2 at 4 p.m.; at least an hour passes between 4.4 and 5.3; 5.6–7 take place at supper time, and 5.9–10 after supper
Place: Finsbury

Geography
Highgate: the Cock and Hen
Paddington: the Red Lion
St Pancras: Pancras Church
Middlesex: Tottenham Court; Kentish Town; Hampstead; Islington; Belsize; Chalcot; Kilburn; Hammersmith; Kingston Bridge; Marylebone; Holloway; St John's Wood; Shoreditch; Canonbury; Hampstead Heath
London: Smithfield; River Thames; Tyburn
Dover: Dover Castle
Kent
[*England*]: Walsingham; Southampton; Warwick Castle; Twyford
France: St Quentin
[*Asia*]: Jericho; Arabia

SOURCES
Narrative: William Shakespeare, *Much Ado About Nothing* (**1148**; the malapropistic constables)
Verbal: Catullus, *Carmina* 22 (t.p. motto); Ovid, *Metamorphoses* 15 (3.7); Plutarch, *Moralia*: De garullitate (1.1); *The Seven Wise Masters of Rome* (1493, repr. *c.* 1555; 5.3); William Lily, *Latin Grammar* (3.7, cited); Laurence Twine, *The Pattern of Painful Adventures* (1576; 3.9); Raphael Holinshed, *Chronicles of England, Scotland, and Ireland* (1577, 2nd edn 1587; 1.3); Sir Philip Sidney, 'My true love hath my heart' (*c.* 1580, printed 1589, repr. 1633; 1.1); Sir Thomas Smith, *De republica Anglorum* (1583, repr. 1584; 4.int.); Thomas Kyd, *The Spanish Tragedy* (**783**; 3.7); Thomas Deloney, *John for the King* (**1030**; 4.int.); John Donne, 'An Epithalamion' (written 1613, printed 1633; 1.1)
Works Mentioned: *Magna Carta* (1215; 1.2); *Bevis of Hampton* (*c.* 1300; 3.6); *Guy of Warwick* (fourteenth century; 3.6); John Skelton, *The Tunning of Elinor Rumming* (*c.* 1517–21; 5.7); Robert Fabyan, *Chronicle* (1516; 1.2); *Mary Ambree* (ballad, after 1584; 1.4); Christopher Marlowe, *Doctor Faustus* (**810**; 4.6); Robert Greene, *Friar Bacon and Friar Bungay* (**822**; 4.6); there is a general reference to the dramatist John Heywood (5.2)

LANGUAGE
English
Latin: 38 words (1.1, 1.3, 1.5, 2.2, 3.1, 3.6–7, 4.int., 5.7, 5.10; Sir Hugh, Scriben, Turf, Medley, Tub)
Greek: 1 word (5.10; Tub)
Italian: 1 word (5.7; Medley)
Spanish: 1 word (3.9; Sir Hugh)
Old English: 1 word (4.int.; Scriben)
Dialect: Hilts, Clench, To-Pan, Scriben, Puppy, Turf, Sibyl, Maid, Clay, Medley, and Audrey all talk consistently or intermittently in 'rustic' dialect.

FORM
Metre: pentameter; a few fourteeners (3.4) and skeltonics (3.5)
Rhyme: blank verse; some couplets
Prologue: 12 lines, in couplets
Act-Division: 5 acts, separated by intermeans
Epilogue: 16 lines, in couplets, spoken by Tub
Lines (Spoken): 2,498 (2,484 verse, 14 prose)
Lines (Written): 2,591

STAGING
Doors: knocked at (3.4, dialogue)

Discovery Space: curtained and set with a tub (5.10, s.d.)
Within: speech (3.4, implicit)
Above: Tub appears or speaks at the window (1.1, s.d.); Medley 'appears above the curtain' (5.10, s.d.)

MUSIC
Music: loud music (5.9–10, s.d.)

PROPS
Weapons: Hilts's dagger (2.2, dialogue); Puppy's weapon (2.2, dialogue; perhaps a sword or wooden staff); Tub's weapon (2.4–5, dialogue); Hilts's sword (2.6, 4.2–3, dialogue)
Musical Instruments: a fiddle (5.9, dialogue)
Money: an angel (1.1, dialogue); two angels (1.5, dialogue); an unspecified sum (2.3, implicit); crowns (2.4, dialogue); ten nobles (3.5, dialogue); an unspecified sum, possibly another ten nobles (3.5, implicit); two bags, each containing fifty pounds (4.5, dialogue)
Small Portable Objects: rosemary and bays (1.4, dialogue; possibly strewn on the stage, since in 3.4 there are said to be herbs on the ground); a handkerchief (3.1, dialogue); a warrant (3.9, dialogue); a key (4.1, 4.2, dialogue); a note (5.9, dialogue); shadow-puppets (5.10, implicit)
Large Portable Objects: seating for eleven characters, including a large chair (5.9–10, s.d.)
Scenery: a curtain (5.10, s.d.); a tub (5.10, s.d.; on its side; the top is covered with fine paper and back-lit to serve as a screen for the puppet show)

COSTUMES AND MAKE-UP
SIR HUGH: a tonsure (dialogue); a cassock (1.1, dialogue); a garment with a pocket (1.5, dialogue); a square cap (3.7, 5.5–6, dialogue); disguised as Captain Thumbs (3.9, s.d.; 4.1, implicit), including bloody scars on his face and his arm in a scarf (dialogue)
TUB: a nightgown (1.1, s.d.); a coat (4.6, dialogue; may be a figure of speech)
HILTS: a false beard (2.2, s.d.; 2.3–4, dialogue); boots and spurs (2.2, s.d.); a sheath (4.2–3, dialogue)
MEDLEY: linen breeches (5.10, dialogue)
PUPPY: a hat (2.1–3, dialogue; doffed on stage); a russet coat (3.8–9, dialogue)
CLAY: swaddling on his legs, yellow stockings, long sausage hose (also called 'pinned-up breeches'), a chamois doublet with long points, and a hat turned up at one side and fastened with a silver clasp (1.4, dialogue; 2.1–2, implicit); a collar (4.6, dialogue)
METAPHOR: a pursuivant's coat with a badge on the front (2.5–6, dialogue); a bloody head (3.7, dialogue); an orange-tawny coat (4.2, 4.4, dialogue); breeches and a hat (4.2, dialogue)
LADY TUB: a velvet gown (1.6–7, 3.4–5, dialogue)
AUDREY: linen clothes (4.4–5, dialogue); fine clothes (5.6, dialogue)

EARLY STAGE HISTORY
1633: presumably performed as licensed, no doubt by Queen Henrietta's Men at the Cockpit.

1634: performed (as *The Tale of the Tub*) by Queen Henrietta's Men at court, presumably at Whitehall Palace, on Tuesday 14 January. The performance took place in the evening, and was 'not liked' by the audience, which probably included: King Charles I; Queen Henrietta Maria. This may have been one of the seven court performances for which Christopher Beeston was later paid £70 by a warrant dated Monday 22 December 1634.

Reported (in 1669) as having been in the repertory of the King's Men at the Blackfriars before 1642.

EARLY TEXTUAL HISTORY
1633: The text was submitted to Sir Henry Herbert for licensing. Inigo Jones heard that the character of Vitruvius Hoop was devised as a personal satire on him, and complained to the Lord Chamberlain, Philip Herbert, 4th Earl of Pembroke and 1st Earl of Montgomery, who ordered Herbert to have the offending role, and the concluding puppet show, removed. Herbert made this proviso when, on Tuesday 7 May, he licensed the text for performance; the licensing fee was £2. It appears that Jonson complied by renaming Hoop, who became Medley.

c. 1637–40: Not long before his death, Ben Jonson placed some of his unpublished works in the hands of Sir Kenelm Digby, with a view to their publication. This play may have been one of the texts in question. After Jonson's death in August 1637, Digby took the texts he had received to Thomas Walkley, who paid Digby £40 and procured a licence to publish them, but did not enter them in the Stationers' Register.

1640: While Walkley's volume was at the printer's, John Benson and Andrew Crooke had some of the masques therein (but not this play) entered to them in the Stationers' Register; the Stationers' Company authorities had no knowledge of Walkley's interest in the matter. Fearful that they were planning to issue their own edition, Walkley complained to a secretary of state, who issued a warrant prohibiting Benson and Crooke from doing so.

1640–1: included in the third volume of Jonson's *Works* ('^{1}F$_1$'), sigs. ^{2}I1^r–^{2}Q2^r, 59 pages on 30 leaves; printed by John Dawson for Thomas Walkley; Latin title-page epigraph; list of roles.

1640–1: The Stationers' Register entry of *The Gypsies Metamorphosed* (**1987**) in Benson's favour misled John Parker, a London stationer, into supposing that the printed copies of Walkley's volume were Benson's property. Benson allegedly owed Parker money, so Parker had the book seized from the printer's. Walkley, who valued the copies at £300 or more, suspected that this was a dishonest move planned by Benson and Crooke in preparation to issuing their own edition, and complained to the Court of Chancery on Wednesday 20 January 1641.

1648: Changes in press licensing arrangements since 1640 meant that Walkley's original licence to print his Jonson works had become void. He attempted to have the texts perused by the new licensers in preparation for having them entered in the Stationers' Register, but one of them, Sir Nathaniel Brent, was out of town and the other, John Langley, claimed to be too busy. He then approached the Stationers' Company, who in turn petitioned the House of Lords on Wednesday 20 December, asking for additional licensers to be appointed.

1653: *The Marrow of Compliments* entered to Humphrey Moseley in the Stationers' Register on Tuesday 20 December.

1654: extract (from 2.3, headed 'A Song At a Wedding') included in Samuel Sheppard's *The Marrow of Compliments*, sigs. C2^r–C3^r; printed (before Saturday 15 July) for Humphrey Moseley.

c. 1655: extracts transcribed from F$_1$ by John Evans in a miscellany, *Hesperides*, intended for publication and entered to Humphrey Moseley in the Stationers' Register on Thursday 16 August 1655. The book remained unpublished in 1660, and Evans continued adding to the collection until at least 1666. Two MS exemplars are known; one was cut up by J. O. Halliwell-Phillipps in the nineteenth century; the other survives (Washington: Folger, MS V. b. 93).

c. 1656: extract (from 3.1) included in *Cupid's Masterpiece*, sigs. B1^v–B2^r; printed for John Andrews.

1658: the third volume of Jonson's *Works* entered to Thomas Walkley in the Stationers' Register on Friday 17 September; the play is individually named.

1658: Walkley's rights to the third volume of Jonson's *Works* transferred to Humphrey Moseley in the Stationers' Register on Saturday 20 November; group transfer of 13 titles, the *Works* being one; the play is individually named.

1660: F$_1$ advertised for sale by Humphrey Moseley.

1667: Moseley's rights to the third volume of Jonson's *Works* transferred by his widow, Ann, to Henry Herringman in the Stationers' Register on Monday 19 August; group transfer of nine titles, the *Works* being one; the play is individually named.

1675: Moseley's rights to *The Marrow of Compliments* transferred from his widow, Ann, to Peter Parker in the Stationers' Register on Wednesday 8 September, by order of a court held on Monday 22 February, and by an assignment dated Thursday 26 September 1672.

1692: included in Jonson's *Works* (^{2}F$_2$), sigs. 3T3^r–3Y2^r, 23 pages on 12 leaves; printed by Thomas Hodgkin for Henry Herringman, Edward Brewster, Thomas Bassett, Richard Chiswell, Matthew Wotton, and George Conyers.

The volumes here designated F$_1$ and F$_2$ are respectively the second and third Jonson Folios.

EDITIONS
Hans Scherer, Materialien 1.39 (Louvain, 1913).

C. H. Herford, Percy Simpson, and Evelyn Simpson, in *Ben Jonson* (Oxford, 1925–52), iii. 1–92, ix. 267–305.

Martin Butler, in *The Selected Plays of Ben Jonson*, ed. Johanna Proctor and Martin Butler, Renaissance and Restoration Dramatists (Cambridge, 1989), ii. 417–518.

Peter Happé, in *The Cambridge Edition of the Works of Ben Jonson*, gen. eds. David Bevington, Ian Donaldson, and Martin Butler (Cambridge, 2012), vi. 543–654.

REFERENCES
Annals 1596, 1633; Bawcutt 254, 283; *Ben Jonson*, ed. Herford & Simpson, ix. 163–6; Bentley, iv. 632–6; Eyre & Rivington, i. 437, ii. 8, iii. 3; Greg 617; Hazlitt, 222; HMC 7, 67; *The Library*, 4th ser., 11 (1930–1), 225–9, 461–5; *The Library*, 5th ser., 28 (1973), 294–308; *The Library*, 7th ser., 10 (2009), 372–404; MSC 6, 84; Allardyce Nicoll, *A History of English Drama*, 4th edn (Cambridge, 1952–9), i. 353; SB 25 (1972), 177–8; Steele, 246.

2404. Royal Entertainment at Welbeck Abbey

TEXT
Two early witnesses:
- F: printed in 1640–1 (STC 14754a);
- MS: London: British Library, MS Harley 4955, fos. 194^r–198^v; transcript from an authorial manuscript.

Additional information derives from a MS account of the performance (Oxford: Bodleian, MS Rawlinson D. 49, fo. 1; cited as R).

GENRE
entertainment
Contemporary: entertainment

TITLE
MS: *The King's Entertainment at Welbeck*
Printed: *The King's Entertainment at Welbeck in Nottinghamshire*
Later Assigned: *Love's Welcome at Welbeck*; *The Entertainment at Welbeck*

AUTHOR
Ben Jonson

DATE
21 May 1633

ORIGINAL PRODUCTION
Earl of Newcastle's household at Welbeck Abbey, Nottinghamshire

2404. Royal Entertainment at Welbeck Abbey

PLOT
All nature greets the King as he arrives for dinner at Welbeck. As he is about to leave, the party is accosted by Accidence and Fitz-Ale. They present a post-wedding event at which Stub the bridegroom and the six Hoods tilt at a quintain. A bride-ale follows, with eating, drinking, singing, and dancing, until an officer rebukes them for detaining the King with unsolicited merriment, and offers a panegyric of the King and royal family.

SCENE DESIGNATION
sc.1–3 (F/MS undivided), as follows:
  SC.1: Doubt, Love, and Affections; during dinner;
  SC.2: rustic wedding; after dinner;
  SC.3: Gentleman.

ROLES
DOUBT
LOVE
The AFFECTIONS, including Joy, Delight, and Jollity (only sing collectively; Jonson removed Jollity in F)
Master A-B-C ACCIDENCE, a Mansfield schoolmaster, Alphabet's father
Humphrey FITZALE, a Derby herald and antiquary, Pem's father; also called Father Fitzale (Jonson removed his first name in F)
STUB, Pem's bridegroom, a very short dwarf; also called Captain Stub and Yeoman Stub (*non-speaking*)
RED-HOOD, a bachelor, descendant of Robin Hood (*non-speaking*)
GREEN-HOOD, a forester and bachelor, descendant of Robin Hood (*non-speaking*)
BLUE-HOOD, a yeoman and bachelor, descendant of Robin Hood (*non-speaking*)
TAWNY-HOOD, a sumner and bachelor, descendant of Robin Hood (*non-speaking*)
MOTLEY-HOOD, a lawyer and bachelor, descendant of Robin Hood (*non-speaking*)
RUSSET-HOOD, a bachelor, descendant of Robin Hood (*non-speaking*)
Two SPECTATORS, who watch the tilting
PEM, Fitz-Ale's daughter, Stub's bride, a very tall woman (*non-speaking*)
Mistress ALPHABET, Accidence's daughter, a maid attending the bride (*non-speaking*)
Five MAIDS attending the bride (*non-speaking*)
Two BRIDE-SQUIRES, the cake-bearer and the bowl-bearer (*non-speaking*)
A GENTLEMAN, a servant or officer of the Lord Lieutenant of Nottinghamshire and Derbyshire

The relative heights of Pem and Stub, crucial to an understanding of this part of the entertainment, are not specified by Jonson, but are mentioned in R.

Speaking Parts: 10 or more
Allegorical Roles: 5 or more (not integrated with the other roles)

Stage Directions and Speech Prefixes
DOUBT: *Doubt* (s.d.s and s.p.s)
LOVE: *Love* (s.d.s and s.p.s)
AFFECTIONS: *Chorus of Affections, Joy, Delight, &c.* (F s.d.s); *Chorus of Affections, Joy, Delight, Jollity* (MS s.d.s); *Chorus* (s.p.s)
ACCIDENCE: *Accidence* (F s.d.s and s.p.s); *A: B: Cee Accidence* (MS s.d.s)
FITZALE: *Fitz-Ale* (F s.d.s); *Fitz<-Ale>* (s.p.s); *Humphrey Fitz-Ale* (MS s.d.s)
STUB: *Stub the Bridegroom* | *Stub* (s.d.s)
RED-HOOD: [one of] *the six Hoods* | *Red-hood* (s.d.s)
GREEN-HOOD: [one of] *the six Hoods* | *Green-hood* (s.d.s)
BLUE-HOOD: [one of] *the six Hoods* | *Blue-hood* (s.d.s)
TAWNY-HOOD: [one of] *the six Hoods* | *Tawny-hood* (s.d.s)
MOTLEY-HOOD: [one of] *the six Hoods* | *Motley-hood* (s.d.s)
RUSSET-HOOD: [one of] *the six Hoods* | *Russet-hood* (s.d.s)
SPECTATORS: *1* | *2* (s.p.s)
PEM: *the Bride* (s.d.s)
ALPHABET: [one of] *Six Maids* | *Mistress Alphabet* (s.d.s)
MAIDS: [five of] *Six Maids* (s.d.s)
BRIDE-SQUIRES: *The two Bride Squires, the Cake-bearer and the Bowl-bearer* | *the Clowns* (s.d.s)
GENTLEMAN: *an Officer, or servant of the Lord Lieutenant's* (s.d.s); *Gentleman* (s.p.s)

OTHER CHARACTERS
The Abbot, Tawny-Hood's master (sc.2)

SETTING
Geography
Nottinghamshire: Sherwood Forest; Mansfield
Derbyshire: Derby; the Peak; St Anne's Well, Buxton; Elden Hole; Poole's Hole; Devil's Arse
England: Kendal
Great Britain: Scotland
France

SOURCES
Narrative: Robert Langham, *A Letter* (1575)
Verbal: Bible: Ezekiel 43.11 (sc.3); Homer, *Iliad* (sc.3; probably via Justus Lipsius, *Politica*, 1589; Jonson owned a copy of the 1623 edition); Seneca, *De consolatione ad Polybium* (sc.3; probably again via Lipsius)

LANGUAGE
English

FORM
Metre: tetrameter, skeltonics, pentameter, and prose
Rhyme: couplets and blank verse
Lines (Spoken): 272 (247 verse, 25 prose)
Lines (Written): 333 (F); 326 (MS)

The spoken length is based on F.

STAGING

Audience: the King is mentioned (sc.1–3); the audience in general is addressed as 'gentlemen of court' (sc.2); the Lord Lieutenant (i.e. Newcastle, the host) is mentioned and addressed directly (sc.2)

MUSIC

Music: trumpet sounds seven flourishes (sc.2, s.d.); bagpipes (sc.2, desc.; accompanies Song 2)
Songs:
1: 'What softer sounds are these salute the ear', sc.1, Doubt, Love, Affections, 30 lines, in parts, *musical setting survives*;
2: 'Let's sing about and say, Hey troll', sc.2, 10 lines, with musical accompaniment.
Dance: the Hoods dance (sc.2, desc.)

PROPS

Weapons: seven lances (sc.2, implicit)
Animals: seven horses with bridles, saddles, and stirrups (sc.2, dialogue)
Food and Drink: a bride-cake (sc.2, desc.; eaten on stage); a bride-bowl (sc.2, desc.; contents drunk on stage)
Small Portable Objects: a pen and inkhorn (sc.2, dialogue); a large embroidered handkerchief with red and blue (sc.2, desc.)
Large Portable Objects: a quintain (sc.2, dialogue)

COSTUMES

ACCIDENCE: a black buckram cassock, a girdle, a hat and hatband, stockings and sandals, all painted with grammatical words and alphabetical letters (sc.2, desc.), with a birch rod in his hat (dialogue)
FITZALE: a herald's buckram tabard of quartered azure and red, lined with yellow, and pasted over with old records and 'fragments of the forest', with a label containing verses (sc.2, desc.)
STUB: a yellow canvas doublet, cut; a forest ranger's green jerkin and hose; a Monmouth cap with a yellow feather; yellow stockings and shoes (sc.2, desc.)
RED-HOOD: a red stammel hood (sc.2, desc./dialogue)
GREEN-HOOD: a green hood (sc.2, desc.)
BLUE-HOOD: a blue hood (sc.2, desc.)
TAWNY-HOOD: a tawny hood (sc.2, desc.)
MOTLEY-HOOD: a multi-coloured hood (sc.2, desc.)
RUSSET-HOOD: a russet hood (sc.2, desc.)
PEM: scarves and 'other habiliments' (sc.2, desc.)
ALPHABET and MAIDS: buckram bride-laces; white sleeves; stammel petticoats (sc.2, desc.)
BRIDE-SQUIRES: yellow leather doublets; russet hose; livery hats; ribbons (sc.2, desc.)
GENTLEMAN: clothes denoting his authority (sc.3, desc.)

EARLY STAGE HISTORY

1633: performed at Welbeck Abbey during and after dinner on Tuesday 21 May, to honour the King's visit on his way to Scotland for his coronation. Much of the performance took place outdoors. Some of the music was composed by William Lawes. The audience included: King Charles I; William Cavendish, Earl of Newcastle (host); lords and courtiers.

A. P. Martinich suggests (in *N&Q* 1998) that the cast may have included Thomas Hobbes (Fitzale).

Production Expenses
The event (including the dinner) cost Newcastle £4,000–£5,000; he later complained of the expense he had incurred.

EARLY TEXTUAL HISTORY

1633: Ben Jonson's payment for writing the entertainment was delivered to him by Robert Payne.

c. 1634–40: transcribed by John Rolleston as part of a **MS** literary collection for William Cavendish, Earl of Newcastle; 5 leaves.

c. 1637–40: Not long before his death, Jonson placed some of his unpublished works in the hands of Sir Kenelm Digby, with a view to their publication. This entertainment may have been one of the texts in question. After Jonson's death in August 1637, Digby took the texts he had received to Thomas Walkley, who paid Digby £40 and procured a licence to publish them, but did not enter them in the Stationers' Register.

1640: While Walkley's volume was at the printer's, John Benson and Andrew Crooke had some of the masques therein (not including this one) entered to them in the Stationers' Register; the Stationers' Company authorities had no knowledge of Walkley's interest in the matter. Fearful that they were planning to issue their own edition, Walkley complained to a secretary of state, who issued a warrant prohibiting Benson and Crooke from doing so.

1640–1: included in the third volume of Jonson's *Works* ('**F₁**'), sigs. 2N4ᵛ–2O4ᵛ, 9 pages on 5 leaves; printed by John Dawson for Thomas Walkley.

1640–1: The Stationers' Register entry of *The Gypsies Metamorphosed* (**1987**) in Benson's favour misled John Parker, a London stationer, into supposing that the printed copies of Walkley's volume were Benson's property. Benson allegedly owed Parker money, so Parker had the book seized from the printer's. Walkley, who valued the copies at £300 or more, suspected that this was a dishonest move planned by Benson and Crooke in preparation to issuing their own edition, and complained to the Court of Chancery on Wednesday 20 January 1641.

c. 1641–5: Song 1 (headed 'A Dialogue between Joy and Delight') included, with a musical setting by William Lawes, in Lawes's autograph MS songbook (London: British Library, Add. MS 31432, fo. 20ᵛ–21ʳ). Lawes later gave the book to Richard Gibbon, whose widow, Anne, gave it away in turn, probably at some time between 1652 and 1656, to one J. R. (probably John Reading).

1648: Changes in press licensing arrangements since 1640 meant that Walkley's original licence to print his Jonson works had become void. He attempted to have the texts perused by the new licensers in preparation for having them entered in the Stationers' Register, but one of them, Sir Nathaniel Brent, was out of town and the other, John Langley, claimed to be too busy. He then approached the Stationers' Company, who in turn petitioned the House of Lords on Wednesday 20 December, asking for additional licensers to be appointed.

1653: *The Marrow of Compliments* entered to Humphrey Moseley in the Stationers' Register on Tuesday 20 December.

1654: extract (from sc.2) included in Samuel Sheppard's *The Marrow of Compliments*, sig. C3^r; printed (before Saturday 15 July) for Humphrey Moseley.

c. 1655: extracts transcribed from F$_1$ by John Evans in a miscellany, *Hesperides*, intended for publication and entered to Humphrey Moseley in the Stationers' Register on Thursday 16 August 1655. The book remained unpublished in 1660, and Evans continued adding to the collection until at least 1666. Two MS exemplars are known; one was cut up by J. O. Halliwell-Phillipps in the nineteenth century; the other survives (Washington: Folger, MS V. b. 93).

1658: rights to the third volume of Jonson's *Works* entered in the Stationers' Register to Thomas Walkley on Friday 17 September; group entry, including a reference to fifteen unnamed masques.

1658: Walkley's rights transferred to Humphrey Moseley in the Stationers' Register on Saturday 20 November.

1660: F$_1$ advertised for sale by Humphrey Moseley.

1667: Moseley's rights to the third volume of Jonson's *Works* transferred by his widow, Ann, to Henry Herringman in the Stationers' Register on Monday 19 August; group transfer of nine titles, the *Works* being one.

1675: Moseley's rights to *The Marrow of Compliments* transferred from his widow, Ann, to Peter Parker in the Stationers' Register on Wednesday 8 September, by order of a court held on Monday 22 February, and by an assignment dated Thursday 26 September 1672.

1692: included in Jonson's *Works* (^{2}F$_2$), printed by Thomas Hodgkin for Henry Herringman, Edward Brewster, Thomas Bassett, Richard Chiswell, Matthew Wotton, and George Conyers, sigs. 4F1^r–4F2^v, 2 leaves.

The books here designated F$_1$ and F$_2$ are respectively the second and third Jonson Folios.

EDITIONS
C. H. Herford, Percy Simpson, and Evelyn Simpson in *Ben Jonson* (Oxford, 1925–52), vii. 787–803, x. 703–9.

James Knowles, in *The Cambridge Edition of the Works of Ben Jonson*, gen. eds. David Bevington, Ian Donaldson, and Martin Butler (Cambridge, 2012), vi. 659–80.

REFERENCES
Annals 1633; Beal JnB 676–7; Bentley, iv. 648–9; Butler, 373; *Chelys* 31 (2003), 3–17; *EMS* 4 (1993), 145–53; Eyre & Rivington, i. 447, ii. 8, iii. 3; Greg 613; Hazlitt, 125; HMC 7, 67; *The Library*, 4th ser., 11 (1930–1), 225–9, 461–5; *The Library*, 5th ser., 7 (1952), 225–34; *The Library*, 5th ser., 28 (1973), 294–308; *The Library*, 7th ser., 10 (2009), 372–404; McGee-Meagher 1625–34, 71–3; *N&Q* 239 (1994), 519–20; *N&Q* 243 (1998), 370–1.

2405. Tottenham Court

TEXT
Printed in 1638 (STC 18344).

GENRE
comedy
Contemporary: 'easy comedy' (prol.); play (prol., S.R.); 'pleasant comedy' (t.p.)

TITLE
Performed/Printed: *Tottenham Court*
Later Assigned: *Tottenham Court Fair*

AUTHOR
Thomas Nabbes

DATE
Limits: 1633–4
Best Guess: May 1633

The year is given on the Q title page, the month in the prologue. There are three factors which combine to make that evidence slightly less than definitive.

The prologue specifically mentions the festivities of May Day, though in practice the fifth-Act allusions to *A Tale of a Tub* (**2403**) mean the play cannot be earlier than 7 May, when Jonson's comedy was licensed; moreover, a reference in 1.2 to a remark about a puppy, said to have been spoken 'last Whitsuntide in a play' might allude to the character of Puppy in Jonson's play. This leaves a very tight turnaround for the completion of the play and its pre-production and licensing, all before the end of May 1633. In consequence, it is worth observing that the reference to witches in Lancashire would have been especially topical in May 1634. The third relevant factor is that a closely associated Nabbes quarto, *Covent Garden* (**2424**), gives on its title page a year of performance that is demonstrably wrong, and this could raise a corresponding doubt about the year given on the *Tottenham Court* title page.

The difference between the cases, however, is that the *Tottenham Court* evidence falls some way short of being secure. To write about Lancashire witches in 1633 did not require preternatural prescience, because there had already been a notorious case in 1612. The puppy reference, meanwhile, could be taken to be ironically self-referential rather than another allusion to Jonson: Whit Sunday fell on 30 May in 1633, which is roughly when the play must have opened if it did indeed open in that month and year. Ultimately, there is enough to make it worth considering an alternative date of early May 1634, but not quite enough to overturn the explicit indicators of late May 1633.

ORIGINAL PRODUCTION
Prince Charles's Men (presumably) at Salisbury Court

In 1633, the acting company at Salisbury Court was Prince Charles's Men. The issue is complicated by the 1639 cancel title page, which removes the year and names the company as Queen Henrietta's Men. The company name might have been mistakenly imported from the cancel title page of *Covent Garden* (**2424**) which was set at the same time; but on the other hand, the removal of the year might also carry significance. In 1633–4, Queen Henrietta's Men were based at the Cockpit, and their repertory there seems to have belonged to the playhouse. In 1637, they moved to Salisbury Court, and their Cockpit plays passed into the repertory of their successors at the theatre, Beeston's Boys. If Salisbury Court had the same arrangement over the ownership of the plays performed there, and if *Tottenham Court* was revived at some time in the years 1637–9, then it may indeed have been performed by Queen Henrietta's Men, making Q's cancel title page accurate after all.

PLOT
Worthgood and Bellamie intend to marry, and have absconded to London with her uncle in pursuit. Bellamie is separated from Worthgood in Marylebone Park. She meets the censorious Cicely, and faints when Cicely voices her suspicions of sexual impropriety. She dreams that she will have Worthgood that very day, and is revived by Cicely's father, the park-keeper, who takes her home and seems interested in the name Worthgood. Worthgood meets the keeper, who promises to reunite him with Bellamie; but she and Cicely have already left for London, exchanging clothes to deceive any pursuers. Worthgood and the keeper follow them.

Bellamie and Cicely arrive at an alehouse in Tottenham Court. Bellamie unexpectedly meets her brother, Sam, but denies her identity when he recognizes her; he infers that she has become a common prostitute. Also at the alehouse is Cicely's unwanted admirer, Frank, who intends to seduce the tailor's wife, Mistress Stitchwell, and has piqued her interest by posing as a misogynist. Mistress Stitchwell intends to cuckold her husband in his presence, but the first attempt backfires: alone in the alehouse bathroom with her, Frank's friend George hides in the tub when Stitchwell arrives, and has water poured over him.

Sam's friend James visits Cicely, thinking her a prostitute too, but hides in a trunk when others arrive. Importuned by Frank, Cicely proposes having herself smuggled to his room in the trunk; she and Bellamie then send it there, with the sleeping James locked inside. Intending to enjoy Cicely himself, George diverts the trunk to his own room. He and Frank fight over it, only to find that it contains James, not Cicely.

Changelove woos Mistress Stitchwell while her husband is in a drunken stupor, but Stitchwell dreams he is being cuckolded and assaults Changelove. The gallant leaves the tailor to pay an inflated alehouse bill when he wakes up. Mistress Stitchwell assures him she was only amusing herself with the gallants, not committing adultery.

Sam tries to engage Bellamie's supposed professional services and, shocked, she admits her identity. Rebuked by her brother, she faints. Worthgood and the keeper locate her, and she wakes to the sound of his voice. Bellamie's uncle also traces her to the alehouse, but when he arrives he finds not only his niece but his nephew planning marriage: Bellamie has interested Sam in Cicely, and he has approved Worthgood as a brother-in-law. The keeper reveals that Cicely is Worthgood's sister, and so of appropriate birth to marry Sam: he adopted her as a child when both her parents died. News arrives that Worthgood's uncle has died and left him a fortune. The couples all leave to get married—including, on the spur of the moment, the keeper and the alehouse hostess.

SCENE DESIGNATION
prol., 1.1–6, 2.1–6, 3.1–6, 4.1–7, 5.1–7, ep. (Q)

The stage is not clear at the following scene-divisions: 1.3–6, 2.1–2, 2.3–4, 2.5–6, 3.1–3, 3.4–5, 4.1–6, 5.1–3, 5.4–7. Verse lines are split across scene-divisions at 4.2–3, 4.3–4, 4.4–5.

ROLES
PROLOGUE
WORTHGOOD, a gentleman, Bellamie's fiancé; formerly a soldier
Mistress BELLAMIE, a chaste gentlewoman, Sam's sister, her guardian's niece, Worthgood's fiancée
The UNCLE and guardian of Bellamie and Sam, a country gentleman
SERVANTS of Bellamie's uncle (1.2, 5.1; only one speaks on stage; any others may speak collectively *within*)
Two TENANTS and neighbours of Bellamie's uncle (1.2, 5.1, 5.6–7)
CICELY, a milkmaid, supposed the Keeper's daughter; in reality Cecilia Worthgood, Worthgood's sister
The KEEPER of Marylebone Park, a widower; supposed Cicely's father
SLIP, the Keeper's man of seven years' service
FRANK, a young courtier, George's friend
GEORGE, a courtier, Frank's friend
Master Will CHANGELOVE, a gallant
Master John STITCHWELL, a tailor, Mistress Stitchwell's husband
MISTRESS STITCHWELL, Stitchwell's wife of more than fifteen years
ROBIN, a tapster at the alehouse

JAMES, a young, lazy law student
SAM, a studious law student, Bellamie's brother, his guardian's nephew
A WENCH at the alehouse, Slip's sweetheart (3.5)
The HOSTESS of the alehouse, a widow
A PORTER, a deaf, married man (4.4, 5.1)
A SERVANT of Worthgood's uncle (5.7)

Speaking Parts: 22

Stage Directions and Speech Prefixes
PROLOGUE: *The Prologue* (heading)
WORTHGOOD: *Worthgood* (s.d.s and s.p.s); *Worthgood. A deserving Gentleman* (d.p.)
BELLAMIE: *Bellamie | [one of] the women* (s.d.s); *Bella<mie>* (s.p.s); *Bellamie. [Worthgood's] Mistress* (d.p.)
UNCLE: *Uncle* (s.d.s and s.p.s); *[Bellamie's] Uncle. An angry country gentleman* (d.p.)
SERVANTS: *servants | [Uncle's] servants* (s.d.s); *Servant* (s.d.s, s.p.s, and d.p.)
TENANTS: *Tenants* (s.d.s); *1 Tenant | 2 Tenant | 1 Neighbour | 2 Neighbour* (s.p.s); *Two Countrymen* (d.p.)
CICELY: *Cicelie | Ciceley | [one of] the women* (s.d.s); *Cice<ley>* (s.p.s); *Ciceley. Sister to Worthgood, but unknown* (d.p.)
KEEPER: *Keeper* (s.d.s and s.p.s); *Keeper of Marrowbone-Park* (d.p.)
SLIP: *Slip* (s.d.s and s.p.s); *Slipp* (s.d.s); *Slip [the Keeper's] Man* (d.p.)
FRANK: *Franke | [one of the] men* (s.d.s); *Frank<e>* (s.p.s); *Franke [one of] Two Courtiers* (d.p.)
GEORGE: *George* (s.d.s and s.p.s); *[one of the] men* (s.d.s); *George [one of] Two Courtiers* (d.p.)
CHANGELOVE: *Changlove | Changelove | [one of the] men* (s.d.s); *Change<love>* (s.p.s); *Changelove. A fantastic Gallant* (d.p.)
STITCHWELL: *Stitchwell* (s.d.s); *Stitch<well> | Stich<well>* (s.p.s); *Stitchwell. A Tailor of the Strand* (d.p.)
MISTRESS STITCHWELL: *[Stitchwell's] Wife* (s.d.s and d.p.); *[one of] the women* (s.d.s); *Wife* (s.d.s and s.p.s); *Mrs St<itchwel>* (s.p.s)
ROBIN: *Tapster* (s.d.s, s.p.s, and d.p.)
JAMES: *James | [one of the] men* (s.d.s); *Jam<es>* (s.p.s); *James. A wild young gentleman of the Inns of Court* (d.p.)
SAM: *Sam* (s.d.s and s.p.s); *[one of the] men* (s.d.s); *Sam. A fine Gentleman of the Inns of Court, and Brother to Bellamie* (d.p.)
WENCH: *a wench* (s.d.s); *Wench* (s.p.s and d.p.)
HOSTESS: *Hostess* (s.d.s, s.p.s, and d.p.); *the Hostess* (s.d.)
PORTER: *Porter* (s.d.s, s.p.s, and d.p.)
SERVANT: *Servant* (s.d.s, s.p.s, and d.p.)

OTHER CHARACTERS
A parson of the Tenants' parish (1.2)

A carter employed by Bellamie's Uncle, who acted in a play (1.2)
A needy poet, Slip's friend, to whom he sent venison (1.5)
The poet's ningle (1.5)
Frank's ancestors (2.1)
Stitchwell's servants, including a finisher (2.2)
A Cornish boy, Stitchwell's apprentice, who is a good wrestler (2.2, 3.3)
A boy from the north east, Stitchwell's servant, who is a good stool-ball player (2.2)
Twelve midwives known to Mistress Stitchwell (2.2)
The fiddlers at Tottenham Court (2.2)
Two constipated citizens, customers at the alehouse (3.1)
Three tailors, customers at the alehouse (3.1)
James's father (3.1)
Deputy Tagg, a citizen (3.3)
An improvident gentleman who ruined his estate, the dead father of Worthgood and Cicely (3.6, 5.5, 5.7)
The dead mother of Worthgood and Cicely (3.6, 5.5, 5.7)
A freeman's widow, the Porter's wife (4.4)
Eighteen virgins seduced by George (4.4)
Bellamie's servant in her Uncle's house (4.5)
Bellamie's dead parents (4.5)
A one-handed costermonger and his wife, who sold expensive prunes (4.7)
Worthgood's rich uncle (5.7)
The Keeper's dead wife (5.7)

SETTING
Period: contemporary
Time-Scheme: the action takes place during a single day, with 1.1–2 taking place just before dawn; dawn breaks in 1.3, and it is still morning in 3.1
Place: Tottenham Court

Geography
Middlesex: the Brick kilns (= Brickhill); Marylebone Park; the Great Oak; St Pancras
London: London Bridge; Bridewell; Barber Surgeons' Hall; the Strand; the Exchange
England: Lancashire; Cornwall; Cranborne Church
France
The Low Countries: Holland
Turkey: Constantinople
Ethiopia
The Indies

SOURCES
Narrative: possibly *Singing Simpkin* (**1006**; trunk sequence)
Works Mentioned: Galen, *De exercitatione parvae pilae* (2.2); Edmund Spenser, unspecified work (3.3); Sir Philip Sidney, *Arcadia* (1580; 3.3); William Shakespeare, unspecified works (3.1); *Swetnam, the Woman-Hater, Arraigned by Women* (**1855**; 2.2); John Harmar, *Praxis grammatica* (1623; 3.5); John Booker,

Almanac (1632; 1.6); Ben Jonson, unspecified works (3.1), *A Tale of a Tub* (**2403**; 5.3, 5.6; possibly also 1.2)

LANGUAGE
English
Latin: 7 words (2.2, 3.5; Changelove, Sam)

FORM
Metre: pentameter and prose
Rhyme: blank verse
Prologue: 28 lines, in couplets
Act-Division: 5 acts
Epilogue: 10 lines, in couplets, spoken by the Hostess
Lines (Spoken): 2,183 (1,176 verse, 1,007 prose)
Lines (Written): 2,423

STAGING
Within: speech (1.1, 2.3, 3.4, s.d.); halloo (1.1, s.d.); singing (1.3, s.d.)
Audience: addressed as 'gentlemen' (prol.); said to have paid for admission (prol.)
Miscellaneous: George has water poured over him on stage (3.5)

MUSIC
Music: unspecified music (3.2, s.d.)
Song: 'What a dainty life the milkmaid leads', 1.3, Cicely within, 8 lines
Other Singing: distant singing within (1.3, s.d.)
Dance: characters, including Changelove and Mistress Stitchwell, dance (3.3, s.d.)

PROPS
Lighting: lights (1.2, s.d.)
Weapons: George's sword (5.3, implicit); Frank's sword (5.3, implicit)
Money: an unspecified sum (3.5, implicit); another unspecified sum (4.4, implicit); half a crown (4.5, dialogue); nine shillings and three pence (4.7, dialogue); an unspecified sum (5.4, dialogue)
Food and Drink: liquor (3.3, implicit; drunk on stage)
Small Portable Objects: a milk-pail (1.4, dialogue); a pail of water (3.5, s.d.); a key (4.3, implicit; 5.1-3, dialogue)
Large Portable Objects: a tub (3.4-5, s.d.); a trunk of feathers (4.1, dialogue; 5.1-3, s.d.; lockable, and large enough to contain a man); a chair (4.7, s.d.)

COSTUMES AND MAKE-UP
BELLAMIE: a brown complexion (dialogue); 'silken' clothes, possibly including petticoats (1.3-5, dialogue); a ring on her little finger (1.3-5, dialogue); Cicely's clothes (2.3, s.d.; 2.6, 3.3, implicit; 4.1-6, dialogue)
CICELY: Bellamie's satin gown (2.3, s.d.; 2.6, 3.3, implicit; 4.1-6, 5.5-7, dialogue)
FRANK: hangers (5.2-3, implicit)
GEORGE: hangers (5.1-3, implicit)
CHANGELOVE: a periwig (4.7, dialogue)

EARLY STAGE HISTORY
Performed at Salisbury Court by 1638.
   1639: possibly performed by Queen Henrietta's Men at Salisbury Court.

EARLY TEXTUAL HISTORY
   1638: entered to Charles Greene in the Stationers' Register on Thursday 5 April; entry names author. Matthew Clay had licensed the book for publication.
   1638: Q printed by Richard Oulton for Charles Greene; collation A-K⁴, 40 leaves; title page names author and playhouse and gives year of performance; authorial dedication to William Mills; list of roles.
   1639: Q reissued with a cancel title page, removing the year of performance and naming Queen Henrietta's Men as the acting company; now said to be printed by John Dawson, apparently for sale by Nicholas Fussell.
   c. 1630s–40s: a copy of the first state of Q was in the possession of John Horne (Vicar of Headington, Oxfordshire). After his death, his entire collection of play-books passed into the possession of John Houghton of Brasenose College, Oxford (c. 1608–77), then to James Herne (died 1685), and then to the library of Ralph Sheldon (1623–84) at Weston, where it was catalogued by Anthony Wood, probably in the late 1670s.
   1640 or later: copies of Q were bound with six other Nabbes quartos to create a collection of Nabbes's *Poems, Masques, &c.* (with a title page dated 1639); possibly sold by Nicholas Fussell. The other plays were *Covent Garden* (**2424**), *Hannibal and Scipio* (**2480**), *Microcosmus* (**2543**), *The Spring's Glory* (**2597**), an edition which also included the text of his Masque of Time and the Almanac-Makers (**2635**), *The Bride* (**2645**), and *The Unfortunate Mother* (**2713**).
   1640–1: Humphrey Moseley was selling copies of Q for 6d each.
   1650: *The Card of Courtship* entered to Humphrey Moseley in the Stationers' Register on Wednesday 6 July.
   1653: extract (from 5.5) included in S. S.'s *The Card of Courtship*, sigs. B5ᵛ–B6ᵛ; printed in January by J. C. for Humphrey Moseley.
   1655: *The English Treasury of Wit and Language* entered in the Stationers' Register to Humphrey Moseley on Tuesday 16 January.
   1655: seven extracts (from 1.3, 2.1, 3.3, 4.3, 4.5, 5.3) included in John Cotgrave's *The English Treasury of Wit and Language*, sigs. E4ʳ, G1ᵛ, L1ʳ, N5ᵛ, O5ʳ, S2ᵛ; printed for Humphrey Moseley.
   1675: Moseley's rights to *The Card of Courtship* transferred from his widow, Ann, to Peter Parker in the Stationers' Register on Wednesday 8 September, by order of a court held on Monday 22 February, and by an assignment dated Thursday 26 September 1672.
   1680: extracts (from 1.3–6, 2.2–4, 3.4, 4.2, 4.4–5, 4.7, 5.1, 5.3–4, with characters renamed and combined with material from 2 *The Honest Whore*, **1459**, and *The Just Italian*, **2282**) appear as the droll, *The Merry*

Milkmaid of Islington, or The Rambling Gallants Defeated, included in *The Muse of Newmarket*, sigs. B2ʳ⁻ᵛ, B3ᵛ–D1ʳ; printed for Daniel Browne, Daniel Major, and James Vade.

1684: Nicholas Cox (Manciple of St Edmund Hall, Oxford) had a copy of Q in his bookshop, as part of a bound collection of Nabbes's plays; the other plays in the volume were *Covent Garden* (**2424**), *The Spring's Glory* (**2597**), an edition which also included the text of his Masque of Time and the Almanac-Makers (**2635**), *The Bride* (**2645**), and *The Unfortunate Mother* (**2713**). It had probably been previously owned by Gerard Langbaine, and appears on a list compiled by Anthony Wood on Saturday 13 December.

1690: a copy of Q was in the library at Petworth House.

EDITION
A. H. Bullen, in *The Works of Thomas Nabbes* (London, 1887), i. 93–184.

REFERENCES
Annals 1634; Bentley, iv. 940–2; Bodleian, MS Wood E. 4, art. 1, p. 45; Eyre & Rivington, i. 347, 463, iii. 3; Greg 540; Hazlitt, 231; *MLR* 13 (1918), 401–11; *National Trust Year Book 1975–6* (London, [1976]), 62–4; *Oxford Bibliographical Society Proceedings and Papers* 2.2 (1929), 132–3; *SP* 40 (1943), 186–203.

2406. The City Shuffler

EVIDENCE
Justinian Pagitt's diary; list of MS plays said to have been in the possession of John Warburton (1682–1759), and destroyed by his cook (London: British Library, MS Lansdowne 807, fo. 1).

In theory, the play recorded by Pagitt could have been the second part (**2415**), which had recently caused controversy and may therefore have been of interest to the Middle Temple audience; however, Pagitt names it simply as '*City Shuffler*', without differentiation of part. The Warburton list also gives the title only as '*City Shuffler*'; there is likewise no knowing whether the baked play was the first or second part (or indeed both). In any event, there must have been a first part for there to have been a second.

GENRE
comedy (?)
Contemporary: play

TITLE
Performed: *The City Shuffler*

DATE
Limits: *c.* 1632–3
Best Guess: 1633

ORIGINAL PRODUCTION
Prince Charles's Men at Salisbury Court (presumably)

ROLES
A dishonest CITIZEN

The predominant sense of the word *shuffler* was a shifty or evasive person.

SETTING
Place: a city (perhaps London)

EARLY STAGE HISTORY
1633: performed in the hall at the Middle Temple on Friday 1 November. The audience included Justinian Pagitt.

REFERENCES
Bentley, v. 1309; *The Library*, 3rd ser., 2 (1911), 225–59; *MRDE* 6 (1993), 191; REED: Inns of Court, 749, 808.

2407. Trappolin Supposed a Prince

TEXT
Printed in 1658 (Wing C4898), probably from authorial copy.

GENRE
comedy
Contemporary: play (prol., ep.); comedy (prol.); 'famous Italian play' (S.R.); 'Italian tragicomedy' (t.p.)

TITLE
Performed: probably *Trappolin Supposed a Prince*
Printed: *Trappolin creduto principe, or Trappolin Supposed a Prince*
Contemporary: *Trappolin*

AUTHOR
Aston Cokayne

DATE
1633

PLOT
Lord Barbarino has lustful designs on Flametta, but she is only interested in Trappolin. Appointed co-deputy during the absence of Lavinio, the Great Duke, who has gone to get married, Barbarino has Trappolin arrested and banished for pimping. Brunetto, a prisoner of war, charitably gives Trappolin a ring to sell. Brunetto is really Horatio, who has fallen in love with Lavinio's sister Prudentia, got himself captured to be near her, and assumed a false identity to avoid being ransomed and sent home. He plans to elope with Prudentia, but they are

overheard, and the deputies forestall the plan by imprisoning Horatio.

Trappolin meets the magician Mago, who gives him an enchanted hat, cloak, and mirror which together will make people believe he is Lavinio, and also a powder which will make someone else seem to be him. He returns to Florence in his new identity, has Horatio released in requital of his generosity, and gives his pseudo-ducal approval to a marriage with Prudentia. Flametta appeals to him for Trappolin to be recalled, and he tests the strength of her feelings by setting a condition: he will rescind Trappolin's banishment in exchange for articles of her clothing; she agrees and strips off, but draws the line at removing her underwear. He eventually agrees that, if she grants Trappolin her sexual favours without his having to marry her, he can come home. The deputies become suspicious of 'Lavinio', but when they question Horatio's release, he has them sent to prison themselves. He hears a series of petitioners' cases, and gives eccentric judgements.

The real Lavinio arrives back in Florence, and he and Trappolin successively reverse one another's decisions: the deputies and Horatio find themselves repeatedly in and out of prison; in the course of this, Lavinio uses his signet ring to reinforce his authority, but it is returned to the impostor. Trappolin explains the apparently inconsistent ducal behaviour by suggesting that he is wont to do strange things when drunk. He uses the magic powder to change Lavinio's appearance: Flametta takes him for Trappolin and welcomes him home, but when he insists that he is the Duke, Trappolin sends him to jail. He uses the ducal signet to allow Horatio and Prudentia to marry.

Mago arrives and offers to sort things out, on condition that Lavinio pardons everything. Upon that promise, he restores Trappolin and Lavinio to their true appearance. He further announces that Horatio's elder brother has died, making him the heir of Savoy; this removes Lavinio's objections to the marriage with Prudentia. Horatio rewards Trappolin with an earldom, Trappolin agrees to marry Flametta, and Mago reveals that he is Trappolin's long-lost father.

SCENE DESIGNATION
prol., 1.1–3, 2.1–3, 3.1–3, 4.1–2, 5.1–5, ep. (Q, corrected)

ROLES
PROLOGUE
TRAPPOLIN, a pimp; also called Trappolino and Trap; turns out to be Mago's son; ultimately created Earl of Vercelli
Mistress FLAMETTA, Trappolin's sweetheart; a young woman; said to be little
Lord BARBARINO, a nobleman, appointed joint Deputy; also called Barbarine
Duke LAVINIO, Great Duke of Tuscany, Duke of Florence and Siena, of the house of Medici; Prudentia's brother; later Isabella's husband; when impersonating him, Trappolin abbreviates his name to Lavin
Princess PRUDENTIA, of the house of Medici; Lavinio's sister; also called Lady Prudentia; later Horatio's wife
Lord MACHIAVEL, a nobleman, appointed joint Deputy
ATTENDANTS on Lavinio (1.2, 4.2, *non-speaking*)
Captain MATTEMOROS, a Spaniard, commander of the Tuscan army; also called Don Mattemoros and Señor Mattemoros
Prince HORATIO of Piedmont; assumes the alias Brunetto, a prisoner of war; later Prudentia's husband
Four OFFICERS (1.2–3)
HIPPOLYTA, Prudentia's lady-in-waiting
A NOTARY (1.3, *non-speaking*)
MAGO, an old conjuror and former galley-slave; turns out to be Trappolin's father
EO, a devil
MEO, a devil (*non-speaking*)
AREO, a devil and tailor
SFORZA, Duke of Milan, Hortensia's husband, Isabella's brother
HORTENSIA, Duchess of Milan, Sforza's wife
Lady ISABELLA, Sforza's sister; later Lavinio's wife and Duchess of Florence
ATTENDANTS at Milan (2.2, *non-speaking*)
HYMEN, god of marriage; a character in the masque
LUNA, a planet, goddess of the moon and Monday; also called Cynthia; a character in the masque
MARS, a planet, god of war and Tuesday; a character in the masque
MERCURY, a planet and god of Wednesday; also called Hermes; a character in the masque
JUPITER, a planet, chief of the gods, god of Thursday; also called Jove; a character in the masque
VENUS, a planet, goddess of love and Friday; a character in the masque
SATURN, a planet, old god of Saturday; a character in the masque
SOL, a planet, god of the sun and Sunday; also called Phoebus and Apollo; a character in the masque
The GUARD (2.3, 4.1, *non-speaking*)
PUCCANELLO, a jailer
Master CALFSHEAD, a Puritan petitioner; also called Goodman Calfshead
Master BULLFLESH, a butcher
Master BARN, a farmer and petitioner
Gaffer TILER, a poor workman
Mistress FINE, a petitioner; a widow and a bereaved mother
Dick WHIP, a coachman
EPILOGUE

Speaking Parts: 36

Stage Directions and Speech Prefixes
PROLOGUE: *The Prologue* (heading)

TRAPPOLIN: *Trappolin* (s.d.s); *Trap<polin>* (s.p.s); *Trappolin Supposed a Prince* (d.p.)
FLAMETTA: *Flametta* (s.d.s and s.p.s); *Flametta Trappoline's sweetheart* (d.p.)
BARBARINO: *Barbarino | Barbarin | Barberino* (s.d.s); *Barba<rino>* (s.p.s); *Barbarine* [one of] *Two noble Florentines* (d.p.)
LAVINIO: *Lavinio the great Duke* (s.d.s); *Lavinio* (s.d.s and s.p.s); *Lavinio The great Duke of Tuskany* (d.p.)
PRUDENTIA: *Prudentia* (s.d.s); *Pruden<tia>* (s.p.s); *Prudentia Horatio's Mistress* (d.p.)
MACHIAVEL: *Machavil | Machiavil | Macchavil* (s.d.s); *Macha<vil> | Macc<havil>* (s.p.s); *Machavil* [one of] *Two noble Florentines* (d.p.)
ATTENDANTS: *others* (s.d.s); *Attendants* (s.d.s and d.p.)
MATTEMOROS: *Mattemores the Spanish Captain | Mattemores | Mattemoros the Spanish Captain | Mattemoros* (s.d.s); *Matte<mores>* (s.p.s); *Mattemores A Spanish Captain* (d.p.)
HORATIO: *Horatio | Brunetto* (s.d.s); *Horat<io>* (s.p.s); *Horatio Son of the Duke of Savoy* (d.p.)
OFFICERS: *Officers* (s.d.s and d.p.); *1 | 2 | 3 | 4 | Officer* (s.p.s)
HIPPOLYTA: *Hipolita* (s.d.s); *Hipol<ita>* (s.p.s); *Hipolita The Captain's Mistress* (d.p.)
NOTARY: *A Notary* (d.p.)
MAGO: *Mago a Conjurer* (s.d.s and d.p.); *Mago* (s.p.s)
EO: *Eo* (s.d.s and s.p.s); *Eo* [one of the] *Devils* (d.p.)
MEO: *Meo* (s.d.s); *Meo* [one of the] *Devils* (d.p.)
AREO: *Areo* (s.d.s and s.p.s); *Areo* [one of the] *Devils* (d.p.)
SFORZA: *Sforza the Duke of Milain* (s.d.s); *Sfor<za>* (s.p.s); *Sforza The Duke of Milain* (d.p.)
HORTENSIA: *Hortentia the Duchess* (s.d.s); *Hort<entia>* (s.p.s); *Hortentia Wife to Sforza* (d.p.)
ISABELLA: *Isabella* [Sforza's] *sister | Isabella the Duchess | Isabella* (s.d.s); *Isab<ella>* (s.p.s); *Isabella Wife to Lavinio* (d.p.)
ATTENDANTS: *Attendants* (s.d.s and d.p.)
HYMEN: *Hymen |* [one of the] *Masquers* (s.d.s); *Hym<en>* (s.p.s); *Hymen* [one of the] *Masquers* (d.p.)
LUNA: *Luna* (s.d.s and s.p.s); [one of the] *Masquers* (s.d.s); *Luna* [one of the] *Masquers* (d.p.)
MARS: *Mars* (s.d.s and s.p.s); *Mars* [one of the] *Masquers* (s.d.s); *Mars* [one of the] *Masquers* (d.p.)
MERCURY: *Mercury |* [one of the] *Masquers* (s.d.s); *Mer<cury>* (s.p.s); *Mercury* [one of the] *Masquers* (d.p.)
JUPITER: *Jupiter |* [one of the] *Masquers* (s.d.s); *Jupit<er>* (s.p.s); *Jupiter* [one of the] *Masquers* (d.p.)
VENUS: *Venus* (s.d.s and s.p.s); [one of the] *Masquers* (s.d.s); *Venus* [one of the] *Masquers* (d.p.)
SATURN: *Saturn |* [one of the] *Masquers* (s.d.s); *Sat<urn>* (s.p.s); *Saturn* [one of the] *Masquers* (d.p.)
SOL: *Sol* (s.d.s and s.p.s); [one of the] *Masquers* (s.d.s); *Sol* [one of the] *Masquers* (d.p.)
GUARD: *the Guard* (s.d.s); *A Guard* (d.p.)

PUCCANELLO: *Pucchanello | Puchanello* (s.d.s); *Pucch<anello> | Puch<anello>* (s.p.s); *Pucannello A Jailer* (d.p.)
CALFSHEAD: [one of the] *petitioners | Calfsheead* (s.d.s); *Calfshead | Calfes<head>* (s.p.s); *Calfshead A Puritan* (d.p.)
BULLFLESH: [one of the] *petitioners* (s.d.s); *Bulflesh* (s.d.s and s.p.s); *Bulflesh A Butcher* (d.p.)
BARN: [one of the] *petitioners* (s.d.s); *Barn* (s.d.s and s.p.s); *Barne* (s.p.s); *Barne A Farmer* (d.p.)
TILER: [one of the] *petitioners* (s.d.s); *Tiler* (s.d.s and s.p.s); *Tiler A poor workman* (d.p.)
FINE: [one of the] *petitioners* (s.d.s); *Mrs Fine* (s.p.s); *Mrs Fine A Plaintiff* (d.p.)
WHIP: [one of the] *petitioners* (s.d.s); *Whip* (s.p.s); *Whip A Coachman* (d.p.)
EPILOGUE: *The Prologue* (heading; *sic*)

OTHER CHARACTERS
The dead father of Lavinio and Prudentia (1.2)
Gonzaga, Duke of Mantua, Horatio's uncle (1.2)
The Tuscan army (1.2)
Trappolin's mother, sisters, uncles, aunts, and kindred (1.2)
The Duke of Savoy, Horatio's father (1.2–3, 3.1, 4.1–2)
People whose friendly letters Trappolin carried (1.3; possibly imaginary)
The Duke of Modena, an unsuccessful suitor to Prudentia (2.3, 4.2)
The Duke of Parma, an unsuccessful suitor to Prudentia (2.3, 4.2)
Calfshead's man, killed by Bullflesh (4.1)
Barn's son, killed when Tiler fell on him (4.1)
Mistress Fine's child, killed when Dick Whip's coach ran over it (4.1)
The people of Florence (4.2, 5.2, 5.4–5)
Gracian of Franckolin, a doctor (5.3)
Prince Filiberto, Horatio's elder brother (5.5)

SETTING
Period: sixteenth or seventeenth century: Calvin is preaching in Geneva (1536–64), but there is also a reference to Baltazar Gracian (1584–1658), and Florence is ruled by the Great Duke of Tuscany, but not the first to bear that style (after 1574)
Time-Scheme: 5.4 probably takes place in the afternoon
Place: Florence; one scene (2.2) takes place at Milan

Geography
Italy: Tuscany; Lombardy; Mantua; Savoy; Siena; Pisa; Piedmont; Turin; Montefiascone; Bologna; Rome; Naples; Venice; Ferrara; Padua; Bergamo; Genoa; Verona; Perugia; Brescia; Rimini; Pistoia; Lucca; Forli; Ravenna; Sinigaglia; Capua; Pesaro; Ancona; Urbino; Ascoli; Recanati; Foligno; the Apennines; Modena; Parma; Campania; Leghorn; Vicenza; Treviso; Vercelli
Spain: Franckolin (i.e. Tarragon)
[*Greece*]: Delphi

[*Europe*]: Geneva; Amsterdam
Cyprus
[*Africa*]: Carthage; Egypt
[*Asia*]: Hyrcania; Turkey
[*Virginia*]: Varina

SOURCES
Narrative: *Il creduto Principe* (improvised *commedia dell'arte* performed by the 'Affezionati', *c.* 1632)
Works Mentioned: Livy, *Roman History* (2.3)

LANGUAGE
English
Latin: 3 words (4.1, ep.; Bullflesh, Epilogue)

FORM
Metre: prose and pentameter
Rhyme: blank verse; the masque is in couplets and ABAB
Prologue: 26 lines, in couplets
Act-Division: 5 acts
Epilogue: 16 lines, in couplets
Lines (Spoken): 2,940 (1,438 verse, 1,502 prose)
Lines (Written): 3,147

STAGING
Doors: characters exit severally (4.1, s.d.)
Within: speech (4.1–2, 5.2, 5.4, s.d.)
Other Openings: characters appear 'in prison' (3.1, 4.2, 5.2, 5.5, s.d.)
Audience: addressed as 'gallants' (prol.), 'ladies and gentlemen' (prol., ep.), and just 'gentlemen' (ep.)
Miscellaneous: The epilogue assumes a performance in England.

MUSIC
Music: unspecified music (2.2, s.d.)
Songs:
  1: 'Since in my orb I shinèd fair', 2.2, Venus, 12 lines;
  2: ''Tis idleness that is the cause', 3.2, Hippolyta, 16 lines; not explicitly marked as a song.
Dance: masquers perform two dances (2.2, s.d.)

PROPS
Clothing: a ring (1.2, dialogue); a signet ring (5.4–5, dialogue)
Small Portable Objects: a paper (1.2, dialogue); pen and ink (1.2, implicit); a book (1.2, implicit; leaves are written on and then torn out on stage); a looking-glass (2.1, 4.1, 5.3, 5.5, dialogue; 3.1, 5.1, implicit); a magic wand (5.5, dialogue)
Large Portable Objects: seating for four characters (2.2, implicit); two chairs (3.1, dialogue)
Miscellaneous: a powder (2.1, 5.4, dialogue)

COSTUMES AND MAKE-UP
TRAPPOLIN: a high-crowned hat and a multi-coloured cloak (2.1, 5.3, dialogue; 2.3, 3.1, 4.1, 5.1, 5.4–5, implicit; put on and removed on stage)
FLAMETTA: shoes, stockings, a gown, and a petticoat (3.1, dialogue; removed on stage); an under-petticoat and a smock (3.1, dialogue)
BARBARINO: a cloak (5.1, dialogue; may be a figure of speech)
MACHIAVEL: breeches (2.3, dialogue); a cloak (5.1, dialogue; may be a figure of speech)
MATTEMOROS: a hat (4.1, dialogue; removed on stage)
HORATIO: richly clothed (4.1, dialogue)
MAGO: a long beard (dialogue)
PUCCANELLO: a dirty face (5.3, dialogue)

EARLY TEXTUAL HISTORY
1633: Aston Cokayne wrote the play while on a tour of Europe: he started in Rome (where he was for three weeks in the spring), continued in Naples (three weeks), and finished it in Paris (two months, May to July).
1657: Cokayne's *Poems of Divers Sorts* entered to William Godbid in the Stationers' Register on Monday 4 May; entry names play (as *Trappolin*).
1658: included in Cokayne's *Small Poems of Divers Sorts* (O), sigs. 2D6^r–2L8^v; 49 leaves; printed by William Godbid; list of roles.
1659: O reissued in or before May as *A Chain of Golden Poems*, with title page naming Isaac Pridmore as the bookseller.
1661: O advertised as for sale by Francis Kirkman, naming this play.
1662: O reissued as *Poems &c.*, with title page naming Philip Stephens, jun., as the bookseller. A variant imprint names Francis Kirkman as the bookseller, and the volume (under the title *Poems Enriched with Wit, Mirth, and Eloquence*) was advertised as being sold by Henry Marsh.
1669: O reissued as *Choice Poems of Several Sorts*, with title page naming Francis Kirkman as the bookseller.
1669–75: O advertised as for sale by Francis Kirkman, naming this play.
1684: Nicholas Cox (Manciple of St Edmund Hall, Oxford) had a copy of O in his bookshop. It had probably been previously owned by Gerard Langbaine, and appears on a list compiled by Anthony Wood on Saturday 13 December.

EDITION
James Maidment and W. H. Logan, in *The Dramatic Works of Sir Aston Cokain*, Dramatists of the Restoration (Edinburgh, 1874), 113–204.

REFERENCES
Annals 1633; Bentley, iii. 170–2; Bodleian, MS Wood E. 4, art. 1, p. 49; Greg 796; Hazlitt, 232; *MLR* 23 (1928), 47–51; *PBSA* 107 (2013), 36–7.

2408. Royal Entry of King Charles I into Edinburgh ~

TEXT
Printed in 1633 (STC 5023). Further details of the event are found in four other principal witnesses:
- **Coch:** letter from William Cochrane of Cowdown to Sir John Maxwell, dated 17 June 1633 (printed in Fraser);
- **Crau:** David Crauford, Memoirs for a History of Edinburgh University (printed in Mill);
- **M:** William Maxwell, eye-witness account (printed in Fraser);
- **R:** Oxford: Bodleian, MS Rawlinson D. 49, fo. 4.

The printed text begins as an account of the entertainment, obviously somewhat unfinished since it leaves gaps for arch measurements which were never supplied; but in the final quire (E) it breaks down into an anthology of unassigned verses. The issue is whether any of these are part of the royal entry, and, if so, where they belong. There are three basic elements: a 20-line poem; a 12-line epigram; and a 180-line panegyric.

In the 1656 edition of William Drummond's poems, the poem is identified as the Muses' song, and in the 1711 edition it is printed in the appropriate place after Caledonia's speech; it is therefore accepted here as part of the text of the royal entry.

The epigram is directly addressed to King Charles, and refers to the substance of the Salt Tron pageant, Apollo and the Muses. We know (from Crauford) that the Muses' song was followed by a panegyric spoken by Apollo. However, the sense of the printed text is incompatible with what was actually performed: the author offers the King a 'song', which is not the one sung by the Muses but the epigram itself; the Muse he mentions is the inspiration of his 'song', and Apollo is not present in person but serves as a metaphorical figure of the King's greatness in comparison with the poet's own unworthy offering. This therefore does not seem to belong to the royal entry.

The panegyric is credited to a different author, Walter Forbes. It too draws on elements of the royal entry performance, this time the Tollbooth pageant: it begins with remarks on the King's noble genealogy, and refers to Mars and Minerva. However, there is no sense that the speaker is a dramatic character (such as Mercury), and the main objective, unconnected with the performance, is to urge the King to intervene on the Protestant side in the Thirty Years War. It too has been treated here as extraneous material; its inclusion may have been patterned after the appearance of Jonson's non-dramatic 'Panegyre' after his contributions to James I's London royal entry of 1604 (**1421**).

The Edinburgh burgh accounts detailing payments in connection with the abortive preparations in 1628–9 indicate that something similar was planned then, though it is true that Edinburgh royal pageantry in general features much thematic overlap with the material presented in 1633: the presentation of the keys to the city in 1561 (**345**), 1579 (**675**), and 1590 (**850**); painted royal genealogies and Bacchus in 1579 and 1590; planets in 1558 (**305**) and 1579. In other words, Edinburgh had tended to be thematically uninventive, or bound by traditional formulas, in devising these events, so the material paid for in 1628–9 and the material performed in 1633 were both primarily continuations of that trend. The props and scenery which were made then were probably put into storage against the day when the King would finally come north; the script was probably newly written in 1633, at which point it seems to have been decided to add a new element (Fame and Honour, at the East Port). This entry records all substantive differences between what was procured in 1628–9 and what was performed in 1633.

GENRE
royal entry
Contemporary: entertainment (t.p.)

TITLE
Printed: *The Entertainment of the High and Mighty Monarch, Charles, King of Great Britain, France, and Ireland, into his Ancient and Royal City of Edinburgh*
Later Assigned: *King Charles's Entertainment at Edinburgh*; *The Entertainment at Edinburgh*; *The Entertainment into Edinburgh*; *The Entertainment of Charles I in Edinburgh*

AUTHORS
John Adamson, Thomas Crawford (?), and William Drummond

Drummond appears to have written the extant speeches (from 1–2 and 5–6). Adamson was the Principal of King James College, Edinburgh. Thomas Crawford was the Rector of the High School from 1630 to 1640. Drummond and Adamson are named as two of the authors by Crauford, who gives the third only as 'the Master of the High School'.

DATE
15 June 1633

ORIGINAL PRODUCTION
City of Edinburgh, in the streets. The route was: West Port; West Bow; Tollbooth; Cross; Salt Tron; Nether Bow; East Port.

PLOT
King Charles formally enters Edinburgh. At the West Port, he meets the nymph Edina, the genius of the city, who is attended with Religion (trampling down Superstition) and Justice (conquering Oppression). She welcomes him and presents him with the keys of the city. At the West Bow, the triumphal arch represents Scotland, with an image of the Romans conquering the Picts. There he sees the Genius of Caledonia, who declares that, in returning at long last to his native land, he brings back a new golden age to this simple, unadorned kingdom, whose glory now extends to the far side of the ocean. Should anyone seek to dispossess him of his crown, she will resist with violence and bloodshed; but she hopes that he will live until the end of time. At the Tollbooth, he meets Mercury, who has brought 107 dead kings of Scotland back from the Elysian fields to celebrate the occasion. One of them, Fergus I, offers him grave advice in Latin: if he proves a righteous, godly, and valiant ruler, he can expect his dynasty to last for another 107 generations.

At the Cross, the King comes upon Bacchus sitting on a hogshead, attended by gods and Satyrs. Venus speaks to him, but when Ceres attempts to do so, she is interrupted by the Satyrs. At the Salt Tron, the Muses sing to him and Apollo gives him a book of poems composed by members of Edinburgh University (or, according to another account, copies of the speeches in the pageants themselves).

At the Nether Bow, the arch represents the heavens with Virgo in the ascendant. The Moon has ordered Endymion to come to Edinburgh to celebrate the King's arrival. The planets too have come down to greet him, and wish him well, as heaven and the Fates ordain. As he leaves the city by the East Port, he sees Fame and Honour.

SCENE DESIGNATION
The entertainment is here divided as follows:
1: Genius of Edinburgh, at the West Port;
2: Caledonia, at the gate of the West Bow;
3: Mercury and Fergus, at the Tollbooth (at the head of Fosters Wynd);
4: Bacchus and gods, at the Cross;
5: Apollo and the Muses, at the Salt Tron;
6: Endymion and planets, at the Nether Bow;
7: Fame and Honour, at the East Port.

ROLES
EDINA, a nymph, the Genius of Edinburgh
RELIGION, a nymph (1, *non-speaking*)
SUPERSTITION, a blind old woman (1, *non-speaking*)
JUSTICE, a woman or nymph (1, *non-speaking*)
OPPRESSION, a fierce-looking person (1, *non-speaking*)
CALEDONIA, a lady, the angel or Genius of the Kingdom of Scotland
NEW SCOTLAND, a native Canadian woman (2, *non-speaking*)
MERCURY, a god (3)
FERGUS I, King of Scotland
Two little BOYS bearing Fergus' mantle (3, *non-speaking*)
BACCHUS, god of wine, a big man (4, *non-speaking*)
SILENUS, attending Bacchus (4, *non-speaking*)
SILVANUS, a god attending Bacchus (4, *non-speaking*)
POMONA, a goddess attending Bacchus (4, *non-speaking*)
VENUS, a goddess attending Bacchus (4)
CERES, a goddess attending Bacchus (4)
SATYRS, or 'Panisques' (4, *non-speaking*)
APOLLO, a god
MELPOMENE, a Muse
CLIO, a Muse
THALIA, a Muse
EUTERPE, a Muse
TERPSICHORE, a Muse
ERATO, a Muse
CALLIOPE, a Muse
URANIA, a Muse
POLYHYMNIA, a Muse
SATURN, a planet and god
JUPITER, a planet and god; also called Jove
MARS, a planet, and god of Thrace

The SUN, a planet and god; also called Hyperion
VENUS, a planet and goddess
MERCURY, a planet and god
The MOON, Empress of the lowest sphere of heaven, a planet and goddess
ENDYMION, an Ionian shepherd
FAME, a female figure (7, *non-speaking?*)
HONOUR, a male figure (7, *non-speaking?*)

It is not clear whether the Scottish worthies in the Mount Parnassus pageant at the Salt Tron were actors or painted scenery. I assume the latter, for three reasons: no speeches seem to be assigned to them; the text says that Apollo and the Muses 'appeared' but that the worthies were 'represented'; and physical representation would add another eight people to a stage that already has to support at least ten actors.

Speaking Parts: 21–3
Allegorical Roles: 8

Stage Directions and Speech Prefixes
EDINA: *the Genius of the town | a Nymph | the Nymph* (s.d.s)
RELIGION: *Religion* (s.d.s)
SUPERSTITION: *Superstition* (s.d.s)
JUSTICE: *Justice* (s.d.s)
OPPRESSION: *Oppression* (s.d.s)
CALEDONIA: *a Lady | the Genius of Caledonia | Caledonia* (s.d.s)
NEW SCOTLAND: *a woman | an American | new Scotland* (s.d.s)
MERCURY: *Mercury* (s.d.s)
FERGUS I: *Fergus the first* (s.d.s)
BACCHUS: *Bacchus* (s.d.s)
SILENUS: *Silenus* (s.d.s)
SILVANUS: *Silvanus* (s.d.s)
POMONA: *Pomona* (s.d.s)
VENUS: *Venus* (s.d.s)
CERES: *Ceres* (s.d.s)
SATYRS: *Panisques | the Satyrs* (s.d.s)
APOLLO: *Apollo* (s.d.s)
MELPOMENE: [one of] *the Muses | Melpomene* (s.d.s)
CLIO: [one of] *the Muses | Clio* (s.d.s)
THALIA: [one of] *the Muses | Thalia* (s.d.s)
EUTERPE: [one of] *the Muses | Euterpe* (s.d.s)
TERPSICHORE: [one of] *the Muses | Terpsichore* (s.d.s)
ERATO: [one of] *the Muses | Erato* (s.d.s)
CALLIOPE: [one of] *the Muses | Calliope* (s.d.s)
URANIA: [one of] *the Muses | Urania* (s.d.s)
POLYHYMNIA: [one of] *the Muses | Polyhymnia* (s.d.s)
SATURN: [one of] *the seven Planets* (s.d.s); *Saturne* (s.d.s and s.p.s)
JUPITER: [one of] *the seven Planets | Jupiter* (s.d.s); *Jove* (s.p.s)
MARS: [one of] *the seven Planets* (s.d.s); *Mars* (s.d.s and s.p.s)
SUN: [one of] *the seven Planets | The Sun* (s.d.s); *Sun* (s.d.s and s.p.s)

VENUS: [one of] *the seven Planets* (s.d.s); *Venus* (s.d.s and s.p.s)
MERCURY: [one of] *the seven Planets* (s.d.s); *Mercury* (s.d.s and s.p.s)
MOON: [one of] *the seven Planets* (s.d.s); *The Moon* (s.d.s and s.p.s)
ENDYMION: *Endymion* (s.d.s and s.p.s)
FAME: *Fame* (s.d.s)
HONOUR: *Honour* (s.d.s)

OTHER CHARACTERS
106 or 107 former Kings of Scotland (3)
Scottish worthies, including: Sedullius Scotus; John Duns Scotus; Bishop William Elphinstone of Aberdeen; Hector Boethius; John Major; Bishop Gavin Douglas; Sir David Lindsay; and George Buchanan (5)
Atlas, Mercury's uncle (6)
The Cyclopes (6)
Thetis, the Moon's handmaid (6)

SETTING
Geography
Edinburgh: Edinburgh Castle; River Leith
Scotland: Grampian mountains; Thule
Great Britain
The Pillars of Hercules
Rome
[Greece]: Thebes; Mount Parnassus; Leucadia; Mount Pindus; Delos
Thrace
The Hellespont
Ionia: Mount Latmus; River Meander; Dindymus
[Asia]: Tyre; Babylon; Arabia
Memphis
Cathay: Quinzay
[The Atlantic Ocean]
Canada: Nova Scotia
Peru
The Antarctic Hemisphere

SOURCES
Verbal: Publilius Syrus, *Sententiae* (5); Virgil, *Georgics* 1 (2), 4 (3), *Aeneid* 1 (5–6), 2 (2, 4), 6 (5–6), 8 (1, 6), 9 (6); Seneca, *Epistulae morales* 37 (5); Lucan, *Pharsalia* (1, 3); Ptolemy, *Geography* (1); Jovianus Pontanus, *Elegies* 13 (fifteenth century; 2); Achille Bocchi, *Symbolarum* 23–4 (1555; 5); Hieronymus Cardanus, *De rerum varietate* (1557; 1)

LANGUAGE
English and Latin

FORM
Metre: pentameter and prose
Rhyme: couplets
Lines (Spoken): 415 (354 verse, 61 prose); incomplete
Lines (Written): 710

STAGING
Audience: the King is addressed directly (1–3, 5–6), and receives gifts from the characters (1, 5); the rest of the audience is directly addressed (2)

MUSIC
Music: organ and 'rare instruments' (5, Coch)
Song: 'At length we see those eyes', 5, Muses, 20 lines

PROPS
Weapons: four scutcheons (1, desc.); a scutcheon (2, desc.); a scutcheon (4, desc.); nine scutcheons (5, desc.); seven scutcheons (6, desc.); Mars's sword (6, desc.)
Musical Instruments: a trumpet (7, desc.)
Clothing: a golden crown (2, desc.; hanging from the arch); Mars's helmet (6, desc.)
Food and Drink: bread (4, M); bowls and glasses of wine (4, R; drunk on stage)
Small Portable Objects: two silver keys (1, desc.; golden in 1629); a basin (1, desc.; the printed text says it was silver, but the other evidence indicates that it was actually gilt); a caduceus (3, desc.); a sceptre (3, M); a gilt book (5, desc.; 1629 also featured a silver book)
Large Portable Objects: a hogshead (4, desc.); a sheep-hook (6, desc.)
Scenery: an arch with battlements (1, desc.); a mountain (1, desc.; the stage; moves as the King approaches); a prospect of the city of Edinburgh (1, desc.; painted on canvas; in 1629 there was an inscription in gold letters); an arch with, on one side, a painted landscape of wild country with human figures, and painted dancers on the other (2, desc.); a curtain (2, desc.; falls to discover Caledonia); an arch with a giant abacus, arms, and painted figures (3, desc.); a curtain (3, desc.; drawn to reveal Mercury); a painting of 107 Scottish kings (3, desc.; painted and gilt in 1629); a hollow mountain stuck with birch and holly (5, desc.; two peaks in a timber frame, with a pyramid in the middle and a glass globe on top with running water; musicians inside); probably a painting of Scottish worthies (5, desc.); an arch with, on one side, a starry sky and figures below, and the Three Graces and Argus on the other side (6, desc.); a throne (6, desc.; seats seven); a verdant grove (6, desc.)

Items procured in 1628–9 with no obvious counterparts in the 1633 event include: two paintings; two large pillars (2?); three large pyramids (3); a stage with 41 pillars (4); 21 pillars and five large balls (6); four large globes.

COSTUMES
EDINA: a sea-green velvet mantle, with blue tissue sleeves and under-robe; blue buskins; a diamond necklace; on her head, a castle with turrets; loose, shoulder-length hair (1, desc.)
RELIGION: white taffeta garments; a blue mantle seeded with stars; a crown of stars (1, desc.)
SUPERSTITION: old, worn garments (1, desc.)

JUSTICE: a red damask mantle; cloth-of-silver undergarments; a golden crown (1, desc.)
OPPRESSION: broken armour (1, desc.)
CALEDONIA: tissue clothes; hair dressed like a cornucopia; two chain baldrics, one of gold and one of pearl (2, desc.)
NEW SCOTLAND: an olive-coloured mask; long black hair; garments made of multi-coloured feathers (2, desc.)
MERCURY: a feathered hat (3, desc.)
FERGUS I: 'a convenient habit' (3, Crau); a red taffeta mantle; a crown (3, M)
BOYS: yellow taffeta (3, M)
BACCHUS: an ivy crown; naked from the shoulders up (4, desc.); 'black' (4, M)
CERES: a straw-coloured mantle (4, desc.)
APOLLO: crimson taffeta clothes with gold purl; a rainbow baldric; a mantle of tissue tied over his left shoulder; a laurel wreath; long golden hair (5, desc.)
MUSES: taffeta, cloth-of-silver, and purl clothes (5, desc.)
MELPOMENE: black clothes; a crimson mantle and buskins (5, desc.)
SATURN: a sad blue mantle embroidered with golden flames; a girdle in the form of an ouroboros snake (6, desc.)
JUPITER: a silver mantle embroidered with lilies and violets (6, desc.)
MARS: red hair and beard; a sword belt; a deep crimson taffeta robe embroidered with wolves and horses; his head bare (6, desc.)
SUN: a crown of flowers, including marigolds and pansies; a tissue mantle (6, desc.)
VENUS: head attire rising like parts in a coronet, and roses; a green damask mantle embroidered with doves; a multi-coloured scarf (6, desc.)
MERCURY: a head-dress of parti-coloured flowers; a parti-coloured mantle (6, desc.)
MOON: a pearl half- or crescent moon; a sad damask mantle fringed with silver and embroidered with chameleons and gourds (6, desc.)
ENDYMION: a long crimson velvet coat; a wreath of flowers on his head; long curly hair; gilt leather buskins (6, desc.)
FAME: a coat full of eyes and tongues; bat's wings at her feet; a golden wreath on her head (7, desc.)
HONOUR: a silvery blue mantle; wavy, shoulder-length hair embroidered with silver (7, desc.)

In 1628–9, six crowns were procured; the 1633 description accounts for only two conventional crowns (worn by Justice and Fergus).

EARLY STAGE HISTORY
Abortive 1629 Entry
Inception: On Wednesday 9 July 1628, King Charles I wrote to the Scottish Privy Council informing them of his intention to visit Edinburgh for his coronation as King of Scots, and to enter the city formally; on Monday 14 July, Edinburgh Council received a similar letter (apparently dated either Tuesday 1 or Saturday 5 July), and ordered a search for records of the previous royal entries in 1561 (**345**) and 1579 (**675**). At this stage, the plan was for the entry and coronation to take place a few days before the Scottish Parliament was due to convene on Monday 15 September 1628. On Thursday 17 July, a committee was appointed to make the arrangements. The members were: David Akenhead (Provost); Thomas Charteris, Alexander Speir, George Suttie, Gilbert Williamson (Bailiffs); Peter Blackburn, John Byres, Alexander Clark, James Cochrane, Patrick Ellis, Mungo Mackall, Archibald Tod, Nicoll Udward (Merchants); Thomas Weir (Pewterer); James Leslie (Tailor); Andrew Scott (Surgeon); the Dean of Guild; the Burgh Treasurer. Also on Thursday 17 July, the Scottish Privy Council asked the local authorities for a loan to defray the expenses of the visit; the following day, they replied, saying they couldn't spare the money. On Friday 18 July, Sir Jerome Lindsay (Lyon King of Arms) was ordered to investigate precedents for the form of coronations, and to report the following Monday, 21 July. On Wednesday 23 July, the Burgh Council agreed that the event should be magnificent, and should be financed by a levy; John Hay was appointed to make the 'speech or harangue' to the King upon his entry at the West Port. (This may mean he was to write it, deliver it, or both; he had previously written a Latin oration for the royal visit of 1617.) On Friday 1 August, the Scottish Privy Council wrote to the King to say that the 'fittest' time for his visit would be the late spring of the following year.

Preparation: On Friday 21 November, the Council ordered the committee (whose membership now also included James Rae, Joseph Marjoribanks, and Laurence Cockburn, apparently in succession to Williamson, Ellis, and Tod) to meet the following Tuesday, 25 November, and to report back. Work had commenced by Saturday 13 December, and continued until around Thursday 17 September 1629. James Mar spent four days making a stage at the West Port for the Provost and Bailiffs to stand on. David Brown and Thomas Younger prepared a banqueting house at the West Port. The painters Alexander Law and George Jameson travelled, respectively from Falkland and Aberdeen, to work on the entertainment: Law painted the stages and Jameson the kings of Scotland. John Smith had painted a prospect of Edinburgh by Tuesday 16 December 1628. William Fairlie turned balls for the pyramids' heads. Thomas Stories and John Stories painted two pictures. A man from Leith made two crowns, and Thomas Duncan another four. The goldsmith Adam Lamb made two keys. The painter John Miller also worked on the entertainment. The pyramid was mounted on wheels to move it from place to place. The stage at the West Port was erected on Friday 3 March 1629. In the event, the King did not come to Scotland that year.

Aftermath: Many of the items prepared for the performance were passed into the keeping of William Gray when he took over as the town's Treasurer in 1630.

Abortive 1632 Entry

Inception: On Saturday 10 December 1631, Edinburgh Council had received notice that King Charles I intended to visit the following spring or summer. A committee was appointed to make arrangements for his reception. Thomas Charteris was named as convener, and the members were: Alexander Clark (Provost); Robert Acheson, William Dick, John Smith (Bailiffs); the Dean of Guild; James Loch (Burgh Treasurer); William Carnegie, James Danielston, Mungo Mackall, John MacNaught, John Rynd, Andrew Simpson, Nicoll Udward. (Mackall and Udward had previously served on the 1628–9 committee.)

Preparation: On Wednesday 25 January 1632, the painter Alexander Law was asked to arrange for the pageant stages to be painted. The stages were apparently set up in the streets, and attended by Thomas Younger. In the event, the King did not come to Scotland that year.

1633 Entry

Inception: On Tuesday 11 December 1632, the King wrote to the Scottish Privy Council announcing his intention to come to Scotland, and appointing William Graham, 7th Earl of Menteith and 1st Earl of Strathearn (President of the Scottish Privy Council) to convey his wishes in detail; he wrote to Menteith on Friday 28 December indicating that he would be arriving the following summer. On Thursday 10 January 1633, the Council wrote to the various local authorities giving notice of the intended royal visit; the Burgh Council of Edinburgh received its copy the following day. Arrangements were made for a magnificent reception, to be financed by a levy. On Saturday 12 January, a committee was appointed to make the arrangements. The members were: Alexander Clark (Provost); George Baillie, William Gray, James Murray, John Sinclair (Bailiffs); the Dean of Guild; James Loch (Burgh Treasurer); Robert Acheson, David Akenhead, Thomas Charteris, James Cochrane, James Danielston, John MacNaught, Joseph Marjoribanks, John Smith, Archibald Tod, Thomas White. (Only White and the Bailiffs had not served on one or other of the previous committees.)

Preparation: On Thursday 14 February, shops at the Tollbooth were ordered to be taken down and a pageant stage erected there. The performance probably used some scenery which had been made for the abortive royal entry of 1629 and kept in storage since then. On Thursday 14 March, the Privy Council ordered the removal from the West Port of the heads of executed criminals, and on Friday 5 April, the Burgh Council ordered the streets to be cleaned. On Thursday 18 April, the Burgh Council decided that the King should be told what preparations had been made, and appointed Alexander Guthrie to go and tell him, with the assistance of Sir John Hay. On Wednesday 12 June, the Privy Council issued orders for the conduct of the procession, and on Thursday 13 June, instructed the Edinburgh authorities and Robert Ker, 1st Earl of Roxburgh, to supply sand to cover the streets. The order of the procession was established on Friday 14 June, when the Privy Council also ordained that guards should stand on each side of the street throughout the King's passage.

Performance: at King Charles I's formal entry into Edinburgh on Saturday 15 June. The musicians included Andrew Sinclair and Stephen Tilliedaff. George Jameson painted the scenery. The cast included the son of Sir James Skene of Curriehill (Edina); Caledonia and the Muses were played by boys.

Audience: The procession included: burgh officers; members of the Burgh Council; fourteen trumpeters; Alexander Clark (Provost of Edinburgh); squires; knights; the King's principal servants; earls' eldest sons (including: Robert Douglas, Lord of Dalkeith; George, Lord Seton; John, Lord Fleming; George, Lord Livingston; John Hamilton, Lord Binning); lords of Parliament (including: John, 10th Lord Lindsay; John, 8th Lord Hay of Yester; Alexander Lindsay, 2nd Lord Spynie; Robert, 2nd Lord Balfour of Burleigh; John, Lord Wemyss of Elcho); Alexander Lindsay (Bishop of Dunkeld); John Leslie (Bishop of the Isles); John Guthrie (Bishop of Moray); Adam Bellenden (Bishop of Dunblaine); John Abernethy (Bishop of Caithness); George Graham (Bishop of Orkney); viscounts; William Kerr, 1st Earl of Lothian; John Maitland, 1st Earl of Lauderdale; John Murray, 1st Earl of Annandale; George Mackenzie, 2nd Earl of Seaforth; Robert Ker, 1st Earl of Roxburgh; James Hamilton, 2nd Earl of Abercorn; John Lyon, 2nd Earl of Kinghorne; John Fleming, 2nd Earl of Wigtown; Charles Seton, 2nd Earl of Dunfermline; John Drummond, 2nd Earl of Perth; Alexander Livingston, 2nd Earl of Linlithgow; Robert Seton, 2nd Earl of Winton; John Kennedy, 6th Earl of Cassilis; Alexander Montgomerie, 6th Earl of Eglinton; James Erskine, 7th Earl of Buchan; William Douglas, 11th Earl of Angus; Patrick Lindsay (Archbishop of Glasgow); Thomas Hamilton, 1st Earl of Haddington (Lord Privy Seal); George Hay, 1st Earl of Kinnoull and Viscount Dupline (Lord Chancellor); William Douglas, 7th Earl of Morton (Lord Treasurer); five sergeants at arms with gilded maces; William Le Neve (York Herald); six Scots heralds; Sir John Burroughs (Norroy King of Arms); Sir James Galloway (Master of Requests); two gentlemen ushers; Sir James Balfour (Lyon King of Arms); William Keith, 6th Earl Marischal; James Stewart, 4th Duke of Lennox (Great Chamberlain); William Hay, 10th Earl of Errol (Great Constable); King Charles I; James Hamilton, 3rd Marquess of Hamilton (Master of the Horse); four gentlemen equerries; English courtiers; Gentlemen of the Privy Chamber; James Howard, 3rd Earl of Suffolk (Captain of the Pensioners); Gentlemen Pensioners; Henry Rich, 1st Earl of Holland (Captain of the Guard); the King's guard (numbering 30 or 34 men). Also present were: William Cochrane of Cowdown; William Maxwell. When the procession was about to move off, it was delayed by a dispute over precedence between five of the earls' eldest sons (those named above) and the lords of Parliament; after some time, the King ruled that the earls' eldest sons should go first.

Aftermath: The Nether Bow was damaged when the stage was removed, and had to be repaired. On Wednesday 28 August, George Jameson was rewarded by being granted free admission as a burgess of Edinburgh. Some items from the performance, including the silver keys presented to the King, were handed over to David McCall when he succeeded James Loch as the town's Treasurer in 1634.

Production Expenses I: 1628–9
The total cost of the abortive event was £7,354.7s.1d. The town Treasurer made the following payments: James Mar (£2.13s.4d); David Brown and Thomas Younger (£16 for two weeks' work, paid in two equal instalments on Saturdays 13 and 20 December 1628); glue to affix the top of the stages (£2); George Jameson's travelling expenses from Aberdeen, paid on Monday 9 February (£17.8s); Alexander Law's travelling expenses from Falkland (£2.18s); Alexander Law's fee for two days' work (£2); a week's wages for Alexander Law and his boy (£7); John Miller's fee for five days' work (£3.6s.8d); setting up the stage (£1.16s); wheels for the pyramid (15s.4d); balls turned by William Fairlie (14s); George Jameson's fee (£800); joists for the pyramid and other materials supplied by Alexander Menteith (£27); sawing of deal-boards to make covers for the bowls of the pyramid (17s.6d); William Bannatyne's fee for attending Law and his boy while the stages were being painted (£29).

Props: payment to John Smith (£100); pillars (£1.4s); nails for pillars (£1); cloth for gold lettering (£6); gold for gilding (£15); Thomas and John Stories (£30); cloth for George Jameson (£31.11s); four great globes supplied by William Fairlie (16s); four pendents (16s); three pyramids (6s); two crowns (£2.18s); two keys supplied by Adam Lamb (£37.6s.4d); two balls (12s); 21 pillars turned by William Fairlie (14s); gold sise bought by Alexander Law (£3); four crowns (£10); 41 pillars (£1.7s.4d); George Jameson's fee for painting the kings of Scotland (£666.13s.4d); gilding of the kings (£33.6s.8d).

Production Expenses II: 1632
The burgh authorities paid fees to Alexander Law (£3.12s) and Thomas Younger (£2.6s).

Production Finance and Expenses III: 1633
Immediate finance was secured by loans totalling £23,333.6s.8d, from the following individuals: Robert Carnegie (£6,666.13s.4d); Alexander Clark (£8,666.13s.4d); Patrick Ellis (£5,333.6s.8d); John MacNaught (£2,666.13s.4d). On Friday 19 July, the Burgh Council ordered that they should be repaid, with interest, on Monday 11 November (Martinmas).

The total cost of the event, including the banquet for the King, was £41,489.7s. The authorities precepted the following payments: on Wednesday 7 August, to Andrew Sinclair (£66.13s.4d) and Stephen Tilliedaff (£133.6s.8d); on Friday 23 August, George Jameson (£15) and his servant (£1.5s). The town Treasurer, James Loch, also paid Alexander Baxter and Thomas Younger for six days' work with two other men erecting scenery (£15.4s). Loch recouped £778.3s by selling various items: deal-boards from the pageants, to John Fleming (£16.13s.4d); costumes, hangings, curtains, and 'other decorations' to James Naismith (£673.6s.8d); cloth from the pageants, to James Nairn (£15.15s); and pewter to 'the neighbours of the town' (£72.8s).

EARLY TEXTUAL HISTORY

1633: the book presented to King Charles I at the performance may have contained the text of the speeches.

1633: ¹Q printed at Edinburgh by John Wreittoun; collation A–E⁴, 20 leaves.

1656: Drummond's contributions included in his *Poems* (²O), sigs. L6ʳ–M6ʳ; 17 pages on 9 leaves; printed at London by William Hunt for Richard Tomlins.

1659: Drummond's *Poems* reissued as his *Most Elegant and Elaborate Poems*, with a cancel title page naming William Rands as the bookseller.

EDITION

L. E. Kastner, in *The Poetical Works of William Drummond of Hawthornden*, University of Manchester Publications 79 (Manchester, 1913), ii. 109–36.

REFERENCES

Annals 1633; Bentley, iii. 289–90; Bergeron, 109–17; Butler, 373; *Documents Relative to the Reception at Edinburgh of the Kings and Queens of Scotland* (Edinburgh, 1822), 69–117; Sir William Fraser, *Memoirs of the Maxwells of Pollok* (Edinburgh, 1863), 226–7, 229–32; Greg 487; Hazlitt, 74; Lancashire 1689; McGee-Meagher 1625–34, 44–5, 66, 73–7; Mill, 80, 207–18; *Register of the Privy Council of Scotland*, 2nd ser., ii. 380–1, 383, v. 49, 112, 114–16; John Spalding, *Memorialls of the Trubles in Scotland and in England*, ed. John Stuart (Aberdeen, 1850–1), i. 32–5; Withington i. 236–7.

2409. *The Seaman's Honest Wife*

TEXT
MS (London: British Library, Egerton MS 1994, fos. 317–49); authorial holograph annotated for theatrical

use and censored. This preserves two distinct states of the text:
- A: original version, with revisions made around the time of composition;
- B: theatrical version, with cuts and further revision in response to censorship. This resulted in the insertion of short substitute passages in 1.1, 3.3, 4.2, and 5.3–4, and the wholesale replacement, on four new MS leaves (fos. 342–5), of one or more scenes in Act 4.

GENRE
'dramatic apologia'
Contemporary: play (ep.)

The play is almost unclassifiable, generically speaking; I have adopted Boas's phrase. Annals lists it as a comedy, but it has no comic process, nor indeed any plot development to speak of.

TITLE
Performed: *The Seaman's Honest Wife*
MS: *The Launching of the Mary, or The Seaman's Honest Wife*

Herbert's use of the second title in the licence probably indicates that this was the acting company's preference.

AUTHOR
Walter Mountfort

DATE
June 1633

ORIGINAL PRODUCTION
either Prince Charles's Men, presumably at Salisbury Court *or* King's Revels Company, presumably at the Fortune

The book-keeper who marked up the surviving MS worked for one or other of these companies at this time.

PLOT
Members of the East India Company explain to the Lord Admiral that trade with the Orient makes a valuable contribution to the English economy, and rebut the claims of the company's detractors.

A new ship is built, the *Mary*. The shipwrights work hard, and it is ready to be launched on the prescribed date, at a ceremony attended by the Queen.

Dorotea, the wife of a seaman absent on one of the East India Company's ships, is unjustly deemed immoral by her friends. Some seamen's wives do indeed behave badly during their husbands' absence: Mary Sparke and Isabel Nutt enjoy themselves with liquor and men whilst pretending to be gainfully and honestly employed with sewing jobs. Dorotea, however, successfully resists all attempts to seduce her. She tells the audience that she is the pattern of seamen's wives, not the exception.

SCENE DESIGNATION
prol., 1.1, 2.1–2, 3.1–4, 4.1–2, 4.C, 5.1–4, ep. (act-division MS, which also has incomplete scene-division, here expanded)

Only the last few lines of 4.C survive, and there is no way of knowing whether it continued directly from 4.2. The stage is not clear during 3.1–3; the Malone edition treats this as a single scene, and so 3.4 is there numbered 3.2.

B-Text
prol., 1.1, 2.1–2, 3.1–4, 4.1–2, 5.1–4, ep. (MS, revised state)

The alterations mainly affect Act 4: A.4.1–2 are marked for omission, A.4.C is replaced with B.4.1, and the new scene B.4.2 overlaps slightly with A.4.1.
MS numbers B.4.1–2 as 4.3–4.

ROLES
PROLOGUE
Lord Admiral HOBAB, an old man
Captain FITZJOHN of the *Mary*, a married man; originally written as Fitzjoseph
NAUPEGUS, a ship-builder
Two or three ATTENDANTS on Hobab (1.1, 3.1, 5.2, non-speaking)
Goodman Thomas TRUNDLE, a shipwright; also called Tom and Gaffer Trundle
Osmond OAKUM, an old shipwright
Goodman Tacklemouth TALLOW, a shipwright; Oakum's acquaintance of more than twenty years
Tarquin TAR, a shipwright; also called Goodman Rufface
Goodman Simon SHEATHING-NAIL, a shipwright and carpenter; a short man; also called Sim
SHAVING, a boy, the drawer at a tavern
The GOVERNOR of the East India Company; at one point Mountford considered designating him the Director instead
The DEPUTY of the East India Company
Two COMMISSIONERS of the East India Company
Mistress DOROTEA Constance, a seaman's wife; a young woman
Mistress MARY Sparke, a seaman's wife; also called Mall
Mistress ISABEL Nutt, a seaman's wife; also called Tib
The CLERK of the Cheque
Voices of 24 SHIPWRIGHTS, named: Peter Pestlehead, Alexander Hogh, Quintilian Quicksilver, Hugh Hugmatee, Roderigo Rawbone, Humphrey Hum, Sempronius Sackful, John of All Trades, Timothy Treadverges, Nathaniel Nip, Valentine Verdigris, William Woolfang, Gregory Greensue, Batt Bendbow, Christopher Clote, Leonard Lourie, Gabriel Goatherd, Philip Fullmouth, Sampson Swabber, Francis Firkin, David ap Owen ap Meredith ap Jenkin, John ap Rhys of Aberhundis,

Llewellyn ap Morgan ap David, and John ap Evan of Llangadock (2.2, *within*)
Miles MENDPRICK, a shipwright (2.2, *non-speaking*)
Edmond ELEPHANT, a shipwright; a very little man (2.2, *non-speaking*)
An ECHO (3.1)
LOCUPLES, a rich man
Hobab's SERVANT (3.2)
A SERVINGMAN, who delivers a letter to Dorotea (4.1, *non-speaking*)
A LAND CAPTAIN, Dorotea's suitor
A BOY, a clergyman's servant, who delivers a letter to Dorotea (4.1)
Captain GOODMAN, a naval commander; a married man; also called Master Goodman
GALLANTS at the launching (5.1; speak collectively)
LADIES at the launching (5.1; speak collectively)
A BOATSWAIN
A VOICE (5.1, *within*)
EPILOGUE

A total of 31 shipwrights' names are called out by the clerk in 2.2, and the s.d. directs for all but two to 'answer within'. The two exceptions presumably appear briefly on stage, since an s.d. indicates what one of them looks like: Elephant is a tiny man with a long beard, an obvious visual joke; one hardly dares imagine why the playwright wanted Mendprick to appear. Five of the remaining 29 names belong to the five shipwrights who feature in the action.

Speaking Parts: 51

Doubling
Presumably the voices of the 24 named off-stage shipwrights in 2.2 are provided by rather fewer actors.

B-Text
SERVINGMAN: *omitted*
LAND CAPTAIN: *omitted*
BOY: *omitted*
GOODMAN: *omitted*

Speaking Parts: 48

Stage Directions and Speech Prefixes
PROLOGUE: *Prologue* (heading)
HOBAB: *the Lord Admiral surnamed Hobab | Lord Admiral* (s.d.); *Hob<ab> | Admiral* (s.p.s); *Lord Admiral surnamed Hobab* (d.p.)
FITZJOHN: *Captain fitzJoseph* (s.d., deleted); *Captain fitzJohn | fitzJ<ohn>* (s.d.s); *Captain* (s.d.s and s.p.s); *fitz Jo<hn>* (s.p.s); *Captain fitz-John* (d.p.)
NAUPEGUS: *Naupegus* (s.d.s and d.p.); *Naup<egus>* (s.p.s)
ATTENDANTS: *an attendant or two | 2 or 3 attendants | attendants* (s.d.s)
TRUNDLE: *Trunnell* (s.d.s and d.p.); *Trun<nell>* (s.p.s)
OAKUM: *Okum* (s.d.s, s.p.s, and d.p.)
TALLOW: *Tallow* (s.d.s, s.p.s, and d.p.)
TAR: *Tarre* (s.d.s, s.p.s, and d.p.)
SHEATHING-NAIL: *Sheathinge nayle* (s.d.s and d.p.); *Sheethinge nayle* (s.d.s); *Shea<thinge nayle>* (s.p.s)
SHAVING: *the drawer* (s.d.s); *Boy | drawer* (s.d.s and s.p.s); *Tapster* (d.p.)
GOVERNOR: *Governor* (s.d.s and s.p.s); *director* (d.p.)
DEPUTY: *deputy* (s.d.s, s.p.s, and d.p.)
COMMISSIONERS: *1 2 Committee* (s.d.s); *Committee 1 | Committee | 1 commissioner* (s.p.s); *1 Committee | 2 Committee* (s.p.s and d.p.)
DOROTEA: *Dorotea Constance | dorotea* (s.d.s); *Doro<tea>* (s.p.s); *dorotea Constance seaman's honest wife* (d.p.)
MARY: *Mary Sparke [one of] two seamen's wives* (s.d.s and d.p.); *Mary Sparke | [one of] the women* (s.d.s); *Spa<rke>* (s.p.s)
ISABEL: *Isabell Nutt [one of] two seamen's wives* (s.d.s and d.p.); *Isabell Nutt | [one of] the women* (s.d.s); *Nutt* (s.d.s and s.p.s)
CLERK: *Clerk of the Cheque* (s.d.s and d.p.); *Clerk* (s.d.s and s.p.s)
MENDPRICK: *Mend<pricke>* (s.d.s)
ELEPHANT: *Ele<phant>* (s.d.s)
ECHO: *Echo* (s.p.s)
LOCUPLES: *Locuples* (s.d.s); *Locu<ples>* (s.p.s)
SERVANT: *Servant* (s.d.s)
SERVINGMAN: *a servingman | servingman* (s.d.s)
LAND CAPTAIN: *Captain* (s.d.s and s.p.s); *Land Captain* (d.p.)
BOY: *boy* (s.d.s and s.p.s); *Messenger* (d.p.)
GOODMAN: *Captain Goodman a sea commander* (s.d.s); *Good<man>* (s.d.s and s.p.s); *Sea Captain* (d.p.)
GALLANTS: *gallants* (s.d.s)
LADIES: *ladies* (s.d.s)
BOATSWAIN: *Boatswain* (s.d.s, s.p.s, and d.p.)
VOICE: *within* (s.p.s)
EPILOGUE: *Epilogue* (heading)

B-Text
HOBAB: *Lord Admiral* (s.d.s and s.p.s)
GOVERNOR: *Governor* (s.d.s and s.p.s)
DEPUTY: *deputy* (s.d.s and s.p.s)
COMMISSIONERS: *1 2 Committee* (s.d.s); *1 Committee | 2 Committee* (s.p.s)
DOROTEA: *doro<tea> Constance* (s.d.s); *doro<tea>* (s.p.s)
TRUNDLE: *Trunnell* (s.d.s and s.p.s); *Trunell* (s.p.s)
TAR: *Tarre* (s.d.s and s.p.s)
OAKUM: *Okum* (s.d.s and s.p.s)
TALLOW: *Tallow* (s.d.s and s.p.s)
SHEATHING-NAIL: *Sheathinge nayle* (s.d.s); *Shea<thinge nayle>* (s.p.s)
FITZJOHN: *Captain fitzJohn* (s.d.s); *fitzJ<ohn>* (s.p.s)

OTHER CHARACTERS
The King (1.1, 3.3)

Goodale, a dead old man mourned by Sheathing-Nail (1.1)

Englishmen murdered by the Dutch at Amboyna, including eleven merchants, a steward, a tailor, and a barber (1.1, 2.2)

Herman van Speult, commander of the Dutch at Amboyna (1.1, 2.2)

The Dutch who perpetrated the Amboyna massacre, including Laurens de Maerschalck, Clement Carseboom, Herman Crayvanger, Pieter van Santen, and Leonard Clock (1.1, 2.2)

Detractors of the East India Company (1.1)

Dorotea's husband, a seaman on an East India Company ship (2.1. 3.1–2, 4.1)

Dorotea's former friends, who accused her of immorality (2.1)

Fitzjohn's wife (2.1)

Isabel Nutt's husband, a seaman (2.1, 3.4)

Mary Sparke's husband, a seaman (2.1)

Three or four grocers' apprentices with whom Isabel Nutt has a date, one of whom kissed Mary Sparke (2.1, 3.4)

The garrison of the Castle of Amboyna, numbering three to four hundred men (2.2)

Queen Mary, descended of the French royal family (2.2, 5.2–3; i.e. Henrietta Maria)

Farmers who object to the East India Company's impact on the corn trade (3.3)

A silkman, Isabel Nutt's acquaintance (3.4; possibly imaginary)

A young milliner, Mary Sparke's acquaintance (3.4; possibly imaginary)

A courtier who wrote importuning Dorotea; his name probably begins 'Ru . . .' (4.1)

A clergyman, Dorotea's suitor (4.1)

Goodman's wife (4.1)

King Henry IV of France and III of Navarre, a Bourbon, the Queen's father (5.3)

B-Text
Matt Maule (4.2)

Dorotea's suitors, including courtiers, captains, cavaliers, linguists, citizens, seamen, and prodigals (4.2)

Charles, son of the Queen (5.3)

Omits: the massacred Englishmen; Herman van Speult; the Dutch at Amboyna; the Amboyna garrison; the King (from 3.3); courtier; Dorotea's husband (from A.4.1); clergyman; Goodman's wife

SETTING

Period: seventeenth century; the play is based around an event which took place in 1626

Time-Scheme: 3.1–3 take place in the early morning. A day passes between 4.2 and 4.C, and another day between 4.C and 5.1 (which takes place on the day of the full moon).

Place: London

Geography
London: Wapping; Ratcliffe; Limehouse; Blackwall; Whittington's Venture tavern by the Six Windmills; the Three Sharks tavern in Field Lane; the Windmill tavern beyond Mile End; the White Lion tavern at Blackman Street; the Ship tavern in Wapping; the Hoop [or Hope] tavern at Limehouse Corner; the Man in the Moon tavern in Whitechapel; the Queen's Head tavern in the Little Minories; West Smithfield; the Tower (*deleted in first revision*); River Thames; Shadwell; Poplar
England: the Goodwin Sands
[*Wales*]: Aberhundis; Llangadock
Great Britain
Ireland
The Low Countries: the United Provinces; Holland; Amsterdam; Antwerp (*added in first revision*); Batavia
France: Marseilles; Valois; Bourbon
Italy: Venice; Leghorn; Genoa
Europe: Spain; Lisbon; Navarre; Poland
[*Mediterranean*]: Candy
Turkey
[*Syria*]: Aleppo
Arabia: Mocha
The Arabian Sea
Persia: Balsera
The Persian Gulf
[*Africa*]: the Cape of Good Hope; Alexandria
India: Calico
The East Indies: Amboyna; the Straits; Bantam

B-Text

Period: The addition of a reference to Prince Charles places the action after 1630.

Time-Scheme: 4.1–2 take place the date before 5.1

Additional Geography
London: the Three Goats' Heads tavern in Ratcliffe Highway
England: Amwell Head
Cyprus

Omits: Amboyna; the Low Countries; the Three Sharks tavern in Field Lane; Amsterdam; Antwerp; Holland; Lisbon; Batavia; Valois; Poland; Navarre; Bourbon

---

SOURCES

Verbal: Bible: 2 Thessalonians 3.10 (3.3); Enea Silvio Piccolomini, unidentified poem (fifteenth century; 5.3); Miguel de Cervantes, *Don Quixote*, tr. Thomas Shelton (1612; 2.1); Thomas Mun, *A Discourse of Trade from England to the East Indies* (1621; 1.1, 3.3); *An Answer unto the Dutch Pamphlet made in Defence of the Unjust and Barbarous Proceedings against the English at Amboyna* (1624; 2.2)

The account of the Amboyna massacre is evidently drawn from the 1624 pamphlet: the names of the Dutch participants appear in both pamphlet and play in the same order and in more or less the same spelling.

> **B-Text**
> **Verbal:** Publilius Syrus, *Sententiae* (4.1); *omits* 1624 Amboyna pamphlet
> **Works Mentioned:** Persius, *Satires* (4.1); Juvenal, *Satires* (4.1); Joseph Swetnam, *The Arraignment of Lewd, Idle, Froward, and Unconstant Women* (1615; 4.2)

LANGUAGE
English
Latin: 9 words (5.3; Fitzjohn)
Dutch: 5 words (1.1; Sheathing-Nail)

> **B-Text**
> **Latin:** now 8 words (4.1; 2nd Commissioner)

FORM
Metre: pentameter and prose
Rhyme: blank verse; some couplets
Prologue: 14 lines, in couplets
Act-Division: 5 acts
Dumb Show: concludes 3.4 (compresses action, possibly as an entr'acte)
Epilogue: 12 lines, in couplets
Lines (Spoken): 2,443 (1,943 verse, 500 prose)
Lines (Written): 2,599

> **B-Text**
> **Lines (Spoken):** 2,421 (1,909 verse, 512 prose)
> **Lines (Written):** 3,023

STAGING
Doors: characters enter at two doors (3.4, 4.1, 5.1, s.d.)
Within: sound effects (2.2, 4.1, s.d.); speech (2.2, 5.1–2, s.d.); great shout (5.1, s.d.)
Above: music aloft (1.1, 5.2, s.d.); gallants and ladies appear above, 'as many ... as the room can well hold' (5.1, s.d.)
Audience: Dorotea asks a favour of the 'kind, courteous women' in the audience (2.1, implicit); directly addressed (3.4, implicit); said to be seated (3.4, s.d.); addressed as 'gentlemen' (5.4, implicit) and 'kind gentlemen' (ep.)

> **B-Text**
> **Doors:** characters enter at two doors (4.1, s.d.); *omits* entry at two doors in A.4.1
> **Within:** *omits* sound effects in A.4.1

MUSIC AND SOUND
Sound Effects: knock within (2.2, 4.1, s.d.); eleven to thirteen gunshots (5.2, s.d.)
Music: bell (1.1, 2.2, s.d.); unspecified music (1.1, 5.2, s.d.); entr'acte music (between Acts 1–2, 2–3, and 4–5, and accompanying the dumb show at the end of 3.4, s.d.); trumpet (5.2, s.d.)
On-Stage Music: boatswain whistles (5.1, s.d.)
Singing: Trundle sings two lines (3.4, s.d.)

Dance: the five shipwrights dance (5.2, s.d.)

> **B-Text**
> **Sound Effects:** *omits* knock within in A.4.1

PROPS
Pyrotechnics: fire (1.1, 2.2, s.d.)
Weapons: the Captain's rapier (4.1, dialogue)
Money: a purse (2.1, s.d.); a purse (3.2, s.d.); an unspecified sum (3.4, dialogue)
Food and Drink: two pots of liquor (1.1, s.d.); a small banquet and wine (1.1, s.d.); five pots of liquor (2.2, s.d.; drunk on stage); three pots of liquor (2.2, s.d.); wine (3.4, s.d.; drunk on stage); bread (3.4, s.d.); a banquet (5.2, s.d.), including liquor (implicit; drunk on stage)
Small Portable Objects: two hand-baskets (2.1, 3.4, s.d.); a paper book (2.2, s.d.); a paper (3.1, s.d.); a paper (3.3, s.d.); a brickbat wrapped in a clean napkin (3.4, s.d.); three or four pieces of painted cloth wrapped in a clean napkin (3.4, s.d.); a towel (3.4, s.d.); a letter (4.1, s.d.; torn up on stage); a letter (4.1, s.d.)
Large Portable Objects: a chair (1.1, dialogue); five three-legged stools (1.1, 2.2, s.d.); a little table (2.2, s.d.); a table (3.4, s.d.); three stools (3.4, s.d.); seating for five characters (5.2, implicit)
Scenery: an alehouse bush (3.4, s.d.); two crabs (5.1, s.d.; i.e. lifting gear); a capstan (5.1, s.d.); cables (5.1, s.d.)
Miscellaneous: perfume (3.4, s.d.)

> **B-Text**
> **Weapons:** Fitzjohn's sword (4.2, implicit); *omits* Captain's rapier (from A.4.1)
> **Money:** a purse (4.2, s.d.)
> **Small Portable Objects:** needlework (4.2, s.d.); *omits* two letters (from A.4.1)
> **Large Portable Objects:** a seat (4.2, implicit)

COSTUMES
TRUNDLE: an emblem on his head representing a trundle or roller (5.2, s.d.)
OAKUM: an emblem on his head representing oakum (5.2, s.d.)
TALLOW: an emblem on his head representing tallow (5.2, s.d.)
TAR: an emblem on his head representing tar (5.2, s.d.)
SHEATHING-NAIL: an emblem on his head representing a sheathing-nail (5.2, s.d.)
ELEPHANT: a long white beard (2.2, s.d.)
LAND CAPTAIN: hangers (4.1, implicit)
GOODMAN: white hair (dialogue)

> **B-Text**
> FITZJOHN: hangers (4.2, implicit)
> TRUNDLE, OAKUM, TALLOW, TAR, and SHEATHING-NAIL: canvas coats (4.2, dialogue)
> DOROTEA: a petticoat and waistcoat (4.2, s.d.)
> LAND CAPTAIN: *omits* his hangers (along with the rest of him)

EARLY STAGE HISTORY
1633: presumably performed, as licensed.

EARLY TEXTUAL HISTORY
1632–3: Mountfort wrote the play aboard the East India Company ship *Blessing* at sea, during the return trip from the East Indies; the ship set sail in April 1632 and the voyage lasted nearly a year.

1632–3: transcribed in **MS**; 28 surviving leaves. (The MS bears the date 1632.)

1633: on Thursday 27 June, Sir Henry Herbert licensed the text for performance, subject to the excision of oaths and the observation of other alterations. Herbert ordered the book-keeper to present him with an expurgated fair copy.

1633 (?): MS was revised, producing **MS (β)**; this entailed replacing one or more leaves with four new ones and adding a slip. It was then marked up by the prompter (who was the same man who marked the extant MS of **1647**).

1640s–50s: MS may have been in the possession of the former actor William Cartwright.

EDITION
John Henry Walter, Malone Society Reprints 73 (Oxford, 1933).

REFERENCES
Annals 1633; Bawcutt, 258; Bentley, iv. 923–4; F. S. Boas, *Shakespeare and the Universities* (Oxford, 1923), 167–238; Hazlitt, 129; *N&Q* 251 (2006), 528–31.

2410. *The Young Admiral*

TEXT
Printed in 1637 (STC 22463).

GENRE
tragicomedy
Contemporary: comedy (Herbert); poem (ded.); play (S.R.); tragicomedy (Abraham Wright, *c.* 1640)

TITLE
Performed/Printed: *The Young Admiral*

AUTHOR
James Shirley

DATE
July 1633

ORIGINAL PRODUCTION
Queen Henrietta's Men at the Cockpit

PLOT
Cesario has provoked a war between Sicily and Naples by wounding the King of Sicily's favourite, Horatio, and by refusing to marry his daughter, Rosinda; he is more interested in Cassandra, the girlfriend of the Neapolitan Admiral Vittori. He pesters her unsuccessfully while Vittori is away fighting the war, then has Vittori's father Alphonso imprisoned. When Vittori returns in triumph, he finds the city gates shut against him on Cesario's orders. Offered a reward by the King, Cesario's father, Vittori asks for Alphonso's freedom; the King agrees only on condition that Vittori and Cassandra go into exile.

The banished pair are shipwrecked on the Neapolitan coast and fall into the hands of the regrouped Sicilian army. Cassandra is taken into Rosinda's custody and Vittori offered a choice: if he agrees to lead the army against Naples, Cassandra's life will be spared. Torn between love and honour, he chooses love. He goes to Naples, disguised as a herald, and tries to persuade the King to surrender; but Cesario complicates his dilemma by sending back the message that Alphonso will be executed if Vittori fights. The threat is a bluff: after the message is sent, Alphonso is appointed to command the Neapolitan army against his son.

Rosinda is with the invasion forces because, despite everything, she loves Cesario. Cassandra writes to him to set up an assignation, intending that Rosinda should go in her place. Cesario agrees to come into the Sicilian camp for the meeting, but the plan is overheard by Horatio, who tells the King. Cesario is arrested on arrival and held as a hostage. Vittori assumes that Cassandra was two-timing him, and decides to fight and save Alphonso. Rosinda corrects his misapprehension, and they go in disguise to Naples, where she offers herself as a reciprocal hostage: now Sicily cannot harm Cesario without Naples harming Rosinda, and vice versa. The war ends with a marriage treaty: Cesario accepts Rosinda and apologises for wounding Horatio.

In the sub-plot, Pazzorello is afraid of battle, and accepts Didimo's offer of magical protection against injury. He meets with a witch—actually Rosinda's waiting-woman in disguise—and, after he has handed over all his money, he is blindfolded for the magical ceremony. Didimo assaults him, telling him that each blow adds to his invulnerability. With his courage reinforced, he picks a fight with a soldier, and comes off worst—because, Didimo explains, the weapons used against him were not included in the spell.

In Naples, Fabio too fears having to fight, and buys his way out of the Neapolitan army by offering Captain Mauritio half his lands—to be handed over only if Mauritio returns from the war alive. When he does, Fabio has to keep his side of the bargain, and Pazzorello, convinced of his invulnerability, goes off in search of adventures as a knight errant.

SCENE DESIGNATION
1.1–2, 2.1–2, 3.1–2, 4.1–5, 5.1–4 (Q has act-division only)

ROLES

Prince CESARIO of Naples, the King's son, a young man
ALBERTO, a Neapolitan, Alphonso' confidant
JULIO, a Neapolitan, Cesario's confidant
Signor FABIO, a Neapolitan courtier
Lord ALPHONSO, an old Neapolitan, Vittori's father; also called Signor Alphonso
A GUARD on Alphonso (1.1, 2.1, *non-speaking*)
Lord VITTORI, the young Admiral of Naples; a gentleman, Alphonso's son; later General of the Sicilian army; poses as a herald
Captain MAURITIO, a Neapolitan
A CAPTAIN in the Neapolitan army (1.2)
SOLDIERS in the Neapolitan army (1.2; three speak individually, any others collectively)
CASSANDRA, a Neapolitan gentlewoman betrothed to Vittori
The King of NAPLES, an old man, Cesario's father
A MESSENGER, who brings news of the renewed Sicilian attack (2.1)
The King of SICILY, Rosinda's father
HORATIO, the King of Sicily's favourite
TRIVULSI, a Sicilian
FABRICCIO, a Sicilian captain and gentleman
ROSINDA, Princess of Sicily, the King's daughter
FLAVIA, Rosinda's waiting-woman; also poses as a Lapland witch, said to be Didimo's aunt
PAZZORELLO, a member of Rosinda's household; a young man
Master DIDIMO, a page; said to be little
SOLDIERS of Sicily (2.2, *non-speaking*)
ATTENDANTS on the King of Sicily (2.2, *non-speaking*)
A SERGEANT in the Sicilian army (4.4)
A GUARD of Sicilians, who arrest Cesario (4.5, *non-speaking*)

Speaking Parts: 23

Stage Directions and Speech Prefixes
CESARIO: *Prince* (s.d.s and s.p.s); *The Prince of Naples* (d.p.)
ALBERTO: *Alberto* (s.d.s and s.p.s); *Alberto* [one of the] *Noblemen of Naples* (d.p.)
JULIO: *Julio* (s.d.s and s.p.s); *Julio* [one of the] *Noblemen of Naples* (d.p.)
FABIO: *Fabio* (s.d.s); *Fab<io>* (s.p.s); *Fabio* [one of the] *Noblemen of Naples* (d.p.)
ALPHONSO: *Alphonso* (s.d.s); *Alp<honso>* (s.p.s); *Alphonso* [Vittori's] *Father* (d.p.)
GUARD: *a Guard* (s.d.s)
VITTORI: *Vittori* (s.d.s); *Vi<ttori>* (s.p.s); *Vittori the Young Admiral* (d.p.)
MAURITIO: *Mauricion | Mauritio* (s.d.s); *Ma<uritio>* (s.p.s); *Mauritio* [one of the] *Captains* (d.p.)
CAPTAIN: *Captain* (s.d.s and s.p.s)
SOLDIERS: *Soldiers* (s.d.s and d.p.s); *1 | 2 | 3 | 1 Soldier* (s.p.s)
CASSANDRA: *Cassandra* (s.d.s); *Cass<andra>* (s.p.s); *Cassandra Vittorie's mistress* (d.p.)

NAPLES: *King of Naples* (s.d.s); *King* (s.ds and s.p.s); *Nap<les>* (s.p.s); *The King of Naples* (s.d.s and d.p.)
MESSENGER: *a Messenger* (s.d.s); *Messenger* (s.p.s)
SICILY: *King of Sicily | King of Scicily* (s.d.s); *King* (s.d.s and s.p.s); *King of Sci<cily> | Sicil<y>* (s.p.s); *The King of Sicily* (s.d.s and d.p.)
HORATIO: *Horatio* (s.d.s); *Hor<atio>* (s.p.s); *Horatio* [one of the] *Noblemen of Sicily* (d.p.)
TRIVULSI: *Trivulsi* (s.d.s); *Tr<ivulsi>* (s.p.s); *Trivulsi* [one of the] *Noblemen of Sicily* (d.p.)
FABRICCIO: *Fabrichio* (s.d.s); *Fab<richio>* (s.p.s); *Fabrichio* [one of the] *Captains* (d.p.)
ROSINDA: *Rosinda* (s.d.s); *Ros<inda>* (s.p.s); *Rosinda the daughter of Sicily* (d.p.)
FLAVIA: *Flavia* (s.d.s); *Fla<via>* (s.p.s); *Flavia, Lady attendant on Rosinda* (d.p.)
PAZZORELLO: *Pazzorello | Pazzorelo* (s.d.s); *Paz<zorello>* (s.p.s); *Pazzorello a servant to Rosinda* (d.p.)
DIDIMO: *Page* (s.d.s and s.p.s); *Didimo a Page to Rosinda* (d.p.)
SOLDIERS: *Soldiers* (s.d.s and d.p.s)
SERGEANT: *Sergeant* (s.d.s and s.p.s)
GUARD: *a Guard* (s.d.s)

OTHER CHARACTERS
The city governor of Naples (1.1)
The people of Naples (1.2, 2.1)
The princes of states neighbouring Naples (2.1)
Didimo's father, a captain (3.1)
An old soldier with whom Pazzorello picked a fight (4.3)
Julio's sister (5.2)

SETTING
Period: Sicily and Naples are distinct kingdoms, pointing to a time after the Sicilian Vespers of 1282
Time-Scheme: 4.4–5 takes place the night following 4.2, and 5.2 the next day
Place: Naples

Geography
Naples: the castle
Sicily
Italy: Rome
Spain
Lapland

SOURCES
Narrative: Lope de Vega, *Don Lope de Cardona* (c. 1611, printed 1618); Ben Jonson, *The Alchemist* (**1621**; 4.1)
Verbal: Horace, *Epodes* 1 (2.2); William Shakespeare, *Hamlet* (**1259**; 1.2); John Webster, *The White Devil* (**1689**; 1.2)
Works Mentioned: Diego Ortúñez de Calahorra, Pedro de la Sierra, and Marcos Martínez, *Espejo de principes y caballeros* (1555–87; English tr., *The Mirror of Princely Deeds and Knighthood*, by Margaret Tyler,

2410. The Young Admiral

R. P., and L. A., 1578–99; 3.1); Christopher Marlowe, *Doctor Faustus* (**810**; 4.1)

LANGUAGE
English
French: 11 words (3.1, 4.3–4; Didimo, Pazzorello, Sergeant, Cesario)
Spanish: 1 word (5.4; Fabio)

FORM
Metre: pentameter and prose; some tetrameter
Rhyme: blank verse; some couplets
Act-Division: 5 acts
Lines (Spoken): 2,223 (1,756 verse, 467 prose)
Lines (Written): 2,623

STAGING
Doors: characters enter 'at several doors' (3.2, s.d.), and 'at one' and 'the other' door (5.4, s.d.)
Within: shout (2.2, s.d.)
Miscellaneous: A stage direction calls for Vittori to chase soldiers whilst carrying the unconscious Cassandra under his arm and also, it is implied, brandishing a sword (2.2).

MUSIC AND SOUND
Sound Effects: thunder (2.2, dialogue); gunfire (4.4, dialogue)
Music: loud music (5.4, s.d.)

PROPS
Pyrotechnics: lightning (2.2, dialogue)
Weapons: Vittori's sword (2.2, implicit); a sword (4.2, dialogue); Pazzorello's sword (5.3, dialogue); Didimo's rapier (5.3, dialogue)
Clothing: a signet ring (1.2, dialogue); a blindfold (4.1, implicit); a ring (4.2, dialogue)
Money: an unspecified amount (4.1, dialogue); gold (4.4–5, dialogue)
Small Portable Objects: a paper (3.1, dialogue); a letter (4.2, dialogue); a letter (4.5, dialogue); a document (5.4, dialogue)
Large Portable Objects: ensigns (1.2, dialogue)

COSTUMES AND MAKE-UP
VITTORI: a scabbard (2.2, implicit); disguised as a herald (3.2, s.d.); a disguise (5.2, s.d.; removed on stage)
CASSANDRA: a mourning habit and a veil (1.2, s.d.)
NAPLES: a crown (2.1, dialogue)
FLAVIA: disguised as a witch (4.1, s.d.)
PAZZORELLO: breeches with a pocket (4.1, dialogue); a garment with a fob (4.1, dialogue); a diamond ring (4.1, dialogue; worn on his little finger; removed on stage); bloody (4.3, s.d.)
DIDIMO: a scabbard (5.3, implicit)

EARLY STAGE HISTORY
1633: presumably performed as licensed, no doubt by Queen Henrietta's Men at the Cockpit.

1633: performed by Queen Henrietta's Men at St James's Palace on Tuesday 19 November (the King's birthday). The audience included: King Charles I; Queen Henrietta Maria. The King and Queen liked the play. Christopher Beeston was later paid £70 for this and six other court performances, by a warrant dated Monday 22 December 1634.

1639: The play was in the repertory of the King's and Queen's Young Company (Beeston's Boys) at the Cockpit. On Saturday 10 August, Philip Herbert, 4th Earl of Pembroke (Lord Chamberlain) issued an order restraining other companies from performing this and 44 other plays.

EARLY TEXTUAL HISTORY
1633: On Wednesday 3 July, Sir Henry Herbert licensed the text for performance.

1637: entered in the Stationers' Register to Andrew Crooke and William Cooke on Thursday 13 April; joint entry with *The Lady of Pleasure* (**2515**); entry names author. Thomas Herbert, Sir Henry Herbert's deputy, had licensed the book for publication.

1637: Q printed by Thomas Cotes for Andrew Crooke and William Cooke; collation A² B–K⁴, 38 leaves; title page names author, acting company, and playhouse; list of roles; authorial dedication to George, 12th Lord Berkeley.

c. 1630s–40s: a copy of Q was in the possession of John Horne (Vicar of Headington, Oxfordshire). After his death, his entire collection of play-books passed into the possession of John Houghton of Brasenose College, Oxford (*c.* 1608–77), then to James Herne (died 1685), and then to the library of Ralph Sheldon (1623–84) at Weston, where it was catalogued by Anthony Wood, probably in the late 1670s. By the time the copy had been bound into a single volume with 21 other plays by Shirley (and, presumably in error, with Henry Shirley's *The Martyred Soldier*, **2030**).

c. 1640: Abraham Wright transcribed extracts into a MS miscellany (London: British Library, Add. MS 22608, fos. 89ʳ–90ʳ). The MS later passed to Wright's son, the antiquarian James Wright (*c.* 1644–*c.* 1717).

1655: *The English Treasury of Wit and Language* entered in the Stationers' Register to Humphrey Moseley on Tuesday 16 January.

1655: five extracts (from 1.2, 3.1, 4.5, 5.2) included in John Cotgrave's *The English Treasury of Wit and Language*, sigs. H2ᵛ, K1ᵛ, R3ᵛ, S5ʳ; printed for Humphrey Moseley.

Mid- to late seventeenth century (before 1689): a copy of Q was owned by Elizabeth Puckering.

1684: Nicholas Cox (Manciple of St Edmund Hall, Oxford) had a copy of Q in his bookshop. It had probably been previously owned by Gerard Langbaine, and appears on a list compiled by Anthony Wood on Saturday 13 December.

EDITIONS
Kenneth J. Ericksen, Garland Renaissance Drama (New York and London, 1979).
Rebecca Bailey, in James Shirley, *The Complete Works*, gen. eds. Eugene Giddens, Teresa Grant, and Barbara Ravelhofer (Oxford, forthcoming).

REFERENCES
Annals 1633; Bawcutt, 259, 272, C98; Beal 2 ShJ 207; Bentley, v. 1168–70; Bodleian, MS Wood E. 4, art. 1, p. 68; *ELR* 14 (1984), 240–1; Eyre & Rivington, i. 463; Robert Stanley Forsythe, *The Relations of Shirley's Plays to the Elizabethan Drama* (New York, 1914), 190–9; Greg 519; Hazlitt, 260; *The Library*, 7th ser., 1 (2000), 376; *MLR* 13 (1918), 401–11; *MP* 66 (1968–9), 256–61; MSC 2.3, 389–90; MSC 6, 84; *SP* 40 (1943), 186–203; Steele, 245.

2411. *The Cunning Lovers*

TEXT
Printed in 1654 (Wing B4850).

GENRE
comedy
Contemporary: comedy (t.p.)

TITLE
Performed/Printed: *The Cunning Lovers*

AUTHOR
Thomas Heywood, possibly with Richard Brome (*attribution*)

Q's title page attributes the play to Alexander Brome (1620–66), but the ascription is deeply problematic, and indeed almost impossible. Brome was primarily a lawyer and poet; his earliest published poem dates from 1641, and this is the only play ever attributed to him. He had one other significant connection with drama: he put together the 1653 and 1658–9 collections of *Five New Plays* by Richard Brome, who was his namesake but not his kinsman.

According to the Oxford *DNB*, he first came to London in c. 1640, the year after the earliest evidence of the play's existence, the Lord Chamberlain's 1639 list of the Cockpit repertory. This would mean that he wrote the play as a teenager and sold it to a London company, either before leaving his native Dorset or, if we take advantage of the inexactitude of the *DNB* date, immediately upon arrival in the capital. It seems circumstantially unlikely, and if in consequence we are disposed to doubt the title page, nothing else about the edition enhances its authority: there is no dedication or epistle, and the one substantial piece of paratext, the list of roles, contains errors (to wit, treating three characters' disguises as separate roles) indicating that it was not compiled by the author. We must, therefore, take seriously the possibility that the title-page ascription is another error.

Strong encouragement to doubt Alexander Brome's authorship comes from the 1639 list. As discussed in **2133**, this includes titles, almost all of them earlier than May 1636, which William Beeston had reason to think might have been in the hands of other companies and were therefore in need of protection. The list seems in part to be organized by playwright; *The Cunning Lovers* appears between *Love's Mistress* (**2451**) and *The Rape of Lucrece* (**1558**), implying the authorship of Thomas Heywood. The play also features Heywood's characteristic Latinate clown, and in particular bears striking tonal similarities with his late romantic plays, notably *A Maidenhead Well Lost* (**2289**) and *A Challenge for Beauty* (**2434**). A preliminary and less than comprehensive investigation found that Heywood's lexical habits in those two plays can also be traced in half of this play's scenes (to wit, 1.1, 1.3, 2.2–3, 3.1, 3.4–5, 4.1–2, 5.1, 5.5). (This used the Brian Vickers method of examining an author's lexis as seen in strings of three or more consecutive words, and ignoring commonplace phrases and formulas. A fuller analysis, using complementary techniques, is desirable.)

The presence of Richard Brome might help to account for the erroneous ascription, with the dead playwright Richard being confused with Alexander the poet and possible supplier of the text. In the mid-1630s, Heywood collaborated with Richard Brome at least once (on **2441**), and probably more often. However, the play contains fewer and less striking lexical traces of Richard Brome; those which were found—based on a comparison with *The Novella* (**2383**), *The Weeding of the Covent Garden* (**2401**), and *The City Wit* (**2419**)—occur mainly in scenes where the Heywood markers are more persuasive. (The scenes in question are: 1.1–2, 1.5, 2.2, 3.1–2, 3.5, 5.5.) The case requires more sustained and systematic research.

DATE
Limits: 1632–9
Best Guess: 1633

If the play was written for the Cockpit by Heywood in collaboration with Richard Brome, then it must antedate Brome's exclusive contract with Salisbury Court from July 1635.

ORIGINAL PRODUCTION
Queen Henrietta's Men at the Cockpit (?)

PLOT
Concerned about the succession, the Duke of Verona arranges for his son Prospero to marry Princess Valentia, heir to the duchy of Mantua. Prospero is at first unwilling to wed, but is persuaded by the sight of Valentia's picture. Then ambassadors from Mantua arrive to break off the engagement; Verona declares war. Prospero is granted permission to spend a year travelling Europe with his friend Monticelso; in fact, they go to Mantua to get a closer look at Valentia. The Duke follows them in disguise.

To keep Valentia away from the many suitors thronging the court, the Duke of Mantua orders the building of a tower in which she will be shut up. Keen to seize both Valentia and power, Julio attempts to assassinate the Duke during a hunt, but he is saved by the newly arrived and incognito Prospero. Monticelso, who professes a skill in architecture, is given the job of finishing the tower, and Prospero is appointed its sentinel, with a lodging immediately next to Valentia's. Monticelso builds a secret door between the two rooms. The Duke further engages the architect to woo the Duchess Lucibell on his behalf; Monticelso wins her for himself, but allows the Duke to suppose otherwise.

Prospero courts Valentia in the tower: though Verona and Mantua are now enemies, she finds him an acceptable suitor because he saved her father's life. The other suitors see him at Valentia's window and report it to the Duke, who becomes suspicious on seeing Valentia's ring on Prospero's finger. He rushes to check Valentia's security, but has to pass through twelve locked doors to reach her; Prospero uses the secret door to get there first and returns the ring in time for the Duke to see it in Valentia's possession.

Monticelso and Prospero plan to spend a night of passion in the tower with their respective lovers. Julio and the disguised Verona overhear them talking and bring the Duke to the tower at midnight, but again the secret door enables a speedy getaway and Julio's story is discredited. Then Prospero invites Mantua to a banquet for his newly arrived girlfriend, a Spanish lady. The Duke is struck by the lady's similarity to Valentia, but again the secret door makes it possible for the lovers to convince him that the two ladies cannot be one and the same person. Finally, he gets the Duke to give the Spanish lady away at their wedding.

Monticelso fakes his own death by drowning to see how Lucibell takes it. She takes it badly: she goes mad. Monticelso sets up in business as a magician with a remarkable knowledge of people's secrets. He gets Valentia's other suitors out of the way at the time of Prospero's wedding by inveigling them into attempting to penetrate the tower in disguise. They are caught in the attempt by guards, and Valentia's absence is discovered. The Duke offers a reward for her discovery, and another for anyone who can cure Lucibell's madness. Prospero thereupon reveals the Spanish lady's true identity, and Monticelso produces Lucibell, restored to sanity on learning that her lover is alive after all. The Duke of Verona brings an army to Mantua to rescue his son, but ends up only having to give his blessing to Prospero's marriage.

There are some problems with the plotting. The strand of action involving the Duke of Verona's disguise is almost superfluous. The continuity of the action goes awry in Act 4: in 4.1, the Clown says that the Duke of Mantua has offered a reward for Lucibell's cure, but the proclamation to that effect is not made until 4.2. Similarly, in 5.1 the disguised Monticelso surprises Prospero with apparently preternatural knowledge of his identity and doings, which is really only the confidential information known to him as the Prince's companion; but the revelations include the Spanish lady trick, which took place after they parted company upon Monticelso's supposed death.

SCENE DESIGNATION
1.1–5, 2.1–4, 3.1–5, 4.1–3, 5.1–5 (Q has act-division only)

ROLES
The Duke of VERONA, Prospero's father, Monticelso's kinsman; an old man; poses as a pilgrim
Prince PROSPERO of Verona, the Duke's son and heir, Monticelso's kinsman; a young man; adopts the alias Antonio, a knight
Lord MONTICELSO, a peer of Verona, kinsman of Prospero and Verona; poses as a magician and a ghost
COSMO, a lord and counsellor of Verona; later appointed the Duke's deputy
AMBASSADORS from Mantua to Verona (1.1–2; one speaks)
The Duke of MANTUA, Valentia's father
The CLOWN, the Duke of Mantua's servant
The Duke of FLORENCE, a suitor to Valentia
The Marquis of FERRARA, a suitor to Valentia
Lord JULIO of Mantua
Princess VALENTIA of Mantua, the Duke's daughter, only child, and heir; also called Lady Valentia; poses as a Spanish lady
LUCIBELL, a duchess and a young widow
A SMITH; called Goodman Padlock, which might be his name (1.5)
A MASON (1.5)
A BRICKLAYER (1.5)
A CARPENTER (1.5)
Prospero's SERVANTS (4.3, *non-speaking*)
A SERVANT (5.1, *non-speaking*)
A BISHOP (5.2, *non-speaking*)
A GUARD (5.3, *non-speaking*)

Speaking Parts: 16

Stage Directions and Speech Prefixes
VERONA: *Verona* (s.d.s); *Ver<ona>* (s.p.s); *Verona, the Duke of Verona | Pilgrim* (d.p.)
PROSPERO: *Prospero* (s.d.s); *Pros<pero>* (s.p.s); *Prospero, the Prince [Verona's] Son* (d.p.)
MONTICELSO: *Montescelso | Montecelso* (s.d.s); *Mont<ecelso>* (s.p.s); *Montecelso, a Peer of Verona | A Necromancer* (d.p.)
COSMO: *Cosmo* (s.d.s); *Cos<mo> | Coz<mo>* (s.p.s); *Cosmo, a Lord of Verona* (d.p.)
AMBASSADORS: *Ambassadors* (s.d.s); *Ambassador* (s.p.s); *Ambassadors from the Mantuan Duke* (d.p.)
MANTUA: *Mantua* (s.d.s); *Man<tua>* (s.p.s); *Mantua, the Duke of Mantua* (d.p.)
CLOWN: *Clown* (s.d.s, s.p.s, and d.p.)
FLORENCE: *Florence | [one of the] Lords* (s.d.s; *Flo<rence>* (s.p.s); *Florence, the Duke of Florence* (d.p.)
FERRARA: *Ferrara | [one of the] Lords* (s.d.s); *Fer<rara>* (s.p.s); *Ferrara, a Marquess* (d.p.)
JULIO: *Julio | [one of the] Lords* (s.d.s); *Jul<io>* (s.p.s); *Julio, a Mantuan Lord* (d.p.)
VALENTIA: *Valentia | the Lady* (s.d.s); *Val<entia>* (s.p.s); *Valentia, Daughter to the Mantuan Duke | A Spanish Lady* (d.p.)

LUCIBELL: *Duchess* (s.d.s, s.p.s, and d.p.)
SMITH: *a Smith* (s.d.s and d.p.); *Smith* (s.p.s)
MASON: *a Mason* (s.d.s and d.p.); *Mason* (s.p.s)
BRICKLAYER: *a Bricklayer* (s.d.s and d.p.); *Bricklayer* (s.p.s)
CARPENTER: *a Carpenter* (s.d.s and d.p.); *Carpenter* (s.p.s)
SERVANT: *Servant* (s.d.s)
BISHOP: *a Bishop* (s.d.s); *Bishop* (d.p.)
GUARD: *Guard* (s.d.s)
D.p. also lists: *Duke of Verona's Army*

OTHER CHARACTERS
The Clown's father, a servant of the Duke of Mantua (1.2, 5.1)
A Jew who sold Julio his disguise (1.4)
Lucibell's parent (2.3)
The people of Verona (3.3)
The Clown's sweetheart (3.5)
The Duke of Mantua's barber (3.5)
The Duke of Mantua's treasurer (4.1)
The Veronese army (5.4–5)

SETTING
Time-Scheme: 1.2 takes place in the morning; 3.4 takes place the evening after 3.3, with compression of time taking the action up to midnight; 5.2 takes place the morning after 5.1
Place: Mantua; the first scene takes place in Verona

Geography
Mantua: St Loretta's chapel
Italy: Florence; Ferrara; Rome
Europe: France; Spain; Greece; Germany
England
[*Turkey*]: Ephesus
The Indies
The North Pole
The South Pole

SOURCES
Narrative: Ser Giovanni Fiorentino, *Il pecorone* 2.5 (c. 1378, printed 1558; English tr., *The Fortunate, the Deceived, and the Unfortunate Lovers*, 1632); Plautus, *Miles gloriosus*
Verbal: William Shakespeare, *Romeo and Juliet* (**987**; 2.4), *Love's Labours Lost* (**1031**; 4.1); Thomas Heywood, *If You Know Not Me, You Know Nobody* (**1427** and **1433**; 2.2); William Rowley, Thomas Dekker, John Webster, and John Ford, *A Late Murder of the Son upon the Mother* (**2136**; 3.4)
Works Mentioned: *Reynard the Fox* (thirteenth century; English tr. 1481; 2.2); Christopher Marlowe, *Doctor Faustus* (**810**; 5.1)

LANGUAGE
English
Latin: 11 words (1.5, 2.2; Clown)
Spanish: 20 words (4.3; Valentia)

FORM
Metre: pentameter and prose; some alexandrines; two passages of fourteeners (3.5, 5.5)
Rhyme: blank verse and couplets
Act-Division: 5 acts
Dumb Show: 5.2 (compresses action)
Lines (Spoken): 2,251 (1,496 verse, 755 prose)
Lines (Written): 2,454

STAGING
Doors: characters enter 'at one door' and 'march over to the church', presumably another door (5.2, s.d.)
Above: characters appear above (2.4, 3.2, 3.4, 4.3, s.d.; a maximum of six at once; passage between the above space and the main stage takes no more than seven lines for an actor simultaneously performing a costume change)
Miscellaneous: characters exit at the end of 4.2 and immediately re-enter at the start of 4.3

MUSIC AND SOUND
Sound Effects: knocking (5.1, s.d.)
Music: flourish (1.1, 5.5, s.d.); hunting horns (1.2–3, s.d.); hautboys (4.3, 5.2, s.d.)

PROPS
Weapons: pole-axes (5.3, dialogue)
Clothing: Monticelso's hat, cloak, and doublet (4.1, dialogue)
Money: gold (2.1, 5.1, dialogue)
Food and Drink: a banquet (4.3, s.d.), including wine (dialogue; drunk on stage)
Small Portable Objects: a picture of Valentia (1.1, dialogue); a builder's rule (2.2, 5.3, s.d.); a builder's line (2.2, s.d.); twelve keys (3.1, 3.4, 4.3, 5.5, dialogue); a book (4.3, dialogue); another book (5.1, s.d.); papers (5.1, s.d.; 5.3, dialogue); a hammer (5.3, implicit)
Large Portable Objects: a chair (3.4, dialogue); seating for six characters (4.3, implicit); a table (5.1, s.d.)
Scenery: an arras (3.4, dialogue)

COSTUMES
VERONA: disguised as a pilgrim (2.2, s.d.; 3.2, 5.1–2, 5.4, implicit)
PROSPERO: Valentia's ring (3.1, dialogue)
MONTICELSO: a hat, cloak, and doublet (3.5, implicit; see also PROPS); disguised (4.1, 5.1, implicit); disguised as a ghost (5.1, s.d.)
MANTUA: a girdle (3.1, dialogue; 4.3, 5.5, implicit)
CLOWN: a beard (dialogue); a girdle (5.1, dialogue)
FLORENCE: disguised as a mason (5.3, s.d.; 5.5, implicit)
FERRARA: disguised as a carpenter (5.3, s.d.; 5.5, implicit), including an apron (dialogue)
JULIO: a disguise (1.4, s.d.; put on on stage; includes a mask); disguised as a smith (5.3, s.d.; 5.5, implicit)
VALENTIA: golden hair (dialogue); a diamond ring 2.4, 3.2, 4.3, dialogue); dressed as a Spanish lady (4.3, s.d.; 5.2, implicit); her own clothes (4.3,

dialogue; she has to change rapidly back and forth between costumes in this scene, whilst on the move between stage levels)

EARLY STAGE HISTORY
1637–9: performed by Beeston's Boys at the Cockpit 'with great applause'.
1639: The play was in the repertory of the King's and Queen's Young Company (Beeston's Boys) at the Cockpit. On Saturday 10 August, Philip Herbert, 4th Earl of Pembroke (Lord Chamberlain) issued an order restraining performances by other companies of this and 44 other plays.

EARLY TEXTUAL HISTORY
1654: Q printed for William Sheares; collation A² B–I⁴ K², 36 leaves; title page names Alexander Brome as author, and the late 1630s acting company and playhouse; list of roles.
1655: *Wit's Interpreter* entered to Nathaniel Brooke in the Stationers' Register on Wednesday 14 March.
1655: two extracts (from 2.3 and 4.3) included in John Cotgrave's *Wit's Interpreter*, sigs. E1ᵛ, E4ᵛ; printed for Nathaniel Brooke. The extracts were omitted from subsequent editions.
1665: Q advertised as for sale by John Playfere.
1684: Nicholas Cox (Manciple of St Edmund Hall, Oxford) had a copy of Q in his bookshop. It had probably been previously owned by Gerard Langbaine, and appears on a list compiled by Anthony Wood on Saturday 13 December.

REFERENCES
Annals 1638; Bentley, iii. 48–9; Bodleian, MS Wood E. 4, art. 1, p. 78; Eyre & Rivington, i. 467; Greg 736; Hazlitt, 55; MSC 2.3, 389–90; *RES* 54 (2003), 601–14.

2412. The Fatal Contract

TEXT
Printed in 1653 (Wing H1422). A version printed in 1687 (Q₃; Wing H1421) has significant revisions which were probably executed after 1674 (and are not detailed here).

GENRE
tragedy
Contemporary: French tragedy (t.p.); poem (ded.)

TITLE
Printed: *The Fatal Contract*
Later Assigned: *The Eunuch*

AUTHOR
William Heminges

DATE
Limits: 1629–38
Best Guess: 1633

The bulk of the previous discussion of the dating centres on a reference in 4.3 to Landri as the Queen's laureate, the issue being who the referent in the English court might be; but there is no good reason to suppose that any contemporary allusion is intended. However, a reference in 2.2 to the Queen's ambition to be an actress seems more pointed, and probably places the play soon after *The Shepherds' Paradise* (**2395**).

ORIGINAL PRODUCTION
Queen Henrietta's Men, presumably at the Cockpit (or, if later, Salisbury Court)

PLOT
Before the start of the action, Queen Fredegund's brother was murdered by the noblemen Du Mayenne and Lamot, who themselves perished by way of revenge. The Queen's vengeance now extends to the next generation. The sons were away at university and not complicit in the crime, but on their return to court they try to protect themselves by posing as soldiers. Fredegund is not taken in by the disguise, but writes that she bears them no malice. In fact, she does. Her other scheme is to dispose of her husband, Childeric, who has discovered her adultery with Landri. Childeric is poisoned and the blame fastened on young Du Mayenne and Lamot, but they flee before they can be arrested. Du Mayenne raises an army of rebellion, but Lamot stays at court disguised as a surgeon, 'Strephon'.

Aphelia privately contracts herself to marry the Queen's younger son, Clovis, but she is also noticed by the new King, his brother Clothair. She is invited to a nocturnal assignation arranged by the Queen's scheming eunuch, Castrato. It is a trap: instead of Clovis, she meets Clothair, who attempts to rape her. Clovis arrives in time to intervene, but is killed in the ensuing fight. Aphelia is imprisoned. In fact, Clovis is not dead: when his body is delivered to 'Strephon' for embalming, the surgeon discovers residual traces of life and brings him back from the brink. This recovery is kept a secret from Clothair's court.

Castrato has his own agenda: his true objective is not to serve the royal family but destroy it. To this end, he starts a fire in Fredegund's lodgings as she is in bed with Landri, and summons Clothair to witness the result. The plan misfires: Landri escapes in a suit of Clovis's armour which Castrato had previously stowed in the Queen's room. Clothair sees the armoured figure and takes it for Clovis's ghost come to demand Aphelia's company in the afterlife; he duly orders Aphelia's execution on the day of Clovis's funeral, but, when Castrato accuses the Queen and Landri, wonders if it has all been a plot to prevent him from marrying Aphelia. At the funeral, Clothair aborts her beheading and makes her his Queen instead. Clovis chooses his moment to reveal himself, but it is too late:

the ambitious Aphelia declares that her marital pre-contract became void when Clovis 'died'.

Fredegund conceals Landri in a hiding-place previously used by her husband for his concubine. Seeking revenge, Clovis has Castrato give Clothair a forged letter suggesting that Aphelia is having an affair with Landri. Clothair jealously decides to murder her in her bed on the wedding night, but she is not there when he arrives (which he takes as corroboration of her guilt). Meanwhile, posing as Childeric's ghost, Clovis breaks in on his mother's assignation with Landri and frightens her into confessing that she poisoned her husband. Clovis hands over the guilty couple to Castrato for torture, and goes to join the rebels. Castrato imprisons and starves them, encouraging them to accept whatever food he offers them; after they have eaten it, he tells them it was poisoned, and they die. Clothair has Aphelia tortured with hot irons. When the castle is besieged by the rebels, Clothair reassures himself that Clovis will see them off, but his hope proves misplaced: Clovis is one of them. Clothair asks Castrato to kill him. It emerges that Aphelia is chaste and the eunuch malicious. Nevertheless, he is unable to finish the job by shooting Clothair, and is stabbed himself just as the rebels arrive. In fact, 'he' is no eunuch but a woman: Du Mayenne's sister, out to avenge herself after Clothair raped her. She, Aphelia, and Clothair all die, Clothair acknowledging that the rebels have just cause against him. Clovis appoints his fellow rebels to Landri's offices.

SCENE DESIGNATION
1.1–3, 2.1–2, 3.1–3, 4.1–3, 5.1–2 (Q, corrected)

The stage is clear during 4.3.

ROLES
LAMOT, a banished nobleman; poses as a soldier, and later adopts the alias Strephon, a surgeon
DU MAYENNE, a banished nobleman, Crotilda's brother; poses as a soldier; later appointed Mayor of the Palace
LANDRI, Fredegund's minion, once her page; Duke of France and Mayor of the Palace
Two or three LORDS attending Landri (1.1, non-speaking)
Three or four PETITIONERS attending Landri (1.1; one speaks individually, the rest collectively)
CASTRATO, a Moorish eunuch and a pagan; in reality, Crotilda, Du Mayenne's sister
FREDEGUND, Queen of France; Childeric's wife (later his widow), mother of Clothair and Clovis; an older woman
CLOVIS, a prince, younger son of Childeric and Fredegund, Clothair's brother; later the Monsieur
APHELIA, Brissac's daughter, Charles's sister; later Clothair's wife, Queen Aphelia of France
Aphelia's PAGE (1.3, 2.1)

CHILDERIC, King of France, Fredegund's husband, father of Clothair and Clovis
CLOTHAIR, elder son of Childeric and Fredegund, Clovis's brother; later King of France; later still, Aphelia's husband
LORDS attending Childeric (1.3, *non-speaking*)
LADIES attending Childeric (1.3, *non-speaking*)
The GUARD; at least six in number (1.3, 2.2, 3.3, 4.2–3; three speak individually, others collectively)
ATTENDANTS at court (1.3, 2.2, *non-speaking*)
Old BRISSAC, a peer and councillor, father of Charles and Aphelia
CHARLES Brissac, Old Brissac's son, Aphelia's brother; a young man; later the rebel general, later still created Duke of France
MARTEL, a rebel nobleman
BOURBON, a rebel nobleman
LANOUE, a rebel nobleman
A CARDINAL at the funeral (3.3, *non-speaking*)
Six YOUNG MEN, who bear the hearse (3.3, *non-speaking*)
Two or three LADIES at the funeral (3.3, *non-speaking*)
A HEADSMAN (3.3, *non-speaking*)
Two NUNS, who sing (3.3)
Two LITTLE BOYS at the funeral (3.3, *non-speaking*)
VIRGINS at the funeral (3.3, *non-speaking*)
ISABEL, a lady attending Aphelia
JULIA, a lady attending Aphelia
A LADY attending Aphelia (4.1, *non-speaking and optional*)
Aphelia's LACKEY (4.1)
MUSICIANS servicing Fredegund's assignation (4.3; at least one sings, the rest speak collectively)
VOICES (5.1, *within*)
ATTENDANTS on Clovis (5.1, *non-speaking*)
Two RUFFIANS (5.2, *non-speaking*)
A TORTURER (5.2, *non-speaking*; but he may be one of the Ruffians)
Two SOLDIERS (5.2)

Speaking Parts: 29–31

Stage Directions and Speech Prefixes
LAMOT: *Lamot | Streph<on>* (s.d.s and s.p.s); *Lamot,* [one of] *two Banished Lords* (d.p.)
DU MAYENNE: *Dumaine | Dumain |* [one of the Monsieur's] *Company* (s.d.s); *Duma<ine>* (s.p.s); *Dumain,* [one of] *two Banished Lords* (d.p.)
LANDRI: *Landrey | Landry | the Ghost* (s.d.s); *Land<rey>* (s.p.s); *Landrey, Favourite to the Queen, and raised by her favour to be Duke of France, and Mayor of the Palace* (d.p.)
LORDS: *two or three insinuating Lords* (s.d.s)
PETITIONERS: *three or four Petitioners* (s.d.s); *Petitioners | 1 Petitioner* (s.p.s)
CASTRATO: *the Eunuch* (s.d.s); *Eunuch* (s.d.s and s.p.s); *Crotilda, by the name of Castrato, as a Eunuch* (d.p.)
FREDEGUND: *Fredigond the Queen* (s.d.s and d.p.); *the Queen* (s.d.s); *Queen* (s.d.s and s.p.s)

CLOVIS: *Clovis the Prince* | *The Monsieur* (s.d.s); *Clovis* (s.d.s and s.p.s); *Monsieur* (s.p.s); *Clovis, the Monsieur* (d.p.)
APHELIA: *Aphelia* (s.d.s); *Aphe<lia>* (s.p.s); *Aphelia, Old Brissac's Daughter* (d.p.)
PAGE: *a Page* | *the Page* (s.d.s); *Page* (s.p.s); *A Page to Brissac Junior* (d.p.)
CHILDERIC: *the King* (s.d.s); *King* (s.d.s and s.p.s); *Childerick, an old King of France* (d.p.)
CLOTHAIR: *Clotaire* | *Clotaire* | *the King* | *King Clotair* | *King* | *the King Clotair* (s.d.s); *Clota<ir>* (s.p.s); *Clotair, the young King* (d.p.)
LORDS: *Lords* (s.d.s); *Lords for Attendants* (d.p.)
LADIES: *Ladies* (s.d.s)
GUARD: *Guard* | *the Guard* | *three or four of the Guard* (s.d.s); *Six of the Guard* (s.d.s and d.p.); *1 Guard* | *2 Guard* | *3 Guard* (s.p.s)
ATTENDANTS: *Attendants* (s.d.s)
BRISSAC: *Old Brissac* (s.d.s); *Old Bris<sac>* | *Bris<sac>* (s.p.s); *Brissac, an old Peer of France* (d.p.)
CHARLES: *Charles Brissac* | *Charles* | *Brissac* | *[one of the Monsieur's] Company* (s.d.s); *Char<les>* | *Bris<sac>* (s.p.s); *Brissac, [Old Brissac's] Son* (d.p.)
MARTEL: *Martell* | *Martel* | *Mart<ell>* (s.p.s); *Martell, [one of the] Noblemen of France, and friends of the banished Lords* (d.p.)
BOURBON: *Bourbon* (s.d.s); *Bourb<on>* (s.p.s); *Bourbon, [one of the] Noblemen of France, and friends of the banished Lords* (d.p.)
LANOUE: *Lanove* (s.d.s and s.p.s); *Lanove, [one of the] Noblemen of France, and friends of the banished Lords* (d.p.)
CARDINAL: *a Cardinal* | *The Cardinal* (s.d.s); *A Cardinal for state, when Aphelia is to be beheaded* (d.p.)
YOUNG MEN: *six young men* (s.d.s); *Six Young men to bear the Hearse* (d.p.)
LADIES: *two or three Ladies* (s.d.s); *Three Ladies for Attendance* (d.p.)
HEADSMAN: *a Headsman* | *the Headsman* | *the Executioner* (s.d.s)
NUNS: *two Nuns* | *Nuns* (s.d.s)
LITTLE BOYS: *two little boys* (s.d.s)
VIRGINS: *more Virgins* (s.d.s)
ISABEL: *[one of] two or three Ladies* | *[one of the] Ladies* | *Isabel* (s.d.s); *1 Lady* | *Isab<el>* (s.p.s); *Isabella, a Lady that waited on Aphelia* (d.p.)
JULIA: *[one of] two or three Ladies* | *[one of the] Ladies* (s.d.s); *2 Lady* (s.p.s)
LADY: *[one of] two or three Ladies* | *[one of the] Ladies* (s.d.s)
LACKEY: *Lackey* (s.d.s and s.p.s); *A Lackey* (d.p.)
MUSICIANS: *Musicians* (s.d.s, s.p.s, and d.p.)
VOICES: *Within* (s.p.s)
ATTENDANTS: *others* (s.d.s)
RUFFIANS: *two Ruffians* (s.d.s)
TORTURER: *man* (s.d.s)
SOLDIERS: *a Soldier* | *another Soldier* | *Soldiers* (s.d.s); *Soldier* | *2 Soldier* (s.p.s)

OTHER CHARACTERS
The Petitioners' wives and children (1.1)
The people of France, the Queen's supporters (1.1)
Old Du Mayenne, father of Du Mayenne and Crotilda (1.1–2, 5.2)
Lamot's father (1.1–2, 5.2)
Clodimir, Fredegund's murdered brother (1.1–2, 5.2)
An Italian artist who painted a picture of Clodimir's murder (1.2)
Isabel, a member of the Lamot or Du Mayenne family (1.2, 5.2)
Maria, a member of the Lamot or Du Mayenne family (1.2, 5.2)
A grandmother of the Lamot or Du Mayenne family (1.2)
Clothair's subjects (2.2)
The rebel army, numbering 30,000 troops (3.2, 4.3, 5.2)
Childeric's concubine, murdered at Fredegund's instigation (3.3)
The priest who married Clothair and Aphelia (4.1)

SETTING
Period: sixth century AD; the first part of the play loosely dramatizes events which took place in 584
Time-Scheme: 1.3, 2.2, 3.1, 4.1 all take place at night; 3.2–3 take place on the same day. There is some compression of time in 4.1: half an hour passes in a few lines.
Place: France

Geography
France: Mayenne; Bourbon
[Europe]: Wittenberg; Italy; Mount Etna; The Low Countries
[Asia]: Tyre; Arabia
[Africa]: Ethiopia
India

SOURCES
Narrative: Jean de Serres, *A General Inventory of the History of France*, tr. Edward Grimestone (1607, repr. 1611, 1624; Heminges probably used one of the later editions); William Shakespeare, *Richard III* (**950**; 3.3), *Hamlet* (**1259**; 1.1), *Macbeth* (**1496**; 5.2); John Webster, *The Duchess of Malfi* (**1726**; 2.1); Thomas Middleton and William Rowley, *The Changeling* (**2010**; 3.1)
Verbal: William Shakespeare, *Richard III* (**950**; 1.1–2, 3.3), *Romeo and Juliet* (**987**; 3.1), *Richard II* (**1002**; 2.1, 5.2), *As You Like It* (**1237**; 1.2, 2.2), *Hamlet* (**1259**; 1.2, 2.1–2, 3.1, 3.3, 4.1, 5.2), *Twelfth Night* (**1297**; 4.3), *Measure for Measure* (**1413**; 1.2), *The Moor of Venice* (**1437**; 2.1–2, 3.3, 4.1, 5.2), *King Lear* (**1486**; 3.1, 4.1, 4.3, 5.2), *Macbeth* (**1496**; 2.2, 4.1), *Coriolanus* (**1589**; 1.1), *The Tempest* (**1652**; 4.3)
Works Mentioned: Ovid, *Metamorphoses* (2.2); there is also a general reference to François Rabelais (4.3)

LANGUAGE
English
Latin: 4 words (2.2, 5.2; Fredegund, Charles, Clothair)
Spanish/Italian: 2 words (4.3; Guard)

FORM
Metre: pentameter and prose
Rhyme: blank verse
Act-Division: 5 acts
Lines (Spoken): 2,354 (2,201 verse, 153 prose)
Lines (Written): 2,525

STAGING
Doors: characters enter at two doors (1.3, 2.2, 3.1, 3.3, s.d.), and exit two ways (3.3, dialogue); beaten at (3.1, dialogue)
Discovery Space: a bed thrust forth (4.1, s.d.); curtained (5.2, implicit); two characters are discovered, sitting at either end of the space (5.2, s.d.)
Stage: mentioned (4.3, s.d.)
Within: music (1.1, 5.2, s.d.); speech (5.1, s.d.)
Above: two characters appear above (3.1, s.d.); music (4.3, s.d.)
Beneath: characters enter through a trapdoor in the stage (4.3, s.d.)
Miscellaneous: 'the bedchamber on fire', apparently intended as a physical effect (3.1, s.d.); Aphelia has her breast seared on stage (5.2, s.d.)

MUSIC
Music: flourish within (1.1, s.d.); alarum bell (2.2, s.d.); sad solemn music (3.3, s.d.); music above (4.3, s.d.); waits play softly (5.2, s.d.); a march softly within (5.2, s.d.); dead march within (5.2, s.d.)
Songs:
  1: 'Come, blest virgins, come and bring', 3.3, Nuns, 10 lines;
  2: 'Wisdom bids us shun the court', 4.3, 9 lines.

PROPS
Lighting: a torch (1.3, s.d.); a wax taper (2.2, s.d.); two or three lights (4.1, s.d.)
Pyrotechnics: fire (3.1, s.d.)
Weapons: a blade weapon (1.2, implicit); Clothair's dagger (2.2, 4.1, s.d.); Clothair's sword (2.2, dialogue; 5.2, s.d.); Clovis's sword (2.2, dialogue); six halberds (3.3, s.d.); an executioner's sword (3.3, s.d.); a knife (5.2, s.d.); a pan and hot irons (5.2, s.d.); a sword (5.2, s.d.); a pistol (5.2, dialogue)
Clothing: a ring (1.3, dialogue); another ring (2.1, dialogue; 3.3, s.d.; broken on stage)
Money: two bags of gold (1.1, s.d.); a purse (3.1, s.d.); an unspecified amount (4.2, implicit)
Food and Drink: wine (5.2, s.d.; drunk on stage); meat (5.2, s.d.; eaten on stage)
Small Portable Objects: a letter (1.1, s.d.); a diamond (1.3, dialogue; perhaps an earring); a book (2.2, s.d.); a miniature picture (3.1, dialogue; called a jewel); a letter (3.2, s.d.); another letter (3.3, 4.1, s.d.); a document (4.3, implicit); binding cords (5.2, implicit); a letter (5.2, implicit)
Large Portable Objects: a picture (1.2, s.d.; stabbed on stage); a hearse (3.3, s.d.), with a coffin (dialogue); two chairs (5.2, s.d./implicit); a third chair (5.2, s.d.)
Scenery: a curtain (1.2, s.d.); a bed (4.1, s.d.); a canopy or curtain (5.2, s.d.)
Miscellaneous: blood (2.2, dialogue)

COSTUMES AND MAKE-UP
LAMOT: disguised as a soldier (1.1, s.d.); dressed 'bravely' (1.2, s.d.); disguised as a surgeon (3.3, s.d.; 4.2–3, implicit); undisguised (4.3, s.d.)
DU MAYENNE: disguised as a soldier (1.1, s.d.); dressed 'bravely' (1.2, s.d.)
LANDRI: armour (3.1, s.d.); 'good clothes', including a a periwig (4.3, dialogue); bound (5.2, implicit); a garment with a sleeve (5.2, s.d.)
CASTRATO: black skin (dialogue)
FREDEGUND: golden hair (dialogue); night attire (3.1, s.d.); a garment with a train (3.3, s.d.); bound (5.2, s.d.)
CLOVIS: disguised (2.1, 3.3, s.d.); a scabbard (2.2, implicit); Childeric's gown and robes (4.3, s.d.; removed on stage)
APHELIA: golden hair (implicit); breasts (s.d.; the dialogue specifies 'globes of flesh'); gold and jewels (1.3, implicit); a garland on her head (3.3, s.d.); in her petticoat (5.2, s.d.); loose hair (5.2, implicit; she is dragged by it, so the wig must be firmly attached)
CLOTHAIR: a beard (dialogue); a cloak (2.2, dialogue); a dagger sheath (2.2, 4.1, implicit); a scabbard (2.2, 5.2, implicit)
BRISSAC: silver hair (dialogue)
LADIES: mourning clothes (3.3, s.d.)
NUNS, BOYS, and VIRGINS: white clothes (3.3, s.d.)

EARLY STAGE HISTORY
Performed by Queen Henrietta's Men, 'with great applause', by 1653 (and presumably before 1642).

EARLY TEXTUAL HISTORY
Before 1653: the play reportedly 'passed through many hands' in private transcripts, perhaps with corrupt texts.
  1653: ¹Q, printed for J. M. (probably John Marriott); collation A² B–I⁴ K², 36 leaves; title page names author and acting company; dedication to James and Isabella Compton, 3rd Earl and Countess of Northampton, signed with the initials of Anthony Turner and Andrew Pennycuicke; list of roles. One surviving copy has a variant dedication to Thomas Wriothesley, 4th Earl of Southampton.
  1654: Q₁ reissued with a cancel title page naming Andrew Pennycuicke as the bookseller.
  1661: ²Q₂ printed (in or before February) for Richard Gammon. The copy was Q₁, but the text is markedly degraded in quire K.

1675: rights transferred in the Stationers' Register from Richard Gammon to William Cademan on Saturday 13 March, in accordance with Gammon's note dated Saturday 2 January, and by order of a court held on Monday 22 February; entry names author; joint transfer with *King John and Matilda* (**2238**).

1687: On Saturday 26 March, Roger L'Estrange licensed a variant text for printing.

1687: ³Q₃ printed (as *The Eunuch*) by either Joseph Bennett or John Bradford for Dorman Newman; collation A² B-H⁴, 30 leaves; omits title-page reference to acting company, dedication.

1687: In June, Q₃ was advertised as for sale by Randolph Taylor.

EDITIONS
Anne Hargrove (Kalamazoo, 1978).
Carol A. Morley, in *The Plays and Poems of William Heminge* (Madison and Teaneck, 2006), 239–401.

REFERENCES
Annals 1639; Bentley, iv. 543–6; Charles R. Forker, *Skull Beneath the Skin* (Carbondale and Edwardsville, 1986), 503–4; Greg 714; Hazlitt, 82; Donald McGinn, *Shakespeare's Influence on the Drama of His Age* (1938), 43–8; *MP* 12 (1914), 51–64; *PBSA* 107 (2013), 42.

2413. The Rebellion

TEXT
Printed in 1640 (STC 20770).

GENRE
tragedy
Contemporary: play (S.R., comm. verses); tragedy (t.p., ded.); work (comm. verses); comedy (William London)

TITLE
Printed: *The Rebellion*

AUTHOR
Thomas Rawlins

DATE
Limits: 1629–36
Best Guess: 1633

The epistle and several of the Q commendatory verses emphasize the author's youth, which poses a problem: if the commendators mean that Rawlins was young in 1640 when he published the play, rather than whenever he wrote it, this discourages a date of composition long beforehand. Perhaps, though, he was simply younger than the men who mentioned his youth, Robert Chamberlain, J. Gough, and J. Knight. His date of birth is commonly given as 'c. 1620', but this seems to be nothing more than an inference from his earliest known work as a medallist, which dates from 1641.

In any event, the play must have been at least 4 years old at the time of its publication, since the company to which it is ascribed on the title page, the King's Revels, wound up its London operation in 1636; one commendator, R. W., explicitly says that he 'ne'er saw' the play, indicating that his opportunity to do so had passed. The claim of a phenomenal initial run followed by performances 'divers times since' also exerts pressure towards an earlier date. It may be relevant that the company included a larger than usual complement of younger men, and seems to have encouraged at least one of them, Thomas Jordan, in his scriptwriting.

The dating is also linked with the question of the original playhouse for which it was written: an early or late date within the limits (1630–2 or 1634–6) would make it a Salisbury Court play, while a date in the middle period (1632–4) would point to the Fortune. The play's soundscape features a level of noise that seems more consistent with the hypothesis of an outdoor playhouse like the Fortune.

ORIGINAL PRODUCTION
King's Revels Company, presumably at either the Fortune or Salisbury Court

PLOT
Machvile envies Antonio his popularity and also covets the crown. When the French, under Raymond the Moor, lay siege to Seville, Machvile engineers Antonio's downfall at a council of war: he speaks for a military strategy, Antonio responds with a proposal to make peace, and the city's Governor accuses Antonio of treason and cowardice; this provokes Antonio into killing the Governor. Antonio flees to his home, where he is appalled to find his sister Evadne kissing the tailor Giovanno. Before he can do more than protest, he is arrested by Machvile, who has succeeded to the governorship; but Giovanno and other tailors rescue him and he goes into hiding among them. Despite Giovanno's help, Antonio is unable to sanction his love for Evadne, being bound by a deathbed promise to his father only to allow her to marry a nobleman.

Machvile's aggressive strategy is put into effect: the Spanish break out of their besieged city and defeat the French; Giovanno captures Raymond, but Machvile takes charge of the prisoner and banishes the heroic tailor. Planning to seize the Spanish throne, he proposes an alliance with Raymond to divide the country between them, planning all the while to kill the Moor once his object is achieved. Meanwhile the captive Raymond looks for a way to communicate with France and ask for additional troops.

Antonio is told in a dream to flee, but is found, arrested, and sentenced to be ground to death in a mill. Aurelia, daughter of the captain of the mill, falls in love with him at first sight, asks for the privilege of executing him herself, and helps him to escape in disguise. Evadne is banished, but Giovanno meets her and rescues her from rape at the hands of bandits. Antonio finds them together, but Aurelia, fleeing with him, identifies Giovanno as her brother Sebastiano: he has adopted the guise of a tailor in order to woo Evadne.

The King comes to Seville incognito and stays with an old tailor, Giovanno's employer, who has overheard Machvile's plotting. Antonio and Sebastiano get confirmation in disguise, Antonio as a physician attending Machvile's wife and Sebastiano as a French cobbler whom Raymond engages as a messenger to the court of France, giving him his ring for authentication (which Sebastiano uses to dismiss the remaining French troops). The grateful King pardons Antonio and agrees to his marrying Aurelia. The plan is to give Machvile enough rope to hang himself. The King witnesses, in hiding, a meeting at which the army colonels, instigated by Antonio, pretend to offer Machvile their support. Thinking himself securely acknowledged as King of Spain, Machvile has Raymond assassinated; but the dying Raymond stabs him, and he in turn kills Antonio. Sebastiano's father permits him to marry Evadne; Aurelia, widowed before her wedding, is to spend the rest of her life in a convent. Only the tailors are unhappy: they don't get to perform *The Spanish Tragedy* for their royal guest.

SCENE DESIGNATION
1.1–4, 2.1–6, 3.1–5, 4.1–11, 5.1–3 (Q has act-division only)

Props remain on stage at 4.2–3 and 4.5–6.

ROLES
Signor ALERZO, a Spanish colonel
FULGENTIO, a Spanish colonel
PANDOLPHO, a Spanish colonel
Count ANTONIO, a young man, Evadne's brother; also called Lord Antonio; poses as a tailor, a hermit, and a physician and astrologer
Count MACHVILE, Auristella's husband; later Governor of Seville
EVADNE, Antonio's sister
Evadne's NURSE, an old woman
GIOVANNO, a young tailor; in reality, Sebastiano, Petruccio's son, Aurelia's brother; said to be little; also called Sebastine; also poses as a French tailor
RAYMOND, a Moor, general of the French, Philippa's husband
PHILIPPA, Raymond's wife
LEONIS, a French colonel
GILBERTI, a French colonel
FIRENZO, a French colonel
FRENCH SOLDIERS (1.3, *within*)
An OLD TAILOR
VIRMINE, a tailor with a theatrical bent; cast as the prologue (and other roles) in the planned performance
Two TAILORS in the Old Tailor's employ
VOICES (2.1, *within*)
The GOVERNOR of Seville
OFFICERS who arrest Antonio (2.2–4; only one speaks)
Two FRENCH SOLDIERS (2.6)
AURISTELLA, Machvile's wife
LOVE, a Cupid (3.3)
AURELIA, Petruccio's daughter, Sebastiano's sister
DEATH (3.3, *non-speaking*)
A JUDGE (3.5)
OFFICERS attending the Judge (3.5, *non-speaking*)
Captain PETRUCCIO, Governor of Filford Mill; a widower, father of Sebastiano and Aurelia
Petruccio' SERVANTS (3.5, *non-speaking*)
BANDITTI who capture Evadne (one or two speak)
The CAPTAIN of the banditti, who is old and impotent
TROTTER, a banditto
ATTENDANTS, who serve a banquet (4.5, *non-speaking*)
Two SERVANTS of Petruccio (4.5–6, *non-speaking*)
A TAILOR, perhaps a boy (4.8, 5.2)
KING PHILIP of Spain
Two SERVANTS of Machvile (4.10, *non-speaking*)
A BRAVO (5.3)
A GUARD (5.3, *non-speaking*)

Speaking Parts: 32–3
Allegorical Roles: 2

Stage Directions and Speech Prefixes
ALERZO: *Alerzo* (s.d.s and s.p.s); [one of] *the Colonels* (s.d.s); *Alerzo* [one of] *Three Spanish Colonels* (d.p.)
FULGENTIO: *Fulgentio* | [one of] *the Colonels* (s.d.s); *Ful<gentio>* (s.p.s); *Fulgentio* [one of] *Three Spanish Colonels* (d.p.)
PANDOLPHO: *Pandolpho* | [one of] *the Colonels* (s.d.s); *Pan<dolpho>* (s.p.s); *Pandolpho* [one of] *Three Spanish Colonels* (d.p.)
ANTONIO: *Antonio* (s.d.s); *Ant<onio>* (s.p.s); *Antonio a Count* (d.p.)
MACHVILE: *Count Machvile* | *Machvile* | *Matchvill* | *Machvill* (s.d.s); *Mach<vile>* (s.p.s); *Machvile a Count* (d.p.)
EVADNE: *Evadne* (s.d.s); *Evad<ne>* (s.p.s); *Evadne Antonio's Sister* (d.p.)
NURSE: *Nurse* (s.d.s and s.p.s); *Nurse Attendant on Evadne* (d.p.)
GIOVANNO: *Giovanno* | *Giavanno* (s.d.s); *Gio<vanno>* | *Gia<vanno>* (s.p.s); *Sebastiano, Petruchio's Son, in the disguise of a Tailor called Giovanno* (d.p.)
RAYMOND: *Raymond* | *Raimond* (s.d.s); *Ray<mond>* (s.p.s); *Raymond a Moor General of the French Army* (d.p.)
PHILIPPA: *Philippa* (s.d.s); *Phil<ippa>* (s.p.s); *Philippa the Moor's wife* (d.p.)
LEONIS: *Leonis* | [one of] *the Colonels* | [one of] *the French Colonels* (s.d.s); *Leo<nis>* (s.p.s); *Leonis* [one of] *Three French Colonels* (d.p.)
GILBERTI: *Gilberty* | [one of] *the Colonels* | [one of] *the French Colonels* (s.d.s); *Gil<berty>* (s.p.s); *Gilberty* [one of] *Three French Colonels* (d.p.)

FIRENZO: *Fyrenzo* | [one of] *the Colonels* | [one of] *the French Colonels* (s.d.s); *Fir<enzo>* (s.p.s); *Firenzo* [one of] *Three French Colonels* (d.p.)
FRENCH SOLDIERS: *Within* (s.p.s)
OLD TAILOR: *Old Tailor* (s.d.s, s.p.s, and d.p.); *the old Tailor* | [one of] *the rest of the Tailors* (s.d.s); *Old* | *1 Tailor* (s.p.s)
VIRMINE: *Virmine* | [one of the] *Tailors* | [one of] *the rest of the Tailors* | *Vermine* (s.d.s); *Virm<ine>* | *3 Tailor* (s.p.s); *Virmine* [the Old Tailor's] *man* (d.p.)
TAILORS: *two more* | *Tailors* | [some of] *the rest of the Tailors* | [two of] *three Tailors* (s.d.s); *2 Tailor* | *3 Tailor* (s.p.s); [two of] *Three Tailors more* (d.p.)
GOVERNOR: *the Governor* (s.d.s); *Governor* (s.p.s)
OFFICERS: *Officers* | *Guard* | *a Officer* (s.d.s; *sic*); *Officer* (s.p.s)
FRENCH SOLDIERS: *a Soldier* | *a second soldier* (s.d.s); *Soldier* | *2 Messenger* (s.p.s)
AURISTELLA: *Auristella* (s.d.s); *Aur<istella>* (s.p.s); *Auristella Machvile's wife* (d.p.)
LOVE: *Love* (s.d.s); *A Cupid* (d.p.)
AURELIA: *Aurelia* | *Aurelius* (s.d.s); *Aur<elia>* (s.p.s); *Aurelia Sebastiano's Sister* (d.p.)
DEATH: *Death* (s.d.s)
JUDGE: *a Criminal Judge* (s.d.s); *Judge* (s.p.s)
OFFICERS: *Officers* (s.d.s)
PETRUCCIO: *Petrucio* | *Petruchio* (s.d.s); *Pet<ruchio>* (s.p.s); *Petruchio, Governor of Filford* (d.p.)
SERVANTS: *servants* (s.d.s); *Attendants* (d.p.)
BANDITTI: *the Banditts* (s.d.s); *Banditto* | *3 Banditto* (s.p.s); *Two Ruffians* (d.p.)
CAPTAIN: [one of] *the Banditos* | *The Captain* (s.d.s); *Captain* (s.p.s); *Captain of the Banditti* (d.p.)
TROTTER: [one of] *the Banditos* | *Trotter* (s.d.s); *Trot<ter>* (s.p.s)
ATTENDANTS: *Attendants* (d.p.)
SERVANTS: *two servants* | *servants* (s.d.s); *Attendants* (d.p.)
TAILOR: [one of] *three Tailors* (s.d.s); *1 Tailor* [?] | *4 Tailor* (s.p.s); [one of] *Three Tailors more* (d.p.)
KING PHILIP: *the King* (s.d.s); *King* (s.p.s); *King of Spaine* (d.p.)
SERVANTS: *two Servants* (s.d.s); *Attendants* (d.p.)
BRAVO: *The Brave* (s.d.s); *Brave* (s.d.s and s.p.s); *a Brave* (d.p.)
GUARD: *a guard* | *guard* (s.d.s)

OTHER CHARACTERS
Belinda, mistress of Fulgentio or Pandolpho (1.1; but possibly generic or imaginary)
The people of Spain (1.1, 2.1, 3.2, 3.4, 4.10)
The French army (1.2–4, 2.1, 2.6, 3.1, 5.1, 5.3)
The Spanish army (1.3, 2.6)
The dead father of Antonio and Evadne (2.2, 2.5, 4.7)
The dead mother of Antonio and Evadne (2.2)
Machvile's father and mother (3.2)
Aurelia's dead mother (4.6)
The Senate (4.10)
The Grand Duchess of Chaves (4.11)
The Queen of France (4.11)
The Queen of Spain (4.11)
The Queen of England (4.11)
An apothecary, who sold Antonio poison (5.1)

SETTING
Period: sixteenth or seventeenth century (?): the King of Spain is named Philip, suggesting a date of either 1504–6 or after 1556
Time-Scheme: 1.1 takes place not long after dawn; 3.3 takes place at night
Place: Seville

Geography
Spain: Filford Mill; Bilbao
[*Portugal*]: Chaves
The Pyrenees
France
Italy: Sicily; Rome; Capri; Naples
The Low Countries: Flanders
England
[*Africa*]: Ethiopia; Egypt
The Antipodes

SOURCES
Narrative: William Shakespeare, *A Midsummer Night's Dream* (**1012**; 5.2); possibly Thomas Dekker, *The Gentle Craft* (**1188**)
Verbal: Bible: Genesis 9.6 (5.3, cited); Horace, *Odes* 4.1 (Chamberlain comm. verses); Thomas Kyd, *The Spanish Tragedy* (**783**; 5.2, cited); William Shakespeare, *Romeo and Juliet* (**987**; 5.3), *King Lear* (**1486**; 5.3)
Works Mentioned: Aesop, *Fables* (3.1); Sophocles, *Antigone* (3.2); Plato, *Republic* (E. B. comm. verses); Ludovico Ariosto, *Orlando furioso* (1516–32; 1.3, 4.4)

LANGUAGE
English
Latin: 4 words (4.8, 5.1; 2 Tailor, Antonio)
French: 18 words (4.11, 5.3; Sebastiano)
Dialect: When disguised as the French tailor, Sebastiano speaks in 'franglais'.

FORM
Metre: pentameter and prose; some tetrameter; Love speaks in trochaic tetrameter catalectic
Rhyme: blank verse; some couplets
Act-Division: 5 acts
Dumb Show: 3.3 (representing Antonio's dream)
Lines (Spoken): 2,134 (1,624 verse, 510 prose)

The verse is sometimes rough and hard to differentiate from prose; moreover, some prose is set as verse.

Lines (Written): 2,304

STAGING
Doors: characters enter severally (1.1, s.d.) and from two sides (3.3, s.d.), and exit severally (3.3, s.d.)

Discovery Space: a character hides behind the hangings (1.1, s.d.); Antonio is discovered 'sitting in a closet' (3.3, implicit); Giovanno and Evadne are discovered (4.7, s.d.)
Within: sound effects (1.2, 2.3, 2.6, 4.5, s.d.); shouts (2.6, s.d.); speech (2.1, 2.3, 4.1, s.d.); music (2.6, s.d.)
Above: Love descends 'halfway' (3.3, s.d.; presumably his speech is delivered while hanging there); five characters appear above (5.3, s.d.; it takes no more than 19 lines to get from above to the main stage)
Beneath: a chair descends into the stage (4.5, s.d.)
Stage Posts: one probably represents the tree to which Evadne is bound (4.4, dialogue)

MUSIC AND SOUND
Sound Effects: knocking within (1.2, s.d.); noise within (2.3, s.d.); confused noise within (2.6, s.d.); thunder (4.4, s.d.); pistol shot within (4.5, s.d.); noise of a mill within (4.5, s.d.); an unspecified noise (4.5, s.d.)
Music: alarum (1.3, 2.6, s.d.); drum (1.3, dialogue); alarum within (2.6, s.d.); soft music (3.3, s.d.)
Song: ' 'Tis a merry life we live', 4.8, three Tailors, solo and chorus, 10 lines

PROPS
Pyrotechnics: lightning (4.4, s.d.)
Weapons: unspecified weapons (2.1, implicit); Raymond's sword (2.6, dialogue; 5.3, implicit); Death's weapon (3.3, implicit); a dagger (4.4, implicit); Captain's sword (4.4, dialogue); a dag (4.5, s.d.; i.e. a pistol); two or more blade weapons (5.3, implicit)
Clothing: a gown (1.2, s.d.; 2.2, dialogue); a scarf or veil (4.2, s.d.; 4.3, dialogue); a gown (4.8, dialogue; also worn by Antonio); French garments (4.8, dialogue; also worn by Giovanno); a ring (4.11, dialogue)
Food and Drink: a banquet (4.5–6, s.d.)
Small Portable Objects: binding cords (4.4, implicit); a key or keys (4.5, dialogue); string (4.5, implicit)
Large Portable Objects: a table (2.1, s.d.); six chairs (2.1, s.d.); a seat (3.3, implicit); a table (4.5, s.d.); a chair (4.5, s.d.); a table (5.3, s.d.); eight stools (5.3, s.d.)
Scenery: hangings (1.1, s.d.); a shop-board (4.8, s.d.)

COSTUMES AND MAKE-UP
ANTONIO: disguised (3.3, s.d.) in tailor's livery (dialogue); a hermit's gown (4.7, s.d.); disguised as a physician (4.10, s.d.), in a gown (dialogue)
EVADNE: long hair (implicit; she is dragged by it in 4.2 and 4.4, so the wig needs to be securely attached); different clothes from those worn earlier in the play (4.2, implicit; 4.4, dialogue)
GIOVANNO: a cloak (1.2, dialogue); disguised as a Frenchman (4.11, 5.3, implicit)
RAYMOND: black skin (implicit); a steel corslet (1.3, dialogue)
LEONIS, GILBERTI, and FIRENZO: steel corslets (1.3, dialogue)
VIRMINE: a cloak (5.3, s.d.)
FIRST FRENCH SOLDIER: bloody (2.6, s.d.)

LOVE: wings (3.3, dialogue)
AURELIA: a hermit's gown (4.7, s.d.)
KING PHILIP: a crown (5.3, s.d.)

EARLY STAGE HISTORY
Performed by the King's Revels Company on nine consecutive days, and 'divers times' after that, 'with good applause'.

EARLY TEXTUAL HISTORY
1639: entered in the Stationers' Register to Daniel Frere on Wednesday 20 November; entry names author. Thomas Wykes had licensed the book for publication.
1640: Q printed by John Okes for Daniel Frere; collation A² ˣA⁴ B–I⁴ K², 40 leaves; title page names author and acting company; list of roles; authorial dedication to Robert Ducie of Aston; address to the reader; commendatory verses by Nathaniel Richards, C. G. (Christopher Gewen?), Robert Davenport, R. W., Robert Chamberlain, Thomas Jordan, J. Gough, E. B. (Edward Benlowes?), John Tatham, J. Knight, and Jo. Meriell.
c. 1640s: a copy of Q was in the possession of John Horne (Vicar of Headington, Oxfordshire). After his death, his entire collection of play-books passed into the possession of John Houghton of Brasenose College, Oxford (c. 1608–77), then to James Herne (died 1685), and then to the library of Ralph Sheldon (1623–84) at Weston, where it was catalogued by Anthony Wood, probably in the late 1670s.
1640–1: Humphrey Moseley was selling copies of Q for 6d.
1652: Q reissued with a cancel title page, omitting acting company and giving only author's initials.
1655: *Wit's Interpreter* entered to Nathaniel Brooke in the Stationers' Register on Wednesday 14 March.
1655: two extracts (from 2.2 and 4.11, entitled 'The French Tailor') and the song (headed 'The Tailors' Song') included in John Cotgrave's *Wit's Interpreter*, sigs. D6ᵛ–D7ʳ, Q7ʳ; printed for Nathaniel Brooke.
c. 1655: extracts transcribed by John Evans in a miscellany, *Hesperides*, intended for publication and entered to Humphrey Moseley in the Stationers' Register on Thursday 16 August 1655. The book remained unpublished in 1660, and Evans continued adding to the collection until at least 1666. Two MS exemplars are known; one was cut up by J. O. Halliwell-Phillipps in the nineteenth century; the other survives (Washington: Folger, MS V. b. 93).
1657: advertised as for sale by the Newcastle-upon-Tyne bookseller William London.
1658–62: advertised as for sale by Nathaniel Brooke.
Mid- to late seventeenth century (before 1689): a copy of Q was owned by Elizabeth Puckering.
1662: *Wit's Interpreter* reprinted (before Thursday 8 June) for Nathaniel Brooke; the extracts and song now appear on sigs. D2ʳ⁻ᵛ, M4ʳ⁻ᵛ.

1668: *The New Academy of Compliments* entered to Samuel Speed in the Stationers' Register on Saturday 2 May.

1669: Song included in *The New Academy of Compliments*, sig. I10^v; printed for Samuel Speed in or before February.

1671: *The New Academy of Compliments* reprinted for Thomas Rookes; the song now appears on sig. K5^{r-v}.

1671: *Wit's Interpreter* reprinted for Nathaniel Brooke and Obadiah Blagrave.

1680: rights to *The New Academy of Compliments* transferred in the Stationers' Register from Mary Rookes, widow and executrix of Thomas Rookes, to George Sawbridge on Wednesday 22 September.

1681: *The New Academy of Compliments* reprinted for George Sawbridge.

1684: Nicholas Cox (Manciple of St Edmund Hall, Oxford) had a copy of Q in his bookshop. It had probably been previously owned by Gerard Langbaine, and appears on a list compiled by Anthony Wood on Saturday 13 December.

1694: *The New Academy of Compliments* reprinted by Ichabod Dawks for Awnsham Churchill and John Churchill.

1698: *The New Academy of Compliments* reprinted by Ichabod Dawks for Awnsham Churchill and John Churchill.

REFERENCES
Annals 1636; Bentley, v. 995–8; Bodleian, MS Wood E. 4, art. 1, p. 4; Eyre & Rivington, i. 467, ii. 8, 386, iii. 95; Greg 582; Hazlitt, 191; *The Library*, 5th ser., 28 (1973), 294–308; *The Library*, 7th ser., 1 (2000), 376; *The Library*, 7th ser., 10 (2009), 372–404; William London, *A Catalogue of the Most Vendible Books in England* (London, 1657), sig. 2F1^v; *MLR* 13 (1918), 401–11; *Oxford Bibliographical Society Proceedings and Papers* 2.2 (1929), 133; *PMLA* 45 (1930), 801–3; *RES* 54 (2003), 601–14.

2414. *The Amazon*

TEXT
MS (London: British Library, Add. MS 88926, fos. 2^r–9^r); unfinished authorial draft.

The MS contains two states of sc.3, one heavily amended and the other a revised but incomplete fair copy, with an unplaceable fragment of dialogue in between.

If we were to hypothesize that the play was intended for court performance and was finished in another, lost draft, then a possible identification might be with **2485**.

GENRE
tragicomedy

TITLE
MS: *The Amazon*

AUTHOR
Edward, Lord Herbert of Cherbury

DATE
Limits: 1624–48

The play might be a *divertissement* of the Civil War years, reflecting Herbert's documented attitudes to divorce at that time, but an earlier date seems preferable in view of the Malone editors' identification of the MS paper as part of a stock in use in Herbert's household in 1623–4, during his time in France. However, the draft cannot have been written then, given that they also identify the unplaceable dialogue fragment as a borrowing from *The Sea Voyage* (**2020**), which Herbert could not have seen before his return to England in August 1624; the paper was, therefore, not a recent purchase when it was used. In any event, the English aristocratic vogue for this type of play is a phenomenon of the 1630s, not the 1620s; courtier play-writing became fashionable after *The Deserving Favourite* (**2262**) in 1629, and even more so after *The Shepherds' Paradise* (**2395**).

PLOT
The Amazons Orithya and Callirrhoe debate the desirability of divorce and the equality of the sexes. Because it is half an hour too early for temple worship, they go to the market place, where they hear a mountebank offering a marvellous unguent. They also read a prophecy engraved on a column, which warns of ruin should a man enter the temple.

Seven years ago, the children of the neighbouring king, Cleobulus, were kidnapped by pirates. The Delphic oracle has promised that they will be restored to him. He sends a messenger to the Amazons to inquire after their new young Queen and her sister, and debates with a counsellor the relative merits of love and war. The counsellor recommends that he should conquer the Amazons: if he tolerates a women's regime so close to his own borders, his other neighbours will infer that he is weak and attack him. Cleobulus, however, rejects the argument.

Polydorus and Aristander discuss the power of love. An unknown character encounters a huntress and falls in love. [*The rest of the play is lost, or unwritten.*]

SCENE DESIGNATION
sc.1–3 (MS undivided)

ROLES
ORITHYA, an Amazon
CALLIRRHOE, an Amazon
AGIRTE, a mountebank (originally written as Thaumasea)
CLEOBULUS, a king and father
A MESSENGER from Cleobulus to the Amazons (sc.2)
Cleobulus' COUNSELLOR (sc.2)
POLYDORUS
ARISTANDER

In the lost or unwritten part of the play
CALLICLEA, young Queen of the Amazons
MYOPS, a pedant

There is no way of knowing whether the lover and huntress in the dialogue fragment are distinct individuals, or identifiable with characters who appear elsewhere in the draft.

Speaking Parts: 8

Stage Directions and Speech Prefixes
ORITHYA: *Orethia* (s.d.s and s.p.s); *Oretheia Amazon* (d.p.)
CALLIRRHOE: *Callerrhoe* (s.d.s); *Call<errhoe>* (s.p.s); *Callerrhoe Amazon* (d.p.)
AGIRTE: *Agirte a Mountebank* (s.d.s and s.p.s); *Agirte* (s.p.s); *Thaumasea* (s.d.s, deleted)
CLEOBULUS: *Cleobulus* (s.d.s); *Cleob<ulus>* | *king* (s.p.s); *Cleobulus a king* (d.p.); *foster father* (d.p., deleted)
MESSENGER: *one* (s.d.s); *The Messenger* (s.p.s)
COUNSELLOR: *a Counsellor* (s.d.s)
POLYDORUS: *Polidorus* (s.d.s)
ARISTANDER: *Aristander* (s.d.s)
CALLICLEA: *Calliclea Amazon Queen* (d.p.)
MYOPS: *Myops a Pedant* (d.p.)

OTHER CHARACTERS
A priest whom Callirrhoe took prisoner at the gate of Thebes, and who asserted the necessity of marriage (sc.1)
A Persian from whom Agirte claims to have won an unguent in battle (sc.1)
A knight who bought the unguent at the price of his sword, or so Agirte claims (sc.1)
A maid who bought the unguent, and reportedly found it a more powerful attractant than her beauty (sc.1)
A priest who praised the superior powers of the unguent (sc.1)
Cleobulus' abducted children (sc.2)
Pirates who kidnapped Cleobulus' children (sc.2)
The recently dead Queen of the Amazons (sc.2; originally written as old but living)
Calliclea's sister (sc.2)
Cleobulus' people (sc.2)
The people of Cleobulus' other neighbouring kingdom (sc.2)

SETTING
Period: antiquity; the action takes place not long after a war between Greece and Persia
Place: Greece

Geography
[*Greece*]: Thebes; Delphos (i.e. Delphi); 'Pylian' (deleted)
Persia

SOURCES
Verbal: John Fletcher and Philip Massinger, *The Sea Voyage* (**2020**; dialogue fragment)

LANGUAGE
English

FORM
Metre: pentameter; some alternating pentameter and trimeter in the mountebank's speech
Rhyme: couplets; a little ABBA
Lines (Spoken): 254
Lines (Written): 310

MUSIC AND SOUND
Sound Effects: a striking clock (sc.1, dialogue)

The Malone editors take the text of sc.3 to be a song. They may be right, but it is not explicitly marked as one.

PROPS
Weapons: probably a bow and arrow (dialogue fragment, implicit)
Small Portable Objects: an unguent (sc.1, dialogue)
Scenery: a column, with a verse inscription (sc.1, dialogue)

EARLY STAGE HISTORY
In the list of roles, Myops appears to be annotated with a remark that the Malone editors take to be a note from Herbert to the producer of the play, recommending himself for this role. This seems unlikely, given that the MS is not a fair copy such as would be shown to a third party, but an incomplete and progressively rougher draft which doesn't even get as far as the first appearance of Myops. If the remark is a request to be cast in a particular role, its phrasing is also impractically opaque: 'If that you me will like, for I think myself to be lovely'. It might just as well be another fragment of dialogue such as appears between the two states of sc.3.

EARLY TEXTUAL HISTORY
1630s (?): partly drafted by Edward, Lord Herbert of Cherbury, in **MS**; the text occupies 12 pages on 8 leaves of a 28-leaf booklet; partial list of roles.

EDITION
Cristina Malcolmson, Matteo Pangallo, and Eugene Hill, MSC 17 (Manchester, 2015), 197–222.

REFERENCES
Around the Globe 44 (2010), 34–5; Beal Online HrE 143.5.

2415. 2 *The City Shuffler*

EVIDENCE
Sir Henry Herbert's office-book; list of MS plays said to have been in the possession of John Warburton (1682–1759), and destroyed by his cook (London: British Library, MS Lansdowne 807, fo. 1).

The Warburton list gives the title only as '*City Shuffler*'; there is no knowing whether the baked play was the first or second part (or indeed both).

GENRE
comedy (?)
Contemporary: play

TITLE
Performed: *The Second Part of The City Shuffler*

DATE
October 1633

ORIGINAL PRODUCTION
Prince Charles's Men (presumably) at Salisbury Court

PLOT
Part of the play may have glanced at a case of 1623 in which a goldsmith dishonestly gave inaccurate weights for items of silver plate in order to buy them at less than their true value.

ROLES
A dishonest CITIZEN

SOURCES
Narrative: The play was a sequel to or continuation of *The City Shuffler* (**2406**).

EARLY STAGE HISTORY
1633: performed at Salisbury Court in October. The goldsmith Edward Sewster complained about the play to Sir Henry Herbert, who forbade further performances until the company gave Sewster satisfaction. This was done the following day, and Sewster certified the same to Herbert.

REFERENCES
Annals 1633; Bawcutt 264; Bentley, v. 1309–10; *The Library*, 3rd ser., 2 (1911), 225–59; Sibley, 27.

2416. *Londini emporia* [London's Markets]

TEXT
Printed in 1633 (STC 13348); contains no substantive description of 4.

GENRE
civic pageant
Contemporary: triumphs, pageants, and shows (t.p.)

TITLE
Printed: *Londini emporia, or London's Mercatura*
Contemporary: *London's Emporia or Mercatura*
Later Assigned: *Device for Ralph Freeman, Clothworker*

AUTHOR
Thomas Heywood

DATE
29 October 1633

ORIGINAL PRODUCTION
London Clothworkers' Company, in the city streets. The route included: River Thames; St Paul's Churchyard; Cheapside; probably the Lord Mayor's house in Cornhill.

PLOT
The Genius of the River Thames is awoken by the arrival of the newly inaugurated Lord Mayor's barge. The Genius thanks the new incumbent for making his streams run clearer than ever, and tells him he will need the virtues symbolized by two nearby griffins. A shepherd encourages him to take care of his metaphorical flock, as he himself protects his sheep from the wolf. Mercury asserts the importance of seaborne trade. The cardinal virtues welcome the Lord Mayor to the Bower of Bliss.

That evening, the Lord Mayor is wished a good night's sleep in readiness for the task of government in the coming year. The signs of the zodiac serve as a conceit to commend him.

SCENE DESIGNATION
The pageant is here divided as follows:
 1: sea-chariot, on the Thames;
 2: Shepherd, at Paul's Churchyard;
 3: Mercury's ship, at the upper end of Cheapside;
 4: 'a model devised for sport to humour the throng' (not described by Heywood);
 5: *The Bower of Bliss*;
 6: Zodiac speech, at night.
Q numbers the shows as the first by water and the first to fourth by land (= 2–5); the final element is unnumbered.

ROLES
Two RIDERS on the griffins (1, *non-speaking*)
THAMESIS, the Genius of the River Thames, an old man
WATER-NYMPHS attending Thamesis (1, *non-speaking*)
A SHEPHERD (2)
MERCURY, god of eloquence, patron of trade, and messenger of the gods; represented as a young man (3)
PRUDENCE, a cardinal virtue (4)
TEMPERANCE, a cardinal virtue (4, *non-speaking*)
JUSTICE, a cardinal virtue (4, *non-speaking*)
FORTITUDE, a cardinal virtue (4, *non-speaking*)
FAITH, a handmaid and theological virtue (4, *non-speaking*)
HOPE, a handmaid and theological virtue (4, *non-speaking*)
CHARITY, a handmaid and theological virtue; also called Love (4, *non-speaking*)
A SPEAKER (5; may be one of the above)

The speaker of the farewell at the Lord Mayor's house would ordinarily have been a figure from one of the main shows. There is no indication of whether, or which, it was this time.

Speaking Parts: 4–5
Allegorical Roles: 7

Stage Directions
RIDERS: *those which ride upon these commixt Birds and Beasts* (s.d.s)
THAMESIS: *Thamesis, or the Genius of the River Thames* (s.d.s)
WATER-NYMPHS: [Thamesis'] *water Nymphs* (s.d.s)
SHEPHERD: *a Shepherd* | *the Shepherd* (s.d.s)
MERCURY: *Mercury* | *Mercurie* (s.d.s)
PRUDENCE: [one of] *the four Cardinal virtues* | *Prudence* (s.d.s)
TEMPERANCE: [one of] *the four Cardinal virtues* | *Temperance* (s.d.s)
JUSTICE: [one of] *the four Cardinal virtues* | *Justice* (s.d.s)
FORTITUDE: [one of] *the four Cardinal virtues* | *Fortitude* (s.d.s)
FAITH: [one of] *the three Theological virtues* | *Faith* (s.d.s)
HOPE: [one of] *the three Theological virtues* | *Hope* (s.d.s)
CHARITY: [one of] *the three Theological virtues* | *Charity* (s.d.s)

OTHER CHARACTERS
Neptune, father of Thamesis (1, 3)
Neptune's other sons (1)
The gods, who sent Mercury (3)

SETTING
Geography
England: River Thames; Staines; River Lea (or possibly Lee, near Barnet)
Italy: Genoa; Lucca; Florence; Naples; Latium
Spain: River Tagus
[*Europe*]: Moscow; Greece; Norway; Denmark; France; the Netherlands
[*Asia*]: Colchis; River Volga; Persia; Turkey; China; Hormuz
The East Indies
The West Indies
The Arctic
The Tropics

SOURCES
Verbal: Plato, *Apology* (desc.; cited); Aristotle, *Politics* (desc.; cited); Cicero, *De officiis* (desc.; cited); Virgil, *Aeneid* 1 (ded.), 'Caesar et Jupiter' (t.p. motto); Horace, *Epistles* 1.1 (desc.; cited); Livy, *Roman History* 4 (ded.; cited); Ovid, *Ex Ponto* 2.7 (desc.; cited); Bible: Matthew 6.19–21 (desc.); John 10.12 (desc.); Pseudo-Seneca, *Liber de moribus* (ded., cited); Plutarch, *Lives*: Solon (desc.); Epictetus, *Discourses* (desc.; cited); St John Chrysostom, *Commentary on Isaiah* (desc.; maxim wrongly ascribed to Plato); Nicholas Ling, *Politeuphuia* (1598; source of maxims ascribed to Hermes, Socrates, Plato, Cicero, and Epictetus)

LANGUAGE
English
Greek: 1 word (2; Shepherd)

FORM
Metre: pentameter
Rhyme: couplets
Dumb Shows: 4 is entirely in dumb show
Lines (Spoken): 204
Lines (Written): 473

STAGING
Stage: two or three pageant stages (2, desc.; 3, 5, implicit)
Audience: the Lord Mayor is directly addressed (1–3, 5–6), including as 'grave Praetor' (2, 5) and by name (2)

PROPS
Money: a golden purse (3, desc.)
Animals: two griffins drawing the chariot (1, desc.; each carries a performer on its back); sheep (2, desc.); a wolf (2, desc.); a dog (2, desc.); a cock (3, desc.)
Small Portable Objects: a caduceus (3, desc.)
Large Portable Objects: two staves with pennants depicting the Sheriffs' arms (1, desc.); a sundial (2, desc.); a sheep-hook (2, desc.)
Scenery: a sea-chariot adorned with shell-fish (1, desc.); a hill with trees and flowers (2, desc.); a ship (3, desc.); a bower (5, desc.; seats seven)

COSTUMES
WATER-NYMPHS: different coloured clothes (1, desc.)
MERCURY: has no beard; wings on his head and heels (3, desc.)

EARLY STAGE HISTORY
Preparation: On Saturday 24 August 1633, the court of the Clothworkers' Company appointed a committee to advise on purchases for the pageant, to select members to process, and to assess members for financial contributions. The five committee members were: Messrs Monger, Burnell, Ferrers, Trussell, Alexander. On Thursday 19 September, the court met with Gerard Christmas to discuss arrangements for the pageants. On Tuesday 24 September, the Court of Aldermen agreed that rooms in the Greenyard in Leadenhall could be used by Christmas and his workmen for completing the preparation of the pageants. The Master and Wardens of the company went to Leadenhall to inspect the pageants, apparently at night (since six torches were provided at a cost of 4s).

Performance: in London on Tuesday 29 October 1633 as part of the celebration of Ralph Freeman's inauguration as Lord Mayor. The performance took place at intervals during the day, from morning to evening; the pageants passed through Cheapside between noon and 3 p.m. The procession included: Vicenzo Gussoni (Venetian Ambassador); Albert Joachimi (Dutch Ambassador); Gouvert Brassert (Dutch Deputy). Also present was Justinian Pagitt.

Production Expenses
The principal cost of the production amounted to £140, which was paid to Thomas Allam and the other wardens of the yeomanry. A further 1s.6d was paid to porters for setting up the two griffins on the pageant house.

EARLY TEXTUAL HISTORY
1633: At some time before the day of the performance, Thomas Heywood read a draft of the text to the organizing committee.
    1633: **Q** printed by Nicholas Okes; collation A–B⁴ C², 10 leaves; title page names author and refers to performance; Latin title-page motto; title-page woodcut (the arms of the Clothworkers' Company); authorial dedication to Ralph Freeman.

EDITION
David M. Bergeron, in *Thomas Heywood's Pageants*, The Renaissance Imagination 16 (New York, 1986), 53–70.

REFERENCES
Annals 1633; Bentley, iv. 576; Bergeron, 226–9; *Cal. Ven.* 1632–6, 163; Greg 483; Hazlitt, 132; McGee-Meagher 1625–34, 77–8; *MRDE* 6 (1993), 191; MSC 5, 11–13; REED: Inns of Court, 808; Withington, ii. 41.

2417. The Guardian

TEXT
Printed in 1655 (Wing M1050), probably from a scribal transcript of authorial papers (by the same scribe who prepared copy for *The Bashful Lover*, **2545**).

GENRE
comedy
Contemporary: play (prol.); comical history (t.p.)

TITLE
Performed/Printed: *The Guardian*

AUTHOR
Philip Massinger

DATE
October 1633

ORIGINAL PRODUCTION
King's Men at the Blackfriars (and perhaps also the Globe)

PLOT
Durazzo is an indulgent guardian to his heavy-spending ward Caldoro, but has doubts about his latest endeavour: to marry into the family of the disgraced Severino, who has fled Naples after murdering his brother-in-law. Unfortunately the girl in question, Severino's daughter Caliste, does not love Caldoro: she would rather marry the libertine Adorio, who himself is only interested in sex with her, not marriage. Overhearing Adorio's insulting treatment of her after a church service, Caldoro intervenes to defend her honour. Caliste is grateful but remains infatuated with Adorio. For his part, Adorio plans to fight a duel with Caldoro, but is frustrated when Durazzo removes his ward to the country. Caliste's mother Iolante is scandalized that she has used religion as a cover to see Adorio, and confines her to the house; but Caliste sends Adorio a message asking his help to escape. Meanwhile, deprived of her husband's company, Iolante is attracted to Laval, a Frenchman in the entourage of the Milanese army, which is passing through Naples en route to attack Rome; she has her neighbour Calypso arrange a date with him.

Caldoro persuades his guardian to help in his love-affair, and they return to Naples on the night planned for Caliste's elopement and Iolante's assignation. In the dark, Caliste mistakes Caldoro for Adorio and leaves with him; Adorio then goes off with Caliste's maid Myrtilla, who was expecting to be summoned to attend on her wedding night. Severino, now leader of a gang of banditti, returns to Naples in disguise to see Iolante, but quickly realizes she is expecting someone else. Disbelieving her claim to be merely celebrating their wedding anniversary, he ties her up and withdraws to consider what action to take; but while he is away, Calypso swaps places with Iolante, enabling her to see Laval. Not noticing the substitution, Severino cuts off Calypso's nose, then searches the house for Caliste. Iolante's meeting with Laval entails a stern lecture about chastity rather than the sex she expected. Afterwards, she and Calypso swap places again, and Severino is amazed to see the severed nose restored as if by miracle, which he takes as confirmation of Iolante's innocence. Ashamed of his jealousy, he takes her to join him in exile as queen of the banditti. Upon hearing that he has dared to enter Naples, King Alfonso pursues him into the woods.

Caliste and Adorio are both disappointed to find that they have eloped with the wrong partners. Adorio's exhausted party fall asleep in the woods. Durazzo comes upon Adorio resting in Myrtilla's lap, and shows Caliste; this puts an end to her feelings for him, and she transfers her love to Caldoro. She also takes back a love-gift, a jewel worn in Adorio's hat; when he wakes, Myrtilla is accused of stealing it. Both eloping parties and King Alfonso are captured by the banditti and forced to hand over their purses. When Alfonso tells how his two sons were captured by pirates after performing heroic deeds against the Turks, Severino offers all the banditti's spoils for their ransom. Even so, Alfonso has sworn never to pardon murder, and intends to exact justice. This proves unnecessary when Laval reveals that he is in fact the missing brother-in-law, who was not murdered at all but went into exile after his quarrel with Severino. Alfonso declares a general pardon and allows the young women to choose their husbands. Caliste selects Caldoro and Myrtilla, Adorio, who becomes less unwilling to marry her upon hearing that she too is of noble birth.

SCENE DESIGNATION
prol., 1.1–2, 2.1–5, 3.1–9, 4.1–3, 5.1–4, ep. (O has act-division only)

Edwards treats the night sequence (3.5–8) as a single scene; he therefore numbers 3.9 as 3.6.

ROLES
PROLOGUE
Lord DURAZZO, Caldoro's uncle and guardian; an old gentleman in his fifties
CAMILLO, a gentleman
Signor LENTULO, a gentleman
DONATO, a gentleman
Two SERVANTS (1.1, *non-speaking*)
Lord ADORIO, a young libertine gentleman
CALISTE, a gentlewoman, daughter of Severino and Iolante, Montecларо's niece; less than 17 years old
MYRTILLA, Caliste's maid; turns out to be of noble birth
CALDORO, Durazzo's nephew and ward, a young man
Madonna IOLANTE, Severino's wife of 17 years, Montecларо's sister, Caliste's mother
CALYPSO, Iolante's neighbour and confidante
ALFONSO, King of Naples, an old man and a father
Duke MONTPENSIER, General of Milan
Monsieur LAVAL, a French gentleman; in reality, Monteclaro, Iolante's brother, Caliste's uncle
ATTENDANTS on Alfonso (2.1, *non-speaking*)
A CAPTAIN of the Neapolitan guard (2.1, 4.3, 5.3)
CARIO, Adorio's servant
CLAUDIO, Severino's servant
Signor SEVERINO, a banished man, captain of the banditti; Iolante's husband, Caliste's father
Six BANDITTI (two may only speak collectively)
Durazzo's SERVANT (3.1, 4.1)
Adorio's SERVANTS (3.3, 3.5, 3.7; one speaks)
COUNTRYMEN, Adorio's tenants; two play Juno and Hymen in the nuptial show (4.2; only two speak)
SINGERS (5.1)
EPILOGUE

Speaking Parts: 29

Stage Directions and Speech Prefixes
PROLOGUE: *Prologue* (heading)

DURAZZO: *Durazzo* | *Durazo* (s.d.s); *Duraz<zo>* (s.p.s; also misprinted *Duzar.*); *Durazzo, the Guardian* (d.p.)
CAMILLO: *Camillo* (s.d.s); *Camil<lo>* (s.p.s); *Camillo, [one of the] Neapolitan Gentlemen* (d.p.)
LENTULO: *Lentulo* (s.d.s); *Lent<ulo>* (s.p.s); *Lentulo, [one of the] Neapolitan Gentlemen* (d.p.)
DONATO: *Donato* (s.d.s); *Donat<o>* (s.p.s); *Donato, [one of the] Neapolitan Gentlemen* (d.p.)
SERVANTS: *two Servants* (s.d.s); *Servants* (d.p.)
ADORIO: *Adorio* (s.d.s); *Ador<io>* (s.p.s); *Adorio, Beloved by Caliste* (d.p.)
CALISTE: *Caliste* (s.d.s and s.p.s); *Caliste,* [Iolante's] *Daughter* (d.p.)
MYRTILLA: *Mirtilla* (s.d.s); *Mirtil<la>* (s.p.s); *Mirtilla, Caliste's Maid* (d.p.)
CALDORO: *Caldoro* (s.d.s); *Cald<oro>* (s.p.s); *Caldoro,* [Durazzo's] *Ward, in love with Caliste* (d.p.)
IOLANTE: *Iolante* (s.d.s); *Iolant<e>* (s.p.s); *Iolantre, Wife to Severino* (d.p.; *sic*)
CALYPSO: *Calypso* (s.d.s); *Calyp<so>* (s.p.s); *Calypso, the Confidante of Iolantre* (d.p.; *sic*)
ALFONSO: *Alphonso* (s.d.s); *Alpho<nso>* (s.p.s); *Alphonso, King of Naples* (d.p.)
MONTPENSIER: *General* (s.d.s and s.p.s); *General of Milain* (d.p.)
LAVAL: *Monteclaro* (s.d.s); *Monte<claro>* (s.p.s); *Monteclaro,* [Severino's] *Brother in law, disguised* (d.p.)
ATTENDANTS: *Attendants* (s.d.s)
CAPTAIN: *Captain* (s.d.s and s.p.s); *Captains* (d.p.)
CARIO: *Cario* (s.d.s); *Car<io>* (s.p.s); *Cario, Servant to Adorio* (d.p.)
CLAUDIO: *Claudio* (s.d.s); *Claud<io>* (s.p.s); *Claudio, Servant to Severino* (d.p.)
SEVERINO: *Severino* (s.d.s); *Sever<ino>* (s.p.s); *Severino, a Nobleman banished* (d.p.)
BANDITTI: *six Banditti* | *all the Banditti* | *two Banditti* (s.d.s); *1* | *2* | *3* | *4* | *1 Bandit* | *2 Bandit* | *3 Bandit* (s.p.s); *Banditti* (s.d.s and d.p.)
SERVANT: *Servant* (s.d.s and s.p.s); [one of the] *Servants* (d.p.)
SERVANTS: *Servants* (s.d.s and d.p.); *Servant* (s.d.s and s.p.s)
COUNTRYMEN: *Country-men* | *Rustici* | *Juno* | *Hymen* (s.d.s)
SINGERS: *Singers* (s.d.s)
EPILOGUE: *Epilogue* (heading)

OTHER CHARACTERS
Durazzo's doctor (1.1; possibly hypothetical)
Durazzo's grandmother (1.1)
Durazzo's huntsmen on his country estate (1.1)
Durazzo's tenants and their sexy daughters (1.1)
Myrtilla's confessor, a learned man (1.2)
A Frenchman who once cured Calypso of a young woman's malady (2.1)
The King of Milan (2.1)
Caliste's dead grandfather (2.3)

A woman whom Durazzo admires but does not aspire to bed (3.1; possibly hypothetical)
A songwriter employed by Cario to write Adorio's nuptial show (3.3)
The Neapolitan watch (3.3, 3.8–9)
The Constable of Naples (3.3)
The porter of the gates of Naples (3.3)
The priest who married Severino and Iolante (3.9)
Durazzo's mother (4.1)
People robbed by the banditti (5.3)
The Queen of Spain (5.4)
Alfonso's twin sons, who are now prisoners of African pirates (5.4)
The master and sailors of the ship on which Alfonso's sons sailed (5.4)
1,000 galley-slaves rescued from Turkish captivity by Alfonso's sons (5.4)
The pirates of Tunis and Argier (5.4)
A noble sea-captain, Myrtilla's father (5.4)

SETTING
Period: The King of Naples is named Alfonso, which might indicate either Alfonso I (reigned 1442–58) or Alfonso II (reigned 1494–5); however, Camillo has read a book by Carranza that was published in 1569.
Time-Scheme: 2.3 takes place in the morning; 3.5–9 take place during the night ensuing 2.5, with 3.5 at 11 p.m. and 3.8 at midnight; three days pass between 1.1 and 4.2, and at least three hours between 3.7 and 4.2; 5.2 takes place at night
Place: Naples

Geography
Naples: the West Gate
Italy: Rome; Milan; Tuscany; Venice
Greece: Sparta
[*Europe*]: Spain; France; [the Alps]; Germany; the Low Countries
England
[*Asia*]: Turkey; Persia; Jerusalem; the Persian Gulf
The East Indies
Africa: Egypt; Tunis; Argier
The West Indies

SOURCES
Narrative: Hendrik van der Putten, *Comus* (1608, repr. 1611)
Verbal: Bible: Isaiah 3.15 (2.4); Ovid, *Ars amatoria* (1.1, cited); Christopher Marlowe, *The Jew of Malta* (**828**; 4.1)
Works Mentioned: *Amadis de Gaul* (fourteenth century; 1.2); Francisco Vazquez, *Palmerin d'Oliva* (1511; English tr. by Anthony Munday, 1588; 1.2); Francisco de Moraes, *Palmerin of England* (1547; English tr. by Anthony Munday, 1581; 1.2); Diego Ortúñez de Calahorra, Pedro de la Sierra, and Marcos Martínez, *Espejo de principes y caballeros* (1555–87; English tr., *The Mirror of Princely Deeds and Knighthood*, by Margaret Tyler, R. P., and L. A., 1578–99; 1.2); Jerónimo de Carranza, *De la filosofía de las armas* (1569; 3.3)

LANGUAGE
English
Latin: 8 words (2.2, 2.5, 3.9, 5.4; Calypso, Durazzo, Caldoro)
Greek: 2 words (3.1; Durazzo)
French: 1 word (4.3; Laval)

FORM
Metre: pentameter; a little prose
Rhyme: blank verse
Prologue: 32 lines, in couplets
Act-Division: 5 acts
Epilogue: 14 lines, in couplets
Lines (Spoken): 2,467 (2,445 verse, 22 prose)
Lines (Written): 3,176

STAGING
Doors: a character listens at the door (3.5, dialogue); a character 'speaks at the door' (3.9, s.d.); doors are thrown open violently (3.9, s.d.; only to admit one character, so the plural may suggest double-doors); characters enter at two or three doors (5.4, s.d.)
Discovery Space: set with a banquet (3.9, implicit)
Within: speech (3.7, s.d.); sound effect (4.1, s.d.); music (4.2, implicit; 5.4, s.d.)
Audience: addressed as 'gentlemen' (prol.)
Miscellaneous: the action is organized to avoid bringing horses on stage (3.1, 4.1, 5.2); a scene begins with a character speaking at length from behind the discovery space curtain, before anyone else enters (3.9); Calypso's nose is cut off on stage (3.9, implicit)

Edwards infers from Calypso's reference to Severino's teeth that he literally bites her nose off. However, the stage direction pointedly equips him with a knife when he enters immediately before doing so, and there is no other reason for him to have it.

MUSIC AND SOUND
Sound Effects: noise within of a horse falling over (4.1, s.d.)
Music: cornett within (4.2, dialogue; 5.4, s.d.); stringed instruments and hautboys (4.2, dialogue)
On-Stage Music: Severino blows a horn (2.4, s.d.)
Songs:
  1: 'Enter a maid, but made a bride', 4.2, Juno and Hymen, in parts, 24 lines;
  2: 'Welcome, thrice welcome, to this shady green', 5.1, Singers, 22 lines.
Dance: Countrymen dance (4.2, s.d.)

PROPS
Lighting: tapers (3.9, s.d.)
Weapons: Adorio's sword (1.1, implicit; 5.2, dialogue); Caldoro's sword (1.1, implicit); Camillo's sword (1.1, implicit; 5.2, dialogue); Lentulo's sword (1.1, implicit;

5.2, dialogue); Donato's sword (1.1, implicit; 5.2, dialogue); a poniard (3.9, s.d.); a knife (3.9, s.d.); three pistols (5.2, s.d.)
Musical Instruments: a horn (2.4, s.d.).
Clothing: a scarf (3.9, dialogue; used to tie up Iolante)
Money: a purse full of crowns (2.2, s.d.); gold (2.3, dialogue; 3.4, implicit); an unspecified sum (4.3, implicit); a bag containing a thousand crowns (5.4, dialogue); seven purses (5.4, s.d.); three bags of gold (5.4, s.d.)
Food and Drink: a rich banquet (3.9, s.d.)
Small Portable Objects: a petition (2.1, s.d.); a jewel (2.2, s.d.); a letter (2.3, s.d.); another jewel (2.3, s.d.; later worn in Adorio's hat); a document (2.4, implicit); table-books (2.4, dialogue); a watch (3.5, dialogue); a key (3.8, dialogue); another key (3.9, s.d.); a casket of jewels (5.4, s.d.)
Large Portable Objects: a chair (3.9, s.d.)
Scenery: a curtain (3.9, s.d.)
Miscellaneous: blood (3.9, dialogue)

COSTUMES AND MAKE-UP
DURAZZO: is fat (implicit); a grey beard (dialogue); a collar (1.1, dialogue); breeches (1.1, dialogue)
CAMILLO, LENTULO, and DONATO: hangers (1.1, implicit)
ADORIO: hangers (1.1, 5.2, implicit); a hat with a jewel in it (5.2, dialogue; the jewel is removed on stage; see also PROPS)
CALISTE: a gown (1.1, implicit); richly habited (3.2, s.d.), in a gown with dressings (dialogue); a veil (4.1, dialogue); a mask (5.4, dialogue)
MYRTILLA: Caliste's gown from the first scene (3.2, s.d.; 3.7, 4.2, implicit); a mask (3.7, implicit; 4.2, s.d.; removed on stage)
CALDORO: curly hair (dialogue); muffled (1.1, s.d.); hangers (1.1, implicit)
IOLANTE: a mantle (3.9, dialogue; removed on stage); Calypso's nightgown (3.9, implicit); an oak-leaf garland (5.1, s.d.)
CALYPSO: a nightgown (3.9, dialogue; removed on stage); Iolante's mantle (3.9, implicit; put on on stage); noseless (3.9, 4.3, dialogue)
ALFONSO: disguised (5.3-4, implicit; removed on stage)
LAVAL: fashionable French clothes (2.1, dialogue)
SEVERINO: an oak-leaf garland (5.1, s.d.)

EARLY STAGE HISTORY
1633: presumably performed by the King's Men, as licensed.
1634: performed at court, presumably at Whitehall Palace, by the King's Men on Sunday 12 January. The audience included: King Charles I; Queen Henrietta Maria. The performance was 'well liked'. John Lowin, Joseph Taylor, and Eliard Swanston were later paid £220 for this and 21 other court performances during the preceding year, by a warrant dated either Sunday 27 or Monday 28 April 1634.

1641: The play was in the repertory of the King's Men. It was later reported (in 1669) as having been performed by them at the Blackfriars before 1642; the 1655 title page says that it was 'often acted' by them there, 'with great applause'.

EARLY TEXTUAL HISTORY
1633: On Thursday 31 October, Sir Henry Herbert licensed the play for performance by the King's Men.
1641: On Saturday 7 August, Robert Devereux, 3rd Earl of Essex (Lord Chamberlain) issued a warrant prohibiting the printing of this and sixty other plays without the consent of the King's Men. On Saturday 14 August, the order was read to the Stationers' Company and instructions issued for its observance.
1653: entered (as a double title with *The City Honest Man*, **2426**) to Humphrey Moseley in the Stationers' Register on Friday 9 September; play and author individually named as part of a group entry of 41 (or 55) plays.
1655: included as the second of Philip Massinger's *Three New Plays* (O), sigs. G5^r–N5^r, 97 pages on 49 leaves; printed by Thomas Newcomb for Humphrey Moseley; title page names author, acting company, and playhouse; list of roles.
1655: George Thomason acquired a copy of O on Thursday 14 June. In c. 1678, some years after his death, his entire collection of books and tracts was acquired by the bookbinder Samuel Mearne, acting as agent for King Charles II; the King never paid him, and the books remained in Mearne's family until 1761.
1657: O advertised as for sale by the Newcastle-upon-Tyne bookseller William London; the list names John Fletcher as the author.
1660: entered to Humphrey Moseley in the Stationers' Register on Friday 29 June; individually named as part of a group entry of 26 plays.
1680: extracts (from 1.1–2, 2.3, 2.5, 3.2, 3.5–7, 4.1–2, 5.2, with some characters renamed and combined with material from *A Very Woman*, **2043**, and *The Bashful Lover*, **2545**) appear as the droll, *Love Lost in the Dark, or The Drunken Couple*, included in *The Muse of Newmarket*, sigs. D4^r–E2^r, E3^v, F1^r–F2^r; printed for Daniel Browne, Daniel Major, and James Vade.
1684: Nicholas Cox (Manciple of St Edmund Hall, Oxford) had a copy of O in his bookshop. It had probably been previously owned by Gerard Langbaine, and appears on a list compiled by Anthony Wood on Saturday 13 December.

Humphrey Moseley's double titles are discussed under **1643**.

EDITION
Philip Edwards, in *The Plays and Poems of Philip Massinger*, ed. Philip Edwards and Colin Gibson (Oxford, 1976), iv. 107–200, v. 242–9.

2418. The Gamester

REFERENCES
Annals 1633; Bawcutt 269, 282; Bentley, iv. 789–90; Bodleian, MS Wood E. 4, art. 1, p. 47; Greg 759; Hazlitt, 99; William London, *A Catalogue of the Most Vendible Books in England* (London, 1657), sig. 2F1ᵛ; MSC 1.4–5, 364–9; MSC 6, 84; Allardyce Nicoll, *A History of English Drama*, 4th edn (Cambridge, 1952–9), i. 354; *PBSA* 107 (2013), 30; Steele, 246.

2418. The Gamester

TEXT
Printed in 1637 (STC 22443).

GENRE
comedy
Contemporary: play (S.R.)

TITLE
Performed/Printed: *The Gamester*

AUTHOR
James Shirley

DATE
November 1633

ORIGINAL PRODUCTION
Queen Henrietta's Men at the Cockpit

PLOT
Wilding is sexually uninterested in his wife, but propositions her ward, Penelope, with the promise that afterwards he will find her a husband. Penelope agrees to sex with him only if Mistress Wilding consents, so Wilding duly asks his wife. Mistress Wilding encourages Penelope to agree—in order to facilitate a plot. Penelope insists on a midnight assignation: Wilding is to come in the dark and neither of them shall speak during the encounter. The plan is for Mistress Wilding to take Penelope's place. When the evening comes, however, Wilding is more interested in a gambling event at an ordinary, and sends Hazard to sleep with Penelope in his place; but after losing his money in the game, he envies Hazard his more pleasurable night. Then Mistress Wilding tells him of the substitution, and he is tormented with the thought of being a cuckold, until he realizes that Hazard still thinks he slept with Penelope. He puts it to Hazard that they should marry, but Hazard is unwilling, until he hears of Penelope's £2,000 estate. He woos and marries her, then tells Wilding that the earlier assignation did not go as expected: both Mistress Wilding and Penelope were there, armed with a light and planning to rebuke Wilding for his lechery. No sex took place, and so Wilding is no cuckold.

In the sub-plot, the friends Delamore and Beaumont fall out in a drunken argument about their respective girlfriends, Leonora and Violante, and Beaumont wounds Delamore. One man is taken to a surgeon, the other to prison. Leonora's father, Sir Richard Hurry, is delighted—he disapproves of Delamore and has a debt of honour to the Beaumont family—and endeavours to find a way of saving Beaumont from prosecution for murder. The terms he puts to Beaumont, however, are that he shall marry Leonora on his release, breaking off his engagement to Violante. Beaumont refuses, and Violante, who has overheard the conversation after bribing the jailer, cannot persuade him to change his mind and save his life. When he continues to refuse, Hurry agrees to his marrying Violante instead of Leonora. It emerges that Delamore is alive, so Beaumont is no longer in danger of capital proceedings.

In the third plot, the rich citizen Barnacle pays Hazard to lose a staged quarrel with his nephew, Young Barnacle, in order to give the youth a dangerous reputation that will allow him to walk the streets safely. Young Barnacle proves ludicrously inept at picking a fight, but Hazard eventually takes his beating. Old Barnacle then talks up the young man's new reputation by offering his services as a fighter to all and sundry. Hazard scares the youth by having Wilding's page pose as a midget soldier; Young Barnacle will not dare to fight even him, but is not cured of his swaggering humour. Old Barnacle worries that his nephew has become too brave, and therefore foolhardy: he provokes quarrels that sooner or later will get him killed. He pays Hazard to humble him again, so Hazard gives the young man a beating, which tames him.

SCENE DESIGNATION
1.1, 2.1–3, 3.1–4, 4.1–2, 5.1–2 (Q has act-division only)

ROLES
Master Jack WILDING, a married man
Mistress PENELOPE, a rich gentlewoman, Mistress Wilding's ward and distant relation; later Hazard's wife; also called Pen
MISTRESS WILDING, formerly a rich widow, now Wilding's wife, Penelope's guardian
Master Will HAZARD, a gentleman gamester; later Penelope's husband
OFFICERS, who take Delamore to a surgeon (1.1; two speak)
Jack DELAMORE, a gentleman, Beaumont's friend (1.1, *non-speaking*)
OFFICERS, who arrest Beaumont (1.1, *non-speaking*)
Master Ned BEAUMONT, a young gentleman of a noble family, Delamore's friend
Master ACRELESS, a gentleman gamester
Master LITTLESTOCK, a gentleman gamester
Master Frank SELLAWAY, a gentleman gamester
OLD Master BARNACLE, a rich citizen, Young Barnacle's uncle

A PAGE, Wilding's servant; poses as Ensign Petard, a soldier
DRAWERS (2.2; one or two speak)
A FIDDLER (2.2)
YOUNG BARNACLE, a would-be gentleman, Old Barnacle's nephew; formerly a university student
DWINDLE, Young Barnacle's man
Mistress LEONORA, Hurry's daughter and heir, Delamore's sweetheart
Mistress VIOLANTE, Beaumont's sweetheart
A SERVANT in Hurry's household (2.3)
Sir Richard HURRY, a knight, Leonora's father
A SERVANT in Hurry's household (3.2; may be the same servant as in 2.3)
Master PROBE, a surgeon
A BOX-KEEPER at the ordinary (3.3)
A LORD (3.3, *non-speaking*)
A KNIGHT (3.3, *non-speaking*)
A COUNTRY GENTLEMAN (3.3, *non-speaking*)
A SERVANT attending Mistress Wilding, Penelope, and Leonora (4.1, *non-speaking*)
A JAILER (4.2)
A SERVANT attending Mistress Wilding (5.2, *non-speaking*)
OFFICERS, who bring Beaumont from prison (5.2, *non-speaking*)

Speaking Parts: 23–5

Stage Directions and Speech Prefixes
WILDING: *Master Wilding | Wilding* (s.d.s); *Wild<ing>* (s.p.s)
PENELOPE: *Mistress Penelope | Penelope* (s.d.s); *Pene<lope>* (s.p.s)
MISTRESS WILDING: *Mistress Wilding* (s.d.s); *Mistress | Mistress Wi<lding>* (s.p.s)
HAZARD: *Hazard | Master Hazard* (s.d.s); *Ha<zard>* (s.p.s)
OFFICERS: *Officers* (s.d.s); *1 Officer | 2 Officer* (s.p.s)
DELAMORE: *Delamore* (s.d.s)
OFFICERS: *Officer* (s.d.s)
BEAUMONT: *Beaumont | Master Beaumont* (s.d.s); *Bea<umont> | Beo<mont>* (s.p.s)
ACRELESS: *Acre-lesse* (s.d.s); *Acr<e-lesse>* (s.p.s)
LITTLESTOCK: *Little-stocke* (s.d.s); *Lit<tle-stock>* (s.p.s)
SELLAWAY: *Sell-away | Sel-away* (s.d.s); *Sel<l-away>* (s.p.s)
OLD BARNACLE: *Master Barnacle | Barnacle | old Barnacle* (s.d.s); *Bar<nacle> | Uncle* (s.p.s)
PAGE: *the Page* (s.d.s); *Page* (s.d.s and s.p.s)
DRAWERS: *Drawers* (s.d.s); *Drawer* (s.d.s and s.p.s)
FIDDLER: *Fiddler* (s.d.s and s.p.s)
YOUNG BARNACLE: *[Barnacle's] Nephew* (s.d.s); *Nephew* (s.d.s and s.p.s)
DWINDLE: *Dwindle* (s.d.s); *Dwi<ndle>* (s.p.s)
LEONORA: *Leonara | Leonora | Mistress Leonora* (s.d.s); *Leo<nora>* (s.p.s)
VIOLANTE: *Violante* (s.d.s); *Vio<lante>* (s.p.s)

SERVANT: *Servant* (s.d.s and s.p.s)
HURRY: *Sir Richard Hurry | Sir Richard* (s.d.s); *Hu<rry>* (s.p.s)
SERVANT: *Servant* (s.d.s and s.p.s)
PROBE: *Surgeon* (s.d.s and s.p.s); *Pr<obe>* (s.p.s)
BOX-KEEPER: *a Box-keeper* (s.d.s); *Box-keeper* (s.p.s)
LORD: *a Lord* (s.d.s)
KNIGHT: *a Knight* (s.d.s)
COUNTRY GENTLEMAN: *a Country gentleman* (s.d.s)
SERVANT: *a Servant* (s.d.s)
JAILER: *[Beaumont's] keeper* (s.d.s); *Keeper* (s.p.s)
SERVANT: *a Servant* (s.d.s)
OFFICERS: *Officers* (s.d.s)

OTHER CHARACTERS
Penelope's dead father (1.1)
Hazard's mother (1.1)
Ladies with whom Wilding consorts (2.1)
Penelope's tailor (3.1)
A merchant who comes to gamble at the ordinary (3.4)
The master of the ordinary (3.4)
The maids in Wilding's household, whom the Page frightened by wearing a false beard (4.1)
Beaumont's father, who gave money to Sir Richard Hurry in time of need (4.2)
The grand jury who committed Beaumont to trial for murder (4.2)
Hurry's friends at court (4.2)
A female pie-seller whom Young Barnacle pushed into the gutter (5.1)
The priest who married Hazard and Penelope (5.2)

SETTING
Period: contemporary
Time-Scheme: The action apparently takes place on two consecutive days: 1.1–3.2 on the same morning (3.2 late in the morning), 3.3–4 the following evening, and 4.1 the next morning; half an hour passes between 5.1 and 5.2.
Place: London

Geography
London: London Bridge; the Exchange; the Strand; Westminster
England: [Oxford or Cambridge]
The Low Countries: Flanders
Europe: Slavonia; Athens
The Mediterranean Sea
Asia: Jerusalem; Turkey; the Mausoleum
The East Indies
Africa
America
The West Indies
The Fortunate Islands

SOURCES
Narrative: *Uranus and Psyche* (c. 1615–30; Wilding plot); possibly John Fletcher and Philip Massinger, *The Little French Lawyer* (**1941**; Barnacle plot)

2418. The Gamester

Verbal: William Shakespeare, *2 Henry IV* (**1083**; 4.1); John Webster, *The White Devil* (**1689**; 4.2)
Works Mentioned: 'Erra Pater', *The Prognostication For Ever* (1536?; 2.2); Diego Ortúñez de Calahorra, Pedro de la Sierra, and Marcos Martínez, *Espejo de principes y caballeros* (1555–87; English tr., *The Mirror of Princely Deeds and Knighthood*, by Margaret Tyler, R. P., and L. A., 1578–99; 3.2); *The Coranto* (1620–33; 3.3)

LANGUAGE
English
Latin: 12 words (3.1, 3.3, 4.1, 5.1; Wilding, Young Barnacle, Dwindle)
Spanish: 1 word (3.3; Wilding)

FORM
Metre: pentameter and prose
Rhyme: blank verse
Act-Division: 5 acts
Lines (Spoken): 2,439 (1,928 verse, 511 prose)
Lines (Written): 2,827

STAGING
Discovery Space: four characters are discovered (2.2, s.d.)
Stage: characters pass over the stage (3.3, s.d.)

MUSIC
Singing: Penelope sings (3.1, s.d.)
Dance: Penelope dances (3.1, s.d.)

PROPS
Weapons: Acreless's sword (1.1, dialogue); Sellaway's sword (1.1, dialogue); Littlestock's sword (1.1, dialogue); a basket-hilt sword (2.2, dialogue); a pistol (4.1, dialogue); a sword (4.1, dialogue); Young Barnacle's blade weapon (5.1, implicit)
Musical Instruments: a fiddle (2.2, implicit)
Clothing: a diamond ring (2.1, dialogue)
Money: one hundred gold pieces (1.1, 2.2, 3.4, dialogue); ten gold pieces (1.1, dialogue); an unspecified sum (4.1, implicit); another unspecified sum (4.2, implicit); one hundred pounds in gold (5.1, dialogue)
Food and Drink: a jug or bottle of wine (2.2, dialogue); four cups of wine (2.2, dialogue; drunk and flung about on stage)
Small Portable Objects: a newsbook (3.3, s.d.); a box (3.4, s.d.); a key (3.4, dialogue)

COSTUMES
WILDING: breeches (3.4, dialogue)
PENELOPE: 'melancholy' clothes (1.1, 2.1, implicit); a new, gayer suit of clothes (3.1, implicit)
PAGE: a false beard (4.1, dialogue; put on on stage)
YOUNG BARNACLE: a cloak (3.3, implicit; 3.4, dialogue)
LORD: probably long hair (dialogue); good clothes (3.3, dialogue)

EARLY STAGE HISTORY
1633: presumably performed as licensed, no doubt by Queen Henrietta's Men at the Cockpit.
1634: performed by Queen Henrietta's Men at court, presumably at Whitehall Palace, on Thursday 6 February, probably in the evening. The audience included: King Charles I; Sir Humphrey Mildmay. The performance was 'well liked'; the King said it was the best play he had seen for seven years, but may not have been entirely objective in his assessment (see EARLY TEXTUAL HISTORY). This might have been one of the seven court performances for which Christopher Beeston was later paid £70 by a warrant dated Monday 22 December 1634.

EARLY TEXTUAL HISTORY
1633: The plot was reportedly devised by King Charles I, who gave it to James Shirley via Sir Henry Herbert.
1633: On Monday 11 November, Sir Henry Herbert licensed the text for performance.
1637: entered in the Stationers' Register to Andrew Crooke and William Cooke on Wednesday 15 November; entry names author. Thomas Wykes had licensed the book for publication.
1637: **Q** printed by John Norton for Andrew Crooke and William Cooke; collation A–I⁴ K², 38 leaves. Norton used standing type from his 1637 edition of *The Example* (**2437**) to print the title page.
c. 1630s–40s: a copy of Q was in the possession of John Horne (Vicar of Headington, Oxfordshire). After his death, his entire collection of play-books passed into the possession of John Houghton of Brasenose College, Oxford (*c.* 1608–77), then to James Herne (died 1685), and then to the library of Ralph Sheldon (1623–84) at Weston, where it was catalogued by Anthony Wood, probably in the late 1670s. By then the copy had been bound into a single volume with 21 other plays by Shirley (and, presumably in error, with Henry Shirley's *The Martyred Soldier*, **2030**).
1640–1: Humphrey Moseley was selling copies of Q for 6d each.
1655: *The English Treasury of Wit and Language* entered in the Stationers' Register to Humphrey Moseley on Tuesday 16 January.
1655: eight extracts (from 1.1, 2.3, 3.1, 4.2, 5.1) included in John Cotgrave's *The English Treasury of Wit and Language*, sigs. D8ʳ⁻ᵛ, G4ʳ⁻ᵛ, N7ʳ, O1ᵛ, P2ᵛ, V3ʳ; printed for Humphrey Moseley.
1657: advertised as for sale by the Newcastle-upon-Tyne bookseller William London.
1684: Nicholas Cox (Manciple of St Edmund Hall, Oxford) had a copy of Q in his bookshop. It had probably been previously owned by Gerard Langbaine, and appears on a list compiled by Anthony Wood on Saturday 13 December.

EDITIONS
William Gifford, in *The Dramatic Works and Poems of James Shirley* (London, 1833), iii. 183–277.

Eugene Giddens, in James Shirley, *The Complete Works*, gen. eds. Eugene Giddens, Teresa Grant, and Barbara Ravelhofer (Oxford, forthcoming).

REFERENCES
Annals 1633; Bawcutt, 270, 289; Bentley, ii. 675, v. 1110–12; Bodleian, MS Wood E. 4, art. 1, p. 68; Eyre & Rivington, i. 463; Robert Stanley Forsythe, *The Relations of Shirley's Plays to the Elizabethan Drama* (New York, 1914), 357–65; Greg 523; Hazlitt, 93; William London, *A Catalogue of the Most Vendible Books in England* (London, 1657), sig. 2F1ᵛ; *MLR* 13 (1918), 401–11; MSC 6, 84; *Oxford Bibliographical Society Proceedings and Papers* 2.2 (1929), 132–3; *Renaissance News* 18 (1965), 1–3; *SP* 40 (1943), 186–203; Steele, 247.

2419. The City Wit

TEXT
Printed in 1653 (Wing B4866), from the prompt-book of a revival.

GENRE
comedy
Contemporary: play, comedy (prol.)

TITLE
Printed: *The City Wit, or The Woman Wears the Breeches*

AUTHOR
Richard Brome

DATE
Limits: 1630–7
Best Guess: 1633

Previous arguments about the play's dating and company ascription amount to a mare's nest. The prologue written for the late 1630s or early 1640s revival claims that it was first performed (perhaps in the same 'round' theatre) 'in former times', during the speaker's childhood. The issue is how literally we take that assertion. The text as it stands cannot have existed before 1624, the date of one of the ballads sampled by Crack. Matthew Steggle suggestively links particular elements with the new rules of court protocol introduced in about 1630, and with the Caroline controversy over whether it was legitimate for women to act in plays, even when the performance was in private.

The most crucial dating evidence, not hitherto adduced, occurs in the court sequence, in which Sarpego is persuaded that he has been appointed 'to be the young Prince's tutor' and the Sneakups attempt to sell the Prince some of Crazy's jewels. The action seems to be contemporary, but there was no Prince in England between 1625 and 1630, except for the 'Prince' whose title was a periphrasis for the King. He might be the 'Prince' to whom the jewels are to be sold, and who is impersonated by Pyannet, but cannot be the 'young' Prince who needs a schoolmaster. However, Prince Charles was felt to need a Latin tutor when he was around 3 years old: Sir Robert Le Grys unsuccessfully offered himself for the post in 1633. This is a year not overburdened with datable work by Brome, and so recommends itself as a much likelier date for the play than the traditional 1630. This is also a year when the issue of women actors was topical, thanks to *The Shepherds' Paradise* (**2395**) and the consequent misfortunes of William Prynne. It is tempting to read Sarpego's hoped-for career as a specific satirical reference to Le Grys, who had probably by now written *Nothing Impossible to Love* (**2388**): this would be an early example of Brome's animus against amateur courtier playwrights, as later exhibited in *The Court Beggar* (**2745**).

ORIGINAL PRODUCTION
Believing that the play was written for a predominantly young cast, Bentley proposes the King's Revels Company at Salisbury Court, with the revival ascribed to Queen Henrietta's Men after they occupied that theatre in 1637. The company ascription is somewhat more credible than the playhouse: Salisbury Court, converted from an agricultural barn or granary, is unlikely to have been a round theatre, though the phrase 'this round' might alternatively refer to the assembled audience rather than the shape of the building they were inside. But during 1632–4, the King's Revels Company were performing at the Fortune, which was said by James Wright in 1699 to have been 'a large, round brick building', unlike its square predecessor that burned down in 1621; the revival, if also in the Fortune, might then have been by Prince Charles's Men in 1640–2.

PLOT
Crazy has trustingly lent money to courtiers, including his brother-in-law Toby, who prove unreliable in making repayments. Now he is bankrupt, unable to raise the money to pay his own debts. His creditors consider giving him an extension, but are dissuaded by his voluble mother-in-law, Pyannet. He temporarily leaves home, determined to be less trusting, and adopts a series of disguises. As a begging soldier, he forces money out of one debtor, the schoolmaster Sarpego, then visits his wife Josina posing as a physician, 'Pulse-Feel'. She asks him for help in procuring her own adultery, under cover of a request to find her a secretary (preferably young, male, and sexy). Attracted by her husband's absence, the courtier-debtors Rufflit and Sir Andrew Ticket begin to court her.

Crazy is asked to help find a new husband for a rich widow, Mistress Tryman, who is lodging at Linsey-Woolsey's house; the actual objective is to establish a money-making alliance of three cheaters modelled on their memories of *The Alchemist*. Several of the courtier-debtors independently show an interest in her. She falls grievously ill and makes her will. 'Pulse-Feel' diagnoses unrequited love for her landlord, and she gets better. This disconcerts the apparently homosexual Linsey-Woolsey, but the prospect of acquiring her wealth reconciles him to a marriage. His problem is that, on his wedding day, he will be contractually obliged to pay Crazy £60 for the ring he has given Tryman. She persuades him to pay the money, but then breaks off the engagement when

Pyannet offers her son Toby as an alternative fiancé. She keeps the ring but leaves her possessions behind in Linsey-Woolsey's house; he finds that her chests of 'treasure' are full of rubbish.

Posing as a courtier, 'Holywater', Crazy convinces Sarpego that he has been appointed a royal tutor. Pyannet proposes to sell the Prince some jewels which Josina has filched from Crazy, and sends her husband, Sneakup, to make the deal posing as Crazy. At court, 'Holywater' takes charge of the jewels, proposing to show them to the Prince himself. Sneakup realizes he has been cheated and, fearful of Pyannet's anger, accepts Sir Andrew's offer of refuge in Lady Ticket's quarters. Lady Ticket writes to tell Pyannet he is there, but Pyannet suspects him of giving her the jewels in exchange for sex and descends on them full of misplaced wrath.

Posing as a dancer, 'Footwell', Crazy persuades Josina that her two courtier-suitors hold her in low regard and must be wooed with gifts, which he offers to carry. He likewise persuades them that they must send her gifts by him. He persuades Josina that 'Pulse-Feel' has betrayed her, and gets Rufflit to visit her posing as the doctor. He gets cudgelled, but 'Footwell' tells him his discomfiture was plotted by Sir Andrew; Rufflit duly enlists his help to cudgel his rival.

Tryman suggests that 'Footwell' may have a prior marital claim on her, so Pyannet pays him off. Toby marries Tryman, and the household performs a wedding play, in the course of which he learns that his bride is a whore and a shrew. Crazy arrives in his own person with his ill-gotten gains, and accepts Josina's explanation that she was only pretending an interest in adultery. Toby asks Crazy to find a way to get him out of his marriage, but it is Tryman who does it, by lifting her skirts to show men's breeches underneath. 'She' is really Jeremy, Crazy's apprentice, who adopted the disguise as a stratagem to help his master get his money back.

SCENE DESIGNATION
1.1–2, 2.1–3, 3.1–4, 4.1–4, 5.1 (O, corrected)

ROLES
SERVANTS, who serve dinner (1.1, *non-speaking*)
Master CRAZY, a bankrupt citizen jeweller, a young man; Josina's husband; variously poses as: a lame soldier; Pulse-Feel, a physician; Master Holywater, a gentleman courtier; and Master Footwell, a dancer; plays Prodigality in the wedding play
JEREMY, Crazy's apprentice, a youth; Crack's elder brother; poses as Mistress Jane Tryman, a young, rich, Cornish tanner's widow who also calls herself Doll; plays Lady Luxury in the wedding play
Master SARPEGO, a schoolmaster, Crazy's debtor; said to be short of stature; plays the prologue in the wedding play
Mistress PYANNET Sneakup, Sneakup's wife, mother of Josina and Toby, Crazy's mother-in-law; also called Mistress Sneakup

Master SNEAKUP, a Justice of the Peace; formerly a grazier; Pyannet's husband, father of Josina and Toby, Crazy's father-in-law
Sir Andrew TICKET, a knight and courtier, Crazy's debtor; Lady Ticket's husband; also called Sir Ticket
Master Jack RUFFLIT, an unmarried courtier and gallant, Crazy's debtor; also called Monsieur Rufflit and Signor Rufflit
LADY TICKET, Sir Andrew's wife
Madam JOSINA Crazy, daughter of Sneakup and Pyannet, Toby's sister, Crazy's wife
Master LINSEY-WOOLSEY, an epicene linen- and woollen-draper and Alderman's deputy; also called Master Woolsey
Master TOBY Sneakup, a courtier, Crazy's debtor; son and heir of Sneakup and Pyannet, Josina's brother; formerly Sarpego's pupil; also called Tobias; plays Folly in the wedding play
BRIDGET, Josina's maid
Jeffery CRACK, a singing boy; Jeremy's younger brother; poses as Tryman's page; also called Jeff
ISABEL, a keeping woman
JOAN, a keeping woman
Lady Ticket's PAGE, who sings (4.2)
Linsey-Woolsey's SERVANT (4.4, *within*)
TORCHBEARERS (5.1, *non-speaking*)
A BOY, Ticket's torchbearer (5.1, *non-speaking*)

Speaking Parts: 17

Stage Directions and Speech Prefixes
CRAZY: *Crasy | Crasie* (s.d.s); *Cras<y>* (s.p.s); *Crasy, a young Citizen, falling into decay* (d.p.)
JEREMY: *Jeremy | the Tryman | Tryman* (s.d.s); *Jer<emy> | Try<man>* (s.p.s); *Jeremy, [Crasy's] Apprentice* (d.p.)
SARPEGO: *Sarpego* (s.d.s); *Sar<pego>* (s.p.s); *Sarpego, a Pedant* (d.p.)
PYANNET: *Pyannet | [Josina's] Mother* (s.d.s); *Py<annet> | Pi<annet>* (s.p.s); *Pyannet, Sneakup's Wife* (d.p.)
SNEAKUP: *Sneakup* (s.d.s); *Sneak<up>* (s.p.s); *Sneakup, Crasye's Father in Law* (d.p.)
TICKET: *Sir Andrew Ticket* (s.d.s); *Ticket* (s.d.s and s.p.s); *Ticket [one of] two Courtiers* (d.p.)
RUFFLIT: *Rufflit* (s.d.s and s.p.s); *Rufflit [one of] two Courtiers* (d.p.)
LADY TICKET: *Lady Ticket* (s.d.s and d.p.); *Lady Tic<ket>* (s.p.s)
JOSINA: *Josina* (s.d.s); *Jos<ina>* (s.p.s); *Josina, Crasye's Wife* (d.p.)
LINSEY-WOOLSEY: *Linsy-Wolsy | Linsy woolsy | Linsey wolsie | Linsy-Wolsie | Linsie Woolsie | Linsie Wolsie* (s.d.s); *Lins<ey-Woolsey>* (s.p.s); *Linsy-Wolsey, a thrifty Citizen* (d.p.)
TOBY: *Tobias | Toby* (s.d.s); *Tob<y>* (s.p.s); *Toby, son to Sneakup* (d.p.)
BRIDGET: *Bridget* (s.d.s); *Bri<dget>* (s.p.s); *Bridget, Josina's Maid* (d.p.)

CRACK: *Crack* (s.d.s and s.p.s); *Crack, a Boy that sings* (d.p.)
ISABEL: *Isabell* (s.d.s); *Isa<bell>* (s.p.s); *Isabell* [one of] *two keeping Women* (d.p.)
JOAN: *Jone* (s.d.s and s.p.s); *Jone* [one of] *two keeping Women* (d.p.)
PAGE: *Page* | *The Page* (s.d.s)
SERVANT: *Servant* (s.p.s)
TORCHBEARERS: *Torches* | *Lights* (s.d.s)
BOY: *Boy* (s.d.s)

OTHER CHARACTERS
Crazy's creditors (1.1)
A tripe-wife, Linsey-Woolsey's mother (1.1)
A rope-maker, Linsey-Woolsey's father (1.1)
Josina's grandmother, who spoke Latin (1.1)
Mistress Parmesan, a cheesemonger's wife (1.1)
Mistress Cauliflower, a herb-woman (1.1)
Mistress Piccadill of Bow Lane (1.1)
An old dry-nurse (1.1)
A London pin-maker, Mistress Tryman's father (2.2; turns out to be imaginary)
A tanner, Mistress Tryman's dead husband (2.3; turns out to be imaginary)
Mistress Tryman's mother (3.1; turns out to be imaginary)
Sir Marmaduke Trevaughan, Mistress Tryman's nephew (3.1; turns out to be imaginary)
Mr Francis Trepton, Mistress Tryman's nephew (3.1; turns out to be imaginary)
Sir Stephen Leggleden, Mistress Tryman's kinsman (3.1; turns out to be imaginary)
Jane Leggleden, Sir Stephen's daughter, Mistress Tryman's goddaughter (3.1; turns out to be imaginary)
Linsey-Woolsey's servants (3.1)
Mistress Tryman's servants (3.1; turns out to be imaginary)
Barbara Tredrite, Mistress Tryman's niece (3.1; turns out to be imaginary)
Sir Gregory Flamstead, Mistress Tryman's brother (3.1; turns out to be imaginary)
The Prince (3.2, 3.4, 5.1)
Mercers visited by Linsey-Woolsey in preparation for the wedding (3.3)
Linsey-Woolsey's special friend (presumably his gay lover) whom he invites to the wedding (3.3)
The players, who lent Crack a false beard (3.3)
Rufflit's elder brother (4.1)
An intelligencer, Lady Ticket's mother (4.2; possibly imaginary)
A bearward with whom Lady Ticket allegedly has sex (4.2; possibly imaginary)
A tripe-wife, Pyannet's mother (4.2)
A hare-finder, Pyannet's father (4.2)
Pyannet's horse-keeper, whom she recommended to Lady Ticket, implicitly for sexual purposes (4.2)
The parish beadle (4.4)
Ticket's barber-surgeon (5.1)

SETTING
Period: contemporary (?)
Time-Scheme: The action takes place over a week. 1.1 begins at dinner-time and ends after 3 p.m. 5.1 takes place at night.
Place: London

Geography
London: Old Fish Street; the Old Exchange; Bow Lane; Clerkenwell; Bridewell (also referred to as St Bride's Nunnery); Christ's Hospital; High Holborn; London Wall; Cheapside; Crooked Lane
Cornwall: Knocker's Hole; St Miniver
England: Tewkesbury
Scotland
Wales
Ireland
[Europe]: France; Germany; Italy; Spain; the Low Countries

SOURCES
Narrative: Thomas Middleton, *A Trick to Catch the Old One* (**1467**); Ben Jonson, *The Silent Woman* (**1603**; 5.1), *The Alchemist* (**1621**)
Verbal: Terence, *Adelphoe* (4.2), *Heautontimorumenos* (2.1, 4.2); Cicero, *In Catilinam* 1 (3.1), 2 (3.2), *Ad familiares* 7.24 (2.1); Virgil, *Eclogues* 5 (2.1), 8 (5.1), *Aeneid* 3 (3.4); Horace, *Epistles* 2.2 (2.1, 5.1), *Odes* 1.22 (2.1); Ovid, *Metamorphoses* 1 (prol.), *Heroides* 3 (4.1); Statius, *Thebais* (4.2); Ben Jonson, *Bartholomew Fair* (**1757**; 4.2); *The Knight and the Shepherd's Daughter* (ballad, 1624; 2.2)
Works Mentioned: Joannes Ludovicus Vives, *Exercitatio linguae Latinae* (1538; 3.4); Robert Greene, *Greene's Groatsworth of Wit* (1592; 1.1); Ben Jonson, *The Alchemist* (**1621**; 3.1, 3.3); *Cupid's Cony-Berry*, *The Park of Pleasure*, and *Christian Love-Letters* (5.1; three unidentified and possibly imaginary pamphlets)

LANGUAGE
English
Latin: 190 words (1.1–2, 2.1, 3.1–2, 3.4, 4.1–2, 5.1; Josina, Sarpego, Crazy, Toby, Pyannet), plus a further 56 words in the revival prologue and epilogue
French: 1 word (1.1; Pyannet)
Greek: 3 words (4.1; Sarpego)
Italian: 1 word (5.1; Toby)

FORM
Metre: prose and pentameter
Rhyme: blank verse
Prologue: 51 lines (24 verse, 27 prose), the verse in couplets, spoken by Sarpego; revival only
Act-Division: 5 acts
Epilogue: 12 lines of trochaic tetrameter catalectic couplets, spoken by Sarpego; revival only
Lines (Spoken): 2,894 (143 verse, 2,751 prose)
Lines (Written): 3,041

STAGING
Doors: mentioned (4.1, s.d.)
Discovery Space: bed thrust out (3.1, implicit); curtained (3.1, dialogue)
Stage: mentioned (prol., dialogue; 1.1, s.d.)
Within: sound effect (2.2, implicit); speech (4.4, 5.1, s.d.)
Above: Crazy appears above (5.1, s.d.; it takes him 9 lines to get up there from the main stage); Sir Andrew is hoisted up by a rope around his middle and left to hang in mid-air while he is cudgelled (5.1, implicit)
Audience: addressed as 'kind gentlemen and men of gentle kind' (prol.)

MUSIC AND SOUND
Sound Effects: knocking within (2.2, s.d.)
Music: unspecified music (5.1, s.d.); flourish (5.1, s.d.)
On-Stage Music: Crack probably plays the lute (5.1, implicit)
Songs:
1: 'He took her by the middle so small', 2.2, Crack, 4 lines;
2: 'The young and the old mun to't, mun to't', 2.2, Crack, 4 lines;
3: 'O she is a matchless piece', 2.2, Crack, 4 lines;
4: 'Along, along where the gallants throng', 2.2, Crack, 4 lines;
5: 'Now, fair maids, lay down my bed', 2.3, Crack, 8 lines;
6: 'Did never truer heart', 2.3, Crack, 3 lines;
7: 'Then let us be friends and most friendly agree', 3.1, Crack, 8 lines;
8: 4.2, Page;
9: 4.4, Crack;
10: 4.4, Crack;
11: 'Then shall a present course be found', 4.4, Crack, 6 lines;
12: 'Io Hymen, Io Hymen, Io Hymen', 5.1, Crack, 14 lines.

PROPS
Lighting: torches (5.1, s.d.); a torch (5.1, s.d.); lights (5.1, s.d.)
Weapons: Crazy's sword (2.1, s.d.); a truncheon (4.2, s.d.); a cudgel (5.1, s.d.); Rufflit's sword (5.1, s.d.)
Musical Instruments: a lute (4.4, 5.1, s.d.)
Clothing: chains (5.1, s.d.)
Money: empty money-bags (1.1, s.d.); a purse (2.1, s.d.); several unspecified amounts (2.1, dialogue); ten pieces (3.2, dialogue); thirty pounds (3.3, dialogue); gold (4.1, dialogue); ten pounds (4.3, dialogue); one hundred pounds (5.1, dialogue); an unspecified amount (5.1, s.d.); bags of money (5.1, s.d.)
Food and Drink: a dinner in covered dishes (1.1, s.d.); a bottle of medicine (3.1, dialogue); a cordial (3.1, dialogue; drunk on stage); a bowl of wine (5.1, s.d.)
Small Portable Objects: bills, bonds, and account-books (1.1, s.d.); a scroll (1.1, s.d.); a handkerchief (1.1, dialogue); a urinal (3.1, s.d.); a will (3.1, s.d.); a table-book (3.2, dialogue); a letter (3.3, dialogue); two jewels (3.4, 4.1, dialogue; 5.1, s.d.); a paper (4.1, s.d.); a letter (4.1, s.d.); two letters (4.1, s.d.); two more jewels (4.1, dialogue; 5.1, s.d.); a carcanet (4.1, dialogue; 5.1, s.d.); music-books (4.4, dialogue)
Large Portable Objects: a table (1.1, s.d.); a basin (3.1, s.d.); seating for three characters (4.2, implicit); a rope (5.1, s.d.)
Scenery: a bed (3.1, s.d.); curtains (3.1, dialogue); hangings (3.4, s.d.)
Miscellaneous: rosemary (5.1, s.d.)

COSTUMES
CRAZY: boots (1.2, s.d.); disguised as a lame soldier (2.1, s.d.), including hangers (implicit); disguised as a physician (2.2, s.d.; 3.1, implicit); disguised as a court messenger (3.2–3, s.d.; 3.4, implicit), including a false beard (dialogue); disguised as a dancer (4.1, s.d.; 4.3, 5.1, implicit); in his own clothes (5.1, s.d.)
JEREMY: cross-dressed as a woman (3.1, 3.3, 5.1, implicit); a ring (3.3, dialogue); 'loosely dressed like a courtesan' (5.1, s.d.); a head-dress (5.1, s.d.; removed on stage); satin breeches under his skirt (5.1, s.d.)
SARPEGO: a goatee beard (dialogue); gorgeous apparel (3.4, s.d.; 4.1, implicit)
PYANNET: a French hood (5.1, dialogue); a gold chain (5.1, s.d.; removed on stage); flagon bracelets (5.1, dialogue)
SNEAKUP: disguised as a citizen (3.4, s.d.)
RUFFLIT: disguised in a doctor's gown (5.1, s.d.); hangers (5.1, implicit; worn under his gown); 'in his own shape' (5.1, s.d.)
LADY TICKET: possibly silk and tiffany clothes (4.2, dialogue)
JOSINA: dark hair (dialogue); night attire (5.1, s.d.)
TOBY: a fool's cap and coat (5.1, s.d.)

EARLY STAGE HISTORY
1637–42 (?): revived, some time after the first production, by a different company, but possibly in the same playhouse.

EARLY TEXTUAL HISTORY
1653: included as a bibliographically independent item in Richard Brome's *Five New Plays* (O), printed by Thomas Roycroft for Richard Marriott and Thomas Dring; collation A–F^8 G^4, 52 leaves; list of roles; the play was the fourth in the collection. At a late stage, Humphrey Moseley also became involved in the project; his name is included as a bookseller on the volume's title page, but not on the play's individual title page.

1653: George Thomason acquired a copy of O on Friday 20 May. In c. 1678, some years after his death, his entire collection of books and tracts was acquired by the bookbinder Samuel Mearne, acting as agent for King Charles II; the King never paid him, and the books remained in Mearne's family until 1761.

1654: O reissued, probably in January (but possibly as early as November 1653), with a cancel title page giving the initials of James Fletcher as the printer and naming John Sweeting as the bookseller. On Wednesday 4 January, Sweeting advertised copies for sale.

1655: *The English Treasury of Wit and Language* entered in the Stationers' Register to Humphrey Moseley on Tuesday 16 January.

1655: nine extracts (from 1.1–2, 2.1–2) included in John Cotgrave's *The English Treasury of Wit and Language*, sigs. E4ʳ, E7ᵛ, E8ᵛ–F1ʳ, G6ᵛ, I2ʳ, K1ʳ, N5ᵛ, P8ʳ⁻ᵛ; printed for Humphrey Moseley.

1657: O advertised as for sale by the Newcastle-upon-Tyne bookseller William London.

1659: rights to *Five New Plays* transferred in the Stationers' Register from Richard Marriott to Humphrey Moseley on Saturday 11 June; part of a group transfer of 21 titles, with the plays in the collection individually named.

1668: *The New Academy of Compliments* entered to Samuel Speed in the Stationers' Register on Saturday 2 May.

1669: *An Antidote against Melancholy* entered to John Playford in the Stationers' Register on Friday 1 January.

1669: Song 7 included in *An Antidote against Melancholy*, sig. N2ᵛ; printed for John Playford.

1669: Songs 7 and 12 included in *The New Academy of Compliments*, sigs. H9ᵛ, H10ʳ–H11ʳ; printed for Samuel Speed in or before February.

1671: *The New Academy of Compliments* reprinted for Thomas Rookes; the songs now appear on sigs. I4ʳ and I5ʳ⁻ᵛ.

1680: rights to *The New Academy of Compliments* transferred in the Stationers' Register from Mary Rookes, widow and executrix of Thomas Rookes, to George Sawbridge on Wednesday 22 September.

1681: *The New Academy of Compliments* reprinted for George Sawbridge.

1684: Nicholas Cox (Manciple of St Edmund Hall, Oxford) had a copy of O in his bookshop. It had probably been previously owned by Gerard Langbaine, and appears on a list compiled by Anthony Wood on Saturday 13 December.

1694: *The New Academy of Compliments* reprinted by Ichabod Dawks for Awnsham Churchill and John Churchill.

1698: *The New Academy of Compliments* reprinted by Ichabod Dawks for Awnsham Churchill and John Churchill.

EDITIONS
Paul Joseph Matte III, unpublished PhD dissertation (Arizona State University, 1976).
Elizabeth Schafer, Richard Brome Online (internet, 2010).

REFERENCES
Annals 1630; Bentley, iii. 59–61; Bodleian, MS Wood E. 4, art. 1, pp. 48–9; Eyre & Rivington, i. 463, ii. 386, 394, iii. 95; Greg 721; Hazlitt, 43; William London, *A Catalogue of the Most Vendible Books in England* (London, 1657), sig. 2F2ʳ; *PBSA* 107 (2013), 25–7; *SP* 40 (1943), 186–203; Matthew Steggle, *Richard Brome* (Manchester, 2004), 28–32, 35–6.

2420. Aristocratic Entertainment: Hospitality and Delight ◯

TEXT
Printed in 1637 (STC 13358).

GENRE
entertainment

AUTHOR
Thomas Heywood

DATE
Limits: 1630–5

This was presumably not written for the same Christmas as **2524**, the New Year masque Heywood also wrote for the Earl of Dover: the venues were different, and in *Pleasant Dialogues and Dramas* the two items are separated by a prologue and epilogue to a Candlemas performance for the Earl. The upper limit is defined by the date of the Earl of Dover's marriage; apart from the direct evidence of the Countess's presence at the entertainment, its avian elements unite the swan from the Hunsdon crest with the cock from the coat of arms of the Countess's first husband, Sir William Cokayne.

ORIGINAL PRODUCTION
Professional actors at the house of Henry Carey, 1st Earl of Dover, Broad Street, London

The likeliest companies are those with which Heywood was otherwise associated at the time: Queen Henrietta's Men and the King's Men. The Carey family had historic connections with the latter, but the structure of the entertainment, wrapped around a play, resembles that of **2326**, which was performed by the former.

PLOT
Hospitality is dismayed to find that he has recently become less popular than Frugality. He has been turned away from many a rich man's door, but heard a cock and a swan which told him where he could be sure of a good welcome: at the Earl of Dover's house.

[*There follows a performance of a tragedy.*]

Delight appears after the play, revived from apparent death. She says she intends to remain at the Earl of Dover's house, and offers her services as a resident handmaid.

Delight's remarks may refer in general terms to the lamentable conclusion of the tragedy, but they might also be interpreted more literally as an indication that the role was played by an actor who had just 'died' in the play. This might suggest that the tragedy was one whose ending encompassed the death of a female character.

SCENE DESIGNATION
prol., ep. (O)

ROLES
HOSPITALITY, an old man, perhaps blind
DELIGHT, a female character

Speaking Parts: 2
Allegorical Roles: 2

Stage Directions
HOSPITALITY: *Hospitality, a frolic old fellow* (heading)
DELIGHT: *delight* (heading)

OTHER CHARACTERS
Frugality, a minion of rich men (prol.)
Old Christmas, Hospitality's former friend (prol.)

SETTING
Period: Christmas

Geography
[*London*]: St Paul's Cathedral; River Thames

LANGUAGE
English

FORM
Metre: pentameter (prol.) and tetrameter (ep.)
Rhyme: couplets
Prologue: 26 lines, spoken by Hospitality
Epilogue: 16 lines, spoken by Delight
Lines (Spoken): 42
Lines (Written): 51

STAGING
Audience: members of the audience are referred to as 'the good lord' and 'kind lady' and their 'guests' (prol.)

PROPS
Food and Drink: a collar of brawn (prol., s.d.); a deep bowl of muscadel (prol., s.d.)

EARLY STAGE HISTORY
1628–35: performed during a 'bountiful' Christmas season, as the prologue and epilogue to a tragedy, at the Earl of Dover's house in Broad Street. The performance took place in the evening. The audience included: Henry Carey, 1st Earl of Dover; Mary Carey, Countess of Dover.

EARLY TEXTUAL HISTORY
1635: *Pleasant Dialogues and Dramas* entered in the Stationers' Register to Richard Hearne on Saturday 29 August; entry names author.
1637: included in Thomas Heywood's *Pleasant Dialogues and Dramas* (**O**), sigs. R1^v–R2^r, 2 pages on 2 leaves; printed by Richard Oulton for Richard Hearne, and to be sold by Thomas Slater.
1684: Nicholas Cox (Manciple of St Edmund Hall, Oxford) had a copy of O in his bookshop. It had probably been previously owned by Gerard Langbaine, and appears on a list compiled by Anthony Wood on Saturday 13 December.

EDITIONS
W. Bang, in Thomas Heywood, *Pleasant Dialogues and Dramma's*, Materialien 3 (Louvain, 1903), 242–3.
David M. Bergeron, in *Thomas Heywood's Pageants*, The Renaissance Imagination 16 (New York, 1986), 143–7.

REFERENCES
Bodleian, MS Wood E. 4, art. 1, p. 31.

1634

2421. The Wits

TEXT
Printed in 1636 (STC 6309); a revised version (not documented here) was printed in 1673 (Wing D320).

GENRE
comedy
Contemporary: comedy (t.p.); play (Herbert, S.R., Carew comm. verses)

TITLE
Performed/Printed: *The Wits*

AUTHOR
William Davenant

DATE
January 1634

ORIGINAL PRODUCTION
King's Men at the Blackfriars (and perhaps also the Globe)

PLOT
Young Pallatine receives insufficient maintenance from his elder brother and lives on handouts from his girlfriend, Lucy, who has sold her jewels to support him. Her aunt assumes this means she has also given him her virginity, and turns her out of the house. She takes refuge with Lady Ample, who accepts her on condition that she reasserts the usual order of things and allows her admirers to support her with their gifts. Lady Ample has been kept on short rations by her guardian, Sir Tyrant Thrift, but is about to come of age and acquire legal independence.

Young Pallatine's elder brother and Sir Morglay Thwack mortgage their country estates for charitable purposes and come to London to chase after women, assuming that city girls are of easy virtue. They present themselves at Lady Ample's, but do not receive the welcome they expected. Meagre and Pert, Young Pallatine's accomplices, persuade the Elder Pallatine to come elsewhere for an assignation, and his younger brother surreptitiously robs him of his finery as he undresses for bed. The bawdy house is raided by the constable, out to secure payment of substantial arrears of rent; Pallatine Senior is arrested on the assumption that he is the tenant rather than just a client. Allowed to send for the true bawd, he uses a pretext to summon Thwack, who is held liable for the unpaid rent, and who pays Young Pallatine all the money he has in order to secure his release.

Thrift is arranging an undesirable marriage for Lady Ample on the final day of her minority, so she feigns a mortal illness. Pallatine Senior is visiting her when Thrift arrives, and is persuaded to hide in a chest. Thrift is told that Ample has made him her heir, so he puts off the marriage in the hope of getting the entire estate. The chest is taken for interment in the family vault with Pallatine Senior still inside. Young Pallatine tells Thwack that the chest has all Ample's gold and jewels inside it, so the old knight goes to rob the tomb. Thrift does likewise on the same information, and a duplicate chest is provided containing a halter, which he finds. It is left to Thwack to find the Elder Pallatine. The constable is tipped off that grave-robbers are at work; Thwack gets away, but both Thrift and Pallatine Senior are arrested and taken to Ample. She agrees to marry Pallatine Senior, on condition that, as a test of love, he seals a document whilst blindfold; it turns out to be a grant of part of his estate to his younger brother. Lady Ample makes a similar grant to Lucy, and Thwack adopts Young Pallatine as his heir.

SCENE DESIGNATION
prol., 1.1–2, 2.1–4, 3.1–4, 4.1–2, 5.1–7, ep. (Q has act-division only)

Maidment and Logan neglect to mark some scene-divisions in Acts 2, 3, and 5 (because, although the stage is clear, the fictional location remains the same); thus their 2.2–3 = 2.3–4, their 3.2–3 = 3.3–4, their 5.1 = 5.2–3, their 5.2 = 5.4–5, and their 5.3 = 5.6–7.

ROLES
PROLOGUE
YOUNG PALLATINE, a young gentleman, the Elder Pallatine's younger brother; also called Pall and Master Pallatine
MEAGRE, a poor soldier; also called Don Meagre
PERT, a poor soldier; also called Don Pert
LUCY, Young Pallatine's girlfriend; less than 20 years old; also called Dame Luce; said to be little; she may be Ample's kinswoman
Sir Morglay THWACK, a rich north-country knight, 50 years old; formerly a sheriff
The ELDER PALLATINE, a gentleman, Young Pallatine's elder brother; also called Sir Pallatine
Lady AMPLE, an heiress, Thrift's ward; she may be Lucy's kinswoman
ENGINE, Thrift's steward
GINET, Ample's woman
Master SNORE, the Constable, Mistress Snore's husband, a father
MISTRESS SNORE, Snore's wife, a mother
Mistress QUEASY, a landlady and mother, the Snores' neighbour

WATCHMEN, at least three in number; one is named Runlet (sing collectively)
ATTENDANTS, who carry on Ample (4.1, *non-speaking*)
Sir Tyrant THRIFT, an old knight, Ample's guardian
EPILOGUE

Speaking Parts: 18 (counting three watchmen)

Stage Directions and Speech Prefixes
PROLOGUE: *The Prologue* (heading)
YOUNG PALLATINE: *Young Pallatine* (s.d.s and s.p.s); *Pallatine the Younger, A Wit too, but lives on his exhibition in Town* (d.p.)
MEAGRE: *Meager* (s.d.s and s.p.s); *Meger* (s.p.s); *Meager, A Soldier newly come from Holland* (d.p.)
PERT: *Pert* (s.d.s and s.p.s); *Pert [Meagre's] Comrade* (d.p.)
LUCY: *Lucy | Luce* (s.d.s and s.p.s); *Lucy, Mistress to the Younger Pallatine* (d.p.)
THWACK: *Sir Morglay Thwack | Thwak* (s.d.s); *Thwack* (s.d.s and s.p.s); *Sir Morglay Thwack, A humorous rich old Knight* (d.p.)
ELDER PALLATINE: *Elder Pallatine | Pallatine | the Elder Pallatine* (s.d.s); *Elder Pallat* (s.p.s); *Pallatine the Elder, Richly Landed, and a Wit* (d.p.)
AMPLE: *the Lady Ample* (s.d.s); *Ample* (s.d.s and s.p.s); *The Lady Ample, An Inheritrix, and Ward to Sir Tirant Thrift* (d.p.)
ENGINE: *Engine* (s.d.s and s.p.s); *Engine, Steward to Sir Tirant Thrift* (d.p.)
GINET: *Ginet* (s.d.s and s.p.s); *Ginet, Woman to the Lady Ample* (d.p.)
SNORE: *Snore* (s.d.s and s.p.s); *Snore, A Constable* (d.p.)
MISTRESS SNORE: *Mistress Snore* (s.d.s and s.p.s); *Mistress Snore, [Snore's] wife* (d.p.)
QUEASY: *Queasie* (s.d.s and s.p.s); *Mistress Queasie, [Mistress Snore's] Neighbour* (d.p.)
WATCHMEN: *Watchmen* (s.d.s and d.p.s)
THRIFT: *Sir Tirant Thrift* (s.d.s); *Thrift* (s.d.s and s.p.s); *Sir Tirant Thrift, Guardian to the Lady Ample* (d.p.)
EPILOGUE: *Epilogue* (heading)

OTHER CHARACTERS
Lucy's old aunt (1.1, 2.1, 3.3, 5.7)
Young Pallatine's surgeon (1.1)
Young Pallatine's tailor (1.1)
The tailor's child, who was given a water pistol by Young Pallatine (1.1)
The dead father of the Pallatine brothers (1.2, 5.6)
John Crump, a country cripple (1.2)
Needy, a country widow (1.2)
Abraham Sloth, a country beadsman (1.2)
Lady Ample's dead father (2.1)
Lady Ample's admirers, who have given her money (2.1)
The mother of the Pallatine brothers (2.4)
The bawd, who has absconded (2.4, 3.1–2)
The local bellman (3.1)
Nock, a nailman (3.1)
Nock's maids (3.1)
Mall, Queasy's daughter (3.1, 4.2)
Queasy's other child or children (3.1)
Samson, the Snores' servant (3.1)
A surgeon, Queasy's son-in-law (3.1)
Boys who knocked over Queasy's stall (3.1)
Goody Tongue, a midwife (3.1)
Mistress Snore's mother (3.1)
Paul, a member of the Snores' family or household (3.2)
Lucy's mercer (3.3)
Lucy's milliner (3.3)
A one-legged, handless gentleman cripple whom Sir Tyrant proposes to marry to Lady Ample (4.1)
The cripple's mother, who fell over while pregnant with him (4.1)
Lady Ample's ancestors, of French extraction (4.1, 5.6)
Thrift's neighbours in St Bartholomew's parish (4.1)
Lady Ample's lawyer (4.1, 5.2)
Lady Ample's dead grandfather (4.1)
Thwack's dead mother (4.2)
Elizabeth Snore, the Snores' daughter (4.2)
A pewterer, Mistress Snore's uncle (4.2)
Lady Ample's dead aunt (4.2, 5.2)
The vicar of St Bartholomew's, London (5.4)
The Elder Pallatine's sister (5.5; possibly imaginary)
Queasy's maid (5.7)
Queasy's clerk (5.7)
A cook in the Temple (5.7)
Mistress Snore's sister (5.7)

SETTING
Period: seventeenth century, after 1603, but not contemporary: there is a King on the throne, Thwack (who is 50 years old) was an adult office-bearer in 1588, and a reference to Ambrogio Spinola in 3.3 places the setting not earlier than the 1620s. The action takes place not long before St George's Day (23 April).
Time-Scheme: the action takes place on three consecutive days, with 3.1–4 during the first night (3.1 after 1 a.m.), 4.1 in the morning, and 5.1–6 on the second night (5.1 before midnight, 5.6 at 2 a.m.)
Place: London

Geography
London: Billingsgate; Finsbury; Fleet Ditch; Spring Garden; Hyde Park; Cheapside; Ratcliffe; Lombard Street; Bow Church; Dowgate; London Bridge; the Counter prison; St Bartholomew's Church and parish; the Temple Garden; Tower Wharf; Covent Garden; the New Exchange; the Old Exchange; Cock Lane; Duck Lane; the [Inner or Middle] Temple
[*Kent*]: Dover; Deal
England: Banbury; Derby; Beggibrigge (unidentified; ?=Begbroke); Moordale (unidentified); Suffolk; Sussex; Devonshire; Ripon

France: Gascony; Paris; Normandy; Boulogne; Frontignan; Brie
The Low Countries: 'Bomball' (?= Zalt Bommel); Brabant; Friesland; Westphalia; Delft; Holland
Germany: Saxony
Switzerland: Geneva; Lake Geneva
Venice: St Mark's; the Lagoon; the Venetian Isles
[*Italy*]: Rome; Leghorn; Turin; Tuscany; Genoa; Carrara; Lucca; Lodi; Sicily
Spain: Biscay
[*Europe*]: Norway; the Alps; Lisbon
[*Asia*]: Assyria; Tartary; Scythia; India; Persia; Turkey; Aleppo
The Indies: the Straits

SOURCES
Narrative: Thomas Middleton and William Rowley, *Wit at Several Weapons* (**1729**; Pallatine plot); Statilius Flaccus, epigram in *The Greek Anthology*, 9.44–5, or Ausonius, *Epigrams* 14, or Sir Thomas Wyatt, 'Against Hoarders of Money', in Richard Tottel (ed.), *Songs and Sonnets* (1557, repr. 1587; 5.4); Giovanni Boccaccio, *Decameron* 7.6 (1348–53; or derivate; 4.1)
Verbal: Sebastian Brandt, *Ship of Fools* (1494; 3.3); William Davenant, *Albovine, King of the Lombards* (**2179**; 5.3)
Works Mentioned: the Bible (general reference; 3.4): Exodus 20.13 (Sixth Commandment; 1.1); Revelation 17.1–8 (2.1); *The Talmud* (5.5); *The Koran* (1.1, 5.5); *Magna Carta* (1215; 4.1); Jacobus de Voragine, *The Golden Legend* (*c*. 1275; 5.5); *Adam Bell, Clim o' the Clough, and William of Cloudesley* (ballad, before 1536; 1.1, 2.2); *Chevy Chase* (ballad, before 1540; 3.4); Henry Cornelius Agrippa, *De occulta philosophia* (1531–3; 3.4); *Little Musgrave and Lady Barnard* (ballad, before 1607; 3.4); George Webbe, *A Posy of Spiritual Flowers* (1610; 4.1). Three titles mentioned in 2.4 are probably imaginary works: *A Pill to Purge Phlebotomy*, *A Balsamum for the Spiritual Back*, and *A Lozenge against Lust*.

LANGUAGE
English
Latin: 1 word (2.3; Pert)
French: 2 words (3.2, 5.4; Elder Pallatine, Pert)
Dutch: 2 words (2.1; Young Pallatine)

FORM
Metre: irregular pentameter; a little prose
Rhyme: blank verse
Prologue: 28 lines, in couplets
Act-Division: 5 acts
Epilogue: 10 lines, in couplets
Lines (Spoken): 2,698 (2,639 verse, 59 prose)
Lines (Written): 2,825

STAGING
Doors: mentioned (2.4, s.d.); knocked at (3.4, s.d.)
Discovery Space: possibly set with a bed (2.4, implicit)
Stage: mentioned (ep., dialogue)
Within: sound effects (2.1, 2.4, s.d.)
Audience: The prologue assumes a large audience.

MUSIC AND SOUND
Sound Effects: knocking within (2.1, 2.4, s.d.)
Song: 'With lantern on stall at tray-trip we play', 5.3, Snore and Watchmen, a catch in four parts, 4 lines; *musical setting survives*
Other Singing: Elder Pallatine sings (4.1, s.d.)
Dance: Thwack 'leaps and frisks' (3.4, s.d.)

PROPS
Lighting: lights (2.4, 3.3, s.d.); a torch (5.1, s.d.); a candle (5.4, s.d.); a dark lantern (5.5, s.d.)
Weapons: Young Pallatine's sword (1.1, dialogue; 5.5, implicit/s.d.); halberds (3.1–2, dialogue; 5.3, implicit); a halter (5.4, s.d.)
Clothing: a ring (2.1, dialogue); another ring (3.2, dialogue; 3.4, s.d.)
Money: a purse (1.1, s.d.); a purse of gold (2.4, implicit); another purse of gold (3.3, s.d.); a pouch containing one hundred pounds (4.2, dialogue); an unspecified sum (4.2 implicit); another unspecified sum (5.3, dialogue); money bags (5.7, s.d.)
Small Portable Objects: a paper (1.1, s.d.); a key (5.1–2, 5.7, dialogue); an iron crowbar (5.5, s.d.)
Large Portable Objects: a couch (4.1, s.d.); a chest with a wicket at one end (4.1, 5.1, 5.5, s.d.; large enough for a character to hide inside); another chest (5.4, implicit)
Scenery: hangings (1.1, 2.1, 2.4, s.d.; 3.2, implicit); a bed (2.4, s.d.; 3.2, dialogue; said to be 'within', so possibly not visible)

COSTUMES
YOUNG PALLATINE: a trim beard (dialogue); possibly a morion (2.1, dialogue; may be a figure of speech); rich, embroidered clothes (4.1, s.d.); stockings (4.1, dialogue)
MEAGRE: a morion (1.1, dialogue); ragged clothes (1.1, dialogue); new clothes (2.3, s.d.)
PERT: a trim beard (dialogue); a morion (1.1, dialogue); ragged clothes (1.1, dialogue); new clothes (2.3, s.d.)
THWACK: grey hair (dialogue); new, rich clothes, fastened with buttons (1.2, s.d.; buttoned up on stage); jewels (1.2, dialogue); enters 'dressing himself' (3.4, s.d.)
ELDER PALLATINE: a beard (dialogue); new, rich clothes, fastened with buttons (1.2, s.d.; buttoned up on stage); jewels (1.2, dialogue); a hat (2.4, s.d.; 3.2, dialogue; removed on stage); a hatband with a row of diamonds (2.4, s.d.; removed on stage); breeches with pockets (2.4, s.d.; 3.2, implicit; removed on stage); shoes or boots (2.4, dialogue; removed on stage); enters 'clothing himself in haste' (3.2, s.d.); ragged clothes (4.1, dialogue)
AMPLE: a veil (4.1, dialogue; removed on stage)

2421. The Wits

EARLY STAGE HISTORY

1634: performed by the King's Men at the Blackfriars on Wednesday 22 January. The audience included Humphrey Mildmay (who paid 1s).

1634: performed at court (presumably at Whitehall Palace) on Tuesday 28 January. The audience included: King Charles I; Queen Henrietta Maria. The play was said to be 'well liked', but the King himself liked only the language, not the plot or the characters. John Lowin, Joseph Taylor, and Eliard Swanston were later paid £220 for this and 21 other court performances during the preceding year, by a warrant dated either Sunday 27 or Monday 28 April 1634.

1634–6: An early audience included Endymion Porter, who enjoyed the play.

EARLY TEXTUAL HISTORY

1633: The play was submitted to Sir Henry Herbert for licensing, and he required some amendments. In December, William Davenant's friend Endymion Porter complained to King Charles I about Herbert's changes. The King refused to deal directly with Porter, but insisted that the play-book should be submitted to Herbert by Porter and collected from him afterwards by Davenant. Herbert duly passed the censored script on to the King for his consideration.

1634: The King met with Herbert on Thursday 9 January and upheld most of the censorship, but ruled that some of the expressions which Herbert had deleted as oaths were to be regarded only as asseverations. (Herbert disagreed with the decision, and noted as much in his office-book.) The following day (Friday 10 January), Herbert returned the script to Davenant.

1634: On Sunday 19 January, Herbert licensed the revised text for performance.

1636: On Tuesday 19 January, Herbert licensed the text ('as it was acted without offence') for the press.

1636: entered to Richard Meighen in the Stationers' Register on Thursday 4 February; entry names author.

1636: ¹Q printed by Marmaduke Parsons for Richard Meighen; collation A–K⁴, 40 leaves; title page names author, acting company, and playhouse; authorial dedication to Endymion Porter; commendatory verses by Thomas Carew; list of roles.

1640: rights to Thomas Carew's works, including poems and masques, entered to Thomas Walkley in the Stationers' Register on Monday 23 March. (This was the same day as Carew's funeral.) Matthew Clay had licensed the book for publication; he reissued the imprimatur on Wednesday 29 April.

1640: Carew's commendatory verses included in his *Poems*, sigs. M2ᵛ–M3ʳ; printed by John Dawson for Thomas Walkley.

c. 1630s–40s: a copy of Q was in the possession of John Horne (Vicar of Headington, Oxfordshire). After his death, his entire collection of play-books passed into the possession of John Houghton of Brasenose College, Oxford (c. 1608–77), then to James Herne (died 1685), and then to the library of Ralph Sheldon (1623–84) at Weston, where it was catalogued by Anthony Wood, probably in the late 1670s.

c. 1640: Abraham Wright transcribed extracts into a MS miscellany (London: British Library, Add. MS 22608, fos. 91ᵛ–93ʳ). The MS later passed to Wright's son, the antiquarian James Wright (c. 1644–c. 1717).

1642: Carew's *Poems* reprinted by John Dawson for Thomas Walkley; the verses now appear on sigs. L4ᵛ–L5ʳ.

1646: Meighen's rights transferred in the Stationers' Register from his widow, Mercy Meighen, to herself and Gabriel Bedell on Saturday 7 November, by order of a court held on Wednesday 21 October; play and author individually named as part of a group transfer of nineteen titles.

1650: Walkley's rights to Carew's *Poems* transferred in the Stationers' Register to Humphrey Moseley on Saturday 8 June.

1651: Carew's *Poems* reprinted for Humphrey Moseley and for sale by John Martin; the verses now appear on sigs. I2ᵛ–I3ʳ.

1653–6: Q advertised as for sale by Mercy Meighen, Gabriel Bedell, and Thomas Collins.

1655: *The English Treasury of Wit and Language* entered in the Stationers' Register to Humphrey Moseley on 16 January.

1655: six extracts (from 1.1, 2.2, 3.4, 5.1) included in John Cotgrave's *The English Treasury of Wit and Language*, sigs. F2ᵛ, F8ᵛ, N3ʳ, O2ᵛ, V5ʳ, X3ᵛ; printed for Humphrey Moseley.

1657: advertised as for sale by the Newcastle–upon–Tyne bookseller William London.

1665: On Friday 3 March, Roger L'Estrange licensed Davenant's *Two Excellent Plays* for printing.

1665: included in Davenant's *Two Excellent Plays* (²O), sigs. A1ʳ– F7ᵛ, 47 leaves; printed for Gabriel Bedell and Thomas Collins by Thursday 8 June. The other play in the collection was *The Platonic Lovers* (**2519**).

1667: Moseley's rights to Carew's *Poems* transferred in the Stationers' Register by his widow, Ann, to Henry Herringman on Monday 19 August.

1667: Song included (as 'The Watchmen's Catch'), with a musical setting, in John Hilton's *Catch that Catch Can*, sig. 2N1ᵛ, printed by William Godbid for John Playford.

1670: Carew's *Poems* reprinted (as *Poems, Songs, and Sonnets*) for Henry Herringman; the verses now appear on sigs. I6ʳ–I7ʳ.

c. 1670s: two extracts (from 2.4) included in MS annotations in an interleaved copy of Cotgrave's *The English Treasury of Wit and Language*, p. 294aʳ. (The copy is now at the British Library, pressmark G.16385.)

1672: Davenant's *Works* entered to Henry Herringman in the Stationers' Register on Thursday 31 October. Roger L'Estrange had licensed the book for the press. On Monday 18 November, it was advertised for sale by Henry Herringman, John Martin,

John Starkey, and Robert Horne; however, it was apparently not issued until the following year.

1673: included, with a revised text, in Davenant's *Works* (³F), sigs. ²X4ʳ–²2F1ʳ, 59 pages on 30 leaves; printed by John Macock for Henry Herringman. The prologue is also included as a separate item on sigs. 2P3ᵛ–2P4ʳ, a part of the book printed by Thomas Newcomb.

1675: Davenant's *Works* advertised as for sale by John Starkey.

1675: the stock of *Two Excellent Plays* had passed to Charles Smith, who was selling copies for 2s.

EDITION
James Maidment and W. H. Logan, in *The Dramatic Works of Sir William D'Avenant*, Dramatists of the Restoration (Edinburgh and London, 1872–4), ii. 107–244.

REFERENCES
Annals 1634; Arber, iv. 504; Bawcutt 281, 285–6, C79; Bentley, ii. 675, iii. 222–5; Eyre & Rivington, i. 344, 463, ii. 380; Greg 507; Hazlitt, 255; William London, *A Catalogue of the Most Vendible Books in England* (London, 1657), sig. 2F1ᵛ; *MLR* 13 (1918), 401–11; *MP* 66 (1968–9), 256–61; MSC 6, 84; *PMLA* 51 (1936), 130; *SP* 40 (1943), 186–203; Steele, 247.

2422. The Pastoral (possibly not a distinct play)

EVIDENCE
Sir Humphrey Mildmay's accounts; Sir Henry Herbert's office-book; John Newdigate's accounts.

Steele and Bentley both propose that the term 'the pastoral' was a generic descriptor rather than a title, and that the Easter Tuesday performance was simply a repeat of *The Faithful Shepherdess* (**1582**), which had been shown at court the previous Twelfth Night. However, the recurrence of the same form of words in three unrelated documents strengthens the case for interpreting it as a title, and the taste for pastorals in mid-1630s court culture makes it unlikely that the phrase in question would refer definitively to any one pastoral (whether *The Faithful Shepherdess* or anything else), unless it was actually called *The Pastoral*, and was deliberately commissioned to capitalize on the vogue. After the court performance of *The Shepherds' Paradise* (**2395**) in 1633, the King's Men had a fine stock of hand-me-down pastoral costumes, some of which were used in *The Faithful Shepherdess*; but the two plays' costume requirements do not correspond exactly, so others would have been destined for other plays, perhaps in the same genre.

GENRE
pastoral
Contemporary: pastoral (title); play (Mildmay); masque (Newdigate)

TITLE
Performed: *The Pastoral*

DATE
1634

ORIGINAL PRODUCTION
King's Men, presumably at the Blackfriars (and perhaps also the Globe)

PLOT
In all likelihood, the play's title simply describes its genre, which in turn defines its action in broad terms: the amours of nymphs and shepherds in an idealized rural landscape. However, it is remotely possible that the production of a pastoral play (at court?) was the focus of the narrative, much as an aristocratic ball is central to *The Ball* (**2389**). If so, the tone would necessarily have been positive, not satirical: *The Pastoral* itself was deemed acceptable for performance at court, and the most prominent fan of pastoral drama was the Queen; nobody would have wanted to emulate William Prynne, who had suffered severe reprisals the year before when a coincidence of timing led his published attack on actresses to be construed as a glancing allusion to her appearance in *The Shepherds' Paradise* (**2395**).

EARLY STAGE HISTORY
1634: possibly performed on Thursday 6 February. If so, the performance probably took place in the afternoon and the audience included Sir Humphrey Mildmay, who recorded expenditure of 2s 'for a book and the play of *Pastoral*'. (That evening, he went to court and saw another play, *The Gamester*, **2418**.)

1634: performed by the King's Men at the Cockpit in Court on Tuesday 8 April (Easter Tuesday). The performance took place in the evening and seems to have featured scenery. The audience included: King Charles I; Queen Henrietta Maria; John Newdigate. Newdigate also paid the stage keeper 1s 'to show the scenes', probably in advance of the performance itself. John Lowin, Eliard Swanston, and Joseph Taylor were paid £220 for this and 21 other court performances during the preceding year, by a Privy Council warrant dated either Sunday 27 or Monday 28 April.

REFERENCES
Bawcutt 293; Bentley, v. 1389–90; Vivienne Larminie, *Wealth, Kinship and Culture* (Woodbridge, 1995), 202; MSC 6, 84; Sibley, 123; Steele, 248.

2423. The Triumph of Peace

TEXT
Two versions, both printed in 1634 (STC 22458.5 and 22459):
  A: authorial pre-performance text, as given in $Q_{\alpha-\beta}$ and the original issue of Q_3; some minor amendments were made for the first performance, which are recoverable with

reference to production documents archived by Bulstrode Whitelocke;

B: the text at the second performance, with a speech by the Genius which appears on an additional leaf inserted into the reissued $Q_{3\beta}$ (STC 22459b); this was presumably substituted for the same character's speech, of the same length, which appears in sc.5 of the original version; Q_3 also omits elements of ant.11, which may indicate that they were not included in the second performance.

A surviving MS cue-sheet for Songs 1–5 (Warminster: Longleat House, Longleat MSS, Parcel 2, No. 9, item 11) contains some minor verbal variants.

Additional information derives from:
- **J:** Inigo Jones's design drawings;
- **M:** Middle Temple records;
- **WM:** Bulstrode Whitelocke's *Memorials of the English Affairs* (1682; Wing W1986);
- **WP:** Bulstrode Whitelocke's papers.

I have not treated the procession as a substantive part of the masque itself, since it is unclear how fictive the pageantry was; the figures who processed but did not appear in the masque proper are accordingly not listed as roles, nor are details included in the records of props and costumes. However, the planning and expenses of the procession cannot be systematically disentangled from those of the masque, so information about it is included in the stage history.

GENRE
masque
Contemporary: triumph (title); masque (t.p.); entertainment (epistle); 'great masque' (Whitelocke); 'great masque or show' (Thomas Crosfield)

TITLE
Printed: *The Triumph of Peace*
Contemporary: *The Masque of the Four Inns of Court*; *The Masque of the Gentlemen of the four Honourable Societies, or Inns of Court*

AUTHOR
James Shirley

According to WM, William Noy the Attorney General made suggestions for the antimasque of projectors (ant.5).

DATE
3 February 1634

ORIGINAL PRODUCTION
Inns of Court at the Banqueting House, Whitehall Palace

PLOT
Fancy, Jollity, and Laughter come to court to help with the masque, only to discover that they are expected to supply the antimasque themselves. They provide one in their own persons, after which most of the party go off to the tavern. Fancy and Opinion stay behind, and Fancy offers another eleven antimasques representing the effects of peace: sexual corruption, sturdy beggars, projectors with mad schemes, cheating prostitutes, highway robbery, attempted rape, folly, and sport; for the sake of variety, Fancy also provides an antimasque of dancing birds, and the antimasques become progressively more fantastical as they go on. His friends return, drunk, and they are all scared off by the arrival of Peace in a cloud.

Peace is joined by Law and Justice: Peace and Law sing of their mutual interdependence, while Justice is initially confused by her surroundings. They present their offspring, the masquers, to the King and Queen in the audience. Dancing ensues.

The stage is invaded by a group of common people who have helped in the production of the masque but have been refused entry to the performance: they are determined to see some dancing, but the masquers will not oblige; so they end up dancing themselves as a further antimasque.

The masquers revel with ladies from the audience. Amphiluche arrives, envious that such entertainment is taking place at night; but her coming heralds the dawn, and brings the masque to an end.

SCENE DESIGNATION
sc.1–6 (Q undivided); the scene-division is defined by the changes of scenery. The antimasques appear during sc.1 (ant.1), sc.2 (ant.2–6), sc.3 (ant.7–9), sc.4 (ant.10–12), and sc.5 (ant.13); the main masque takes place during sc.4–6 (and is interrupted by ant.13).

ROLES
OPINION, Novelty's husband, Admiration's father
CONFIDENCE, Fancy's male companion
Lady NOVELTY, Opinion's wife, Admiration's mother; also called Madam Novelty
ADMIRATION, daughter of Opinion and Novelty
Signor FANCY, a hermaphrodite gentleman (who is consistently spoken of using masculine pronouns), said to be begotten by Mercury and Venus and to be a cross between an owl and a bat; Confidence's companion (and nominal master)
JOLLITY, probably a male figure
LAUGHTER, a male figure
The MASTER of a tavern (ant.2, *non-speaking*)
The Master's WIFE (ant.2, *non-speaking*)
The Master's SERVANTS (ant.2, *non-speaking*)
A MAQUERELLE, a fat bawd (ant.3, 6, *non-speaking*)
Two WENCHES (ant.3, 6, *non-speaking*)
Two wanton GAMESTERS (ant.3, 6, *non-speaking*)
A GENTLEMAN (ant.4, *non-speaking*)
Four BEGGARS, feigned cripples (ant.4, *non-speaking*)
A JOCKEY, a projector (ant.5, *non-speaking*)
A COUNTRY FELLOW, a projector (ant.5, *non-speaking*)
Two More PROJECTORS (ant.5, *non-speaking*)
A PHYSICIAN, a projector (ant.5, *non-speaking*)
A SEAMAN, a projector (ant.5, *non-speaking*)
An OWL (ant.7, *non-speaking*)

A CROW (ant.7, *non-speaking*)
A KITE (ant.7, *non-speaking*)
A JAY (ant.7, *non-speaking*)
A MAGPIE (ant.7, *non-speaking*)
A MERCHANT (ant.8, *non-speaking*)
Two THIEVES (ant.8, *non-speaking*)
A CONSTABLE (ant.8, *non-speaking*)
OFFICERS (ant.8, *non-speaking*)
Four NYMPHS (ant.9, *non-speaking*)
Three SATYRS (ant.9, *non-speaking*)
Four HUNTSMEN (ant.9, *non-speaking*)
Three DOTTERELS (ant.10, *non-speaking*)
Three DOTTEREL-CATCHERS (ant.10, *non-speaking*)
A WINDMILL (ant.11, *non-speaking*)
A fantastic KNIGHT (ant.11, *non-speaking*)
The Knight's SQUIRE (ant.11, *non-speaking*)
A COUNTRY GENTLEMAN (ant.11, *non-speaking*; possibly omitted from the second performance)
The Country Gentleman's SERVANT (ant.11, *non-speaking*; possibly omitted from the second performance)
Four BOWLERS (ant.12, *non-speaking*)
Irene or PEACE, one of the Hours, sister of Law and Justice, daughter of Jove and Themis, mother of some of the masquers
A CHORUS of 25 singers
Eunomia or LAW, one of the Hours, sister of Peace and Justice, daughter of Jove and Themis, mother of some of the masquers
Dice or JUSTICE, one of the Hours, sister of Law and Peace, daughter of Jove and Themis, mother of some of the masquers; also called Astraea
Thirteen MUSICIANS (*non-speaking*; includes the stringer, who appeared and may have played an instrument)
Sixteen MASQUERS, the sons of Peace, Law, and Justice (*non-speaking*)
A GENIUS, a male angel
A CARPENTER (ant.13)
A PAINTER (ant.13)
One of the BLACK GUARD (ant.13)
A TAILOR, a married man (ant.13)
The TAILOR'S WIFE (ant.13)
An EMBROIDERER'S WIFE (ant.13)
A FEATHER-MAKER'S WIFE (ant.13)
A PROPERTY MAN'S WIFE (ant.13)
Two GUARDS (ant.13)
AMPHILUCHE, the forerunner of the morning, a young maid
CONSTELLATIONS, who sing the final song (scripted for four, but cast for five in production; members of the chorus)

Whitelocke's account (in WM) claims that some the projectors were 'of the Scotch and northern quarters'; there is no indication of this in the text, so it is impossible to say which ones he meant.

Speaking Parts: 51–2 (counting the chorus as 25)
Allegorical Roles: 7 (or 10 including the Hours)

Stage Directions and Speech Prefixes
OPINION: *Opinion* (s.d.s and s.p.s); [one of] *the presenters* (s.d.s)
CONFIDENCE: *Confidence* (s.d.s and s.p.s); [one of] *the presenters* (s.d.s)
NOVELTY: *Novelty* (s.d.s and s.p.s); *Lady Novelty* | [one of] *the presenters* (s.d.s)
ADMIRATION: *Admiration* (s.d.s and s.p.s); [one of] *the presenters* (s.d.s)
FANCY: *Fancy* (s.d.s and s.p.s); [one of] *the presenters* (s.d.s)
JOLLITY: *Jollity* (s.d.s and s.p.s); [one of] *the presenters* (s.d.s)
LAUGHTER: *Laughter* (s.d.s and s.p.s); [one of] *the presenters* (s.d.s)
MASTER: *the Master of the Tavern* (s.d.s)
WIFE: [the Master's] *Wife* (s.d.s)
SERVANTS: [the Master's] *Servants* (s.d.s)
MAQUERELLE: *A Maquerelle* | *The Maquerelle* (s.d.s)
WENCHES: *two Wenches* | *Wenches* (s.d.s)
GAMESTERS: *two wanton Gamesters* | *Gentlemen* | *The Gallants* (s.d.s)
GENTLEMAN: *A Gentleman* | *The Gentleman* (s.d.s)
BEGGARS: *Beggars 4* | *the Beggars* | *The Cripples* (s.d.s)
JOCKEY: [one of] *six Projectors* | [one of] *the Projectors* | *A Jockey* | *Jockey* (s.d.s)
COUNTRY FELLOW: [one of] *six Projectors* | [one of] *the Projectors* | *a Country Fellow* | *The Country Fellow* (s.d.s)
PROJECTORS: [two of] *six Projectors* | [two of] *the Projectors* | *a grim Philosophical faced fellow* | *another Projector* | *The third Projector* | *The fourth Projector* (s.d.s)
PHYSICIAN: [one of] *six Projectors* | [one of] *the Projectors* | *a Physician* | *The fifth Projector* (s.d.s)
SEAMAN: [one of] *six Projectors* | [one of] *the Projectors* | *a Seaman* | *the sixth Projector* (s.d.s)
OWL: *An Owl* (s.d.s)
CROW: [one of] *The Birds* | *A Crow* (s.d.s)
KITE: [one of] *The Birds* | *A Kite* (s.d.s)
JAY: [one of] *The Birds* | *A Jay* (s.d.s)
MAGPIE: [one of] *The Birds* | *A Magpie* (s.d.s)
MERCHANT: *A Merchant* (s.d.s)
THIEVES: *Two Thieves* (s.d.s)
CONSTABLE: *A Constable* (s.d.s)
OFFICERS: *Officers* (s.d.s)
NYMPHS: *Four Nymphs* | *the Nymphs* | *One Nymph* (s.d.s)
SATYRS: *Three Satyrs* | *the Satyrs* (s.d.s)
HUNTSMEN: *Four Huntsmen* (s.d.s)
DOTTERELS: *Three Dotterels* (s.d.s)
DOTTEREL-CATCHERS: *Three Dotterel catchers* (s.d.s)
WINDMILL: *A Windmill* | *The Windmill* (s.d.s)
KNIGHT: *A fantastic Knight* | *The Fantastic Adventurer* | *the Knight* (s.d.s)
SQUIRE: [the Knight's] *Squire* (s.d.s)
COUNTRY GENTLEMAN: *A Country Gentleman* (s.d.s)
SERVANT: [the Country Gentleman's] *Servant* (s.d.s)
BOWLERS: *Bowlers, 4* (s.d.s)

PEACE: *Irene* | *Irene, or Peace* (s.d.s); *Ir<ene>* (s.p.s)
CHORUS: [part of] *the whole train of Musicians* (s.d.s); *Chorus* (s.p.s)
LAW: *Eunomia* | *Eunomia or Law* (s.d.s); *Eu<nomia>* (s.p.s)
JUSTICE: *Diche* | *Diche or Justice* (s.d.s); *Dich<e>* (s.p.s)
MUSICIANS: [part of] *the whole train of Musicians* | *the Musicians* (s.d.s)
MASQUERS: *the grand Masquers* | *the Masquers* (s.d.s)
GENIUS: *Genius* (s.d.s and s.p.s); *a Genius or Angelical person* (s.d.s)
CARPENTER: *A Carpenter* (s.d.s); *Carpenter* (s.p.s)
PAINTER: *A Painter* (s.d.s); *Painter* (s.p.s)
BLACK GUARD: *One of the Black-guard* (s.d.s); *Black guard* (s.p.s)
TAILOR: *A Tailor* (s.d.s); *Tailor* (s.p.s)
TAILOR'S WIFE: *The Tailor's wife* (s.d.s); *Tailor's Wife* (s.p.s)
EMBROIDERER'S WIFE: *An Embroiderer's Wife* (s.d.s); *Emb<roiderer's Wife>* (s.p.s)
FEATHER-MAKER'S WIFE: *A Feather-maker's wife* (s.d.s); *Fea<ther-maker's Wife>* (s.p.s)
PROPERTY MAN'S WIFE: *A Property-man's wife* (s.d.s); *Pro<perty-man's Wife>* (s.p.s)
GUARDS: *1 Guard* | *2 Guard* (s.p.s)
AMPHILUCHE: *Amphiluche* | *a young Maid* (s.d.s); *Am<philuche>* (s.p.s)
CONSTELLATIONS: *other voices* (s.d.s); *1* | *2* | *3* | *4* (s.p.s)

OTHER CHARACTERS
The guard at court (sc.1)
Mercury, god of wit, Fancy's father (sc.1)
Venus, goddess of love, Fancy's mother (sc.1)
Jove, father of the Hours (sc.4; identified with the King in the audience)
Themis, mother of the Hours (sc.4; identified with the Queen in the audience)
The Lord Chamberlain (sc.5)
A property man who made the owl and other props for the masque, a husband (sc.5)
A feather-maker who sold feathers used in the masque, a husband (sc.5)
An embroiderer who worked on two costumes in the masque, a husband (sc.5)

SETTING
Geography
The Goodwin Sands
[Scotland]

SOURCES
Narrative: possibly François Desprez, *Les songes drolatiques de Pantagruel* (1565; ant.5); Miguel de Cervantes, *Don Quixote* (1605, English tr. by Thomas Shelton printed 1612, repr. 1620; ant.11); possibly Ben Jonson, *Neptune's Triumph* (**2080**; sc.1)

Verbal: Virgil, *Eclogues* 10 (t.p. motto)
Design: the Arundel Marbles (proscenium); Léonard Thiry, *Livre de la conqueste de la toison de l'or* (1563; proscenium); Odoardo Fialetti, *Il vero modo et ordine* (1608; Sons of Peace); Jacques Callot, *Capitano Spagnuolo* and *Pantalone* (c. 1618–20; Forum of Peace), *The Fair at Impruneta* (after 1622; Forum of Peace); Alessandro Francini, *Livre de l'Architecture* (1631; proscenium frieze)
Works Mentioned: François Rabelais, unspecified work (sc.2); possibly George Chapman, Masque of the Princes of Virginia (**1699**; sc.2)

Opinion, commenting on the antimasques, says that hitherto he has seen 'baboons | in quellios' (i.e. ruffs). This sounds like an 'in' reference to a specific earlier court masque, such as often featured in Jacobean masque librettos. It is at the very least striking that the two previous major joint Inns of Court masques presented at court, the wedding masques of 1613 (**1699–1700**), both featured baboons, that no known court masque since had done so, and that in **1699**, presented by the Middle Temple and Lincoln's Inn, the baboons were wearing ruffs. This was, it is true, a very long time ago, and it is tempting to suppose that the allusion refers instead to the apes in *Tempe Restored* (**2359**), even though the surviving design indicates that they, unlike their asinine teacher, did not wear ruffs. On the other hand, several senior members of the Inns of Court who had been involved in some capacity with **1699** also contributed to the organization of *The Triumph of Peace*. Notable among these was William Noy, who was said to have given Shirley some ideas; perhaps the baboon allusion was one of them.

LANGUAGE
English
Latin: 3 words (sc.5; Property-Man's Wife)

FORM
Metre: pentameter, tetrameter, and prose; a little trimeter
Rhyme: blank verse and couplets
Presenter: Opinion and Fancy present the antimasques
Lines (Spoken): 385 (335 verse, 50 prose)
Lines (Written): 865 (890 in $Q_{3\beta}$)

STAGING
Stage: a great stage with steps descending into the room (desc.; the lowest part of the structure is 'painted in rustic work'); mentioned (sc.5, desc.)
Within: music (sc.3, desc.); voices (sc.5, desc.)
Above: the three Hours descend on clouds (sc.4, desc.); Amphiluche ascends on a cloud (sc.6, desc.)
Beneath: Amphiluche rises on a cloud (sc.6, desc.; apparently, she starts under the stage and goes all the way to the uppermost level)
Other Openings: characters exit through a door at the back of the tavern set (sc.2, implicit); the Owl enters out of an ivy-bush (sc.3, desc.)
Audience: the King and Queen are mentioned (sc.1, 4) and directly addressed (sc.4, desc.); Laughter refers to ladies in the audience (sc.1), and the masquers dance with them (sc.5, implicit)

Miscellaneous: the first scene change is said to take less than two minutes to accomplish (sc.1–2); there is an effect in which the audience is encouraged to believe that the stage machinery is about to collapse (sc.5, desc.)

MUSIC AND SOUND

Sound Effects: a crack (sc.5, desc.)
Music: hunting horns within (sc.3, desc.); heavenly music (sc.4, dialogue); loud music (sc.5, desc.); violins (sc.5, desc.); *some of the instrumental music survives.*
On-Stage Music: Peace and Law probably play lutes (sc.4, dialogue; accompanies Song 3); the musicians and chorus play the harp, treble lutes, viols, bass viols, bass lute, and theorboes (WP)
Songs:
  1: 'Hence, ye profane, far hence away', sc.4, Peace and Chorus, in parts, 12 lines; *musical setting survives;*
  2: 'Wherefore do my sisters stay?', sc.4, Peace and Chorus, in parts, 12 lines; *musical setting survives;*
  3: 'Think not I could absent myself this night', sc.4, Law, Peace, and Chorus, in parts, 22 lines, with lute accompaniment; *musical setting survives;*
  4: 'Swiftly, O swiftly, I do move too slow!', sc.4, Justice, Law, Peace, and Chorus, in parts, 27 lines;
  5: 'To you, great King and Queen, whose smile', sc.4, 16 lines;
  6: 'They that were never happy Hours', sc.5, Justice, Law, Peace, and Chorus, 15 lines;
  7: 'Why do you dwell so long in clouds', sc.5, 12 lines; *musical setting survives;*
  8: 'In envy to the night', sc.6, Amphiluche, 10 lines; *musical setting survives;*
  9: 'Come away, away, away', sc.6, Constellations, 20 lines; *musical setting survives.*
Dance: Opinion, Confidence, Novelty, Admiration, Fancy, Jollity, and Laughter dance in the first antimasque (sc.1, desc.); the Maquerelle, Wenches, and Gamesters dance in the third and sixth antimasques (sc.2, desc.); the Beggars dance in the fourth antimasque (sc.2, desc.); the six Projectors each dance separately and then together in the fifth antimasque (sc.2, desc.); the Gentlemen dance alone in the sixth antimasque (sc.2, desc.); the Birds dance in the seventh antimasque (sc.3, desc.); the Nymphs dance both alone and with Huntsmen in the ninth antimasque (sc.3, desc.); the masquers dance an entry dance, with violin accompaniment (sc.5, desc.); the masquers dance a main dance (sc.5, desc.); the characters in the thirteenth antimasque dance, with violin accompaniment (sc.5, desc.); masquers dance the revels with ladies from the audience (sc.5, desc.). No dancing is specified in ant.2, 8, 10–12. *Some of the dance music survives.*

PROPS

Lighting: a lamp (sc.2, desc.); a dim torch (sc.6, desc.)
Weapons: four javelins (sc.3, desc.); a lance (sc.4, desc.); possibly two halberds (sc.5, dialogue)

Musical Instruments: up to four hunting horns (sc.3, implicit); two lutes (sc.4, dialogue); harp, bass viol, six treble lutes, one or two bass lutes, two viols, violin, eleven or twelve theorboes, five mean lutes (unknown scenes, WP)
Clothing: an imperial crown (sc.4, desc.)
Money: an unspecified sum (sc.2, implicit)
Animals: a capon (sc.2, desc.); a horse (sc.3, desc.; probably a hobby-horse worn by the Merchant)
Small Portable Objects: a line and plummet (sc.2, desc.); a bridle (sc.2, desc.; see also COSTUMES: JOCKEY); a flail (sc.2, desc.); a palm branch (sc.4, desc.); a small white rod (sc.5, desc.)
Large Portable Objects: a staff (sc.1–4, desc.); four or more crutches (sc.2, desc.); a portmanteau (sc.3, desc.)
Scenery: a proscenium with figures and painted foliage (desc.; *design drawing survives*); a curtain (desc.; raised to reveal the action; *design drawing survives*); a street with buildings, trees, and grounds, with the Forum of Peace at the back (sc.1, desc.); a tavern with a red lattice, several drinking rooms, a functional back door, a conceited sign and a bush (sc.2, desc.); a woody landscape with bushes, one of which, an ivy-bush, functions as an entry point (sc.3, desc.); a landscape (sc.4, desc.); a white cloud bearing a golden chariot (sc.4, desc.; descends with Peace on board); an orient [i.e. red] cloud bearing a silver chariot (sc.4, desc.; descends with Law on board); a cloud of a third colour (sc.4, desc.; descends with Justice on board); a hill with carved steps (sc.5, desc.; the Whitelocke cue-sheet establishes that there is a room within the scene to which the musicians retire); an arbour with silver foliage, human figures for terms, and an architrave (sc.5, desc.; *design drawing survives*); sky (sc.5, desc.); sixteen seats, arranged pyramidally (sc.5, desc.); open country stretching to the horizon, a dark sky with dusky clouds and a new moon (sc.6, desc.); a strangely shaped and coloured cloud (sc.6, desc.; rises with a character sitting on it)
Miscellaneous: vapour (sc.6, desc.; rises and drops again on cue, so it needs to be controllable)

COSTUMES AND MAKE-UP

OPINION: an old-fashioned black velvet doublet; trunk hose; a short black velvet cloak; an antique cape; a black velvet cap with a fall (sc.1–4, desc.)
CONFIDENCE: a slashed parti-coloured doublet; matching breeches with points at the knees; favours on his breast and arm; a broad-brimmed hat tied up on one side and banded with a feather; a long lock of hair trimmed with ribbons of several colours; wide boots; big spurs with bells (sc.1–2, 4, desc.)
FANCY: a suit of several coloured feathers; bat's wings; a hood (sc.1–4, desc.)
JOLLITY: a flame-coloured suit; scarves and napkins like a morris dancer's; a conical hat with a little fall (sc.1–2, 4, desc.)
LAUGHTER: a long, multi-coloured side coat with laughing vizards on his breast and back; a cap with

two grinning faces and feathers between them (sc.1–2, 4, desc.)

MAQUERELLE: is fat; a broad-brimmed hat (sc.2, J); *design drawing survives*

JOCKEY: a bonnet with a whip on top (sc.2, desc.); a bridle and bit on his head (sc.2, WM; in the desc., however, the bridle is in his hand; see PROPS)

COUNTRY FELLOW: a leather doublet; grey trunk hose; on his head a perpetual-motion wheel (sc.2, desc.)

PROJECTORS: one is bearded (dialogue), and wears a furred, girdled gown and a furnace on his head (sc.2, desc.); the other has a black leather diving suit, vast in the middle and round on top, with glass eyes and bellows under each arm (sc.2, desc.)

PHYSICIAN: a hat with a bunch of carrots (sc.2, desc.)

SEAMAN: a ship on his head (sc.2, desc.)

MERCHANT: see PROPS: **Animals**

KNIGHT and SQUIRE: armour (sc.4, implicit)

PEACE: a flowery vesture with puffs around her neck and shoulders; a garland of olives on her head; green taffeta buskins (sc.4, desc.)

CHORUS: nine wear purple garments, seven or eight, white garments, and seven, carnation garments (sc.4–6, WP)

LAW: a purple satin robe decorated with golden stars; a carnation mantle with gold lace and fringe; a coronet of light (possibly representing stars); purple buskins inlaid with yellow (sc.4, desc.)

JUSTICE: long fair hair; a white robe; a satin mantle; a coronet of silver pikes; white wings; white buskins (sc.4, desc.; the wings are also said to be silver)

MUSICIANS: sky-coloured taffeta robes and fish-coloured satin mantles, studded with stars; coronets set with stars; another list specifies groups dressed in purple (twelve or thirteen characters), azure or watchet (ten or twelve characters), and crimson (ten or possibly twelve characters); at least one wears sarcenet, and two wear satin mantles (sc.4–6, WP)

MASQUERS: carnation habits (including doublets and trunk hose) made of satin, taffeta, and taffeta sarcenet, with silver knots and white and carnation scallops at the shoulders, white and carnation labels at the shoulders, white under-sleeves, a puffed sleeve to the elbow, a small scallop and a slender girdle around the waist, and carnation and white under-bases with labels, all embroidered with silver spangles; carnation hats (or caps) with low crowns and double brims, quartered, lined with white and embroidered with silver, with olive wreaths, white feather plumes, and falls, the longest at the back; long white silk stockings; white shoes and roses (sc.5–6, desc., WP, and M); masks (M; may have been worn in sc.5–6, or only in the procession); *design drawings survive*, including two possible alternative designs for the head-dresses

GENIUS: long yellow hair; wings of several coloured feathers; a carnation robe tucked up; a silver coronet; white buskins (sc.5, desc.)

AMPHILUCHE: olive-coloured skin (visible at face, arms, and breast); a 'curious dressing' on her head; a string of pearls around her neck; a transparent garment with a dark blue ground decorated with silver spangles; white buskins trimmed with gold (sc.6, desc.)

EARLY STAGE HISTORY

Inception

In the first few days of October 1633, the King communicated with Thomas, 1st Baron Coventry (Lord Keeper), to signal his wish that the Inns of Court should present a masque at court. By Thursday 17 October, four masquers had been appointed from each Inn, and dancing practice had begun (to the detriment of their legal studies); there was some anxiety among the participants that their inexperience would be a cause for mockery by the courtiers. The ostensible purpose of the masque was to celebrate the birth of Prince James, the Duke of York, which did not occur until Monday 14 October, after the masque was first mooted by the King; it was also noted that the Inns of Court had not yet performed a masque at court during the present King's reign (though an offering from the Inner Temple, **2227**, had at least been envisaged in 1628). But the real purpose was to dissociate the Inns from the controversial antitheatrical opinions expressed by one of their members, William Prynne, in his *Histriomastix*, published earlier that year.

Scheduling

Initially it was planned to have the performance on Monday 6 January 1634 (Twelfth Night), but during the day rather than in the evening; on Friday 6 December it was rumoured that the performance would also include a combat at barriers (such as the Inns of Court had previously offered in 1616, **1808**). At some time after Friday 27 December, the performance was deferred (instead there was a performance of *The Faithful Shepherdess*, **1582**, by the King's Men), with the projected date now being Sunday 2 February (Candlemas). At some time after Friday 17 January it was postponed again, reportedly at the request of the performers. By Friday 24 January, the date of the performance had been fixed as Monday 3 February.

Organization

The Inns of Court established a committee of eight to oversee the production. Its members were: Edward Hyde and Bulstrode Whitelocke of the Middle Temple, Sir Edward Herbert and John Selden of the Inner Temple, William Noy and Nathaniel Gurlyn of Lincoln's Inn, and Sir John Finch and another member of Gray's Inn (probably either Peter Brereton, Clement Spelman, or Ralph Whitfield). This committee then appointed four sub-committees to supervise the different aspects of the occasion: the 'Grand Masque'

(Sir John Banks, Robert Caesar, William Hakewill, John Herne, Sir Richard Shelton, Robert Thorpe, Ralph Whitfield); the Antimasques (Sir John Amy, William Hakewill, Lewis Hele, Robert Mason, William Noy, John Rutter, John Selden; Bulstrode Whitelocke deputized in Hele's absence); the Music (headed by Bulstrode Whitelocke, with Peter Brereton, Robert Caesar, and Thomas Gardiner); and the Procession (John Daniell, Ralph Davison, Sir John Finch, Timothy Pollard, Sir Walter Pye, Philip Rhys, and Bulstrode Whitelocke, assisted by John Herne).

James Shirley was admitted as a member of Gray's Inn on Thursday 23 January 1634, presumably in recognition of his contribution.

Gray's Inn

On Friday 8 November, the authorities appointed a committee of three members (Peter Brereton, Ralph Davison, Ralph Whitfield) to supervise Gray's Inn's contribution. On Tuesday 26 November, John Rutter was appointed to assist them.

Lincoln's Inn

On Thursday 7 November, the Council of Lincoln's Inn appointed as their commissioners William Hakewill, John Herne, and Thomas Styles. On Thursday 14 November, they appointed Thomas Escourt as their Master of the Revels and asked him to select the four masquers in association with Edward [or John?] Herne and Thomas Styles.

Casting

Wishing to save expense, Sir Walter Pye refused to allow his son (either Walter, jun., or Robert, of the Middle Temple) to be one of the masquers. At an early stage (Thursday 17 October), one of the Gray's Inn masquers was to have been one Davenport. The eventual masquers were: James Aiskoughe, John Crawley, Edward Page, and John Reade of Gray's Inn; Arthur Baker, Edmund Carew, John Farwell, and Reginald Foster of the Inner Temple; Robert Cole, Martyn Harvey, Philip Morgan, and Robert Owen of the Middle Temple; and Edward Herne, Stephen Jay, Henry Maxey, and John North of Lincoln's Inn.

The other performers included: John Lanier (Peace); Walter Porter's boy (Law); Maturin Mari (Justice); the Lord Chamberlain's boy (Amphiluche); Thomas Holmes, Thomas Day, John Frost, Henry Lawes, Thomas Day's boy (Constellations). The antimasque birds were played by little boys.

The role of Amphiluche was originally to have been played by Thomas Holmes, a bass, but was subsequently assigned to a boy soprano; it appears that the text was then amended to create a role for Holmes (by adding a fifth Constellation). The role of Law was originally assigned to one of Thomas Day's boys. The name John Squire, assigned the role of Peace in one document, may be a simple error for John Lanier, or may be a superseded casting (though Squire appears nowhere else in the surviving documents; if he was a real person, he was dropped altogether).

Music

Bulstrode Whitelocke selected the principal musical contributors, and may also have written some of the music himself. The main composers were William Lawes (including the music for Songs 1–3 and 7–9) and Simon Ives. Davis Mell contributed some music for the antimasques. The choreography was by Stephen de Nau and Sebastian la Pierre, and they too may also have composed some of the music.

In all there were 29 singers (including those playing named roles): seven or eight boys (three belonging to Thomas Day, one each to Walter Porter, William Lawes, Charles Coleman, and [Bulstrode?] Whitelocke, and possibly also the Lord Chamberlain's boy) and Maturin Mari (trebles); William Lawes, John Wilson, Charles Coleman, Simon Ives, Anthony Roberts, Thomas Lawton, Nicholas Ham, Henry Lawes, John Kellaway (counter-tenors); Walter Porter, John Lanier, Thomas Day, Robert Tomkins, William Smegergil (a.k.a. William Caesar), William Webb (tenors); Nicholas Duvall, John Lawes, Thomas Holmes, Roger Nightingale, John Frost, John Drew (basses); the singers accompanied themselves on theorboes. The chorus members who performed in Song 2 were Henry Lawes, Drew, and Webb.

There were thirteen principal instrumental musicians: John Jenkins (bass viol); William Tomkins and Dietrich Stoeffken (viols); John Woodington (violin); Thomas Bedowes (harp); William Page (bass lute); Jacques Gaultier, John Kelly, John Lawrence, Peter Jacob, Robert Keith, Richard Miller (treble lutes); Francis Dickinson (unknown instrument); Dickinson was also the 'stringer' responsible for maintenance of the stringed instruments. A smaller group was also used during the masque, consisting of seven instrumentalists: Bedowes (harp); Coleman and Jenkins (treble viols); Page and William Tomkins (bass viols); Wilson and Smegergil (theorboes). Dance music was played by members of the King's violins: Richard Darny, John Hopper, Robert Kindersley, Thomas Warren (bass); John Heydon, James Johnston, Leonard Mell (tenor); Theophilus Lupo (counter-tenor), Thomas Lupo, Robert Parker (low tenor); Davis Mell, Stephen de Nau, Nicholas Picart (treble); Simon Hopper (unknown). Some music was probably played by members of the King's loud music (wind instruments): John Adson, Anthony Bassano, Alfonso Ferrabosco, Henry Ferrabosco, Clement Lanier, and Davis Mell. Bulstrode Whitelocke later wrote that he also employed a musician named Pierre de la Mare, whose name does not appear in any surviving production document; perhaps he was replaced by Jacques Gaultier, or perhaps Whitelocke was misremembering the name of Maturin Mari. Antimasque music may have been played by Thomas Bassett (bagpipe), John Seywell (shawm), Thomas

Rudstone (Jew's harp), John Fidler (tongs), and Robert Davis and John Morton (bird whistles).

The musicians were assigned their own messenger, Richard Griffith; he also served as a lute carrier. The harpist Jean de la Flelle was initially to have participated, but he was replaced by Thomas Bedowes. During pre-production it was considered necessary to recruit more treble singers and lutenists. Plans to use the wind musicians of the Blackfriars and Cockpit playhouses were abandoned.

The musicians rehearsed frequently at Whitelocke's house in Salisbury Court. Davis Mell attended rehearsals for the main masque and played for the masquers on the treble violin.

Procession Planning

The masquers were to process through the streets of London on their way to court. The hundred gentlemen to attend them had been chosen by Thursday 17 October. On Monday 18 and Thursday 21 November, Justinian Pagitt of the Middle Temple was engaged on business connected with the procession. The authorities of the Middle Temple apparently had difficulty gathering their 25 representatives to instruct them on their role in the procession, because the Second Butler, Francis Chafin, failed to summon them but passed on the task to one of the under butlers; on Tuesday 28 January, Chafin was fined £2 for his negligence.

In a letter of Wednesday 29 January, the Privy Council ordered Ralph Freeman, the Lord Mayor of London, to arrange for cleaning of the streets through which the procession had to travel, especially Aldersgate Street (which was presumably noticeably dirty), and to have watch strictly kept to prevent disorder on the way, not only in the city itself but the liberties as well; the city's Common Council issued orders to that effect the following day, Thursday 30 January. Also on Wednesday 29 January, Inigo Jones was instructed 'to make passages for the masquers through the wall of the Tiltyard'.

Anticipatory rumours about the procession imagined it as a second, equestrian masque to complement the masque on foot; on Saturday 1 February, William Crofts sardonically opined that the horses would probably make the better dancers.

Members of the organizing committees were instructed to be at the starting-point on the day of the procession from 2 p.m. Specific responsibilities were assigned as follows: *provision of horses*, Peter Brereton, Robert Caesar, Nathaniel Gurlyn, Edward Hyde, Timothy Pollard, John Rutter, Thomas Styles, Bulstrode Whitelocke; *musicians' horses*, John Herne, Robert Thorpe, Bulstrode Whitelocke; *antimasquers' horses*, Nathaniel Gurlyn; *masquers' chariots*, Sir John Finch, John Herne, Bulstrode Whitelocke, Ralph Whitfield; *musicians' chariots*, Sir John Finch, Bulstrode Whitelocke; *antimasquers*, John Herne; *antimasque musicians' horses and costumes*, Thomas Styles; *trumpeters*, Ralph Whitfield; *drummer*, Thomas Styles; *marshal's men and torchbearers* (including ensuring they had costumes and taking their names and addresses), Peter Brereton, William Hakewill, Lewis Hele, John Herne, Mr Hunt, Robert Thorpe, Ralph Whitfield, Thomas Willis; *delivery and distribution of torches*, John Herne, Robert Thorpe, Ralph Whitfield, Thomas Willis. The masquers were asked to wear cloaks during the procession, but were given the option not to do so.

On Tuesday 28 January, it was planned for Ralph Whitfield's servant and Bulstrode Whitelocke's coachman to give order for the charioteers' coats and buskins to be made. Whitfield ordered the servant to stay in until the afternoon, but it appears that the coachman didn't turn up. The following day, with time pressing and his servant otherwise engaged, Whitfield wrote asking Whitelocke to issue notes of authorization, and to send one of the charioteers to be measured.

Preparation of Venue

Edward Hyde and Bulstrode Whitelocke liaised with the Lord Chamberlain (Philip Herbert, 4th Earl of Pembroke and 1st Earl of Montgomery) and the Comptroller of the King's Household (Sir Henry Vane) about the preparation of the venue. Whitelocke's meeting with Vane resulted in an argument which was settled by the intervention of the Lord Chamberlain. A gallery behind the King's chair of state was reserved for members of the Inns of Court.

On Saturday 28 December 1633, Inigo Jones was instructed to make 'a scene' in the Banqueting House. Eight men worked for ten days and nights preparing the Banqueting House, commissioned by William Penrin, who was paid £13.6s.8d by the Exchequer. The carpenters Ralph Brice, John Barton, and John Sinsbury were paid £35 for erecting a stage (seven feet high, 40′ × 27′, with double stairs) at the lower end of the Banqueting House for this masque and *Coelum Britannicum* (**2428**); John Davenport, who supervised the work, was paid a gratuity of £4.

Invitations

Before the performance, Sir John Finet (Master of Ceremonies) paid his usual round of visits to ambassadors and agents to see whether they would like to come. As usual, they were concerned about the protocol of formal invitation and placement in the auditorium, and wary of the possible presence of other hostile ambassadors. In the end, Finet arranged 24 tickets for members of the diplomats' retinues, while the ambassadors themselves opted to watch the procession instead.

Procession

On Monday 3 February 1634, the masque was preceded by a procession of the performers through the streets of London. The order of precedence between the Inns was decided randomly (using a dice), and was: Gray's

Inn, then the Middle Temple, then the Inner Temple, then Lincoln's Inn. The procession was marshalled by Thomas Dayrell of Lincoln's Inn (who was knighted the following day in recognition of his work).

The participants met in the afternoon. The torchbearers were dressed at Furnivall's Inn. The procession began in the evening at Ely House and Hatton House, and travelled through the city to Whitehall between 7 and 9 p.m.; they passed through Aldersgate Street, Chancery Lane, and the Strand. Many of the participants rode on horseback; the horses were provided by the royal stables. The antimasquers were supplied with 'the poorest, leanest jades that could be gotten out of the dirt-carts or elsewhere'. Trumpeters attended the gentlemen on horseback, and the antimasquers were preceded by percussionists playing tongs and keys 'snapping and yet playing in a consort before them'.

The principal masquers and musicians rode in specially-made chariots, which (at Bulstrode Whitelocke's suggestion) were oval in shape so that the passengers could sit in a circle and avoid any dispute over precedence. The first two chariots were for the musicians; the charioteers were coachmen in the service of Sir Henry Vane and Algernon Percy, 10th Earl of Northumberland. Four other chariots (the first orange and silver, the second blue and silver, the third crimson and silver, and the fourth white and silver) carried the masquers; the charioteers were John Crafts, Bulstrode Whitelocke's man, Ralph Whitfield's man, and John Herne's man. Whitelocke also supplied the coach-horses for the Middle Temple chariot.

The procession was slowed down by the crowds in the streets who had turned out to see it; this enabled Bulstrode Whitelocke and Edward Hyde to rush ahead of it by coach, using an alternative route to Whitehall, to make final preparations at the Banqueting House; then the Lord Chamberlain escorted them to the chamber of his daughter, Anne Sophia Dormer, Countess of Carnarvon, to be entertained by her while they waited. The King and Queen had supper at Salisbury House and watched the procession from the windows; they were then taken by water to Whitehall, and saw the masquers arrive there at the Tiltyard; they asked the procession to parade around the yard before coming in.

Participants
As well as the cast and musicians who were to appear in the masque itself, the procession included one hundred gentlemen of the Inns of Court (25 from each Inn), each attended by two torchbearers and a page from his own liveried servants. At the head of the procession were twenty footmen to clear the streets. Dayrell the Marshal had forty attendants, two lackeys, and a page. Bringing up the rear were the two Marshals of London and a guard of two hundred halberdiers.

The gentlemen riders included, from the Inner Temple, [William?] Carew, John Finch, John Johnson, [Dudley or George] Pope, Rowland Reinoldes; and from the Middle Temple, Charles Adderly (who insisted on obtaining his mother's permission before agreeing to take part), John Bramston, John Cole, Sir Simonds D'Ewes, Robert Napper, Justinian Pagitt.

Costumed torchbearers attended the performers and musicians on horseback. They were: William Auckland; Thomas Baker; Thomas Baldock; Peter Bastable; William Berry; Epiphaneus Bird; John Butterfield; Catlyn [first name unknown]; Richard Clarke; William Cooper; Edward Cripps; Oliver Dring; John Dupper; Thomas Evans; another Thomas Evans; William Evans; John Fiddler; William Fisher; John Francis; James Franklin; Thomas Gawen; Thomas Gillett; Robert Goodhart; Robert Greene; Gunter [first name unknown]; John Guy; Thomas Guy; James Hargrave; Thomas Hayward; Edward Hopper; Hurst [first name unknown]; George Hynde; Edward Jones; Robert Jones; Thomas Kifford; John Ladman; Joseph Leigh; John May; Walter May; Samuel Milton; Matthew Morrell; Richard Newton; William Odson; John Page; Philpott [first name unknown]; John Philpott; Philip Philips; Thomas Philips; Roger Powell; William Price; Edward Prust; Thomas Ranger (or Langer); Richard Raynsford; William Rogers; Rookwood [first name unknown]; Richard Rotherham; William Seare; Christopher Sicklyn; Robert Slaughter; John Smith; John Steward; George Stokes; Oliver Stringer; Richard Stutesbury; Thomas Swanson; William Taylor; Robert Venning; John Walden (replacing William Hyde); Richard Weatherhead; Thomas Wiggan; Jeremy Wilkins. The horses were led by: Francis Browne; Anthony Crowe; Leonard Greene; Richard Holmes; Henry Joy; William Kentsey (replacing Matthew Walker); John Leech; Richard Lunt; John Ranger; Robert Sayers; Jacob Smith; Thomas Taylor; Titus Warne; Thomas Wayte; Thomas White; John Wilkinson.

The flambeau-bearers attending the chariots were: Joseph Alpert; Thomas Anott; Walter Ashe; Edward Baldock; Thomas Barker; John Bennen; William Best; Henry Carvagnion; Thomas Chapman; James Collett; Richard Davis; Thomas Deane; Thomas Dixon; Thomas Dodd; John Donster; Thomas Fisher; William Graham; Thomas Harrison; Thomas Harsnett; Richard Hartley; John Hawkins; William Holmes, sen.; John Jolley; Emanuel Jones; William Locke; Arthur Minthorne; Andrew Musket; Harsnett Norton; James Parry; Robert Parry; James Pasley; Richard Philips; William Seare; Richard Shelton; Thomas Shepster; Richard Slaughter; Nicholas Turner; Roger Twist; Thomas Upston; John Vinte; Hersey Wayte; Richard Weekson; William Williams; Christopher Woodson. The horses drawing the masquers' chariots were led by: Henry Anott; Thomas East; Richard Golding; Thomas Hatch; David Jones; John Patericke; Edward Strickson; William Ward.

2423. The Triumph of Peace

First Performance
The masque was performed at the Banqueting House, Whitehall, on Monday 3 February 1634 by gentlemen of the four Inns of Court. The design was by Inigo Jones. The performance took place at night, and continued until it was nearly morning.

The Banqueting House was very crowded; the audience was seated on degrees, and the gallery behind the throne was reserved for members of the Inns of Court. Those present included: King Charles I; Queen Henrietta Maria; Philip Herbert, 4th Earl of Pembroke and 1st Earl of Montgomery (Lord Chamberlain); Thomas Howard, 14th Earl of Arundel; Bulstrode Whitelocke; Edward Hyde; Thomas May; Sir Humphrey Mildmay; Lord George Digby; William Crofts; possibly Lady Jane Mildmay; Monsieur Bobarre; William Gawdy; Susanna Newdigate; probably also Anne Sophia Dormer, Countess of Carnarvon, Algernon Percy, 10th Earl of Northumberland (who paid £2 for tickets), Sir Henry Vane, Sir William Jones, Robert Bentley, Sir George Croke, and Sir Richard Hutton; possibly also Vincenzo Gussoni (Venetian Ambassador), Sir Simonds D'Ewes, George Garrard, and Robert Reade. The Queen danced with some of the masquers.

Lady Joan Pye was refused admission to the performance because of her husband's unwillingness to allow their son to appear in the masque. Thomas May was assaulted by the Lord Chamberlain, who did not know who he was; the King witnessed the incident and recognized May; the following day the Lord Chamberlain apologized to May and gave him £50. Digby and Crofts had a quarrel when the former went to take a lady's hand and the latter barged in. (This developed into a feud that culminated in Digby's imprisonment in the Fleet at the end of May.)

Aftermath
The masquers were given a banquet by the King and Queen which other lords and ladies were forbidden to touch before the masquers had finished. On Wednesday 5 February, the Lord Chamberlain wrote to the Lord Keeper signifying the King's pleasure and inviting 120 members of the Inns of Court to the King's masque (*Coelum Britannicum*, **2428**) later that month; the letter was read at Lincoln's Inn the following day, Thursday 6 February; Sir Edward Clarke and William Hakewill were asked to reply on behalf of the Inn. Francis Lenton later published a book of verses based on anagrams of the masquers' names, some of which were rather rude.

Second Performance
The King and Queen enjoyed the masque and the Queen asked for a second performance at the Lord Mayor of London's house; the procession was also to be repeated, with twenty more people involved. It was initially intended that the royal visit should take place on Tuesday 11 February; but eventually the King postponed it until Thursday 13 February, owing to the Queen's indisposition on the Tuesday. The postponement was made at very short notice: on Monday 10 February, the Lord Mayor still expected his royal guest the following day and issued a series of orders in connection with the event.

Venue: On Thursday 6 February, the London civic authorities decided that the Lord Mayor's house in Cornhill was too small for the masque; the royal party was therefore to move on to Merchant Taylors' Hall after supper. A committee was appointed to supervise the preparation of the hall (headed by Sir Hugh Hamersley, with Sir Robert Ducie, Richard Venn, Sir Maurice Abbott, Henry Garraway, Sir William Acton, Humphrey Smith, Anthony Abdy, Hugh Perry, and Henry Pratt); Hamersley and Venn were appointed to liaise with the Earl Marshal (Thomas Howard, 14th Earl of Arundel) and the Lord Chamberlain, with an initial meeting set for the morning of Friday 7 February. On Saturday 8 February, the Court of the Merchant Taylors' Company gave order for the gunpowder stored at the Hall to be removed.

Musical Arrangements: For the second performance, John Adson persuaded Bulstrode Whitelocke to hire twelve city waits to play during the procession; they were Adson himself, Ambrose Beeland, Jeffrey Collins, Henry Field, Thomas Hunter, Thomas Hutton, John Levasher, Francis Parker, Ralph Strachey, John Strong, Nicholas Underhill, and Edward Wright. However, this supplanted the King's musicians, and on Wednesday 12 February Nicholas Lanier protested to Whitelocke, who immediately reversed the decision, explaining that he had thought it beneath the dignity of the King's musicians to process. The disappointed waits were subsequently paid £6.10s for their trouble (£6 of this was paid by Whitelocke to Field and Strachey on Sunday 23 February).

Rehearsals: At some time between the two performances, one or more music rehearsals took place at Bulstrode Whitelocke's house. The instruments, which had been taken from Whitehall to the house of either Mr Riley or Richard Griffith, had to be brought there specially; they were then taken directly to Merchant Taylors' Hall for the second performance.

Procession: The masquers again processed through the streets of London before the performance, this time to Merchant Taylors' Hall. A scaffold was erected in Cornhill for the King and Queen to view the procession.

Performance: at Merchant Taylors' Hall on Thursday 13 February 1634. The performance took place in the evening after supper. The audience included: King Charles I; Queen Henrietta Maria; seventy lords and ladies; the Aldermen of London (some or all of: Sir Maurice Abbott, Anthony Abdy, Sir William Acton, Rowland Backhouse, Sir Edward Barkham, Edward Bromfield, Sir James Campbell, Robert Campbell, Christopher Clitherow, Samuel Cranmer, Sir Richard Deane, Sir Robert Ducie, Henry Garraway, Sir John

Gore, Sir Hugh Hamersley, Sir Martin Lumley, Thomas Moulson, Robert Parkhurst, Hugh Perry, Henry Pratt, Sir Nicholas Rainton, Humphrey Smith, Richard Venn, Sir George Whitmore, Edmund Wright); the Aldermen's wives and daughters, and other citizens. The Lord Mayor, Ralph Freeman, was ill and may have missed the masque (though he did greet the King on arrival and also presented himself during supper; he died just over a month later). Admission was by ticket, and two turnstile doors (one for the nobility and one for citizens) were installed to restrict entrance. After the performance, the masquers were given a cold supper; the antimasquers were given a barrel of beer at Drapers' Hall.

Aftermath: A little while after the masque, Finch, Gurlyn, Hyde, and Whitelocke were appointed to visit the King and thank him for graciously accepting the masque and deigning to be present at it. Both the King and Queen thanked them for their work, and the Queen told them 'that she never saw any masque more noble nor better performed than this was'.

Production Finance
By Friday 25 October 1633, a budget of £2,400 had been decided, with each Inn contributing £600. By Thursday 23 January, the projected expenses had doubled to £4,800: a further £600 had been requested from each Inn. (However, an undated document connected with the planning of the procession suggests a different escalation to the same total: each house had already levied £900, and they were now to be asked to raise another £300 each.)

Middle Temple
On Friday 25 October 1633, the Middle Temple authorities decided to levy £3 from each bencher, £2 from each barrister, and £1 from all other members; since it was recognized that the money might take a long time to collect, £300 was to be provided for immediate payment, borrowed by the Under-Treasurer John Bayliffe. Robert Thorpe was appointed the treasurer for the masque; he eventually received a payment of £5 for his services (paid before Friday 16 October 1635). On Friday 24 January the authorities decided to borrow money for their additional £600 contribution; John Barker (Chief Butler), John Bayliffe, and William Lane (Steward) were to make the arrangements, and to be indemnified by the house.

The Inn continued to levy its members in subsequent years to pay for the expenses; a masque roll is extant dated Friday 16 October 1635, recording receipts totalling £46 (including contributions of £1 each from John Barton, sen., John Bingham, Robert Boothby, Anthony Dering, Henry Lewis, John Lister, Richard Lydall, Richard Skippe, John Southcott; Thomas Morse was also listed but apparently paid nothing), of which £5 was paid to Francis Chafin for his assistance in collecting the money. Further masque roll receipts are extant for 1638-9 (£2, in equal sums from Gervase Holles and John Mitchell), 1640-1 (£11), and 1641-2 (£2), but these may pertain to the costs of *The Triumphs of the Prince D'Amour* (**2532**), or indeed to both masques.

Gray's Inn
On Friday 8 November 1633, it was formally agreed to finance the masque with a levy on members, with the rates set at £4 from each reader, £3 from each ancient, £2 from each barrister, and £1 from each gentleman. (These rates were already known to members, however; Thomas Coke reported them in a letter dated Thursday 17 October.) Ralph Whitfield was elected treasurer, with various members appointed to collect the money: John Godbold, Joseph Gulston, Richard Newdigate, Edward Rumsey, John Rutter, William Ward, and Samuel Wentworth. On Thursday 14 November, special rates were determined for named individuals, including the attorneys William Hooker, Mr Jones, and Edward Page (£3 each); Page was evidently not the Gray's Inn masquer of the same name, since the masquers were to be exempt from payment. On Monday 18 November, penalties were decreed against members who had not paid by Thursday 21: those in chambers would be ejected from them and put out of commons, while those not in chambers would be expected to pay double. On the Thursday, the collectors were ordered to present defaulters' names the following Saturday, 23 November.

On Thursday 23 January 1634, a second levy was agreed to defray the additional costs; this was to be half as much again as the first levy (i.e. £2, £1.10s, £1, and 10s), with exemption granted to the masquers and those who were to ride in the procession. When this proved insufficient, a third levy was agreed on Wednesday 5 February, again at half as much as the previous (second) assessment (i.e. £1, 15s, 10s, and 5s). John Heilen was appointed as a collector in place of Samuel Wentworth, who was out of town. Again, there were difficulties collecting the money, and on Monday 12 May, non-payers were given until Thursday 15 to pay up or lose their chambers.

Richard Gibbs made a loan of £50, which was repaid in four instalments on Monday 21 December 1635 (£25), Saturday 20 May 1637 (£10), Tuesday 20 June 1637 (£5), and Tuesday 24 October 1637 (£10).

On Wednesday 12 November 1634, the authorities reissued orders for contributions, requiring defaulters to pay up, and appointed Lambert Osbaldeston and Edward Rumsey to meet with the representatives of the other Inns about the outstanding masque money.

Inner Temple
On Tuesday 12 November 1633, the Inner Temple set its levy at £5 from each bencher, £2.10s from each senior barrister, £2 from junior barristers, and £1 from other members. Individual office-holders were levied as follows: Matthew Cradock, Francis Williamson (£2); Richard Barringer, Humphrey Streete (£3.6s.8d);

Richard Brownlowe (£5); Thomas Fanshawe, William Rolfe (£6.13s.4d); Robert Henley, Samuel Wightwick, Hugh Audley, William Blage (£10). Thomas Willis was appointed to collect the Inner Temple's financial contribution, and he, Thomas Caesar, and Timothy Pollard were appointed to supervise its disbursement.

By Sunday 9 February 1634, it was known that too little money had been raised. Thomas Willis had already received payments from 'the stock of the house' as well as from subscriptions, and now the authorities decided to draw further on their stock: he was paid an overall total of £626. On the same date, Edward Bulstrode, William Farrar, and Edward Trotman were appointed as a committee to audit expenditure and recommend how much more needed to be raised. They reported on Sunday 22 June that at least £100 more would be required, and a payment was authorized from stock; but it remained unpaid at the end of the Inner Temple's accounting year on Monday 3 November, and on Sunday 23 November the authorities ordered £170 to be paid to Willis. On the same date, the committee was asked to consider what rewards should be paid to Willis's and Sir Richard Shelton's men for their part in the masque arrangements.

Thomas Nash contributed £2.10s, on an unknown date apparently between Monday 21 July and Saturday 1 November 1634.

Lincoln's Inn

On Thursday 14 November 1633, William Hakewill informed the Council of Lincoln's Inn that a contribution of £600 was required. The Council agreed to a per capita levy at the following rates: benchers and associates, £6; senior barristers, £3; junior barristers, £2; other members, £1. The four masquers themselves, 25 assistants, and freshmen, were to be exempt; all others had to pay on pain of exclusion from commons. John Greene was appointed the treasurer for the masque, and the following were to collect the money: Humphrey Chambers, William Glinne, Matthew Hales, Richard Mason.

Before Tuesday 7 January 1634, [Eusebius?] Wright agreed to lend £250 towards the expenses, to be repaid with interest in seven annual instalments of £50 (but with the last £50 remitted if he should die before the loan had been repaid). By Thursday 6 February, Edward Wendover offered to lend £100 interest-free, to be repaid in three annual instalments of £33.6s.8d; at the same time, Sir Edward Clarke also offered a £100 loan, repayable over five years in £20 instalments due each succeeding 14 February (1635–9).

Sir Robert Rich was assessed to pay £6 towards the masque, but failed to do so. The chief butler was sent to ask him for the money, but he refused because he was not resident in the Inn, nor did he eat there. The butler was sent a second time to ask him to pay or attend the Council meeting on Thursday 6 February to explain his reasons for not doing so. Instead, he sent a letter which was read at the meeting, in which he said he hadn't time to come to them but would receive any bencher they sent to him. The Council took offence at the letter, and expelled him from membership of Lincoln's Inn.

Later, the house had to borrow £450 to make up its revised contribution, and on Tuesday 6 May, John Greene reported that there was still a deficit of £200. After an audit of expenditure, Mr [Samuel?] Taylor reported on Tuesday 11 November 1634 that a number of assessed contributions were unpaid. The Council ordered the collectors to identify the defaulters, and on Thursday 20 November instructed them to pay by the following day; it was also agreed that no further contributions would be ordered over and above the existing assessments.

On Thursday 12 November 1635, Greene reported that he was in possession of a surplus; the Council ordered him to render accounts, including a note of those who had not paid their assessments. In consequence it was discovered that one of the benchers, Edmund Escourt, had neglected to pay, and on Thursday 19 November he was ordered to do so.

On Tuesday 20 June 1637, John Herne was asked to consult with the other three Inns in the question of the masque's finance.

Production Expenses

Expenses were estimated in advance as (on Friday 6 December) £4,000–£5,000, and (on Thursday 9 January) £20,000. After the event, Bulstrode Whitelocke's estimate was £21,000. Surviving Inns of Court financial records, however, indicate a total payment by all four Inns of only £5,003.18s.8d, though this may not be comprehensive. The rest of the cost probably fell on the individual participants. (It is therefore relevant that gossip at the time, recorded in William Whiteway's diary, put the cost to the performers at £17,000.)

On Thursday 20 and Friday 21 February, the committees passed decisions relating to the payment of the attendants in the procession. Payments were made by Lincoln's Inn, and the cost divided equally between the four Inns; John Herne was the Lincoln's Inn payee for the others' contributions (and the extant warrants are for payments to him of the Middle Temple's share). The four French musicians (Maturin Mari, Nicholas Duvall, Jacques Gaultier, and Anthony Roberts) were paid in an unusual way: Bulstrode Whitelocke invited them to dine with him at St Dunstan's tavern on Saturday 1 March, and each man had set before him a covered dish, which turned out to contain £40 in gold coins.

Antimasque Costumes: The following payments were made, totalling £824.13s: priests', antimasquers', torchbearers', and trumpeters' costumes, made by John Weaver, John Walker, and William Patten (£820, paid in seven instalments of £100, £80, £100, £120, £100, £120, and £200, Middle Temple warrants dated

Monday 13, Wednesday 15, Thursday 23, Tuesday 28, and Friday 31 January, and Saturday 8 and Monday 17 February; the total bill is recorded as £800, but the total recorded payment is £20 more); masks and torches for the antimasquers, supplied by William Greenhawe (£4.13s, Middle Temple warrant dated Thursday 20 February).

Main Masque Costumes: The following payments were made, totalling £1,331.15s.10d: 104 yards of incarnadine Florence satin, 88 yards of white Florence satin, 49 ells of white taffeta, and 40 ells of white Florence taffeta sarcenet, for the masquers' costumes, supplied by Edmund Griffith and James Bencroft (£196.15s.8d, Middle Temple warrant dated Monday 13 January); making, cutting, and trimming of the masquers' suits and hats by Peter le Huc (£193.15s, Middle Temple warrant dated Thursday 20 February; only £193.14s.2d was paid); embroidering the masquers' costumes (£528, paid in two instalments of £160 and £368, Middle Temple warrants dated Saturday 4 and Monday 20 January); sixteen pairs of roses, supplied by William Gumbleton (£20, Middle Temple warrant dated Monday 13 January); plumes, supplied Mr [William?] Audley and his partner, presumably Peter le Knite (£72, Middle Temple warrant dated Wednesday 15 January); bands, cuffs, and strings for the masquers' costumes, supplied by Mr Basse (£95.10s, paid in two instalments of £88 and £7.10s, Middle Temple warrants dated Thursday 23 January and Thursday 20 February); silk stockings for the masquers' costumes, supplied by Mr Robinson (£32, Middle Temple warrant dated Friday 31 January); coats, scarves, and banners for two trumpeters, and taffeta sarcenet for the masquers' trousers, supplied by Edmund Griffith (£9.2s, Middle Temple warrant dated Tuesday 4 February); feathers for the masquers, Marshal's men, trumpeters, chariots, and horses, supplied by Mr [William?] Audley and Peter le Knite (£111.12s, Middle Temple warrant dated Wednesday 19 February); copper points and tinsels supplied by Mr Spencer (£23.12s, Middle Temple warrant dated Thursday 20 February; £26 was actually paid); masquers' masks, supplied by John King (£12.16s, Middle Temple warrant dated Thursday 27 February); masquers' silk stockings for the second performance, supplied by Mr Tooken (£32, Middle Temple warrant dated Friday 21 November 1634); a pair of silk stockings for [Edward?] Herne (£2.6s, paid by the Middle Temple on Wednesday 17 June 1635).

Design: Inigo Jones was paid a total of £200, and Anthony Jarman the carpenter £100 for making the scenery; half the total sum (i.e. £150) was pre-paid to them in December (Middle Temple warrant dated Friday 20 December 1633; however, the later account dates it Tuesday 17 December).

Performers: Payments totalling £240 were made: antimasque actors (£80, in two instalments of £50 and £30, Middle Temple warrant dated Friday 28 February); antimasque dancers (£160, Middle Temple warrant dated Friday 28 February. However, the total paid to the antimasquers, possibly including actors, was also recorded as £132.12s).

Music: William Lawes and Simon Ives were to have been paid £100 each: an initial payment of £65 was to have been made to each of them on Tuesday 25 February, but this payment was cancelled; they eventually received £55 each in two instalments (£35 on Monday 17 March and £20 on Wednesday 16 April). The other musicians were paid as follows: Maturin Mari, Nicholas Duvall, Jacques Gaultier, and Anthony Roberts (£40 each); Thomas Day (£30, including £10 for the services of his three boys); Henry Lawes, John Lanier, Thomas Holmes, Davis Mell, John Kellaway, and John Wilson (£20 each); John Drew, John Frost, John Lawes, William Webb, Peter Jacob, Dietrich Stoeffken, and Thomas Bedowes (£15 each); Charles Coleman and Walter Porter (£15 each, including £5 each for the services of their boys); Roger Nightingale, Thomas Lawton, Nicholas Ham, John Lawrence, Robert Keith, Robert Tomkins, William Tomkins, William Smegergil, William Page, Richard Miller, John Kelly, John Jenkins, and John Woodington (£10 each); fourteen violinists (£120, paid to John Heydon, John Hopper, and Thomas Warren on Saturday 22 February); twelve members of the King's loud music (£20; paid to Anthony Bassano and Henry Bassano on Monday 24 February); Francis Dickinson (£35, in two instalments of £5 and £30); the Lord Chamberlain's boy (£5, paid to William Lawes); Walter Porter's boy and Charles Coleman's boy (£1 each). The messenger Richard Griffith was paid £2 (in two equal instalments). Mr Riley was paid 13s for the loan of instruments 'and for things the first night'.

The total itemized sum laid out for music in Bulstrode Whitelocke's accounts (including the £6.10s payment to the disappointed waits, but excluding the deferred payments to Ives and William Lawes) was £766.3s; but the Middle Temple warrant dated Friday 21 February records a total payment of £845. Most of the payments to individual musicians were made on Monday 24 and Tuesday 25 February, but some outstanding fees were paid on Tuesday 4 March (Jenkins), Monday 10 March (Woodington, Kelly, Henry Lawes, and the Lord Chamberlain's boy), and Wednesday 16 April (Jacob).

Whitelocke later estimated costs of about £1,000, and John Herne recorded a total payment of £925; the latter total includes a payment to the musicians who attended the masquers at their rehearsals (£80, Middle Temple warrant dated Monday 24 February). Stephen de Nau and Sebastian la Pierre were paid £100 each (Middle Temple warrant dated Tuesday 25 February; this covered choreography, composition of music, and attendance at rehearsals). La Pierre was also due to be reimbursed expenses of £12.10s connected with the antimasque, and a warrant for the Middle Temple's share was issued on Friday 21 November 1634. The money, however, seems not to have reached la Pierre and was reportedly still unpaid in 1637; on Tuesday 9 May, two benchers of Lincoln's Inn, John Greene and John Herne, were asked to investigate. A payment of £12 for antimasque music was made, apparently without a warrant; and £10 was paid to Thomas Bassett, John Seywell, Thomas Rudstone, John Fidler, Robert Davis and John Morton (Middle Temple warrant dated Monday 17 February). A bill is extant, apparently for work undertaken in connection with the second performance, amounting to £11.14s, including charges for the loan of treble lutes (£2) and for carrying the instruments (10s).

Lefkowitz (in *JAMS*) suggests that the record of a payment of £120 to fourteen violinists is in error and that there were actually fifteen (which would mean that they got a round sum of £8 each). There were indeed fifteen members of the King's violins, as listed elsewhere in the Whitelocke papers, but one of them was John Woodington, who was one of the musicians playing in the 'symphony' and who was presumably therefore not available to join his fourteen colleagues accompanying the main masque dances; he was paid separately. This means that one violinist, Davis Mell, was paid twice, as an individual and as one of the fourteen violinists; but the individual payment was clearly for other services such as composing music and playing at dance rehearsals.

Lighting: The total sum recorded for torches for both performances was £132.16s.8d, but payments made in 1634 amount to £163.12s.8d, as follows: flambeaux and torches supplied by Matthew Fox (£28.10s, Middle Temple warrant dated Monday 17 February); 504 torches and fifteen flambeaux (£28.16s.8d, Middle Temple warrant dated Friday 21 February); 840 torches and sixty flambeaux used in the first performance, supplied by William Lovell and Henry Bishop (£46.18s, Middle Temple warrant dated Friday 21 February); 500 torches and fifteen flambeaux used in the second performance, supplied by William Lovell (£28.12s, Middle Temple warrant dated Tuesday 25 February); reimbursement of Thomas Willis for torches and flambeaux he purchased for use in the masque (£30.16s, Middle Temple warrant dated Wednesday 26 February). A further £1 for torches on the first night was paid by the Middle Temple on Wednesday 17 June 1635.

Gratuities: The following payments were made, totalling £114.10s or £114: servants of Francis White, Bishop of Ely, and Lady Elizabeth Hatton for attending the masquers at Ely House and Hatton House (£20, half to each household, Middle Temple warrant dated Monday 17 February; paid by William Noy); the officers of Lincoln's Inn (£20, Middle Temple warrant dated Friday 21 November 1634); officers of Southampton House for attending the masquers (£10, Middle Temple warrant dated Friday 28 February; paid by Robert Mason); John Hillyard, the messenger attending the production committee (£4.10s, in two instalments: £1, Middle Temple warrant dated Tuesday 24 December 1633; £3.10s, Middle Temple warrant dated 21 November 1634; the audited accounts, however, seem to indicate that he was paid £4); servants and others attending at the masque (£40); Guillaume la Pierre (£20, Middle Temple warrant dated Friday 21 November 1634).

Sundry: The following payments were made, totalling £107.15s.10d: candles, wine, and coal for the masque committees (14s.10d, paid by Sir Edward Clarke, Treasurer of Lincoln's Inn, to the steward, Samuel Taylor); wine, bread, and beer for the masquers, supplied by George Smythson (£25, Middle Temple warrant dated Monday 17 February); cotton for the Banqueting House floor and cloth for the Marshal's men, supplied by Mr Newman (£73.11s, Middle Temple warrant dated Thursday 20 February); payment to the printer Thomas Walkley (£5; Middle Temple warrant dated Friday 21 November 1634); payment to one Dadly (£1.5s, without warrant); payment to Sir Laurence Hyde's man (5s, paid before Friday 16 October 1635); payment to John Pepys (£2, on Tuesday 16 February 1636). In addition, the authorities of the Inner Temple hired four watchmen to watch the premises on the nights of the two performances, at a total cost of 4s.

Court: The total cost to the Works Office of preparing the Banqueting House for both this masque and *Coelum Britannicum* (**2428**) was £254.3s.7d.

Corporation of London: On Tuesday 25 February, the Corporation of London instructed its committee responsible for the second performance to present its accounts. Payments were authorized as follows: Tuesday 25 February (£7.16s); Thursday 27 February (£65.15s.10d); Friday 28 March (£122.11s.4½d); Tuesday 15 April (£502.2s.11d, including the carpenter's bill for work done at Merchant Taylors' Hall); Tuesday 22 April (£115); Tuesday 6 May (£470); Tuesday 24 June (£4.1s.7d). The total cost to the city (including the culinary as well as the dramatic part of the entertainment) was thus £1,287.7s.8½d. Specific production-related expenses include: hire of 52 lighting branches from William Penrin, and replacement of those which were lost (£31.11s); candles and three flambeaux supplied by Henry Box (£2.15s); 240 wax lights and 228 torches supplied by Bartholomew Hitche (£20.4s); 216 wax lights and 120 torches supplied by Stafford Clare (£13.15s); payment to John Spiller for wax candles, carriage of stools to and from the hall, personal attendance, and reimbursement of money disbursed (£2.9s.3d; £1.10s of this covered his attendance).

Procession Expenses

The one hundred gentlemen in the procession paid for the clothes which they and their attendants wore; the cost was estimated at £100 for each suit.

Chariots: The following payments were made, totalling £449.2s.2d: six chariots, reins for the horses, and other services supplied by Rowland Buckett (£272.17s, paid in three instalments of £80, £80, and

£112.17s, Middle Temple warrants dated Saturday 11 and Thursday 23 January, and Friday 21 February); chariots, clothing, and caparison for the horses, supplied by Mr Smith of St Martin's (£120, Middle Temple warrant dated Thursday 23 January); stuffs for the horses, chariots, and charioteers, supplied by Mr Smith of St Martin's (£24.5s.2d, Middle Temple warrant dated Wednesday 19 February); caparisons and saddle covers supplied by Mr Abbott the saddler, and for his attendance at the procession (£32, Middle Temple warrant dated Thursday 20 February); see also under main *Costume* expenses.

Horse Hire: The following payments were made, totalling a maximum of £37.1s.4d: antimasquers' horses, supplied by Thomas Styles (£11, Middle Temple warrant dated Thursday 20 February); James Willett, for care of the antimasquers' horses, attendance at Ely House by Garrett, and 'other petty payments' (£1.6s.8d, Middle Temple warrant dated Thursday 20 February); hire of horses and coach, with associated labour, supplied by Hugh Roberts (£1.10s, paid by Thomas Lane on Tuesday 25 February); coach hire from Robert Day (12s, paid by Thomas Lane on Tuesday 4 March); reimbursement of Nathaniel Gurlyn's horse-hire expenses (£16.19s.8d; may include some of the above payments); horse hire (£2.13s, without warrant); hire of a saddle from Thomas Smithsby (£3, paid by the Middle Temple on Wednesday 17 June 1635). John Johnson of the Inner Temple paid £5 for his own horse, and was never reimbursed.

Torchbearers: The costumes, made by John Wood, plus feathers and masks, cost £94 (paid in two instalments of £40 to John Wood and £54 to Thomas Wood, Middle Temple warrants dated Monday 13 January and Monday 17 February); see also under main *Costume* expenses.

On Thursday 20 February 1634, the organizing committee agreed that each of the torchbearers who attended the procession on both days should be paid 2s.6d, with each Inn taking responsibility for paying its own appointees. On Wednesday 26 February, Robert Thorpe was asked in error to submit the Middle Temple's share, reckoned at £10, but the original plan held and the Inns paid the torchbearers themselves; the total amount paid was reckoned to be £10 per Inn, but exact figures are not available. A further payment was made to seventeen watermen who carried torches twice (£8.10s, paid before Friday 16 October 1635).

Musicians: The following payments were made, totalling £120.19s: twelve coats, scarves, and banners for the trumpeters and drummers, supplied by Edmund Griffith (£43.19s, Middle Temple warrant dated Thursday 23 January); payments to trumpeters and drummer (£5 each, totalling £75, agreed by the organizing committee on Thursday 20 February; Middle Temple warrant dated Friday 21 February); payment for music at Denmark House (£2, without warrant); see also under main *Costume* expenses and under *Marshal's Men*.

Marshal's Men: The following payments were made, totalling £92.7s.8d: eight or more suits, hats, feathers, and belts, plus twenty ells of cloth, supplied by Nicholas Maunder (£26.14s.4d, paid in two instalments of £16 and £10.14s.4d, Middle Temple warrants, the first dated only February, the second Tuesday 18 February); ten suits, supplied by Bridle the tailor (£6, Middle Temple warrant dated 19 February); lining of the suits, plus making of six coats for the charioteers, by George Norbury (£19, Middle Temple warrant dated Wednesday 12 February); lace for the suits, supplied by Thomas Chapman (£10.13s.4d, Middle Temple warrant dated Saturday 22 February; in the Middle Temple's account there is also a record of a payment of £10.13s.8d to one Pory for lace for the suits, which may be the same one despite the 4d discrepancy); 63 hats and bands for the Marshal's men and trumpeters, and a Monmouth cap for the drummer, supplied by Thomas Tyler (£21, Middle Temple warrant dated Wednesday 19 February); belts, supplied by Nicholas Clement (£5, Middle Temple warrant dated Monday 17 February); eighty truncheons, supplied by [Francis] Tipsley (£4, in two equal instalments, Middle Temple warrants dated Friday 24 January and Monday 17 February); see also under main *Costume* and *Sundry* expenses.

Charioteers: Six pairs of buskins, supplied by Abraham Ewre, cost £1.16s (Middle Temple warrant dated Friday 14 February); see also under *Marshal's Men*.

Gratuities: On Thursday 20 February 1634, the organizing committee agreed the following gratuities, totalling £9.10s: the Bishop of Ely's grooms (£2); the grooms employed by Sir William Jones, Sir George Croke, Sir Robert Berkeley, Sir Francis Ashley, and Serjeant John Hoskyns (10s each, totalling £2.10s); Thomas Willis's groom (£1); and the housekeeper's man at Denmark House (£3.10s); they also made a 10s allowance 'for the dog'.

Further gratuities, totalling £25, were paid to the Marshals of London (£10, Middle Temple warrant dated Friday 21 November 1634), and, before Friday 16 October 1635, to the following: Sir William Jones's men, Sir George Croke's men, and Sir Robert Berkeley's men (£9); Serjeant John Hoskyns's men (£2); Henry Anott (£4).

Audit and Reimbursement

On Friday 10 October 1634, the authorities of Gray's Inn appointed a committee to take Ralph Whitfield's accounts, comprising Mr Brickenden, William Gerrard, Mr Pheasant, and Edward Rumsey. Whitfield eventually presented his accounts on Friday 29 January 1636; on the same day, the authorities appointed [Augustine or Henry] Reve and [Joseph or William] Bryan to take Edward Rumsey's account.

John Greene presented his accounts to Lincoln's Inn, and on Tuesday 4 November 1634 the Council appointed Edward Fettiplace, Mr Taylor, John

Wakering, and Mr Wright to audit them and make a report.

At the Inner Temple, Thomas Willis's accounts were verified on Sunday 25 January 1635 and he was discharged from all further obligation. On Sunday 8 February, the authorities ordered the reimbursement of subscriptions and expenses for hiring saddles (for use in the procession) to [Dudley or George] Pope and John Finch; Pope was eventually reimbursed £2.15s (including £1.15s for saddle hire) and Finch £1; reimbursements also went to Rowland Reinoldes (£4.6s) and [William?] Carew (£1).

The Middle Temple was still reimbursing John Herne and Edward Hyde as late as 1638: on Saturday 19 May, Herne was paid £12.10s (the Middle Temple's share of an outstanding debt of £50). On the same date, Hyde was paid £9.4s (for torches and silk stockings; the full debt, if owed by all four Inns, may have been £50; a previous instalment of £3.6s had been paid before Friday 16 October 1635).

EARLY TEXTUAL HISTORY

1633–4: For writing the masque, James Shirley was paid £100 by the Inns of Court (an initial payment of £40 in December 1633, the balance of £60 in February, Middle Temple warrant dated Monday 3 February).

1634: extracts from Songs 1–5, apparently in early versions, appear on a **MS** cue-sheet written out by Bulstrode Whitelocke.

1634: entered (as *The Masque of the Four Inns of Court*) to William Cooke in the Stationers' Register on Friday 24 January. (This was ten days before the first performance.) Sir John Finch had licensed the book for publication.

1634: $^1Q_\alpha$ and $^2Q_\beta$ printed by John Norton for William Cooke, before Monday 24 March; collation a^2 A–D^4, 18 leaves; title page names author; Latin title-page motto; epistle to the Inns of Court signed by the author. The text for the two editions was set in simultaneous duplicate and the copies assembled indiscriminately from the sheets of the two settings.

1634: $^3Q_3$ printed by John Norton for William Cooke, before Monday 24 March; the edition was printed partly from standing type set for the first two editions.

1634: At some time during the week ending Monday 10 February, Justinian Pagitt sent a copy of the masque to his kinsman, one Tremyll.

1634: At some point between Tuesday 4 and Thursday 13 February, Shirley wrote new material for inclusion in the second performance. This extra work may have been the reason he later received a supplementary payment of £20 (Middle Temple warrant dated Friday 21 November).

1634: On Wednesday 19 February, William Gawdy sent a copy of the masque to his father, Framlingham Gawdy.

1634: Q_3 reissued (as $Q_{3\beta}$) with an additional leaf containing a speech added in the second performance. The book now has 19 leaves, but the placement of the added leaf varies between surviving copies.

1634: In July, John Newdigate bought 'a book of the masque', probably this one (but possibly **2428**); in any event he eventually owned copies of both masques.

1638: William Lawes's musical settings for Songs 1–3 included in a MS virginal-book (London: Museum of London, MS 46.78/748, fos. 16^v, 24^r, 29^r) owned by Anne Cromwell of Upwood, Huntingdonshire (a cousin of Oliver Cromwell). The MS was later owned by her grandson.

1638–45: incipits and settings of Songs 1–3 and 9 included in William Lawes's autograph songbook (Oxford: Bodleian, MS Mus. Sch. b. 2, pp. 34–41.

c. 1641–45: Song 8 (headed 'Amphiluche in a Masque') included, with Lawes's setting, in his autograph music MS (London: British Library, Add. MS 31432, fo. 26^r). Lawes later gave the book to Richard Gibbon, whose widow, Anne, gave it away in turn, probably at some time between 1652 and 1656, to one J. R. (probably John Reading).

c. 1640: Song 8 included, with Lawes's musical setting, in a MS songbook (New York Public Library, Music Division, MS Drexel 4041, No. 20, fo. 16).

1646: Cooke's rights transferred in the Stationers' Register to Humphrey Moseley on Saturday 12 December; masque and author individually named as part of a group transfer of two titles. (The other was *The Contention for Honour and Riches*, **2274**.)

c. 1640s–50s: Lawes's settings for Songs 1–3 included in a set of MS musical part-books, of which the bass part survives (Oxford: Christ Church, MS Mus. 1022, p. 27, nos. 60–2); the MS was probably compiled in Oxford.

After 1648: Song 7 included, with Lawes's setting, in a set of four MS musical part-books (New York Public Library, MS Mus. Res. *MNZ (Chirk)).

1649: music for Song 1 included, in an arrangement by Pieter Pers, in Paulus Matthysz, *'t Uitnemend Kabinet von Pavanen, Almanden, Sarabanden, Couranten, Balleten, Intraden, Airs, &c.*, fos. 17^r–18^r; printed at Amsterdam.

c. 1650s: Song 7 included, with Lawes's musical setting, in a set of MS songbooks compiled by Edward Lowe, of which two treble parts survive (Oxford: Bodleian, MS Mus. d. 238, pp. 196–5 rev.; Edinburgh University Library, MS Dc 1.69, fo. 109).

1652: music for Song 1 included in Richard Mathew, *The Lute's Apology*, no. 21; printed by Thomas Harper for Livewell Chapman.

1653–60: $^4Q_4$ may have been printed for Humphrey Moseley, who advertised it; but no copy is known to survive.

1654: Song 1 included in a MS music-book (Oxford: Bodleian, MS Mus. d. 220, fo. 83^r (no. 70).

After *c.* 1655: instrumental music, and the settings for Songs 1–3, included in five MS part-books (London: British Library, Add. MS 18940–4).

1656: three pieces of Lawes's music for the masque (including settings for Songs 1 and 2) included in a MS virginal-book (London: British Library, Add. MS 10337, fo. 4ᵛ–5ʳ, 19ᵛ) belonging to Elizabeth Rogers.

1657: advertised as for sale by the Newcastle-upon-Tyne bookseller William London.

1671: dance music by Simon Ives included in a MS music-book (Cambridge University Library, MS Dd VI 48, fos. 30–1).

1673: settings for Songs 1 and 2 included in MS musical part-book (Oxford: Bodleian, MS Mus. d. 245–6, fo. 211ʳ) compiled by William Isles.

1678: *New Airs and Dialogues* received an imprimatur on Saturday 4 May.

1678: Lawes's music for Songs 1 and 3 (signed with the composer's initials) included in John Banister and Thomas Low, *New Airs and Dialogues*, nos. 12, 27, sigs. 2B4ᵛ, 2E4ᵛ; printed (probably in the autumn) by Andrew Clark and Mary Clark for Henry Brome.

1679: *New Airs and Dialogues* entered to Henry Brome in the Stationers' Register on Thursday 2 October.

1684: Nicholas Cox (Manciple of St Edmund Hall, Oxford) had a copy of Q₃ in his bookshop. It had probably been previously owned by Gerard Langbaine, and appears on a list compiled by Anthony Wood on Saturday 13 December.

EDITIONS

Clifford Leech, in T. J. B. Spencer and Stanley Wells (eds.), *A Book of Masques* (Cambridge, 1967), 275–313.

Murray Lefkowitz, in *Trois Masques a la Cour de Charles Iᵉʳ D'Angleterre* (Paris, 1970), 27–109.

Orgel and Strong, ii. 536–65.

Sabol, nos. 36–9, 384, 414, 416; see also nos. 209–10, 222, 228, 236, 382–3, 385, 428 (songs and music only).

Alan H. Nelson and John R. Elliott, jun., in REED: Inns of Court (Cambridge, 2010), 591–612.

Barbara Ravelhofer, in James Shirley, *The Complete Works*, gen. eds. Eugene Giddens, Teresa Grant, and Barbara Ravelhofer (Oxford, forthcoming).

REFERENCES

Annals 1634; Bawcutt 288; Beal 2 ShJ 197–204; Bentley, ii. 675–6, v. 1154–63; Bodleian, MS Wood E. 4, art. 1, p. 7; Butler, 298–310, 373; *Cal. Dom, 1633–4*, 464; *Cal. Dom. 1634–5*, 81; *Cal. Ven. 1632–6*, 180, 195; *Chelys* 11 (1982), 25–6; *Chelys* 31 (2003), 3–17; *ELH* 51 (1984), 422–4; *EMS* 3 (1988), 192–215; Eyre & Rivington, iii. 88; Reginald J. Fletcher (ed.), *The Pension Book of Gray's Inn* (London, 1901), i. 317–20, 323, 326; Robert Stanley Forsythe, *The Relations of Shirley's Plays to the Elizabethan Drama* (New York, 1914), 398–9; A. Wigfall Green, *The Inns of Court and Early English Drama* (New Haven, 1931), 123–32; Greg 488; Hazlitt, 234; HMC Cowper, ii. 34; *The Honour of the Inns of Court Gentlemen* (London, 1634; English Broadside Ballad Archive 33486); Charles Henry Hopwood (ed.), *A Calendar of the Middle Temple Records* (London, 1903), 64–5, 67, 95; Charles Henry Hopwood (ed.), *Middle Temple Records* (London, 1904–5), ii. 812, 814–15, 852–3, 997; David Howarth, *Lord Arundel and his Circle* (New Haven and London, 1985), 114; F. A. Inderwick, *A Calendar of the Inner Temple Records* (London, 1896–1901), ii. 210–14, 217, 219–20; *Journal of the American Musicological Society* 18 (1965), 42–60; Vivienne Larminie, *Wealth, Kinship and Culture* (Woodbridge, 1995), 202; Francis Lenton, *The Inns of Court Anagrammatized* (London, 1634); *The Library*, 5th ser., 1 (1946–7), 113–26; *The Library*, 5th ser., 7 (1952), 225–34; David Lindley (ed.), *The Court Masque* (Manchester, 1984), 161–2; William London, *A Catalogue of the Most Vendible Books in England* (London, 1657), sig. 2F1ᵛ; Loomie, 148–50; McGee-Meagher 1625–34, 78–90; *MRDE* 5 (1991), 309–42; *MRDE* 6 (1993), 191; *MRDE* 7 (1995), 341–2; MSC 1.1, 99–100; MSC 2.3, 362; MSC 3, 179–80; MSC 10, 46; MSC 12, 31–84; MSC 13, 127; MSC 15, 177–9; *Music and Letters* 47 (1966), 10–26; John Peacock, *The Stage Designs of Inigo Jones* (Cambridge, 1995), 92–3, 96–7, 129, 135, 250–1, 253–4, 305–8, 331 n. 38; REED: Dorset, 204–5; REED: Inns of Court, 234–342, 344–6, 348, 352, 355, 360, 362, 699–707, 720–4, 739–40, 768, 776–7, 808; REED: Oxford, 513; *REED Newsletter* 12.2 (1987), 14; *REED Newsletter* 13.2 (1988), 2–9; Reyher, 505, 530–1, Steele, 247–8; Sullivan, 144; *Theatre Survey* 20 (1979), 19–20; J. Douglas Walker (ed.), *The Records of the Honourable Society of Lincoln's Inn: The Black Books* (London, 1897–1902), ii. 312, 314–18, 320, 342–3; Bulstrode Whitelocke, *The Diary*, ed. Ruth Spalding (Oxford, 1990), 73–6, 86; Bulstrode Whitelocke, *Memorials of the English Affairs* (Oxford, 1853), i. 53–62; Withington, i. 117–18.

2424. Covent Garden

TEXT
Printed in 1638 (STC 18339).

GENRE
comedy
Contemporary: play (prol., ep., S.R.); 'pleasant comedy' (t.p.)

TITLE
Printed: Covent Garden

AUTHOR
Thomas Nabbes

DATE
Limits: 1633–4
Best Guess: February 1634

2424. Covent Garden

The Q title page gives the date of performance as 1632, and Bentley infers from the pre-Lenten setting that the play must have opened in February 1633 (which was still 1632 by the old style). However, this cannot be right. Dobson's remark in the first scene, wishing he 'had stayed still in the country, now sports are tolerated', clearly places the play shortly after the reissue of the King's *Book of Sports* in October 1633; in striking contrast, the play to which this one responds, *The Weeding of the Covent Garden* (**2401**), written some time before October, includes an observation that 'holiday sports are cried up [i.e. decried] in the country'. It is unlikely that the reference to toleration was an interpolation for a later performance, since Nabbes indicates in the Q dedication that the play was not especially successful on stage: it received only 'some partial allowance'. Parts of the Q title page appear to have been set from standing type for the equivalent parts on the title page of *Tottenham Court* (**2405**), which would have been set not more than eight weeks earlier; but there is some tinkering in the line containing the date, and this was presumably the point at which the error was introduced. One possible explanation is that copy was marked to change the year MDCXXXIII to MDCXXXIV, but the correction was misread and the final letter simply deleted rather than II being turned into V. Applying Bentley's reasoning to the new (albeit partly hypothetical) data, the pre-Lenten setting would also support a date in early 1634; the effect would be to narrow the hiatus between this and Nabbes's next known play, *Hannibal and Scipio* (**2480**).

ORIGINAL PRODUCTION
Queen Henrietta's Men at the Cockpit

PLOT
Dungworth comes to London from the country with his servants, Ralph and Dobson, intending to sell some of his lands and buy himself a knighthood. Artlove aims to woo Dorothy Worthy, and Mistress Tongueall offers her services as matchmaker—but also helps the foolish Littleword to the same ends. Hugh Jerker's objective is to cuckold Dorothy's father, Sir Generous Worthy: Lady Worthy was Jerker's mistress before she was forced to marry Sir Generous to get her away from him.

Warrant and Spruce are both interested in the waiting-woman, Susan, and meet to fight a duel over her. Warrant has taken the precaution of procuring an advance pardon for killing Spruce, and Spruce anticipates that, if he kills Warrant, Susan will save his life with a gallows wedding. In the event, both are too cowardly to fight, and Susan and Dorothy, who are watching, engage Dobson and Ralph to attack them. Both talk their way out of a beating, leaving behind clothes and money. The servants consider taking up robbery as a profession. They have an altercation with Dorothy's brother, but Artlove intervenes and sees them off. Young Worthy vets his rescuer as a potential brother-in-law, and recommends him to Dorothy. She resents this interference, but eventually accepts Artlove.

At the tavern, Ralph and Dobson are arrested for the robbery and brought before Sir Generous; but Warrant refuses to admit that he was robbed, and the case collapses. Ralph and Dobson conduct a mock-trial, with themselves as judge and constable, and use the opportunity to pass satirical comment on several characters.

Lady Worthy arranges an assignation with Jerker, and asks Susan to be the lookout. Instead, Susan fetches the jealous Sir Generous, who arrives to see his wife kissing Jerker. Jerker suggests that he should divorce her; but she explains that the assignation was set up to cure her husband's jealousy. It does.

SCENE DESIGNATION
prol., 1.1–6, 2.1–7, 3.1–5, 4.1–6, 5.1–6, ep. (Q)

The stage is only clear between the acts.

ROLES
PROLOGUE
Roger DUNGWORTH, a country landowner
RALPH, Dungworth's servant
John DOBSON, Dungworth's servant
Mistress TONGUEALL, a match-maker
Master Theodore ARTLOVE, a gentleman heir
Master LITTLEWORD, a foolish gentleman
Master Hugh JERKER, a young man, Jeffrey's kinsman
JEFFREY Jerker, Jerker's kinsman; a youth just under the age of majority; said to be little
Mistress DOROTHY Worthy, a gentlewoman, Sir Generous's daughter, Young Worthy's sister
Mistress SUSAN, Dorothy's waiting-woman; also called Mistress Secretary (but it is unclear whether this is her name or her office)
Master WARRANT, Sir Generous's clerk
Master SPRUCE, Lady Worthy's gentleman usher; formerly a tailor
LADY WORTHY, a young woman, Sir Generous's second wife, stepmother of Dorothy and Young Worthy; formerly Hugh Jerker's mistress
SIR GENEROUS Worthy, an old knight and judge; Lady Worthy's husband, father of Dorothy and Young Worthy
YOUNG WORTHY, Sir Generous's son, Dorothy's brother
A DRAWER at Dasher's tavern, a boy (4.1)
Master DASHER, a vintner, perhaps a married man
WILLIAM, a drawer at Dasher's tavern (4.5, *non-speaking*)
A BOY, Dasher's servant (4.5; may be the Drawer from 4.1)
A CONSTABLE (4.6, 5.6)
OFFICERS (4.6, *non-speaking*)
MUSICIANS, Sir Generous's servants (5.5, *non-speaking*)
EPILOGUE

Speaking Parts: 20–1

Stage Directions and Speech Prefixes
PROLOGUE: *The Prologue* (heading)
DUNGWORTH: *Dungworth* | *Dungwell* (s.d.s); *Dungw<orth>* (s.p.s); *Dungworth. A Country Gentleman* (d.p.)

RALPH: *Ralph* (s.d.s and s.p.s); *Ralph* [one of Dungworth's] *Servants* (d.p.)
DOBSON: *Dobson* (s.d.s and s.p.s); *Dobson* [one of Dungworth's] *Servants* (d.p.)
TONGUEALL: *Mrs Tongall* (s.d.s and s.p.s); *Mrs Tongall. A busy Gossip* (d.p.)
ARTLOVE: *Art-love | Artlove* (s.d.s); *Artl<ove>* (s.p.s); *Theodore Artlove. A complete Gentleman* (d.p.)
LITTLEWORD: *Littleword | Little-word* (s.d.s); *Little<word>* (s.p.s); *Littleword. A reputed Wit* (d.p.)
JERKER: *Jerker* (s.d.s and s.p.s); *Hugh Jerker. A wild Gallant* (d.p.)
JEFFREY: *Jeffery* (s.d.s); *Jeffrey* (s.d.s and s.p.s); *Jefferey Jerker. A lad of the same humour* [as Hugh Jerker] (d.p.)
DOROTHY: *Dorothy* (s.d.s); *Doroth<y>* (s.p.s); *Dorothy Worthy. Daughter to Sir Gene<rous>* (d.p.)
SUSAN: *Susan* (s.d.s and s.p.s); *Secre<tary>* (s.p.s); *Susan. A Waiting-woman to the Lady* (d.p.)
WARRANT: *Warrant* (s.d.s); *Warr<ant>* (s.p.s); *Warrant. Clerk to Sir Generous* (d.p.)
SPRUCE: *Spruce* (s.d.s and s.p.s); *Spruce. Gentleman Usher to the Lady* (d.p.)
LADY WORTHY: *Lady* (s.d.s and s.p.s); *Lady Worthy* (d.p.)
SIR GENEROUS: *Sir Generous Worthy | Sir Generous Worthy* (s.d.s); *Sir Gener<ous>* (s.p.s); *Sir Generous Worthy* (d.p.)
YOUNG WORTHY: *Young Worthy* (s.d.s); *Young Worth<y>* (s.p.s); *Young Worthy* [Sir Generous Worthy's] *Son* (d.p.)
DRAWER: *a Drawer* (s.d.s); *Boy* (s.p.s); *Drawer* (d.p.)
DASHER: *Dasher* (s.d.s and s.p.s); *Dasher. A complimenting Vintner* (d.p.)
WILLIAM: *Drawer* (s.d.s)
BOY: *a Boy* (s.d.s); *Boy* (s.p.s)
CONSTABLE: *Constable* (s.d.s, s.p.s, and d.p.)
OFFICERS: *Officers* (s.d.s)
MUSICIANS: *Music* (s.d.s)
EPILOGUE: *The Epilogue* (heading)

OTHER CHARACTERS
Gillian, Dungworth's dairymaid, Dobson's sweetheart (1.1)
A troupe of ragged players who visited Dungworth's house last Christmas (1.1)
The players of the Cockpit (1.1)
Justice Troublesome, a country justice who is maliciously opposed to sport (1.1)
Dungworth's ancestors (1.1, 5.6)
Mistress Tongueall's neighbours (1.2)
Jinny, Mistress Tongueall's daughter (1.2-3, 2.5, 4.5-6, 5.6)
Mistress Tongueall's husband, an attorney, the only surviving man in his family (1.2, 2.5)
Rowland Dungworth, Dungworth's father (1.2)
Jeffrey Jerker's uncle (1.4)
An old country waiting-woman who fell in love with every man she saw (1.6)
Lady Worthy's friends, who made her marry Sir Generous (1.6)
A gentlewoman who has an entrée with a lord at court (2.1)
Littleword's ancestors, reputedly philosophers (2.5)
The only girl in seven generations of Littlewords, who died in infancy (2.5)
The Worthys' cook (2.6)
A citizen who became proud when his wife sought his permission to kiss a lord, and who insisted that in future only lords should cuckold him (2.6)
A cutler, who supplied Warrant with a sword (3.1)
Lady Worthy's chambermaid (3.1)
Joan, the Worthys' kitchen-wench (3.1)
Dasher's wife (4.1; possibly imaginary)
Jeffrey Jerker's mistress (4.2; possibly imaginary)
Dasher's customers, including lords and gentlemen (4.4)
Ralph's former master, who kept a music school (4.5)
An honourable lady, Jinny's mistress (4.6)
Nicholas, Worthy's butler, who gives Susan sack (5.1)
The wenches at Dasher's tavern (5.6)

SETTING
Period: contemporary. The action takes place shortly before Lent.
Time-Scheme: 3.1-5 take place before supper on the night following 2.1; 5.1-6 take place the afternoon or evening following 4.3
Place: Covent Garden, London

Geography
Covent Garden: the Piazza
London: Cockpit playhouse; Long Lane; Houndsditch; Tyburn; Ludgate; Cheapside; Bankside
[Surrey]: Cuckolds' Haven
Sussex: Carterton; Dirtall Farm
England: Warwick; Banbury; Dunstable; Cornwall
France
Spain
[Africa]: Guinea
The Indies
The Antipodes

SOURCES
Verbal: Horace, *Ars poetica* (ded.)
Works Mentioned: Plato, *Timaeus* (3.4); Sir Philip Sidney, *Arcadia* (1580; 1.6, 3.2); possibly Christopher Marlowe and George Chapman, *Hero and Leander* (1593-8; 1.5); *Guy of Warwick* (play; **1666** or **1944**?; 1.1); George Ruggle, *Ignoramus* (**1768**; 5.6); Richard Brome, *The Weeding of the Covent Garden* (**2401**; prol.); Sir John Suckling, *Aglaura* (**2567**; ded.)

LANGUAGE
English
Latin: 5 words (2.2, 5.6; Spruce, Warrant, Ralph)

2424. Covent Garden

FORM
Metre: prose and pentameter
Rhyme: blank verse
Prologue: 26 lines, in couplets
Act-Division: 5 acts
Epilogue: 12 lines, in couplets
Lines (Spoken): 2,323 (825 verse, 1,498 prose)
Lines (Written): 2,468

STAGING
Doors: three doors: 'the right scene' (1.2–4, 3.3, s.d.); 'the middle scene' (1.6, 2.1–7, 3.2, 3.5, 5.1–4, 5.6, s.d.); 'the left scene' (1.2, 1.6, 3.3–5, 4.1–6, s.d.)
Above: two characters appear on 'the balcony' (1.5, 3.1–3, s.d.); a glove is dropped from the balcony to the main stage (1.5); it takes 17 lines to descend from balcony to main stage

MUSIC
On-Stage Music: musicians play (5.5, implicit)
Dance: Artlove, Dorothy, and others dance (5.5, s.d.)

PROPS
Weapons: Warrant's sword (3.2–3, dialogue); Spruce's sword (3.2–3, implicit); Artlove's sword (3.4–5, implicit)
Musical Instruments: unspecified instruments (5.5, implicit)
Clothing: a glove (1.5, dialogue)
Money: an unspecified amount (3.3, dialogue)
Food and Drink: wine (4.1, dialogue; drunk on stage); sack (4.2–3, 4.5, dialogue; drunk on stage); a bottle of sack (5.1, 5.3, 5.6, dialogue)
Small Portable Objects: pen and ink (4.5–6, implicit); a table-book (4.5–6, dialogue)
Large Portable Objects: a staff of office (5.6, dialogue)

In 3.5, Young Worthy says he has come out without a sword; but later in the scene, Artlove tells him to draw. The likeliest explanation of the discrepancy arises from the fact that the scene takes place at night: Artlove assumes, but cannot see, that Young Worthy is wearing a sword, when in fact he is not. (This is also the basis for the inference that Artlove himself is armed.)

COSTUMES
SUSAN: possibly an apron (5.1–3, dialogue)
WARRANT and SPRUCE: cloaks and beaver hats (3.2–3, dialogue; removed on stage)
YOUNG WORTHY: a silk garment with pockets (3.5, dialogue)

EARLY STAGE HISTORY
1633–4: performed by Queen Henrietta's Men at the Cockpit, perhaps in February 1634. The play may not have met with the acclaim that its author felt it deserved.

EARLY TEXTUAL HISTORY
1633–4: Thomas Nabbes says in the prologue that the play was written in the course of a few weeks.

1638: entered to Charles Greene in the Stationers' Register on Monday 28 May; entry names author. Matthew Clay had licensed the book for publication.

1638: **Q** printed by Richard Oulton for Charles Greene; collation A–K⁴ L², 42 leaves; title page names author and acting company, and gives (incorrect) year of performance; authorial dedication to Sir John Suckling; list of roles.

1639: Q reissued with a cancel title page, removing the performance year; now said to be printed by John Dawson, apparently for sale by Nicholas Fussell.

c. 1630s–40s: a copy of the reissued state of Q was in the possession of John Horne (Vicar of Headington, Oxfordshire). After his death, his entire collection of play-books passed into the possession of John Houghton of Brasenose College, Oxford (c. 1608–77), then to James Herne (died 1685), and then to the library of Ralph Sheldon (1623–84) at Weston, where it was catalogued by Anthony Wood, probably in the late 1670s.

1640 or later: copies of Q were bound with six other Nabbes quartos to create a collection of Nabbes's *Poems, Masques, &c.* (with a title page dated 1639); possibly sold by Nicholas Fussell. The other plays were *Tottenham Court* (**2405**), *Hannibal and Scipio* (**2480**), *Microcosmus* (**2543**), *The Spring's Glory* (**2597**), an edition which also included the text of his Masque of Time and the Almanac-Makers (**2635**), *The Bride* (**2645**), and *The Unfortunate Mother* (**2713**).

1655: *The English Treasury of Wit and Language* entered in the Stationers' Register to Humphrey Moseley on Tuesday 16 January.

1655: seven extracts (from 1.3, 2.4, 2.6–7, 3.4–5) included in John Cotgrave's *The English Treasury of Wit and Language*, sigs. D4ʳ, F1ʳ, F7ᵛ, K2ʳ, M5ᵛ, Q7ᵛ; printed for Humphrey Moseley.

1684: Nicholas Cox (Manciple of St Edmund Hall, Oxford) had a copy of Q in his bookshop, as part of a bound collection of Nabbes's plays (but not the same as the Fussell collection of 1640 or later); the other plays in the volume were *Tottenham Court* (**2405**), *The Spring's Glory* (**2597**), an edition which also included the text of his Masque of Time and the Almanac-Makers (**2635**), *The Bride* (**2645**), and *The Unfortunate Mother* (**2713**). It had probably been previously owned by Gerard Langbaine, and appears on a list compiled by Anthony Wood on Saturday 13 December.

EDITION
A. H. Bullen, in *The Works of Thomas Nabbes* (London, 1887), i. 1–91.

REFERENCES
Annals 1633; Bentley, iv. 932–4; Bodleian, MS Wood E. 4, art. 1, p. 45; Eyre & Rivington, i. 463; Greg 542; Hazlitt, 52; *MLR* 13 (1918), 401–11; *SP* 40 (1943), 186–203.

2425. Play with a Flamen

EVIDENCE
Sir Henry Herbert's office-book.

DATE
February 1634

ORIGINAL PRODUCTION
Prince Charles's Men at Salisbury Court

ROLES
A FLAMEN, a heathen priest

SETTING
If the reference to a flamen were taken literally, the play might have been set in ancient Rome.

COSTUMES
FLAMEN: a robe

EARLY STAGE HISTORY
1634: probably performed by Prince Charles's Men at Salisbury Court in February. The company borrowed a robe for the Flamen from one Cromes, a broker (probably William Cromes of Long Lane); it was an ecclesiastical vestment with the name of Jesus on it, which apparently caused some negative comment.
Aftermath: On Sunday 16 February, Sir Henry Herbert committed Cromes to the Marshalsea Prison for lending the robe. He was released the following day after acknowledging his fault.

REFERENCES
Bawcutt 313; MSC 2.3, 408.

2426. The City Honest Man

EVIDENCE
Stationers' Register.

GENRE
comedy (?)
Contemporary: play

TITLE
Contemporary: *The City Honest Man*

There are no good grounds for speculation (in *ELR*) that this play might have been *The City Madam* (**2373**) under an alternate title. First, *The City Madam* has unbroken continuity of title from the performance licence in 1632 to the Q title page in 1658, via the King's Men's repertory list of 1641: there is no reason to suppose that it was ever called anything else. Secondly, it was published by Andrew Pennycuicke, whereas *The City Honest Man* was entered by Humphrey Moseley, who did not subsequently dispose of his rights (and indeed, since he was apparently trying to build up a portfolio of dramatic copy, he had good reason not to do so).

AUTHOR
Philip Massinger (?)

Ascriptions associated with Humphrey Moseley's double titles are especially uncertain: even if the ascription is correct, the named author could apply to one title or both. *The Guardian* (**2417**) was a Massinger play; it follows that *The City Honest Man* might not have been.

DATE
Limits: 1626–40 (?) if by Massinger, 1610–42 if not
Best Guess: 1634

If the play was a reaction to *The City Shuffler* (**2406**; see PLOT), then it would probably have been staged at the end of 1633 or the early months of 1634; there seems, moreover, to have been a fad for 'City' titles in the second quarter of the 1630s. In terms of Massinger's career, this would put the play comfortably between *The Guardian* (**2417**) and two jobs of revision, to *Cleander* (**2077**) and *A Very Woman* (**2043**) in May and June 1634, after which he probably started work on *The Orator* (**2460**). See also **2225** for discussion of the general problems associated with Massinger's lost and undatable plays.

ORIGINAL PRODUCTION
King's Men at the Globe and/or Blackfriars (?)

The majority of the Massinger titles registered by Humphrey Moseley in 1653 were King's Men plays; this admits a strong presumption about the company ascription of the others.

PLOT
The title bears three possible but incompatible interpretations which might suggest something about the play's tone and content. It could be a title like *The Just Italian* (**2282**) or *The Honest Lawyer* (**1754**) which emphasizes a rare aberration, in which case the play was grounded in a sardonic attitude towards citizens. But it may, alternatively, have been assertively reactive to another play, such as *The City Shuffler* (**2406**), in which case the emphasis was instead on the general probity of citizens who had been libelled by the other satirical play. Thirdly, it may bear remembering that 'the town's honest man' in Ben Jonson's poem (*Epigrams* 115) is actually a hypocrite and knave.

ROLES
A CITIZEN, probably honest

EARLY TEXTUAL HISTORY
1653: entered (as a double title with *The Guardian*, **2417**) to Humphrey Moseley in the Stationers' Register on Friday 9 September; play and author individually named as part of a group entry of 41 (or 55) plays.

Moseley's double titles are discussed under **1643**.

REFERENCES
Annals 1633; Bentley, iv. 770–1; *ELR* 7 (1977), 368–81; Greg Θ82.

2427. The London Merchant

EVIDENCE
Stationers' Register; list of MS plays said to have been in the possession of John Warburton (1682–1759), and destroyed by his cook (London: British Library, MS Lansdowne 807, fo. 1).

GENRE
comedy
Contemporary: comedy

TITLE
Contemporary: *The London Merchant*

AUTHOR
John Ford

DATE
Limits: 1619–40
Best Guess: 1634

The only basis for the 1624 dating in *Annals* is a wish to identify the play, in defiance of English geography, with *The Bristol Merchant* (**2142**). Before the late 1620s, Ford seems mainly to have worked in collaboration, whereas (for whatever it may be worth) he is the only named author associated with this play in the 1660 Stationers' Register entry. In the second half of the decade, he seems to have written exclusively for the King's Men, and may have been under contract. This may not have been a King's Men play, since it does not appear in either the 1641 repertory list or the 1653 Stationers' Register entry which seems to have recorded the bulk of Humphrey Moseley's acquisitions from the company. In the 1630s he wrote mainly or exclusively for the Cockpit companies, though only his first two plays for them (**2329** and **2360**) had been retained in the repertory when it was protected in 1639.

This is also not one of the plays which Ford released for printing in 1633–4 in what looks like a systematic programme of publishing what he may have considered to be his best work. There is an unexplained gap in his output between *Perkin Warbeck* (**2399**) and *The Fancies* (**2528**). (The other significant gap, of 1636–7, is probably attributable to the long plague closure of the London theatres.) It may therefore be significant that there are also two otherwise undatable Ford plays, this one and *The Royal Combat* (**2470**), in the 1660 Stationers' Register entry and the Warburton list. If we assume that they belong in the 1634–5 gap, then perhaps *The London Merchant* might be more appropriately placed in 1634 than in the year when the same company revived *The Knight of the Burning Pestle* (**1562**) with its satire of an imaginary play of the same title. It is perhaps also relevant that James Shirley's output suggests that the Cockpit company was buying London comedies in 1633–4, but more romantic fare in 1634–5.

ROLES
A MERCHANT of London

SETTING
Geography
London

The play may actually have been set in London, but in that case it might as well have been called just *The Merchant*: specifying his origins could indicate that he was represented out of that context.

EARLY TEXTUAL HISTORY
1660: entered in the Stationers' Register to Humphrey Moseley on Friday 29 June; play and author individually named as part of a group entry of 26 plays.

REFERENCES
Annals 1624; Bentley, iii. 447–8; Greg Θ174; Hazlitt, 131; *The Library*, 3rd ser., 2 (1911), 225–59; Sibley, 93.

2428. Coelum Britannicum [The British Heaven]

TEXT
Printed in 1634 (STC 4618). Additional information derives from:
- **J:** Inigo Jones's design drawings;
- **K:** George Kirke's account for the supply of costumes (Kew: National Archives, AO 3/910, 2 and 4);
- **LC:** Lord Chamberlain's warrant for the purchase of musical instruments (printed in Lafontaine, *The King's Musick*);
- **MS:** description of the masque (London: British Library, MS Harley 4931, fo. 28).

GENRE
masque
Contemporary: masque (Q heading); 'royal masque' (*Lismore Papers*)

TITLE
Performed/Printed: *Coelum Britannicum*

AUTHOR
Thomas Carew

DATE
18 February 1634

ORIGINAL PRODUCTION
English Court in the Banqueting House, Whitehall

PLOT
Mercury comes to Britain from a heavenly court whose morals have been reformed through following the example of King Charles and Queen Henrietta Maria. He announces that Jove is so ashamed of his former life of sexual incontinence that he has removed from the night sky the stellified memorials of his former girlfriends, and intends to replace them with images of the King and Queen.

Mercury is interrupted by Momus, who complains that he never gets to appear in any court masques, and describes critically the newly chaste court of heaven. Mercury conjures down the monsters from the constellations, then Cancer, the highest sign of the zodiac, then the constellations representing vices, and each group dances in turn. At last the sky is emptied. Momus invites applicants to fill the stellar vacancies. Plutus, Poverty, Fortune, and Pleasure all express interest, introduce antimasque dances, and are rejected. Momus leaves to prevent further suitors from entering. Mercury explains that only the King and Queen are worthy to be the new constellations. Britain's heroic past is celebrated in dance, and the British worthies appear as new stars in the heavens, with the King pre-eminent among them. Allegorical virtues sing their praises, and further dancing ensues.

SCENE DESIGNATION
sc.1–4 (Q undivided), defined by the changes of scenery. The eight numbered antimasques take place during sc.2 (ant.1–7) and sc.3 (ant.8), and the main masque during sc.3–4.

ROLES
MERCURY, god of theft, Jove's ambassador to Britain, Momus' kinsman; also called Don Mercury, Cyllenius, and Hermes
MOMUS, a god, Mercury's kinsman; he gives his full name as Momus-ap-Somnus-ap-Erebus-ap-Chaos-ap-Demogorgon-ap-Eternity, and his offices as Supreme Theomastix, Hypercritic of Manners, Protonotary of Abuses, Arch-Informer, Dilator General, Universal Calumniator, Eternal Plaintiff, and Perpetual Foreman of the Grant Inquest
Eight MONSTERS from constellations: the Hydra, the Bear (Ursa Major), the Dragon (Draco), the Whale (Cetus), the Centaur (Centaurus), Capricorn, the Gorgon (part of Perseus), and Sagittarius (ant.1, non-speaking)
The CRAB, the constellation of Cancer (ant.2, non-speaking)
CONSTELLATIONS, including the great and little Dogs (Canis Major and Canis Minor), the Hare (Lepus), the Eagle (Aquila), the Ship (Argo Navis), the Goblet (Crater), the Dart (Sagitta), the Scorpion (Scorpio), Hercules, the Lion (Leo), and Cassiopeia, representing the various vices (ant.3, non-speaking)
PLUTUS, the god of gold, represented as an old man; also called Riches and Wealth
COUNTRY PEOPLE: ploughmen, shepherds, miners, and country lasses (ant.4, non-speaking)
POVERTY, represented as a woman; also called Poenia
GYPSIES (ant.5, non-speaking)
Dame FORTUNE, also called Tiche
SOLDIERS (ant.6, non-speaking)
PLEASURE, represented as a young woman; also called Lady Hedone
The five SENSES (ant.7, non-speaking)

PICTS, soldiers (ant.8, non-speaking)
ANCIENT SCOTS, soldiers (ant.8, non-speaking)
IRISHMEN, soldiers (ant.8, non-speaking)
ENGLAND, one of the kingdoms of Britain
SCOTLAND, one of the kingdoms of Britain
IRELAND, one of the kingdoms of Britain
The GENIUS of the three kingdoms of Britain
DRUIDS, aged British priests, part of a chorus of singers (sing collectively)
RIVERS, represented as old men, part of a chorus of singers (sing collectively)
Fifteen MASQUERS, representing ancient British heroes (non-speaking)
Ten TORCHBEARERS attending the masquers (non-speaking)
RELIGION, a female figure; also called Eusebia
TRUTH, a female figure; also called Alethia
WISDOM, a female figure; also called Sophia
CONCORD, a female figure; also called Homonoia
GOVERNMENT, a female figure; also called Dicaearche
REPUTATION, represented as a young man; also called Euphemia
ETERNITY, a male figure

Speaking Parts: 17
Allegorical Roles: 18

Stage Directions and Speech Prefixes
MERCURY: *Mercury* (s.d.s and s.p.s)
MOMUS: *Momus* (s.d.s and s.p.s)
CONSTELLATIONS: *several vices* (s.d.s)
PLUTUS: *Plutus* (s.d.s); *Plut<us>* (s.p.s)
COUNTRY PEOPLE: *Country People* (s.d.s)
POVERTY: *Poenia* (s.d.s); *Poverty* (s.p.s)
GYPSIES: *Gypsies* (s.d.s)
FORTUNE: *Tiche* (s.d.s); *Fortune* (s.p.s)
PLEASURE: *Hedone* (s.d.s); *Pleasure* (s.p.s)
SENSES: *the five senses* (s.d.s)
PICTS: *Picts* (s.d.s)
ANCIENT SCOTS: *ancient Scots* (s.d.s)
IRISHMEN: *Irish* (s.d.s)
ENGLAND: *England* | [one of the] *Kingdoms* (s.d.s); *Kingdoms* | *1* (s.p.s)
SCOTLAND: *Scotland* | [one of the] *Kingdoms* (s.d.s); *Kingdoms* | *2* (s.p.s)
IRELAND: *Ireland* | [one of the] *Kingdoms* (s.d.s); *Kingdoms* | *3* (s.p.s)
GENIUS: *a young man . . . representing the Genius of these kingdoms* | *the Genius of the three kingdoms* (s.d.s); *Genius* (s.p.s)
DRUIDS and RIVERS: *the Chorus* (s.d.s); *Chorus of Druids and Rivers* | *Chorus* (s.p.s)
MASQUERS: *the Masquers* (s.d.s)
TORCHBEARERS: *a troop of young lords and noblemen's sons* (s.d.s)
RELIGION: *Religion* (s.d.s); *Eusebia* (s.p.s)
TRUTH: *Truth* (s.d.s); *Alethia* (s.p.s)
WISDOM: *Wisdom* (s.d.s); *Sophia* (s.p.s)
CONCORD: *Concord* (s.d.s); *Homonoia* (s.p.s)

2428. Coelum Britannicum

GOVERNMENT: *Government* (s.d.s); *Dicaearche | Dicaearches* (s.p.s)
REPUTATION: *Reputation* (s.d.s); *Euphemia* (s.p.s)
ETERNITY: *Eternity* (s.d.s and s.p.s)

OTHER CHARACTERS
Jove or Jupiter, god of thunder, ruler of the gods, Juno's husband, who sent Mercury (sc.1–2, 4)
Juno, Queen of the gods, Jove's wife (sc.1–2)
Unchaste women seduced by Jove (sc.1–2)
Mars, a god, Venus' lover (sc.1)
Venus, a goddess, mother of Cupid and adulterous wife of Vulcan (sc.1–2)
Vulcan, a god reformed by the new regime in heaven, Venus' deformed husband (sc.1–2)
Saturn, former ruler of the gods (sc.1–2)
Saturn's father, whom he castrated (sc.1)
Cynthia, a goddess (sc.1)
Phoebus, a god (sc.1)
Hebe, a goddess whom Momus caused to fall over and expose her private parts (sc.1)
Bacchus, a once drunken god reformed by the new regime in heaven (sc.2)
Cupid, Venus' son, a once naked god reformed by the new regime in heaven (sc.2)
Ganymede, a secretly unchaste god reformed by the new regime in heaven (sc.2)
Pan, a piping god reformed by the new regime in heaven (sc.2)
Proteus, a juggling god reformed by the new regime in heaven (sc.2)
Danaë, once courted by Jove (sc.2)
Minerva, who showed herself naked to Paris (sc.2)
Other suitors for a place in the heavens, intercepted by Momus before they can get on stage (sc.2)

SETTING
Geography
England: Windsor Castle
Britain: Ireland; Scotland
[*Greece*]: Mount Olympus; Mount Parnassus; Lake Lerna; River Eridanus
[*Italy*]: Calabria; Puteolum
[*Europe*]: France; Germany
[*Asia*]: Colchis; Mount Ida; Scythia
[*Africa*]: Ethiopia; Mount Atlas
[*America*]: New England; the West Indies
[*Hades*]: River Styx; River Lethe

SOURCES
Narrative: Giordano Bruno, *Spaccio de la bestia trionfante* (1584); Guillaume Colletet, *Ballet de l'Harmonie* (1632)
Verbal: Ausonius, *Praefatiunculae* 1 (t.p. motto)
Design: Federigo Zuccaro, *The Coronation of the Virgin* (c. 1570; Proscenium Arch); Battista Pittoni, illustrations to Vincenzo Scamozzi, *Discorsi sopra l'antichita di Roma* (1582; Ruined City); Cesare Ripa, *Iconologia* (1593, repr. 1611; Momus and Poverty); Giulio Parigi, *Il giudizio di Paride* (1608; Mountain Scene; Roman City); Francesco Albani, *Hercules Bearing the Globe* (before 1616; Atlas); Willem van Nieulandt (1584–1635), *The Flight into Egypt* (Ruined City), *Temples in the Forum* (Ruined City), *Temple of Peace* (Ruined City), *Temple of Jupiter Stator* (Ruined City); Antonio Tempesta, *Un giardino* (before 1630; Garden and Villa)
Works Mentioned: *Bevis of Hampton* (c. 1300; sc.4); *Guy of Warwick* (fourteenth century; sc.4); Richard Allestree, *Almanac* (annually from 1617; sc.2); John Booker, *Telescopium Uranium* (1631; sc.2); also general references to Pietro Aretino (sc.1) and François Rabelais (sc.1)

LANGUAGE
English
Latin: 6 words (sc.1–2; Momus)
French: 1 word (sc.1; Momus)

FORM
Metre: pentameter and prose
Rhyme: blank verse, occasional couplets
Lines (Spoken): 958 (607 verse, 351 prose)
Lines (Written): 1,230

STAGING
Stage: at least six feet high (desc.; some performance records say seven feet)
Above: Mercury descends in a chariot (sc.1, desc.); the Genius ascends in a cloud (sc.3, desc.); seven characters ascend and descend in clouds (sc.4, desc.)
Beneath: a mountain rises out of the earth (sc.3, desc.)
Other Openings: the Picts, Irish, and Scots come out of the woods at the foot of the mountains (sc.3, desc.); the masquers enter through a cave which opens in the mountain (sc.3, desc.)
Audience: Mercury approaches the throne and addresses the King and Queen directly (sc.1, desc.); addressed by Momus as 'mortals' and 'gay people' (sc.1); the masquers dance the revels with ladies from the audience (sc.4, desc.); the King and Queen are mentioned (sc.4)

The text assumes the King to be in the audience during the opening scene, even though later he is one of the masquers.

MUSIC
Music: loud music (sc.1, desc.; accompanying Mercury's descent); rural music (sc.2, desc./MS; accompanying ant.4); probably viols (sc.3, dialogue; accompanying Song 2); treble lutes (LC)
Songs:
  1: 'Raise from these rocky cliffs your heads', sc.3, Genius and the three kingdoms, in parts, 50 lines;
  2: 'Here are shapes formed fit for heaven', sc.3, Genius and the three kingdoms, in parts, 39 lines, probably with musical accompaniment;

- **3:** 'Whilst thus the darlings of the gods', sc.4, Chorus, 24 lines;
- **4:** 'Be fixed, you rapid orbs, that bear', sc.4, Eternity, Religion, Truth, Wisdom, Concord, Government, Reputation, in parts, 51 lines.

Dance: eight antimasque dances (sc.2–3, desc.), including Cancer the Crab, danced backwards (sc.2, desc.), rustics' measures (sc.2, desc.) and morris dances (MS), soldiers' dance representing a battle (sc.2, desc.), and martial dance of Picts, ancient Scots, and Irish (sc.3, desc.); torchbearers dance (sc.3, desc.); masquers' entry dance (sc.3, desc.); masquers' main dance (sc.3, desc.); masquers dance the revels with ladies (sc.4, desc.); masquers' final dance (sc.4, desc.).

PROPS

Lighting: wax torches (sc.3, desc.)
Pyrotechnics: a flame of fire (sc.3, desc.)
Weapons: a shield with a Medusa's head (sc.4, desc.); a lance (sc.4, desc.)
Musical Instruments: a cithera (sc.4, desc.)
Animals: a crowing cock (sc.1, desc.; may be just decoration on the chariot); a serpent in a circle with its tail in its mouth (sc.4, desc.)
Food and Drink: a cornucopia containing corn and fruit (sc.3, desc.)
Small Portable Objects: a caduceus (sc.1, desc.); Fortune's wheel (sc.2, desc.); a book (sc.4, desc.); a palm (sc.4, desc.); 'a little faggot of sticks bound together', with a heart on top (sc.4, desc.)
Large Portable Objects: an iron chain attached to a heavy stone (sc.2, desc.; the other end is attached to Poverty's hand); the ancient arms of England, of Scotland, and of Ireland (sc.3, desc.)
Scenery: a proscenium decorated with foliage, two golden vases, allegorical and grotesque figures, two impresas with Latin mottos, and a box containing the title (desc.; *design drawing survives*); a curtain with watchet blue and pale yellow panels (desc.; raised to reveal the scene, falls at the end of the performance); a ruined city (sc.1, desc.; *design drawing survives*); a chariot (sc.1, desc.; descends); heaven, with the stars in constellations, and a globe carried by a naked Atlas (sc.2, desc.; *design drawing survives*; the stars are progressively extinguished, leaving the heavens darkened); high mountains, their peaks above the clouds (sc.3, desc.; *design drawing survives*; also apparently a rejected design); a hill that rises out of the earth to become a huge mountain, and sinks back again (sc.3, desc.; it has seating in the middle for three characters, and opens at the base to admit the masquers; it is significantly more than six feet high, and exceeds the available under-stage headroom); a bright, transparent cloud which descends and ascends again (sc.3, desc.; carries up one character); a garden with walks, parterres, trees, fountains, and grottoes, and a palace in the distance, with high walks on arches, terraces, and cypress tress (sc.4, desc.; *design drawing survives*); a large, multi-coloured cloud (sc.4, desc.; opens; *design drawing survives*); two more clouds, each seating three characters (sc.4, desc.); a globe (sc.4, desc.; inside the large cloud; seats one character on top); fifteen stars (sc.4, desc.; appear in the sky); a prospect of Windsor Castle (sc.4, desc.; appears in the background)

COSTUMES AND MAKE-UP

MERCURY: a flame-coloured coat with a girdle; a white mantle trimmed with gold and silver; a wreath with small falls of white feathers; wings at his heels (sc.1, desc.)
MOMUS: a long darkish robe embroidered with poniards, snakes' tongues, eyes, and ears; particoloured hair and beard; a wreath stuck with feathers, with a porcupine on the front (sc.1, desc.); *design drawing survives*
PLUTUS: wrinkles; bald-headed; a thin white beard; spectacles; hunched back; a robe of cloth of gold (sc.2, desc.)
POVERTY: a pale face; a large hat-brim with no crown; disordered hair; a dark, patched robe (sc.2, desc.)
FORTUNE: head bald at the back and with a large forelock; wings on her shoulders; naked to the waist; a skirt embroidered with crowns, sceptres, books, and other objects (sc.2, desc.); a veil over her eyes (sc.2, dialogue)
PLEASURE: a 'light, lascivious habit' with silver and gold adornments; a garland of roses on her head, and above that a rainbow hanging down to her shoulders (sc.2, desc.)
ENGLAND, SCOTLAND, and IRELAND: each wears a crown and regal habit (sc.3, desc.)
GENIUS: a white embroidered robe; wings at his shoulders; fair hair; an olive garland (sc.3, desc.)
MASQUERS: yellow clothes embroidered with silver; antique plumed helms (sc.3, desc.); the King's costume has aurora-coloured satin under-sleeves, bodice, and upper bases, and white satin watchet upper sleeves and under-bases, all embroidered with silver purls, plates, and silver Os (sc.3, K); *five design drawings survive*
TORCHBEARERS: white, square-collared, full-gathered, girdled coats embroidered with silver; round caps with a white feather round them (sc.3, desc.); ruffs; cuffs; gloves; buskins; stockings; tiffany gorgets (sc.3, K); shoes with large roses (sc.3, J); *three design drawings survive*
RELIGION: white clothes; a light veil (sc.4, desc.)
TRUTH: a watchet blue robe; a sun on her forehead (sc.4, desc.)
WISDOM: a mantle embroidered with eyes and hands; golden rays around her head (sc.4, desc.)
CONCORD: a carnation habit; a garland of corn (sc.4, desc.)
GOVERNMENT: a coat of armour; a plumed helm (sc.4, desc.)
REPUTATION: a purple robe embroidered with gold; a laurel wreath (sc.4, desc.)

ETERNITY: a long, light-blue garment embroidered with gold stars (sc.4, desc.)

Miscellaneous: K records payments for materials (taffeta, taffeta sarcenet, white and yellow ribbon, tinsel, tinsel ribbon, copper lace and fringe) and clothing items (epaulettes decorated with lions' heads, an embroidered cap with a feather and sprig, a spangled headpiece covered with tinsel and flowers, band and cuffs, embroidered gloves, *bas d'attache* silk hose, long *bas d'attache* silk hose, aurora-coloured stockings, shoes and roses, masks) which were probably part of the King's or another masquer's costume.

EARLY STAGE HISTORY

Inception: The masque was intended by the King as a gift to the Queen in return for her gift of a Twelfth Night production of *The Faithful Shepherdess* (**1582**).

Preparation: By Thursday 9 January 1634, Shrove Tuesday had been set as the date of the performance. On Sunday 19 January, a warrant was issued to pay John Kelly and John Lawrence £16 for two treble lutes to be used in the masque. The masque was performed on the stage which had already been erected for *The Triumph of Peace* (**2423**). Eight men worked eight days and two nights preparing the Banqueting House; the job was commissioned by William Penrin, who was paid a total of £6.13s.4d (1s.8d per man per day).

Rehearsals: Rehearsals had begun by Friday 24 January. Viscount Cranborne paid a 2s gratuity to a page of the presence at a rehearsal on or after Tuesday 11 February.

Invitations: On Wednesday 5 February, the Lord Chamberlain (Philip Herbert, 4th Earl of Pembroke and 1st Earl of Montgomery) wrote to the Lord Keeper (Thomas, 1st Baron Coventry) inviting 120 members of the Inns of Court to attend, in acknowledgement of the King's pleasure in *The Triumph of Peace* (**2423**).

Performance: in the Banqueting House, Whitehall, on Tuesday 18 February 1634 (Shrove Tuesday). The performance took place in the evening. The cast included: King Charles I; James Stewart, 4th Duke of Lennox; William Cavendish, 3rd Earl of Devonshire; Henry Rich, 1st Earl of Holland; Mountjoy Blount, 1st Earl of Newport; Thomas Bruce, 1st Earl of Elgin; William Villiers, 2nd Viscount Grandison; Robert, Lord Rich of Holland; Basil, Lord Feilding; Robert, 1st Baron Digby; Richard Boyle, Viscount Dungarvan; Randall MacDonnell, Viscount Dunluce; Philip, 4th Baron Wharton; William, 5th Baron Paget; Alexander Abernethy, 9th Baron Saltoun (Masquers); James Howard, Lord Walden; Charles Cecil, Viscount Cranbourne; John Egerton, 2nd Viscount Brackley; George Brydges, 6th Baron Chandos; William Herbert; Thomas Howard; Thomas Egerton; Charles Cavendish; Robert Howard; Henry Spencer (Torchbearers). The design was by Inigo Jones. The music may have been composed by Henry Lawes (or possibly William Lawes, or both). The stage was 6 or 7 feet high and measured 40 x 27 feet, with double stairs. The audience included: Queen Henrietta Maria; Thomas Howard, 14th Earl of Arundel; Sir Humphrey Mildmay; members of the Inns of Court. Admission was by ticket only (which cost Mildmay 6d) and a turnstile arrangement was used to restrict admission. No ambassadors were formally invited, and none came, though some members of their retinues were present. The King and Queen were pleased by the masque; the Queen told Sir Henry Herbert that she had never seen better costumes. Herbert himself thought it 'the noblest masque' produced during his term as Master of the Revels, with 'the best poetry, best scenes, and the best habits'. On the evening of the performance, George Weal fell over and hurt himself while he was busy doing something for the King; he was later paid a £2 gratuity.

Aftermath: The King hoped for a repeat performance of the masque at Easter (which fell on Sunday 6 April that year), but there is no record that it took place.

The use of a turnstile was evidently considered an innovation in 1634. It had a precedent at the second (city) performance of *The Triumph of Peace* (**2423**) five days earlier; the Revels Office probably decided to adopt the idea because of difficulties about admission at the first (court) performance of *The Triumph of Peace*, when a (wrongly) suspected gatecrasher was assaulted by the Lord Chamberlain.

It has been claimed that this masque was performed in Germany before Thomas Howard, 14th Earl of Arundel. This arises from confusion with the non-Catalogue play, *Pax in Anglia, diu exul in Germaniam postliminio reditura*, performed for him at the Clementina, Prague, in July 1636 (see Appendix 2). The Prague play is introduced by Mercury, but has no other similarity with the masque.

Production Finance and Expenses

Edmund Taverner was paid £1,200 to cover expenses, in two instalments (£800 on Saturday 15 February and £400 on Friday 21 February).

Costumes: The Exchequer's total recorded expenditure on costumes was £141.12s.5d. George Kirke was paid £120 on Thursday 27 February for supplying masquing apparel for the King and others.

The King's Costume: The pattern cost at least £11.2s.10d, as follows: aurora-coloured sarcenet (£1.1s) and white and carnation calico (£1.6d), supplied by Patrick Black; yellow taffeta sarcenet, supplied by Robert Austen (£1.5s); silver tassels, girdle, and flowers supplied by Peter le Huc (£1); Peter le Huc, for cutting the pattern suit (£1); Patrick Black, for making the pattern and supply of canvas stiffening, buckram, bays, ribbon, buttons, and silk (£3.3s.4d); John Knight, for making and painting the patterns in colours (£2.13s). The final costume cost at least £74.1s.11d, as follows: aurora and white satin (£9.1s.3d), taffeta (£1.11s.6d) and Florence taffeta sarcenet (£2.12s.6d), all supplied by Richard Miller; French tinsel (£1.10s) and silver tassels and girdle, flowers for the breast (£3), all supplied by Peter le Huc;

Peter le Huc, for marking, cutting, and sizing the suit (£1.6s.8d); Patrick Black, for making the suit (£5); Edmund Harrison, for embroidering the suit (£50).

Torchbearers' Costumes: The total cost was £10.1s.10d, as follows: Patrick Black, for making patterns, and supply of canvas buckram stiffening, bays, ribbon, buttons, and silk (£2.10s); tinsel (£1.8s); white and carnation calico (12s), plate, lace edging, lace, and fringe (£1.10s), all supplied by Patrick Black; tassels and girdle (15s), ruff and cuffs (12s), a tiffany gorget (2s.6d), cap, feather, and band (£1), gloves (1s), buskins and stockings (12s), and tinsel ribbon (6s), all supplied by Peter le Huc; Peter le Huc, for cutting the suits (13s.4d).

Materials: The total cost was £5.6s, as follows: white and yellow ribbon, supplied by Thomas Robinson (£2.8s); counterfeit tinsel (£1.12s) and copper lace and fringe (£1) supplied by Patrick Black; tinsel ribbon, supplied by Peter le Huc (6s). (Some of these may have been for the King's costume, but they are not explicitly assigned to it in the account.)

Other Garments: The total cost was £38.12s, as follows: two pairs of epaulettes decorated with gilt and spangled lions' heads, made by Francis Tipsley (£5); Nicholas Stone, for embossing the first patterns of the lions' heads, and making moulds (£3); an embroidered cap, with feather and sprig (£3), band and cuffs (£1.2s), aurora-coloured stockings (15s), shoes and silver roses (£1), and a pair of gloves (1s.6d), all supplied by Peter le Huc; Elizabeth Lovedey, for making a spangled headpiece covered with tinsel and flowers (£5); a plume of white feathers with a sprig of aigrettes, and the pattern for the headpiece, supplied by Robert Jones (£6.10s); a plume of white feathers and a sprig of aigrettes, supplied by Thomas Church (£3); a pair of gloves with embroidered, aurora-coloured satin tops, supplied by Joseph Atkinson (£2); two pairs of *bas d'attache* silk hose (£5), one pair of long *bas d'attache* silk hose (18s), and a pair of rich spangled roses (£1.13s.4d), all supplied by Thomas Robinson; three masks lined with white sweet leather, supplied by John King (£3). (Some of these may have been for the King's or torchbearers' costumes, but they are not explicitly assigned to them in the account.)

Private: On Wednesday 19 February, the day after the performance, Viscount Dungarvan drew £600 from Captain Gerard Fookes, apparently for his expenses, to be repaid on Sunday 25 May following by his father, Richard Boyle, 1st Earl of Cork; the Earl, who was in Ireland, was told of the debt on Saturday 12 April and on Thursday 17 April wrote to John Walley ordering the money to be paid on the due date.

The total cost of Viscount Cranborne's costume was £20.14s.6d, including: carnation satin (£4.2s.6d); white taffeta (£2.2s); white Florence sarcenet (10s); silver buttons and silk (9s); embroidering the suit, cap, and buskins (£5); 2½ yards of white calico (2s.6d); Peter le Huc, for making the suit (£6.8s.6d); the tailor's bill for making up the suit (£2). The payments are dated to the day of the performance. Cranborne also paid a 2s.6d gratuity to a servant of Sir Thomas Jarman who assisted him at his costume fitting, apparently during the week before the performance; he also incurred expenses of 1s for the carriage of his trunk to Whitehall.

Though it seems likely that Kirke records expenditure only on the costumes specified, i.e. for the King and 'pages' (i.e. torchbearers), this is not entirely clear from the document.

EARLY TEXTUAL HISTORY

1634: **¹Q** printed for Thomas Walkley; collation A² B–E⁴ F², 20 leaves; Latin title-page motto; most of the book was reset during printing.

1634: In July, John Newdigate bought 'a book of the masque', possibly this one (but more probably **2423**); in any event he eventually owned copies of both masques.

1640: Thomas Carew's works, including poems and masques, entered in the Stationers' Register to Thomas Walkley on Monday 23 March; general entry, not naming the individual masque. (This was the same day as Carew's funeral.) Matthew Clay had licensed the book for publication; he reissued the imprimatur on Wednesday 29 April.

1640: included in Carew's *Poems* (²O₁), sigs. O8ʳ–S4ᵛ, 29 leaves; printed by John Dawson for Thomas Walkley.

1642: included in Carew's *Poems* (³O₂), sigs. P2ʳ–S6ᵛ, 29 leaves; printed for Thomas Walkley.

1650: Walkley's rights to Carew's *Poems* transferred in the Stationers' Register to Humphrey Moseley on Saturday 8 June; general entry, naming no individual work.

1650–60: Carew's *Poems* advertised as for sale by Humphrey Moseley.

1651: included in Carew's *Poems* (⁴O₃), sigs. L7ʳ–O8ᵛ, 26 leaves; printed for Humphrey Moseley.

1651: O₃ reissued (probably in early May) with a cancel title page naming John Martin as the bookseller.

1656: *The English Parnassus* entered to Evan Tyler, Thomas Johnson, and Thomas Davies in the Stationers' Register on Wednesday 24 December.

1657: two extracts (from sc.2) included in Joshua Poole's *The English Parnassus*, sigs. 2F5ʳ, 2R6ᵛ; printed for Thomas Johnson.

1667: Moseley's rights transferred in the Stationers' Register by his widow, Ann, to Henry Herringman in the Stationers' Register on Monday 19 August; individually named as part of a group transfer of nine titles.

1668: O₃ advertised as for sale by Henry Herringman.

1670: included in Carew's *Poems* (⁵O₄), sigs. M3ʳ–P1ᵛ, 23 leaves; printed for Henry Herringman.

1671: O₄ reissued with a cancel title page naming Hobart Kemp as the bookseller.

1672: William Davenant's *Works* entered to Henry Herringman in the Stationers' Register on Thursday 31 October. Roger L'Estrange had licensed the book

2429. Cornelianum dolium

for the press. On Monday 18 November, it was advertised for sale by Henry Herringman, John Martin, John Starkey, and Robert Horne; however, it was apparently not issued until the following year.

1673: included in William Davenant's *Works* (⁶F), sigs. 2Z1ᵛ–3B4ᵛ, 13 pages on 7 leaves; printed by Thomas Newcomb for Henry Herringman; probably included in error for Davenant's *Britannia triumphans* (**2589**).

1675: Davenant's *Works* advertised as for sale by John Starkey.

1677: *The English Parnassus* reprinted by Henry Brome for Thomas Bassett and John Wright; the extracts now appear on sigs. 2F1ʳ, 2R2ᵛ.

1679–86: O₄ advertised as for sale by Henry Herringman.

EDITIONS
Rhodes Dunlap in Thomas Carew, *The Poems* (Oxford, 1949), 151–85.
Orgel and Strong, ii. 566–97.
David Lindley, in *Court Masques*, Oxford English Drama (Oxford, 1995), 166–93.

REFERENCES
Annals 1634; Ashbee, iii. 76; Bawcutt 290; Bentley, ii. 676, iii. 108–10, v. 1450; Butler, 310–18, 373; *Cal. Ven. 1632–6*, 190; Cecil Papers, Accounts 127/6, pp. 7, 26; Henry Cart de Lafontaine (ed.), *The King's Musick* (London, 1909), 88; Eyre & Rivington, ii. 103; Fletcher, 416; Greg 496; Alexander B. Grosart (ed.), *The Lismore Papers* (London, 1886), iv. 23; Hazlitt, 44; HMC Portland, ii. 124; HMC Salisbury, xxii. 271; Charles Henry Hopwood (ed.), *Middle Temple Records* (London, 1904), ii. 997; David Howarth, *Lord Arundel and his Circle* (New Haven and London, 1985), 114–15; Vivienne Larminie, *Wealth, Kinship and Culture* (Woodbridge, 1995), 202; Loomie, 150; McGee-Meagher 1625-34, 91–5; *MRDE* 7 (1995), 341; MSC 2.3, 361–2; MSC 10, 46; MSC 12, 34; MSC 13,128; *PBSA* 107 (2013), 18; John Peacock, *The Stage Designs of Inigo Jones* (Cambridge, 1995), 16–17, 315–24; REED: Inns of Court, 701–3, 707, 723–4; Reyher, 516–18, 531; Steele, 248; *Theatre Survey* 20 (1979), 20–1; J. Douglas Walker (ed.), *The Records of the Honourable Society of Lincoln's Inn: The Black Books* (London, 1897–1902), ii. 315; Enid Welsford, *The Court Masque* (Cambridge, 1927), 229.

2429. Cornelianum dolium [The Tub of Cornelius]

TEXT
Printed in 1638 (STC 20691).

GENRE
comedy

Contemporary: comedy (S.R.); *comoedia lepidissima* (t.p.)

TITLE
Printed: *Cornelianum dolium*

AUTHOR
T. R. (*probably* Thomas Ryley, *but perhaps* Thomas Randolph)

Randolph and Ryley, both actively involved in drama at Trinity College, Cambridge, are the only two plausible candidates with names to fit the 1638 title-page initials, but the case operates largely in negative terms: in effect, if not Randolph, then Ryley. The grounds for doubting Randolph's authorship, helpfully summarized by Sutton, include the points that he wrote no other plays in Latin, might not have recycled his own material from *The Jealous Lovers* (**2365**) quite so blatantly, and might have been considered worth a more explicit identification on the title page. One point on the other side of the argument is that the dedication seems to refer to the author as a 'posthumus vates'; and in 1638, Randolph was dead, and Ryley was not.

Although the evidence is compelling that the play originated in 1630s Cambridge, we cannot entirely pass over the argument, first proposed by James Crossley in 1861, that it may also have some connection with the older, Oxford-educated Richard Brathwaite. The strongest elements of the case are that: Brathwaite knew the dedicatee, Sir Alexander Radcliffe, and had previously dedicated his *Whimsies* to him in 1631; the terms 'candide, condite, cordate', which appear in the dedication's heading, were previously used by Brathwaite in the dedication of his *Essays on the Five Senses* (1635); the publisher, Thomas Harper, also printed three of Brathwaite's books in 1634–6; the frontispiece engraver, William Marshall, also executed engravings for several of Brathwaite's books, including his 1638 *Survey of History* and also one of his Harper publications, *The Arcadian Princess* (1636); and the verses heading the erratum list echo those attached to the similar list in Brathwaite's *Barnabae itinerarium* (1636).

All these points relate to the play's publication in 1638, and the associated paratext, rather than its original composition. But it is striking that two of the dialogue's Latin tags of unknown origin are associated with works which Brathwaite published in the 1650s: 'vincit qui patitur' (quoted in 3.2) is the title of a 1653 pamphlet, *Vincit qui patitur, or Colonel John Lilburne Deciphered*; and 'in noxam sectatur et umbra' (quoted in 3.3) is used as a motto in Brathwaite's 1658 *The Honest Ghost*. This still falls far short of a case for authorship—*Cornelianum dolium* could itself have been Brathwaite's source for the phrases in question—but it is hard to dismiss outright the view that he had some connection with the play. If the author was indeed dead, then the basis for speculative hypothesis on the point becomes marginally more stable. Might Brathwaite have facilitated the play's publication?

DATE
Limits: 1633–8
Best Guess: 1634

Sutton plausibly detects traces of the Trinity-Queens' animosity ensuing the royal visit of 1632, making this probably a Trinity play written soon afterwards. The only recorded Trinity performance of the mid-1630s which has not been securely assigned a play is that of 4 February 1636 for the visit of the Elector Palatine, the King's nephew; the play is sometimes thought to have been *Senilis amor* (**2474**). That occasion seems a little late for the topical jibes in *Cornelianum dolium*, however. Moreover, Thomas Harper, the 1638 publisher, evidently went to some trouble to make the book attractive to purchasers, including having a frontispiece specially engraved; one might expect him not to have passed up the opportunity to mention a significant royal performance on the title page.

The borrowing from *The White Devil* (**1689**) establishes the author's attention to the London commercial theatre, but has no dating implications in that the play was revived and reprinted in 1631. However, two other possible links with London plays both suggest a date after 1633. First, the odd focus on the sweating-tub in the title of this overtly Jonsonian play might allude to Jonson's most recent (and last complete) play, *A Tale of a Tub* (**2403**), licensed in May 1633. The same month saw the revival of *The Night-Walkers* (**1772**), which may have influenced the scene partly played as if in complete darkness, and also the name Latrunculus (= 'little thief').

ORIGINAL PRODUCTION
Trinity College, Cambridge (?)

PLOT
After a life of debauchery, Cornelius is dying. He sends for the priest Opilio to make his will, and appoints him and the schoolmaster Priscian as his executors. On the point of death, he says, he will reveal where his buried treasure may be found. The executors want to keep him alive long enough to hear the secret, but the servants want to ensure that he dies quickly and painlessly, so that they can collect their legacies. To that end, they engage Peregrine, a Neapolitan physician who has come to town looking for patronage. He is an honest doctor, however, and seeks to cure Cornelius with a prolonged and painful session in a sweating-tub. When the servants protest that this is killing him too slowly, the doctor assures them that he is only being tormented with false hope.

The servants pose as ghosts to scare Priscian and Opilio into resigning as executors, passing on the job to the steward, Grincome. The whore Pocadilla also tricks Opilio into giving her his wife Prunella's best dress, leading her to suspect that he is having an affair. Grincome tells him that he is Cornelius' sole heir, and Prunella is pacified with the promise that she will have full control of the estate. Priscian is likewise assured that he will be the only legatee.

Peregrine tells the servants that Cornelius is on the point of death. In fact, he is getting better, but the joy of his restored health is alloyed with dismay upon finding what false friends and rascally servants he has. To get his own back, he has Peregrine put it about that he is dead, and will be buried with his treasure. After Peregrine ensures that he will be able to breathe inside the coffin, he is duly interred. His servants engage two grave-robbers to retrieve the rumoured treasure, and they get a scare when they open the coffin and Cornelius comes back to life. Priscian and Opilio struggle to find reasons not to have to give back the estate, but in the end they are obliged to go back to their old lives, the poorer for the expenses of their legacy-hunting. The grave-robbers are sent to a madhouse, and the whores and Grincome to a house of correction.

SCENE DESIGNATION
prol., 1.1–5, 2.1–10, 3.1–8, 4.1–9, 5.1–14, ep. (D)

The stage is not clear at the following scene-divisions: 1.2–3, 1.4–5, 2.1–6, 2.7–10, 3.1–8, 4.1–9, 5.1–6, 5.7–8, 5.12–14.

ROLES
PROLOGUE
POCADILLA, Cornelius' whore
GRINCOME, Cornelius' steward
OPILIO, a priest, Prunella's husband
PRISCIAN, a schoolmaster
TUBERCULA, Cornelius' whore; said to be little
SCIATICA, Cornelius' maid
CORNELIUS, a wealthy old debauchee
SYRINGE, a surgeon
ATTENDANTS carrying Cornelius (1.4–5; one may speak *within*, but it could be Syringe)
PEREGRINE, a Neapolitan physician
SIMPLICIUS, Opilio's parishioner
BALBUTIUS, Opilio's parishioner
PRUNELLA, Opilio's wife
A SEXTON (5.2)
LURCANIO, a grave-robber
LATRUNCULUS, a grave-robber
LICTORS (5.14; one speaks)
EPILOGUE

Speaking Parts: 18–19

Stage Directions and Speech Prefixes
PROLOGUE: *Prologus* (heading)
POCADILLA: *Pocadilla* | [one of the] *famuli* (s.d.s); *Poc<adilla>* (s.p.s); *Pocadilla,* [one of] *Cornelii meretriculae* (d.p.)
GRINCOME: *Grinchamus* | [one of the] *famuli* (s.d.s); *Grinc<hamus>* (s.p.s); *Grinchamus, Cornelii servus* (d.p.)
OPILIO: *Opilio* (s.d.s); *Opil<io>* (s.p.s); *Opilio, Pastor gregis* (d.p.)
PRISCIAN: *Priscianus* (s.d.s); *Prisc<ianus>* (s.p.s)
TUBERCULA: *Tubercula* | [one of the] *famuli* (s.d.s); *Tub<ercula>* (s.p.s); *Tubercula,* [one of] *Cornelii meretriculae* (d.p.)
SCIATICA: *Ciatica* | [one of the] *famuli* (s.d.s); *Ciat<ica>* (s.p.s); *Ciatica, Cornelii Ancilla* (d.p.)
CORNELIUS: *Cornelius* (s.d.s and d.p.); *Corn<elius>* (s.p.s)
SYRINGE: *Syringius Chyrurgus* (s.d.s and d.p.); *Syringius* (s.d.s); *Syring<ius>* (s.p.s)

ATTENDANTS: *famuli* (s.d.s)
PEREGRINE: *Peregrinus, Neapolitanus Medicus* | *Peregrinus* (s.d.s); *Peregrin<us>* (s.p.s); *Peregrinus Neapolitanus, Medicus* (d.p.)
SIMPLICIUS: *Simplicius* (s.d.s); *Simp<licius>* (s.p.s); *Simplicius,* [one of the] *Parochiani Opilionis* (d.p.)
BALBUTIUS: *Balbutius* (s.d.s); *Balb<utius>* (s.p.s); *Balbutius,* [one of the] *Parochiani Opilionis* (d.p.)
PRUNELLA: *Prunella* (s.d.s); *Prun<ella>* (s.p.s); *Prunella,* [Opilius'] *Marita* (d.p.)
SEXTON: *Vespilo* (s.d.s and s.p.s); *Vespilo, sepulchralem curam agens* (d.p.)
LURCANIO: *Lurcanio* (s.d.s); *Lurc<anio>* (s.p.s); *Lurcanio,* [one of the] *Meretricii Consortes* (d.p.)
LATRUNCULUS: *Latrunculus* (s.d.s); *Latr<unculus>* (s.p.s); *Latrunculus,* [one of the] *Meretricii Consortes* (d.p.)
LICTORS: *Lictores* (s.d.s); *Lictor* (s.p.s)
EPILOGUE: *Epilogus* (heading)

OTHER CHARACTERS
Scholars who regularly dine with Opilio (1.2)
Cornelius, eldest bastard son of Cornelius (1.5)
The dead mother of the younger Cornelius (1.5)
Polypater, Cornelius' second bastard son (1.5)
Clea, Polypater's nursemaid (1.5)
Other candidates for Polypater's paternity, including a senior clergyman (1.5)
Licinia, Polypater's mother (1.5)
Perfidis, Cornelius' bastard daughter (1.5)
Fiddlers from whom Cornelius took Perfidis (1.5)
Cornelius' younger bastards, infants at nurse (1.5)
A physician from Tarento, who overcharged for chamber pots (1.5)
Opilio's parishioners, mostly butchers, bawds, and cowherds (2.8)
Syringe's mother (2.9)
Opilio's mother (2.9)
The parish bell-ringer (2.10)
Lectella, a prostitute (3.3)
Spitella, a prostitute (3.3)
Lazarella, a prostitute (3.3)
Sisters with whom Prunella went out drinking (3.7)
Knights whose requests for sex with Prunella have hitherto been denied (3.7)
Numerous girls debauched by Cornelius (3.7)
Marges, a deceased debauchee (4.9)
Cornelius' forebears (5.6)
Priscian's ancestors (5.13)

SETTING
Time-Scheme: 4.1–9 take place the day after 3.2, which is a Thursday; 5.7 takes place at bed-time and 5.8 at night
Place: Genoa

Geography
Genoa: Silver Street (actually in Cambridge); Duck Lane (actually in London); Platea Lasciviana

[*Italy*]: Tarento; Naples; Venice
Greece: Haemonia (i.e. Thessaly)
[*Mediterranean*]: 'the Amalthean Sea' (i.e. off Crete?)
France
[*London*]: Turnbull Street; Clerkenwell
[*Middlesex*]: Bloomsbury
[*Surrey*]: Cuckold's Haven
England: Oxford; [Bath]; Somerset
Ireland
[*Asia Minor*]: River Meander; Phrygia
Arabia
Ethiopia

SOURCES
Narrative: Ben Jonson, *Volpone* (**1493**); William Shakespeare, *Hamlet* (**1259**; 5.2); John Fletcher (revised James Shirley), *The Night-Walkers* (**1772**; 5.8); Thomas Randolph, *The Jealous Lovers* (**2365**; 5.7); William Davenant, *The Wits* (**2421**; grave robbery)
Verbal: Bible (Vulgate): Psalms 102.15 (4.2, 4.5, 4.8, 5.1), 129.1 (1.2, 5.2); Ecclesiastes 9.4 (5.2); Matthew 3.7 (3.4); Aristophanes, *Clouds* (2.10); Hippocrates, *De aeris, aquis, et locu* (3.2, cited), *Regimen* (4.5, cited); Terence, *Andria* (1.5, 3.6, 4.2), *Adelphoe* (3.4); Cicero, *Pro Cluentio* (the name Balbutius); Catullus, *Carmina* 3 (3.2); Sallust, *Catiline* (1.5); Virgil, *Aeneid* 3 (2.8), 4 (1.3); Horace, *Epistles* 1.19 (ded.); Ovid, *Heroides* 1 (1.5), 7 (1.5), *Ars amatoria* (4.5), *Metamorphoses* 1 (3.7); Suetonius, *Twelve Caesars*: Vespasian (1.5); *The Book of Common Prayer*: Litany (1549, rev. 1552; 3.5); Thomas Legge, *3 Richardus tertius* (**666**; 4.5); John Webster, *The White Devil* (**1689**; 3.6); Vincentius Fabricius, *Elegies* 4.7 (1632; 3.3)
Works Mentioned: Plautus, *Curculio* (3.7); Terence, *Eunuchus* (4.6); Virgil, *Georgics* (5.6); Galen, unspecified English translation (probably Thomas Gale's *Certain Works of Galen's,* 1566; 4.6); Arnaldus de Villanova, *Regimen sanitatis Salernitanum* (1480; 4.5); Pietro Aretino, *Postures* (1524; 1.5); William Shakespeare, *Venus and Adonis* (1593; 1.5); Albertus Magnus, *The Book of Secrets* (1595; 4.6); John Gerard, *Herbal* (1597; 4.6); Thomas Fougasses, *The General History of Venice* (1612; 3.2)

Sutton suggests that Grincome's reference in 4.1 to his playing the ambidexter ('Ambidextrum personam me acturum') refers to the title character of *Ignoramus* (**1768**), whose first name is Ambidexter. This is an unnecessarily specific reading: Ignoramus is called Ambidexter because of the general connotations of the word which also lie behind Grincome's remark; there is no reason to think he is named after any particular character who bears that name, whether in *Ignoramus* or *Cambyses* (**480**).

LANGUAGE
Latin
English: 91 words (1.2, 1.5, 3.3, 3.5, 5.2; Opilio, Priscian, Cornelius, Prunella)
Greek: 1 word (1.2; Opilio)

FORM
Metre: prose and Terentian pseudo-metre; a little English tetrameter
Rhyme: couplets
Prologue: 18 lines
Act-Division: 5 acts
Epilogue: 10 lines
Lines (Spoken): 3,762 (99 true verse, 419 pseudo-verse, 3,244 prose)
Lines (Written): 4,215

STAGING
Doors: said to creak (1.3, dialogue); mentioned (5.8, s.d.)
Discovery Space: Cornelius is discovered in the tub (3.2, s.d.), and on his couch (4.6, s.d.)
Stage: mentioned (5.8, s.d.)
Within: speech (1.3–4, s.d.); sound effects (4.6, s.d.)
Beneath: a grave is dug on stage (5.2, s.d.); the grave is opened (5.8, s.d.)
Audience: the prologue gives the audience permission, between the acts, to crack nuts, smoke tobacco, and kiss women; apparently asked to bear witness to events on stage in a previous scene (3.7, implicit); addressed as 'candidi' (fair ones; ep.)
Miscellaneous: Part of 5.8 is played as if in total darkness.

MUSIC AND SOUND
Sound Effects: noise within (4.6, s.d.)
Songs:
1: 'Quis tam dives, cui datur', 5.2, Sexton, 12 lines;
2: 'Functo Cornelio laetantur omnes', 5.4, antiphonal chorus of men and women, 12 lines;
3: 'Per abyssos et lacunos', 5.10, Latrunculus and Lurciano, with Pocadilla, Tubercula, and Sciatica as chorus, 16 lines.

PROPS
Lighting: two lanterns (5.8, s.d.)
Musical Instruments: a drum (5.13, s.d.)
Clothing: a gold bracelet (4.2, dialogue)
Money: coins (4.1, dialogue); a coin (5.2, dialogue)
Small Portable Objects: a will (1.5, implicit; written on stage); pen and ink (1.5, implicit); a box (2.1–6, dialogue); funeral flowers (5.1–2, s.d.)
Large Portable Objects: a couch (1.4–5, 4.6–9, s.d.); a tub (3.2–8, s.d.; large enough to contain a man); a spade (5.2, implicit); a coffin (5.8, s.d.)
Scenery: an arbour (2.1–6, 3.1–8, s.d.); a curtain (3.2, s.d.); a stone (5.8, s.d.; covering the grave)
Miscellaneous: ash and bones (5.2, s.d.)

COSTUMES
POCADILLA and GRINCOME: ghost masks (3.3–4, 3.6, s.d.); funeral bands (5.1–2, s.d.; presumably black)
OPILIO: ecclesiastical dress (2.8–10, 3.5–8, dialogue); a shirt (3.3–4, dialogue); a funeral band (5.1–2, s.d.)
TUBERCULA and SCIATICA: ghost masks (3.3–4, 3.6, s.d.); funeral bands (5.1–2, s.d)
PEREGRINE: a funeral band (5.1–2, s.d.)
PRUNELLA: a new dress (4.2–3, implicit); a funeral band (5.1–2, s.d.)

EARLY TEXTUAL HISTORY
1638: entered in the Stationers' Register to Thomas Harper and Thomas Slater on Friday 30 March; entry gives author's initials. Thomas Wykes had licensed the book for publication.

1638: **D** printed for Thomas Harper, for sale by Thomas Slater and Laurence Chapman; collation A–G¹², 84 leaves; engraved frontispiece by William Marshall; title page gives author's initials; Latin title-page motto; dedication to Sir Alexander Radcliffe; address 'omnibus et singulis' (to all and sundry), written in the person of the principal character, Cornelius; list of roles; argument.

1660: Samuel Pepys bought a copy in a shop in St Paul's Churchyard on Wednesday 14 November, and read it, 'with great pleasure', on the evening of Monday 3 December.

EDITION
Dana Sutton, The Philological Museum (internet, 2003).

REFERENCES
Annals 1638; Bentley, v. 962–4; Greg L16; Hazlitt, 50; Samuel Pepys, *Diary*, ed. Robert Latham and William Matthews (London, 1970–83), i. 292, 308; REED: Cambridge, 939; *RES* 1 (1925), 311–19; Smith, 95; Stratman, 303–4.

2430. *Confessor utinam feliciter nata* [Would That the Confessor Were Well Born]

TEXT
MS (Oxford: Bodleian, MS Rawlinson poet. 77); presentation copy. There is a brief lacuna in the text of 2.5.

GENRE
comedy
Contemporary: *comoedia* (MS)

TITLE
MS: *Confessor utinam feliciter nata*
Contemporary: *Confessor*

AUTHOR
Thomas Sparrow

DATE
Limits: 1629–41

2430. Confessor utinam feliciter nata

Best Guess: 1634

The conferral of Sparrow's Cambridge B.A. in 1633 is, as Bentley says, 'the last certain record of the man', though a man of the same name was admitted to Gray's Inn in 1635. It seems unwise to date the play much later than the B.A.: if he was the Gray's Inn Sparrow, then he left Cambridge not later than two years afterwards, and if he was not, then the fact that he took no M.A. still indicates that he left, either through displacement or mortality. However, the play's imitations of 'Tis Pity She's a Whore (**2329**), some of which are unmistakable, makes it far more likely that Sparrow wrote his comedy after Ford's play was published, also in 1633.

PLOT

It is understood that Antonius, balked of his hope to marry Clarinda, has gone off to fight the Turks, but was drowned on the way. Clarinda's father Lucentius is sorry not to have him for a son-in-law, but sets about making alternative arrangements: Clarinda is now to marry the foolish heir Morosus.

In fact, Antonius faked his own death, and has merely gone into hiding in the woods. Clarinda's sister Asphalia pretends that she is entering a nunnery, but actually disguises herself as a nymph, visits Antonius, and gets him to return to town, where he watches his own funeral. Seeking to frustrate Morosus' wedding plans, he poses as a hermit and presents Lucentius with Fidelio, a young Ethiopian who will be able to act as Clarinda's tutor (and who is really Asphalia in disguise). His friend Calliodorus also inveigles his way into the household: he wants to marry Asphalia, but plans to do it while she is posing as Fidelio, and so disguises himself as a woman.

The disguised Antonius hears confessions in the household. Lucentius admits to being uneasy about the proposed marriage to Morosus, and Antonius warns him that it would be an unpardonable sin to make his daughter wed a fool. When Clarinda visits the confessional, he reveals his identity and imposes a penance in the form of kisses. 'Fidelio' further courts her on Antonius' behalf under cover of a Greek lesson, and arranges to dispose of Morosus under the pretence of an elopement. When Morosus keeps his date, Asphalia and her allies disguise themselves as ghosts and scare him, after which he is apparently killed, driving his uncle insane with grief. In fact, the assassins only wounded him, having treated their swords with a sleeping potion. Morosus is deluded into thinking that he is in the underworld, and is offered an option: marry instantly or suffer the torments of the damned. He chooses the wedding, and has to select the only available bride, an old nurse. With him out of the way, Clarinda marries the hermit, causing her father some annoyance until he reveals who he really is. Asphalia washes off her make-up and agrees to marry Calliodorus.

SCENE DESIGNATION

1.1–6, 2.1–7, 3.1–6, 4.1–6, 5.1–5 (MS, corrected)

MS neglects to mark a new scene when the stage is clear at the end of 5.2, and consequently misnumbers the last two scenes as 5.3–4.

The stage is not clear at the following scene-divisions: 2.1–4, 2.6–7, 3.2–3, 3.4–5, 5.1–2, 5.4–5.

ROLES

ASPHALIA, Lucentius' daughter, Clarinda's sister; poses as Fidelio, an Ethiopian youth

DOLLABELLA, Asphalia's nursemaid, nearly 60 years old; poses as Lachesis, one of the Fates; later Morosus' wife

PISANIUS, Antonius' father, Lucentius' friend

Three SAILORS (1.2)

GELAXIUS, a priest, Lucentius' servant

ANTONIUS, Pisanius' son; a young man; poses as a hermit, and as Clotho, one of the Fates; later Clarinda's husband

MOROSUS, Gryphus' nephew, about 20 years old; later Dollabella's husband

BUBULO, Morosus' servant; claims to be 60 years old (but may be joking)

CALLIODORUS, Diaphantus' son; poses as Calliparea, a young woman, and as Atropos, one of the Fates

DIAPHANTUS, an Italian physician, Calliodorus' father

MUSICIANS at Antonius' funeral; one seems to be a lutenist (2.2; including one soloist)

MOURNERS at Antonius' funeral (2.2, *non-speaking*)

LUCENTIUS, father of Clarinda and Asphalia, Pisanius' friend

CLARINDA, Lucentius' daughter, Asphalia's sister; later Antonius' wife

GRYPHUS, an old miser, Morosus' uncle

A PRIEST (2.2)

Four MUSICIANS accompanying Morosus (3.6; three speak)

Two ASSASSINS (4.6)

Two SERVANTS of Lucentius (5.1)

A BOY, a servant in Lucentius' household (5.5)

Speaking Parts: 24–5

Stage Directions and Speech Prefixes

ASPHALIA: *Asphalia* (s.d.s and d.p.); *Fidelio* (s.d.s); *Asp<halia>* | *Fid<elio>* (s.p.s)

DOLLABELLA: *Dollabella* (s.d.s); *Dol<labella>* (s.p.s); *Dolabella nurus* (d.p.)

PISANIUS: *Pisanius* (s.d.s); *Pisan<ius>* (s.p.s); *Pisanius pater Antonii* (d.p.)

SAILORS: *Tres Nautae* (s.d.s and d.p.); *Nauta 1* | *Nauta 2* | *Nauta 3* (s.p.s)

GELAXIUS: *Gelaxius* (s.d.s); *Gel<axius>* (s.p.s); *Gelaxius Sacerdos Lucentii servus* (d.p.)

ANTONIUS: *Antonius* (s.d.s); *Eremita* (s.d.s and s.p.s); *Ant<onius>* (s.p.s); *Antonius Clarindae Amator* (d.p.)

MOROSUS: *Morosus* (s.d.s); *Mor<osus>* (s.p.s); *Morosus stultus Amator Clarin<dae>* (d.p.)

BUBULO: *Bubulo* (s.d.s); *Bub<ulo>* (s.p.s); *Bubulo servus Morosi* (d.p.)

CALLIODORUS: *Calliodorus* | *Calliparea* (s.d.s); *Call<iodorus>* (s.p.s); *Calliodorus Asph<aliae> amator mutatio deinde nomine Calliparea* (d.p.)
DIAPHANTUS: *Diaphantus* (s.d.s); *Diaph<antus>* (s.p.s); *Diaphantus pater Calliodori* (d.p.)
MUSICIANS: *Chorus cantatium* | *Cytharista* (s.d.s); *Chorus* (s.p.s)
MOURNERS: *pompa lugubri* (s.d.s)
LUCENTIUS: *Lucentius* (s.d.s); *Lucen<tius>* (s.p.s); *Lucentius pater Clarindae et Asphaliae* (d.p.)
CLARINDA: *Clarinda* (s.d.s and d.p.); *Clar<inda>* (s.p.s)
GRYPHUS: *Gryphus* (s.d.s); *Gry<phus>* (s.p.s); *Gryphus, Avarus Avunculus Morosi* (d.p.)
PRIEST: *Sacerdos* (s.d.s and s.p.s)
MUSICIANS: *cytharistum choro* (s.d.s); *1 Tibicen* | *3 Tibicen* | *2 Tibicen* (s.p.s); *Quatuor Tibicines* (d.p.)
ASSASSINS: *2° Sicarii* | *Sicarii* (s.d.s); *Sicarius 1* | *Sicarius 2* (s.p.s); *Duo Sicarii* (d.p.)
SERVANTS: *servoli 2°* (s.d.s); *Servus 1* | *Servus 2* (s.p.s)
BOY: *Puer* (s.p.s)

OTHER CHARACTERS
Men who mocked Clarinda's grief for Antonius (3.3)
Clarinda's many suitors (3.4–5)

SETTING
Period: contemporary (?)
Time-Scheme: 2.4 and 2.7 end at a mealtime (probably the same mealtime), and 3.6 takes place at 10 p.m. the ensuing evening; 4.4 and 4.6 take place late at night
Place: a Mediterranean coastal town in a Catholic country, possibly not Italy

The town where the action takes place is never named, but the play assumes several things about it. The sailors in 1.2 establish that it is on the coast, and, since Antonius was supposedly drowned on the way to fight the Turks, it is probably the Mediterranean coast in particular. Diaphantus is not a native, let alone Italian; therefore the play may not be set in Italy (or he may just be from a different Italian state). The plot partly turns on auricular confession, so the country is Catholic.

Geography
Britain: Wales
[Europe]: Italy; Greece; France
[Asia]: The Dead Sea; Turkey; Arabia; River Meander; Tyre; Lebanon; Caucasus
[Africa]: Ethiopia

SOURCES
Narrative: William Shakespeare, *The Taming of the Shrew* (**916**; 4.1); John Ford, *'Tis Pity She's a Whore* (**2329**; especially 4.6)
Verbal: Homer, *Iliad* (4.1, cited); Plautus, *Amphitruo* (5.2), *Captivi* (2.4, cited), *Miles gloriosus* (3.3), *Persa* (2.5), *Pseudolus* (3.6), *Truculentus* (3.3); Terence, *Andria* (3.3–4, 5.1), *Eunuchus* (3.3), *Heautontimorumenos* (3.3, 3.5–6), *Phormio* (4.1); Publilius Syrus, *Sententiae* (1.3, 1.6); Sallust, *Ad Caesar de re publica* (2.1); Virgil, *Georgics* 4 (4.6), *Eclogues* 10 (1.4), *Aeneid* 2 (3.3), 4 (2.7), 5 (1.3), 10 (5.4); Horace, *Ars poetica* (2.5), *Odes* 3.4 (3.3); Seneca, *Hippolytus* (3.2); Bible: Luke 4.23 (2.1); John Ford, *'Tis Pity She's a Whore* (**2329**; 2.5, 3.3, 4.6)
Works Mentioned: Aesop, *Fables* (1.5); there are general references to Homer (3.6), Demosthenes (2.5), and Cicero (1.3)

The general situation of a father trying to arrange his daughter's marriage, and giving serious consideration to a booby with a rich uncle, has obvious parallels with *'Tis Pity She's a Whore*. What clinches Ford's play as a definite source is the joke in 2.5 whereby the fool writes a love-letter and plans to deliver it in person: 'Tute scribis et eris tabellarius?' asks Gryphus, translating Donado's 'wouldst thou write a letter and carry it thyself?' (*TP* 2.4). The first stage of the gulling of Morosus, in 4.6, is a riff on the murder of Bergetto (*TP* 3.7): the fool is attacked and stabbed, apparently to death, during an attempted nocturnal elopement. In the same scene, the assassins are paid off in language which echoes Soranzo's 'Here's gold—here's more—want nothing' (*TP* 5.4): 'Hem aureos—cape sis—plures.' The description of 'dead' Antonius in 3.3, 'iuvenem omnibus naturae dotibus instructum', echoes that of dead Annabella in Ford's penultimate line: 'one so young, so rich in Nature's store'.

LANGUAGE
Latin
Greek: 17 words (4.1; Clarinda, Asphalia)

FORM
Metre: Terentian pseudo-metre
Act-Division: 5 acts
Lines (Spoken): 2,068 (65 true verse)
Lines (Written): 2,186

STAGING
Doors: knocked at (4.4, s.d.)
Stage: characters watch from opposite sides of the stage (2.2, s.d.)
Above: Clarinda's window (3.6, 4.4, s.d.; it is serenaded in the former scene, but only in the latter does anyone appear at it)
Audience: directly addressed (5.5, implicit)
Miscellaneous: 'Calliparea' exits from the window above at the end of 4.4 and immediately re-enters on the main stage at the start of 4.5.

MUSIC
On-Stage Music: a musician plays a stringed instrument (3.6, dialogue)
Songs:
  1: 'Errans, vagansque anima', 2.2, soloist and chorus, 14 lines;
  2: 'Ad fenestram vitae languens', 3.6, 2 Musician, Morosus, and everyone on stage, 20 lines, some repeated;
  3: 'Arthurum cum primo regem', 3.6, Morosus, 4 lines;
  4: 'Ab Oberone lemurem', 5.4, Gryphus, 20 lines.

PROPS
Lighting: torches (3.3, s.d.); a torch (4.6, s.d.)
Weapons: Fidelio's sword (3.4–5, s.d.); two swords (4.6, dialogue)
Musical Instruments: possibly a lute (2.2, implicit); a stringed instrument (3.6, dialogue); lutes (3.6, implicit)
Money: gold (4.6, s.d.)
Small Portable Objects: a fan (1.5, 2.7, dialogue); a letter (2.5, dialogue); a garland of roses (3.3, s.d.); a handkerchief (3.6, dialogue); a book (4.1, s.d.); a goblet (5.2, dialogue); a jar (5.3, s.d.; used to distort 'Fidelio's' voice and make 'him' sound spectral)
Large Portable Objects: a walking-stick (2.3, dialogue); a seat (2.2–3, dialogue); a basin of water (5.5, dialogue)
Scenery: a tomb (2.2, s.d.)
Miscellaneous: blood (4.6, dialogue)

COSTUMES AND MAKE-UP
ASPHALIA: disguised as a nymph (1.4, s.d.); cross-dressed as a man (2.1, 2.6–7, s.d.; 3.2–5, 4.1, 4.3, 4.5–6, 5.3, 5.5, implicit); black facial make-up (2.6–7, s.d.; 3.2–5, 4.1, 4.3, 4.5–6, 5.3, implicit; 5.5, dialogue; washed off on stage); a scabbard (3.4–5, implicit); disguised as a ghost (4.6, 5.3, s.d.)
DOLLABELLA: disguised as a ghost (4.6, 5.3, 5.5, s.d.)
PISANIUS: white hair (dialogue)
ANTONIUS: disguised as a hermit (2.6–7, 3.2–3, 3.6, 4.2, 4.6, 5.3, 5.5, s.d.; removed on stage), including a hood (dialogue); disguised as a ghost (4.6, 5.3, s.d.)
MOROSUS: a beard and a mole on his face (dialogue); fine clothes trimmed with gold (1.5, dialogue); shoes (1.5, dialogue); a cloak and garters (1.5, 2.7, dialogue); a plume of ostrich feathers (2.3, 2.5, dialogue); dressed as a ghost (5.3, 5.5, s.d.)
CALLIODORUS: has no beard (dialogue; at least from 3.1 onwards); cross-dressed as a woman (3.1, 3.6, s.d.; 4.1, 4.4–6, 5.3, 5.5, implicit; removed on stage); disguised as a ghost (4.6, 5.3, s.d.)
CLARINDA: white clothes (3.3, s.d.)
GRYPHUS: tears his garments on stage (4.6, s.d.)

EARLY TEXTUAL HISTORY
Before 1641: transcribed in **MS**; 49 leaves; authorial dedication to a bishop (probably John Williams); list of roles.
  1666: MS was in the possession of Richard Walden of the Inner Temple.
  1675: MS was in the possession of Johannes Ludovicus.

EDITIONS
Sabine U. Bückmann-de Villegas, Renaissance Latin Drama in England 2.12 (Hildesheim, Zurich, and New York, 1991).
Dana Sutton, The Philological Museum (internet, 2001).

REFERENCES
Annals 1634; Bentley, v. 1180–1; Hazlitt, 46; REED: Cambridge, 936; Smith, 96.

2431. *The Spartan Ladies*

EVIDENCE
Sir Henry Herbert's office-book; Sir Humphrey Mildmay's diary; Stationers' Register; Lord Chamberlain's list of former Blackfriars plays assigned to the Theatre Royal in January 1669 (Kew: National Archives, LC 5/12, p. 212).

GENRE
Contemporary: play (Mildmay)

TITLE
Performed: *The Spartan Ladies*
Contemporary: *The Spartan Lady*

AUTHOR
Lodowick Carlell

DATE
April 1634

ORIGINAL PRODUCTION
King's Men at the Blackfriars (and perhaps also the Globe)

ROLES
One or more LADIES from Sparta

SETTING
Period: antiquity (?)

Geography
[*Greece*]: Sparta

EARLY STAGE HISTORY
1634: performed (as *The Spartan Ladies*) by the King's Men at the Blackfriars in April. The audience included Queen Henrietta Maria.
  1634: performed on the afternoon of Thursday 1 May; the play was then still a new one. The audience included Sir Humphrey Mildmay (who paid 1s.3d and gave the title as *The Spartan Lady*).

EARLY TEXTUAL HISTORY
1646: entered to Humphrey Robinson and Humphrey Moseley in the Stationers' Register between Friday 4 and Tuesday 15 September; group entry of 105 titles, play and author individually named. John Langley had licensed the book for publication.
  1656: In an advertisement, Moseley declared his intention to publish this and other plays 'very speedily'.
  1673: Robinson's rights transferred in the Stationers' Register by his executor (also named Humphrey Robinson) to John Martin and Henry Herringman on Thursday 30 January, as part of a list of 105 titles, by assignment of Saturday 13 May 1671.

1683: Martin's rights transferred in the Stationers' Register from his widow, Sarah, to Robert Scott, on Tuesday 21 August, by assignment of Tuesday 14 June 1681 and order of a court of Monday 7 November 1681; individually named as part of a group transfer of 360 titles.

REFERENCES
Annals 1634; Bawcutt 291; Bentley, ii. 676, iii. 124; Greg Θ54; Hazlitt, 217; William van Lennep, *The London Stage, 1660–1800*, Part 1: 1660–1700 (Carbondale, 1965), 152; Allardyce Nicoll, *A History of English Drama*, 4th edn (Cambridge, 1952–9), i. 354; Sibley, 152.

2432. The Seven Champions of Christendom

TEXT
Printed in 1638 (STC 15014), possibly from authorial papers.

GENRE
romance
Contemporary: play (S.R., ded.); work, history (ded.)

TITLE
Printed: *The Seven Champions of Christendom*

AUTHOR
John Kirke

DATE
Limits: 1625–34
Best Guess: Spring 1634

John Freehafer (in *SP*) makes a very detailed but ultimately unconvincing case for limits of 1612–14, in support of a reading of the play as a parody of *The Tempest* (**1652**). The argument frequently depends on general references which are taken to be more precise and chronologically significant than they really are: for example, a mention of shows and fireworks does not necessarily refer to the Palatine marriage celebrations, and green men featured in many London civic shows other than that of 1612 (**1687**).

In any event, Q's 'never printed until 1638' tag need not mean that this is a very old play; it more probably means that, for sales and rights purposes, the bookseller was keen to avoid confusion with the Richard Johnson romance of the same title, which had been in print a long time. Moreover, imitation of a Shakespeare play need not indicate a date close to the composition of the original work; a number of indisputably 1630s plays, such as *The Bashful Lover* (**2545**) and *The Goblins* (**2592**), also draw on *The Tempest*.

The allusion in 3.6 to the stage conjuror Hocus Pocus, which Freehafer advances as another Jacobean reference (on the basis of third-hand evidence), actually fixes the play as almost certainly Caroline: the earliest *OED* citation of Hocus Pocus is dated 1625,

and the records of his activities mainly belong to the 1620s and 1630s. Such a dating is also consistent with the tension in 2.2 between the shepherds and the priest over the legitimacy or otherwise of setting up a maypole.

Although the reference to the Lancashire witches (in 1.1) could be to the 1612 case, the subject acquired new topicality in 1633–4, which would date the play to the first half of 1634. This would also be consistent with the borrowing from *The Faithful Shepherdess* (**1582**), revived at court in January 1634, and presumably in the King's Men's commercial venues during the ensuing months. *The Seven Champions* cannot be later than that, because Kirke's company then moved from the Red Bull to the Fortune.

ORIGINAL PRODUCTION
Red Bull Company

PLOT
Years ago, the witch Calib stole a child, George, intending to bathe in his blood; but she fell in love with the baby and brought it up with her own son, Suckabus. She has always refused to let him know the identity of his real parents, but after much importunity she relents and tells George that he was a bastard whom she saved from infanticide. She asks her diabolic lover Tarpax how long she has to live; the demon prophesies that she will die only when love causes her to lose control of her magical powers. She shows George six Christian champions whom she keeps in her cave, and grants him their ransom. When George feels pity for them but pretends severity, she gives him her magic wand. The ghosts of his parents visit him, and he learns that Calib poisoned them, and that he is really of noble birth. He uses the magic wand to kill Calib, but agrees to take on Suckabus as a servant; Tarpax encourages Suckabus to spread his seed widely around the earth by taking every opportunity for procreation. George joins the six champions, bringing them up to the number prophesied by a Sibyl, seven. They go their separate ways into pagan lands.

Trebizond is troubled by monsters: a dragon and a lion terrorize the land and kill knights who attempt to dispose of them. The Emperor proclaims a reward for anyone who will deal with the menace. The champions Andrew and Anthony arrive in Trebizond, and the Princess and Carintha fall in love with them; but their welcome evaporates when the Emperor discovers their religion. An oracle has decreed that any Christians who set foot in Trebizond must convert to paganism or be executed. The Emperor allows them to choose their own executioners; they choose the ladies, who refuse to comply; so they offer to relieve the ladies of the responsibility and execute one another. The Emperor allows them to be rearmed so that they can do so, and this enables them to fight their way to freedom.

The champion David accidentally causes the death of Prince Arbasto in a joust. David has helped the King of Tartary, Arbasto's father, in his war with the Persians, and cannot honourably be executed, so the King offers him a pardon, half the kingdom, and the succession if he will bring back the head of his enemy, Ormandine. The expectation is that Ormandine will kill him. Ormandine was once a duke, but was deposed by the Kings of Tartary and Arabia, and took up magic to avenge himself. A prophecy assures him of his security until the arrival of a British knight; but David is not the knight in question, and Ormandine conjures him into a deep sleep. Meanwhile, George has killed a dragon on the promise of marriage to Sabrina, but her father reneges and throws him in a dungeon; after seven years, he kills the jailer and escapes. He confronts Ormandine, who is struck dead by a thunderbolt; George then allows David to sever the enchanter's head for delivery to the King.

The enchanter Argalio has shrouded his island in darkness using the black emanations of Hell. His friend Leonides has failed to bury the bodies of his family, and their ghosts urge him to do so. The Queen of the island asks James, Denis, and Patrick to expel Argalio. They find a prophecy that only the union of Spain, France, and Ireland can do this, and realize that they are the solution to the riddle. On learning of their approach, Argalio escapes in a flying throne: the land is free.

Tarpax is displeased with Suckabus' progress in wickedness, but gives him a document with magic words on it. He leaves George's service and transports himself magically to the castle of the giant Brandron, where he expects to get a good meal. The man-eating Brandron plans to make a good meal of him, but Suckabus uses magic to make the giant amiable. Brandron is the terror of Macedon: he kidnapped the King's daughters, but they turned themselves into swans to avoid rape, and have been in the castle fountain ever since. The King asks six of the champions to deal with Brandron, and they besiege the castle. Suckabus tricks them into coming inside unarmed: he claims that George is inside and has killed Brandron, but is worried that their weapons will frighten the ladies. The champions are imprisoned and, when George really does arrive, Brandron makes them fight against him in single combat. He defeats them all and the seven champions reunite to take on the giant; but Brandron, refusing to be beaten, kills himself. Due to be hanged for his treachery, Suckabus saves his life by revealing the whereabouts of the missing daughters. The King of Macedon converts to Christianity, and the swans turn back into women. The King gives them as wives to the three unmarried champions.

SCENE DESIGNATION

1.1–3, 2.1–2, 3.1, Cho., 3.2–7, 4.1–3, 5.1–8 (Q has act-division only)

ROLES

CALIB, a, old witch, Suckabus' mother; said to be the Queen of Limbony and Duchess of Witchcordia

TARPAX, a spirit of the air and prince of the north; Calib's lover, Suckabus' father

SUCKABUS, the clown, son of Tarpax and Calib; said to be the Duke of Styx, Sulphur, and Helvetia; later George's servant

GEORGE of England, a young man and an orphan, dead Coventry's son; later a champion of Christendom; also called Master George

JAMES, a Spanish knight of the Golden Fleece; a champion of Christendom

ANTHONY, a knight of Italy; a Roman and a champion of Christendom

ANDREW, a knight of Scotland; a champion of Christendom; he is unmarried

PATRICK, a knight of Ireland; a champion of Christendom; he is unmarried

DAVID, a knight of Britain and of Wales (though he is also said to be English); a champion of Christendom

DENIS, a knight of France; a champion of Christendom; he is unmarried

The Earl of COVENTRY, George's father, a ghost

George's MOTHER, a ghost

SPIRITS, who attempt to defend Calib (1.2, *non-speaking*)

The EMPEROR of Trebizond, Violeta's father

VIOLETA, Princess of Trebizond, the Emperor's daughter; initially written as Carinthia

CARINTHA, Violeta's maid; initially written as Violeta

ANCETES, a lord of Trebizond

Three ATTENDANTS on the Emperor (2.1–2, *non-speaking*)

Three COUNTRY SWAINS, shepherds of Trebizond

The PRIEST of Pan

BAPTISTO, a shepherd of Trebizond

Three VIRGINS of Diana (2.2, *non-speaking*)

ALMENO, a Tartarian nobleman; also called Almene

Lord LENON, a Tartarian nobleman

VOICES, spectators at the joust (3.1, *within*)

A MESSENGER, who reports Arbasto's death (3.1)

The King of TARTARY, an old man, Arbasto's father; may be named Tartaria

Two KNIGHTS attending the King of Tartary (3.1, *non-speaking*)

Prince ARBASTO of Tartary, the King's son (3.1, *non-speaking*; only appears as a dead body, and may alternatively be represented by a prop)

CHORUS

CORYDON, a shepherd (3.2)

ORMANDINE, a magician, formerly a duke; also called Ormand and Ormandy

Two LORDS, Ormandine's friends in magic (one may be *non-speaking*)

SPIRITS serving Ormandine (3.3, 3.5–6, *non-speaking*)

FREE EXCESS, conjured by Ormandine against David; also called Excess (3.5, *non-speaking*)

IMMODEST MIRTH, conjured by Ormandine against David (3.5, *non-speaking*)

DELIGHT, conjured by Ormandine against David (3.5, *non-speaking*)

DESIRE, conjured by Ormandine against David (3.5, *non-speaking*)

LUST SATED, conjured by Ormandine against David (3.5, *non-speaking*)
SICKNESS, conjured by Ormandine against David (3.5, *non-speaking*)
ARGALIO, an enchanter
LEONIDES, a young man, Argalio's friend; a brother
SPIRITS who serve Argalio (4.1, possibly 4.3; only one speaks)
Leonides' FATHER, a ghost (4.1, *non-speaking*)
Leonides' MOTHER, a ghost (4.1, *non-speaking*)
Leonides' SISTER, a ghost (4.1, *non-speaking*)
BRANDRON, a giant
The King of MACEDON, an old man, father of three daughters; possibly named Tenopas (if it is not a place name)
A DRUMMER attending the King of Macedon (5.8, *non-speaking*)
SOLDIERS attending the King of Macedon (5.8, *non-speaking*)
Three LADIES, daughters of the King of Macedon; sisters (only speak collectively)

Speaking Parts: 37–9
Allegorical Roles: 6 (spirits)

Stage Directions and Speech Prefixes
CALIB: *Calib the Witch* (s.d.s and d.p.); *Witch* (s.d.s); *Calib* (s.p.s)
TARPAX: *Tarpax* (s.d.s); *Tarp<ax>* (s.p.s); *Tarpax the Devil* (d.p.)
SUCKABUS: *Clown* (s.d.s and s.p.s); *fool | Suckabus | the Clown* (s.d.s); *Suckabus, the Clown* (d.p.)
GEORGE: *George* (s.d.s and s.p.s); [one of the] *Champions | [one of] the Champions* (s.d.s); *St George of England* [one of] *The seven Champions* (d.p.)
JAMES: *James* (s.d.s and s.p.s); [one of the] *Champions | [one of] the six Champions | [one of] the Champions* (s.d.s); *James of Spaine* [one of] *The seven Champions* (d.p.)
ANTHONY: *Anthony | [one of the] Champions | [one of] the six Champions | [one of] the Champions* (s.d.s); *Anton<y> | Anthon<y>* (s.p.s); *Anthony of Italy* [one of] *The seven Champions* (d.p.)
ANDREW: *Andrew | [one of the] Champions | [one of] the six Champions | [one of] the Champions* (s.d.s); *Andr<ew> | [one of] 3 Knights* (s.p.s); *Andrew of Scotland* [one of] *The seven Champions* (d.p.)
PATRICK: *Patricke | [one of the] Champions | [one of] the six Champions | [one of] the Champions* (s.d.s); *Pat<rick> | [one of] 3 Knights* (s.p.s); *Patrick of Ireland* [one of] *The seven Champions* (d.p.)
DAVID: *David* (s.d.s and s.p.s); [one of the] *Champions | [one of] the six Champions | [one of] the Champions | Knight* (s.d.s); *David of Wales* [one of] *The seven Champions* (d.p.)
DENIS: *Denis* (s.d.s and s.p.s); [one of the] *Champions | [one of] the six Champions | [one of] the Champions* (s.d.s); *[one of] 3 Knights* (s.p.s); *Denis of France* [one of] *The seven Champions* (d.p.)

COVENTRY: *the ghost of George's father* (s.d.s); *Father* (s.p.s)
MOTHER: *the ghost of George's . . . mother* (s.d.s); *Mother* (s.p.s)
SPIRITS: *other spirits | the spirits* (s.d.s); *Three Spirits* (d.p.)
EMPEROR: *Emperor of Trebizond* (s.d.s); *Emperor* (s.d.s and s.p.s); *The Emperor of Trebozand* (d.p.)
VIOLETA: *Violeta | [the Emperor's] daughter* (s.d.s); *Princess* (s.p.s); *Violeta, the Princess* (d.p.)
CARINTHA: *Carinthia the Princess* (s.d.s; *sic*); *Car<intha>* (s.p.s); *Carintha, [Violeta's] maid* (d.p.)
ANCETES: *Ancetes a Lord* (s.d.s); *Ancet<es>* (s.p.s); *Ancetes* [one of] *Three Lords* (d.p.)
ATTENDANTS: *attendance | attendants* (s.d.s); *Three attendants on the Emperor* (d.p.)
COUNTRY SWAINS: *Country Swains* (s.d.s); *1 | 2 | 3* (s.p.s); *Three Shepherds* (d.p.)
PRIEST: *Priest* (s.d.s and s.p.s); *A priest of Pan* (d.p.)
BAPTISTO: *Baptisto* (s.d.s); *Bap<tisto>* (s.p.s); [one of] *Three messengers* (d.p.)
VIRGINS: *three other Virgins* (s.d.s)
ALMENO: *Almona* (s.d.s); *Almon<a>* (s.p.s); *Almeno* [one of] *Three Lords* (d.p.)
LENON: *Lenon* (s.d.s and s.p.s); *Lenon* [one of] *Three Lords* (d.p.)
MESSENGER: *Messenger* (s.d.s and s.p.s); [one of] *Three messengers* (d.p.)
TARTARY: *the King of Tartary* (s.d.s); *King* (s.p.s); *The King of Tartary* (d.p.)
KNIGHTS: *two Knights* (s.d.s); *Two armed Knights* (d.p.)
ARBASTO: *the body of the Prince Arbasto* (s.d.s)
CHORUS: *Chorus* (s.p.s)
CORYDON: *Shepherd* (s.d.s and s.p.s)
ORMANDINE: *the Enchanter Ormandine | Ormandine | Ormand* (s.d.s); *Orm<andine>* (s.p.s); *Ormandine, a Magician* (d.p.)
LORDS: *some selected friends | Lords | [Ormandine's] friends* (s.d.s); *Lord* (s.p.s); *2 Lords [Ormandine's] friends* (d.p.)
SPIRITS: *[Ormandine's] spirits | spirits | Devils* (s.d.s)
FREE EXCESS: *free Excess | Excess* (s.d.s)
IMMODEST MIRTH: *immodest Mirth* (s.d.s)
DELIGHT: *Delight* (s.d.s)
DESIRE: *Desire* (s.d.s)
LUST SATED: *Lust sated* (s.d.s)
SICKNESS: *sickness* (s.d.s)
ARGALIO: *Argalio* (s.d.s); *Arg<alio>* (s.p.s); *Argalio, an Enchanter* (d.p.)
LEONIDES: *Leonides | Leopides* (s.d.s); *Leon<ides>* (s.p.s); *Leonides, [Argalio's] friend* (d.p.)
SPIRITS: *Spirits* (s.d.s); *Spirit* (s.p.s)
FATHER: *father* (s.d.s); [one of] *Three Ghosts; the Father . . . of Leonides* (d.p.)
MOTHER: [one of] *Three Ghosts; the . . . Mother . . . of Leonides* (d.p.)
SISTER: *sister* (s.d.s); [one of] *Three Ghosts; the . . . Sister of Leonides* (d.p.)

BRANDRON: *Brandron* | *The Giant* (s.d.s); *Bran<dron>* (s.p.s); *Brandron the Giant* (d.p.)
MACEDON: *the King* (s.d.s); *Mac<edon>* (s.p.s); *King of Macedon* (d.p.)
DRUMMER: *Drum* (s.d.s)
SOLDIERS: *Soldiers* (s.d.s)
LADIES: *3 Ladies* (s.p.s); *Three Daughters to Macedon* (d.p.)

OTHER CHARACTERS
The Sibyls, who prophesied that there would be a total of seven champions of Christendom (1.3)
The Emperor of Trebizond's army (2.1)
Travellers and knights eaten by the Trebizond lion (2.1)
Niger, Pallemon, and Antigonus, three young knights who fought the Trebizond monsters and were killed (2.1–2)
The people of Trebizond, the Emperor's subjects (2.1–2)
The priests of Apollo in Trebizond (2.1)
The Persian army, enemies of the Tartars (3.1)
Sabrina, who was promised in marriage to George if he killed a dragon (Cho.)
Pomil, Sabrina's father, who imprisoned George (Cho.)
The King of Morocco, George's rival for Sabrina (Cho.)
The jailer, whose neck George broke (Cho.)
A giant killed by George and Suckabus (3.2)
The guard in Corydon's country, tall men (3.2)
Corydon's master (3.2)
Old Dick, a knight errant who employed Corydon's master as a page (3.2)
A lord, Suckabus' first alternative master during George's imprisonment (3.2)
The lord's cook (3.2)
A young lady whom Suckabus served as a gentleman usher, but whom he left on account of her dislike of new fashions (3.2)
A young heir, whom Suckabus served, but whom he considered excessively hospitable (3.2)
A usurer, who habitually got drunk and gave away money, much to Suckabus' disapproval (3.2)
A proctor, whose conscientious dining habits caused Suckabus to leave his service (3.2)
A scrivener, Suckabus' final interim master, who was pilloried (3.2)
The King of Arabia (3.3, 3.7)
Brute, ancestor of both David and George (3.3, 3.5)
Aurela, Queen of the dark island (4.1, 4.3)
The people of the dark island (4.3; heard shouting within)
The people of Macedon (5.1)

SETTING
Period: medieval; 2.2 takes place in the month of May
Time-Scheme: 2.1 takes place in the morning, and 2.2 later the same day; more than seven years pass between 1.3 and 3.2

Place: outside Christendom, including Trebizond (apparently thought to be in Greece), Tartary, a dark island, and Macedon

Geography
London: Tothill Fields
England: Lancashire; Coventry; Devil's Arse; the Peak; River Thames; Ware
Britain: Scotland; Ireland; Wales
France: Normandy
Italy: Rome; Mount Etna
Macedon: Tenopas (unidentified; may alternatively be a character name)
Europe: Spain; Greece; the Low Countries; Thrace
[Africa]: Morocco; Barbary; Libya; Ethiopia
Asia: Persia; Arabia; Turkey; Sabaea
India
The West Indies
The Antipodes
The North Pole
The South Pole
Hell: River Styx; Avernus; River Cocytus

SOURCES
Narrative: Richard Johnson, *The Seven Champions of Christendom* (1596–7, repr. 1626); Lucian, *A True History* (5.1); John Fletcher, *The Faithful Shepherdess* (**1582**; Priest of Pan)
Verbal: William Shakespeare, *Hamlet* (**1259**; 1.1); Thomas Ravenscroft, *Pammelia* (1609; 5.8)

LANGUAGE
English
Latin: 2 words (3.1–2; Messenger, Suckabus)
Gibberish: 12 magic words (3.6, 5.1; Tarpax, Suckabus)

FORM
Metre: pentameter and prose; some hexameter and fourteeners
Rhyme: blank verse; some couplets
Chorus: appears between 3.1 and 3.2
Act-Division: 5 acts
Lines (Spoken): 2,660 (1,979 verse, 681 prose)
Lines (Written): 2,764

STAGING
Doors: characters enter severally (5.8, s.d.)
Discovery Space: possibly represents a cave (1.1, implicit)
Stage: mentioned (Cho., dialogue; 3.6, s.d.)
Within: speech (1.1, 4.2, s.d.; 3.1, implicit); music (1.1, 3.1, s.d.); sound effect (1.2, 3.1, s.d.); shout (4.3, s.d.); a great cry (3.6, s.d.)
Above: Tarpax descends (1.1, s.d.); characters appear above (3.5, 5.5, 5.8, s.d.; at least eight simultaneously; it takes only 2 lines to get down to the main stage); a throne descends, possibly with spirits aboard, then goes back up again with Argalio and Leonides (4.3, implicit)

Beneath: Calib 'sinks' through a cleft rock (1.2, s.d.)
Audience: Suckabus threatens Tarpax with attack by 'all the prentices in the house' (1.2)
Miscellaneous: a brazen pillar magically appears (3.3, implicit; the obvious options would be the trap or the discovery space); Ormandine is struck by a thunderbolt on stage (3.7, s.d.); Brandron 'beats out his own brains' on stage (5.8, s.d.); three swans metamorphose into women on stage (5.8, s.d.)

MUSIC AND SOUND

Sound Effects: thunder (1.1–2, 3.5–7, 4.1, s.d.); noise within (1.2, 3.1, s.d.)
Music: horn within (1.1, s.d.); soft music (1.1, 3.5, s.d.); unspecified music (1.2, s.d.; 3.6, dialogue); loud music (2.2, 3.3, s.d.); flourish (2.2, s.d.); charges (3.1, s.d.); a dead march within (3.1, s.d.); sweet music (3.5, s.d.); a lazy tune (3.5, s.d.)
On-Stage Music: drum (5.8, dialogue)
Song: 'I have a love, as white as a raven', 5.3, Suckabus, 15 lines
Other Singing: Suckabus sings two lines (5.8, s.d.)
Dance: the vices dance (3.5, s.d.); spirits dance (4.1, s.d.); champions dance (5.8, s.d.)

PROPS

Pyrotechnics: lightning (1.1–2, 3.5–6, 4.1, s.d.); flames from inside the cloven rock (1.2, dialogue)
Weapons: George's falchion (1.2–3, dialogue); three bows, arrows, and quivers (2.2, s.d.); Andrew's sword (2.2, 5.6, dialogue); Anthony's sword (2.2, 5.6, dialogue); a golden sword (3.5, 3.7, dialogue; 3.6, s.d.; stuck in the brazen pillar); fiery clubs (3.5, s.d.); David's sword (3.5, s.d.; 5.6, dialogue); George's sword (3.7, 5.8, dialogue); Leonides' sword (4.3, dialogue); an iron mace or club (5.1, s.d.); Denis's, James's, and Patrick's weapons (5.6, dialogue); unspecified weapons (5.8, s.d.)
Musical Instruments: a drum (5.8, s.d.)
Animals: three swans (5.8, s.d.; they are seen to turn into human beings on stage, so may be costumes for the daughters)
Food and Drink: two carrots, a turnip, and a piece of bean-bread (3.2, dialogue; eaten on stage); bread and meat (5.1, s.d.)
Small Portable Objects: Calib's magic wand (1.1–2, dialogue); binding cords (2.2, implicit); a book (3.3, dialogue); Ormandine's magic wand (3.5, s.d.); a paper (3.6, dialogue); possibly a jewel (3.6, dialogue; may be a figure of speech); keys (5.5, 5.8, dialogue)
Large Portable Objects: a hearse (3.1, s.d.); a dead body (3.1, s.d.; may be represented by an actor); possibly a sheep-hook (3.2, dialogue; may be just a figure of speech); a canopy (3.3, s.d.); a magic mirror (3.3, dialogue); seating for one character (5.8, implicit); military colours (5.8, s.d.)
Scenery: a rock (1.1, dialogue; 1.2, s.d.; large enough for a character to climb; splits on cue so that she drops through it); a brazen pillar with an engraved golden tablet (3.3, 3.5–6, dialogue); a pillar with an inscribed tablet (4.2, dialogue); a throne (4.3, dialogue; seats two; descends and ascends)
Miscellaneous: blood (1.1, s.d.); a thunderbolt (3.7, implicit)

COSTUMES AND MAKE-UP

TARPAX: wings (dialogue)
SUCKABUS: a mole on his cheek (dialogue); blood on his head (1.1, s.d.); dressed as a poor shepherd (3.2, s.d.); clothes of good cloth (3.6, dialogue)
GEORGE: armour (1.3, 3.6, 5.8, s.d.; 3.7, implicit); a plume (1.3, s.d.); a poor habit (3.2, s.d.); a red cross on his breast (3.6, implicit; 3.7, dialogue); a burgonet (5.8, dialogue)
JAMES: armour (1.3, 5.8, s.d.); a plume (1.3, s.d.); a helmet (4.2, dialogue)
ANTHONY and **ANDREW:** armour (1.3, 2.2, 5.8, s.d.; removed on stage); a plume each (1.3, s.d.)
PATRICK: armour (1.3, 5.8, s.d.); a plume (1.3, s.d.)
DAVID: armour (1.3, 5.8, s.d.); a plume (1.3, s.d.); bound (3.1, s.d.); 'armed cap-a-pie' (3.4, s.d.; 3.5, implicit), including a black corselet and a black plume (dialogue)
DENIS: armour (1.3, 5.8, s.d.); a plume (1.3, s.d.)
CALIB'S SPIRITS: armed (1.2, s.d.)
LENON: a coat (3.1, dialogue)
TARTARY: a large crown (3.1, dialogue)
KNIGHTS: armour (3.1, s.d.)
ARGALIO'S SPIRITS: are black (dialogue)
MACEDON: steel armour (5.8, dialogue)

EARLY STAGE HISTORY

Acted at both the Red Bull and the Cockpit by 1638, 'with a general liking'. The Red Bull Company's performances were probably before July 1634 (when the company transferred to the Fortune). The Cockpit performance would have been by either Queen Henrietta's Men (up to 1636) or the King and Queen's Young Company (Beeston's Boys; 1637–8).

EARLY TEXTUAL HISTORY

1638: entered in the Stationers' Register to John Okes on Friday 13 July; entry names author. The entry bundles in a separate work, *The Life and Death of Jack Straw and Wat Tyler*, as if it were a subtitle for the play. Thomas Wykes had licensed the book for publication.

1638: **Q** printed by John Okes, and for sale by James Beckett; collation A–L⁴, 44 leaves; title page gives author's initials, and refers to two playhouses; dedication to John Waite signed by John Kirke; list of roles.

c. 1630s–40s: a copy of Q was in the possession of John Horne (Vicar of Headington, Oxfordshire). After his death, his entire collection of play-books passed into the possession of John Houghton of Brasenose College, Oxford (*c.* 1608–77), then to James Herne (died 1685), and then to the library of Ralph Sheldon (1623–84) at Weston, where it was catalogued by Anthony Wood, probably in the late 1670s.

1673: rights transferred in the Stationers' Register on Monday 30 June from Anne Oakes, the widow of Edward Oakes, to Thomas Vere and John Wright, in accordance with Oakes's will dated Monday 16 June; individually named as part of a group transfer of 21 titles.

1684: Nicholas Cox (Manciple of St Edmund Hall, Oxford) had a copy of Q in his bookshop. It had probably been previously owned by Gerard Langbaine, and appears on a list compiled by Anthony Wood on Saturday 13 December.

EDITION
Giles Edwin Dawson, Western Reserve University Bulletin NS 32.16 (Cleveland, Ohio, 1929).

REFERENCES
Annals 1635; Bentley, iv. 712–14; Bodleian, MS Wood E. 4, art. 1, p. 19; Greg 545; Hazlitt, 206; *The Library*, 5th ser., 33 (1978), 226–30; *MLR* 13 (1918), 401–11; *SP* 66 (1969), 87–103.

2433. *Arcades* [The Arcadians]

TEXT
Two substantive witnesses:
- **MS:** Cambridge: Trinity College, MS R.34, pp. 1–3: holograph transcript with authorial revisions; includes a false start; possibly first transcribed in advance of the performance;
- **O:** printed in 1645 (Wing M2160).

GENRE
entertainment
Contemporary: masque (MS, deleted heading); entertainment (MS heading)

TITLE
MS/Printed: *Arcades*

AUTHOR
John Milton

DATE
Limits: 1630, 1632–4
Best Guess: May 1634

ORIGINAL PRODUCTION
Dowager Countess of Derby's household at Harefield House, Middlesex

The Genius refers to a wood, which is usually taken to indicate an *al fresco* performance, and the specification that all the characters 'appear', rather than 'enter', might be consistent with this. The hypothesis has implications for the dating and occasion, in that an outdoor performance would be likelier during the summer, and would tend against the hypothesis that the performance was associated with the Dowager Countess's birthday, when there would still be the risk of post-April showers.

However, the Genius also says that the entertainment takes place, or at least continues, in the evening, which would suggest an indoor venue, perhaps with pictorial scenery for the wood. **2177** is a precedent for an indoor performance with scenery representing an outdoor part of the venue; Milton's next Egerton commission, **2445**, does the same more pointedly in its final scene. The opening s.d., moreover, speaks of the Nymphs and Shepherds 'on the scene', implying a stage.

PLOT
Arcadian nymphs and shepherds identify the Dowager Countess of Derby (in the audience) as the goddess whom they have sought on their travels. Attended by the Genius of the Wood, they approach and do her honour, and are adopted into her household.

ROLES
NYMPHS of Arcadia
SHEPHERDS of Arcadia
The GENIUS of the Wood, a lesser god, appointed by Jove

Speaking Parts: 1 or more

Stage Directions and Speech Prefixes
GENIUS: *The Genius of the Wood* (s.d.s); *Genius* (s.p.s)

OTHER CHARACTERS
Jove, who assigned the Genius to the wood

SETTING
Geography
Arcadia: River Alpheus; River Ladon; Mount Lycaeus; Mount Cyllene; Mount Erymanthus; Mount Maenalus

SOURCES
Verbal: Bible: 1 Kings 10.6–7; Plato, *Republic*; Virgil, *Aeneid* 6; Ben Jonson, *Royal Entertainment at Althorp* (**1407**)

LANGUAGE
English

FORM
Metre: iambic pentameter
Rhyme: couplets
Lines (Spoken): 109
Lines (Written): 111 (MS, ignoring marginalia and deleted lines); 119 (O)

STAGING
Audience: the Dowager Countess is mentioned, and is seated on a 'seat of state' (s.d.), which the performers approach

MUSIC
On-Stage Music: the Genius may play a stringed instrument

Songs:
1: 'Look, nymphs and shepherds, look', 25 lines; marked as a song in O but not in MS;
2: 'O'er the smooth enamelled green', Genius, 12 lines;
3: 'Nymphs and shepherds, dance no more', probably the Genius, 14 lines.

PROPS
Musical Instruments: possibly a stringed instrument ('warbled string', dialogue)

COSTUMES
NYMPHS: 'pastoral habit' (s.d.s); silver buskins (dialogue)
SHEPHERDS: 'pastoral habit' (s.d.s)

EARLY STAGE HISTORY
Early 1630s: performed at Harefield House, Middlesex. The cast included members of the Egerton family (Nymphs and Shepherds). The music was probably by Henry Lawes. The audience included Alice Egerton, Dowager Countess of Derby. The performance may have taken place in early May 1634 in honour of the Dowager Countess's 75th birthday, but probably not on the birthday itself, 4 May, which was a Sunday.

EARLY TEXTUAL HISTORY
1632–8: transcribed and revised by John Milton in **MS**, 3 pages on 2 leaves.
1645: Milton's *Poems* entered to Humphrey Moseley in the Stationers' Register on Monday 6 October. Sir Nathaniel Brent had licensed the book for publication.
1645: included in Milton's *Poems* ('**O₁**'), sigs. D2ʳ–D4ᵛ, 3 leaves; printed by Ruth Raworth for Humphrey Moseley.
1645: O₁ reissued.
1646: George Thomason bought a copy of O₁ on Friday 2 January. In *c.* 1678, some years after his death, his entire collection of books and tracts was acquired by the bookbinder Samuel Mearne, acting as agent for King Charles II; the King never paid him, and the books remained in Mearne's family until 1761.
1650–60: O₁ advertised as for sale by Humphrey Moseley.
1673: included in Milton's *Poems, &c. Upon Several Occasions* (²O₂), sigs. E3ᵛ–E6ʳ, 6 pages on 4 leaves; printed during Michaelmas Term, probably by William Rawlins, for Thomas Dring.
1673: O₂ reissued twice.
1691: MS was probably given to Trinity College, Cambridge, by Sir Henry Puckering; at that time the MS was a collection of unbound papers.
1695: included in Milton's *Poems Upon Several Occasions* (³F), sigs. †D2ᵛ–E1ʳ, 2 pages on 2 leaves; printed for Jacob Tonson.
1697: F incorporated into Jacob Tonson's edition of Milton's *Poetical Works*.
1697: *Poetical Works* reissued twice.
1700: *Poetical Works* advertised as for sale by Jacob Tonson.

EDITIONS
Frank Allen Patterson, in *The Works of John Milton*, Columbia edn (New York, 1931–8), i.1. 72–6.
H. F. Fletcher, in *John Milton's Complete Poetical Works Reproduced in Photographic Facsimile*, vol. 1 (Urbana, 1943), 384–9.
Helen Darbishire, in John Milton, *The Poetical Works* (Oxford, 1952–5), ii. 159–62.
Geoffrey Bullough and Margaret Bullough, *Milton's Dramatic Poems* (London, 1958), 64–7, 175–8.
John T. Shawcross, in John Milton, *The Complete English Poetry* (New York, 1963), 83–6.
John Carey, in John Milton, *The Poems*, ed. John Carey and Alistair Fowler, Longman Annotated English Poets (London and New York, 1968), 155–61.
Scolar Press facsimile of Trinity MS (Menston Ilkley, 1970).

REFERENCES
Annals 1633; Beal 2 MnJ 56; Bentley, iv. 912–13; Cedric C. Brown, *John Milton's Aristocratic Entertainments* (Cambridge, 1985); Butler, 372; Greg 625; Hazlitt, 17; *JEGP* 58 (1959), 627–36; McGee-Meagher 1625–34, 49–50; *MLN* 11 (1973), 46–7; *N&Q* 204 (1959), 359–64; *RES* NS 37 (1986), 542–9; Reyher, 530; John T. Shawcross, *Milton: A Bibliography for the Years 1624–1700* (Binghamton, New York, 1984) 35, 70–1, 313–15, 380–3.

2434. *A Challenge for Beauty*

TEXT
Printed in 1636 (STC 13311).

The blunder over Leonora's identity in Q's d.p. makes it clear that the list was not prepared by Heywood; this raises questions about whether the rest of the copy was authorial (though it is also worth noting that the title page has Heywood's usual motto from Horace).

GENRE
tragicomedy
Contemporary: play (S.R.)

TITLE
Printed: *A Challenge for Beauty*

AUTHOR
Thomas Heywood

DATE
Limits: 1634–6
Best Guess: 1634

The upper limit is defined by the allusion in 3.3 to the pillorying of William Prynne in May 1634, which is said to have happened 'not long since'; an early date is also supported by the prologue's allusion to the recent import of *commedia dell'arte* onto the London stage (as exemplified by **2407**). It follows that Heywood probably completed this play in the early summer of 1634 before proceeding to work with Brome on *The Witches of Lancashire* (**2441**).

ORIGINAL PRODUCTION
King's Men at the Globe and Blackfriars

PLOT
The marriage of Sebastian and Isabella unites the crowns of Portugal and Spain. Covetous of excessive praise, the proud Isabella solicits flattery from her courtiers. Two comply, but Bonavida criticizes her arrogant self-regard and is banished: he may return only when he can produce a woman who is Isabella's equal in beauty, so he travels the world in search of one. Petrocella thinks she might be in with a chance, and is disappointed when her next caller is not Bonavida but her suitor Valladaura, who has returned injured from a sea-battle. She disparages his exploits and rejects him, but speaks well of the Englishman who wounded him. The soldier in question, Ferrers, has been captured by the Turks; Valladaura finds him in a slave market and buys him and his friend, Manhurst. Though Ferrers is suspicious of his motives, Valladaura frees them both: Manhurst goes back to England, and Ferrers is introduced to Petrocella, in the hope that he will testify to Valladaura's bravery and court her on his behalf.

In England, Bonavida finds the beautiful woman he is searching for: Helena. He proposes marriage, but plans to go home to have his banishment rescinded before bringing Helena there as his wife. They exchange tokens, and Bonavida takes his leave; but when he arrives in Spain, he is imprisoned for breaking his exile, having returned without the woman he was charged to find. Isabella sends her two flatterers to England to get the ring Bonavida left with Helena, and they trick her maid into stealing it. Pursued by his creditors, Manhurst enters Helena's household in disguise, and tells her that her brother, Ferrers, is still in prison and must be ransomed; she sets off for Spain.

Ferrers falls for Petrocella himself, declares his love for her, and finds that she loves him too. He tells her that he may only marry a woman who agrees unconditionally to his first request, and she swears to do so; he then asks her to love and marry Valladaura. At Valladaura's request, he first disguises himself as a priest and performs the marriage, then substitutes himself for the bridegroom on the wedding night, observing Valladaura's stipulation that there should be no sex. Valladaura tells his new father-in-law that Petrocella is spending the night with another man; but Petrocella has stabbed the man in bed with her, taking him for Valladaura. Or so it seems, for in fact Ferrers is not dead, and Valladaura can see his plan through: to test his friend's fidelity and then (having ensured that his own marriage would be invalid because performed by a layman) to give him Petrocella as his wife.

The flatterers return to Spain and produce Helena's ring; Isabella has Bonavida temporarily released from prison to hear their story, and it makes him a confirmed misogynist. Helena arrives in Spain on the day set for his execution, and intervenes after her maid identifies the flatterers as the ones who had her steal the ring: she accuses them of stealing a slipper after a night of sex, and their denial that they have ever seen her before establishes her innocence—and, by extension, Bonavida's. The penitent Isabella acknowledges Helena her equal in beauty.

SCENE DESIGNATION
prol., 1.1–2, 2.1–3, 3.1–5, 4.1–3, 5.1–3, ep. (Q has act-division only)

ROLES
PROLOGUE
King SEBASTIAN of Portugal, Isabella's husband
Queen ISABELLA of Spain, Sebastian's wife
Lord BONAVIDA, a Spanish lord; also called Bonavide
CENTELLA, a flattering lord of the Spanish court; adopts the alias Master Oracle
PINEDA, a flattering lord of the Spanish court
ATTENDANTS at Sebastian's court, a great train (1.1, 2.3, 4.2, 5.3, *non-speaking*)
The CLOWN, Bonavida's servant
PETROCELLA, Aldana's daughter
ALDANA, Petrocella's father, a widower
Aldana's SERVANT (1.2)
VALLADAURA, a noble gentleman and knight, Petrocella's suitor; also called Valladaur
LEONORA, an old Englishwoman, mother of Helena and Ferrers
HELENA, a young Englishwoman, Leonora's daughter, Ferrers's sister; also called Lady Ferrers
A TURKISH CAPTAIN
FERRERS, an English soldier and gentleman; Leonora's son, Helena's brother; also called Montferrers; poses as a priest
MANHURST, an English soldier, Ferrers's friend
Three ENGLISH PRISONERS (2.2, *non-speaking*)
Valladura's SERVANT (2.2, *non-speaking*)
A LORD, who announces Bonavida's return (2.3)
ROSARA, Helena's maid; poses as a page
OFFICERS at the execution (5.3, *non-speaking*)
An EXECUTIONER (5.3, *non-speaking*)
EPILOGUE

Speaking Parts: 19

Stage Directions and Speech Prefixes
PROLOGUE: *The Prologue* (heading)
SEBASTIAN: *the King of Portugall* | *Sebastian* (s.d.s); *King* | *Sebast<ian>* (s.p.s); *King Sebastian King of Portugal* (d.p.)

ISABELLA: *Isabella the Queen* (s.d.s); *Isabella* (s.d.s and s.p.s); *Queen Isabella* [Sebastian's] *proud Queen* (d.p.)
BONAVIDA: *the Lord Bonavida* | *Lord Bonavida* | *Bonavida* (s.d.s); *Bonavid<a>* (s.p.s); *Lord Bonavida A noble and honest Spanish Lord* (d.p.)
CENTELLA: [one of] *two other lords* (s.d.s); *Centella* (s.ds and s.p.s); *Centella* [one of] *Two Spanish Sycophants* (d.p.)
PINEDA: [one of] *two other lords* (s.d.s); *Pineda* (s.d.s and s.p.s); *Pyn<eda>* (s.p.s); *Pineda* [one of] *Two Spanish Sycophants* (d.p.)
ATTENDANTS: *a great train of attendants* | *other attendants and followers* | *other Followers and Attendants* | *&c.* (s.d.s)
CLOWN: *the Clown* | [Bonavida's] *man* (s.d.s); *Clown* (s.p.s); *The Clown Servant to the Lord Bonavida* (d.p.)
PETROCELLA: *Petrocella* (s.d.s); *Petro<cella>* (s.p.s); *Petrocella A fair Spanish Lady* (d.p.)
ALDANA: *Aldana* [Petrocella's] *father* | *Aldana* (s.d.s); *Alda<na>* (s.p.s); *Aldana Father to Petrocella* (d.p.)
SERVANT: *Servant* (s.d.s and s.p.s)
VALLADAURA: *Valladaura* (s.d.s); *Valladau<ra>* (s.p.s); *Valladaura A noble Spanish Sea Captain* (d.p.)
LEONORA: *Leonora* (s.d.s); *Leo<nora>* (s.p.s); *Leonora An ancient Lady, wife to Aldana* (d.p.; sic)
HELENA: [Leonora's] *daughter* | *Hellena* | *Hellen* (s.d.s); *Helle<na>* | *Ellen* (s.p.s); *Hellena Sister to Ferrers, of incomparable Virtue and Beauty* (d.p.)
TURKISH CAPTAIN: *Turkish Captain* (s.d.s); *Turk* (s.p.s)
FERRERS: *Mont Ferars* (s.d.s); *Ferrers* (s.d.s and s.p.s); *Fera<rs>* (s.p.s); *Mont Ferrers A noble English Sea Captain* (d.p.)
MANHURST: *Monhurst* | *Manhurst* (s.d.s); *Manh<urst>* | *Mon<hurst>* (s.p.s); *Manhurst, Ferrers's friend* (d.p.)
ENGLISH PRISONERS: *others* (s.d.s); *Three Englishmen Sold for Slaves in Spain* (d.p.)
SERVANT: *a servant* (s.d.s)
LORD: *a Lord* (s.d.s); *Lord* (s.p.s)
ROSARA: [Helena's] *Maid* | *the Maid* (s.d.s); *Maid* (s.d.s and s.p.s); *Rosa<ra>* (s.p.s); *Rosara, Maid to Hellena* (d.p.)
OFFICERS: *Officers* (s.d.s)
EXECUTIONER: *executioner* (s.d.s)
EPILOGUE: *The Epilogue* (heading)

OTHER CHARACTERS
Bonavida's mother (1.1)
A Spanish princess named Isabella, whose hair caught fire when she looked at the sun (2.3)
Petrocella's ladies (3.1, 4.3)
Petrocella's dead mother (4.1)
The father of Ferrers and Helena (5.3)

SETTING
Period: unspecified, but England is at war with Spain

Time-Scheme: Bonavida leaves Spain in 1.1 and, after considerable European travel, arrives in England in 2.1; Pineda and Centella set out from Spain in 2.3, and arrive in England three days before 3.2; 5.1 takes place the night after 4.3; 5.2–3 take place three days after 4.2 and one day after 4.3; 5.3 takes place at 10 a.m.
Place: Seville and London

Geography
Seville: the castle
Spain: the Pillars of Hercules; Cadiz
Portugal
London: St Martin's parish
England: the white cliffs of Dover
Wales: Monmouth
[*British Isles*]: Ireland; Scotland
France: Orleans
The Low Countries: Flushing; Middleburg; Brussels; Sluys; Nijmegen; Ostend; the Hague; Rotterdam; Nieuport; Bergen
Germany: Lübeck
Italy: Tuscany; Rome; Lombardy; Venice
Europe: the Alps; Greece; Russia
Asia: Persia; Turkey; Arabia Felix
Africa
India
The West Indies
The Antipodes

SOURCES
Narrative: William Shakespeare, *King Lear* (**1486**; 1.1), *Cymbeline* (**1623**; the ring); Philip Massinger, *The Picture* (**2273**; 2.3)
Verbal: Horace, *Ars poetica* (t.p. motto); William Lily, Latin Grammar (4.2, 5.2); Thomas Heywood, *The Rape of Lucrece*, B-text (**1558**; 5.2); John Webster, *The White Devil* (**1689**; 4.3)
Works Mentioned: Aesop, *Fables* (1.2); Baptista Mantuanus, *Eclogues* 4 (written c. 1465, printed 1498; 1.1)

LANGUAGE
English
Latin: 13 words (1.2, 2.1, 3.1, 5.2; Aldana, Valladaura, Clown, Manhurst)
Greek: 1 word (1.2; Petrocella)
Italian: 2 words (1.2; Petrocella)

FORM
Metre: pentameter and prose
Rhyme: blank verse
Prologue: 28 lines, in couplets
Act-Division: 5 acts
Epilogue: 6 lines, in couplets
Lines (Spoken): 2,151 (1,515 verse, 636 prose)
Lines (Written): 2,433

MUSIC
Music: unspecified music (4.3, s.d.); trumpets (5.3, s.d.)

2435. The Triumph of Beauty

Songs:
1: 3.2, Rosara;
2: 'The Spaniard loves his ancient slop', 5.2, Manhurst, 40 lines.

PROPS
Weapons: a bloody poniard (5.1, s.d.); an axe (5.3, dialogue)
Clothing: a ring (2.1, 3.3, 4.2, 5.3, dialogue; also worn by Helena); a carcanet with a miniature of Helena (2.1, 2.3, dialogue; 4.2, implicit; also worn by Isabella); a false beard (3.4, s.d.; probably later worn by Manhurst); a slipper (5.3, dialogue)
Money: bags of money (2.2, s.d.)
Small Portable Objects: a paper (2.2, dialogue)
Large Portable Objects: a basin of water (3.2, s.d.; later brought back empty); seating for at least six people (5.3, implicit); a headsman's block (5.3, implicit)
Scenery: a throne (5.3, dialogue)

COSTUMES AND MAKE-UP
SEBASTIAN: a crown (5.3, dialogue)
ISABELLA: a crown (5.3, dialogue); Helena's carcanet (5.3, dialogue; see also PROPS)
PINEDA: 'very good clothes' (3.3, dialogue)
PETROCELLA: an expensive dress, possibly cloth of gold (1.2, dialogue)
ALDANA: a beard (dialogue)
VALLADAURA: open wounds (1.2, dialogue)
HELENA: Bonavida's ring (3.2, s.d.; removed on stage; see also PROPS)
FERRERS: 'gallant' clothes (3.1, s.d.); perhaps a single gyve on his leg (3.1, dialogue; but this may be a figure of speech); disguised as a priest (4.3, s.d.)
MANHURST: disguised (3.5, s.d.; 5.2–3, implicit; probably including a false beard)
ROSARA: cross-dressed as a page (5.2, s.d.; 5.3, implicit)

EARLY STAGE HISTORY
Performed by the King's Men at the Blackfriars and Globe by 1636.

EARLY TEXTUAL HISTORY
1636: entered to Robert Raworth in the Stationers' Register on Friday 17 June; entry names author. Sir Henry Herbert had licensed the book for publication.
1636: **Q** printed (probably after Monday 1 August) by Robert Raworth for James Beckett; collation A⁴ (–A1) B–I⁴ K1, 36 leaves; title page names author, acting company, and playhouses; Latin title-page motto; list of roles. Some quires are O (in Q format) rather than Q.
Before 1640: a copy of Q was owned by Robert Burton.
c. 1630s–40s: a copy of Q was in the possession of John Horne (Vicar of Headington, Oxfordshire). After his death, his entire collection of play-books passed into the possession of John Houghton of Brasenose College, Oxford (c. 1608–77), then to James Herne (died 1685), and then to the library of Ralph Sheldon (1623–84) at Weston, where it was catalogued by Anthony Wood, probably in the late 1670s.
1640–1: Humphrey Moseley was selling copies of Q for 6d each.
1657: advertised as for sale by the Newcastle-upon-Tyne bookseller William London.
c. 1678: Abraham Hill saw a MS (now lost or untraced).
1684: Nicholas Cox (Manciple of St Edmund Hall, Oxford) had a copy of Q in his bookshop. It had probably been previously owned by Gerard Langbaine, and appears on a list compiled by Anthony Wood on Saturday 13 December.

For the subsequent textual history of Song 2, see *The Rape of Lucrece* (**1558**), where it is Song 9A.

EDITION
R. H. Shepherd (?), in *The Dramatic Works of Thomas Heywood* (London, 1874), v. 1–78.

REFERENCES
Annals 1635; Bawcutt C80; Bentley, iv. 562–3; Bodleian, MS Wood E. 4, art. 1, p. 3; Greg 509; Hazlitt, 37; Nicolas K. Kiessling, *The Library of Robert Burton* (Oxford, 1988) 802; *The Library*, 4th ser., 20 (1939), 94; William London, *A Catalogue of the Most Vendible Books in England* (London, 1657), sig. 2F1ᵛ; *MLR* 13 (1918), 401–11; *Oxford Bibliographical Society Proceedings and Papers* 2.2 (1929), 132–3.

2435. The Triumph of Beauty

TEXT
Printed in 1646 (Wing S3488), presumably from authorial papers.

GENRE
entertainment
Contemporary: masque (1650 advertisement)

TITLE
Printed: *The Triumph of Beauty*

AUTHOR
James Shirley

DATE
Limits: 1624–46
Best Guess: 1634

Peter Walls summarizes the usual understanding of this entertainment's origins when he says that it was written 'almost certainly after the closing of the theatres', before the death of William Lawes in 1645, at a time when Shirley was working as a schoolteacher, and probably for performance by his pupils. All of these points are open to question.

The first thing to emphasize is that the 'young gentlemen' who performed the entertainment were not necessarily schoolboys and still less necessarily Shirley's own charges. If they were, then the entertainment might date from the 1620s, during the periods when Shirley was teaching at St Albans and then Holborn. He cannot be securely shown to have returned to teaching before 1646—the first definite indication of this career move is the publication of his first Latin grammar in 1649—and if, as seems likely, the publication of the 1646 collection of his *Poems &c.* was motivated by financial need, then he had probably not yet found other employment by then. If the 'young gentlemen' were not Shirley's own pupils, then, whether they were schoolboys or not, all that can be said for sure is that the entertainment was written as a private commission.

Lawes set Song 1, but the original production would also have needed settings for the other three songs; so either Lawes set them all and three of them are lost, or more than one composer was engaged to service a relatively small-scale private production, or Lawes did not set the song for the production at all but as an independent lyric. The last possibility would mean that it was either extracted from or subsequently incorporated into *The Triumph of Beauty*; it is notable that Lawes also set lyrics from *The Widow* (**1787**) and *The Mad Lover* (**1809**), both likewise unpublished in his lifetime (though in each case he might have produced the settings for a theatrical revival). If we admit the possibility that he did set the song for the production, then he is likelier to have undertaken the job during the period when he was actively engaged in writing theatre music, 1633–41. His opportunities to do so after 1642, or indeed to cross Shirley's path at all, were limited by his activity in the Civil War, based initially at Oxford, then in Wales, and finally at Chester, where he was killed.

The same argument applies to Shirley's opportunities to write the text after 1642: by the end of the year, he had joined his patron, William Cavendish, Earl of Newcastle, and remained in the royalist army, presumably in the north-east of England, until Cavendish's defeat and exile in 1644. We cannot absolutely rule out the possibility that a group of young men, either serving in the royalist army or avoiding it, either in search of a respite from military duties or determined to carry on as if nothing untoward was happening, engaged Shirley to write them a piece for a recreational performance. The balance of probability, however, leans towards a pre-War origin, in common with most of the other items collected in the 1646 *Poems &c.*

Conceptual links with other plays in the Shirley canon cluster in the 1630s: the story of the Judgement of Paris is also an important element in *The Ball* (**2389**) and *The Constant Maid* (**2629**), while *The Triumph of Peace* (**2423**)—on which Shirley worked with Lawes—features both the Hours and a group of antimasque characters trying to put together a court entertainment and discussing what elements should go into it. *A Midsummer Night's Dream* (**1012**) was also in Shirley's mind in 1631, when he borrowed from it in *The Duke* (**2339**), and 1635, when he did likewise in *The Arcadia* (**2481**).

Another relevant but problematic literary connection is with a 1634 Christmas masque (**2457**) written by Cavendish, which presents virtually the same scenario as sc.1 of *The Triumph of Beauty*: a rustic discussion, echoing *A Midsummer Night's Dream*, concerning what dramatic entertainment should be offered to a noble patron, which ends up having to be just a dance. Given that Shirley had himself devised a previous version of the same scenario in *The Triumph of Peace*, it seems unlikely that he subsequently borrowed it back at second hand from Cavendish. Cavendish and Shirley were close literary acquaintances in 1641, when the professional dramatist helped the aristocratic amateur with his plays; but if Cavendish knew *The Triumph of Beauty* through Shirley, rather than through its original private performance, the timescale for him to acquire that knowledge is, though not impossible, uncomfortably tight. Shirley's first contact with Cavendish seems to have been the dedication of *The Traitor* (**2337**), which was published in 1635 but must have been written no later than the start of November 1634, when the book was entered in the Stationers' Register. (However, the later case of *The Royal Master*, **2581**, shows that in some instances Shirley wrote his dedications very early.) If, hypothetically, he then showed Cavendish some other (recent?) examples of his unpublished work, Cavendish would still have had a month or so in which to appropriate Shirley's idea in response to his family's importunate demands for a masque at Christmas.

The Triumph of Peace seems not only to have set a fashion for antimasque scenarios involving artisans (also found in **2439**, another entertainment linked to Cavendish) but also to have brought Shirley and William Lawes into professional juxtaposition. Its effect might have been to make Shirley an attractive candidate to write a private masque, and in the ensuing months he also seems to have had the leisure to do so: the rate of his commercial work slackens in 1634, perhaps cushioned by the generous fee the Inns of Court paid him for *The Triumph of Peace*. The circumstantial case that *The Triumph of Beauty* was also written in 1634 is heavy on hypothesis and far from unassailable, but seems the likeliest interpretation of what evidence there is.

ORIGINAL PRODUCTION
'young gentlemen'

PLOT

Unacknowledged by his royal father and brought up in a wood by a bear, Prince Paris is melancholy. The local shepherds decide to present him with an entertainment to cheer him up, and exchange some ideas about content. They decide on the story of the Golden Fleece, but don't have the props or costumes for it, and have to do an antic dance instead.

Paris is in fact rather irritated by the shepherds' attentions, but *noblesse oblige* makes him watch their rustic show. Mercury arrives, sends him to sleep, and tells him he must judge between three goddesses, each of whom claims to be most deserving of a golden ball. The goddesses make their pitches: Juno offers Paris wealth, power, and luxury; Pallas, knowledge, valour, and victory; and Venus, love. Paris awards the ball to Venus, offending the others. Venus summons her nymphs to entertain him, including the Graces and Hours. Dancing ensues, after which the Hours steal away to Elysium. Paris pursues them.

SCENE DESIGNATION
sc.1–2 (O undivided)

ROLES

BOTTLE, a married shepherd; cast as the Golden Fleece in the play
CRAB, a shepherd; cast as Jason in the play
CLOUT, a shepherd; cast as the ship in the play

TOADSTOOL, a shepherd; cast as Lady Medea in the play
SHRUB, a shepherd; cast as Hercules in the play
SCRIP, a married shepherd; cast as the dragon in the play
Goodman HOBBINOL, a shepherd; cast as Absyrtus in the play
PARIS, Prince of Troy; a young man
MERCURY, messenger of the gods
JUNO, a goddess, Queen of Heaven; also called Saturnia
PALLAS, goddess of arts and arms; also called Minerva
VENUS, a goddess, Queen of love and beauty, Cupid's mother; also called Cytherea
A KING attending Juno (sc.2, *non-speaking*)
A SENATOR attending Juno (sc.2, *non-speaking*)
A SOLDIER attending Pallas (sc.2, *non-speaking*)
A PHILOSOPHER attending Pallas (sc.2, *non-speaking*)
HYMEN, Venus' servant
CUPID, young god of love, Venus' blind son
DELIGHT, Venus' servant
The three GRACES, Venus' servants (one or two speak)
The HOURS, Venus' nymphs; named Eunomia, Dice, and Irene (*non-speaking*)

Speaking Parts: 16–17
Allegorical Roles: 1

Stage Directions and Speech Prefixes
BOTTLE: *Bottle* [one of the] *Shepherds* | [one of] the *Shepherds* (s.d.s); *Bottle* (s.d.s and s.p.s)
CRAB: *Crab* [one of the] *Shepherds* | [one of] *The Shepherds* (s.d.s); *Crab* (s.p.s)
CLOUT: *Clout* [one of the] *Shepherds* | [one of] *The Shepherds* (s.d.s); *Clout* (s.p.s)
TOADSTOOL: *Toad-stoole* [one of the] *Shepherds* | [one of] *The Shepherds* (s.d.s); *Toad<-stoole>* (s.p.s)
SHRUB: *Shrub* [one of the] *Shepherds* | *Shrub* | [one of] *The Shepherds* (s.d.s); *Shr<ub>* (s.p.s)
SCRIP: *Scrip* [one of the] *Shepherds* | [one of] *The Shepherds* (s.d.s); *Scrip* (s.p.s)
HOBBINOL: *Hobbinoll* [one of the] *Shepherds* | [one of] *The Shepherds* (s.d.s); *Hob<binoll>* (s.d.s and s.p.s)
PARIS: *Paris* (s.d.s); *Par<is>* (s.p.s)
MERCURY: *Mercury* (s.d.s); *Mer<cury>* (s.p.s)
JUNO: *Juno* (s.d.s and s.p.s)
PALLAS: *Pallas* (s.d.s and s.p.s); *Min<erva>* (s.p.s)
VENUS: *Venus* (s.d.s and s.p.s)
KING: *a King* (s.d.s)
SENATOR: *a Senator* (s.d.s)
SOLDIER: *a Soldier* (s.d.s)
PHILOSOPHER: *a Philosopher* (s.d.s)
HYMEN: *Hymen* (s.d.s); *Hym<en>* (s.p.s)
CUPID: *Cupid* (s.d.s); *Cup<id>* (s.p.s)
DELIGHT: *Delight* (s.d.s and s.p.s)
GRACES: *The Graces* (s.d.s); *1 Grace* | *Grace* (s.p.s)
HOURS: *The Hours* (s.d.s)

OTHER CHARACTERS
Bottle's wife (sc.1)
Scrip's wife (sc.1)
Priam, King of Troy, Paris's father (sc.2)
Paris's mother (sc.2)
Bottle's father, who thrashed him for being in love (sc.2)
Jove, King of the gods, Juno's brother and husband (sc.2)
Neptune, god of the sea (sc.2)

SETTING
Period: antiquity
Place: Mount Ida

Geography
Asia Minor: Troy; River Pactolus
[*Greece*]: Mount Rhodope; Mount Olympus
[*Mediterranean*]: Paphos
Europe: River Tagus; River Iberus [i.e. Ebro]
Asia: Colchos; Babylon; Assyria [misprint for Arabia?]
Egypt: the Pyramids
India: River Ganges
The Orchard of Hesperides

SOURCES
Narrative: Lucian, *Dearum iudicium* (sc.2); William Shakespeare, *A Midsummer Night's Dream* (**1012**; sc.1); probably James Shirley, *The Triumph of Peace* (**2423**; sc.1)

LANGUAGE
English

FORM
Metre: pentameter and prose
Rhyme: blank verse and couplets
Lines (Spoken): 749 (449 verse, 300 prose)
Lines (Written): 807

STAGING
Doors: the three Goddesses appear 'at several places' (sc.2, s.d.)
Above: Mercury descends and ascends (sc.2, s.d.)
Within: speech (sc.2, s.d.); song (sc.2, s.d.)

MUSIC
Music: bagpipes (sc.2, s.d.); unspecified music (sc.2, s.d.); soft music (sc.2, s.d.)
Songs:
   1: 'Cease, warring thoughts, and let his brain', sc.2, 16 lines; *two early musical settings survive*;
   2: 'Jove sent thee, Paris, what is mine', sc.2, Juno Pallas, Venus, and Chorus, within, 24 lines, *an early musical setting survives*;
   3: 'Come, ye Graces, come away', sc.2, Hymen and Delight, in parts, 18 lines; *an early musical setting survives*;
   4: 'How dully all your joys do move', sc.2, 10 lines.
Dance: antic dance by the Shepherds (sc.2, s.d.); the Goddesses and their attendants dance (sc.2, s.d.);

Hymen, Delight, Graces, and Hours dance (sc.2, s.d.; possibly also Venus, Cupid, and Paris)

PROPS
Small Portable Objects: a golden ball (sc.2, s.d.; with an inscription)

COSTUMES
MERCURY: wings (dialogue)

EARLY STAGE HISTORY
Before 1646: first performed at a 'private recreation' by 'some young gentlemen'. Some music may have been composed by William Lawes.

EARLY TEXTUAL HISTORY
1638–45: Song 1 included, with a musical setting, in William Lawes's autograph songbook (Oxford: Bodleian, MS Mus. Sch. b. 2, pp. 35–6); the song was later deleted.
1646: rights to James Shirley's *Poems &c.* transferred in the Stationers' Register from Francis Constable to Humphrey Moseley on Saturday 31 October.
1646: **O** printed by Susan Islip for Humphrey Moseley as a bibliographically independent part of Shirley's *Poems &c.*; collation A–B^8, 16 leaves; title page names author and refers in general terms to performance.
After 1648: Song 1 included, with Lawes's setting, in a set of four MS musical part-books (New York Public Library, MS Mus. Res. *MNZ (Chirk)).
1650: *Poems &c.* advertised as for sale by Humphrey Moseley; the entertainment is individually named.
1650s: Song 1 included, with Lawes's musical setting, in a set of MS songbooks (Oxford: Bodleian, MS Mus. d. 238, pp. 200–199 (rev.); Edinburgh University Library MS Dc. 1 69, fos. 112^v–111^v rev.) compiled by Edward Lowe, of which two, both for treble parts, survive. The latter MS also includes a version of the setting scored for three voices.
1657: *Poems &c.* advertised as for sale by the Newcastle-upon-Tyne bookseller William London.
1659: Songs 1 (headed 'A Calm'), 2, and 3 (headed 'A Pastoral Dialogue') included, with musical settings, in John Gamble's *Airs and Dialogues*, sigs. D1^r, P2^v–Q1^r, Y1^r–Y2^v; printed by William Godbid for Nathaniel Ekin.
1674: Song 1 (headed 'On his Mistress Asleep') included in C. F.'s *Wit at a Venture*, sigs. D3^v–D4^r; printed for Jonathan Edwin.

EDITIONS
William Gifford, in *The Dramatic Works and Poems of James Shirley* (London, 1833), vi. 315–41.
Barbara Ravelhofer, in James Shirley, *The Complete Works*, gen. eds. Eugene Giddens, Teresa Grant, and Barbara Ravelhofer (Oxford, forthcoming).

REFERENCES
Annals 1646; Beal 2 ShJ 194–6; Beal Online ShJ 196.5; Bentley, v. 1153–4; Eyre & Rivington, i. 250; Robert Stanley Forsythe, *The Relations of Shirley's Plays to the Elizabethan Drama* (New York, 1914), 400–1; Greg 627; Hazlitt, 233; *Journal of the American Musicological Society* 16 (1963), 246; William London, *A Catalogue of the Most Vendible Books in England* (London, 1657), sig. 2F1^r; Peter Walls, *Music in the English Courtly Masque, 1604–1640* (Oxford, 1996), 334–5.

2436. *Christianetta*

EVIDENCE
Stationers' Register; Abraham Hill's list of MS plays (London: British Library, MS Sloane 2893).

GENRE
Contemporary: play

TITLE
MS (Lost): *Christianetta, or Marriage and Hanging Go by Destiny*
Contemporary: *Christianetta*

AUTHOR
Richard Brome, *possibly in collaboration with* Henry Glapthorne (or George Chapman)

The MS Hill saw attributed the play to Brome and Chapman, which seems very unlikely indeed: so far as we know, Chapman's commercial play-writing years were over well before Brome's began. There are two possible explanations. First, the name of Chapman may have been jotted on the MS by an early owner in the same way as **1655** is variously ascribed to him, Shakespeare and Goffe. Alternatively, the name 'Chapman' might be an error for Glapthorne; a comparable mistake may lie behind the misattribution of Glapthorne's *Revenge for Honour* (**2824**) to Chapman.

DATE
Limits: 1623–35

Brome must have written the play before he was contracted to Salisbury Court, the fruits of which are all accounted for. It cannot have been very much before if his collaborator was indeed Glapthorne, who was born in 1610.

PLOT
The subtitle is proverbial (Tilley W232); if taken literally, it suggests that some of the characters may be married, and at least one other hanged.

ROLES
CHRISTIANETTA

PROPS
Weapons: perhaps a halter

EARLY TEXTUAL HISTORY
1640: entered (as *Christianetta*) to Andrew Crooke in the Stationers' Register on Tuesday 4 August; play and author (Brome) individually named as part of a group

entry of six Brome plays. Thomas Wykes had licensed the book for publication.

c. 1678: Abraham Hill saw a MS (now lost or untraced), bearing both titles and an ascription to Brome and Chapman.

REFERENCES
Annals 1633; Bentley, iii. 58–9; Greg Θ48; Hazlitt, 40; *The Library*, 4th ser., 20 (1939), 81; Sibley, 26.

2437. The Example

TEXT
Printed in 1637 (STC 22442), probably from authorial papers.

GENRE
comedy
Contemporary: play (prol., S.R.)

TITLE
Performed/Printed: *The Example*

AUTHOR
James Shirley

DATE
June 1634

ORIGINAL PRODUCTION
Queen Henrietta's Men at the Cockpit

PLOT
Money troubles have driven Sir Walter Peregrine to go to war in Europe to keep him away from his creditors in England. In his absence, his wife Bellamia is being pursued by Lord Fitzavarice, who plies her with rich gifts. She chastely refuses him, but he feels that, since he is known to have courted her, it is a matter of honour that the seduction should succeed. He pursues her to her chamber and offers to surrender her husband's mortgage if she will sleep with him, then pay off her debts £100 a time in return for subsequent nights of passion. When she still refuses him, he threatens rape, and she faints. The experience converts him from his louche ways: he is relieved to learn that she is not dead, and returns the mortgage anyway, impressed with her virtue.

A captain comes from the Netherlands on a recruiting mission. Sir Walter takes the opportunity to accompany him and pays a flying visit to his wife. She proposes to pay his debts with Lord Fitzavarice's gifts, but he assumes that these are the rewards of adultery and challenges the Lord to a duel. Fitzavarice, recognizing that he is obliged to answer the challenge, appoints Confident as his second. But Confident's reputation for valour is undeserved: rather than have to prove it by fighting, he tips off Sir Walter's creditors and has him arrested for his debts before the duel can take place. Lord Fitzavarice disowns the ploy and secures Sir Walter's release by paying his debts. Sir Walter realizes that his suspicions must be false—an adulterer would find it more convenient to keep him in jail—but the Lord insists on going through with the duel. Both men are slightly wounded, and honour is satisfied.

In the sub-plot, Vainman and Pumicestone have both borrowed heavily to finance their courtship of Bellamia's sister, Jacintha. They agree that whichever of them wins her will cover the other's expenses. Jacintha is not disposed to marry anyone, but asks them to demonstrate which of them loves her best. Rather than send them to do dangerous deeds, she imposes difficult conditions: they must both visit her every day for six months, during which time Vainman must not speak a word and Pumicestone must do the opposite of everything she asks. She then contrives a situation in which their compliance is embarrassing. At her instigation they also visit her uncle, the plot-obsessed Sir Solitary, and pretend to be agents of a foreign power; Jacintha also arranges for servants to pose as officers come to arrest them. The shock cures Sir Solitary of his humour, and the two would-be suitors give up their objective. Jacintha has a new love: Lord Fitzavarice has impressed her with his new virtue, honour, and magnanimity, and he agrees to marry her.

SCENE DESIGNATION
prol., 1.1, 2.1–3, 3.1, 4.1–3, 5.1–3, ep. (Q has act-division only)

ROLES
PROLOGUE
SIR SOLITARY Plot, Lady Plot's husband, uncle of Bellamia and Jacintha
DORMANT, Sir Solitary's servant; poses as an officer
OLDRAT, Sir Solitary's servant; poses as an officer
Master CONFIDENT Rapture, a gentleman
LADY PLOT, Sir Solitary's wife; also called Madam Plot
Lady BELLAMIA Peregrine, Sir Walter's wife, Jacintha's younger sister, Sir Solitary's niece
A WAITING-WOMAN, Lady Peregrine's servant
A PAGE, Lord Fitzavarice's servant
Lord FITZAVARICE, a young nobleman and former soldier; also called Lord Fitzamorous
Master VAINMAN, a gentleman
Master PUMICESTONE, a gentleman
A SCRIVENER, Sir Walter's creditor (2.1, 4.1–3)
Mistress JACINTHA, Bellamia's elder sister, Sir Solitary's niece
SIR WALTER Peregrine, a knight, Bellamia's husband
A CAPTAIN, Sir Walter's friend, a recruiting officer
A VOICE from the tavern (4.1, *within*)
OFFICERS (4.1; one or two speak)
The UNDER-SHERIFF of London (4.3)
EPILOGUE

The form 'Lord Fitzamorous' appears in the dialogue once at an early stage, before the character has made his first appearance in person. Jones explains it as a joke, and he may be right. But it is striking that an early reader systematically corrected 'Fitzavarice' to 'Fitzamorous' in the University of Michigan copy of Q, so an alternative explanation might be that 'Fitzavarice' is a recurrent compositorial error. Since the character is a debauchee who reforms, he might fittingly be called 'Fitzamorous'; whereas his willingness to pay Sir Walter's debts, both for sexual purposes before his reformation and as an honourable act afterwards, means that 'Fitzavarice' is never apt.

Speaking Parts: 20–1

Stage Directions and Speech Prefixes
PROLOGUE: *Prologue* (heading)
SIR SOLITARY: *Sir Solitary Plott | Sir Solitary | Sir Solitarie* (s.d.s); *Sol<itary> | Plo<tt> | Sir | Sir Sol<itary>* (s.p.s)
DORMANT: *Dormant |* [one of the] *Servants* (s.d.s); *Dor<mant>* (s.p.s)
OLDRAT: *Oldrat |* [one of the] *Servants* (s.d.s); *Old<rat>* (s.p.s)
CONFIDENT: *Master Confident | Confident* (s.d.s); *Con<fident>* (s.p.s)
LADY PLOT: *Lady Plott |* [Sir Solitary's] *Lady* (s.d.s); *Lady | Plo<tt> | Lady Plo<tt>* (s.p.s)
BELLAMIA: *Lady Peregrine | Lady Bellamia | Bellamia* (s.d.s); *Lady* (s.d.s and s.p.s); *Bel<lamia>* (s.p.s)
WAITING-WOMAN: [Lady Peregrine's] *woman | waiting woman | waiting-woman* (s.d.s); *Woman* (s.d.s and s.p.s)
PAGE: *a Page* (s.d.s); *Page* (s.d.s and s.p.s)
FITZAVARICE: *Lord Fitzavarice | Fitzavarice | the Lord Fitzavarice* (s.d.s); *Lord* (s.d.s and s.p.s)
VAINMAN: *Vayne-man | Vaine-man | Vaineman* (s.d.s); *Va<yne-man>* (s.p.s)
PUMICESTONE: *Pumicestone | Pumiceston* (s.d.s); *Pu<micestone>* (s.p.s)
SCRIVENER: *Scrivener* (s.d.s and s.p.s)
JACINTHA: *Jacintha* (s.d.s); *Ja<cintha>* (s.p.s)
SIR WALTER: *Sir Walter Peregrine | Sir Walter* (s.d.s); *Sir | Sir Wal<ter>* (s.p.s)
CAPTAIN: *a Captain* (s.d.s); *Captain* (s.d.s and s.p.s)
VOICE: *Within* (s.p.s)
OFFICERS: *Officers* (s.d.s); *Officer* (s.p.s)
UNDER-SHERIFF: *under-Sheriff* (s.d.s); *Sheriff* (s.d.s and s.p.s)
EPILOGUE: *Epilogue* (heading)

OTHER CHARACTERS
Lady Plot's footman (1.1)
The porter at Sir Solitary's house (1.1)
Sir Walter's servants (1.1)
Lord Fitzavarice's father (3.1)
Sir Walter's creditors (3.1, 4.1, 4.3)

SETTING
Period: contemporary, after the assassination of Wallenstein (25 February 1634)

Time-Scheme: 1.1 takes place at 2 a.m.; 3.1 takes place at night
Place: London

Geography
[*London*]: Westminster; the Exchange; the Bermudas
England
The Netherlands: Bergen
[*Europe*]: Italy; Tilly; Germany
Egypt
The Indies
Virginia

SOURCES
Narrative: Ben Jonson, *Volpone* (**1493**; Sir Solitary)
Verbal: William Shakespeare, *1 Henry IV* (**1059**; 2.2, cited)
Works Mentioned: Statute of Bigamy (1603; 1 James I c. 11; 3.1, 4.2); Gervase Markham and Lewis Machin, *The Dumb Knight* (**1563**; 4.2); *Mercurius Gallobelgicus* (periodical, from 1594; 4.1)

LANGUAGE
English
Latin: 13 words (2.1–2, 5.1, 5.3; Scrivener, Fitzavarice, Sir Solitary, Oldrat)

FORM
Metre: pentameter and prose
Rhyme: blank verse
Prologue: 42 lines, in couplets
Act-Division: 5 acts
Epilogue: 10 lines, in couplets
Lines (Spoken): 2,281 (1,930 verse, 351 prose)
Lines (Written): 2,579

STAGING
Within: speech (3.1, 4.1, s.d.); sound effects (5.1, s.d.); song (5.3, implicit)
Above: a character appears above (3.1, s.d.)
Miscellaneous: the epilogue assumes a performance in (or at least ending in) the evening

MUSIC AND SOUND
Sound Effects: knocking (1.1, s.d.); noise within (5.1, s.d.)
Music: unspecified music (5.3, s.d.; accompanying the song)
Song: 'Welcome, welcome, again to thy wits', 5.3, Lady Plot and Sir Solitary, in parts, 16 lines
Dance: characters exit dancing (2.2, s.d.; it is not specified precisely who dances, but those on stage are Fitzavarice, Lady Plot, Confident, Jacintha, Vainman, and Pumicestone)

PROPS
Weapons: a poniard (3.1, s.d.); Sir Walter's sword (3.1, 4.1, 4.3, 5.2, dialogue); Lord Fitzavarice's sword (5.2, implicit)

Money: five pieces (2.1, dialogue); one hundred pieces (4.3, dialogue); a purse of gold (5.2, dialogue)
Small Portable Objects: jewels (1.1, dialogue); a paper (1.1, dialogue); a document (3.1, dialogue); a paper (4.1, dialogue); a letter (4.3, dialogue)
Scenery: an arras (1.1, dialogue)
Miscellaneous: blood (5.2, dialogue)

COSTUMES
SIR SOLITARY: in his shirt (3.1, s.d.)
DORMANT and OLDRAT: false beards (5.1, s.d.; removed on stage)
SIR WALTER: a feather (3.1, dialogue); hangers (5.2, implicit)
CAPTAIN: a jerkin (3.1, dialogue)

EARLY STAGE HISTORY
1634: presumably performed as licensed, no doubt by Queen Henrietta's Men at the Cockpit (as mentioned on the 1637 title page).

1639: The play was in the repertory of the King's and Queen's Young Company (Beeston's Boys) at the Cockpit. On Saturday 10 August, Philip Herbert, 4th Earl of Pembroke (Lord Chamberlain) issued an order restraining performances by other companies of this and 44 other plays.

EARLY TEXTUAL HISTORY
1634: On Tuesday 24 June, Sir Henry Herbert licensed the text for performance.

1637: entered in the Stationers' Register to Andrew Crooke and William Cooke on Wednesday 18 October; entry names author. The following day, Thursday 19 October, the book was licensed for publication by Thomas Wykes (even though this had already been mentioned in the Stationers' Register entry).

1637: Q printed by John Norton for Andrew Crooke and William Cooke; collation A–I⁴ (I4 signed *2, apparently for insertion between A1 and A2), 36 leaves; title page names author, acting company, and playhouse.

c. 1630s–40s: a copy of Q was in the possession of John Horne (Vicar of Headington, Oxfordshire). After his death, his entire collection of play-books passed into the possession of John Houghton of Brasenose College, Oxford (c. 1608–77), then to James Herne (died 1685), and then to the library of Ralph Sheldon (1623–84) at Weston, where it was catalogued by Anthony Wood, probably in the late 1670s. By then the copy had been bound into a single volume with 21 other plays by Shirley (and, presumably in error, with Henry Shirley's *The Martyred Soldier*, **2030**).

1640–1: Humphrey Moseley was selling copies of Q for 6d.

1645: Song included in the fourth edition of 'Philomusus', *The Academy of Compliments*, sig. I6ᵛ; printed by Thomas Badger for Humphrey Moseley.

1646: *The Academy of Compliments* reprinted by Moses Bell for Humphrey Moseley; the song now appears on sig. K9ʳ.

1646: rights to James Shirley's *Poems &c.* transferred in the Stationers' Register from Francis Constable to Humphrey Moseley on Saturday 31 October.

1646: Song (headed 'Melancholy Converted') included in Shirley's *Poems &c.*, sig. C2ʳ⁻ᵛ, printed for Humphrey Moseley.

1650: *The Academy of Compliments* reprinted for Humphrey Moseley; the song now appears on sig. K5ʳ⁻ᵛ.

1655: *The English Treasury of Wit and Language* entered in the Stationers' Register to Humphrey Moseley on Tuesday 16 January.

1655: three extracts (from 1.1, 3.1, 4.3) included in John Cotgrave's *The English Treasury of Wit and Language*, sigs. K8ᵛ, O5ᵛ, S2ʳ; printed for Humphrey Moseley.

1655: *Wit's Interpreter* entered to Nathaniel Brooke in the Stationers' Register on Wednesday 14 March.

1655: extract (from 3.1) included in John Cotgrave's *Wit's Interpreter*, sig. F8ʳ⁻ᵛ; printed for Nathaniel Brooke.

1657: advertised as for sale by the Newcastle-upon-Tyne bookseller William London.

1658: *The Academy of Compliments* reprinted for Humphrey Moseley.

1661: Song included in N. D.'s *An Antidote against Melancholy*, sig. L2ᵛ; printed (before Friday 19 April) by 'Mercurius Melancholicus'. The song was omitted from subsequent editions.

1662: *Wit's Interpreter* reprinted (before Thursday 8 June) for Nathaniel Brooke; the extract now appears on sigs. E4ᵛ–E5ʳ, and is entitled 'Resolute Resistance'.

1663: *The Academy of Compliments* reprinted by Thomas Leach and Thomas Child.

1671: Song included in *Windsor Drollery*, sig. M11ʳ; printed for John Macock.

1671: *Wit's Interpreter* reprinted for Nathaniel Brooke and Obadiah Blagrave.

1672: *Windsor Drollery* reprinted for John Macock; the song now appears on sig. E12ᵛ.

1684: Nicholas Cox (Manciple of St Edmund Hall, Oxford) had a copy of Q in his bookshop. It had probably been previously owned by Gerard Langbaine, and appears on a list compiled by Anthony Wood on Saturday 13 December.

EDITION
William F. Jones, *The Renaissance Imagination* 33 (New York and London, 1987).

Hester Lees-Jeffries and Ian Burrows, in James Shirley, *The Complete Works*, gen. eds. Eugene Giddens, Teresa Grant, and Barbara Ravelhofer (Oxford, forthcoming).

REFERENCES
Annals 1634; Bawcutt 299; Bentley, v. 1108–10; Bodleian, MS Wood E. 4, art. 1, p. 68; Eyre & Rivington, i. 250, 463, 467; Robert Stanley Forsythe, *The Relations of Shirley's Plays to the Elizabethan Drama* (New York,

1914), 365–71; Greg 521; Hazlitt, 78; William London, *A Catalogue of the Most Vendible Books in England* (London, 1657), sig. 2F1ᵛ; *MLR* 13 (1918), 401–11; *MSC* 2.3, 389–90; *Oxford Bibliographical Society Proceedings and Papers* 2.2 (1929), 132; *RES* NS 54 (2003), 601–14; *SP* 40 (1943), 186–203.

2438. A Dialogue between Policy and Piety ~

TEXT
Three MSS:
- F: Washington: Folger, MS V. a. 313; holograph presentation copy;
- O: New Haven: Yale University Library, Beinecke Library, Osborn MS b 52, vol. 2, pp. 191–4;
- W: reported in the nineteenth century as having been in the possession of John Withorn (or Wittern) of Broomhead; now untraced.

The dialogue was evidently not designed for performance: there is a long third-person descriptive passage about Hibernia, which is in couplets integrated with the rhyme scheme of the spoken parts of the text, and which begins and ends part-way through a verse line.

GENRE
dialogue
Contemporary: dialogue

TITLE
MS: *A Dialogue between Policy and Piety*
Contemporary: *A Plain Familiar Dialogue between Piety and Policy*

AUTHOR
Robert Davenport

DATE
Limits: 1634–9
Best Guess: 1634

The upper limit is the date of the dedicatee John Bramhall's translation to Londonderry. Davenport was resident in Ireland for some time during the mid-1630s, and the dialogue was evidently written then; but Tricomi establishes that the stock of paper on which he wrote MS F has a London watermark, which might indicate composition either before he moved to Ireland or early in his residency there, when he was still using paper he had brought with him from London. He surfaces again in London with a burst of publication activity in early 1639, which establishes a definite terminus for his Irish period and may have been the actual time of his return (with the new publications as an attempt to re-establish himself).

PLOT
Policy and Piety meet and fall in love. Hibernia is pleased to hear of their forthcoming wedding and calls the banns. The couple are married and plan to set up a home, with each spouse bringing appropriate allegorical furniture: wisdom, counsel, art, foresight, prevention, and safety from Policy; zeal, prayers, desire, and mercy from Piety. The chosen location for their home is in the true statesman's heart. Hibernia optimistically looks forward to an end to her woes.

ROLES
PIETY, later Policy's wife
POLICY, later Piety's husband
HIBERNIA, a female figure

Speaking Parts: 3
Allegorical Roles: 3

Stage Directions and Speech Prefixes
PIETY: *Piety* (s.p.s)
POLICY: *Policy* (s.p.s)
HIBERNIA: *Hibernia* (s.d.s); *Hib<ernia>* (s.p.s)

OTHER CHARACTERS
The people of Hibernia
Piety's master (i.e. Christ)

SETTING
Place: Ireland

Geography
England: London
Europe
The Holy Land

SOURCES
Verbal: *The Book of Common Prayer*: Marriage service (1549, rev. 1552)

LANGUAGE
English

FORM
Metre: pentameter and tetrameter
Rhyme: couplets; one unrhymed line
Lines (Spoken): 147

Because of the interruption of the spoken verse (see under TEXT), this is a factitious figure incorporating the two separate half-lines where the long verse 'stage direction' intersects with the speeches.

Lines (Written): 173

PROPS
Musical Instruments: a harp (s.d.)
Animals: a greyhound (s.d.)
Food and Drink: a bottle of usquebaugh (s.d.); a small box of tobacco (s.d.)
Large Portable Objects: a baby (s.d.)

2439. Royal Entertainment at Bolsover Castle

COSTUMES
PIETY: a white habit (desc.)
POLICY: a comely purple habit (desc.)
HIBERNIA: a large red mantle fringed with green (s.d.); big breasts (s.d.)

EARLY TEXTUAL HISTORY
c. 1634: transcribed by Robert Davenport in MS (**F**); 7 leaves; authorial dedication to John Bramhall, Bishop of Londonderry; verses 'to the book'; verse description of two speakers.

Mid-seventeenth century: transcribed in another MS (**W**); dedication to Sir John Kaye; list of roles; couplet on the theme of the dialogue.

c. 1678–88: included in a MS miscellany (**O**) compiled by Sir John Pye; 2 leaves.

The dedicatee of the lost MS W could have been either Sir John Kaye, M.P. for Eye (knighted 27 May 1607, died 9 March 1641) or his son of the same name (1616–62; knighted 24 May 1641, created a baronet 4 February 1642); the family seat was Woodsome Hall, Yorkshire, not far from what seems to have been the home of the MS's nineteenth-century owner, in the region of Broomhead Moor.

EDITION
Albert H. Tricomi, *ELR* 21 (1991), 190–203.

REFERENCES
Annals 1635; Bentley, iii. 228–9; *N&Q* 170 (1936), 295.

2439. Royal Entertainment at Bolsover Castle

TEXT
Two substantive witnesses:
- **F**: printed in 1640–1 (STC 14754a), with minor revisions, presumably by Jonson;
- **MS**: London: British Library, MS Harley 4955, fos. 199ʳ–202ʳ; probably a transcript from the original acting copy.

The most substantial differences between the two texts are the inclusion in F of sharper satire against Inigo Jones in sc.2, and a second banquet served to the royal guests in sc.3. Knowles argues that F represents Jonson's original conception of the entertainment and MS the toned-down version that was actually performed. However, the stage directions in MS are in the present tense, whereas in F they are in the past, and MS is markedly vague about aspects of the staging. The location of the Vitruvius sequence is referred to in MS as 'a garden' (when there is only the Fountain Garden at Bolsover, so it should be 'the garden'); the phrase is absent from F. The Cupids sequence is assigned no certain place of performance, just 'a fit place selected for the purpose'; again the phrase is not in F. This indicates that MS represents a pre-production state of the text, before decisions had been taken about precisely where particular elements of the entertainment would be staged. It does not follow that the elements unique to F were necessarily additions rather than cuts, still less that they were additions specifically for the performance; but F's status remains, *prima facie*, post-production.

GENRE
entertainment
Contemporary: entertainment (title)

TITLE
MS: *The King and Queen's Entertainment at Bolsover*
Printed: *Love's Welcome: The King and Queen's Entertainment at Bolsover*
Later Assigned: *Love's Welcome at Bolsover*

AUTHOR
Ben Jonson

DATE
30 July 1634

ORIGINAL PRODUCTION
Earl of Newcastle's household at Bolsover Castle, Derbyshire

PLOT
During a banquet, singers welcome the King and Queen and declare the metaphysical importance of love. After dinner, they are entertained by a dance of eight artisans, supervised by Colonel Vitruvius.

As the King and Queen are leaving, Eros and Anteros serve a second banquet. They quarrel over a palm bough but end up dividing it between them; their love is a perfect symbol of that between the King and Queen. Philalethes intervenes, advising them to stop speaking in rhyme, which has no more credit at court. He concludes by once again celebrating the mystical, mutual love of the King and Queen.

SCENE DESIGNATION
sc.1–4 (F/MS undivided), as follows:
- **SC.1:** song at the banquet;
- **SC.2:** Vitruvius, after the banquet;
- **SC.3:** Eros and Anteros;
- **SC.4:** Philalethes.

ROLES
Three SINGERS, two tenors and a bass
Colonel VITRUVIUS, a surveyor, supervisor of the artisans; also called Iniquo Vitruvius (*in F only*)
Captain SMITH, a blacksmith ('Smith' may be his occupation rather than his name); also called Vulcan (*non-speaking*)
Three CYCLOPES accompanying Captain Smith (*non-speaking*)
CHISEL, a carver (*non-speaking*)
Master MAUL, a freemason (*non-speaking*)
Squire SUMMER, a carpenter; the name Summer does not appear in MS; perhaps alternatively named Square (*non-speaking*)

TWYBILL, Summer's man (*non-speaking*)
DRESSER, a plumber (*non-speaking*)
QUARREL, a glazier (*non-speaking*)
FRET, a plasterer (*non-speaking*)
BEATER, a mortar-man (*non-speaking*)
EROS or Cupid, son of Venus, brother of Anteros, and smaller than him; also called Love
ANTEROS or Cupid, son of Venus, brother of Eros, and bigger than him; also called Love-Again
PHILALETHES, presumably a lover of truth

Speaking Parts: 7

Stage Directions and Speech Prefixes
SINGERS: *two Tenors and a Bass* (s.d.s); *1 Tenor | 2 Tenor | Bass* (s.p.s)
VITRUVIUS: *Coronell Vitruvius* (s.d.s); *Vit<ruvius>* (s.p.s)
SMITH: [one of the] *mechanics* (s.d.s); *Captain Smith* (F s.d.s); *Captain Smyth or Vulcan* (MS s.d.s)
CYCLOPES: [three of the] *mechanics | three Cyclopes* (s.d.s)
CHISEL: [one of the] *mechanics | Chesil, The Carver* (s.d.s)
MAUL: [one of the] *mechanics | Maul, The Free-Mason* (s.d.s)
SUMMER: [one of the] *mechanics* (s.d.s); *Squire Summer, The Carpenter* (F s.d.s); *Squire the Carpenter* (MS s.d.s)
TWYBILL: [one of the] *mechanics | Twybil,* [Squire Summer's] *Man* (s.d.s)
DRESSER: [one of the] *mechanics | Dresser, The Plumber* (s.d.s)
QUARREL: [one of the] *mechanics | Quarel, The Glazier* (s.d.s)
FRET: [one of the] *mechanics | Fret, The Plasterer* (s.d.s)
BEATER: [one of the] *mechanics | Beater, The Mortar-man* (s.d.s)
EROS: [one of] *two Cupids* (MS s.d.s); [one of] *two Loves* (F s.d.s); *Eros* (s.d.s and F s.p.s); *Ero<s>* (MS s.p.s)
ANTEROS: [one of] *two Cupids* (MS s.d.s); [one of] *two Loves* (F s.d.s); *Anteros* (s.d.s and F s.p.s); *Ant<eros>* (MS s.p.s)
PHILALETHES: *Philalethes* (s.p.s)

OTHER CHARACTERS
Venus, mother of Eros and Anteros (sc.3–4)
The Graces, nurses of Eros (sc.3)
Themis, who prophesied about Eros (sc.3)

SOURCES
Narrative: Vincenzo Cartari, *Le imagini degli dei antichi* (1566; repr. 1603; also available in a Latin translation by Antoine du Verdier, *Imagines deorum*, 1581; sc.3); Ben Jonson, *A Challenge at Tilt* (**1732** and **1735**; sc.3)
Verbal: Bible: Judges 14.14 (sc.4); Aristotle, *De anima* (sc.1); Geoffrey Chaucer, *Canterbury Tales*: General Prologue (*c.* 1387; printed 1478, repr. 1602; sc.2, cited; Jonson owned a copy of Thomas Speght's 1602 edn)

LANGUAGE
English
Latin: 3 words (sc.2; Vitruvius)

FORM
Metre: prose and pentameter
Rhyme: couplets
Lines (Spoken): 158 (78 verse, 80 prose)
Lines (Written): 180 (F); 202 (MS)

The spoken length is based on F.

STAGING
Above: the second banquet may be let down from above (sc.3, implicit; *not in MS*)
Audience: the King and Queen are mentioned (sc.2–4) and directly addressed (sc.4); the host is mentioned (sc.2, 4); at least some of the audience are said to be seated (sc.4, dialogue)

MUSIC
On-Stage Music: percussion of hammers on anvil, played by the Cyclopes (sc.2, dialogue)
Song: 'If love be called a lifting of the sense', sc.1, Singers, in parts, 28 lines
Dance: the artisans dance in two groups of four: Chisel, Maul, Summer, and Twibill; Dresser, Quarrel, Fret, and Beater (sc.2, desc.)

PROPS
Weapons: two bows and two quivers of arrows (sc.3. desc.)
Food and Drink: a second banquet (sc.3, desc.; served to the King and Queen by the Cupids; *not in MS*)
Small Portable Objects: a cleft palm bough (sc.3, desc.; split in two on stage; in MS, it is cleft 'to the bottom', in F only 'a little at the top')
Large Portable Objects: three blacksmiths' hammers (sc.2, dialogue); an anvil (sc.2, dialogue)
Scenery: possibly clouds (sc.3, desc.; *not in MS*)

COSTUMES
SMITH: a polt-foot (dialogue)
EROS and ANTEROS: both are winged; each wears an identical cassock, breeches, buskins, gloves, and a peruke (sc.3, desc.); the King's Cupid wears a garland of white and red roses, and the Queen's, a garland of lilies interwoven with purple, gold, silver, and other colours (sc.3, desc.)

EARLY STAGE HISTORY
Inception: After his return from his coronation in Scotland, the King asked William Cavendish, Earl of Newcastle, to prepare an entertainment for the Queen comparable to that which he had himself received in the Earl's household in May 1633 (which had included a dramatic element, **2404**).

2440. Entertainment at Chirk Castle

Performance: at Bolsover Castle on Wednesday 30 July 1634. The performance took place mainly or entirely in the afternoon during the visit to the Castle of the King and Queen (who were staying at Welbeck Abbey nearby); part of it took place during dinner, and part in the garden afterwards. The audience included: King Charles I; Queen Henrietta Maria; William Cavendish, Earl of Newcastle (host).

The first part of the entertainment (during the first banquet) may have taken place in the Pillar Parlour (as argued in *RenQ*); the Vitruvius sequence took place in the Fountain Garden; the Cupids sequence must also have taken place outside, if the second banquet was let down from above (there is no appropriate multi-level room inside).

Production Expenses
The event (including the dinner) reportedly cost Newcastle £14,000–£15,000.

EARLY TEXTUAL HISTORY
c. 1634–40: transcribed by John Rolleston as part of a MS literary collection for William Cavendish, Earl of Newcastle; 4 leaves.

c. 1637–40: Not long before his death, Ben Jonson placed some of his unpublished works in the hands of Sir Kenelm Digby, with a view to their publication. This entertainment may have been one of the texts in question. After Jonson's death in August 1637, Digby took the texts he had received to Thomas Walkley, who paid Digby £40 and procured a licence to publish them, but did not enter them in the Stationers' Register.

1640: While Walkley's volume was at the printer's, John Benson and Andrew Crooke had some of the masques therein (not including this one) entered to them in the Stationers' Register; the Stationers' Company authorities had no knowledge of Walkley's interest in the matter. Fearful that they were planning to issue their own edition, Walkley complained to a secretary of state, who issued a warrant prohibiting Benson and Crooke from doing so.

1640–1: included in the third volume of Jonson's *Works* ($^1F_1$), sigs. 2P1^r–2Q1^r, 5 pages on 3 leaves; printed by John Dawson for Thomas Walkley.

1640–1: The Stationers' Register entry of *The Gypsies Metamorphosed* (**1987**) in Benson's favour misled John Parker, a London stationer, into supposing that the printed copies of Walkley's volume were Benson's property. Benson allegedly owed Parker money, so Parker had the book seized from the printer's. Walkley, who valued the copies at £300 or more, suspected that this was a dishonest move planned by Benson and Crooke in preparation to issuing their own edition, and complained to the Court of Chancery on Wednesday 20 January 1641.

1648: Changes in press licensing arrangements since 1640 meant that Walkley's original licence to print his Jonson works had become void. He attempted to have the texts perused by the new licensers in preparation for having them entered in the Stationers' Register, but one of them, Sir Nathaniel Brent, was out of town and the other, John Langley, claimed to be too busy. He then approached the Stationers' Company, who in turn petitioned the House of Lords on Wednesday 20 December, asking for additional licensers to be appointed.

c. 1655: extracts transcribed from F_1 by John Evans in a miscellany, *Hesperides*, intended for publication and entered to Humphrey Moseley in the Stationers' Register on Thursday 16 August 1655. The book remained unpublished in 1660, and Evans continued adding to the collection until at least 1666. Two MS exemplars are known; one was cut up by J. O. Halliwell-Phillipps in the nineteenth century; the other survives (Washington: Folger, MS V. b. 93).

1658: the third volume of Jonson's *Works* entered to Thomas Walkley in the Stationers' Register on Friday 17 September; the listing of its contents includes fifteen unnamed masques.

1658: Walkley's rights to the third volume of Jonson's *Works* transferred to Humphrey Moseley in the Stationers' Register on Saturday 20 November; group transfer of 13 titles, the *Works* being one.

1660: F_1 advertised for sale by Humphrey Moseley.

1667: Moseley's rights to the third volume of Jonson's *Works* transferred by his widow, Ann, to Henry Herringman in the Stationers' Register on Monday 19 August; group transfer of nine titles, the *Works* being one.

1692: included in Jonson's *Works* ($^2F_2$), sig. 4F3^{r-v}, 1 leaf; printed by Thomas Hodgkin for Henry Herringman, Edward Brewster, Thomas Bassett, Richard Chiswell, Matthew Wotton, and George Conyers.

The books here designated F_1 and F_2 are respectively the second and third Jonson Folios.

EDITIONS
C. H. Herford, Percy Simpson, and Evelyn Simpson in *Ben Jonson* (Oxford, 1925–52), vii. 805–14, x. 709–10.
James Knowles, in *The Cambridge Edition of the Works of Ben Jonson*, gen. eds. David Bevington, Ian Donaldson, and Martin Butler (Cambridge, 2012), vi. 681–96.

REFERENCES
Annals 1634; Beal JnB 680; Bentley, iv. 653–4; Butler, 373; *EMS* 4 (1993), 145–53; Eyre & Rivington, ii. 8; Greg 614; Hazlitt, 144; HMC 7, 67; *The Library*, 4th ser., 11 (1930–1), 225–9, 461–5; *The Library*, 5th ser., 28 (1973), 294–308; *The Library*, 7th ser., 10 (2009), 372–404; McGee-Meagher 1634–42, 26–7; *RenQ* 52 (1999), 402–39; *SB* 25 (1972), 177–8.

2440. Entertainment at Chirk Castle

TEXT
MS (London: British Library, MS Egerton 2623, art. 13), scribal copy.

1634

GENRE
entertainment
Contemporary: entertainment (MS heading)

TITLE
MS: <...> *at Chirk Castle 1634*
Later Assigned: *The Entertainment at Chirk Castle*; *The Masque of the Four Seasons*; *The Four Seasons*
Alternative Modernization: *The Entertainment at Chirke Castle*

The MS title was erased in the nineteenth century by J. P. Collier, presumably with a view to removing evidence which contradicted his claim that this was a Jacobean court masque. Parts of it were subsequently legible under ultra-violet light.

AUTHOR
Brown suggests that the author may have been Sir Thomas Salusbury.

DATE
August 1634

ORIGINAL PRODUCTION
Sir Thomas Myddelton's household at Chirk Castle, Denbighshire

PLOT
New arrivals cause a change in the local climate which amazes the Genius of the country. He initially assumes that the visitors must be Mars and Venus; in fact, they are the Earl and Countess of Bridgewater. Orpheus welcomes them with a song praising the civilization, government, and prosperity they bring with them. The four seasons serve the guests a three-course meal, followed by sweet water.

Afterwards, Genius calls back the seasons to show how they celebrate May Day and Midsummer. Seasonal dances ensue. Genius offers further entertainment and wishes the audience goodnight.

SCENE DESIGNATION
sc.1–6, ep. (MS undivided); sc.2–5 correspond with the courses of the dinner.

ROLES
GENIUS, a male figure, the good angel of the country
ORPHEUS, a musician
WINTER, an old man
AUTUMN, a male figure (*non-speaking*)
SUMMER, of uncertain gender (*non-speaking*)
SPRING, a female figure (*non-speaking*)
GAMBOLS, Christmas dancers (sc.6, *non-speaking*)
DRUNKARDS, who dance (sc.6, *non-speaking*)
REAPERS, who dance (sc.6, *non-speaking*)
MORRIS DANCERS (sc.6, *non-speaking*)

Summer is referred to using the feminine pronoun in s.d.s, but the masculine pronoun in the dialogue.

Speaking Parts: 3
Allegorical Roles: 4

Stage Directions and Speech Prefixes
GENIUS: *Genius or the Country's better Angel* (s.d.s); *Genius* (s.p.s)
ORPHEUS: *Orpheus* (s.d.s)
WINTER: *Winter* (s.d.s and s.p.s)
AUTUMN: *Autumn* (s.d.s)
SUMMER: *Summer* (s.d.s)
SPRING: *Spring | the Spring* (s.d.s)
GAMBOLS: *Gambols* (s.d.s)
DRUNKARDS: *drunkards* (s.d.s)
REAPERS: *hay-maker or reapers* (s.d.s)

OTHER CHARACTERS
Mars, a god (sc.1)
Venus, a goddess (sc.1)
Diana, a goddess (sc.1)
Jove, a god (sc.1)
Hebe, cupbearer of the gods (sc.1)

SETTING
Geography
[*Wales*]: the mountains

SOURCES
Verbal: Juvenal, *Satires* 2 (sc.4; cited in MS margin)

LANGUAGE
English

FORM
Metre: pentameter and tetrameter
Rhyme: couplets
Epilogue: 4 lines, in couplets, spoken by Genius
Lines (Spoken): 149
Lines (Written): 182

STAGING
Audience: addressed as 'ladies' (sc.4)
Miscellaneous: The entertainment coincides with the serving of dinner to the guests at the castle, in several courses.

MUSIC
Music: unspecified music (sc.6, dialogue)
On-Stage Music: Orpheus plays the lyre (sc.1, dialogue; accompanying Song 1)
Songs:
 1: 'Canst thou in judgement be so slow', sc.1, Orpheus, 16 lines, with musical accompaniment;
 2: 'Your beauties, ladies, far more bright', sc.3, Orpheus, 20 lines;
 3: 'Summer was offering sacrifice', sc.4, Orpheus, 14 lines;
 4: 'The nightingale, the lark, the thrush do sing', sc.5, Orpheus, 21 lines.

Dance: Gambols dance a single antic (sc.6, s.d.); an antic of Drunkards (sc.6, s.d.); a country dance of Reapers (sc.6, s.d.); a morris dance (sc.6, s.d.).

It appears that the original intention may have been for the seasons to sing their own songs, but the task was instead given to a single performer, playing Orpheus. Thus, Orpheus is said in the MS to sing Song 2 'in [Autumn's] name', and Song 4 is introduced with the s.d., 'The last of Orpheus' songs is in the person of Spring'. The clearest indicator of a change of plan during pre-production pertains to Song 3 (Summer), where the pronouns were initially written in the first person and then amended to the third.

PROPS
Musical Instruments: a lyre (sc.1, dialogue)
Food and Drink: the meal's first course (sc.2, s.d.; possibly venison); the meal's second course of bake-meat and wine (sc.3, s.d.); the meal's third course of summer fruits (sc.4, s.d.; probably including cherries); sweet water (sc.5 dialogue; in the ewer)
Large Portable Objects: the dinner tables (sc.2–5, s.d.); a basin (sc.5, s.d.); a ewer (sc.5, s.d.); a form (sc.6, s.d.).

It is striking that the courses served by Winter and Autumn include foodstuffs associated with those seasons but available all the year round, whereas Summer's fruit course would presumably have been available only in the summer itself.

EARLY STAGE HISTORY
1634: performed in early August at Chirk Castle, Denbighshire, in honour of the visit of the President of the Council of Wales and his family. The entertainment took place in the evening during dinner. The audience included: John Egerton, 1st Earl of Bridgewater (President); Frances Egerton, Countess of Bridgewater; presumably Sir Thomas Myddelton (host); probably also Lady Alice Egerton, John Egerton, 2nd Viscount Brackley, Thomas Egerton.

EARLY TEXTUAL HISTORY
1634: transcribed in **MS**; 3 leaves. The MS was presented to John Egerton, 1st Earl of Bridgewater.

EDITIONS
Cedric C. Brown, *Milton Quarterly* 11 (1977), 76–86.
David N. Klausner, REED: Wales (Toronto, 2005), 141–6.

REFERENCES
Annals 1634; Bentley, v. 1303–5; Butler, 373; Hazlitt, 90; McGee-Meagher 1634-42, 27–8; *N&Q* 197 (1952), 96–7; Steele, 227.

2441. The Witches of Lancashire

TEXT
Printed in 1634 (STC 13373), from copy with some theatrical annotation. Additional information derives from a letter from Nathaniel Tomkyns to Sir Robert Phelips dated Saturday 16 August 1634.

GENRE
comedy
Contemporary: play (Tomkyns, S.R.); comedy (Tomkyns, t.p.)

TITLE
Performed: *The Witches of Lancashire*
Printed: *The Late Lancashire Witches*
Contemporary: *The Lancashire Witches*; possibly *The Witches and Devil of Lancashire*

AUTHORS
Thomas Heywood and Richard Brome

DATE
August 1634

ORIGINAL PRODUCTION
King's Men at the Globe

PLOT
Arthur hopes for a subvention from his uncle, Seely, to help him redeem a mortgage, but strange things are going on in the Seely household: the father is dominated by the son, Gregory, who is mastered in turn by his servant, Lawrence; there is a similar inversion of hierarchy among the women of the house. Gregory disapproves of his father's plans to help Arthur, so the money is not forthcoming; but fortunately Arthur's friend Generous helps out instead.

The truth is that the Seelys have been bewitched in reprisal for some harsh words spoken to an old woman. Many other supernatural events are going on. Mall Spencer, owner of an amazing self-propelled milk-pail, gives Generous's groom Robert a high-speed horse so that he can fetch wine from his master's favourite London tavern in a single overnight journey. Anyone who spends the night in a haunted mill is assaulted, so Gretty the miller gives up his tenancy, and Generous gives it to a poor, demobilized soldier. A witch and her spirit take the form of greyhounds; when Gretty's son tries to whip the dogs, they scare and then abduct him. Lawrence marries his fellow servant Parnell, but a spirit turns the wedding cake into crumbs, and the rest of the meal magically becomes even less appetizing; the real food is taken to supply the witches' feast. Mall Spencer gives Lawrence a codpiece point, which makes him impotent, causing marital difficulties. He and Parnell are mocked with a skimmington, but the relationship returns to normal when they burn the codpiece point.

Mistress Generous has developed the habit of riding out alone at night. Acting on her husband's orders, Robert refuses her a horse, so she rides him instead. It turns out that she is meeting with the witches: she is their leader. Gretty's son escapes from their feast and tells his father about them. The new miller has a bad night, but cuts off the paw of one of the cats who are attacking him. What is found on the ground, however, is a severed human hand wearing rings identifiably belonging to Mistress Generous. She falls sick, and is found to have a stump where her hand should be. Generous orders her arrest. The witches are rounded up, confronted with their magical misdeeds, and sent for trial.

SCENE DESIGNATION

prol., 1.1–2, 2.1–6, 3.1–3, 4.1–5, 5.1–5, ep. (Q has act-division only)

ROLES

PROLOGUE

Master ARTHUR, a gentleman, Seely's nephew; reputedly Robert's natural son
Master Tom SHAKSTONE, a gentleman; reputedly the Tailor's natural son
Master BANTAM, a gentleman; reputedly the Pedant's natural son
Master WHETSTONE, a bastard, reputedly the Gallant's; nephew of Generous and Anne; also called Master Byblow
Master GENEROUS, Anne's husband, Whetstone's uncle (by marriage); 50 years old
Old Master SEELY, Joan's husband, father of Gregory and Winny, Arthur's uncle
Master DOUGHTY, an old bachelor, Seely's neighbour, godfather of Gretty's son
Master GREGORY Seely, son of Old Seely and Joan, Winny's brother, Arthur's cousin
LAWRENCE, Gregory's groom, Mall's former sweetheart; later Parnell's husband; also called Lall and (in mocking allusion to his temporary impotence) Master Donought
JOAN, Old Seely's wife, mother of Gregory and Winny
WINNY, daughter of Old Seely and Joan, Gregory's sister, Arthur's cousin; also called Win
PARNELL, Winny's maid, later Lawrence's wife; also called Pall
MEG, a witch; also called Peg, Mother Johnson, and Granny Johnson
MAUD, a witch; probably surnamed Hargrave
Goody DICKISON, an old, thin witch; also called Gillian
A WITCH (2.1; only speaks collectively)
Four SPIRITS attending the witches, named Mamillion, Mawsy, Puckling (in the form of a boy), and possibly Suckling (only one speaks)
ROBERT, Generous's groom, reputed to be Arthur's biological father; also called Robin
A begging SOLDIER from Yorkshire; a former miller
GRETTY, a miller, Generous's tenant; a father (2.2)
Gretty's SON, a boy, Doughty's godson; said to be little
An INVISIBLE SPIRIT leading a brace of greyhounds (2.3, *non-speaking*)
MALL Spencer, Robin's sweetheart, a young witch

MUSICIANS, fiddlers at the wedding (3.1, 3.3; one or two speak individually)
Two COUNTRY LASSES at the wedding (3.1, 3.3; only speak collectively)
A SPIRIT at the wedding; in the form of a bagpiper (3.3, *non-speaking*)
MISTRESS [Anne] GENEROUS, Generous's wife, Whetstone's aunt, a witch; also called Lady Nan
WITCHES at the feast (4.1; three speak)
RUSTICS in the skimmington (4.3; speak collectively)
A DRUMMER in the skimmington (4.3, *non-speaking*)
A HUSBAND in the skimmington (4.3, *non-speaking*)
A WIFE in the skimmington (4.3, *non-speaking*)
SERVANTS, who bring on a banquet (4.5, *non-speaking*)
A PEDANT, Bantam's former teacher, reputed to be his biological father (4.5, *non-speaking*)
A TAILOR in the household of Shakstone's mother, reputed to be his biological father (4.5, *non-speaking*)
A GALLANT reputed to be Whetstone's father (4.5, *non-speaking*)
The CONSTABLE (5.5, *non-speaking*)
OFFICERS (5.5, *non-speaking*)
EPILOGUE

There is some uncertainty about the identity of the different witches and spirits in different parts of the play. The first thing to remember is that s.d.s referring to 'all the witches' mean 'all the witches we can represent on stage' rather than 'every member of the coven': in 5.2, when 'all the witches' are directed to enter, dialogue follows at once establishing that two or three named witches are not in fact present (and one of these, moreover, is Peg/Meg, one of the principal witches). This means that names ascribed to absent witches in some scenes do not need to be identified with unnamed witches who are present in other scenes; thus Tib, Nab, and Jug are here listed as 'other characters' rather than identified with the three unnamed speaking witches in 4.1. (Two of them may in any event be the names of familiars rather than witches.)

The issue is partly tied up with the identification of the witches' familiar spirits. The four witches who appear in 2.1 each have a named familiar, but two of the names seem to be linked to different witches at different points in the action. In 2.1, 4.4, and 5.5, Mamillion is Meg/Peg's familiar; but in the separately printed song in 2.1, he belongs to the singer (whom the main text identifies as Maud); and in 4.1 he is associated with the second unnamed speaking witch. Similarly, in 2.1, Puckling belongs to Goody Dickison (and her dialogue in that scene further identifies him with the boy spirit who appears with her in 2.5); but in 5.5 Puckling is the name of Maud's familiar.

Ultimately the text is more concerned with matters of theatrical function from scene to scene than with overall fictional consistency, so in all likelihood there is no overall order to be discovered and imposed. The defining scene for the full complement of witches seems to be their feast in 4.1; I have assumed that no new witches appear thereafter, but up to and including that scene I have avoided identifying unnamed witches with named ones who appear elsewhere. I have also assumed that most of the spirits' activity is covered by the four who make their first appearance in 2.1, except for the invisible spirit in 2.3, who has a specific actor assigned to play him, and the piper spirit in 3.3, who must be played by a musician; since the named actor in 2.3, John Adson, was also a musician, he may have handled both scenes. It is always possible that additional spirits might be introduced at the feast.

Speaking Parts: 28–30

Stage Directions and Speech Prefixes
PROLOGUE: *The Prologue* (heading)
ARTHUR: *Master Arthur* | [one of the] *Gentlemen* (s.d.s); *Arthur* (s.d.s and s.p.s)
SHAKSTONE: *Mr Shakstone* | *Shakstone* | *Shakston* | [one of the] *Gentlemen* (s.d.s; also misprinted *Shakson*); *Shak<stone>* (s.p.s)
BANTAM: *Mr Bantam* | [one of the] *Gentlemen* (s.d.s); *Bantam* (s.d.s and s.p.s); *Bantham* (s.p.s)
WHETSTONE: *Whetstone* | [one of the] *Gentlemen* (s.d.s); *Whet<stone>* (s.p.s)
GENEROUS: *Mr Generous* | *Generous* (s.d.s); *Gener<ous>* (s.p.s)
SEELY: *old Seely* (s.d.s); *Seely* (s.d.s and s.p.s)
DOUGHTY: *Doughty* (s.d.s and s.p.s); [one of the] *Gentlemen* (s.d.s)
GREGORY: *Gregory* (s.d.s); *Greg<ory>* (s.p.s)
LAWRENCE: *Lawrence* (s.d.s and s.p.s)
JOAN: *Joane* (s.d.s and s.p.s); *Joane* [old Seely's] *wife* (s.d.s); *Joan* (s.p.s)
WINNY: *Winny* (s.d.s); *Win* (s.d.s and s.p.s)
PARNELL: *Parnell* (s.d.s); *Parn<ell>* (s.p.s)
MEG: [one of] *4 Witches* | [one of] *the Witches* | [one of the] *Witches* (s.d.s); *Meg* | *Peg* (s.p.s)
MAUD: [one of] *4 Witches* | [one of] *the Witches* | [one of the] *Witches* | [one of the] *Witches* (s.d.s); *Mawd* | *Maud* (s.p.s)
DICKISON: [one of] *4 Witches* | [one of] *the Witches* | [one of the] *Witches* (s.d.s); *Goody Dickison* (s.d.s and s.p.s); *Gill<ian>* | *Dickis<on>* (s.p.s)
WITCH: [one of] *4 Witches* (s.d.s)
SPIRITS: *four Spirits* | *the Boy* | *The Spirit* | *A Spirit* | [the witches'] *Spirits* (s.d.s); *Sprite* (s.p.s)
ROBERT: *Robert* (s.d.s); *Robin* (s.d.s and s.p.s); *Rob<in>* (s.p.s)
SOLDIER: *a soldier* (s.d.s); *Soldier* (s.p.s)
GRETTY: *Miller* (s.d.s and s.p.s)
SON: *Boy* (s.d.s and s.p.s); *the Boy* (s.d.s)
INVISIBLE SPIRIT: *an invisible spirit* (s.d.s)
MALL: *Mall* | *Mal Spencer* | *Mall Spencer* (s.d.s); *Mal* (s.d.s and s.p.s)
MUSICIANS: *Musicians* | *The Fiddlers* | *Fiddlers* (s.d.s); *Fiddler* (s.p.s)
COUNTRY LASSES: *two Country Lasses* | *Maids* (s.d.s)
SPIRIT: *the piper* (s.d.s)
MISTRESS GENEROUS: *Mrs Generous* | *Mistress Generous* (s.d.s); *Mrs* | *Mrs Gener<ous>* (s.p.s)
WITCHES: [some of] *the Witches* (s.d.s); *2* | *1* | *3* (s.p.s)
RUSTICS: *Divers country rustics* | *The hoydens* | *the clowns* (s.d.s); *Within* | *Rabble* (s.p.s)
DRUMMER: *drum* (s.d.s)
HUSBAND: *a Skimington* | *Skimington* (s.d.s)
WIFE: [the Skimmington's] *wife* | *Skimington's wife* (s.d.s)
PEDANT: *a Pedant* (s.d.s)
TAILOR: *a nimble Tailor* (s.d.s)
GALLANT: *a Gallant* (s.d.s)
CONSTABLE: *Constable* (s.d.s)
OFFICERS: *Officers* (s.d.s)
EPILOGUE: *The Epilogue* (heading)

OTHER CHARACTERS
Whetstone's mother, of the Whetstone family; possibly dead (1.1)
Whetstone's father, said to be of the Byblow family (1.1; but the name may be just a joke about illegitimacy)
Generous's cook (1.1)
A usurer to whom Arthur has mortgaged a manor (1.1)
Doughty's father (1.2)
The local curate (1.2)
Seely's gambling companions (1.2)
The Seely family, Gregory's landed ancestors (1.2)
Generous's neighbours (2.2)
Generous's butler (2.2)
Master Robinson, the owner of two greyhounds (2.3, 2.5)
Parson Knitknot, who performs the marriage (3.1, 4.3)
The bellringers (3.1)
Jack Paine, the drawer at the Mitre tavern in London (3.2)
Mall Spencer's father, a husbandman (3.3)
Bantam's father (4.5)
Bantam's mother (4.5)
Shakstone's mother (4.5)
Shakstone's father (4.5)
Arthur's father (4.5)
The Lord President of the North (4.5)
Tib, a witch or familiar (4.5)
Nab, a witch or familiar (4.5, 5.2)
Jug, a witch (4.5, 5.2)
Gretty's wife, the mother of his son (5.1)
A club-footed horse-courser (5.1)
Arthur's mother (5.1)
An old woman, presumably a witch, to whom Seely spoke harshly (5.5; but she may be one of the witches who appear on stage)
The witch's disobedient son (5.5)
The justice (5.5)

SETTING
Period: contemporary; the play is loosely based on events which took place in 1633–4; the action takes place during the summer months
Time-Scheme: 1.1 takes place at around noon, and 2.2 later the same day; 3.1–3 take place the day after 2.2 and 2.6; 4.1 takes place the following night, and 4.2 the next morning; 4.5 takes place at midnight, and 5.3 before 5 a.m. the following morning
Place: Lancashire

Geography
Lancaster: the Market Cross
London: the Mitre tavern, Fleet Street
England: Yorkshire; Tutbury; York

Scotland
[Europe]: Paris; Russia; Poland; Lapland; Bilbao
New England
The Indies

SOURCES
Narrative: The play is based on contemporary legal depositions in the case of the alleged Lancashire witches of 1633–4. It also draws on: Jean Bodin, *De la Demonomanie des Sorciers* (1580; 5.2–4; the authors probably used a Latin translation); Henri Boguet, *Discours des Sorciers* (1590; 5.2–4).
Verbal: Horace, *Ars poetica* (t.p. motto); William Lily, Latin Grammar (1.1)
Music: 'Sellenger's Round' (3.3)
Works Mentioned: Aesop, *Fables* (4.1); Ovid, *Metamorphoses* (2.2); Pliny, *Natural History* (2.2); William Shakespeare, *Macbeth* (**1496**; 1.2)

The magical fetching of liquor may draw on one of the stories told about John Lambe, and possibly dramatized in *Doctor Lambe and the Witches* (**2252**).

LANGUAGE
English
Latin: 26 words (1.1, 3.1, 4.3, 4.5, 5.4–5; Whetstone, Arthur, Seely, Gregory, Doughty)
Dialect: Lawrence and Parnell speak in a thick northern dialect.

FORM
Metre: prose and pentameter; the witches speak mainly in trochaic tetrameter
Rhyme: blank verse; the witches speak in couplets
Prologue: 11 lines, in couplets and one triplet
Act-Division: 5 acts
Epilogue: 18 lines, in couplets
Lines (Spoken): 2,615 (957 verse, 1,658 prose)
Lines (Written): 2,820

STAGING
Doors: characters enter at several doors (2.1, 4.1, 5.2, s.d.); mentioned (3.1, s.d.); characters exit severally (5.5, s.d.).
Discovery Space: a bed thrust out (5.4, s.d.)
Within: sound effects (3.1, 4.1, 5.4, s.d.); music (3.3, implicit); shout (4.1, s.d.); speech (4.3, s.d.)
Above: a spirit appears above a door (3.1, s.d.); musicians appear above (3.3, s.d.)
Miscellaneous: the greyhounds are transformed on stage into Goody Dickison and Puckling (2.5, s.d.; the dogs 'go in' and the human characters 'appear'); Mall vanishes (3.3, s.d.); food is 'flown' down to the witches when they pull on cords (4.1, Tomkyns); the Soldier exits and immediately re-enters in the middle of a scene (5.2, s.d.)

MUSIC AND SOUND
Sound Effects: knocking within (3.1, 5.4, s.d.); a great noise within (4.1, s.d.)
Music: bells ringing backwards (3.1, dialogue); 'Sellenger's Round' within (3.3, s.d.; *a traditional, extant tune*); another tune within (3.3, s.d.); each individual musician simultaneously plays a different tune within (3.3, s.d.); music in the air (4.1, s.d.); dance music (4.5, s.d.); flourish (5.5, s.d.)
On-Stage Music: fiddles (3.1, s.d.); drum, including an alarum (4.3, s.d.)
Songs:
  1: 'There was a deft lad and a lass fell in love', 1.2, Joan, 8 lines;
  2: 'Come Mawsy, come Puckling', 2.1, Maud, 16 lines;
  3: 4.1; Gretty's son speaks during the song.
Dance: the witches dance (2.1, dialogue); Doughty, Mall, Lawrence, and Parnell dance (3.3, s.d.); Lawrence and Parnell dance a reel (3.3, s.d.); witches dance (4.1, s.d.); the Pedant dances (4.5, s.d.); the Tailor dances (4.5, s.d.)

'Sellenger's Round' may be found in Claude M. Simpson, *The British Broadside Ballad and its Music* (New Brunswick, 1966), 643–6.

PROPS
Lighting: two tapers (4.5, s.d.)
Weapons: the Soldier's sword (2.2, 5.2–3, dialogue); a switch (2.3, s.d.; 2.5, dialogue); Arthur's sword (4.3, implicit; 5.3, dialogue); Bantam's sword (4.3, implicit); Shakstone's sword (4.3, implicit); a riding switch (4.5, s.d.)
Musical Instruments: fiddles (3.1, 3.3, implicit); a bagpipe (3.3, implicit); a drum (4.3, s.d.)
Money: a shilling (2.5, dialogue)
Animals: two greyhounds (2.3, 2.5, s.d.), with collars and leashes (dialogue); live birds (3.1, dialogue; inside the pie); kittens (3.1, Tomkyns; inside the pie); a horse (4.3, s.d.)
Food and Drink: a cake (3.1, s.d.); bran (3.1, s.d.); a pie (3.1, dialogue; opened on stage); a feast, including a sirloin of beef, poultry, fowl, and fish (4.1, dialogue); bottles of wine and beer (4.1, dialogue); a posset (4.1, dialogue); a banquet (4.5, s.d.); wine (4.5, s.d.)
Small Portable Objects: keys (2.2, dialogue); a milk-pail (2.6, s.d.; moves of its own accord); a bill of fare (3.1, dialogue); dishes (3.1, s.d.; probably covered), containing unappetizing items, including horns (dialogue), bones, and stones (Tomkyns); a paper (3.2, s.d.); a bridle (3.2, 4.2, s.d.; 4.1, dialogue; fitted onto Robert); a key (4.2, dialogue); a curry-comb (4.5, s.d.); a severed hand with rings on it (5.3, s.d.)
Large Portable Objects: a millstone (5.2, dialogue)
Scenery: a bed (5.4, s.d.)
Miscellaneous: blood (5.3, dialogue; on the tip of the Soldier's sword)

COSTUMES AND MAKE-UP
ARTHUR, SHAKSTONE, and BANTAM: hangers (4.3, implicit)

GENEROUS: enters 'making him ready' (4.2, s.d.)
LAWRENCE: wedding clothes (3.1, 3.3, 4.3, implicit); slops with a codpiece (3.3, dialogue; 4.3, implicit); a codpiece point (3.3, dialogue; 4.3, implicit; tied on on stage); a garment with a pocket (3.3, dialogue); the costume he originally wore in 1.2 (5.5, s.d.)
JOAN: homely clothes (1.2, dialogue)
PARNELL: wedding clothes (3.1, 3.3, 4.3, implicit); the costume she originally wore in 1.2 (5.5, s.d.)
SOLDIER: a sword-belt (2.2, dialogue)
GRETTY: his face and hands scratched and bloody (2.2, s.d.)
GRETTY'S SON: a cap (5.1, s.d.)
MISTRESS GENEROUS: appears in the form of a cat (5.2, Tomkyns); a stump at her wrist rather than a hand (5.4, dialogue)
RUSTICS: bonnets (4.3, s.d.; doffed on stage)

EARLY STAGE HISTORY
Preparation: The King's Men discovered that rival companies were attempting to pre-empt their production by inserting episodes involving witches into old plays. On Sunday 20 July 1634, they petitioned the Revels Office to disallow this until their own play had been licensed and performed. The case was referred to the Deputy Master, William Blagrave, in the absence of the Master, Sir Henry Herbert.
1634: performed by the King's Men at the Globe on three consecutive days in mid-August. The cast included John Adson (Invisible Spirit). On the third day the audience included Nathaniel Tomkyns and a friend, and many 'fine folk, gentlemen, and gentlewomen'.

Two other early performances may have been of this play, but are more likely to have been a puppet show on the same subject (**2478**):
1635: performed on an unknown date between Saturday 11 July and Friday 31 July (possibly Monday 13 July) at Oxford near the King's Head.
1646: performed in London (before Tuesday 8 December) as *The Witches and Devil of Lancashire*. The audience included Ralph Trumbull.

EARLY TEXTUAL HISTORY
1634: entered (as *The Witches of Lancashire*) in the Stationers' Register to Benjamin Fisher on Tuesday 28 October. Sir Henry Herbert had licensed the book for publication.
1634: **Q** printed by Thomas Harper for Benjamin Fisher; collation A² B-L⁴, 42 leaves; title page names authors, acting company, and playhouse; Latin title-page motto.
1637: Fisher's rights transferred in the Stationers' Register to Robert Young, by deed of mortgage, on Monday 27 March; individually named as part of a group transfer of eighty titles.
Before 1640: a copy of Q was owned by Robert Burton.
c. 1630s–40s: a copy of Q was in the possession of John Horne (Vicar of Headington, Oxfordshire). After his death, his entire collection of play-books passed into the possession of John Houghton of Brasenose College, Oxford (c. 1608–77), then to James Herne (died 1685), and then to the library of Ralph Sheldon (1623–84) at Weston, where it was catalogued by Anthony Wood, probably in the late 1670s.
1642: a half-share in Young's rights transferred in the Stationers' Register to Miles Flesher on Tuesday 14 June; individually named as part of a group transfer of eighty titles.
1644: Young's remaining share transferred posthumously in the Stationers' Register to James Young on Monday 22 July; individually named as part of a group transfer of 130 titles.
1684: Nicholas Cox (Manciple of St Edmund Hall, Oxford) had a copy of Q in his bookshop. It had probably been previously owned by Gerard Langbaine, and appears on a list compiled by Anthony Wood on Saturday 13 December.

EDITIONS
Laird H. Barber, Garland Renaissance Drama (New York and London, 1979).
Gabriel Egan, Globe Quartos (London, 2002).
Helen Ostovitch, Richard Brome Online (internet, 2010).

REFERENCES
Annals 1634; Bawcutt 301, C73; Bentley, iii. 73–6; Bodleian, MS Wood E. 4, art. 1, p. 15; Thomas Crosfield, *The Diary*, ed. Frederick S. Boas (London, 1935), 79; Greg 494; Hazlitt, 128; Nicolas K. Kiessling, *The Library of Robert Burton* (Oxford, 1988) 811; *MLR* 13 (1918), 401–11; *MRDE* 1 (1984), 211–30; MSC 2.3, 410; *N&Q* 251 (2006), 92–4, 531–3; REED: Oxford, 518; REED: Somerset, 416; *The Trumbull Papers* (Sotheby's catalogue, 14 December 1989), 115.

2442. Masque at Holdenby House

EVIDENCE
Letter from James Howell to Philip Warwick, dated 3 June 1634; Sir John Finet's notebooks; letter from Nathaniel Tomkyns to Sir Robert Phelips, dated 29 July 1634; Queen Henrietta Maria's debenture accounts (Kew: National Archives, LR 5/66).

Howell's letter was hitherto taken to be the first intimation of plans for *The Temple of Love* (**2469**); but that was more than eight months later, whereas the Holdenby masque was being prepared the month after Howell wrote.

GENRE
masque
Contemporary: masque, ballet (Finet); *galanteria* (Tomkyns)

TITLE
Later Assigned: *The Masque at Holdenby; The Queen's Galanteria*

DATE
17 August 1634

ORIGINAL PRODUCTION
Queen Henrietta Maria's Court at Holdenby House, Northamptonshire

PLOT
The masque probably dealt with Platonic love.

ROLES
Seven MASQUERS

MUSIC
Dance: the masquers dance (Finet)

COSTUMES
MASQUERS: do not wear masks (Finet); buckram caps bound with white ribbon and decorated with silver bone-lace; kersey chips [i.e. hats?]; suits; scarves; pairs of roses (accounts)
Miscellaneous: six fine straw hats; four hats; four pairs of holland linings with ribbon; a coat (accounts)

EARLY STAGE HISTORY
Inception: The masque was apparently contemplated by Tuesday 3 June 1634; a letter written by James Howell on this date refers to the court craze for Platonic love, and reports rumours that the Queen and her maids of honour will shortly have a masque on the subject. It was certainly in active preparation by Tuesday 29 July.
Preparation: In July, John White arranged for the manufacture of some costumes. On Tuesday 5 August, William Geeres delivered lace and silk to Peter le Huc for use in making caps. On or after Friday 15 August, Robert Ramsey started work making costumes.
Rehearsal: The masque was said to have been 'casually prepared'.
Performance: at Holdenby House on Sunday 17 August 1634. The performance took place in the evening after supper, and ended about midnight. The cast included: Queen Henrietta Maria; ladies, lords, and gentlemen. The audience included: Gianfrancesco San Martino (Savoy Ambassador); Sir John Finet (Master of Ceremonies); Henry Grey, 1st Earl of Stamford.

Production Expenses
The total recorded expenses amount to £23.1s.6d. On Monday 21 March 1636, William Geeres was paid £3.6d, for lace and silk. On the same day, Robert Ramsay was paid for the following: kersey (18s.6d); stitching (10s.6d); buttons (5s); four hats (£1); cutting (£4.10s); making garments (£5); ribbon (8s); travelling expenses to London (£2). On Wednesday 23 March, Peter le Huc was paid for six straw hats (£3) and seven caps (£2.9s).

REFERENCES
Butler, 373; *ELR* 19 (1999), 79; Loomie, 166; McGee-Meagher 1634–42, 27; *MRDE* 1 (1984), 225.

2443. Possible Play of the Battle of Lepanto

EVIDENCE
Registrum Audomarensis Anglorum gymnasii (London: British Library, Add. MS 9354, fo. 49ᵛ).

McCabe infers that the *Registrum*'s reference to the Virgin's victory over barbarians refers to the subject of the prize-giving play that year. It is a reasonable interpretation, but the lack of an explicit statement means that this stops short of absolute certainty.

GENRE
history

TITLE
Later Assigned: *Virgineque magna matre saltus insolentiaeque barbarae aeternum victrice*

DATE
August 1634

ORIGINAL PRODUCTION
English Jesuit College, St Omers

PLOT
Aided by the Virgin Mary, the forces of Christianity rout the barbarian Turks at the Battle of Lepanto.

ROLES
The Virgin MARY, Our Lady of Victory
DON JOHN, commander of the Christian navy
The TURKS

SETTING
Period: sixteenth century; the play dramatizes events which took place in 1571.
Place: Lepanto

Geography
Turkey

EARLY STAGE HISTORY
1634: possibly performed at the English Jesuit College, St Omers, at the annual prize-giving in August.

REFERENCES
Bentley, v. 1450; McCabe, 89; *Revue de littérature comparée* 17 (1937), 366.

2444. Comedy of an Eccentric Magistrate ⌒

TEXT
Two early MS witnesses:
- **Ar:** authorial working draft (Arbury Hall, Warwickshire, MS A.414, fos. 104ᵛ–143ʳ), with corrections and amendments made during composition and also extensive, intermittent deletions and reworkings made subsequently;
- **w:** revised and cut fair copy (Calgary: University Library, MS C 132.27); the 'Watnall Hall' MS.

This reflects three states of the text:
- **A:** original composition, in the uncorrected state of Ar;
- **B:** intermediate working revision, in the corrected state of Ar;
- **C:** final revision, in W; this does not derive directly from B, since it includes material both deleted and added in B.

In this entry, asterisks mark the small number of C-text elements which were previously introduced in the B-text.

GENRE
comedy
Contemporary: play (ep.)

TITLE
Later Assigned: *The Humorous Magistrate*

> **C-Text**
> **Later Assigned:** *Marriage upon Marriage, or As I Told You Before*

AUTHOR
John Newdigate

DATE
Limits: 1632–42
Best Guess: 1634

> **C-Text**
> **Limits:** 1640–2
> **Best Guess:** 1641

A date in or close to the 1630s is supported by allusions in 4.3 to enclosures and the encroachment of provincial antitheatricalism (itinerant musicians are said to have been whipped for singing); an apparent reference to the 1632 proclamation ordering the gentry back to their country estates (identified in *Early Theatre*, 2009) establishes the upper limit. The author died in 1642, so unsurprisingly there are no Civil War period references. Kidnie establishes that the epilogue is written on paper with a watermark also found elsewhere in the collection, a leaf (fo. 70) in Newdigate's hand containing a MS poem dated August 1637. However, this establishes only an affinity, not a date, and in any event it pertains only to the epilogue: the rest of the play is written on paper with a different watermark. The substitution of Dyer for Coke in a joke about literary and legal works in 2.2 might suggest that the play was first drafted before Coke's death in September 1634, but amended afterwards (though it is impossible to tell whether the alteration was part of the B revision, an isolated amendment made earlier, or a change of mind during the original composition).

The C-text is certainly later than mid-1640, as indicated by the addition of an allusion to the 'etcetera oath'. It is striking that all but one of the references to the King are omitted, but a post-1642 date is ruled out by the fact that the MS appears to be in the author's hand.

PLOT
Spruce wants to marry Justice Thrifty's daughter, Constance, but Thrifty thinks him too poor, and puts him off. He asks his mother, Mistress Mumble, to give him his inheritance now, and gets around her reluctance by threatening suicide. He visits Thrifty's house, knocks out the housekeeper, Jennet, with drugged sweets, and elopes with Constance in a coach. Thrifty identifies Spruce and his associates as the prime suspects.

Mistress Mumble and her daughter, Sophia, both have suitors. Mumble disposes of Strife the lawyer, thinking him a fortune-hunter. Sophia's suitor, Wild, is wooing her when Thrifty arrests him for complicity in Constance's disappearance. At Sophia's request, Thrifty agrees to release him, but asks in return to marry Mumble. The old woman agrees.

Spruce and Constance are on their way to Welcome Hall, his uncle's home, when they take a break and are attacked by thieves. Spruce loses his money and is separated from Constance, who meets a group of shepherds. One of them is employed by Welcome, and takes her to Welcome Hall. Spruce learns that she is safe and marries her there.

Thrifty marries Mumble, much to Strife's disappointment. He gives his consent to Wild's marrying Sophia, and accepts Spruce as his son-in-law.

> **C-Text**
> This version omits Strife's reaction to Mumble's marriage.

SCENE DESIGNATION
prol., 1.1–2, 2.1, 3.1–3, 4.1–4, 5.1–5, ep. (MS has act-division only)

> **C-Text**
> 1.1–3, 2.1–2, 3.1–3, 4.1–3, 5.1–5 (MS has act-divisions only). This corresponds with the A-text acts and scenes as follows: A.1.1 = C.1.1; A.1.2 = C.1.3; A.2.1 = C.2.1; A.3.2 = C.2.2; A.4.1a = C.3.1; A.3.3 = C.3.2; A.4.1b = C.3.3; A.4.2–4 = C.4.1–3; A.5.1–5 = C.5.1–5. The prologue, epilogue, and A.3.1 are omitted altogether, and C.1.2 is entirely new.

ROLES
PROLOGUE

Master THRIFTY, an old Middlesex Justice of the Peace, Constance's father; later Mumble's third husband; also called Justice Thrifty

Master Christopher SPRUCE, Mumble's son, Sophia's elder half-brother, Welcome's nephew; later Constance's husband; also called Kit and Kester

PETER Parchment, Thrifty's clerk of seven years' standing, Jennet's husband, a father; formerly a scrivener's boy; also called Master Parchment

Master WILD, a young man and elder brother, Spruce's friend; later Sophia's fiancé

JOHNNY, Wild's Scottish servant

Mistress MUMBLE, an old, deaf, rich widow, Welcome's sister, Thrifty's neighbour; mother of Spruce and Sophia; later Thrifty's wife

Mistress SOPHIA, Mumble's daughter, Spruce's younger half-sister, Welcome's niece; later Wild's fiancée

Mistress CONSTANCE, a gentlewoman, Thrifty's daughter; later Spruce's wife; also called Lady Constance

Mistress JENNET, Peter's wife, Thrifty's housekeeper, a mother; formerly Constance's dry nurse

Dick CRISP, Spruce's barber; also called Richard

GODFREY, Mumble's servant

Master STRIFE, a lawyer and member of the Inns of Court; originally written as Thomas Strife

A CONSTABLE (4.1, 5.1)

OFFICERS (4.1, non-speaking)

Will CATCH, a thief

Tom SNAP, a thief

Ned CARELESS, a thief

Jack KILLMAN, a thief

Hodge DINGTHRIFT, a thief

The KING of the shepherds, Welcome's employee

Five SHEPHERDS; two are named Will Goodman and Dick Hopper (originally written as Dick Shepherd)

MUSICIANS (4.3; up to three speak; originally written as just one musician)

The musicians' BOY, who attempts to sing (4.3)

Six COUNTRY WENCHES, named Tib, Madge White, Bess Blackabye, Kit Harrison, Gillian (also called Gill), and Kate (only Tib speaks individually; the rest may sing collectively)

Goodman Thomas CRUTCH, an old man, Margery's husband; also called Father Crutch

MARGERY, an old woman, Crutch's wife; a mother

Master WELCOME, an old gentleman, Mumble's brother, Mistress Welcome's husband, uncle of Spruce and Sophia

BEADLES (5.1; one speaks)

MISTRESS WELCOME, Welcome's wife, aunt of Spruce and Sophia

Two COUNTRY MEN, suitors to Thrifty (5.5; only one speaks)

Two COUNTRY WOMEN, one of them a grandmother (5.5)

EPILOGUE

Speaking Parts: 37–44

C-Text
PROLOGUE: *omitted*
THRIFTY: no reference to his county of jurisdiction
PETER: no reference to his length of service as a clerk, nor to his fatherhood
WILD: not said to be an elder brother
JOHNNY: *omitted*
JENNET: no reference to her motherhood
CONSTABLE: now also appears in 1.2
STRIFE: his Inns of Court membership is not mentioned; also called Master Contention
KILLMAN: is now *non-speaking*
DINGTHRIFT: is now *non-speaking*
SHEPHERDS: none are given names
BOY: *omitted*
WENCHES: none have surnames, and Gillian is only Jill; all are now *non-speaking*; Tib is referred to as Queen of the Shepherds
CRUTCH: is not called Goodman Crutch, and not named Thomas
MARGERY: is now unnamed; no reference to her motherhood
BEADLES: are now *non-speaking*
MISTRESS WELCOME: is now *non-speaking*
EPILOGUE: *omitted*

Speaking Parts: 28–30

Stage Directions and Speech Prefixes
PROLOGUE: Prologue (heading)
THRIFTY: *Mr Thrifty* | *Justice Thrifty* (s.d.s); *Thrifty* (s.d.s and s.p.s); *Mr Thrifty a Justice of Peace* (d.p.)
SPRUCE: *Mr Spruse* | *Spruse* (s.d.s); *Spr<use>* (s.p.s); *Mr Christopher Spruce son to Mrs Mumble* (d.p.)
PETER: *Peter Parchm<en>t* | *Parchm<en>t* (s.d.s and s.p.s); *Peter Parchment Thriftye's Clerk* (d.p.)
WILD: *Mr Wild* (s.d.s); *Wild* (s.d.s and s.p.s); *Mr Wild [Spruce's] companion* (d.p.)
JOHNNY: *Jony* (s.d.s and s.p.s); *Jonye* (s.d.s); *Jony Wild's man* (d.p.)
MUMBLE: *Mrs Mumble* (s.d.s); *Mum<ble>* (s.p.s); *Mrs Mumble a deaf rich widow* (d.p.)
SOPHIA: *Sophia* | *Mrs Sophia* (s.d.s); *Sop<hia>* (s.p.s); *Sophia [Mrs Mumble's] daughter* (d.p.)
CONSTANCE: *Mrs Constance* | *Constance* (s.d.s); *Con<stance>* (s.p.s); *Constance Thriftye's daughter* (d.p.)
JENNET: *Mrs Jennet* | *Jennet* (s.d.s); *Jen<net>* (s.p.s); *Jennet Parchm<en>t's wife Thriftye's housekeeper* (d.p.)
CRISP: *Crisp, [Spruce's] barber* (s.d.s); *Crisp* (s.d.s and s.p.s); *Dick Crisp a barber Spruce's man* (d.p.)
GODFREY: *a servant* (s.d.s); *Godfrye* (s.d.s and d.p.); *Godf<rye>* (s.p.s)
STRIFE: *Mr Strife* (s.d.s); *Strife* (s.d.s and s.p.s); *Strife a Lawyer* (d.p.)

CONSTABLE: *A Constable* (s.d.s); *Constable* (s.d.s, s.p.s, and d.p.)
OFFICERS: *officers* (s.d.s and d.p.)
CATCH: *Will Catch* (s.d.s); *Catch* (s.d.s and s.p.s); *Will Catch* [one of] *2 thieves* (d.p.)
SNAP: *Tom Snap* (s.d.s); *Snap* (s.d.s and s.p.s); *Tom Snap* [one of] *2 thieves* (d.p.)
CARELESS: [one of] *the other 3 thieves* | *Careles* (s.d.s); *Care<les>* (s.p.s); *Ned Careles* [one of] *3 other thieves* (d.p.)
KILLMAN: [one of] *the other 3 thieves* | *Kilman* (s.d.s); *Kil<man>* (s.p.s); *Jack Killman* [one of] *3 other thieves* (d.p.)
DINGTHRIFT: [one of] *the other 3 thieves* | *Dingthrift* (s.d.s); *Ding<thrift>* (s.p.s); *Hodge Dingthrift* [one of] *3 other thieves* (d.p.)
KING: [one of] *some shepherds* | *king of Shepherds* | [*Mr Welcome's*] *shepherd* (s.d.s); *King* (s.p.s); *Shepherd* (s.d.s and s.p.s); [one of the] *Shepherds* (d.p.)
SHEPHERDS: *some shepherds* (s.d.s); *1 Shepherd* | *2 Shepherd* | *3 Shepherd* | *4 Shepherd* | *5 Shepherd* (s.p.s); *Shepherds* (d.p.)
MUSICIANS: *A musician* (s.d.s); *Musician* (s.p.s)
BOY: *Boy* (s.d.s and s.p.s)
COUNTRY WENCHES: *2 or 3 country wenches* | *as many country wenches as shepherds* (s.d.s); *Tib* (s.d.s and s.p.s)
CRUTCH: *Cruch* (s.d.s and s.p.s); *Cruch an old country man* (d.p.)
MARGERY: [*Crutch's*] *wife* (s.d.s); *Old Woman* (s.p.s); *Cruch's wife* (d.p.)
WELCOME: *Mr Wellcome* (s.d.s); *Well<come>* (s.p.s); *Mr Wellcome brother to Mrs Mumble* (d.p.)
BEADLES: *officers* (s.d.s and d.p.); *1 Officer* (s.p.s)
MISTRESS WELCOME: *Mrs Wellcome* (s.d.s); *Mrs Well<come>* (s.p.s); *Mrs Wellcome* (d.p.)
COUNTRY MEN: [two of] *4 country people* | [two of] *4 country men and women* | [two of Thrifty's] *strangers* | [two of] *The country folks* | [two of] *the suitors* | [two of the] *Country Folks* (s.d.s); *Countryman* | *1 Country Man* (s.p.s); *Country men* (d.p.)
COUNTRY WOMEN: [two of] *4 country people* | [two of] *4 country men and women* | [two of Thrifty's] *strangers* | [two of] *The country folks* | [two of] *the suitors* | [two of the] *Country Folks* (s.d.s); *1 Country Woman* | *2 Country Woman* (s.p.s); *Country . . . women* (d.p.)
EPILOGUE: *Epilogue* (heading)

C-Text

THRIFTY: *Mr Thrifty* | *Thrifty* | *Thriftye* (s.d.s); *Thrif<ty>* (s.p.s); *Mr Thrifty, a Justice of peace* (d.p.)
SPRUCE: *Mr Spruce* | *Spruce* (s.d.s); *Spr<uce>* (s.p.s); *Mr Christopher Spruce Son to Mrs Mumble* (d.p.)
PETER: *Peter* (s.d.s); *Pet<er>* (s.p.s); *Peter Parchment Thriftie's Clerk* (d.p.)
WILD: *Mr Wild* (s.d.s); *Wild* (s.d.s and s.p.s); *Mr Wild Spruce's friend* (d.p.)

CONSTABLE: *a Constable* (s.d.s); *Constable* (s.d.s, s.p.s, and d.p.)
MUMBLE: *Mrs Mumble* | *Mumble* (s.d.s); *Mum<ble>* (s.p.s); *Mrs Mumble, a deaf rich widow* (d.p.)
SOPHIA: *Sophia* | *Mrs Sophia* (s.d.s); *Soph<ia>* (s.p.s); *Sophia,* [*Mrs Mumble's*] *daughter* (d.p.)
CONSTANCE: *Constance* | *Mrs Constance* (s.d.s); *Const<ance>* (s.p.s); *Constance Thriftye's daughter* (d.p.)
JENNET: *Jenet* (s.d.s and s.p.s); *Jenet Peter's wife Thriftye's housekeeper* (d.p.)
CRISP: *Crisp* (s.d.s and s.p.s); *Crisp a barber Spruce's man* (d.p.)
GODFREY: *Godfrye* (s.d.s); *Godf<rye>* (s.p.s); *Godfry Mrs Mumble's man* (d.p.)
STRIFE: *Mr Strife* (s.d.s); *Strife* (s.d.s and s.p.s); *Mr Strife a lawyer* (d.p.)
OFFICERS: *officers* (s.d.s and d.p.)
CATCH: *Catch* [one of] *two thieves* (s.d.s); *Catch* (s.d.s and s.p.s); *Will Catch* [one of] *two thieves* (d.p.)
SNAP: *Snap* [one of] *two thieves* (s.d.s); *Snap* (s.d.s and s.p.s); *Tom Snap* [one of] *two thieves* (d.p.)
CARELESS: [one of] *3 other thieves* | *Careless* (s.d.s); *Care<less>* (s.p.s); *Ned Careless* [one of] *three other thieves* (d.p.)
KILLMAN: [one of] *3 other thieves* | *Killman* (s.d.s); *Jack Killman* [one of] *three other thieves* (d.p.)
DINGTHRIFT: [one of] *3 other thieves* | *Dingthrift* (s.d.s); *Hodge Dingthrift* [one of] *three other thieves* (d.p.)
KING: *King of shepherds* | [*Welcome's*] *shepherd* (s.d.s); *King* (s.d.s and s.p.s); *Shepherd* (s.p.s); [one of the] *Shepherds* (d.p.)
SHEPHERDS: *5 other shepherds* | *The Shepherds* (s.d.s); *1 Shepherd* | *2 Shepherd* | *3 Shepherd* | *4 Shepherd* | *5 Shepherd* (s.p.s); *Shepherds* (d.p.)
MUSICIANS: *Musicians* (s.d.s and d.p.); *Musician* (s.p.s)
COUNTRY WENCHES: *6 country wenches* (s.d.s)
CRUTCH: *Crutch* (s.d.s and s.p.s); *Crutch, an old man* (d.p.)
WIFE: [*Crutch's*] *wife* (s.d.s); *Cr<utch>'s wife* (s.p.s); *Cruche's wife* (d.p.)
WELCOME: *Mr Wellcome* | *Mr Wellcom* (s.d.s); *Well<come>* (s.p.s); *Mr Wellcome brother to Mrs Mumble* (d.p.)
BEADLES: *officers* (s.d.s and d.p.)
MISTRESS WELCOME: *Mrs Wellcom* (s.d.s and d.p.)
COUNTRYMEN: [two of] *four country men and women* | [two of the] *Country folks* | [two of the] *Country people* (s.d.s); *Countryman* (s.p.s); *Some Country men* (d.p.)
COUNTRYWOMEN: [two of] *four country men and women* | [two of the] *Country folks* | *the women* | [two of the] *Country people* (s.d.s); *1 Countrywoman* | *2 Countrywoman* (s.p.s); *Country women* (d.p.)

OTHER CHARACTERS
Justices, Thrifty's colleagues, one of whom interrupted Thrifty's animadversions upon alehouses (1.1, 3.3)
Mistress Yardley, keeper of an ordinary (1.1)
Lory Spence, with whom Johnny claims to have been brought up (1.1; possibly the name of a horse)
The Sheriff of the county, a well-dressed man (1.2, 4.3)
A sow-gelder, who blows his horn in search of work (1.2)
Bridget, Mumble's chambermaid (1.2)
Constance's music master (2.1)
The assistant to the Clerk of the Assizes, who had difficulty reading Peter's handwriting (2.1)
Take-all, Thrifty's former clerk, Peter's predecessor (2.1)
The children of Jennet and Peter (2.1)
Wild's page (3.1; possibly Johnny)
Sir William Brokage, a scrivener (3.1)
Men to whom Wild mortgaged his non-existent manor (3.1)
A countess, Sophia's mistress (3.2)
Thomas Mumble, a London merchant, Mumble's dead second husband, Sophia's father (3.2–3)
Squire Spruce of Norfolk, Mumble's dead first husband, Spruce's father (3.2)
A scrivener who prepared a document for Wild's signature (3.3; possibly imaginary)
Wild's adversary in a legal matter (3.3; possibly imaginary)
An Inns-of-Court man against whom Wild agreed to run a race (3.3; possibly imaginary)
Country people who told Jennet to expect Thrifty's imminent return home (3.3)
A young woman who became pregnant out of wedlock (4.1)
The gentleman who made the young woman pregnant (4.1)
The young woman's parents (4.1)
The butler, who got the blame for the unplanned pregnancy (4.1)
The Second Shepherd's landlord, a Justice of the Peace (4.3; possibly Thrifty)
A lord, the landlord's next-door neighbour, who enclosed the commons (4.3)
Mother Brewer, an alewife (4.3)
Grace, Margery's daughter, who married a London waterman thirty years ago (4.3)
Captain Pouch, possibly Grace's second husband (4.3)
The local Constable, a fool (4.3)
The person appointed to be the next Justice of the Peace, an unworthy successor for reasons which cannot be named (4.3)
The Lord of the Manor, an elder brother (4.3)
Thomas, a servingman named in a warrant (5.1)
Jennet's neighbours (5.1, 5.4)
Wild's tailor (5.2)
A scrivener, Peter's former master (5.3)
Strife's laundress, to whom he owes money (5.4)
The parish clerk (5.4)
Sophia's physician (5.4)
A tanned lady who took offence when a gentleman called her fair (5.4)
The First Countrywoman's daughter, whom Thrifty saved from a whipping, and her bastard child (5.5)
Thrifty's neighbours (5.5)

B-Text
A gentleman who encouraged Peter to treat his buckram bag as a relic of antiquity (2.1)

varies
Justices: omits reference in 1.1

C-Text
Wild's dead father (1.1)
A gentleman who encouraged Peter to treat his buckram bag as a relic of antiquity (2.1)*
Mumble's dead uncle (2.2)
Mumble's midwife (3.3)
Mumble's physician (3.3)

varies
Bridget: no reference in A.1.2/C.1.3, but a new reference in C.3.3
Assistant to Clerk of the Assizes: now his associate
Landlord: his tenant is now the Third Shepherd, not the Second
Encloser of commons: now a great man rather than a lord
Jennet's neighbours: no reference in 5.4

omits: Mistress Yardley; Lory Spence; children of Jennet and Peter; Wild's page; Brokage; Wild's mortgage lenders; Sophia's countess; scrivener; Wild's adversary; Inns-of-Court man; country people; pregnant girl, gentleman, parents, and butler; Mother Brewer; Grace and her husband; Captain Pouch; Thomas the servingman; Wild's tailor; Strife's laundress; parish clerk; Sophia's physician; tanned lady and complimentary gentleman

SETTING
Period: seventeenth century (roughly contemporary); the action takes place at a time when there is a king on the throne, who maintains a troupe of travelling players (mentioned in 1.2), and during the first quarter of the year, before April
Time-Scheme: 1.2 takes place relatively early in the day, 3.2 in the morning, and 5.4 late in the day, but apparently not all the same day
Place: London and the country

Geography
London: the Phoenix tavern; Hyde Park; the Stillyard; the Bear Garden; St Antholin's church; Westminster; Fleet Street; Mile End; Moorfields

England: Banstead; Lincoln (*deleted*); Kiplingcotes; Coventry; Oxford; Norfolk; Middlesex; Welcome Hall
[*Europe*]: France; Mount Etna; the Holy Roman Empire; Flanders
Turkey
The Indies

B-Text
Period: not necessarily contemporary; whereas in A the thieves propose that the coin to be given to Spruce be either a Carolus or a Jack (i.e. minted in the reigns of Charles I or James I), in B only the Jack is mentioned

Additional Geography
[*Europe*]: Arcadia
The Torrid Zone
The North Pole

Omitted Geography
Coventry; Oxford

C-Text
Period: *omits* references to the King and the time of year; the period is now non-specific
Time-Scheme: at least a night passes between 5.1 and 5.2
Place: now no more specific than England.

Additional Geography
London: Piccadilly
England: Winchester
[*Europe*]: Naples; Arcadia*
*The Torrid Zone**
*The North Pole**

omits: Phoenix tavern; Hyde Park; Bear Garden; St Antholin's; Westminster; Fleet Street; Mile End; Moorfields; Banstead; Lincoln; Kiplingcotes; Coventry; Oxford; Etna; Middlesex

---

SOURCES
Verbal: Terence, *Adelphoe* (5.4); Ovid, *Heroides* 15 (1.1); *The Noble Acts of Arthur of the Round Table* (ballad, before 1597; 3.2); John Newdigate, *Tragedy of the Imperial Favourite Crispinus* (**2382**; 1.2)
Works Mentioned: Sir Thomas Littleton, *Les Tenures* (1481; 3.2); Sir James Dyer, *Reports* (1513–82, printed 1585; 3.2, replacing deleted reference to Coke); Jean Bodin, *Six Livres de la République* (1576; 2.1); Sir Philip Sidney, *Arcadia* (1580; 3.2); William Shakespeare, *Hamlet* (**1259**; 1.1); John Dowland, *The Second Book of Songs or Airs* (1600), 2: Lachrymae (4.2); Statute of Vagabonds (1572; 14 Elizabeth I c. 5; 4.3); Sir Edward Coke, unspecified work (before 1634; 3.2, deleted)

C-Text
Verbal: Cicero, *De officiis* (3.2; cited); Ovid, *Fasti* 4 (1.2); Athanasius, *Contra gentes* (1.2); 'Come hear, lady Muses, and help me to sing' (ballad, 1627; 4.2); *varies*: Terence, *Adelphoe* (the quotation is omitted from 5.4, but the same passage quoted in 2.2)
Music: 'King Arthur' (3.2)
Works Mentioned: *omits*: *Hamlet*; Lachrymae

The tune 'King Arthur', also known as 'Flying Fame', is traditional, and may be found in Claude M. Simpson, *The British Broadside Ballad and its Music* (New Brunswick, 1966), 97.

LANGUAGE
English
Latin: 66 words (1.1, 2.1, 3.1, 3.3, 4.1–2, 5.1, 5.4–5; Thrifty, Peter, Wild, Spruce, Crisp, Catch, Constance)
Dialect: Johnny speaks in Scots throughout.

B-Text
Latin: 57 words (1.1, 2.1, 3.1, 3.3, 4.1–2, 5.1, 5.4–5; Wild, Thrifty, Peter, Crisp, Catch, Constance)

C-Text
Latin: 70 words (1.1–2, 2.1–2, 3.1–2, 5.1, 5.4–5; Thrifty, Peter, Wild, Crisp)
Dialect: *omitted*

FORM
Metre: prose and pentameter
Rhyme: blank verse
Prologue: 24 lines, in couplets
Act-Division: 5 acts
Epilogue: 14 lines, in couplets
Lines (Spoken): 3,154 (1,153 verse, 2,001 prose)
Lines (Written): 3,291

The written length is markedly different from the Malone edition's count of 3,492 lines (including the d.p.), owing to the editor's decision, understandable in presenting such a heavily worked-over MS, to number interlineations as if they were substantive lines.

B-Text
Lines (Spoken): 3,072 (1,127 verse, 1,945 prose)

C-Text
Prologue: *omitted*
Epilogue: *omitted*
Lines (Spoken): 1,960 (694 verse, 1,266 prose)
Lines (Written): 2,080

STAGING
Doors: a second door, different from the one used for an immediately precedent exit, is specified for entrance (1.2, 4.4, s.d.)

Stage: mentioned (5.1, s.d.)
Miscellaneous: Spruce's soliloquy is overheard (1.1). The shepherds 'make a shepherds' table' with their spades, presumably a mound of earth (4.3, s.d.; in the C-text they are explicitly said to 'dig' it). The duration of the performance is said to have been two hours (ep.).

> **C-Text**
> **Doors:** in this version, the second door is specified for entrance in different scenes (2.2, 3.2, 4.3, 5.5, s.d.); characters exit at two doors (2.2, s.d.)

MUSIC AND SOUND
Sound Effects: knocking (2.1, s.d.)
Music: sow-gelder's horn (1.2, s.d.)
On-Stage Music: Musicians play their fiddles (4.3, s.d.)
Song: 'While harmless shepherds watch their flocks', 4.3, King of Shepherds with Shepherds in chorus, 33 lines

The six wenches' names are here treated as spoken interpolations into the song. If they were taken as part of the song lyric, then it would be 30 lines longer. 14 of these lines are not written out in the MS but have been included in the calculation for spoken prose.

Other Singing: Mumble sings one line (3.2, s.d.; the C-text specifies the tune as 'King Arthur'); the King of Shepherds sings a tune (4.3, s.d.); the Boy attempts to sing the song at various pitches (4.3, s.d.)
Dance: five Shepherds and five Wenches dance (4.3, s.d.; Tib is excluded)

> **C-Text**
> **Song:** now only 28 lines
> **Other Singing:** *omits* preliminary singing by King of Shepherds and Boy

PROPS
Weapons: Spruce's sword (2.1, 4.2, implicit); two pistols (4.2, s.d.); up to three more pistols (4.3, dialogue); thieves' swords (4.2, implicit); a truncheon (5.3, s.d.)
Musical Instruments: fiddles (4.3, dialogue)
Clothing: a ring (3.3, dialogue)
Money: gold (2.1, s.d.); an unspecified amount, including a coin (4.2, dialogue/C s.d.); an unspecified sum (4.3, s.d.); half a crown (5.4, dialogue)
Animals: four chickens (5.5, s.d./dialogue); two capons (5.5, s.d./dialogue)
Food and Drink: a maudlin cup (3.2, s.d.), containing liquor (implicit; drunk on stage); sweetmeats (3.3, s.d.); a box of comfits (3.3, dialogue); wine (4.1, s.d.); biscuit bread (4.1, s.d.); a chest of wine bottles (4.2, s.d.); ale (4.3, dialogue; drunk on stage); cheesecake (4.3, dialogue; eaten on stage)
Small Portable Objects: an almanac (1.1, s.d.); keys (1.2, dialogue); a napkin (3.2, dialogue); writing materials (3.3, 5.5, implicit); a letter (4.1, implicit/C dialogue); a damask drinking napkin (4.1, dialogue); a silver tankard (4.1, dialogue); a box of barber's tools (4.2, dialogue); a jewel (4.2, s.d.); five cuts (4.3, dialogue); a letter (4.4, implicit); a warrant (5.1, s.d.; torn up on stage); a letter (5.2, 5.4, dialogue/C s.d.); a muff (5.3, s.d.); possibly unspecified gifts (5.5, s.d.; if anything is offered beyond the chickens and capons); a document (5.5, s.d.)
Large Portable Objects: a staff (3.2, dialogue; 4.1, s.d.); a chair (3.3, s.d.); spades (4.3, dialogue)
Scenery: a cart (5.1, s.d.)

> **B-Text**
> **Small Portable Objects:** *varies*: silver tankard *becomes* silver spout-pot (4.1, dialogue)

> **C-Text**
> **Weapons:** *varies*: truncheon *becomes* a rope's end (5.3–4, s.d.); *omits*: three pistols, thieves' swords
> **Money:** *omits*: unspecified sum (from A 4.3/C 4.2), half-crown
> **Food and Drink:** *varies*: maudlin cup *becomes* a silver tankard (2.2, s.d.); the shepherds' feast is not specified as ale and cheesecake; *omits*: sweetmeats, wine (from A 4.1/C 3.3), biscuit bread
> **Small Portable Objects:** *varies*: napkin *becomes* a handkerchief (2.2, dialogue); box of barber's tools includes a jointed syringe (4.1, dialogue); muff *becomes* a handkerchief (5.3, dialogue); *omits*: damask napkin, silver tankard (from A.4.1/C.3.3), cuts, letter (from A.4.4/C.4.3), warrant
> **Large Portable Objects:** *omits* staff (only from A 4.1/C 3.3)

COSTUMES
THRIFTY: a tufftaffeta jerkin (3.3, s.d.; removed on stage); a judicial robe (5.5, dialogue)
SPRUCE: a bandstring and a hat (1.1, dialogue); a curled periwig (2.1, dialogue); a cloak (2.1, dialogue; removed on stage); hangers (2.1, 4.2, implicit); a doublet (4.2, s.d.; removed and replaced on stage); breeches with a buttoned pocket (4.2, dialogue)
PETER: grogram garments (2.1, dialogue); a hat (5.3, s.d.; removed on stage)
WILD: possibly a hat (1.1, dialogue)
CRISP: a hat (4.2, dialogue)
STRIFE: a beard (dialogue)
CATCH: breeches (4.2, dialogue); hangers (4.2, implicit)
SNAP: a doublet (4.2, dialogue); hangers (4.2, implicit)
CARELESS, KILLMAN, and DINGTHRIFT: hangers (4.2, implicit)

> **C-Text**
> SPRUCE: *omits* cloak
> STRIFE: *omits* beard

2445. Masque of Lost Children and Comus

EARLY STAGE HISTORY
The prologue assumes performance on 'the public stage'.

EARLY TEXTUAL HISTORY
Mid-1630s (?): original version (A) written out in MS (**Ar**), probably by John Newdigate; 78 pages on 40 leaves; list of roles.

After 1634 (?): MS Ar (or a lost, cognate MS) was seen and commented upon by one 'Dr S.' (probably Gilbert Sheldon).

After 1634 (?): MS Ar was amended with reference to another MS (not now known to be extant), producing a revised version (B).

1640-2: a version with further revision (C) transcribed in MS (**W**); 27 leaves; list of roles.

The two extant MSS were later in the possession of, respectively, the Newdigate family of Arbury Hall, Warwickshire (Ar) and probably the Rolleston family of Watnall Hall, Nottinghamshire (W).

EDITIONS
Margaret Jane Kidnie, Malone Society Reprints 177 (Manchester, 2012).

C-Text
Jacqueline Jenkins and Mary Polito, Malone Society Reprints 178 (Manchester, 2012).

REFERENCES
Annals Supp. I; *Early Theatre* 12.1 (2009), 92–118; *Early Theatre* 14.2 (2011), 257–83; *EMS* 13 (2007), 187–211; *Renaissance Papers* (1989), 51–62.

2445. Masque of Lost Children and Comus

TEXT
Five substantive witnesses:

Br: MS (London: British Library, Loan MS 76); the 'Bridgewater MS'; derives from Trinity MS α, with further revisions; also includes music for five songs; has been presumed to be the state of the text used in the production;

O₁: printed in 1645 (Wing M2160); includes one minor revision and some errors;

O₂: printed in 1673 (Wing M2161); Milton's final revision of the text, with minor changes from the Q text and one line deleted;

Q: printed in 1637 (STC 17937); derives from Trinity MS β;

T: MS (Cambridge: Trinity College, MS R.34, pp. 13–29); the 'Trinity MS'; authorial working copy, possibly transcribed from an earlier draft, with three distinct states of revision: (α) early version, perhaps pre-performance; (β) revision conducted before the publication of Q in 1637; (γ) further minor revisions undertaken after 1637.

There are therefore essentially two versions of the masque as a public artefact:

A: performed version, represented in Br;
B: literary version, represented initially in Q, with minor revisions and variants in O₁ and O₂.

In addition, MS T represents a number of preliminary and intermediate states of textual development; in this entry, the record of variants in T is mostly limited to elements which are not present in either of the two public versions.

GENRE
pastoral masque
Contemporary: masque (t.p.); poem (Q epistle); 'dainty piece of entertainment' (Wotton)

TITLE
MS: *A Masque*
Later Assigned: *Comus*; *A Masque at Ludlow Castle*; *The Masque at Ludlow Castle*

Trinity MS
MS: *A Masque*

B-Text
Printed: *A Masque Presented at Ludlow Castle*
Contemporary: *A Masque performed before the President of Wales at Ludlow*

AUTHOR
John Milton

DATE
29 September 1634

ORIGINAL PRODUCTION
Earl of Bridgewater's household at Ludlow Castle, Shropshire

PLOT
A peer's children, two brothers and a lady, get lost in the woods on their way to join their father at his new court. Comus the enchanter is wont to tempt travellers in the wood, offering them his magic drink that will turn them into monsters. The Lady, separated from her brothers, follows the sound of merriment and meets Comus, who creates the magical illusion that he is a shepherd. Attracted to her, he offers her help and shelter, which she accepts.

Recognizing the danger, a guardian daemon has come down to earth to help. He too disguises himself as a shepherd, and warns the brothers that the Lady has been captured; they will be unable to rescue her with brute force alone, but need to carry a magic herb.

2445. Masque of Lost Children and Comus | 249

1634

At his palace, Comus traps the Lady in a magic chair and tempts her with arguments for hedonism; she offers counter-arguments for chastity. As he urges her to drink his liquor, her brothers rush in, break the vessel, and drive him and his followers away. Without Comus' wand to free her, the Lady remains stuck in the chair, but she is released by the river-goddess Sabrina, whom the daemon summons. The children are reunited with their parents: the daemon praises their ability to resist temptation, then returns home to the heavens.

SCENE DESIGNATION
sc.1–6 (all early texts undivided). The divisions reflect the clearing of the stage; scenery changes occur at sc.4–5 and sc.5–6.

> B-Text
> *adds* an epilogue

ROLES
A guardian DAEMON or attendant spirit; poses as a shepherd named Thyrsis
COMUS, a sorcerer, son of Bacchus and Circe; poses as a shepherd
MONSTERS, Comus' followers; male and female beings with human bodies and animal heads (sc.2, 5, *non-speaking*)
The LADY, a virgin, daughter of a peer, and a sister
The ELDER BROTHER of the Lady, son and heir of a peer
The SECOND BROTHER of the Lady, son of a peer
SABRINA, a virgin nymph; once daughter of King Locrine, now goddess of the River Severn
WATER NYMPHS attending Sabrina (sc.5, *non-speaking*)
SHEPHERDS, country dancers (sc.6, *non-speaking*)

> B-Text
> DAEMON: now primarily represented as a SPIRIT

Speaking Parts: 6

Stage Directions and Speech Prefixes
DAEMON: *A Guardian spirit, or Demon* | *the guardian demon* | *the Demon* (s.d.s); *Daemon* | *Demon* (s.p.s)
COMUS: *Comus* (s.d.s); *Co<mus>* (s.p.s)
MONSTERS: *a rout of monsters* | *[Comus'] rabble* (s.d.s)
LADY: *the Lady* (s.d.s); *Lady* (s.p.s)
ELDER BROTHER: [one of] *The two brothers* | [one of] *the brothers* | [one of] *The 2 brothers* (s.d.s); *Elder Brother* (s.p.s)
SECOND BROTHER: [one of] *The two brothers* | [one of] *the brothers* | [one of] *The 2 brothers* (s.d.s); *2 Brother* (s.p.s)
SABRINA: *Sabrina* (s.d.s); *Sab<rina>* (s.p.s)
WATER NYMPHS: *the water nymphs* (s.d.s)

Trinity MS
DAEMON: *A Guardian spirit, or Daemon* | *the guardian Daemon* | *the Daemon* (s.d.s); *Daemon* (s.p.s); *Shepherd* (deleted s.p.)
COMUS: *Comus* (s.d.s and s.p.s)
MONSTERS: *[Comus'] rout* | *komazontes* | *[Comus'] rabble* | *the shapes* (s.d.s); *the monsters* (deleted s.d.)
LADY: *the Lady* (s.d.s); *Lady* (s.p.s)
ELDER BROTHER: [one of] *the two brothers* | [one of] *The brothers* (s.d.s); *1 Brother* (s.p.s)
SECOND BROTHER: [one of] *the two brothers* | [one of] *The brothers* (s.d.s); *2 Brother* (s.p.s)
SABRINA: *Sabrina* (s.d.s); *Sa<brina>* (s.p.s)
WATER NYMPHS: *the water nymphs* (s.d.s)

B-Text
SPIRIT: *the attendant Spirit* | *the Spirit* (s.d.s); *Spirit* (s.p.s); *The attendant Spirit afterwards in the habit of Thyrsis* (O₁ d.p.)
COMUS: *Comus* (s.d.s, s.p.s, and O₁ d.p.)
MONSTERS: *a rout of Monsters* | *[Comus'] rabble* (s.d.s); *[Comus'] crew* (O₁ d.p.)
LADY: *the Lady* (s.d.s and O₁ d.p.); *Lady* (s.p.s); (O₁ d.p.)
ELDER BROTHER: [one of] *The two Brothers* | [one of] *The brothers* (s.d.s); *Elder Brother* (s.p.s); *1 Brother* (O₁ d.p.)
SECOND BROTHER: [one of] *The two Brothers* | [one of] *The brothers* (s.d.s); *2 Brother* (s.p.s and O₁ d.p.)
SABRINA: *Sabrina* (s.d.s); *Sab<rina>* (s.p.s); *Sabrina the Nymph* (O₁ d.p.)
WATER NYMPHS: *water Nymphs* (s.d.s)
SHEPHERDS: *Country Dancers* (s.d.s)

OTHER CHARACTERS
Jove, [ruler of the gods], who sent the Daemon to protect the lost children (sc.1)
Neptune, god of the sea (sc.1, 4)
Nether Jove, [god of the underworld] (sc.1)
The tributary gods, subsidiary rulers of Neptune's dominions (sc.1)
The father of the Lady and her Brothers, a peer, who rules nearby (sc.1, 4–6; represents the Earl of Bridgewater in the audience)
Bacchus, god of wine, Comus' father (sc.1, 4)
Mariners of Tuscany who landed on Circe's island (sc.1)
Circe, a nymph and enchantress, daughter of the Sun, Comus' mother (sc.1–4)
The three Sirens, Circe's attendants (sc.3)
Naiades, Circe's attendants (sc.3)
Thyrsis, a shepherd employed by the Lady's father; the Attendant Spirit assumes his identity (sc.4)
A shepherd lad, said to have taught herbal lore to the Daemon (sc.4)
Meliboeus, an old shepherd said to have told the Daemon about Sabrina (sc.5)

King Locrine, Sabrina's father (sc.5)
King Brut, Locrine's father (sc.5)
Gwendolen, Sabrina's wicked stepmother (sc.5)
Water-nymphs who rescued the drowning Sabrina (sc.5)
Nereus, who took pity on the drowned Sabrina (sc.5)
Nereus' daughters, who revived Sabrina (sc.5)
Shepherds, who laud and honour Sabrina at their festivals (sc.5)
Amphitrite, in whose bower Sabrina attends (sc.5)
Anchises, Sabrina's ancestor (sc.5)

SETTING
Period: implied to be contemporary
Time-Scheme: the action takes place during a single night
Place: woods near Ludlow

Geography
[*England*]: River Severn
Greece: Arcadia
[*Europe*]: the Celtic Fields (i.e. France); the Iberian Fields (i.e. Spain); Tuscany; Carpathian mountains
[*Mediterranean*]: the Tyrrhenian Sea; Circe's island (i.e. Aeaea)
The Atlantic Ocean
[*Asia*]: River Meander; Tyre
Africa: Egypt
India
The North Pole

> B-Text
> *Varies*: which pole is not specified

SOURCES
Narrative: Bible: Matthew 18.10–14 (Parable of the Lost Sheep; central conceit; it was the canonical reading for Michaelmas); Ovid, *Metamorphoses* 3 (sc.1; the George Sandys translation, printed in 1632, may have contributed some features of the Circe myth); Edmund Spenser, *The Faerie Queene* 2 (1590, repr. 1617; Sabrina); possibly George Peele, *The Old Wife's Tale* (**913**); Erycius Puteanus (Hendrik van der Putten), *Comus* (1608, repr. 1634); John Fletcher, *The Faithful Shepherdess* (**1582**; Sabrina); possibly Ben Jonson, *Pleasure Reconciled to Virtue* (**1854**; Comus); Aurelian Townshend, *Tempe Restored* (**2359**); Thomas Carew, *Coelum Britannicum* (**2428**; sc.6)
Verbal: Aeschylus, *Suppliants* (sc.1); Plato, *Phaedo* (sc.4); Cicero, *De finibus* (sc.5); Virgil, *Eclogues* 1 (sc.4), *Aeneid* 1 (sc.1), 9 (sc.1); Horace, *Odes* 2.3 (sc.4), 3.1 (sc.1); William Shakespeare, *The Tempest* (**1652**; sc.5)

> B-Text
> **Verbal:** Virgil, *Eclogues* 2 (Q t.p. motto), *Aeneid* 6 (ep.); Horace, *Odes* 1.34 (sc.5); Ovid, *Fasti* 5 (sc.3)

LANGUAGE
English

FORM
Metre: iambic pentameter; trochaic tetrameter (some of it catalectic); some trimeter and alexandrines; some stichomythia
Rhyme: blank verse and couplets; a little ABBA and ABAB
Lines (Spoken): 908
Lines (Written): 948

> Trinity MS
> **Lines (Spoken):** 951 (α); 991 (β)
> **Lines (Written):** 1,120

> B-Text
> **Epilogue:** 48 lines, in trochaic tetrameter catalectic couplets, spoken by the Spirit; *replaces Song 7*
> **Lines (Spoken):** 1,023 (Q & O_1); 1,022 (O_2)
> **Lines (Written):** 1,069 (Q)

STAGING
Within: halloo (sc.4, implicit/T s.d.)
Above: the Daemon may descend (sc.1, s.d. says he 'descends or enters')
Beneath: Sabrina and the Water Nymphs rise and descend again (sc.5, s.d.)
Audience: obliquely mentioned by the Daemon (sc.1, 5); the Earl and Countess of Bridgewater are directly addressed (sc.6)

MUSIC
Music: soft music (sc.5, s.d.)
Songs:
1: 'From the heavens now I fly', Daemon, 20 lines; there is an option either to sing or speak the lines; *musical setting survives*;
2: 'Sweet Echo, sweetest nymph that liv'st unseen', sc.3, Lady, 14 lines; *musical setting survives*;
3: 'Sabrina fair', sc.5, Daemon, 8 or 31 lines (the MS gives the option not to sing the last 23 lines); the longer version is sung by the Daemon and Brothers in parts; *musical setting survives*;
4: 'By the rushy-fringèd bank', sc.5, Sabrina and Daemon, in parts, 48 lines;
5: 'Back, shepherds, back, enough your play', sc.6, Daemon, 8 lines; *musical setting survives*;
6: 'Noble lord and lady bright', sc.6, Daemon, 10 lines; *musical setting survives*;
7: 'Now my task is smoothly done', sc.6, Daemon, 12 lines; there is an option either to sing or speak the lines; *musical setting survives*.
Dance: a measure danced by Comus and the Monsters, 'a wild, rude, and wanton antic' (sc.2, s.d.); the Shepherds dance (sc.6, implicit); unspecified characters dance (sc.6, s.d.)

Trinity MS
Songs:
  3: the notation 'to be said' appears after the first 8 lines, establishing where the song ends;
  7: now 34 (α) or 48 (β) lines; both states are marked with an option either to sing or speak the lines.

B-Text
Music: *omitted*
Songs:
  1: *omitted*;
  3: only the first 8 lines are explicitly marked as a song; the remaining 23 are spoken (or sung) by the Spirit alone;
  4: only the first 12 lines, sung by Sabrina, are explicitly marked as a song;
  7: *omitted*.
Dance: the measure in sc.2 is not specified as wild, rude, or wanton

PROPS
Lighting: torches (sc.2, s.d.)
Weapons: Brothers' swords (sc.4, dialogue; sc.5, s.d.)
Food and Drink: a glass of liquor (sc.2, 5, s.d.; broken on stage); dainties (sc.5, s.d.)
Small Portable Objects: a charming rod (sc.2, s.d.; sc.5, dialogue); 'magic dust' (sc.2, dialogue, sc.3, implicit)
Large Portable Objects: two or more tables (sc.5, s.d.); a marble chair (sc.5, s.d.)
Scenery: perhaps a curtain (sc.1, implicit; the first scene is said to be discovered); a wild wood (sc.1–4, s.d.); a stately palace (sc.5, s.d.); a prospect of Ludlow town and castle (sc.6, s.d.)
Miscellaneous: water drops (sc.5, dialogue)

COSTUMES
DAEMON: possibly sky-coloured or rainbow-coloured robes (sc.1, dialogue); dressed as a shepherd (sc.4, s.d.)
COMUS: possibly disguised as a shepherd or villager (sc.3, dialogue)
MONSTERS: animal heads (s.d.; dialogue specifies the animals as a wolf, bear, lynx, tiger, hog, and goat); 'glistering' clothes (sc.2, s.d.)
BROTHERS: have no facial hair (dialogue); hangers (sc.4–5, implicit)

Does Comus visibly adopt a disguise? There is no s.d. to say so (whereas the Daemon's costume change is specified), but it is also said that mere mortals will need a magic herb to see through his rustic appearance. The central issue is whether or not the audience is put in the position of sharing the Lady's visual delusion.

EARLY STAGE HISTORY
1634: performed on Monday 29 September (Michaelmas) in the Great Hall at Ludlow Castle. The cast included: Lady Alice Egerton (Lady); John Egerton, 2nd Viscount Brackley (Elder Brother); Thomas Egerton (Second Brother); Henry Lawes (Daemon). (Lawes was Lady Alice's music teacher.) The audience included: John Egerton, 1st Earl of Bridgewater (Lord Lieutenant of Wales); Frances Egerton, Countess of Bridgewater. Local town officials were invited, probably including Edward Colbatch (High Bailiff) and Thomas Crowther (Low Bailiff), and possibly Edward Berry. (Colbatch incurred expenses in connection with the visit: a 2s.6d gratuity to officers, and 16s.7d for a sugarloaf supplied by Berry; it is unclear whether the phrase 'being one of those was presented to the Countess' refers to Berry himself or the comestible, nor whether Berry was its procurer or the confectioner.)

It has been suggested that the cast also included Lady Mary Villiers as Sabrina, but (as discussed by John Creaser in *Milton Quarterly*, 2012) the hypothesis is problematic.

EARLY TEXTUAL HISTORY
1634 or 1637: John Milton transcribed an early draft in MS (**T**); 17 pages on 9 leaves. This may have been either shortly before the original production or in the autumn of 1637 with a view to publication.
  1634–7: MS (**Br**) made by a professional scribe; includes a note of the occasion and performers (the names of the latter being added in Henry Lawes's hand); later, John Egerton, 2nd Viscount Brackley, added the author's name to the title page. The copy was an early (α) state of MS T, or a transcript thereof.
  c. 1637: Milton made revisions to MS T.
  1634–7: a number of MS copies were made by Henry Lawes (who then sponsored the publication of the masque in order to satisfy the demand); none of these copies are now known to be extant.
  1637 (or possibly early 1638, before Sunday 25 March): ¹Q printed for Humphrey Robinson; collation A² B–E⁴ F², 20 leaves; dedicatory epistle to John Egerton, 2nd Viscount Brackley, signed by Henry Lawes; list of principal actors. The copy was an intermediate (β) state of MS T, or a transcript thereof.
  1637 or later; an unidentified hand (possibly Milton's) made nine MS corrections in a copy of Q (formerly owned by the Egerton family, and now at the University of Texas, Austin, pressmark Pforzheimer 714).
  1638: on Friday 6 April, Milton sent a copy of the masque, presumably Q, to Sir Henry Wotton, who had recently been his host at Eton College. Wotton had received it by Friday 13 April, when he wrote to thank Milton and commented on the poetry. He had already read the masque, he said, having been sent a copy by their mutual friend, 'Mr R.' (John Rouse, Bodley's Librarian?), bound in with a copy of the 1638 edition of Thomas Randolph's *Poems*.
  c. 1630s–40s: a copy of Q was in the possession of John Horne (Vicar of Headington, Oxfordshire). After

his death, his entire collection of play-books passed into the possession of John Houghton of Brasenose College, Oxford (c. 1608–77), then to James Herne (died 1685), and then to the library of Ralph Sheldon (1623–84) at Weston, where it was catalogued by Anthony Wood, probably in the late 1670s.

1637–45: Milton made further revisions to MS T, producing a third (γ) state of the text.

1639: On Monday 10 June, during a visit to Geneva, Milton wrote an extract (from sc.6, the last two lines of the masque) in the *liber amicorum* of Camillus Cardonius, a.k.a. Camillo Cerdagni of Naples (Cambridge, Mass.: Harvard, MS Sumner 84 (Lobby XI. 3. 43), p. 110).

1645: Milton's *Poems* entered in the Stationers' Register to Humphrey Moseley on Monday 6 October. Sir Nathaniel Brent had licensed the book for publication.

1645: included in Milton's *Poems* ($^2O_1$), sigs. $E2^r$–$H4^v$, 27 leaves; printed by Ruth Raworth for Humphrey Moseley; printed from an annotated copy of Q; adds letter to the author by Sir Henry Wotton and list of roles.

1645: *Poems* reissued.

1646: George Thomason bought a copy of O_1 on Friday 2 January. In c. 1678, some years after his death, his entire collection of books and tracts was acquired by the bookbinder Samuel Mearne, acting as agent for King Charles II; the King never paid him, and the books remained in Mearne's family until 1761.

Mid-seventeenth century (c. 1637–62): Songs 1–3, 5–7, with musical settings, included in Henry Lawes's autograph MS songbook (London: British Library, Add. MS 53723, fos. 37^r–39^v); includes MS notes the original context of the songs.

1650–60: Milton's *Poems* advertised as for sale by Humphrey Moseley.

c. 1655: extracts transcribed by John Evans in a miscellany, *Hesperides*, intended for publication and entered to Humphrey Moseley in the Stationers' Register on Thursday 16 August 1655. The book remained unpublished in 1660, and Evans continued adding to the collection until at least 1666. Two MS exemplars are known; one was cut up by J. O. Halliwell-Phillipps in the nineteenth century; the other survives (Washington: Folger, MS V. b. 93).

1658: transcribed from O_1 into a MS miscellany (New Haven: Yale, Osborn Collection b63, pp. 197–240); 22 leaves.

1673: included in Milton's *Poems, &c. Upon Several Occasions* ($^3O_2$), sigs. $F2^v$–$I1^r$, 46 pages on 24 leaves; printed during Michaelmas Term, probably by William Rawlins, for Thomas Dring; this edition removes all explicit reference to the Egerton family, and all the paratext (epistle, lists of roles and of actors, Wotton letter). The copy was O_1.

1673: *Poems, &c. upon Several Occasions* reissued twice.

1684: Nicholas Cox (Manciple of St Edmund Hall, Oxford) had a copy of Q in his bookshop. It had probably been previously owned by Gerard Langbaine, and appears on a list compiled by Anthony Wood on Saturday 13 December.

1691: MS T was probably given to Trinity College, Cambridge, by Sir Henry Puckering; at that time the MS was a collection of unbound papers.

Late seventeenth century: transcribed from a printed source into a MS verse miscellany (Montreal: McGill University, MS M90 Bd. 84, fos. 2–24); 23 leaves.

1695: included in Milton's *Poems Upon Several Occasions* (^4F), sigs. $C1^v$–$†D2^v$, 11 pages on 6 leaves; printed for Jacob Tonson.

1697: F incorporated into Jacob Tonson's edition of Milton's *Poetical Works*.

1697: *Poetical Works* reissued twice.

1698: translated into Latin by William Hog; ^TQ printed (as *Comoedia Ioannis Miltoni*); collation A–G^4, 28 leaves; title page names author and translator; translator's dedication and verses addressed to Sir Robert Harley.

1700: *Poetical Works* advertised as for sale by Jacob Tonson.

EDITIONS

Harris Francis Fletcher, in *John Milton's Complete Poetical Works Reproduced in Photographic Facsimile* (Urbana, 1943–8), i. 300–44.

John S. Diekhoff, in *A Maske at Ludlow: Essays on Milton's Comus* (Cleveland, Ohio, 1968), 207–40.

S. E. Sprott (Toronto, 1973).

Sabol, nos. 40–4 (songs and music only).

Trinity MS
Scolar Press facsimile (Menston Ilkley, 1970).
S. E. Sprott (Toronto, 1973).

B-Text

Frank Allen Patterson, in *The Works of John Milton*, Columbia edn (New York, 1931–8), i.1. 85–123.

Harris Francis Fletcher, in *John Milton's Complete Poetical Works Reproduced in Photographic Facsimile* (Urbana, 1943–8), i. 398–433.

Helen Darbishire, in John Milton, *The Poetical Works* (Oxford, 1952–5), ii. 171–203.

Geoffrey Bullough and Margaret Bullough, *Milton's Dramatic Poems* (London, 1958), 68–106, 178–96.

John T. Shawcross, in John Milton, *The Complete English Poetry* (New York, 1963), 87–115.

John Carey, in John Milton, *The Poems*, ed. John Carey and Alistair Fowler, Longman Annotated English Poets (London and New York, 1968), 168–229.

S. E. Sprott (Toronto, 1973).

REFERENCES

Annals 1634; Beal MnJ 57–64; Bentley, iv. 913–16; Bodleian, MS Wood E. 4, art. 1, p. 99; Cedric C. Brown,

John Milton's Aristocratic Entertainments (Cambridge, 1985); Butler, 374; Eyre & Rivington, ii. 8; Greg 524; Hazlitt, 46; *The Library*, 5th ser., 28 (1973), 294–308; *The Library*, 7th ser., 10 (2009), 372–404; David Lindley (ed.), *The Court Masque* (Manchester, 1984), 111–34; McGee-Meagher 1634–42, 28–31; *Milton Quarterly* 21 (1987), 24–34; *Milton Quarterly* 46 (2012), 15–20; *MLR* 13 (1918), 401–11; *N&Q* 204 (1959), 364; *PBSA* 54 (1960), 38–56, 293–4; *PMLA* 52 (1937), 705–27; *PMLA* 58 (1943), 948–57; REED: Shropshire, 113; *RES* 8 (1932), 170–6; Reyher, 531; John T. Shawcross, *Milton: A Bibliography for the Years 1624–1700* (Binghamton, New York, 1984) 35–8, 40, 70–1, 261, 313–15, 380–3, 394; Sir Henry Wotton, *Life and Letters*, ed. Logan Pearsall Smith (Oxford, 1907), ii. 381.

2446. Truth's Triumph

EVIDENCE
John Greene's diary.

TITLE
Performed: *Truth's Triumph*
Later Assigned: *Truth's Triumphs*

DATE
Limits: 1614–35

There is no way of knowing how old the play was when John Greene saw it in February 1635. If the play were dated to within a range set by the other datable plays Greene saw during the period covered by his diary, then the upper limit could extend as far back as 1597: most of his choices were old plays, ranging from *The Inconstant Lady* (**2293**) back to *The Merry Wives of Windsor* (**1079**); only in November, on a special occasion, did he certainly opt for newer fare. However, the only two Elizabethan plays on his list were performed by the King's Men, whereas this seems to have been a Cockpit play; the oldest play he saw there was *Wit without Money* (**1758**), which might pull the upper limit forward to 1614. An alternative procedure would be to date the play within a period defined by either the inception of its acting company (1625) or, since they inherited some of their repertory from their predecessors, the opening of the theatre itself (1616). The earliest of the three possible company- and playhouse-specific dates is adopted here as the upper limit.

The only grounds for guesswork within the resultant 21-year limits lie, paradoxically, in the very obscurity that makes the play so difficult to date inductively. It has left no other evidential traces, so there is no positive reason to believe that it was an 'old favourite' which had been a long time in the repertory. It was also not among the plays that William Beeston protected as part of the Cockpit repertory in 1639. It is theoretically possible that it was owned by the company or one of its members rather than the playhouse, and that they took it with them when they moved on in 1636; but there is no general evidence to support that hypothesis, and if Beeston's objective was to protect Cockpit plays he suspected might be in other hands (see **2133**), then the non-inclusion of this one suggests it may have been relict by 1639. The play's absence from the repertory in 1639 might therefore have been a matter of choice, perhaps because it was deemed to be of no further commercial value. This might support the view that it was a play with a relatively short lifespan, which Greene may have seen some months into its run.

ORIGINAL PRODUCTION
Queen Henrietta's Men at the Cockpit (?)

EARLY STAGE HISTORY
1635: performed on Saturday 21 February, probably by Queen Henrietta's Men at the Cockpit. The audience included John Greene.

REFERENCES
Annals 1635; Bentley, v. 1425–6; *English Historical Review* 43 (1928), 386; *MRDE* 6 (1993), 192; REED: Inns of Court, 810.

2447. Charles, Duke of Bourbon

EVIDENCE
Stationers' Register.

It is possible, but far from certain, that this is the same play as *Bourbon* (**1076**).

GENRE
tragedy
Contemporary: play, tragedy

TITLE
Contemporary: *Charles, Duke of Bourbon*

DATE
Limits: before 1641

See discussion under **2323**. If the play originated in the commercial theatre, the plot, which turns in part on treason plotted during the King's absence at war, might have hit censorship difficulties during the Bishops' Wars in 1639 or 1640.

PLOT
The King of France passes over Charles, Duke of Bourbon, for an honourable military office. The resentment this causes is compounded when Bourbon's legal claim to inherit the duchy's lands as well as its title is denied by the Crown. He conspires with the Holy Roman Emperor to bring an invading army into France while the King is away at war in Italy. The King learns of the plot and confronts Bourbon, who denies it, but then leaves France disguised as a servant and rendezvouses with the Imperial lance-knights. In the ensuing battles, the French King is taken prisoner by the Emperor. Bourbon subsequently leads the Imperial troops to conquer Rome, but is shot dead during the siege.

The reconstruction assumes that the title character was the third Duke of Bourbon to be named Charles. His two predecessors held the title respectively in 1434–56 and 1488, but offer less promising material for dramatization.

ROLES
FRANCIS, King of France
Charles, Duke of BOURBON, Constable of France; poses as a servant
The Holy Roman EMPEROR

SETTING
Period: sixteenth century; the play dramatizes events from the life of Charles, Duke of Bourbon (1490–1527)
Place: France and Italy

Geography
France: Bourbon
Germany
Italy: Milan; Rome

SOURCES
Narrative: probably Jean de Serres, *A General Inventory of the History of France*, tr. Edward Grimestone (1607, rev. 1622)

PROPS
Weapons: an arquebus

EARLY TEXTUAL HISTORY
1641: entered in the Stationers' Register to John Nicholson on Thursday 15 April; individually named as part of a group entry of three plays. Thomas Wykes had licensed the book for publication.

REFERENCES
Annals 1641; Bentley, v. 1302; Greg Θ50.

2448. The Triumphs of Fame and Honour

TEXT
Printed in 1634 (STC 23808).

GENRE
civic pageant
Contemporary: 'the Lord Mayor's show' (S.R.); pageants, shows, and triumphs (t.p.)

TITLE
Printed: *The Triumphs of Fame and Honour*
Later Assigned: *Device for Robert Parkhurst, Clothworker*

AUTHOR
John Taylor

DATE
29 October 1634

ORIGINAL PRODUCTION
London Clothworkers' Company, in the city streets. Route: River Thames, near Paul's Wharf; St Paul's Churchyard; Little Conduit, Cheapside; Lawrence Lane End in Cheapside; the Lord Mayor's house.

PLOT
En route by river to his inauguration, the new Lord Mayor of London is met by a barge containing Thetis, who sends London imported merchandise with every tide. She promises to continue her bounty if the Lord Mayor will have the Thames dredged to clear her of shelves and sandbanks. The barge returns to Paul's Wharf while the Lord Mayor makes his way to Westminster.

After his return, he meets Time and Mercury in St Paul's Churchyard. Time commends his love for Truth, and hopes he will continue to defend her during his year in office. In his honour, Mercury has endowed the author of the entertainment with wit and eloquence, and given creativity to the scenic artists who made the pageants. In the next pageant, London remarks on her own freedom from war and tyranny, in contrast with Germany, and encourages the city apprentices to work hard. The next pageant is the Tower of Honour, which shows the hierarchy of city, church, law, and army under the King. Honour explains that, through obedience, patience, diligence, and virtue, lowly members of these estates can eventually attain high office, and encourages the Lord Mayor to rule with both justice and mercy.

The Lord Mayor proceeds along Cheapside, and meets Endymion, who asserts the honour and economic importance of both shepherds and clothworkers. There is a dance of shepherds.

All the pageants follow the Lord Mayor home from St Paul's Cathedral that night. Fame blows a silver trumpet to commemorate former Lord Mayors of the Clothworkers' Company. Time names them, and encourages the new Lord Mayor to rule with honour so that he may join their company.

SCENE DESIGNATION
1–6 (O numbers 1–3 only), as follows:
  1: Thetis, on the Thames;
  2: Time and Mercury, in St Paul's Churchyard;
  3: London, in St Paul's Churchyard;
  4: the Tower of Honour, at the Little Conduit;
  5: Endymion, at Lawrence Lane End;
  6: The Monument of Fame, at night.

ROLES
THETIS, goddess of the sea
THAMES, one of Thetis' fairest daughters; also called Thamesis (1, *non-speaking*)
Two SAILORS, who row Thetis' barge (1, *non-speaking*)

1634

Two WATERMEN, who row Thetis' barge (1, *non-speaking*)
TIME, an old man
MERCURY, messenger of the gods; also called Hermes (2, *non-speaking*)
ANTIQUITY (3, *non-speaking*)
RECORD (3, *non-speaking*)
MEMORY (3, *non-speaking*)
WISDOM (3, *non-speaking*)
Unspecified ALLEGORICAL FIGURES (3, *non-speaking*)
LONDON, Queen of Cities, an ancient matron
A KING (4, *non-speaking*)
A LORD MAYOR (4, *non-speaking*)
A BISHOP (4, *non-speaking*)
A JUDGE or lawyer (4, *non-speaking*)
A GENERAL or captain (4, *non-speaking*)
HONOUR, a male figure attending the Lord Mayor
PIETY, or the Fear of God, attending the Bishop (4, *non-speaking*)
POWER, attending the Judge (4, *non-speaking*)
VICTORY, attending the General (4, *non-speaking*)
An APPRENTICE, placed under the Lord Mayor (4, *non-speaking*)
OBEDIENCE, attending the Apprentice (4, *non-speaking*)
A SCHOLAR, placed under the Bishop (4, *non-speaking*)
PATIENCE, attending the Scholar (4, *non-speaking*)
A CLERK, placed under the Judge (4, *non-speaking*)
DILIGENCE, attending the Clerk (4, *non-speaking*)
A COMMON SOLDIER, placed under the General (4, *non-speaking*)
VIRTUE, attending the Common Soldier (4, *non-speaking*)
JUSTICE, a cardinal virtue (4, *non-speaking*)
FORTITUDE, a cardinal virtue (4, *non-speaking*)
TEMPERANCE, a cardinal virtue (4, *non-speaking*)
PRUDENCE, a cardinal virtue (4, *non-speaking*)
ENDYMION, a shepherd
SHEPHERDS, who dance (5, *non-speaking*)
FAME (6, *non-speaking*)

The text is inconsistent about the gender of Fame: a feminine pronoun is used in the description, but a masculine one in the dialogue.

Speaking Parts: 5
Allegorical Roles: 20 (plus the unspecified ones)

Stage Directions
THETIS: *Thetis (the Goddess of the Sea)* | *Thetis* (s.d.s)
THAMES: *Thames, or Thamisis (one of* [Thetis'] *fairest daughters)* | *Thamisis* (s.d.s)
SAILORS: [two of] *the Rowers* | *two Sailors* (s.d.s)
WATERMEN: [two of] *the Rowers* | *two watermen* (s.d.s)
TIME: *Time* (s.d.s)
MERCURY: *Mercury* (s.d.s)
ANTIQUITY: *Antiquity* (s.d.s)
RECORD: *Record* (s.d.s)
MEMORY: *Memory* (s.d.s)
WISDOM: *Wisdom* (s.d.s)
ALLEGORICAL FIGURES: *others* (s.d.s)
LONDON: *an ancient Matron* | *London* (s.d.s)
KING: *one in royal robes* (s.d.s)
LORD MAYOR: *a Lord Mayor* | *the Lord Mayor* (s.d.s)
BISHOP: *a Bishop* | *the Bishop* (s.d.s)
JUDGE: *a Lawyer* | *the Judge* (s.d.s)
GENERAL: *a warlike Captain or General* | *the General or Captain* | *the Lord General* (s.d.s)
HONOUR: *Honour* (s.d.s)
PIETY: *piety or the fear of God* (s.d.s)
POWER: *a figure representing power* (s.d.s)
VICTORY: *victory* (s.d.s)
APPRENTICE: *an apprentice* (s.d.s)
OBEDIENCE: *obedience* (s.d.s)
SCHOLAR: *a scholar* (s.d.s)
PATIENCE: *patience* (s.d.s)
CLERK: *a clerk* (s.d.s)
DILIGENCE: *diligence* (s.d.s)
COMMON SOLDIER: *a Common Soldier* (s.d.s)
VIRTUE: *virtue* (s.d.s)
JUSTICE: [one of] *the four prime or Cardinal Virtues* | *Justice* (s.d.s)
FORTITUDE: [one of] *the four prime or Cardinal Virtues* | *Fortitude* (s.d.s)
TEMPERANCE: [one of] *the four prime or Cardinal Virtues* | *Temperance* (s.d.s)
PRUDENCE: [one of] *the four prime or Cardinal Virtues* | *Prudence* (s.d.s)
ENDYMION: *Endimion, or a shepherd* | *the shepherd* | *Endimion* (s.d.s)
SHEPHERDS: *shepherds* (s.d.s)
FAME: *Fame* (s.d.s)

OTHER CHARACTERS
The daughters of Thetis: Danubius, Ister, Rhine, Po, Maine, Seine, Volga, Ems, Elve, Tanais, Tigris, Nilus, Ganges, Euphrates, Tiber, Jordan, Xanthus, Indus, and Tagus (1)
Truth, Time's loveliest daughter (2)

SETTING
Geography
London: River Thames
England
Germany: River Rhine; River Maine; River Ems; River Elbe
[France]: River Seine
[Italy]: River Po; River Tiber; Rome
[Spain]: River Tagus; Numantia
[Greece]: Thebes; Arcadia
[Europe]: River Danube (a.k.a. Ister); River Volga; River Tanais
[Africa]: River Nile; Carthage
Turkey: River Xanthus; Constantinople
[The Holy Land]: River Jordan; the Dead Sea; Jerusalem
[Asia]: River Tigris; River Euphrates; Babylon
[India]: River Ganges; River Indus

2448. The Triumphs of Fame and Honour

SOURCES
Verbal: John Taylor, *Taylor's Pastoral* (1624; 5)
Works Mentioned: Edmund Spenser, *The Shepherd's Calendar* (1579; 5); Christopher Marlowe, *Tamburlaine* (**784**; 5)

LANGUAGE
English

FORM
Metre: pentameter
Rhyme: couplets
Lines (Spoken): 246
Lines (Written): 476

STAGING
Stage: pageant stages (3–6)
Audience: addressed as 'worthy troop' (1); the Lord Mayor is directly addressed, including as 'my lord' (2–4, 6) and 'my honoured lord' (5)

MUSIC
Music: drums and trumpets (4, dialogue)
On-Stage Music: Fame plays the trumpet (6, desc.)
Dance: the Sailors and Watermen dance a rugged friskin (1, desc.); Shepherds dance (5, desc.)

PROPS
Weapons: a scythe (2, desc.)
Musical Instruments: a silver trumpet (6, desc.)
Animals: a large whelk adorned with strange fishes 'and other significant representations' (1, desc.); two gryphons (2, desc.; mounts for Time and Mercury); a ram crested with gold (5, desc.; Endymion's mount)
Food and Drink: cans of liquor (1, desc.; drunk during the action); leather bottles of liquor (5, desc.; drunk during the action)
Small Portable Objects: a caduceus (2, desc.); an orb (4, desc.)
Large Portable Objects: four oars (1, desc.); a sceptre (4, desc.)
Scenery: a barge with arms and impresas of the City of London and the Clothworkers' Company, and loaded with packs, dryfats, and other mercantile cargo (1, desc.; rowed by four men, seats two other characters; later carried as a pageant through the streets); a city, with walls, battlements, gates, churches, towers, steeples, tall buildings, shops, human figures, and scutcheons of the City of London and the Clothworkers' Company on the walls (3, desc.; the pageant carries at least seven characters, one of whom is seated in one of the gates); a square pageant with a round three-storey tower (4, desc.; carries 21 characters, including at least eight seated in the tower, four seated at the four corners, the rest standing in the tower); an ancient, ruined monument of fame, decorated with arms and scutcheons of nine former Lord Mayors (5–6, desc.)

Taylor says the pageants are 'six in number', presumably including the barge and two gryphons as well as the three conventional pageants.

COSTUMES
THETIS: a sea-green mantle, with a coronet of different kinds of sea-shells (1, desc.)
THAMES: a white or silver robe; a chaplet of green reeds, flowers, and rushes; sedge, bulrushes, and flags around her feet (1, desc.)
TIME: a blue robe (2, desc.)
MERCURY: wings on his head and feet (2, desc.)
LONDON: a civil grave robe, and long dishevelled hair down her back (3, desc.)
KING: a royal robe and crown (4, desc.)
JUSTICE, FORTITUDE, TEMPERANCE, and **PRUDENCE:** emblematic robes (4, desc.)

EARLY STAGE HISTORY
Preparation: On Sunday 10 August 1634, the Clothworkers' Company appointed a committee to help and advise on the entertainment. The members were: Edward Claxton (Warden), Mr Heath, Thomas Austen, Mr Browne, Mr Holmes, Mr Hodges, Mr Evans, and Mr Hough. At the same time, another committee (consisting of Hodges, Evans, Hough, and Mr Monger) was appointed to choose members of the Company to attend on the day and to contribute towards the cost of the production. On an unspecified date, the Master and Wardens, with Evans, Hodges, and Hough, met with Robert Norman, Zachary Taylor, and others to discuss the pageants, and afterwards dined at Clothworkers' Hall at a cost of £1.4s.5d. There was a subsequent meeting at the hall with Taylor and Norman, with Claxton, Monger, Hodges, Evans, and Hough in attendance; the committee then dined at Foyes' Ordinary, at a cost of £1.8s.2d. On Thursday 4 September, the Court of Aldermen agreed that rooms in the Greenyard in Leadenhall could be used for the preparation of the pageants.

Invitations: Anzolo Correr (incoming Venetian Ambassador) was invited to be present, but excused himself on the grounds that he had not yet taken up his appointment. (He had arrived in England only a fortnight before the event.) Juan de Necolalde (Spanish Agent) and Henry Taylor (Flemish Agent) were also invited, but did not attend. Jacques d'Angennes, Marquis of Pougny (French Ambassador) was invited and intended to come, but failed to provide himself with a house or stand in Cheapside to watch the pageants. On Tuesday 28 October he asked Sir John Finet (Master of Ceremonies) to help him find one; but Finet was only able to provide a stand for him to watch the procession to St Paul's Cathedral after the formal dinner at the Guildhall; he was allowed to watch the water pageant from Denmark House.

Performance: in London on Wednesday 29 October 1634 at the inauguration of Robert Parkhurst as Lord Mayor. The production designer was Robert Norman, who was assisted by the sculptor Zachary Taylor. The performance took place at intervals throughout the day, from morning to evening. The audience included: Jean d'Angennes, Marquis of Pougny (French Ambassador); Albert Joachimi (Dutch Ambassador).

Presumably Thomas Heywood, the usual writer of Lord Mayors' pageants at this time, did not tender this year because he was otherwise engaged with his court commission for *Love's Mistress* (**2451**).

Production Expenses
The total cost of the production was £147.12s.8d.

EARLY TEXTUAL HISTORY
1634: entered in the Stationers' Register to Henry Gosson on Tuesday 14 October; entry names author.
1634: **O** printed for Henry Gosson; collation presumably A–B⁸, 16 leaves (though the only surviving copy lacks A1 and B7–8, which were probably blank); title page refers to performance and names author; verse dedication to Robert Parkhurst; explanatory notes on the mythological and geographical allusions.

EDITION
J. Caitlin Finlayson, MSC 17 (Manchester, 2016 for 2015), 111–50.

REFERENCES
Annals 1634; Arber, iv. 328; Bentley, v. 1225; Bergeron, 212–16; *Bulletin of the John Rylands Library* 41 (1958–9), 501–31; *Cal. Ven.* 1632–6, 296; Greg 495; Hazlitt, 234; Loomie, 168–9; McGee-Meagher 1634–42, 31–3; MSC 5, 13–14; Withington, ii. 41–2.

2449. *The Queen's Exchange*

TEXT
Printed in 1657 (Wing B4882), probably from authorial foul papers.

The clearest sign of foul papers is the inconsistency in the identification of the lords. Elfride (of Wessex) does not appear in the opening s.d., and disappears after 1.1; his name only ever appears unabbreviated in the d.p. (which is not authorial, as is clear from the inclusion of Alberto and the hermit as two distinct characters). The Northumbrian lords are sometimes named and sometimes numbered, and the lord consistently named Ethelbert in the first four acts becomes Ethelred in the fifth.

GENRE
tragicomedy
Contemporary: play (prol.); comedy (t.p.); poem (epistle)

TITLE
Printed: *The Queen's Exchange*
Later Assigned: *The Royal Exchange*

AUTHOR
Richard Brome

DATE
Limits: 1633–5
Best Guess: 1634

The sequence in 2.2 in which the country Clowns are forbidden their sports by royal command is a sardonic inversion of the contemporary toleration of pastimes in the *Book of Sports* promulgated in October 1633.

ORIGINAL PRODUCTION
King's Men at the Blackfriars (?)

In his epistle, the stationer says of the play, 'when 'twas written, or where acted, I know not', so some doubt necessarily attaches to the Stationers' Register and title-page assertion of its Blackfriars provenance. Even so, there is a striking concentration of narrative overlap with plays from the King's Men's back catalogue, which means it 'feels' like a part of their repertory—which might, of course, be the basis for a mistaken attribution as well as a correct one. An alternative hypothetical attribution, proposed by Marion O'Connor, is Prince Charles's Men at the Red Bull, which is not implausible save for the fact that Brome is not otherwise known to have worked for that company.

PLOT
Bertha succeeds to the throne of Wessex, and, contrary to her father's will, accepts a proposal of marriage from Osric, King of Northumbria. Segebert urges the danger of subjecting one nation's laws to another's, and Bertha banishes him. Taking his leave of his family, he decrees that his younger son, Offa, shall inherit his estate after his death (the elder son, Anthynus, is only to receive an annuity), and he commands his daughter, Mildred, to give up her liaison with the Northumbrian ambassador, Theodric. Anthynus chooses to join his father in exile.

Bertha and Osric have exchanged pictures; but when Theodric shows Osric Mildred's picture, he finds her more beautiful, starts to have second thoughts about the marriage, and falls into a melancholy. Celebratory bonfires are cancelled, and one of the local clowns, Jeffrey, is appointed court fool in an attempt to cheer up the gloomy King. Osric banishes Theodric for causing his malady, recalls the banished Lord Ethelswick to court, and plans to go on a pilgrimage, which is really cover for a visit to Mildred; Ethelswick is appointed to rule in his absence.

Segebert and Anthynus make their way to Northumbria so that Segebert can speak his mind to Osric, but they are attacked en route by Offa and his men. Anthynus beats off the attackers and takes Offa's sword, but Segebert is wounded, and Anthynus goes for help. Recognizing the sword, Segebert realizes that he has misjudged his two sons. He is taken away by a hermit. Anthynus returns to find him gone, sees a vision of the past kings of Wessex, who point to him as the next in line, and then falls into a deep sleep. He is found by two courtiers who mistake him for Osric, and is brought to court. Osric sees the opportunity for a substitution: while he is away, Anthynus can sleep in his bed and continue to be taken for him. When Anthynus eventually wakes up, the Northumbrian courtiers take his protestations about his true identity as insanity. Ethelswick is banished for driving the King mad, and Bertha summoned in an effort to cure him. Anthynus' genius encourages him to go along with it, and when Bertha arrives they are married.

After receiving assurance that his father and brother are dead, Offa locks his accomplices in a dungeon. He tries incestuously to seduce Mildred, who says she would commit suicide rather than submit. Her nurse tells Offa that she is not really his sister, but another noblewoman's daughter substituted for a stillborn baby. Osric arrives, but is taken for Anthynus and imprisoned for Segebert's murder. That night, three burglars, dressed as devils, attempt to rob Offa's jewel-house, but only find the starving outlaws. They meet Mildred, who is trying to abscond, and hide her under their costumes to smuggle her out of the house; then they meet Offa, on his way to rape Mildred, and their diabolic appearance drives him mad with fear. Ethelswick and his allies arrive in Wessex to find Osric in prison, thought to be Anthynus and accused of Segebert's murder. Mildred is attracted to him and, believing herself not to be Anthynus' sister, asks to marry him, but her nurse tells her that the story of her adoption was a lie to discourage Offa's incestuous passion: Anthynus really is her brother, so she cannot marry him. The real Anthynus arrives in Wessex with Bertha and reveals his true identity. Segebert arrives with the hermit who healed his wounds, and who is actually his banished friend Alberto. The sentences are repealed and the true malefactors are granted mercy; Anthynus becomes King of Wessex, and Osric is to marry Mildred.

SCENE DESIGNATION
prol., 1.1–2, 2.1–4, 3.1–3, 4.1–2, 5.1–4 (Q has full act-division and scene-division up to 2.3; remaining scene-division O'Connor)

The stage is clear during 2.4.

ROLES
PROLOGUE
CELERIC, a lord of Wessex
ELKWIN, a lord of Wessex
ELFRIDE, a lord of Wessex
Lord SEGEBERT, a baron of Wessex, an old widower, father of Anthynus, Offa, and Mildred
Queen BERTHA of Wessex, Kenwalcus' daughter; betrothed to Osric, later Anthynus' wife
ATTENDANTS on Bertha (1.1, 4.2; only speak collectively in 1.1, if at all)
THEODRIC, a young, unmarried courtier, Osric's favourite, Northumbrian ambassador to Wessex

Lord ANTHYNUS, Segebert's elder son and rightful heir, brother of Offa and Mildred; he is physically similar to Osric (but the parts cannot be doubled); later Bertha's husband and King of Wessex
OFFA, Segebert's younger son and appointed heir, brother of Anthynus and Mildred
Lady MILDRED, Segebert's daughter, sister of Anthynus and Offa; 16 years old
King OSRIC of Northumbria; betrothed to Bertha, and later to Mildred; he is physically similar to Anthynus
THEODWALD, a lord of the Northumbrian council, Theodric's enemy
Lord EAUFRIDE of Northumbria
ALFRIDE, a lord of Northumbria, a gentleman and a courtier
ETHELBERT, a lord of Northumbria; Brome may also have considered the alternative name Ethelred
Two LORDS of the Northumbrian court (2.1; may be coextensive with two of the preceding four lords)
ATTENDANTS at Osric's court (2.1, 4.2; one speaks in 2.1, or all collectively)
Four CLOWNS of Northumbria
JEFFREY, a Northumbrian clown; later Osric's fool
A CONSTABLE of Northumbria
Three OUTLAWS, Offa's accomplices
An old HERMIT; in reality Lord Alberto, a banished lord of Wessex; also called Albert
The Hermit's SERVANT (2.3–4)
An ECHO (2.4, within)
Lord ETHELSWICK of Northumbria, an old man, court favourite of Osric's father
A PHYSICIAN attending Osric
The ghosts of six SAXON KINGS of Wessex, including King Kenwalcus, Bertha's father (3.2, non-speaking)
Two ATTENDANTS on Alfride and Ethelbert (3.2, non-speaking)
EDITH, Mildred's old nurse
A GUARD at the Northumbrian court (4.2, non-speaking)
Two ATTENDANTS at the Northumbrian court (4.2, non-speaking)
Anthynus' GENIUS (4.2; whispers, but has no scripted lines)
USHERS at the wedding (4.2, non-speaking)
A CARDINAL at the wedding (4.2, non-speaking)
Two LADIES at the wedding (4.2, non-speaking)
Four SERVANTS in Offa's household (5.1; only one speaks)
ARNOLD, an old man, Offa's servant
A CARPENTER, a thief
A MASON, a thief
A SMITH, a thief
The KEEPER of the prison (5.3–4)
A GUARD on Osric (5.4, non-speaking)

Speaking Parts: 36–9

Stage Directions and Speech Prefixes
PROLOGUE: *Prologue* (heading)

CELERIC: *Celerick | Kelriick |* [one of] *the four Lords |* [one of] *the Lords | Kelrick* (s.d.s); *Celr<ick>* (s.d.s and s.p.s); | *Kelr<ick>* (s.p.s; also misprinted *Colr.*); *Kelrick,* [one of] *three sycophant Lords* (d.p.)

ELKWIN: *Elkwin |* [one of] *the four Lords |* [one of] *the Lords* (s.d.s); *Elkw<in>* (s.p.s); *Elkwine,* [one of] *three sycophant Lords* (d.p.)

ELFRIDE: *Elf<ride>* (s.d.s); *Elfr<ride>* (s.p.s); *Elfride,* [one of] *three sycophant Lords* (d.p.)

SEGEBERT: *Segebert* (s.d.s); *Seg<ebert>* (s.p.s); *Segebert,* [one of] *two banished Lords* (d.p.)

BERTHA: *Bertha | the Queen | the Queen Bertha* (s.d.s); *Bert<ha> | Bart<ha>* (s.p.s); *Bertha, Queen of West Saxons* (d.p.)

ATTENDANTS: *Attendants | Followers* (s.d.s)

THEODRIC: *Ambassador* (s.d.s and s.p.s); *Theodrick* (s.d.s); *Theodr<ick>* (s.p.s); *Theodrick,* [Osric's] *Favourite and Ambassador* (d.p.)

ANTHYNUS: *Anthynus* (s.d.s; also misprinted *Apthynus*); *Anth<ynus>* (s.p.s); *Anthynus,* [one of] *Segebert's Sons* (d.p.)

OFFA: *Offa* (s.d.s and s.p.s); *Offa,* [one of] *Segebert's Sons* (d.p.)

MILDRED: *Mildred |* [one of] *the women* (s.d.s); *Mild<red>* (s.p.s); *Mildred, Segebert's daughter, Osriick's Queen* (d.p.)

OSRIC: *Osriick the King | the King | Osriick* (s.d.s); *King* (s.d.s and s.p.s); *Osr<iick>* (s.p.s); *Osriick, King of Northumbria* (d.p.)

THEODWALD: *Theodwald |* [one of] *the four Lords |* [one of] *the Lords* (s.d.s); *Theodw<ald> | 1 Lord or 2 Lord* (s.p.s); *Theodwald,* [one of the] *lords of* [Osric's] *Council* (d.p.)

EAUFRIDE: *Eaufrid | Eaufride |* [one of] *the four Lords |* [one of] *the Lords* (s.d.s); *2 Lord or 1 Lord | Eaufr<ide>* (s.p.s); *Eaufride,* [one of the] *lords of* [Osric's] *Council* (d.p.)

ALFRIDE: *Alfrid | Alfride* (s.d.s); *Alfr<ide> | 3 Lord* (s.p.s); *Alfride,* [one of the] *lords of* [Osric's] *Council* (d.p.)

ETHELBERT: *Ethelbert | Edelbert | Edelred* (s.d.s); *4 Lord | Edel<bert>* (s.p.s); *Edelbert,* [one of the] *lords of* [Osric's] *Council* (d.p.)

LORDS: *2 Lords | Lords* (s.d.s); *1 Lord | 2 Lord* (s.p.s)

ATTENDANTS: *Attendants* (s.d.s); *Attendant* (s.p.s)

CLOWNS: *4 Clowns* (s.d.s and d.p.s); *1 | 2 | 3 | 4* (s.p.s)

JEFFREY: *Jeffrey* (s.d.s); *Jeff<rey>* (s.p.s); *Jeffrey, the King's fool* (d.p.)

CONSTABLE: *a Constable* (s.d.s); *Constable* (s.p.s)

OUTLAWS: *Outlaws | the other | the Outlaws | 2 Outlaws | Outlaw | an Outlaw* (s.d.s); *1 Outlaw* (s.d.s and s.p.s); *Outlaw | 2 Outlaw | 1 | 2* (s.p.s)

HERMIT: *a Hermit | Alberto* (s.d.s); *Hermit* (s.d.s, s.p.s, and d.p.); *Alberto,* [one of] *two banished Lords* (d.p.)

SERVANT: *Servant* (s.d.s and s.p.s); [Hermit's] *Servant* (d.p.)

ECHO: *Echo* (s.p.s)

ETHELSWICK: *Ethelswick* (s.d.s); *Eth<elswick>* (s.p.s); *Ethelswick,* [Osric's] *Substitute* (d.p.)

PHYSICIAN: *Physician* (s.d.s and s.p.s); *A Physician* (d.p.)

SAXON KINGS: *six Saxon Kings' ghosts | the first | the second | the third | the last* (s.d.s)

ATTENDANTS: *two followers* (s.d.s)

EDITH: *Edith |* [one of] *the women* (s.d.s); *Ed<ith>* (s.p.s); *Edith, Mildred's Nurse* (d.p.)

GUARD: *Guard* (s.d.s)

ATTENDANTS: *2 Attendants* (s.d.s)

GENIUS: *Genius* (s.d.s)

USHERS: *Ushers* (s.d.s)

CARDINAL: *a Cardinal | the Cardinal* (s.d.s)

LADIES: *two Ladies* (s.d.s)

SERVANTS: *four Servants* (s.d.s); *Servant* (s.p.s)

ARNOLD: *Arnold* (s.d.s); *Arn<old>* (s.p.s); *Arnold, an old servant of Offa* (d.p.)

CARPENTER: *Carpenter* (s.d.s and s.p.s); *A Carpenter,* [one of] *three Thieves* (d.p.)

MASON: *Mason* (s.d.s and s.p.s); *A Mason,* [one of] *three Thieves* (d.p.)

SMITH: *Smith* (s.d.s and s.p.s); *A Smith,* [one of] *three Thieves* (d.p.)

KEEPER: *Keeper* (s.d.s and s.p.s); *Keeper of Prison* (d.p.)

GUARD: *Guard* (s.d.s)

In 3.1, the four named Northumbrian lords—Theodwald, Eaufride, Alfride, and Ethelbert—are given speech prefixes identifying them by number ('1 Lord', etc.) rather than by name. The third is addressed as Alfride, and the fourth is addressed as Ethelbert, in dialogue which sets up the hunting expedition on which they are seen in the following scene. There is no clue as to which of the remaining two is which.

OTHER CHARACTERS
The people of Wessex, Bertha's subjects (1.1)
The ladies of Bertha's court (1.1, 2.1)
Waiters and officers appointed by Osric to serve Bertha's picture (1.1)
Segebert's neighbours, friends, and enemies (1.2)
Segebert's dead wife, mother of his children (1.2, 4.1)
The people of Northumbria, Osric's subjects (2.1, 3.3)
Bertha's limner (2.1)
Osric's doctors (2.1, 3.1; one appears on stage)
The churchwarden of the Clowns' parish (2.2)
The curate of the Clowns' parish (2.2)
The Clowns' masters, who begrudged them wood for the bonfires (2.2)
The local Northumbrian girls (2.2, 4.2)
The Third Clown's mother (2.2)
A guard on Theodric (3.1)
The former King of Northumbria, Osric's dead father (3.1)
Osric's ancestors (3.3)
Offa's butler, reputed to be a Lothario (5.2)
Offa's dairymaid (5.2)
The Mason's three bastard children (5.2)
A pregnant woman carrying the Mason's fourth bastard (5.2)

A priest in the prison (5.3)
Prisoners who made merry with the priest (5.3)

SETTING
Period: eighth century AD; the action nominally takes place during the reign of King Osric of Northumbria (718–29)
Time-Scheme: enough time passes between 1.1 and 2.1 for Theodric to travel from Wessex to Northumbria; 3.2 takes place three days after 2.3–4 and at least four days after 2.1; 3.3 takes place at night; 4.1 and 5.1 take place on the same day, and 5.2 the following night; a few days pass between 4.2 and 5.4
Place: England

Geography
England: Wessex; Northumbria
Africa

SOURCES
Narrative: William Shakespeare, *King Lear* (**1486**; Segebert plot, Jeffrey), *Macbeth* (**1496**; 3.2); John Webster, *The Duchess of Malfi* (**1726**; 4.2); Thomas Middleton, *Women, Beware Women* (**1981**; 4.1); Philip Massinger, *The Picture* (**2273**; 1.1, 2.1, 5.2); possibly James Shirley, *The Triumph of Peace* (**2423**; 4.2)
Verbal: Virgil, *Aeneid* 1 (Latin motto at foot of text); Horace, *Ars poetica* (epistle); Ovid, *Fasti* 6 (t.p. motto, adapted); Baptista Mantuanus, *Eclogues* 3 (written *c.* 1465, printed 1498; t.p. motto); William Shakespeare, *Macbeth* (**1496**; 3.1)
Works Mentioned: Thomas Lupton, *A Dream of the Devil and Dives* (**742**; 3.3); Richard Brome, *The Northern Lass* (**2277**), *The Sparagus Garden* (**2479**), *The Antipodes* (**2591**), *A Jovial Crew* (**2843**), *Five New Plays* (1653 publication of *The Novella*, **2383**, *The City Wit*, **2419**, *The Demoiselle*, **2601**, *A Mad Couple Well Matched*, **2694**, and *The Court Beggar*, **2745**; all in the epistle); Richard Brome and Thomas Heywood, *The Witches of Lancashire* (**2441**; epistle)

LANGUAGE
English
Latin: 3 words (2.2; Jeffrey)

FORM
Metre: pentameter and prose
Rhyme: blank verse; one passage of couplets (5.4)
Prologue: 14 lines, in couplets
Act-Division: 5 acts
Dumb Shows: 2 (3.2, representing supernatural events; 4.2, compresses action)
Lines (Spoken): 2,753 (1,760 verse, 993 prose)
Lines (Written): 4,148

Because the play is printed in narrow double columns, the figures for written length and spoken prose are somewhat inflated.

STAGING
Doors: characters enter at two doors (3.1, implicit; 5.1, s.d.)
Discovery Space: a bed thrust out (4.2, s.d.)
Within: shout (2.2, 5.3, s.d.); speech (2.4, 3.3, s.d.); sound effects (3.3, s.d.)
Beneath: the Outlaws 'sink' into the stage (4.1, s.d.); the Carpenter climbs down on a rope and comes back up with an Outlaw hanging onto him (5.2, s.d.; the trapdoor must therefore be conveniently close to the stage post on which the pulley is fastened)
Stage Posts: one may represent the oak beside which Anthynus leaves his father (2.4); the pulley is fastened to one (5.2, s.d.)

MUSIC AND SOUND
Sound Effects: knocking within (3.3, s.d.)
Music: hautboys (1.1, 5.4, s.d.); unspecified music (2.2, s.d.; probably fiddles); bells (2.2, s.d.); recorders (3.2, s.d.); loud music (3.2, s.d.; accompanying the dance)
On-Stage Music: Jeffrey winds a horn (4.2, s.d.)
Dance: the Saxon Kings dance (3.2, s.d.)

PROPS
Lighting: two dark lanterns (5.2, s.d.); a light (5.2, s.d.)
Weapons: Offa's sword (2.3, 5.4, dialogue); Segebert's sword (2.3, dialogue); two Outlaws' swords (4.1, implicit); a dagger (5.2, s.d.)
Musical Instruments: a horn (4.2, s.d.)
Clothing: an unspecified wearable object (1.1, implicit)
Money: gold (2.2, dialogue); an unspecified sum (4.1, dialogue)
Animals: hawks (3.2, dialogue)
Food and Drink: two crusts of bread (5.2, dialogue)
Small Portable Objects: a picture of Osric (1.1, dialogue); a miniature of Bertha (2.1, s.d.; 4.2, dialogue); a miniature of Mildred (2.1, 4.2, dialogue); possibly a handkerchief (2.4, implicit); six sceptres (3.2, s.d.); a bunch of picklocks (5.2, s.d.); binding cords (5.4, implicit)
Large Portable Objects: agricultural tools (2.2, s.d.); a basket (2.3, s.d.); a pickaxe (5.2, s.d.); a rope and pulley (5.2, s.d.); a chair (5.4, s.d.)
Scenery: a bed (4.2, s.d.)
Miscellaneous: blood (2.3–4, dialogue)

COSTUMES AND MAKE-UP
SEGEBERT: white hair (dialogue); disguised (2.3, dialogue, 2.4, implicit); blood on his head (2.4, dialogue)
BERTHA: a dress with a train (4.2, s.d.)
ANTHYNUS: disguised in pilgrim's weeds (2.3, 3.2, dialogue; 2.4, implicit); bound (4.2, s.d.) with manacles and gyves (dialogue; removed on stage); different garments from previous scenes (4.2, dialogue); a hat, feather, and cloak (4.2, s.d.; put on on stage)
OFFA: disguised (2.3, s.d.)
OSRIC: a crown (2.1, dialogue); pilgrim's weeds (3.1, dialogue)

JEFFREY: a long coat (3.1, dialogue)
OUTLAWS: two wear hangers (4.1, implicit)
PHYSICIAN: a coat (3.3, dialogue)
SAXON KINGS: crowns (3.2, s.d.)
CARPENTER, MASON, and SMITH: devil costumes (5.2, s.d.; they are voluminous enough to hide Mildred and Edith underneath)

EARLY STAGE HISTORY
Said to have been 'acted with general applause' by the King's Men at the Blackfriars before 1657 (and presumably by 1642). This may, however, be untrue.

EARLY TEXTUAL HISTORY
1656: entered to Randolph Taylor in the Stationers' Register on Thursday 20 November; entry names author, acting company, and playhouse.

1657: Q printed (in or before June) for Henry Brome; collation A² B–F⁴ G², 24 leaves; title page names author, acting company, and playhouse; Latin title-page motto; stationer's epistle; list of roles. The text is printed in double columns.

1657 (?): George Thomason bought a copy of Q, and annotated it with the date Monday 3 November 1656 (which was before the book can have been issued, and is presumably an error). In c. 1678, some years after his death, his entire collection of books and tracts was acquired by the bookbinder Samuel Mearne, acting as agent for King Charles II; the King never paid him, and the books remained in Mearne's family until 1761.

1659: advertised as for sale by Henry Brome.

1661: Q reissued with a cancel title page giving the title as *The Royal Exchange*.

1664: the reissued Q, under its new title, advertised as for sale by Henry Brome.

1684: Nicholas Cox (Manciple of St Edmund Hall, Oxford) had a copy of Q in his bookshop. It had probably been previously owned by Gerard Langbaine, and appears on a list compiled by Anthony Wood on Saturday 13 December.

EDITION
Marion O'Connor, Richard Brome Online (internet, 2010).

REFERENCES
Annals 1631; Bentley, iii. 86–7; Bodleian, MS Wood E. 4, art. 1, p. 79; Greg 772; Hazlitt, 189; *PBSA* 107 (2013), 31.

2450. *A Projector Lately Dead*

EVIDENCE
Henry Burton, *A Divine Tragedy Lately Acted* (1636; STC 4140.7).

GENRE
comedy
Contemporary: merry comedy

TITLE
Performed: *A Projector Lately Dead*

DATE
Autumn 1634

PLOT
A lawyer and projector dies and is dissected, presumably in an anatomy theatre. (This was then thought to be a dreadful posthumous dishonour.) When he is opened up, he is found to have numerous papers inside him; his belly is full of white soap (referring to a notorious monopoly of the 1630s), but it has failed to keep his body clean inside.

ROLES
A PROJECTOR and lawyer, representing the recently deceased Attorney General, William Noy
A SURGEON

STAGING
Miscellaneous: The lawyer is dissected on stage, and objects are removed from his head, maw, and belly.

PROPS
Weapons: surgeons' knives
Small Portable Objects: numerous proclamations; a moth-eaten records
Large Portable Objects: a dissecting table
Miscellaneous: an abundance of white soap

COSTUMES
PROJECTOR: lawyer's robes; the inner recesses of his body are 'very black and foul'.

EARLY STAGE HISTORY
1634: performed in London during Michaelmas Term (Wednesday 1 October to Sunday 21 December).

REFERENCES
Annals 1636; Bentley, v. 1398; Henry Burton, *A Divine Tragedy Lately Acted* (London, 1636), sig. *2ʳ (p. 45); Hazlitt, 186; Sibley, 128.

2451. *Love's Mistress*

TEXT
Two early witnesses:
  Q_1: printed in 1636 (STC 13352), presumably from authorial papers (though some indications of prompt copy have been noticed);
  Q_2: printed in 1640 (STC 13353), from an annotated copy of Q_1, with scattered minor amendments of spelling, punctuation, and word order.

2451. Love's Mistress

Additional information derives from likely costume and set designs by Inigo Jones (cited as J).

GENRE
classical legend; allegory
Contemporary: play (Cho.1, S.R.); masque (title); poem, drama (ded.); dramatic poem (epistle); 'a very pretty comedy' (Cotgrave, *Wit's Interpreter*, 1655)

TITLE
Performed: *Love's Mistress*
Printed: *Love's Mistress, or The Queen's Masque*
Contemporary: *The Queen's Masque, or Love's Mistress*; *Cupid's Mistress, or Cupid and Psyche*

Q indicates that *The Queen's Masque* was the title assigned at the second performance. It is a reasonable inference that the original performance was therefore as *Love's Mistress*, which is also the title under which it was protected in 1639. The evidence implies that *The Queen's Masque* was the court title and *Love's Mistress* the playhouse title, in which case Heywood's emphasis on the former in Q needs little explanation.

AUTHOR
Thomas Heywood

DATE
November 1634

ORIGINAL PRODUCTION
Queen Henrietta's Men at the Cockpit

PLOT
Apuleius, formerly an ass but now restored to human form, meets the surly Midas, challenges him to hear a story, and interprets the allegory during the act-divisions.

Admetus undertakes a pilgrimage to Delphos to learn the marital destiny of his daughter Psyche. The oracle declares that she will marry no human being, will become immortal, and will see Hell. Venus envies the attention being paid to Psyche, and recruits her fellow gods to assist in her revenge, but they all follow their own ends instead. Cupid abducts and seduces Psyche, whilst remaining invisible, and gives her a life of luxury. Her sisters envy her good luck, and try to 'save' her from her fate by advising her to murder her invisible husband as he sleeps. In the attempt she discovers his identity; he sends her home punished with disfigurement.

Apollo and Pan contend which is the better musician, but Pan has a sore throat, so they have to compete with proxy singers. Apollo is the clear winner, but Midas foolishly judges in Pan's favour. Apollo withdraws his music from Arcadia and wishes Midas long ears.

The pregnant Psyche returns to her family, but they do not recognize her. When Cupid identifies her, Admetus sentences her to banishment. She is arrested by Mercury and handed over to Venus, who imposes a penance: she must manually separate mingled grain by nightfall. Mercury releases Cupid, imprisoned by Venus, and they send ants to do Psyche's task for her; Cupid then persuades his father Vulcan to knock off his fetters. Venus sets Psyche a second labour: to fetch water from one of the rivers of the underworld. Cupid helps her with that, too, so Venus finally sends her to fetch a box of beauty from Hell. After Hell's rulers cannot persuade her to eat, and thereby trick her into having to remain there, Proserpine hands over the box. Psyche decides to use it to restore her own lost looks, but Corydon the clown plans to steal the beauty for his girlfriend. Cupid intervenes: the stolen box is switched for a duplicate as Corydon sleeps, and the beauty extracted by Psyche put back. Corydon's attempts to beautify himself with the contents of the box have the opposite effect, and he goes off deluded to his wedding. Jove restores Psyche's beauty with a cup of immortality, and she goes to heaven. Her two sisters are forgiven.

Midas doesn't like the play Apuleius has shown him. Cupid rewards them both: laurels to Apuleius, ass's ears to Midas.

SCENE DESIGNATION
ind., 1.1–5, Cho.1, 2.1–4, Cho.2, 3.1–2, Cho.3, 4.1–2, Cho.4, 5.1–3, Cho.5 (Q has act-division only)

The stage is not clear at 5.3–Cho.5.

Shady's edition marks the induction as 1.1, and neglects to mark a new scene where the stage is clear at 1.4–5; thus in his edition 1.1–3 are 1.2–4 and 1.4–5 are 1.5. He treats all of the choruses as the final scene of their respective acts, so that Cho.1 is 1.6, and so on.

ROLES
APULEIUS, a poet, the author of the story; representing art
MIDAS, an old man, Corydon's father; formerly King of Phrygia; now a shepherd, and calls himself the king of beasts; representing ignorance
ADMETUS, King of Thessaly and Arcadia, father of Psyche, Petrea, and Astioche
MENOETIUS, Petrea's husband, Psyche's brother-in-law
ZELOTIS, Astioche's husband, Psyche's brother-in-law
ASTIOCHE, Admetus' daughter, Zelotis' wife, sister of Psyche and Petrea; representing sin
PETREA, Admetus' daughter, Menoetius' wife, sister of Psyche and Astioche; representing sin
PSYCHE, Admetus' daughter, sister of Astioche and Petrea, later Cupid's wife; representing the soul
APOLLO, the sun-god; also god of archery, arts, medicine, and poetry; son of Jove and Latona, Proserpine's twin brother; also called Phoebus and Hyperion
VENUS, goddess of love, Vulcan's wife, Cupid's mother, Mercury's sister; also named Cytherea and styled Queen of Love and of Paphos; representing lust

CUPID, boy god of love, son of Venus and Vulcan, later Psyche's husband; also called Love; said to be little; representing true desire; he also speaks the prologue and epilogue in performances where they are included
PAN, a shepherd god
ZEPHYRUS, a gentle wind, Cupid's servant; representing celestial pleasure (*non-speaking*)
Three ECHOES, the voices of Psyche's invisible attendants
A PROUD ASS, a male character (Cho.1, *non-speaking*)
A PRODIGAL ASS, a male character (Cho.1, *non-speaking*)
A DRUNKEN ASS, a male character (Cho.1, *non-speaking*)
A USURER, an old man and a covetous ass (Cho.1, *non-speaking*)
A YOUNG GENTLEWOMAN, a she-ass (Cho.1, *non-speaking*)
An IGNORANT ASS, said to be Midas's brother (Cho.1, *non-speaking*)
EVEMORE, an attendant at Admetus' court
CORYDON, the clown; a rustic, son of Midas
SWAINS, shepherds of Arcadia; three are named Colin, Dickon, and Hobbinol; there may be a fourth (who may be *non-speaking*)
COUNTRY WENCHES (*non-speaking*)
BOREAS, the north wind; also called Aquilon (*non-speaking*)
AMARYLLIS, an old, ugly, dowdy she-swain (*non-speaking*)
Apollo's PAGE (3.2)
MERCURY, a young god, Venus' brother; also called Hermes
A KING (Cho.3, *non-speaking*)
A BEGGAR (Cho.3, *non-speaking*)
A YOUNG MAN (Cho.3, *non-speaking*)
An OLD WOMAN (Cho.3, *non-speaking*)
A LEAN MAN (Cho.3, *non-speaking*)
A FAT WOMAN (Cho.3, *non-speaking*)
VULCAN, a crook-backed blacksmith god, Venus' husband, Cupid's father
Four CYCLOPES employed by Vulcan; one is named Pyracmon
PLUTO, a god, King of Hell, Proserpine's husband
PROSERPINE, Queen of Hell, Pluto's wife; also identified as the moon goddess, Apollo's twin sister; also called Proserpina
MINOS, a judge of Hell
AEACUS, a judge of Hell
RHADAMANTH, a judge of Hell
CHARON, the churlish ferryman of Hell
CERBERUS, the porter of Hell
The FURIES, hags of Hell (*non-speaking*)

The status of Proserpine is confused: she is both Queen of Hell and moon goddess, the daughter of both Ceres and Latona; in each case the former attribute is mythologically accurate and the latter associated with Diana. Perhaps there was an early intention to include Diana among the goddesses, which had to be scrapped (for casting reasons?) and some of her functions reassigned.

Speaking Parts: 34–5

The variable is the possible fourth swain. No scene requires more than three speaking swains, but no swain is identifiable as a consistent figure from scene to scene; the numbers 1–3 may thus be scene-specific rather than play-specific. The first stage direction for these characters calls for 'three or four swains', and the Q character list specifies four.

Stage Directions and Speech Prefixes
APULEIUS: *Apuleius* (s.d.s); *Ap<uleius>* (s.p.s); *Apuleus* [one of] *The Chorus* (d.p.)
MIDAS: *Midas* (s.d.s); *Mid<as>* (s.p.s); *Midas* [one of] *The Chorus* (d.p.)
ADMETUS: *Admetus* (s.d.s); *Ad<metus>* (s.p.s); *Admetus, King of Thessaly* (d.p.)
MENOETIUS: *Menetius* | [one of Petrea's and Astioche's] *two husbands* (s.d.s); *Mene<tius>* (s.p.s); *Menetius Husband to Petrea* (d.p.)
ZELOTIS: *Zelotis* | [one of Petrea's and Astioche's] *two husbands* | *Zelotes* (s.d.s); *Zelo<tis>* (s.p.s); *Zelotes Husband to . . . Astioche* (d.p.)
ASTIOCHE: *Astioche* | [one of] *the two Sisters* (s.d.s); *Astio<che>* (s.p.s); *Astioche* [one of Admetus'] *three Daughters* (d.p.)
PETREA: *Petrea* | [one of] *the two Sisters* (s.d.s); *Petre<a>* (s.p.s); *Petrea* [one of Admetus'] *three Daughters* (d.p.)
PSYCHE: *Psiche* (s.d.s); *Psi<che>* (s.p.s); *Psiche* [one of Admetus'] *three Daughters* (d.p.)
APOLLO: *Apollo* (s.d.s and d.p.); *Phoebus* | [one of] *the gods* (s.d.s); *Apol<lo>* (s.p.s)
VENUS: *Venus* (s.d.s and d.p.); [one of] *the goddesses* (s.d.s); *Ven<us>* (s.p.s)
CUPID: *Cupid* (s.d.s and d.p.); *Cup<id>* (s.p.s)
PAN: *Pan* (s.d.s, s.p.s, and d.p.); [one of] *the gods* (s.d.s)
ZEPHYRUS: *Zephirus* (s.d.s and d.p.)
ECHOES: *Echo | 2 | 3* (s.p.s)
PROUD ASS: *a Proud Ass* (s.d.s)
PRODIGAL ASS: *a Prodigal Ass* (s.d.s)
DRUNKEN ASS: *a Drunken Ass* (s.d.s)
USURER: *a Usurer* (s.d.s)
YOUNG GENTLEWOMAN: *A Young Gentlewoman* (s.d.s)
IGNORANT ASS: *an Ignorant Ass* (s.d.s)
EVEMORE: *Evemore* (s.d.s); *Eve<more>* (s.p.s)
CORYDON: *Clown* (s.d.s and s.p.s); *The Clown* (d.p.)
SWAINS: *three or four Swains* | *Swains* (s.d.s); *1 Swain* | *2 Swain* | *3 Swain* (s.p.s); *Four Swains* (d.p.)
COUNTRY WENCHES: *Country Wenches* (s.d.s)
BOREAS: *Boreas* (s.d.s and d.p.); *Boreus* (s.d.s)
AMARYLLIS: *Amarillis* (s.d.s); *Amarillis a she Swain* (d.p.)
MERCURY: *Mercury* (s.d.s and d.p.); [one of] *the gods* (s.d.s); *Mer<cury>* (s.p.s)
KING: *a King* (s.d.s)
BEGGAR: *a Beggar* (s.d.s)
YOUNG MAN: *a Young man* (s.d.s)

OLD WOMAN: *an Old woman* (s.d.s)
LEAN MAN: *a Lean man* (s.d.s)
FAT WOMAN: *a Fat woman* (s.d.s)
VULCAN: *Vulcan* (s.d.s and d.p.); [one of] *the gods* (s.d.s); *Vul<can>* (s.p.s)
CYCLOPES: *1 Ciclop* | [Vulcan's] *Ciclopps* (s.d.s); *Ciclop* | *2 Ciclop* | *3 Ciclop* | *4 Ciclop* (s.p.s); *Four Ciclops* (d.p.)
PLUTO: *Pluto* (s.d.s and d.p.); *Plu<to>* (s.p.s)
PROSERPINE: *Proserpine* (s.d.s and d.p.); [one of] *the goddesses* (s.d.s); *Pros<erpine>* (s.p.s)
MINOS: *Minos* (s.d.s and d.p.); *Mino<s>* (s.p.s)
AEACUS: *Eacus* (s.d.s and d.p.); *Eac<us>* (s.p.s)
RHADAMANTH: *Rhadamant* (s.d.s and d.p.); *Rha<damant>* (s.p.s)
CHARON: *Charon* (s.d.s and d.p.); *Cha<ron>* (s.p.s)
CERBERUS: *Cerberus* (s.d.s and d.p.); *Cer<berus>* (s.p.s)
FURIES: *Furies* (d.p.)

OTHER CHARACTERS
The nine Muses (ind., 1.1, 2.3, 5.3)
Bacchus, god of wine, who rewarded Midas with the golden touch (ind., 5.3)
Apollo's sibyls (1.1)
Latona, Apollo's mother; also said to be Proserpine's mother (1.1, 3.2, 5.1, 5.3)
Jove, a god, Apollo's father, Cupid's uncle (1.1–2, 2.3, 3.2, Cho.3, 4.1, 5.1–3)
Juno, a goddess, Jove's wife, Pluto's mother, Cupid's aunt (1.2, 4.1, 5.1)
Queen Ceres, goddess of harvest and fertility, Proserpine's mother (1.2, 4.1, 5.1, 5.3)
Jove's paramours (1.2)
Ganymede, Jove's page (1.2, 4.1, 5.2–3)
Satyrs, followers of Pan (1.2, 2.3, 4.1, 5.3)
Former pilgrims to Paphos, who no longer worship Venus, but Psyche instead (1.2–3)
Berenice, whose hair Venus intends to use for Cupid's coronet (1.2)
Flora, goddess of flowers (1.2, 2.1; but she may be merely metaphorical)
The Prodigal Ass's father (Cho.1)
The Young Gentlewoman's mother (Cho.1)
Heirs who were offered as prospective husbands for the Young Gentlewoman, but whom she foolishly refused (Cho.1)
The Young Gentlewoman's father (Cho.1)
The Young Gentlewoman's husband, formerly her father's servingman (Cho.1)
Fauns, who fear Cupid (2.3, 4.2)
Susanna, a fair nymph of Arcadia (2.3)
Neptune, a god (2.3, 3.2, 4.1)
Mars, a god, Venus' paramour (2.3, 4.1)
Nymphs of Arcadia, who recognize Cupid's sovereignty; some may be named Doll, Jug, and Peg (2.3, 4.2, 5.2–3)
Orithyia, Boreas' beloved (3.1)
Marsyas, who was flayed for competing with Apollo (3.2)
Daphne, Apollo's beloved (3.2)
Syrinx, a nymph, Pan's beloved (3.2, 5.3)
Phyllis, Pan's beloved (3.2)
Adonis, Venus' dead beloved, whom she turns posthumously into a hyacinth (3.2, 4.1, 5.2)
Achilles, Venus' paramour (4.1)
One of Ceres' husbandmen, who has come to Vulcan's smithy for a ploughshare (4.1)
Mars's lackey, who has come to Vulcan's smithy to have a piece of armour mended (4.1)
A clown, who has come to Vulcan's smithy for hobnails (4.1; may be Corydon)
Vulcan's journeymen, twelve or more in number (4.1)
Vulcan's apprentices (4.1)
Oblivion, an old man who swims in the River Styx and tempts souls to dive in after him (4.1, Cho.4, 5.1)
Old, wrinkled hags who spin on the banks of the Styx (4.1, Cho.4, 5.1)
Folly, a male character, who reels up what the hags spin (4.1, Cho.4, 5.1)
Mopsa, an unprepossessing girl (4.2)
Maia, Mercury's mother (5.1)
The Sicilians, including virgins, old wives, young children, soldiers, citizens, princes, and prelates (5.1)
Iambe, a Sicilian maid (5.1)
Metaneira, Iambe's mistress (5.1)
The Furies (5.1)
Pallas, Pluto's sister (5.1)
Phaon, a famously beautiful Sicilian ferryman (5.2)
Hymen, god of marriage (5.2)
Cannae, a nymph to whom Pan is attracted (5.3)
Saturn, Pluto's father (5.3)
The Graces (5.3)

SETTING
Period: classical antiquity
Time-Scheme: enough time passes between Cho.1 and 4.1 for Psyche's pregnancy to become visible
Place: Arcadia and other parts of Greece; one scene (1.1) is set at Delphos (i.e. Delphi), and one (5.1) in Hell

Geography
Asia: Phrygia; Lydia; Troy; Mount Ida
[*Greece*]: Mount Helicon; Aganippe; Taenarus; Thessaly (only mentioned in d.p.)
[*Aegean Sea*]: Delos
Cyprus: Paphos
Sicily: River Cephissus (actually in Greece; but Q reads Cissephus); Pisma
Spain
Hell: River Cocytus; River Styx; River Phlegethon; River Acheron

SOURCES
Narrative: Apuleius, *The Golden Ass* 4–6 (cited in epistle); probably Thomas Dekker, Henry Chettle, and John Day, *Cupid and Psyche* (**1247**); Ovid, *Metamorphoses* 5 (5.1), 9 (3.2)

Verbal: Virgil, *Eclogues* 1 (2.3); Horace, *Ars poetica* (t.p. motto); Suetonius, *Twelve Caesars*: Julius Caesar (4.2); Nemesianus, *Eclogues* 1 (ded.; cited); William Lily, Latin Grammar (2.3); Natalis Comes, *Mythologia* (1551; widely reprinted in several European countries, but not in England; also available in a 1597 French translation by Jean de Montliard; 5.1); William Shakespeare, *2 Henry VI* (**888**; 4.1); *King Cophetua and the Beggar Maid* (ballad; Cho.3); Thomas Dekker, Henry Chettle, and John Day, *Cupid and Psyche* (**1247**; ind., 2.1)

Works Mentioned: Homer, *Iliad* (2.3); Plato, *Timaeus* (prol., first Denmark House performance only); there are also general references to Homer (4.2), Hesiod (4.2), Virgil (4.2), Ovid (2.3, 4.2), Persius (4.2), Martial (4.2), and Juvenal (4.2)

LANGUAGE
English
Latin: 32 words (Cho.1, 2.3, 3.2, 4.2, 5.1; Apuleius, Corydon, Midas, Cerberus)

The prologue used for the first Denmark House performance has 2 additional words of Latin and 3 of French.
In 2.3, Corydon describes the vernacular as 'plain Arcadian'.

FORM
Metre: pentameter and prose; a few trimeters; Apollo's prophecy is in tetrameter (1.1)
Rhyme: blank verse and couplets; the prophecy rhymes ABACBCDACDD (1.1)
Prologue: three prologues, each for a specific royal performance:
  1: 18 lines, in couplets, spoken by Cupid; first performance;
  2: 24 lines, in couplets, spoken by Cupid; first Denmark House performance;
  3: 20 lines, in couplets, spoken by Cupid; second Denmark House performance.
Induction: establishes the choric figures of Apuleius and Midas
Chorus: Apuleius and Midas; they speak at the end of each act
Act-Division: 5 acts, separated by chorus scenes
Epilogue: 18 lines, in couplets, spoken by Cupid, at the first Denmark House performance only
Lines (Spoken): 2,081 (1,794 verse, 287 prose)
Lines (Written): 2,272

STAGING
Discovery Space: contains a bed in which Cupid is discovered (3.1, s.d); a silken curtain hangs across it (3.1, dialogue)
Stage: mentioned (Cho.1, dialogue); may have a magic circle drawn on it (1.5, dialogue; but this could be just a figure of speech)
Within: speech (1.2, 4.1, s.d.)
Above: Cupid descends in a cloud (*first performance only*, prol., s.d.); a character may climb between stage levels in vision (1.3, implicit; but the 'rock' climbed may also be a piece of scenery); Cupid descends and ascends (3.2, s.d.)

Audience: asked for information (ind.; it is assumed that they will not reply); said to be seated (ind., dialogue); directly addressed (ind., 5.2, implicit; including as 'kind gentlemen' (Cho.1), 'gentlemen' (Cho.4), and 'judicious' (Cho.5); mentioned (Cho.2–3, dialogue) and called 'spectators' (Cho.4, dialogue) and 'gentlemen' (Cho. 5, dialogue); in the first Denmark House performance, the King is addressed as 'great King' (prol.) and the King and Queen as 'royal princes' (ep.); in the second Denmark House performance, the King and Queen are directly addressed (prol.)

Miscellaneous: Apuleius invites Midas to sit and watch the play, but they do not do so on stage (ind.; the characters exit at the end of the induction and enter and exit in each subsequent chorus scene); the banquet 'miraculously' appears on a bare table (1.5, dialogue); Corydon is shot on stage with an arrow (2.3, implicit)

MUSIC AND SOUND
Sound Effects: a storm (3.1–2, s.d.); a great storm (3.1, s.d.)
Music: recorders (1.1–2, 2.1, 3.2, s.d.); loud music (2.1, s.d.); still music (2.1, s.d.); a flourish (3.2, s.d.); hideous music (5.1, s.d.)
On-Stage Music: Apollo plays the harp (3.2, implicit; accompanying Song 1); Pan plays the pipe (3.2, implicit; accompanying Song 2); the Cyclopes play percussively on the anvil to accompany their dance (Cho.4, dialogue)
Songs:
  1: 'Phoebus unto thee we sing', 3.2, Page, 13 lines, with musical accompaniment;
  2: 'Thou that art called the bright Hyperion', 3.2, Corydon, 28 lines, with musical accompaniment.
Dance: six entry dances by each of the six Asses (Cho.1, s.d.); exit dance, presumably by the Asses (Cho.1, s.d.); Pan, Clown, Swains, and Country Wenches dance (Cho.2, s.d.); the King, Beggar, Young Man, Old Woman, Lean Man, and Fat Woman dance (Cho.3, s.d.); Vulcan and the Cyclopes dance (Cho.4, s.d.; with quasi-musical accompaniment); Cupid and Psyche, Mercury and Proserpine, Venus and Vulcan dance in pairs (5.3, s.d.)

PROPS
Lighting: a lighted oil lamp (3.1, s.d.; some of the oil is spilt on Cupid)
Weapons: a quiver of arrows (1.2, 3.1, dialogue; 2.3, implicit; the arrows have gold, silver, and leaden tips); two or more swords (1.3, dialogue); a bow (2.3, implicit; 3.1, dialogue); a razor (3.1, s.d.); another bow (3.2, 4.1, dialogue); another quiver of arrows (4.1, dialogue; possibly also 3.2)
Musical Instruments: a harp (3.2, implicit); a pipe (3.2, implicit)

Clothing: possibly a laurel wreath (Cho.5, s.d.; may be a figure of speech); a pair of ass's ears (Cho.5, dialogue; also worn by Apuleius)
Money: bags of gold (2.1, s.d.); a coin or two (4.1, implicit; 5.1, dialogue)
Food and Drink: a banquet of delicates (1.5, s.d.); wine (1.5, s.d.; filled from a pitcher into a cup or other smaller vessel); five measures of grain (3.2, s.d.); two sops (5.1, dialogue); a banquet (5.1, s.d.), including wine (dialogue)
Small Portable Objects: blacksmith's tools (4.1, implicit); a vial (4.1, s.d.; first empty, then filled with water); a box (5.1, 5.3, dialogue; 5.2, s.d.); a duplicate box (5.2, s.d.; contains cosmetics)
Large Portable Objects: a table (1.5, implicit); a seat (1.5, implicit); a sheep-hook (Cho.1, dialogue); another sheep-hook (2.3, dialogue); an anvil (Cho.4, dialogue)
Scenery: a cloud (*first performance only,* prol. s.d.; descends with Cupid on board); possibly a rock (1.3–5, s.d.; sturdy enough for Psyche to climb, and stuck with brambles; may alternatively be represented by the permanent architecture of the theatre); a silk curtain (3.1, dialogue); a bed (3.1, s.d.); *some set designs probably survive*
Miscellaneous: water (4.1, dialogue); ugly cosmetics (5.2, s.d.; daubed on a character's face)

COSTUMES AND MAKE-UP
APULEIUS: ass's ears (ind., s.d.; removed on stage; see also PROPS)
MIDAS: silver hair (dialogue); a woollen crown (ind., dialogue; probably a hat)
ADMETUS: a crown (2.2, dialogue)
ASTIOCHE and PETREA: probably each wears a skirt with a pocket or pouch in the lap (2.1–2, 2.4, implicit; gold is poured into the pockets)
PSYCHE: long hair (implicit); mourning clothes (1.3, implicit); silk clothes (2.1, 2.4, dialogue); night attire (3.1, s.d.; possibly made of silk); torn rags (3.2, dialogue; 4.1, 5.1–2, implicit); deformed, leprous make-up (3.2, 4.1, 5.1–2, implicit); visibly pregnant (4.1, dialogue; 5.1–3, implicit); a crown (5.3, dialogue; put on on stage)
APOLLO: yellow hair (dialogue)
CUPID: wings (dialogue); a ring (1.5, dialogue); golden fetters on his ankles (4.1, s.d.; removed on stage)
PAN: horns and a beard (dialogue)
ZEPHYRUS: silver, feathered wings (1.4–5, dialogue; it is also implied that he is *not* wearing wings in 1.2)
PROUD ASS: ears (Cho.1, s.d.)
PRODIGAL ASS: 'fantastic habits and gay clothes' (Cho.1, dialogue)
USURER: a grey beard (dialogue; but this may be a figure of speech); patched clothes (Cho.1, dialogue)
CORYDON: ugly make-up (5.2, s.d.; put on on stage)
AMARYLLIS: wrinkled; a long nose (dialogue)
LEAN MAN: probably a pointed beard (Cho.3, J); *costume design probably survives*
FAT WOMAN: probably a hat and ruff (Cho.3, J); *costume design probably survives*
VULCAN: a club foot (dialogue); sooty black make-up (4.1, dialogue)

EARLY STAGE HISTORY
1634: performed by Queen Henrietta's Men at the Cockpit, probably on Saturday 15 November (or, alternatively, Thursday 13 November); first performance (or a private dress rehearsal). The audience included Queen Henrietta Maria.

1634: performed by Queen Henrietta's Men at Denmark House on the King's birthday, Wednesday 19 November; second performance; the play was retitled *The Queen's Masque* and supplied with a different prologue. In this version, the concluding dance of the gods, or planets, featured three gods who do not otherwise appear in the play (Juno, Ceres, and Jove; taking Apollo to be the Sun and Proserpina the Moon), followed by a new epilogue. The scenery was designed by Inigo Jones. The performance took place in the evening, and was expected to end late at night. The audience included: King Charles I; Queen Henrietta Maria; possibly sundry foreign ambassadors.

1634: performed by Queen Henrietta's Men at court, probably again at Denmark House, between Thursday 20 and Wednesday 26 November (most probably either the Thursday, Friday, or Saturday); a third prologue was performed. The audience included: King Charles I; Queen Henrietta Maria; possibly sundry foreign ambassadors. By a warrant dated either Tuesday 10 February 1635 or Tuesday 24 March 1635, Christopher Beeston was paid £90 for eight plays acted at court during 1634; this may have included £10 or £20 for one or both of the court performances of *Love's Mistress* (though the 19 November performance may alternatively have been paid for from the Queen's purse).

1639: The play was in the repertory of the King's and Queen's Young Company (Beeston's Boys) at the Cockpit. On Saturday 10 August, Philip Herbert, 4th Earl of Pembroke (Lord Chamberlain) issued an order restraining performances by other companies of this and 44 other plays.

It is possible that some of Inigo Jones's surviving but unidentified scenic and costume designs may relate to the court performances, particularly those for the Temple of Apollo (Orgel and Strong no. 452; compare 1.1), a mountainous valley (no. 453; compare 1.2–5), Cupid's palace (no. 113; compare 2.1 and 2.4), a bed in an inner chamber (two drafts, nos. 454–5; compare 3.1; annotated as 'the 4th scene a chamber—a shutter set back so that one might pass by' on the later draft), costumes for a lean man and a fat woman (no.473; compare Cho.3) and a hell scene (no. 447; compare 5.1); there are also various pastoral and forest settings (nos. 456–7, 459–62, 465) which may be relevant.

There is no direct evidence of the venue for the second court performance, but in the prologue Cupid infers from the presence of the Queen in the audience that he is back in the

1634

same place, which would support the inference that the play was again at Denmark House. This would have obviated the need to move and install the scenery elsewhere (perhaps with adjustments to fit it to the dimensions of a different space).

EARLY TEXTUAL HISTORY

1635: *Pleasant Dialogues and Dramas* entered in the Stationers' Register to Richard Hearne on Saturday 29 August; entry names author.

1635: entered (as *The Queen's Masque, or, Love's Mistress*) in the Stationers' Register to John Crouch on Wednesday 30 September; entry names author. William Blagrave, Sir Henry Herbert's deputy, had licensed the book for publication.

1636: $^1Q_1$ printed by Robert Raworth for John Crouch, and to be sold by Jasper Emery; collation π^2 A–L^4 M^2, 48 leaves; title page names author, acting company, and playhouse, and refers to court performances; Latin title-page motto; authorial dedication to Edward Sackville, 4th Earl of Dorset (the Queen's Lord Chamberlain); authorial epistle to the reader; list of roles. The outer forme of quire B was reset during printing, possibly as a result of a late decision to increase the number of copies to be printed.

1637: the court prologues and epilogue included in Thomas Heywood's *Pleasant Dialogues and Dramas*, sigs. Q7^v–Q8^v; printed by Richard Oulton for Richard Hearne, and to be sold by Thomas Slater.

c. 1630s–40s: a copy of Q$_1$ was in the possession of John Horne (Vicar of Headington, Oxfordshire). After his death, his entire collection of play-books passed into the possession of John Houghton of Brasenose College, Oxford (c. 1608–77), then to James Herne (died 1685), and then to the library of Ralph Sheldon (1623–84) at Weston, where it was catalogued by Anthony Wood, probably in the late 1670s.

1640: $^2Q_2$ printed by John Raworth for John Crouch; collation A–I^4, 36 leaves. The title page claims that the text has been 'corrected by the author'; the principal copy was Q$_1$.

1640–1: Humphrey Moseley was selling copies of Q$_1$ for 6d each.

c. 1661: $^3Q_3$ printed with a false imprint duplicating that of Q$_2$, possibly by Thomas Johnson for circulation by Francis Kirkman; collation A–G^4, 28 leaves. The copy was Q$_2$.

1661: advertised as for sale by Francis Kirkman.

1662: advertised as having been 'published this term' and for sale by Henry Marsh. (It is unclear which of the four law-terms this means.)

c. 1663–5: Henry Oxinden of Barham, Kent, had a copy of Q$_1$ in his possession.

1678?: advertised by Francis Kirkman as having been printed for Obadiah Blagrave.

1684: Nicholas Cox (Manciple of St Edmund Hall, Oxford) had a copy of Q$_2$ in his bookshop. It had probably been previously owned by Gerard Langbaine, and appears on a list compiled by Anthony Wood on Saturday 13 December.

EDITION
Raymond C. Shady, Salzburg Studies in English Literature: Jacobean Drama Studies 65 (Salzburg, 1977).

REFERENCES
Annals 1634; Bawcutt C91; Bentley, iv. 579–82; Bodleian, MS Wood E. 4, art. 1, p. 15; Greg 504; Hazlitt, 56, 142; *The Library*, 4th ser., 15 (1935), 445–56; *MLR* 13 (1918), 401–11; MSC 2.3, 389–90; Orgel and Strong, i. 328–9, ii. 792–3, 796–7, 800, 816–17, 826; *Oxford Bibliographical Society Proceedings and Papers* 2.2 (1929), 132–3; Steele, 278–9, 282–3; *Theatre Survey* 18.2 (1977), 86–95.

2452. Love's Riddle

TEXT
Printed in 1638 (STC 5904).

GENRE
pastoral
Contemporary: play (ep.); pastoral comedy (S.R., t.p.); pastoral (Robert Creswell)

TITLE
Printed: *Love's Riddle*

AUTHOR
Abraham Cowley

DATE
Limits: 1630–6
Best Guess: 1634

The play cannot be precisely dated in Cowley's career at Westminster School, but seems likely to have been written later rather than sooner. O's engraved frontispiece portrait shows him at the age of 13, being crowned with bays by a Cupid; this probably accounts for John Aubrey's statement that he wrote the play at that age, and probably also influenced the *Annals* dating. However, the plate had previously been used on the 1636 edition of Cowley's *Poetical Blossoms*, and was a copy of the engraving used on the book's first edition of 1633.

There are two specific literary connections that might narrow the limits at either end. One of Cowley's sources was *The Shepherds' Holiday* (**2402**), which was published in or after mid-January 1635; dating *Love's Riddle* after that would make it possible for Cowley to have read the play. It was performed, however, at the Cockpit, little more than a stone's throw from the school, and Cowley could have seen it there; he certainly knew the playhouse, and satirically mentions one of its clientele in 'A Poetical Revenge', published in *Sylva* (1637).

The hedging of bets, and so a date in 1635 or 1636, might still have been desirable were it not for the other, also uncertain, connection. William Cartwright's *The Ordinary* (**2468**), likely to have been performed at Oxford in early 1635 but not printed until 1651, contains an uncommonly close parallel with Cowley's play. In *Love's Riddle*, it is said that Truga 'hast nothing left thee of a woman | But lust and tongue'; Cartwright's version, addressed to Potluck, says that she has 'nothing left thee that may style thee | Woman but lust and tongue'. Cartwright's editor, G. Blakemore Evans, drily remarks that the two playwrights probably drew on 'a common classical source for this elevating comment'; but two writers adapting independently from a source in Latin or Greek would be unlikely to use identical English words in the same order. One dramatist seems therefore to have borrowed from the other, and the question of the direction of the influence turns on that of access. Since both plays were unpublished, the debtor either saw a manuscript or a performance of the lender. Cartwright was a former and Cowley a current King's scholar at Westminster; the school is the common factor, and the schoolboy seems likely to have had less opportunity to see or read the rising Oxford academic's play than vice versa.

PLOT

Before the start of the action, Callidora was the victim of an attempted rape when she was alone in her absent parents' house: Aphron, who was obsessed with her, broke into the house, but she hid in a corner and evaded him. Afraid of a second encounter, she borrowed a suit of her brother's clothes and fled into the forest. Aphron went mad, and initially believed every woman he met to be Callidora.

In the forest, the cross-dressed Callidora becomes 'Callidorus'. She meets Alupis, a shepherd who sold his inheritance to see the city and came home penniless but with a witty devotion to pleasure. She takes him on as her man, and asks him to teach her indifference to love. She sets up home in the country, only to find that, seeming to be a beautiful youth, she attracts the amorous attentions of the local women, young and old.

Palaemon is interested in marrying Hylace, but her father Melarnus refuses the match, thinking him too poor. But Hylace has only been leading him on, more interested in his gifts than in him. Alupis encourages him to turn the tables: she will come to heel if he treats her with masterful disdain; but when this doesn't bring about her immediate devotion, he loses his nerve and tells her it was all a joke. Alupis decides to recruit her mother, the ancient but amorously inclined Truga, to support Palaemon's suit. Though infatuated with 'Callidorus', Truga transfers her affections to Alupis when he speaks politely to her, and gives him a ring as a lover's token. Alupis uses the ring to blackmail her: he will show it to her husband, as evidence of adultery, if she doesn't ensure that Palaemon and Hylace are married before the end of the day. When he brings Palaemon to Truga's cottage to arrange the wedding, Hylace eavesdrops on the meeting and decides to cross the plan. Palaemon and Alupis meet with Melarnus. The problem of Palaemon's relative poverty is resolved when Aegon pretends to adopt him as his heir, disinheriting his daughter Bellula for her unseemly interest in 'Callidorus'; so Melarnus accepts Palaemon, though he still has reservations about the young man's habit of writing poetry. Before the wedding, however, he changes his mind and pretends that Hylace is to marry someone else—Hylace has had a word with him.

Florellus, Callidora's brother, returns home after five years' travel, and goes to look for his missing sister. In the forest, he sees Bellula and falls for her; but she is more interested in 'Callidorus', and urges the difference in their rank. He dresses as a shepherd to woo her, but the result is a love-triangle: Bellula tells him that she cannot love him while 'Callidorus' is alive. Florellus decides to kill his rival, and fights 'him'; they are interrupted by Philistus, Callidora's fiancé, and then by Bellula. The sight of Philistus brings Florellus to his senses, but the two women faint.

Clariana, Philistus' sister, finds the exhausted and insane Aphron, takes him in, and falls in love with him. Dismayed to learn that he is the man responsible for Callidora's disappearance, she locks him up. Aphron's affections turn from Callidora to Clariana. Callidora and Florellus are identified and reunited with their parents. Aegon admits that Bellula is not really his daughter: he found her as a baby with her dying nurse, abandoned after an attack by pirates, and has brought her up as his own. It turns out that she is Aphron's long-lost sister: there is no impediment of rank between her and Florellus. Aphron is forgiven for the attempted rape, and the day is to be marked with multiple marriages: Philistus to Callidora, Florellus to Bellula, Aphron to Clariana, and—now that Aegon really does adopt him and Hylace sees that 'Callidorus' is female—Palaemon to Hylace. Philistus invites everyone to join him for a wedding dinner.

SCENE DESIGNATION

1.1–2, 2.1–4, 3.1–2, 4.1–6, 5.1–5, ep. (O has act-divisions only)

ROLES

CALLIDORA, daughter of Demophil and Spodaia, Florellus' sister, Philistus' fiancée; poses as Callidorus, a gentleman
ALUPIS, a shepherd; later Callidora's man
PALAEMON, a shepherd
MELARNUS, an old shepherd; Truga's husband, Hylace's father
TRUGA, Melarnus' wife, Hylace's mother; 90 years old
AEGON, a wealthy shepherd, supposed Bellula's father
BELLULA, a shepherdess, supposed Aegon's daughter and only child, but in fact of noble birth and Aphron's sister; a little over 15 years old
Mistress HYLACE, daughter of Melarnus and Truga
APHRON, a noble madman; turns out to be Bellula's brother
DEMOPHIL, an old nobleman, Spodaia's husband, father of Callidora and Florellus
SPODAIA, Demophil's wife, old mother of Callidora and Florellus
PHILISTUS, Callidora's fiancé, Clariana's brother
CLARIANA, a gentlewoman, Philistus' sister
FLORELLUS, Callidora's brother, son of Demophil and Spodaia
Clariana's MAID and confidante

Speaking Parts: 15

Stage Directions and Speech Prefixes
CALLIDORA: *Callidora | Callidorus* (s.d.s); *Call<idora>* (s.p.s); *Callidora* [one of Demophil and Spodaia's] *Children* (d.p.)
ALUPIS: *Alupis* (s.d.s); *Alu<pis>* (s.p.s); *Alupis a merry Shepherd* (d.p.)
PALAEMON: *Palaemon* (s.d.s); *Pal<aemon>* (s.p.s); *Palaemon a young Swain in love with Hylace* (d.p.)
MELARNUS: *Melarnus* (s.d.s); *Mel<arnus>* (s.p.s); *Melarnus, a crabbed old Shepherd* (d.p.)
TRUGA: *Truga* (s.d.s); *Trug<a>* (s.p.s); *Truga* [Melarnus'] *Wife* (d.p.)
AEGON: *Aegon* (s.d.s and s.p.s); *Aegon an ancient Countryman* (d.p.)
BELLULA: *Bellula* (s.d.s); *Bell<ula>* (s.p.s; also misprinted *Ball.*); *Bellula* [Aegon's] *supposed Daughter* (d.p.)
HYLACE: *Hylace* (s.d.s); *Hyl<ace> | Hil<ace>* (s.p.s); *Hylace* [Melarnus and Truga's] *Daughter* (d.p.)
APHRON: *Aphron* (s.d.s); *Aph<ron>* (s.p.s); *Aphron* [one of] *two Gentlemen both in love with Callidora* (d.p.)
DEMOPHIL: *Demophil* (s.d.s); *Demo<phil>* (s.p.s); *Demophil* [one of] *two old folk of a Noble family* (d.p.)
SPODAIA: *Spodaia* (s.d.s); *Spo<daia>* (s.p.s); *Spodaia* [one of] *two old folk of a Noble family* (d.p.)
PHILISTUS: *Philistus* (s.d.s); *Phi<listus>* (s.p.s); *Philistus* [one of] *two Gentlemen both in love with Callidora* (d.p.)
CLARIANA: *Clariana* (s.d.s); *Cla<riana>* (s.p.s); *Clariana, sister to Philistus* (d.p.)
FLORELLUS: *Florellus* (s.d.s); *Flo<rellus>* (s.p.s); *Florellus* [one of Demophil and Spodaia's] *Children* (d.p.)
MAID: [Clariana's] *Maid* (s.d.s); *Maid* (s.d.s and s.p.s); *Clariana's Maid* (d.p.)

OTHER CHARACTERS
Alupis's dead father (1.1, 3.1)
Alupis's mother (1.1)
Court beauties whom Alupis saw in the city, but whose charms he resisted (1.1)
Damon, a woodland artist who gave Bellula a cup he made (2.3)
Galla, probably Menalca's daughter, said to be more beautiful than Hylace (3.2)
Menalca, probably Galla's father (3.2; if not, his daughter is a separate unnamed personage and is also said to be more beautiful than Hylace)
Amaryllis, said to be more beautiful than Hylace (3.2)
A handsome young shepherd who gave Truga a ring 80 years ago (3.2)
Servants in Clariana's household (4.4)
Dametas, a young shepherd (5.1, 5.5)
Men who helped Aphron to break into Demophil's house (5.5)

Demophil's servants (5.5)
Bellula's nurse (5.5)
Pirates who kidnapped Bellula as a baby, said variously to be Turkish and from Argier (5.5)
The Governor of Pachynus, a Sicilian nobleman, father of Bellula and Aphron (5.5)
Aegon's wife (5.5)

SETTING
Period: the reference to Argier and Turkish pirates suggests a period between the fifteenth and seventeenth centuries, but there is no other significant historical context
Time-Scheme: 3.2, 4.2–3, 4.5, 4.6, and 5.1 all take place on the same day, 3.2 in the morning; less than an hour passes between 4.5 and 5.1.
Place: Sicily

Geography
Sicily: Pachynus
[*Italy*]: Paestum
[*London*]: the Bear Garden
Wales
[*Greece*]: Mount Pelion; Mount Ossa; Mount Olympus; Mount Helicon; Anticyra; Paros
[*Spain*]: Castile; River Tagus
Europe: the Alps; Poland
[*Africa*]: Argier
[*Asia*]: Persia; Arabia; Scythia; Turkey
The Indies
The North Pole

SOURCES
Narrative: William Shakespeare, *As You Like It* (**1237**), *Twelfth Night* (**1297**; 5.3); Thomas Randolph, *Amyntas* (**2321**); Joseph Rutter, *The Shepherds' Holiday* (**2402**; 2.3).
Verbal: possibly William Cartwright, *The Ordinary* (**2468**; 1.2; but the influence is more likely to have been vice versa).

LANGUAGE
English
Latin: 2 words (3.2; Alupis)
Spanish: 10 words (3.2; Aphron, Alupis)

FORM
Metre: pentameter; a little prose; intermittent dimeter, trimeter, and tetrameter lines
Rhyme: blank verse
Act-Division: 5 acts
Epilogue: 16 lines, in couplets, spoken by Alupis
Lines (Spoken): 2,606 (2,517 verse, 89 prose)
Lines (Written): 2,813

Alupis's incessant singing creates a problem in calculating the spoken length. Here I have adopted the following principles. Whenever he breaks into song, he starts a new verse line. The text usually prints only the first words or line of what he sings, but when this is followed by '&c.', I assume that he goes on to sing the remainder of the refrain in full, and include the unprinted lines in the calculation. However, when no '&c.' appears after a complete line of the song, I assume that this is all he sings.

STAGING
Doors: one represents the door to Melarnus' cottage: it is knocked on (4.2, implicit), and mentioned (5.1, s.d.)
Within: Melarnus speaks to Hylace 'within his door' (5.1, s.d.)
Audience: said to be seated (ep.)
Miscellaneous: Aphron exits and immediately re-enters in 5.4.

MUSIC
Songs:
  1: 'Rise up, thou mournful swain', 1.1, Alupis, 8 lines;
  2: 'The merry waves dance up and down and play', 1.1, Alupis, 12 lines;
  3: ' 'Tis better to dance than sing', 1.2, Alupis, 6 lines;
  4: 'It is a punishment to love', 4.1, Bellula, 8 lines; *musical setting survives*.
Other Singing: Alupis continually sings snatches from Song 1 (1.1–2, 2.2, 3.1–2, 4.2–3, 4.5–6, 5.1, 5.5, ep., implicit)
Dance: Alupis dances (1.2, s.d.)

PROPS
Weapons: two swords (5.3, s.d.)
Clothing: a garland of flowers (2.3, dialogue); a ring (3.2, dialogue); an ebony ring (3.2, 4.2, dialogue)
Food and Drink: apples (2.3, 2.4, dialogue)

COSTUMES AND MAKE-UP
CALLIDORA: cross-dressed in a man's suit (1.1, s.d.; 1.2, 2.3, 4.1, 5.3, implicit)
TRUGA: wrinkled face (implicit)
BELLULA: golden hair (dialogue)
FLORELLUS: a fine suit (3.1, dialogue); shepherd's clothes (4.1, 4.6, 5.3, dialogue; loose enough to carry two swords underneath); a hat (4.6, dialogue)

EARLY TEXTUAL HISTORY
1630–6: The play was written when Abraham Cowley was a pupil at Westminster School.
1638: entered to Henry Seile in the Stationers' Register on Wednesday 14 March; entry names author. Thomas Wykes had licensed the book for publication.
1638: **'O** printed by John Dawson for Henry Seile; collation A–F^8, 48 leaves; title page names author; portrait of author facing title page; authorial verse dedication to Sir Kenelm Digby; list of roles.
c. 1630s–40s: a copy of O was in the possession of John Horne (Vicar of Headington, Oxfordshire). After his death, his entire collection of play-books passed into the possession of John Houghton of Brasenose College, Oxford (*c.* 1608–77), then to James Herne (died 1685), and then to the library of Ralph Sheldon (1623–84) at Weston, where it was catalogued by Anthony Wood, probably in the late 1670s.
1640–1: Humphrey Moseley was selling copies of O for 6d.
c. 1640s: Song 4 included, with a musical setting by William Webb, in a MS songbook (Oxford: Bodleian, MS Don. c. 57, fo. 40^r).
1656: *The English Parnassus* entered to Evan Tyler, Thomas Johnson, and Thomas Davies in the Stationers' Register on Wednesday 24 December.
1657: seventeen extracts (from 1.1–2, 2.3–4, 3.1–2, 4.1, 4.4, 5.2–3) included in Joshua Poole's *The English Parnassus*, sigs. Q5^v, S3^r, S6^v, V6^r, Y3^r, 2A1^r, 2G6^r, 2H1^v, 2I1^{r-v}, 2L4^v, 2M1^r, 2N2^v; printed for Thomas Johnson.
c. 1659: Song 4 included, with a musical setting, in a MS music-book (New York Public Library, MS Drexel 4257, no. 164) owned and partly compiled by John Gamble.
1677: *The English Parnassus* reprinted by Henry Brome for Thomas Bassett and John Wright; the extracts now appear on sigs. Q1^v, R7^r, S2^v, V2^r, X7^r, Z5^r, 2G2^r, 2G5^v, 2H5^{r-v}, 2K8^v, 2L5^r, 2M6^v.
1678: *New Airs and Dialogues* received an imprimatur on Saturday 4 May.
1678: Song 4 included, with Webb's setting, in John Banister and Thomas Low, *New Airs and Dialogues*, sig. S1^r; printed (probably in the autumn) by Andrew Clark and Mary Clark for Henry Brome.
1679: *New Airs and Dialogues* entered to Henry Brome in the Stationers' Register on Thursday 2 October.
1681: included in the second part of Cowley's *Works* (^{2}F$_1$), sigs. I1^r–R1^r, 65 pages on 33 leaves; printed by Mary Clark for Charles Harper and Jacob Tonson.
1682: included in a pirated overseas edition of the second part of Cowley's *Works* (^{3}D), sigs. c9^r–f12^v, 40 leaves.
1684: included in the second part of Cowley's *Works* (^{4}F$_2$), printed by Mary Clark for Charles Harper and Abel Swalle. The copy was F$_1$.
1689: included in the second part of Cowley's *Works* (^{5}F$_3$), printed by Mary Clark for Charles Harper.
1700: included in the second part of Cowley's *Works* (^{6}F$_4$), printed by Mary Clark for Charles Harper.

EDITION
A. R. Waller, in Abraham Cowley, *Essays, Plays, and Sundry Verses* (Cambridge, 1906), 67–148.

REFERENCES
Annals 1633; John Aubrey, *Brief Lives*, ed. Oliver Lawson Dick (London, 1949), 75, 98; Beal 2 CoA 207–8; Bentley, iii. 179–80; Eyre & Rivington, ii. 103, iii. 88; Greg 539; Hazlitt, 143; *MLR* 13 (1918), 401–11; *Oxford Bibliographical Society Proceedings and Papers* 2.2 (1929), 133; REED: Cambridge, 858; *RES* 4 (1928), 1–8.

2453. *Love and Honour*

TEXT
Printed in 1649 (Wing D329).

GENRE
tragicomedy
Contemporary: play (prol.)

TITLE
Performed/Printed: *Love and Honour*
Contemporary: *The Courage of Love*; *The Nonpareils, or The Matchless Maids*

AUTHOR
William Davenant

DATE
November 1634

ORIGINAL PRODUCTION
King's Men at the Blackfriars (and perhaps also the Globe)

PLOT
Savoy has just vanquished Milan in a war, in which Count Prospero has taken prisoner Evandra, the heir of Milan. He sends her hastily back to Turin, unaware of two things: the old Duke of Savoy has sworn to avenge an old affront—the execution of his brother by Milan ten years before—by beheading a member of the Milanese royal family, and Prince Alvaro has fallen in love with her. By the time Prospero learns this, it is too late to fetch her back, so he and Alvaro hatch a scheme together to conceal her in a hidden cave beneath Prospero's house, and smuggle her out of the city later.

The Duke decrees that Evandra shall indeed lose her head, but that all other female prisoners of war will be allowed to return home after a year, without having to pay any ransom, unless their captors can persuade them to marriage. However, he cannot induce Alvaro to reveal Evandra's whereabouts. Prospero falls for Evandra himself, and gives her another prisoner, Melora, to keep her company and woo her on his behalf. In fact, Melora broaches the suit of her brother, Leonell, but Evandra isn't interested. On learning that Alvaro will be executed if he does not produce her by nightfall, she tricks him into entering the cave and locks him in; Prospero gets the same treatment when he proposes dying in Alvaro's place. She intends to present herself to the Duke for execution, but Melora attempts to forestall her by giving herself up under Evandra's name. The courtier to whom she surrenders, Calladine, falls in love with her and decides to save her by, in effect, the same plan: replace the Princess with her lady-in-waiting (with Evandra taken to be Melora and so substituted for herself). The upshot is that both Melora and Evandra go to court independently, both claiming to be Evandra and both offering themselves for execution. The Duke decides to play safe and behead them both.

Ambassadors arrive from Milan, but are unable to persuade the Duke to grant a stay of execution. Leonell offers himself as a substitute: he is not the knight he seems to be, but the Prince of Parma, an incognito scion of the Milanese royal family whose father was responsible for the capture of the Duke's brother in the first place. The Duke accepts his offer, but the ambassadors forestall the alternative execution by revealing that they are in fact the Duke of Milan and the lost brother, who is not dead after all: Milan kept him a prisoner, in a life of comfortable contemplation, in order to disable the military might of Savoy. Melora reminds Alvaro that he promised to marry her if the enmity between Milan and Savoy were ever resolved. Leonell in turn gets Evandra, and Prospero devotes himself to a soldier's life.

In the sub-plot, the soldier Vasco realizes that, under the Duke's decree, there is only one way he will get his hands on his captive's money: to woo and marry her. She is not the perfect match: an old widow who has sworn not to remarry for another ten years. Eventually he marries her, but finds her averse to dying, and ends up requesting a divorce, which is granted.

SCENE DESIGNATION
prol., 1.1–2, 2.1–3, 3.1–4, 4.1–5, 5.1–3, ep. (Q has act-division only)

ROLES
PROLOGUE
Captain VASCO, a soldier; later the Widow's husband; also said to be a colonel
ALTESTO, an officer
FRIVOLO, an officer; also called Lord Frivolo, presumably in jest
Signor TRISTAN, an officer
Count PROSPERO, a young nobleman and soldier, Alvaro's minion; also called Lord Prospero
EVANDRA, Princess of Milan, the Duke of Milan's daughter and heir
CALLADINE, an old counsellor
Prince ALVARO of Piedmont, the Duke of Savoy's elder son; he is no longer young
SOLDIERS of Savoy (1.1, *non-speaking*)
Sir LEONELL, a young Milanese knight, Melora's brother; in reality, the Prince and heir of Parma, a kinsman of the Milanese royal house
LELIA, a poor Milanese woman, Tristan's prisoner; later the Widow's maidservant
MELORA, Evandra's lady-in-waiting, Leonell's sister, Altesto's prisoner; a young woman
The DUKE of Savoy, Alvaro's father; an old man
ATTENDANTS on the Duke (3.2, 4.4, 5.3, *non-speaking*)
A WIDOW, an old Milanese woman, deaf and toothless, Vasco's prisoner, later his wife; said to be coming up to 110 years old

Calladine's SERVANT (4.1, 4.4)
MUSICIANS (4.2; some or all sing collectively)
A BOY, who sings (4.2, 5.2)
The Duke's GUARD (4.4, 5.3, *non-speaking*)
An AMBASSADOR from Milan; in reality, the Duke of Milan, Evandra's father
An AMBASSADOR from Milan; in reality, the Duke of Savoy's brother, Alvaro's uncle
EPILOGUE

Speaking Parts: 19

Stage Directions and Speech Prefixes
PROLOGUE: *Prologue* (heading)
VASCO: *Vasco* (s.d.s and s.p.s); *Vasco, a Colonel* (d.p.)
ALTESTO: *Altesto* (s.d.s and s.p.s); *Altesto* [one of the] *Officers and Soldiers* (d.p.)
FRIVOLO: *Frivolo* (s.d.s and s.p.s); *Frivolo* [one of the] *Officers and Soldiers* (d.p.)
TRISTAN: *Tristan* (s.d.s and s.p.s); *Tristan* [one of the] *Officers and Soldiers* (d.p.)
PROSPERO: *Prospero* (s.d.s); *Prosp<ero>* (s.p.s); *Prospero, a young Count* (d.p.)
EVANDRA: *Evandra* (s.d.s); *Evand<ra>* (s.p.s); *Evandra, Heir of Millaine* (d.p.)
CALLADINE: *Calladine* | *Caladine* (s.d.s); *Call<adine>* (s.p.s); *Caladine, an old Counsellor* (d.p.)
ALVARO: *Alvaro* (s.d.s); *Alva<ro>* (s.p.s); *Alvaro, Prince of Savoy* (d.p.)
SOLDIERS: *Soldiers* (s.d.s and d.p.)
LEONELL: *Leonell* (s.d.s and s.p.s); *Leonel* (s.d.s); *Leonell, Prince of Parma* (d.p.)
LELIA: *Lelia* (s.d.s and s.p.s); *Lelia,* [the Widow's] *Maid* (d.p.)
MELORA: *Melora* (s.d.s); *Melor<a>* (s.p.s); *Melora, Sister to Leonell* (d.p.)
DUKE: *The Duke* (s.d.s); *Duke* (s.d.s and s.p.s); *The old Duke of Savoy* (d.p.)
ATTENDANTS: *Attendants* (s.d.s)
WIDOW: *the Widow* (s.d.s); *Widow* (s.d.s and s.p.s); *An old Widow* (d.p.)
SERVANT: *a Servant* (s.d.s); *Servant* (s.d.s and s.p.s); *Servants* (d.p.)
MUSICIANS: *Musicians* (s.d.s and d.p.); *Music* (s.d.s); *Chorus* (s.p.s)
BOY: *Boy* (s.d.s, s.p.s, and d.p.)
GUARD: *a Guard* | *The Guard* | *Guard* (s.d.s)
AMBASSADOR: [one of] *2 Ambassadors* | [one of the] *Ambassadors* | *Millaine* (s.d.s); *1 Ambassador* (s.p.s); *The Duke of Millaine* (d.p.)
AMBASSADOR: [one of] *2 Ambassadors* | [one of the] *Ambassadors* (s.d.s); *2 Ambassador* (s.p.s); [The old Duke of Savoy's] *brother* (d.p.)
EPILOGUE: *Epilogue* (heading)

OTHER CHARACTERS
The Milanese army, some of whom have been maimed in battle (1.1–2)

The ladies of Evandra's train (1.1)
The Savoy army, including cavalry (1.1, 2.2, 5.1, 5.3)
Altesto's mother (1.1, 2.1)
The Milanese general (1.1)
Vasco's father (1.1)
Vasco's ensign (1.2)
The Widow's dead husband, who made his fortune from a monopoly of dead women's hair (2.1)
Vasco's barber (2.1, 2.3)
Prospero's servant (2.2)
The people of Savoy (2.3, 3.2, 5.1)
The Duke of Savoy's younger son (3.2)
Lelia's mother, probably an alewife or tavern hostess, but said (ironically) to be a wealthy dowager (3.3)
The Duke of Parma, father of Leonell and Melora (3.4, 5.3)
Frivolo's grandmother, who died at the spinning wheel (4.2)
A diminutive baker whom Altesto once knew (5.1)
A carman who died of food poisoning (5.1)
The Widow's grandmother (5.1)

SETTING
Period: seventeenth century (?); the Great Turk is named as Achmet, which would suggest a time in or after the reign of Ahmed I (1603–17)
Time-Scheme: 2.3 takes place in the morning; 4.1 takes place before dawn, and 4.2 in the early morning; a day passes between 4.4 and 5.1; 5.1–3 take place on the same day
Place: Savoy

Geography
Savoy: Turin; Piedmont
Milan: the citadel; St Magdalen's Wall
Italy: Sicily; Venice; Parma
Europe: Flanders; Paros; Paris; Westphalia; Cordoba; Delphos (i.e. Delphi)
[*Africa*]: Algiers; Egypt
[*Asia*]: Turkey; Assyria; Scythia; Arabia
India
Japan

SOURCES
Works Mentioned: *A Lady's Daughter of Paris* (ballad, 1586; 2.3); *Fortune, My Foe* (ballad, before 1590; 2.1); 'John, Come Kiss Me Now' (song; 2.1); *Queen Guinevere's Death* (**H39**; 5.1); there is a general reference to Pietro Aretino (3.3)

LANGUAGE
English
Latin: 2 words (3.3; Frivolo)
French: 1 word (5.1; Vasco)

FORM
Metre: rough and irregular pentameter; a little prose
Rhyme: blank verse

Prologue: 14 lines, in couplets
Act-Division: 5 acts
Epilogue: 8 lines, in couplets
Lines (Spoken): 2,474 (2,436 verse, 38 prose)
Lines (Written): 3,488

STAGING
Doors: mentioned (2.2, s.d.; 4.1, dialogue); characters enter at two doors (3.4, 5.3, s.d.)
Discovery Space: covered with an arras (3.4, s.d.)
Stage: mentioned (2.2, s.d.)
Within: sound effect (2.2, s.d.)
Above: a bay window (4.2, dialogue); two characters appear above (5.2, s.d.)
Beneath: 'the stage opens' and Evandra is lifted up from 'the cave' beneath (2.2, s.d.); characters descend into 'the cave' (2.2, 3.4, s.d.)
Audience: addressed as 'gentlemen' (ep.)
Miscellaneous: the playwright is said to be waiting 'below' at the entrance to the theatre to hear the audience's first reactions to the play (ep.; the Blackfriars auditorium was upstairs)

MUSIC AND SOUND
Sound Effects: knock within (2.2, s.d.)
Music: distant retreat (1.1, s.d.); distant drum march (1.1, s.d.); distant cornett flourish (1.1, s.d.)
On-Stage Music: fiddles (4.2, dialogue)
Songs:
  1: 'With cable and thong he drew her along', 3.3, Altesto, 4 lines;
  2: 'No morning red and blushing fair', 4.2, Boy and Chorus of Musicians, 30 lines;
  3: 'O draw your curtains and appear', 5.2, Boy, 8 lines; *musical setting survives.*
Other Singing: Vasco may sing a snatch of a ballad (2.3, implicit)

PROPS
Lighting: lights (2.2, 3.4, s.d.); a light (3.1, s.d.)
Weapons: Alvaro's sword (1.1, s.d.); Leonell's sword (4.5, dialogue; 5.2, s.d.); Prospero's sword (4.5, dialogue; 5.2, s.d.)
Musical Instruments: fiddles (4.2, dialogue)
Small Portable Objects: a key (2.2, 3.1, s.d.; 3.4, 4.1, dialogue); letters (3.2, 4.4, 5.1, s.d.); a bottle (3.4, s.d.); a bag (3.4, s.d.); binding cords (4.4, implicit)
Large Portable Objects: a table (3.4, s.d.); a seat (3.4, implicit); seating for at least three characters (5.3, implicit)
Scenery: an arras (3.4, s.d.)

COSTUMES AND MAKE-UP
PROLOGUE: a long cloak (dialogue)
VASCO: a garment with small point tags (2.1, dialogue); 'fantastically accoutred' (3.3, s.d.), with a ribboned lock of hair on his left side (dialogue); enters dressing himself (4.2, s.d.)
ALTESTO: a bonnet (2.1, dialogue; doffed on stage)
FRIVOLO: a glove (4.2, dialogue)
PROSPERO: wounded (1.1, s.d.); muffled (3.4, s.d.); a sheath (4.5, 5.2, implicit)
EVANDRA: her arms pinioned in a scarf (1.1, s.d.); bound (5.3, dialogue)
CALLADINE: a nightgown (4.1, s.d.)
ALVARO: a corselet (1.1, s.d.; removed on stage); a sheath (1.1, implicit)
LEONELL: wounded (1.2, s.d.); a sheath (4.5, dialogue; 5.2, implicit)
LELIA: mean clothes (3.3, dialogue)
MELORA: mourning clothes (4.1, s.d.); a veil (4.1, s.d.; removed on stage); bound (5.3, dialogue)
WIDOW: a hood (3.3, dialogue; 4.2, implicit); petticoats (3.3, dialogue)
AMBASSADORS: false beards (5.1, implicit; 5.3, s.d.; removed on stage)
Miscellaneous: one unidentifiable character wears red (4.4, dialogue)

EARLY STAGE HISTORY
1634: presumably performed, as licensed, no doubt by the King's Men. Music for the production was probably contributed by William Lawes.

1634: performed on Friday 12 December, presumably by the King's Men at the Blackfriars. The audience included Sir Humphrey Mildmay and 'the 2 Southlands'; Mildmay paid 4s.6d for his party.

1637: performed by the King's Men at Hampton Court on Sunday 1 January. The performance took place in the evening. The audience included: King Charles I; Queen Henrietta Maria. John Lowin and Joseph Taylor were later paid £210 for this and twenty other court performances, by a warrant dated either Sunday 12 or Wednesday 15 March 1637.

1641: The play was in the repertory of the King's Men.

EARLY TEXTUAL HISTORY
1634: On Thursday 20 November, Sir Henry Herbert licensed the play for performance. Originally it was entitled *The Courage of Love*; at some later date, at William Davenant's request, Herbert retitled it *The Nonpareils, or The Matchless Maids*. By Friday 12 December, however, the title had stabilized as *Love and Honour*.

c. 1630s: Song 2 included in a MS volume of state papers (London: British Library, MS Egerton 2026, fo. 66ᵛ) at various times owned by Robert Drake and by Stephen Foster.

c. 1630s: Song 2 included in a MS miscellany (London: British Library, MS Harley 6931, fo. 52ᵛ).

1638: On Monday 26 February, Matthew Clay granted an imprimatur to Davenant's *Madagascar and Other Poems*.

1638: Davenant's *Madagascar and Other Poems* entered to Thomas Walkley in the Stationers' Register on Tuesday 13 March.

1638: epilogue included in Davenant's *Madagascar and Other Poems*, sig. F10ʳ; printed by John Haviland for Thomas Walkley.

c. 1639–45: Song 3 included, with a musical setting by William Lawes, in Lawes's autograph MS songbook (London: British Library, Add. MS 31432, fo. 39^r). Lawes later gave the book to Richard Gibbon, whose widow, Anne, gave it away in turn, probably at some time between 1652 and 1656, to one J. R. (probably John Reading).

c. 1640: Song 3 included, with Lawes's setting, in a MS songbook (New York Public Library, MS Drexel 4041 no. 10, fo. 9^{r-v}).

1641: On Saturday 7 August, Robert Devereux, 3rd Earl of Essex (Lord Chamberlain) issued a warrant prohibiting the printing of this and sixty other plays without the consent of the King's Men. On Saturday 14 August, the order was read to the Stationers' Company and instructions issued for its observance.

1646: entered to Humphrey Robinson and Humphrey Moseley in the Stationers' Register between Friday 4 and Tuesday 15 September; group entry, play and author individually named. John Langley had licensed the book for publication.

1648: Walkley's rights to *Madagascar and Other Poems* transferred in the Stationers' Register to Humphrey Moseley on Tuesday 22 February.

1648: *Madagascar and Other Poems* reprinted for Humphrey Moseley; the epilogue now appears on sig. E12^v.

1649: 'Q printed for Humphrey Robinson and Humphrey Moseley; collation A–E^4, 20 leaves; title page names author, acting company, and playhouse; list of roles. The text is printed in double columns.

1650–60: Q advertised as for sale by Humphrey Moseley.

Mid-seventeenth century: Song 2 included in a MS verse miscellany (London: British Library, MS Egerton 2421, fos. 26^v–27) variously owned by Francis Norreys (?= Sir Francis Norris) and by Henry Balle.

Mid-seventeenth century (before 1677): a copy of Q was owned by Frances Wolfreston.

c. 1640s–50s: Song 2 included in a MS verse miscellany (Oxford: Bodleian, MS Rawlinson poet. 62, fo. 33) compiled by a Cambridge man.

1653: *The Marrow of Compliments* entered to Humphrey Moseley in the Stationers' Register on Tuesday 20 December.

1654: Song 3 included in Samuel Sheppard's *The Marrow of Compliments*, sig. G2^{r-v}; printed (before Saturday 15 July) for Humphrey Moseley.

1657: advertised as for sale by the Newcastle-upon-Tyne bookseller William London.

Mid- to late seventeenth century (before 1689): a copy of Q was owned by Elizabeth Puckering.

1667: Moseley's rights to Davenant's *Masques, Plays, and Poems* transferred from his widow, Ann, to Henry Herringman in the Stationers' Register on Monday 19 August; group transfer of nine titles, the Davenant collection being one, with the play individually named.

1668: advertised as for sale by Henry Herringman.

1672: advertised as for sale by Thomas Dring.

1672: Davenant's *Works* entered to Henry Herringman in the Stationers' Register on Thursday 31 October. Roger L'Estrange had licensed the book for the press. On Monday 18 November, it was advertised for sale by Henry Herringman, John Martin, John Starkey, and Robert Horne; however, it was apparently not issued until the following year.

1673: Robinson's rights transferred in the Stationers' Register by his executor (also named Humphrey Robinson) to John Martin and Henry Herringman on Thursday 30 January, as part of a list of 105 titles, by assignment of Saturday 13 May 1671.

1673: included in in Davenant's *Works* (^{2}F), sigs. ^{2}2F1^v– ^{2}2M1^v, 49 pages on 25 leaves; printed by John Macock for Henry Herringman. The epilogue is also included separately on sig. 2H4^r, and Song 3 (headed 'On Two Lovers Condemned to Die') on sig. 2Q4^r, both in parts of the book printed by Thomas Newcomb.

1675: Davenant's *Works* advertised as for sale by John Starkey.

1675: Moseley's rights to *The Marrow of Compliments* transferred from his widow, Ann, to Peter Parker in the Stationers' Register on Wednesday 8 September, by order of a court held on Monday 22 February, and by an assignment dated Thursday 26 September 1672.

1678: *New Airs and Dialogues* received an imprimatur on Saturday 4 May.

1678: Song 3 included, with Lawes's musical setting, in John Banister and Thomas Low, *New Airs and Dialogues*, sigs. Q6^v–Q7^r; printed (probably in the autumn) by Andrew Clark and Mary Clark for Henry Brome.

1679: *New Airs and Dialogues* entered to Henry Brome in the Stationers' Register on Thursday 2 October.

1683: Martin's rights transferred in the Stationers' Register from his widow, Sarah, to Robert Scott, on Tuesday 21 August, by assignment of Tuesday 14 June 1681 and order of a court of Monday 7 November 1681; individually named as part of a group transfer of 360 titles.

Late seventeenth century: Song 2 included in a MS verse miscellany (London: British Library, MS Harley 3991, fo. 65^{r-v}); the heading ascribes the song to the play.

c. 1690s: Song 2 included in a MS commonplace book (Austin: University of Texas at Austin, MS (Killigrew, T) Works B Commonplace book, fos. 25^v–26^r).

EDITIONS

James W. Tupper, in *Love and Honour and The Siege of Rhodes*, The Belles Lettres Series (Boston and London, 1909), 1–177.

A. M. Gibbs, in Sir William Davenant, *The Shorter Poems* (Oxford, 1972), 66, 156, 208–9, 294–5 (epilogue, songs, and music only).

REFERENCES
Adams, 76; *Annals* 1634; Arber, iv. 41; Bawcutt 305, 355; Beal 2 DaW 87–93; Beal Online DaW 91.5; Bentley, ii. 676, iii. 205–6; *Chelys* 31 (2003), 3–17; Eyre & Rivington, i. 290, 437, 463, iii. 3, 88; Greg 684; Hazlitt, 138; *The Library*, 5th ser., 7 (1952), 225–34; *The Library*, 6th ser., 11 (1989), 213; *The Library*, 7th ser., 1 (2000), 377; William London, *A Catalogue of the Most Vendible Books in England* (London, 1657), sig. 2F1^v; MSC 1.4–5, 364–9; MSC 2.3, 382; Steele, 258, 264.

2454. The Proxy

EVIDENCE
Sir Henry Herbert's office-book; Stationers' Register.

GENRE
Contemporary: play

TITLE
Performed: *The Proxy, or Love's After-Game*
Contemporary: *Love's After-Game*

DATE
November 1634

ORIGINAL PRODUCTION
King's Revels Company (presumably) at Salisbury Court

PLOT
The subtitle implies either that a lover has been rejected by the object of their desire, but tries again, or that he or she deliberately holds back in the early stages of courtship with the intention of acting more effectively later on. Perhaps the process involves using a stand-in either in the early courtship or as part of the second strike.

ROLES
A PROXY

EARLY STAGE HISTORY
1634: possibly performed at Salisbury Court on Monday 24 November. (However, this is more likely to be a misunderstanding of the licence.)
  1636: performed (as *Love's Aftergame*) at St James's Palace by the Salisbury Court players (i.e. the King's Revels Company) on Wednesday 24 February. The audience included: King Charles I; Queen Henrietta Maria. Richard Heton was later paid £50 for this and two other court performances, by a warrant dated Friday 17 or Saturday 18 February 1637.

EARLY TEXTUAL HISTORY
1634: On Monday 24 November, Sir Henry Herbert probably licensed the text for performance at Salisbury Court.

  1653: entered to Richard Marriott in the Stationers' Register on Thursday 29 December (?; recorded as Tuesday 29 November); group entry of 21 plays; play individually named.

REFERENCES
Annals 1634; Bawcutt 306, 341; Bentley, v. 1399; Greg Θ104; Hazlitt, 186; MSC 6, 86; Sibley, 97; Steele, 256.

2455. The Opportunity

TEXT
Printed in 1640 (STC 22451), probably from authorial copy.

GENRE
comedy
Contemporary: play (S.R.); comedy (t.p.); poem (ded.)

TITLE
Performed/Printed: *The Opportunity*

AUTHOR
James Shirley

DATE
November 1634

ORIGINAL PRODUCTION
Queen Henrietta's Men at the Cockpit

PLOT
Arriving in Urbino for the first time, Aurelio is surprised to find the inhabitants greeting him as a long-lost friend. It turns out that he looks identical to Borgia, who had been banished for killing the brother of Ursini, a court favourite. Accepted by Borgia's father Mercutio, he seizes his opportunity and steps into his alter-ego's shoes. They are summoned to court, where Ursini, in love with Borgia's sister Cornelia, has procured a pardon for Borgia in order to gain the family's favour. Complications arise when Aurelio falls in love with Cornelia himself, while the Duchess falls in love with him and appoints him her secretary. Aurelio decides to keep his options open, maintains his assumed identity, and pursues both ladies, circumventing any suspicion of incest by telling Cornelia that he is acting on Aurelio's behalf: Aurelio fell for her on seeing her picture, he says, and engaged him to woo her.
  Other suitors have come to woo the Duchess, including the Duke of Ferrara, posing as his own ambassador; he takes offence at the favours shown to 'Borgia'. There is a mix-up in the dark: posing as the Duchess, Cornelia tells 'Borgia' that she will marry Ferrara; then the Duchess arrives, 'Borgia' takes her for Cornelia, and, on hearing she is to marry Ursini,

admits his true identity. Having overheard Cornelia's comments, Ferrara arrives in Urbino in his own person to claim the Duchess as his bride, but she denies ever promising herself to him. Aurelio's servant Pimponio poses as another potential suitor to the Duchess. Initially he pretends to be a Spanish don, but is advised to adopt an Italian identity instead when he is introduced at court. He duly claims to be the Duke of Ferrara, which infuriates the real Duke further.

'Borgia' asks the Duchess directly whether she loves him. She tartly reminds him of the unbridgeable distance between them, then dictates him a love-letter to be delivered to the person who loves her best, asking the recipient to come to an assignation in the garden. Discouraged, Aurelio gives the letter to Ferrara, but then realizes that the Duchess meant it for him. She sets Mercutio to guard the garden gate and let in none but 'Borgia', but he mistakenly admits Ferrara instead. Realizing that he has lost his opportunity to court the Duchess, Aurelio turns his attentions to Cornelia; but his friend Pisauro, eager to get the girl for himself, tells her that 'Borgia' is incestuously in love with her, and will claim, untruthfully, that he is not really her brother. When he tells her just that, she gives herself to Ursini. The Duchess, meanwhile, has contracted herself to Ferrara. Aurelio's true identity emerges, and, having won neither lady, he prepares to go off to war in Germany. The real Borgia is recalled from his exile.

SCENE DESIGNATION
1.1–2, 2.1–3, 3.1–3, 4.1, 5.1–2 (Q has act-division only)

ROLES
Signor AURELIO Andreozzi of Milan, a young gentleman; adopts the identity of Signor Borgia; later appointed the Duchess's chief secretary
Signor PISAURO of Milan, a member of a noble family, Aurelio's companion
PIMPONIO, Aurelio's footman; poses as a Spanish prince; also called Pimp
LUCIO, a gentleman
PIETRO, Ursini's creature
JULIO, a gentleman, Borgia's friend
Signor MERCUTIO, an old widower, father of Borgia and Cornelia; later appointed Comptroller of the Duchess's household and called Lord Mercutio
The DUCHESS of Urbino; a widow
Signor URSINI, a court favourite
CORNELIA, the Duchess's waiting-woman; Mercutio's daughter, Borgia's sister
MELINDA, a lady attending the Duchess
Madam LAURA, a lady attending the Duchess
ASCANIO, a boy, Grutti's son; said to be little; poses as a Switzer
GRUTTI, an innkeeper, Ascanio's father
The DUKE of Ferrara; poses as his own ambassador
SERVANTS at the inn (3.1; two speak)

Speaking Parts: 17

Stage Directions and Speech Prefixes
AURELIO: *Aurelio | Borgia* (s.d.s and d.p.); *Aur<elio> | Bor<gia>* (s.p.s)
PISAURO: *Pisauro* (s.d.s and d.p.); *Pis<auro>* (s.p.s)
PIMPONIO: *Pimponio* (s.d.s, s.p.s, and d.p.)
LUCIO: *Lucio* (s.d.s and d.p.); *Luc<io>* (s.p.s)
PIETRO: *Pietro* (s.d.s and d.p.); *Pie<tro>* (s.p.s)
JULIO: *Julio* (s.d.s and d.p.); *Ju<lio>* (s.p.s)
MERCUTIO: *Mercutio* (s.d.s and d.p.; also misprinted *Mecutio*); *Mer<cutio>* (s.p.s)
DUCHESS: *Duchess* (s.d.s, s.p.s, and d.p.)
URSINI: *Ursini* (s.d.s and d.p.); *Urs<ini>* (s.p.s)
CORNELIA: *Cornelia* (s.d.s and d.p.); *Cor<nelia>* (s.p.s)
MELINDA: *Melinda | [one of the] Ladies* (s.d.s and d.p.); *Mel<inda>* (s.p.s)
LAURA: *Laura | [one of the] Ladies* (s.d.s and d.p.); *Lau<ra>* (s.p.s)
ASCANIO: *Ascanio, a Boy* (s.d.s and d.p.); *Ascanio* (s.d.s); *Asc<anio>* (s.p.s); *Asca<nio>* (d.p., second entry)
GRUTTI: *Grutty* (s.d.s and d.p.); *Grutti* (s.d.s); *Gr<utti>* (s.p.s)
DUKE: *Ferrara* (s.d.s and d.p.); *Duke* (s.d.s); *Fer<rara>* (s.p.s)
SERVANTS: *Servants* (s.d.s); *1 Servant | 2 Servant* (s.p.s)

OTHER CHARACTERS
Signor Borgia, a banished man, Mercutio's son, Cornelia's brother (1.1–2, 2.2–3, 3.2–3, 4.1, 5.1–2)
Borgia's dead uncle (1.1)
Ursini's brother, a gentleman killed by Borgia (1.1–2, 5.2)
The dead Duke of Urbino, the Duchess's husband (1.1–2)
Ascanio's dead mother (3.1)
The Duke of Ferrara's train (3.3)
Borgia's dead mother (4.1)
Ferrara's groom (4.1)
Paulo Andreozzi, Aurelio's father, major domo to the Duchy of Milan (5.2)

SETTING
Period: seventeenth century, after the outbreak of the Thirty Years War (1618)
Time-Scheme: 2.2–3 take place at night (2.2 at bed-time), and 3.3 the following morning; 5.1–2 take place the evening after 4.1 (5.1 at around dusk)
Place: Urbino

Geography
Italy: Naples; Milan; Ferrara
Spain
Europe: Orange; Germany; Switzerland; Lake Lerna
Arabia

SOURCES
Narrative: Tirso de Molina, *El castigo del penséque* (1613); William Shakespeare, *The Comedy of Errors*

(**944**; 1.1); John Webster, *The Duchess of Malfi* (**1726**; 4.1, 5.2)
Verbal: Thomas Kyd, *The Spanish Tragedy* (**783**; 1.1); William Shakespeare, *The Taming of the Shrew* (**916**; 3.1), *The Comedy of Errors* (**944**; 1.2); John Webster, *The White Devil* (**1689**; 5.2)
Works Mentioned: Ben Jonson, *Pleasure Reconciled to Virtue* (**1854**; 2.1)

LANGUAGE
English
Italian: 2 words (1.1; Pisauro)
Spanish: 3 words (2.1; Pimponio)

FORM
Metre: irregular pentameter and prose; one passage of skeltonics (5.2)
Rhyme: blank verse
Act-Division: 5 acts
Lines (Spoken): 2,275 (1,858 verse, 417 prose)
Lines (Written): 2,656

STAGING
Doors: two characters enter at several doors (4.1, s.d.)
Stage: characters pass over the stage (3.3, s.d.)
Within: speech (5.2, s.d.)
Above: Cornelia and the Duchess appear above (2.3, s.d.; they interact with characters on the main stage)

MUSIC
Music: unspecified music (3.1, dialogue); loud music (3.3, s.d.)
Song: 2.3, Cornelia
Dance: unspecified dance (3.1, s.d.)

PROPS
Lighting: a light (2.3, s.d.); a light above (2.3, dialogue)
Clothing: a glove (4.1, implicit)
Money: gold (2.1, 3.1, dialogue); an unspecified sum (2.1, implicit); a bag of gold (2.1, dialogue)
Food and Drink: two bottles of wine (3.1, dialogue; drunk on stage)
Small Portable Objects: a pardon (1.2, dialogue); pen and ink (1.2, 4.1, implicit); keys (4.1, dialogue); letters patents (4.1, implicit); a letter (4.1, dialogue; written on stage)
Large Portable Objects: a portmanteau (2.1, dialogue)
Scenery: hangings (5.2, dialogue)

COSTUMES
AURELIO: a thin beard, or none at all (dialogue); a hat (4.1, implicit; doffed on stage)
PIMPONIO: mean clothes (2.1, implicit); dressed as a Spanish don (3.1, s.d.; 4.1, dialogue; removed on stage); an undergarment (4.1, implicit)
LUCIO and JULIO: bare-headed (2.2, dialogue)
MERCUTIO: probably a hat (4.1, implicit)
ASCANIO: dressed as a Switzer (3.1, s.d.; 4.1, implicit)

EARLY STAGE HISTORY
1634: presumably performed, as licensed, no doubt by Queen Henrietta's Men at the Cockpit, to whom the play was ascribed in 1640.
1639: The play was in the repertory of the King's and Queen's Young Company (Beeston's Boys) at the Cockpit. On Saturday 10 August, Philip Herbert, 4th Earl of Pembroke (Lord Chamberlain) issued an order restraining performances by other companies of this and 44 other plays.
Before 1660 (possibly before 1642, but more probably in 1659–60): reportedly performed at the Red Bull. At one performance, a father and son were present in the audience; the boy's favourite character was Pimponio.

EARLY TEXTUAL HISTORY
1634: On Saturday 29 November, Sir Henry Herbert licensed the text for performance.
1639: entered in the Stationers' Register to Andrew Crooke and William Cooke on Thursday 25 April; named individually as part of a group entry of five plays. Thomas Wykes had licensed the book for publication.
1640: Q printed (probably in April) by Thomas Cotes for Andrew Crooke and William Cooke; collation A² B–K⁴, 38 leaves; title page names author, acting company, and playhouse; authorial dedication to Captain Richard Owen; list of roles. Two variant imprints name Andrew Crooke alone as publisher, for sale in London and Dublin respectively. (Crooke is not otherwise known to have traded in Dublin, but his brother, Edmond Crooke, did.)
c. 1640s: a copy of Q was in the possession of John Horne (Vicar of Headington, Oxfordshire). After his death, his entire collection of play-books passed into the possession of John Houghton of Brasenose College, Oxford (*c.* 1608–77), then to James Herne (died 1685), and then to the library of Ralph Sheldon (1623–84) at Weston, where it was catalogued by Anthony Wood, probably in the late 1670s. By then the copy had been bound into a single volume with 21 other plays by Shirley (and, presumably in error, with Henry Shirley's *The Martyred Soldier*, **2030**).
1655: *The English Treasury of Wit and Language* entered in the Stationers' Register to Humphrey Moseley on Tuesday 16 January.
1655: an extract (from 2.2) included in John Cotgrave's *The English Treasury of Wit and Language*, sig. S5ᵛ; printed for Humphrey Moseley.
c. 1655: extracts transcribed by John Evans in a miscellany, *Hesperides*, intended for publication and entered to Humphrey Moseley in the Stationers' Register on Thursday 16 August 1655. The book remained unpublished in 1660, and Evans continued adding to the collection until at least 1666. Two MS exemplars are known; one was cut up by J. O. Halliwell-Phillipps in the nineteenth century; the other survives (Washington: Folger, MS V. b. 93).

1657: advertised as for sale by the Newcastle-upon-Tyne bookseller William London.

1662: extracts (from 2.1, 3.1, 4.1, 5.2) appear as the droll *A Prince in Conceit* in *The Wits*, sigs. E4^r–E7^r; printed for Henry Marsh.

1672: *The Wits* reprinted by Edward Crouch for Francis Kirkman.

1684: Nicholas Cox (Manciple of St Edmund Hall, Oxford) had a copy, presumably of Q, in his bookshop. It had probably been previously owned by Gerard Langbaine, and appears on a list compiled by Anthony Wood on Saturday 13 December.

EDITION
Mary J. Mekemson, *The Renaissance Imagination* (New York and London, 1991).
Peter Happé, in James Shirley, *The Complete Works*, gen. eds. Eugene Giddens, Teresa Grant, and Barbara Ravelhofer (Oxford, forthcoming).

REFERENCES
Annals 1634; Bawcutt 307; Bentley, v. 1134–7; Bodleian, MS Wood E. 4, art. 1, p. 68; *ELR* 14 (1984), 241–2; Eyre & Rivington, i. 463, ii. 8; Robert Stanley Forsythe, *The Relations of Shirley's Plays to the Elizabethan Drama* (New York, 1914), 297–304; Greg 575; Hazlitt, 171; *The Library*, 5th ser., 28 (1973), 294–308; *The Library*, 7th ser., 10 (2009), 372–404; William London, *A Catalogue of the Most Vendible Books in England* (London, 1657), sig. 2F1^v; *MLR* 13 (1918), 401–11; MSC 2.3, 389–90; *SB* 1 (1948–9), 151–82.

2456. The City Find . . .

EVIDENCE
John Greene's diary.

TITLE
Performed: [*A* or *The*] *City Find<. . .>*

Assuming that the last word of the title is indeed incomplete, there are four possible expansions: *Findal* (meaning invention or discovery), *Finder*, *Find-Fault*, or *Finding*.

DATE
Limits: 1597–1635

See **2446**.

SETTING
Place: London (?)

EARLY STAGE HISTORY
1635: performed in London on Friday 27 February. The audience included John Greene.

REFERENCES
REED: Inns of Court, 810.

2457. Christmas Masque

TEXT
The masque survives in five MS fragments, three of them authorial and two scribal, which add up to a more or less complete draft of the whole text:

A: antimasque and coda (University of Nottingham, Portland Collection, MS Pw V 26, fos. 155^r–159^r); authorial;
B1: ballad (University of Nottingham, Portland Collection, MS Pw V 25, fo. 61^{r-v}); authorial;
B2: ballad (University of Nottingham, Portland Collection, MS Pw V 25, fo. 62^{r-v}); scribal;
B3: ballad (University of Nottingham, Portland Collection, MS Pw V 25, fo. 64^{r-v}); scribal;
M: main masque (University of Nottingham, Portland Collection, MS Pw V 26, fo. 160^{r-v}); authorial.

The ballad and associated material in the antimasque were a late addition.

GENRE
masque
Contemporary: country masque, Christmas toy (Cavendish's letter to his daughters)

TITLE
Later Assigned: *The Christmas Antimasque*

AUTHOR
William Cavendish, Earl of Newcastle

DATE
Christmas 1634–5

ORIGINAL PRODUCTION
Earl of Newcastle's household, probably at Welbeck Abbey, Nottinghamshire

'Norton', the Vicar's parish, is almost certainly Norton Cuckney, just south of Welbeck.

PLOT
The vicar and his parishioners want to offer their lord and lady some Christmas entertainment. They can't mount a play: they don't have enough time and the vicar isn't able to write one. They can't put on a proper masque because they have no fine clothes, but the vicar thinks he may be able to write around this. He is offended by the others' scepticism and haughtily describes his pedigree. Other ideas are floated and rejected: a dancing bear will frighten the ladies, dancing apes are too commonplace, classical gods too unoriginal, virtues and vices too old-fashioned, and a ballad mocking romances, when performed, is considered too topical. Finally, they settle on a dance, and perform it.

The main masque follows. Three ladies have been sent away to the country by their jealous husbands: they seek sympathy from the audience, then dance.

The vicar returns: he failed to acknowledge the audience at the start, and is allowed to expiate his discourtesy by speaking the epilogue.

SCENE DESIGNATION
The masque is here divided as follows:
sc.1: antimasque;
sc.2: main masque;
sc.3: coda.

ROLES
Ap Thomas ap Richard, the Welsh VICAR of Norton
SNIP Razor, a barber; originally to have been called Coxcomb
Cellidide LAST, a shoemaker; originally to have been called Widgeon Last
Hammer KETTLEMAN, a tinker
Master FERARIUS Anvil, a farrier
GILES Goose, a tailor
CHEVEREL Conscience, a glover
Robin PUFFED-PASTE, a cook
Tom RYE-WHEAT, a baker
Three LADIES, the masquers, all wives

Speaking Parts: 12

Stage Directions and Speech Prefixes
VICAR: *The Vicar* (s.d.s); *Vicar* (s.p.s); *Up Thomas upp Ritchard A Weltch vicar* (d.p.)
SNIP: *3* (s.p.s); *A Barber snip rasor | Coxe Come* [deleted] (d.p.)
LAST: *Widgin-Laste A Shoemaker* (d.p.)
KETTLEMAN: *A Tinker Hamer Ketleman* (d.p.)
FERARIUS: *Ferarius* (s.p.s); *ferarius Anvill A Farrier* (d.p.)
GOOSE: *A Tailor Giles Goose* (d.p.)
CHEVEREL: *Cheferill Contience A Glover* (d.p.)
PUFFED-PASTE: *A Cook Robin Pufte Paste* (d.p.)
RYE-WHEAT: *Baker | The Baker* (s.p.s); *Tom Rie-wheate A Baker* (d.p.)
LADIES: *The Ladies* [amended] | *The Lady masquers* (s.d.s); *1 | 2 | 3* (s.p.s)

Several antimasque speeches are assigned to numbered rather than named speakers, and numbers are also assigned in the character list at the head of the text. However, the two sets of numbers don't match: in the text, 3 is Snip Razor, who is numbered 2 in the character list; and in the list the Vicar is numbered 1, whereas in the text 1 is an (unidentifiable) interlocutor of his.

OTHER CHARACTERS
The Vicar's father (sc.1)
A Dutchman, who may teach apes to dance (sc.1)
A Frenchman, who taught the Dutchman to dance (sc.1)
Projectors, the three ladies' husbands (sc.2)

SETTING
Geography
[London]: the Exchange; St Paul's Cathedral; the Banqueting House
England: Norton [Cuckney]; Southampton
Wales
The Netherlands
France

SOURCES
Narrative: Ben Jonson, *Royal Entertainment at Bolsover* (**2439**; sc.1); probably James Shirley, *The Triumph of Beauty* (**2435**; sc.1)
Verbal: William Shakespeare, *A Midsummer Night's Dream* (**1012**; sc.1)
Music: 'Bessy Bell' (before 1621; Song); 'The Morris' (unidentified; Song)
Works Mentioned: Bible: Proverbs (sc.1), Song of Solomon (sc.1); the Talmud (sc.1); the Koran (sc.1); *Le Chanson de Roland* (twelfth century; sc.1; probably Jacobus de Voragine, *The Golden Legend* (*c.* 1275; sc.1); *Bevis of Hampton* (*c.* 1300; sc.1); *Amadis de Gaul* (fourteenth century; sc.1); *Guy of Warwick* (fourteenth century; sc.1); Sir Thomas Malory, *Le Morte D'Arthur* (1470; sc.1); *Robin Hood* (1500; sc.1); Diego Ortúñez de Calahorra, Pedro de la Sierra, and Marcos Martínez, *Espejo de principes y caballeros* (1555–87; English tr., *The Mirror of Princely Deeds and Knighthood*, by Margaret Tyler, R. P., and L. A., 1578–99; sc.1); Francisco Vazquez, *Palmerin d'Oliva* (1511; English tr. by Anthony Munday, 1588) or Francisco de Moraes, *Palmerin of England* (1547–8, English tr. by Anthony Munday, 1581; sc.1); Puppet Play of the Virtues and Vices (**H22**, possibly imaginary; sc.1); Miguel de Cervantes, *Don Quixote* (1605–15; English tr. by Thomas Shelton, 1612–20; sc.1); Aurelian Townshend, *Tempe Restored* (**2359**; sc.1)

LANGUAGE
English
Latin: 10 words (sc.1, 3; Vicar)
Dialect: The Vicar speaks consistently in a stage 'Welsh' accent.

FORM
Metre: prose and tetrameter
Rhyme: couplets
Epilogue: 4 lines, spoken by the Vicar
Lines (Spoken): 374 (108 verse, 266 prose)
Lines (Written): 350-4 (three segments of 229, 48–52, and 73 lines respectively)

The variable is the lengths of the three ballad MSS; the shortest of the three is the one in Cavendish's own hand.

STAGING
Audience: addressed as 'noble lords and ladies' (sc.2)

MUSIC
Music: fiddles (sc.1, dialogue; accompanies the first dance); unspecified music (sc.2, implicit; accompanies the second dance)

2457. Christmas Masque

Song: 'Some do not lie, I'll tell you why', sc.1, Rye-Wheat, 48 lines; sung twice to different tunes (respectively 'Bessy Bell' and 'The Morris'); *the former tune is extant*
Other Singing: the Vicar speaks the epilogue 'in a continued tune' (sc.3, s.d.)
Dance: the antimasquers dance (sc.1, s.d.; with musical accompaniment); the masquers dance (sc.2, implicit; with musical accompaniment)

The tune of 'Bessy Bell', which is traditional, may be found in Claude M. Simpson, *The British Broadside Ballad and its Music* (New Brunswick, 1966), 298–9.

PROPS
Small Portable Objects: a handkerchief (sc.3, s.d.)

COSTUMES
VICAR: a coat (sc.1, dialogue; removed on stage); a hat (sc.3, s.d.; removed on stage)

EARLY STAGE HISTORY
The dialogue assumes a Christmas performance in the country in the presence of a lord and lady, presumably William Cavendish, Earl of Newcastle, and Elizabeth Cavendish, Countess of Newcastle.

EARLY TEXTUAL HISTORY
1634: William Cavendish was asked by his daughters, Jane and Elizabeth, aged 12 and 7, to write the masque. His draft MSS survive (**A**, 9 pages on 5 leaves; **B1**, 1 leaf; **M**, 1 leaf).

One, or possibly two further copies of the masque were in existence, but are now lost: Cavendish asked for verses about the masque, addressed to his daughters, to be copied into 'my book' (which may or may not have contained the text of the masque itself), and 'before' (i.e. in the front of 'the masque book', which presumably did).

The ballad was copied twice by Cavendish's secretary, John Rolleston (**B2–3**, 1 leaf each); B3 is dated 1634, but this may refer to the date of the text rather than of its transcription.

EDITION
Lynne Hulse, in William Cavendish, *Dramatic Works*, Malone Society Reprints 158 (Oxford, 1996), 10–29.

REFERENCES
Butler, 374; McGee-Meagher 1634–42, 33–4.

1635

2458. The Antiquary

TEXT
Printed in 1641 (Wing M703).

GENRE
comedy
Contemporary: comedy (S.R., t.p.)

TITLE
Printed: The Antiquary

AUTHOR
Shackerley Marmion

DATE
Limits: 1634–6
Best Guess: 1635

ORIGINAL PRODUCTION
Queen Henrietta's Men at the Cockpit

PLOT
The Duke plans to go through his city in disguise to see how the common people behave.

The rich fool Petrutio returns home from foreign travels, ambitious to secure a place at court. He offends Lionel by refusing his request for a loan, and Lorenzo by refusing to marry his daughter Lucretia. Lionel and Lorenzo plan to get even; Lionel tells Lorenzo that his page is the key to it, and asks Lorenzo to look after the boy for the time being.

Lionel has tried unsuccessfully to get money from his uncle, the antiquary Veterano. Even a visit from the disguised Duke to see his collection of antiquities cannot sway the old man. Posing as a scholar, Lionel brings him some books purporting to be lost classical texts, along with a document recording an old family debt, which Veterano decides to pay; but he will still give nothing to his nephew. The disguised Duke scares Veterano by producing a warrant sequestering his relics for the state, but then revokes it.

Lorenzo's wife Aemilia takes a fancy to Lionel's page, and proposes adultery. She is overheard by Lorenzo, who angrily intervenes. Assured by Lionel that things will be alright, Aemilia accuses her husband of slander and points out that the 'page' is really a girl, perhaps brought to the house by Lorenzo for immoral purposes. Lionel confirms the girl's gender, and the balance of power in the marriage shifts.

Lionel and the disguised Duke speak well of Petrutio, knowing him to be eavesdropping. Petrutio is so pleased with the prospect of preferment at court that he invites everyone to a fantastical banquet in which the dishes are signs of the zodiac. Veterano gets drunk, and falls asleep when Petrutio recites a poem he has written in honour of the occasion. Petrutio takes offence. As Veterano sleeps it off, the Duke dresses him in a fool's coat. Petrutio gets his preferment: Lionel poses as the Duke and allows him to marry into the ducal family. Petrutio goes off to his wedding, but discovers afterwards that the bride is not the Duke's sister but Lionel's, who had previously posed as the page and whom he once jilted.

In the other plot, Lucretia is playing hard-to-get with Aurelio, accepting his attentions and gifts at one moment and rejecting him with disdain at another. This pleases her father, who intends to marry her to the old, wealthy Moccinigo. She is averse to such a husband, and tries to dissuade Moccinigo: she cannot love him and will only drive him mad with jealousy. When he persists, she tells him that he will need to get rid of Aurelio, his rival; he engages a bravo to have him murdered. Lucretia tries to prevent the killing, but the bravo seems implacable: neither an appeal to conscience nor a threat to expose him to the authorities will change his purpose. The certainty of hellfire does the trick, however, and she secures his assistance in an alternative plot. She warns Aurelio to flee for his life, but he sneaks into her bedroom and, when spotted by passers-by at the window, claims he is now her husband. Meanwhile the bravo pretends to have committed the murder and gone mad with remorse. He publicly accuses Moccinigo as the procurer of the crime, and Aurelio, disguised as an officer, arrests them both.

Aurelio presents Moccinigo and the bravo to receive the supposed Duke's justice. Moccinigo agrees to hand over his entire estate to whomever Lucretia should marry, and signs a bond to that effect; she chooses the arresting officer, who then reveals himself to be Aurelio. The bravo too has a secret identity: he is actually Aurelio's father, who posed as a hired killer to save his son after Lucretia told him of Moccinigo's plot. Finally, the Duke discovers himself and approves the proceedings.

SCENE DESIGNATION
1.1–3, 2.1–3, 3.1–4, 4.1–8, 5.1–4 (Q has act-division only)

ROLES
Signor LIONEL, a young man, Angelia's brother, Veterano's nephew and heir; poses as the Duke; also called Master Lionel
Signor PETRUTIO, a gentleman, Gasparo's son; later Angelia's husband
Lionel's PAGE; said to be little; turns out to be his sister Angelia, Veterano's niece; later Petrutio's wife

GASPARO, an old magnifico, Petrutio's father
LORENZO, an old gentleman; Aemilia's husband, Lucretia's father
Signor MOCCINIGO, a rich old gentleman; a praetor and *clarissimo*
The DUKE of [Venice]; poses as a foreigner
LEONARDO, a courtier
Signor AURELIO, a young gentleman and citizen; poses as a *commandatore*; also called Master Aurelio
MUSICIANS (2.1; one sings)
Mistress LUCRETIA, a gentlewoman, daughter of Lorenzo and Aemilia; 16 years old
Mistress AEMILIA, Lorenzo's wife, Lucretia's mother
Signor VETERANO, an old antiquary, uncle of Lionel and Angelia
Master PETRO, Veterano's boy
A BRAVO; in reality, Aurelio's father
A BOY, the Bravo's attendant
Aurelio's SERVANT (3.3)
A COOK, who prepared Petrutio's banquet (4.4)
Mistress JULIA, Lucretia's waiting-woman
BACHA, a waiting-woman
Two SERVANTS, who pose as officers (5.3–4, non-speaking)

Speaking Parts: 20

Stage Directions and Speech Prefixes
LIONEL: *Lionell* (s.d.s and s.p.s); *Lionell, Nephew to the Antiquary* (d.p.)
PETRUTIO: *Petrutio* (s.d.s); *Pet<rutio>* (s.p.s); *Petrutio a foolish Gentleman, son to Gasparo* (d.p.)
PAGE: *Angelia* (s.d.s); *Ang<elia>* (s.p.s); *Angelia sister to Lionell, in the disguise of a Page* (d.p.)
GASPARO: *Gaspero | Gasparo* (s.d.s); *Gasp<aro>* (s.p.s); *Gasparo a Magnifico of Pisa* (d.p.)
LORENZO: *Lorenzo* (s.d.s); *Lor<enzo>* (s.p.s); *Lorenzo an old Gentleman* (d.p.)
MOCCINIGO: *Moccinigo* (s.d.s); *Moc<cinigo>* (s.p.s); *Moccinigo, an old Gentleman that would appear young* (d.p.)
DUKE: *Duke* (s.d.s and s.p.s); *The Duke of Pisa* (d.p.)
LEONARDO: *Leonardo* (s.d.s); *Leon<ardo>* (s.p.s); *Leonardo* [one of] *2 Courtiers* (d.p.)
AURELIO: *Aurelio* (s.d.s); *Aur<elio>* (s.p.s); *Aurelio a young Gentleman* (d.p.)
MUSICIANS: *Musicians* (s.d.s)
LUCRETIA: *Lucretia* (s.d.s); *Luc<retia>* (s.p.s); *Lucretia daughter to Gasparo* (d.p.; *sic*)
AEMILIA: *Aemilia* (s.d.s); *Aemil<ia>* (s.p.s); *Aemilia wife to Gasparo* (d.p.; *sic*)
VETERANO: *Antiquary* (s.d.s and s.p.s); *the Antiquary* (s.d.s); *Veterano the Antiquary* (d.p.)
PETRO: *Petro* (s.d.s); *Pet<ro>* (s.p.s); *Petro the Antiquary's boy* (d.p.)
BRAVO: *Bravo* (s.d.s and s.p.s); *Aurelio's father, in the disguise of a Bravo* (d.p.)
BOY: *Boy* (s.d.s and s.p.s); [the Bravo's] *Boy* (d.p.)
SERVANT: *Servant* (s.d.s and s.p.s)

COOK: *Cook* (s.d.s and s.p.s); *A Cook* (d.p.)
JULIA: *Julia* (s.d.s); *Jul<ia>* (s.p.s); *Julia* [one of] *2 Waiting women* (d.p.)
BACHA: *Bacha* (s.d.s); *Ba<cha>* (s.p.s); *Baccha* [one of] *2 Waiting women* (d.p.)
SERVANTS: *two Servants | Officers* (s.d.s); *2 Servants* (d.p.)
D.p. also lists: *Donato* [one of] *2 Courtiers*

OTHER CHARACTERS
Gallants, sons of the *clarissimi*, with whom Petrutio intends to dine (1.1–2)
A courtesan who twice refused to sleep with Moccinigo (1.2)
The customers in a tippling house visited by the disguised Duke (2.3)
Men who have been killed by the Bravo's rapier (3.1; probably imaginary)
Signor Jovanno Veterano de Montenegro, Veterano's great-grandfather (3.4)
Lionel's creditors (3.4)
The Duke's daughter (4.4; possibly imaginary)
The Duke's niece (4.4; possibly imaginary)
Aemilia's family (4.7)
Aemilia's friends (4.7)

SETTING
Period: sixteenth or seventeenth century: Machiavelli (died 1527) and King Harry of England (died 1547, if the referent is Henry VIII) belong to a former age
Time-Scheme: 1.1 takes place not long before noon, 2.1 at dawn, and 4.3 in the morning; a day passes between 3.2 and 4.4
Place: Venice (but Q's character list says Pisa)

Geography
Venice: the Rialto
Italy: Padua; Florence; Rome; Aquileia
The Adriatic Sea
Greece: Crete; Athens; Delphi
[*Europe*]: England; Spain; France; the Pyrenees; Montenegro
[*Africa*]: River Nile
The Indies

SOURCES
Narrative: William Shakespeare, *Measure for Measure* (**1413**; Duke); Thomas Middleton, *No Wit, No Help Like a Woman's* (**1644**; 4.4)
Verbal: Ovid, *Metamorphoses* 15 (5.1, cited); Petronius, *Satyricon* (2.2); Seneca, *Hippolytus* (4.1); Persius, *Satires*, Prologue (3.2); Juvenal, *Satires* 8 (2.2); Geoffrey Chaucer, *Canterbury Tales*: The Merchant's Tale (*c.* 1387, printed 1478, repr. 1602; 1.2); William Shakespeare, *Romeo and Juliet* (**987**; 2.1), *Love's Labours Lost* (**1031**; 3.1); Thomas Heywood, *The Escapes of Jupiter* (redaction of **1637** and **1645**; 4.7); Philip Massinger, *A New Way to Pay Old Debts* (**2180**; 3.4); John Earl, *Microcosmography* (1628; 3.4)

Works Mentioned: Plato, *Timaeus* (1.1); Terence, 150 lost comedies (1.1); Cicero, *De republica* (3.4); Virgil, *Aeneid* 3 (5.3); Horace, *Satires* 1.8 (5.4); Ptolemy, *Mathematics* (3.4); Sir Philip Sidney, *Arcadia* (c. 1580; 3.2); Ben Jonson, *Sejanus' Fall* (**1412**; 5.4); Honoré d'Urfé, *L'Astrée* (1607–28; 3.2); Thomas Heywood, *Love's Mistress* (**2451**; 4.4)

LANGUAGE
English
Latin: 6 words (3.4, 5.1; Veterano, Duke, Lorenzo)
Italian: 5 words (2.1, 3.1, 3.4, 5.4; Lorenzo, Bravo, Veterano, Aemilia)
French: 1 word (5.1; Lorenzo)

FORM
Metre: prose and pentameter
Rhyme: blank verse
Act-Division: 5 acts
Lines (Spoken): 2,526 (1,013 verse, 1,513 prose)
Lines (Written): 2,706

STAGING
Stage: characters pass over the stage (4.3, s.d.)
Above: Lucretia appears at a window above (2.1, implicit; s.d. misplaced); Aurelio and Lucretia both appear there (4.3, s.d.); there is interaction between characters at the window and on the main stage

MUSIC
Music: flourish (5.4, s.d.)
On-Stage Music: one of the Musicians plays the fiddle (2.1, dialogue)
Song: 2.1, Musician

PROPS
Weapons: the Bravo's rapier (3.1, dialogue)
Musical Instruments: a fiddle (2.1, dialogue)
Money: a groat (2.3, dialogue); twenty livres (3.1, dialogue)
Food and Drink: two bottles (4.5, s.d.)
Small Portable Objects: papers (3.2, dialogue and implicit); two books (3.4, s.d.); a document (3.4, implicit); a warrant (3.4, dialogue); a document (4.4, implicit); a cup (4.5, dialogue); a paper (4.6, implicit); a bond (5.4, dialogue); a seal (5.4, dialogue)
Large Portable Objects: a chair (4.6, dialogue)

Although Veterano's various antiquities are described by Petro in 2.2 using the gestural word 'this', they are not in fact present on stage; Petro is rehearsing his descriptive patter, and when the Duke arrives later in the scene it is clear that there are no antiquities to be seen until he goes inside.

COSTUMES
LIONEL: disguised as a scholar (3.4, s.d.); disguised as the Duke (5.4, s.d.)
ANGELIA: cross-dressed as a page (1.1–2, 2.1, 4.1, implicit); women's clothes (5.4, s.d.)
LORENZO: a beard (dialogue)
MOCCINIGO: a dyed beard (1.2, dialogue); white hair (dialogue; it has been either dyed or covered up in 1.2, and perhaps elsewhere)
AURELIO: disguised as an officer (5.3, s.d.; 5.4, implicit)
LUCRETIA: golden hair (dialogue)
VETERANO: big breeches and a hat (4.6, dialogue); spectacles (4.6, dialogue; put on on stage); a fool's coat (4.8, s.d.; 5.4, dialogue)
PETRO: cross-dressed in women's clothes (4.8, s.d.; 5.4, dialogue)
BRAVO: hangers (3.1, implicit)

EARLY STAGE HISTORY
Performed by Queen Henrietta's Men at the Cockpit by 1641 (and presumably by 1636).

EARLY TEXTUAL HISTORY
1640: entered in the Stationers' Register to John Williams and Francis Eglesfield on Wednesday 11 March; individually named as part of a group entry of two plays; entry apparently names James Shirley as author (but this might pertain only to *Look to the Lady*, **1946**, which is named second). Thomas Wykes had licensed the book for publication.

1641: **Q** printed by Felix Kingston for John Williams and Francis Eglesfield; collation A² B–K⁴ L², 40 leaves; title page names author, acting company, and playhouse; list of roles.

c. **1640s**: a copy of Q was in the possession of John Horne (Vicar of Headington, Oxfordshire). After his death, his entire collection of play-books passed into the possession of John Houghton of Brasenose College, Oxford (*c.* 1608–77), then to James Herne (died 1685), and then to the library of Ralph Sheldon (1623–84) at Weston, where it was catalogued by the antiquarian Anthony Wood, probably in the late 1670s.

1655: *The English Treasury of Wit and Language* entered in the Stationers' Register to Humphrey Moseley on Tuesday 16 January.

1655: three extracts (from 1.1–2, 5.1) included in John Cotgrave's *The English Treasury of Wit and Language*, sigs. B8ʳ, R8ᵛ–S1ʳ, V4ʳ; printed for Humphrey Moseley.

1676–93: eighteen extracts (from 1.1, 2.1, 3.2–3, 4.3, 4.6, 5.1) copied into a MS miscellany (Oxford: Bodleian, MS Sancroft 29, pp. 107–8) compiled by William Sancroft.

1684: Nicholas Cox (Manciple of St Edmund Hall, Oxford) had a copy of Q in his bookshop. It had probably been previously owned by Gerard Langbaine, and appears on a list compiled by Anthony Wood on Saturday 13 December.

Late seventeenth century (before 1695): a copy of Q was owned by Anthony Wood.

EDITIONS
W. Carew Hazlitt, in *A Select Collection of Old Plays* (London, 1874–6), xiii. 411–523.

James Maidment and W. H. Logan, in *The Dramatic Works of Shackerley Marmion* (Edinburgh, 1875), 197–295.

REFERENCES
Annals 1635; Bentley, iv. 739–41; Bodleian, MS Wood E. 4, art. 1, p. 31; Eyre & Rivington, i. 463; Greg 601; Hazlitt, 15; Nicolas K. Kiessling, *The Library of Anthony Wood* (Oxford, 2002) 4373; *MLR* 13 (1918), 401–11; *SP* 40 (1943), 186–203.

2459. The Conspiracy

TEXT
Two early versions:
- **A:** printed in 1653 (F; Wing K444A); authorized edition;
- **B:** printed in 1638 (Q; STC 14958); unauthorized edition, allegedly from a surreptitious transcript; lays out the text mainly as prose; adds induction, prologue, two new scenes, epilogue, and extended passages in 1.1, 2.1–2, B.2.7–9, 3.1, 4.1, 4.4–5, 5.1–3.

The central textual issue is the relationship and sequence of the two versions. Bentley believed that F was a revision undertaken in the 1650s, partly because the 1653 publisher's assertion of Q's corruption understates the extent of the differences between the texts and misrepresents their nature. The case is closely analogous to that of a better-known Folio with prefatory matter damning previous quarto editions as piracies; but we no longer dismiss all pre-1623 exemplars of Shakespeare's plays on the word of Heminges and Condell alone. It scarcely needs to be spelt out that a publisher could have a commercial motive for talking down an earlier edition.

The 1653 epistle places Q, irrespective of its precise nature, later in the chain of textual transmission than F, printed from the author's own copy. One variant seems to confirm this definitively, while others are suggestive. In the Q version of 1.1, Polyander enters early to talk to the servants setting out the banquet at the start, after which the King and his courtiers enter in a group (in both Q and F); the entry direction for the King must have come first, because it includes Polyander, and the reviser neglected to delete his name when adding the new material in Q. There is no evidence to support the hypothesis of an authorial revision in the 1650s, and it is striking that the publisher, rather than the author, wrote the epistle to the 1653 edition.

The Q text appears to have been prepared for performance; one recurrent type of variant is the systematic provision of non-speaking attendants. It may also have been expurgated: for example, in 1.2, F's 'some god give me temper' becomes Q's 'ease, my breast'. The addition of an induction pertaining to an aristocratic wedding and a royal audience strongly indicates that the performance in question was the York House premiere. F's text may therefore be understood as, in essence, a pre-performance state of the play, but with a retrospectively appended note of the occasion of the premiere, which describes the spectacle in 5.5 (whereas Q gives only the text of the song).

GENRE
tragedy

Contemporary: tragedy (B ind., Q and F t.p.); play (Greene, epistle, S.R.)

TITLE
Performed: *The Conspiracy*
Printed: *Pallantus and Eudora*

B-Text
Printed: *The Conspiracy*

AUTHOR
Henry Killigrew

DATE
January 1635

ORIGINAL PRODUCTION
York House

PLOT
Two foreign princes arrive on Crete after a storm. One is Clearchus, who is finding an excuse to land with a shipful of troops which he intends to use to rescue the Princess Hianthe from a forced marriage to the usurping King's son, Timeus. The other is Pallantus, whose ship has been wrecked. Afterwards he discovers that this was a lucky escape: Timeus suborned the sailors to kill him. He disguises himself as a soldier and both he and Clearchus fall in with a group of courtiers who are conspiring to restore the rightful King, Cleander, to the throne. (Cleander disappeared in infancy when the present King seized power sixteen years ago, and was wrongly presumed murdered.)

Timeus learns of the plot, but open rebellion breaks out before he can do anything about it: Clearchus' troops storm the city, Hianthe is rescued, and Pallantus kills the usurping King. In the ensuing sack, Pallantus encounters the Princess Eudora, the King's daughter, and falls in love with her. He later returns to her in his own person, and counters her objections to him as her father's killer by producing the evidence that Timeus attempted to have him murdered. Meanwhile, Timeus and his associates take refuge in the fort. Pallantus is sent to parley with them, and succeeds in persuading him to abandon villainy and accept Cleander's mercy. Timeus and Eudora are reunited, and Timeus shows remorse for the attempted murder of Pallantus. Eudora agrees to marry Pallantus, and the dead King is cremated.

SCENE DESIGNATION
1.1–4, Cho.1, 2.1–7, Cho.2, 3.1–5, Cho.3, 4.1–6, Cho.4, 5.1–5 (F has act-division only)

B-Text
ind., prol, 1.1–4, Cho.1, 2.1–9, Cho.2, 3.1–4, Cho.3, 4.1–7, Cho.4, 5.1–5, ep. (Q has act-division only)

This corresponds to the A-text as follows: A.1.1–4 = B.1.1–4; A.2.1–2 = B.2.1–2; A.2.3–4 = B.2.5–6; A.2.5 = B.2.8; A.2.6a = B.2.7; A.2.6b = B.2.3; A.2.7 = B.2.9; A.3.1–4 = B.3.1–4; A.4.1–6 = B.4.1–6; A.5.1–5 = B.5.1–5. A.3.5 is omitted. The induction, prologue, B.2.4, 4.7, and epilogue are B-text additions in their entirety.

ROLES

The KING of Crete, a usurper; father of Timeus and Eudora; an old man
Lord COMASTES, a young buffoon
Lord ARATUS, a conspirator, Pallantus' kinsman
POLYANDER, a lord of the King's faction
PHRONIMUS, a lord and conspirator
EURYLOCHUS, a lord and conspirator
MENETIUS, a lord of the King's faction
Lord TIMEUS, the King's son, Eudora's brother; a young man
HARPASTES, a villain
MELAMPUS, a villain
Prince PALLANTUS, a young prince, a kinsman of Aratus, Cleander, and Hianthe; formerly the First Prince of Crete; also called Lord Pallantus
Prince CLEARCHUS, a young foreign soldier
Lord HAIMANTUS, Admiral of Clearchus' fleet
Clearchus' SERVANT (1.3)
CORACINUS, Timeus' servant
RODIA, Eudora's waiting-woman
EUDORA, the Princess, the King's daughter, Timeus' sister
CHORUS of priests and people
Two COURTIERS (2.1, *non-speaking*)
MELISSA, Hianthe's waiting-woman
Princess HIANTHE, Cleander's sister, Pallantus' kinswoman
Two LADIES attending Hianthe (2.2, 2.7)
Two WAITERS attending Hianthe (2.2)
A POET and playwright (2.2)
CLEANDER, rightful King of Crete (his age is given as 17 in the epistle); a young man; Hianthe's brother, Pallantus' kinsman
ACATES, Cleander's tutor
A FLAMEN, an accomplice in the conspiracy (3.1)
ARGESTES, Timeus' servant (*non-speaking*)
A SERVANT at court (3.3)
The GUARD (3.3, 4.2–4; two or three speak)
A SERVANT, who delivers a letter (4.1)
The CAPTAIN of the guard (4.2–3, 5.3)
A CAPTAIN in the King's army (4.4)
A LADY attending Eudora (4.6, 5.1)
SOLDIERS, including captains, in Cleander's faction (4.6, *non-speaking*)
The PEOPLE of Crete (5.2, 5.5; speak collectively; may be the same as the Chorus)
A GUARD accompanying Pallantus (5.3, *non-speaking*)
PRIESTS (5.5; two sing individually; may be the same as the Chorus)

Speaking Parts: 37–8

B-Text
Induction
DIANA, goddess of hunting and chastity; also called Phoebe: *new role*
NYMPHS of Diana, more than two in number (*non-speaking*): *new roles*
JUNO, a goddess; *new role*
TRAGEDIA, a female figure who speaks the prologue; *new role*

Main Action
Two SERVANTS, who set out the banquet (1.1): *new roles*
ATTENDANTS on the King (1.1, 3.3–4, *non-speaking*): *new roles*
ATTENDANTS on the conspirators (1.2–3, 3.1, *non-speaking*): *new roles*
SERVANT (1.3): now described as a MESSENGER
CORACINUS: now described as one of Timeus' guard
CHORUS: not now identified as priests and people
Hianthe's LADIES: now also appear in 5.2
WAITERS attending Haimantus (2.3, *non-speaking*): *new roles*
ARGESTES: now described as one of Timeus' guard
ATTENDANTS on Timeus (3.3, *non-speaking*): *new roles*
GUARD: not now in 3.3
SERVANT (4.1): now named DEMOPHILUS
CAPTAIN of the Guard: now also appears in 4.7; but he may be split into two roles, the Captain who commands the guard in 4.2–3 and the Captain who joins Timeus in the fort in 4.7 and 5.3
ATTENDANTS on Polyander, including a boy (4.4, *non-speaking*): *new roles*
Six SOLDIERS (4.4; only one speaks): *new roles*
ATTENDANTS on Cleander (4.5, 5.2, 5.4, *non-speaking*): *new roles*
Eudora's LADY (4.6): now LADIES, probably two in number (one may speak only collectively); one now also appears in 5.4
PRIESTS (5.5): now Three FLAMENS
EPILOGUE: *new role*

Speaking Parts: 46–7
Allegorical Roles: 1

Stage Directions and Speech Prefixes
KING: *the King* (s.d.s); *King* (s.d.s and s.p.s); *The King a Usurper* (d.p.)
COMASTES: *Comastes* (s.d.s); *Com<astes>* (s.p.s); *Comastes a buffoonish Lord* (d.p.)
ARATUS: *Aratus* (s.d.s and s.p.s); *Arates* (s.d.s); *Aratus* [one of] *three great Lords* (d.p.)
POLYANDER: *Polyander* | [probably one of Timeus'] *Party* (s.d.s); *Poly<ander>* (s.p.s); *Polyander* [one of] *two Lords* (d.p.)

PHRONIMUS: *Phronimus* (s.d.s); *Phro<nimus>* (s.p.s); *Phronimus* [one of] *three great Lords* (d.p.)
EURYLOCHUS: *Eurylochus | Eurilochus* (s.d.s); *Eury<lochus>* (s.p.s); *Eurylochus* [one of] *three great Lords* (d.p.)
MENETIUS: *Menetius* | [probably one of Timeus'] *Party* (s.d.s); *Mene<tius>* (s.p.s); *Minetius* [one of] *two Lords* (d.p.)
TIMEUS: *Timeus* (s.d.s and s.p.s); [Eudora's] *Brother* (s.d.s); *Timeus* [the King's] *Son* (d.p.)
HARPASTES: *Harpastes* (s.d.s); *Harp<astes>* (s.p.s); *Harpastes* [one of] *two Villains* (d.p.)
MELAMPUS: *Melampus* (s.d.s); *Melam<pus>* (s.p.s); *Melampus* [one of] *two Villains* (d.p.)
PALLANTUS: *Pallantus | Palantus* | [one of Clearchus'] *Party* (s.d.s); *Pallan<tus>* (s.p.s); *Pallantus first Prince of Crete, disguised* (d.p.)
CLEARCHUS: *Clearchus* (s.d.s); *Clear<chus>* (s.p.s); *Clearchus a stranger Prince* (d.p.)
HAIMANTUS: *Haimantus* | [one of Clearchus'] *Party* (s.d.s); *Haim<antus>* (s.p.s); *Haimantus Admiral of Clearchus' Fleet* (d.p.)
SERVANT: *a Servant* (s.d.s); *Servant* (s.p.s)
CORACINUS: *Coracinus* (s.d.s); *Cora<cinus>* (s.p.s); *Coracinus* [one of the] *Servants to Timeus* (d.p.)
RODIA: *Rodia* (s.d.s and s.p.s); [one of] *the Ladies* (s.d.s); *Rodia* [Eudora's] *Woman* (d.p.)
EUDORA: *Eudora* (s.d.s); *Eudo<ra>* (s.p.s); *Eudora Sister to Timeus* (d.p.)
CHORUS: *Chorus* (s.d.s); *Chorus of Priests and People* (d.p.)
COURTIERS: *one | another* (s.d.s)
MELISSA: *Melissa* | [one of] *The Ladies* (s.d.s); *Mel<issa>* (s.p.s); *Melissa* [Hianthe's] *Woman* (d.p.)
HIANTHE: *Hianthe | the Princess* (s.d.s); *Hian<the>* (s.p.s); *Hianthe Sister to Cleander* (d.p.)
LADIES: *two Ladies | The Ladies | Ladies* (s.d.s); *1 Lady | 2 Lady* (s.p.s); *2 Ladies* (d.p.)
WAITERS: *Waiters* (s.d.s and d.p.); *1 Waiter | 2 Waiter* (s.p.s)
POET: *The Poet* (s.d.s); *Poet* (s.p.s and d.p.)
CLEANDER: *Cleander | the King* (s.d.s); *Clean<der> | King* (s.p.s); *Cleander the true King of Crete, a Youth* (d.p.)
ACATES: *Acates* (s.d.s); *Aca<tes>* (s.p.s); *Acates Tutor to Cleander* (d.p.)
FLAMEN: *a Flamen | the Flamen* (s.d.s); *Flamen* (s.p.s and d.p.)
ARGESTES: *Argestes* (s.d.s); *Argestes* [one of the] *Servants to Timeus* (d.p.)
SERVANT: *a Servant* (s.d.s); *Servant* (s.d.s and s.p.s)
GUARD: *Guard* (s.d.s, s.p.s, and d.p.); *a Guard | The Guard | one of the Guard* (s.d.s); *1 Guard | 2 Guard* (s.p.s)
SERVANT: *a Servant* (s.d.s); *Servant* (s.p.s)
CAPTAIN: [one of] *the Guard | the Captain of the Guard* (s.d.s); *Captain* (s.d.s and s.p.s)
CAPTAIN: *a Captain* (s.d.s); *Captain* (s.d.s and s.p.s)

LADY: *another Lady* | [one of] *the Ladies* (s.d.s); *Lady* (s.d.s and s.p.s); *2 Ladies* (d.p.)
SOLDIERS: *other Soldiers | Captain and Soldiers* (s.d.s); *Soldiers* (d.p.)
PEOPLE: *the People* (s.d.s); *People* (s.p.s)
GUARD: *a Guard* (s.d.s); *Guard* (d.p.)
PRIESTS: *the Priests of the Land* (s.d.s); *1 Priest | 2 Priest* (s.p.s)

B-Text

DIANA: *Diana* (s.d.s and s.p.s)
NYMPHS: *Nymphs | two of the Nymphs* (s.d.s)
JUNO: *Juno* (s.d.s and s.p.s)
TRAGEDIA: *Tragedia* (s.d.s and s.p.s)
SERVANTS: *two servants* (s.d.s); *1 | 2* (s.p.s)
POLYANDER: *Polyander | Poliander* | [one of] *the Captains* (s.d.s); *Poli<ander> | Poly<ander>* (s.p.s)
KING: *King* (s.d.s and s.p.s); *the King* | [Timeus'] *father* (s.d.s)
MENETIUS: *Menetius* | [one of] *the Captains* (s.d.s); *Mene<tius>* (s.p.s)
COMASTES: *Comastes* | [one of] *the Captains* (s.d.s); *Comast<es>* (s.p.s)
ARATUS: *Aratus* (s.d.s); *Ara<tus>* (s.p.s)
PHRONIMUS: *Phronimus* (s.d.s); *Phro<nimus>* (s.p.s)
EURYLOCHUS: *Eurylochus | Eurilochus* (s.d.s); *Euril<ochus> | Eury<lochus>* (s.p.s)
ATTENDANTS: *attendants* (s.d.s)
TIMEUS: *Timeus* (s.d.s and s.p.s); *Tymeus* (s.d.s)
HARPASTES: *Harpastes* (s.d.s); *Har<pastes>* (s.p.s)
MELAMPUS: *Melampus* (s.d.s); *Mel<ampus>* (s.p.s)
PALLANTUS: *Pallantus* (s.d.s and s.p.s)
ATTENDANTS: *others | attendants* (s.d.s)
CLEARCHUS: *Clearchus* (s.d.s); *Clear<chus>* (s.p.s)
HAIMANTUS: *Haimantus* (s.d.s; also misprinted *Hiamantus*); *Haim<antus>* (s.p.s)
MESSENGER: *a Messenger* (s.d.s); *Messenger* (s.p.s)
CORACINUS: *Coracinus* | [one of Timeus'] *guard* (s.d.s; also misprinted *Coarcinus*); *Cora<cinus>* (s.p.s)
RODIA: *Rodia* (s.d.s and s.p.s)
EUDORA: *Eudora* | [Rodia and the Ladies'] *Lady* (s.d.s); *Eudo<ra>* (s.p.s)
CHORUS: *Chorus* (s.p.s)
COURTIERS: *Courtier | Another something fat Courtier* (s.d.s)
MELISSA: *Mellissa | Melissa* (s.d.s); *Mell<issa>* (s.p.s)
HIANTHE: *Hianthe | the Princess* (s.d.s); *Hian<the>* (s.p.s)
LADIES: *Ladies | other Ladies | the Ladies | The other Ladies* (s.d.s); *1 Lady | 2 Lady* (s.p.s)
POET: *a Poet* (s.d.s); *Poet* (s.d.s and s.p.s)
WAITERS: *1 Waiter | 2 Waiter* (s.p.s)
WAITERS: *Waiters* (s.d.s)
CLEANDER: *Cleander | Cleander the young Prince | the King | Cleander the young King* (s.d.s); *Clean<der> | King* (s.p.s)
ACATES: *Achates* (s.d.s); *Acha<tes>* (s.p.s)

FLAMEN: *a Flamen* | *the Flamen* (s.d.s); *Flamen* (s.p.s)
ARGESTES: [one of Timeus'] *guard* | *Argestes* (s.d.s)
ATTENDANTS: *others* (s.d.s)
SERVANT: *a Servant* (s.d.s); *Servant* (s.p.s)
DEMOPHILUS: *Demophilus* (s.d.s); *Demo<philus>* (s.p.s)
GUARD: *the Guard* | *two* | *one* (s.d.s); *Guard* | *1 Guard* | *2 Guard* (s.p.s)
CAPTAIN: *the Captain of the guard* | *a Captain* (s.d.s); *Captain* (s.d.s and s.p.s)
CAPTAIN: *a Captain* | [one of] *the Captains* | *the Captain* (s.d.s); *Captain* (s.d.s and s.p.s)
ATTENDANTS: *others* | *one* (s.d.s)
SOLDIERS: *Six Soldiers* | *The Soldiers* (s.d.s); *1 Soldier* (s.p.s)
ATTENDANTS: *others* (s.d.s)
LADIES: *Ladies* | *the Ladies* | *a Lady* (s.d.s); *Lady* (s.d.s and s.p.s)
SOLDIERS: *a Captain, and Soldiers* | *The Soldiers* (s.d.s)
PEOPLE: *People* (s.p.s)
GUARD: *a guard* | *the guard* (s.d.s)
FLAMENS: *1 Flamen* | *2 Flamen* | *3 Flamen* (s.p.s)
EPILOGUE: *Epilogue* (heading)

OTHER CHARACTERS
The neighbouring princes (1.1, 1.3, 2.1)
The sailors on the wrecked ship (1.2)
Pallantus' dead father (1.2, 3.1, 5.1)
Mariners, captains, and soldiers in Clearchus' fleet, numbering more than 300 men (1.3, 3.3–4, 4.1)
Timeus' mother (2.5)
The former King of Crete, Cleander's dead father (3.1, 4.4, 5.1)
Innocent people murdered to achieve the King's usurpation (3.1)
Two rebels taken prisoner by the King's forces (4.1)
The King's army (4.2, 4.4–5, 5.3)
Charasius, Timeus' attendant (4.3)
Erastus, Timeus' attendant (4.3)
Acmanthes, Timeus' attendant (4.3)
The Praetor of the city (4.5)
Comastes' dead father (5.3)

B-Text
Woodmen who assist Diana and her nymphs in the hunt (ind.)
A nymph whom Diana has lost (i.e. the bride; ind.)
Endymion, a fair youth (ind.)
Hippolytus, a fair youth (ind.)
Jove, a god (ind.)
A Satyr who has ensnared the lost nymph (i.e. the bridegroom; ind.)
Cupid, god of love (ind.)
The parents of the bride and groom (ind.)
Minerva, goddess of wisdom (ind.)
Phoebus, the sun-god (ind.)

Comedy, Tragedia's sister (ind.)
The wine merchant (1.1)
The Governor of the city (3.4)
Two messengers from the conspirators to the King, one of whom was beheaded (4.1)
Clitus, Timeus' attendant (4.3)
A messenger who reported the King's death to the city (5.1)

Varies
Mariners, captains, and soldiers: references omitted from 3.3–4, but a new one added in 4.5; numbers now unspecified
Former King of Crete: reference omitted from 4.4
King's army: references omitted from 4.2 and 5.3, but a new one added in 5.1

Omits: Praetor; Comastes' father

SETTING
Period: unspecified, but later than the first century BC
Time-Scheme: 2.1 takes place the night ensuing 1.3
Place: Crete

Geography
[*Mediterranean*]: Chios; Paphos
[*Italy*]: Falernum; Rome
India

B-Text
Additional Geography
Greece
Africa

omits: India; Rome

SOURCES
Narrative: William Shakespeare, *Macbeth* (**1496**; 1.2)
Verbal: Martial, *Epigrams* 6.61 (F t.p. motto), 9.99 (motto at foot of F epistle); William Shakespeare, *2 Henry IV* (**1083**; 1.1); maxim by unidentified philosopher (5.3); Walter Montagu, *The Shepherds' Paradise* (**2395**; the name Pallantus)
Works Mentioned: Virgil, *Aeneid* (4.3)

B-Text
Verbal: *omits* Martial

LANGUAGE
English
Latin: 2 words (2.2; Melissa)
Italian: 2 words (4.4; Comastes)
Spanish: 1 word (2.2; Melissa)
Gibberish: 14 magic words (2.4; Comastes)

B-Text
Spanish: *omitted*
Gibberish: now 20 words

2459. The Conspiracy

FORM
Metre: rough pentameter; a little prose
Rhyme: blank verse
Chorus: People and Priests; appears between the acts
Act-Division: 5 acts, separated by chorus
Lines (Spoken): 3,613 (3,548 verse, 65 prose)
Lines (Written): 3,740

A fundamental problem in comparing the two versions is the relationship between A's verse and B's prose renderings of corresponding passages. A's verse is typical of 1630s courtier drama in having no discernible metre. B cannot be treated simply as 'verse' misprinted as prose, because there are numerous small verbal variants which alter the sequence and rhythm; moreover, even when it prints passages in verse, the lineation is often not the same as in A. Accordingly, the spoken length for each version has been calculated without reference to the other.

> **B-Text**
> **Metre:** prose and rough pentameter
> **Rhyme:** blank verse
> **Prologue:** 33 lines, mainly in couplets, spoken by Tragedia
> **Induction:** Diana, Juno, and Tragedia
> **Chorus:** now non-specific, not the People and Priests
> **Epilogue:** 15 lines, mainly in couplets
> **Lines (Spoken):** 3,522 (944 verse, 2,578 prose)
> **Lines (Written):** 3,763

STAGING
Doors: characters exit severally (2.1, 4.6, s.d.), and enter at two doors (2.4, 5.3, s.d.); mentioned (3.4, 4.2, s.d.); characters enter 'at another door' from the previous exit (3.5, s.d.)
Discovery Space: Cleander is discovered sleeping (2.3, s.d.); set with a table (4.1, s.d.)
Stage: mentioned (3.2, s.d.)
Within: speech (3.3–4, 4.6, s.d.); shout (4.4, implicit)

> **B-Text**
> **Doors:** mentioned (5.1, s.d.); *omits*: exit severally; mention (from 3.4); use of 'another door'
> **Discovery Space:** characters are discovered 'as in their tent' (4.1, 4.4, s.d.)
> **Stage:** *omits* mention
> **Within:** *omits* speech (from 3.4)
> **Audience:** said to be seated (ind., dialogue); the King and Queen in the audience are called a 'royal pair' (ind.), and addressed as 'great princes' (prol.)

MUSIC AND SOUND
Sound Effects: volley of 'great shot' (3.4, s.d.); tumultuous noise of fighting (3.4, s.d.); an uproar (4.2, s.d.); noise of an assault (4.6, s.d.); sound of doors being forced (4.6, s.d.)
Music: loud music (1.1, s.d.); drum (4.6, s.d.)
Songs:
  1: 'While Morpheus thus doth gently lay', 2.3, 20 lines;
  2: 'Sacred paeans to Mars sing', 5.5, People and Two Priests, 28 lines.

> **B-Text**
> **Sound Effects:** a mutinous noise (4.1, s.d.); knocking (5.1, s.d.); *omits*: volley; tumult; assault
> **Music:** *omitted*
> **Songs:** Song 2 is now sung by three Flamens.

PROPS
Lighting: a torch (5.5, s.d.)
Pyrotechnics: smoke and fire (5.5, s.d.)
Weapons: Pallantus' sword (3.1, dialogue; 3.4, 4.6, s.d.; 4.2, implicit); Clearchus' sword (3.3–4, s.d.); Aratus' sword (3.3, s.d.); Timeus' sword (3.3, implicit; 4.3, 5.3, s.d.); Haimantus' sword (3.4, s.d.); guards' swords (4.2, implicit/B s.d.); Polyander's sword (4.4, s.d.; 5.3, implicit); Menetius' sword (4.4, s.d.; 5.3, implicit); Comastes' sword (4.4, s.d.; 5.3, implicit); a dagger (4.6, s.d.); Captain's sword (5.3, implicit)
Clothing: a false beard (1.2, dialogue); black patches (1.2, dialogue; later worn by Pallantus)
Food and Drink: a banquet (1.1, s.d.), including cups of wine (drunk on stage), fowl, boar meat, and apples (dialogue); a cup of poison (5.3, s.d.; the liquid is spilt on stage)
Small Portable Objects: a letter (1.2, 5.1, s.d.; 5.4, dialogue/B s.d.); a large goblet (2.1, s.d.); a roll of paper (2.2, s.d.); an image (3.1, s.d.); a letter (3.2, s.d.); pen and ink (4.1, s.d.); paper (4.1, s.d.); mathematical instruments (4.1, s.d.); a letter (4.1, s.d.); a paper (5.1, s.d.); a document (5.3, s.d.)
Large Portable Objects: seven seats (1.1, dialogue); a table (1.1, dialogue 4.1, 5.3, s.d.); seating for four characters (2.2, implicit), for two characters (4.1, implicit), and for five characters (5.3, implicit)
Scenery: hangings (2.4, dialogue; 5.4, s.d.); a throne (3.1, implicit/B s.d.); a funeral pile with the King's body on top (5.5, s.d.; apparently burnt on stage); a curtain (5.5, s.d.)
Miscellaneous: blood (1.2, 4.2, dialogue); perfumes (5.5, s.d.; burnt on stage)

> **B-Text**
> **Lighting:** *omitted*
> **Pyrotechnics:** *omitted*
> **Weapons:** Pallantus' sword (3.2, implicit); Timeus' sword (3.2, implicit); soldiers' swords (4.6, s.d.); *omits* dagger
> **Clothing:** a wig (1.2, dialogue); armour (4.4, s.d.; see also COSTUMES: COMASTES); a helmet (4.4, implicit)
> **Food and Drink:** wine (4.4, s.d.; drunk on stage)
> **Small Portable Objects:** a cup (4.4, s.d.); a great goblet (4.4, s.d.); *varies*: the single image is now multiple images of gods (3.1, dialogue); *omits*: pen, ink, and paper (from 4.1); mathematical instruments; paper (from 5.1)
> **Large Portable Objects:** a table (4.4, s.d.); *omits*: table, seating (from 4.1)
> **Scenery:** *omits* funeral pile
> **Miscellaneous:** *omits* perfumes

COSTUMES AND MAKE-UP
COMASTES: a beard (dialogue); a sheath (4.4, 5.3, implicit)
ARATUS: a sheath (3.3, dialogue)
POLYANDER and MENETIUS: sheaths (4.4, 5.3, implicit)
TIMEUS: bloody (3.3, s.d.); a sheath (3.3, 5.3, implicit); mourning clothes (5.5, s.d.)
MELAMPUS: a garment with a pocket (1.2, s.d.)
PALLANTUS: disguised as a soldier (2.2, 2.4, 3.1–2, 3.4, 4.1–2, 4.6, implicit), with boots, a buff coat, and black patches on his face (dialogue; including a velvet eye-patch); richly habited (5.1, s.d.)
CLEARCHUS: disguised as a Flamen (2.6–7, s.d.; removed on stage); a sheath (3.3, implicit)
HAIMANTUS: disguised as a sailor (3.3, s.d.)
CORACINUS: bloody (3.3, s.d.)
EUDORA: a dress (1.4, dialogue)
CLEANDER: a black habit (3.1, s.d.; removed on stage); a rich robe and a crown (3.1, s.d.; put on on stage)
ARGESTES: bloody (3.3, s.d.)
CAPTAIN: a sheath (5.3, implicit)
Miscellaneous: all the main characters (unspecified) wear mourning clothes (5.5, s.d.)

> B-Text
> TRAGEDIA: a robe, a crown, and buskins (ind., dialogue)
> COMASTES: armour (4.4, s.d.; put on on stage)
> ARATUS, PHRONIMUS, and EURYLOCHUS: headgear (3.1, implicit; doffed on stage)
> TIMEUS: a sheath (3.2, implicit); *omits* mourning clothes (from 5.5)
> PALLANTUS: headgear (3.1, implicit; doffed on stage); a sheath (3.2, implicit)
> HAIMANTUS: a holy habit (2.7, s.d.); *omits* sailor disguise
> SECOND COURTIER (2.1): is now fat (s.d.)
> CLEANDER: robe is now specified as scarlet (3.1, s.d.)
> **Miscellaneous:** *omits* mourning clothes

EARLY STAGE HISTORY
1635: performed at York House as part of the celebrations of the wedding of Lord Charles Herbert and Lady Mary Villiers on Thursday 8 January. (The house was the residence of the bride's mother, Katherine Villiers, Dowager Duchess of Buckingham.) The play was performed with scenery throughout. The priests in 5.5 were played by a consort of musicians. The audience also included: King Charles I; Queen Henrietta Maria.
1635: performed by the King's Men at the Blackfriars. The audience at the first performance included Lucius Cary, 2nd Viscount Falkland, who rebuked another member of the audience for criticizing the precocious characterization of Cleander.
1635: On Thursday 5 or Friday 6 November, a group of bachelors celebrating the marriage of Edward and Margaret Bysshe, including Margaret's brother John Greene, went to the theatre; some went to see *The Lady of Pleasure* (**2515**) at the Cockpit, the others *The Conspiracy* at the Blackfriars.

EARLY TEXTUAL HISTORY
Before 1637: Ben Jonson reportedly read the play, and spoke well of it.
1638 or later: Henry Killigrew reportedly took his copy of the text with him to Italy.
1638: entered to Andrew Crooke in the Stationers' Register on Tuesday 13 March; the clerk making the entry left a blank for the author's name, which was never inserted. Thomas Wykes had licensed the book for publication.
1638: ^{1}Q printed (as *The Conspiracy*) by John Norton for Andrew Crooke; collation A–N^4, 52 leaves; title page names author and refers to performance occasion.
c. 1630s–40s: a copy of Q was in the possession of John Horne (Vicar of Headington, Oxfordshire). After his death, his entire collection of play-books passed into the possession of John Houghton of Brasenose College, Oxford (c. 1608–77), then to James Herne (died 1685), and then to the library of Ralph Sheldon (1623–84) at Weston, where it was catalogued by Anthony Wood, probably in the late 1670s.
1653: ^{2}F printed for John Hardesty; collation A–R^2, 34 leaves; title page now omits performance occasion; adds Latin title-page motto, publisher's address to the reader, list of roles. Hardesty himself decided to change the title to *Pallantus and Eudora*.
1655: *The English Treasury of Wit and Language* entered in the Stationers' Register to Humphrey Moseley on Tuesday 16 January.
1655: fifteen extracts (from the B-text, Cho.1, 2.2, 2.7–8, 3.2, 3.4, Cho.3, 4.1–2, 4.4, 4.6, Cho.4, 5.2, 5.5) included in John Cotgrave's *The English Treasury of Wit and Language*, sigs. B2^v, C7^v, E2^v, F6^{r-v}, G4^v, I4^v, K2^r, K4^v, L4^v–L5^r, N2^{r-v}, P5^r, R1^r, R3^v, V1^r; printed for Humphrey Moseley.
1660: advertised as for sale by Simon Miller.
1684: Nicholas Cox (Manciple of St Edmund Hall, Oxford) had copies of both Q and F in his bookshop. It had probably been previously owned by Gerard Langbaine, and appears on a list compiled by Anthony Wood on Saturday 13 December.

REFERENCES
Annals 1635; Bentley, iv. 691–4; Gerald Eades Bentley, *Shakespeare and Jonson* (Chicago, 1945), ii. 85; Bodleian, MS Wood E. 4, art. 1, pp. 18, 103; *English Historical Review* 43 (1928), 389; Eyre & Rivington, i. 463; Greg 537; Hazlitt, 47; Philip Major (ed.), *Thomas Killigrew and the Seventeenth-Century English Stage* (Farnham and Burlington, 2013), 94–108; *MLR* 13 (1918), 401–11; *MRDE* 6 (1993), 192; REED: Inns of Court, 812; *SP* 40 (1943), 186–203; Steele, 250–1; *Theatre Survey* 20 (1979), 21.

2460. The Orator

EVIDENCE
Sir Henry Herbert's office-book; Stationers' Register

GENRE
Contemporary: play

TITLE
Performed: *The Orator*

AUTHOR
Philip Massinger

DATE
January 1635

ORIGINAL PRODUCTION
King's Men, presumably at the Blackfriars and/or Globe

ROLES
An ORATOR

EARLY STAGE HISTORY
1635: presumably performed, as licensed, by the King's Men.

EARLY TEXTUAL HISTORY
1635: On Saturday 10 January, Sir Henry Herbert licensed the text for performance by the King's Men.
  1653: entered (as a double title with *The Noble Choice*, **2664**) to Humphrey Moseley in the Stationers' Register on Friday 9 September; play and author individually named as part of a group entry of 41 (or 55) plays.

Moseley's double titles are discussed under **1643**.

REFERENCES
Annals 1635; Bawcutt 310; Bentley, iv. 803–4; Greg ⊖71; Hazlitt, 167; Sibley, 111–12.

2461. Tragedy of Prince Alexander and Lorenzo

TEXT
MS fragment (Melbourne Hall; on deposit at the British Library, as Loan MS 98), probably authorial foul papers; the first leaf is numbered '2', implying that the fragment may be from an early point in the action.

I. A. Shapiro suggests (in *TLS* 4344) that the fragment is a rejected early draft of a scene (1.2) in Shirley's *The Traitor* (**2337**). That there is some link is evident in shared detail: both texts include references to Castruccio and Salviati, and both include the same allusion to Gonzales and Ferdinand and the bill for spies. On the other hand, there are significant differences. In *The Traitor*, the scene happens in front of the courtiers, whereas in the fragment they have been sent away and the action takes place in private. In *The Traitor*, the identity of Lorenzo's accuser as an exile furnishes him with part of his rebuttal, whereas in the fragment the signature is torn off the letter before it is given to Lorenzo, to protect the informant. One especially interesting difference is that, in the fragment, Lorenzo starts by admitting that he is a traitor, then claims to be a double agent, whereas in *The Traitor* the denial comes first and the statement, 'I am a dangerous man', comes afterwards as a kind of modesty device.

If there is a direct relationship between the two texts, rather than simply dependence on a common source, then both the direction of the debt and the process of the influence is suggested by the treatment of proper names: Shirley's Alonso becomes Alphonso, Gonzales becomes 'Consales', and Salviati becomes 'Salviatto'. The last is especially telling, for two reasons: Shirley's rendering of the name is historically accurate, and the passage about him employs wording too similar to be a coincidence—the phrase 'for his cardinal's cap' recurs verbatim. It follows that the fragment cannot be an early draft of *The Traitor* scene, but may well be an imitation of it, probably undertaken by an author who did not have access to Shirley's play in written form, and relied on his aural memory (of the play in performance?) for at least some of the proper names. Perhaps he was writing before the publication of the first quarto in 1635, or perhaps he had no access to a copy for some other reason (such as because he was in prison—see under AUTHOR).

GENRE
tragedy (?)

TITLE
Later Assigned: *The Duke of Florence*

AUTHOR
Pryor made a weak case for John Webster, which was over-dependent on subjective literary associations; Shapiro's identification requires the author to have been James Shirley. The most that can be said is that the MS is not written in the identifiable hand of any dramatist of the period (including Shirley), and that we have no specimens of the handwriting of a number of known major dramatists; as well as Webster, these include Beaumont, Ford, and William Rowley, though none of them are likely candidates and only Ford was alive at the time the play must have been written. The possibility also remains that this is the work of a minor or otherwise unknown playwright.

One tentative line of enquiry, albeit a highly speculative one, is opened up by an odd statement in the 1692 edition of Shirley's *The Traitor* (**2337**): the dedication says that 'the author was Mr Rivers'. A notice by Peter Motteux in *The Gentleman's Journal* the same year expands: 'The author of it was one Mr Rivers, a Jesuit, who wrote it in his confinement in Newgate, where he died.' The evidence for Shirley's authorship of *The Traitor* is sound; yet it is a striking coincidence that there was an English Catholic priest named John Rivers (c. 1588–c. 1650; real name John Abbot), who was a non-dramatic poet with works published in 1623 and 1647, and who was imprisoned in Newgate from 1637 until his death. One explanation might be that Rivers was in fact the author of a different play on the same subject, which was, somehow, later confused with *The Traitor*.

In any event, in the absence of secure palaeographical evidence, any case for authorship must provide an adequate circumstantial explanation for the fact that the manuscript ended up as a document wrapper in the papers of Sir John Coke (1563–1644), where it was found in 1985. Shapiro proposes a link to Shirley through Gray's Inn. Alternatively, perhaps it is relevant that William Prynne, whose *Hidden Works of Darkness Brought to Public Light* (1645) includes a reference to John Rivers, also remarks in *Rome's Masterpiece* (1643) that Coke was actively opposed to the Jesuits and inquired deeply into their factions. Might the MS have been passed to him by his spies?

DATE
Limits: 1631–40
Best Guess: 1635

Five partly contradictory criteria bear on the dating: the palaeographical judgement that the handwriting belongs to the first quarter of the seventeenth century; the debt to *The Traitor* (**2337**); the dates of the documents which the MS was used to wrap (1601–30); MacDonald P. Jackson's identification (in *MRDE*) of stylistic and vocabulary links with the drama of the first half of the 1630s; and the outside chance that John Rivers may have been the author. The best guess is arrived at partly as a mid-point between the limits, and partly because it is the latest date when a printed text of *The Traitor* would not have been available.

PLOT
[*The start of the play is lost.*] Prince Alexander sends away his courtiers and confronts his favourite Lorenzo, who intends to assassinate him, with a letter exposing the plot. Lorenzo admits it, but claims to have been acting as a double agent to discover the enemy's secrets. He emphasizes his previous good services, and offers to execute himself. [*The rest of the play is lost, but presumably Lorenzo eventually murders Alexander.*]

ROLES
Prince ALEXANDER (presumably of Florence), Lorenzo's kinsman
ALPHONSO, a courtier close to the Prince
COURTIERS (*non-speaking*)
LORENZO Medici, Alexander's kinsman and favourite

Speaking Parts: 3

Stage Directions and Speech Prefixes
ALEXANDER: *the Prince* (s.d.s); *Prince* (s.p.s)
ALPHONSO: *Alp<honso>* (s.p.s)
LORENZO: *Lorenz<o>* (s.p.s)

OTHER CHARACTERS
Castruccio, a banished man who wrote to warn Prince Alexander; he may appear on stage in the complete play
Lorenzo's tailor, to whom he owes money
A taverner, to whom Lorenzo owes money
Salviato, a cardinal who conspired against Prince Alexander, and was exposed by Lorenzo

SETTING
Period: sixteenth century; the play dramatizes events which took place in 1537
Place: Florence (presumably)

Geography
Italy

SOURCES
Narrative: James Shirley, *The Traitor* (**2337**)
Verbal: Sophocles, *Oedipus Rex*
Works Mentioned: Cato, *Sentences* (probably meaning the *Disticha Catonis*); Boethius, *De consolatione philosophiae* (sixth century)

LANGUAGE
English
Latin: 1 word (Lorenzo)
Spanish: 1 word (Lorenzo)

FORM
Metre: pentameter and prose
Lines (Spoken): 134 (72 verse, 62 prose)
Lines (Written): 144

PROPS
Weapons: a blade weapon (dialogue)
Small Portable Objects: a letter (dialogue; the bottom is torn off on stage)

EARLY TEXTUAL HISTORY
1630s: written in **MS**; 2 surviving leaves.

EDITIONS
Felix Pryor, Bloomsbury Book Auctions Catalogue (London, 1986).
Antony Hammond and Doreen DelVecchio, *SB* 41 (1988), 1–32.

REFERENCES
Beal ShJ 192; Bentley, v. 1152; *MRDE* 19 (2006), 21–44; *TLS* 4341 (13 June 1986), 651; *TLS* 4344 (4 July 1986), 735–6; *TLS* 4346 (18 July 1986), 787; *TLS* 4349 (8 August 1986), 865; *TLS* 4351 (22 August 1986), 913–14; *TLS* 4352 (29 August 1986), 939.

2462. The Apprentice's Prize

EVIDENCE
Stationers' Register.

GENRE
Contemporary: play

TITLE
Contemporary: *The Apprentice's Prize*
Alternative Modernization: *The Apprentices' Prize*

2463. Eumorphus

AUTHOR
The play is sometimes ascribed to Richard Brome and Thomas Heywood, which determines its *Annals* dating (by attraction to the 1634 Heywood/Brome collaboration on *The Witches of Lancashire*, **2441**). In fact, the Stationers' Register entry clearly applies the ascription only to the other play entered at the same time, *Sir Martin Schenck* (**2473**): it is named first, followed by the ascription; *The Apprentice's Prize* then follows on a new line, without ascription even though there is enough room for one to have been included. The entry is the last of a series of nine made by Humphrey Moseley that day. Since the others were all individual works, the grouping of 'two plays' in a single entry might be taken to imply a connection between them, which might (and might not) be one of common authorial origin; on the other hand, the previous entry but one is of *The Maiden's Holiday* (**1464**), bearing an authorial ascription which is impossible. There is also a chance that Moseley and the clerk bundled the last two plays together merely to hasten the end of what would have been a lengthy process; the same motive might have led them to omit any authorial ascription, whether to Brome and Heywood or anyone else.

DATE
Limits: 1630–5 if by Brome and Heywood, 1587–1648 if not

If the play were by Brome and Heywood, it is very unlikely to have been written in 1634, the date favoured by *Annals* and Bentley, because Heywood was so heavily committed to other work in that year, but it would probably have been written in an adjacent year. The possibilities are limited: there was good reason for a collaborative arrangement to be initiated by the King's Men in the summer of 1634 (for **2441**), and it may have been resumed with *Sir Martin Schenck* (**2473**) the following year; but both authors' other commitments in the first half of that year (Brome to **2479**, Heywood to the compilation of *Pleasant Dialogues and Dramas*, including **2490–2510**) leave little room for manoeuvre. If, as seems more likely, *The Apprentice's Prize* was a play of unknown authorship, then the only context for it is the miscellaneous group of plays among which Moseley entered it in 1654.

PLOT
The title invites an analogy with *The Welshman's Prize* (**1115**), *The Woman's Prize* (**1609**), and *The Widow's Prize* (**2157**). All four titles ascribe success to an individual from a group with a lower status in terms of esteem, economic power, or the period's conventional social hierarchy. It is likely, therefore, that the apprentice wins his probably metaphorical prize at the expense of his master.

ROLES
One or more APPRENTICES

EARLY TEXTUAL HISTORY
1654: entered to Humphrey Moseley in the Stationers' Register on Saturday 8 April; joint entry with *Sir Martin Schenck* (**2473**).

REFERENCES
Annals 1634; Bentley, iii. 58; Greg Θ125; Hazlitt, 16; Sibley, 9.

2463. Eumorphus

TEXT
MS (London: British Library, Add. MS 14047, fos. 60^r–97^v); scribal copy.

GENRE
comedy
Contemporary: *comoedia* (prol.)

TITLE
MS: *Eumorphus, sive Cupido adultus*

AUTHOR
George Wilde

DATE
February 1635

ORIGINAL PRODUCTION
St John's College, Oxford

PLOT
Eumorphus is a magnet for amorous women, but utterly uninterested in them. His would-be paramours include: the wizened and wealthy Maleola; Antiphila, whose husband Zelotypus is so jealous that he never allows her out of the house; and Pasithea, whose concern for her reputation causes her to adopt the alias Charissa. Maleola is offended when she overhears Eumorphus' misogyny, but the servant Panergus tells her he was only shamming to put off his other suitors; in fact, he wants to marry the rich crone himself. Eumorphus gets rid of 'Charissa' by offering her his love if she will swear two things; she agrees without knowing what they are, but the boons turn out to be neither to love nor see Eumorphus. Panergus gets into a fight with Pasithea's servant, Anoetus.

Zelotypus, alerted to his wife's passion after she talks about Eumorphus in her sleep, makes her load a gun. Pasithea's suitor, the braggart soldier Polymachaeroplacides, also intends revenge against Eumorphus. Panergus poses as Eumorphus in order to visit and marry Maleola; meanwhile, Eumorphus tries to avoid female attention by dressing as a woman, purportedly his own sister, Lucina. Zelotypus and the braggart both come looking for a fight, and Zelotypus fires his gun at Panergus, only to find that Antiphila didn't load it as ordered. Maleola brings officers to break up the fight.

Pasithea writes to Eumorphus, but Anoetus, taking servant for master, delivers it to Panergus. Panergus gets him drunk, and Anoetus boasts of sleeping with his mistress; Panergus sends him back with a forged, abusive letter purportedly from Eumorphus. After delivering it, he falls into a drunken stupor. Pasithea faints upon reading the letter, and is revived by Paracelsius, who offers to administer a love philtre to

Eumorphus. Paracelsius' assistant, Capo, puts a false beard on Anoetus and persuades him that he has slept for fifty years, then gets him a new job, as a soldier under Polymachaeroplacides in the war against France.

Eumorphus finds that his feminine disguise only means that he attracts the attentions of men rather than women. Zelotypus abandons his objection to Antiphila's loving Eumorphus, and invites him to dinner, so long as he brings his sister along with him. Eumorphus falls ill and Paracelsius is summoned to cure him; but he too falls in love with his apparently female patient. He inadvertently gives 'her' the love philtre that will make the recipient fall for 'Charissa', and, realizing this, returns with one brewed for himself; but Panergus, entrusted with the drug, is so impressed with Paracelsius' claims for its prophylactic powers that he takes it himself to ensure that he will never again suffer from a hangover, and instantly falls in love with the doctor.

To make himself less attractive, Eumorphus disfigures his face with a dagger and poison, then takes Paracelsius' supposed medicine (the love philtre) to prevent the effects being fatal. He falls in love with 'Charissa', but she rejects him now that he is ugly. Paracelsius offers to restore his good looks in return for marriage to Lucina. Panergus persuades Maleola's waiting-woman, Glycerium, to pose as Lucina for the wedding. Under the influence of Paracelsius' medicine, Eumorphus' face seems to be healing, and 'Charissa' seems ready to take him back. But Pamphilus, Eumorphus' friend, recognizes her as Pasithea, his love: she had taken him for dead.

Infuriated to learn that he has been duped into marrying a servant, Paracelsius retaliates by telling Eumorphus that his love for 'Charissa' is only philtre-induced and will soon wear off—so that's alright. Panergus marries Maleola, who reveals that Glycerium is in fact her granddaughter, and gives her a dowry—so that's alright too. Pamphilus and Pasithea are to be married, and Eumorphus looks forward with relief to a life of celibacy.

SCENE DESIGNATION
prol., 1.1–4, 2.1–4, 3.1–7, 4.1–3, 5.1–6, ep. (MS)

The stage may not be clear at 1.1–3.
The stage direction 'Scena Saltantium' in 5.6 could imply that a new scene, 5.7, begins there. But in general the MS only marks new scenes when the stage is clear (the exceptions in Act 1 arise from the presence of characters hidden somewhere), and generally gives the act as well as the scene in its scene headings; so this seems to be just a stage direction for a dancing set piece.

ROLES
PROLOGUE
MALEOLA, an old, rich woman; turns out to be Glycerium's grandmother; later Panergus' wife
GLYCERIUM, Maleola's maid, and in reality her granddaughter; later Paracelsius' wife, and addressed as Mistress Glycerium
PANERGUS, Eumorphus' servant; later Maleola's husband
ANTIPHILA, Zelotypus' wife
Master EUMORPHUS, a beautiful young man; poses as Lucina, his own (imaginary) sister
PAMPHILUS, Eumorphus' friend
PARACELSIUS, a French empiric or quack-doctor; later Glycerium's husband
PASITHEA, a noble lady; assumes the alias Charissa
ANOETUS, Charissa's servant
ZELOTYPUS, Antiphila's jealous husband, a citizen jeweller and goldsmith
POLYMACHAEROPLACIDES, a soldier
SCLOPO, Polymachaeroplacides' servant
Two OFFICERS (2.4)
Johannes CAPO, Paracelsius' servant
A DRUMMER following Polymachaeroplacides (5.1, 5.6, non-speaking)
Nine DANCERS (5.6, non-speaking)
A SERVANT, who whispers to Paracelsius (ep., non-speaking)

Speaking Parts: 16

Stage Directions and Speech Prefixes
PROLOGUE: *Prologus* (heading)
MALEOLA: *Maleola* (s.d.s and s.p.s); *Maleola Vetula Eumorphum amans* (d.p.)
GLYCERIUM: *Glycerium* (s.d.s); *Glycer<ium>* (s.p.s); *Glycerium Maleolae ancilla* (d.p.)
PANERGUS: *Panergus* (s.d.s); *Panerg<us>* (s.p.s); *Panergus Eumorphi servus* (d.p.)
ANTIPHILA: *Antiphila* (s.d.s); *Antiph<ila>* (s.p.s); *Antiphila Uxor Zelotipi* (d.p.)
EUMORPHUS: *Eumorphus* (s.d.s); *Eumorph<us>* (s.p.s); *Eumorphus illustris formae Juvenis* (d.p.)
PAMPHILUS: *Pamphilus* (s.d.s); *Pamph<ilus>* (s.p.s); *Pamphilus Eumorphi Amicus* (d.p.)
PARACELSIUS: *Paracelsius* (s.d.s); *Paracel<sius>* (s.p.s); *Paracelsius Empiricus* (d.p.)
PASITHEA: *Charissa* (s.d.s); *Chariss<a>* (s.p.s); *Pasithea sive Charissa Illustris Domina* (d.p.)
ANOETUS: *Anoetus* (s.d.s); *Anoet<us>* (s.p.s); *Anoetus Charissae servus* (d.p.)
ZELOTYPUS: *Zelotipus | Zelotypus* (s.d.s); *Zelot<ypus>* (s.p.s); *Zelotipus Civis* (d.p.)
POLYMACHAEROPLACIDES: *Polymachaeroplacides | Polymacheroplacides* (s.d.s); *Polyma<chaeroplacides>* (s.p.s); *Polymachaeroplacides miles* (d.p.)
SCLOPO: *Sclopo* (s.d.s and s.p.s); *Sclopo servus Polymachaee&c.* (d.p.)
OFFICERS: 2^{bus} *officiariis* (s.d.s); *Officiarius* 1^s | *Officiarius* 2^s (s.p.s)
CAPO: *Johanne Capo | Joannes Capo* (s.d.s); *Capo* (s.d.s and s.p.s); *Johannes Capo Paracelsi servus* (d.p.)
DRUMMER: *Tympanista* (s.d.s)
DANCERS: *Novem saltatores* (s.d.s)
SERVANT: *servolus* (s.d.s)

OTHER CHARACTERS
Eumorphus' other servants (1.1, 1.3)
Zelotypus' friend, whom he would not trust to test Antiphila's chastity (1.2)
Signor Angelo, a painter who tried to sell Zelotypus a picture of Jupiter (1.2)
Virgins whom Pamphilus claims to have defended against rapists (1.3)
Pasithea's lovers, whom she mocked (1.3)
Antiphila's mother (1.4, 3.6)
The Sultan, with whom Polymachaeroplacides claims to have fought a duel (2.1)
Hans van den Mater Steimach Cotienolem bogel Suartansnout, a legate from the Batavian Senate, who brought a letter to Polymachaeroplacides (2.1; possibly imaginary)
Diana, Polymachaeroplacides' chaste sister (2.1; possibly imaginary)
Pasithea's servants (2.1)
Eugenius, a sick friend of Eumorphus (2.3)
An old beggar-woman, who refused Eumorphus' money and asked only to be allowed to look at him instead (2.3; may refer to Maleola)
Clora, Pamphilus' dead sister (2.3)
The Duke of Florence (2.4, 3.1)
A girl impregnated by Paracelsius, who asked him for drugs to procure an abortion (3.1)
Antiphila's father (3.6)
Zelotypus' customers (3.6)
Paracelsius' wealthy family (4.3; possibly imaginary)
The King of France (4.3)
Oxford scholars who received the visiting Paracelsius with honour (5.3; possibly imaginary)
Paracelsius' 25 servants when he practised in England (5.3; possibly imaginary)
Paracelsius' numerous English patients (5.3; possibly imaginary)

SETTING
Period: roughly contemporary (after the time of King Philip II of Spain, who died in 1598). The action takes place in the 'mensis secundi' (the second month; presumably February).
Time-Scheme: The action takes place during two consecutive days. 1.1–3 take place in the morning, and 2.1 at 'hora ... secunda' (the second hour); an hour passes between 2.1 and 3.1; 3.7–4.1 take place at night, and 4.2–3 the ensuing morning; about an hour passes between 5.3 and 5.6.
Place: Florence

Geography
Florence: [Our Lady of] Loreto (a church); the bull-ring
Italy
England: Tyburn; Oxford
Scotland
France: Paris
Greece: Mount Olympus; Delphi; Thessaly

[*Europe*]: Batavia; Germany
The Hellespont
Turkey: Lydia
The Dead Sea
Africa: Ethiopia
India
China
The Straits of Magellan
Unidentified: Aula Grenarcha

SOURCES
Narrative: Plautus, *Mostellaria* (3.1), *Stichus* (2.4), *Miles gloriosus* (Polymachaeroplacides)
Verbal: Plautus, *Asinaria* (1.3–4, 3.1–2, 3.4), *Aulularia* (1.3, 3.1), *Bacchides* (1.3, 2.1, 2.4), *Captivi* (2.4, 4.2), *Casina* (1.3–4, 2.2, 3.6), *Cistellaria* (1.1), *Curculio* (1.3), *Epidicus* (2.2), *Miles gloriosus* (2.1), *Mostellaria* (4.2), *Persa* (1.3, 3.3), *Poenulus* (1.3), *Pseudolus* (1.1, 2.1, 2.4; also the name Polymachaeroplacides), *Stichus* (2.4); Terence, *Andria* (4.3, and the name Glycerium), *Adelphoe* (1.1, 2.4), *Heautontimorumenos* (4.2); Cicero, *De officiis* (5.6); Virgil, *Aeneid* 3 (5.6); Horace, *Epodes* 1 (3.3), 4 (1.4), *Odes* 1.3 (3.4), 2.1 (3.3); Ovid, *Ars amatoria* (1.3), *Ex Ponto* 1.3 (4.2); Pliny the Younger, *Epistles* 1.5 (1.1); Juvenal, *Satires* 13 (5.1), 14 (5.2); Nicolaus Pergamenus, *Dialogus creaturarum* 23 (1480; 5.1); Edward Forcett, *Pedantius* (**697**; 2.4); Edmund Stubbes, *Fraus honesta* (**1887**; 4.2); Peter Hausted, *Senile odium* (**2296**; 1.3)
Works Mentioned: Terence, *Eunuchus* (3.6); George Chapman, *Bussy D'Amboise* (**1428**; 2.4)

LANGUAGE
Latin
Greek: 1 word (1.3; Panergus)
French: 3 words (2.4; Polymachaeroplacides)

FORM
Metre: Terentian pseudo-metre
Prologue: 12 lines
Act-Division: 5 acts
Epilogue: 28 lines, spoken by Paracelsius and Capo
Lines (Spoken): 2,701 (including 17 true verse)
Lines (Written): 2,782

STAGING
Doors: two stage houses, one for Pasithea and one for Eumorphus (the latter is explicitly mentioned in 5.5, s.d.); Eumorphus' door is knocked at with a strap, which may be attached as a knocker (1.3, s.d.)
Above: characters appear at a window above (1.1, 5.5, s.d.; it takes only two lines to get down to the main stage)
Audience: addressed as 'spectatores perbenevoli' (prol.; most benevolent spectators) and as 'auditores' (ep.); said to be seated (prol.)
Miscellaneous: Three characters are concealed on stage in an area which appears to be elevated (1.1–3,

implicit; one of them coming out of hiding is asked to descend). A gun is fired at a character on stage (2.4).

MUSIC
Music: lyres (2.1, dialogue)
On-Stage Music: lyre, played by Glycerium (5.5, s.d.; accompanying the song); drum (5.6, implicit)
Song: 'Cor mihimet Cupido laesit', 5.5, Glycerium, 6 lines, repeated; with musical accompaniment
Other Singing: Anoetus sings 3 lines (2.4, s.d.)
Dance: Dancers dance ridiculously (5.6, s.d.)

PROPS
Lighting: a candle (4.1, s.d.)
Weapons: Pamphilus' sword (1.3, 4.3, dialogue; 5.6, s.d.); Anoetus' sword (1.3, s.d.); a dagger (1.4, dialogue); an arquebus (1.4, 3.6, dialogue; 2.4, s.d.); Panergus' dagger (2.2, dialogue); Polymachaeroplacides' sword (2.4, dialogue); Polymachaeroplacides' dagger (2.4, dialogue); a spear (2.4, dialogue); a knife (3.6, dialogue); a dagger (3.7, dialogue)
Musical Instruments: a drum (5.1, 5.6, implicit); a lyre (5.5, s.d.)
Clothing: 'Lucina's' clothes (5.2, dialogue; also worn by Eumorphus and Glycerium)
Money: a purse (1.3, dialogue); two gold pieces (1.3, dialogue); a coin (1.3, dialogue); eighty minas (2.4, dialogue); gold (3.5, dialogue); more gold (3.6, dialogue); a purse (5.1, dialogue); four farthings (5.1, dialogue); a gold coin (5.1, dialogue)
Food and Drink: a flask of cordial (1.1, 1.3, dialogue; drunk on stage); poison (1.4, dialogue); wine (2.4, dialogue; drunk on stage); a flask of medicine (3.1, dialogue; drunk on stage); a love philtre (3.3–4, dialogue; 3.7, s.d.); a second love philtre in a phial (3.5, dialogue); poison (3.7, dialogue)
Small Portable Objects: a letter (2.1, dialogue; 2.2, s.d.); another letter (2.1, dialogue); a third letter (2.4, 3.1, dialogue); a jewel (2.4, dialogue); a picture of a bearded man (2.4, dialogue; probably a miniature); four letters (3.1, dialogue); a diary (3.1, dialogue); a pen and ink (4.1, implicit); a letter (4.1–2, dialogue; written on stage); medicines, including a plaster, a balsam, and an antidote (5.1, dialogue)
Large Portable Objects: a walking-stick (1.1, implicit); seating for three characters (1.1–3, implicit); a strap (1.3, s.d.; may be permanently attached to a door); a bag (2.2, s.d.; 3.1, dialogue); a chair (3.1, dialogue); another bag (3.1, dialogue)

COSTUMES AND MAKE-UP
MALEOLA: wrinkled skin (dialogue); spectacles (2.4, s.d.; put on on stage)
GLYCERIUM: dressed in the woman's clothes previously worn by Eumorphus (5.4, s.d.; 5.5–6, implicit; see also PROPS)
PANERGUS: has no beard (dialogue); Eumorphus' clothes (2.2, s.d.; 2.4, dialogue; 5.6, implicit), including breeches (dialogue); a glove (2.4, dialogue)
EUMORPHUS: pale yellow hair, and no beard (dialogue); cross-dressed as a woman (2.4, s.d.; 3.4, dialogue; see also PROPS); face disfigured with a black wound (4.1, 4.3, 5.6, dialogue; in the last scene, the wound has abated but is still visible); a brimmed hat (4.3, dialogue)
PAMPHILUS: a scabbard (5.6, implicit)
ANOETUS: a mantle and a belt (2.2, dialogue); a cap (2.2, dialogue; removed and replaced on stage); a white false beard (5.1, s.d.; removed on stage)
POLYMACHAEROPLACIDES: a silk eye-patch (2.1, s.d.; removed on stage); armour, probably including a helmet, breastplate, and greaves (2.4, dialogue)

Panergus exits dressed in Eumorphus' clothes at the end of 2.2, and Eumorphus immediately enters in his own person and clothes at the start of 2.3; when they are both on stage in 5.6, Eumorphus' clothes are said to be similar to those worn by Panergus. Therefore, there need to be two (presumably identical) sets of Eumorphus' clothes.

EARLY STAGE HISTORY
Preparation: A stage and scaffolds were made and erected at St John's College, Oxford, for the performance of a comedy and a tragedy (perhaps **2465**), at a cost of £24.15s.

Performance: at St John's College, Oxford, on Thursday 5 February 1635.

EARLY TEXTUAL HISTORY
After 1660 (?): included in a MS collection of plays and poems; 38 leaves; title page names author and refers to performance; list of roles. The scribe may possibly have had the initials W. B. The other plays in the volume are *The Converted Robber* (**2475**) and *The Hospital of Lovers* (**2551**).

EDITIONS
Heinz J. Vienken, Humanistische Bibliothek 2.19 (Munich, 1973).
Heinz J. Vienken, Renaissance Latin Drama in England 1.3 (Hildesheim and New York, 1981).

REFERENCES
Annals 1635; Bentley, v. 1259–60; Hazlitt, 77, 105, 124; REED: Oxford, 517, 809–10; *Shakespeare Jahrbuch* 47 (1911), 84–7; Sibley, 74.

2464. The Coronation

TEXT
Printed in 1640 (STC 22440).

GENRE
tragicomedy
Contemporary: play (prol., ep.)

2464. The Coronation

TITLE
Performed/Printed: *The Coronation*

AUTHOR
James Shirley

DATE
February 1635

ORIGINAL PRODUCTION
Queen Henrietta's Men at the Cockpit

PLOT
When King Theodosius seized power in Epirus, he agreed to make his opponent Cassander the next heir should he himself die without issue. Now his daughter Sophia is Queen and Cassander the Lord Protector during her minority. She appears to favour Cassander's son Lysimachus as a potential husband, but this is only a stratagem to secure Cassander's support for her forthcoming installation as Queen regnant.
    Wishing to find a legitimate way of killing Arcadius, Seleucus proposes settling a family feud by single combat with themselves acting as champions. Sophia agrees, and schedules the fight immediately after her coronation; but the two heads of the families disapprove and prevent it by announcing that they have settled their differences. Sophia now declares her choice of husband: not Lysimachus as expected, but Arcadius. Arcadius accepts, even though he has sworn a vow of constancy to Polydora. Seleucus is imprisoned when he protests, and the disappointed Cassander plots treachery. Macarius, Arcadius' uncle, produces documentary evidence that the proposed marriage would be incestuous: Arcadius is really Sophia's brother, Demetrius, Theodosius' younger son, who was bestowed on Macarius in infancy for fear of Cassander's ambition; his claim to the throne is therefore better than Sophia's. He and Sophia both try to reactivate their former relationships, but Polydora and Lysimachus are both less than compliant.
    Cassander plans to pull off the same trick twice: he arranges Seleucus' release, claims him to be Theodosius' elder son, Leonatus, and installs him as King. Demetrius takes refuge in Polydora's house, happy to be deposed and so eligible to win back her love. But Cassander has overestimated the ease with which his new King can be controlled: 'Leonatus' refuses to reinstate him as Lord Protector, so he plots first to assassinate Demetrius and then admit the ruse, deposing Seleucus. The scheme backfires when it emerges that Seleucus really is Leonatus after all, and so the rightful King.

SCENE DESIGNATION
prol., 1.1, 2.1–3, 3.1–2, 4.1–3, 5.1–3, ep. (Q has act-divisions only)

ROLES
SOPHIA, Queen of Epirus; sister of Leonatus and Demetrius; a young woman; later known as Princess Sophia
PHILOCLES, a gentleman
LYSANDER, a gentleman
Lord CASSANDER, the Lord Protector, Lysimachus' father, an old man
Lord LYSIMACHUS, Cassander's son, a noble young gentleman
ANTIGONUS, a gentleman
ARCADIUS, a young courtier, supposed Macarius' nephew; turns out to be Demetrius, younger brother of Leonatus and Sophia; for a time installed as King of Epirus
Lord MACARIUS, an old man, supposed Arcadius' uncle
SELEUCUS, a young gentleman soldier, supposed Eubulus' son; turns out to be Leonatus, elder brother of Demetrius and Sophia, and rightful King of Epirus
CHARILLA, Sophia's servant
POLYDORA, Nestorius' daughter, Arcadius' girlfriend
A SERVANT who tells Arcadius he is summoned to court (2.1)
NESTORIUS, Polydora's father
Nestorius' SERVANT (2.1, *non-speaking*)
Lord EUBULUS, supposed Seleucus' father
LADIES attending Sophia (2.2, *non-speaking*)
ATTENDANTS on Sophia (2.2, *non-speaking*)
GENTLEMEN attending Sophia (2.2, *non-speaking*)
A GENTLEMAN, Seleucus' man (2.3, *non-speaking*)
Two PAGES bearing Arcadius' and Seleucus' targets (2.3, *non-speaking*)
Polydora's SERVANT (3.1–2, 5.2)
A BISHOP (3.2, 5.3)
A SOLDIER (4.1)
POLEANUS, captain of the castle
FORTUNE, a queen; a character in the masque (4.3)
YOUTH, a character in the masque (4.3, *non-speaking*)
HEALTH, a character in the masque (4.3, *non-speaking*)
PLEASURE, a character in the masque (4.3, *non-speaking*)
FAME, a character in the masque (4.3)
LOVE, a male character in the masque; also called Cupid; said to be little (4.3)
HONOUR, Fortune's servant; a male character in the masque (4.3)
ATTENDANTS on Leonatus (5.1, *non-speaking*)
A MESSENGER, who brings news of Demetrius' flight (5.1)

Speaking Parts: 22–3
Allegorical Roles: 7 (the characters in the masque)

Stage Directions and Speech Prefixes
SOPHIA: *Queen* (s.d.s, s.p.s, and d.p.); *Sophia* (s.d.s and d.p.); *Sop<hia>* (s.p.s)
PHILOCLES: *Philocles* (s.d.s and d.p.); *Phil<ocles>* (s.p.s)

LYSANDER: *Lisander* (s.d.s and d.p.); *Lisa<nder>* (s.p.s)
CASSANDER: *Cassander* (s.d.s and d.p.); *Casander* (s.d.s); *Cas<sander>* (s.p.s)
LYSIMACHUS: *Lisimachus* (s.d.s and d.p.); *Lisi<machus>* (s.p.s)
ANTIGONUS: *Antigonus* (s.d.s and d.p.); *Ant<igonus>* (s.p.s)
ARCADIUS: *Arcadius | Demetrius* (s.d.s and d.p.); *Arc<adius> | Dem<etrius>* (s.p.s)
MACARIUS: *Macarius* (s.d.s and d.p.); *Mac<arius>* (s.p.s)
SELEUCUS: *Seleucus | Selucus | Leonatus* (s.d.s); *Sel<eucus> | Leo<natus>* (s.p.s)
CHARILLA: *Charilla* (s.d.s and d.p.); *Charia* (s.d.s); *Cha<rilla>* (s.p.s)
POLYDORA: *Polidora* (s.d.s and d.p.); *Pol<idora>* (s.p.s)
SERVANT: *a servant* (s.d.s); *Servant* (s.p.s); [one of the] *Servants* (d.p.)
NESTORIUS: *Nestorius* (s.d.s and d.p.); *Nes<torius>* (s.p.s)
SERVANT: *a servant* (s.d.s); [one of the] *Servants* (d.p.)
EUBULUS: *Eubulus* (s.d.s and d.p.); *Eub<ulus>* (s.p.s)
LADIES: *Ladies* (s.d.s); *Gentlewomen* (d.p.)
ATTENDANTS: *attendants* (s.d.s and d.p.)
GENTLEMEN: *Gentlemen* (s.d.s and d.p.)
GENTLEMAN: *Gentleman* (s.d.s); *Gentlemen* (d.p.)
PAGES: [Seleucus' and Arcadius'] *pages* (s.d.s)
SERVANT: *a Servant | [Polydora's] servant* (s.d.s); *Servant* (s.d.s and s.p.s); [one of the] *Servants* (d.p.)
BISHOP: *a Bishop* (s.d.s and d.p.); *Bishop* (s.d.s and s.p.s)
SOLDIER: *Soldier* (s.d.s and s.p.s)
POLEANUS: *Poleanus* (s.d.s); *Pol<eanus>* (s.p.s); *Polianus* (d.p.)
FORTUNE: *Fortune* (s.d.s and s.p.s)
YOUTH: *Youth* (s.d.s)
HEALTH: *Health* (s.d.s)
PLEASURE: *Pleasure* (s.d.s)
FAME: *Fame* (s.d.s and s.p.s)
LOVE: *Love* (s.d.s and s.p.s)
HONOUR: *Honour* (s.d.s and s.p.s)
ATTENDANTS: *Attendants* (d.p.)
MESSENGER: *Messenger* (s.d.s and s.p.s)

OTHER CHARACTERS
Theodosius, dead King of Epirus, a foreigner; father of Leonatus, Demetrius, and Sophia (1.1, 2.2, 3.2, 4.1–2, 5.1, 5.3)
Members of Macarius' and Eubulus' families, who fomented a feud (1.1)
Macarius' father (1.1, 2.2)
Eubulus' father (1.1, 2.2)
The people of Epirus (2.3, 4.1, 4.3, 5.1–2)
Lysimachus' mother, Cassander's wife (3.2)
Seleucus' supposed mother (4.1)
The Epirot army (5.1)
Eubulus' dead son (5.3)

SETTING
Period: antiquity (presumably)
Time-Scheme: 2.1–3 take place the morning after 1.1; 3.2 takes place the day after 2.3
Place: Epirus

Geography
The Alps
Arabia

SOURCES
Narrative: Francis Beaumont and John Fletcher, *A King and No King* (**1636**)
Verbal: William Shakespeare, *Coriolanus* (**1589**; 1.2)

LANGUAGE
English

FORM
Metre: pentameter; a few alexandrines and tetrameters; a little prose
Rhyme: blank verse
Prologue: 44 lines, in couplets, spoken by Sophia
Act-Division: 5 acts
Epilogue: 14 lines, in couplets, spoken by Sophia
Lines (Spoken): 2,129 (2,029 verse, 100 prose)
Lines (Written): 2,558

STAGING
Doors: characters enter at two doors (2.3, s.d.)
Within: shout (2.3, 5.2, s.d.)
Audience: assumed to include both sexes, and to be seated (prol.); referred to as 'these gentlemen' and 'the ladies' (prol.); addressed as 'noble gentlewomen' (prol.) and 'gentlemen' (ep.)

MUSIC
Music: melancholy music (3.2, dialogue); unspecified music (4.3, dialogue)
Dance: Fortune, Youth, Health, Pleasure, Fame, and Love dance (4.3, s.d.)

PROPS
Weapons: Arcadius' sword (2.2–3, dialogue); two targets (2.3, s.d.); Seleucus' sword (2.3, dialogue)
Clothing: a diadem or crown (3.2, dialogue; 4.3, s.d.)
Small Portable Objects: a letter (3.1, implicit; 3.2, dialogue); a paper (3.2, implicit); a mourning cushion (4.3, s.d.); a document (5.3, implicit)
Large Portable Objects: a seat (3.2, implicit)
Scenery: an arras (1.1, dialogue); a chair of state (2.3, s.d.)

COSTUMES AND MAKE-UP
SOPHIA: a crown (2.3, dialogue)
LYSIMACHUS: is 'black', i.e. a swarthy complexion (dialogue)
ARCADIUS and SELEUCUS: a plume each (2.3, dialogue)
POLYDORA: black mourning clothes (4.3, s.d.)
FORTUNE: a crown (4.3, s.d.)

2465. Tragedy of Pedro the Cruel

EARLY STAGE HISTORY

1635: presumably performed, as licensed, no doubt by Queen Henrietta's Men at the Cockpit, to whom the play was ascribed in 1640.

1639: The play was in the repertory of the King's and Queen's Young Company (Beeston's Boys) at the Cockpit. On Saturday 10 August, Philip Herbert, 4th Earl of Pembroke (Lord Chamberlain) issued an order restraining performances by other companies of this and 44 other plays.

EARLY TEXTUAL HISTORY

1635: on Friday 6 February, Sir Henry Herbert licensed the text for performance; entry names author.

1639: entered in the Stationers' Register to Andrew Crooke and William Cooke on Thursday 25 April; named individually as part of a group entry of five plays. Thomas Wykes had licensed the book for publication.

1640: ¹Q printed (probably in the spring) by Thomas Cotes for Andrew Crooke and William Cooke; collation A² B-I⁴ K², 36 leaves; title page names John Fletcher as author, and also the acting company and playhouse; list of roles.

1646: rights to James Shirley's *Poems &c.* transferred in the Stationers' Register from Francis Constable to Humphrey Moseley on Saturday 31 October.

1646: prologue (in an abridged version) and epilogue included in Shirley's *Poems &c.*, sigs. ²D2ʳ–²D3ʳ, ²D4ʳ; printed by Ruth Raworth for Humphrey Moseley.

1653: The play was included in a catalogue of Shirley's works in print, appended to his *Six New Plays*; the title is annotated, 'Falsely ascribed to John Fletcher'.

1655: *The English Treasury of Wit and Language* entered in the Stationers' Register to Humphrey Moseley on Tuesday 16 January.

1655: two extracts (from 4.1 and 4.3) included in John Cotgrave's *The English Treasury of Wit and Language*, sigs. C5ʳ and T7ᵛ; printed for Humphrey Moseley.

1679: included in Beaumont and Fletcher's *Fifty Comedies and Tragedies* (²F), sigs. ²2P1ᵛ–²2R3ʳ, 20 pages on 11 leaves; printed by Thomas Newcomb for John Martin, Henry Herringman, and Richard Marriott.

EDITIONS

William Gifford, in *The Dramatic Works and Poems of James Shirley* (London, 1833), iii. 455–540.

Eleanor Collins, in James Shirley, *The Complete Works*, gen. eds. Eugene Giddens, Teresa Grant, and Barbara Ravelhofer (Oxford, forthcoming).

REFERENCES

Annals 1635; Bawcutt 312; Bentley, v. 1098–9; Eyre & Rivington, i. 250, 463; Robert Stanley Forsythe, *The Relations of Shirley's Plays to the Elizabethan Drama* (New York, 1914), 304–13; Greg 572; Hazlitt, 50; MSC 2.3, 389–90; *SB* 1 (1948–9), 151–82; *SP* 40 (1943), 186–203.

2465. Tragedy of Pedro the Cruel

EVIDENCE

Edmund Gayton, *Pleasant Notes upon Don Quixote* (1654; Wing G415).

The play may not be irretrievably lost: the 34-leaf MS of a seventeenth-century Latin play about Pedro the Cruel was sold at Sotheby's in 1938; it was bought by Maggs for a client with the initials V. S., but its present whereabouts are unknown. This might, however, be the text of a Jesuit play on the same subject, performed at Hamburg in 1655, for which a playbill survives. An alternative candidate is **2466**, which draws on the story of Pedro the Cruel and fits the evidence, but which changes some of the names, including that of the King.

GENRE

tragedy
Contemporary: tragedy, play

TITLE

Later Assigned: *Spanish Tragedy*; *A Spanish Tragedy of Petrus Crudelis*; *Don Pedro the Cruel King of Castile*; *Don Pedro*

DATE

Limits: before 1648
Best Guess: 1635

Gayton entered St John's College, Oxford, in 1625, and he was active in university theatre. The *Annals* date is assigned simply by attraction to his known appearance as an actor in *The Hospital of Lovers* (**2551**), by which time he was quite senior (he became a college Fellow in 1633 and was appointed a university bedell in 1636). But the anecdote of the spooked spooks could relate to an incident from before, rather than during, his time at Oxford.

If we want to do better than that, we must begin with an assumption which, while it may be reasonable, is in no way secure: that Gayton's anecdote pertained to a performance by his own college. Its dramatic activities, or at least the College's financial contributions thereto, seem to have been markedly more extensive in the period 1635–42 than during the preceding decade, when the only records pertain to the traditional New Year's Day 'founder's show' (though it is always possible that other performances left no financial trace, such as, perhaps, **2331**). There was a particularly heavy outlay in the Christmas Day to Lady Day quarter of the academic year 1634–5, with expenditure of £24.15s on the erection of a stage and scaffolds, followed by a £36.5s reimbursement of the actors in the week of Monday 2 to Sunday 8 March (REED: Oxford, 517). This would be consistent with a more prestigious performance before the university; it is also the only record of this period specifying that one of the plays performed was a tragedy.

PLOT

The King of Castile commits atrocities, including the murder of two noblemen, who return as ghosts. In all likelihood, he himself comes to a bad end.

ROLES

Don PEDRO the Cruel, King of Castile; also called Petrus Crudelis
Two GHOSTS of Pedro's victims

SETTING
Period: fourteenth century; the play dramatizes events from the life and reign of Peter the Cruel, King of Castile (born 1334, reigned 1350–69)
Place: Spain

SOURCES
Narrative: Pedro López de Ayala, *Chronicle* (fourteenth century, printed 1495), or derivate

STAGING
Stage: The ghosts enter from two ends of the stage.

PROPS
Lighting: two torches
Pyrotechnics: flashes of sulphur when the ghosts appear
Scenery: hangings

COSTUMES AND MAKE-UP
GHOSTS: long white robes; pale faces (achieved with meal)

EARLY STAGE HISTORY
Preparation: The play was intended for public performance at Oxford before the university, perhaps by members of St John's College. However, the actors were asked first to give a private performance to ensure that they were good enough; any who were found wanting would be replaced. This trial performance was the first time the actors appeared in costume, and the two who were playing the ghosts scared each other so much that they forgot their lines and so lost their parts.

REFERENCES
Annals 1636; Bentley, v. 1322, 1411–12; Edmund Gayton, *Pleasant Notes upon Don Quixote* (London, 1654), sigs. N3ᵛ–N4ʳ; David McInnis and Matthew Steggle, *Lost Plays in Shakespeare's England* (Basingstoke, 2014), 273–4; REED: Oxford, 835; Sibley, 151–2.

2466. Tragedy of Alfonso of Castile

TEXT
MS (Oxford: Bodleian, MS Don. d. 102); scribal copy apparently with authorial corrections.

The play has a number of suggestive points of overlap with what is known about **2465**: both dramatize the story of Pedro the Cruel and both feature the ghosts of his victims, including two who are such minor parts that they could easily be replaced if needs be. However, the fact that the anecdote pertains to a plan about Pedro, whereas the extant play renamed the character as Alfonso, renders any identification unavoidably uncertain.

If the two plays were one and the same, an ascription to St John's College, Oxford, is possible. It may therefore be relevant that the play's use of dancers resembles that of another St John's play, *Eumorphus* (**2463**), and that the author of the possible source, John Speed, was the father of a known St John's dramatist.

GENRE
tragedy

DATE
Limits: 1620–40 (?)

The watermark resembles Heawood 577 and 585, which are found in paper used in England in the 1620s and 1630s; this is consistent with the italic hand.

PLOT
Having murdered his father and brothers and seized the throne, Alfonso now rules tyrannically. His councillors see his vices as the evils of peace, and so hope for war. What they get instead is a royal wedding: Alfonso marries Isabella, to the chagrin of his supplanted mistress Padilla. Renewed persecution of the Castilian Jews is attributed to Isabella's influence.

Isabella's wedding present to Alfonso is a jewelled girdle. Padilla's brother Sancho, entrusted with its safe keeping, has it enchanted by the vengeful Jewish magician Mermuthus, so that when Alfonso wears it, he will imagine it to be a poisonous snake. The objective is to discredit Isabella and so restore Padilla to favour. The charm takes effect, and the court dissolves into mutual recrimination; even the goldsmith who made the girdle is to be executed, and Alfonso murders the man's son when he comes to plead for clemency. In his mind, only Sancho is free of suspicion. Telius, a philanderer who claims he merely follows the example of the King's own vices, is sent to recall Padilla to court, and he attempts to chat her up on his own account, but is rebuffed. Upon her return to court, the King reaffirms his devotion to her.

Phalantus of Aragon has come to court with a view to marrying Larinda, Alfonso's ward, but Alfonso takes his time to name the nuptial day. Sancho also plots to secure his downfall, and picks a fight about admission to the royal presence, which induces Alfonso to stab Phalantus. Sancho tries to ingratiate himself with the newly available Larinda; but she has made common cause with Isabella, the good councillors, and Alfonso's brother Alvarez, who are all opposed to Sancho's influence over the King, and she lures him into a trap. Alfonso is haunted by the ghosts of his victims, then assassinated by Alvarez and the conspirators.

SCENE DESIGNATION
Cho.1, 1.1–5, Cho.2, 2.1–4, Cho.3, 3.1–4, Cho.4, 4.1–3, Cho.5, 5.1–5, Cho.6, ep. (MS, corrected)

The stage is not clear at 1.1–2.

2466. Tragedy of Alfonso of Castile

ROLES
The GENIUS of Castile
The ghost of ALBERTO, Alfonso's father
The ghosts of Alberto's two SONS, Alfonso's younger brothers (only speak collectively)
TELIUS, a lustful courtier
GARCIA, a councillor
CAPITO, a councillor
SANCHO, a bawd, Padilla's brother
PADILLA, a whore, Sancho's sister and Alfonso's mistress
PHALANTUS, Prince of Aragon, Larinda's fiancé; also appears as a ghost
LARINDA, Princess of Biscay, Alfonso's ward, Phalantus' fiancée
MERMUTHUS, a Jewish magician
A citizen BARBER
A TAILOR, a citizen and a married man
A GOLDSMITH, a citizen and father
A BOY, the goldsmith's son
ALFONSO, King of Castile, Isabella's husband, Alvarez's brother, Alberto's son
ISABELLA, Queen of Castile, Alfonso's wife
ALVAREZ, Alfonso's brother and heir presumptive, Alberto's son
XIMENIA, Isabella's maidservant
PSECAS, Isabella's maidservant
Six DANCERS (4.1, *non-speaking*)
Two ATTENDANTS (5.5, *non-speaking*)
VOICES (ep., *within*)
EPILOGUE

Speaking Parts: 22

Stage Directions and Speech Prefixes
GENIUS: *Genius Castellensis* (s.d.s); *Genius* (s.d.s and s.p.s); *Genius Castellae* (d.p.)
ALBERTO: *Umbr<a> Alberti patris Alphonsi* | [one of the] *Umbrae* | *Umbra Alberti* | *Alberti Umbra* (s.d.s); *Alber<tus>* (s.p.s); [one of the] *Chorus Umbrarum Alberti Patris Alphonsi Regis* (d.p.)
SONS: *Umbrae ... fratrum duorum* | [two of the] *Umbrae* | *Filii* | [Alberti] *Filiorum* | *Umbrae ... 2* [Alberti] *Filiorum* | *Umbrae Fratrum* (s.d.s); (s.p.s); [two of the] *Chorus Umbrarum* | *Filiorum 2 a fratre occisorum* (d.p.)
TELIUS: *Telius* (s.d.s and s.p.s); *Telius Aulicus lascivus* (d.p.)
GARCIA: *Garsias* (s.d.s); *Gars<ias>* (s.p.s); *Garsias* [one of the] *Consiliarii* (d.p.)
CAPITO: *Capito* (s.d.s); *Capi<to>* (s.p.s); *Capito* [one of the] *Consiliarii* (d.p.)
SANCHO: *Santius Leno* (s.d.s); *Santius* (s.d.s and d.p.); *Sant<ius>* (s.p.s)
PADILLA: *Padilla Pellex* | *Padilla* (s.d.s); *Pad<illa>* (s.p.s); *Padilla Pellex Regis* (d.p.)
PHALANTUS: *Phalantus* | *Phalanti Umbra* | [one of the] *Umbrae* (s.d.s); *Phal<antus>* (s.p.s); *Phalantus Princeps Arragoniae* (d.p.)

LARINDA: *Larinda* (s.d.s); *Larin<da>* (s.p.s); *Larinda Principessa Biscay pupilla Regis* (d.p.)
MERMUTHUS: *Mermuthus* (s.d.s); *Merm<uthus>* (s.p.s); *Mermuthus Judaeus, Magus* (d.p.)
BARBER: *Tonsor* (s.d.s and s.p.s); [one of] *Cives 3* | *Tonsor* (d.p.)
TAILOR: *Scissor* (s.d.s and s.p.s); [one of] *Cives 3* | *Scissor* (d.p.)
GOLDSMITH: *Aurifaber* (s.d.s and s.p.s); [one of] *Cives 3* | *Aurifaber* (d.p.)
BOY: *Puer* (s.d.s and s.p.s); *Puer filius Aurifabri* (s.d.s); *Puer Aurifabri filius* (d.p.)
ALFONSO: *Alphonsus* | *Rex* (s.d.s); *Alph<onsus>* (s.p.s); *Alphonsus Rex Castella* (d.p.)
ISABELLA: *Isabella* (s.d.s); *Isab<ella>* (s.p.s); *Isabella Regina* (d.p.)
ALVAREZ: *Alvarus* (s.d.s); *Alva<rus>* (s.p.s); *Alvarus Frater Regis* (d.p.)
XIMENIA: *Ximenia* (s.d.s); *Xim<enia>* (s.p.s); *Ximenia* [one of the] *Famulae Reginae* (d.p.)
PSECAS: *Psecas* (s.d.s and s.p.s); *Psecas* [one of the] *Famulae Reginae* (d.p.)
DANCERS: *Saltatores 6* (d.p.)
ATTENDANTS: *Satellitio* | *Satellites due* (s.d.s); *Satellites* (d.p.)
EPILOGUE: *Epilogus* (heading)

OTHER CHARACTERS
Phyllis (or Philotis), Telius' would-be lover (1.1, 3.4)
Telius' other, jilted lovers, including Cloris, Aegle, Galla, Lycoris, Fulvia, Sempronia, and Amaryllis (1.1, 3.4)
The Jews of Castile, whom Alfonso has expelled from court (1.1, 1.4, Cho.2, 2.1, 2.3)
The Tailor's wife (1.5)
The people of Castile (2.1, 3.2, 4.1, 5.2)
Ferdinand, Alfonso's enemy (2.1)
Aguilar (2.1)

SETTING
Period: fourteenth century (?); the play is very loosely based on events which took place in 1353–69, but some of the personages' names have been changed
Time-Scheme: 2.4 takes place in the morning, and 5.5 at night
Place: Castile

Geography
Iberia: River Tagus; Aragon; Biscay
France
The Underworld: River Styx; Orcus

SOURCES
Narrative: probably John Speed, *The Theatre of the Empire of Great Britain* (1612, repr. 1632; girdle episode); possibly John Ford, *The Broken Heart* (**2281**; 2.4)

Speed's brief account was the only one available in English at the time the play was probably written; but the dramatist could alternatively have used a Continental source (such as, perhaps,

Ayala's *Chronicle*). Telius' unsuccessful attempt to seduce Isabella's maids may be modelled on the behaviour of Lemophil and Groneas in Ford's play (1.2).

LANGUAGE
Latin

FORM
Metre: iambic senarius; a little prose
Act-Division: 5 acts, separated by chorus
Chorus: Alberto and his Sons; appears at the start of the play and after each act
Epilogue: 16 lines
Lines (Spoken): 1,399 (1,381 verse, 18 prose)
Lines (Written): 1,691

STAGING
Within: song (3.4, implicit); three characters watch the on-stage action 'in postscenium' (from behind the scene; 5.4, s.d.); shouted dialogue (ep., s.d.)
Above: the Genius appears above (Cho.1, s.d.)
Miscellaneous: the ghosts 'disparent' (disappear; Cho.1, 5, s.d.); no provision is made to remove the dead bodies of Phalantus and the Boy at the end of 4.1

MUSIC AND SOUND
Sound Effects: thunder (Cho.5, s.d.)
Song: 'Dulce quid canent labella', 3.4, Padilla within, 16 lines
Dance: Dancers dance (4.1, s.d.)

PROPS
Lighting: torches (5.5, dialogue)
Pyrotechnics: lightning (Cho.5, s.d.)
Weapons: Alfonso's sword (4.1, s.d.); Alvarez's, Capito's, and Garcia's swords (5.3, 5.5, dialogue)
Clothing: a golden, jewelled girdle (2.1, 2.3, dialogue; also worn by Alfonso)
Small Portable Objects: a letter (1.1, dialogue); a box of jewels (1.5, dialogue); binding cords (5.4, implicit)
Scenery: a little cloud (Cho.6, s.d.)

COSTUMES AND MAKE-UP
SONS: bloody wounds (5.5, dialogue)
TELIUS: splendid clothes (2.4, dialogue)
GARCIA and CAPITO: scabbards (5.3, implicit)
PADILLA: possibly pregnant (5.2, dialogue; 5.5, implicit)
ALFONSO: a beard (dialogue); a jewelled girdle (3.1, dialogue; ripped off on stage; see also PROPS)
ALVAREZ: a scabbard (5.3, implicit)

EARLY TEXTUAL HISTORY
1620s–30s (?): transcribed in **MS**; 34 leaves; list of roles.

EDITION
Elizabeth Sandis and Martin Wiggins, The Philological Museum (internet, forthcoming).

REFERENCES
Falconer Madan and H. H. E. Craster, *A Summary Catalogue of Western Manuscripts in the Bodleian Library at Oxford* (Oxford, 1895–1953) 39065.

2467. Comedy of Geometry

TEXT
MS (Rome: English College, MS Scrittura 35.1); scribal fair copy, showing some signs of late authorial revision. MS deterioration at the foot of fo. 1 has resulted in the loss of a line and a half of the dialogue.

It is evident that the MS from which the text was copied featured Rhombus (spelt 'Rombus') in the role finally assigned to Quadro, and that the scribes were instructed to apply the correction as they copied. This is apparent at a point where the text reads 'Romulus' (Malone TLN 477): the scribe read the first three letters, assumed the word was 'Rombus', and made an unthinking substitution of 'Quadro' before realizing the error and reverting to copy. The instruction was probably issued after the text on fos. 1–2ʳ had been copied, since on those pages the correction is made by deletion and substitution, whereas from fo. 2ᵛ Quadro is correctly named throughout.

GENRE
comedy
Contemporary: possibly *comedia* (English College performance records of 1635)

TITLE
Later Assigned: *Blame Not Our Author*

AUTHOR
said to be male

DATE
Limits: 1613–35
Best Guess: February 1635

ORIGINAL PRODUCTION
English College, Rome

PLOT
The square Quadro wants to become a circle, and to that end enlists the help of Compass. The treatment partly involves a change of diet to make him rotund, but partly also being physically constrained in hoops to force a change of shape. This latter procedure is so painful that Quadro has himself released and seeks revenge on Compass. Circulus too has a grudge against Compass: he finds it undignified to be subject to one who is handled by base artisans.

Rectangulum makes mischief. First, he arrests Compass on a fictitious warrant; but, acknowledging favours done him by Compass in the past, helps him to escape instead and hides him in a press. The next victim is Quadro: Rectangulum tells him that he has been banished for harbouring strumpets and encouraging dice-play, and hides him in the press too. Then Rectangulum tells Line that Circulus must be apprehended for the murder of Compass.

Line passes the news about Circulus on to Triangulum, who doubts its veracity. His suspicions are confirmed when he overhears Circulus plotting to kill Compass—which establishes that Compass is not yet dead—and he initiates a counter-plot. He tells Circulus that Compass has died of a broken heart because of Circulus' unkindness, and that Line has a warrant for Circulus' arrest. Rectangulum confirms that Compass is dead: he killed him on Circulus' behalf, and now he abets Circulus' escape by hiding him in the press. Rectangulum is triumphant: if he can only capture Triangulum as well, all the principal polygons will be out of the way, and he can expect promotion.

Regulus, the melancholy ruler, hears of Compass's murder, and sentences Circulus to death in his absence; but Triangulum intervenes and accuses Rectangulum of the murder. Rectangulum is arrested as he is practising elevated speech for his anticipated new station in life. Under threat of torture, he admits that he has the missing characters imprisoned in the press, and throws himself on Regulus' mercy. Compass, Quadro, and Circulus are released, and reconcile their differences. Regulus cheers up.

SCENE DESIGNATION
prol., 1.1–5, 2.1–9, 3.1–6 (MS)

The stage is only clear between the acts.

ROLES
PROLOGUE
Sir QUADRO, a square; originally written as Rhombus
RECTANGULUM, Quadro's man
Sir COMPASS, who has long legs
Master LINE, a Protestant; also called Linea
Sir CIRCULUS, also called Sir Circle
TRIANGULUM, a male character
SEMICIRCULUS, the Constable; also called Master Horseshoe and Sir Semicircle
RHOMBUS, a male character
REGULUS, governor of the mathematical sphere

Speaking Parts: 10
Allegorical Roles: 9

Stage Directions and Speech Prefixes
QUADRO: *Quadro* (s.d.s and s.p.s); *Rhombus* (deleted s.d.s and s.p.s)
RECTANGULUM: *Rectangulum* (s.d.s and s.p.s)
COMPASS: *Compass* (s.d.s and s.p.s)
LINE: *Line* (s.d.s and s.p.s)
CIRCULUS: *Circulus* (s.d.s and s.p.s)
TRIANGULUM: *Triangulum* (s.d.s and s.p.s)
SEMICIRCULUS: *Semicirculus* (s.d.s and s.p.s)
RHOMBUS: *Rhombus* (s.d.s and s.p.s)
REGULUS: *Regulus* (s.d.s and s.p.s)

OTHER CHARACTERS
One of Compass's pupils, who performed many marvellous feats (1.3)
Cord, Line's cousin (1.5)
People who sought Compass's help, including a group of tailors, a London ale-inspector, a fastidious astronomer, a gentlewoman concerned about her farthingale, two courtiers, and Euclid (2.4)
A courtier's mistress (2.4)
People who sought Line's help, including a group of rope-makers and a company of sailors (2.6)
Bible, a minister who asked Line to translate the Psalms (2.6)
The under-officers of the mathematical sphere, including Prismat, Conum, Scalenum, Rhomboides, Isosceles, Pyramides, Cylindrum, Pentagonon, Poliagonon, and others (2.7)
Pentalpa, a lesser shape (2.9)

SETTING
Period: The action takes place during Carnival (i.e. Shrovetide).
Time-Scheme: 1.1 takes place at night, and 1.2 at 9 a.m. the following morning; about an hour passes between 2.7 and 2.8. (However, in both cases the action is continuous.)
Place: Rome

Geography
Italy: the Apennines; Venice
London: Bridewell, the New River; Wapping; St Andrew's parish
[*England*]: Norfolk; Banbury; River Thames
Ireland
Greece: Mount Olympus; Athens; Arcadia; Delphos (i.e. Delphi)
Egypt: Memphis
[*Asia*]: Bashan; Assyria; Babylon
The Antipodes
The Arctic Circle: the North Pole
The Antarctic Circle: the South Pole

SOURCES
Verbal: Euclid, *Elementa* (the author probably used the 1591 Latin edition by Christopher Clavius; 1.5)
Works Mentioned: Bible: Psalms (2.6); Aesop, *Fables* (2.4); Aristotle, *Mechanica* (2.1)

LANGUAGE
English
Latin: 107 words (1.2–5, 2.1–7, 3.1, 3.5; Quadro, Rectangulum, Compass, Line, Circulus, Triangulum, Semicirculus)
Greek: 5 words (1.3, 2.2, 2.4, 2.9; Compass, Triangulum, Rectangulum)
Italian: 4 words (2.4, 3.1; Compass, Rectangulum, Semicirculus, Rhombus)

FORM
Metre: prose and pentameter; some trimeter, occasional alexandrines
Rhyme: blank verse; some couplets
Prologue: 12 lines, partly in couplets
Act-Division: 3 acts
Lines (Spoken): 1,021 (429 verse, 592 prose)
Lines (Written): 1,077

MUSIC AND SOUND
Sound Effects: possibly a clock striking nine (1.2, dialogue)
Song: 'Bring the juice of Hebe', 2.6, Rectangulum, 42 lines
Other Singing: Rectangulum may sing intermittently (2.4, implicit)
Dance: Quadro attempts to dance (1.3, s.d.; he can't because he is bound in the hoops)

PROPS
Money: two unspecified sums (3.3, implicit)
Food and Drink: a potion (1.3, dialogue; drunk on stage); a bottle of liquor (2.5, s.d.); a sausage (3.1, s.d.)
Small Portable Objects: a warrant (2.7, dialogue); a patent (2.9, s.d.; 3.6, dialogue); a warrant (3.3, s.d.; signed on stage); pen and ink (3.3, implicit)
Large Portable Objects: two hoops (1.3–4, s.d.)
Scenery: a press (2.4, s.d.; 2.5, 2.9, dialogue; large enough to accommodate three characters)

EARLY STAGE HISTORY
Probably performed at the English College, Rome, during Carnival, possibly in 1635 (when Shrovetide fell, in the Gregorian Calendar, from Sunday 18 to Tuesday 20 February).

EARLY TEXTUAL HISTORY
Early seventeenth century (1635?): transcribed in **MS**; 16 leaves; primarily in two hands, with addenda in two others.

c. 1635: The MS was in the possession of Thomas Turrett.

EDITION
Suzanne Gossett, MSC 12 (Oxford, 1983), 85–132.

REFERENCES
Annals Supp. I.

2468. The Ordinary

TEXT
Printed in 1651 (Wing C714).

GENRE
comedy
Contemporary: comedy (prol., t.p.); tragicomedy (S.R.)

TITLE
Printed: *The Ordinary*
Contemporary: *The City Cozener, or The Ordinary*

AUTHOR
William Cartwright

DATE
Limits: 1634–5
Best Guess: 1635

The setting during the regnal year 10 Charles I establishes the likely limits. Evans speculates that the play might have been performed to mark Cartwright's M.A. graduation on Wednesday 15 April 1635; however, there is no evidence of this, it would place the play some weeks after the regnal year in question, and at Christ Church it was the custom for a graduand to write a play for his B.A., not his M.A. (see **2749**).

PLOT
Before the start of the action, Littleworth's wooing of his girlfriend Jane was cut short by the disapproval of her avaricious father, Sir Thomas Bitefig, who thought him too poor for a prospective son-in-law; to add to his misfortunes, his father was imprisoned for debt by the usurer Credulous. He has adopted the alias Meanwell and fallen in with a gang of cheaters who have set up base in a city ordinary, each having insincerely promised himself in marriage to the owner, Mistress Potluck.

Credulous plans to marry his wastrel son Andrew to Jane, and to that end brings him to the ordinary to receive tuition in appropriate behaviour. The cheaters do their best to convince Credulous that they are men of the world and therefore suitable for the job: Slicer poses as a military hero, and Hearsay as an experienced traveller and spy. Bitefig agrees that an intermediary may be sent as a go-between to woo Jane on Andrew's behalf. 'Meanwell' takes on the task, but Jane rejects the suit because she prefers Littleworth. During the visit, Priscilla, Jane's chambermaid, falls for 'Meanwell' and writes to him proposing an assignation. Littleworth arranges for Andrew to keep the date, and he woos Priscilla, mistaking her for Jane. Priscilla corrects him, and he transfers his attentions to Jane, but when he keeps eyeing up Priscilla, Jane proposes that he should woo blindfold. The cheater Shape then imitates her voice, makes conditions for marriage, and takes some jewels from him as lover's tokens.

The cheaters have other plots and other clients. Have-at-All consults Slicer for instruction on how to fight. He is persuaded that he can eat his way to valour if he chooses the correct menu in the right order: the meal must be an allegory of an army. Caster wants to learn how to win at cards, and fantasizes about how munificent he will be as a result, but he ends up a most unsuccessful gambler. Credulous arranges to buy his farm, but Shape poses as Caster's bailiff and misappropriates the payment. Shape tells a creditor that he will be paid by a barber-surgeon, but tells the barber-surgeon that the creditor is a pox patient, and an encounter at cross-purposes ensues. The cheaters invite all their clients to dine at the ordinary, convincing each that he is the guest of one of the others. To escape their obligations to Mistress Potluck, they arrange a suitable husband for her, the antiquarian Moth.

Bitefig falls ill after his food disagrees with him. Shape visits him, posing as a confessor, and gets him to admit all his miserly villainies. Littleworth reveals his identity and lets Bitefig know the truth, but when he arrives with a constable to raid the ordinary, the birds have flown; they have, in fact, disguised themselves as the watchmen conducting the raid. Andrew is arrested after being caught having sex with Priscilla, whom he has married. Littleworth helps Bitefig to take possession of the cheaters' ill-gotten gains, and Bitefig consents to his marrying Jane after all. The cheaters escape arrest, but decide that London is too hot for them: they plan to emigrate to America, where they will continue to practise their trickery on the Puritan population.

SCENE DESIGNATION
prol., 1.1–5, 2.1–5, 3.1–6, 4.1–5, 5.1–5, ep. (O)

The stage is not clear at the following scene-divisions: 1.2–5, 2.4–5, 5.1–2, 5.4–5.

ROLES
PROLOGUE
Master Frank HEARSAY, a cheater; less than 40 years old; claims to be an intelligencer and a eunuch
Master SLICER, a cheater; claims to be a soldier; also called Lieutenant Slicer and 'D. Slicer' ('D' for 'Dominus'?)
Master SHAPE, a cheater; poses as a countryman, Caster's bailiff
Master MEANWELL, a cheater; in reality, Littleworth, a debtor's son; a young man
Mistress Joan POTLUCK, an old, toothless matron and vintner's widow, landlady of the ordinary
ANDREW Credulous, Credulous's son; later Priscilla's husband; also called Young Master Credulous
Master Simon CREDULOUS, an old citizen, grocer, and usurer, Andrew's father; also called Sim
Master HAVE-AT-ALL, a gamester
Robert MOTH, an old antiquary of Aldersgate; later chooses the name Master Geoffrey
Master CASTER, a gamester and landowner
Sir Thomas BITEFIG, an old, miserly knight and landowner, Jane's father
PRISCILLA, Jane's chambermaid; later Andrew's wife; also called Mistress Pris
Mistress JANE, Bitefig's daughter; also called Janie
RHYMEWELL, a poet
BAGSHOT, a lawyer's clerk; said to be little
Vicar CATCHME, a cathedral chorister
SIR CHRISTOPHER, a Puritan curate; also called Master Christopher, Sir Kit, and (in derision) Israel Inspiration

JAMES, a servant at the ordinary (3.5)
A SURGEON and barber (4.4)
A MERCER, Shape's creditor (4.4)
A CONSTABLE (4.5, 5.4)
The Constable's ASSISTANTS (4.5, non-speaking)
WATCHMEN (5.4; two speak)

Speaking Parts: 24

Stage Directions and Speech Prefixes
PROLOGUE: *The Prologue* (heading)
HEARSAY: *Hearesay | Hearsay* (s.d.s); *Hear<say>* (s.p.s); *Heare-say An Intelligencer* [one of the] *Complices in the Ordinary* (d.p.)
SLICER: *Slicer* (s.d.s); *Slic<er>* (s.p.s); *Slicer A Lieutenant* [one of the] *Complices in the Ordinary* (d.p.)
SHAPE: *Shape* (s.d.s); *Shap<e>* (s.p.s); *Shape A Cheater* [one of the] *Complices in the Ordinary* (d.p.)
LITTLEWORTH: *Meanewell | Meanwell | Meanwel | Mr Meanwell* (s.d.s); *Mean<well>* (s.p.s); *Meanewell, Littleworth disguised, a decayed Knight's son* [one of the] *Complices in the Ordinary* (d.p.)
POTLUCK: *Mrs Potlucke | Mrs Potluck | Potluck* (s.d.s); *Potl<uck>* (s.p.s); *Joane Pot-lucke A Vintner's Widow* (d.p.)
ANDREW: *Andrew* (s.d.s); *And<rew>* (s.p.s); *Andrew* [Credulous's] *Son, Suitor to Mrs Jane* (d.p.)
CREDULOUS: *Credulous* (s.d.s); *Cred<ulous>* (s.p.s); *Simon Credulous A Citizen* (d.p.)
HAVE-AT-ALL: *Have-at-all | Haveatall* (s.d.s); *Have<atall>* (s.p.s); *Have-at-all* [one of the] *Gamesters* (d.p.)
MOTH: *Moth* (s.d.s and s.p.s); *Robert Moth, An Antiquary* (d.p.)
CASTER: *Caster* (s.d.s); *Cast<er>* (s.p.s); *Caster* [one of the] *Gamesters* (d.p.)
BITEFIG: *Sir Thomas Bitefig | Sir Thomas Bitefigg | Sir Thomas* (s.d.s); *Sir Tho<mas>* (s.p.s); *Sir Tho<mas> Bitefigg A covetous Knight* (d.p.)
PRISCILLA: *Priscilla* (s.d.s); *Prisc<illa>* (s.p.s); *Priscilla* [Mistress Jane's] *Maid* (d.p.)
JANE: *Mrs Jane* (s.d.s); *Jane* (s.d.s and s.p.s); *Mrs Jane Daughter to Sir Thomas* (d.p.)
RHYMEWELL: *Rimewell* (s.d.s); *Rime<well>* (s.p.s); *Rimewell A Poet* [one of the] *Clubbers at the Ordinary* (d.p.)
BAGSHOT: *Bagshot* (s.d.s); *Bagsh<ot>* (s.p.s); *Bag-shot A decayed Clerk* [one of the] *Clubbers at the Ordinary* (d.p.)
CATCHME: *Vicar Catchmey | Catchmey* (s.d.s); *Catch<mey>* (s.p.s); *Vicar Catchmey A Cathedral Singing-man* [one of the] *Clubbers at the Ordinary* (d.p.)
SIR CHRISTOPHER: *Sir Christopher* (s.d.s); *Chris<topher>* (s.p.s); *Sir Christopher A Curate* [one of the] *Clubbers at the Ordinary* (d.p.)
JAMES: *a Servant* (s.d.s); *Servant* (s.d.s and s.p.s); *Servants* (d.p.)

SURGEON: *Surgeon* (s.d.s, s.p.s, and d.p.)
MERCER: *Mercer* (s.d.s and s.p.s); *Shopkeeper* (d.p.)
CONSTABLE: *Constable* (s.d.s and s.p.s)
ASSISTANTS: *Assistants* (s.d.s); *Officers* (d.p.)
WATCHMEN: *Watchmen | other Watchmen* (s.d.s); *1 Watchman | 2 Watchman* (s.d.s and s.p.s); *Officers* (s.d.s and d.p.)

OTHER CHARACTERS
Sir Robert Littleworth, an old knight imprisoned for debt, Littleworth's father (1.1, 2.5, 5.4)
Vintner Potluck, Mistress Potluck's dead husband, who neglected her (1.2, 2.2, 5.4)
The women of Mistress Potluck's parish (1.2)
A bankrupt ballad-man, who received charity from the women of the parish (1.2)
The King (1.2, 5.4–5)
Andrew's mother (2.5)
Timothy Credulous, a liveryman, Credulous's father, Andrew's grandfather (2.5)
Bitefig's tenants (5.3)
Children, whose peas Bitefig ate (5.3)
Bitefig's man (5.3)
Servants in Bitefig's lodgings, with whom he sang psalms (5.3)
A chandler, in whose shop Bitefig secretly ate bread (5.3)
A tailor, whose black puddings Bitefig stole (5.3)

The cheaters tell their dupes that they have had professional dealings with a variety of people (such as, for example, the Great Turk, who supposedly had Hearsay castrated); these figures are surely imaginary.

SETTING
Period: contemporary; the action takes place in the regnal year 10 Charles I (Thursday 27 March 1634–Thursday 26 March 1635)
Time-Scheme: 3.2 takes place in the morning, and 4.1 later the same day; 3.4 takes place the day after 2.5; 4.5 takes place in the morning
Place: London

Geography
London: St Antholin's Church; the Tower; the [Inner or Middle] Temple; St Paul's Cathedral; Aldersgate; the Sign of the Half Moon; Cheapside; Queenhithe
England: [Oxford]; Banbury; Salisbury Plain
Ireland
France: River Seine
The Low Countries: Holland; Brussels; the Hague
Germany: Bavaria
Italy: Naples; Venice
[*Europe*]: Spain; Russia
[*Asia*]: Turkey; Tartary; China
[*Africa*]: Ethiopia
India
[*America*]: Newfoundland; New England

SOURCES
Narrative: Aristophanes, *Plutus* (1.2); William Shakespeare, *1 Henry IV* (**1059**; 1.2); Ben Jonson, *The Alchemist* (**1621**; 2.3, 4.3, 5.4), *The Devil is an Ass* (**1810**; 1.2); John Fletcher and Philip Massinger, *Beggars' Bush* (**1799**; 5.5); possibly *The Fairy Knight* (**2078**; but the debt could be vice versa; 4.2); Thomas Middleton and John Webster, *Anything for a Quiet Life* (**2005**; 4.4); Philip Massinger, *The Bondman* (**2074**; 4.3); James Shirley, *The Beauties* (**2396**; 3.3), *The Gamester* (**2418**; 1.4)
Verbal: Bible: Judges 3.17 (3.5), 15.16 (3.5); Terence, *Adelphoe* (5.4); Virgil, *Aeneid* 6 (3.5); Boethius, *Consolation of Philosophy*, tr. Geoffrey Chaucer (1370s–80s, printed 1477–8, repr. 1602; 3.1); Geoffrey Chaucer, *The Book of the Duchess* (early 1370s, printed 1532, repr. 1602; 4.2), *The Legend of Good Women*: Thisbe (1370s–80s, printed 1532, repr. 1602; 5.4), *Troilus and Criseyde* (1380s, printed c. 1483, repr. 1602; 2.2, 3.1, 4.2), *Canterbury Tales* (c. 1387–1400, printed 1478, repr. 1602): General Prologue (2.2); The Knight's Tale (2.2, 3.1), The Miller's Tale (2.2, 3.1, 4.2), The Reeve's Tale (2.2, 3.1, 5.4, cited), The Man of Law's Tale (2.2), The Clerk's Tale (2.2), The Merchant's Tale (2.2, 3.1), Chaucer's Tale of Sir Thopas (3.1), The Monk's Tale (4.2), The Nun's Priest's Tale (5.4), The Canon's Yeoman's Tale (3.1); *The Romaunt of the Rose* (late fourteenth century, printed 1532, repr. 1602; 5.4); George Peele, *Edward I* (**881**; 5.4); William Shakespeare, *1 Henry IV* (**1059**; 1.1–2); Ben Jonson, *The Arraignment* (**1296**; 3.5), *The Staple of News* (**2174**; 2.1, 5.3); possibly John Webster, *The White Devil* (**1689**; 5.4); probably Abraham Cowley, *Love's Riddle* (**2452**; 1.2; but the debt might be vice versa)
Works Mentioned: Sappho, lyrics (general reference; 3.3); Strabo, *Geography* (1.3); Ovid, *Metamorphoses* (2.2); Ptolemy, *Geography* (1.3); Geoffrey Chaucer, *Canterbury Tales*: The Nun's Priest's Tale (3.1); Robert Wisdom, *Psalms* (c. 1544; 3.5); *The Book of Common Prayer* (1549, rev. 1552; 1.1); Thomas Sternholt and John Hopkins (tr.), *Psalms* (1549–62; 3.5); John Foxe, *Acts and Monuments* (1563; 1.3); Philip Stubbes, *The Life and Death of Katherine Stubbes* (1591; 3.5); Robert Stafford, *A Geographical and Anthological Description of All the Empires and Kingdoms* (1607; 1.3); Ben Jonson, *The Alchemist* (**1621**; 4.1); John Mico, *A Pill to Purge Out Popery* (1623; 3.5); Francis Bacon, Lord Verulam, *New Atlantis* (written 1625, printed 1627; 2.3); Charles I, *Book of Sports* (1633; 1.1); *A Judgement Shown upon a Knot of Drunkards* (unidentified; 3.5)

A passage in 2.1 is sometimes said to derive from *Neptune's Triumph* (**2080**), but the same source words appear in *The Staple of News*; given the relative accessibility of the two texts, the latter is likelier to be the source.

LANGUAGE
English

Latin: 34 words (2.1–2, 3.5, 5.3–4; Slicer, Moth, Sir Christopher, Shape, Hearsay, Bitefig)
Italian: 3 words (1.4; Slicer)
French: 3 words (2.1–2; Slicer, Moth)
Dialect: Moth speaks throughout in a version of Middle English.

FORM
Metre: pentameter; some alexandrines
Rhyme: blank verse; some couplets
Prologue: 24 lines, in couplets
Act-Division: 5 acts
Epilogue: 10 lines, in couplets, spoken by Shape
Lines (Spoken): 2,512 (2,510 verse, 2 prose)
Lines (Written): 3,004

Two halves of a single verse line are separated by two verses of Song 1.

STAGING
Doors: characters exit several ways (3.3, s.d.)
Discovery Space: there may be a discovery space above (5.3, implicit)
Within: music and song (3.3, s.d.)
Above: two characters discover themselves above (5.3, s.d.; it takes four lines to get up there from the main stage)
Other Openings: a window (4.5, s.d.)

MUSIC
Music: lute within (3.3, s.d.; accompanying Song 1)
Songs:
   1: 'Come, O come, I brook no stay', 3.3, Priscilla within, 20 lines, with lute accompaniment; *musical setting survives*;
   2: 'Then our music is in prime', 3.5, Catchme, Bagshot, Rhymewell, Sir Christopher, in parts, 36 lines;
   3: 'My name's not Tribulation', 4.1, Credulous, 4 lines;
   4: 'Whiles early light springs from the skies', 4.5, Catchme, Bagshot, Rhymewell, Sir Christopher, 36 lines;
   5: 'Now thou, our future brother', 4.5, Sir Christopher, 30 lines.

PROPS
Weapons: Slicer's sword (1.4–5, dialogue); Have-at-All's sword (2.1, 4.2, dialogue); a baton or cudgel (2.1, 4.2, dialogue)
Clothing: a ring (3.1, dialogue); another ring (3.3, dialogue)
Money: two unspecified sums (1.2, implicit and dialogue); ten pieces (1.4, dialogue); eighty pounds (2.3, dialogue); one hundred pounds (3.2, dialogue); an unspecified sum (5.4, implicit)
Food and Drink: beer (3.5, s.d.; drunk on stage)
Small Portable Objects: a letter (3.5, dialogue); an inkhorn (3.5, s.d.); a letter (3.6, s.d.); a handkerchief (4.3, dialogue; used to blindfold Andrew)
Large Portable Objects: seating for one or two characters (4.4, implicit); the Constable's staff (4.5, dialogue); a chair (5.3, dialogue)
Scenery: possibly pictorial hangings (3.3, dialogue; but they may be imagined rather than literal)

COSTUMES AND MAKE-UP
HEARSAY and SLICER: beards (dialogue); disguised as a watchman (5.4, implicit)
SHAPE: a beard (dialogue); a confessor's habit (5.3, s.d.); disguised as a watchman (5.4, implicit; removed on stage)
MEANWELL/LITTLEWORTH: has no beard (dialogue); disguised, possibly with a false beard (1.1, 1.3, 1.5, 2.2, 2.4–5, 3.3, 3.6, 4.3, implicit; 5.2, dialogue; enough is removed on stage to reveal his true identity)
POTLUCK: white hair, a red nose, and a yellow complexion (dialogue); one or more plasters on her face (1.2, dialogue)
ANDREW: hose and doublet, without a cloak (2.4–5, dialogue; a cloak may be worn in his earlier scenes); a ruby ring (4.3, dialogue; removed on stage); a bandstring with a diamond in it (4.3, dialogue)
HAVE-AT-ALL: a sheath (2.1, implicit; 4.2, dialogue)
MOTH: white or grey hair and a beard (dialogue)
RHYMEWELL and BAGSHOT: neither has a beard (dialogue)
CATCHME: a long, rough beard (dialogue)
SIR CHRISTOPHER: a clerical coat (3.5, dialogue); a hat and spectacles (3.5, s.d.; removed on stage)

EARLY TEXTUAL HISTORY
c. 1630s: Song 1, ascribed to 'W. C.', included in a MS verse miscellany (Oxford: Bodleian, MS Rawlinson poet. 199, p. 16).

Mid-seventeenth century (*c.* 1637–62): Song 1 transcribed by Henry Lawes, with his own musical setting, in his autograph MS songbook (London: British Library, Add. MS 53723, fo. 54ᵛ).

c. 1640: Song 1 included in a MS verse miscellany (Oxford: Bodleian, MS Rawlinson D. 1092, fos. 270ᵛ–271ʳ) compiled by an Oxford man.

1648: Cartwright's *Poems and Plays* entered to Humphrey Moseley in the Stationers' Register on Thursday 4 May; play individually named as *The City Cozener, or The Ordinary*. Sir Nathaniel Brent had licensed the book for publication.

Mid-seventeenth century: Song 1 included in a MS verse miscellany (London: British Library, MS Harley 3511, fo. 9ᵛ) compiled by Arthur Capell.

1651: included, with an independent title page naming the author, in William Cartwright's *Comedies, Tragicomedies, with Other Poems* (**O**), sigs. A1ʳ–F7ᵛ; 47 leaves; printed for Humphrey Moseley; list of roles.

1651: George Thomason acquired a copy of O on Monday 23 June. In *c.* 1678, some years after his death, his entire collection of books and tracts was acquired by the bookbinder Samuel Mearne, acting as agent for King Charles II; the King never paid him, and the books remained in Mearne's family until 1761.

1653: *The Marrow of Compliments* entered to Humphrey Moseley in the Stationers' Register on Tuesday 20 December.

1654: four extracts (from 1.2, 3.1, and 4.3; one headed 'The Consecration of a New-Built Fabric') and Songs 2, 4, and 5 included in 'Philomusus', *The Marrow of Compliments*, sigs. C1^v, C8^r–C9^r, C12^v–D1^r, D2^v–D3^r, D8^{r-v}, D10^v–D12^r; printed (before Saturday 15 July) for Humphrey Moseley.

1655: *Wit's Interpreter* entered to Nathaniel Brooke in the Stationers' Register on Wednesday 14 March.

1655: four extracts (from 1.2 and 4.3; one entitled 'The Old Widow') and Song 2 included in John Cotgrave's *Wit's Interpreter*, sigs. G1^r–G3^v, G4^v–G5^v, R2^r; printed for Nathaniel Brooke.

c. 1655: extracts transcribed by John Evans in a miscellany, *Hesperides*, intended for publication and entered to Humphrey Moseley in the Stationers' Register on Thursday 16 August 1655. The book remained unpublished in 1660, and Evans continued adding to the collection until at least 1666. Two MS exemplars are known; one was cut up by J. O. Halliwell-Phillipps in the nineteenth century; the other survives (Washington: Folger, MS V. b. 93).

1657: O advertised as for sale by the Newcastle-upon-Tyne bookseller William London.

c. 1659: Song 1 included, with Lawes's setting, in a MS music book (New York Public Library, MS Drexel 4257, no. 103) owned and partly compiled by John Gamble.

1659: Song 1 included, with Lawes's setting, in John Playford's *Select Airs and Dialogues*, sig. Q2^r; printed by William Godbid for John Playford.

After 1660: extracts included in a MS miscellany (Oxford: Bodleian, MS Rawlinson D. 951, fos. 63^v–64^v), probably compiled by a member of the University of Cambridge.

1662: *Wit's Interpreter* reprinted (before Thursday 8 June) for Nathaniel Brooke; the extracts now appear on sigs. E5^v–F1^r and M7^r; two are entitled 'The Fantastic Scholar' and 'The Widow's Complaint'.

1666: Song 1 included, with Lawes's setting, in John Playford's *Music's Delight*, sig. G3^r; printed by William Godbid for John Playford.

1668: *The New Academy of Compliments* entered to Samuel Speed in the Stationers' Register on Saturday 2 May.

1669: Song 2 included in *The New Academy of Compliments*, sig. G5^{r-v}; printed for Samuel Speed.

1669: *Select Airs and Dialogues* reissued as *The Treasury of Music*.

1671: *Wit's Interpreter* reprinted for Nathaniel Brooke and Obadiah Blagrave.

1671: *The New Academy of Compliments* reprinted for Thomas Rookes.

1672: On Monday 15 January, Sir Henry Herbert licensed the text for performance; Herbert wrote his licence on the prompt-book, a marked-up copy of O.

1672: *Westminster Drollery, The Second Part* entered to William Gilbert in the Stationers' Register on Monday 3 June.

1672: Song 1 (headed 'An Invitation to Enjoyment') included in *Westminster Drollery, The Second Part*, sig. F8^r; printed for William Gilbert and Thomas Sawbridge.

1675: Moseley's rights to *The Marrow of Compliments* transferred from his widow, Ann, to Peter Parker in the Stationers' Register on Wednesday 8 September, by order of a court held on Monday 22 February, and by an assignment dated Thursday 26 September 1672.

1680: rights to *The New Academy of Compliments* transferred in the Stationers' Register from Mary Rookes, widow and executrix of Thomas Rookes, to George Sawbridge on Wednesday 22 September.

1681: *The New Academy of Compliments* reprinted for George Sawbridge.

1684: Nicholas Cox (Manciple of St Edmund Hall, Oxford) had a copy in his bookshop, presumably of O but without the other contents of the volume. It had probably been previously owned by Gerard Langbaine, and appears on a list compiled by Anthony Wood on Saturday 13 December.

1694: *The New Academy of Compliments* reprinted by Ichabod Dawks for Awnsham Churchill and John Churchill.

1697: extract (from Song 2) included in William Winstanley's *Poor Robin*, sig. C3^{r-v}; printed by J. R. (John Rawlins? John Richardson?) for the Company of Stationers. (The first part of the book was printed by John Leake; the second part has its own title page crediting a different printer.)

1698: *The New Academy of Compliments* reprinted by Ichabod Dawks for Awnsham Churchill and John Churchill.

EDITION

G. Blakemore Evans, in *The Plays and Poems of William Cartwright* (Madison, 1951), 255–331.

REFERENCES

Annals 1635; Bawcutt R93; Beal Online CaW 76–9; Bentley, iii. 132–4; Bodleian, MS Wood E. 4, art. 1, p. 29; Eyre & Rivington, i. 437, 467, ii. 8, 386, 443, iii. 3, 95; Friedrich Gerber, *The Sources of William Cartwright's Comedy The Ordinary* (Berne, 1909); Greg 702; Hazlitt, 171; *The Library*, 5th ser., 28 (1973), 294–308; *The Library*, 7th ser., 10 (2009), 372–404; William London, *A Catalogue of the Most Vendible Books in England* (London, 1657), sig. 2E4^v; REED: Oxford, 816; *RES* 15 (1939), 293n.; *RES* NS 54 (2003), 601–14; Stratman, 254–7, 348–50.

2469. *Templum amoris* [The Temple of Love]

TEXT
Printed in 1635 (STC 14719). Additional information derives from Inigo Jones's design drawings (cited as J), and from bills presented for goods and services supplied in connection with the masque (Kew: National Archives, LR 5/66).

GENRE
masque
Contemporary: masque (t.p.)

TITLE
Performed: *Templum amoris*
Printed: *The Temple of Love*
Contemporary: *The Queen's Masque of Indians*; *The Queen's Masque of Indamora*

AUTHOR
William Davenant

DATE
10 February 1635

ORIGINAL PRODUCTION
English Court at the Banqueting House, Whitehall

PLOT
The Temple of Chaste Love is hidden from the world, and magicians have set up a false temple and have tempted noble youths to lust. Now Indamora is to re-establish the Temple in Britain, a nation which consecrates the love of souls rather than of bodies. Divine Poesy proclaims her return with the assistance of a group of dead poets. Learning that their reign of error is coming to an end, the magicians call up elemental spirits to hinder the process. Nine noble Persian youths arrive to worship at the Temple, having failed to be seduced by the magicians. Orpheus calms the seas, and Queen Indamora arrives in a chariot drawn by sea-monsters; her coming dispels the mists which conceal the Temple. Dancing ensues. Thelema and Sunesis, will and understanding, join together, and King Charles and his Queen are invoked as an example of chaste love.

SCENE DESIGNATION
sc.1–4 (Q undivided), according to the changes of scenery; the seven numbered antimasque entries (ant.1–7) take place during sc.2, and the main masque during sc.3–4.

ROLES
DIVINE POESY, a beautiful woman, the secretary of Nature
A CHORUS of the spirits of ancient Greek poets, including Demodocus, Phemius, Homer, Hesiod, Terpander, and the poetess Sappho
Four MAGICIANS; one is lean and one fat
FIERY SPIRITS (ant.1–2, *non-speaking*)
AIRY SPIRITS (ant.1, 3–4, *non-speaking*)
WATERY SPIRITS (ant.1, 5, *non-speaking*)
EARTHY SPIRITS (ant.1, 6, *non-speaking*)
Debauched and QUARRELLING MEN (ant.2, *non-speaking*)
A loose WENCH (ant.2, *non-speaking*)
AMOROUS MEN and WOMEN (ant.3, *non-speaking*)
ALCHEMISTS (ant.4, *non-speaking*)
Drunken Dutch SKIPPERS (ant.5, *non-speaking*)
WITCHES (ant.6, *non-speaking*)
USURERS (ant.6, *non-speaking*)
FOOLS (ant.6, *non-speaking*)
A modern DEVIL, representing discord, rumour, libel, and faction (ant.7, *non-speaking*)
FOLLOWERS of the modern devil (ant.7, *non-speaking*)
Three INDIANS of quality, members of Indamora's train (*non-speaking*)
A Persian PAGE
Nine Persian YOUTHS, said to be noble knights (*non-speaking*)
ORPHEUS, chief priest of Divine Poesy (only sings collectively)
SEAMEN, the pilots of Indamora's barque (*non-speaking*)
BRAHMINS of the Temple of Love (only sing collectively)
PRIESTS of the Temple of Love (only sing collectively)
INDAMORA, Queen of Narsinga, the principal masquer (*non-speaking*)
Fourteen LADIES attending Indamora, the masquers (*non-speaking*)
The Great CHORUS (only sings collectively)
SUNESIS, a man, representing understanding
THELEMA, a young woman, representing free will; the character was originally written as Gnome (divine will)
AMIANTEROS, a male figure; also called Chaste Love

Speaking Parts: 10
Allegorical Roles: 4

Stage Directions and Speech Prefixes
DIVINE POESY: *Divine Poesy* (s.d.s, s.p.s, and arg.); *a beautiful woman ... representing Divine Poesy* (s.d.s)
CHORUS: *a company of ancient Greeke Poets, as Demodicus, Foemius, Homer, Hesiod, Terpander, and Sapho a Poetess* | *the Chorus of Poets* (s.d.s); *The Poets* (s.d.s and s.p.s)
MAGICIANS: *the Magicians* | *three Magicians* | *another Magician* (s.d.s); *1* | *2* | *3* | *4* (s.p.s); *certain Magicians* | *the Magicians* | *the false Magicians* (arg.)
FIERY SPIRITS: [some of] *the Spirits* | *The fiery Spirits* (s.d.s)
AIRY SPIRITS: [some of] *the Spirits* | *The Airy Spirits* | *the Spirits of Air* (s.d.s)
WATERY SPIRITS: [some of] *the Spirits* | *The Watery Spirits* | *the Spirits of Water* (s.d.s)
EARTHY SPIRITS: [some of] *the Spirits* | *The Earthy Spirits* | *the Spirits of Earth* (s.d.s)

QUARRELLING MEN: *debauched and quarrelling men* (s.d.s)
WENCH: *a loose Wench* (s.d.s)
AMOROUS MEN and WOMEN: *amorous men and women* (s.d.s)
ALCHEMISTS: *Alchemists* (s.d.s)
SKIPPERS: *drunken Dutch skippers* (s.d.s)
WITCHES: *Witches* (s.d.s)
USURERS: *Usurers* (s.d.s)
FOOLS: *Fools* (s.d.s)
DEVIL: *a Modern Devil* (s.d.s)
FOLLOWERS: [the Modern Devil's] *factious followers* (s.d.s)
INDIANS: *three Indians of quality, of Indamora's train* (s.d.s)
PAGE: *A Persian Page* | *The Page* (s.d.s)
YOUTHS: *the Noble Persian youths* (s.d.s); *a company of noble Persian youths* (arg.)
ORPHEUS: *Orpheus* (s.d.s); *Orpheus,* [Divine Poesy's] *chief Priest* (s.p.s)
SEAMEN: *other persons* (s.d.s)
BRAHMINS: *the Brachmani* (s.d.s); *the Brachmans and Priests of the Temple* (arg.)
PRIESTS: *the Priests of the Temple of Love* (s.d.s)
INDAMORA: [one of] *the Masquers* | *Indamora, Queen of Narsinga* | *the Queen* (s.d.s); *Indamora* (s.d.s and arg.); *the glorious Indian Queen* (arg.)
LADIES: *the Masquers* (s.d.s); [Indamora's] *Contributary Ladies* (s.d.s and arg.); [Indamora's] *train* (arg.)
CHORUS: *the Chorus* | *the Music* | *the Chori* | *the great Chorus* (s.d.s); *Chorus* (s.p.s)
SUNESIS: *Sunesis* (s.d.s, s.p.s, and arg.)
THELEMA: *Thelema* (s.d.s, s.p.s, and arg.)
AMIANTEROS: *Amianteros, or Chaste Love* (s.d.s and s.p.s); *Chaste Love* (s.d.s and arg.)

OTHER CHARACTERS
Nature, to whom Divine Poesy is secretary (arg., sc.2)
An old witch, beloved of the leading magician (sc.2)
The grand fiend of hell (sc.2)
The gods, whom Divine Poesy entertains with music (sc.2)
Young lords of the British court who were initially unimpressed by Platonic love, but have since been converted (sc.2)

SETTING
Geography
India: Narsinga
Asia: River Meander
Persia: River Tigris
Britain
[*Europe*]: Spain; Italy; Greece; the Netherlands

SOURCES
Narrative: *Il Tempio d'amore* (performed at Ferrara, 1565; printed 1566; repr. 1567); Plato, *Timaeus* (antimasque); Giulio Parigi, *Il giudizio di Paridi* (1616; Indamora)
Design: Giulio Romano, *Battle of the Romans and Persians* (sixteenth century, before 1546; proscenium arch; Jones probably used an engraving by Cornelis Cort), Fresco from the Palazzo del Tè, Mantua (1524–34; Jones may have used an engraving by Diana Ghisi; proscenium arch); Alfonso Chacón, *Historia utriusque belli Dacici a Traiano Caesare gesti* (1576; Airy Spirit); Cesare Vecellio, *Habiti antichi e moderni di tutto il mondo* (1590; Jones used the 1598 edn; Persian Youths, Indamora's headdress); William Shakespeare, *1 Henry IV* (**1059**; one of the Brahmins is said on the design drawing to be 'like a Sir John Falstaff'); Antonio Tempesta, Print of a Palace and its Gardens (1598; back shutter); Giulio Parigi, *Il giudizio di Paridi* (1608; Indian Shore); Giacomo Cicognini, *Amore pudico* (Wedding masque for Michele Peretti, 8 February 1614); Daniel Rabel, *Le ballet de la Douairière le Billebahaut* (1622; Earthy Spirit), *Le ballet du Château du Bicêtre* (1632; Watery Spirit); Alfonso Parigi, *La Flora* (1628; Grove)

LANGUAGE
English

FORM
Metre: tetrameter and pentameter
Rhyme: ABAB, AABCCB, couplets, triplets, and blank verse
Lines (Spoken): 307
Lines (Written): 575

STAGING
Stage: mentioned (desc.)
Above: Divine Poesy descends in a cloud, which then goes back up (sc.1, desc.); a cloud descends, then opens to admit Amianteros, then closes and goes back up (sc.3, desc.; he may thus descend in the cloud or enter through a concealed aperture behind it)
Beneath: the Magicians enter out of underground caves (sc.2, desc.)
Audience: Divine Poesy approaches the state and addresses the King (sc.1, desc.); ladies in the audience are directly addressed, and are said to be equipped with fans (sc.2, implicit); the Queen, in the cast, goes and sits by the King, in the audience (sc.3, desc.); the King and Queen are mentioned (sc.4); the masquers dance with lords from the audience, including the King (sc.4, desc.)

MUSIC
Music: unspecified music (sc.3, desc.; accompanying Songs 5–6)
On-Stage Music: the Poets play their instruments (sc.1, desc.; accompanying Song 3); Orpheus plays the harp (sc.3, desc.; *the music may survive*); the Brahmins play their instruments (sc.3, desc.)
Songs:
  1: 'As cheerful as the morning's light', sc.1, Divine Poesy and Poets, in parts, 30 lines;

2: 'Thou monarch of men's hearts, rejoice!', sc.1, Divine Poesy and Poets, in parts, 14 lines;
3: 'Take leave now of thy heart', sc.1, Poets, 14 lines, with musical accompaniment;
4: 'Hark! Orpheus is a seaman grown', sc.3, Brahmins, 24 lines;
5: 'She comes! Each princess in her train hath all', sc.3, Chorus, 18 lines; with musical accompaniment;
6: 'The planets, though they move so fast', sc.3, Chorus, 18 lines, probably with musical accompaniment;
7: 'Come, melt thy soul in mine, that, when unite', sc.4, Sunesis, Thelema, and Chorus, in parts, 10 lines;
8: 'Whilst by a mixture thus made one', sc.4, Amianteros, Sunesis, and Chorus, in parts, 21 lines.

Other Singing: other parts of the dialogue may be sung, even though not explicitly identified as song

Dance: seven antimasque dances (sc.2, desc.); three Indians dance (sc.2, desc.); the Persian Page enters 'leaping', which may signify a dance (sc.2, desc.); the Persian Youths dance (sc.2, desc.); masquers' entry dance (sc.3, desc.); masquers' second dance (sc.3, desc.); revels (sc.4, desc.).

PROPS

Musical Instruments: Poets' unspecified instruments (sc.1, desc.); a harp (sc.3, desc.); Brahmins' unspecified instruments (sc.3, desc.);

Clothing: two laurel garlands (sc.4, desc.)

Animals: a swan (sc.1, desc.)

Small Portable Objects: a white sceptre (sc.2, dialogue); a green wand (sc.3, J); a rod (sc.3?, J); a parchment scroll (sc.3?, J)

Scenery: a proscenium with figures and the title of the masque (desc.; *design drawing survives*); a curtain (desc.; raised to reveal the first scene); a grove of trees with a mount and a bower on top (sc.1, desc.; *design drawing survives*); a rosy cloud (sc.1, desc.; descends with a character visible on board; later closes and goes back up empty; *design drawing survives*); mist and clouds with glimpses of a temple (sc.2, desc.); a calm sea with islands and moving billows, a shore, and an Indian landscape of broken grounds and rocks, a mountainous country with strange trees, arbours, beasts, and birds (sc.3, desc.; the downstage part of the sea later transforms itself into dry land; *design drawing survives*); an antique barque embossed with silver and gold, with a sea-god figurehead (sc.3, desc.; moves across the sea; *design drawing survives*); a maritime chariot made of spongy rock with shells, seaweed, coral, and pearl, golden rimless wheels, flat oar-shaped spokes, containing a throne backed with a giant scallop shell, and drawn by sea-monsters (sc.3, desc.; large enough for fourteen characters; moves across the sea); the Temple of Chaste Love, with satyrs as terms and golden decoration, including architrave, frieze, cornice, pilasters, niches, statues, and a gate (sc.4, desc.); a bright, transparent cloud (sc.4, desc.; descends, then opens to admit a character)

COSTUMES AND MAKE-UP

DIVINE POESY: a sky-coloured garment with gold stars; a veil hanging down behind; artificial curly hair (sc.1, desc.); *design drawing survives (for her cloud)*

CHORUS: laurel wreaths; garments of various colours (sc.1, desc.); *design drawing of headgear survives*

MAGICIANS: the first three have deformed bodies and wear 'strange fashions' (sc.2, desc.; *two design drawings survive*); one has dog's ears, one is lean, and one is fat (sc.2, J); the fourth has a different shape and habit (sc.2, desc.), including a conical hat (J; *design drawing survives*)

FIERY SPIRITS: suits resembling flames; vizards of choleric complexion (sc.2, desc.); *two design drawings survive*

AIRY SPIRITS: sanguine vizards; garments and caps made of feathers (sc.2, desc.); *two design drawings survive*

WATERY SPIRITS: fishes' heads and fins; scaly garments (sc.2, desc.); *two design drawings survive*

EARTHY SPIRITS: garments decorated with leafless trees and bushes, serpents and little animals; barren rocks on their heads (sc.2, desc.); black cloth wound around a skin-coat, which is open at various places revealing dark flesh colour underneath; long black hair and long thin beards (sc.2, J); *five design drawings survive*

AMOROUS MEN and WOMEN: ridiculous habits (sc.2, desc.)

INDIANS: 'several strange habits' (sc.2, desc.)

PAGE: shoes (sc.2, bill)

YOUTHS: sea-green Asian coats, embroidered, with buttons and loops in front, cut square to the hips and two short skirts to above the knee; large short sleeves with a long train and trimmed with buttons, with a sleeve of embroidered white satin and white satin bases; Persian turbans silvered underneath and wound about with white cypress, and one fall of a white feather in front (sc.2, desc.); narrow sashes (sc.2, J); *two design drawings survive*

ORPHEUS: a white robe and girdle; a carnation mantle; a laurel garland (sc.3, desc.); a scarf (sc.3, J); *two design drawings survive*

BRAHMINS: 'extravagant habits' (sc.3, desc.), including, for at least two different Brahmins: (a) a short cloak, (b) light green straight sleeves; and possibly for at least three: (c) a cap; a Persian mitre; large spectacles; a long red and white beard hanging in locks; (d) a russet robe girt low; a great belly; long moustache; 'skin-coat' sleeves and leggings representing fat arms and legs; buskins, a peaked cap, a bald head; (e) a close suit, black trousers with a flap and a large button; a cloak; a long square cape; a physician's cap; a girdle (sc.3, J; it is possible that

the descriptions of (c–e) may not refer to the Brahmins); *two design drawings survive*
PRIESTS: 'extravagant habits' (sc.3, desc.), including sleeves (J); *design drawing survives*
INDAMORA: a watchet and greyish yellow satin habit, embroidered with copper Os around the gorget and wings; embroidered bases cut through in panes; silver headgear with a fall of white feathers tipped in watchet (sc.3, desc./bills); gloves decorated with rich yellowish-brown and silver ribbon, trimmed and lined with taffeta (sc.3, bills); *three design drawings survive*
LADIES: watchet and greyish yellow habits, with embroidered bases cut through in panes; silver headgear with falls of white feathers tipped in watchet (sc.3, desc.).
SUNESIS: a cloth-of-gold garment reaching to the below the knees, girt at the waist, with wide, turned-up sleeves; a watchet mantle hanging down behind; a garland of sinope with a flame; yellow buskins wrought with gold (sc.4, desc.); *two design drawings survive*
THELEMA: a robe of changeable silk girt under her breast and at the waist; leaves of silver on her shoulders and hanging down to mid-arm; a garland of marigold and puffs of silvered lawn; angels' wings on her shoulders (sc.4, desc.); *two design drawings survive*
AMIANTEROS: carnation and white clothes, and a garland of laurel (sc.4, desc.).

EARLY STAGE HISTORY
Preparation: The masque was in preparation by no later than Saturday 6 December 1634. By Friday 19 December, the Queen had not yet decided on the masquers, so the performance was delayed until Shrovetide, but on Sunday 3 January 1635, a performance at Candlemas (Monday 2 February) was mooted. The masquers were chosen by Sunday 11 January; Lucy Hay, Countess of Carlisle, and Anne Percy, Countess of Northumberland, were excused from performing because they were in mourning.
Design Preparation: Amerigo Salvetti probably showed Inigo Jones a copy of Alfonso Parigi's designs for *La Flora* (1628).
Costume Preparation: On Monday 10 November 1634, Matthew Jumper delivered cloth for the masque. On Tuesday 27 January 1635, the mercers Richard Miller and Rhys Williams delivered cloth for masquing suits. On Saturday 7 February, the embroiderer Charles Gentile worked on the Queen's masquing gown, and made two other gowns (for Victoria Cary and Mrs Neville). Deliveries were made on Tuesday 10 February, the day of the performance, by the shoemaker John Fausse (a pair of dancing shoes), Matthew Jumper (ribbon and tinsel), and Peter Lermitt (feathers, delivered to the tirewoman Sara Gretton). On Thursday 12 February, the milliner Humphrey Bradborne delivered ribbon and taffeta for the Queen's masquing gloves (presumably for use in the third performance, if the delivery is correctly dated in the bill).
Preparation of Venue: The Banqueting House was made ready by carpenters and labourers; the whole process took at least 28 days. The six-foot-high stage was set up at the lower end. The turning door, installed the previous year (for **2428**), was lined by the Great Wardrobe by a warrant dated Saturday 7 February, which also ordered two close stools to be given to Mr [Clement?] Kinnersley for use at the performance.
Rehearsals: Rehearsals had begun by Friday 23 January; at that stage the number of lady masquers attending the Queen was reported as fifteen, not fourteen. By Friday 30 January rehearsals were taking place daily.
First Performance: in the Banqueting House, Whitehall, on Tuesday 10 February 1635 (Shrove Tuesday). The cast included: James Stewart, 4th Duke of Lennox; Mountjoy Blount, 1st Earl of Newport; George Feilding, 1st Earl of Desmond; William Villiers, 2nd Viscount Grandison; William, Lord Russell; James Hay, 2nd Viscount Doncaster; Thomas Weston; George Goring; Henry Murray (Persian Youths); Jeffery Hudson (Page?); Queen Henrietta Maria (Indamora); Mary Hamilton, Marchioness of Hamilton; Beatrice de Vere, Countess of Oxford; Elizabeth Howard, Countess of Berkshire; Anne Sophia Dormer, Countess of Carnarvon; Ann Blount, Countess of Newport; Lady Mary Herbert; Lady [Mary?] Herbert [of Shurland?]; Lady Katherine Howard; Lady Ann Carr; Lady Elizabeth Feilding; Lady Elizabeth Thimbleby; Dorothy Savage; Victoria Cary; Mrs [Sophia?] Neville (Ladies); possibly Jean de la Flelle (Orpheus). The design was by Inigo Jones. The audience included: King Charles I; George Brydges, 6th Baron Chandos (who incurred expenses of £8.2s.6d); Sir Thomas Roe (who found the masque wearisome, but admired the lady masquers); John Greene. Anzolo Correr (Venetian Ambassador) was present at this or one of the next two performances; Gregorio Panzani (Papal Agent) may have been present at one or more of the performances, and later wrote to Cardinal Francesco Barberini that the design resembled that of the 1614 Peretti wedding masque that Jones had seen when in Italy.
Repeat Performances: there were two or three further performances, all in the Banqueting House, Whitehall: Wednesday 11 February (Ash Wednesday); Thursday 12 February; and possibly Saturday 14 February (St Valentine's Day). For one of these performances (probably Ash Wednesday), the Queen gave a ticket to Thomas Knyvett. If the Valentine's Day performance took place, it was in the evening as an adjunct to a French comedy, and the audience included: Sir Humphrey Mildmay; probably Lady Jane Mildmay; Lady Cooke (wife of Sir Francis Cooke).
Aftermath: The scenery was still standing in the Banqueting House on Sunday 22 March.

There is some confusion about the number of masquers. Orgel and Strong list only fourteen, but both Sir Thomas Roe (in a letter of 30 January) and Amerigo Salvetti (in a dispatch of 2 February Gregorian) say that there are to be fifteen. The problem arises because two of them have similar titles: Q lists not only Lady Mary Herbert but also Lady Herbert. They probably, indeed, had the same name: Lady Mary Herbert was presumably the wife of Richard Herbert, the future 2nd Baron Herbert of Cherbury, and the other was probably the 12-year-old newlywed bride of Lord Charles Herbert of Shurland, who had until the month before been Lady Mary Villiers.

Production Finance and Expenses
Edmund Taverner was paid £1,400 towards the cost of the masque by a warrant dated Sunday 18 January.
Costumes: Payments were made from the Queen's Purse totalling £246.7s.3d; a saving of £37.15s was made by unilaterally reducing three bills. On Thursday 19 March, Charles Gentile was paid for: embroidering the Queen's gown (£50; £10 less than billed); making two other gowns (£100; £20 less than billed); cutting and gluing the gowns (£6; £3 less than billed). On the same day, Peter Lermitt was paid for: making four patterns of feathers (£1; half what was billed); tops of watchet and white feathers (15s; 5s less than billed); the Queen's fall (15s); twelve falls (£6; £3 less than billed). Also on Thursday 19 March, Richard Miller and Rhys Williams were paid for watchet satin (£24.15s) and Isabella satin (£19.16s). On Saturday 21 March, Humphrey Bradborne was paid for ribbon (16s.3d) and Matthew Jumper was paid for broad tinsel ribbon (£6.6s), narrow tinsel ribbon (13s.6d), and tinsel stuff (£12). On Sunday 22 March, the tirewoman Sara Gretton was paid £9 for dressing the Queen, Victoria Cary, and Mrs Neville. On Monday 23 March, John Fausse was paid for Jeffery Hudson's dancing shoes (£1), and Gilbert Morette was paid for stiffening (£1) and making three gowns (£4.10s; 10s less than billed).
Preparation of Venue (Works): The total recorded cost was £254.14s.7d, which broke down as follows: supplies (£101.16s.1d); carriage of supplies (£1.12s.6d); wages (£151.6s). However, the account seems to have been negligently calculated: the stated total for supplies was 4d less than the sum of the itemized amounts, and for wages, 5d more, so the actual overall cost was a penny less than the declared total. Specific materials used were: deal boards (£23.13s.4d); fire timber (£10.6s.3d); burlings (£5); bomespars (£4); nails (£30.15s.6d); base rope (£1.2s.2d); candles (£4.10s); lines (12s); cords (7s.6d); baskets (8s.4d); birch besoms (2s); brass pulleys (12s); wooden pulleys (6s.5d); soap (7s.6d); leather (2s.6d) ironworks (£19.8s.11d); mops (2s). Specific wage costs were: carpenters (£119.5s.5d); labourers (£19.5s); Andrew Durdant, Clerk of the Works (£2.9s for fourteen days' work); John Williams, Purveyor (£2.6s.8d for 28 days' work); sawyers (£7.19s.6d).
Preparation of Venue (Revels): The Revels Office made the following payments to William Penrin, totalling £18.13s.4d: 24 small branches (£12); eight men working eight days and two nights in February 'for the King's masque' (£6.13s.4d).

EARLY TEXTUAL HISTORY
1635: William Davenant was paid £50 for writing the masque; the payment was made through Henry Jermyn.
1635: ¹Q printed (in February) for Thomas Walkley; collation A⁴ B⁴ (–B4) C⁴ D², 13 leaves; title page names Jones and Davenant as authors (in that order, with Davenant's name initially in smaller type, though the title page was reset during printing to enlarge it). Leaf B4 was found to be defective during printing (the Persian Page had been omitted), so the leaf was cancelled (although it is still present in some surviving copies) and quire C set to continue the text from the end of sig. B3ᵛ.
1635: In February, John Newdigate bought a copy.
1635: This may have been the masque whose text was copied out for Edward, 2nd Viscount Conway, at a cost of 1s.6d; the transcript was made and paid for no later than Thursday 19 March.
Late 1630s (after 1637): Bullen Reymes transcribed four pieces of music, probably Orpheus' harp solos, into a MS lute-book (Paris: Bibliothèque du Centre Nationale de la Recherche Scientifique, MS [no pressmark], fos. 59ᵛ–60ʳ); the heading notes that they were played by Jean de la Flelle in 'the Queen's masque'.
1640–1: This may have been the 'Temple Masque', copies of which were being sold for 6d each by Humphrey Moseley.
1658: rights transferred in the Stationers' Register from Thomas Walkley to Humphrey Moseley on Saturday 6 March; individually named as part of a group transfer of four masques; entry names author.
1660: advertised as having been printed for Humphrey Moseley.
1667: Moseley's rights to Davenant's *Masques, Plays, and Poems* transferred from his widow, Ann, to Henry Herringman in the Stationers' Register on Monday 19 August; group transfer of nine titles, the Davenant collection being one, with the masque individually named.
1672: Davenant's *Works* entered to Henry Herringman in the Stationers' Register on Thursday 31 October. Roger L'Estrange had licensed the book for the press. On Monday 18 November, it was advertised for sale by Henry Herringman, John Martin, John Starkey, and Robert Horne; however, it was apparently not issued until the following year.
1673: included in Davenant's *Works* (²F), sigs. 3B4ᵛ–3D2ᵛ; printed by Thomas Newcomb for Henry Herringman.
1675: Davenant's *Works* advertised as for sale by John Starkey.

Greg identifies the 'Temple Masque' of Moseley's 1640 or 1641 bill as a duplicate entry for *The Triumphs of the Prince D'Amour* (**2532**). However, the first entry for that masque is dated 1636, whereas the copy of the 'Temple Masque' is dated 1635. The problem is that both masques' title pages bear old-style dates, 1634 and 1635; so Moseley acted inconsistently if the entries are duplicates for the same masque, but updated both, ignoring the imprint dates, if the entries pertain to two different masques.

EDITION
Orgel and Strong, ii. 598–629.
John H. Robinson, *Lute News* 67 (October 2003), Supplement, 20–1 (music only).

REFERENCES
Annals 1635; Ashbee, iii. 81; Bentley, ii. 677, iii. 216–18; Karen Britland, *Drama at the Courts of Queen Henrietta Maria* (Cambridge, 2006), 141–9; Butler, 335–7, 374; *Cal. Dom.* 1634–5, 482, 510, 591; *Cal. Ven.* 1632–6, 334, 475; *Early Music* 15 (1997), 188–203; Greg 497; Hazlitt, 225; HMC Hastings, i. 377; David Howarth, *Lord Arundel and His Circle* (New Haven, 1985), 47–8, 230 n. 41; *JWCI* 61 (1998), 176–97; Vivienne Larminie, *Wealth, Kinship and Culture* (Woodbridge, 1995), 203; David Lindley (ed.), *The Court Masque* (Manchester, 1984), 159; Loomie, 174; McGee-Meagher 1634–42, 34–9; Joanna Moody (ed.), *The Private Correspondence of Jane, Lady Cornwallis Bacon, 1613–1644* (Madison, 2003), 245; *MRDE* 6 (1993), 192; MSC 2.3, 374–5; MSC 10, 47–8; MSC 13, 133; *Oxford Bibliographical Society Proceedings and Papers* 2.2 (1929), 132–3; John Peacock, *The Stage Designs of Inigo Jones* (Cambridge, 1995), 144–9, 192–5, 252; REED: Inns of Court, 810; Reyher, 531; Bertram Schofield (ed.), *The Knyvett Letters* (London, 1949), 88; *ShS* 11 (1958), 111; Steele, 251–2; *Theatre Survey* 20 (1979), 21–2; *TN* 30 (1976), 109–14; Erica Veevers, *Images of Love and Power* (Cambridge, 1989), 133–42.

2470. The Royal Combat

EVIDENCE
Stationers' Register; list of MS plays supposedly in the possession of John Warburton (1682–1759), and destroyed by his cook (London: British Library, MS Lansdowne 807, fo. 1).

GENRE
comedy
Contemporary: comedy

TITLE
Contemporary: *The Royal Combat*

AUTHOR
John Ford

DATE
Limits: 1620–39
Best Guess: 1635

See **2427**.

ROLES
One or more ROYAL PERSONAGES, probably male

EARLY TEXTUAL HISTORY
1660: entered in the Stationers' Register to Humphrey Moseley on Friday 29 June; play and author individually named as part of a group entry of 26 plays.

REFERENCES
Annals 1638; Bentley, iii. 458; Greg Θ172; *The Library*, 3rd ser., 2 (1911), 225–59; Sibley, 137.

2471. The Italian Night Masque

EVIDENCE
Undated letter from Sir Henry Wotton to Sir Gervase Clifton; Stationers' Register.

Although the last word of the title differs in the two sources (*Masque* in Wotton, *Piece* in S.R.), the wording is otherwise too similar and distinctive to admit a hypothesis that the evidence relates to two separate plays. Indeed, the appearance of similar titles in two independent pieces of testimony decades apart presents better than usual evidence for the play's existence. However, John Freehafer (in *JEGP*) offers an inventive and tendentious argument which identifies *The Italian Night-Piece* of Humphrey Moseley's 1653 Stationers' Register entry as an alternative title for *Luminalia* (**2599**), and *The Italian Night Masque* of the Wotton letter as a confused reference to a production of *Aglaura* (**2567**) which, he suggests, reused scenery that had been made for *Luminalia*.

The argument is problematic in five ways. First, its starting-point is the assumption that the two variant titles must belong to an extant text better known as something else. The case made for the *Luminalia* identification is simply that no other dramatic text of the period could more aptly be termed *The Italian Night-Piece*. The possibility is never admitted that the recorded title or titles belong to a lost work, so the aptness of the identification is secondary to the belief that an identification needs to be made: *Luminalia* only recommends itself to a scholar who is already looking for candidates.

Secondly, the argument interprets the evidence using hypotheses which it then treats as secure facts. The last-minute rehearsal call which prevented Richard Robinson from receiving Wotton might have been because the production was organized at short notice, as Freehafer proposes, but there could just as well have been other reasons for a schedule change. Likewise, the information Wotton got from Robinson only says that the play will be 'the rarest thing ... that hath ever been seen on a stage'. It is supposition, not fact, that the performance was going to be special because it was going to use scenery; yet the proposition that scenery was involved is then treated as the clinching factor which identifies the play being rehearsed as *Aglaura*. In any event, *Aglaura* was not, in fact, the first play in the London commercial theatre to use scenery: it had previously featured in *Microcosmus* (**2543**).

The third problem is the way aspects of the evidence that don't fit the theory are ignored or disbelieved. It does not add up that *The Italian Night-Piece*, if it were *Luminalia*, would appear in

Moseley's 1653 entry, which is, or seems to be, exclusively a listing of plays: *Luminalia* would be anomalous as the only masque. (See also under GENRE.) Moreover, Moseley acquired the rights to *Luminalia*, under its own title, by transfer from another stationer in 1658, which would not have been necessary if he had already registered it in his own name five years earlier. Furthermore, although the entry's ascription to Massinger is admittedly insecure, it might *not* be fraudulent, whereas it *must* be for Freehafer's argument to work. Similarly, when Robinson named the play as *The Italian Night Masque*, the theory demands that the information must be garbled, and that he muddled up the play with the masque from which it had supposedly recycled its scenery.

Robinson's putative error illustrates the argument's fourth weakness: it requires human behaviour that is fundamentally implausible. The actor's confusion, it is proposed, arose because the play had been unexpectedly sprung on him. Yet the argument also requires it to have been a restaging, with a revised text, of a play the company had performed only a few weeks earlier during the Christmas season at court: if it was *Aglaura*, we could be reasonably sure that Robinson would have known what it was. It follows that, on the contrary, we can be reasonably sure that it was not *Aglaura*, and it is therefore a good bet that it really was *The Italian Night Masque*.

The fifth problem with the case turns that bet into a racing certainty: at the time of the *Aglaura* performance in early April 1638, Sir Henry Wotton was at Eton College, where he was Provost, and was visited there by John Milton, who wrote to thank him shortly afterwards on Friday 6 April; but he was in London when he wrote the letter to Clifton about *The Italian Night Masque*.

GENRE
Contemporary: play (Wotton, S.R.)

The title need not imply that the play was, or was perceived as, a 'night masque'; it is at least as likely that it was *about* a masque, in the same way that *The Ball* (**2389**) is about a ball. 'Night-piece' might also be generic terminology, a literary composition about the night; but another available meaning (*OED* 2) was 'a mistress' (in the sexual sense).

TITLE
Performed: *The Italian Night Masque*
Contemporary: *The Italian Night-Piece*

AUTHOR
Philip Massinger (?)

Ascriptions associated with Moseley's double titles are especially uncertain: even if the ascription is correct, the named author could apply to one title or both. This play's Register-mate, *The Unfortunate Piety* (**2340**), was a play by Massinger; it is therefore possible that *The Italian Night-Piece* might not have been his at all.

DATE
Limits: 1624–39

See **2225** for general discussion of the dating of the ten lost Massinger plays registered in 1653 and 1660. If Massinger was not the author, the lower limit could extend to 1642.

The play must date from the period when Sir Henry Wotton was back in England, after his long term as a diplomat abroad. His letters reveal that he spent much of that time in Eton and Canterbury, whereas the letter pertaining to the play was written in London. His other datable London letters were written in April 1626, November 1628, February 1629, February to June 1633, and March and November 1635. His known correspondence with Clifton (including letters from Eton as well as London) runs from April 1628 to June 1635.

ORIGINAL PRODUCTION
King's Men at the Blackfriars and/or the Globe (?)

ROLES
A LADY, perhaps a courtesan (?)

See under GENRE.

SETTING
Time-Scheme: at least some of the action probably takes place at night

Geography
Italy

EARLY STAGE HISTORY
Performed by the King's Men. The play was rehearsed, and had its first public performance on the ensuing Wednesday. The cast included Richard Robinson. The afternoon rehearsal seems to have been arranged at a day's notice; in consequence, Robinson had to put off a visit Sir Henry Wotton was to make to his home to view some pictures. He told Wotton that he thought the play was 'the rarest thing . . . that hath ever been seen on a stage'.

EARLY TEXTUAL HISTORY
1653: entered (as a double title with *The Unfortunate Piety*, **2340**) to Humphrey Moseley in the Stationers' Register on Friday 9 September; play and author individually named as part of a group entry of 41 (or 55) plays.

Moseley's double titles are discussed under **1643**.

REFERENCES
Bentley, iv. 792–3; Greg Θ74; Hazlitt, 118; *JEGP* 67 (1965), 249–65; Sir Henry Wotton, *Life and Letters*, ed. Logan Pearsall Smith (Oxford, 1907), ii. 333, 450–2.

2472. Messalina, the Roman Empress

TEXT
Printed in 1640 (STC 21011), probably from authorial papers.

GENRE
tragedy
Contemporary: tragedy (title, prol.); play (prol., ep.); Roman tragedy (Bradwell comm. verses)

2472. Messalina, the Roman Empress

TITLE
Printed: *The Tragedy of Messalina, the Roman Empress*
Contemporary: *The Tragedy of Messalina*
Later Assigned: *The Tragedy of Messalina, the Insatiate Roman Empress*
Alternative Modernization: *Messallina*

AUTHOR
Nathaniel Richards

DATE
Limits: 1634–6
Best Guess: 1635

ORIGINAL PRODUCTION
King's Revels Company, probably at Salisbury Court

PLOT
Having successfully competed with the prostitute Calpurnia to see which of them can sleep with more men in 24 hours, the Empress Messalina sets her sights on the chaste Silius as her lover. He is summoned to the brothel and successfully seduced.

The Emperor Claudius leaves Rome for an annual religious ceremony. While he is away, Messalina's debauchery has free rein. Romans are summoned to court to participate: the actor Mnester is tortured into compliance, and three women taking refuge with Lepida, Messalina's mother, are murdered when they refuse to come. Messalina invokes the Furies to make her sexy, and resists Lepida's attempts to persuade her to a chaste life; Lepida goes mad. Silius is sent to murder his wife, Silana, but finds himself unable to go through with it; instead he conceals from Messalina the fact that she is still alive.

Messalina's seduction programme is not universally successful: she identifies Montanus as a desirable sexual partner, but he resists her and flees Rome. She decides to go through a ceremony of marriage with Silius, and has a document of approval drawn up, and authenticated with the imperial seal. A wedding masque is planned, in which the Vestal Virgins are to be raped; but Lepida overhears the arrangements being discussed, and rescues the Virgins through a secret passage before they are called on to perform. They are pursued by Messalina's agents, but the earth swallows them and the Virgins are saved; the pander Saufellus is confronted by the ghosts of the three murdered women and shot with a thunderbolt before he goes down.

Claudius' minions inform him of Messalina's sexual misconduct, and he sends in the guard. The palace is raided and Messalina's favourites killed. Silana arrives too late to help Silius, and dies kissing his dead lips. Claudius orders Messalina to be tried before the Senate, but his minion Narcissus fears his susceptibility to her feminine wiles, and sends an executioner to kill her. She is visited by the ghosts of her victims, agents, and favourites, and pre-empts the executioner by taking her own life. Claudius decides not to marry again.

SCENE DESIGNATION
prol., 1.1–4, 2.1–3, 3.1–3, 4.1–3, 5.1–5, ep. (Q has act-division only)

ROLES
PROLOGUE
Caius SILIUS, a chaste gentleman, Silana's husband; also appears as a ghost
Vectius VALENS, Silius' friend; also appears as a ghost
PROCULUS, Silius' friend; also appears as a ghost
VENERIA, an old bawd; also appears as a ghost
CALPURNIA, a prostitute
HEM, a pander and ruffian; also appears as a ghost
STITCH, a pander and ruffian; also appears as a ghost
Lord SAUFELLUS Trogus, Messalina's court pander; also appears as a ghost
Valeria MESSALINA, Empress of Rome, Lepida's daughter, Claudius' wife and the mother of his children
CLAUDIUS, Emperor of Rome, Messalina's husband, father of her children; also called Caesar
NARCISSUS, Claudius' minion
PALLAS, Claudius' minion
CALLISTUS, Claudius' minion
ATTENDANTS on Claudius (1.3, 5.5, *non-speaking*)
MNESTER, an actor; also appears as a ghost
A GUARD, who tortures Mnester (1.4, *non-speaking*)
Madam LEPIDA, Messalina's mother
Three Roman DAMES, summoned to court; later appear as ghosts
MANUTIUS, Lepida's servant (he or Folio may be *non-speaking*)
FOLIO, Lepida's servant (he or Manutius may be *non-speaking*)
Three FURIES, who sing and dance
SILANA, Silius' wife
Annaeus MELA, brother of the banished Seneca
MONTANUS, a knight
COURTIERS (3.2, *non-speaking*)
VIRGILIANUS, a senator
CALPURNIANUS, a senator
ATTENDANTS on Messalina (4.1, *non-speaking*)
The AUSPICES (4.3, *non-speaking*)
VIBIDIA, Matron of the Vestal Virgins
An ANGEL (5.3, *non-speaking*)
SULPICIUS, commander of Messalina's soldiers
A GUARD of soldiers (5.4; two speak)
SENATORS (5.4, *non-speaking*)
Eight BACCHANALIANS in the antimasque (5.4, *non-speaking*)
Three COURTESANS, who play queens in the masque (5.4; only speak collectively)
SOLDIERS accompanying Claudius (5.4, *non-speaking*)
EVODIUS, commander of Claudius' soldiers
Two SPIRITS, who sing (5.5)
A HEADSMAN (5.5, *non-speaking*)
A GUARD attending the headsman (5.5, *non-speaking*)
EPILOGUE

2472. Messalina, the Roman Empress

Speaking Parts: 39–40

Stage Directions and Speech Prefixes
PROLOGUE: *The Prologue* (heading)
SILIUS: *Silius* (s.d.s); *Sil<ius>* (s.p.s); *Silius chief Favourite to the Empress* (d.p.)
VALENS: *Valens* | [one of the] *Favourites* | [one of Messalina's and Silius'] *faction* | [one of the] *Ghosts* (s.d.s); *Vall<ens>* (s.p.s); *Valens* [one] *of the same faction* [as Saufellus] *and* [one of the] *favourites* (d.p.)
PROCULUS: *Proculus* | [one of the] *Favourites* | [one of Messalina's and Silius'] *faction* | [one of the] *Ghosts* (s.d.s); *Pro<culus>* (s.p.s); *Proculus* [one] *of the same faction* [as Saufellus] *and* [one of the] *favourites* (d.p.)
VENERIA: *Veneria the Bawd* | [one of the] *Ghosts* (s.d.s); *Bawd* (s.d.s and s.p.s)
CALPURNIA: *Calphurnia* (s.d.s); *Calph<urnia>* (s.p.s); *Calphurnia a Courtesan* (d.p.)
HEM: [one of the] *Panders* | [one of] *the two Ruffians* | [one of] *two Ruffians* | [one of the] *Ghosts* (s.d.s); *Hem* (s.d.s and s.p.s); *Hem* [one of] *two Panders* (d.p.)
STITCH: [one of the] *Panders* | [one of] *the two Ruffians* | [one of] *two Ruffians* | [one of the] *Ghosts* (s.d.s); *Stitch* (s.d.s and s.p.s); *Stitch,* [one of] *two Panders* (d.p.)
SAUFELLUS: *Saufellus* | [one of Messalina's and Silius'] *faction* | [one of the] *Ghosts* (s.d.s); *Sauf<ellus>* (s.p.s); *Saufellus chief of Counsel to Silius and Messalina* (d.p.)
MESSALINA: *Messallina* (s.d.s); *Empress* (s.d.s and s.p.s); *Mess<allina>* (s.p.s); *Messallina Empress* (d.p.)
CLAUDIUS: *Emperor Claudius* (s.d.s); *Emperor* (s.d.s and s.p.s); *Claudius Emperor* (d.p.)
NARCISSUS: *Narcissus* (s.d.s); *Nar<cissus>* (s.p.s); *Narcissus* [one of the] *Minions to the Emperor of his faction* (d.p.)
PALLAS: *Pallas* (s.d.s); *Pall<as>* (s.p.s); *Pallas* [one of the] *Minions to the Emperor of his faction* (d.p.)
CALLISTUS: *Calistus* (s.d.s); *Cal<istus>* (s.p.s); *Calistus* [one of the] *Minions to the Emperor of his faction* (d.p.)
ATTENDANTS: *attendance* | *attendants* (s.d.s)
MNESTER: *Menester* | [one of the] *Favourites* | [one of Messalina's and Silius'] *faction* | [one of the] *Ghosts* (s.d.s); *Men<ester>* (s.p.s); *Menester an actor and Favourite compelled by the Empress* (d.p.)
GUARD: *Guard* (s.d.s)
LEPIDA: *Lepida* (s.d.s); *Lep<ida>* (s.p.s); *Lepida mother to Messalina* (d.p.)
DAMES: *three Roman dames* | *three murdered Dames* | *the ghosts of the murdered Roman Dames* | [three of the] *Ghosts* (s.d.s); *1* | *2* | *3* (s.p.s); *Three murdered Roman Dames* (d.p.)
MANUTIUS: [one of Lepida's] *two Servants* (s.d.s); *Servant* (s.p.s); *Manutius* [one of the] *Servants to Lepida* (d.p.)
FOLIO: [one of Lepida's] *two Servants* (s.d.s); *Servant* (s.p.s); *Folio* [one of the] *Servants to Lepida* (d.p.)
FURIES: *three Furies* (s.d.s; also misprinted as *Eight Furies*); *1* | *2* | *3* (s.p.s); *Three Spirits* (d.p.)
SILANA: *Syllana* (s.d.s); *Syll<ana>* (s.p.s); *Syllana wife to Silius* (d.p.)
MELA: *Annaeus Mela* (s.d.s); *Mela* (s.d.s and s.p.s); *Mela Seneca's Brother* (d.p.)
MONTANUS: *Montanus* (s.d.s); *Mon<tanus>* (s.p.s); *Montanus a knight in Rome defence virtuously inclined* (d.p.; sic)
COURTIERS: *others* (s.d.s)
VIRGILIANUS: *Virgilianus* (s.d.s); *Vir<gilianus>* (s.p.s); *Virgilianus* [one of the] *Senators of Messalina's Faction* (d.p.)
CALPURNIANUS: *Calphurnianus* (s.d.s); *Calp<hurnianus>* (s.p.s); *Calphurnianus* [one of the] *Senators of Messalina's Faction* (d.p.)
ATTENDANTS: *attendants* (s.d.s)
AUSPICES: *the Auspices* (s.d.s)
VIBIDIA: *Vibidea* | *Vibidia* (s.d.s); *Vib<idia>* (s.p.s); *Vibidia matron of the Vestals* (d.p.)
ANGEL: *Angel* (s.d.s)
SULPICIUS: *Sulpitius* (s.d.s); *Sulp<itius>* (s.p.s); *Sulpitius of* [Messalina's] *Faction* (d.p.)
GUARD: *a Guard* (s.d.s); *1 Guard* | *2 Guard* (s.p.s)
SENATORS: *Senate* (s.d.s)
BACCHANALIANS: *eight Bachinalians* | *The Antimasque* (s.d.s); *Bachinalls* (d.p.)
COURTESANS: *three Courtesans* | *Courtesans* (s.d.s)
SOLDIERS: *Soldiers* (s.d.s)
EVODIUS: [one of the] *Soldiers* | *Evodius* (s.d.s); *Evod<ius>* (s.p.s); *Evodius a Soldier* (d.p.)
SPIRITS: *Two Spirits* (s.d.s); *1 Spirit* | *2 Spirit* (s.p.s); *Spirits* (d.p.)
HEADSMAN: *Headsman* (s.d.s)
GUARD: *a Guard* (s.d.s)
EPILOGUE: *The Epilogue* (heading)

OTHER CHARACTERS
Seneca, a banished philosopher, Mela's brother (1.1, 3.1)
25 men who slept with Messalina in 24 hours (1.2, 4.2, 5.1)
Messalina's doctors (1.4)
The murdered parents and husbands of the three Roman Dames (2.1)
Silana's noble family (2.3)
Messalina's brother (3.1; possibly only figurative)
Montanus' father (3.1)
The people of Rome (4.1–2, 5.1)
Silius' father, who committed suicide in the Senate (4.1)
The Emperor Tiberius (4.1)
100 Vestal Virgins whom Messalina commanded to appear in the wedding masque and be raped (4.3, 5.2–4)
Geta, Captain of the Guard (5.1)
The soldiers in Claudius' guard at Ostia (5.1)
Lucullus, in whose garden Messalina is held prisoner (5.4)

Britannicus, son of Claudius and Messalina (5.4)
Octavia, daughter of Claudius and Messalina (5.4)

SETTING

Period: first century AD; the play dramatizes events which took place in AD 47–8
Time-Scheme: 1.4, 2.1, and 2.3 take place at night; 4.3 takes place the day after 4.1; 5.4–5 take place on the same day
Place: Rome; one scene (5.1) takes place at Ostia

Geography
Rome: Pompey's Theatre; the Forum; the Porta Collina
[Sicily]: Mount Etna
[Mediterranean]: Corcyra; Corsica; the Tyrrhenian Sea
[Greece]: Sparta; Barathrum; Mount Pindus; Mount Ossa; Lerna
[Europe]: the Alps; France
[Africa]: River Nile; Ethiopia
[Asia]: Caucasus
The Atlantic Ocean

SOURCES

Narrative: Tacitus, *Annals* (cited in footnotes in 1.4, 2.2–3, 3.2, 4.1–2, 5.1, 5.4–5); Pliny, *Natural History* (1.2; cited in footnote); Juvenal, *Satires* 6; Suetonius, *Twelve Caesars*: Claudius (4.1; cited in footnote); Thomas Nashe and William Shakespeare, *1 Henry VI* (**919**; 5.4); John Marston, *The Dutch Courtesan* (**1434**; Silius plot)
Verbal: Sallust, *Catiline* (2.2); Ovid, *Metamorphoses* 7 (2.3); unidentified Latin maxim ascribed (wrongly?) to Seneca (1.1); Juvenal, *Satires* 10 (t.p. motto); 'Heu mihi domine' (medieval Latin responses; 5.5); Thomas Kyd, *The Spanish Tragedy* (**783**; 2.2, 5.3); William Shakespeare, *Richard II* (**1002**; 2.2, 5.4), *Julius Caesar* (**1198**; 4.1), *Hamlet* (**1259**; 3.1, 5.4), *Macbeth* (**1496**; 2.2); Ben Jonson, *Sejanus' Fall* (**1412**; 1.2, 3.1, 4.1, 5.4); Thomas Middleton, *The Revenger's Tragedy* (**1520**; 4.2–3, 5.1, 5.4); William Barksted, Lewis Machin, and John Marston, *The Insatiate Countess* (**1605**; 3.3); Georg Carolides, *Farraginis symbolicae* 2.72 (1612; 5.4); John Webster, *The White Devil* (**1689**; 5.4), *The Duchess of Malfi* (**1726**; 5.4); Nathaniel Richards, *The Celestial Publican* (1630): The Celestial Publican (3.3), The Spiritual Sea-Fight (5.4), The World (3.1), The Flesh (1.2), The Vicious Courtier (4.2–3), The Devil (2.2), *Poems Sacred and Satirical* (printed 1641): Man's Misery (5.4), Mercy's Miracle (5.4), The Single and Married Life (2.2)
Works Mentioned: Plutarch, unspecified historical work (wrongly mentioned as a source in ded.)

LANGUAGE

English
Latin: 48 words (1.1, 2.2–3, 4.2, 5.3–5; Silius, Valens, Saufellus, Lepida, Calistus, Mnester, Messalina)
Italian: 1 word (5.4; Messalina)

FORM

Metre: pentameter and prose; some alexandrines
Rhyme: blank verse; some couplets
Prologue: 26 lines, in couplets
Act-Division: 5 acts
Epilogue: 8 lines, in couplets
Lines (Spoken): 2,107 (1,989 verse, 118 prose)
Lines (Written): 2,427

STAGING

Doors: mentioned (2.1, s.d.); two characters enter 'meeting each other' (5.2, s.d.; implying two doors)
Discovery Space: a bed is drawn out (2.3, s.d.)
Stage: characters pass over the stage (4.3, s.d.)
Within: sound effects (2.1, s.d.); speech (2.1, 5.2, s.d.); music (5.4, s.d.)
Above: two characters appear above (3.1, s.d.; it takes only two lines to get down to the main stage, but the time may be extended with fighting); Messalina and Silius appear in a cloud aloft (5.4, s.d.); Narcissus enters aloft and leaves a burning torch fixed there (5.4, s.d.)
Beneath: the earth gapes and gradually swallows Hem, Stitch, and Saufellus (5.3, s.d.)
Miscellaneous: the action is arranged to avoid showing Lepida and Vibidia descending (5.2; perhaps to avoid compromising the next scene's stage image of the murderers falling into hell rather than for theatrical reasons); Saufellus is shot with a thunderbolt on stage (5.3, s.d.).

MUSIC AND SOUND

Sound Effects: knocking within (2.1, s.d.); thunder (5.3, s.d.)
Music: unspecified music (1.2, 2.2, 5.4, s.d.; in 5.4, the first strain is played four times); hautboys (1.3, 3.2, s.d.); distant bell (2.1, s.d.); bell near at hand (2.1, s.d.); solemn music (3.2, 5.4, s.d.); cornetts (4.3, s.d.); cornetts sound a flourish (5.4, s.d.); alarum within (5.4, s.d.); horrid music (5.5, s.d.); treble violin and lute (5.5, s.d.; accompanying Song 2)
Songs:
  1: 'From these blue flames burning dim', 2.2, Furies, in parts, 11 lines;
  2: 'Helpless wretch, despair, despair', 5.5, Spirits, in parts, 20 lines, with musical accompaniment.
Dance: Furies dance an antic (2.2, s.d.); Messalina and Saufellus dance a coranto (2.2, s.d.); Bacchanalians dance (5.4, s.d.); Messalina and her favourites dance (5.4, s.d.).

PROPS

Lighting: a torch (1.4, s.d.); a lighted taper (2.1, s.d.); a lighted torch (2.3, s.d.); lights (5.3, s.d.); a burning torch (5.4, s.d.); eleven torches (5.5, s.d.)
Pyrotechnics: lightning (5.3, s.d.); a thunderbolt (5.3, s.d.; strikes a character on stage)
Weapons: a knife (2.1, s.d.); three arrows (2.2, s.d.); a pistol (2.2, s.d.); Silius' poniard (2.2–3, s.d.); Mela's sword (3.1, s.d.); Montanus' weapon (3.1, s.d.); Valens' sword (3.1, implicit); Proculus' sword (3.1, implicit); Mnester's sword (3.1, implicit); Sulpicius' sword (5.4,

s.d.); Claudius' sword (5.4, s.d.); Narcissus' sword (5.4, s.d.); Callistus' sword (5.4, s.d.); Soldiers' swords (5.4, s.d.); Evodius' sword (5.5, s.d.); an executioner's axe (5.5, implicit)
Clothing: a gag (2.1, s.d.); a ring (5.1, s.d.)
Money: a purse of gold (2.1, dialogue)
Food and Drink: a bottle of liquor (1.2, dialogue; drunk on stage); a cup of liquor (1.2, s.d.; drunk on stage); a banquet (3.2, s.d.); eight cups of wine (5.4, s.d.; drunk on stage)
Small Portable Objects: a book (1.1, s.d.); a book (2.1, s.d.); a book (3.1, dialogue); a document (4.1, s.d.)
Large Portable Objects: stools and cushions (1.2, dialogue); extensive seating (5.4, implicit); a seat (5.5, implicit); an execution block (5.5, s.d.)
Scenery: a rack (1.4, s.d.); a bed (2.3, s.d.); an 'arch-glittering cloud' (5.4, s.d.; carries two characters, and descends); a scaffold (5.5, s.d.)
Miscellaneous: blood (3.1, implicit; 5.4, dialogue)

COSTUMES
SILIUS: a crown (4.3, 5.4, s.d.)
VALENS and PROCULUS: scabbards (3.1, implicit)
VENERIA: is fat (dialogue)
MESSALINA: a crown (4.3, 5.4, s.d.)
MNESTER: a scabbard (3.1, implicit)
LEPIDA: night attire (2.1, s.d.); her hair dishevelled (4.3, s.d.)
MONTANUS: disguised (3.1, s.d.)
BACCHANALIANS: girt with vine leaves and shaped in the middle with tun vessels (5.4, s.d.)
COURTESANS: dressed as queens, with coronets of state (5.4, s.d.)

EARLY STAGE HISTORY
Performed by the King's Revels Company before 1640 (and presumably by May 1636). The cast included: John Barrett (Messalina); William Cartwright, sen. (Claudius); Christopher Goad (Silius); William Hall (Mela); Richard Johnson (Montanus); Thomas Jordan (Lepida); Mathias Morris (Silana); John Robinson (Saufellus); Samuel Thomson (Mnester). Song 2 was omitted because nobody in the company could sing in parts as required. The play met with 'general applause' from 'honourable personages' and others; John Carey, Viscount Rochford, expressed a wish to see it performed, but was prevented from doing so by 'serious occasions'.

EARLY TEXTUAL HISTORY
1639: entered to Daniel Frere in the Stationers' Register on Thursday 3 October; entry gives author's initials. Thomas Wykes had licensed the book for publication.
1640: O printed by Thomas Cotes for Daniel Frere; collation A–F⁸, 48 leaves; title page names acting company and author; Latin title-page motto; engraved portrait of the author by Thomas Rawlins; engraved secondary title page including images of Claudius, Messalina, Silius, a goat, a stage, and a lamb; authorial dedication to John Carey, Viscount Rochford; English commendatory verses by Stephen Bradwell, Robert Davenport, John Robinson, Thomas Jordan, Thomas Rawlins; Latin commendatory verses by Thomas Combes; list of roles and actors.
1640–1: Humphrey Moseley was selling copies of O for 6d.
1658–62: advertised as for sale by Nathaniel Brooke.
1684: Nicholas Cox (Manciple of St Edmund Hall, Oxford) had a copy of O in his bookshop. It had probably been previously owned by Gerard Langbaine, and appears on a list compiled by Anthony Wood on Saturday 13 December.
1688: A copy of O was owned by Roger Harling.

EDITION
A. R. Skemp, Materialien 1.30 (Louvain, 1910).

REFERENCES
Annals 1635; Bentley, v. 1002–4; Bodleian, MS Wood E. 4, art. 1, p. 23; Greg 578; Hazlitt, 156; *N&Q* 221 (1976), 221–2; *N&Q* 258 (2013), 43–5; *Oxford Bibliographical Society Proceedings and Papers* 2.2 (1929), 133.

2473. Sir Martin Schenck

EVIDENCE
Stationers' Register.

GENRE
history
Contemporary: play

TITLE
Contemporary: *The Life and Death of Sir Martin Schenck, with the Wars of the Low Countries*
Alternative Modernization: *Sir Martin Skink*

AUTHORS
Richard Brome and Thomas Heywood

DATE
Limits: 1620–35, 1640–1
Best Guess: 1635

If the play is correctly attributed, the two authors' other certainly known collaboration, *The Witches of Lancashire* (**2441**) exerts some chronological attraction. On the face of it, Brome and Heywood are surprising collaborators, but they may also have already worked together on *The Cunning Lovers* (**2411**). One plausible reason for the King's Men to put them together for *The Witches of Lancashire* would have been the need to create a topical script quickly; if *Sir Martin Schenck* was a subsequent project, it would not have followed immediately, since, after completing *The Witches of Lancashire*, Heywood was tied up until mid-November working on *Love's Mistress* (**2451**). Conversely, by the late spring of 1635, Brome would have been engaged in writing *The Sparagus Garden* (**2479**), and Heywood in compiling

Pleasant Dialogues and Dramas; thereafter, Brome was under contract to Salisbury Court until 1639, and his entire output is accounted for. As it happens, the interim between *Love's Mistress* and *The Sparagus Garden* supplies a plausible topical context for *Sir Martin Schenck*, the renewal of hostilities in the Low Countries after the Franco–Dutch alliance of February 1635.

PLOT
Martin Schenck, a mercenary, at first fights for the Spanish against the Dutch, but then changes sides. He is knighted by the Earl of Leicester, but treated poorly by the Dutch. His property is seized by the Spanish when the town of Grave capitulates, but his wife and children are allowed to go free. Schenck attacks Nijmegen, but is wounded and cornered inside the city. He attempts to take the only escape route, across the river, but is pulled down by his armour, and drowns.

ROLES
Martin SCHENCK, a mercenary soldier; a married man and a father; later knighted and styled Sir Martin
SPANISH soldiers
DUTCH soldiers
The Earl of LEICESTER
ENGLISH soldiers under Leicester
Schenck's WIFE, the mother of his children
Schenck's CHILDREN

SETTING
Period: sixteenth century; the play dramatizes events from the life of Sir Martin Schenck (1550–89)
Place: the Low Countries and Germany

Geography
The Low Countries: Grave; Nijmegen
Spain
England: Leicester

COSTUMES
SCHENCK: armour

EARLY TEXTUAL HISTORY
1654: entered to Humphrey Moseley in the Stationers' Register on Saturday 8 April; joint entry with *The Apprentices' Prize* (**2462**); entry names authors.

REFERENCES
Annals 1634; Bentley, iii. 76; Greg Θ124; Hazlitt, 212; Matthew Steggle, *Richard Brome* (Manchester, 2004), 62–4.

2474. *Senilis amor* [Love in Old Age]

TEXT
MS (Oxford: Bodleian, MS Rawlinson poet. 9, fos. 46–80); scribal copy, probably from an authorial text; the leaves are bound in the wrong order, and some are missing. In the later stages of the play the action is partly incoherent, suggesting that the text as it survives represents an interim state of composition, before the play was completed. (There is, of course, no evidence that it ever was.)

GENRE
comedy
Contemporary: *comoedia* (MS)

TITLE
MS: *Senilis amor*

DATE
Limits: 1635–6
Best Guess: April 1635

PLOT
Castruccio is in love with a courtesan, Amida. After trying to dissuade him, the servant Gemulo abets him by wooing her on his behalf: he pays Dorpius the pimp for access, using counterfeit coins, and tells Amida that he himself loves her and has murdered Castruccio for her sake. This has the desired effect: she goes off to find the body. Meanwhile Castruccio admits his love for Amida to his father, Antoninus, and the scandalized old man puts him into a monastery.

Colossus helps to rob and defraud visitors to the brothel: the foolish Vincentius is forced to hand over his purse when the prostitutes claim he has stolen money from them, and the Puritan tobacconist Nicot loses a large roll of tobacco, given to Colossus as a sample for which he then refuses to pay. Nicot fetches an officer, Nicolaus, but the crooks try to bully him too, until Antoninus intervenes. Nicot and Nicolaus visit the brothel, but their clothes are stolen. Alcon too is robbed, and seeks revenge; Gemulo sees the chance to rescue Castruccio from the monastery. At his suggestion, Alcon returns to the brothel disguised as a devil, and Dorpius runs to fetch the monks to exorcise the house; the disturbance gives Castruccio the chance to escape. In Dorpius' absence, Alcon retrieves his stolen gold, but meets an Ethiopian servant and takes him for a real devil (because the blackness of his face won't wipe off); Alcon flees in terror, leaving the gold behind.

Two of the monks are seduced by a prostitute, and they smuggle her back into the monastery with them. Colossus is challenged to a duel by Lopez, but proves too cowardly to accept: when he fails to bully Lopez or buy him off, he runs away. He acquires some chickens from Nicolaus' wife to supply a feast at the brothel, and refuses to pay her for them. [*A lacuna in the text follows. The feast takes place; Colossus and Tytubus the sea-captain get drunk and are put in the stocks, but are later released.*]

Gemulo loves Catharina, his master's daughter. Antoninus plans to put a stop to this by marrying her to the Spanish merchant Aquila, and sets Lopez, who is Aquila's associate, to spy on the servant. Gemulo plans to have Catharina smuggled to his room in a chest, but Alcon, whom he engages as his accomplice, cannot keep his mouth shut and Aquila learns of it. While sitting in the privy, Alcon overhears Aquila arranging with Vincentius to divert the chest, so he makes new arrangements: Catharina leaves her father's house dressed as an old man. [*A lacuna in the text follows. Catharina gets into the chest after all.*] Aquila and his accomplices carry off the chest and break it open to find Catharina inside.

Dorpius is frustrated that he has been unable to force Amida into prostitution, but Castruccio overhears him bullying her and intervenes. Believing Castruccio to be a ghost, Amida faints, but when he revives her he is able to convince her that he is alive. He takes her away from the brothel. Gemulo, Alcon, and Colossus come to rescue her, but Colossus runs away when it appears that a fight will ensue. [*A lacuna in the text follows.*]

D'Amburgio arrives in search of his twin children, who were stolen at the age of thirteen by his ne'er-do-well brother. He recognizes Amida as the image of his dead wife, and Dorpius acknowledges that, despite his best efforts, she has remained chaste in the brothel; Gemulo turns out to be her brother. The two fathers give their blessing to a double marriage: Castruccio to Amida and Gemulo to Catharina.

SCENE DESIGNATION
[prol.], 1.1–7, 2.1–8, 3.1–12, fragment from Act 3 or Act 4, 4.A–B, 5.1–4, 5.E–F (numbered scenes as in MS; the unnumbered scenes are here assigned letters)

The stage is not clear at the following scene-divisions: 1.1–3, 1.4–5, 2.2–7, 3.1–2, 3.3–6, 3.7–8, 3.11–12, 4.A–B, 5.1–3, 5.E–F. However, the stage is clear during 3.5.

ROLES
PROLOGUE (*missing from extant text*)
CASTRUCCIO, Antoninus' son, Catharina's brother
Master GEMULO, Antoninus' servant, a young man; in reality, D'Amburgio's son and Amida's twin brother
DORPIUS, a pimp
AMIDA, a courtesan; in reality, D'Amburgio's daughter and Gemulo's twin sister
COLOSSUS, a braggart soldier
VINCENTIUS, a foolish young merchant; a younger son, but claims nevertheless to be an heir
COXINA, an old prostitute
FINLASSA, a prostitute
SHUREK, an Ethiopian, Dorpius' servant
NICOT, a Puritan tobacconist
NICOLAUS, a Puritan officer; Mildred's husband, Nicot's neighbour
Master TYTUBUS, a sea-captain
ANTONINUS, an old magistrate; a widower, father of Castruccio and Catharina

ARTHUR, a monk
VOLGE, a monk
MILDRED, a chicken-breeder, Nicolaus' wife
ALCON, a rustic
CATHARINA, Antoninus' daughter, Castruccio's sister
MUSICIANS (2.7, *non-speaking*)
Four MONKS (2.7)
Master LOPEZ, a Jew
Petrus de AQUILA, a Spanish merchant
Signor D'AMBURGIO, a wealthy widower, father of Gemulo and Amida

Speaking Parts: 25 (excluding the prologue)

Stage Directions and Speech Prefixes
PROLOGUE: *Prologus* (d.p.)
CASTRUCCIO: *Castruchio* (s.d.s); *Castru<chio>* (s.p.s); *Castruchio Filius Anto<nini>* (d.p.)
GEMULO: *Gemulo* (s.d.s); *Gemul<o>* (s.p.s); *Gemulo Servus Antoni<ni>* (d.p.)
DORPIUS: *Dorpius* (s.d.s and s.p.s); *Dorpius Leno* (d.p.)
AMIDA: *Amida* (s.d.s); *Amid<a>* (s.p.s); *Amida Filia D Amburgio* (d.p.)
COLOSSUS: *Collossus* (s.d.s); *Collos<sus>* (s.p.s); *Collossus Miles gloriosus* (d.p.)
VINCENTIUS: *Vincentius* (s.d.s); *Vincent<ius>* (s.p.s); *Vincentius Stultus Mercator* (d.p.)
COXINA: *Coxina* | [one of the] *meretrices* (s.d.s); *Coxin<a>* (s.p.s); *Coxina* [one of the] *Meretrices* (d.p.)
FINLASSA: *Finlass<a>* | [one of the] *meretrices* (s.d.s); *Finl<assa>* (s.p.s); *Finlassa* [one of the] *Meretrices* (d.p.)
SHUREK: *Shurek* | *Shureck* (s.d.s); *Shure<k>* (s.p.s); *Shurek Aethiops* (d.p.)
NICOT: *Nicot* (s.d.s and s.p.s); *Nicot Paetivendulus* (d.p.)
NICOLAUS: *Nicolaus* (s.d.s and s.p.s); *Nicolaus, officiarius Amsellodami* (d.p.)
TYTUBUS: *Tytubus* (s.d.s); *Tytub<us>* (s.p.s); *Titubus Nauta aebrius* (d.p.)
ANTONINUS: *Antoninus* (s.d.s); *Antoni<nus>* (s.p.s); *Antoninus Praetor* (d.p.)
ARTHUR: *Arthur<us>* (s.d.s); *Arth<urus>* (s.p.s); *Arthurus* [one of the] *Monachi* (d.p.)
VOLGE: *Volge* (s.d.s); *Volg<e>* (s.p.s); *Volge* [one of the] *Monachi* (d.p.)
MILDRED: *Mildre<da>* (s.d.s); *Mild<reda>* (s.p.s); *Mildreda Uxor Nicolai avicularia* (d.p.)
ALCON: *Alcon* (s.d.s and s.p.s); *Alcon Rusticus Antonini* (d.p.)
CATHARINA: *Catharina* (s.d.s); *Cathari<na>* (s.p.s); *Catharina Filia Antonini* (d.p.)
MUSICIANS: *choro musicorum* (s.d.s); *Tibicines* (d.p.)
MONKS: *1 | 2 | 3 | 4* (s.p.s)
LOPEZ: *Lopez* (s.d.s and s.p.s); *Lopez Hebreus* (d.p.)
AQUILA: *Aquil<a>* (s.d.s and s.p.s); *Petrus de Aquila Mercator hispanus* (d.p.)

D'AMBURGIO: *D'Amburgio* | *D Amburgio* (s.d.s); *D Ambur<gio>* (s.p.s); *Signor D'Amburgio Nobilis pater Gem<uli>* (d.p.)

OTHER CHARACTERS
Clients at Dorpius' brothel (1.1)
The fathers of Dorpius' clients (1.1)
Vincentius' father, a rich man (1.4)
Merchants in the market at Amsterdam (1.6)
Antoninus' dead wife, mother of Castruccio and Catharina (1.7, 3.2, 5.F)
Alcon's serving boys (2.7)
The pastor of Nicot and Nicolaus's church, who knows no Greek (3.7)
Johannes Johnson, a printer (3.7)
An English author of books against church rites and bishops (3.7)
Twelve Hungarian women seduced by Colossus (3.10)
The British roaring boys, who allowed Colossus to join them (3.10)
Maria de Crumena Scissa (i.e. Moll Cutpurse), queen of the roaring boys (3.10)
The cook in Dorpius' brothel (3.12)
D'Amburgio's dead wife, mother of Amida and Gemulo (5.2, 5.E–F)
Dorpius' servants (5.2)
D'Amburgio's dead father (5.E)
D'Amburgio's dead brother, a wastrel who abducted Gemulo and Amida as children, but died a penitent (5.E)
The ancestors of D'Amburgio's wife (5.E)
Italian bravoes hired by D'Amburgio's brother to assassinate him (5.E)

SETTING
Period: probably contemporary: Tytubus has coins bearing the heads of the Emperor Ferdinand (presumably Ferdinand II, reigned 1619–37) and [Gustavus] Adolphus (reigned 1611–32). The action takes place in early April.
Time-Scheme: 3.4 and 3.9 take place during the same night.
Place: Amsterdam

Geography
Britain: England
Rome: the Port Esquiline
Italy: Mount Etna
[*Greece*]: Marpesia
[*Europe*]: Spain; Flanders; France; Hungary
[*The Aegean Sea*]: [Rhodes]
The Hellespont
Jerusalem: the Sepulchre
[*Asia*]: the Dead Sea; Caucasus; Turkey; Persia
The Red Sea
[*Africa*]: Ethiopia; the Cape of Good Hope; Libya
The Torrid Zone
India
The Antipodes

SOURCES
Narrative: Peter Hausted, *Senile odium* (**2296**)
Verbal: Plautus, *Pseudolus* (1.7); Terence, *Adelphoe* (1.7, 3.11); Cicero, *De officiis* (3.12); Virgil, *Aeneid* 1 (5.2–3); Horace, *Ars poetica* (4.A); Ovid, *Metamorphoses* 1 (1.4); Pliny the Younger, *Epistles* 1.8 (3.9); Edward Forcett, *Pedantius* (**697**; 4.A); William Shakespeare, *Hamlet* (**1259**; 1.5)
Works Mentioned: Ovid, *Ars amatoria* (3.11), satirical poems (3.1, general reference); Christopher Marlowe, *Tamburlaine* (**784**; 3.1); William Shakespeare, *Comedies, Histories, and Tragedies* (1623; 3.7, oblique allusion)

LANGUAGE
Latin
Gibberish: 16 words, supposed to be the Ethiopian vernacular (1.5; Shurek)

FORM
Metre: Terentian pseudo-metre
Prologue: yes, but missing from the extant MS
Act-Division: 5 acts
Lines (Spoken): 1,992 (including 2 true verse)
Lines (Written): 2,055

STAGING
Doors: three doors, representing Dorpius' brothel (1.2, 1.6, 2.6, 5.4; probably central), Antoninus' house (1.7), and the monastery (2.2, 2.4); characters exit severally (1.6, s.d.); mentioned (1.7, 2.3, 2.6, dialogue; 5.4, s.d.); knocked at (1.6–7, 2.2, dialogue; 2.4, s.d.) and rattled (2.6, dialogue)
Stage: has a corner (2.2, s.d.); mentioned (5.2, s.d.)
Within: speech (1.6, implicit)
Above: Dorpius appears above (1.2, implicit); he is able to descend to stage level rapidly, in mid-speech

MUSIC
Song: in a missing scene, sung by Tytubus and Colossus.
Other Singing: Tytubus sings two lines (5.F, dialogue; possibly an extract from the earlier song in the missing scene)

PROPS
Weapons: Vincentius' sword (1.4, dialogue); Colossus' sword (1.5, 3.1, dialogue); Gemulo's sword (3.9, s.d.); Castruccio's sword (5.1–3, dialogue); a cannon and other artillery equipment (5.4, s.d.)
Musical Instruments: lutes (2.7, dialogue)
Clothing: a jewelled ring (1.1–3, dialogue; 5.2, implicit); Nicot's and Nicolaus' clothes, including breeches (2.3, s.d.); a second ring (5.2, dialogue; possibly worn by Amida)
Money: counterfeit gold coins (1.1–2, dialogue); a purse (1.4, dialogue); a purse of silver (1.7, dialogue); coins (2.6, dialogue); gold (2.8, dialogue); gold coins (3.4, dialogue); coins (3.6, dialogue)

Food and Drink: cups of liquor (1.4, dialogue; drunk on stage); a roll of tobacco (1.5, implicit); aqua vitae (3.4, dialogue; in a large vessel; poured into a smaller vessel and drunk on stage); fruit, including pears and apples (3.4, dialogue); chestnuts (3.4, dialogue); chickens (3.12, dialogue); a hare (3.12, dialogue)

Small Portable Objects: a letter (1.1–3, s.d.); binding cords (2.2, dialogue; 2.8, implicit); a gag (2.2–3, implicit); a wallet (2.3, dialogue); an almanac (2.3, dialogue); a censer (2.7, implicit); a note (3.1, implicit; 3.3–4, 3.6, dialogue; written on stage); pen and ink (3.1, implicit); a key (3.6, dialogue)

Large Portable Objects: a walking-stick (1.7, dialogue); planks (3.4, dialogue); a chest (3.9, implicit; 4.A, s.d; large enough to contain a woman); stocks (fragment, implicit)

Miscellaneous: holy water (2.7, dialogue); consecrated oil (2.7, dialogue)

COSTUMES AND MAKE-UP

CASTRUCCIO: a cloak (2.7, s.d.; removed on stage); a scabbard (5.1–3, implicit)

GEMULO: a scabbard (3.9, implicit)

DORPIUS: a wig (1.2, 1.4–6, 2.2–3, 2.6–7, 5.1–3, implicit; 5.F, s.d.; removed on stage); bald-headed under the wig (5.F, dialogue); a cloak (5.F, dialogue)

AMIDA: possibly a ring (5.2, dialogue)

COLOSSUS: a moustache (dialogue); headgear made of peacock feathers (3.12, dialogue)

FINLASSA: Castruccio's cloak (2.7, dialogue)

SHUREK: black skin (dialogue); a cap (5.3, dialogue)

NICOT: a beard (dialogue); naked (2.3, s.d.); a cloak (3.7–8, dialogue); a dirty face (4.A, dialogue); see also PROPS: **Clothing**

NICOLAUS: long hair (dialogue); naked (2.3, s.d.); see also PROPS: **Clothing**

TYTUBUS: possibly spectacles (1.6, dialogue; put on on stage); a cloak (3.3–4, dialogue)

ANTONINUS: grey hair and a long beard (dialogue)

ARTHUR and VOLGE: tonsures (dialogue)

MILDRED: may be fat (dialogue)

ALCON: a devil mask (2.6–7, implicit; pun on on stage)

CATHARINA: cross-dressed as an old man (3.9, s.d.), including silver hair and a toga (dialogue), and presumably a beard like Antoninus' (implicit)

MONKS: tonsures (dialogue)

LOPEZ: dirty fingers (3.1, dialogue); disguised as a liquor seller (3.4, s.d.)

AQUILA: disguised as a fruit seller (3.4–5, s.d.)

D'AMBURGIO: a long beard (dialogue)

EARLY STAGE HISTORY

1636: it has been speculated that this might possibly have been the Latin comedy performed at Trinity College, Cambridge, on Thursday 4 February in connection with the visit of Charles Louis, the Elector Palatine. Sir Simonds D'Ewes avoided attending the performance because he objected to transvestism. However, there is no positive evidence to support the identification, which rests solely on the mistaken belief that this is the only extant Cambridge play written at about this time. The case for *Cornelianum dolium* (**2429**), is only stronger in that its ascription to Cambridge is more secure. Moreover, academic comedies of this period usually match the fictional time of the action, where specified, to the actual time of the performance; the action of *Senilis amor* takes place in April.

In fact, we don't even know for sure that this *was* a Cambridge play. That being so, it may not be irrelevant to observe a striking (but perhaps coincidental) correspondence of source usage between this play and *Eumorphus* (**2463**), an Oxford comedy of the same year: they are two of only four plays of the 1630s to draw on *Senile odium* (**2296**), two of three to draw on *Pedantius* (**697**), and the only two in which borrowings from Pliny the Younger have been noticed.

EARLY TEXTUAL HISTORY

1630s (?): transcribed in **MS**; 35 leaves; list of roles. The MS bears the date 1635, probably the year of original composition rather than transcription (if different).

EDITIONS

Laurens J. Mills, Indiana University Publications: Humanities Series 27 (Bloomington, 1952).

Michael P. Steppat, Renaissance Latin Drama in England 2.17 (Hildesheim, Zurich, and New York, 1991).

REFERENCES

Annals 1636; Bentley, v. 1407–8; Hazlitt, 206; Loomie, 194; REED: Cambridge, 923; *Shakespeare Jahrbuch* 47 (1911), 81–3; Smith, 109; Stratman, 189–91.

2475. *The Converted Robber*

TEXT

MS (London: British Library, Add. MS 14047, fos. 44ᵛ–59ᵛ); transcript.

The case for identifying *The Converted Robber* with Speed's play *Stonehenge*, mentioned by Anthony Wood, is overwhelming. The main problem with the identification is that the MS dates the performance 1637, whereas Wood dates *Stonehenge* to a specific occasion in 1635. The extant play's collocation of Stonehenge with Salisbury Cathedral is a good fit for that occasion, the return of the College's President after his installation as Dean of Salisbury. It follows that either the MS date is in error or the play was revived. The likely late date of the MS might account for the former possibility.

It is less plausible to identify the play with the comedy *Salisbury Plain* (**2681**) entered in the Stationers' Register by Richard Marriott in 1653, on the basis of nothing more than a coincidence of setting.

GENRE
pastoral
Contemporary: pastoral (MS)

TITLE
MS: *The Converted Robber*
Later Assigned: *Stonehenge*

AUTHOR
John Speed (*attribution*)

The attribution rests on Wood's testimony. The only basis for the alternative ascription to George Wilde that appears in some scholarly works is the fact that he wrote the other two plays in the MS; but the volume's unifying principle is institutional rather than authorial.

DATE
Spring 1635

ORIGINAL PRODUCTION
St John's College, Oxford

PLOT
The robbers of Salisbury Plain plan a raid on the local shepherds, and to this end their leader Alcinous inveigles himself and his boy Alexis into their community by pretending to be a shepherd looking for his lost sheep. Alexis is actually a shepherdess, Clarinda, whom Alcinous saved from rape, and who is now in love with him; she has adopted this disguise to be able to follow him. They meet the old shepherd Iarbus, who tells them at length about local mythology, including the origins of Salisbury Cathedral and Stonehenge, and invites them to a shepherds' festival in honour of the shepherdesses.
 Both Castina and Avonia fall in love with Alcinous, and he woos Castina. When she refuses his advances, he threatens to rape her, she attempts to kill herself, and he repents all his evil intentions. His fellow thieves rob Iarbus and smear tar on his face, but Alcinous persuades them to follow his example and repent; the robbers all become shepherds. Alexis reveals her true identity, and shepherds and shepherdesses pair off.

SCENE DESIGNATION
sc.1–6, ep. (MS undivided)

ROLES
ALCINOUS, a thief, leader of the robbers
ALEXIS, supposed a boy, but actually a shepherdess, Clarinda, Castina's sister
IARBUS, an old shepherd
Two BOYS, who sing (sc.1)
PALAEMON, a shepherd
Dame CASTINA, a shepherdess, Clarinda's sister
AVONIA, a shepherdess
DORUS, a shepherd
AUTOLYCUS, a thief
CONTO, a thief
SHEPHERDS, who dance (sc.6, *non-speaking*)
MASQUERS (sc.6, *non-speaking*)

Speaking Parts: 11

Stage Directions and Speech Prefixes
ALCINOUS: *Alcinous* (s.d.s); *Alcino<us>* (s.p.s); *Alcinous, a robber turned by Castina to an Innocent shepherd* (d.p.)

ALEXIS: *Alexis* (s.d.s and s.p.s); *Clarinda, Sister to Castina, enamoured of Alcinous, follows him by fame | Alexis, Clarinda in A boy's Apparel* (d.p.)
IARBUS: *Iarbus* (s.d.s); *Iarb<us>* (s.p.s); *Iarbus, an old shepherd* (d.p.)
BOYS: *2 boys* (s.d.s)
PALAEMON: *Palaemon* (s.d.s); *Palaem<on>* (s.p.s); *Palaemon, Enamoured of Castina* (d.p.)
CASTINA: *Castina* (s.d.s and s.p.s); *Castina,* [one of two] *Shepherdesses* (d.p.)
AVONIA: *Avonia* (s.d.s and s.p.s); *Avonia,* [one of two] *Shepherdesses* (d.p.)
DORUS: *Dorus* (s.d.s and s.p.s); *Dorus, A shepherd loving Avonia* (d.p.)
AUTOLYCUS: *Autolicus* (s.d.s); *Autolic<us>* (s.p.s); *Autolicus,* [one of] *Two Robbers* (d.p.)
CONTO: *Conto* (s.d.s and s.p.s); *Conto,* [one of] *Two Robbers* (d.p.)
SHEPHERDS: *an antic of shepherds* (s.d.s)
MASQUERS: *the masque* (s.d.s)

OTHER CHARACTERS
Travellers robbed by Alcinous on Salisbury Plain (sc.1)
Alexis' mother (sc.1; possibly imaginary)
Chromus, father of Clarinda and Castina (sc.1, 6)
Four clothiers robbed by Autolycus and Conto (sc.2)
The parson, robbed by Autolycus and Conto (sc.2)
The churchwarden, whose head was broken by the parson's over-enthusiastic gesticulation during a sermon against thieves (sc.2)
Six (or fewer) women raped by Conto in the last six months (sc.2)
Conto's twenty children, all thieves (sc.2)
The shoemaker who made Iarbus' shoes (sc.4)
Daphne, Iarbus' beloved (sc.4)

SETTING
Period: well after the foundation of Salisbury Cathedral (here dated 1222)
Time-Scheme: sc.1 ends as the evening is drawing in; sc.6 takes place in the morning
Place: Salisbury Plain

Geography
[*Wiltshire*]: Salisbury; Salisbury Cathedral; Stonehenge
Britain: Ireland; Wales

SOURCES
Verbal: William Shakespeare, *The Winter's Tale* (**1631**; the name Autolycus)

LANGUAGE
English
Latin: 3 words (sc.6, Conto, Autolycus)
Dialect: Iarbus speaks entirely in rustic dialect.

FORM
Metre: tetrameter and prose; some pentameter and long lines

Rhyme: couplets and blank verse
Epilogue: 16 lines, in pentameter couplets, spoken by Alexis
Lines (Spoken): 924 (748 verse, 176 prose)
Lines (Written): 945

STAGING
Discovery Space: the scene opens to reveal Stonehenge (sc.1, s.d.)
Audience: addressed as 'fair nymphs or, rather, goddesses' (ep.)

MUSIC AND SOUND
Sound Effects: horse's hoofs and bells (sc.2, dialogue)
Music: pipes and cornetts, first soft, then louder (sc.1, s.d./dialogue); wind music (sc.1, s.d.); unspecified end-of-scene music (sc.1, 3, 5, s.d.)
Song: sc.1, two Boys, with musical accompaniment
Dance: dance of shepherds (sc.6, dialogue); two masques, at least one of which includes dancing (sc.6, s.d.)

PROPS
Weapons: possibly Conto's and Autolycus' swords (sc.4, dialogue; may be a figure of speech); a knife (sc.5, s.d.)
Food and Drink: bread and meat (sc.4, dialogue; found in Iarbus' pockets)
Small Portable Objects: a shepherd's tar-box (sc.4, dialogue); a ribbon (sc.4, s.d.; worn in Iarbus' button-hole); an almanac (sc.4, dialogue)
Large Portable Objects: a sheep-hook (sc.6, dialogue); possibly seating for up to nine characters (sc.6, implicit; but they could sit on the ground)
Scenery: Stonehenge, inside openable scenery (sc.1, s.d.; sc.6, implicit)
Miscellaneous: tar (sc.4, s.d.; put on Iarbus' face; probably in a tar-box carried by Iarbus)

COSTUMES AND MAKE-UP
ALCINOUS: probably has no beard (dialogue; but may be a figure of speech); disguised as a shepherd (sc.1–2, 5–6, dialogue)
ALEXIS: cross-dressed as a shepherd boy (sc.1, 3, 6, implicit)
IARBUS: high shoes (sc.4, dialogue; removed on stage); a garment with pockets and a button-hole (sc.4, s.d.); tar on his face (sc.4, s.d.; applied on stage; possibly also in sc.6)
AUTOLYCUS and CONTO: possibly scabbards (sc.4, implicit)

EARLY STAGE HISTORY
1635: performed in the common refectory of St John's College, Oxford, to mark the return of the College President, Dr Richard Baylie, after his installation as Dean of Salisbury. (The installation took place on Friday 10 April.) The audience included Baylie and the Fellows of the College; the epilogue also assumes the presence of ladies (perhaps including Baylie's wife, Elizabeth).

1637: said to have been 'acted by St John's College'.

EARLY TEXTUAL HISTORY
After 1660 (?): included in a **MS** collection of plays and poems; 31 pages on 16 leaves; heading refers to a performance; list of roles. The scribe may possibly have had the initials W. B. The other plays in the volume are *Eumorphus* (**2463**) and *The Hospital of Lovers* (**2551**).

1691–2: Reportedly the play 'is not printed, but goes about in MS from hand to hand'.

REFERENCES
Annals 1635; Bentley, v. 1181–4, 1259; Hazlitt, 49, 220; REED: Oxford, 807–8; Sibley, 154.

2476. Floral Play

TEXT
Only the prologue is extant in an autograph MS (Oxford: Corpus Christi College, 325, fos. 125^r–126^r), with minor revisions.

The extant text is usually taken to be a standalone work, a verse prologue to the Florists' Feast itself (and so not inherently dramatic). However, it says that what follows will be inspired by the Muses and will feature flowers in human form; it cannot be anything other than the prologue to a play whose main text does not survive.

AUTHOR
William Strode

He may have written only the prologue, but the fact that he was selected to write the leading play for the royal visit of 1636 (**2550**) suggests that he was not entirely inexperienced in such matters.

DATE
Limits: 1633–5

Strode's association with Norwich was as the chaplain to the Bishop, Richard Corbet, whose appointment was confirmed in May 1632, and who died in office in July 1635. Since the Florists' Feast, and the performance, took place in early May, Strode could not have written for it in 1632.

ORIGINAL PRODUCTION
Norwich

ROLES
PROLOGUE
VER, the spring, a male character
TULIP, a flower; a speaking part
Other FLOWERS

The identity of some of the other flowers might be implied by allusions in Matthew Stevenson's prologue to a later Florists'

Feast entertainment (printed in 1654; **H44**). In particular, he mentions the King and Queen of the flowers, the rose and the lily, and says that on that occasion they will not be present. This cannot allude to the play at the inaugural Feast of 1631, *Rhodon and Iris* (**2335**), since Rhodon (the rose) is a shepherd, not a king, and his love is the iris, not the lily. If it has a referent at all (rather than being merely a random conceit), it must therefore be to a later play at the annual Feast; this is the only one known, though that need not rule out the possibility that there was yet another flower play that has left no other trace.

Allegorical Roles: at least 1

SOURCES
Works Mentioned: Puppet Play of Queen Elizabeth (**2379**)

LANGUAGE
English
French: 1 word (Prologue)

FORM
Prologue: 56 lines, in pentameter couplets
Lines (Spoken): 56
Lines (Written): 56

STAGING
Stage: mentioned
Audience: assumed to include ladies; addressed as 'my friends'

COSTUMES
PROLOGUE: crowned with flowers (s.d.)

EARLY STAGE HISTORY
1633–5: performed at the Florists' Feast, Norwich, in early May.

EARLY TEXTUAL HISTORY
1635–7: prologue transcribed by William Strode in a MS notebook of his poetry.

EDITIONS
Margaret Forey, in 'A Critical Edition of the Poetical Works of William Strode', unpublished B.Litt. thesis (Oxford, 1966).
Amy M. Charles, in Ralph Knevet, *The Shorter Poems* (Columbus, 1966), 25–7.

REFERENCES
Beal 2 StW 675.

2477. Freewill

TEXT
MS (Washington: Folger, MS V. b. 221); fair copy.

In 1799, according to the *Biographia Dramatica*, a MS translation of Negri's *Freewill*, made by Francis Bristowe from an intermediate French text, and dated 1635, was offered for sale in 'Mr Barker's Catalogue of plays'. This may have been a catalogue issued by James Barker, whose supplementary *The Drama Recorded* (1814, p. 95) refers erroneously to *King Farewill*, giving the date 1799 and the name Bristowe.

Was this the same MS which is now in the Folger? The latter was likewise prepared using the French version of the play, and once contained a flyleaf ascription to Bristowe, since deleted. However, the MS nowhere gives the title as *King Freewill*, nor does it bear the date 1635. Confusingly, a later hand has annotated the title page, wrongly identifying the translation as that of Henry Cheke (**471**): in fact, the two translations are markedly different, partly because Cheke worked from the original Italian version of the play. The title page is in two hands, one apparently older than the other, but both using archaic orthography; the Cheke ascription is in the more recent hand. (Both, however, seem to be modelled on the title page of the 1572–3 edition of the Cheke translation.) The anomalies suggest that the Folger MS may not be the one reported in 1799, but even so, the two MSS could well have been copies of the same translation; the common French source is suggestive, and the shared association with Bristowe even more so.

GENRE
Reformation allegory
Contemporary: tragedy (MS)

TITLE
MS: *Freewill*
Later Assigned: *King Freewill*
Alternative Modernization: *Free Will*

AUTHOR
Francis Bristowe (?), *translating* Francesco Negri de Bassano

The abbreviation 'Fr. Br. Gent.' appears on the cover of a 1638 translation of another Italian work (STC 3474.5), but this is a red herring, since the referent is Francesco Bracciolini, author of the translated work. If we accept the only available date, 1635, then the text is probably too late to identify the translator with the Francis Bristowe (born 1565–6) who matriculated from Christ Church in 1582, and was the fourth son of Nicholas Bristowe of Herefordshire (1537–1616). Identification with the seventeenth-century London glass manufacturer of the same name seems even more unlikely.

DATE
1635 (?)

This is simply the reported date of the manuscript seen in 1799, and could of course be the date of transcription rather than of translation.

PLOT
Fabian, returning from a pilgrimage, learns of a rebellion which has broken out among some of Freewill's subjects. Diaconat tells him how Freewill came to power about three hundred years ago, and explains the clerical orders of the kingdom. Fabian is puzzled: he does not understand how clergymen can also be rich.

Clergy hosts a dinner at which visiting theologians discuss the nature and foundation of papal authority;

Hermes, the interpreter, is sent to obtain bulls granting the guests benefices in reward for their loyalty to the Pope.

A full geographical, political, and cultural survey of Freewill's kingdom has been prepared, and is read aloud for purposes of checking. Bertaut the barber makes sceptical comments throughout. Freewill discusses the rebellion with the Pope, and they agree to set up an inquisition to extirpate heresy. Bertaut is engaged to obtain an official pardon for a corrupt monk, and is shocked by how much it costs.

The apostles Peter and Paul come to Rome to investigate disturbing reports from a new arrival in heaven; to ensure their welcome, they disguise themselves as pilgrims. Peter, who has never been to Rome before, is aghast at the city's inappropriate opulence. They meet Bertaut and convince him, by extensive scriptural citation, that Freewill is a usurping tyrant, and that the true interpretation of Christianity is a good deal simpler than the rituals of the Catholic church.

God sends Grace Justifying and the angel Raphael to Rome. Their mission is to punish Freewill for his presumption and declare the Pope's true identity as Antichrist, Satan's agent on Earth. They seek out Peter and Paul, who in turn warn Bertaut. Meanwhile Grace creeps into Freewill's palace and beheads him, and sends Raphael to promulgate a divine proclamation sentencing the Pope to death. Bertaut wants to change his allegiance from Freewill to Christ, and Grace promises to recommend him; he also gets a lecture on the vanity of popish ceremonies and sacraments. The apostles are shocked to hear how their writings have been misinterpreted by the church to provide scriptural authority for such dubious practices. Once Raphael returns, they all leave Rome together.

SCENE DESIGNATION
1.1–4, 2.1–3. 3.1–4, 4.1–3, 5.1–5 (MS)

ROLES
FABIAN, a pilgrim; a married man and a father
Signor HUMAN DISCOURSE, Freewill's secretary, a father; also called Signor Discourse
Signor DIACONAT, Clergy's steward
Signor HERMES, an interpreter; a poor and married man
FELIN, a dispenser or clerk of the kitchen
King FREEWILL, ruler of Goodworks; born an infidel with two mothers and no father; a married man and a father
Signor ACT ILLICIT, Freewill's household steward
BERTAUT, Freewill's barber
Signor AMON, a chancellor
TRIFON, a notary
ORBILE, a servant
Messier CLERGY, the Pope's son
Clergy's CHAPLAIN
PAUL the Apostle

PETER the Apostle
Lady GRACE JUSTIFYING, also called Lady Justifying Grace and Madam Justifying Grace
RAPHAEL, an angel

Speaking Parts: 17
Allegorical Roles: 5

Stage Directions and Speech Prefixes
FABIAN: *Fabian* (s.d.s and s.p.s); *Fabian a Pilgrim of Ostia* (d.p.)
HUMAN DISCOURSE: *Human-discourse* (s.d.s and s.p.s); *Discourse* (s.p.s); *Human-discourse Secretary* (d.p.)
DIACONAT: *Diaconat* (s.d.s and s.p.s); *Diaconat steward to Messier Clergy* (d.p.)
HERMES: *Hermes* (s.d.s and s.p.s); *Hermes Interpreter* (d.p.)
FELIN: *Felin the dispenser* | *Felin dispenser* (s.d.s); *Felin* (s.d.s and s.p.s); *Felin Dispenser* (d.p.)
FREEWILL: *King Free-will* (s.d.s and d.p.); *Free-will* | *Freewill* (s.p.s)
ACT ILLICIT: *Act-illicit* | *Act illicit* (s.d.s); *Act* (s.p.s); *Act-Illicit steward of the King's court* (d.p.)
BERTAUT: *Bertaut the Barber* (s.d.s); *Bertaut* (s.d.s and s.p.s); *Bertaut Barber to the Court* (d.p.)
AMON: *Amon the Chancellor* (s.d.s); *Amon* (s.p.s); *Amon Chancellor* (d.p.)
TRIFON: *Trifon the Notary* (s.d.s); *Trifon* (s.p.s); *Trifon Notary* (d.p.)
ORBILE: *Orbile servitor* (s.d.s); *Orbile* (s.p.s); *Orbile a servant* (d.p.)
CLERGY: *Messier Clergy* (s.d.s and d.p.); *Clergy* (s.p.s)
CHAPLAIN: *Chaplain* (s.d.s and s.p.s); *Chaplain to Messier Clergy* (d.p.)
PAUL: *Paul the Apostle* | *Paul Apostle* (s.d.s); *Paul* (s.p.s); *Paul Apostle* (d.p.)
PETER: *Peter the Apostle* | *Peter Apostle* (s.d.s); *Peter* (s.p.s); *Peter Apostle* (d.p.)
GRACE JUSTIFYING: *Grace-justifying* | *Justifying-Grace* (s.d.s); *Grace* (s.p.s); *Grace Justifying* (d.p.)
RAPHAEL: *The Angel Raphael* (s.d.s); *Raphael* | *Ralph<ael>* (s.p.s); *Raphael Angel* (d.p.)

OTHER CHARACTERS
Fabian's wife and children (1.1)
Fabian's friends in Ostia (1.1–2)
Heretics, Freewill's rebellious subjects (1.1, 1.3, 3.1)
Pelagius, a monk who helped Freewill in his rise to power (1.2, 3.3)
Celestin, who helped Freewill in his rise to power; also called Celestius (1.2, 3.3)
Divines of the universities and schools, who helped in Freewill's rise (1.2)
Natural Illumination, a noble lady, regent of the schools (1.2)
The Pope, Clergy's father, who is really Antichrist (1.2–3, 2.2–3, 3.1, 3.3, 4.1–3, 5.1–3, 5.5)
The King of Spain (1.2)

Lady Grace of Congruity, a princess, the Pope's kinswoman, Freewill's wife (1.2–3, 4.3, 5.5)
Grace of Condignity, daughter of Freewill and Grace of Congruity (1.2–3, 4.3, 5.5)
A Jewish woman, Clergy's mother (1.2)
Lord Opus Operatum, governor of the province of the Mass, a lord and baron of the Popish monarchy; also called Monsieur Opus Operatum (1.2, 2.2, 5.5)
Fabian's servant (1.2)
Morgant Cross, the master of the boat that will take Fabian to Ostia (1.2)
Foreign divines who dined with Clergy, including: Monsieur Fabri, Bishop of Vienne; Pelargus; Cocleus; Empserus; and two divines of the Sorbonne, Friar Ambrose Catherin and Friar Corneille of Piacenza (1.2–4, 2.1, 3.1–4)
Doctor Eccius, a foreign divine who dined with Clergy (1.2–4, 3.1–4)
The papal Datary in Rome (1.3, 5.5)
Signor Chrysostom, the Treasurer (1.3–4)
An astrologer friend of Human Discourse (1.3)
Regina Pecunia, the Pope's mother; also called Lady Pecunia (1.3, 5.5)
The Emperor Charles of Austria (1.3)
Dame Reason, one of Freewill's mothers (1.3)
Dame Will, one of Freewill's mothers (1.3)
Augustine Guigi, a banker who left a legacy to Clergy to enable masses to be said for his soul (1.3)
Cardinal Sadolet, a Ciceronian (1.4)
King Ferdinand, who sent the Pope news of heresy in Germany (2.1, 3.1)
Ferdinand's officers (2.1)
The Lutherans, rebels against Freewill (2.1–2, 3.1, 3.3, 4.2)
Fugitives from Freewill's dominions, including monks (2.1, 3.1)
Good Intention, a duchess, Lady Regent and Lieutenant General of the kingdom of Good Works (2.2, 4.1)
The Countess of Guastilla, Good Intention's lieutenant (2.2)
Signor Error (2.2)
Signor Desperation (2.2)
Signor Andrea Dores, a war leader (2.2)
Barbarossa, Dores's antagonist (2.2)
Madam Hypocrisy, ruler of the province of Moynery, or Monkery (2.2, 4.2)
Dame Discord, Hypocrisy's companion (2.2)
Dame Envy, Hypocrisy's companion (2.2)
Dame Ambition, Hypocrisy's companion (2.2)
Pasquil, Bertaut's recently dead cousin and fellow barber, who told the apostles in heaven about the lamentable state of Rome (2.2, 4.1)
Quieti, a prospective inquisitor, who called Pasquil a knave (2.2, 3.1, 4.2–3)
Dame Superstition, governess of the provinces of Saint Worship and Building (2.2)
Master Omnius Utriusque Sexus, a hermaphrodite architect (2.2)
Lord Shrovetide, a chief baron of the papal monarchy (2.2)
Signor Montanus, governor of the province of Fasting (2.2)
The Bishop of Trent, who recently moved to the province of the Mass and spent a great deal of money which might have been put to better use (2.2)
Madam Indulgence, a shameless quean; also called Dame Indulgence and Lady Indulgence (2.2, 4.3, 5.5)
Friar Cipoulle, master of the novices of Aracaeli, for whom Bertaut is seeking a papal pardon (2.2–3, 4.1–2)
Lady Truth (2.2)
Truth's heirs (2.2)
Lord An Jubilee, a Jew, Indulgence's husband (2.2, 4.3)
Dame Supererogation (2.2)
A novice of Aracaeli assaulted by the novice-master (2.3)
Lord Peter (2.3)
Lewis, Lord Peter's son, who received an easy absolution (2.3)
The Bishop of Fano (2.3)
Freewill's deceased predecessors, the rulers of Good Works (3.1)
Cruel monks appointed as inquisitors of the faith (3.1)
Five men appointed as senior inquisitors: the Cardinal of Eugl<os>, Monsieur Burgos, Monsieur Teatin, Monsieur Parisius, and Monsieur Guidiction (3.1–2, 4.2)
Hermes' wicked mother-in-law (3.3)
Hermes' kindred (3.3)
Alpine people, makers of stone vessels (3.3)
The host who gave the travelling foreign divines accommodation in the Alps (3.3)
An Alpine advocate, who disputed the papal supremacy with Dr Eccius (3.3)
Corrupt, rapacious Roman courtiers (4.1)
Master Gratis Acceptis, an honest man who has left Rome (4.1)
Master Gratis Date, an honest man who has left Rome (4.1)
The Great Penitentioner, the Pope's merchant and broker (4.1)
A French bishop, a true minister of God, with whom Paul discussed scripture (4.1)
The father of Clergy's chaplain, from whom he inherited only moveable property (4.2)
Human Discourse's son, Quieti's secretary (4.2)
The General of the monastic order of Sabottiers (4.2)
A citizen of Venice who discussed theology with his friends (4.3)
God, who sent Grace Justifying and Raphael to Rome (5.1–2, 5.5)
Madam Faustine, a penitent whore who shelters Grace Justifying (5.1–2, 5.4)
Jesus Christ, the Apostles' master (5.2, 5.5)
The other angels (5.2)
Satan, the devil, Lying's father (5.2, 5.5)
A friend of Bertaut, who told him of the political upheavals in Rome (5.3)
The Pope's courtiers (5.3)

Clergy's clericature, including academics (5.3)
Sin, a lewd fellow, Antichrist's father (5.5)
Perdition, a quean, Antichrist's mother (5.5)
Lying, an old woman, Satan's daughter, Antichrist's nurse (5.5)

SETTING

Period: sixteenth century; the action takes place at some time between 1540 and 1543
Place: Rome

Geography
Rome: Aracaeli monastery; River Tiber; St Peter's; the Appian Way; Porte de Populi
Florence: the Church of St Miniato
Italy: Ostia; Padua; Piacenza; Venice; Milan; Aquino; Trent; Vercelli; Fano; Ravenna; Lombardy; Siena; Fiesole; Assisi
France: Sorbonne; Boulogne; Vienne; Marseilles; Nice; Amiens; Tours; Lorraine; Aquitaine; Auvergne; Paris; Meaux; Meyronnes; Molesmes
Spain: Calatrava; Montesa; Castile
England: Canterbury; Cornwall; Hales
The Alps: Rhaetia; Grison; St Gall
Germany: Constance; Saxony; Frankfurt; Cologne
Greece: Salamina; Nemea; Mount Pieria
Europe: the Low Countries; Austria; Sweden (Suecia); Avers
[*Aegean Sea*]: Samos; Rhodes; Delos; Seriphos
Cyprus
Turkey: Constantinople; Hierapolis
Palestine: Bethlehem; Caesarea; Cappadochia; Antioch
Jerusalem: the Sepulchre; Mount Sion
Chaldea: Babylon
Asia: Persia
Egypt: Thebes; Alexandria; Cairo
Africa: Carthage; Hippo
The New World
Unidentified: Alega; Montgranel
Heaven

SOURCES

Narrative: Francesco Negri de Bassano, *Libero arbitrio* (1546; Bristowe used the 1558 French tr., possibly by Jean Crespin, *Le Tragédie du Roi Franc-Arbitre*)
Verbal: Bible: Genesis 1.26 (4.3), 3.9 (2.2), 6.6 (4.3, cited in side-note), 11.5 (4.3); Exodus 20.4 (2.2, 5.5), 20.7–17 (5.5); Deuteronomy 17.8–12 (3.3, cited); 1 Samuel 2.8 (1.2, cited), 15.11 (4.3, cited in side-note as 1 Kings 15), 15.23 (4.1, cited); Psalms 69.1 (Vulgate; 2.2), 143.2 (5.5, cited); Ecclesiastes 9.1 (4.3, cited in side-note); Jeremiah 10.23 (4.1, cited); Joel 3.16? (4.3, cited in side-note); Ecclesiasticus 15.14–17 (4.1, cited); Matthew 5.14 (4.3, cited in side-note), 6.12 (2.2, cited), 16.16 (3.3), 16.18 (1.3, 3.3, cited), 16.19 (3.3), 18.17 (5.5), 18.20 (3.3), 19.25–6 (4.1), 20.16 (4.3), 20.25–8 (4.1), 21.31 (5.4), 24.23 (2.2), 25.34 (4.3, cited in side-note), 26.15 (3.3), 26.27 (5.5), 28.19 (5.5); Luke 1.52 (5.3, cited), 2.14 (Vulgate; 3.3), 15.7 (5.4), 22.17 (2.2), 22.19 (5.5), 22.32 (3.3), 24.47 (4.3, cited in side-note); John 3.16 (5.5, cited in side-note), 4.24 (2.2, 4.3, cited in side-note), 6.40 (2.2), 8.12 (4.3, 5.5, wrongly cited in side-notes as John 1 and 8.13), 12.8 (5.5, cited in side-note), 12.31 (5.2, cited), 14.6 (4.3, cited), 14.30 (5.2, cited), 20.21 (3.3), 20.23 (4.3, cited in side-note), 21.16 (3.3, 5.2); Acts 1.11 (5.5, cited in side-note), 4.12 (4.3), 5.35–9 (4.2, cited), 10.43 (4.3, cited in side-note), 19.18 (3.3, cited in side-note); Romans 1.23 (4.3, wrongly cited in side-note as Romans 11), 2.6 (4.3, cited), 5.8 (4.3, cited), 8.30 (4.3, cited); 1 Corinthians 1.13 (2.2, cited), 1.30 (4.3, cited in side-note), 3.12–13, 15 (5.5, wrongly cited in side-note as chapter 2), 7.9 (3.3, cited), 7.12–13 (5.5, cited), 12.6 (4.1, cited in side-note), 14.9 (5.5); Galatians 1.8 (5.5); Ephesians 1.4 (4.3, cited in side-note), 1.22 (3.3, cited), 2.3 (4.3); Philippians 2.13 (4.1, cited in side-note); Colossians 2.14–16 (5.5, cited), 3.1 (5.5, cited); 2 Thessalonians 2.4 (5.5, cited in side-note); 1 Timothy 2.5 (2.2, 5.5, cited in side-note), 3.1 (4.2, cited), 4.1–4 (5.5, cited); 2 Timothy 4.1 (5.5, cited), 4.16 (4.1, cited); Hebrews 1.3 (5.5, cited), 6.17–18 (4.3), 13.17 (3.3); James 5.14 (5.5, cited), 5.16 (3.3, cited in side-note); 1 Peter 1.2 (5.5, cited), 1.10 (5.5, cited), 1.16 (3.3, cited), 1.22 (4.3, cited), 2.9 (5.5, cited in side-note); 2 Peter 1.20 (5.5, cited in side-note); Revelation 1.5 (5.5, cited), 9.3 (2.2, cited), 13.17 (3.3, cited in side-note), 16.2 (5.5, cited); Lucan, *Pharsalia* (2.2, cited); Apostles' Creed (2.2); Augustine, *Sermons* 169 (1.3; wrongly cited in side-note as Sermon 17); St Thomas Aquinas, *Summa theologiae* (1265–73; 2.2, 3.3, cited)

Works Mentioned: Bible: general reference (1.3, 2.2, 4.1, 4.3, 5.5); Old Testament (1.2, 2.2, 3.3, 4.1); Genesis 48.14 (5.5, side-note; wrongly cited as chapter 28); Exodus 20.3 (5.5, side-note), 20.4 (2.2, 3.3, side-note); Leviticus 18 (5.5, side-note); Isaiah (5.5); Daniel 7 (5.5, side-note); New Testament (2.2, 3.3); Matthew 9.29 (5.5, side-note), 16.24 (5.5, side-note), 26.27 (5.5, side-note); Mark (general reference, 5.5), 7.33 (5.5, side-note); Acts 7.17 (5.5, side-note), 28 (4.1, side-note); Paul's Epistles (4.1, 4.3, 5.5); Romans (4.1); 1 Timothy 3 (5.5, side-note); Peter's epistles (5.5); Hesiod, *Theogony* (2.2); Ovid, *Metamorphoses* (3.3); 'Salve Regina' (5.5, side-note); Nicene Creed (3.3); *Corpus juris canonici* (1.2–3, 2.2, 3.3, 5.5, cited in side-notes); Eutropius, *Breviorum historiae Romanae* (3.3, side-note); Isidore of Seville, unidentified work on councils (3.3); Paulus Diaconus, *Historia Romana* (eighth century; 3.3, side-note); Anastasius Bibliothecarius (ascr.), *Liber pontificalis* (ninth century; 3.3, side-note); *Augsburg Chronicles* (3.3, side-note); St Antoninus, *Chronicon* (fifteenth century; 3.3, side-note); Enea Silvio Piccolomini (Pope Pius II), unidentified historical work (3.3, side-note); Bartholomeus Platina, *Vitae pontificum* (1479; 3.3, side-note); Marcus Antonius Sabellicus, *Enneades* (1504; 3.3, side-note); Johannes Nauclerus, *Chronicon* (1500–10, printed 1516; 3.3, side-note); Raphael Maffei Volaterranus, *Vitae pontificum* (1518; 3.3, side-note); Johann Eck, *Loci communes adversus Lutherum et alios histes ecclesiae* (1525; 3.3; title given as *Enchiridion contra Lutheranos*)

LANGUAGE
English
Latin: 116 words (1.2–3, 2.2, 3.1–3, 4.1–3, 5.5; Diaconat, Hermes, Trifon, Act Illicit, Bertaut, Clergy, Chaplain, Felin, Paul, Grace)
Greek: 4 words (1.2, 3.3, 5.5; Diaconat, Hermes, Grace)
French: 4 words (1.4, 3.3; Felin, Hermes)
Popish Gibberish: 2 words (5.5; Grace)

FORM
Metre: prose
Act-Division: 5 acts
Lines (Spoken): 6,387
Lines (Written): 6,430

STAGING
Doors: one represents the palace (1.2, 5.1, dialogue), another Amon's house (2.2, dialogue)

PROPS
Small Portable Objects: a letter (2.1, dialogue); a document (2.2, dialogue); a book (2.2, dialogue); a papal bull (4.2, dialogue); copies of a proclamation (5.4–5, dialogue)
Large Portable Objects: barber's tools bound up in a fardel (5.5, dialogue)

COSTUMES
FABIAN: pilgrim's weeds (1.1–2, dialogue)
PETER and PAUL: dressed as pilgrims (4.1, dialogue)
RAPHAEL: heavenly apparel (5.1–2, dialogue)

EARLY TEXTUAL HISTORY
1630s (?): transcribed in MS; 78 leaves; title page (written in two later hands) gives author's initials and wrongly ascribes the translation to Henry Cheke; index of topics; argument; explanation of terminology; list of roles.
  1635 (?): transcribed (as *King Freewill*?) in perhaps another MS (unlocated); flyleaf names translator.

REFERENCES
Annals 1635; *Annals* 3 Supp. I; David Erskine Baker, Isaac Reed, and Stephen Jones, *Biographia Dramatica* (London, 1812), ii. 250; Bentley, iii. 46–7; Hazlitt, 125.

2478. The Witches of Lancashire

EVIDENCE
Thomas Crosfield's diary; Georg Rudolph Weckherlin, letter to Sir William Trumbull, dated 8 December 1646.

Crosfield lists the show among 'things [that] were to be seen for money', and Weckherlin among 'plays'. One cannot rule out altogether the possibility that the evidence pertains to performances of **2441**, but there are several reasons to think otherwise. First, Crosfield's list is of things 'besides the plays at the King's Arms'. Secondly, none of the other items on either list is a non-puppet play. Crosfield records: rope-dancing at the racket court by the Blue Boar; a stage conjurer, Hocus Pocus, below the Flower de Luce; three exotic animals (a lion by All Hallows' Church, camels at the Crown, and a wolf); a display of waterworks by the Bear; a person with a cloven foot by the Moot Hall; and two other puppet shows (**1398** and either **1588** or **1638**). Weckherlin also mentions Hocus Pocus, along with 'virginals and virgins showed by some Germans', and 'other things'.

GENRE
puppet show (?)

TITLE
Performed: *The Witches of Lancashire*
Contemporary: *The Witches and Devil of Lancashire*

DATE
Limits: 1634–5

PLOT
The Witches of Lancashire meet one another, conjure up the devil, and then play magical tricks on others.

ROLES
WITCHES of Lancashire
The DEVIL
The Witches' VICTIMS

SETTING
Period: contemporary; the play is based on events which took place in 1633–4 (or, possibly, 1612)
Place: Lancashire

PROPS
Small Portable Objects: puppets

EARLY STAGE HISTORY
1635: probably performed on an unknown date between Saturday 11 July and Friday 31 July (possibly Monday 13 July) at Oxford near the King's Head. However, this might alternatively have been the King's Men play on the same subject (**2441**).
  1646: probably performed in London (before Tuesday 8 December) as *The Witches and Devil of Lancashire*. The audience included Ralph Trumbull. This too may have been the King's Men play (**2441**).

REFERENCES
REED: Oxford, 518; *The Trumbull Papers* (Sotheby's catalogue, 14 December 1989), 115.

2479. The Sparagus Garden

TEXT
Printed in 1640 (STC 3820), probably from authorial papers.

2479. The Sparagus Garden

GENRE
comedy
Contemporary: play (prol., ep., S.R.); comedy (t.p.)

TITLE
Performed/Printed: *The Sparagus Garden*
Alternative Modernization: *The 'Sparagus Garden*

AUTHOR
Richard Brome

DATE
Spring or early Summer 1635

ORIGINAL PRODUCTION
King's Revels Company at Salisbury Court

PLOT
There is a family feud of long standing between Touchwood and his neighbour, the now sickly Striker. Touchwood's son, Samuel, is advised to join the hostilities rather than lose his inheritance; but he would rather marry Striker's granddaughter, Annabell, whom Striker has taken in to keep her property out of the hands of her impecunious father, Sir Hugh Moneylacks. Striker is enraged to hear that she has allowed Samuel to court her, especially since Touchwood has now sent Samuel abroad to prevent any chance of a marriage. Thirty years ago, in similar circumstances, Striker threw out his pregnant sister Audrey and refused to pay her marriage portion, but he is persuaded not to repeat the sanction.

Brittleware and his wife Rebecca have been married for five years but, to her annoyance, have not yet produced any children. Sir Hugh, their lodger, recommends an asparagus diet as a way of inducing pregnancy, so they go to a local asparagus garden, in which Sir Hugh happens to have a financial interest, and which is also a high-class venue for adulterous assignations. Sir Hugh and Brittleware also bring a pupil there: they have undertaken to give a makeover to the country-born Tim Hoyden, whose dying mother told him of her brother in the city and sent him to London to make himself a gentleman before presenting himself to his uncle, Striker. Another visitor to the garden is Sir Arnold Cautious, who simply likes to look at women. His nephew Walter asks for his help in arranging a marriage to Annabell.

Hoyden's half-brother Tom follows him to London and presents himself at Striker's house, attempting to pass himself off as a long-lost nephew in the hope of being adopted as the old man's heir; but Striker asks him for proof of identity. He is eager to arrange for Annabell's marriage, believing her to be pregnant by Samuel, and responds to Sir Arnold's proposal on his nephew's behalf with a frank admission that she is no longer a virgin and an offer to make her his sole heir. Sir Arnold decides to have her himself, and Rebecca goes to help dress her as a bride. Noticing her absence, Brittleware jealously supposes she has gone off in a sedan chair for adulterous purposes, but the occupant of the sedan in question turns out to be Tim Hoyden, who has been cheated by Sir Hugh of his money and clothes and sent out dressed in Rebecca's garments.

Sir Arnold changes his mind about marrying Annabell when he first sees her, apparently very pregnant indeed, and asks his nephew to take her off his hands; Walter won't do so himself, but procures a willing friend, who is actually Samuel in disguise. Once the marriage is agreed, Annabell reveals that her pregnancy was simulated with a cushion. Touchwood explains that his quarrel with Striker arose over Audrey: he had married her and fathered the unborn child with whom Striker sent her into the country; so he is really Tim Hoyden's father. Tim produces evidence confirming this: a jewel of his mother's, given by Touchwood. Rebecca is reconciled to Brittleware on condition that he ceases to be jealous.

SCENE DESIGNATION
prol., 1.1–6, 2.1–6, 3.1–11, 4.1–11, 5.1–13, ep. (Q, corrected)

The stage is not clear at the following scene-divisions: 1.1–2, 1.3–6, 2.1–3, 2.4–6, 3.1–5, 3.7–11, 4.1–8, 4.9–11, 5.1–3, 5.4–6, 5.7–13. A verse line is split across 2.4–5. Q includes an erroneous and otiose scene heading (for 4.2) halfway through 4.7.

ROLES
PROLOGUE
Master WALTER Camlet, a young, unmarried gentleman; a younger brother, Goldwire's brother-in-law, Cautious's nephew; also called Wat
Master GILBERT Goldwire, a young, married gentleman, Walter's brother-in-law
Master Samson TOUCHWOOD, an old magistrate, Samuel's father (and, as it turns out, Tim Hoyden's)
Master SAMUEL Touchwood, Samson Touchwood's son and heir; turns out to be Tim Hoyden's half-brother; also called Sam; adopts the alias Master Bounce, a gentleman poet and soldier
Master Will STRIKER, a magistrate and esquire; an old widower, Annabell's grandfather; also called Master Justice Striker
Sir Hugh MONEYLACKS, a knight and widower; Annabell's father, Striker's son-in-law, the Brittlewares' lodger
Mistress FRISWOOD, Striker's old housekeeper of thirty years' service, Annabell's nurse, Rebecca's aunt; also called Fris, Fid, and Mistress Flibbertigib
Mistress ANNABELL, Moneylacks's daughter, Striker's granddaughter (also called his niece); a young woman
Master John BRITTLEWARE, keeper of a china shop; formerly a barber-surgeon; Rebecca's husband of five years; also called Jack
Mistress REBECCA Brittleware, Brittleware's wife, Friswood's niece; also called Beck

Master SPRINGE, Moneylacks's accomplice
Master TIM HOYDEN of Taunton, a young would-be gentleman, in his late 20s; supposed Tom Hoyden's younger half-brother; turns out to be Touchwood's son and Samuel's half-brother; also called Timothy
COULTER, Tim Hoyden's man
A GARDENER, keeper of the asparagus garden, Martha's husband; his name may actually be Master Gardner
MARTHA, a Dutchwoman, the Gardener's wife; also called Mat
A GENTLEMAN, a client at the asparagus garden (3.2)
A GENTLEWOMAN, a client at the asparagus garden (3.2; may be *non-speaking*)
Two BOYS, servants at the asparagus garden (3.4; only one speaks)
Three COURTIERS, clients at the asparagus garden (3.5, *non-speaking*)
Lady STATELY, a client at the asparagus garden (3.5, *non-speaking*)
Lady HANDSOME, a client at the asparagus garden (3.5, *non-speaking*)
Lady PEERLESS, a client at the asparagus garden (3.5, *non-speaking*)
Sir Arnold CAUTIOUS, a bachelor knight and voyeur, Walter's uncle; about 50 years old; also called Sir Cautious
Two COURTIERS, clients at the asparagus garden (3.6; may be two of those from 3.5)
Two LADIES, clients at the asparagus garden (3.6; may be two of the named ladies from 3.5)
A GENTLEMAN, a client at the asparagus garden (3.9–10)
Mistress HOLLYHOCK, a city draper's wife, a client at the asparagus garden (3.9–10)
A SERVANT at the asparagus garden, a young man (3.10)
Master TOM HOYDEN, a rustic, supposed Tim's elder half-brother; also called Thomas
ATTENDANTS who carry on Striker in his chair (4.4, *non-speaking*)
Master PANCRAS, a curate
Master Ambodexter TRAMPLER, a lawyer
A SERVANT (5.2, *non-speaking*)
Two LITTERMEN (5.6; one may be *non-speaking*)
EPILOGUE

Speaking Parts: 31–3

Stage Directions and Speech Prefixes
PROLOGUE: *The Prologue* (heading)
WALTER: *Walter* (s.d.s); *Wat* (s.d.s and s.p.s); *Walt<er>* (s.p.s); *Walter* [one of two] *young Gentlemen and friends* (d.p.)
GILBERT: *Gilbert* (s.d.s); *Gil<bert>* (s.p.s); *Gilbert* [one of two] *young Gentlemen and friends* (d.p.)
TOUCHWOOD: *Touchwood* | *Touch-wood* (s.d.s); *Touch<wood>* (s.p.s); *Touch-wood* [one of the] *Old adversaries, and Justices* (d.p.)

SAMUEL: *Samuel* (s.d.s); *Sam* (s.d.s and s.p.s); *Samuel, Son to Touch-wood* (d.p.)
STRIKER: *Striker* (s.d.s); *Stri<ker>* (s.p.s); *Striker* [one of the] *Old adversaries, and Justices* (d.p.)
MONEYLACKS: *Mony-lacks* | *Mony-lacke* | *Money-lacke* | *Money-lacks* | *Monylacks* (s.d.s); *Mon<y-lacks>* (s.p.s); *Mony-lacks, a needy Knight, that lives by shifts* (d.p.)
FRISWOOD: *Friswood* (s.d.s); *Fris<wood>* (s.p.s); *Friswood, [Annabell's] nurse: and Housekeeper to Striker* (d.p.)
ANNABELL: *Annabell* (s.d.s); *Ann<abell>* (s.p.s); *Annabel, Daughter to Mony-lacks, and Grandchild to Striker* (d.p.)
BRITTLEWARE: *Brittle ware* | *Brittle-ware* | *Brittleware* | *Britleware* (s.d.s); *Brit<tleware>* (s.p.s); *Brittleware* [one of the] *Confederates with Mony-lacks* (d.p.)
REBECCA: *Rebecca* (s.d.s); *Wife* (s.d.s and s.p.s); *Reb<ecca>* (s.p.s); *Rebecca, wife to Brittle-ware* (d.p.)
SPRINGE: *Springe* (s.d.s); *Sprin<ge>* (s.p.s); *Springe* [one of the] *Confederates with Mony-lacks* (d.p.)
TIM HOYDEN: *Hoydon* | *Hoyden* (s.d.s); *Hoy<den>* (s.p.s); *Tim Hoyden, the new made Gentleman* (d.p.)
COULTER: *Coulter* (s.d.s); *Coult<er>* (s.p.s); *Coulter, [Tim Hoyden's] Man* (d.p.)
GARDENER: *Gardener* (s.d.s and s.p.s); *A Gardener* (d.p.)
MARTHA: *Martha [the Gardener's] wife* | *Martha* (s.d.s); *Mat* (s.p.s); *Martha, the Gardener's wife* (d.p.)
GENTLEMAN: *Gentleman* (s.d.s and s.p.s)
GENTLEWOMAN: *Gentlewoman* (s.d.s)
BOYS: *two boys* (s.d.s); *Boy* (s.p.s)
COURTIERS: *three Courtiers* (s.d.s and d.p.)
STATELY: [one of the] *Ladies* (s.d.s); [one of] *Three Ladies* (d.p.)
HANDSOME: [one of the] *Ladies* (s.d.s); [one of] *Three Ladies* (d.p.)
PEERLESS: [one of the] *Ladies* (s.d.s); [one of] *Three Ladies* (d.p.)
CAUTIOUS: *Cautious* (s.d.s); *Caut<ious>* (s.p.s); *Sir Arnold Cautious, a stale Bachelor, and a ridiculous Lover of women* (d.p.)
COURTIERS: *Courtiers* (s.d.s); *1 Courtier* | *2 Courtiers* (s.p.s)
LADIES: *Ladies* (s.d.s); *1 Lady* | *2 Lady* (s.p.s)
GENTLEMAN: *a Gentleman* (s.d.s); *Gentleman* (s.p.s)
HOLLYHOCK: *a City Wife* (s.d.s); *Woman* (s.p.s)
SERVANT: *Servant* (s.d.s and s.p.s)
TOM HOYDEN: *Tom Hoyden* (s.d.s); *Tom* (s.d.s and s.p.s); *Thomas Hoyden, Tim Hoyden's brother* (d.p.)
PANCRAS: *Curate* (s.d.s, s.p.s, and d.p.)
TRAMPLER: *Trampler* (s.d.s); *Tram<pler>* (s.p.s); *Trampler, a Lawyer* (d.p.)
SERVANT: *Servant* (s.d.s)
LITTERMEN: *Litter-man* (s.p.s)
EPILOGUE: *The Epilogue* (heading)

OTHER CHARACTERS
Walter's dead father, Touchwood's friend and neighbour (1.1)
Gilbert's dead father, Touchwood's friend and neighbour (1.1)
Gilbert's wife, Walter's sister (1.1, 3.5)
Touchwood's friends (1.1)
Samuel's virtuous mother (1.2)
Moneylacks's dead wife, Striker's daughter, Annabell's mother (1.3–4)
Striker's dead wife (1.4, 2.5)
Doctor Thou-Lord, a physician to the aristocracy (2.2)
Card-sharpers who cheated Tim (2.3)
Hoyden, a Somerset yeoman, father of Tom, and supposed father of Tim (2.3, 3.7, 4.1–2, 5.11)
Card-sharps who cheated Tim at Hammersmith (2.3)
Audrey Hoyden, née Striker, Tim Hoyden's dead mother, Striker's sister (2.3, 2.6, 3.7, 4.1–2, 4.5, 4.11, 5.3, 5.11–13)
The curate of the Hoydens' parish in Taunton (2.3, 4.1, 4.5)
Striker's physicians (2.5–6, 4.3, 4.7, 5.12)
Clients at the asparagus garden, including a rich old merchant, a poor young gentleman's wife, a knight, and a bankrupt citizen and his wife and servingmen (3.1)
Hoyden's first wife, Tom Hoyden's mother (3.7, 4.1–2)
Hollyhock, a city draper, Mistress Hollyhock's husband (3.9)
The so-called Countess of Copt Hall, apparently a commercial competitor of the asparagus garden (3.10)
The minister of Touchwood's parish, who asked him to visit the dying Striker (4.3)
Brittleware's mother (5.6)
Touchwood's wife, Samuel's mother (5.12)
Striker's neighbours (5.13)

SETTING
Period: contemporary; the action takes place during the spring
Time-Scheme: ten days pass between 2.3 and 3.7, and less than a fortnight between 2.3 and 4.10
Place: London

Geography
London: the Sparagus Garden; Smithfield; St Paul's Cathedral; River Thames; Bankside; the Strand; St Giles's; Bridewell
[*Middlesex*]: Hammersmith; Brentford
[*Essex*]: Copt Hall
Somerset: Taunton; Taunton Deane
England: Ware; the Fens; Windsor
The Low Countries
France: Burgundy; Languedoc
[*Europe*]: Germany; Italy

SOURCES
Narrative: Thomas May, *The Heir* (**1943**); Ben Jonson, *Volpone* (**1493**; 4.6–7); James Shirley, *Hyde Park* (**2367**; structure)

Verbal: Virgil, *Aeneid* 3 (5.6), 7 (4.4); Horace, *Epistles* 1.19 (5.6); Martial, *Epigrams* 11.15 (t.p. motto); William Lily, Latin Grammar (2.5); *The Book of Common Prayer*: Marriage service (1549, rev. 1552; 5.11); 'Love Will Find Out the Way' (ballad, 1620s or earlier; 1.2, cited); [Samuel?] Rowley, *A Match or No Match* (**2087**; 4.8)
Works Mentioned: Homer, *Iliad* (3.5); Francis Beaumont, *The Knight of the Burning Pestle* (**1562**; 2.2); Ben Jonson, *The Alchemist* (**1621**; 2.2), *The New Inn* (**2263**; 1.3)

LANGUAGE
English
Latin: 21 words (2.2, 4.4, 4.9–10, 5.6, 5.9; Moneylacks, Touchwood, Pancras, Tim Hoyden)
French: 3 words (3.4; Boy)
Dialect: Coulter and Tom Hoyden both speak with 'rustic' accents.

FORM
Metre: prose and pentameter; some tetrameter and alexandrines
Rhyme: blank verse; some couplets
Prologue: 22 lines, in couplets
Act-Division: 5 acts
Epilogue: 8 lines, in couplets
Lines (Spoken): 2,875 (726 verse, 2,149 prose)
Lines (Written): 2,995

MUSIC
Music: dance music (3.6, dialogue)
On-Stage Music: Cautious whistles (4.7, s.d.)
Dance: Courtiers and Ladies dance (3.6, s.d.)

PROPS
Weapons: Samuel's sword (1.2, implicit); a dagger (3.3–5, s.d.)
Musical Instruments: a whistle (4.7, dialogue)
Money: a piece (1.3, s.d.); another piece (1.4, dialogue); four hundred pounds (2.3, dialogue); one hundred pieces (2.4, dialogue); twelve pieces (3.7, dialogue; including a crown); a piece worth twenty shillings (3.10, dialogue); two shillings (3.10, dialogue); two pieces (3.11, dialogue); an unspecified amount (4.10, dialogue); another unspecified amount (5.3, implicit); forty pieces (5.9, dialogue); a purse (5.10, s.d.)
Food and Drink: two bottles of wine (3.4, s.d.); dishes of sugar (3.4, s.d.); a dish of asparagus (3.4, s.d.)
Small Portable Objects: a paper (1.6, s.d.); a document (2.2–3, implicit); a book (2.3, dialogue); a pen or pencil (2.3, 4.9–11, implicit); a coulter (2.3, dialogue; 4.11, implicit); a letter (4.8, s.d.); a table-book (4.9–11, s.d.); a paper (5.12, dialogue); a document (5.13, dialogue); a small jewel (5.13, dialogue)
Large Portable Objects: a table (3.4, s.d.); a table cloth (3.4, implicit); a chair (4.4–8, s.d.); a seat (5.10–13, implicit)
Scenery: a sedan chair (5.6, s.d.; has the number 21 on the back)

COSTUMES
GILBERT: his arm in a scarf (4.8, s.d.)
SAMUEL: hangers (1.2, implicit); disguised (3.3–5, s.d.; 5.11–12, implicit)
STRIKER: a cap and gown (4.6–8, dialogue; put on on stage; may also be worn in 4.4)
MONEYLACKS: mourning clothes (1.3, dialogue)
FRISWOOD: a French hood (1.4, dialogue)
ANNABELL: a veil (4.6, dialogue); a mourning habit and willow garland (5.12–13, dialogue; one of the garments is fastened with laces); a cushion under her dress to simulate pregnancy (5.12, dialogue; removed on stage)
TIM HOYDEN: a new suit (3.7, dialogue); a cloak and hat (4.9, dialogue; removed on stage); a silk jacket (4.9–11, dialogue); cross-dressed in women's clothes (5.6, s.d.; 5.13, dialogue)
COURTIERS: rich garments, perhaps of cloth of gold (3.5, implicit)

EARLY STAGE HISTORY
1635–6: performed at Salisbury Court by the King's Revels Company. Richard Brome later claimed that the company's profits from the play amounted to approximately £1,000.

EARLY TEXTUAL HISTORY
1640: entered to Francis Constable in the Stationers' Register on Thursday 19 March; individually named in a group entry of three plays, at least two of them by Richard Brome. Thomas Wykes had licensed the book for publication.
1640: **Q** printed by John Okes for Francis Constable; collation A–L⁴, 44 leaves; title page names author, acting company, and playhouse, and gives year of first performance; Latin title-page motto; authorial dedication to William Cavendish, Earl of Newcastle; commendatory verses by C. G. (Christopher Gewen?) and R. W.; list of roles. Parts of the title page were printed from the same setting of type used in *The Antipodes* (**2591**). In the first copies printed, the epilogue appeared at the start of the play, beneath the prologue; during printing, it was moved to the end.
c. 1640s: a copy of Q was in the possession of John Horne (Vicar of Headington, Oxfordshire). After his death, his entire collection of play-books passed into the possession of John Houghton of Brasenose College, Oxford (*c.* 1608–77), then to James Herne (died 1685), and then to the library of Ralph Sheldon (1623–84) at Weston, where it was catalogued by Anthony Wood, probably in the late 1670s.
1648: Constable's rights transferred in the Stationers' Register (by Anthony Savage, Mary Constable, Frances Constable, and Rachael Constable, the administrators of his deceased widow, Alice Constable, and by assignment of Edwin Bush) to Richard Thrale on Thursday 17 February, by consent of a court held on Monday 6 December 1647; individually named as part of a group transfer of twenty titles.
1655: *The English Treasury of Wit and Language* entered in the Stationers' Register to Humphrey Moseley on Tuesday 16 January.
1655: six extracts (from 2.4, 3.4–5, 4.9, 5.7) included in John Cotgrave's *The English Treasury of Wit and Language*, sigs. F1ʳ, I2ʳ⁻ᵛ, Q2ᵛ, T3ʳ⁻ᵛ; printed for Humphrey Moseley.
1681: Thrale's rights assigned in the Stationers' Register by his widow, Dorothy, to Benjamin Thrale on Monday 11 April (or on an unknown date between then and Monday 9 May), by assignment of Monday 28 March; individually named as part of a group transfer of 42 titles.
1684: Nicholas Cox (Manciple of St Edmund Hall, Oxford) had a copy of Q in his bookshop. It had probably been previously owned by Gerard Langbaine, and appears on a list compiled by Anthony Wood on Saturday 13 December.

EDITIONS
Donald S. McClure, Garland Renaissance Drama (New York, 1980).
Julie Sanders, Richard Brome Online (internet, 2010).

REFERENCES
Annals 1635; Bentley, iii. 87–9; Bodleian, MS Wood E. 4, art. 1, p. 79; Eyre & Rivington, i. 463; Greg 587; Hazlitt, 217; *MLR* 13 (1918), 401–11; *SP* 40 (1943), 186–203; Matthew Steggle, *Richard Brome* (Manchester, 2004), 67–83.

2480. *Hannibal and Scipio*

TEXT
Printed in 1637 (STC 18341), from authorial copy.

GENRE
tragedy
Contemporary: tragedy, piece (prol.); play (prol., S.R.); history (S.R.); historical tragedy (t.p.)

TITLE
Printed: *Hannibal and Scipio*

AUTHOR
Thomas Nabbes

DATE
1635

ORIGINAL PRODUCTION
Queen Henrietta's Men at the Cockpit

PLOT
Having conquered Capua, Hannibal's troops are enjoying the sensual pleasures the town affords. Wanting to get on with the campaign in Italy, Hannibal

rebukes them, but finds himself attracted to one of the local ladies. News from Spain snaps him out of it: Scipio has taken several Carthaginian cities. He decides to attack Rome, but is recalled to Carthage before he can do so.

Carthage has recently lost an African ally, Masinissa, who has been wooed to the side of Rome. In an effort to counterbalance him, Hannibal goes to Numidia to seek an alliance with its king, Syphax. He also finds Scipio there, and suspects Syphax of treachery, but makes the offer anyway: Syphax's military support in return for marriage to Sophonisba, who was previously promised to Masinissa. The lady herself is reluctant—she still loves Masinissa and thinks herself above a petty king like Syphax—but Syphax is agreeable and the marriage goes ahead. The alliance does not help the Carthaginians: Masinissa defeats Syphax's forces in battle, takes Sophonisba prisoner, and marries her (even though Syphax, her husband, is still alive). Scipio wants her to be sent to Rome, but she takes poison rather than be handed over.

Hannibal meets with Scipio and offers him a peace, but Scipio refuses, and Hannibal is routed in the ensuing battle. When he returns to Carthage, the Senate rebukes him for initiating unauthorized peace negotiations, and also suspects him of attempting to set himself up as a king. He leaves Carthage in disgust. When Scipio arrives in triumph, the senators order a pre-emptive announcement that Hannibal has been banished, but their disloyalty to their general only wins Scipio's contempt.

Hannibal takes refuge at the court of King Prusias in Bithynia, and offers his services in a policy of resistance to Rome's territorial ambitions. Prusias refuses, preferring not to jeopardize his diplomatic relations with the Romans. A legation arrives from Rome, with Scipio on its personnel. Hannibal learns that the exits from the palace are being guarded, and infers that he is about to be surrendered to the Romans. He forestalls this by taking poison. Scipio plans to retire to country seclusion.

SCENE DESIGNATION
prol., 1.1–6, 2.1–5, 3.1–5, 4.1–5, 5.1–3, ep. (Q)

The stage is clear only between the acts. Verse lines are split across the following scene-divisions: 1.1–2, 1.2–3, 1.5–6, 2.1–2, 2.2–3, 2.4–5, 3.1–2, 3.3–4, 3.4–5, 4.1–2, 4.2–3, 4.3–4, 4.4–5, 5.1–2, 5.2–3.

ROLES
PROLOGUE
MAHARBAL, a Carthaginian captain
HIMILCO, a Carthaginian captain
A COMMON SOLDIER in Hannibal's army (1.2)
A LADY of Capua (1.2)
HANNIBAL, the Carthaginian general, Bomilcar's kinsman
Two LADIES, one a married woman, the other from Salapia (1.4–5)

A MESSENGER, who brings news from Spain (1.5)
BOMILCAR, Hannibal's kinsman
SYPHAX, King of Numidia, a young, unmarried man; later Sophonisba's first husband
PISTON, Syphax's counsellor
CRATES, Syphax's counsellor
ATTENDANTS on Syphax (2.1, non-speaking)
A MESSENGER, who announces Scipio's arrival (2.1)
SCIPIO, the Roman general and Consul
LAELIUS, a Roman
A MESSENGER, who announces Sophonisba's arrival (2.4)
SOPHONISBA, a Carthaginian lady, Masinissa's fiancée; later Syphax's wife, then (polyandrously) Masinissa's
LADIES attending Sophonisba (2.5, non-speaking)
Roman SOLDIERS (3.1–2, 4.4–5, non-speaking)
MASINISSA, King of Massulia; a young man, Sophonisba's fiancé, later her second husband
Masinissa's SOLDIERS (3.2, non-speaking)
A MESSENGER, who brings wine (3.4, non-speaking)
HANNO, a Carthaginian senator, Hannibal's enemy
GISCO, a Carthaginian senator
BOSTAR, a wealthy Carthaginian senator
Carthaginian SENATORS (4.1–4, non-speaking)
A MESSENGER from Hannibal to the Senate (4.1–3)
Carthaginian SOLDIERS following Hannibal (4.2, 4.5, non-speaking)
LUCIUS, Prince of the Celtiberians, a young man
A YOUNG LADY, a Spanish captive
ROMAN CAPTAINS, who dance (4.5, non-speaking)
CARTHAGINIAN CAPTAINS, who dance (4.5, non-speaking)
PRUSIAS, King of Bithynia
ATTENDANTS on Prusias (5.1–3, non-speaking)
FLAMINIUS, a Roman legate (non-speaking)
Roman LEGATES (5.2–3, non-speaking)

Speaking Parts: 26

Doubling
Four actors doubled in the 1635 production:
   1: Bomilcar, Gisco;
   2: Maharbal, Prusias;
   3: Messenger (1.5), Syphax;
   4: Common Soldier (1.2), Bostar.

Stage Directions and Speech Prefixes
PROLOGUE: *The Prologue* (heading)
MAHARBAL: *Maharball* (s.d.s and d.p.); *Mahar\<ball\>* (s.p.s)
HIMILCO: *Himulco* (s.d.s and d.p.); *Himul\<co\>* (s.p.s)
COMMON SOLDIER: *a common Soldier* (s.d.s); *Soldier* (s.p.s and d.p.)
LADY: *a fair Lady* (s.d.s); *Lady* (s.p.s); *A Lady* (d.p.)
HANNIBAL: *Hanniball* (s.d.s); *Hannibal* (s.d.s and d.p.); *Hanni\<bal\>* (s.p.s)
LADIES: *two Ladies* (s.d.s); *1 Lady | 2 Lady* (s.p.s); *2 other Ladies* (d.p.)

MESSENGER: *Nuntius* (s.d.s, s.p.s, and d.p.)
BOMILCAR: *Bomilcar* (s.d.s and d.p.); *Bom<ilcar>* (s.p.s)
SYPHAX: *Syphax* (s.d.s and d.p.); *Syph<ax>* (s.p.s)
PISTON: *Piston* (s.d.s and d.p.); *Pist<on>* (s.p.s)
CRATES: *Crates* (s.d.s and d.p.); *Crat<es>* (s.p.s)
ATTENDANTS: *Attendants* (s.d.s and d.p.)
MESSENGER: *Messenger* (s.d.s, s.p.s, and d.p.)
SCIPIO: *Scipio* (s.d.s and d.p.); *Scip<io>* (s.p.s)
LAELIUS: *Lelius* (s.d.s, s.p.s, and d.p.)
MESSENGER: *Messenger* (s.d.s and s.p.s)
SOPHONISBA: *Sophonisba* (s.d.s and d.p.); *Sopho<nisba>* (s.p.s)
LADIES: *Ladies* (s.d.s and d.p.)
SOLDIERS: *Soldiers* (s.d.s and d.p.); *some Soldiers | The Soldiers* (s.d.s)
MASINISSA: *Massanissa* (s.d.s and d.p.); *Massa<nissa>* (s.p.s)
SOLDIERS: *Soldiers* (s.d.s and d.p.)
MESSENGER: *Messenger* (s.d.s)
HANNO: *Hanno* (s.d.s, s.p.s and d.p.); [one of the] *Senators* (s.d.s)
GISCO: *Gisgon* (s.d.s and d.p.); [one of the] *Senators* (s.d.s); *Gisg<on>* (s.p.s)
BOSTAR: *Bostar* (s.d.s and d.p.); [one of the] *Senators* (s.d.s); *Bost<ar>* (s.p.s)
SENATORS: *a full Senate* (s.d.s); *Senators* (s.d.s and d.p.)
MESSENGER: *Nuntius* (s.d.s and s.p.s)
SOLDIERS: *some Soldiers | The Soldiers* (s.d.s); *Soldiers* (d.p.)
LUCIUS: *Lucius* (s.d.s and d.p.); *Luci<us>* (s.p.s)
YOUNG LADY: *a young Lady* (s.d.s and d.p.); *Lady* (s.p.s)
ROMAN CAPTAINS: [the Soldiers'] *Captains* (s.d.s)
CARTHAGINIAN CAPTAINS: [the Soldiers'] *Captains* (s.d.s)
PRUSIAS: *Prusias* (s.d.s and d.p.); *Prus<ias>* (s.p.s)
ATTENDANTS: *Attendants* (s.d.s and d.p.)
FLAMINIUS: *Flaminius* (s.d.s)
LEGATES: *other Roman Legates* (s.d.s)

OTHER CHARACTERS
Boys who serve banquets to the Carthaginians in Capua (1.1)
Capuan ladies who entertain the Carthaginians (1.1)
Himulco's mistress (1.2)
Romans killed in battle by Himulco (1.2)
The Senators of Rome (1.3)
Hannibal's father (1.3, 4.2)
The First Lady's husband (1.5)
Fishermen whose information helped Scipio conquer New Carthage (1.5)
Scipio's Roman army, including cavalry and infantry legions (1.5, 2.1, 2.3, 3.1, 3.5, 4.1)
Hannibal's Carthaginian army of 40,000 men, 39,500 of whom were killed at Zama (1.6, 2.3–4, 4.1–2)
Six Roman consuls killed in the war: Scipio's father and uncle, Sempronius, Terentius, Flaminius (father of the Flaminius who appears on stage), and Marcellus (2.2, 4.2)
Piston's family (2.2)
Hasdrubal, a Carthaginian military leader (3.1)
Syphax's troops, including 2,000 taken prisoner by the Romans (3.1)
Sophonisba's father (3.4)
Sophonisba's uncle (3.4)
Roman spies among the Carthaginians (3.5)
A messenger from Hannibal inviting Scipio to a conference at Zama (3.5)
Masinissa's Numidian cavalry (4.1)
Hanno's family, Hannibal's enemies (4.1)
Hannibal's family (4.1–2)
Hannibal's faction in Carthage (4.1–3)
Human sacrifices immolated on the Carthaginians' altar (4.2)
A hundred Roman senators killed by Hannibal at Cannae (4.2)
The people of Carthage (4.4)
The King of the Celtiberians, Lucius' father (4.5)
Antiochus, an Asian potentate (4.5, 5.1)
The people of Bithynia (5.1)
Soldiers guarding the entrance to Prusias' court (5.3)
Prusias' physicians (5.3)

SETTING
Period: third and second centuries BC; the play dramatizes events which took place between 216 and 183
Place: Capua, Cirta, Utica, Carthage, Bithynia

Geography
Rome: the Capitol; River Tiber; the seven hills
Italy: Campania; the Apennines; Salapia; Cannae; Lake Trasimene; Locri; River Arno; Mount Vesuvius; River Eridanus [i.e. Po]; Linturnum
Sicilia: Mount Etna
The Alps
Spain: New Carthage; Sagunt; Tarragon
Africa: Numidia; Massulia; Mount Atlas; Zama; Hadrumentum
[*Greece*]: Corinth; Othris mountains; Dodona; Thessaly; Tempe; Mount Oeta; Thebes
Macedonia
[*Aegean Sea*]: Rhodes; Samos
Bithynia: Chalcedon
Cyprus
Asia: Tyre; Persia; Scythia; Pontus; River Phasis; Arabia; Ephesus; Colchis
Panchaia
India

SOURCES
Narrative: Livy, *Roman History*; Plutarch: *Lives*: Scipio, tr. Thomas North (1579, repr. 1631)
Verbal: Cicero, *Ad Quintum fratrem* 1.1 (Act 5, arg.); Virgil, *Aeneid* 1 (t.p. motto)
Works Mentioned: Xenophon, *Cyropaedia* (5.3); Silius Italicus, *Punica* (prefatory verses); Lucian, *Dialogues of the Dead*: Alexander, Hannibal, Minos,

and Scipio (prefatory verses); Petrarch, *Africa* (fourteenth century, printed 1501; prefatory verses); unidentified play on the same subject (prol.; probably **2370**, or, less plausibly, either John Marston, *The Wonder of Women*, **1485**, or Richard Hathway and William Rankins, *Hannibal and Scipio*, **1274**)

LANGUAGE
English
Latin: 1 word (3.3; Scipio)

FORM
Metre: pentameter
Rhyme: blank verse
Prologue: 30 lines, in couplets
Act-Division: 5 acts, separated by music
Epilogue: 8 lines, in couplets, spoken by Scipio
Lines (Spoken): 2,071
Lines (Written): 2,474

STAGING
Stage: mentioned (prol., dialogue)
Within: shout (2.4, s.d.)
Other Openings: a song is heard 'as from some window' (1.3, s.d.)
Audience: said to include both sexes (prol.); addressed as 'ladies' (prol.)
Miscellaneous: the performance is said to be of two hours' duration (prol.)

MUSIC
Music: music plays between the acts (dialogue); unspecified music (1.3, 2.3–5, 4.5, s.d.); flourish (2.1, 2.3, 3.1, s.d.)
Songs:
  1: 'March on, my merry mates', 1.3, 16 lines;
  2: 'Beauty no more the subject be', 2.5, 11 lines;
  3: 'On, bravely on, the foe is met', 4.5, 10 lines.
Dance: Sophonisba and Ladies dance (2.5, s.d.); Soldiers and Captains dance, 'expressing a fight' (4.5, s.d.)

PROPS
Weapons: Masinissa's sword (3.2–5, dialogue)
Food and Drink: wine (3.4, s.d.; drunk on stage); poison (5.3, s.d.; taken on stage; a pill, small enough to be concealed in a ring)
Large Portable Objects: seating for the Senate (4.1–5, dialogue); ensigns (4.5, s.d.)

A different setting is specified at the head of each act. It is unlikely that this refers to five different pictorial scenery pieces, but not impossible given that Nabbes's next play (**2543**) was written for performance with scenery, albeit at a different playhouse.

COSTUMES AND MAKE-UP
MAHARBAL and HIMULCO: silken clothes; jewels at their necks (1.1–6, dialogue)
COMMON SOLDIER: buff clothes (1.2, dialogue)

HANNIBAL: a wrinkled brow, and only one eye (dialogue); a ring (5.1–3, implicit)
SYPHAX: bound (3.2, s.d.)
SOPHONISBA: golden hair with curls on her forehead (dialogue); all in white (2.5, s.d.); a veil (2.5, s.d.; removed on stage)
LADIES: all in white (2.5, s.d.); veils (2.5, s.d.; removed on stage)
HANNO and BOSTAR: purple gowns (4.1–4, dialogue)
GISCO and SENATORS: purple gowns (4.1–4, implicit)
SOLDIERS and CAPTAINS: differentiated armour for Romans and Carthaginians (4.5, s.d.)

EARLY STAGE HISTORY
1635: performed by Queen Henrietta's Men at the Cockpit. The cast included: William Allen (Hannibal); Robert Axen (Bomilcar, Gisco); Theophilus Bird (Masinissa); Michael Bowyer (Scipio); Hugh Clark (Messenger, Syphax); Ezekiel Fenn (Sophonisba); John Page (Laelius); Richard Perkins (Hanno); William Shurlock (Maharbal, Prusias); George Stutfield (Common Soldier, Bostar); John Sumner (Himulco); Anthony Turner (Piston).

EARLY TEXTUAL HISTORY
1636: entered in the Stationers' Register to Charles Greene on Saturday 6 August; entry names author. William Blagrave, Sir Henry Herbert's deputy, had licensed the book for publication.
1637: **Q** printed by Richard Oulton for Charles Greene; collation A–K^4, 40 leaves; title page names author, acting company, and playhouse, and gives year of performance; Latin title-page motto; verses addressed by the author to the ghosts of Hannibal and Scipio, and by them to him; list of roles and actors; arguments at the head of each act.
c. 1630s–40s: a copy of Q was in the possession of John Horne (Vicar of Headington, Oxfordshire). After his death, his entire collection of play-books passed into the possession of John Houghton of Brasenose College, Oxford (*c.* 1608–77), then to James Herne (died 1685), and then to the library of Ralph Sheldon (1623–84) at Weston, where it was catalogued by Anthony Wood, probably in the late 1670s.
1640 or later: copies of Q were bound with six other Nabbes quartos to create a collection of Nabbes's *Poems, Masques, &c.* (with a title page dated 1639); possibly sold by Nicholas Fussell. The other plays were *Tottenham Court* (**2405**), *Covent Garden* (**2424**), *Microcosmus* (**2543**), *The Spring's Glory* (**2597**), an edition which also included the text of his Masque of Time and the Almanac-Makers (**2635**), *The Bride* (**2645**), and *The Unfortunate Mother* (**2713**).
c. 1647–8: extracts included in a MS notebook (Oxford: Bodleian, MS Ashmole 420) compiled by the astrologer William Lilly. Later, probably after his death in 1681, in the MS passed into the possession of Elias Ashmole; after Ashmole died in turn, in 1692, the MS passed to the Ashmolean Museum, Oxford.

1655: *The English Treasury of Wit and Language* entered in the Stationers' Register to Humphrey Moseley on Tuesday 16 January.

1655: eight extracts (from 1.4, 3.2, 3.5, 4.1, 4.4, 5.2, 5.3) included in John Cotgrave's *The English Treasury of Wit and Language*, sigs. B1^{r-v}, G7^v, M2^v, N3^r, O1^v, Q8^v, T8^r; printed for Humphrey Moseley.

1684: Nicholas Cox (Manciple of St Edmund Hall, Oxford) had a copy of Q in his bookshop. It had probably been previously owned by Gerard Langbaine, and appears on a list compiled by Anthony Wood on Saturday 13 December.

EDITION
A. H. Bullen, in *The Works of Thomas Nabbes* (London, 1887), i. 185–270.

REFERENCES
Annals 1635; Bawcutt C92; Bentley, iv. 934–6; Bodleian, MS Wood E. 4, art. 1, p. 21; Eyre & Rivington, i. 463; Greg 513; Hazlitt, 101; *MLR* 13 (1918), 401–11; *SEL* 11 (1971), 327–43; *SP* 40 (1943), 186–203.

2481. The Arcadia

TEXT
Printed in 1640 (STC 22453). The text contains some early music cues, but omits the words of all three songs.

GENRE
pastoral romance
Contemporary: pastoral (S.R., t.p.); comedy (d.p.)

TITLE
Printed: *The Arcadia*

AUTHOR
James Shirley

DATE
Limits: 1630–6
Best Guess: Summer 1635

Between *The Coronation* (**2464**) and *The Lady of Pleasure* (**2515**), there is an otherwise unexplained 8-month gap in Shirley's output, at a time when he was usually writing three plays a year. 1634–5 is a period when the Cockpit seems to have been buying tragicomedies set in romantic versions of antiquity. It is striking, and may be relevant, that one of the character names in *The Coronation* that Shirley did not draw from his main source of nomenclature, the Diadochi, was Arcadius.

There are two less likely alternative options. One is the period between *The Gamester* (**2418**) in November 1633 and *The Example* (**2437**) in June 1634; but in the early months of that period Shirley was writing *The Triumph of Peace* (**2423**), for which he was handsomely paid, which would temporarily have reduced his economic need to write for the commercial stage.

The other possibility is the period after *The Duke's Mistress* (**2526**), which was licensed in January 1636, after which there is no new play by Shirley until *The Royal Master* (**2581**); but since *The Arcadia* was performed by Queen Henrietta's Men at the Cockpit, the schedule is uncomfortably tight given that they left that playhouse during the plague closure that began in May 1636.

ORIGINAL PRODUCTION
Queen Henrietta's Men at the Cockpit

PLOT
King Basilius understands an oracle to have foretold that his daughters' marriage will result in his death and the usurpation of his throne by a foreigner; it has also indicated that he will commit adultery with his own wife. In an effort to thwart destiny, he has decided to keep the girls unmarried virgins: he leaves court, placing the kingdom under the rule of his deputy, Philanax, and lodges his elder daughter Pamela in the forest with Dametas.

Pyrocles and Musidorus are amorously interested in Basilius' daughters, Pamela and Philoclea, and come to Arcadia in disguise. Musidorus poses as a shepherd, takes a job under Dametas, and, to enable him to elope with Pamela, gets the family out of the way with a series of ruses: Dametas is told a story of buried gold, Miso of her husband's philandering, and Mopsa of a wishing tree which will enable her to become whatever she wants. (She wants to be a queen, with no obligation to obey anyone.) Pyrocles, meanwhile, gets access to Philoclea by disguising himself as an Amazon, Zelmane, only to find that in his new identity he has attracted interest from Basilius.

'Zelmane' helps to quell a rebellion by the people of Arcadia, who are dissatisfied with Basilius' retirement from government, then arranges an assignation with the King at a nearby cave. Queen Gynecia sees through Pyrocles' disguise and falls for him herself. He arranges for Gynecia to take his place at the date with Basilius, and approaches Philoclea while they are away. Basilius meets Gynecia in the cave and so fulfils part of the oracle: he commits 'adultery' with his own wife. Realizing her identity and his folly, he swears constancy, and she gives him what she takes to be a love philtre—which causes him to pass out, apparently dead. The defeated rebels take refuge in the forest, and encounter Musidorus and Pamela. Despite Pamela's insistence that he should fight and die with honour, Musidorus persuades the rebels to release them. When they realize Pamela's identity, however, they suspect treason and take the couple to court in an attempt to purge their own crimes. Meanwhile Pyrocles and Philoclea are found asleep together by Dametas, who has come looking for the missing Pamela.

Philanax is now faced with what appears to be a royal crime wave—a poisoner queen, and two princesses guilty of sexual misconduct—and, despite Pamela's insistence that her father's death makes her Queen of Arcadia, he has them all imprisoned. King

Euarchus comes to visit Basilius, and stays in Arcadia as its Lord Protector. He tries Gynecia for Basilius' murder and sentences her to be buried alive with her husband's corpse. Pyrocles and Musidorus are sentenced to death for complicity, and Euarchus refuses to rescind the sentence on learning that they are in fact his son and nephew. But then Basilius comes back to life: the supposed poison was only a sleeping potion, so no crime has been committed and the sentences are quashed. The oracle is fulfilled, and the princes are allowed to marry their princesses.

SCENE DESIGNATION
1.1–3, 2.1, 3.1–5, 4.1–3, 5.1–2 (Q has act-divisions only)

I treat 4.1–2 as two scenes because there is a change of location, albeit only to 'another part of the forest'; but Q marks no exit for the rebels at the end of 4.1, and it is alternatively possible that they simply skulk around the stage while Pamela and Musidorus enter and speak.

ROLES
BASILIUS, King of Arcadia; an old man, Gynecia's husband, father of Pamela and Philoclea
Lord PHILANAX, Basilius' deputy; later ruler of Arcadia and called King Philanax
CALANDER, a lord
GYNECIA, Queen of Arcadia, Basilius' wife, mother of Pamela and Philoclea; formerly of Argos
Lady PHILOCLEA, younger daughter of Basilius and Gynecia, Pamela's sister
PYROCLES, Prince of Macedon, Euarchus' son, Musidorus' cousin; poses as Lady Zelmane, an Amazon (and ignorantly called Lady Salamander); later claims to be Daiphantus of Lycia
Madam PAMELA, the Princess, elder daughter of Basilius and Gynecia, Philoclea's sister
MOPSA, daughter and only child of Dametas and Miso
MUSIDORUS, Prince of Thessaly, Euarchus' nephew, Pyrocles' cousin; poses as Dorus, a shepherd, Dametas's servant; later claims to be Palladius of Iberia
DAMETAS, a shepherd, Miso's husband, Mopsa's father, Pamela's governor
A SHEPHERD in the play (1.3, *non-speaking*)
CUPID, god of love; a character in the play
MISO, Dametas's wife, Mopsa's mother
The CAPTAIN of the rebels
Four REBELS, one of them a haberdasher
THUMB, a miller; also called Tom (but this may not be his real name); said to be little
A GUARD, who beat off the rebels (3.1, *non-speaking*)
A SHEPHERD accompanying Dametas (4.3)
A GUARD attending Philanax (4.3, *non-speaking*)
A MESSENGER, who brings news of Euarchus' visit (4.3)
SYMPATHUS, the jailer (identified as a lord in the d.p.)
A VOICE summoning Dametas to court (5.1, *within*)
King EUARCHUS of Macedon; Pyrocles' father, Musidorus' uncle; assumes the title Lord Protector of Arcadia

GUARDS on Pyrocles and Musidorus (5.2, *non-speaking*)
CALODOULUS, Musidorus' servant

Speaking Parts: 24

Stage Directions and Speech Prefixes
BASILIUS: *Basilius* (s.d.s; also misprinted *Basilus*); *Bas<ilius>* (s.p.s); *Basilius King of Arcadia* (d.p.)
PHILANAX: *Philonax* (s.d.s); *Philon<ax>* (s.p.s); *Philonax* [one of] *3 Arcadian Lords* (d.p.)
CALANDER: *Calander* | *Callander* (s.d.s); *Cala<nder>* (s.p.s); *Calander* [one of] *3 Arcadian Lords* (d.p.)
GYNECIA: *Gynaecia* | *Gynecia* (s.d.s); *Gyne<cia>* (s.p.s); *Gynecia the Queen* (d.p.)
PHILOCLEA: *Philoclea* (s.d.s); *Phi<loclea>* (s.p.s); *Philoclea* [one of the] *Daughters to Basilius and Gynecia* (d.p.)
PYROCLES: *Pyrocles* (s.d.s); *Pyr<ocles>* (s.p.s); *Pyrocles a Prince disguised as an Amazon, lover of Philoclea* (d.p.)
PAMELA: *Pamela* (s.d.s); *Pam<ela>* (s.p.s); *Pamela* [one of the] *Daughters to Basilius and Gynecia* (d.p.)
MOPSA: *Mopsa* (s.d.s); *Mop<sa>* (s.p.s); *Mopsa daughter to Dametas and Miso* (d.p.)
MUSIDORUS: *Musidorus* | *Musedo<rus>* (s.d.s); *Mus<idorus>* (s.p.s); *Musidorus a Prince disguised as a Shepherd, lover of Pamela* (d.p.)
DAMETAS: *Dametas* (s.d.s); *Dame<tas>* (s.p.s); *Dametas a Rustic shepherd and Guardian to Pamela and Philoclea* (d.p.)
SHEPHERD: *a Shepherds* [sic] | *Shepherd* (s.d.s); [one of the] *Masquers* (d.p.)
CUPID: *Cupid* (s.d.s, s.p.s, and d.p.)
MISO: *Miso* (s.d.s and s.p.s); *Miso wife to Dametas* (d.p.)
CAPTAIN: [one of the] *Rebels* (s.d.s); *Captain* (s.p.s); *Captain of the Rebels* (d.p.)
REBELS: *Rebels* (s.d.s, s.p.s, and d.p.); *the Rebels* | *4 Rebel* (s.d.s); *2* | *3* | *4* | *1* | *Rebel* (s.p.s)
THUMB: *Thumbe* (s.d.s); *Thu<mbe>* (s.p.s); *Thumbe a miller* (d.p.)
GUARD: *a guard* (s.d.s)
SHEPHERD: *a Shepherd* (s.d.s); *Shepherd* (s.p.s)
GUARD: *a guard* | *guard* (s.d.s)
MESSENGER: *Messenger* (s.d.s and s.p.s); *A Messenger* (d.p.)
SYMPATHUS: *Simpathus* (s.d.s); *Sim<pathus>* (s.p.s); *Simpathus* [one of] *3 Arcadian Lords* (d.p.)
VOICE: *Within* (s.p.s)
EUARCHUS: *Euarchus* (s.d.s); *Eua<rchus>* (s.p.s; also misprinted *Euax*.)
CALODOULUS: *Calodoulus* (s.d.s); *Calo<doulus>* (s.p.s); *Caladolous servant to Musidorus* (d.p.)

In 3.1, the Captain seems to be the first rebel, so that the speech prefixes refer to them as 'Captain' and '2–4'; in 4.1, however, they appear to be two separate roles, and the speech prefix '1' first appears.

OTHER CHARACTERS
Menalcus, Musidorus' brother (1.2)
Aristomenes, a rich man who was banished from Arcadia (2.1)
Charita, with whom Miso suspects Dametas of adultery (2.1)
Charita's father (2.1)
Gynecia's mother (4.3)
Musidorus' mother (5.2)

SETTING
Period: antiquity (?)
Time-Scheme: 3.3–5 take place at night
Place: Arcadia

Geography
Arcadia: Mantinea; Oudemion Street; Enispe
Greece: Argos; Lycia; Iberia; Thessaly
Macedon
[*Asia*]: Tyre

SOURCES
Narrative: Sir Philip Sidney, *Arcadia* (c. 1580, printed 1590, repr. 1633)
Verbal: William Shakespeare, *A Midsummer Night's Dream* (**1012**; 3.1)
Works Mentioned: Statute of Drunkenness (1603 or 1623; 1 James I c. 9 or 21 James I c. 7; 3.1); Statute of Bigamy (1603; 1 James I c. 11; 3.1); William Shakespeare and George Wilkins, *Pericles, Prince of Tyre* (**1555**; 1.2); *Tom Thumb* (1621; 3.1)

LANGUAGE
English
Dialect: Mopsa speaks with a light rustic accent.

FORM
Metre: pentameter and prose
Rhyme: blank verse; some couplets
Act-Division: 5 acts
Lines (Spoken): 2,243 (1,398 verse, 845 prose)
Lines (Written): 2,381

STAGING
Doors: characters enter at two doors (4.3, s.d.)
Within: music (2.1, implicit); song (2.1, implicit; 3.2, s.d.); speech (3.5, 5.1, s.d.)
Beneath: Dametas digs in the stage by the 'tree' and finds a parchment in the hole (3.2, dialogue); Dametas enters 'as from a vault' (3.5, s.d.)
Stage Posts: possibly representing trees (3.1–2, 4.1–2, implicit)
Miscellaneous: Mopsa falls out of a tree on stage (3.2, s.d.)

MUSIC
Music: lute within (2.1, s.d.; accompanying Song 1); bell (3.1, s.d.); lutes (3.4, s.d.); recorders (3.4, 5.2, s.d.); flourish (5.2, s.d.)

Songs:
  1: 2.1, Pyrocles within, with lute accompaniment;
  2: 3.2, Dametas within;
  3: 5.1, Pyrocles and Musidorus within.

PROPS
Lighting: a taper (3.3, s.d.)
Weapons: Cupid's bow and arrow (1.3, dialogue); a two-handed sword (3.1, s.d.); Pyrocles' sword (3.5, dialogue); Musidorus' sword (4.2, dialogue); the Captain's sword (4.2, dialogue)
Clothing: possibly a mantle (3.3, dialogue; if not part of Pyrocles' costume)
Money: gold (2.1, dialogue)
Food and Drink: a golden vial (3.3, s.d.; 4.3, dialogue)
Small Portable Objects: a paper (1.1, dialogue); a jewel shaped like a crab (1.2, dialogue); a parchment (3.2, dialogue); jewels (4.2, dialogue); binding cords (4.2–3, implicit)
Large Portable Objects: seating for at least five characters (1.2, implicit); a bier (5.2, s.d.)
Scenery: a tree (3.2, 4.2, dialogue; must be climbable; possibly represented by a stage post); a bar (5.2, s.d.)

COSTUMES
BASILIUS: white hair (dialogue)
GYNECIA: Pyrocles' mantle (3.3, 4.3, implicit; put on on stage)
PHILOCLEA: a veil (3.5, dialogue; put on on stage)
PYROCLES: cross-dressed as a woman (1.1, 1.3, 2.1, 3.1, possibly 3.3, implicit); a mantle (3.3, dialogue; only worn if cross-dressed, and removed on stage; otherwise carried on and given to Gynecia); breeches (3.5, dialogue)
MOPSA: a cloak with a hood (3.2, dialogue; removed on stage)
MUSIDORUS: a hat (2.1, dialogue; put on on stage)
REBELS: at least one wears a scabbard (4.2, dialogue)

EARLY STAGE HISTORY
Performed by Queen Henrietta's Men at the Cockpit before 1640 (and presumably by May 1636).

EARLY TEXTUAL HISTORY
1639: entered in the Stationers' Register (with *Love's Cruelty*, **2349**) to John Williams and Francis Eglesfield on Friday 29 November; entry names author. Thomas Wykes had licensed the book for publication.
  1640: **Q** printed by John Dawson for John Williams and Francis Eglesfield; collation A² B–I⁴, 34 leaves; title page names author, acting company, and playhouse; list of roles.
  c. 1640s: a copy of Q was in the possession of John Horne (Vicar of Headington, Oxfordshire). After his death, his entire collection of play-books passed into the possession of John Houghton of Brasenose College, Oxford (*c*. 1608–77), then to James Herne (died 1685), and then to the library of Ralph Sheldon (1623–84) at Weston, where it was catalogued by Anthony Wood,

probably in the late 1670s. By then the copy had been bound into a single volume with 21 other plays by Shirley (and, presumably in error, with Henry Shirley's *The Martyred Soldier*, **2030**).

1655: *The English Treasury of Wit and Language* entered in the Stationers' Register to Humphrey Moseley on Tuesday 16 January.

1655: extract (from 1.1) included in John Cotgrave's *The English Treasury of Wit and Language*, sig. L8^r; printed for Humphrey Moseley.

1684: Nicholas Cox (Manciple of St Edmund Hall, Oxford) had a copy of Q in his bookshop. It had probably been previously owned by Gerard Langbaine, and appears on a list compiled by Anthony Wood on Saturday 13 December.

EDITIONS
Alexander Dyce, in *The Dramatic Works and Poems of James Shirley* (London, 1833), vi. 169–251.
Robert Carver, in James Shirley, *The Complete Works*, gen. eds. Eugene Giddens, Teresa Grant, and Barbara Ravelhofer (Oxford, forthcoming).

REFERENCES
Annals 1640; Bawcutt 148a; Bentley, v. 1073–6; Bodleian, MS Wood E. 4, art. 1, p. 68; Eyre & Rivington, i. 463; Robert Stanley Forsythe, *The Relations of Shirley's Plays to the Elizabethan Drama* (New York, 1914), 268–79; Greg 583; Hazlitt, 17; John Johnson, *The Academy of Love* (1641), sig. O1^r; *MLR* 13 (1918), 401–11; *SP* 40 (1943), 186–203.

2482. *Icon ecclesiastici* [The Image of a Churchman]

TEXT
MS (London: British Library, MS Sloane 1767, fos. 2–4).

GENRE
dialogue
Contemporary: *concertatio* (title)

TITLE
MS: *Icon ecclesiastici, sive Concertatio Divum Thomae in regiam cruce armiti cum Henrico Principe et tenebrarum principis*

DATE
Limits: 1635–7
Best Guess: 1635

PLOT
St Thomas meets King Henry and tries to inculcate piety in him by drawing his attention to a cross with the figure of Christ crucified. The King is irked by the bishop's arrogance, and asserts the wide extent of his military conquests and political power; by what right does Thomas upbraid him? Thomas points out that, for all his worldly greatness, and for all the luxury with which he surrounds himself, Henry is still mortal. Soon he will grow old, then die; his body will rot away to nothingness and his soul be tormented in hell, and his only hope is to change his attitude to the church. But, on the contrary, Henry becomes more insistent that the clergy must be brought to obedience, by violent means if necessary. Thomas points out that, although his cross is physically no match for the King's sword, spiritually it will secure his admission into heaven.

ROLES
King HENRY, a mature man
Saint THOMAS, a bishop

Speaking Parts: 2

Speech Prefixes
HENRY: *Henric<us>* (s.p.s)
THOMAS: *Thom<as>* (s.p.s)

OTHER CHARACTERS
Henry's subjects

SETTING
Period: twelfth century; the action takes place during the reign of Henry II (1154–81), but the precise time is contradictory, since Thomas Becket (1118–70) is alive, but England has invaded Ireland (1171)
Place: a palace

Geography
[*Britain*]: Scotland; Ireland
[*France*]: Aquitaine
[*Asia*]: Phrygia; Arabia; Tyre
The Red Sea

LANGUAGE
Latin

FORM
Metre: iambic senarius
Lines (Spoken): 209
Lines (Written): 215

PROPS
Weapons: a sword
Small Portable Objects: a crucifix (dialogue)

COSTUMES
HENRY: a crown (dialogue); a scabbard (implicit)
THOMAS: a mitre (dialogue)

EARLY TEXTUAL HISTORY
c. 1635: transcribed in a **MS** literary miscellany connected with the English College, Douai; 3 leaves.

The collection also includes *Andronicus Comnenus* (**2547**).

EDITION
Dana Sutton and Martin Wiggins, *The Philological Museum* (internet, 2018).

REFERENCES
Annals 1635; *The Library*, 6th ser., 10 (1988), 68.

2483. Love's Changelings' Change

TEXT
MS (London: British Library, MS Egerton 1994, fos. 293–316); possibly an authorial transcript.

GENRE
pastoral

TITLE
Performed/MS: *Love's Changelings' Change*
Alternative Modernizations: *Love's Changeling's Change*; *Love's Changelings Change*

DATE
Limits: 1621–40
Best Guess: 1635

The upper limit is established by the use of material first published in the 1621 edition of *Arcadia*. The *Annals* date is no more than a medial position within Greg's assessment of the MS handwriting as belonging to the 1630s; the play's vast scope and uncertain metrics also seem to align it with that decade's courtier drama. Cutts remarks cryptically that there may be significance in the dramatist's systematic excision of the Argalus and Parthenia narrative, in view of the fact that this material was used by Henry Glapthorne in his own *Argalus and Parthenia* (**2579**). I take this to be a tentative suggestion that *Love's Changelings' Change* might have been written soon after *Argalus and Parthenia*, and that the dramatist was seeking to avoid duplication. However, the hypothesis is complicated by the existence of Shirley's *The Arcadia* (**2481**), which condenses Sidney in a somewhat similar way, only more efficiently: the *Love's Changelings' Change* dramatist was obviously not worried about duplication there, and the avoidance of mutual toe-treading might more plausibly be ascribed to Shirley and Glapthorne, who at least were both working in the same professional milieu, albeit for different companies. (The *Love's Changelings' Change* dramatist seems, on the contrary, to have been untroubled by practical considerations of length and cast size.) On balance it seems best to leave this play where it is, uncertainly positioned in the middle of the 1630s.

PLOT
After abandoning a burning ship, Musidorus is separated from his friend Pyrocles and washed up on the coast of Laconia, where two shepherds find him. He tells them he is a commoner, not the prince he truly is. At first he believes that Pyrocles has drowned, but then catches sight of him aboard a ship which is about to be attacked by pirates. The shepherds take him to Arcadia and he receives the hospitality of Kalander. On hearing that his host's son Clytophon has been taken a prisoner of war, Musidorus goes to rescue him, and engages one of the enemy soldiers in single combat. This is broken off as soon as his opponent realizes his identity—for he is fighting the lost Pyrocles. Clytophon is returned home, and is soon to be married.

King Basilius has taken his family into bucolic retirement, lodging his elder daughter Pamela separately from the rest. Pyrocles falls in love with the younger daughter, Philoclea, and gives himself the opportunity to meet her by disguising himself as an Amazon, Zelmane. The upshot is that Basilius is attracted to 'Zelmane', while Gynecia, the Queen, sees through the disguise and also falls in love with Pyrocles. Musidorus, meanwhile, falls for Pamela and takes on the identity of a shepherd, Dorus. He enters the service of Dametas, Pamela's keeper, and the daughter of the household, Mopsa, falls in love with him.

Pamela realizes who 'Dorus' really is, and 'Zelmane' admits to Philoclea that he is in fact Pyrocles. The two princesses and 'Zelmane' go for a picnic, but are kidnapped by agents of Cecropia, whose son, Amphialus, is the next in line to the throne after Philoclea. Philoclea refuses to marry Amphialus. He launches a military coup, and captures one of Basilius' lords, but releases him at Philoclea's entreaty. Musidorus absconds from Dametas' household, takes on the identity of a black knight, and does valiant deeds in battle. Finally, he takes on Amphialus in single combat: the rebellion is quashed and Amphialus grievously wounded. Cecropia sends Basilius an ultimatum: if he does not capitulate, his daughters will be killed. When Basilius is unmoved, Cecropia makes it appear that the princesses have been beheaded. Amphialus kills her in revenge for Philoclea, then kills himself in remorse. His surviving allies attempt to rape the lady prisoners, but 'Zelmane' kills them, and the princesses are returned home.

Upon realizing that 'Dorus' is wealthier than he seems, Dametas tries to force him to marry Mopsa. Musidorus tells him where he can find buried gold, then tells his wife that her husband has gone out whoring. In the confusion, he and Pamela are able to elope, but are captured by thieves and taken back to court. Meanwhile, Basilius sets up a nocturnal assignation with 'Zelmane', but it is kept by Gynecia, who has borrowed the Amazon costume. While the parents are occupied, Pyrocles spends the night chastely in bed with Philoclea, but Dametas assumes the worst when he catches them together.

The dead body of Basilius is found: the courtiers infer a murder conspiracy between Gynecia, Musidorus, and Pyrocles. Since Pamela is not yet old enough to succeed to the throne, Euarchus is appointed Lord Protector. He is obliged by law to try the murder case before the victim can be interred; the other misdemeanours are also raised in the same session. Pyrocles exonerates Philoclea of unchastity, but she is sent to a nunnery anyway. Gynecia confesses to poisoning Basilius and is sentenced to be buried alive. Pyrocles and Musidorus are found guilty and sentenced to death, but the sentence is revoked when it emerges that they are princes, not commoners, and so not subject to the laws of a foreign land. Basilius wakes up inside his coffin: he is not dead after all, so none of the sentences need be carried out. Musidorus and Pyrocles are to marry the princesses.

SCENE DESIGNATION
prol., 1.1–8, 2.1–8, 3.1–27, 4.1–16, 5.1–6, ep. (MS has act-division only)

This maps onto Rota's scene-division as follows: 1.1–5 = Rota 1.1–5; 1.6–8 = Rota 1.6; 2.1–5 = Rota 2.1; 2.6–8 = Rota 2.2–4; 3.1 = Rota 3.1–2; 3.2–3 = Rota 3.3; 3.4 = Rota 3.4; 3.5–8 = Rota 3.5; 3.9–10 = Rota 3.6–7; 3.11–12 = Rota 3.8; 3.13–14 = Rota 3.9–10; 3.15–16 = Rota 3.11; 3.17–23 = Rota 3.12–18; 3.24–5 = Rota 3.19; 3.26–7 = Rota 3.20; 4.1–7 = Rota 4.1–7; 4.8–10 = Rota 4.8; 4.11–16 = Rota 4.9–14; 5.1–6 = Rota 5.1–6.

ROLES
PROLOGUE
STREPHON, a singing shepherd
KLAIUS, a shepherd
ATTENDANTS, who drag on the half-drowned Musidorus (1.1, *non-speaking*)
Prince MUSIDORUS, Duke of Thessaly; Pyrocles' cousin, Euarchus' nephew; a young man; also called Lord Thessalia; assumes the alias Palladius of Iberia, a commoner; later poses as Dorus, a shepherd
A FISHERMAN (1.1)
Prince PYROCLES of Macedon, Euarchus' son, Musidorus' cousin; assumes the alias Diaphantus of Lycia, a commoner; later poses as Lady Zelmane, an Amazon
Lord KALANDER, Clytophon's father, an old man
A BOY, who brings a letter (1.2, *non-speaking*)
Kalander's SERVANT (1.2)
Kalander's COUNSEL (1.2, *non-speaking*)
Helot SOLDIERS (1.3, *non-speaking*)
PRISONERS of the Helots (1.3, *non-speaking*)
CLYTOPHON, Kalander's son
Two ATTENDANTS in Kalander's household (1.4)
Two HUNTSMEN (1.6–7)
A SHRILL VOICE (2.1, *above* and presumably *within*)
Master DAMETAS, a swineherd; Miso's husband, Mopsa's father
King BASILIUS of Arcadia, an old man, Gynecia's husband, father of Pamela and Philoclea; also called Prince Basilius and Lord Basilius
GYNECIA, Queen of Arcadia, Basilius' wife, mother of Pamela and Philoclea
Lady PAMELA, elder daughter and heiress of Basilius and Gynecia, Philoclea's sister, Cecropia's niece, Amphialus' cousin; younger than 21 years

Lady PHILOCLEA, younger daughter of Basilius and Gynecia, Pamela's sister, Cecropia's niece, Amphialus' cousin
DORUS, a singing shepherd (2.6)
SHEPHERDS, who dance (2.6; sing collectively)
Mistress MOPSA, daughter of Dametas and Miso
MISO, Dametas' wife, Mopsa's mother; an old woman
CECROPIA, Amphialus' mother, aunt of Pamela and Philoclea, [Gynecia's sister]
CLINEAS, Amphialus' counsellor
Four MAIDS (3.1; two speak)
Four MEN who kidnap the princesses and Zelmane (3.1, *non-speaking*)
A MESSENGER, who reports the kidnapping (3.2)
Lord AMPHIALUS, Cecropia's son, cousin of Pamela and Philoclea
Amphialus' SOLDIERS (3.5–7, *non-speaking*)
Lord PHILANAX, of Basilius' faction
A CAPTAIN in Amphialus' army (3.8, *non-speaking*)
An OLD KNIGHT of Amphialus' faction (3.8)
Two LORDS of Amphialus' faction (3.9)
A GUARD at the execution (3.9, *non-speaking*)
Philanax's JAILERS (3.9; one speaks)
An EXECUTIONER (3.9; his only speech was originally written for a jailer and reassigned)
NOBLES of Basilius' faction (3.11, 3.18, 4.2, 5.2, 5.6; one speaks in 3.18, and one in 4.2)
Dametas' SQUIRE (3.12, 3.14)
A PAGE, who brings a letter (3.14)
TRUMPETERS (3.14, *non-speaking*)
Two JUDGES of the duels (3.14, 3.17, 4.3)
ATTENDANTS on Cecropia (3.15, 3.19, *non-speaking*)
A MESSENGER from Amphialus to Cecropia (3.15)
ANAXIUS, brother of Lycurgus and Zoilus, Amphialus' ally
LYCURGUS, brother of Anaxius and Zoilus, Amphialus' ally
ZOILUS, brother of Lycurgus and Anaxius, Amphialus' ally
Two KNIGHTS attending Musidorus (3.16–17, *non-speaking*)
A MESSENGER from the camp (3.16)
Musidorus' SQUIRE (3.17)
Four OLD WOMEN, who whip the princesses (3.21; speak collectively)
Philoclea's KEEPERS (3.23, *non-speaking*; may be the same as the Old Women)
Zelmane's KEEPER (3.24)
A MESSENGER (3.26, *non-speaking*)
Anaxius' PAGE (4.1–2)
A LORD (4.3)
ATTENDANTS, who remove the dead bodies of Zoilus and Lycurgus (4.3, *non-speaking*)
A CAPTAIN in the rebel army (4.4)
Musidorus' PAGE (4.4)
A WAITING-MAID attending Pamela and Philoclea (4.5)
A MESSENGER from Basilius to his daughters (4.5)
Five or more SHEPHERDS (4.14; four speak)

Four THIEVES (4.15–16)
SYMPHATHUS, a lord
A GENTLEMAN, a messenger (5.1)
Prince EUARCHUS of Macedon, Lord Protector of Arcadia; Pyrocles' father, Musidorus' uncle; also called Lord Euarchus
A CRIER (5.4, *within*)
Kalander's SERVANT (5.5, *non-speaking*)
A GUARD on Gynecia (5.6, *non-speaking*)
KALODOLUS, Musidorus' servant
EPILOGUE

Speaking Parts: 70–1

Stage Directions and Speech Prefixes
PROLOGUE: *Prologus* (heading)
STREPHON: [one of] 2 *Shepherds* | [one of the] *Shepherds* | [one of] *two shepherds Shepherd* | | *the Shepherd* | *th'other Shepherd* | [one of] *the Shepherds* (s.d.s); *Strephon* | 1 *Shepherd* (s.p.s); *Strephon* [one of the] *Shepherds* (d.p.)
KLAIUS: [one of] 2 *Shepherds* | [one of the] *Shepherds* | [one of] *two shepherds* | *Shepherd* (s.d.s); *Claius* (s.p.s); *Claius* [one of the] *Shepherds* (d.p.)
ATTENDANTS: *Attendants* (d.p.)
MUSIDORUS: *Musidorus* (s.d.s and s.p.s); *Dorus* | *Musidorus the Black knight* (s.d.s); *Musidorus* [one of] *two princes disguised for the love of* [Basilius'] *daughters* (d.p.)
FISHERMAN: *a Fisherman* (s.d.s); *Fisherman* (s.p.s); *Fishermen* (d.p.)
PYROCLES: *Pyrocles* (s.d.s and s.p.s); [the Helots'] *captain* | [one of] *the Ladies* | *Zelmane* (s.d.s); *Zelm<ane>* (s.p.s); *Pyrocles* [one of] *two princes disguised for the love of* [Basilius'] *daughters* (d.p.)
KALANDER: *Kalander* (s.d.s); *Kalan<der>* (s.p.s); *Kalander* [one of] *three Arcadian Lords* (d.p.)
BOY: *a boy* (s.d.s)
SERVANT: *Kalander's servant* (s.d.s); *Servant* (s.d.s and s.p.s)
COUNSEL: [Kalander's] *Counsel* (s.d.s)
SOLDIERS: *the poor soldiers* | *the Helots* (s.d.s)
PRISONERS: [the poor soldiers'] *prisoners* (s.d.s)
CLYTOPHON: *Clitophon* (s.d.s); *Clito<phon>* (s.p.s); *Clitophon Kalander's son* (d.p.)
ATTENDANTS: *Attendants* (s.d.s and d.p.); 1 *Attendant* | 2 *Attendant* (s.p.s)
HUNTSMEN: *two huntsmen* (s.d.s); 1 *Huntsman* | 2 | 1 *Huntsman* (s.p.s); 2 *Huntsmen* (d.p.)
SHRILL VOICE: *shrill voice* (s.d.s)
DAMETAS: *Dametas* (s.d.s); *Dam<etas>* (s.p.s); *Dametas a Clown and guardian to the 2 Sisters* (d.p.)
BASILIUS: *Basilius* (s.d.s); *Basil<ius>* | *Bass<ilius>* (s.p.s); *Basilius King of Arcadia* (d.p.)
GYNECIA: *Gynecia* | *the Queen* | *Gynec<ia>* (s.p.s); *Gynecia Queen and Basilius' wife* (d.p.)
PAMELA: *Pamela* (s.d.s and s.p.s); [one of Gynecia's] *daughters* | [one of] *the Ladies* | [one of] *the Sisters* | [one of the] *Sisters* | [one of] 2 *Sisters* (s.d.s); *Pamela* [one of Gynecia's] *daughters* (d.p.)
PHILOCLEA: *Philoclea* | [one of Gynecia's] *daughters* | [one of] *the Ladies* | [one of] *the Sisters* | [one of the] *Sisters* | [one of] 2 *Sisters* (s.d.s); *Philoc<lea>* (s.p.s); *Philoclea* [one of Gynecia's] *daughters* (d.p.)
DORUS: [one of] *the Shepherds* (s.d.s); *Dorus* (s.d.s and s.p.s)
SHEPHERDS: *the Shepherds* (s.d.s); *Chorus* (s.p.s); *Shepherds* (d.p.)
MOPSA: *Mopsa* (s.d.s and s.p.s); *Mopsa* [Dametas' and Miso's] *daughter* (d.p.)
MISO: *Misoe* (s.d.s); *Miso* (s.d.s and s.p.s); *Miso wife to Dametas* (d.p.)
CECROPIA: *Cecropia* (s.d.s); *Cecrop<ia>* (s.p.s); *Cecropia mother to Amphialus* (d.p.)
CLINEAS: *Clineas* (s.d.s); *Cline<as>* (s.p.s); *Clinea counsellor to Amphialus* (d.p.)
MAIDS: 4 *Maids* | *maids* (s.d.s); 1 *Maid* | 2 *Maid* (s.p.s); *Maids as attendants* (d.p.)
MEN: 4 *men* (s.d.s)
MESSENGER: *a messenger* (s.d.s)
AMPHIALUS: *Amphialus* (s.d.s); *Amph<ialus>* (s.p.s); *Amphialus nephew to Basilius* (d.p.)
SOLDIERS: *Soldiers* (s.d.s)
PHILANAX: *Philinax* (s.d.s); *Phil<i>n<ax>* | *Phil<ina>x* (s.p.s); *Philonax* [one of] *three Arcadian Lords* (d.p.)
CAPTAIN: *a Captain* (s.d.s)
OLD KNIGHT: *an old knight* (s.d.s); *knight* (s.p.s)
LORDS: *Lords* (s.d.s); 1 *Lord* | 2 *Lord* (s.p.s)
GUARD: *a guard* (s.d.s); *Guard* (s.p.s)
JAILERS: [Philanax's] *Jailers* (s.d.s); *Jailer* (s.p.s)
EXECUTIONER: *Executioner* | *the executioner* (s.d.s)
NOBLES: *nobles* | *Lords* | *other Lords* | *t'other Lords* | 2 *other lords* | *the other Lords* (s.d.s); 1 *Lord* (s.p.s)
SQUIRE: *a Esquire* | [Dametas'] *Squire* (s.d.s); *Squire* (s.d.s and s.p.s)
PAGE: *a Page* (s.d.s); *Page* (s.p.s)
TRUMPETERS: *Trumpet* (s.d.s)
JUDGES: *Judges* (s.d.s and d.p.); *the Judges* (s.d.s); 1 *Judge* | 2 *Judge* (s.p.s)
ATTENDANTS: *Attendants* (s.d.s and d.p.)
MESSENGER: *a messenger* (s.d.s); *Messenger* (s.p.s)
ANAXIUS: *Anaxius* (s.d.s); *Anax<ius>* (s.p.s); *Anaxius* [one of the] *brothers and friends to Amphialus* (d.p.)
LYCURGUS: *Lycurgus* | [one of Anaxius'] *brothers* | [one of Anaxius'] *brethren* (s.d.s); *Lycur<gus>* (s.p.s); *Lycurgus* [one of the] *brothers and friends to Amphialus* (d.p.)
ZOILUS: *Zoylus* (s.d.s and s.p.s); [one of Anaxius'] *brothers* | [one of Anaxius'] *brethren* (s.d.s.); *Zoylus* [one of the] *brothers and friends to Amphialus* (d.p.)
KNIGHTS: *two other knights* | 2 *other knights* | *the 2 other knights* (s.d.s)
MESSENGER: *a messenger from the camp* (s.d.s)
SQUIRE: [Musidorus'] *Squire* (s.d.s); *Squire* (s.p.s)
OLD WOMEN: 4 *old women* (s.d.s); *women* (s.p.s); *women Keepers* (d.p.)

KEEPERS: [Philoclea's] *keepers* (s.d.s)
KEEPER: *Zelmane's keeper* (s.d.s); Keeper (s.d.s and s.p.s)
MESSENGER: *a messenger* | *the messenger* | *messenger* (s.d.s)
PAGE: [Anaxius'] *Page* | *Anaxius' page* (s.d.s); Page (s.d.s and s.p.s); [one of] 2 Pages (d.p.)
LORD: *a Lord* | *the Lord* (s.d.s); Lord (s.p.s)
ATTENDANTS: *Attendants* (d.p.)
CAPTAIN: *a Captain* (s.d.s); Captain (s.d.s and s.p.s)
PAGE: [Musidorus'] *page* (s.d.s); *Attendant* (s.p.s); [one of] 2 Pages (d.p.)
WAITING-MAID: *a waiting maid* (s.d.s); Maid (s.d.s and s.p.s)
MESSENGER: *a messenger* (s.d.s); Messenger (s.d.s and s.p.s)
SHEPHERDS: *Shepherds* (s.d.s and d.p.s); *more shepherds* (s.d.s); 1 *Shepherd* | 2 | 3 | 4 (s.p.s)
THIEVES: *Thieves* (s.d.s and d.p.s); 1 *Thief* | 2 *Thief* | 3 *Thief* | 4 *Thief* | *Thief* (s.p.s)
SYMPATHUS: *Sympathus* (s.d.s); *Symph<athus>* (s.p.s); *Sympathus* [one of] *three Arcadian Lords* (d.p.)
GENTLEMAN: *a messenger and a gentleman* | *Gentleman* (s.d.s); *Messenger* (s.p.s)
EUARCHUS: *Evarchus* (s.d.s); *Evar<chus>* (s.p.s); *Evarchus father to Pyrocles* (d.p.)
CRIER: *from within* (s.p.s)
SERVANT: *a servant* (s.d.s)
GUARD: *a Guard* | *the Guard* (s.d.s); *Guard* (d.p.)
KALODOLUS: *Kalodolus* (s.d.s); *Kalo<dolus>* (s.p.s); *Kalodolus servant to Musidorus* (d.p.)
EPILOGUE: *Epilogus* (heading)

OTHER CHARACTERS
Urania, loved unrequitedly by Strephon and Klaius (1.1)
Lacon, a notorious pirate and slave-trader (1.1–2, 1.8)
Pirates, Lacon's followers (1.2)
Basilius' predecessors (1.2)
The King of Argos, Gynecia's father, Amphialus' uncle (1.2, 3.3)
The gentlemen of Lacedaemon, who fought in the war against the Helots (1.2)
Clytophon's bride (1.5)
Lady Zelmane, whom Pyrocles once loved, and whose name he borrows (2.1)
The local parson (2.1)
Queen Synecia, ruler of the Amazons, said to be Zelmane's aunt (2.1)
Menalcas, a shepherd whose clothes Musidorus borrows (2.5)
The citizens, Basilius' subjects (3.3, 3.27, 5.6)
Basilius' soldiers (3.8, 4.3)
The pioneers in Basilius' army (3.11)
Dametas' father (3.14)
A shepherd, who brought Dametas a message from Musidorus (4.6)
Aristomanes, a rich man (4.7)
Charita, a loose woman (4.7, 4.12)
Charita's uncle (4.7)
Dametas' dead grandfather (4.16)
The nuns of Arcadia (5.6)
Pyrocles' dead mother (5.6)

SETTING
Period: antiquity
Time-Scheme: 4.10 takes place at night; 5.6 takes place the day after 5.2
Place: Arcadia; a few scenes (1.1–2a) take place in Laconia

Geography
Arcadia: Oudemion Street; Mantinea
Greece: Argos; Delphos (i.e. Delphi); Lacedaemon; Thessaly; Athens
[*Europe*]: France; Macedon
Asia: Parthia; Lycia; Iberia

SOURCES
Narrative: Sir Philip Sidney, *Arcadia* (1580, printed 1590, repr. 1633); Sir William Alexander, 'Supplement' to the *Arcadia* (1621, repr. 1633; 4.4–6)
Verbal: Terence, *Eunuchus* (epigraphic couplet); Sir Philip Sidney, *Arcadia*: First Eclogues (2.5), 'Transformed in show' (2.1), 'We love and are beloved again' (2.6); perhaps William Shakespeare, *Love's Labours Lost* (**1031**; title); probably *Hic mulier* (1620; 5.6)
Works Mentioned: Ovid, *Metamorphoses* (1.4); Robert Greene, *Friar Bacon and Friar Bungay* (**822**; 3.12); also a general reference to Homer (1.2)

LANGUAGE
English
Latin: 8 words (2.5, 4.16, 5.1, 5.6; Musidorus, Philanax, Kalander, Euarchus, Dametas)
French: 3 words (4.5–6; Pamela, Dametas)

FORM
Metre: loose pentameter and alexandrines, and prose
Rhyme: blank verse and couplets
Prologue: 12 lines, in couplets
Act-Division: 5 acts
Epilogue: 6 lines, in couplets
Lines (Spoken): 3,067 (2,088 verse, 979 prose)
Lines (Written): 3,354

STAGING
Doors: characters enter (1.3, 3.3, 3.7, 3.14, 3.26, 4.7, s.d.) and exit (1.4, 1.8, 5.4, s.d.) at two doors; characters exit at three doors (4.12, s.d.)
Discovery Space: curtained (1.2, 4.13, s.d.); set with pictures (1.2, implicit); Pyrocles and Philoclea are discovered asleep (4.13, implicit)
Stage: mentioned (4.4, s.d.)
Within: noise (1.3, s.d.); whoop (1.7, 3.8, 4.4, s.d.); speech (2.1, implicit; 3.8, 3.17, 4.3, 4.7, 5.4, s.d.); song

(2.1, 2.5, s.d.); music (3.5, s.d.); sound effects (3.6, implicit); shout (3.15, s.d.); shriek (3.23, 3.25, s.d.)
Above: characters appear above (1.1, 4.12, s.d.; one at a time); music (2.1, 2.6, 3.1, 4.1, s.d.); Mopsa falls from above onto the main stage (4.12, s.d.)
Beneath: smoke rises from underneath (1.1, s.d.); Dametas digs (4.11, s.d.)
Stage Posts: possibly represent a tree (4.11, implicit)
Miscellaneous: Characters exit at the end of one scene and immediately re-enter at the start of the next on four occasions (Musidorus, 1.1–2; Cecropia, 3.2–3; Amphialus, 3.8–9; Dametas, 4.11–12 and 4.12–13). In 1.2, the fictional location shifts without the stage being cleared.

MUSIC AND SOUND
Sound Effects: clashing weapons within (3.6, s.d.)
Music: retreat (1.3, 3.16, s.d.); still music from above (2.1, s.d.); unspecified music above (2.6, 3.1, s.d.); drum within (3.5, s.d.); unspecified music (3.16, s.d.); drums and trumpets (3.16, 4.3, s.d.); a retreat (3.16, s.d.); trumpets (3.17, s.d.); loud music from above (4.1, s.d.)
On-Stage Music: Helot Soldiers play bagpipes (1.3, s.d.); Huntsmen wind 'their horn' (1.6, s.d.); Dametas whistles (2.6, s.d.); trumpets (3.14, s.d.); Trumpeters sound a retreat (3.14, dialogue)
Songs:
  1: 'Transformed in show, but more transformed in mind', 2.1, Pyrocles within, 14 lines;
  2: 'These weeds will become my mind', 2.5, Musidorus within, 4 lines;
  3: 'We love and are beloved again', 2.6, Strephon and Dorus, in parts, 16 lines.
Dance: shepherds dance (2.6, s.d.)

PROPS
Lighting: a lighted candle (2.8, s.d.); a lamp (4.13, s.d.)
Weapons: Pyrocles' long sword (1.1, 4.4, 4.13, dialogue; 1.3, 2.1, 4.10, s.d.); Musidorus' sword (1.3, implicit; 3.8, dialogue; 4.15, s.d.); a coach-whip (2.6, s.d.); Old Knight's sword (3.8, implicit); an axe (3.9, s.d.); a shield with an impresa (3.14, s.d.); Dametas' buckler (3.14, dialogue; possibly the same as the heraldic shield); Dametas' sword (3.14, dialogue); Clineas' sword (3.14, dialogue); four whips (3.21, s.d.); Messenger's sword (3.26, s.d.); Anaxius' sword (3.27, dialogue; 4.3, dialogue; 4.4, implicit); Zoilus' sword (4.3, s.d.); Lycurgus' sword (4.3, s.d.)
Musical Instruments: bagpipes (1.3, s.d.); a hunting horn (1.6, s.d.; or two, perhaps); unspecified instruments (2.6, implicit); trumpets (3.14, s.d.)
Clothing: bloody shirts hanging on staves (1.3, s.d.; carried like military colours); clothing (5.5, s.d.; also worn by Musidorus and Pyrocles)
Money: a bag of gold (2.5, s.d.)
Food and Drink: a supper (1.2, dialogue); medicine (2.6, dialogue); liquid (3.1, implicit; drunk on stage)

Small Portable Objects: a letter (1.2, s.d.); a jewel (1.2, s.d.); a letter (1.2, s.d.); a box of jewels (1.4, s.d.); a letter (1.8, s.d.); jewels (1.8, s.d.); a gallipot (2.6, s.d.); a picture of a crab, with a motto (2.6, dialogue); a letter (2.8, s.d.); a gag (3.1, s.d.); binding cords (3.1, implicit); letters (3.3, s.d.); a looking-glass (3.4, dialogue); a letter (3.9, s.d.); two documents (3.12, s.d.); a letter (3.13, dialogue; 3.14, s.d.); a letter (3.16, s.d.); an unspecified gift (3.25, s.d.); a letter (4.1, s.d.); a document (4.2, s.d.); a cabinet (5.5, s.d.); a key (5.6, s.d.)
Large Portable Objects: a chest (1.1, s.d.; 1.2, dialogue); a rope (1.1, s.d.; too short to reach from the main stage to the above space); pictures of women (1.2, dialogue); a picture of the royal family (1.2, s.d.); two seats (1.2, 2.6, implicit); a table (1.2, 3.1, s.d.); a hedge bill (2.1, s.d.); seating for four characters (2.6, 3.1, implicit); a shepherd's crook (2.6, s.d.); a seat (2.8, implicit); an execution block (3.9, s.d.); a woman's severed head in a bloody basin (3.25, s.d.); a digging tool (4.11, implicit); a hearse covered with velvet (5.6, s.d.)
Scenery: a curtain (1.2, 2.1, 4.10, 4.13, s.d.); a bar covered with black (5.6, s.d.); a throne (5.6, s.d.)
Miscellaneous: water (1.1, s.d.; runs out of Musidorus' mouth); smoke (1.1, s.d.); blood (4.15, s.d.; on Musidorus' sword)

COSTUMES AND MAKE-UP
MUSIDORUS: wet (1.1, s.d.); a helmet (1.3, s.d.; falls off on stage); 'clothed like the sun' (1.5, dialogue); a hunting habit (1.6–7, s.d.); a shepherd's habit (2.5, dialogue; 2.6, implicit); black armour (3.7–8, implicit); rags (5.5, dialogue); fine clothes (5.6, implicit; probably the same costume as in 1.5)
PYROCLES: has no beard (dialogue); a helmet (1.3, s.d.; removed on stage); a pilgrim's habit (1.4, dialogue); 'clothed like the sun' (1.5, dialogue); a hunting habit (1.6–7, s.d.); cross-dressed as an Amazon (2.1, s.d.; 2.5–8, 3.1, 3.25, 4.1, 4.3–8, implicit); a scabbard (2.1, implicit); a veil (2.6, dialogue); a hood (3.1, s.d.; put on on stage); a mantle (4.8, s.d.; removed on stage); man's clothing (4.10, s.d.; 4.13, implicit), including a codpiece (dialogue); richly clad, with jewels (5.6, dialogue; probably the same costume as in 1.5)
KALANDER: grey hair (dialogue); a hunting habit (1.6–7, s.d.)
SOLDIERS: rusty armour (1.3, s.d.)
PRISONERS: chains (1.3, s.d.; removed on stage)
CLYTOPHON: a hunting habit (1.6–7, s.d.)
DAMETAS: shoes (4.7, dialogue); chains (5.4, s.d.)
PAMELA: a cypress veil (2.1, 2.8, dialogue); a hood (3.1, s.d.; put on on stage)
PHILOCLEA: a hood (3.1, s.d.; put on on stage)
MAIDS: shepherdesses' habits, with laurel crowns (3.1, s.d.)
AMPHIALUS: bandages (3.26, s.d.)
SOLDIERS: bloody (3.6, s.d.; 3.7, implicit)
PHILANAX: chains (3.9, s.d.)
ZOILUS: a scabbard (4.3, implicit)
MESSENGER: a scabbard (3.26, implicit)

2484. News of Plymouth

EARLY TEXTUAL HISTORY
1630s (?): transcribed in **MS**, probably by the author; 24 leaves; list of roles; epigraphic couplet.
　1640s–50s: MS was apparently in the possession of the former actor William Cartwright.

EDITIONS
Felicina Rota, in *L'Arcadia di Sidney e il Teatro*, Biblioteca di Studi Inglesi 6 (Bari, 1966), 193–379.
John P. Cutts, North American Mentor Texts and Studies 2 (Fennimore, Wisconsin, 1974).

REFERENCES
Annals 1635; Beal SiP 111, 117, 120; Beal Online SiP 168.3; Bentley, v. 1367; Martin Garrett (ed.), *Sidney: The Critical Heritage* (London and New York, 1996), 204–7; Hazlitt, 141.

2484. News of Plymouth

TEXT
Printed in 1673 (Wing D320); the text may have been altered from the play as first written in the 1630s. A variant version of the epilogue was printed in 1638 (STC 6304).

GENRE
comedy
Contemporary: play (prol., ep.); vacation play (*Madagascar*)

TITLE
Performed: News of Plymouth
Printed: News from Plymouth

AUTHOR
William Davenant

DATE
August 1635

ORIGINAL PRODUCTION
King's Men at the Globe, and perhaps also the Blackfriars

PLOT
Three sea-captains, Seawit, Topsail, and Cable, are stranded in Plymouth by a contrary wind. Hearing that the rich young Lady Loveright is a guest in the rich young Widow Carrack's house, Topsail and Cable set their amorous sights on her. Topsail decides that the way to win the lady is to cultivate her uncle, Sir Solemn Trifle, but this means that he has to endure the knight's ultra-boring conversation. Cable finds himself targeted by the widow, and rebuffs her with the claim that he is not disposed to marry. He hears of a visiting lady from London and goes off to seek her favours; but she insists on marriage before sex (and, in any event, she is Carrack in disguise), so he goes away unsatisfied.
　Topsail finds that Trifle has been so busy sending out fabricated pro-Protestant news to the Continent that he has done nothing to help woo his niece; he is further told that Lady Loveright holds her uncle in low esteem anyway. In revenge, he gives Trifle a scare and makes it seem as if he is about to be arrested for treason in connection with his newsletters. Cable finds himself sought by creditors, and realizes that he will have to marry Carrack for her money.
　Lady Loveright is more interested in Seawit. Her kinswoman, Jointure, sets out to cross the supposed match and win him for herself. He believes the ladies are mocking him, and is also infuriated to find that one of Loveright's other suitors, Warwell, is eavesdropping on their meeting. A duel is only prevented when news arrives that the wind has changed. Loveright resolves to stop playing hard-to-get and offers herself to Seawit in marriage. Carrack agrees to pay Cable's debts if he marries her. Topsail remains unclaimed, and is left with only the honour to be won by feats of valour at sea.

SCENE DESIGNATION
prol., 1.1–2, 2.1–4, 3.1–5, 4.1–5, 5.1–5, ep. (F has act-division, but discontinues scene-division after 2.2)

ROLES
PROLOGUE
Captain SEAWIT, a sailor
Captain TOPSAIL, a sailor
Captain CABLE, a sailor
Widow CARRACK, a rich young woman
A PORTER, a married man; formerly a collector for the poor
SMOOTHALL, Carrack's maid
Sir Solemn TRIFLE, a knight and Justice of the Peace; Loveright's uncle; also called Sir Trifle
Lady LOVERIGHT, an earl's daughter, Trifle's niece, Jointure's kinswoman; also called Madam Marchpane
Mistress JOINTURE, Loveright's kinswoman
Mistress NIGHTINGALE, Loveright's waiting-woman; also called Mistress Magpie
The BOATSWAIN on Seawit's ship (2.4, 5.5)
Sir Furious INLAND, a young Staffordshire knight and landowner
Sir Studious WARWELL, a gentleman, Loveright's admirer
Hans van BUMBLE, a Dutch skipper; also called Captain Bumble
SAILORS, one of them named Houndsfoot (3.1, *non-speaking*)
MUSICIANS (3.3; one or more sing)
A DUTCH BOATSWAIN on Bumble's ship (4.1)
DASH, Trifle's clerk
SCARECROW, an intelligencer, Trifle's client
ZEAL, an intelligencer, Trifle's client
PRATTLE, an intelligencer, Trifle's client

SERVANTS who bring a banquet (4.3, *non-speaking*)
An ENGLISH SKIPPER on Bumble's ship (4.4, 5.3)

Speaking Parts: 22

Stage Directions and Speech Prefixes
PROLOGUE: *Prologue* (heading)
SEAWIT: *Seawit* (s.d.s and s.p.s); *Seawit,* [one of the] *Sea-Captains* (d.p.)
TOPSAIL: *Topsaile | Topsail* (s.d.s and s.p.s); *Topsal* (s.p.s); *Topsaile,* [one of the] *Sea-Captains* (d.p.)
CABLE: *Cable* (s.d.s and s.p.s); *Cable,* [one of the] *Sea-Captains* (d.p.)
CARRACK: *Carack | Carracke* | [one of] *the Women* (s.d.s); *Carrack* (s.d.s and s.p.s); *Carracks | Carrak* (s.p.s); *Carrack, A Rich Widow* (d.p.)
PORTER: *a Porter* (s.d.s); *Porter* (s.d.s, s.p.s, and d.p.)
SMOOTHALL: *Smoothall* (s.d.s and s.p.s); *Smoothall,* [*Carrack's*] *Maid* (d.p.)
TRIFLE: *Sir Solemne Trifle* (s.d.s); *Trifle* (s.d.s and s.p.s); *Sir Solemne Trifle A Foolish old Knight* (d.p.)
LOVERIGHT: *Loveright* (s.d.s and s.p.s); [one of] *the Ladies |* [one of] *the Women* (s.d.s); *Lady Loveright, Niece to Trifle* (d.p.)
JOINTURE: *Jointure | Joynture* (s.d.s and s.p.s); [one of] *the Ladies |* [one of] *the Women* (s.d.s); *Mrs Joynture, Cousin to Loveright* (d.p.)
NIGHTINGALE: *Loveright's Woman |* [one of] *the Women* (s.d.s); *Nightingale | Woman* (s.d.s and s.p.s); *Nightingale, Loveright's Waiting-woman* (d.p.)
BOATSWAIN: *Boatswain* (s.d.s, s.p.s, and d.p.)
INLAND: *Sir Furious Inland | Sir Furious* (s.d.s); *Inland | Furious* (s.d.s and s.p.s); *Sir Furious Inland A Country Knight* (d.p.)
WARWELL: *Warwell | Warwel* (s.d.s and s.p.s); *Wurwell, A Gentleman Servant to Loveright* (d.p.; *sic*)
BUMBLE: *Bumble* (s.d.s and s.p.s); *Bumble A Dutch Captain* (d.p.)
SAILORS: *Sailors* (s.d.s and d.p.s)
MUSICIANS: *Musicians* (s.d.s)
DUTCH BOATSWAIN: *Dutch Boatswain* (s.d.s); *Boatswain* (s.d.s and s.p.s)
DASH: *Dash* ([*Trifle's*] *Clerk*) (s.d.s); *Dash* (s.d.s and s.p.s); *Dash, Clerk to Trifle* (d.p.)
SCARECROW: *Scarcrow* (s.d.s); *Scarr<crow>* (s.p.s); *Scarcrow,* [one of the] *Intelligencers* (d.p.)
ZEAL: *Zeale* (s.d.s and s.p.s); *Zeale,* [one of the] *Intelligencers* (d.p.)
PRATTLE: *Pratle* (s.d.s); *Prattle* (s.d.s and s.p.s); *Prattle,* [one of the] *Intelligencers* (d.p.)
ENGLISH SKIPPER: *an English Skipper | English-Skipper* (s.d.s); *Skipper | Eng<lish> Skipper* (s.p.s)

OTHER CHARACTERS
Cable's purser (1.1)
Moneylenders in Plymouth (1.1)
Cable's boatswain (1.1)
Cable's girlfriend (1.1; possibly imaginary)
Biscay matrons left in Plymouth by the Spaniards in 1588 (1.1)
The hostess of the Hoop (1.1)
The hostess's daughter, who tried to cadge an old sail to make herself some modest underwear (1.1)
A wise woman who advised Carrack about the flatteries gold attracts (1.2)
A farmer, Smoothall's father (1.2)
Lady Loveright's dead grandmother (1.2)
The Earl, Lady Loveright's father, a former soldier (1.2, 2.1, 3.4)
Goody Smoothall, Smoothall's mother (1.2)
The King, who cured Inland of scrofula (1.2, 2.4, 3.1, 3.3–4, 4.1, 5.1, 5.3, 5.5)
Trifle's fellow justices (1.2)
Carrack's dead husband, a sea-captain (1.2, 2.3, 5.1, 5.5)
Captain Carrack's ship-boys, sailors, and boatswain, all of them well acquainted with the lash (1.2)
An admiral and his mistress, Carrack's guests at her house in Portsmouth (1.2)
Trifle's scrivener (1.2)
Topsail's uncle (2.1)
Inland's kinsmen, who placed him with Seawit (2.1)
Lady Loveright's mother (2.1)
Trifle's stationer (2.2, 3.3)
Topsail's sailors and ship-boys (2.2, 3.3)
A glazier sent for to fix a broken window at Carrack's house (2.3)
Carrack's baker (2.3)
Seawit's officers and sailors, including the ship-master, purser, gunner, and gunner's mate (2.4)
A man who asked Inland the time in the street, and got beaten up for it (2.4)
Inland's father (3.1)
The Porter's wife (3.2)
Seawit's old aunt, from whom he has modest expectations (3.5)
The Mayor of Plymouth (3.5)
A merchant to whom Trifle has sent libellous gossip about Seawit (4.2, 5.3)
Scarecrow's correspondents, including a man in Geneva and a Fleming (4.2)
Cable's mother (4.3)
Cable's creditors (5.1)
Gregory Thimble, one of Cable's creditors (5.1)
Thimble's wife and children (5.1)
The sergeants of London, who know Cable inconveniently well (5.1)
An apprentice sent by one of Cable's creditors to find him in Plymouth (5.1)
Inland's falconers, huntsmen, and women (5.2)
Inland's tenants (5.5)
The Admiral of the fleet (5.5)

SETTING
Period: contemporary; the action takes place during the summer vacation, after 5 July

Time-Scheme: 1.2 ends at dinner-time; 3.3 takes place in the morning, and 4.1 later the same day (which is not a Sunday); an hour passes between 4.1 and 5.2
Place: Plymouth

Geography
Plymouth: the High Street; the Hoop tavern
London: Cheapside; St Antholin's; the Pickt Hatch; Paris Garden; Smithfield; Rotherhithe; the Exchange; Kent Street; Bedlam; Fleet Ditch
Staffordshire: Stafford
England: Essex; Portsmouth (but this may be a misprint for Plymouth)
The Low Countries: Brabant; Bouillon; Delft; Holland; Flanders; Breda; Amsterdam; Antwerp; Brussels; Louvain; the Hague
France: Boulogne; Orange; La Rochelle
[Germany]: Saxony; Hamburg
Spain: Biscay; Bilbao; Gibraltar; Cadiz
Italy: Genoa; Rome; Florence
Switzerland: Geneva
Europe: Greece; Portugal; Norway
[Africa]: Libya; Barbary
[The Middle East]: Jerusalem; Turkey; Persia
China
Amboyna
Brazil

SOURCES
Narrative: Ben Jonson, *Volpone* (**1493**; Trifle, 5.3), *The Alchemist* (**1621**; Inland); William Davenant, *Love and Honour* (**2453**; 5.5)
Verbal: Ben Jonson, *The Alchemist* (**1621**; 3.4, 4.2)
Works Mentioned: Galen, *De alimentorum facultatibus* (3.3); *The Tale of Troy* (i.e. John Lydgate's *Troy Book*?, 1420; 3.4); Diego Ortúñez de Calahorra, Pedro de la Sierra, and Marcos Martínez, *Espejo de principes y caballeros* (1555–87; English tr., *The Mirror of Princely Deeds and Knighthood*, by Margaret Tyler, R. P., and L. A., 1578–99; 3.1); William Wisdom, *Metres* (unidentified; 3.4); also a general reference to Ovid (2.1)

The debt to *Love and Honour* lies in the denouement: Davenant recycles the ending in which two of the three suitors end up with brides and the third, like Topsail, is left unmarried to pursue further martial glory.

LANGUAGE
English
Latin: 9 words (1.2, 2.1, 3.3–4, 5.1; Carrack, Seawit, Trifle, Loveright, Cable)
French: 4 words (3.3, 5.1, 5.5; Topsail, Cable, Seawit)
Dutch: 231 words (3.1, 4.1, 4.4, 5.2; Bumble, Dutch Boatswain, Seawit, English Skipper)
Dialect: Bumble speaks English throughout in a heavy 'Dutch' accent.

FORM
Metre: rough pentameter; a little prose
Rhyme: blank verse
Prologue: 14 lines, in couplets
Act-Division: 5 acts
Epilogue: 12 lines, in couplets, spoken by Inland
Lines (Spoken): 2,512 (2,371 verse, 141 prose)
Lines (Written): 3,834

STAGING
Doors: characters exit several ways (2.3, 4.5, s.d.)
Discovery Space: curtained (4.2, s.d.); Trifle is discovered in his study (4.2, s.d.)
Within: speech (5.3, s.d.)
Audience: called 'a noble company' (prol.); addressed as 'dear hearts' (ep.; 'poor souls' in the variant version); presumed to include both men and women (ep.), with both 'rich gaudy sirs' and men of judgement among the former (prol.)

MUSIC
Music: unspecified music (4.3, s.d.)
On-Stage Music: Musicians accompany Song 1 (3.3, implicit)
Songs:
  1: 'O thou that sleepst like pig in straw', 3.3, Topsail, 24 lines, with musical accompaniment;
  2: 'Thrice happy he who, cares laid by', 4.3, 18 lines.

PROPS
Lighting: a taper (4.2, s.d.)
Weapons: Seawit's sword (4.5, implicit; 5.5, s.d.); Warwell's sword (5.5, dialogue); Inland's sword (5.5, ep., dialogue)
Musical Instruments: unspecified instruments (3.3, implicit); a bell (4.2, s.d.)
Clothing: Topsail's glove (3.3, dialogue); Cable's glove (3.3, dialogue)
Money: coins (3.1, dialogue)
Food and Drink: cans of liquor (3.1, s.d.; drunk on stage; one of the cans is broken over Inland's head); a banquet (4.3, s.d.), including a glass of wine (dialogue; drunk on stage)
Small Portable Objects: a table-book (2.2, s.d.); a paper (3.2, implicit); a letter (3.3, dialogue); a letter (4.1, dialogue); papers (4.2, s.d.); a seal and sealing-wax (4.2, s.d.); a letter (4.2, dialogue); a paper (4.5, s.d.); letters (5.1, s.d.)
Large Portable Objects: a chair (3.3, s.d.); a desk (4.2, implicit)
Scenery: a curtain (4.2, s.d.); hangings (4.5, s.d.)

COSTUMES
SEAWIT: in his shirt (5.5, s.d.); hangers (5.5, implicit)
CABLE: is fat and bearded (dialogue); typically wears a buff jerkin (dialogue); a garment with pockets (1.1, dialogue; may be a figure of speech); a feather (5.1, dialogue; presumably in his hat)
CARRACK: sexy clothes, including a gown, a silk stocking, and shoes with roses (3.2, dialogue)

PORTER: disguised (3.2, 4.3, dialogue; 4.1, implicit); disguised as a pursuivant (5.3, s.d.)
TRIFLE: a beard (dialogue)
WARWELL: a garment with pockets (3.4, dialogue); in his shirt (5.5, s.d.)
BUMBLE: a beard (dialogue); long slops (3.1, dialogue)

EARLY STAGE HISTORY
1635: presumably performed by the King's Men at the Globe, as licensed, probably during the summer vacation (whose last day was Monday 28 September).
1641: The play was in the repertory of the King's Men, by now entitled *News from Plymouth*.

EARLY TEXTUAL HISTORY
1635: On Saturday 1 August, Sir Henry Herbert licensed the play for performance.
1638: On Monday 26 February, Matthew Clay granted an imprimatur to William Davenant's *Madagascar and Other Poems*.
1638: Davenant's *Madagascar* entered in the Stationers' Register to Thomas Walkley on Tuesday 13 March.
1638: epilogue included in Davenant's *Madagascar and Other Poems*, sig. F10^v; printed by John Haviland for Thomas Walkley.
1641: On Saturday 7 August, Robert Devereux, 3rd Earl of Essex (Lord Chamberlain) issued a warrant prohibiting the printing of this and sixty other plays without the consent of the King's Men. On Saturday 14 August, the order was read to the Stationers' Company and instructions issued for its observance.
1646: entered to Humphrey Robinson and Humphrey Moseley in the Stationers' Register between Friday 4 and Tuesday 15 September; group entry, play and author individually named. John Langley had licensed the book for publication.
1648: Walkley's rights to *Madagascar and Other Poems* transferred in the Stationers' Register to Humphrey Moseley on Tuesday 22 February.
1648: *Madagascar and Other Poems* reprinted for Humphrey Moseley; the epilogue now appears on sig. F1^r.
1656: Song 1 included in John Phillips's *Wit and Drollery*, sig. L3^v; printed (in or before mid-January) for Nathaniel Brooke.
1656: *Wit and Drollery* entered in the Stationers' Register to Nathaniel Brooke on Wednesday 30 January.
1656–60: Humphrey Moseley included the play on a list of books he intended to print in the near future.
1661: *Wit and Drollery* reprinted for Nathaniel Brooke.
1672: Moseley's rights transferred in the Stationers' Register by his widow, Ann, to Henry Herringman on Monday 14 October, by an assignment dated Thursday 26 September; individually named as part of a group transfer of four Davenant plays.
1672: Davenant's *Works* entered to Henry Herringman in the Stationers' Register on Thursday 31 October. Roger L'Estrange had licensed the book for the press. On Monday 18 November, it was advertised for sale by Henry Herringman, John Martin, John Starkey, and Robert Horne; however, it was apparently not issued until the following year.
1673: Robinson's rights transferred in the Stationers' Register by his executor (also named Humphrey Robinson) to John Martin and Henry Herringman on Thursday 30 January, as part of a list of 105 titles, by assignment of Saturday 13 May 1671.
1673: included in Davenant's *Works* (F), sigs. ^{2}4A1^r–^{2}4E1^r, 33 pages on 17 leaves; printed for Henry Herringman by an unidentified printer; list of roles. The volume also includes the epilogue as a separate item on sig. 2H4^r, in a part of the book printed by Thomas Newcomb.
1675: Davenant's *Works* advertised as for sale by John Starkey.
1683: Martin's rights transferred in the Stationers' Register from his widow, Sarah, to Robert Scott, on Tuesday 21 August, by assignment of Tuesday 14 June 1681 and order of a court of Monday 7 November 1681; individually named as part of a group transfer of 360 titles.

EDITION
James Maidment and W. H. Logan, in *The Dramatic Works of Sir William D'Avenant*, Dramatists of the Restoration (Edinburgh and London, 1872–4), iv. 105–99.

REFERENCES
Annals 1635; Arber, iv. 41; Bawcutt 323; Bentley, iii. 209–11; Sir William Davenant, *The Shorter Poems and Songs from the Plays and Masques*, ed. A. M. Gibbs (Oxford, 1972), 127, 288; Eyre & Rivington, i. 290, ii. 27; Greg 831; Hazlitt, 166; MSC 1.4–5, 364–9; *RES* 16 (1940), 436.

2485. Pastoral (possibly not a Catalogue item)

EVIDENCE
Debenture accounts of Queen Henrietta Maria (Kew: National Archives, LR 5/66); Venetian diplomatic correspondence (Anzolo Correr to the Doge Francesco Erizzo and the Senate, 31 August 1635 Gregorian).

GENRE
pastoral
Contemporary: comedy (Gentile's bill); pastoral (Knight's bill)

TITLE
Later Assigned: *The Pastoral at Oatlands*

2486. Court Masque at Oatlands Palace

DATE
August 1635

ORIGINAL PRODUCTION
Queen Henrietta Maria's Court at Oatlands Palace, Surrey

COSTUMES
Jeffery Hudson's character wore a suit decorated with white copper lace. Mrs La Bredache's character wore a suit decorated with white and yellow copper lace and white copper lace 'O's (spangles). Four characters wore beaver hats with gold and silver bands.

EARLY STAGE HISTORY
Preparation: On Thursday 30 July 1635, the embroiderer Charles Gentile supplied lace.
  Performance: performed at Oatlands on Sunday 2 August 1635. The cast included: Jeffery Hudson; four ladies, one of whom may have been Mrs La Bredache.

Production Expenses
Payments for costumes from the Queen's Purse amounted to £10.10s, with a saving of £5 made by unilaterally reducing the tradesmen's bills. On Saturday 19 March 1636, the haberdasher Arthur Knight's bill was paid, including £2.10s (10s less than billed) for the supply of hats used in the pastoral, and for two journeys to Oatlands to deliver them. On the same day, Charles Gentile's bill was paid for embroidering Jeffery Hudson's costume (£3, £1 less than billed) and Mrs La Bredache's costume (£5, 10s less than billed); a further sum of £3, in respect of Mrs La Bredache's costume, was disallowed.

REFERENCES
Butler, 374; *Cal. Ven. 1632–6*, 445; *ELR* 19 (1999), 79; Steele, 252–3.

2486. Court Masque at Oatlands Palace

EVIDENCE
Debenture accounts of Queen Henrietta Maria (Kew: National Archives, LR 5/66).

The four documents relating to costumes for performances at Oatlands in August 1635 refer variously to a comedy, a pastoral, and a masque. Unless the tradesmen's terminology was inexact, this indicates two distinct dramatic works. Pastoral and comedy can readily define a single work; but, although in the mid-1630s 'masque' was being used in respect of plays (notably *Love's Mistress*, **2451**), it is also true that a discrete masque might be staged as an afterpiece to a separate play—the masques that followed *Artenice* in 1626 (**2177**) and *Florimène* in 1635 (**2522**) are cases in point. It is therefore safest to treat the records of a masque and those of a pastoral or comedy (**2485**) as relating to two potentially distinct works, with the caveat that they might in fact have been one and the same. It may or may not be significant that the two bills relating to a comedy or pastoral were both paid on 19 March, and the two relating to a masque were both paid on 22 March.

GENRE
masque
Contemporary: masque

DATE
August 1635

ORIGINAL PRODUCTION
Queen Henrietta Maria's Court at Oatlands Palace, Surrey

ROLES
Eight female MASQUERS
A DWARF or child

COSTUMES
MASQUERS: fine silk stockings
DWARF: a carnation calico suit with bases

EARLY STAGE HISTORY
Preparation: On Wednesday 29 July, the tailor Gilbert Morette made a masquing suit for Jeffery Hudson.
  Performance: by Queen Henrietta Maria's court at Oatlands Palace in August 1635, possibly on Sunday 2. The cast included Jeffery Hudson (Dwarf or Child).

Production Expenses
Payments for costumes from the Queen's Purse amounted to £13.10s.6d, with a saving of £1.4s made by unilaterally reducing the tradesmen's bills. On Tuesday 22 March 1636, Gilbert Morette was paid £1.10s.6d for making Hudson's suit. On the same day, Thomas Robinson was paid £12 for supplying stockings (£1.4s less than billed).

REFERENCES
Butler, 374.

2487. The Prisoners

TEXT
Printed in 1640–1 (Wing K452), probably from authorial papers; two place names are censored in 2.3 and 5.3. A revised version (not documented here) was printed in 1663–4 (Wing K450).

GENRE
tragicomedy
Contemporary: tragedy (S.R.); tragicomedy (t.p.); play (1641 comm. verses)

2487. The Prisoners

TITLE
Printed: *The Prisoners*
Contemporary: *The Prisoner*

AUTHOR
Thomas Killigrew

DATE
Limits: 1632–5
Best Guess: 1635

The limits are defined by the publication of the source in France and Killigrew's departure from England in October 1635. (The play was, therefore, written before the publication of the source's English translation in 1636.) The best guess adopted here is the *Annals* date, which places the play close to the rest of Killigrew's mid-1630s burst of play-writing; the most sustained study of the play, by Eleanor Collins (in Major), dates it a few years earlier, to c. 1633, but does not say why. The avoidance of naming the King's territory may reflect the acting company's caution over aristocratic names in the wake of their troubles over *The Ball* (**2389**); but this lasted at least until the time Killigrew left England, as is apparent in the vagueness over the Lord's identity in *The Lady of Pleasure* (**2515**).

ORIGINAL PRODUCTION
Queen Henrietta's Men at the Cockpit

PLOT
Sardinia's constitution seeks to avoid the hazards of ambition that go with monarchy by vesting power in two officials, a priest and a judge chosen by lot rather than by faction. Before the start of the action, the priest Memnon and the judge Theagines wanted to send their sons abroad to learn the art of government; but since this was illegal, Memnon invented an oracle exempting himself and Theagines from the restriction. Everything went wrong: the sons were lost overseas, the oracle itself denounced Memnon, and both fathers were banished, leaving their daughters Eucratia and Lucanthe as the effective rulers of the island.

The King approaches the Sardinians for military aid against his enemies, but the island's laws forbid the people to take up arms except in self-defence, and they are obliged to refuse. He takes offence and musters a punitive expedition against them. His sister Cecilia is captured by the pirate Gallippus, but rescued by the slave Pausanes and his supposed brother Hipparchus. When the King intervenes, the two slaves are taken prisoner, but Cecilia persuades him to release them into her custody rather than send them to the galleys. Gallippus escapes and offers his services to the Sardinians.

Cecilia realizes that she is attracted to Pausanes, and sends the two slaves to join the King's army; she later disguises herself as a boy and follows them. After a battle, the King is victorious over Sardinia, and Eucratia surrenders, but Gallippus abducts Lucanthe, sails away, and attempts to rape her; she is saved when the ship is caught in a tempest. The King gives chase, but his ship too encounters the storm. Both groups are forced to abandon their respective ships and go ashore, where they gravitate towards a fire lit by the local hermit. Hipparchus rescues Lucanthe, but is wounded in the fight. Theagines, who has also been shipwrecked and is living with the hermit, heals Hipparchus and realizes that Lucanthe is his daughter. Cecilia is found unconscious and the hermit cures her. It emerges that Pausanes and Hipparchus are not brothers but cousins, the sons of Theagines and Memnon. It was Gallippus who was responsible for their disappearance: he captured them, enslaved them, and killed their guardian, taking from him the evidence of their identity, two gold medals that he still wears around his neck. The hermit reveals that he is Memnon: the scattered families are reunited.

SCENE DESIGNATION
1.1–5, 2.1–3, 3.1–8, 4.1–4, 5.1–3 (D, corrected and completed)

D omits scene headings for 1.3 and 3.6–8.
  The stage is not clear at 1.4–5.

ROLES
The KING of a Mediterranean island (presumably Sicily or Corsica), Cecilia's brother
SORTANES, the King's courtier
EUMENES, the King's courtier
CLEON, the King's courtier
CECILIA, the King's sister; Killigrew may have originally named, or intended to rename, her Lissemella (or Lyssimella)
PHILON, a kinsman of Cecilia (and presumably of the King)
EUGENE, a beautiful woman accompanying Cecilia
Three SOLDIERS accompanying Cecilia (1.2, non-speaking)
PIRATE SOLDIERS following Gallippus (1.2–3, 1.5; only speak collectively and *within*)
GALLIPPUS, a pirate captain
HIPPARCHUS, Gallippus' slave, a young man; supposed Pausanes' brother, but actually his cousin, Memnon's son, Eucratia's brother, Theagines' nephew
PAUSANES, Gallippus' slave; a young man; supposed Hipparchus' brother, but actually his cousin, Theagines' son, Lucanthe's brother, Memnon's nephew
Gallippus' SLAVE (1.4, *non-speaking*)
ZENON, a Sardinian pirate; his real name is Pelius
The KING'S SOLDIERS (1.5, 3.4, 3.8; only speak collectively and *within*)
A GUARD attending the King (2.1, *non-speaking*)
EUCRATIA, Princess of Sardinia; also called the Queen; said to be Lucanthe's sister, but actually her cousin, Memnon's daughter, Hipparchus' sister, Theagines' niece
Princess LUCANTHE of Sardinia; said to be Eucratia's sister, but actually her cousin, Theagines' daughter, Pausanes' sister, Memnon's niece
DION, a Sardinian courtier

CREMNOFIELD, a Sardinian courtier
PROCLES, an old common soldier in the King's army
A SOLDIER, who reports the abduction of Lucanthe (3.8)
An old HERMIT, a father; turns out to be Memnon, the Priest of Sardinia, Theagines' brother, father of Eucratia and Hipparchus, uncle of Lucanthe and Pausanes
The HERMIT'S SON (4.2, 5.3)
THEAGINES, the Judge of Sardinia, Memnon's brother, father of Lucanthe and Pausanes, uncle of Eucratia and Hipparchus
Gallippus' three SLAVES (4.3; one speaks individually, the others collectively)
The HELMSMAN of Gallippus' ship, the *Pluto* (4.3)
The MASTER of the *Pluto* (4.3)
A SAILOR aboard the *Pluto* (4.3, *within*)
The HELMSMAN of the King's galley (4.4)
The BOATSWAIN of the King's galley (4.4)

Killigrew did in fact rename the character of Cecilia in the 1663–4 version of the text; the alternate name appears only once in the 1640–1 printing (in the first stage direction of 4.1). It is possible that he named the character after Cecilia Crofts (died 1638), in whom he was interested at the time of writing, and momentarily had second thoughts in 1640 when he was her widower. Alternatively, he may have systematically made the opposite change to honour her memory, but reverted to the original name in the 1660s, when he was married to his second wife, Charlotte.

The family relationship of the Hermit's Son to Memnon's children and in-laws is undefined in the play.

Speaking Parts: 28

Stage Directions and Speech Prefixes
KING: *King* (s.d.s and s.p.s); *the King* (s.d.s); *King of ——* (d.p.)
SORTANES: *Sortanes* | *Certanes* | *Sor<tanes>* (s.p.s); *Sortanes Of the King's party* (d.p.)
EUMENES: *Eumenes* | *Eum<enes>* (s.p.s; also misprinted *Em.*); *Eumenes,* [one of] *Two Nobles* (d.p.)
CLEON: *Cleon* (s.d.s); *Cle<on>* (s.p.s); *Cleon,* [one of] *Two Nobles* (d.p.)
CECILIA: *Cecillia* | *Cecilla* | *Lissemella* | *Cicillia* (s.d.s); *Cecill<ia>* | *Cicil<lia>* (s.p.s); *Cecilia, Sister to the King* (d.p.)
PHILON: *Philon* (s.d.s); *Phil<on>* (s.p.s); *Philon, Kinsman to Cecilia* (d.p.)
EUGENE: *Eugene* (s.d.s); *Eu<gene>* (s.p.s); *Eugene Of the King's party* (d.p.)
SOLDIERS: *three Soldiers* | [*Philon's*] *party* (s.d.s)
PIRATE SOLDIERS: *Soldiers* (s.d.s)
GALLIPPUS: *Gilipus* | *Gallippus* | *Gillippus* (s.d.s); *Gill<ippus>* | *Gall<ippus>* (s.p.s); *Gilippus, Captain of the Pirates* (d.p.)
HIPPARCHUS: *Hiparcus* | *Hipparchus* | *Hiparchus* | [one of] *The slaves* | *Hipercus* (s.d.s); *Hip<parchus>* | *Hyp<archus>* (s.p.s); *Hipparchus,* [one of] *The Prisoners, son to Theagines* (d.p.)

PAUSANES: *Pausanes* | [one of] *The slaves* (s.d.s); *Paus<anes>* (s.p.s); *Pausanes,* [one of] *The Prisoners, son to Memnon* (d.p.)
SLAVE: *a slave* (s.d.s); [one of] *Four Slaves* (d.p.)
ZENON: *Zenon* (s.d.s); *Zen<on>* (s.p.s); *Zenon, a Gentleman of Lucanthe's party* (d.p.)
KING'S SOLDIERS: *Soldiers* | *the King's party* (s.d.s)
GUARD: *a Guard* (s.d.s)
EUCRATIA: *Eucratia* (s.d.s); *Eucra<tia>* (s.p.s); *Eucratia, Daughter to Memnon, beloved of the King* (d.p.)
LUCANTHE: *Lucanthe* (s.d.s); *Lucan<the>* (s.p.s); *Lucanthe Daughter to Theagines* (d.p.)
DION: *Dion* (s.d.s and s.p.s); *Dion* [one of] *Two Sardinian Commanders* (d.p.)
CREMNOFIELD: *Cremnofield* (s.d.s); *Crem<nofield>* (s.p.s); *Cremnofeild* [one of] *Two Sardinian Commanders* (d.p.)
PROCLES: *Procles* (s.d.s); *Proc<les>* (s.p.s); *Procles a common Soldier* (d.p.)
SOLDIER: *a Soldier* (s.d.s); *Soldier* (s.p.s)
HERMIT: *a Hermit* | *the Hermit* (s.d.s); *Hermit* (s.d.s and s.p.s); *Memnon the Priest, now the Hermit* (d.p.)
HERMIT'S SON: [the Hermit's] *Son* (s.d.s); *Son* (s.p.s)
THEAGINES: *an old man* | *The Judge* (s.d.s); *Judge* (s.d.s and s.p.s); *Theagines, judge of Sardinia* (d.p.)
SLAVES: *three slaves* | *the Slave* (s.d.s); *Slaves* (s.d.s and s.p.s); *Slave* (s.p.s); [three of] *Four Slaves* (d.p.)
HELMSMAN: *Helmsman* (s.p.s)
MASTER: *Master* (s.d.s and s.p.s)
SAILOR: *Within* (s.p.s)
HELMSMAN: *Helmsman* (s.p.s)
BOATSWAIN: *Boatswain* (s.d.s, s.p.s, and d.p.)

OTHER CHARACTERS
The captain of Eumenes' galley (1.1)
The King's slaves (1.1; possibly galley-slaves)
A slave of Cecilia's, sent to fetch help (1.2)
Perseus, Theagines' friend, guardian of Pausanes and Hipparchus, killed in battle by Gallippus (1.5, 4.2, 5.3)
Officers in the King's galleys (2.1)
The King's enemies in war (2.2)
The Sardinian Princesses' guard (3.2, 3.4)
Zenonia, a woman loved by both Zenon/Pelius and Eumenes (3.6)
Cecilia's dead mother (4.1)
The people of Sardinia (4.2)

SETTING
Period: antiquity (?)
Time-Scheme: 2.2 takes place late in the day, and 2.3 in the morning
Place: Sardinia and the Mediterranean

Geography
Rhodes
[*Mediterranean*]: The Rocks of Asilara (unidentified)

Tunis
The Indies

SOURCES
Narrative: Armand Desmarets de Saint-Sorlin, *Ariane* (1632)
Verbal: Heliodorus, *Aethiopica* (the names Theagines and Memnon); William Shakespeare, *Romeo and Juliet* (**987**; 3.8); John Webster, *The Duchess of Malfi* (**1726**; 5.3)
Works Mentioned: Bible: Exodus 20.1–17 (Ten Commandments; 4.1, oblique allusion)

LANGUAGE
English

FORM
Metre: rough pentameter
Rhyme: blank verse
Act-Division: 5 acts
Lines (Spoken): 1,721 (1,647 verse, 74 prose)
Lines (Written): 2,041

STAGING
Stage: mentioned (3.5, 4.2, s.d.)
Within: speech (1.2, 3.4, 3.8, 4.3–4, s.d.); music and song (2.3, implicit); groaning (4.3, s.d.)
Above: four characters appear above (5.2, s.d.)
Miscellaneous: Philon exits at the end of 1.2 and immediately re-enters at the start of 1.3. A fire is lit on stage (four lines from the end of 4.2), and apparently remains there until 5.3, even though the fictional location is elsewhere in the interim.

MUSIC AND SOUND
Sound Effects: storm (4.1–4, s.d.)
Music: lute within (2.3, dialogue; accompanying the song); alarums (3.1, 3.4, s.d.)
On-Stage Music: the Master whistles (4.3, s.d.)
Song: 'Fond Pausanes, let not thy love aspire', 2.3, Pausanes or Hipparchus within, 24 lines, with lute accompaniment

PROPS
Pyrotechnics: a fire (4.2, 5.3, s.d.; lit on stage)
Weapons: Pausanes' sword (1.3, dialogue; 1.4–5, 3.1, s.d.; 3.7, implicit); Hipparchus' sword (1.4–5, 3.8, 5.3, dialogue; 3.1, s.d.); Gallippus' sword (1.5, 4.3, implicit; 3.5, s.d.; 5.3, dialogue); Zenon's sword (1.5, implicit; 3.6, 3.8, dialogue); the King's sword (3.5, implicit; 3.8, s.d.); Eumenes' sword (3.6, implicit); Procles' sword (3.7, s.d.); King's Soldiers' swords (3.8, dialogue)
Musical Instruments: a whistle (4.3, implicit)
Clothing: a chain (2.3, s.d.); a ring (3.6, dialogue)
Food and Drink: 'strong water' (5.3, dialogue)
Small Portable Objects: binding cords (1.4–5, 2.1, implicit); a cabinet (2.3, s.d.); a rope (5.1, implicit); a balsam (5.3, dialogue)
Miscellaneous: blood (5.3, dialogue)

COSTUMES AND MAKE-UP
CECILIA: cross-dressed as a boy (4.1, s.d.; 5.3, implicit), including a doublet (dialogue); a loose robe (5.3, dialogue; put on on stage)
GALLIPPUS: a scabbard (1.5, implicit); wounded (3.6, dialogue); two golden medals around his neck (5.3, s.d.; removed on stage)
HIPPARCHUS: a scabbard (1.4–5, implicit); disguised as a common soldier (2.3, s.d.); wet clothes (5.3, dialogue)
PAUSANES: has no beard (dialogue); a scabbard (1.4–5, implicit); disguised as a common soldier (2.3, s.d.); wounded (3.3, 3.8, s.d.)
ZENON: a scabbard (1.5, 3.8, implicit)
LUCANTHE: wet clothes (5.3, dialogue)
PROCLES: silver hair (dialogue)
HERMIT: a priest's habit (4.2, dialogue)
THEAGINES: white hair (dialogue); a rich habit suggestive of a religious order (4.2, dialogue; it is wet; removed on stage); probably a grey coat (4.2, dialogue; put on on stage)

EARLY STAGE HISTORY
1632–6 (?): performed at the Cockpit by Queen Henrietta's Men.

EARLY TEXTUAL HISTORY
1640: entered (with *The Swaggering Damsel*, **2668**) in the Stationers' Register to Andrew Crooke on Thursday 2 April; entry names author and gives the title as *The Prisoner*. Thomas Wykes had licensed the book for publication.

1640–1: included in Thomas Killigrew's *Two Tragicomedies* ('**D**'), sigs. A3r–C11r, 65 pages on 33 leaves; printed by Thomas Cotes for Andrew Crooke; the play has a separate title page, which names author, acting company, and playhouse; list of roles. The other play in the collection was *Claracilla* (**2529**). The volume also contains commendatory verses, pertaining to both plays, by Henry Bennet, the author's nephew-in-law (in English), Robert Waring (in Latin), and William Cartwright (in Latin and English).

c. 1640s: a copy of D was in the possession of John Horne (Vicar of Headington, Oxfordshire). After his death, his entire collection of play-books passed into the possession of John Houghton of Brasenose College, Oxford (*c.* 1608–77), then to James Herne (died 1685), and then to the library of Ralph Sheldon (1623–84) at Weston, where it was catalogued by Anthony Wood, probably in the late 1670s.

1655: *The English Treasury of Wit and Language* entered in the Stationers' Register to Humphrey Moseley on Tuesday 16 January.

1655: two extracts (from 2.3, 4.2) included in John Cotgrave's *The English Treasury of Wit and Language*, sigs. F7r, S1r; printed for Humphrey Moseley.

1663: Killigrew's *Comedies and Tragedies* entered to Henry Herringman in the Stationers' Register on Saturday 24 October. Sir John Berkenhead had licensed the book for publication.

1663–4: included, in a revised text, in Killigrew's *Comedies and Tragedies* (²**F**), sigs. f4ʳ–k4ᵛ, 17 leaves; printed (by Thursday 28 January 1664) by John Macock for Henry Herringman; the play has an individual title page with a dedication to Lady [Catherine?] Crompton; list of roles. The book was issued in January 1664.

1664: F reissued, probably in May, with a cancel title page.

1665: an O edition of *The Prisoners* and *Claracilla* (**2529**) was advertised as printed by John Playfere.

1684: Nicholas Cox (Manciple of St Edmund Hall, Oxford) had a copy of F in his bookshop. It had probably been previously owned by Gerard Langbaine, and appears on a list compiled by Anthony Wood on Saturday 13 December.

c. 1690s: Song included in a MS commonplace book (Austin: University of Texas at Austin, MS (Killigrew, T) Works B Commonplace book, pp. 1–2).

Lady Crompton, the dedicatee of F, is described as the author's 'niece', but is likely to have been his great-niece by marriage. Among the sisters of his first wife, Cecilia Crofts, was Frances Crompton (d. 1661), who had many sons and at least two daughters. The daughters were either dead or married by 1663, but the only child of the eldest surviving son, Sir Robert Crompton (1613–69), was Catherine Crompton (d. 1669). Another of Cecilia's sisters, Anne Wentworth, was the mother of another 'niece' who received a dedication in F, Lady Anne Wentworth.

REFERENCES
Annals 1635; Beal Online KiT 10; Bentley, iv. 708–9; Bodleian, MS Wood E. 4, art. 1, p. 81; Eyre & Rivington, i. 463; Greg 619; Hazlitt, 185; Philip Major (ed.), *Thomas Killigrew and the Seventeenth-Century English Stage* (Farnham and Burlington, 2013), 21–44; *MLR* 13 (1918), 401–11; *PBSA* 107 (2013), 45–6; *PMLA* 51 (1936), 129; *SP* 40 (1943), 186–203.

2488. *Adrasta*

TEXT
Printed in 1635 (STC 14721).

GENRE
tragicomedy
Contemporary: play (ind., ded.); work (prol., ep.); tragicomedy (t.p.); poem (ded.)

TITLE
Printed: *Adrasta, or The Woman's Spleen and Love's Conquest*
Contemporary: *The Woman's Spleen and Love's Conquest*

AUTHOR
John Jones

DATE
1635

This is the only solid date associated with the play, that of publication. In the dedication, Jones says that the play was completed 'long since', and was then offered to and rejected by an acting company, so it may well have been written in an earlier year. Even so, it is a striking coincidence that this play contains a citizen tradesman whose name is, for no very good reason, Frailware, while another play of the first half of 1635, *The Sparagus Garden* (**2479**), features the owner of a china shop named Brittleware. If there is a connection, and if aptness of nomenclature defines originality, one might expect *Adrasta* to be the debtor play.

PLOT
Adrasta, Duchess of Florence, objects to the amours between her son Lucilio and Althea, a woman of lower rank. She forges a letter from Lucilio to Althea which describes a plan to murder the Duke; Althea's reply provides evidence to have her arrested for treason. Lucilio visits her in prison, convinces her that the original letter was a fake, and arranges her escape. Dressed in women's clothes, he takes her place in the cell, stands trial as her, and is sentenced to death. The substitution is discovered only just before the execution; Lucilio attempts to kill himself anyway, but is prevented by his friend Antonio. He leaves Florence, fearful of his parents' reprisals, and asks Antonio to assume his name and go to Greece, hoping that his father's agents will follow this false trail and so leave him in peace. Worried that he may yet take his own life, Antonio passes on the responsibility to the villainous servant Alastor, and shadows Lucilio in disguise.

Consulted by Adrasta, the witch Micale conjures up spirits, who locate Althea living as a shepherdess in the mountains and supply poison to dispose of her. Micale is magically transported there and tries to share food with her, but Althea is melancholy and only her friend Camilla will drink the poisoned wine. Micale's second strategy entails getting her to despair and kill herself, so she claims that both Lucilio and Althea's mother Julia have been executed. Camilla dies, and Althea covers her face with a scarf she was given by Lucilio. Shepherds find and bury her body, and show the scarf to Antonio, who infers that the dead girl is Althea and duly notifies Julia. Julia blames Lucilio for her daughter's death and hires Assassino to murder him. Assassino tracks Lucilio to the port where he is about to take ship for Greece, not knowing it is really Alastor whom he is following; he kills the supposed Prince and disposes of the body in the sea, but is arrested and sent back to Florence for trial. The corpse is later recovered, but is so decomposed that only the clothes are identifiable.

Assassino confesses, and implicates Julia in the hope of being spared himself. Antonio offers Julia his help to lie low, but plans to attend Assassino's execution with her in disguise. Althea goes to the place of execution, intending to throw herself off the rock and be reunited with Lucilio in death; but on the edge she sees the living Lucilio coming with the same intention. They are found together when Assassino is brought there for execution. The Duke and Duchess take them for vengeful ghosts, and beg their forgiveness. Once it emerges that they are alive, Assassino is reprieved and banished, since his true victim was a person of no account.

In the sub-plot, Ambrosia, wife of the city grocer Frailware, invites the philosopher Damasippus to her home. The messenger, Rigazzo, warns Frailware that his wife plans to cuckold him in his absence, so he interrupts the liaison by unexpectedly bringing Damasippus' wife Abigail to supper. Ambrosia hides Damasippus under the table, where he overhears the conversation between Abigail and Frailware: he makes advances and she consents, admitting that she has little love for her husband. Later Frailware takes further revenge by engaging a barber to pose as a devil and shave off Damasippus' beard.

SCENE DESIGNATION
ind., prol., 1.1–7, 2.1–4, 3.1–6, 4.1–5, 5.1–4, ep. (Q has act-division only; corrected)

Props remain on stage between 2.3 and 2.4.

ROLES
A GENTLEMAN, a member of the audience (ind.)
PROLOGUE
Signor ANTONIO, a courtier, Lucilio's friend
RIGAZZO, Lucilio's page; said to be little; also called Galateo; poses as Tigellinus, a fiddler
COSMO, Duke of Florence, Adrasta's husband, Lucilio's father; an old man
ADRASTA, Duchess of Florence, Cosmo's wife, Lucilio's mother
Lord LUCILIO, the Prince, son of Cosmo and Adrasta; poses as a poor husbandman
Lady JULIA, an old widow, Althea's mother
ALTHEA, a gentlewoman, Julia's daughter
ATTENDANTS on Cosmo (1.2, 2.4; one speaks)
Mistress AMBROSIA Frailware, Frailware's wife
ALASTOR, a court servant; also appears as a dead body
Mistress ABIGAIL, Damasippus' wife
Master FRAILWARE, a grocer and constable, Ambrosia's husband; said to be little
Frailware's MAN (2.1, non-speaking)
A SERVANT at court (2.3)
A PURSUIVANT at arms (2.4, non-speaking)
GUARDS at the trial and execution (2.4, 3.1, non-speaking)
Master DAMASIPPUS, a Stoic philosopher and university teacher, Abigail's husband
An EXECUTIONER (3.1)
A SERVANT at the execution (3.1)
MICALE, a witch, Sarvia's mother; poses as a shepherdess
SARVIA, a witch, Micale's daughter
ASSASSINO, a murderer
DEBORAH, Ambrosia's maid
Three SPIRITS, the first in the shape of a young gentlewoman and prostitute, the second in the shape of an old gentlewoman and vendor of sex aids, the third in male shape (3.6, non-speaking)
CAMILLA, Julia's waiting-woman
DAMON, a shepherd
ARMINIO, a shepherd
LAURINDA, a shepherdess
A BARBER, who poses as a devil (4.3)
A ship's CAPTAIN (4.5)
NAVARCHUS, master of a ship
A SHIPMAN (4.5)
A MESSENGER, who brings news of the murder (5.1)
FIORETTA, Julia's waiting-woman
TORCHBEARERS at the funerals (5.2, non-speaking)
MOURNERS at the funerals (5.2, non-speaking)
Four MAIDS, pallbearers at Althea's funeral (5.2, non-speaking)
OFFICERS at Assassino's execution (5.4, non-speaking)
EPILOGUE

Speaking Parts: 32–3

Stage Directions and Speech Prefixes
GENTLEMAN: *one of the Actors* | *a stranger* (s.d.s); *Gentleman* (s.p.s)
PROLOGUE: *the Prologue* (s.d.s); *Prologue* (s.p.s, heading, and d.p.)
ANTONIO: *Antonio* (s.d.s); *Anton<io>* (s.p.s); *Antonio a Courtier and friend to Lucilio* (d.p.)
RIGAZZO: *Rigazzo the Page* | *the Page* (s.d.s); *Page* (s.d.s and s.p.s); *Rigazzo a Page to Lucilio* (d.p.)
COSMO: *Cosmo the Duke* | *the Duke* (s.d.s); *Duke* (s.d.s and s.p.s); *Cosmo a Duke* (d.p.)
ADRASTA: *Adrasta [Cosmo's] Duchess* (s.d.s and d.p.); *the Duchess* (s.d.s); *Duchess* (s.d.s and s.p.s)
LUCILIO: *Lucilio [Cosmo's and Adrasta's] Son* (s.d.s and d.p.); *Lucilio* (s.d.s); *Lucil<io>* (s.p.s)
JULIA: *Lady Julia* | *the Lady Julia* | *[Althea's] Mother* (s.d.s); *Julia* (s.d.s and s.p.s); *Lady Julia a widow* (d.p.)
ALTHEA: *Althea* (s.d.s and s.p.s); *Althea [Julia's] daughter* (d.p.)
ATTENDANTS: *&c.* | *other Attendants* (s.d.s); *Attendant* (s.p.s)
AMBROSIA: *Mistress Frailware* (s.d.s); *Mistress Frail<ware>* (s.p.s); *Mistress Ambrosia Frailware [Frailware's] wife* (d.p.)
ALASTOR: *Alastor* | *the corpse of the Duke's supposed Son* (s.d.s); *Alast<or>* (s.p.s); *Alastor a villain but a Coward* (d.p.)
ABIGAIL: *Mistress Abigail* (s.d.s); *Mistress Abig<ail>* | *Abig<ail>* (s.p.s); *Mistress Abigail [Damasippus'] wife* (d.p.)
FRAILWARE: *Master Frailware* | *Frailware* (s.d.s); *Master Frail<ware>* | *Frail<ware>* (s.p.s); *Mr Frailware a Grocer and Constable* (d.p.)

MAN: [Frailware's] *man* | *man* (s.d.s)
SERVANT: *another Servant* (s.d.s); *Servant* (s.p.s)
PURSUIVANT: *a Pursuivant at Arms* (s.d.s)
GUARDS: *others* | *one more* (s.d.s)
DAMASIPPUS: *Damasippus* (s.d.s and s.p.s); *Mr Damasippus a lecherous Stoic* (d.p.)
EXECUTIONER: *the executioner* (s.d.s); *Executioner* (s.p.s)
SERVANT: *Servant* (s.d.s and s.p.s)
MICALE: *Mycale a Witch* | *Micale* (s.d.s); *Mical<e>* (s.p.s); *Micale a Witch* (d.p.)
SARVIA: *Sarvia* (s.d.s); *Sar<via>* (s.p.s); *Sarvia* [Micale's] *daughter* (d.p.)
ASSASSINO: *Assassino* (s.d.s); *Assass<ino>* (s.p.s); *Assassino a Blade or desperate fellow* (d.p.)
DEBORAH: *Debora* (s.d.s); *Debor<a>* (s.p.s); *Debora* [Mistress Frailware's] *maid* (d.p.)
SPIRITS: *The first Spirit* | *The second Spirit* | *The third Spirit* | *The Spirit* (s.d.s)
CAMILLA: *Camilla* (s.d.s); *Camill<a>* (s.p.s); *Camilla* [one of] *the Lady Julia's women* (d.p.)
DAMON: *Damon* [one of] *two Shepherds* (s.d.s and d.p.); [one of the] *Shepherds* (s.d.s); *Dam<on>* (s.p.s)
ARMINIO: *Arminio* [one of] *two Shepherds* (s.d.s and d.p.); [one of the] *Shepherds* (s.d.s); *Armin<io>* (s.p.s)
LAURINDA: *Laurinda a Shepherdess* (s.d.s and d.p.); [one of the] *Shepherds* (s.d.s); *Laur<inda>* (s.p.s)
BARBER: *one disguised like a Devil Barber* (s.d.s); *Barber* (s.p.s)
CAPTAIN: *a Captain of a Ship* (s.d.s); *Captain* (s.p.s)
NAVARCHUS: *Navarchus a Master of a Ship* (s.d.s and d.p.); *Navar<chus>* (s.p.s)
SHIPMAN: *a Shipman* (s.d.s); *Shipman* (s.p.s); *One Mariner of Shipman* (d.p.)
MESSENGER: *a Messenger* (s.d.s and d.p.); *Messenger* (s.p.s)
FIORETTA: *Fioretta* (s.d.s); *Fior<etta>* (s.p.s); *Fioretta* [one of] *the Lady Julia's women* (d.p.)
TORCHBEARERS: *Torches* | *the Torchbearers* (s.d.s)
MOURNERS: *Mourners* | *others* (s.d.s)
MAIDS: *four maids* (s.d.s)
OFFICERS: *Officers* (s.d.s)
EPILOGUE: *The Epilogue* (heading and d.p.)

OTHER CHARACTERS
Rigazzo's tutors at Athens, sober graduates (1.1)
Donna Fiozza, a lady who acquired an ague after her monkey fell off a table (1.1)
An Italian count, Fiozza's lord, who may have the pox (1.5)
The people of Florence, Cosmo's subjects (1.7, 2.4, 5.2)
Ambrosia's courtier friends, one of whom told her about Althea's arrest (2.1)
Ambrosia's lovers in her youth, including a nobleman and a knight (2.1)
The court ladies, who are fans of bear-baiting (2.1)
The court ladies' waiting-gentlewomen, who are crowded out of the bear-baitings (2.1)
The Court Servant's former schoolmaster (2.3)

Boys in the Frailwares' household (3.5)
The Frailwares' friends and neighbours (3.5)
Frailware's fellow magistrates (3.5)
Women who consulted Micale to know whether they would outlive their husbands (3.6)
Althea's dead father (4.4)
Two merchants who saw the murder of Alastor (4.5)
The people of the port, who arrested Assassino (4.5)
The Governor of the port (4.5)
Julia's family (5.3–4)

SETTING
Period: The action takes place in the month of May.
Time-Scheme: 1.2 takes place late in the evening; 2.4 and 3.2 take place on the same day, and 3.4–6 the ensuing night (with 3.6 ending at dawn); 4.1 takes place around noon and 4.5 in the evening.
Place: Florence

Geography
Italy: Naples; Lombardy; the Apennines
The Tyrrhenian Sea
Greece: Athens
[*London*]: Merchant Taylors' Hall; the Counter prison
The Low Countries: Amsterdam
Egypt: [River Nile]
Brazil

SOURCES
Narrative: Giovanni Boccaccio, *Decameron* 8.8 (1348–53; 3.5)
Verbal: Virgil, *Eclogues* 1 (4.3), 10 (motto at foot of text); Horace, *Ars poetica* (t.p. motto, ded.), *Satires* 1.10 (ded.), *Epistles* 2.2 (ded.); Ovid, *Metamorphoses* 1 (1.5); Juvenal, *Satires* 1 (ind., 2.3), 3 (4.5); Nicholas Trevet, commentary on *Hercules furens* (thirteenth or fourteenth century; 3.2); J. H., *The Devil of the Vault* (1606; 3.5)
Works Mentioned: Aesop, *Fables* (2.3); Pietro Aretino, *Postures* (1524; 3.6); John Ryder, *Dictionary* (1589; 4.5)

LANGUAGE
English
Latin: 42 words (ind., 1.2, 1.5, 2.2–3, 3.2, 3.4–5, 4.3, 4.5; Prologue, Lucilio, Servant, Rigazzo, Damasippus, Frailware, Barber, Alastor)
Italian: 1 word (1.1; Rigazzo)
French: 2 words (3.6; Micale)

The characters understand themselves to be speaking Italian.

FORM
Metre: pentameter and prose; some stichomythia
Rhyme: blank verse; some couplets
Prologue: 6 lines, in couplets
Induction: an altercation between the Prologue and a gentleman of the audience
Act-Division: 5 acts
Epilogue: 24 lines, in couplets

Lines (Spoken): 2,795 (1,664 verse, 1,131 prose)
Lines (Written): 2,996

STAGING

Doors: characters enter at two doors (2.4, 5.2, s.d.); mentioned (3.5, dialogue)
Stage: mentioned (ind., 3.6, s.d.)
Within: speech (3.5, s.d.); cry (4.3, s.d.)
Above: Althea appears above at a window, then climbs down on a rope ladder, after which Lucilio climbs up (2.2, s.d.); characters go 'up to the rock', which appears to be a raised area on stage accommodating at least four people, without interruption of the action as they ascend (3.1, 5.4, s.d.; Julia ascends in the middle of her own speech)
Beneath: spirits rise from under the stage (3.6, s.d.); a grave is dug and Camilla buried in it (4.1, s.d.)
Audience: the play assumes a theatre where members of the audience ordinarily sit on the stage (ind.); referred to as 'auditors' (ind.); addressed as 'judging spectators' (ep.)

MUSIC

Music: cornetts or hautboys (1.1, s.d.)
On-Stage Music: Rigazzo plays the fiddle (3.5, implicit)
Songs:
  1: 'Sarvia! Mother! Take thy flight', 3.3, Micale and Sarvia, in parts, 20 lines;
  2: 'Die, die, ah, die', 4.1, Laurinda, 16 lines;
  3: 'Come, lovers, bring your cares', 5.2, Fioretta, 8 lines, sung to 'some mournful tune'.
Other Singing: four other lines of Fioretta's in 5.2 may be sung

PROPS

Lighting: torches (5.2, s.d.)
Weapons: two halberds (2.1, 2.4, 3.1, s.d.); more halberds (2.4, 3.1, s.d.); Alastor's sword (3.4, dialogue); a razor (4.3, dialogue)
Musical Instruments: a fiddle (3.5, implicit)
Clothing: a bag of clothes (2.2, s.d.); a scarf (2.2, dialogue; later worn by Lucilio); another scarf (4.1, dialogue; 4.4, 5.2, s.d.; it has blood on it in 4.4, presumably from contact with Camilla's corpse in 4.1)
Money: an unspecified amount (1.6, s.d.)
Food and Drink: supper (3.5, s.d.); canary wine (3.5, dialogue; drunk on stage); a bottle of liquor (4.1, s.d.; drunk on stage); viands (4.1, s.d.)
Small Portable Objects: a letter with a seal (1.4, dialogue); another letter with a different seal (1.6, 2.4, s.d.); a stone (2.2, s.d.); binding cords (3.1, implicit); a looking-glass (3.6, s.d.); a vial (3.6, s.d.); a bag (4.1, s.d.); 'green strewings' (4.1, s.d.), including flowers (dialogue); a cloth (4.1, s.d.); green herbs and flowers (5.2, s.d.)
Large Portable Objects: a seat (ind., implicit); a line (2.2, s.d.; strong enough to support the bag of clothes as it is drawn up to the window); a rope ladder with hooks at one end (2.2, s.d.); a seat of judgement (2.3–4, implicit); cushions (2.3–4, s.d.); a table covered with a cloth (3.5, s.d.); seating for at least two (3.5, implicit); a seat (3.6, implicit); two digging tools (4.1, dialogue); a chair (4.3, s.d.); two hearses (5.2, s.d./dialogue)
Scenery: a bar (2.3–4, s.d.)
Miscellaneous: blood (4.1, implicit)

COSTUMES

ANTONIO: disguised (4.1, 5.4, s.d.)
RIGAZZO: disguised as a fiddler (3.5, 4.3, s.d.)
COSMO: mourning robes (5.2, s.d.)
ADRASTA: disguised (3.3, s.d.); mourning robes (5.2, s.d.)
LUCILIO: cross-dressed as Althea (2.4, s.d.; 3.1, implicit); a scarf over his face (2.4, 3.1, s.d.; removed on stage); disguised as a countryman (4.2, 5.2, s.d.); his own habit (5.4, s.d.)
JULIA: grey or white hair (implicit); her hair dishevelled (3.1, s.d.); disguised (5.4, s.d.)
ALTHEA: a disguise (2.2, dialogue; the actor has a 9-line quick change into the new costume off stage during the scene); disguised as a shepherdess (4.1, 5.4, s.d.; in 5.4, the costume is worn over her own clothes, and removed on stage)
ALASTOR: disguised in rich apparel (4.5, s.d.)
DAMASIPPUS: a beard (s.d.; shaved off on stage in his last scene, 4.3)
MICALE: disguised as a shepherdess (4.1, s.d.)
ASSASSINO: disguised (4.5, s.d.)
DEBORAH: large buttocks (dialogue)
CAMILLA: disguised as a shepherdess (4.1, s.d.)
BARBER: disguised as a devil (4.3, s.d.)
FIORETTA: her hair down (5.2, s.d.); a mourning habit (5.2, implicit)
MOURNERS: mourning robes (5.2, s.d.)
MAIDS: black clothes; dishevelled hair; garlands of dead myrtle or other leaves (5.2, s.d.)

EARLY STAGE HISTORY

1635 or earlier: The play was rejected by the acting company to which the author offered it.

EARLY TEXTUAL HISTORY

1635 or earlier: At the time of publication, the play was said to have been 'long since finished'. It was read to John Jones's friends, including members of the universities of Oxford and Cambridge, who reportedly liked it. Jones offered it to an acting company, but they rejected it after what Jones considered to be only a cursory examination. The play was subsequently revised.

1635: Jones was encouraged by his friends to publish the play.

1635: Q printed, probably by Miles Flesher, for Richard Royston; collation A–L⁴, 44 leaves; Latin title-page motto; general authorial dedication to the author's friends, collectively styled 'Musophilus'; list of roles; Latin motto at foot of text.

c. 1630s–40s: a copy of Q was in the possession of John Horne (Vicar of Headington, Oxfordshire). After his death, his entire collection of play-books passed into the possession of John Houghton of Brasenose

College, Oxford (c. 1608–77), then to James Herne (died 1685), and then to the library of Ralph Sheldon (1623–84) at Weston, where it was catalogued by Anthony Wood, probably in the late 1670s.

1640–1: Humphrey Moseley was selling copies of Q for 6d each.

1655: *The English Treasury of Wit and Language* entered in the Stationers' Register to Humphrey Moseley on Tuesday 16 January.

1655: three extracts (from 2.2, 4.1, 5.2) included in John Cotgrave's *The English Treasury of Wit and Language*, sigs. E3^{r-v}, L4^{r-v}, R6^v; printed for Humphrey Moseley.

1684: Nicholas Cox (Manciple of St Edmund Hall, Oxford) had a copy of Q in his bookshop. It had probably been previously owned by Gerard Langbaine, and appears on a list compiled by Anthony Wood on Saturday 13 December.

REFERENCES
Annals 1635; Bentley, iv. 603; Bodleian, MS Wood E. 4, art. 1, p. 30; Eyre & Rivington, i. 463; Greg 501; Hazlitt, 3; *MLR* 13 (1918), 401–11; *Oxford Bibliographical Society Proceedings and Papers* 2.2 (1929), 132–3; *SP* 40 (1943), 186–203.

2489. Puppet Play of Susanna and the Elders

EVIDENCE
James Shirley, *The Lady of Pleasure* (**2515**); Edmund Gayton, *Pleasant Notes upon Don Quixote* (1654; Wing G415); 'An Ancient Song of Bartholomew Fair' (1655; printed 1719).

Shirley's allusion seems to indicate that the story was the central focus of the play, but it might alternatively have been just an episode in a broader play, such as **1472**.

GENRE
puppet show
Contemporary: 'canvas tragedy' (Shirley)

TITLE
Contemporary: *The History of Susanna*; *Chaste Susanna, or The Court of Babylon*

DATE
1635 or earlier

PLOT
Two wicked elders become sexually obsessed with the chaste Susanna, and contrive to spy on her when she bathes in the privacy of a locked garden. Overcome by lust, they demand sex from her. When she refuses, they charge her with the capital crime of adultery. They are believed and Susanna condemned, but Daniel is inspired to question the elders separately and establishes that the details of their stories do not match up: they are false witnesses. Susanna is released and the elders put to death.

The subject matter initially seems hard to reconcile with the two-handed exigencies of staging a play with glove-puppets: the fact that there are two elders peeping at the abluting Susanna is central to the operation of the narrative. A possible solution is that the voyeurism episode centred on the elders, and that the Susanna puppet was not on stage at the time: a glove-puppet with no clothes on is, after all, just a hand, so it was prudent of Gayton to counsel, 'let Susanna's bathing be by chorus'. Alternatively, the play may have been designed for performance by more than one puppeteer (and perhaps by marionettles).

ROLES
SUSANNA, a married woman; possibly also called Susan
TWO ELDERS
DANIEL, a prophet

OTHER CHARACTERS
God

SETTING
Period: sixth century BC, during the Jews' Babylonian captivity, at the time of the prophet Daniel
Place: Babylon

SOURCES
Narrative: Bible: Daniel 13 (Apocrypha)

PROPS
Small Portable Objects: puppets

EARLY STAGE HISTORY
1635: said in the autumn to have been performed at a recent fair (probably London's Bartholomew Fair, Monday 24 to Thursday 27 August).

REFERENCES
Edmund Gayton, *Pleasant Notes upon Don Quixote* (London, 1654), sig. 2M2^v; James Shirley, *The Lady of Pleasure*, ed. Ronald Huebert (Manchester, 1986), 3.2.230–6; George Speaight, *The History of the English Puppet Theatre*, 2nd edn (London, 1990), 282, 327.

2490. *Naiagaion* [The Shipwreck]

TEXT
Printed in 1637 (STC 13358).

GENRE
dialogue
Contemporary: dialogue

TITLE
Printed: *Naiagaion, or Naufragium*
Contemporary: *Naufragium*; *The Shipwreck*

AUTHOR
Thomas Heywood, *translating* Desiderius Erasmus

DATE
Limits: 1630–7
Best Guess: 1635

PLOT
Adolphos tells Antonius of a shipwreck he survived. At night, a fiery sphere appeared alongside the ship, a prodigy of disaster. The sea grew stormy, the pilot lost control, and the ship's tackling burst. The passengers' baggage was thrown overboard, followed by the mainmast. The passengers prayed, some to the Virgin Mary, some to the sea, some to various saints; but Adolphos addressed his prayers to God alone. The passengers and crew abandoned ship: Adolphos used the remnants of the mast to float, and was one of the very few survivors. Washed up on the shores of Holland, he has resolved not to go to sea again in a hurry.

ROLES
ANTONIUS
ADOLPHOS

Speaking Parts: 2

Speech Prefixes
ANTONIUS: Anthon<ius> (s.p.s); Antonius (d.p.)
ADOLPHOS: Adol<phos> (s.p.s); Adolphos (d.p.)

OTHER CHARACTERS
The pilot of the wrecked ship
Sailors aboard the wrecked ship
Passengers aboard the wrecked ship
A rich Italian, sent as ambassador to Scotland, a passenger on the ship
An Englishman, a passenger on the ship
A fat man from Zeeland, a passenger on the ship
A woman and her baby, passengers on the ship
The master of the wrecked ship
Adam, a 60-year-old priest, a passenger on the ship
A Dominican friar, a passenger on the ship
The inhabitants of a coastal community, who attempted to direct the ship to the safest landing place
Thirty people drowned when the lifeboat disintegrated
A man who helped Adolphos free the remains of the mast, but was drowned
People on the shore of Holland, who pulled Adolphos from the sea

SETTING
Period: The action apparently takes place at a time when Scotland is diplomatically separate from England (i.e. before 1603), and when there was still a shrine at Walsingham (i.e. before 1538)
Place: presumably Holland

Geography
[*The Low Countries*]: Zeeland
The English Channel
England: Walsingham
Scotland
[*France*]: Paris
The Alps
Italy: Rome

SOURCES
Narrative: Desiderius Erasmus, *Colloquies*: Naufragium (1523)
Verbal: Bible: Matthew 6.9; Luke 1.28
Works Mentioned: the Bible (general reference); Jean de Gerson, *Requête pour les condamnés à mort* (early fifteenth century)

LANGUAGE
English
Latin: 1 word (Adolphos)

FORM
Metre: pentameter
Rhyme: couplets; a few triplets
Lines (Spoken): 437
Lines (Written): 504

EARLY TEXTUAL HISTORY
1635: *Pleasant Dialogues and Dramas* entered in the Stationers' Register to Richard Hearne on Saturday 29 August; entry names author. Thomas Wykes had licensed the book for publication.
  1637: included in Thomas Heywood's *Pleasant Dialogues and Dramas* (O), sigs. B1^r–B8^r; 15 pages on 8 leaves; printed by Richard Oulton for Richard Hearne, and to be sold by Thomas Slater; verse argument; list of roles.
  1684: Nicholas Cox (Manciple of St Edmund Hall, Oxford) had a copy of O in his bookshop. It had probably been previously owned by Gerard Langbaine, and appears on a list compiled by Anthony Wood on Saturday 13 December.

EDITION
W. Bang, in Thomas Heywood, *Pleasant Dialogues and Dramas*, Materialien 1.3 (Louvain, 1903), 1–15.

REFERENCES
Annals 1635; Bodleian, MS Wood E. 4, art. 1, p. 52.

2491. *Procus et puella* [The Suitor and the Girl]

TEXT
Printed in 1637 (STC 13358).

GENRE
dialogue
Contemporary: dialogue (heading); colloquy (argument)

2492. The Dialogue betwixt Earth and Age

TITLE
Printed: *Procus et puella*
Contemporary: *Procus and Puella*

AUTHOR
Thomas Heywood, *translating* Desiderius Erasmus

DATE
Limits: 1630–7
Best Guess: 1635

PLOT
Maria does not love Pamphilus, and undermines all the conventional lover's poses he adopts. He argues that, because his soul is not in his body but with her, he is dead for love and she the murderess; but she retorts that he has committed suicide by freely choosing to love her. Since the sight of her is so dangerous, she asks, would he rather she didn't look at him? He threatens the wrath of Cupid, and tells the story of a young woman who rejected her suitor and was forced to fall in love with a hideously ugly hunchback. Maria argues for the virtues of virginity, Pamphilus for the pleasures of having children. Finally, she accepts him, subject to her parents' consent, but his hope of pre-marital sex is not fulfilled. She sends him away with a gift, but no kiss, arguing that with a kiss she risks sucking out the little of his soul that remains in his body.

ROLES
PAMPHILUS, a bachelor
MARIA, also called Mary

Speaking Parts: 2

Speech Prefixes
PAMPHILUS: *Pam<philus>* (s.p.s); *Pamphilus* (d.p.)
MARIA: *Mar<ia>* (s.p.s); *Mary* (d.p.)

OTHER CHARACTERS
Pamphilus' rival in love
A beautiful virgin of Aurelia, who suffered unrequited love
Mauritius Aglaius, a lawyer, the virgin's father
Sophronia, the virgin's recently dead mother
Pamphilus, a young suitor whom the virgin refused (not the same as the Pamphilus in the dialogue)
An ugly hunchback whom the virgin loved, perhaps named Thersites
The hangman, who cut off the hunchback's ear
Pamphilus' ancestors, allies of Maria's ancestors
Pamphilus' parents
Maria's parents

SETTING
Time-Scheme: The action apparently takes place in the evening.

Geography
'Aurelia' (unidentified; Orleans in the Latin source)

SOURCES
Narrative: Desiderius Erasmus, *Colloquies*: Proci et Puellae (1523)
Verbal: Homer, unidentified work (notes, cited; possibly via George Pettie, *A Petite Palace of Pettie's Pleasure*, 1576, repr. 1613); Euripides, *Andromache* (notes); Menander, unidentified fragment (notes); Ovid, *Heroides* 18 (notes); Bible: Luke 6.43; Statius, *Sylvae* 5 (notes); 'Dion' (Dio Chrysostom? Dio Cassius? Dionysius the Areopagite?), unidentified work (notes); Boethius, *Consolation of Philosophy* (notes)

LANGUAGE
English

FORM
Metre: pentameter
Rhyme: couplets
Lines (Spoken): 658
Lines (Written): 722

PROPS
Small Portable Objects: a sweet-ball (dialogue)

EARLY TEXTUAL HISTORY
1635: *Pleasant Dialogues and Dramas* entered in the Stationers' Register to Richard Hearne on Saturday 29 August; entry names author. Thomas Wykes had licensed the book for publication.

1637: included in Thomas Heywood's *Pleasant Dialogues and Dramas* (**O**), sigs. B8^v–D3^r; 22 pages on 12 leaves; printed by Richard Oulton for Richard Hearne, and to be sold by Thomas Slater; verse argument; list of roles. Annotations to the text appear on sig. T7^{r-v}.

1684: Nicholas Cox (Manciple of St Edmund Hall, Oxford) had a copy of O in his bookshop. It had probably been previously owned by Gerard Langbaine, and appears on a list compiled by Anthony Wood on Saturday 13 December.

EDITION
W. Bang, in Thomas Heywood, *Pleasant Dialogues and Dramas*, Materialien 1.3 (Louvain, 1903), 16–37.

REFERENCES
Annals 1635; Bodleian, MS Wood E. 4, art. 1, p. 52.

2492. The Dialogue betwixt Earth and Age

TEXT
Printed in 1637 (STC 13358).

GENRE
dialogue
Contemporary: dialogue (title)

1635   2492. *The Dialogue betwixt Earth and Age* | 361

TITLE
Printed: *The Dialogue betwixt Earth and Age*

AUTHOR
Thomas Heywood, *translating* Ravisius Textor

DATE
Limits: 1630–7
Best Guess: 1635

PLOT
Like any mother, Earth is upset to see her offspring dying—but her grief is the greatest of all, because she is the mother of everything. Age defends this as the will of the gods, and recommends that Man be advised to leave the Earth if he is to evade it. Various historical figures describe their common end in death to illustrate the supreme power of Age: neither heroism nor beauty, learning nor political power are proof against it. To his mother's consternation, Man decides he'd better enjoy himself while he can.

ROLES
Mother EARTH, Man's mother
AGE, a female character
MAN, Earth's son
HECTOR, a Trojan warrior; a married man and a father
ACHILLES, a Greek warrior
ALEXANDER Macedon, a conqueror
SAMSON, a strong man
HELEN, a beautiful Greek woman; a wife
LAIS, a Corinthian prostitute
THISBE, a Babylonian noblewoman
LUCRETIA, a sexy woman; also called Lucrece
VIRGIL, a pre-eminent poet
XERXES, a mighty king of Persia
NERO, a Roman tyrant
SARDANAPAL, a hedonistic sensualist and transvestite

Speaking Parts: 15
Allegorical Roles: 3

Speech Prefixes
EARTH: *Earth* (s.p.s)
AGE: *Age* (s.p.s)
MAN: *Man* (s.p.s)
HECTOR: *Hector* (s.p.s)
ACHILLES: *Achilles* (s.p.s)
ALEXANDER: *Alexander* (s.p.s)
SAMSON: *Sampson* (s.p.s)
HELEN: *Hellen* (s.p.s)
LAIS: *Lais* (s.p.s)
THISBE: *Thisbe* (s.p.s)
LUCRETIA: *Lucretia* (s.p.s)
VIRGIL: *Virgil* (s.p.s)
XERXES: *Xerxes* (s.p.s)
NERO: *Nero* (s.p.s)
SARDANAPAL: *Sardanapal* (s.p.s)

OTHER CHARACTERS
Priam, Hector's father; also called Priamus
Patroclus, slain by Hector
The Greek army, put to flight by Hector
Andromache, Hector's widow
Hector's son
Paris, who abducted Helen and killed Achilles
Darius, conquered by Alexander
Porus, a tall Indian conquered and then freed by Alexander
1,000 people whom Samson slew with the jawbone of an ass
Menelaus, Helen's husband, one of the Atrides
Theseus, who raped Helen
[Agamemnon], one of the Atrides
Helen's father
Juno, who was jealous of Thisbe
Xerxes' soldiers
Nero's mother
Lucan, killed by Nero
Seneca, killed by Nero
St Paul, killed by Nero
St Peter, killed by Nero
The Senate, mostly killed by Nero
The people of Rome, who hated Nero
Common prostitutes, with whom Sardanapal spent his time

SETTING
Geography
Greece: Ascra; Thebes; Sparta; Corinth; Leucadia
Macedon
The Aegean Sea: Rhodes
[*Asia Minor*]: [the Mausoleum of Halicarnassus]; Troy; Colossae; Cilicia; Paphlagonia; River Cayster
[*Jerusalem*]: the Temple of Solomon
Phoenicia
[*Egypt*]: Pharos; the Pyramids; Memphis; River Nile
[*Africa*]: Numidia
Spain: the Pillars of Hercules; Calpe
[*Italy*]: Cannae
Rome: the Tarpeian Rock; [the Colosseum]
[*Asia*]: Babylon; Nineveh; Persia
India: River Ganges; River Hydaspes

SOURCES
Narrative: Ravisius Textor, *Dialogi aliquot*: Terra, Aetas, Homo, et alii plerique (1530, repr. 1616)
Verbal: Ovid, *Tristia* 1.1 (notes, cited)
Works Mentioned: Hesiod, *Works and Days* (text); Virgil, *Aeneid* (text and notes); Ovid, *Metamorphoses* 1–2, 8 (notes); Varro, lost work quoted by Lactantius (notes); Aulus Gellius, *Attic Nights* (notes); Aelius Spartianus, *Life of Caracalla* (notes); Lactantius, *Divinarum institutionum* (notes); Augustine, *City of God* (notes); 'Suidas', *Lexicon* (c. 1100; notes); Natalis Comes, *Mythologiae* (1551; notes); Abraham Ortelius, *Synonyma geographia* (1578; notes); Joseph Justus

Scaliger, *De emendatione temporum* (1583; notes); Sethus Calvisius, *Opus chronologicum* (1605; notes); Christophorus Helveticus, *Theatrum historicum* (1609–10; notes)

LANGUAGE
English

FORM
Metre: pentameter
Rhyme: couplets; a few triplets
Lines (Spoken): 513
Lines (Written): 545

EARLY TEXTUAL HISTORY
1635: *Pleasant Dialogues and Dramas* entered in the Stationers' Register to Richard Hearne on Saturday 29 August; entry names author. Thomas Wykes had licensed the book for publication.

1637: included in Thomas Heywood's *Pleasant Dialogues and Dramas* (**O**), sigs. D3^v–E3^r; 16 pages on 9 leaves; printed by Richard Oulton for Richard Hearne, and to be sold by Thomas Slater; verse argument. Annotations to the text appear on sigs. T7^v–V3^r.

1684: Nicholas Cox (Manciple of St Edmund Hall, Oxford) had a copy of O in his bookshop. It had probably been previously owned by Gerard Langbaine, and appears on a list compiled by Anthony Wood on Saturday 13 December.

EDITION
W. Bang, in Thomas Heywood, *Pleasant Dialogues and Dramas*, Materialien 1.3 (Louvain, 1903), 38–53.

REFERENCES
Annals 1635; Bodleian, MS Wood E. 4, art. 1, p. 52.

2493. *Misanthropos* [The Man-Hater]

TEXT
Printed in 1637 (STC 13358).

GENRE
dialogue
Contemporary: dialogue

TITLE
Printed: *Misanthropos, or The Man-Hater*
Contemporary: *The Man-Hater*; *Timon Misanthropos*
Alternative Modernization: *Misanthropus*

AUTHOR
Thomas Heywood, *translating* Lucian

DATE
Limits: 1630–7
Best Guess: 1635

PLOT
Timon has brought himself to poverty through his excessive generosity to the Athenians, whereupon his former friends deserted him; now he works tilling the fields. He challenges Jupiter to prove his existence—for if there is no God, humanity has nothing to fear. Recognizing that he is a pious man who has done sacrifice, Jupiter pities him and plans to give him gold; but Plutus is unwilling to go back to Timon, having been ill-treated by him in the past. Jupiter retorts that Timon's liberality gave Plutus liberty, but Plutus is truculent: hard to control and reluctant to obey orders.

Mercury brings Plutus to Timon and drives away Poverty and her associates; but Timon does not want Plutus' company and tries to get rid of him with violence. He is also uninterested in Mercury's offer of political power in Athens: he has found virtue in a simple life, and asks for Plutus to be taken back to Jupiter. But when he sets to work at his digging, Mercury and Plutus arrange for him to find treasure.

The newly enriched Timon renounces poverty and instead embraces solitude: now he hates humanity and gives no thought to charity or kinship. The news of his wealth spreads round Athens, and draws crowds to visit him: all his old parasites want their share of the loot. He abuses and assaults them, driving them away by throwing stones at them.

ROLES
TIMON, an Athenian; later assumes the name Misanthropos
JUPITER, god of thunder, Mercury's father; also called Jove
MERCURY, a god, Jupiter's son; also called Hermes
PLUTUS, god of wealth; an old, lame, blind man
Mistress POVERTY, Timon's companion in penury
LABOUR, a rough fellow, Timon's companion in penury (*non-speaking*)
WISDOM, Timon's companion in penury (*non-speaking*)
HEALTH, Timon's companion in penury (*non-speaking*)
FORTITUDE, Timon's companion in penury (*non-speaking*)
KNOWLEDGE, Timon's companion in penury (*non-speaking*)
GNATHONIDES, a flatterer, Timon's former friend and sycophant
PHILIADES, a father, Timon's former friend and sycophant
DEMEAS, an unmarried orator, Timon's kinsman, former friend, and sycophant; also called Demect
THRASYCLES, a gluttonous sophist, Timon's former friend and sycophant
BLEPSIAS, Timon's former friend and sycophant
LACHES, Timon's former friend and sycophant (*non-speaking*)

GNIPHON, Timon's former friend and sycophant (non-speaking)

Speaking Parts: 10
Allegorical Roles: 6; interact with others

Speech Prefixes
TIMON: *Timon* (s.p.s)
JUPITER: *Jupiter* (s.p.s)
MERCURY: *Mercury* (s.p.s)
PLUTUS: *Plutus* (s.p.s)
POVERTY: *Poverty* (s.p.s)
GNATHONIDES: *Gnaton<ides>* (s.p.s)
PHILIADES: *Philiades* (s.p.s)
DEMEAS: *Demeas* (s.p.s)
THRASYCLES: *Thrasicles* (s.p.s)
BLEPSIAS: *Bleps<ias>* (s.p.s)

OTHER CHARACTERS
Echecratides, Timon's father
Disputants in the schools of Athens
Anaxagoras, a sophist who preached atheism
Anaxagoras' pupils
Pericles, who bestrode Anaxagoras' body and caused Jupiter's thunderbolt to miss
Misers, whom Plutus despises
The Cyclopes, who repair Jupiter's thunderbolts
Dis, divine ruler of hell, whom Plutus gladly obeys
Aristides, to whom Plutus was sent
Base Athenians, including Hipponicus and Callias, to whom Plutus went instead of Aristides
Hyperbolus and Cleon, whom it would be inappropriate for Plutus to visit
The Corybantes, friends of Timon
Timon's cousins and nephews
Timon's former domestic servants
Thousands of Athenians coming to visit Timon
Philiades' daughter
Erechtheiades, governor of the treasury
The Acharnanian army, defeated by the Athenians
The Spartans, defeated by the Athenians in two battles

SETTING
Period: fifth century BC; the dialogue's central character reputedly lived during the Peloponnesian War (431–404 BC)
Place: Athens

Geography
Athens: Collytus
Greece: Mount Licoris (i.e. Parnassus); Mount Olympus; Mount Oeta; Mount Hymettus; Delphos (i.e. Delphi); Acharnania; Sparta; Aegina
Crete
[*Sicily*]: Mount Etna
[*Asia*]: Persia; Tyre

SOURCES
Narrative: Lucian, *Timon*

Works Mentioned: Homer, *Iliad*; Bible: Titus 1.12 (notes); Theodore Beza, *Annotationes majores in novum testamentum* (1594; notes); Christophorus Helveticus, *Theatrum historicum* (1609–10; notes)

LANGUAGE
English

FORM
Metre: pentameter
Rhyme: couplets
Lines (Spoken): 1,432
Lines (Written): 1,456

STAGING
Above: Mercury flies away (dialogue)
Beneath: Timon digs gold out of the ground (dialogue)

PROPS
Weapons: stones (dialogue)
Money: gold coins (dialogue)
Large Portable Objects: a spade (dialogue); a scrip (dialogue; capacity said to be two bushels)
Scenery: a rock (dialogue; sturdy enough to be climbed by Timon)

COSTUMES AND MAKE-UP
TIMON: a goat-skin coat (dialogue)
MERCURY: a cloak; wings (dialogue)
PLUTUS: a pale complexion (dialogue)
PHILIADES: a bald head (dialogue)
THRASYCLES: shoulder-length hair; a bushy beard and eyebrows; a threadbare cloak (dialogue)

EARLY TEXTUAL HISTORY
1635: *Pleasant Dialogues and Dramas* entered in the Stationers' Register to Richard Hearne on Saturday 29 August; entry names author. Thomas Wykes had licensed the book for publication.
1637: included in Thomas Heywood's *Pleasant Dialogues and Dramas* (O), sigs. E3ᵛ–G8ʳ; 40 pages on 21 leaves; printed by Richard Oulton for Richard Hearne, and to be sold by Thomas Slater; verse argument. Annotations to the text appear on sigs. V3ʳ–V4ᵛ.
1684: Nicholas Cox (Maniciple of St Edmund Hall, Oxford) had a copy of O in his bookshop. It had probably been previously owned by Gerard Langbaine, and appears on a list compiled by Anthony Wood on Saturday 13 December.

EDITION
W. Bang, in Thomas Heywood, *Pleasant Dialogues and Dramas*, Materialien 1.3 (Louvain, 1903), 54–95.

REFERENCES
Annals 1635; Bentley, iv. 584; Bodleian, MS Wood E. 4, art. 1, p. 52.

2494. Jupiter and Ganymede

TEXT
Printed in 1637 (STC 13358).

GENRE
dialogue
Contemporary: dialogue

TITLE
Printed: *Jupiter and Ganymede*
Contemporary: *A Dialogue ... betwixt Jupiter and Ganymede*

AUTHOR
Thomas Heywood, *translating* Lucian

DATE
Limits: 1630–7
Best Guess: 1635

PLOT
In the guise of an eagle, Jupiter abducts Ganymede and attempts to seduce him. Ganymede is unconvinced that Jupiter truly is the god he claims to be, but offers to sacrifice to him in return for being taken back home. Jupiter has other ideas: he will make Ganymede divine, and his only duties will be to serve as the gods' cupbearer and to sleep with Jupiter. Ganymede warns that he is a sprawling bedfellow, but Jupiter says he'll enjoy that.

ROLES
JUPITER, King of the gods; also called Jove
GANYMEDE, a beautiful young Trojan shepherd

Speaking Parts: 2

Speech Prefixes
JUPITER: *Jupiter* (s.p.s)
GANYMEDE: *Ganimed* (s.p.s)

OTHER CHARACTERS
Pan, a rural god
Ganymede's father, who sacrificed to Jupiter
Cupid, a boy god
Ganymede's mother
Mercury, a god (would appear if the dialogue were staged)

SETTING
Period: antiquity
Place: heaven

Geography
[*Phrygia*]: Troy; Gargarus; Mount Ida

SOURCES
Narrative: Lucian, *Dialogues of the Gods* 4: Zeus and Ganymede

LANGUAGE
English

FORM
Metre: pentameter
Rhyme: couplets
Lines (Spoken): 122
Lines (Written): 135

EARLY TEXTUAL HISTORY
1635: *Pleasant Dialogues and Dramas* entered in the Stationers' Register to Richard Hearne on Saturday 29 August; entry names author. Thomas Wykes had licensed the book for publication.

1637: included in Thomas Heywood's *Pleasant Dialogues and Dramas* (**O**), sigs. G8ᵛ–H2ᵛ; 5 pages on 3 leaves; printed by Richard Oulton for Richard Hearne, and to be sold by Thomas Slater; verse argument.

1684: Nicholas Cox (Manciple of St Edmund Hall, Oxford) had a copy of O in his bookshop. It had probably been previously owned by Gerard Langbaine, and appears on a list compiled by Anthony Wood on Saturday 13 December.

EDITION
W. Bang, in Thomas Heywood, *Pleasant Dialogues and Dramas*, Materialien 1.3 (Louvain, 1903), 96–100.

REFERENCES
Annals 1635; Bodleian, MS Wood E. 4, art. 1, p. 52.

2495. Jupiter and Juno

TEXT
Printed in 1637 (STC 13358).

GENRE
dialogue
Contemporary: dialogue

TITLE
Printed: *Jupiter and Juno*
Contemporary: *A [Dialogue] betwixt Jupiter and Juno*

AUTHOR
Thomas Heywood, *translating* Lucian

DATE
Limits: 1630–7
Best Guess: 1635

PLOT
Juno is jealous of Jupiter's interest in Ganymede. She criticizes him for his lechery, but he is unrepentant.

ROLES
JUNO, Jupiter's wife

JUPITER, King of the gods, Juno's husband, god of thunder; also called Jove

Speaking Parts: 2

Speech Prefixes
JUNO: *Juno* (s.p.s)
JUPITER: *Jupiter* (s.p.s)

OTHER CHARACTERS
Ganymede, cupbearer of the gods, formerly a young Trojan shepherd (would appear if the dialogue were staged)
Earthly prostitutes visited by Jupiter (Europa and Danaë are alluded to, but not named)
Ganymede's father
Hebe, former cupbearer of the gods
Vulcan, a lame god, Juno's son

SETTING
Period: antiquity

Geography
Phrygia: Troy

SOURCES
Narrative: Lucian, *Dialogues of the Gods* 5: Zeus and Hera

LANGUAGE
English

FORM
Metre: pentameter
Rhyme: couplets
Lines (Spoken): 104
Lines (Written): 107

COSTUMES
JUPITER: a long beard (dialogue)

EARLY TEXTUAL HISTORY
1635: *Pleasant Dialogues and Dramas* entered in the Stationers' Register to Richard Hearne on Saturday 29 August; entry names author. Thomas Wykes had licensed the book for publication.
  1637: included in Thomas Heywood's *Pleasant Dialogues and Dramas* (**O**), sigs. H3^r–H4^v; 2 leaves; printed by Richard Oulton for Richard Hearne, and to be sold by Thomas Slater; verse argument.
  1684: Nicholas Cox (Manciple of St Edmund Hall, Oxford) had a copy of O in his bookshop. It had probably been previously owned by Gerard Langbaine, and appears on a list compiled by Anthony Wood on Saturday 13 December.

EDITION
W. Bang, in Thomas Heywood, *Pleasant Dialogues and Dramas*, Materialien 1.3 (Louvain, 1903), 101–4.

REFERENCES
Annals 1635; Bodleian, MS Wood E. 4, art. 1, p. 52.

2496. *Jupiter and Cupid*

TEXT
Printed in 1637 (STC 13358).

GENRE
dialogue
Contemporary: dialogue

TITLE
Printed: *Jupiter and Cupid*
Contemporary: *A [Dialogue] betwixt Jupiter and Cupid*

AUTHOR
Thomas Heywood, *translating* Lucian

DATE
Limits: 1630–7
Best Guess: 1635

PLOT
Cupid's influence has made Jupiter transform himself into a variety of humiliating disguises. Jupiter is offended, but Cupid advises him that, if he wishes to woo in his own shape, he should smarten himself up. Jupiter has no wish to appear effeminate, but equally is unwilling to renounce love.

ROLES
CUPID, a boy god of very advanced years; also called Love
JUPITER, god of thunder, a married deity; also called Jove

Speaking Parts: 2

Stage Directions and Speech Prefixes
CUPID: *Cupid* (s.p.s)
JUPITER: *Jupiter* (s.p.s)

OTHER CHARACTERS
Iapetus, an old man
Juno, Queen of heaven, Jupiter's wife
Jupiter's earthly paramours
Hyacinthus, a lover of Apollo
Branchus, a lover of Apollo
Apollo, [a god]
Daphne, who resisted Apollo's advances
Maenads who attend [Bacchus]
[Bacchus], god of wine

SETTING
Period: antiquity

Geography
Sidon

SOURCES
Narrative: Lucian, *Dialogues of the Gods* 2: Eros and Zeus

LANGUAGE
English

FORM
Metre: pentameter
Rhyme: couplets
Lines (Spoken): 54
Lines (Written): 60

COSTUMES
CUPID: has no beard (dialogue)

EARLY TEXTUAL HISTORY
1635: *Pleasant Dialogues and Dramas* entered in the Stationers' Register to Richard Hearne on Saturday 29 August; entry names author. Thomas Wykes had licensed the book for publication.
    1637: included in Thomas Heywood's *Pleasant Dialogues and Dramas* (**O**), sigs. H5ʳ–H6ʳ; 3 pages on 2 leaves; printed by Richard Oulton for Richard Hearne, and to be sold by Thomas Slater; verse argument. Annotations to the text appear on sig. V6ʳ.
    1684: Nicholas Cox (Manciple of St Edmund Hall, Oxford) had a copy of O in his bookshop. It had probably been previously owned by Gerard Langbaine, and appears on a list compiled by Anthony Wood on Saturday 13 December.

EDITION
W. Bang, in Thomas Heywood, *Pleasant Dialogues and Dramas*, Materialien 1.3 (Louvain, 1903), 105–7.

REFERENCES
Annals 1635; Bodleian, MS Wood E. 4, art. 1, p. 52.

2497. *Vulcan and Apollo*

TEXT
Printed in 1637 (STC 13358).

GENRE
dialogue
Contemporary: dialogue

TITLE
Printed: *Vulcan and Apollo*
Contemporary: *A [Dialogue] betwixt Vulcan and Apollo*

AUTHOR
Thomas Heywood, *translating* Lucian

DATE
Limits: 1630–7
Best Guess: 1635

PLOT
Mercury has only just been born, but proves a precocious child. He has already invented the lyre, and begun to steal things from the other gods: Apollo has lost his bow and arrows, and Vulcan his tongs.

ROLES
VULCAN, a god
APOLLO, a god

Speaking Parts: 2

Speech Prefixes
VULCAN: *Vulcan* (s.p.s)
APOLLO: *Apollo* (s.p.s)

OTHER CHARACTERS
Mercury, a new-born god; also called Cyllenius
Maia, Mercury's mother
Iapetus, an old man
Neptune, a god, whose trident was stolen by Mercury
Mars, a god, whose sword was stolen by Mercury
Cupid, a god, whom Mercury bested at wrestling
Venus, a goddess, whose girdle was stolen by Mercury
Jove, a god, whose sceptre was stolen by Mercury

SETTING
Period: antiquity

SOURCES
Narrative: Lucian, *Dialogues of the Gods* 7: Hephaestus and Apollo

LANGUAGE
English

FORM
Metre: pentameter
Rhyme: couplets
Lines (Spoken): 74
Lines (Written): 84

EARLY TEXTUAL HISTORY
1635: *Pleasant Dialogues and Dramas* entered in the Stationers' Register to Richard Hearne on Saturday 29 August; entry names author. Thomas Wykes had licensed the book for publication.
    1637: included in Thomas Heywood's *Pleasant Dialogues and Dramas* (**O**), sigs. H6ᵛ–H7ᵛ; 3 pages on 2 leaves; printed by Richard Oulton for Richard Hearne, and to be sold by Thomas Slater; verse argument.
    1684: Nicholas Cox (Manciple of St Edmund Hall, Oxford) had a copy of O in his bookshop. It had probably been previously owned by Gerard Langbaine,

and appears on a list compiled by Anthony Wood on Saturday 13 December.

EDITION
W. Bang, in Thomas Heywood, *Pleasant Dialogues and Dramas*, Materialien 1.3 (Louvain, 1903), 108–10.

REFERENCES
Annals 1635; Bodleian, MS Wood E. 4, art. 1, p. 52.

2498. Mercury and Apollo

TEXT
Printed in 1637 (STC 13358).

GENRE
dialogue
Contemporary: dialogue

TITLE
Printed: *Mercury and Apollo*
Contemporary: A [*Dialogue*] betwixt Apollo and Mercury

AUTHOR
Thomas Heywood, *translating* Lucian

DATE
Limits: 1630–7
Best Guess: 1635

PLOT
Jupiter has sent Mercury to ask Apollo not to drive the chariot of the sun for three days, to give him the opportunity to seduce Alcmena. He will need all that time because the product of this mighty bout of sex is to be Hercules.

ROLES
MERCURY, messenger of the gods
APOLLO, god of light; also called Phoebus

Speaking Parts: 2

Speech Prefixes
MERCURY: *Mercury* (s.p.s)
APOLLO: *Apollo* (s.p.s)

OTHER CHARACTERS
Jupiter, a god; also called Jove
Amphitryo of Boeotia
Alcmena, Amphitryo's wife
Alcides (i.e. Hercules), the son whom Jupiter is to beget on Alcmena
Saturn and Rhea, gods of old

SETTING
Period: antiquity

Geography
[*Greece*]: Boeotia; Thebes

SOURCES
Narrative: Lucian, *Dialogues of the Gods* 10: Hermes and Helios

LANGUAGE
English

FORM
Metre: pentameter
Rhyme: couplets
Lines (Spoken): 58
Lines (Written): 61

EARLY TEXTUAL HISTORY
1635: *Pleasant Dialogues and Dramas* entered in the Stationers' Register to Richard Hearne on Saturday 29 August; entry names author. Thomas Wykes had licensed the book for publication.

1637: included in Thomas Heywood's *Pleasant Dialogues and Dramas* (**O**), sigs. H8ʳ–I1ʳ; 3 pages on 2 leaves; printed by Richard Oulton for Richard Hearne, and to be sold by Thomas Slater; verse argument.

1684: Nicholas Cox (Manciple of St Edmund Hall, Oxford) had a copy of O in his bookshop. It had probably been previously owned by Gerard Langbaine, and appears on a list compiled by Anthony Wood on Saturday 13 December.

EDITION
W. Bang, in Thomas Heywood, *Pleasant Dialogues and Dramas*, Materialien 1.3 (Louvain, 1903), 111–13.

REFERENCES
Annals 1635; Bodleian, MS Wood E. 4, art. 1, p. 52.

2499. Mercury and Maia

TEXT
Printed in 1637 (STC 13358).

GENRE
dialogue
Contemporary: dialogue

TITLE
Printed: *Mercury and Maia*
Contemporary: A [*Dialogue*] betwixt Maia and Mercury

AUTHOR
Thomas Heywood, *translating* Lucian

2500. Vulcan and Jupiter

DATE
Limits: 1630–7
Best Guess: 1635

PLOT
Mercury complains to his mother about his excessive workload: he has to clean heaven, wait on the gods, and do Jove's errands to his mortal paramours. Maia tells him he must do the work, not least because Jove is in love and therefore volatile.

ROLES
MERCURY, a young god, Maia's son, the messenger of the gods; also called Hermes
MAIA Atalantiades, Mercury's mother

Speaking Parts: 2

Speech Prefixes
MERCURY: *Merc<ury>* (s.p.s)
MAIA: *Maia* (s.p.s)

OTHER CHARACTERS
The gods
Jove, a god, Mercury's father; also called Jupiter
A Phrygian, Jove's cupbearer (i.e. Ganymede)
Pluto, ruler of the underworld
Leda's sons (i.e. Castor and Pollux)
Mortal women in whom Jove took an amorous interest, including Leda, Alcmena, Semele, Danaë (whom Jove visited in a golden shower), and Antiope
Cadmus, Semele's father

SETTING
Period: antiquity

Geography
[*Greece*]: Argos; Boeotia
[*Asia*]: Phrygia; Sidon

SOURCES
Narrative: Lucian, *Dialogues of the Gods* 24: Hermes and Maia

LANGUAGE
English

FORM
Metre: pentameter
Rhyme: couplets
Lines (Spoken): 72
Lines (Written): 74

EARLY TEXTUAL HISTORY
1635: *Pleasant Dialogues and Dramas* entered in the Stationers' Register to Richard Hearne on Saturday 29 August; entry names author. Thomas Wykes had licensed the book for publication.
  1637: included in Thomas Heywood's *Pleasant Dialogues and Dramas* (**O**), sigs. I1ᵛ–I2ᵛ; 3 pages on 2 leaves; printed by Richard Oulton for Richard Hearne, and to be sold by Thomas Slater; verse argument. Annotations to the text appear on sig. V6ʳ.
  1684: Nicholas Cox (Manciple of St Edmund Hall, Oxford) had a copy of O in his bookshop. It had probably been previously owned by Gerard Langbaine, and appears on a list compiled by Anthony Wood on Saturday 13 December.

EDITION
W. Bang, in Thomas Heywood, *Pleasant Dialogues and Dramas*, Materialien 1.3 (Louvain, 1903), 114–16.

REFERENCES
Annals 1635; Bodleian, MS Wood E. 4, art. 1, p. 52.

2500. Vulcan and Jupiter

TEXT
Printed in 1637 (STC 13358).

GENRE
dialogue
Contemporary: dialogue

TITLE
Printed: *Vulcan and Jupiter*
Contemporary: [*A Dialogue*] *betwixt Jupiter and Vulcan*

AUTHOR
Thomas Heywood, *translating* Lucian

DATE
Limits: 1630–7
Best Guess: 1635

PLOT
Jupiter has a headache, so he orders Vulcan to chop his head open with an axe. Vulcan does so, and Minerva jumps out of the cloven head. He asks Jupiter to give him Minerva as his wife, but Jupiter refuses and ordains that she is to remain a virgin. Vulcan decides to rape her instead, but Jupiter assures him that he will find this impossible.

ROLES
VULCAN, a god
JUPITER, a god; also called Jove
MINERVA, a virgin goddess; also called Pallas (non-speaking)

Speaking Parts: 2

Speech Prefixes
VULCAN: *Vulcan* (s.p.s)
JUPITER: *Jupiter* (s.p.s)

1635

SETTING
Period: antiquity

SOURCES
Narrative: Lucian, *Dialogues of the Gods* 8: Hephaestus and Zeus

LANGUAGE
English
Latin: 2 words (Vulcan)

FORM
Metre: pentameter
Rhyme: couplets
Lines (Spoken): 52
Lines (Written): 56

STAGING
Miscellaneous: The action cannot be literally represented on stage: Jupiter has his head cut open and Minerva is inside.

MUSIC
Dance: Minerva dances a matachin (dialogue)

PROPS
Weapons: an axe (dialogue); a lance and shield (dialogue)

COSTUMES
MINERVA: armour (dialogue)

EARLY TEXTUAL HISTORY
1635: *Pleasant Dialogues and Dramas* entered in the Stationers' Register to Richard Hearne on Saturday 29 August; entry names author. Thomas Wykes had licensed the book for publication.
  1637: included in Thomas Heywood's *Pleasant Dialogues and Dramas* (O), sigs. I3^r–I4^r; 3 pages on 2 leaves; printed by Richard Oulton for Richard Hearne, and to be sold by Thomas Slater; verse argument.
  1684: Nicholas Cox (Manciple of St Edmund Hall, Oxford) had a copy of O in his bookshop. It had probably been previously owned by Gerard Langbaine, and appears on a list compiled by Anthony Wood on Saturday 13 December.

EDITION
W. Bang, in Thomas Heywood, *Pleasant Dialogues and Dramas*, Materialien 1.3 (Louvain, 1903), 117–19.

REFERENCES
Annals 1635; Bodleian, MS Wood E. 4, art. 1, p. 52.

2501. *Neptune and Mercury*

TEXT
Printed in 1637 (STC 13358).

GENRE
dialogue
Contemporary: dialogue

TITLE
Printed: *Neptune and Mercury*
Contemporary: *A [Dialogue] betwixt Mercury and Neptune*

AUTHOR
Thomas Heywood, *translating* Lucian

DATE
Limits: 1630–7
Best Guess: 1635

PLOT
Neptune wants to see Jove, but Mercury tells him that Jove can't see anyone: he is too busy giving birth to Bacchus, whom he has incubated in his thigh after incinerating the pregnant Semele with his lightning.

ROLES
NEPTUNE, a god, Mercury's uncle
MERCURY, a god, Neptune's nephew

Speaking Parts: 2

Speech Prefixes
NEPTUNE: *Nep<tune>* (s.p.s)
MERCURY: *Merc<ury>* (s.p.s)

OTHER CHARACTERS
Jove, Neptune's brother
Juno, Jove's jealous wife
Ganymede, a boy, Jove's catamite
Pallas, Jove's daughter
Semele, Jove's dead paramour
Cadmus, Semele's father
Bacchus Bimater, son of Semele and Jove; also called Dionysus
The nymphs of Nisa

SETTING
Period: antiquity

Geography
[*Greece*]: Thebes
[*Asia Minor*]: Nisa

SOURCES
Narrative: Lucian, *Dialogues of the Gods* 9: Poseidon and Hermes

LANGUAGE
English

FORM
Metre: pentameter
Rhyme: couplets
Lines (Spoken): 62
Lines (Written): 71

EARLY TEXTUAL HISTORY
1635: *Pleasant Dialogues and Dramas* entered in the Stationers' Register to Richard Hearne on Saturday 29 August; entry names author. Thomas Wykes had licensed the book for publication.

1637: included in Thomas Heywood's *Pleasant Dialogues and Dramas* (**O**), sigs. I4^v–I5^v; 3 pages on 2 leaves; printed by Richard Oulton for Richard Hearne, and to be sold by Thomas Slater; verse argument.

1684: Nicholas Cox (Manciple of St Edmund Hall, Oxford) had a copy of O in his bookshop. It had probably been previously owned by Gerard Langbaine, and appears on a list compiled by Anthony Wood on Saturday 13 December.

EDITION
W. Bang, in Thomas Heywood, *Pleasant Dialogues and Dramas*, Materialien 1.3 (Louvain, 1903), 120–2.

REFERENCES
Annals 1635; Bodleian, MS Wood E. 4, art. 1, p. 52.

2502. *Diogenes and Mausolus*

TEXT
Printed in 1637 (STC 13358).

GENRE
dialogue
Contemporary: dialogue

TITLE
Printed: *Diogenes and Mausolus*
Contemporary: A [*Dialogue*] betwixt Mausolus and Diogenes

AUTHOR
Thomas Heywood, *translating* Lucian

DATE
Limits: 1630–7
Best Guess: 1635

PLOT
Mausolus has built up an empire, conquered barbarous nations, and built himself a magnificent tomb, but Diogenes disputes his claim to superiority on that account. In death he will be tormented by the memory of the pleasures he has left behind, whereas Diogenes himself will be famous for his wisdom.

ROLES
DIOGENES, a dead philosopher
MAUSOLUS, the dead King of Caria

Speaking Parts: 2

Speech Prefixes
DIOGENES: *Diogenes* (s.p.s)
MAUSOLUS: *Maus<olus>* (s.p.s)

OTHER CHARACTERS
Mausolus' army
Artists who decorated the mausoleum
Mausolus' sister
Mausolus' queen

SETTING
Period: antiquity; the action nominally takes place after the deaths of both Mausolus (353 BC) and Diogenes (323 BC)
Place: the underworld

Geography
Halicarnassus: the Mausoleum
[*Asia Minor*]: Caria; Synope; Lydia; Ionia; Miletus

SOURCES
Narrative: Lucian, *Dialogues of the Dead* 24: Diogenes and Mausolus

LANGUAGE
English

FORM
Metre: pentameter
Rhyme: couplets
Lines (Spoken): 76
Lines (Written): 79

COSTUMES
DIOGENES and MAUSOLUS: each is lipless and noseless, with a bald head (dialogue; i.e. their faces are now skulls)

EARLY TEXTUAL HISTORY
1635: *Pleasant Dialogues and Dramas* entered in the Stationers' Register to Richard Hearne on Saturday 29 August; entry names author. Thomas Wykes had licensed the book for publication.

1637: included in Thomas Heywood's *Pleasant Dialogues and Dramas* (**O**), sigs. I6^r–I7^r; 3 pages on 2 leaves; printed by Richard Oulton for Richard Hearne, for sale by Thomas Slater; verse argument.

1684: Nicholas Cox (Manciple of St Edmund Hall, Oxford) had a copy of O in his bookshop. It had probably been previously owned by Gerard Langbaine, and appears on a list compiled by Anthony Wood on Saturday 13 December.

EDITION
W. Bang, in Thomas Heywood, *Pleasant Dialogues and Dramas*, Materialien 1.3 (Louvain, 1903), 123–5.

REFERENCES
Annals 1635; Bodleian, MS Wood E. 4, art. 1, p. 52.

2503. *Crates and Diogenes*

TEXT
Printed in 1637 (STC 13358).

GENRE
dialogue
Contemporary: dialogue

TITLE
Printed: *Crates and Diogenes*
Contemporary: [*A Dialogue*] *betwixt Diogenes and Crates*

AUTHOR
Thomas Heywood, *translating* Lucian

DATE
Limits: 1630–7
Best Guess: 1635

PLOT
Crates tells Diogenes about two rich men who made a pact to make each other their heirs, but who drowned together so that neither inherited anything. Diogenes argues that virtue is more important than money.

ROLES
CRATES, a dead philosopher
DIOGENES, a dead philosopher

Speaking Parts: 2

Speech Prefixes
CRATES: *Crat<es>* (s.p.s)
DIOGENES: *Diog<enes>* (s.p.s)

OTHER CHARACTERS
Moerichus, a rich Corinthian, cousin and heir of Aristeas
Aristeas, a rich man, cousin and heir of Moerichus
Thrasycles and Eunomius, who inherited the money
Antisthenes, [a philosopher]

SETTING
Period: antiquity; the action nominally takes place after the deaths of Diogenes (323 BC) and Crates (c. 285 BC)
Place: the underworld

Geography
[*Greece*]: Corinth; Sicyon; Cirrha
[*Italy*]: Iapygium
[*Asia*]: Chaldea; Persia

SOURCES
Narrative: Lucian, *Dialogues of the Dead* 11: Crates and Diogenes
Verbal: Homer, *Iliad* (cited)

FORM
Metre: pentameter
Rhyme: couplets
Lines (Spoken): 94
Lines (Written): 97

EARLY TEXTUAL HISTORY
1635: *Pleasant Dialogues and Dramas* entered in the Stationers' Register to Richard Hearne on Saturday 29 August; entry names author. Thomas Wykes had licensed the book for publication.

1637: included in Thomas Heywood's *Pleasant Dialogues and Dramas* (O), sigs. I7^v–K1^r; 4 pages on 3 leaves; printed by Richard Oulton for Richard Hearne, and to be sold by Thomas Slater; verse argument. Annotations to the text appear on sig. V6^{r-v}.

1684: Nicholas Cox (Manciple of St Edmund Hall, Oxford) had a copy of O in his bookshop. It had probably been previously owned by Gerard Langbaine, and appears on a list compiled by Anthony Wood on Saturday 13 December.

EDITION
W. Bang, in Thomas Heywood, *Pleasant Dialogues and Dramas*, Materialien 1.3 (Louvain, 1903), 126–9.

REFERENCES
Annals 1635; Bodleian, MS Wood E. 4, art. 1, p. 52.

2504. *Charon, Menippus, Mercury*

TEXT
Printed in 1637 (STC 13358).

GENRE
dialogue
Contemporary: dialogue

TITLE
Printed: *Charon, Menippus, Mercury*

Contemporary: A [Dialogue] betwixt Charon, Menippus, and Mercury

AUTHOR
Thomas Heywood, *translating* Lucian

DATE
Limits: 1630–7
Best Guess: 1635

PLOT
Menippus cannot pay the ferryman Charon for his passage into the underworld, so he asks for help from Mercury, who guided him down there. Mercury doesn't want to be burdened with paying dead men's fares for them. Menippus tells Charon that, having helped to row the boat, he has worked his passage and owes nothing. In any event, the dead cannot be taken back to the land of the living, so Charon simply has to accept the situation.

ROLES
CHARON, ferryman of the underworld
MENIPPUS, a shade
MERCURY, a god; also called Hermes

Speaking Parts: 3

Speech Prefixes
CHARON: *Char<on>* (s.p.s)
MENIPPUS: *Menip<pus>* (s.p.s)
MERCURY: *Merc<ury>* (s.p.s)

OTHER CHARACTERS
Aeacus, [judge of the underworld, Charon's master]
Hecate, [goddess of the underworld]
The passengers aboard Charon's boat

SETTING
Period: antiquity; the action takes place shortly after the death of Menippus (third century BC)
Place: the underworld

Geography
[*Hades*]: River Phlegethon

SOURCES
Narrative: Lucian, *Dialogues of the Dead* 22: Charon and Menippus

LANGUAGE
English

FORM
Metre: pentameter
Rhyme: couplets
Lines (Spoken): 52
Lines (Written): 62

PROPS
Large Portable Objects: a rope (dialogue); a staff (dialogue); a scrip (dialogue; said to contain pulse)

EARLY TEXTUAL HISTORY
1635: *Pleasant Dialogues and Dramas* entered in the Stationers' Register to Richard Hearne on Saturday 29 August; entry names author. Thomas Wykes had licensed the book for publication.
1637: included in Thomas Heywood's *Pleasant Dialogues and Dramas* (**O**), sigs. K1ᵛ–K2ᵛ; 3 pages on 2 leaves; printed by Richard Oulton for Richard Hearne, and to be sold by Thomas Slater; verse argument.
1684: Nicholas Cox (Manciple of St Edmund Hall, Oxford) had a copy of O in his bookshop. It had probably been previously owned by Gerard Langbaine, and appears on a list compiled by Anthony Wood on Saturday 13 December.

EDITION
W. Bang, in Thomas Heywood, *Pleasant Dialogues and Dramas*, Materialien 1.3 (Louvain, 1903), 130–2.

REFERENCES
Annals 1635; Bodleian, MS Wood E. 4, art. 1, p. 52.

2505. Menippus, Aeacus, Pythagoras, Empedocles, and Socrates

TEXT
Printed in 1637 (STC 13358).

GENRE
dialogue
Contemporary: dialogue

TITLE
Printed: *Menippus, Aeacus, Pythagoras, Empedocles, and Socrates*
Contemporary: A [Dialogue] betwixt Menippus, Aeacus, Pythagoras, Empedocles, and Socrates

AUTHOR
Thomas Heywood, *translating* Lucian

DATE
Limits: 1630–7
Best Guess: 1635

PLOT
Aeacus gives the newly arrived Menippus a guided tour of the underworld and its inhabitants. He meets three illustrious sages, but is uninterested in staying with them for an eternity of philosophical discussion: he would rather spend his time deriding the damned.

ROLES
MENIPPUS, a shade
AEACUS the Great, Judge of the dead
PYTHAGORAS, a dead philosopher
EMPEDOCLES, a dead philosopher
SOCRATES, a dead Athenian philosopher

Speaking Parts: 5

Speech Prefixes
MENIPPUS: *Menip<pus>* (s.p.s)
AEACUS: *Aeac<us>* (s.p.s)
PYTHAGORAS: *Pythag<oras>* (s.p.s)
EMPEDOCLES: *Emped<ocles>* (s.p.s)
SOCRATES: *Socrat<es>* (s.p.s)

OTHER CHARACTERS
Pluto, the infernal King
The ferryman of the underworld
The Furies
The infernal Queen (i.e. Proserpina)
The dead Greek heroes, including Agamemnon, Achilles, Idomen (i.e. Idomeneus), Ulysses, Ajax, Diomede, Nestor, Palamedes
Dead rulers, including Cyrus, Croesus, Sardanapalus (also called Sardanapal), Midas, and Xerxes
Dead sages, including Solon, Thales, Pittacus, Aristippus, and Plato
Ercecestides, Solon's father (*sic*; i.e. Execestides)
Socrates' dead companions, Charmides, Phaedrus, and Clinias' son [i.e. Alcibiades]
Athenian sophists
The tyrant of Sicily

SETTING
Period: antiquity; the action takes place shortly after the death of Menippus (third century BC)
Place: the underworld

Geography
The Underworld: River Pyriphlegethon; Lake Styx
Greece: Athens
The Hellespont
Sicily: Mount Etna

SOURCES
Narrative: Lucian, *Dialogues of the Dead* 20: Menippus and Aeacus
Works Mentioned: Homer, *Iliad*

LANGUAGE
English

FORM
Metre: pentameter
Rhyme: couplets
Lines (Spoken): 128
Lines (Written): 144

PROPS
Large Portable Objects: a scrip (dialogue; said to contain pulse)

COSTUMES AND MAKE-UP
EMPEDOCLES: sandals; covered with ash (dialogue)
SOCRATES: bald and noseless (dialogue)

EARLY TEXTUAL HISTORY
1635: *Pleasant Dialogues and Dramas* entered in the Stationers' Register to Richard Hearne on Saturday 29 August; entry names author. Thomas Wykes had licensed the book for publication.
1637: included in Thomas Heywood's *Pleasant Dialogues and Dramas* (O), sigs. K3ʳ–K5ʳ; 5 pages on 3 leaves; printed by Richard Oulton for Richard Hearne, and to be sold by Thomas Slater; verse argument. Annotations to the text appear on sigs. V6ᵛ–V7ʳ.
1684: Nicholas Cox (Manciple of St Edmund Hall, Oxford) had a copy of O in his bookshop. It had probably been previously owned by Gerard Langbaine, and appears on a list compiled by Anthony Wood on Saturday 13 December.

EDITION
W. Bang, in Thomas Heywood, *Pleasant Dialogues and Dramas*, Materialien 1.3 (Louvain, 1903), 133–7.

REFERENCES
Annals 1635; Bodleian, MS Wood E. 4, art. 1, p. 52.

2506. Nireus, Thersites, Menippus

TEXT
Printed in 1637 (STC 13358).

GENRE
dialogue
Contemporary: dialogue

TITLE
Printed: *Nireus, Thersites, Menippus*
Contemporary: *A [Dialogue] betwixt Nireus, Thersites, and Menippus*
Alternative Modernization: *Nereus, Thersites, Menippus*

AUTHOR
Thomas Heywood, *translating* Lucian

DATE
Limits: 1630–7
Best Guess: 1635

PLOT
Nireus and Thersites quarrel over which of them is the more beautiful. They appoint Menippus as arbiter, but

Menippus cannot tell which of them is which: the dead all look alike.

ROLES
NIREUS, a fair Athenian
MENIPPUS, a cynic philosopher
THERSITES, a deformed and ugly Greek captain

Speaking Parts: 3

Speech Prefixes
NIREUS: *Ner<eus>* (s.p.s)
MENIPPUS: *Menip<pus>* (s.p.s)
THERSITES: *Thers<ites>* (s.p.s)

OTHER CHARACTERS
Aglaea, Nireus' mother
Charopes, Nireus' forebear

SETTING
Period: antiquity; the action takes place after the death of Menippus (third century BC)
Place: the underworld

Geography
Greece: Athens
Troy

SOURCES
Narrative: Lucian, *Dialogues of the Dead* 25: Nireus, Thersites, Menippus
Works Mentioned: Homer, *Iliad*; Diogenes Laertius, *Lives* 6: Menippus (notes); Varro, *Satyra Menippea* (notes)

LANGUAGE
English

FORM
Metre: pentameter
Rhyme: couplets
Lines (Spoken): 36
Lines (Written): 41

COSTUMES
NIREUS and THERSITES: physically identical, including bald heads (dialogue; in effect, they are both just skeletons)

EARLY TEXTUAL HISTORY
1635: *Pleasant Dialogues and Dramas* entered in the Stationers' Register to Richard Hearne on Saturday 29 August; entry names author. Thomas Wykes had licensed the book for publication.
1637: included in Thomas Heywood's *Pleasant Dialogues and Dramas* (**O**), sigs. K5ᵛ–K6ʳ; 2 pages on 2 leaves; printed by Richard Oulton for Richard Hearne, and to be sold by Thomas Slater; verse argument. Annotations to the text appear on sig. V5ʳ.

1684: Nicholas Cox (Manciple of St Edmund Hall, Oxford) had a copy of O in his bookshop. It had probably been previously owned by Gerard Langbaine, and appears on a list compiled by Anthony Wood on Saturday 13 December.

EDITION
W. Bang, in Thomas Heywood, *Pleasant Dialogues and Dramas*, Materialien 1.3 (Louvain, 1903), 138–9.

REFERENCES
Annals 1635; Bodleian, MS Wood E. 4, art. 1, p. 52.

2507. *Deorum iudicium* [The Judgement of the Gods]

TEXT
Printed in 1637 (STC 13358).

GENRE
dialogue
Contemporary: dialogue

TITLE
Printed: *Deorum iudicium*
Alternative Modernization: *Deorum judicium*

AUTHOR
Thomas Heywood, *translating* Lucian

DATE
Limits: 1630–7
Best Guess: 1635

PLOT
A golden apple is to be awarded to the most beautiful of three goddesses, Juno, Minerva, and Venus. Jupiter is unable to judge the beauty contest himself, because he knows that, whoever he chooses, the two losers will resent him for it; so he appoints Paris to do the job.

Mercury brings the contestants to Paris, who asks all three to take their clothes off so that he can judge correctly. Dazzled by the array of naked beauty, he asks to see them individually. Each offers him a bribe: Juno offers world domination, Minerva military and artistic glory, and Venus a beautiful bride, Helen of Sparta. Paris is only interested in Venus' offer. Venus gives him detailed instructions on how to seduce Helen, and Paris gives Venus the golden apple.

ROLES
JUPITER, a god, Juno's husband and brother, father of Venus and Minerva; also called Jove
Lord MERCURY, a young god; also called Hermes
VENUS, a goddess, Queen of Beauty, Jupiter's daughter
JUNO, a goddess, Jupiter's wife and sister

MINERVA, a virgin goddess, Jupiter's daughter; also called Pallas
PARIS, a young, unmarried Trojan shepherd

Speaking Parts: 6

Speech Prefixes
JUPITER: *Jupit<er>* (s.p.s)
MERCURY: *Merc<ury>* (s.p.s)
VENUS: *Venus* (s.p.s)
JUNO: *Juno* (s.p.s)
MINERVA: *Minerva* (s.p.s)
PARIS: *Paris* (s.p.s)

OTHER CHARACTERS
Ate, sender of the golden apple (arg.)
Priam, Paris's father, a ruler
Ganymede, Paris's cousin, a Trojan shepherd abducted by Jupiter for sexual purposes
Minos, a judge
Mars, Venus' lover
Paris' companion, a young woman of Ida (i.e. Oenone)
Vulcan, a god
Anchises, Venus' lover
Maia, Mercury's mother
Helen, Jupiter's daughter, a beautiful Spartan woman, Menelaus' wife
Leda, Helen's mother
Theseus, who raped Helen during her childhood
Princes and potentates who woo Helen
Menelaus, a king and a Pelopidan, Helen's husband
Cupid and Amability, Venus' children, who are to abet Paris's wooing of Helen
The Graces, whom Venus will ask to attend Paris
Desire and Hymen, whom Venus offers as agents in the seduction of Helen

SETTING
Period: antiquity
Place: Phrygia

Geography
Phrygia: Troy; Mount Ida; Gargarus
Asia: Lydia
Greece: Argos; Corinth; Sparta (also called Lacena and Lacedaemon)

SOURCES
Narrative: Lucian, *Dearum iudicium*

LANGUAGE
English

FORM
Metre: pentameter
Rhyme: couplets
Lines (Spoken): 464
Lines (Written): 489

STAGING
Miscellaneous: If the dialogue were staged, the three goddesses would appear nude.

PROPS
Weapons: a goad (dialogue); a truncheon (dialogue)
Small Portable Objects: a golden apple (dialogue)

COSTUMES AND MAKE-UP
VENUS: painted cheeks (dialogue); a girdle (dialogue); gay, rich, coloured clothes (dialogue); strips naked on stage, and dresses again (dialogue)
JUNO: strips naked on stage, and dresses again (dialogue)
MINERVA: a plumed helmet with a brim covering her forehead (dialogue); strips naked on stage, and dresses again (dialogue)

EARLY TEXTUAL HISTORY
1635: *Pleasant Dialogues and Dramas* entered in the Stationers' Register to Richard Hearne on Saturday 29 August; entry names author. Thomas Wykes had licensed the book for publication.
1637: included in Thomas Heywood's *Pleasant Dialogues and Dramas* (**O**), sigs. K6^v–L5^v; 15 pages on 8 leaves; printed by Richard Oulton for Richard Hearne, and to be sold by Thomas Slater; verse argument.
1684: Nicholas Cox (Manciple of St Edmund Hall, Oxford) had a copy of O in his bookshop. It had probably been previously owned by Gerard Langbaine, and appears on a list compiled by Anthony Wood on Saturday 13 December.

EDITION
W. Bang, in Thomas Heywood, *Pleasant Dialogues and Dramas*, Materialien 1.3 (Louvain, 1903), 140–54.

REFERENCES
Annals 1635; Bentley, iv. 564–5; Bodleian, MS Wood E. 4, art. 1, p. 52.

2508. Jupiter and Io

TEXT
Printed in 1637 (STC 13358).

There is dispute about the origins and status of the three original compositions (the others being **2509–10**) that follow the translated dialogues in the 1637 collection. Heywood himself is inconsistent in his assumptions about them: in the table of contents and epistle to the reader he treats them as generically distinct, 'dramas' and 'stage-poetry' rather than 'dialogues'; yet in the annotations he calls *Jupiter and Io* a 'dialogue', and the presentation of all three pieces, with verse arguments and (in the first two cases) titles drawn from their principal speakers, is consistent with the translations that have gone before. Thus, there are grounds for seeing them as either literary or theatrical pieces.

2508. Jupiter and Io

Greg suggested (after Fleay) that *Jupiter and Io* began as part of a 1590s Admiral's Men play, because a number of relevant items appear in an inventory taken by Philip Henslowe in March 1598: a coat for Juno, wings for Mercury, a head for Argus. Since there is no appropriate title in Henslowe's records, the hypothesis generates further speculation, supported by no evidence whatever, that the play originated as part of an anthology, *Five Plays in One* (**1063**). The principal problem with this suggestion is that it cherry-picks the overlapping elements of the inventory and ignores others, such as Iris's head and rainbow, which are associated with related subject matter but have no connection with *Jupiter and Io*. A further weakness is the absence of any interim evidence of the play's existence: if it had existed as early as the 1590s, and if Heywood recycled his work as systematically as is often suggested, one might well wonder why the material did not find its way into *The Silver Age* (**1645**).

The three playlets are brief and rather static; they are unlikely to have a basis in commercial theatre, but sit neatly in Heywood's development towards more literary modes of writing in the final phase of his career. *Jupiter and Io* and *Apollo and Daphne* (**2509**) might just as well be a second phase of the renewed interest in the amours of the classical gods evidenced in *Love's Mistress* (**2451**), while *Amphrisa the Forsaken Shepherdess* (**2510**) obviously appeals to another strand of 1630s courtly taste.

GENRE
classical myth
Contemporary: drama (O contents); dialogue (annotation)

TITLE
Printed: *Jupiter and Io*

AUTHOR
Thomas Heywood

DATE
Limits: 1630–7
Best Guess: 1635

The limits are those of the other datable items included in *Pleasant Dialogues and Dramas*, which seems to be a collection of Heywood's early 1630s writings, mostly on classical themes.

PLOT
Io boasts of her superiority to her fellow nymphs: they only have mortals for their suitors, whereas she is loved by a god, Jupiter. The nymphs think this an idle vaunt until Jupiter appears and confirms Io's story. Jupiter conjures up a fog to shroud their love-making, but this makes jealous Juno suspicious. Jupiter turns Io into a cow to conceal his adultery, but Juno asks him to give her the cow, for use as a sacrificial offering. Jupiter has no choice: he hands over the cow, and Juno sets Argus to guard her and treat her harshly.

Io's disappearance worries her father Inachus. He and his friends see Argus maltreating the cow, and notice that she weeps like a human being; she also uses her hoofs to write her name on the ground. Hearing Inachus' laments, Jupiter sends Mercury to release Io. Argus boasts to Mercury about the tricks his cow can do. Mercury sings him to sleep and decapitates him; Juno finds his body and turns him into a peacock. Jupiter and Juno reach a compromise: Juno will release Io, who will then go into exile in Egypt; Jupiter will leave her alone, but the Egyptians will worship her as a goddess.

SCENE DESIGNATION
sc.1–6 (O undivided)

ROLES
IO, a water-nymph, Inachus' daughter
DAPHNE, a water-nymph, Peneus' daughter
NAIADES, water-nymphs (sc.1, *non-speaking*)
JUPITER, god of thunder, King of the gods, Juno's husband and brother; also called Jove
Queen JUNO, a goddess, Jupiter's wife and sister; also called Saturnia
ARGUS, a herdsman, Juno's servant
River INACHUS, Io's old father
PENEUS, a river, Daphne's father
APIDANUS, a river, Amphrysus' neighbour; also called Apidan
AMPHRYSUS, a river, Apidanus' neighbour
MERCURY, a crafty god, Jupiter's son and servant

Speaking Parts: 10

Stage Directions and Speech Prefixes
IO: *Io* (s.d.s and s.p.s)
DAPHNE: *Daphne* (s.d.s and s.p.s)
NAIADES: *other Nymphs called Naiades, the daughters of the Rivers near adjacent* | *the other Nymphs* (s.d.s)
JUPITER: *Jupiter* (s.d.s); *Jupit<er>* (s.p.s)
JUNO: *Juno* (s.d.s and s.p.s)
ARGUS: *Argus* (s.d.s and s.p.s)
INACHUS: *Inachus the father of Io* (s.d.s); *Inachus* (s.p.s)
PENEUS: *Peneus* [one of the] *Rivers* | [one of] *the other Rivers* (s.d.s); *Peneus* (s.p.s)
APIDANUS: *Appidanus* [one of the] *Rivers* | [one of] *the other Rivers* (s.d.s); *Apid<anus>* (s.p.s)
AMPHRYSUS: *Amphrisus* [one of the] *Rivers* | [one of] *the other Rivers* (s.d.s); *Amphr<isus>* (s.p.s)
MERCURY: *Mercury* | *Mercurie* (s.d.s); *Merc<ury>* (s.p.s)

OTHER CHARACTERS
Satyrs, fauns, and shepherds, the nymphs' admirers (sc.1)
Daphne's suitors, gallants from both city and court (sc.1)
Saturn, a melancholy god, deposed by his son Jupiter (sc.1)
Phoebus, the sun-god; also called Apollo (sc.1, 6)
Neptune, god of the sea (sc.1–2)
The Nereae and Dorides, water-goddesses and Neptune's prostitutes (sc.2)

Jupiter's early paramours, including Danaë, Alcmena, Semele, Callisto, and Leda (sc.2)
Hercules, who overcame the dog of Hell (sc.3)
Aristor, Argus' father (sc.6)
The Pierides, or Muses, who tell of the war of the giants (sc.6)
The rebellious giants, led by Typhon (sc.6)
Bacchus, a god (sc.6)
Diana, a goddess; also called Dian (sc.6)
Venus, a goddess (sc.6)
Mars, a god (sc.6)
Pan, god of shepherds (sc.6)
Syrinx, a nymph of Diana pursued by Pan and turned into a reed (sc.6)
Ladon, who transformed Syrinx into a reed (sc.6)

SETTING
Period: antiquity
Place: Tempe

Geography
Greece: River Peneus; Mount Pindus; Mount Haemon; River Apidanus; River Epineus; River Amphrysus; River Aeas; River Inachus; Argos; Thebes; Pelagia; Sparta; Thessaly; Mount Ossa; Mount Pelion; Mount Parnassus; Arcadia
[Africa]: Libya; Egypt
[Asia]: Caucasus

SOURCES
Narrative: Ovid, *Metamorphoses* 1
Verbal: Ovid, *Metamorphoses* 1 (sc.2)

LANGUAGE
English
Latin: 6 words (sc.2; Juno)

FORM
Metre: pentameter; a few trimeters
Rhyme: blank verse; some couplets
Lines (Spoken): 655 (654 verse, 1 prose)
Lines (Written): 746

STAGING
Miscellaneous: 'a great damp ariseth' (sc.1, s.d.; i.e. mist); Argus is beheaded on stage (sc.6, s.d.; perhaps facilitated by the mask; see COSTUMES)

MUSIC AND SOUND
Sound Effects: thunder (sc.1, s.d.)
Music: pipes (sc.6, s.d.)
Song: 'Syrinx, one of Dian's train', sc.6, Mercury, 30 lines.

PROPS
Pyrotechnics: a burning 'trisull' (i.e. thunderbolt; sc.1, s.d.)
Weapons: a goad (sc.6, dialogue); a blade weapon (sc.6, implicit)

Animals: a white, long-horned cow (sc.3, s.d.; sc.4, 6, dialogue)
Small Portable Objects: a halter (sc.4, dialogue; sc.6, s.d.; around the cow's neck); flowers (sc.4, dialogue); probably a caduceus (sc.5, dialogue); Argus' severed head (sc.6, implicit)
Scenery: possibly a rock (sc.6, dialogue)

COSTUMES
IO: curled golden hair (dialogue)
DAPHNE: curled hair (dialogue)
ARGUS: a hundred eyes all around his head (s.d.; presumably the actor wears a mask)
MERCURY: a petasus and winged sandals (sc.5, dialogue); disguised as 'a young, formal shepherd' (sc.6, s.d.)

EARLY TEXTUAL HISTORY
1635: *Pleasant Dialogues and Dramas* entered in the Stationers' Register to Richard Hearne on Saturday 29 August; entry names author. Thomas Wykes had licensed the book for publication.
1637: included in Thomas Heywood's *Pleasant Dialogues and Dramas* (**O**), sigs. L6ʳ–M8ᵛ; 11 leaves; printed by Richard Oulton for Richard Hearne, and to be sold by Thomas Slater; verse argument. Annotations to the text appear on sigs. V5ʳ⁻ᵛ.
1684: Nicholas Cox (Manciple of St Edmund Hall, Oxford) had a copy of O in his bookshop. It had probably been previously owned by Gerard Langbaine, and appears on a list compiled by Anthony Wood on Saturday 13 December.

EDITION
W. Bang, in Thomas Heywood, *Pleasant Dialogues and Dramas*, Materialien 1.3 (Louvain, 1903), 155–76.

REFERENCES
Annals 1635; Bentley, iv. 574; Bodleian, MS Wood E. 4, art. 1, p. 52; Greg 528.

2509. Apollo and Daphne

TEXT
Printed in 1637 (STC 13358).

GENRE
classical myth
Contemporary: drama (O contents)

TITLE
Printed: *Apollo and Daphne*

AUTHOR
Thomas Heywood

2509. Apollo and Daphne

DATE
Limits: 1630–7
Best Guess: 1635

The limits are those of the other datable items included in *Pleasant Dialogues and Dramas*, which seems to be a collection of Heywood's early 1630s writings, mostly on classical themes. The play's composition, or at least its transcription, probably followed immediately after that of *Jupiter and Io* (**2508**): on sig. N3ʳ, Peneus is mistakenly assigned the speech prefix *Inach.*, indicating that the author or copyist has momentarily confused one nymph's father with another—Inachus being Io's father in *Jupiter and Io*.

PLOT
Peneus encourages Daphne to marry and procreate, and introduces two suitors. Evasive and unwilling to commit herself, she asks for a few months' respite to study men and marriage.

In his role as the sun, Apollo has revealed Venus' adultery with Mars, and she has sworn vengeance. At her instigation, Cupid makes him fall in love with Daphne. Daphne runs away, and Apollo gives chase; but Daphne prays to the chaste goddesses, and is transformed into a laurel tree before Apollo can catch her.

Apollo's infatuation has affected his work as the sun-god, and time has gone haywire: Aurora has to get up early (which displeases her husband), the seasons are beginning to meld into one another, and Day and Night are not getting their proper quota of hours. Apollo asserts his authority over them, but promises to do a better job in future.

SCENE DESIGNATION
sc.1–4 (O undivided)

ROLES
River PENEUS, Daphne's father
DAPHNE, a young nymph, Peneus' daughter
AMPHRYSUS, a river, Daphne's suitor, Apidanus' friend
APIDANUS, a river, Daphne's suitor, Amphrysus' friend; also called Apidane
Two NYMPHS, Daphne's attendants
VENUS, a goddess, Cupid's mother
CUPID, boy god of love, Venus' little son
APOLLO, the sun, god of light and archery; also called Phoebus
AURORA, the dawn, a married woman
Two of the HOURS
SPRING, a season; also called Ver
SUMMER, a female season
AUTUMN, a male season
WINTER, a male season
DAY, the sun's mistress

Speaking Parts: 17
Allegorical Roles: 7 (interact with Apollo and Aurora)

Stage Directions and Speech Prefixes
PENEUS: *the river Peneus the father of Daphne* (s.d.s); *Peneus* (s.p.s; also, in error, *Inach<us>*)
DAPHNE: *Daphne* (s.d.s); *Daph<ne>* (s.p.s)
AMPHRYSUS: *Amphrisus* [one of] *two Rivers that were Suitors to* [Daphne] (s.d.s); *Amph<risus>* (s.p.s)
APIDANUS: *Apidanus* [one of] *two Rivers that were Suitors to* [Daphne] (s.d.s); *Appid<anus>* (s.p.s)
NYMPHS: *two Nymphs Attendants on Daphne* (s.d.s); *1 Nymph | 2 Nymph* (s.p.s)
VENUS: *Venus* (s.d.s and s.p.s)
CUPID: *Cupid* (s.d.s and s.p.s)
APOLLO: *Apollo* (s.d.s and s.p.s); *Phoeb<us>* (s.p.s)
AURORA: *Aurora* (s.d.s and s.p.s)
HOURS: *the Hours* (s.d.s); *1 Hour | 2 Hour* (s.p.s)
SPRING: [one of] *the four Seasons* (s.d.s); *Spring* (s.d.s and s.p.s)
SUMMER: [one of] *the four Seasons* (s.d.s); *Summer* (s.d.s and s.p.s)
AUTUMN: [one of] *the four Seasons* (s.d.s); *Autumn* (s.d.s and s.p.s)
WINTER: [one of] *the four Seasons* (s.d.s); *Winter* (s.d.s and s.p.s)
DAY: *Day* (s.d.s and s.p.s)

OTHER CHARACTERS
Mars, Venus' lover (arg., sc.2)
Vulcan, a smith, Venus' husband (arg.)
The gods, who laughed at the discomfiture of Venus and Mars (arg.)
Peneus' parents (sc.1)
Daphne's mother (sc.1)
Diana, the moon, Apollo's sister (sc.1, 3)
Endymion, loved by the Moon (sc.1)
Jove, Apollo's father (sc.3)
The nine Muses, Apollo's daughters (sc.3)
Juno, a goddess, queen of chaste marriage (sc.3)
Tython, Aurora's old husband (sc.4)
Night, a female character who can never be in the same place as Day (sc.4)

SETTING
Period: antiquity
Place: Greece

Geography
Greece: River Peneus; River Amphrysus; River Apidanus; Mount Eryx (actually in Sicily); Delphos (i.e. Delphi)
[Cyprus]: Paphos
[Asia Minor]: Tenedos
[Africa]: Ethiopia; Pharos
The Antipodes

SOURCES
Narrative: Ovid, *Metamorphoses* 1

LANGUAGE
English

Latin: 12 words (sc.1, 4; Apollo, Aurora, Hours, Spring, Summer, Autumn, Winter, Day)

FORM
Metre: pentameter; a little prose
Rhyme: blank verse
Lines (Spoken): 419 (412 verse, 7 prose)
Lines (Written): 474

STAGING
Miscellaneous: an arrow is fired at Apollo on stage, and hits him (sc.1, s.d.); Daphne is transformed into a laurel on stage (sc.3, s.d.)

MUSIC
Music: sudden music (sc.3, s.d.)
Song: 'Howsoe'er the minutes go', sc.4, Aurora, Hours, Spring, Summer, Autumn, Winter, Day, 12 lines

PROPS
Weapons: a bow and a quiver of gold-tipped arrows (sc.1, dialogue)
Scenery: a laurel tree (sc.3, s.d.; sc.4, dialogue)

COSTUMES
APOLLO: golden hair (dialogue); glittering beams (sc.1, s.d.)

EARLY TEXTUAL HISTORY
1635: *Pleasant Dialogues and Dramas* entered in the Stationers' Register to Richard Hearne on Saturday 29 August; entry names author. Thomas Wykes had licensed the book for publication.
1637: included in Thomas Heywood's *Pleasant Dialogues and Dramas* (O), sigs. N1ʳ–N8ʳ, 15 pages on 8 leaves; printed by Richard Oulton for Richard Hearne, and to be sold by Thomas Slater; verse argument.
1684: Nicholas Cox (Manciple of St Edmund Hall, Oxford) had a copy of O in his bookshop. It had probably been previously owned by Gerard Langbaine, and appears on a list compiled by Anthony Wood on Saturday 13 December.

EDITION
W. Bang, in Thomas Heywood, *Pleasant Dialogues and Dramas*, Materialien 1.3 (Louvain, 1903), 177–91.

REFERENCES
Annals 1635; Bentley, iv. 558–9; Bodleian, MS Wood E. 4, art. 1, p. 52; Greg 529; Hazlitt, 16.

2510. *Amphrisa, the Forsaken Shepherdess* ◈

TEXT
Printed in 1637 (STC 13358).

GENRE
pastoral
Contemporary: pastoral drama (O contents)

TITLE
Printed: *Amphrisa, the Forsaken Shepherdess*
Contemporary: *Amphrisa, or The Forsaken Shepherdess*; *Pelopaea and Alope*

AUTHOR
Thomas Heywood

DATE
Limits: 1630–7
Best Guess: 1635

The limits are defined by the other datable items included in *Pleasant Dialogues and Dramas*, which seems to be a collection of Heywood's early 1630s writings, mostly on classical themes. This playlet obviously appeals to the period's courtly taste for pastoral.

PLOT
Jilted by her lover, Amphrisa has become melancholy, but accepts her fellow shepherdesses' attempts to cure her. Out hunting, the Queen and her nymphs overhear their conversation, and show themselves. The shepherdesses entertain the Queen with song and dance and are rewarded with jewels.

ROLES
PELOPAEA, a shepherdess
ALOPE, a shepherdess
AMPHRISA, a shepherdess
The QUEEN of Arcadia
Two NYMPHS attending the Queen

Speaking Parts: 6

Stage Directions and Speech Prefixes
PELOPAEA: [one of] *two Shepherdesses* | *Pelopaea* (s.d.s); *Pelop<aea>* (s.p.s)
ALOPE: [one of] *two Shepherdesses* | *Alope* (s.d.s); *Alop<e>* (s.p.s)
AMPHRISA: *Amphrisa* (s.d.s and s.p.s)
QUEEN: [the shepherdesses'] *Queen* (s.d.s); *Queen* (s.p.s)
NYMPHS: *two Nymphs* (s.d.s); *1 Nymph* | *2 Nymph* (s.p.s)

OTHER CHARACTERS
Amphrisa's false lover
Swains of Arcadia

SETTING
Period: antiquity (?)
Time-Scheme: The action takes place before noon.
Place: Arcadia

SOURCES
Verbal: Ovid, *Ars amatoria*

2511. *Byrsa basilica*

LANGUAGE
English

FORM
Metre: pentameter; one passage of tetrameter
Rhyme: blank verse, some couplets
Lines (Spoken): 295
Lines (Written): 346

MUSIC
Music: unspecified music (s.d.)
Song: 'We that have known no greater state', Amphrisa, 14 lines (with a further 12 spoken by Amphrisa and Alope)
Dance: all characters dance a measure (s.d.)

PROPS
Small Portable Objects: jewels (s.d.)
Scenery: boughs (dialogue)

COSTUMES
PELOPAEA and ALOPE: coarse, plain clothing (dialogue)
AMPHRISA: coarse, plain clothing (dialogue); a willow wreath (s.d.; put on and removed on stage)

EARLY TEXTUAL HISTORY
1635: *Pleasant Dialogues and Dramas* entered in the Stationers' Register to Richard Hearne on Saturday 29 August; entry names author. Thomas Wykes had licensed the book for publication.
 1637: included in Thomas Heywood's *Pleasant Dialogues and Dramas* (**O**), sigs. N8^v–O5^v, 11 pages on 6 leaves; printed by Richard Oulton for Richard Hearne, and to be sold by Thomas Slater; verse argument.
 1684: Nicholas Cox (Manciple of St Edmund Hall, Oxford) had a copy of O in his bookshop. It had probably been previously owned by Gerard Langbaine, and appears on a list compiled by Anthony Wood on Saturday 13 December.

EDITION
W. Bang, in Thomas Heywood, *Pleasant Dialogues and Dramas*, Materialien 1.3 (Louvain, 1903), 192–202.

REFERENCES
Annals 1635; Bentley, iv. 558; Bodleian, MS Wood E. 4, art. 1, p. 52; Greg 530; Hazlitt, 12.

2511. *Byrsa basilica* [The Imperial Burse]

TEXT
MS (Oxford: Bodleian, MS Tanner 207); either an authorial fair copy, or a scribal transcript. The transcription contains many errors, but is in the same hand as the parish register of All Saints, Worcester, which was begun in 1641 during the author's incumbency; it follows that the careless transcriber was either the author or his parish clerk.

GENRE
comedy
Contemporary: *fabula* (prol.)

TITLE
MS: *Byrsa basilica, seu Regale excambium*

AUTHOR
John Rickets

DATE
1635

Annals puts the play in 1633, based on the apparent date of the forged letter in 1.7, which Bowers read as 20 August 1633. However, the final, heavily inked digit seems to be a 3 corrected to a 5, and the news in 3.5 establishes that the play was written after May 1635 and probably before November.

ORIGINAL PRODUCTION
Jesus College, Cambridge (?)

Rickets was a member of the college, but was appointed to a rectorship in Worcester on 14 October 1633. He might have sent the play back to his *alma mater* for production, or might have merely intended it for or imagined it in performance in a university context.

PLOT
Rialto completes the building of a Royal Exchange in London. Merchants congregate there, and Dequoy sees new opportunities for villainy. The public insurer Doso is concerned that many ships have failed to come in, leaving him liable to pay out on the owners' insurance policies; but, having heard nothing from Emporius, his factor in Venice, he has no money with which to pay. Emporius arrives in London incognito, hoping to woo Doso's niece Virginia, and brings forged letters of credit establishing his alternative identity as Cosmopolites. He finds he has a rival for Virginia, the French trader Cap-a-Pie, who fights a duel with him, and scares him off by fixing a piece of cheese, which Emporius detests, on the end of his sword. But Emporius turns the tables by forcing Cap-a-Pie to eat a black pudding, and the Frenchman signs a contract formally renouncing any claim to Virginia. Emporius plans to elope with her; she intends to fund their journey by stealing money from Doso.
 Despite his contract, Cap-a-Pie continues to pursue Virginia. Dequoy gives him some pills to render him immune to the effects of alcohol, so that he will be able to out-drink Emporius and take the chance to steal Virginia from him. The pills don't work, and Cap-a-Pie staggers away drunk. Virginia steals his clothes, disguises herself, and asks Dequoy to take her to

Emporius, but he lets her down. When Cap-a-Pie wakes up, he has to put on Virginia's abandoned clothes. Doso takes him for Virginia herself, and locks 'her' up for stealing his jewels. Formicoso is set to guard 'her', and gets a surprise when he tries to take advantage of 'her' sexually.

News arrives that English shipping is embargoed in Venice, but Doso tries to argue his way out of liability. When his clients try to have him arrested for the money he owes on the policies, he produces a royal indemnity protecting him from arrest. Emporius sends Doso the forged letter reassuring him that his finances are secure. Doso is so pleased that he decides to marry Virginia to Emporius; so Emporius resumes his own identity. Doso is elected to a consulship.

Meanwhile, Perdu the merchant returns home after a long, troubled voyage, only to find that his wife, Peregrina, has given him up for dead, and doesn't recognize him when they meet. As a rich widow, she is a magnet for suitors. One of them is Formicoso, who has fathered a child on Ursula, but denies paternity.

Ursula abandons her baby on Doso's doorstep in the expectation that Formicoso will have to accept his responsibilities. Two lictors find the child and give it back to Ursula's bawd, who tries to foist it on the cross-dressed Virginia. Virginia protests that she cannot possibly be the father. The matter is brought to trial before Doso, who is satisfied that Formicoso is the father; he is forced to marry Ursula. Doso has the false 'Virginia' brought before him and tries to give 'her' to Emporius; but on learning that Emporius played him false as Cosmopolites, he changes his mind and tries to bestow his daughter, now correctly identified, on Cap-a-Pie. Emporius produces the contract debarring Cap-a-Pie from marrying Virginia, and her pleas make her father relent. Perdu identifies himself to Peregrina, and she happily accepts him.

In a subsidiary action, one of Dequoy's scams involves borrowing signet rings: he brings them to the owner's household and asks for money. One of the victims is Rialto, who has Dequoy's villainy publicly proclaimed—but Dequoy has already absconded with his ill-gotten gains. Most of Rialto's ships come in, and he is so pleased that he is unconcerned by his captain's tall tale of adventure and pirate attacks.

SCENE DESIGNATION
prol., 1.1–13, 2.1–16, 3.1–9, int., 4.1–13, 5.1–14, ep. (MS)

The stage is not clear at the following scene-divisions: 1.1–2, 1.6–9, 1.10–13, 2.1–2, 2.3–6, 2.7–9, 2.10–11, 2.12–16, 3.1–9, 4.1–8, 4.9–11, 4.12–13, 5.1–4, 5.5–13.

ROLES
MERCURY, a god, presenter of the play
RIALTO, a Crown agent, founder of the Exchange
CICADILLO, a parasite
FORMICOSO, Doso's steward, father of Ursula's baby
Signor DEQUOY, a false merchant and a bankrupt
MERCURIUS GALLO-BELGICUS, a mountebank trader and almanac-maker
MERCURIUS BRITANNICUS, a messenger-boy
PERDU Redux, an unfortunate merchant, Peregrina's husband
Master DOSO, the public insurer, an old miser; Heroina's husband, Virginia's uncle; later elected Consul (here a chief magistrate, an office held annually; probably signifying Sheriff); also called Signor Doso
EMPORIUS, Doso's factor, a young man; adopts the alias Cosmopolites
Mistress VIRGINIA, Doso's niece; assumes the name Virago when cross-dressed as a man
Signor FRISCO, a Venetian trader, Heroina's kinsman
Monsieur CAP-A-PIE, a French trader
Mistress HEROINA, a young woman of noble birth, Doso's wife, Frisco's kinswoman
Mistress PEREGRINA, Perdu's wife (and supposed his widow), a tavern keeper
Mistress MAQUERELLA, an old bawd; claims also to be a nurse and midwife
MERCURIUS ANTWERPIENSIS, a messenger-boy
Three MERCHANTS, Doso's creditors; one of them is a married man and a father, another may be German (3.9)
A COURTIER (3.9)
Two LICTORS (3.9)
Morning CROWDS at the Exchange (int., *non-speaking*)
DEMAGOGUS, a supposedly celibate clergyman
PIOVANO, a Protestant clergyman
Two LICTORS accompanying Rialto (4.13, *non-speaking*)
A CIVIC OFFICER (5.2)
URSULA, a chambermaid, mother of Formicoso's bastard; formerly a country girl
Two LICTORS, who find Ursula's baby (5.6–9, 5.11–12)
Captain MERCATANTUCCIO, a braggart sailor, captain of Rialto's ship
Three SAILORS from Rialto's ship (5.14)
Afternoon CROWDS at the Exchange (5.14, *non-speaking*)

Speaking Parts: 31–3

Stage Directions and Speech Prefixes
MERCURY: *Mercurius* (s.d.s and d.p.)
RIALTO: *Rialto* (s.d.s and s.p.s); *Rialto Negotiator Regius & Dominus Fundator Byrsa* (d.p.)
CICADILLO: *Cicadillo* (s.d.s and s.p.s); *Cicadillo Parasitaster* (d.p.)
FORMICOSO: *Formicoso* (s.d.s and s.p.s); *Formicoso Dosoni a Rationibus* (d.p.)
DEQUOY: *Dequoy Pseudo-Mercator | Dequoy decoctor et convasator* (s.d.s); *Dequoy* (s.d.s and s.p.s); *Dequoy Mercator-Fraudulentus; Banccae-Ruptor Profugus* (d.p.)

MERCURIUS GALLO-BELGICUS: *Mercurius Gallobelgicus* (s.d.s); *Mercurius Gallo-Belgicus* (s.d.s and s.p.s); *Mercurius Gallo-Belgicus Operator Circumforaneus* (d.p.)

MERCURIUS BRITANNICUS: *Mercurius Britannicus* (s.d.s); *Merc<urius> Britannicus* (s.p.s); *Mercurius Britannicus Puer Cursorius* (s.d.s and d.p.)

PERDU: *Perdu Redux Mercator infeliciter negotians* | *Perdu Redux* (s.d.s); *Perdu* (s.d.s and s.p.s); *Perdu Redux Maritus Peregrinae, Mercator Infeliciter Negotians* (d.p.)

DOSO: *Doso assecurator publicus* (s.d.s); *Doso* (s.d.s and s.p.s); *Doso Assecurator publicus* (d.p.)

EMPORIUS: *Emporius Dosonis Negotiator* | *Cosmopolites alias Emporius* (s.d.s); *Emporius* (s.d.s and s.p.s); *Cosmop<olites> alias Emporius* | *Cosmopolites* | *Empor<ius> alias Cosmop<olites>* (s.p.s); *Emporius alias Cosmopolites Donsonis Negotiator Redux* (d.p.)

VIRGINIA: *Virginia* | *Virago alias Virginia* (s.d.s and s.p.s); *Virago* (s.p.s); *Virginia alias Virago Neptis Dosonis* (d.p.)

FRISCO: *Signor Frisco* | *Frisco* (s.d.s and s.p.s); *Frisco Negotiator Venetus, Prodigus; Heroina Cognatus* (d.p.)

CAP-A-PIE: *Monsieur Cap-a-pe* | *Cap-a-pe* (s.d.s and s.p.s); *Monsieur Cap-a-pe Negotiator Gallus Rivalis Emporii* (d.p.)

HEROINA: *Heroina* (s.d.s and s.p.s); *Heroina Dosonis uxorcula Formosula* (d.p.)

PEREGRINA: *Peregrina Relicta & Oenopola* | *Peregrina Hospita* (s.d.s); *Peregrina* (s.d.s and s.p.s); *Peregrina Relicta et Oenopola* (d.p.)

MAQUERELLA: *Maquerella* (s.d.s and s.p.s); *Maquerella Lena & Obstetrix* (d.p.)

MERCURIUS ANTWERPIENSIS: *Mercurius Antuerpiensis Puer Cursorius* (s.d.s); *Merc<urius> Antuerp<iensis>* (s.p.s)

MERCHANTS: *Chorus Mercatorum* (s.d.s); *1 Mercator* | *2 Mercator* | *3 Mercator* (s.p.s); *Chorus ... Mercatorum* (d.p.)

COURTIER: *unius Aulici* (s.d.s); *Aulicus* (s.p.s); *Chorus Aulicorum* (d.p.)

LICTORS: *2 Lictorum* (s.d.s); *1 Lictor* | *2 Lictor* (s.p.s)

CROWDS: *Prima & Anti-meridiana Frequentia Subbasilicana* (s.d.s); *Frequentia 1ª Antemeridiana Subbasilicana* (d.p.)

DEMAGOGUS: *Demagogus* (s.d.s and s.p.s); *Demagogus* [one of] *2 Clerici* (d.p.)

PIOVANO: *Piovano* (s.d.s and s.p.s); *Piovano* [one of] *2 Clerici* (d.p.)

LICTORS: *duo Lictoribus* (s.d.s)

CIVIC OFFICER: *Praetorianus Ensifer* (s.d.s and s.p.s); *Ensifer Praetorianus* (d.p.)

URSULA: *Ursula* (s.d.s and s.p.s); *Ursula Virgo Cubicularia* (d.p.)

LICTORS: *Lictores 2* (s.d.s); *2 Lictores* (s.d.s and s.p.s); *1 Lictor* | *2 Lictor* (s.p.s)

MERCATANTUCCIO: *Capitaneo Mercatantuccio* (s.d.s); *Capitaneo Mercant<uccio>* (s.p.s; sic); *Capitaneo Mercatantuccio Navarcha Gloriosus* (d.p.)

SAILORS: *Turba Nautica* (s.d.s and d.p.); *1º Nauta* | *2º Nauta* | *3º Nauta* | *1ᵘˢ Nauta* | *2ᵘˢ Nauta* | *3ᵘˢ Nauta* (s.p.s)

CROWDS: *Secunda & Pomeridiana Frequentia Subbasilicana* (s.d.s); *Frequentia 2ª Pomeridiana Subbasilicana* (d.p.)

OTHER CHARACTERS

Argenti-Extenibronide, Rialto's grandfather (1.1; but possibly just a figure of speech)

A girl known to Mercurius Britannicus, who regrets being no longer a virgin (1.4; may refer to Ursula)

Perdu's creditors (1.5)

People who were unable to give Peregrina news of her missing husband, including merchants, the public messenger, and customers both native and foreign (2.1)

Peregrina's many suitors (2.1)

Myrmidonulus, Ursula's illegitimate baby son (2.7, 5.5–9, 5.11; represented on stage by a prop)

Heroina's family, who forced her to marry Doso (2.10)

Doso's servants (2.10, 4.5)

Courtiers, kinsmen of Heroina, who dine well and free of charge at Doso's table (2.10)

Heroina's fashionable dressmakers, mercers, and tailors (2.10)

A dishonest sea-captain who absconded with his ship and its cargo (3.2)

The Venetians, reported to have embargoed some English ships (3.5)

The Third Merchant's creditors (3.9)

The Third Merchant's wife and children (3.9)

Dequoy's creditors (4.11)

The customs officer, whom Emporius claims to have bamboozled (5.1)

The Mayor, who has sent congratulations on Doso's elevation (5.1)

Ursula's family (5.5)

SETTING

Period: contemporary: the action takes place in 1635, after 20 August (Gregorian?)

Time-Scheme: the action takes place during a single day: 2.14 takes place before noon, int. still in the morning, and 5.14 in the afternoon

Place: London

Geography

London: the Royal Exchange; the Trireme (or perhaps just the Ship); the Golden Cross

England

Venice: the Rialto

Italy: Falernum

[Sicily]: Mount Etna

Greece: Attica; Anticyra
[*Aegean Sea*]: Delos
Europe: the Alps; Spain; France; Antwerp; Portugal; Germany; Bohemia
The Mediterranean Sea: Crete
Asia: Arabia
The Red Sea
Africa: Syrtes
America
The Antipodes

SOURCES
Narrative: William Shakespeare, *Henry V* (**1183**; 1.12; black pudding episode); either Nathan Field, *Amends for Ladies* (**1615**) or John Fletcher, *Love's Cure* (**1779**; 1.10–12; the cheese episode inverts an anecdote from both earlier plays); either Athenaeus, *Deipnosophists* or Thomas Heywood, *The English Traveller* (**2098**; 5.3); possibly Thomas Middleton, *A Chaste Maid in Cheapside* (**1715**; 5.5–6)
Verbal: Plautus, *Amphitruo* (4.13, 5.6), *Aulularia* (1.1, 3.1, 3.9, 4.4, 4.8), *Bacchides* (3.5), *Captivi* (2.7, 4.5), *Casina* (1.7, 2.3), *Cistellaria* (2.7, 3.7, 5.8), *Epidicus* (3.7), *Mercator* (4.5), *Mostellaria* (3.9, 4.4), *Persa* (1.1, 2.3), *Poenulus* (3.9), *Rudens* (2.4), *Stichus* (5.2); Terence, *Andria* (2.9), *Adelphoe* (2.13), *Heautontimorumenos* (4.8), *Phormio* (1.8); Cicero, *Ad familiares* 7.6 (2.3), *De oratore* (2.9), *Paradoxia* (1.4); Caesar, *De bello Gallico* (2.8); Catullus, *Carmina* 5 (5.14); Virgil, *Eclogues* 1 (4.12), *Aeneid* 1 (int.), 2 (1.5, 5.13), 5 (5.5); Horace, *Epistles* 1.12 (4.12), 2.1 (3.3), *Odes* 3.30 (4.11), 4.12 (2.12), *Satires* 1.2 (5.14), 2.3 (5.2); Ovid, *Metamorphoses* 3 (2.1, 3.9); Bible: Matthew 6.13 (1.12); Seneca, *Quaestiones naturales* (4.11); Pliny, *Natural History* (ep.); Suetonius, *Twelve Caesars*: Julius Caesar (1.12–13); Juvenal, *Satires* 1 (4.11), 2 (1.8), 3 (3.2), 6 (4.5); Martial, *Epigrams* 2.18 (1.12), 9.27 (2.8); Hadrian, *To His Soul* (5.5); Edmund Stubbes, *Fraus honesta* (**1887**; prol.); Peter Hausted, *Senile odium* (**2296**; 1.1, 2.6, 2.12, 3.5, 3.9); *The Swedish Intelligencer* 7 (1635; 3.5)
Works Mentioned: Hesiod, *Works and Days* (5.2; oblique allusion); *Magna Carta* (1215; 1.13); Sebastian Brandt, *Ship of Fools* (1494; 5.12); 'Erra Pater', *The Prognostication For Ever* (1536?; 3.5); Hieronymus Cardanus, *De subtilitate* (1551; 1.4); Tycho Brahe, unspecified work (3.5)

LANGUAGE
Latin
French: 6 words (1.12; Cap-a-Pie, Emporius)
Italian: 9 words (3.2, 3.5, 4.10; Rialto, Dequoy)
Spanish: 1 word (1.12; Cap-a-Pie)
German: 2 words (3.9; 1 Merchant)
Arabic: 2 words (3.5; Dequoy, Rialto)

FORM
Metre: Terentian pseudo-metre; a little prose
Prologue: 47 lines, spoken by Mercury

Presenter: Mercury; speaks the prologue and epilogue, and an entr'acte speech between Acts 3 and 4
Chorus: The non-speaking crowds at the Exchange are described as a Chorus (but obviously have no choric function).
Act-Division: 5 acts
Epilogue: 46 lines, spoken by Mercury
Lines (Spoken): 2,875 (including 26 true verse, 54 true prose)
Lines (Written): 3,137

STAGING
Doors: knocked at (1.10, 4.4, implicit; 4.5, dialogue); mentioned (4.5, s.d.)
Stage: mentioned (ep., dialogue)
Above: Formicoso speaks from a window above (4.5, s.d.; it takes him almost no time at all to descend to main stage level)
Audience: addressed as 'academici' (prol., ep.); Dequoy cannot see the audience when he checks whether it is safe to soliloquize (4.11); Mercury offers gifts to two members of the audience (ep.)
Miscellaneous: the stage needs somewhere to hang up a notice (1.4, s.d.; 4.13, 5.8, dialogue)

MUSIC
Song: 'Io Bacchae nunc—feri tuo thyrso', 2.11, Mercurius Britannicus, 16 lines
Dance: Mercurius Britannicus dances (2.11, s.d.)

PROPS
Weapons: Cap-a-Pie's sword (1.10–13, dialogue; 4.9–10, implicit); Emporius' sword (1.12–13, dialogue); a fasces (3.9, dialogue); Civic Officer's sword (5.2, implicit)
Clothing: Frisco's ring (2.4, 2.12, dialogue; 2.11, s.d.); half a ring (2.13, dialogue)
Money: coins (1.1, s.d.); an unspecified sum (1.2, dialogue); an unspecified sum (1.11, dialogue); three gold coins (2.5, dialogue); gold coins (2.6, dialogue); more gold coins (2.7, dialogue); thirty gold coins (2.11, dialogue); an unspecified sum (2.11, dialogue); one hundred pounds (3.5, s.d.); a thousand pounds (4.2, dialogue); an unspecified amount (4.11, dialogue); Dequoy's ill-gotten gains, not less than £1,900); a purse containing about five hundred minas (5.2, dialogue); a purse (ep., dialogue)
Food and Drink: a small piece of cheese (1.10–12, dialogue); a black pudding (1.12, s.d.; eaten on stage); a box of pills (2.5–6, dialogue)
Small Portable Objects: possibly a caduceus (prol., dialogue); documents (1.4, dialogue); pens (1.4, dialogue); paper (1.4, dialogue); a tablet (1.4, s.d.; i.e. a notice to be hung up); a letter (1.4, dialogue); another letter (1.6, dialogue); a forged letter (1.7, 4.7, s.d.; 5.1, dialogue); documents (1.7, dialogue); a contract (1.12, 5.10, implicit; written on stage); pen and ink (1.12, implicit); three golden cups (2.12, s.d.); Rialto's insurance policy (3.2, implicit); Dequoy's insurance

policy (3.3, dialogue); letters (3.5, s.d.); an almanac (3.5, dialogue); a wallet (3.5, dialogue); an inventory (3.6–7, s.d.); a document (3.9, dialogue); a tablet (4.13, 5.8, dialogue; it probably hangs on stage throughout the intervening scenes); insignia of office (5.2, dialogue)
Large Portable Objects: a baby (2.7, 5.6–9, dialogue; 5.5, s.d.); a bag (4.3, dialogue); a basket (5.5, s.d.; 5.6–9, implicit); a seat (5.9, implicit)
Miscellaneous: blood (4.5, dialogue)

COSTUMES
MERCURY: a petasus (ep., dialogue)
RIALTO: a jewelled ring (3.4, 4.10, dialogue; 3.5, s.d.; removed and put on on stage)
MERCURIUS GALLO-BELGICUS: a hat and cloak (1.4, dialogue)
PERDU: disguised (1.5, 2.2, 2.9, implicit); undisguised (5.13, s.d.)
DOSO: fine merchant's clothes (1.6–9, implicit)
EMPORIUS: a scabbard (1.12–13, dialogue)
VIRGINIA: cross-dressed in Cap-a-Pie's clothes (4.3–4, s.d.; 4.9–10, dialogue; 5.8–13, implicit), including his scabbard (4.9–10, implicit)
FRISCO: a ring (2.4, dialogue; removed on stage; see also PROPS)
CAP-A-PIE: a scabbard (1.10–13, implicit); a cap (2.5–6, dialogue); cross-dressed in Virginia's clothes (4.4, 5.10–13, s.d.)
HEROINA: a mean gown (2.10–11, dialogue)

EARLY TEXTUAL HISTORY
1630s: transcribed in **MS**; 48 leaves; list of roles; author named at foot of text. The title page bears the date 23 January 1570, but this is the date of the historical event which suggested the plot (i.e. the opening of the Royal Exchange in London), not the date of the MS itself (or indeed of the action). If the MS is a scribal transcript, it was probably made in Worcester.

EDITIONS
R. H. Bowers, Materialien 2.17 (Louvain, 1939).
Sabine U. Bückmann-de Villegas, Renaissance Latin Drama in England 2.12 (Hildesheim, Zurich, and New York, 1991).

REFERENCES
Annals 1633; Bentley, v. 1005–6; Churchill-Keller, 281–5; Hazlitt, 32; *N&Q* 239 (1994), 522–4; REED: Cambridge, 935; Smith, 95; Stratman, 191–5, 298.

2512. *The Strange Discovery*

TEXT
Printed in 1640 (STC 12133).

GENRE
romance
Contemporary: play, history (prol.); tragicomedy (S.R., t.p.)

TITLE
Performed/Printed: *The Strange Discovery*

AUTHOR
J. Gough

Bentley's identification of the variant title page's 'J. Gough' with John Goffe the clergyman, who matriculated at Oxford in 1624, enables him to narrow the date limits; he is tentative, however, in identifying Goffe with the 'J. Gough' who contributed commendatory verses to *The Rebellion* (**2413**) in 1640. It seems to me that his confidence and caution are the wrong way round: there is no positive reason to link the preacher with the play, and the Oxford *DNB* entry for Goffe the clergyman makes no suggestion that he was a dramatist; but the verses connect J. Gough with drama and place him in a literary network which also includes the playwrights Thomas Rawlins (author of *The Rebellion*), Robert Davenport, Thomas Jordan, Nathaniel Richards, John Tatham, and Robert Chamberlain (fellow contributors of commendatory verses). The playwright may, of course, have been named John whether or not he was the cleric, though he could equally well have been (say) James or Joseph, or indeed Isaac.

DATE
Limits: 1606–40
Best Guess: 1635

The central problem in dating the play is the complete absence of any external evidence about its provenance prior to publication. The *Annals* dating in the year of publication rests on the assumption that it is a 'closet', literary play, which depends solely on the doubtful identification of the author as John Goffe. The writing seems theatrical, notably when the clown speaks to the audience at the end of the first Act. The verse is more competent than that usually perpetrated by the cavalier amateur playwrights of the 1630s. I have noticed no topical allusions.

Since, as discussed under AUTHOR, the only other context for Gough is among a group of writers of verses, many of whom were dramatists of the 1630s, this seems the likeliest period for the play. Other, equally tentative indicators are the absence of any company ascription from the title page and the relatively large number of roles. Although the practice of doubling means that the latter has no implications for company size, it is notable that the principal 1630s companies whose repertory routinely exceeded 30 speaking parts per play were the King's Men and the King's Revels Company. (Too little survives of the Red Bull Company's repertory to allow a generalisation.) It would be odd for the 1640 title page to omit any mention of the premier London acting company, whereas there might have been less commercial incentive to name a company that had been defunct for years. This may add to the significance of Gough's 'network' of fellow authors, at least three of whom (Jordan, Richards, Rawlins) had also written for the King's Revels Company. If this was a play for them, then its chronological limits would narrow to 1629–36, and it would have been performed at either Salisbury Court (1629–32, 1634–6) or the Fortune (1632–4). Its specific context might be the turn of commercial-theatre fashion towards classical and pseudo-classical romance in 1635.

PLOT

After the death of his daughter, Charicles decides to leave Egypt and return to Greece so that he can die at home. Before he can go, the Ethiopian legate entrusts him with the care of a maiden, whom he adopts as a daughter and names Chariclea; but the legate is expelled from Egypt before he can reveal more of the girl's history.

Back in Greece, Chariclea seems uninterested in men until she meets Theagenes, who has come to Delphos to participate in a religious ceremony. After that, they are both stricken with love-melancholy. A physician diagnoses Chariclea with green-sickness and prescribes sex, so Charicles plans to introduce her to his nephew, whom he hopes she will marry. The visiting Egyptian priest Calasiris realizes otherwise and helps her to abscond with Theagenes to Africa, taking with them a fascia which explains her origins. Chariclea is really the daughter of the King and Queen of Ethiopia. Her fortunes arise from her skin colour: her mother was looking at a picture of a white woman at the moment of conception, so the child too was born white; fearing a charge of adultery, she disposed of the baby and reported her dead.

In Egypt, Theagenes attracts the interest of Arsace while her husband, the Deputy, is away at war with Ethiopia, but she is impervious to her advances, even when she has him imprisoned and scourged. Realizing that the problem lies in his love for Chariclea, Arsace plots to poison her, but the poisoned cup goes astray and it is the bawd Cybele who is killed. Chariclea is tried for the murder and found guilty after Arsace provides five false witnesses; but when she is thrown into the fire, it refuses to burn her because she is wearing a magical fire-repelling ring. The Deputy hears of her beauty and has her brought to him along with Theagenes. Arsace commits suicide. Chariclea and Theagenes are captured by the Ethiopians on the way to the Deputy's camp. It is customary for prisoners of war to be sacrificed, but Chariclea saves herself by producing the fascia describing her origins, and she and Theagenes are appointed Ethiopian priests in succession to her parents.

In the sub-plot, Demeneta attempts to seduce her stepson Cnemon, but when he rejects her, she tells his father, Aristippus, that he assaulted her and thereby gets the young man a thrashing. To further her revenge, she asks Thisbe, her maid, to lead him on. Thisbe encourages him to regain his father's favour by catching his stepmother in the act of adultery. When he bursts into the bedroom with a drawn sword, however, it is Aristippus himself whom he finds there. Cnemon is brought to trial and banished, but stays secretly with the courtesan Arsinoe. Thisbe learns of this and suggests making another opportunity for Demeneta with a double-substitution bed-trick: she will ask Arsinoe for a night with Cnemon, and then arrange for her mistress to take her place. She then arranges for Aristippus to catch Demeneta in the act, but for Cnemon to get away; Demeneta kills herself. Thisbe confesses her part in the deception of Cnemon, and takes poison. Aristippus has his son formally cleared of all wrongdoing.

SCENE DESIGNATION

prol., 1.1–5, 2.1–10, 3.1–8, 4.1–7, 5.1–6 (Q, corrected; Q fails to mark the start of 3.6, and consequently misnumbers 3.7–8 as 3.6–7)

The stage is clear during 3.1.

ROLES

PROLOGUE

CHARICLES, formerly the Priest of Apollo at Delphos; a widower; Chariclea's adoptive father; an old man

NEBULO, Charicles' servant, Nebulona's husband; a lean man (or so he hungrily says)

SISIMITHRES, a Gymnosophist, Legate of Ethiopia

Mistress DEMENETA, Aristippus' second wife, Cnemon's stepmother; a young woman

CNEMON, Aristippus' son, Demeneta's stepson; a youth

ARISTIPPUS, a citizen of Athens; Demeneta's husband, Cnemon's father; an old man

CHARICLEA, adopted as a daughter (and named) by Charicles; 17 years old; in reality, the daughter of Hydaspes and Persinna; poses as Theagenes' sister

THISBE, Demeneta's maid, a bondwoman

Aristippus' SERVANTS (1.4, non-speaking)

CALASIRIS, Priest of Isis at Memphis

NEBULONA, Nebulo's wife

Thessalian YOUTHS, also called Aenians (2.7, non-speaking)

Thessalian VIRGINS (2.7, non-speaking)

THEAGENES, Captain of the Thessalians; a young man; poses as Chariclea's brother

GALLANTS attending Theagenes (2.7, non-speaking)

The ORACLE of Apollo (2.7; presumably within)

Four JUDGES of Athens (2.8)

The PEOPLE of Athens (2.8; only speak collectively)

ATTENDANTS at the feast (3.2, non-speaking)

ARSINOE, a musical courtesan, Thisbe's friend

KINSFOLK of Chariclea (3.7, non-speaking)

ACESTINUS, a physician

ARSACE, a Persian lady, wife of the Deputy of Egypt

CYBELE, an old bawd, Arsace's chamberlain and nurse

Two JUDGES of Athens (4.6; may be two of those who appeared in 2.8)

AURA, Cybele's servant

Arsace's SERVANTS (4.7, 5.2, non-speaking)

King HYDASPES of Ethiopia; Persinna's husband, Chariclea's father; a priest

ATTENDANTS on Hydaspes (5.1, 5.6, non-speaking)

Three Persian MAGISTRATES (5.2)

Five WITNESSES suborned by Arsace (5.2; only speak collectively)

BAGOAS, a Persian officer

PERSINNA, Queen of Ethiopia, Hydaspes' wife, Chariclea's mother; a priestess
A GENTLEMAN ATTENDANT at the Ethiopian court (5.6)
The PEOPLE of Ethiopia (5.6; speak collectively)

Speaking Parts: 34–6

Stage Directions and Speech Prefixes
PROLOGUE: *The Prologue* (heading)
CHARICLES: *Caricles, sometimes Apollo's Priest at Delphos* | *[one of] the Priests* | *the gentleman* (s.d.s); *Caricles* (s.d.s and s.p.s); *Caricles, Apollo's Priest* (d.p.)
NEBULO: *Nebulo [Charicles'] man* (s.d.s); *Nebulo* (s.d.s and s.p.s); *Nebulo, Caricles' man* (d.p.)
SISIMITHRES: *Sisimethres, Legate of Aethiopia* | *Sysimethres* (s.d.s); *Sisimet<hres>* | *Sysim<ethres>* (s.p.s); *Sysimethres, a Gymnosophist, Ambassador for the King* (d.p.)
DEMENETA: *Demeneta* (s.d.s); *Demen<eta>* (s.p.s); *Demeneta, [Aristippus'] wife* (d.p.)
CNEMON: *young Cnemon [Demeneta's] son in Law* | *Cnemon* (s.d.s); *Cnem<on>* (s.p.s); *Cnemon, Aristippus' son* (d.p.)
ARISTIPPUS: *Aristippus* | *[Cnemon's] father* | *the old man* (s.d.s); *Aristip<pus>* (s.p.s); *Aristippus, a Citizen of Athens* (d.p.)
CHARICLEA: *Cariclea* (s.d.s and s.p.s); *Cariclea [Hydaspes' and Persinna's] daughter* (d.p.)
THISBE: *Thisbe [Demeneta's] maid* | *Thisbe* (s.d.s); *This<be>* (s.p.s); *Thisbe, Demeneta's maid* (d.p.)
SERVANTS: *[Aristippus'] servants* (s.d.s)
CALASIRIS: *Calasiris Isis' priest at Memphis* | *[one of] the Priests* (s.d.s); *Calasiris* | *Calasires* (s.d.s and s.p.s); *Calasiris, Isis' Priest* (d.p.)
NEBULONA: *Nebulona* (s.d.s and s.p.s); *Nebulona, [Nebulo's] wife* (d.p.)
YOUTHS: *the Thessalians* | *The Thessalian youths* (s.d.s)
VIRGINS: *virgins of Thessalia* | *the maids* (s.d.s)
THEAGENES: *Theagines Captain of the Thessalians* | *Theagenes* | *Theagenes [The Thessalian youths'] Captain* (s.d.s); *Theagines* (s.d.s and s.p.s); *Theagines, a Thessalian Captain* (d.p.)
GALLANTS: *many gallants* (s.d.s)
ORACLE: *The Oracle* (s.d.s)
JUDGES: *the judges … of Athens* (s.d.s); *1 Judge* | *2 Judge* | *3 Judge* | *4 Judge* (s.p.s); *4 Judges* (d.p.)
PEOPLE: *people of Athens* (s.d.s); *The people* (s.p.s)
ATTENDANTS: *attendants* (s.d.s and d.p.)
ARSINOE: *Arsinoe* (s.d.s); *Ars<inoe>* (s.p.s); *Arsinoe, a Courtesan* (d.p.)
KINSFOLK: *[Chariclea's] kinsfolks* (s.d.s)
ACESTINUS: *Acestinus a skilful physician* | *Acestinus* (s.d.s); *Acestin<us>* (s.p.s)
ARSACE: *Arsace* (s.d.s); *Arsa<ce>* (s.p.s); *Arsace, wife to the Deputy of Aegypt* (d.p.)
CYBELE: *[Arsace's] old bawd Cibile* (s.d.s); *Cibile* (s.d.s and s.p.s); *Cibile, [Arsace's] Chamberlain, nurse, and bawd* (d.p.)
JUDGES: *two Judges* (s.d.s); *1 Judge* | *2 Judge* (s.p.s)
AURA: *Aura* (s.d.s and s.p.s); *Aura, Cibile's maid* (d.p.)
SERVANTS: *servants* | *Arsace's servants* (s.d.s)
HYDASPES: *Hydaspes* | *The King* (s.d.s); *Hydasp<es>* (s.p.s); *Hydaspes, King of Aethiopia* (d.p.)
ATTENDANTS: *attendants* (s.d.s and d.p.)
MAGISTRATES: *the Persian magistrates* (s.d.s); *1 Magistrate* | *2 Magistrate* | *3 Magistrate* | *3* | *1* (s.p.s); *Magistrates of Persia* (d.p.)
WITNESSES: *All 5* (s.p.s)
BAGOAS: *an Officer* | *Bogoas the officer* (s.d.s); *Officer* (s.p.s)
PERSINNA: *Persina [Hydaspes'] Queen* (s.d.s and d.p.); *the Queen* (s.d.s); *Pers<ina>* (s.p.s)
GENTLEMAN ATTENDANT: *a gentleman attendant* | *the gentleman* (s.d.s); *Gentleman* (s.p.s); *attendants* (d.p.)
PEOPLE: *the people* (s.d.s); *All the people* (s.p.s)

OTHER CHARACTERS
Chariclea's dead daughter (1.1, 1.3, 5.3)
Oroondates, Deputy of Egypt, Arsace's husband (1.1, 1.3, 1.5, 4.2, 4.4, 5.1, 5.4–5)
Cnemon's tutor (1.2)
The wise men of Ethiopia (1.3)
Shepherds whom Sisimithres charged with Chariclea's upbringing (1.3)
Rhodopis, beloved by Calasiris (2.1)
Thyamis, eldest son of Calasiris (2.1)
Chariclea's sister, Alcamenes' mother, (2.3, 3.8)
Alcamenes, Chariclea's nephew, a young man to whom he hopes to marry Chariclea (2.3, 2.10, 3.7–8)
Achilles, Theagenes' ancestor (2.3, 2.7, 3.7)
Nebulona's lover, whom she has considered marrying in her husband's prolonged absence (2.6)
Nebulona's doctor (2.6)
The people of Delphos (2.9)
Guests at Theagenes' feast (2.10)
Ormenes, who competed with Theagenes in a race, and lost (3.3)
Feledemus, a dancer (3.5)
Aristippus' friends (3.6)
Euphrates, Arsace's eunuch (4.5)
The Ethiopian army (4.5, 5.1–2, 5.6)
The Egyptian army (5.1)
The people of Syene (5.1)
Archers in Syene (5.1)
The King of Persia (5.1)
Hydaspes' royal guard (5.1)
Chariclea's dead wife (5.3)
The executioners who attempted to burn Chariclea (5.4)
People present at the execution (5.4)
Arsace's guard (5.4)
Fifty horsemen sent to escort Chariclea (5.4)
Two advance riders of the Ethiopian army, who captured Chariclea and Theagenes (5.6)

SETTING

Period: antiquity; Egypt is part of the Persian Empire (525–404 BC), but there are anomalous past-tense references to Cleopatra and Ovid (first century BC)
Time-Scheme: In the main plot, 1.3 takes place the morning after 1.1; 3.3 takes place early in the morning after 3.2; a day passes between 3.7 and 3.8. In the sub-plot's separate and unrelated time-scheme, 1.2 takes place at about 10 a.m.; 2.5 takes place late at night; three days pass between 3.1 and 3.5, and 3.6 takes place the ensuing night.
Place: Egypt, Athens, Delphos (i.e. Delphi), and Ethiopia

Geography
Egypt: Catadupa; River Nile; [the Nile cataracts]; Memphis; Thebes; Philae; Syene; Elephantine
Greece: Mount Parnassus; Castalia; Thessaly
[*Aegean Sea*]: Lesbos
[*Asia*]: Arabia; Sidon; Lydia; Persia
India
The Equator

SOURCES

Narrative: Heliodorus, *Aethiopica*, tr. Thomas Underdown (1569); Thomas Middleton, *The Revenger's Tragedy* (**1520**; 2.5)
Verbal: Homer, *Iliad* (3.7, cited); Christopher Marlowe, *The Jew of Malta* (**828**; 5.6)
Works Mentioned: Ovid, *Ars amatoria* (1.2)

LANGUAGE
English
Latin: 4 words (1.2, 4.1; Demeneta, Calasiris)

FORM
Metre: pentameter and prose; a few fourteeners
Rhyme: blank verse; some couplets
Prologue: 21 lines, mainly in couplets
Act-Division: 5 acts
Lines (Spoken): 2,762 (2,426 verse, 336 prose)
Lines (Written): 3,192

STAGING
Doors: banged loudly (3.6, s.d.); characters enter at two doors (3.8, s.d.)
Stage: mentioned (3.6, s.d.)
Within: speech (2.7, 3.3, implicit)
Beneath: Demeneta falls into a pit in the stage (3.6, s.d.)
Audience: addressed as 'gentlemen' (1.5, implicit)
Miscellaneous: Calasiris exits at the end of 3.2 and immediately re-enters at the start of 3.3; Thisbe does likewise at 3.4–5. No provision is made to remove Arsace's dead body at the end of 5.5.

MUSIC AND SOUND
Sound Effects: knocking (1.1, dialogue; 3.3, 4.2, s.d.)
Music: unspecified music accompanying the song (2.7, s.d.); dance music (3.2, dialogue)
Song: 'O Nereus, god in surging seas', 2.7, 24 lines, with musical accompaniment
Dance: Thessalian Virgins dance (2.7, s.d.); Theagenes and the Thessalian Youths dance (3.2, s.d.)

PROPS
Lighting: a candle (2.5, 3.6, s.d.); a burning taper (2.7, s.d.)
Pyrotechnics: the sacrifice is burned on the altar (2.7, s.d.); fire (3.7, dialogue)
Weapons: rods (1.4, s.d.); Cnemon's sword (2.5, s.d.); a gilded bow and a quiver of arrows (2.7, s.d.); a bastinado (2.10, s.d.); Theagenes' sword (3.8, dialogue); a sword (5.5, s.d.)
Animals: a hecatomb sacrifice (2.7, s.d.; burned on stage)
Food and Drink: a banquet (3.2, s.d.); wine (3.2, dialogue; drunk on stage); poison (4.3, s.d.; drunk on stage); unspecified food (4.7, dialogue; eaten on stage); a cup of wine (4.7, s.d.; drunk on stage); a second cup of wine (4.7, dialogue)
Small Portable Objects: a little bag of precious stones (1.1, 5.6, s.d.); flowers (2.7, s.d.); fruit (2.7, s.d.); baskets of knacks and perfumes (2.7, s.d.); laurel (3.7, s.d.; presumably leaves; enough to cover a human body from top to toe); a fascia with an inscription (4.1, 5.6, s.d.); a pen and ink (4.3, implicit); a document (4.3, implicit; 4.6, dialogue; written on stage); binding cords (4.7, 5.2, implicit); a seal (5.1, dialogue)
Large Portable Objects: a seat (1.2, implicit); a table (3.2, 4.7, dialogue); a three-legged stool (3.7, dialogue); a table (4.7, dialogue); seating for two characters (4.7, implicit); seating for three characters (5.2, implicit); a picture of Andromeda (5.6, s.d.)
Scenery: a bed (1.4, 2.5, 2.10, 3.7, s.d.; 3.6, implicit); the tomb of Pyrrhus (2.7, s.d.); an altar (2.7, s.d.); a throne (5.6, s.d.)
Miscellaneous: ashes (2.8, s.d.); frankincense (3.7, s.d.; burned on stage)

COSTUMES AND MAKE-UP
CHARICLES: a pilgrim's habit (1.1, s.d.)
SISIMITHRES: dark skin (dialogue)
CNEMON: robes and a crown (1.4, s.d.); bound (2.8, s.d.)
ARISTIPPUS: white hair (dialogue)
CHARICLEA: long yellow hair (s.d.); a mask (1.3, s.d.; put on on stage); her hair loose at the back, with a garland of young laurel (2.7, s.d.); sumptuously adorned (2.7, s.d.); a ring with a jewel (5.4, 5.6, dialogue); a garment with a sleeve (5.6, dialogue); a black mole above her elbow (5.6, s.d.); Persinna's mitre (5.6, dialogue; put on on stage)
NEBULONA: visibly pregnant (2.6, dialogue)
THESSALIAN YOUTHS: white garments knit about them (2.7, s.d.); armour (3.2, s.d.)

THESSALIAN VIRGINS: their hair loose about their ears (2.7, s.d.)
THEAGENES: 'very richly apparelled' (2.7, s.d.); armour (3.2, s.d.); a cloak (3.8, s.d.); Hydaspes' mitre (5.6, s.d.); put on on stage)
HYDASPES: dark skin (implicit); a white mitre (5.6, s.d.; removed on stage)
PERSINNA: dark skin (implicit); a white mitre (5.6, dialogue; removed on stage)
ETHIOPIANS: dark skin (implicit)

EARLY TEXTUAL HISTORY
1640: entered to William Leake in the Stationers' Register on Friday 31 January; entry gives author's initials. Thomas Wykes had licensed the book for publication.

1640: **Q** printed by Edward Griffin for William Leake; collation A1 B–L⁴ M⁴ (–M4), 44 leaves; title page gives author's initials; list of roles. During printing, the title page was reset to expand the author's second initial into a surname.

c. 1640s: a copy of Q was in the possession of John Horne (Vicar of Headington, Oxfordshire). After his death, his entire collection of play-books passed into the possession of John Houghton of Brasenose College, Oxford (*c.* 1608–77), then to James Herne (died 1685), and then to the library of Ralph Sheldon (1623–84) at Weston, where it was catalogued by Anthony Wood, probably in the late 1670s.

1640–1: Humphrey Moseley was selling copies of Q for 6d.

1652–62: advertised as for sale by William Leake.

1655: *Wit's Interpreter* entered to Nathaniel Brooke in the Stationers' Register on Wednesday 14 March.

1655: extract (from 2.6) included in John Cotgrave's *Wit's Interpreter*, sigs. F6ʳ–ᵛ; printed for Nathaniel Brooke.

c. 1656: extract (from 2.6) included in *Cupid's Masterpiece*, sigs. A8ᵛ–A9ʳ; printed for John Andrews.

1662: *Wit's Interpreter* reprinted (before Thursday 8 June) for Nathaniel Brooke; the extract now appears on sigs. E2ᵛ–E3ʳ, and is entitled 'The Country Bumpkin'.

1671: *Wit's Interpreter* reprinted for Nathaniel Brooke and Obadiah Blagrave.

1684: Nicholas Cox (Manciple of St Edmund Hall, Oxford) had a copy, presumably of Q, in his bookshop. It had probably been previously owned by Gerard Langbaine, and appears on a list compiled by Anthony Wood on Saturday 13 December.

1691–4: advertised as for sale by Richard Bentley.

REFERENCES
Annals 1640; Bentley, iv. 515–16; Bodleian, MS Wood E. 4, art. 1, p. 95; Eyre & Rivington, i. 467; Greg 584; Hazlitt, 220; *MLR* 13 (1918), 401–11; *Oxford Bibliographical Society Proceedings and Papers* 2.2 (1929), 132.

2513. The Partial Law

TEXT
MS (Washington: Folger, MS V. a. 165); fair copy, probably scribal.

GENRE
tragicomedy
Contemporary: tragicomedy (MS)

TITLE
MS: *The Partial Law*

DATE
Limits: 1609–42 (?)
Best Guess: 1635

Dobell dated the MS 1615–30; but in style and preoccupation the play could just as well belong to the 'high' Caroline period of the 1630s. Literary associations, some more certain than others, provide the only evidence on which to base a more precise dating. The play cannot be earlier than *Philaster* (**1597**), from which it draws the situation of the unsympathetic foreign prince visiting to woo the princess, and some of the consequences. There are also a striking number of minor points of contact with John Ford's work: the jewellery which a woman's dead mother charged her only to give to her true love (1.3; compare *'Tis Pity She's a Whore*, **2329**, 2.6); the evening 'which doth crown the day' (2.2; compare *'Tis Pity* 2.6 again); the oath taken by two people using identical words (2.2; compare *'Tis Pity* 1.2); aspects of the father–daughter–suitors dynamic resemble *The Broken Heart* (**2281**), and some aspects of the final scene resemble *The Queen* (**2224**). None of this amounts to a case for the play's authorship: the tone and style are markedly unlike Ford's work. However, the similarities, if accepted, might help to confirm a date no earlier than the 1630s, probably after the Ford plays had been published in 1633. The reference to *The Soldier's Delight*, which was registered on 16 March 1635, might conclusively set the upper limit, were it not for the fact that the ballad is also mentioned in *The Unnatural Combat* (**2185**) and might therefore have had an earlier incarnation (or namesake).

PLOT
The King of Corsica, who has always been famous for ruling impartially, now has a favourite, Bellamour. Philocres has come to Corsica to woo Princess Florabella; the King is agreeable, but requires that Florabella should also consent. However, Florabella detests Philocres and loves Bellamour; when Philocres overhears this, he swears vengeance. Florabella offers to elope to Italy with Bellamour, and gives him a chain of pearl her mother left her, to be given only to the man she loves.

The King gives Philocres the chance to display his chivalry in a tilt, defending the premise that it is base to persist in a neglected love, but he is unhorsed by Bellamour. Florabella's companion Lucina is herself interested in Philocres, but he agrees to a nocturnal assignation only if she dresses up in Florabella's clothes. After he picks a fight with Bellamour, the King makes them swear friendship. Bellamour agrees to give up Florabella in his rival's favour if he has a better claim on her. Philocres alleges that he has already slept with the Princess, and offers Bellamour the ocular proof that night. Bellamour is joined by Garamont, who is out on amorous business, and they watch as Philocres climbs into Florabella's chamber and embraces Lucina, dressed in Florabella's clothes. Bellamour becomes suicidal and throws himself into the sea. When Florabella hears the news, she falls sick.

Garamont tells the King that Florabella is unchaste. By law, he must support the charge in a trial by combat: he will be executed if he loses, but Florabella will die if he wins. Philocres refuses to take up the challenge, and arranges to silence Lucina: he offers to take her to Majorca and marry her, but the servants he sends to escort her out of the city have been suborned to murder her. She is wounded, but saved by the intervention of Sylvander.

Bellamour did not drown: he was fortuitously saved by a fishing boat, and plans to return in disguise to prove himself worthy of Florabella's love. He finds that Florabella is to be beheaded if no champion defends her honour, and puts himself forward. He is selected over the only other contender, a little gentleman, but the fight is averted when Sylvander produces Lucina, exposes Philocres, and vindicates both sides in the combat: Florabella is chaste, but Garamont's accusation was honestly made. The King forgives Lucina and offers both would-be champions a boon. Bellamour reveals himself, but the woman on the scaffold turns out to be Florabella's maid Fiducia, and the King has her sent for torture. The little gentleman claims his boon: Fiducia's freedom. 'He' is in fact Florabella, ready to fight in her own defence if necessary. Bellamour reveals his own true identity as the Prince of Cyprus: he left incognito to escape a forced marriage, but Sylvander has come to fetch him back urgently to succeed to the throne. The King agrees that he and Florabella should marry.

SCENE DESIGNATION
1.1–5, 2.1–5, 3.1–5, 4.1–6, 5.1–4 (MS, corrected)

MS marks no scene headings for 3.4 and 4.6, and consequently misnumbers 3.5 as 3.4.
The stage is not clear at the following scene-divisions: 1.1–4, 2.1–2, 5.2–4.

ROLES
FEREDO, a wealthy gentleman of the court, Philocres' friend
ARGALES, a gentleman of the court
The KING of Corsica; an old widower, Florabella's father (claims to be three times Florabella's age)
Princess FLORABELLA, the King's daughter; poses as a little gentleman; also called Florabell and Lady Florabella
Prince PHILOCRES of Majorca; also called the Duke of Majorca

BELLAMOUR, an Italian gentleman, the King's favourite; in reality the Prince of Cyprus, later its King
Lord GARAMONT, a young lord of the Council
Lord MONTALTO, a young lord of the Council; later appointed Lord High Constable
Lord ARNALDO, a young lord of the Council; later appointed Lord Marshal (and possibly Lord High Chamberlain)
Lady LUCINA, Florabella's companion and bedfellow
ATTENDANTS at court (1.2, 3.1, 3.5 *non-speaking*)
ROGER, a servingman; also called Hodge; claims to have been a soldier
A SERVINGMAN (1.5, 2.4, 3.4, 5.1–3)
A SERVINGMAN, who may be named Dicky; also called Goodman Jobernoll (1.5, 2.4, 3.4, 5.1–3)
JOAN, a country woman and mother
ROSE, a country woman
MADGE, a country woman
FIDUCIA, Florabella's maid; poses as Florabella
Five PAGES attending the challenger and tilters (1.5, *non-speaking*)
Five SQUIRES attending the challenger and tilters (1.5, *non-speaking*)
A GROOM at court (3.1)
NIGRETTA, Florabella's maid, Garamont's girlfriend; also addressed as Mistress Minx
A MESSENGER, who brings news of Bellamour's death (3.2–3)
A MESSENGER, who summons Nigretta and Fiducia to the Council (4.1)
FRANCISCO, Philocres' servant; also called Frank
PONTO, Philocres' servant
SYLVANDER, a traveller and gentleman of Cyprus
ATTENDANTS at the trial by combat (5.2, 5.4, *non-speaking*)
PEOPLE who help set up the scaffold (5.3, *non-speaking*)

The naming and designation of the Servingmen and Countrywomen is inconsistent, and this is reflected below in the record of the stage directions and speech prefixes. In 2.4, Roger is the first man; in 5.3 he is the second man. In 2.4 'Woman 1' is Joan, but in 5.1 she appears to be Madge. (Madge could alternatively be 'Woman 2', but in 2.4 she was named Rose.) It is possible (though not certain) that two of the three women in 2.4 are not the same as in 1.5, but consistency of character seems otherwise intended. In the tilt, Philocres is the challenger and Bellamour the fifth tilter; the other three tilters are Garamont, Montalto, and Arnaldo, but there is no way of identifying which is which.

Speaking Parts: 24

Stage Directions and Speech Prefixes
FEREDO: *Feredo* (s.d.s); *Fer<edo>* (s.p.s); *Feredo*, [one of] *two Gentlemen of the Court* (d.p.)
ARGALES: *Argales* (s.d.s); *Arg<ales>* (s.p.s); *Argales*, [one of] *two Gentlemen of the Court* (d.p.)
KING: *The King* (s.d.s); *King* (s.d.s and s.p.s); *The King of Corsica* (d.p.)
FLORABELLA: *Florabell* [the King's] *daughter* | *Florabella* | *The Princess* | [one of the] *Ladies* | [one

of] *The Champions* | [one of the] *Champions* | [one of] *The two champions* | [one of] *the combatants* | *the lesser champion* | [the King's] *daughter* (s.d.s); *Flor<abella>* (s.p.s); *Florabella, daughter to the King of Carsica* (d.p.)

PHILOCRES: *Philocres* | *The Challenger* (s.d.s); *Phil<ocres>* (s.p.s); *Philocres, Prince of Majorca* (s.d.s and d.p.)

BELLAMOUR: *Bellamour the Italian* | *Bellamour* | *Another Tilter* | [one of] *The Champions* | [one of the] *Champions* | [one of] *The two champions* | [one of] *the combatants* | *the taller* [champion] | *Prince of Cyprus* (s.d.s); *Bell<amour>* (s.p.s); *Bellamour, a supposed Gentleman of Italy, but Prince of Cyprus* (d.p.)

GARAMONT: *Garamont*, [one of] *three young Lords* | *Garamont* | *Tilter* | [one of the] *Lords* (s.d.s); *Gar<amont>* (s.p.s); *Garamont*, [one of] *three Court Lords* (d.p.)

MONTALTO: *Montalto*, [one of] *three young Lords* | *Montanto* | *Tilter* | [one of the] *Lords* (s.d.s); *Mont<alto>* (s.p.s); *Montalto*, [one of] *three Court Lords* (d.p.)

ARNALDO: *Arnaldo*, [one of] *three young Lords* | *Arnaldo* | *Tilter* | [one of the] *Lords* (s.d.s); *Arn<aldo>* (s.p.s); *Arnaldo*, [one of] *three Court Lords* (d.p.)

LUCINA: *Lucina, companion to the Princess* | *Lucina* | [one of the] *Ladies* (s.d.s); *Luc<ina>* (s.p.s); *Lucina, a Lady of the Court, companion to Florabella* (d.p.)

ATTENDANTS: *Attendants* (s.d.s)

ROGER: [one of] *Three serving-men* | [one of] *Three Men* | [one of the] *servingmen* | [one of] *three servants* | *the . . . second man* (s.d.s); *1 Man* | *2 Man* (s.p.s); [one of the] *servants* (d.p.)

SERVINGMAN: [one of] *Three serving-men* | [one of] *Three Men* | [one of the] *servingmen* | [one of] *three servants* | [probably] *the first . . . man* (s.d.s); *2 Man* | [probably] *1 Man* (s.p.s); [one of the] *servants* (d.p.)

SERVINGMAN: [one of] *Three serving-men* | [one of] *Three Men* | [one of the] *servingmen* | [one of] *three servants* | [probably] *the third man* (s.d.s); *3 Man* (s.p.s); [one of the] *servants* (d.p.)

JOAN: [one of] *Three Women* (s.d.s); *1 Woman* (s.p.s); [one of the] *country women* (d.p.)

ROSE: [one of] *Three Women* (s.d.s); *2 Woman* (s.p.s); [one of the] *country women* (d.p.)

MADGE: [one of] *Three Women* (s.d.s); *3 Woman* | *1 Woman* (s.p.s); [one of the] *country women* (d.p.)

FIDUCIA: [one of the] *Ladies* | [one of] *two women* | *the Princess* | [the King's daughter's] *maid Fiducia* (s.d.s); *Fiducia* (s.d.s and s.p.s); *1 Lady* (deleted s.p.); *Fiducia*, [one of] *Florabella's waiting women* (d.p.)

PAGES: [the Challenger's] *Page* | *The Page* | [another Tilter's] *page* (s.d.s)

SQUIRES: [the Challenger's] *Squire* (s.d.s)

GROOM: *Groom* (s.d.s and s.p.s); *A Groom* (d.p.)

NIGRETTA: [one of] *two women* | *Nigretta* | [the Princess's] *woman* (s.d.s); *Nigret<ta>* (s.p.s); *Nigretta*, [one of] *Florabella's waiting women* (d.p.)

MESSENGER: *Messenger* (s.d.s and s.p.s); *A Messenger* (d.p.)

MESSENGER: *Messenger* (s.d.s and s.p.s)

FRANCISCO: *Francisco* (s.d.s); *Franc<isco>* (s.p.s); *Francisco*, [one of the] *servants to Philocres* (d.p.)

PONTO: *Ponto* (s.d.s); *Pont<o>* (s.p.s); *Ponto*, [one of the] *servants to Philocres* (d.p.)

SYLVANDER: *Sylvander* (s.d.s); *sylv<ander>* (s.p.s); *sylvander, a Gentleman of Cyprus* (d.p.)

ATTENDANTS: *Attendants* (s.d.s)

PEOPLE: *people* (s.d.s)

OTHER CHARACTERS
Feredo's clients (1.1)
Florabella's dead mother (1.4, 2.2)
Joan's 15-year-old daughter (1.5, 2.4, 3.4)
A taborer the Countrywomen brought with them (2.4)
Philocres' man (3.1; but he could be Francisco or Porto)
Bellamour's man (3.1)
Nigretta's tailor (3.2; possibly imaginary)
The King of Majorca, Philocres' father (4.2)
The people of Majorca (4.2)
Young lads of the town (5.2)
A carpenter who erected the scaffold (5.3)
Fiducia's young brother (5.4)
The King of Cyprus, Bellamour's recently dead father (5.4)
49 gentlemen of Cyprus, Sylvander's associates, who seek Bellamour through the world (5.4)
Sylvander's footboy, who provided Lucina with boy's clothes (5.4)
Princes of neighbouring states (5.4)

SETTING
Time-Scheme: One day passes between 1.1–4 and 1.5. 2.1–4 take place the day after that (2.2–3 in the evening), and 2.5 at about 2 a.m. that night. 3.1–5 take place the following day (which is not a Sunday). 4.5–6 take place the day after 4.2–4 (4.4 at night and 4.5 in the early morning), and no more than three days pass between 3.5 and 5.1–4.
Place: Corsica

Geography
Corsica: the Forest of Disaster
Mediterranean: Majorca; Malta; Cyprus
[*Europe*]: France; Italy
[*Asia*]: Media; Persia

SOURCES
Narrative: Francis Beaumont and John Fletcher, *Philaster* (**1597**); Ludovico Ariosto, *Orlando furioso* 5 (1516) and/or William Shakespeare, *Much Ado About Nothing* (**1148**); William Shakespeare and George Wilkins, *Pericles, Prince of Tyre* (**1555**; 1.5)
Verbal: Bible: Daniel 6.15 (1.3)

Works Mentioned: John Dowland, *The Second Book of Songs or Airs* (1600), 2: Lachrymae (3.4); *The Soldier's Delight* (ballad, 1635?; 2.4)

At the level of diction, there is also a great deal of low-level lexical imitation of Shakespeare.

LANGUAGE
English
Latin: 19 words (1.5, 2.3, 3.5, 4.5; King, Lucina, Montalto, Sylvander)
Italian: 10 words (1.5; King)
French: 5 words (1.5; King)

FORM
Metre: pentameter and prose
Rhyme: blank verse; occasional couplets
Act-Division: 5 acts
Lines (Spoken): 3,154 (2,873 verse, 281 prose)
Lines (Written): 3,234

STAGING
Doors: characters enter at two doors (1.5, s.d.; 5.1, implicit)
Stage: the scaffold is placed on one side of the stage (5.3, s.d.; the stage needs to be large enough to have a combat area on the other side)
Within: music (1.5, s.d.)
Above: characters appear 'above in the window' (1.5, 2.5, s.d.; this area accommodates at least four people); Philocres climbs from the main stage up to the window using a rope ladder (2.5, s.d.; the area above must therefore have somewhere to fasten the ladder)

MUSIC
Music: trumpets within (1.5, s.d.); still music (1.5, s.d.); a tabor (2.4, s.d.); trumpets (5.4, s.d.)
Song: 'A catch, a match, in faith, a catch, a match', 3.4, Servingmen, 13 lines, a catch
Dance: the Servingmen and Countrywomen dance (2.4, s.d.)

PROPS
Lighting: a closed lantern (2.5, s.d.)
Weapons: five scutcheons with mottos and emblems (1.5, s.d.); five lances (1.5, s.d.); Philocres' sword (2.2, 5.4, implicit); Bellamour's sword (2.2, 5.4, dialogue; 2.5, s.d.); Bellamour's dagger (2.2, implicit); Garamont's sword (2.5, 5.4, dialogue); Francisco's sword (4.6, dialogue); Ponto's sword (4.6, dialogue); Sylvander's sword (4.6, 5.4, implicit)
Clothing: a chain of pearl (1.4, 3.2, dialogue; also worn by Bellamour); a glove (5.4, s.d.)
Small Portable Objects: two sets of letters patents (4.4, dialogue); a box of balsam (4.6, s.d.)
Large Portable Objects: a rope ladder (2.3, implicit; 2.5, s.d.)
Scenery: a throne of state on degrees (1.2, implicit; 5.3–4, s.d.); a scaffold (5.3–4, s.d.; brought on stage manually and set up, not discovered ready-made); a bar (5.4, dialogue)
Miscellaneous: blood (4.6, dialogue)

COSTUMES
FLORABELLA: cross-dressed in a boy's suit (5.4, dialogue); her own clothes (5.4, s.d.); she has 65 lines in which to change costume off stage
PHILOCRES: a sheath (2.2, 5.4, implicit); muffled in a cloak (2.5, s.d.)
BELLAMOUR: a sheath (2.2, dialogue; 2.5, implicit); a chain of pearls (1.5, implicit; 2.2, dialogue; see also PROPS); disguised (4.5, 5.3–4, s.d.)
GARAMONT: a sheath (2.5, 5.4, implicit)
LUCINA: Florabella's clothes (2.5, dialogue); cross-dressed as a man, including a hat and a false beard (5.4, s.d.; the hat and beard are removed on stage)
FIDUCIA: a veil (5.4, s.d.; removed on stage); Florabella's clothes (5.4, implicit)
FRANCISCO and PONTO: sheaths (4.6, implicit)
SYLVANDER: a sheath (4.6, 5.4, implicit)

EARLY TEXTUAL HISTORY
1630s (?): transcribed in **MS**; 55 leaves; list of roles.

EDITION
Bertram Dobell (London, 1908).

Dobell silently omits the words of the catch sung in 3.4, no doubt because the whole song is an extended vagina joke.

REFERENCES
Annals 1625; Bentley, v. 1388–9.

2514. Unused London Lord Mayor's Pageant

EVIDENCE
Records of the London Ironmongers' Company.

GENRE
civic pageant
Contemporary: pageants; show

AUTHOR
John Taylor

DATE
October 1635

SCENE DESIGNATION
The device consisted of five pageants.

EARLY TEXTUAL HISTORY
1635: On Friday 2 October, the painter Robert Norman and the poet John Taylor presented the Court of the

London Ironmongers' Company with a proposed device for the next Lord Mayor's inaugural pageant. They set their minimum price at £190, so the Court opted for a cheaper alternative proposal (**2517**). However, Norman and Taylor were paid £1 for their trouble.

REFERENCES
MSC 3, 122–3.

2515. *The Lady of Pleasure*

TEXT
Printed in 1637 (STC 22448), probably from authorial fair copy.

GENRE
comedy
Contemporary: play (Greene, S.R.); comedy (t.p.); poem (ded.); 'rare play' (Mildmay)

TITLE
Performed/Printed: *The Lady of Pleasure*

AUTHOR
James Shirley

DATE
October 1635

ORIGINAL PRODUCTION
Queen Henrietta's Men at the Cockpit

PLOT
Bored with country life, Aretina forces her husband, Sir Thomas Bornwell, to sell up their estate and come to live in London. There she lives extravagantly, buying expensive luxuries and gay clothes, and keeping up with her equally prodigal neighbour, the young widow Celestina. She summons her nephew Frederick home from university, unhappy that he has been turned into a serious scholar, and she asks her fashionable friends Kickshaw and Littleworth to teach him the conventions of social behaviour. Bornwell decides that all he can do is match his wife's profligacy, and visits Celestina as one of her many suitors. He invites her back to his house as a guest.

A formerly promiscuous lord has lost all interest in sex since the death of his mistress. Decoy the bawd offers to procure Aretina for him, but Aretina is his kinswoman: he refuses, and sends Decoy to Aretina with a letter purporting to be a testimonial, but which is actually a warning against the bearer. But Aretina, seeking an extra-marital liaison, treats the letter as a positive recommendation, and engages Decoy to procure Kickshaw for her. She also asks Kickshaw and Littleworth to provoke her unwanted guest Celestina, but their disparaging remarks have no effect, other than to annoy Bornwell when he overhears them; he encourages Celestina to insult them back at length.

Kickshaw is invited to an assignation, which turns out to be with Decoy, disguised as a crone. She proposes a nocturnal meeting for sex, promising that she will seem much younger in the dark (primarily, of course, because she will be a different woman, Aretina incognito). That night, Aretina gives him money and rich presents, but makes him promise not to talk about his lover; instead, when he visits her at home, he boasts about his mistress and unwittingly gives her back her own gifts.

The Lord's friends introduce him to Celestina in the hope that she will rekindle his interest in women. It does, but she refuses him unless he commits himself to an honourable chastity.

Bornwell has started to gamble and to lose large sums of money. Husband and wife compete with one another in conspicuous consumption—dinner parties, playgoing, balls—until Bornwell tells Aretina that they have enough left for one more month of this lifestyle, after which they will lead a life of poverty. Aretina comes to her senses and insists they return to the country; Bornwell reassures her that he has not in fact been spending money, so they are financially secure after all. Frederick goes back to the university: at least he has got a new suit out of his stay in London.

SCENE DESIGNATION
1.1–2, 2.1–2, 3.1–2, 4.1–3, 5.1 (Q has act-division only)

ROLES
Lady ARETINA, a noblewoman; Bornwell's wife, Frederick's aunt, the Lord's kinswoman
Aretina's STEWARD, a gentleman
Sir Thomas BORNWELL, a knight, Aretina's husband, Frederick's uncle
Madam DECOY, a gentlewoman and bawd; poses as an old woman
Master Alexander KICKSHAW, a young gentleman
Master John LITTLEWORTH, a lean gentleman gallant; also called Jack
A SERVANT in Bornwell's household (1.1; may be one of the servants in 5.1)
Lady CELESTINA, a widow; by marriage, Lady Bellamour; 15 years old; kinswoman of Mariana and Isabella; also called Mistress Celestina
Celestina's STEWARD
Master HAIRCUT, the Lord's barber; an unmarried gentleman and would-be courtier
Master FREDERICK, nephew of Aretina and Bornwell, a young university man; said to be little
MARIANA, Isabella's sister, Celestina's kinswoman; either she or Isabella is Lady Novice
ISABELLA, Mariana's sister, Celestina's kinswoman
Celestina's GENTLEWOMAN (2.2)

Sir William SCENTLOVE, a knight and a bachelor; also called Will
A LORD, a courtier; Aretina's kinsman
The Lord's SECRETARY (3.1)
A SERVANT, who brings Madam Decoy's letter to Kickshaw (3.2, *non-speaking*)
Two MEN, who abduct Kickshaw (4.1, *non-speaking*)
Aretina's SERVANT (5.1; may be the servant in 1.1)
Bornwell's SERVANTS (5.1; one speaks, and may be the servant in 1.1)
The Lord's SERVANT (5.1)

Speaking Parts: 18–20

Stage Directions and Speech Prefixes
ARETINA: *Aretina* (s.d.s); *Are<tina>* (s.p.s); *Aretina, Sir Thomas Bornwell's Lady* (d.p.)
STEWARD: *[Aretina's] Steward* (s.d.s); *Steward* (s.d.s and s.p.s); *Steward to the Lady Aretina* (d.p.)
BORNWELL: *Sir Thomas Bornewell* (s.d.s and d.p.); *Sir Thomas Bornwell* | *sir Thomas* | *Bornewell* | *Bornwell* (s.d.s); *Bor<newell>* (s.p.s)
DECOY: *Madam Decoy* (s.d.s and d.p.); *Decoy* (s.d.s); *Dec<oy>* (s.p.s)
KICKSHAW: *Alexander* | *Kickshaw* (s.d.s); *Alex<ander>* | *Kic<kshaw>* (s.p.s); *Mr Alex<ander> Kickshaw* (d.p.)
LITTLEWORTH: *Littleworth* (s.d.s); *Lit<tleworth>* (s.p.s); *Mr John Littleworth* (d.p.)
SERVANT: *Servant* (s.d.s and s.p.s); *Servants* (d.p.)
CELESTINA: *Celestina* (s.d.s); *Cel<estina>* (s.p.s); *Celestina, a young Widow* (d.p.)
STEWARD: *[Celestina's] Steward* (s.d.s); *Steward* (s.d.s and s.p.s); *Steward to the Lady Celestina* (d.p.)
HAIRCUT: *Haircut* (s.d.s); *Mr Haircut* (s.d.s and d.p.); *Hair<ecut>* (s.p.s)
FREDERICK: *Mr Fredericke* (s.d.s and d.p.); *Fredericke* (s.d.s); *Fre<dericke>* (s.p.s)
MARIANA: *Mardana* | *Marcana* (s.d.s); *Mariana* (s.d.s and d.p.); *Mar<iana>* (s.p.s)
ISABELLA: *Isabella* (s.d.s and d.p.); *Issabella* (s.d.s); *Is<abella>* (s.p.s)
GENTLEWOMAN: *Celestinae's gentlewoman* (s.d.s); *Gentlewoman* (s.d.s and s.p.s)
SCENTLOVE: *Sir Will<iam> Sentlove* | *Sentlove* (s.d.s); *Sent<love>* (s.p.s); *Sir William Sentlove* (d.p.)
LORD: *Lord* (s.d.s, s.p.s, and d.p.)
SECRETARY: *Secretary* (s.d.s, s.p.s, and d.p.)
SERVANT: *servant* (s.d.s); *[one of the] Servants* (d.p.)
MEN: *two men* (s.d.s)
SERVANT: *Servant* (s.d.s and s.p.s); *[one of the] Servants* (d.p.)
SERVANTS: *Servant* (s.p.s); *Servants* (d.p.)
SERVANT: *Servant* (s.d.s and s.p.s); *[one of the] Servants* (d.p.)

OTHER CHARACTERS
Bornwell's tenants (1.1, 2.1)
Aretina's kinsmen, powerful men in the state (1.1)
Kickshaw's jeweller, a goldsmith (1.1)
Lord Bellamour, a knight, Celestina's dead husband (1.1–2, 2.2, 3.2)
Bornwell's footmen (1.1, 2.1)
Bornwell's wine merchant (1.1)
A Dutch or Belgian painter for whom Aretina sits (1.1, 2.1)
Ladies who visit Celestina (1.2)
The Countess, Celestina's aunt (1.2)
Frederick's tutor (2.1)
Frederick's dead father, Aretina's brother or brother-in-law (2.1)
Aretina's physician (2.1)
The poor of the country parish, whom Bornwell used to entertain to dinner (2.1)
Bornwell's country footmen and coachmen (2.1)
Three fiddlers who used to play at Bornwell's country house at holidays (2.1)
Aretina's chambermaids (2.1)
Celestina's tailor (2.2)
People who can offer testimonials as to the state of Bornwell's body (2.2)
Waiting-women who know Scentlove (2.2)
Bella Maria, the Lord's dead mistress (3.1, 4.3)
Noblemen who have used Decoy's house for sexual assignations (3.2)
A French tailor who made Frederick's new clothes (3.2, 4.2)
A pie-wench and carrier of clandestine messages (4.2)
A female ballad vendor (4.2)
A drawer at the Bear tavern (4.2)
Celestina's father (4.3)
Women whom the Lord once courted (4.3)
People who gambled at dice with Bornwell (5.1; possibly imaginary)
The master of the gaming house (5.1; possibly imaginary)
Bornwell's jeweller (5.1)
Aretina's waiting-woman (5.1)
Ladies and gentlemen whom Bornwell invited to eat out with him (5.1; possibly imaginary)
Courtiers whom Aretina invited to dine with her (5.1; possibly imaginary)
The host of the Italian ordinary (5.1)
Kickshaw's clerk of the kitchen (5.1)
Kickshaw's footman (5.1)
A man known to Celestina, who wants to buy a coat of arms (5.1)

SETTING
Period: contemporary
Time-Scheme: The action takes place on two consecutive days: 1.1–2.2 in the morning, 3.1 at 3 p.m., and 3.2 and 4.1 later the same day; 5.1 takes place the next day.
Place: London

Geography
London: Hyde Park; Mile End; the Strand; Charing Cross; Temple Bar; Westminster; Tyburn; Long

Lane; the Bear Tavern at Bridge Foot; London Bridge; River Thames; Strand Bridge; the Stillyard
[*Middlesex*]: Islington
England: Banstead Downs; Windsor; [Oxford or Cambridge]
Ireland
The Low Countries: Belgia; Flanders; Westphalia
Italy: Venice; Lombardy
[*Europe*]: France; Spain; Greece
[*Africa*]: Barbary; Ethiopia
Peru

SOURCES
Verbal: Catullus, *Carmina* 5 (3.2); Bible: John 8.44 (4.1); James Shirley, *Hyde Park* (**2367**; 1.2)
Works Mentioned: Bible: Luke 15.11–32 (prodigal son; 1.2); John Dowland, *The Second Book of Songs or Airs* 2: Lachrymae (1600; 5.1); Statute of Bigamy (1603; 1 James I c. 11; 2.2); James Shirley, *The Ball* (**2389**; 1.1); Puppet Play of Susanna and the Elders (**2489**; 3.2)

LANGUAGE
English
French: 201 words (2.1, 3.2; Aretina, Celestina)
Latin: 5 words (3.2, 5.1; Frederick, Bornwell)
Spanish: 1 word (4.2; Littleworth)

FORM
Metre: pentameter and prose
Rhyme: blank verse
Act-Division: 5 acts
Lines (Spoken): 2,528 (2,035 verse, 493 prose)
Lines (Written): 2,591

MUSIC
Music: unspecified music (4.1, 5.1, dialogue)
Singing: Bornwell sings (3.2, 5.1, implicit)
Dance: Bornwell, Celestina, Scentlove, Mariana, Haircut, and Isabella dance (2.2, s.d.)

PROPS
Lighting: a light (4.1, s.d.)
Weapons: possibly Littleworth's rapier (1.1, 2.1, 3.2, 4.2, dialogue); Haircut's sword (5.1, dialogue)
Clothing: a ruby ring (1.1, dialogue; contains more than one ruby); a periwig (3.1, s.d.; see also COSTUMES: LORD); a jewel (3.2, 5.1, dialogue); a chain (5.1, dialogue)
Money: a purse containing one hundred pieces (2.1, dialogue; only five of the pieces are taken out); gold (4.1, 5.1, dialogue)
Food and Drink: sugar plums (1.1, 3.2, dialogue)
Small Portable Objects: a looking-glass (3.1, s.d.); a pen (3.1, dialogue); ink (3.1, implicit); a letter (3.1, implicit; 3.2, s.d.; written on stage); a picture of a woman (3.1, implicit; probably a miniature); a fan (3.2, dialogue); a letter (3.2, s.d.); unspecified trinkets (5.1, dialogue)
Large Portable Objects: a table (3.1, s.d.)

Scenery: arras hangings (1.2, dialogue); possibly a bed (4.1, dialogue)

COSTUMES
ARETINA: curled hair (dialogue); a gown (5.1, dialogue); a white glove (5.1, dialogue; possibly removed on stage)
DECOY: disguised as an old woman (4.1, s.d.), with coarse clothing (dialogue)
KICKSHAW: is fat (dialogue); silk clothes (3.2, implicit); a blindfold (4.1, s.d.; removed on stage); rich clothes (4.2, dialogue); silk stockings, garters, a beaver hat, roses on his shoes, and clothing made of gold and silver (5.1, dialogue)
LITTLEWORTH: silk clothes (3.2, implicit); possibly hangers (implicit); wet clothes (5.1, s.d.); a shirt (5.1, dialogue; probably removed on stage); he is undressed on stage, apparently to his skin (5.1, dialogue)
FREDERICK: black clothes, including a satin doublet and a hat (2.1, dialogue); new clothes (4.2, implicit), including a hat with a feather, a doublet, a shirt, breeches, and a hip-length cloak (dialogue)
SCENTLOVE: a periwig (5.1, dialogue; removed on stage; underneath it he is bald)
LORD: 'unready' (3.1, s.d.); a periwig (4.3, dialogue; see also PROPS)

EARLY STAGE HISTORY
1635: On Thursday 5 or Friday 6 November, a group of bachelors celebrating the marriage of Edward and Margaret Bysshe, including Margaret's brother John Greene, went to the theatre; some went to see *The Lady of Pleasure* at the Cockpit, the others *The Conspiracy* (**2459**) at the Blackfriars.
1635: performed in the afternoon on Tuesday 8 December. The audience included Sir Humphrey Mildmay (who paid 1s, and enjoyed the play).
1639: The play was in the repertory of the King's and Queen's Young Company (Beeston's Boys) at the Cockpit. On Saturday 10 August, Philip Herbert, 4th Earl of Pembroke (Lord Chamberlain) issued an order restraining performances by other companies of this and 44 other plays.

EARLY TEXTUAL HISTORY
1635: On Thursday 15 October, Sir Henry Herbert licensed the text for performance.
1637: entered in the Stationers' Register to Andrew Crooke and William Cooke on Thursday 13 April; joint entry with *The Young Admiral* (**2410**), entry names author. Thomas Herbert, Sir Henry Herbert's deputy, had licensed the book for publication.
1637: Q printed by Thomas Cotes for Andrew Crooke and William Cooke; collation A² B–I⁴ K², 36 leaves; title page names author, acting company, and playhouse; list of roles; authorial dedication to Richard, 1st Baron Lovelace of Hurley (died 1634; perhaps in error for his son, John, 2nd Baron Lovelace of Hurley).

Before 1640: a copy of Q was owned by Robert Burton.

c. 1630s–40s: a copy of Q was in the possession of John Horne (Vicar of Headington, Oxfordshire). After his death, his entire collection of play-books passed into the possession of John Houghton of Brasenose College, Oxford (c. 1608–77), then to James Herne (died 1685), and then to the library of Ralph Sheldon (1623–84) at Weston, where it was catalogued by Anthony Wood, probably in the late 1670s. By then the copy had been bound into a single volume with 21 other plays by Shirley (and, presumably in error, with Henry Shirley's *The Martyred Soldier*, **2030**).

1640–1: Humphrey Moseley was selling copies of Q for 6d each.

c. 1640: Abraham Wright transcribed extracts into a MS miscellany (London: British Library, Add. MS 22608, fos. 99ᵛ–101ᵛ). The MS later passed to Wright's son, the antiquarian James Wright (c. 1644–c. 1717).

Mid-seventeenth century: MS amendments were made on a copy of Q (now in the Library of Congress, Washington), perhaps for use as copy for a projected reprint.

1655: *The English Treasury of Wit and Language* entered in the Stationers' Register to Humphrey Moseley on Tuesday 16 January.

1655: nine extracts (from 1.1, 2.1–2, 3.2, 5.1) included in John Cotgrave's *The English Treasury of Wit and Language*, sigs. E4ʳ⁻ᵛ, G4ᵛ, I2ᵛ–I3ʳ, K4ʳ, M6ʳ, Q5ᵛ, S3ʳ, V5ʳ; printed for Humphrey Moseley.

EDITIONS

Marilyn J. Thorssen, Garland Renaissance Drama (New York and London, 1979).

Ronald Huebert, Revels Plays (Manchester, 1986).

Julie Sanders, in James Shirley, *The Complete Works*, gen. eds. Eugene Giddens, Teresa Grant, and Barbara Ravelhofer (Oxford, forthcoming).

REFERENCES

Annals 1635; Bawcutt 329, C97; Beal 2 ShJ 182–3; Bentley, ii. 677, v. 1125–7; *English Historical Review* 43 (1928), 389; Eyre & Rivington, i. 463; Greg 518; Robert Stanley Forsythe, *The Relations of Shirley's Plays to the Elizabethan Drama* (New York, 1914), 371–9; Hazlitt, 128; Nicolas K. Kiessling, *The Library of Robert Burton* (Oxford, 1988) 1475; *MLR* 13 (1918), 401–11; *MP* 66 (1968–9), 256–61; *MRDE* 6 (1993), 192; MSC 2.3, 389–90; *Oxford Bibliographical Society Proceedings and Papers* 2.2 (1929), 132–3; REED: Inns of Court, 812; *SP* 40 (1943), 186–203.

2516. The Lady Mother

TEXT

MS (London: British Library, MS Egerton 1994, fos. 186–211); scribal transcript of authorial foul papers, subsequently censored, revised, and marked for use as a prompt-book. This preserves broadly two states of the text:

A: original version, with a first round of minor authorial alterations and corrections;

B: version revised by the author for performance, with cuts and further revision in response to censorship, and also brief passages inserted in A.2.1 (which becomes, through a change to the scene order, B.2.2).

GENRE

comedy

Contemporary: play (Blagrave)

TITLE

Performed/MS: *The Lady Mother*

Alternative Modernization: *The Lady-Mother*

AUTHOR

Henry Glapthorne (*attribution*)

DATE

October 1635

ORIGINAL PRODUCTION

King's Revels Company at Salisbury Court (?)

PLOT

Thorogood and Bonville both want to marry into the Marlove family, respectively to the mother and one of the daughters, saving wedding expenses by doing it on the same day. But they have rivals: Belizea is courted by Crackby and Sucket, Lady Marlove by both her steward, Alexander, and Crackby's rich uncle, Sir Geoffrey. The other daughter, Clariana, is being wooed by Thurston.

Lady Marlove interferes in her daughters' love-lives. She lets Bonville know, via Thorogood, that Belizea is unchaste, causing him to break off the engagement; when he offers himself to Lady Marlove instead, she tells him that it was a test of his love for Belizea—and that he has failed. He asks Belizea's forgiveness, and she grants it on condition that he names her traducer, but when he does, it only makes matters worse. Lady Marlove also persuades Clariana to jilt Thurston, because she secretly wants him for herself. When the rejected Thurston offers himself to her, she accepts, only to be told that it was a test of her chastity—and that she has failed. Piqued, she orders her daughters to marry Sir Geoffrey and Crackby, on pain of being disinherited. The men woo aggressively, and Belizea is reconciled with Bonville when he rescues her from Crackby, who is trying to steal her ring.

Lady Marlove asks Clariana to court Thurston on her behalf, facing Thurston with a problem: should he accept the love of a woman he hates in order to accommodate the one he loves? Thorogood brings news that Belizea and Bonville have eloped, only to be thrown by their horses and drowned in the river; their bodies have been swept away by the current. Lady Marlove sends Alexander to procure her son to murder Thurston. Young Marlove is pursued and arrested for the murder, and names Alexander as the instigator. At the trial, Lady Marlove tries to take the blame, insisting that her son acted only out of filial obedience; Thorogood in turn attempts to save her by claiming to have instigated the murder. She, Alexander, and Young Marlove are all sentenced to death. A masque of death arrives to bring Lady Marlove to mortification, but it is sent away by a masque of Hymen. The two pairs of masked lovers in the latter turn out to be Clariana and Thurston (who has been married, not murdered) and Belizea and Bonville (whose reported drowning was only a ruse).

In a subsidiary episode, Alexander gets drunk and falls asleep; Crackby and his accomplices bloody and bandage his face, and, when he wakes, try to convince him that he has been brawling with prostitutes in a brothel.

SCENE DESIGNATION
1.1–3, 2.1–2, 3.1, 4.1–3, 5.1 (MS has act-division only)

B-Text
1.1–3, 2.1–2, 3.1, 4.1–2, 5.1–2

Most of the scenes are the same, but the sequence of 2.1 and 2.2 is reversed (A.2.1 = B.2.2 and A.2.2 = B.2.1), and the final act-division moved (A.4.3 = B.5.1, A.5.1 = B.5.2).

ROLES
Master THOROGOOD, Lady Marlove's suitor
Master BONVILLE, Belizea's suitor
GRIMES, a servant; plays Death in the masque
Master ALEXANDER Lovell, Lady Marlove's steward; formerly a tailor
LADY MARLOVE, a widow, mother of Belizea, Clariana, and Young Marlove
MAGDALEN, Lady Marlove's waiting-woman
TIMOTHY, Lady Marlove's butler; also called Tim; plays Hymen in the masque
SUCKET, a soldier and captain
Master CRACKBY, a young citizen, Sir Geoffrey's nephew
SIR GEOFFREY, an old knight, Crackby's rich uncle
BUNCH, Sir Geoffrey's servant
CLARIANA, Lady Marlove's daughter, sister of Belizea and Young Marlove; less than 20 years old; later Thurston's wife
BELIZEA, Lady Marlove's daughter, sister of Clariana and Young Marlove
Six MUSICIANS, the town waits, including a boy, who sings treble (2.1; only the boy speaks)
Young MARLOVE, Lady Marlove's son, brother of Belizea and Clariana
Master THURSTON, a young gentleman, Young Marlove's friend; later Clariana's husband

The CONSTABLE
OFFICERS accompanying the Constable (4.3; only speak collectively)
The RECORDER
FURIES in the masque (5.1, *non-speaking*)

B-Text
RECORDER: altered to a Judge by the censor and named SIR HUGH

Speaking Parts: 18
Allegorical Roles: Death (in the masque)

Stage Directions and Speech Prefixes
THOROGOOD: *Thorowgood* | *Thorogood* | *Thorougood* (s.d.s); *Thoro<good>* (s.p.s)
BONVILLE: *Bonvill* | [one of] *the lovers* | *Bonvil* (s.d.s); *Bon<vill>* (s.p.s)
GRIMES: *Grimes* | *Death* (s.d.s); *Gri<mes>* (s.p.s)
ALEXANDER: *Alexander* | *Lovell* | *Alexander Lovell* | [one of the] *Prisoners* (s.d.s); *Lov<ell>* | *Alex<ander>* (s.p.s)
LADY MARLOVE: *Lady* (s.d.s and s.p.s); *Lady Marlove* | [one of the] *Prisoners* (s.d.s)
MAGDALEN: *Maudlin* | *Magdalen* (s.d.s); *Mag<dalen>* (s.p.s)
TIMOTHY: *Timothy* | *Tymothy* | *Timothie* | *Hymen* (s.d.s); *Tim<othy>* (s.p.s)
SUCKET: *Sucket* | *Suckett* (s.d.s); *Suc<ket>* (s.p.s)
CRACKBY: *Crackby* | *Crackbie* | *Crakby* (s.d.s); *Crack<by>* (s.p.s)
SIR GEOFFREY: *Sir Gefferie* | *Sir Geffery* | *Sir Geffry* (s.d.s); *Sir Geff<ery>* (s.p.s)
BUNCH: *Bunch* | *Bunche* (s.d.s); *Bun<ch>* (s.p.s)
CLARIANA: *Clariana* | [one of] *the lovers* (s.d.s); *Clari<ana>* (s.p.s)
BELIZEA: *Bell<izea>* | *Belizea* | *Belisea* | [one of] *the lovers* | *Belisia* (s.d.s); *Bel<izea>* (s.p.s)
MUSICIANS: *Music* (s.d.s); *Mu<sician>* (s.p.s)
MARLOVE: *Young Marlove* | [one of the] *Prisoners* (s.d.s); *Young Mar<love>* (s.p.s)
THURSTON: *Thurston* | *Turston* | [one of] *the lovers* (s.d.s); *Thur<ston>* (s.p.s)
CONSTABLE: *Constable* (s.d.s and s.p.s)
OFFICERS: *Officers* (s.d.s); *Within* (s.p.s)
RECORDER: *Recorder* (s.d.s and s.p.s); *the Recorder* (s.d.s)
FURIES: *furies* (s.d.s)

B-Text
SIR HUGH: *Judge* (s.d.s); *Sir Hu<gh>* (s.p.s)

OTHER CHARACTERS
Lady Marlove's dead husband, an old knight, father of Young Marlove and Clariana (1.1, 3.1, 4.1–3)
Crackby's father (1.2, 3.1)
A country chambermaid who laughed at Crackby when he tried to seduce her (1.2)
A county treasurer responsible for paying soldiers' pensions (1.2)

Bonville's dead mother (1.3, 4.1)
A poet, the author of the Boy's song, who has agreed with the actors to limit its promulgation (2.1)
Women who have asked for Crackby's picture, including a merchant's daughter (3.1; possibly imaginary)
Nan, Crackby's schoolfellow (3.1; possibly imaginary)
Thurston's friends (3.1)
An astrologer who warned Clariana not to marry too young (3.1)

SETTING
Period: contemporary. The action takes place during neither Lent nor Advent.
Place: England, in the country

Geography
London: Whitefriars theatre (i.e. Salisbury Court); the Artillery Garden; Bedlam
[*Middlesex*]: Pimlico
The Low Countries: Busse [= 'sHertogenbosch]; Maastricht
Italy: Mount Etna
Spain: Bilbao
[*Europe*]: France; Russia
[*Asia*]: Turkey; Scythia; Arabia
[*Africa*]: Ethiopia
India
The East Indies
The West Indies

B-Text
Additional Geography
Heidelberg

SOURCES
Narrative: William Shakespeare, *Twelfth Night* (**1297**; Alexander)
Verbal: William Shakespeare, *Hamlet* (**1259**; 4.1); George Wilkins, John Day, and William Rowley, *The Travels of the Three English Brothers* (**1534**; 3.1)
Works Mentioned: Homer, *Iliad* (4.1); *The Koran* (1.3)

Brown proposes borrowings from *The Wedding* (**2184**), *The Jealous Lovers* (**2365**), and *A Fine Companion* (**2378**), but gives no details; in narrative terms, the similarities seem no more than superficial. There are perhaps a few hints of *The Duchess of Malfi* (**1726**) in Young Marlove's attachment to his father's sword and the concluding device of sending a masque to mortify the condemned Lady Marlove.

LANGUAGE
English
Latin: 13 words (1.1, 3.1, 5.1; Alexander, Clariana, Sir Geoffrey)
Spanish: 2 words (1.2; Sir Geoffrey)
French: 1 word (1.2; Sir Geoffrey)

FORM
Metre: pentameter and prose
Rhyme: blank verse
Act-Division: 5 acts
Lines (Spoken): 2,534 (1,361 verse, 1,173 prose)
Lines (Written): 2,608

B-Text
Lines (Spoken): 2,287 (1,338 verse, 949 prose)
Lines (Written): 2,622

STAGING
Within: speech (4.3, s.d.); shout (5.1, s.d.)
Miscellaneous: Grimes pricks his finger on stage and it is said to bleed (2.1, dialogue)

MUSIC
Music: unspecified music (2.1, s.d.; 5.1, dialogue); flourish (5.1, s.d.); horrid music (5.1, s.d.); recorders (5.1, s.d.)
Song: 2.1, Boy
Dance: musicians dance (2.1, s.d.); Furies dance (5.1, dialogue); everyone on stage dances (5.1, s.d.)

PROPS
Weapons: Bonville's sword (1.3, implicit; 3.1, dialogue); Sucket's sword (3.1, dialogue); a cudgel (3.1, dialogue); Young Marlove's sword (4.2–3, dialogue); Thorogood's sword (5.1, implicit)
Clothing: a garter (2.1, dialogue); a veil (4.3, dialogue)
Money: half a piece (2.1, dialogue); an unspecified sum (2.1, implicit); a purse of gold (4.1–2, dialogue)
Food and Drink: a bottle of sack (2.1, s.d.; drunk on stage); a cup (2.1, s.d.); a flagon of wine (2.1, s.d.); tobacco (2.1, dialogue)
Small Portable Objects: pen and ink (1.1, s.d.); paper (1.1, implicit; written on on stage); a letter (1.1, dialogue); a jewel (4.1–2, dialogue)
Large Portable Objects: a chair (2.1, dialogue); a table (5.1, s.d.)
Scenery: an arras (2.1, dialogue)
Miscellaneous: salvatory (2.1, dialogue); blood (2.1, dialogue)

COSTUMES
THOROGOOD: hangers (5.1, implicit)
BONVILLE: hangers (1.3, implicit); a mask (5.1, implicit; removed on stage)
GRIMES: disguised (2.1, s.d.); a blue garment (3.1, dialogue); a mask (5.1, implicit; removed on stage)
ALEXANDER: fine clothes, including a doublet with a satin front and buckram back, a cloak, a cap, garters, and roses (1.1, 2.1, dialogue); a plaster (2.1, dialogue); a napkin on his head (2.1, dialogue)
LADY MARLOVE: probably dressed in widow's black clothes (4.1, dialogue; may be figurative)
SUCKET: a scabbard (3.1, implicit)
SIR GEOFFREY: grey hair (dialogue); a garter with a rose (1.2, dialogue); a cloak (5.1, dialogue)

CLARIANA: a mask (5.1, implicit; removed on stage)
BELIZEA: a jewelled ring (3.1, dialogue); a glove (3.1, dialogue); a mask (5.1, implicit; removed on stage)
THURSTON: a mask (5.1, implicit; removed on stage)
RECORDER: a grey beard (dialogue)

B-Text
ALEXANDER: a codpiece (2.1, dialogue)

EARLY STAGE HISTORY
1635: probably performed by the King's Revels Company, perhaps at Salisbury Court. The cast included: Thomas Sandes (Musician); Harry (Magdalen); possibly < >assingar (Young Marlove or Thurston).

The company attribution derives from the appearance of Thomas Sandes in the cast. See **1796** for further details. It is possible that the actor whose name ended with 'assingar' may have been named Massinger; see **2699**.

EARLY TEXTUAL HISTORY
1635: transcribed in MS, 26 leaves. The scribe's work was corrected by the author.
1635: MS was submitted for censorship to William Blagrave (Deputy Master of the Revels), and on Thursday 15 October, he licensed it for performance, subject to the observation of alterations.
1640s–50s: MS may have been in the possession of the former actor William Cartwright.

EDITION
Arthur Brown, Malone Society Reprints 109 (Oxford, 1959 for 1958).

REFERENCES
Annals 1635; Bawcutt, 330; Bentley, iv. 923–4; Hazlitt, 128; *N&Q* 13th ser., 1 (1923), 503–5.

2517. *Londini sinus salutis* [London's Harbour of Health]

TEXT
Printed in 1635 (STC 13348a); contains no substantive description of 3. Additional information derives from the court books of the London Ironmongers' Company.

GENRE
civic pageant
Contemporary: triumphs, pageants, and shows (t.p.)

TITLE
Printed: *Londini sinus salutis, or London's Harbour of Health and Happiness*
Contemporary: *London's Sinus Salutis*

Later Assigned: *Device for Christopher Clitherow, Ironmonger*
Alternative Modernization: *Device for Christopher Cletherow, Ironmonger*

AUTHOR
Thomas Heywood

DATE
29 October 1635

ORIGINAL PRODUCTION
London Ironmongers' Company, on the River Thames and in the city streets

PLOT
Three goddesses offer the new Lord Mayor of London the gifts of power, wisdom, and love. The centaur Sagittarius comes, attended by lady constellations, and an astrologer explicates his bow as a symbol of the justice the Lord Mayor will wield. Mars is in readiness to defend him, and describes the essential importance of metal in the workings of the world. The Lord Mayor is commended to observe eight virtues, who appear in person.
That evening, Mars recapitulates the lessons of the show.

SCENE DESIGNATION
The event is here divided as follows:
   1: the Celestial Goddesses, on the Thames;
   2: Sagittarius;
   3: 'antic pageant for pleasure' (not described by Heywood);
   4: the Castle of Mars;
   5: *Sinus salutis* (or 'the Harbour of Happiness');
   6: Mars's final speech at night.
Q numbers them the first, next, third, fourth, and last pageants; the final speech is unnumbered (and is not included in the list of the pageants in the records of the Ironmongers' Company).

ROLES
JUNO, Queen of heaven, a celestial goddess, representing power and state (1, *non-speaking*)
PALLAS, a celestial goddess, representing arms and arts; also called Minerva (1, *non-speaking*)
VENUS, Queen of love, a celestial goddess, Cupid's mother; representing beauty and love
CUPID, god of love, Venus' young son; also called Love (1, *non-speaking*)
SAGITTARIUS, a centaur and constellation; also called Croton and Sagittary (2, *non-speaking*)
VIRGO, a female constellation (2, *non-speaking*)
ARIADNE, a female constellation (2, *non-speaking*)
CASSIOPEIA, a female constellation (2, *non-speaking*)
ANDROMEDA, a female constellation (2, *non-speaking*)
An ASTROLOGER
MARS, a god

FORTITUDE, a virtue; also called Fortitudo Togata (5, *non-speaking*)
GENTLENESS, a virtue; also called Mansuetudo (5, *non-speaking*)
SINCERITY, a virtue; also called Candor (5, *non-speaking*)
PATIENCE, a virtue; also called Patientia Philosophica (5, *non-speaking*)
PLACABILITY, a virtue (5, *non-speaking*)
CONCORD, a virtue; also called Philosuchia (5, *non-speaking*)
FIDELITY, a virtue; also called Humanity and Ethos (5, *non-speaking*)
ZEAL, a virtue; also called Nemesis (5, *non-speaking*)
A SPEAKER (5)

The virtues in the fifth pageant are principally named in Latin in Heywood's description, but in English in the spoken text. The seventh virtue is Fidelity in the spoken text but Humanity in the description.

Speaking Parts: 4
Allegorical Roles: 8

Stage Directions
JUNO: [one of] *the Three Celestial Goddesses | Juno* (s.d.s)
PALLAS: [one of] *the Three Celestial Goddesses | Pallas | Minerva* (s.d.s)
VENUS: [one of] *the Three Celestial Goddesses | Venus* (s.d.s)
CUPID: [Venus'] *Son Cupid | Love* (s.d.s)
SAGITTARIUS: *Sagitarius called Croton* (s.d.s)
VIRGO: *Virgo* (s.d.s)
ARIADNE: *Ariadne* (s.d.s)
CASSIOPEIA: *Cassiopeia* (s.d.s)
ANDROMEDA: *Andromeda* (s.d.s)
ASTROLOGER: *an Astrologian* (s.d.s)
MARS: *Mars* (s.d.s)
FORTITUDE: *Fortitudo togata* (s.d.s)
GENTLENESS: *Mansuetudo or gentleness* (s.d.s)
SINCERITY: *Candor, or sincerity* (s.d.s)
PATIENCE: *Patientia Philosophica* (s.d.s)
PLACABILITY: *Placability* (s.d.s)
CONCORD: *Philosuchia, or study of Peace, and Concord* (s.d.s)
FIDELITY: *Humanity* (s.d.s)
ZEAL: *Nemesis, or Zeal* (s.d.s)

OTHER CHARACTERS
Jove (also called Jupiter), Pallas's father, who sent the goddesses (1)

SETTING
Geography
India
The Pole (there is no indication which one)

SOURCES
Verbal: Cicero, *Pro Cluentio* (ded.); Virgil, 'Caesar et Jupiter' (t.p. motto); Pliny, *Natural History* (desc.); Dio Cassius, *Roman History* (ded.; cited); Lactantius, *Divine Institutions* (ded.); Eutropius, *Breviarum historiae Romanae* (desc.); Pierre Bersuire, *Ovidius moralizatus* (fourteenth century; desc.); Desiderius Erasmus, *Apophthegmata* (1531; ded., cited)
Works Mentioned: Anthony Munday, *Camp Bell* (**1595**; desc.)

LANGUAGE
English

FORM
Metre: pentameter
Rhyme: couplets
Lines (Spoken): 182
Lines (Written): 459

STAGING
Stage: four pageant stages (2–5)
Audience: The Lord Mayor is directly addressed throughout, including as 'grave Praetor' (1), 'great lord' (2), 'great Praetor' (2), 'sir' (4), and 'great sir' (5).

MUSIC
Music: trumpets, fifes, and drums (court books)

PROPS
Weapons: a bow (2, desc.); an arrow headed with a star (2, desc.); ordnance (4, desc.; fired during the pageant); Mars's sword (4, desc.)
Animals: peacocks, owls, swans, and turtle-doves (1, desc.)
Scenery: a floating rock (1, desc.); a platform with four corners (2, desc.; seats five); a platform (3, desc.); a castle with a seat in front (4, desc.); a platform (5, desc.; seats eight or nine)

COSTUMES
ARIADNE: probably a golden crown (2, desc)
MARS: possibly a plumed helmet (4, desc.; but the description is translated from Bersuire and does not necessarily represent what the actor wore); possibly a scabbard (4, implicit)
FORTITUDE: a gown (5, desc.); a palm crown (5, dialogue)
Miscellaneous: mockado and silk scarves (court books)

EARLY STAGE HISTORY
Inception: Two rival bids for the Lord Mayor's show were considered by the Court of the London Ironmongers' Company on Friday 2 October. One (**2514**) was by Robert Norman and John Taylor, who had handled the previous year's show (**2448**); it consisted of five pageants and would have cost £190. This was underbid by John Christmas and Thomas Heywood, who were duly appointed to prepare the show.
Preparation: On Thursday 8 October, the Court of Aldermen agreed that the Greenyard in Leadenhall

should not be used for preparing the pageants, as it had been in previous years; the Christmas brothers were required to find somewhere else for their workshop. The authorities viewed work on the pageants twice, and spent 12s.1d, probably given to the workmen as a *pourboire*.

Performance: in London on Thursday 29 October 1635 as part of the celebration of the inauguration of Christopher Clitherow as Lord Mayor. The design was by John Christmas and Mathias Christmas. The performance took place at intervals during the day, from morning to evening. At least some of the performers were children. The procession was marshalled by Richard Allnut, and included Izaak Walton. Also taking part were green men, ten fencers (supplied by John Bradshaw and Thomas Jones), two men on horseback in white armour, 32 trumpeters, seven drummers, and four fifers. Anzolo Correr (Venetian Ambassador) either processed or watched; other ambassadors were invited and may have attended.

Production Finance and Expenses
The Ironmongers' Company financed the event in part by a levy on members processing, including twelve bachelors in foins (£5 each).

Ralph Hudson and Mr Sarracold (a warden) took responsibility for disbursements. The total cost of the event was £550.10s.9d. The budget agreed with Christmas and Heywood was £180, £80 of which was paid in advance by an order dated Friday 9 October. This was to cover fees to performers, costumes, carriage by land and water, green men and fireworks, and music. Selected expenses included: hire of two horses and the children's breakfast (£3); payment to the keeper of Blackwell Hall, presumably Mr Dunne (£1); drums (£6.6s, of which 3s was paid in advance on Wednesday 7 October); fifes (£3.12s, of which 17s was paid in advance on Wednesday 7 October); gratuity to trumpeters (10s); city marshals' fee (£4); Richard Allnut's fee (£4.10s, of which £1 was paid in advance on Wednesday 7 October).

EARLY TEXTUAL HISTORY
1635: John Christmas and Thomas Heywood contracted to supply the Ironmongers' Company with 500 copies of the text.

1635: O printed by Robert Raworth; collation A⁸ B⁴, 12 leaves; title page names author and refers to performance; Latin title-page motto; woodcut (the arms of the Ironmongers' Company) on the verso of the title page; authorial dedication to Christopher Clitherow.

1656: *The English Parnassus* entered to Evan Tyler, Thomas Johnson, and Thomas Davies in the Stationers' Register on Wednesday 24 December.

1657: extract (from 4) included in Joshua Poole's *The English Parnassus*, sig. 2Q3ᵛ; printed for Thomas Johnson.

1677: *The English Parnassus* reprinted by Henry Brome for Thomas Bassett and John Wright; the extract now appears on sig. 2P7ᵛ.

EDITION
David M. Bergeron, in *Thomas Heywood's Pageants*, The Renaissance Imagination 16 (New York, 1986), 71–88.

REFERENCES
Annals 1635; Bentley, iv. 576–7; Bergeron, 229–31; *Cal. Ven.* 1632–6, 475; Eyre & Rivington, ii. 103; Greg 500; Hazlitt, 132; McGee-Meagher 1634–42, 39–40; MSC 3, 122–5; John Nicholl, *Some Account of the Worshipful Company of Ironmongers*, 2nd edn (London, 1866), 222–6; Withington, ii. 42.

2518. The Queen and Concubine

TEXT
Printed in 1659 (Wing B4872).

GENRE
tragicomedy
Contemporary: comedy (t.p.)

TITLE
Printed: *The Queen and Concubine*

AUTHOR
Richard Brome

DATE
Limits: 1635–6
Best Guess: 1635

ORIGINAL PRODUCTION
King's Revels Company at Salisbury Court

PLOT
When Eulalia married King Gonzago of Sicily, her countryman Sforza became a Sicilian subject and displaced the general, Petruccio, who was placed under long-term house arrest. Now the King has just won a war, after Sforza saved his life in battle. But the praises heaped on Sforza make Gonzago jealous; he also suspects an improper relationship between Eulalia and Sforza. In her husband's absence, Eulalia brought Sforza's daughter Alinda to court for company; but in agreeing to come, Alinda broke a promise to her father. Now she catches Gonzago's amorous eye, but when Sforza attempts to defend her honour, he is arrested for treason. Petruccio is recalled and Eulalia too is arrested, tried for adultery, and convicted by false testimony. The laws of Sicily prohibit the execution of a person of royal blood, but she is stripped of her title

and possessions and banished to live without aid or comfort from the King's subjects; her former servants are expelled from the court. Parliament grants Gonzago permission to take a new wife, Alinda, and Eulalia dutifully voices her approval before she leaves. The courtiers Horatio and Lodovico worry that, without Eulalia's restraining influence, Gonzago's natural viciousness will make him a tyrant. Lodovico decides to leave court and follow Eulalia along with her faithful fool Andrea; but Horatio, self-consciously loyal to the crown, stays put.

Eulalia goes to the province of Palermo, traditionally the Queen of Sicily's dowry, and is visited in her sleep by her good genius, who endows her with gifts of prophecy, medicine, and pedagogical skill to help the country folk around her. A plague has fallen upon the land, which the rustics at first attribute to the Queen's adultery; but Eulalia is able to cure them.

Alinda begins a reign of terror. She sends Strozza and Fabio, two of the false witnesses, into the country to assassinate Eulalia. She also orders Petruccio to supervise her father's execution. Petruccio becomes convinced that Sforza is innocent of the charges against him, and feels dishonoured by the job. He brings back not Sforza's head as ordered but his ear-ring, which Alinda accepts as adequate proof of his death. She persuades the King that his first wife must die.

Eulalia's medical gifts dispose of the plague and restore health to Palermo. The people engage her to educate their daughters, thus ensuring that she lives by her own labour and not, contrary to the proclamation, on their charity. Strozza and Fabio fail in their assassination mission, but Eulalia intervenes to save them from execution, and has them imprisoned instead. Further assassins from court meet with no better success. The people encourage Eulalia to become their ruler, independently of the King, but she refuses. Alinda fabricates a letter inviting Eulalia to join Horatio and Lodovico in a plot against her. Eulalia weighs up her options: should she betray her misguided allies and save Alinda, or use the conspiracy to bring about her restoration? She chooses the virtuous, self-denying course.

At court, the Prince's devotion to his mother displeases Gonzago, and Petruccio reports that the boy has died of a broken heart; in fact, he has been sent to Eulalia in the country. The King hears rumours of a rebellion in Palermo, and tries to raise an army, but his soldiers mutiny in support of their executed general, Sforza. The riot is quelled only when Sforza reveals that he is still alive, saved by Petruccio; the King realizes that he is innocent and Eulalia blameless.

Although Alinda has gone mad with bloodlust, Gonzago intends to keep a promise to grant her three boons in public at Palermo. They visit Eulalia, who regretfully reveals the treason in the forged letter; Horatio and Lodovico are arrested. Alinda asks her boons: that Lodovico and Horatio be executed, the Prince disinherited, and Eulalia blinded. Gonzago realizes her wickedness, banishes her, and takes Eulalia back as his queen; he has not broken his oath, because he swore to grant the boons to his lawful queen, and that is Eulalia. Alinda faints.

Eulalia intervenes to save the imprisoned miscreants from country justice, and one of them admits that the evidence against her was perjured. Gonzago is presented with a rustic entertainment in which one of the performers turns out to be the missing Prince. At Eulalia's request, the offenders are pardoned, including even Alinda, whose fainting fit has brought her to her senses. She opts to enter a nunnery, and the King abdicates to become a monk, leaving his son to govern under the kindly direction of Eulalia.

SCENE DESIGNATION

1.1–9, 2.1–8, 3.1–11, 4.1–10, 5.1–9, ep. (O, corrected)

The stage is not clear at the following scene-divisions: 1.1–3, 1.4–5, 1.7–8, 2.1–2, 2.4–5, 2.6–8, 3.1–7, 3.8–9, 4.1–2, 4.3–6, 4.7–10, 5.1–2, 5.3–5, 5.6–7, 5.8–9. A verse line is split across a scene-division at 4.7–8.

ROLES

HORATIO, an old courtier; a married man
LODOVICO, a courtier; also called Lodowick
FLAVELLO, a peer, Alinda's sycophant; adopts the alias Alphonso
Prince GONZAGO, young son of King Gonzago and Eulalia
Queen EULALIA of Sicily, King Gonzago's wife of nearly 20 years, the Prince's mother; born a Neapolitan
ALINDA, Sforza's daughter; later King Gonzago's second wife, styled Queen Alinda
ATTENDANTS on Eulalia (1.2–3, *non-speaking*)
A CAPTAIN in the Sicilian army (1.3; speaks collectively)
A DRUMMER in the Sicilian army (1.3, *non-speaking*)
Gonzago, KING of Sicily, Eulalia's husband, the Prince's father; later Alinda's husband
Lord SFORZA, the Sicilian general and Lord Marshal; born a Neapolitan; Alinda's father; an old man; also called General Sforza
SOLDIERS of the Sicilian army (1.3, 4.9; speak collectively)
Lord PETRUCCIO, the disgraced former Sicilian general, later reappointed; also the Lord Marshal
PETRUCCIO'S SERVANT (1.4)
The GUARD (1.5–6, 2.5, 2.7–8, 5.4; one speaks in 2.7)
The CAPTAIN of the Guard (1.6, *non-speaking*)
Four LORDS of the Parliament (2.1; speak collectively; but they may include Horatio, Lodovico, and Flavello)
Two BISHOPS of the Parliament (2.1; speak collectively)
Two FRIARS (2.1, *non-speaking*)
Eulalia's DOCTOR, a false witness

Eulalia's MIDWIFE, a false witness (only speaks collectively)
STROZZA, a cashiered lieutenant, mutineer, and false witness; a young man
FABIO, a cashiered lieutenant, mutineer, and false witness; a young man
Two VIRGINS attending Alinda (2.2, *non-speaking*)
PETITIONERS (2.3, *non-speaking*)
ANDREA, Eulalia's fool, a Neapolitan; later appointed a rustic magistrate and addressed as Judge Andrea
JAGO, Eulalia's servant
RUGIO, Eulalia's servant
Two or three GENTLEMEN (2.5, *non-speaking*)
The KEEPER of the prison
The GENIUS, Eulalia's guardian spirit
PEDRO, a gentleman of Palermo and rustic magistrate
POGGIO of Palermo, a rustic magistrate and a father
LOLLIO of Palermo, a rustic magistrate and a father; formerly a sexton
Four RUSTICS, respectively deaf, blind, lame, and dumb (3.4)
Four to eight COUNTRYMEN of Palermo (3.5, 4.1–4, 4.6; four to six speak individually, and all collectively; may be the same as the sick rustics in 3.4)
A CURATE and schoolmaster of Palermo
A CRIER (3.7)
GUARDS, countrymen (4.3, 5.7; one or two speak)
Four or seven GIRLS, Eulalia's pupils (4.4, 5.4, 5.9; two speak)
A CAPTAIN at court (4.9)
Two CAPTAINS in the Sicilian army (4.9)
A SERVANT attending Petruccio (4.9; may be the same servant as in 1.4)
ATTENDANTS on the King (5.3–4; only speak collectively, if at all)
A TIPSTAFF (5.6, *non-speaking*)
SCHOOLBOYS (5.9, *non-speaking*)

Speaking Parts: 38–50

Stage Directions and Speech Prefixes
HORATIO: *Horatio* (s.d.s); *Hor<atio>* (s.p.s); *Horatio An old humorous Courtier* (d.p.)
LODOVICO: *Lodovico* (s.d.s); *Lod<ovico>* (s.p.s); *Lodovico Eulalia's faithful Counsellor* (d.p.)
FLAVELLO: *Flavello | Favello | Flavello, alias Alphonso | Alphonso | Alphanso* (s.d.s); *Flav<ello>* (s.p.s); *Alphonso* (s.d.s and s.p.s); *Flavello alias Alphonso, Alinda's Sycophant* (d.p.)
GONZAGO: *the Prince | Gonzago | Conzago* (s.d.s and s.p.s); *Gonza<go>* (s.p.s); *Gonzago [Gonzago's] Son the Prince* (d.p.)
EULALIA: *the Queen Eulalia | the Queen | Eulalia* (s.d.s); *Eul<alia> | Queen* (s.p.s); *Eulalia, The Banished Queen* (d.p.)
ALINDA: *Alinda* (s.d.s); *Alind<a>* (s.p.s); *Alinda, the veiled Concubine* (d.p.)
ATTENDANTS: *Attendants* (s.d.s)

CAPTAIN: *Captain* (s.d.s)
DRUMMER: *Drum* (s.d.s)
KING: *King* (s.d.s and s.p.s); *The King* (s.d.s); *Gonzago King of Sicilie* (d.p.)
SFORZA: *Sforza* (s.d.s); *Sfor<za>* (s.p.s); *Sforza [one of] Two Rival Generals* (d.p.)
SOLDIERS: *Soldiers* (s.d.s, s.p.s, and d.p.); *a Rabble of Soldiers* (s.d.s)
PETRUCCIO: *Petruccio* (s.d.s); *Petr<uccio>* (s.p.s); *Petruccio [one of] Two Rival Generals* (d.p.)
SERVANT: *Servant* (s.d.s and s.p.s); *Petruccio's Servant* (d.p.)
GUARD: *Guard* (s.d.s and s.p.s); *King's Guard* (d.p.)
CAPTAIN: *Captain* (s.d.s)
LORDS: *four Lords* (s.d.s and d.p.); *the Lords* (s.d.s)
BISHOPS: *two Bishops* (s.d.s and d.p.); *the Bishops* (s.d.s)
FRIARS: *two Friars* (s.d.s)
DOCTOR: *a Doctor of Physic | [one of the] offenders* (s.d.s); *Doctor* (s.d.s and s.p.s); *A Doctor [one of the] Suborned false witnesses against Eulalia* (d.p.)
MIDWIFE: *a Midwife | [one of the] offenders* (s.d.s); *Midwife* (s.d.s and s.p.s); *A Midwife [one of the] Suborned false witnesses against Eulalia* (d.p.)
STROZZA: *[one of] two Soldiers | [one of] two Lieutenants | [one of the] Lieutenants | Strozza | [one of the] offenders* (s.d.s); *Stroz<za>* (s.p.s); *Strozza [one of] Two cashiered Lieutenants* (d.p.)
FABIO: *[one of] two Soldiers | [one of] two Lieutenants | [one of the] Lieutenants | Fabio | [one of the] offenders* (s.d.s); *Fab<io>* (s.p.s); *Fabio [one of] Two cashiered Lieutenants* (d.p.)
VIRGINS: *two Virgins* (s.d.s)
PETITIONERS: *divers Petitioners* (s.d.s)
ANDREA: *Andrea* (s.d.s); *Andr<ea>* (s.p.s); *Andrea Eulalia's fool* (d.p.)
JAGO: *Jago* (s.d.s); *Jag<o>* (s.p.s); *Jago [one of] Two other [Eulalia's] Servants* (d.p.)
RUGIO: *Rugio* (s.d.s); *Rug<io>* (s.p.s); *Rugio [one of] Two other [Eulalia's] Servants* (d.p.)
GENTLEMEN: *two or three Gentlemen* (s.d.s)
KEEPER: *Keeper* (s.d.s and s.p.s); *the Jailer* (s.d.s); *Jailer* (d.p.)
GENIUS: *Genius | the Genius* (s.d.s); *Genius of Eulalia* (d.p.)
PEDRO: *Pedro | [one of the] Rustici | Petro* (s.d.s); *Pedr<o>* (s.p.s); *Pedro A Gentleman of Palermo* (d.p.)
POGGIO: *Poggio | [one of the] Rustici* (s.d.s); *Pogg<io>* (s.p.s); *Poggio [one of] Two chief Inhabitants of Palermo* (d.p.)
LOLLIO: *Lollio | [one of the] Rustici* (s.d.s); *Loll<io>* (s.p.s); *Lollio [one of] Two chief Inhabitants of Palermo* (d.p.)
RUSTICS: *four Others | Rustici* (s.d.s); *1 | 2 | 3 | 4* (s.p.s)
COUNTRYMEN: *three or four Country-men | two Country-men | one of the Countrymen | three country-men | Countrymen* (s.d.s); *1 | 2 | 3 | Countryman* (s.p.s); *Three or four Country-men of Palermo* (d.p.)

CURATE: *Curate* (s.d.s and s.p.s); *Curate of Palermo* (d.p.)
CRIER: *Crier* (s.d.s and s.p.s); *Crier of Palermo* (d.p.)
GUARDS: *Guard* (s.d.s and s.p.s); *Guard of Palermo* (d.p.)
GIRLS: *2 Girl* | *4 Girls* | *Girls* | *three or four Lasses* | *Lasses* (s.d.s); *1 Girl* | *3 Girls* (s.d.s and s.p.s); *Three or four Girls* (s.d.s and d.p.)
CAPTAIN: *a Captain* (s.d.s); *Captain* (s.p.s)
CAPTAINS: *two Captains* (s.d.s); *1 Captain* | *2 Captain* (s.p.s); *Two other Captains* (d.p.)
SERVANT: *a Servant* (s.d.s); *Servant* (s.p.s)
ATTENDANTS: *Attendants* (s.d.s)
TIPSTAFF: *a Tipstaff* | *Tipstaff* (s.d.s)
SCHOOLBOYS: *many School Boys* (s.d.s)

OTHER CHARACTERS
Peers and princes whom Sforza defeated in the tournament celebrating the wedding of the King and Eulalia (1.2)
The enemy army (1.2)
People who praised Sforza as the army returned home (1.3)
Alinda's dead mother (1.6)
People killed by Sforza in defence of the King's life (2.8)
Divines and augurs who advised the sickly people of Palermo to visit the court (3.4)
A woman who murdered her husband for castrating a priest (3.8)
The King's predecessors (3.9)
The people of Sicily, the King's subjects (3.11)
Lollio's daughter (4.1; may be one of the girls who appear on stage)
Poggio's daughter (4.1; may be one of the girls who appear on stage)
The children of Palermo (4.1, 4.3, 4.5, 5.7)
Two men-at-arms who accused Eulalia of witchcraft, but dropped dead before they could kill her (4.3)
The miller's wife, with whom one of the Countrymen had 'naughty' dealings (4.3)
Horatio's wife (4.8)

SETTING
Time-Scheme: 2.4 takes place at dinner-time; 22 days pass between 1.6 and 2.8; two weeks pass between 3.7 and 4.3; ten days pass between 3.11 and 4.9
Place: Sicily

Geography
Sicily: Palermo; Nicosia
[Italy]: Naples; Lucera; Soleto
[Europe]: France; Ireland
Egypt

SOURCES
Narrative: Robert Greene, *Penelope's Web* 1 (1587, repr. 1601); William Shakespeare, *The Winter's Tale* (**1631**); John Fletcher and William Shakespeare, *All is True* (**1674**)

Verbal: Terence, *Andria* (3.7, 4.2); Cicero, *De officiis* (3.7); Sallust, *Catiline* (3.7), *Jugurtha* (4.2); Virgil, *Aeneid* 1 (motto at foot of text), 2 (4.2); Ovid, *Metamorphoses* 2 (4.2); Persius, *Satires* 1 (3.7); Seneca, *Hercules furens* (4.2); Juvenal, *Satires* 1 (3.7); Claudian, *In Eutropium* (t.p. motto), *Panegyricus de quartu consulatu Honorii Augusti* (5.9); William Lily, *Latin Grammar* (3.7, 5.5); William Shakespeare, *Hamlet* (**1259**; 4.9); Thomas Campion, 'What if a day, or a month, or a year' (song, printed in Richard Alison, *An Hour's Recreation in Music*, 1606, no. 17; 4.4)
Music: Thomas Campion, 'What if a day, or a month, or a year' (setting in Richard Alison, above, and reprinted in Thomas Robinson, *New Cithaeren Lessons*, 1609, no. 45; Song 1)

LANGUAGE
English
Latin: 164 words (1.6, 3.3, 3.7, 4.2–3, 5.5, 5.9; Sforza, Lodovico, Curate, Andrea)
French: 7 words (2.5, 3.7, 5.6; Andrea, Curate)

FORM
Metre: pentameter and prose; the Genius speaks in trochaic tetrameter
Rhyme: blank verse; some couplets
Act-Division: 5 acts
Dumb Shows: 2 (2.1, compresses action; 3.2, represents a vision)
Epilogue: 6 lines, in couplets, spoken by Lodovico
Lines (Spoken): 3,868 (2,792 verse, 1,076 prose)
Lines (Written): 4,460

STAGING
Doors: characters enter at two doors (2.1, s.d.); Sforza enters 'at the other end' (3.2, s.d.; i.e. of the stage)
Stage: characters pass over the stage (5.9, s.d.)
Within: speech (1.2, 4.3–4, 4.9–10, s.d.); shout (4.9, implicit)
Miscellaneous: Horatio and Lodovico exit at the end of 2.2 and immediately re-enter at the start of 2.3. Sforza enters 'as in prison' in 2.6, and apparently remains on stage unseen while Petruccio arrives to see him, for there is no direction for him to exit or to enter when he next appears in 2.7; presumably he is either in the discovery space, under a trapdoor, or in some other opening.

MUSIC AND SOUND
Sound Effects: birds chirp (3.1, s.d.)
Music: hautboys (1.2, s.d.); loud music (2.1, s.d.); flourish (2.4, s.d.); a post-horn (4.10, s.d.); soft music (5.3, s.d.); dance music (5.4, s.d.); recorders (5.8–9, s.d.); shawms (5.8, s.d.)
On-Stage Music: drum (1.3, dialogue); a Girl plays the lute, accompanying Song 1 (4.4, dialogue); the Curate plays the fiddle (5.9, s.d.)

Songs:
  1: 'What if a day, or a month, or a year', 4.4, Third Girl, 16 lines, with musical accompaniment; *musical setting survives*;
  2: 'How blessed are they that waste their wearied hours', 5.4, Girls, 12 lines;
  3: 5.9.

Dance: Andrea capers and turns (3.4, s.d.); dance (5.4, s.d.); Girls and Schoolboys dance (5.9, s.d.)

PROPS
Weapons: Petruccio's sword (1.4–5, implicit); Guards' bills (1.5, dialogue); Sforza's sword (1.6, dialogue); Fabio's sword (3.6–7, dialogue); Strozza's sword (3.6–7, dialogue); a knife (4.5, dialogue)
Musical Instruments: a drum (1.3, s.d.); a lute (4.4, dialogue); a fiddle (5.9, s.d.)
Clothing: a fool's coxcomb, bells, and coat (2.5, s.d.); a signet ring (2.7, dialogue; 3.2, s.d.); Sforza's ear-ring (3.11, s.d.; see also COSTUMES); embroidered nightcaps, coifs, and stomachers (5.4, s.d.); scarves (5.9, s.d.)
Money: an unspecified amount (1.3, implicit); another, smaller unspecified sum (1.4, implicit); another unspecified sum (5.4, implicit); a purse of one hundred ducats (5.9, dialogue)
Food and Drink: unspecified food (3.3, dialogue; eaten on stage); a bottle of drink (3.3, dialogue; drunk on stage)
Small Portable Objects: a golden wand (2.1–2, s.d.); four sets of papers (2.1–2, s.d.); books (2.1–2, s.d.); a white wand (2.1–2, s.d.); a fool's bauble (2.5, s.d.); keys (2.7, dialogue); a warrant (2.7–8, implicit; 3.2, s.d.); a document (3.8, implicit); pen and ink (3.9, implicit); a letter (3.9, implicit; 4.6, s.d.; written on stage); a sampler with an embroidered flower (4.4, dialogue); a writing book (4.4, dialogue); letters (4.10, s.d.); more letters (5.1, s.d.); needlework, including sale-work, day-work, night-work (5.4, s.d.); a book (5.4, dialogue); nosegays (5.9, s.d.)
Large Portable Objects: military colours (1.3, s.d.); seating for at least three characters, probably nine (2.1–2, dialogue and implicit); a box or pack (2.4–5, s.d.; presumably a trunk); a seat (5.4, dialogue); a chair (5.9, s.d.)

COSTUMES
LODOVICO: disguised (3.3–7, dialogue)
FLAVELLO: bare-headed (1.2–3, s.d.); fine clothes (5.7, dialogue)
PRINCE: cross-dressed as a queen, with a crown (5.9, s.d.)
EULALIA: black clothes (2.1–2, s.d.); a crown (2.1, s.d.; removed on stage); a cypress wreath (2.1–2, s.d.; put on on stage); homely attire (3.1–7, implicit)
ALINDA: dressed as a bride (2.2, s.d.); a veil (5.9, s.d.; removed and replaced on stage)
SFORZA: a jewelled ear-ring (1.6, dialogue; see also PROPS); hangers (1.6, implicit); disguised (4.9, s.d.; removed on stage)
PETRUCCIO: hangers (1.4–5, implicit)
DOCTOR: a false beard (4.5, dialogue; removed on stage)
MIDWIFE: muffled (4.5, dialogue; unmuffled on stage)
STROZZA and FABIO: false beards (3.6–7, dialogue; removed on stage)
ANDREA: disguised (3.3–7, dialogue)
POGGIO and LOLLIO: possibly hobnailed shoes (5.6–7, dialogue)
CURATE: richly robed with a crown of bays (5.9, s.d.)
GIRLS: veils (5.9, s.d.)

EARLY STAGE HISTORY
1635–6: performed by the King's Revels Company at Salisbury Court.

EARLY TEXTUAL HISTORY
1659: included as a bibliographically independent item in Richard Brome's *Five New Plays* (O); collation A² B–I⁸ K², 68 leaves; printed in January (possibly by John Taylor or John Twyn) for Andrew Crooke and Henry Brome; Latin mottos on the play's individual title page and at the foot of the text; list of roles; the play was the fifth item in the collection.

1659: George Thomason acquired a copy of O in January. In *c.* 1678, some years after his death, his entire collection of books and tracts was acquired by the bookbinder Samuel Mearne, acting as agent for King Charles II; the King never paid him, and the books remained in Mearne's family until 1761.

1659: O reissued.

1684: Nicholas Cox (Manciple of St Edmund Hall, Oxford) had a copy of O in his bookshop. It had probably been previously owned by Gerard Langbaine, and appears on a list compiled by Anthony Wood on Saturday 13 December.

EDITION
Lucy Munro, Richard Brome Online (internet, 2010).

REFERENCES
Annals 1635; Bentley, iii. 85–6; Bodleian, MS Wood E. 4, art. 1, p. 55; Greg 810; Hazlitt, 188.

2519. *The Platonic Lovers*

TEXT
Printed in 1636 (STC 6305).

GENRE
tragicomedy
Contemporary: play (Herbert, S.R.); tragicomedy (t.p.)

TITLE
Performed/Printed: *The Platonic Lovers*

AUTHOR
William Davenant

DATE
November 1635

ORIGINAL PRODUCTION
King's Men at the Blackfriars (and perhaps also the Globe)

PLOT
Duke Theander returns after three years of war, intending to cement an alliance with the neighbouring Duke, Phylomont. Phylomont visits Theander's sister Ariola in her bedroom at night, but she refuses him sex and insists that their marriage must be deferred until Theander consents. Theander also pays a nocturnal visit to his fiancée Eurythea, but not for sexual purposes, because they are devotedly Platonic lovers. Moreover, Theander so disapproves of sex that he refuses Ariola's request to marry and imprisons her. Phylomont issues an ultimatum: Theander has three days to change his mind, release Ariola, and allow the marriage; otherwise they will be at war. Also returning home is Gridonell, who has been a soldier since childhood; in accordance with his father's directions, he has not been taught to read or write, and has never seen a woman: when he sees one, the old waiting-woman Amadine, he takes her for an angel.

Concerned that Theander should marry and secure the succession by begetting an heir, his courtiers plan to introduce him to sex, and have the physician Buonateste administer an aphrodisiac. Fredeline has more personal reasons for wanting to see Eurythea married to the Duke: he wants to be her lover, whilst leaving to her husband the financial responsibility for keeping her; he procures from Buonateste a medicine that will make the taker irresistible to women. Meanwhile Amadine's brother Castraganio wants to raise their family's fortunes by procuring a marriage to Gridonell, so he too gets a dose of Buonateste's medicine. At first, neither patient responds: Gridonell proves an unapt pupil in amatory matters, and Theander continues to play chaste pastoral games with Eurythea. But the effect has only been delayed because of the recipients' sexual inexperience. Theander consents to Ariola's marriage, and himself marries Eurythea. Gridonell cannot attend the wedding: he has become so frisky that there is a danger he might rape the bride, and he has to be locked up.

Ariola is so shocked by the reverse in her brother's character that she breaks off her engagement to Phylomont. Eurythea is shocked, too, that Theander wants sex on their wedding night, but the aphrodisiac wears off before the night itself. Theander goes to visit her in her bedroom to tell her so, but sees Castraganio apparently coming out and infers adultery; Eurythea is disgraced. In fact, Castraganio has been bribed to be there: Fredeline offered him public office in return for his help in making Theander jealous. Castraganio is asked to sign a document admitting sex with Eurythea; the prospect of marriage to Gridonell induces Amadine to affirm that she witnessed the event. Fredeline then tells them that there is no vacancy in the proffered office and that he has never broached the marriage with Gridonell. He locks them up pending their departure into exile, then shows Eurythea the confession and promises her that he will keep Theander from seeing it.

Fredeline has dosed himself with love-medicine, but it does not have the intended effect; instead it makes him sick. Buonateste explains that it was actually a poison, and forces him to confess his villainies on the promise of an antidote. The ill effects then wear off and Fredeline is arrested. Eurythea is vindicated and reconciled with Theander. Buonateste persuades Ariola to give up her aversion to marrying Phylomont, so the courtiers ask him to have a word with Theander and Eurythea too.

SCENE DESIGNATION
prol., 1.1, 2.1–5, 3.1–5, 4.1–5, 5.1–6, ep. (Q has act-division only)

ROLES
PROLOGUE
Lord SCIOLTO, Gridonell's father; an old widower
ARNOLDO, a young gentleman, Theander's attendant
JASPERO, a young gentleman, Theander's attendant
ATTENDANTS on Sciolto (1.1, *non-speaking*)
Signor FREDELINE, a courtier
CASTRAGANIO, a Florentine gentleman, Amadine's brother; later commissioned as an officer and styled Captain Castraganio
Fredeline's SERVANT (1.1, *within*)
GRIDONELL, a young soldier, Sciolto's son and heir
Duke THEANDER of Palermo, Ariola's brother, Eurythea's fiancé, later her husband; a young man
Duke PHYLOMONT of Mazara, Eurythea's brother; a young man
ATTENDANTS on Theander (1.1; one speaks *within*)
Princess EURYTHEA, Phylomont's sister, Theander's fiancée, later his wife and Duchess of Palermo; a young woman
ARIOLA, Theander's sister
AMADINE, Eurythea's chief woman, Castraganio's sister; older than Gridonell, and poor
ROSELLA, Ariola's waiting-woman
Signor BUONATESTE, an old physician and philosopher
EPILOGUE

Speaking Parts: 17

Stage Directions and Speech Prefixes
PROLOGUE: *Prologue* (heading)
SCIOLTO: *Sciolto* (s.d.s and s.p.s); *Sciolto, An old Lord, friend to Theander* (d.p.)

ARNOLDO: *Arnoldo* (s.d.s); *Arnold<o>* (s.p.s); *Arnoldo [one of the] Attendants on Theander* (d.p.)
JASPERO: *Jaspero* (s.d.s); *Jasp<ero>* (s.p.s); *Jaspero [one of the] Attendants on Theander* (d.p.)
ATTENDANTS: *Attendants* (s.d.s and d.p.)
FREDELINE: *Fredeline* (s.d.s); *Fred<eline>* (s.p.s); *Fredeline, Creature to Theander* (d.p.)
CASTRAGANIO: *Castraganio* (s.d.s); *Castrag<anio>* (s.p.s); *Castraganio, Creature to Fredeline* (d.p.)
SERVANT: *Within* (s.p.s)
GRIDONELL: *Gridonell* (s.d.s); *Grido<nell>* (s.p.s); *Gridonell, A young Soldier, Son to Sciolto* (d.p.)
THEANDER: *Theander* (s.d.s); *Theand<er>* (s.p.s); *Theander, A young General* (d.p.)
PHYLOMONT: *Phylomont* (s.d.s); *Phylom<ont>* (s.p.s); *Phylomont, A young Duke that borders by* [Theander] (d.p.)
ATTENDANTS: *Attendants* (s.d.s and d.p.); *Within* (s.p.s)
EURYTHEA: *Eurithea* (s.d.s); *Eurith<ea>* (s.p.s); *Eurithea, Mistress to Theander, sister to Phylomont* (d.p.)
ARIOLA: *Ariola* (s.d.s and s.p.s); *Ariola, Mistress to Phylomont, sister to Theander* (d.p.)
AMADINE: *Amadine* (s.d.s); *Amad<ine>* (s.p.s); *Amadine, Woman to Eurithea, sister to Castraganio* (d.p.)
ROSELLA: *Rosella* (s.d.s); *Rosell<a>* (s.p.s)
BUONATESTE: *Buonateste* (s.d.s); *Buonat<este>* (s.p.s); *Buonateste, A generous Artist* (d.p.)
EPILOGUE: *Epilogue* (heading)

OTHER CHARACTERS
The train accompanying the two dukes (1.1)
Waiters and grooms at court (1.1)
The troops of Theander and Phylomont (1.1, 3.1)
A colonel, Gridonell's governor (1.1)
The old Sicilian kings, Theander's ancestors (1.1)
Gridonell's dead mother (2.1)
The father of Castraganio and Ariola (2.1)
Phylomont's dead mother (3.1)
The enemy against whom Theander's troops fought (3.1)
Theander's regiment at Messina, in which Castraganio is promised a command (3.2, 5.2)
Gridonell's corporal, a womanizer (3.3, 4.2)
A damsel about whom the corporal told stories (3.3)
The priest who marries Theander and Eurythea (4.1, 4.5)
Phylomont's newly levied troops (4.1)
Jaspero's sister, a six-month-old baby (4.2)
The nurse to Jaspero's sister (4.2)
Arnoldo's dead sister (4.2)
A priest who is to marry Phylomont and Ariola (4.3)
Theander's mother (5.1)
Fredeline's brother (5.1; possibly hypothetical)
Two shaggy murderers hired by Fredeline as enforcers (5.2; possibly imaginary)
A captain in the Messina regiment, who is wrongly reported dead (5.2)
The people of Palermo (5.6)

SETTING
Period: sixteenth or seventeenth century; the action is unhistorical, but paintings by Titian (died 1576) and Tintoretto (died 1594) are available
Time-Scheme: 2.1–5 take place at night, with 2.1 at dusk and 2.3–5 leading up to dawn; around two hours pass between 2.5 and 3.5; 4.4–5 take place at bed-time, and 5.1 not long before dawn the next morning
Place: Sicily

Geography
Sicily: Palermo; Mazara; Messina
[*Mediterranean Sea*]: Crete; Corsica; Sardinia
Italy: Rome; Naples; Tuscany; the Vatican; Florence; Capua
The Alps
France: Paris
Greece: Arcadia; Athens
[*Europe*]: Denmark; Vienna; Spain; Flanders; the Baltic Sea; Geneva; Moscow; Thrace
[*Cyprus*]: Paphos; Nicosia
[*Asia*]: Tartary; Arabia; Scythia; Persia; Assyria; Phrygia; Turkey
India
[*Africa*]: Barbary; Ethiopia
The Southern Sea
The Bermudas

SOURCES
Verbal: William Shakespeare, *The Moor of Venice* (**1437**; 2.1)
Works Mentioned: Plato, *Symposium* (1.1, 2.1, 2.4); Aristotle, works (general reference; 3.4), *De memoria et reminiscia* (2.4); *The Seven Wise Masters* (fourteenth century; 2.4); Edmund Spenser, *The Shepherd's Calendar* (1579; 1.1); also general references to Aeschylus, Empedocles, Gorgias, Euclid, Archimedes, and Diodorus Siculus (all 1.1)

LANGUAGE
English
French: 9 words (3.3, 4.1, 5.5; Gridonell, Fredeline)

FORM
Metre: pentameter; a little tetrameter and alexandrines
Rhyme: blank verse
Prologue: 30 lines, in couplets
Act-Division: 5 acts
Epilogue: 12 lines, in couplets
Lines (Spoken): 2,895 (2,849 verse, 46 prose)
Lines (Written): 2,949

STAGING
Doors: characters exit severally (1.1, 2.3–4, s.d.); two characters enter at several doors (5.4, s.d.)
Discovery Space: canopied (2.3, s.d.); Eurythea is discovered asleep on a couch (2.3, s.d.)
Within: speech (1.1, s.d.)

Audience: potentially contains both courtiers and citizens (prol.), and both men and women (ep.)
Miscellaneous: The prologue refers to playbills on city posts to advertise the performance.

MUSIC
Music: flourish afar off (1.1, s.d.)

PROPS
Lighting: tapers (2.2, s.d.); a taper (2.3, s.d.); lights (2.5, 4.5, s.d.)
Weapons: Sciolto's sword (4.2, dialogue); Fredeline's sword (5.6, dialogue)
Musical Instruments: a lute (2.3, s.d.)
Money: a purse of five hundred crowns (1.1, 2.1, dialogue)
Food and Drink: two papers (2.4, s.d./implicit) containing powder (dialogue)
Small Portable Objects: a letter (1.1, s.d.); a key (1.1, 4.1–2, dialogue; 3.1, implicit); another letter (1.1, dialogue); a fan (2.2, dialogue); a document (3.2, dialogue); a paper (4.4, s.d.); a parchment patent (5.2, s.d.); a pocket inkhorn (5.2, s.d.); a pen (5.2, s.d.); a paper (5.2, 5.4, s.d.; signed on stage)
Large Portable Objects: a table (2.2, 4.5, s.d.); a couch (2.3, s.d.); stools (4.5, s.d.)
Scenery: a canopy (2.3, s.d.); an arras (5.1, 5.6, dialogue; 5.2, implicit)

COSTUMES
PROLOGUE: a cloak (prol., dialogue)
SCIOLTO: white hair and a grey beard (dialogue); hangers (4.2, implicit)
FREDELINE: hangers (5.6, implicit)
CASTRAGANIO: in a nightgown unready (5.1, s.d.); a garment with a pocket (5.2, dialogue)
THEANDER: dressed as a noble shepherd (3.5, s.d.); dressed as a pilgrim (5.4, dialogue; 5.6, s.d.)
PHYLOMONT: probably a beard (dialogue)
EURYTHEA: a veil (2.3, 3.5, 4.1 s.d.; put on and removed on stage); dressed as a shepherdess (3.5, s.d.)
ARIOLA: she is partially undressed on stage (2.2, implicit); pendants (2.2, dialogue; removed on stage); night-linen (2.2, s.d.; put on on stage), including a cambric nightcap and a lawn nightgown (dialogue); dishevelled hair (2.2, dialogue)
AMADINE: a garment with cambric and bone-lace wings at the shoulders (1.2, dialogue); taffeta petticoats (2.1, dialogue)
BUONATESTE: a beard (dialogue)

EARLY STAGE HISTORY
1635–6: performed by the King's Men at the Blackfriars; the production appears not to have met with universal applause. The prologue was written for performance by an actor of thirty years' experience with the company; if taken literally, this could only be John Lowin.

EARLY TEXTUAL HISTORY
1635: On Monday 16 November, Sir Henry Herbert licensed the play for performance.
1636: On Tuesday 19 January, Sir Henry Herbert licensed the play for the press.
1636: entered to Richard Meighen in the Stationers' Register on Thursday 4 February; entry names author.
1636: ¹Q printed by Marmaduke Parsons for Richard Meighen; collation A⁴ (–A4) B–K⁴ L1, 40 leaves; title page names author, acting company, and playhouse; authorial dedication to Henry Jermyn; list of roles.
c. 1630s–40s: a copy of Q was in the possession of John Horne (Vicar of Headington, Oxfordshire). After his death, his entire collection of play-books passed into the possession of John Houghton of Brasenose College, Oxford (c. 1608–77), then to James Herne (died 1685), and then to the library of Ralph Sheldon (1623–84) at Weston, where it was catalogued by Anthony Wood, probably in the late 1670s.
c. 1640: Abraham Wright transcribed extracts into a MS miscellany (London: British Library, Add. MS 22608, fos. 90ʳ–91ᵛ). The MS later passed to Wright's son, the antiquarian James Wright (c. 1644–c. 1717).
1640–1: Humphrey Moseley was selling copies of Q for 6d each.
1646: Meighen's rights transferred in the Stationers' Register from his widow, Mercy Meighen, to herself and Gabriel Bedell on Saturday 7 November, by order of a court held on Wednesday 21 October; play and author individually named as part of a group transfer of nineteen titles.
1653–6: advertised as for sale by Mercy Meighen, Gabriel Bedell, and Thomas Collins.
1655: *The English Treasury of Wit and Language* entered in the Stationers' Register to Humphrey Moseley on Tuesday 16 January.
1655: nine extracts (from 1.1, 2.1, 3.4–5, 4.5) included in John Cotgrave's *The English Treasury of Wit and Language*, sigs. B8ʳ⁻ᵛ, F5ʳ, M5ᵛ, O5ʳ, P6ᵛ, P6ᵛ–P7ʳ, P8ᵛ, S4ʳ, V5ᵛ; printed for Humphrey Moseley.
1655: *Wit's Interpreter* entered to Nathaniel Brooke in the Stationers' Register on Wednesday 14 March.
1655: extract (from 2.1) included in John Cotgrave's *Wit's Interpreter*, sigs. C8ʳ–D1ʳ; printed for Nathaniel Brooke.
1657: advertised as for sale by the Newcastle-upon-Tyne bookseller William London.
1662: *Wit's Interpreter* reprinted (before Thursday 8 June) for Nathaniel Brooke; the extract now appears on sigs. C3ᵛ–C4ᵛ, and is entitled 'The Platonic'.
1665: On Friday 3 March, Roger L'Estrange licensed William Davenant's *Two Excellent Plays* for printing.
1665: included in Davenant's *Two Excellent Plays* (²O), sigs. F8ʳ–M7ᵛ, 48 leaves; printed for Gabriel Bedell and Thomas Collins by Thursday 8 June. The copy was Q. The other play in the collection was *The Wits* (**2421**).

c. 1670s: two extracts (from 2.3, 3.4) included in MS annotations in an interleaved copy of John Cotgrave's *The English Treasury of Wit and Language*, pp. 28aᵛ, 222aʳ. (The copy is now at the British Library, pressmark G.16385.)

1671: *Wit's Interpreter* reprinted for Nathaniel Brooke and Obadiah Blagrave.

1672: Davenant's *Works* entered to Henry Herringman in the Stationers' Register on Thursday 31 October. Roger L'Estrange had licensed the book for the press. On Monday 18 November, it was advertised for sale by Henry Herringman, John Martin, John Starkey, and Robert Horne; however, it was apparently not issued until the following year.

1673: included in Davenant's *Works* (³F), sigs. ²3C1ᵛ–²3F4ᵛ, 31 pages on 16 leaves; printed by John Macock for Henry Herringman; omits dedication. The text was mostly set as prose.

1675: Davenant's *Works* advertised as for sale by John Starkey.

1675: the stock of *Two Excellent Plays* had passed to Charles Smith, who was selling copies for 2s.

1676–93: 23 extracts and paraphrases (from 1.1, 2.1, 2.3–4, 3.4–5, 4.1–2, 4.4, 5.2, 5.4–6) copied into a MS miscellany (Oxford: Bodleian, MS Sancroft 29, pp. 108–9) compiled by William Sancroft.

EDITION
Wendell W. Broom, jun., The Renaissance Imagination 23 (New York and London, 1987).

REFERENCES
Annals 1635; Bawcutt 332, C78; Beal Online DaW 102.4, 102.6; Bentley, iii. 211–12; Eyre & Rivington, i. 463, 467; Greg 506; Hazlitt, 181; William London, *A Catalogue of the Most Vendible Books in England* (London, 1657), sig. 2F1ᵛ; *MLR* 13 (1918), 401–11; *MP* 66 (1968–9), 256–61; *Oxford Bibliographical Society Proceedings and Papers* 2.2 (1929), 132–3; *PMLA* 51 (1936), 130; *RES* NS 54 (2003), 601–14; *SP* 40 (1943), 186–203.

2520. Philenzo and Hippolyta

EVIDENCE
Stationers' Register; list of MS plays said to have been in the possession of John Warburton (1682–1759), and destroyed by his cook (London: British Library, MS Lansdowne 807, fo. 1).

See **959** on the remote possibility of a surviving MS.

GENRE
tragicomedy
Contemporary: tragicomedy

TITLE
Contemporary: *Philenzo and Hippolyta*
Alternative Modernization: *Philenzo and Hypollita*

AUTHOR
Philip Massinger

DATE
Limits: *c.* 1613–40

See **2225** for general discussion of the dating of the ten lost Massinger plays registered in 1653 and 1660.

ROLES
PHILENZO
HIPPOLYTA

SETTING
Place: Italy (?)

EARLY TEXTUAL HISTORY
1660: entered in the Stationers' Register to Humphrey Moseley on Friday 29 June; play and author individually named as part of a group entry of 26 plays.

REFERENCES
Annals 1620; Bentley, iv. 808; Greg Θ162; *The Library*, 3rd ser., 2 (1911), 225–59; Sibley, 121.

2521. Wit's Triumvirate

TEXT
MS (London: British Library, Add. MS 45865); scribal fair copy with extensive amendments in two other hands. The scribe left some blank spaces, apparently because he could not read his copy.

The completed MS was initially worked over by, apparently, the author, who filled in most of the scribe's blanks (but left one in 5.3, resulting in a brief textual lacuna), and made extensive corrections and amendments (including the addition of passages of more than a word or two in 1.1, 1.3–4, 2.1–3, 3.1, 4.1, 4.3–4, 5.1). Afterwards the text was revised by a third hand, whose interventions were mainly concentrated in Act 5 (including additions in 2.2, 5.1, 5.3–4). The text was also cut by one or both of the non-scribal hands: substantial passages are removed from 2.2, 5.1, and 5.3–4, and there are also shorter trims in 1.4, 2.1, 2.3, 3.1–2, 5.1, and 5.3; the cuts were apparently for content rather than length, since they do not address the issue of the prolix fourth Act. The process of revision and cutting seems to have been left incomplete: one of the intended effects was to excise the characters of Bead and Narrowit, but they still appear in 3.1; another was to rename Jealousia, but again this was not carried through consistently.

The reviser's work demonstrably came after the author's interventions in at least some cases. The issue—undecidable in our present state of knowledge—is whether the two sets of interventions were made at distinct stages of the text's development, thereby defining an A- and a B-text, or whether they are part of the same process. The incompleteness of the revisions might suggest the former interpretation (with the B-text an unfinished intention), but a case for the latter might rest in part on the fact that William Cavendish had professional assistance in the composition of some of his later plays (**2796** and **2828**).

GENRE
comedy
Contemporary: play (prol., royal ep.); comedy (prol., d.p. heading)

TITLE
MS: *Wit's Triumvirate, or The Philosopher*
Contemporary: *The Philosopher, or Wit's Triumvirate*

The sequence of the two titles is reversed for the putative royal performance.

AUTHOR
William Cavendish, Earl of Newcastle (*attribution*)

The main, scribal hand is that of John Rolleston, Cavendish's secretary; the 'authorial' hand is Cavendish's. The identity of the third, revising hand has not been established; it is not that of, among playwrights associated with Cavendish, Ben Jonson, James Shirley, or William Davenant, but it is impossible to rule out Richard Brome, Jasper Mayne, or Robert Stapylton.

DATE
Limits: 1634–6
Best Guess: 1635

PLOT
Expelled from their college, Clyster and Silence are now working for Bond the pettifogging attorney. The three of them set up a phoney advice agency to cozen clients: Clyster handles medical problems, Silence spiritual ones, and Bond legal ones.

Clyster treats: Fright for nervous incontinence; Sir Cupid Fantasy, who is amorous and prone to speak in rhyming couplets; Sickly, who is excessively worried about his minor ailments; and Jealousia, who is initially reluctant to mention his problem of obsessive marital jealousy. Silence deals with the excessively superstitious Ominous, and, in a single consulting session, proffers diametrically opposed religious advice to Bead the Catholic and Narrowit the Puritan. Clyster refers Fright to Silence, who recommends a course of devotional reading; and Silence refers Ominous to Clyster, who diagnoses melancholy.

Patients continue to arrive for Clyster. Conquest is a timid man who has daydreams of duelling prowess and military glory, so Clyster prescribes abstinence from violent entertainment and reading. Jealousia's excessive sexual imagination is diagnosed as the cause of his malady, and he is advised to do everything he can to externalize his thoughts, including wearing a merkin on his head instead of a periwig. After an unsuccessful attempt to render Fantasy prosaic by making him read chronicles—he simply tries to versify them—Clyster recommends something even duller: legal textbooks.

Concerned about the statute against usury, Caution consults Bond in search of a loophole. His acquaintance Algebra is convinced that the consultants are cheaters. Aiming to expose them, he consults all three, posing as a man obsessed with astronomical theories and big ideas, such as the notion that the planet Earth is a giant animal. Clyster identifies him as a fellow student at their college, and worries that they may be recognized. However, it is the roarer Damme, brought by Sickly, who exposes them after they rob him of his clothes and persuade him he is dying. The clients all demand their money back, and appoint Algebra to judge the case. He declares that the victims' misfortunes are partly their own fault. Clyster and Silence reveal their true identities to Algebra. Acknowledging their own credulity, the gulls reward Algebra with the money due to them; but, as a philosopher, he has no use for money and gives it back to the cheaters, who make him a present of astronomical instruments.

SCENE DESIGNATION
prol., 1.1–4, 2.1–4, 3.1–4, 4.1–4, 5.1–4, ep. (MS)

The stage is not clear at the following scene-divisions: 1.1–4, 2.3–4, 4.1–4, 5.1–3; it is clear, however, during 4.2 and 5.3.

ROLES
PROLOGUE
Doctor CLYSTER, a physician; also called Doctor Merriman, Doctor Merdurinous, and Doctor Conniver; in reality, Hodge Hurebrave, a cashiered musketeer
Master SILENCE, a Puritan divine; in reality, Nick Nograne, a petty schoolmaster; also claims to be a Roman Catholic priest in disguise
Master Bill BOND, an attorney; also called Crop-Ear and Master Bramble; perhaps representing William Prynne
Master FRIGHT, a nervous man
Master OMINOUS, a superstitious man; a husband
Sir Cupid FANTASY, an amorous knight; a would-be poet and playwright
Master ALGEBRA, a poor philosopher
Master Usurious CAUTION, a rich usurer and Justice of the Peace
Master SICKLY, a rich gentleman; a hypochondriac and a married man; 60 years old
Signor JEALOUSIA, a jealous husband; renamed Doubtall by the second reviser
Master BEAD, a Roman Catholic; a married man and a father
Master NARROWIT, a Puritan; a married man and a father
Master CONQUEST Shadow, a coward and a married man; also called Sir Conquest

Master DAMME de Bois, a roarer and a soldier
Three SERVANTS (5.1; only two speak)

The avoidance of female characters—every role is male—is in line with Cavendish's mid-1630s practice as a household dramatist, insofar as we can judge it from the only substantially extant exemplar, his 1634 Christmas masque (**2457**), in which the only women performers are masquers.

Speaking Parts: 17

Stage Directions and Speech Prefixes
PROLOGUE: *Prologue* (heading)
CLYSTER: *Clyster | [one of] the Cheaters | the Physician | [one of] the three Cheaters | [one of the] Cheaters* (s.d.s); *Cly<ster>* (s.p.s); *Mr Clyster: A Physician* (d.p.)
SILENCE: *Silence | [one of] the Cheaters | [one of] the three Cheaters | [one of the] Cheaters* (s.d.s); *Sile<nce>* (s.p.s); *Mr Silence: A Puritan Divine* (d.p.)
BOND: *Bond | [one of] the Cheaters | [one of] the three Cheaters | [one of the] Cheaters* (s.d.s); *Bon<d>* (s.p.s); *Bill Bond: An Attorney* (d.p.)
FRIGHT: *Fright* (s.d.s); *Fri<ght>* (s.p.s); *Mr Fright: A man fearful of Hobgoblins* (d.p.)
OMINOUS: *Ominous* (s.d.s); *Om<inous>* (s.p.s); *Mr Ominous: A man fearful of Superstitious Accidents* (d.p.)
FANTASY: *Phantsy* (s.d.s); *Pha<ntsy>* (s.p.s); *Sir Cupid Phantsy: A Lover* (d.p.)
ALGEBRA: *Algebra | the Philosopher* (s.d.s); *Alg<ebra>* (s.p.s); *Mr Algebra: A Philosopher* (d.p.)
CAUTION: *Caution* (s.d.s); *Cau<tion>* (s.p.s); *Mr Caution: A man fearful of Penal Statutes* (d.p.)
SICKLY: *Sickly | Mr Sickly | the Sick man* (s.d.s); *Sic<kly>* (s.p.s); *Mr Sickly: One overcareful of his health* (d.p.)
JEALOUSIA: *Jealousie | Jelosia | Jealosia | the Jealous Man* (s.d.s); *Jeal<ousie>* (s.p.s); *Signor Jealousia: A Jealous man* (d.p.)
BEAD: *Bead* (s.d.s); *Bea<d>* (s.p.s); *Mr Bead: A Scrupulous Papist* (d.p.)
NARROWIT: *Narrowitt* (s.d.s); *Nar<rowitt>* (s.p.s); *Narrowitt: A Precise Puritan* (d.p.)
CONQUEST: *Conquest* (s.d.s); *Con<quest>* (s.p.s); *Sir Conquest Shaddow: Imaginary Valour* (d.p.)
DAMME: *Dammy | The Roarer* (s.d.s); *Dam<my>* (s.p.s); *Damy de Bois: A Roarer* (d.p.)
SERVANTS: *Servant* (s.d.s); *1 Servant | 2 Servant* (s.p.s); *three Servants* (d.p.)

OTHER CHARACTERS
Senior university men under whom Clyster and Silence served (1.1)
Officers in the Low Countries under whom Clyster served (1.1)
A barber, Bond's neighbour (1.1)
A physician who told Fright that the medical profession was a religious denomination (1.2)
Ominous's wife (1.3, 3.3)
Ominous's grandmother (1.3)
Ominous's mother-in-law (1.3)
A great prince, who died soon after the appearance of a comet (1.3)
A poor London cobbler, who also died after the comet (1.3)
A preacher whose sermon made Ominous weep (1.3)
Fantasy's mistress (1.4, 4.4, 5.3–4)
Doctor Lecture, a glover (1.4)
Unthrifts to whom Caution lends money (2.1)
Doctors, mountebanks, and quacks, both English and foreign, including Dutch empirics, whom Sickly has consulted without success (2.2)
London sick-nurses, whose comments on death were overheard by Sickly (2.2)
Sickly's tailor's wife, whom Sickly kissed (2.2)
Jealousia's wife, formerly a widow (2.4, 4.3, 5.4)
Jealousia's men (2.4)
Jealousia's doctor (2.4)
A man who travels with Jealousia in his coach, to give him early warning of the sight of horns (2.4)
Jealousia's family (2.4)
Fiddlers who played songs about cuckoldry in Jealousia's hearing (2.4)
A bishop, whom Narrowit treated with respect (3.1)
The Bishop of Chalcedon, whom Bead treated with inadvertent disrespect (3.1; a real person)
Narrowit's dead father, whom he prayed for, just a little (3.1)
Bead's dead friends, whom he neglected to pray for (3.1)
Narrowit's wife (3.1)
A sexton who sold Narrowit's wife a surplice (3.1)
Bead's wife (3.1)
The heir of a common lawyer, who sold Bead's wife embroidered cushions (3.1)
A common lawyer who rifled an old abbey (3.1)
Narrowit's son, who learned philosophy at a university (3.1)
Bead's son (3.1)
The minister who baptised Narrowit (3.1)
A Puritan minister who baptised Bead (3.1)
An Arminian whom Narrowit pledged at a christening (3.1)
A Puritan whom Bead pledged at a christening (3.1)
A Puritan of the Low Countries who confirmed the authenticity of Foxe's *Acts and Monuments* to Narrowit (3.1)
Narrowit's pastor (3.1)
A man whom Narrowit heard swearing (3.1)
Fright's men (3.2)
A man who sleeps [in the room or bunk] beneath Fright, who became incontinent in the night for fear of an owl (3.2)
A laundress who charged extra for cleaning a filthy nightshirt (3.2)
Fright's barber (3.2)
A Puritan upholsterer, to whom Fright sold his bedroom hangings (3.2)
A maid who picked up a pin the wrong way round and became pregnant (3.3)

Condemned prisoners whom Ominous went to see being executed (3.3)
A company of fiddlers, whose arrival at Fright's door caused him to say his prayers to music (3.4)
Fiddlers engaged by Fright to play at mealtimes (3.4)
Fright's father (3.4)
The minister of Fright's church (3.4)
A man who killed a drawer, and with whom Conquest imagines himself fighting (4.1)
A famous fencer whom Conquest imagines himself disarming (4.1)
A man who beat Conquest with a straw, and a friend skilled in fighting who restored his reputation (4.1)
A schoolboy who scared Conquest with a pop-gun (4.1)
The boy's schoolmaster (4.1)
Conquest's wife, formerly a widow (4.1)
A soldier in the wars, Conquest's correspondent (4.1)
Conquest's father and mother (4.1)
Booker, an almanac-maker, who was punished for his opinions (4.2; a real person)
Jealousia's groom (4.3)
The chambermaid of Jealousia's wife (4.3)
Women who refused to sleep with Jealousia when he was a bachelor, including waiting-women, chambermaids, and cook-maids (4.3)
Men whom Jealousia hears boasting of their sexual prowess (4.3)
A married woman whom Jealousia loved, and who made a fool of him (4.3)
The husband of Jealousia's lover (4.3)
A person who played at rhyming with Fantasy, and gave him a difficult word (4.4)
A wife whom Fantasy wanted to woo, and her husband with whom he mistakenly played footsie under the table (4.4)
Fantasy's dead grandmother (4.4)
Fantasy's aunt (4.4)
Two doctors, who gave Damme contradictory advice about tobacco and wine (5.1)
Young men whom Damme cheats (5.1)
A broker in Long Lane who has three suits of Damme's clothes (5.1)
A boy whom the roarers have in common (5.1)
Surgeons, Damme's friends (5.1)
Damme's 'best beloved' in Turnbull Street, presumably a whore (5.1)
The anatomy reader at the Physicians' College (5.1)
Damme's creditors (5.1)
Higgenbotham, Damme's father (5.3)

SETTING
Period: contemporary
Place: London

Geography
London: Westminster; Bridewell; Leather Lane; Philpot Lane; the New Exchange; St Bartholomew's Hospital; Westminster Hall; Fleet Bridge; Fetter Lane; Bedlam; Turnbull Street; Cheapside; Cheapside Cross; St Paul's Cathedral; the Pope's Head tavern; the Mitre tavern; Blackfriars House; Tyburn; St George's Fields; Lincoln's Inn Fields; Hyde Park; Milford Lane; the Strand; Bedford's Buildings (near the New Exchange; a brothel?); the Lady Chambers (in the Strand; a brothel?); St Thomas Apostle's church; Snow Hill; Birchin Lane; Long Lane; Yardly's Ground; the Artillery Yard; Barber Surgeons' Hall; Christ's Hospital; Smithfield; the Physicians' College; Furnivall's Inn; Newgate prison
Middlesex: Holborn
[Kent]: Greenwich; Margate
St Albans: the Bull inn; the Saracen's Head inn; the White Greyhound inn; the bridge
Oxford: the Bodleian Library
England: Lancashire; Tutbury; Sheffield; River Trent; Newcastle; Cambridge
Scotland
The Low Countries: Holland; Flanders; Amsterdam; Douai; St Omers; Dunkirk; the United Provinces; Bouillon
Germany: Saxony
France: Bouteville; Tilly; Bucquoy
Spain: Toledo
Italy: Padua; Rome; the Vatican Library
Europe: Poland; Geneva; Sweden; Denmark
[Asia]: Chalcedon; Turkey; the Holy Land; Arabia; Aleppo
[Africa]: Fez, Morocco
The Cape of Good Hope
[America]: New England

SOURCES
Narrative: Ben Jonson, *The Alchemist* (**1621**); possibly Henry Glapthorne, *The Lady Mother* (**2516**; 5.1; but the alternative possibility of a common source cannot be ruled out)
Verbal: Bible: Genesis 3.7 (Geneva trans.; 1.3); Ecclesiastes 1.2 (2.1); Daniel 6.12 (2.3); Joel 2.28 (1.3); Matthew 5.37 (1.3), 6.9 (Lord's Prayer; 3.1, 4.2); Acts 26.28–9 (4.2); 1 Timothy 3.8 (Vulgate text; 2.1); 1 Peter 5.8 (1.2); Aesop, *Fables* (2.4); Cicero, *Paradoxa stoicorum* (2.1); Geoffrey Chaucer, *Canterbury Tales*: General Prologue (c. 1387; printed 1478, repr. 1602; 1.2, cited); Leo Africanus, *Description of Africa* (1526, English tr. by John Pory, 1600; 4.2); William Lily, *Latin Grammar* (5.2); Christopher Marlowe, *2 Tamburlaine* (**789**; 2.1); Tommaso Campanello, *De sensu rerum* (c. 1593; 4.2, cited); William Shakespeare, *1 Henry IV* (**1059**; 4.2), *King Lear* (**1486**; 1.2), *Macbeth* (**1496**; 3.2); Statute of Usury (1624; 21 James I c. 17; 2.3, cited); Galileo Galilei, *Dialogo* (1632; 4.2, cited); unidentified work by a Dutchman (2.1, cited)
Works Mentioned: Bible (general references, 1.2, 5.1; Geneva tr., 3.1): Psalms (Geneva tr.; 3.1); John (3.1, deleted); Aristotle, *Astronomy* (4.2); Euclid, *Elementa* (4.2); Cicero, *De divinatione* (1.3); Jacobus de

Voragine, *Legenda aurea* (c. 1275; 3.1); Sir John Mandeville, *Travels* (1356-7; 3.2); Statute of Hunting Game (1389-90; 13 Richard II c. 13; 2.3); Sir Thomas Littleton, *Les Tenures* (1481; 4.4); Sir Anthony Fitzherbert, *La Grande Abbregement de la Ley* (c. 1516; 4.4); Sir Thomas More, *Utopia* (1516; 2.1); Paracelsus, unspecified work (sixteenth century, before 1541; 5.1); Francesco Guicciardini, *Storia di Italia* (written 1537-40, printed 1561; 1.4); Statute of Game (1540; 32 Henry VIII c. 8; 2.3); Statute of Maintenance and Embracery (1540; 32 Henry VIII c. 9; 2.3); Statute of Great Horses (1541; 33 Henry VIII c. 5; 2.3); Nicolaus Copernicus, *De revolutionibus orbium coelestium* (1543; 4.2); Statute of Leather (1548; 2-3 Edward VI c. 9; 2.3); Statute of Hail-Shot (1548; 2-3 Edward VI c. 14; 2.3); John Foxe, *Acts and Monuments* (1563; 3.1, 3.4); William Lambarde, *Eirenarchia* (1582; 4.4); Thomas Kyd, *The Spanish Tragedy* (**783**; 4.4); Christopher Marlowe, *Tamburlaine* (**784**; 4.4); Tycho Brahe, *Astronomiae instauratae progymnasmata* (1588; 4.2); Richard Hakluyt, *Principal Navigations* (1589; 4.1); Richard Crompton, *L'authoritie et jurisdiction des Courts* (1594; 4.4); Johannes Kepler, unspecified astronomical work (4.2); William Shakespeare, *Hamlet* (**1259**; 4.4); John Dowland, *The Second Book of Songs or Airs* (1600), 2: Lachrymae (3.4); John Donne, poems (general reference; 1.4); Sir Edward Coke, *Reports* (1600-15; 4.4); Statute of Game (1603-4; 1 James I c. 27; 2.3); William Perkins, *The Cases of Conscience* (1608; 3.1, deleted); Francis Beaumont and John Fletcher, *Philaster* (**1597**; 4.4); John Speed, *History of Great Britain* (1611; 1.4, 4.4); Thomas Brightman, *A Revelation of the Apocalypse* (1611; 2.4); Lewis Bayly, *The Practice of Piety* (1612; 3.4); Samuel Purchas, *Purchas's Pilgrimage* (1613; 3.2, 4.1); Ben Jonson, *Bartholomew Fair* (**1757**; 5.3); John Selden, *De diis Syris* (1617; 1.3); James I, *The Declaration of Sports* (1617-18, reissued 1633; 3.1); Ferdinand Pulton, *The Statutes at Large* (1618; 4.4); Richard Allestree, *Almanac* (annually from 1621; 2.1); *Tom Thumb* (1621; 3.2); Augustine Vincent, *A Discovery of Errors in the First Edition of the Catalogue of Nobility* (1622; 1.3); Michael Dalton, unspecified work (4.4); Michael Sparke, *The Crumbs of Comfort* (1623; 3.4); Statute of Hawking and Hunting (1623-4; 21 James I c. 28; 2.3); John Andrewes, *A Sovereign Salve to Cure a Sick Soul* (1624; 3.4); John Booker, *Almanac* (1631-4; 4.2); Galileo Galilei, *Dialogo*, tr. probably Joseph Webbe (c. 1635; 4.2); *The Merry Cuckold* (ballad; 2.4); 'I prithee neighbour, lend me thy wife' (ballad?; 2.4); *The Bull's Feather* (ballad; 2.4); *A Marvellous Medicine for the Maladies of the Mind* (unidentified; 3.4); there is also a general reference to Ben Jonson as 'our best poet' (4.4).

Nelson annotates a mention of platonic lovers as an allusion to *The Platonic Lovers* (**2519**). In fact, it is nothing more than a general reference, topically alluding to courtly fashion surrounding Henrietta Maria in 1635.

LANGUAGE

English
French: 19 words (1.1, 2.3, 3.3, 4.1, 4.3; Silence, Caution, Clyster, Conquest, Jealousia)
Latin: 87 words (1.2-3, 2.1-4, 3.1, 3.4, 4.1-2, 4.4, 5.1-3; Fright, Clyster, Silence, Caution, Algebra, Sickly, Bond, Jealousia, Conquest, Fantasy, Damme), plus 1 word of *faux*-Latin (2.2; Clyster)
Greek: 2 words (3.4; Fright)
Italian: 8 words (4.1; Conquest)
***Faux*-Dutch:** 2 words (4.2; Conquest)
Spanish: 3 words (5.1, 5.3; Damme)

FORM

Metre: prose and pentameter
Rhyme: couplets
Prologue: 26 lines, in couplets; alternative, 12-line prologue for court performance
Act-Division: 5 acts
Epilogue: 6 lines, in couplets, spoken by Algebra; alternative epilogue (also 6 lines) for court performance
Lines (Spoken): 5,358 (231 verse, 5,127 prose)
Lines (Written): 5,490

STAGING

Doors: characters exit severally (1.4, s.d.; 3.1, dialogue); one door represents Bond's house (2.1, 2.3, 3.2-4, s.d.); mentioned (2.2, 5.3, s.d.); knocked on (5.1, implicit; 5.4, s.d.)
Stage: large enough for Silence to hold two separate consultations simultaneously, walking between the two clients, without either hearing the other (3.1); mentioned (5.1, s.d.)
Within: noise (5.3, implicit)
Above: characters speak from above (5.4, s.d.)
Audience: said to be seated and to include 'gallants' (prol.); called a 'worthy company' (5.4) and addressed as 'noble spectators' (ep.); the court prologue is initially addressed to one member of the audience (i.e. the King) who is called 'sir', and later broadens to include the Queen ('madam'); they are mentioned by name as 'Charles the Great' and 'Mary'
Miscellaneous: Clyster exits at the end of 3.2 and immediately re-enters at the start of 3.3.

MUSIC AND SOUND

On-Stage Music: Fantasy 'hums', which may or may not be musical (1.4, s.d.)
Sound Effects: knocking (1.1-2, 2.2-4, s.d.; 3.1, 4.2, 5.3, dialogue); noise within (5.3, implicit)

PROPS

Lighting: a candle (5.1, s.d.)
Weapons: possibly a dagger (5.1, s.d.); a cudgel (5.4, dialogue)
Clothing: a pair of bracelets (4.4, dialogue); a little glove (4.4, dialogue)
Money: ten angels (1.2, dialogue); two pieces (1.3, dialogue); three unspecified sums (1.4, 3.3, implicit;

3.4, dialogue); fifty gold pieces (2.2, dialogue); twenty gold crowns (2.3, dialogue); a leather purse (2.3, dialogue); ten pieces (2.4, dialogue); ten pieces (3.1, dialogue); eighty shillings (3.1, dialogue); a sovereign (3.1, dialogue); ten pounds (4.1, dialogue); ten pieces (4.3, dialogue); a purse containing twenty pieces (4.4, dialogue); forty pounds (5.3, dialogue); twenty pounds (5.3, dialogue); ten pounds (5.3, dialogue); five pieces (5.3, dialogue; deleted)
Food and Drink: a little glass of powdered sugar candy (2.2, s.d.); a pipe of tobacco (5.1, s.d.; smoked on stage); hot water (5.1, s.d.; drunk on stage)
Small Portable Objects: a looking-glass (1.1, dialogue); pen and ink (1.2, 4.4, s.d.; 5.1, dialogue); books (1.2, s.d.); papers (1.2, s.d.); urinals (1.2, s.d.); vial glasses (1.2, s.d.); gold weights (1.2, s.d.); a mortar and pestle (2.2, s.d.); a urinal containing water (2.4, s.d.); a straw on a ribbon (3.1, dialogue; there is blood on the straw); a purse (3.1, dialogue; 5.3, implicit; said to contain a severed human ear; can be hung around a character's neck); paper (4.4, s.d.; 5.1, dialogue; written on on stage); ribbons (4.4, dialogue); feathers (4.4, dialogue); unspecified trinkets (4.4, dialogue); possibly a key (5.1, s.d.)
Large Portable Objects: a little table (1.2, s.d.); seating for four characters (4.2, implicit); a table (4.4, s.d.); two chairs (4.4, dialogue); seating for five characters (5.1, implicit), including at least one chair (dialogue); a trunk (5.4, s.d.); seating for one character (5.4, implicit)

COSTUMES AND MAKE-UP
CLYSTER: dressed as a physician (1.1, dialogue; 1.2, 1.4, 2.2–4, 3.2–3, 4.1–4, 5.1–4, implicit; put on on stage), including a gown and cap (5.3, dialogue) and a false beard (s.d.; removed on stage)
SILENCE: dressed as a Puritan divine (1.1, dialogue; 1.2–3, 2.3, 3.1, 3.4, 4.2, 5.1–4, implicit; put on on stage), including a false beard (s.d.; removed on stage)
BOND: has no ears (dialogue)
FANTASY: fine clothes (1.4, dialogue); two rings (4.4, dialogue; removed on stage); a garment with extensive pockets (4.4, s.d.)
ALGEBRA: a philosopher's habit (4.2, dialogue)
CAUTION: there is no lace in his costume (2.3, dialogue)
SICKLY: a red pimple on the bridge of his nose (2.2, dialogue)
DAMME: a beard (dialogue); a cloak, a hat, doublet, breeches, stockings, and boots (5.1, dialogue; removed on stage); old clothes (5.1, 5.3, s.d.; put on on stage), including a coat and a greasy cap (s.d.; removed on stage); calzoons (i.e. underwear; 5.3, dialogue; 5.4, implicit)

EARLY STAGE HISTORY
c. 1635: the play was written with a view to performance both in a playhouse and at court, the latter in the evening with King Charles I and Queen Henrietta Maria in the audience; an alternative prologue and epilogue are supplied for the court occasion. There is no evidence that any such commercial or court performances took place.

EARLY TEXTUAL HISTORY
1635: transcribed in **MS** by John Rolleston; 96 leaves; list of roles.

EDITION
Cathryn Anne Nelson, Salzburg Studies in English Literature: Jacobean Drama Studies (Salzburg, 1975).

REFERENCES
Annals 1635; *EMS* 4 (1993), 150–2; *SEL* 4 (1964), 227–37.

2522. Pastoral Court Masque

TEXT
Printed (in 1635?; San Marino: Huntington, 13016), presumably for distribution for the audience at the performance; spoken text only with headings.

GENRE
masque
Contemporary: masque (Q); poem (Q verses)

TITLE
Later Assigned: *The Ante-Masques*; *A Pastoral Masque*
Alternative Modernization: *The Antimasques*

The Ante-Masques is only the heading of one Q section; its use as the title of the whole masque is a modern misunderstanding.

AUTHOR
Aurelian Townshend

DATE
21 December 1635

ORIGINAL PRODUCTION
English Court at Whitehall Palace

PLOT
Men come from all over the world, drawn by the fame of four French shepherdesses. Among them are four shepherds, who are required to submit themselves to chaste love if they are to dance with the shepherdesses. The deity of the grove points out one of them (or possibly the Queen in the audience) as a bride; the others must merely hope to achieve such a state. A pygmy points out that the remainder of the night is even shorter than he is: it should not be wasted in a mannerly abstention from dancing.

SCENE DESIGNATION
The action includes four numbered antimasque entries (ant.1–4), but is otherwise undivided.

ROLES
A MAN OF CANADA (ant.1)
Two EGYPTIANS, prophets (ant.2; presumably one is *non-speaking*)
Three PANTALOONS from Bergamo (ant.3; presumably two are *non-speaking*)
Four SPANIARDS (ant.4; presumably three are *non-speaking*)
Four SHEPHERDESSES of France (*non-speaking*)
SHEPHERDS, the masquers, possibly of England or Arcadia (*non-speaking*)
A PYGMY

Probably also
PRIESTS (who sing)
A HIGH PRIEST (who speaks)

Speaking Parts: 5–12

The maximum of 12 would apply if all the antimasquers spoke (in unison?) and the 'subject of the masque' speech were spoken by a high priest or other such role.

Stage Directions
MAN OF CANADA: *a Man of Canada* (s.d.s)
EGYPTIANS: *2 Aegyptians* (s.d.s)
PANTALOONS: *3 Pantaloones* (s.d.s)
SPANIARDS: *4 Spaniards* (s.d.s)
PYGMY: *A Pygmy* (s.d.s)

OTHER CHARACTERS
The deity of the grove

SETTING
Geography
France: Beauce
[Italy]: Bergamo
Spain
Arcadia
Egypt: Memphis
Canada
The Indies

SOURCES
Works Mentioned: François le Metel, Sieur de Boisrobert, *Florimène* (oblique allusion)

LANGUAGE
English

FORM
Metre: tetrameter, dimeter, pentameter
Rhyme: ABBACCDD and ABABCCDD stanzas, couplets
Lines (Spoken): 98
Lines (Written): 106

MUSIC
Song: 'Draw near! And let not your condition', 12 lines
Dance: probably the antimasquers and masquers dance at different points

PROPS
Scenery: a grove (dialogue)

The scene would presumably have been one of those for *Florimène*, perhaps the back shutter for the standing scene, for which a design is extant (Orgel and Strong 327).

COSTUMES
MAN OF CANADA: bare feet (ant.1, dialogue)

EARLY STAGE HISTORY
Preparation: A performance of *Florimène*, presumably with this associated masque, was planned for the King's birthday, Thursday 19 November 1635. On Saturday 24 October, Inigo Jones was ordered to set up a stage and degrees in the hall at Whitehall Palace for the performance; the cost amounted to £87.10s.2d. Lighting branches were hung in the hall. The standby carpenter for the play and masque was John Davenport.

Postponement: The intended birthday performance of *Florimène* was postponed and replaced with a play by a commercial acting company, with a special prologue and epilogue by Thomas Heywood.

Performance: in the hall at Whitehall Palace on Monday 21 December 1635. The performance took place in the evening after a play (the French pastoral *Florimène*). The raked stage was 4′6″ high at the front, rising to 5′6″ at the back shutters, and 23′ deep. The audience included: King Charles I; Queen Henrietta Maria (who was heavily pregnant, and gave birth eight days later); Prince Charles; Charles Louis, Elector Palatine; Mary Hamilton, Marchioness of Hamilton; Alethea Howard, Countess of Arundel; Inigo Jones; Sir Thomas Edmondes. (The Marchioness, Countess, Jones, and Edmondes were each assigned their own box.)

Production Expenses
Sir Roger Palmer (Cofferer of the Household) was reimbursed £73.19s.1½d for expenses incurred in feeding the masquers, by a warrant dated Wednesday 18 January 1637. The cost of hanging the lighting branches and attendance was £9.10s. In 1638, John Davenport was paid £2 for his work.

EARLY TEXTUAL HISTORY
1635 (?): **Q** printed; collation A⁴, 4 leaves; includes closing verses addressed to the King and Queen, subscribed by the author. The surviving copy (Huntington Library 136016) is corrected in a contemporary hand, possibly Aurelian Townshend's.

EDITIONS
Stephen Orgel, *RenD* 4 (1971), 149–53.

Orgel and Strong, ii. 636–7.
Cedric C. Brown, in Aurelian Townshend, *The Poems* (Reading, 1983), 109–14.

REFERENCES
Annals 1636; Bentley, v. 1231, 1334; Butler, 374; *Cal. Dom.* 1636–7, 371; *Cal. Ven.* 1632–6, 499; McGee-Meagher 1634–42, 40–2; MSC 2.3, 376; MSC 10, 48, 50; MSC 13, 141; *N&Q* 210 (1965), 343–5; Orgel and Strong, ii. 638–59; John Orrell, *The Theatres of Inigo Jones and John Webb* (Cambridge, 1985), 128–48; *RenD* 4 (1972), 135–53; Steele, 254–5; *Theatre Survey* 20 (1979), 22.

2523. The Christmas Ordinary

TEXT
Two early witnesses:
- **MS:** London: British Library, MS Sloane 1458, fos. 36ᵛ–42ʳ; incomplete copy of the first half of the play (up to sc.5a), with revisions; supplies a line and half missing from the Q version of the prologue;
- **Q:** printed in 1682 (Wing R1375).

(A second MS was owned by Raymond Richards in 1948, but its current whereabouts is unknown; it appears to have been textually independent of the other two witnesses.)

This amounts to two substantive texts of the entertainment:
- **A:** Q, early version;
- **B:** MS, revised version, possibly post-Catalogue (and, as it stands, incomplete).

Although the MS text has been revised to change the characters' names, it seems to have been transcribed from copy that was in other respects close to that used for the printing of Q; for example, the wording of the statement of performance is nearly identical.

GENRE
academic entertainment
Contemporary: comedy (S.R.); private show (Q t.p.)

TITLE
Printed/MS: *The Christmas Ordinary*

AUTHOR
Henry Birkhead (?)

DATE
Limits: 1633–6
Best Guess: Christmas 1635–6

ORIGINAL PRODUCTION
Trinity College, Oxford

PLOT
Roger absconds from his master, a surgeon who is doing poor business, to go off drinking with Drink-Fight. They are joined by Astrophil, taking a break from his studies, and also bully the hermit Austin into accompanying them. They entertain one another with wit and poems, Drink-Fight teaches his companions the technique of smoking as if it were army drill, and Austin is drunk under the table.

Astrophil's father, Makepeace, is distressed to find his son missing, and sends the servant Humphrey to find him. Humphrey tracks down the drinking party and gets into their company disguised as a traveller full of tales. Together they watch a Christmas show in which the four seasons contend for supremacy over the entire year, but end up being given equal shares by Apollo. Next, they gamble, and, using false dice, Humphrey cheats them of their clothes and money, reasoning that this is the best way to make his young master come home.

With no money left, the drinkers refuse to pay their bill, so the host has them arrested. They are brought before the justice, who turns out to be Makepeace. Delighted at his son's return, he refuses to punish any of them. With his new taste for liquor, Austin the hermit becomes the host's apprentice.

SCENE DESIGNATION
prol., sc.1–10, ep. (Q)

ROLES
PROLOGUE
DRINK-FIGHT, a military captain
ROGER, Shab-Quack's apprentice
ASTROPHIL, an astronomer and scholar, Makepeace's son; a young man
AUSTIN, a hermit
Master MAKEPEACE, a country justice, Astrophil's father
HUMPHREY, Makepeace's servant; poses as a traveller
A TAPSTER at the ordinary (possibly not a role)
An ALEWIFE at the ordinary (possibly not a role)
A DRAWER at the ordinary (possibly not a role)
WIN-ALL, the host of the ordinary
APOLLO, a god, visitor and overseer of the year; a character in the show
TERRA, the earth; a female character in the show
VER, the spring; a female character in the show
AESTAS, also called Summer; a female character in the show
AUTUMNUS, also called Autumn; a male character in the show
HIEMS, also called Winter; a character in the show
Master SHAB-QUACK, a poor surgeon
Two SERGEANTS (*non-speaking*)
EPILOGUE

Drink-Fight says he has procured Song 1 from the Tapster, Alewife, and Drawer, and they are then listed in turn above their sections of the song; but it is possible that the singers are actually the drinkers themselves, assuming for the purposes of the song the identities of those who serve their liquor. (They are evidently the singers of the final stanza, though not specified as such.)

> B-Text
> DRINK-FIGHT: *renamed* COMASTES
> ROGER: *renamed* ADRASTA
> ASTROPHIL: *renamed* POLYASTER
> AUSTIN: *renamed* MYSEDONUS
> MAKEPEACE: *renamed* DICASTES
> HUMPHREY: *renamed* CALINOUS
> WIN-ALL: *renamed* MINNALL
> SHAB-QUACK: *renamed* PTOCHO-CHIRURGUS

Speaking Parts: 16–19
Allegorical Roles: 5 (in the show)

Stage Directions and Speech Prefixes
PROLOGUE: *The Prologue* (heading)
DRINK-FIGHT: *Drink-fight | Drink fight* (s.d.s and s.p.s); *Drink-Fight, A Jovial Soldier* (d.p.)
ROGER: *Roger* (s.d.s and s.p.s); *Roger, An Apprentice to Shab-Quack* (d.p.)
ASTROPHIL: *Astrophil* (s.d.s and s.p.s); *Astrophil, An Astronomer,* [Makepeace's] *Son* (d.p.)
AUSTIN: *Austin | Hermit* (s.d.s and s.p.s); *Austin, A Hermit* (d.p.)
MAKEPEACE: *Mr Make-peace* (s.d.s and s.p.s); *Make-peace* (s.p.s); *Mr Make peace* (s.p.s); *Mr Make Peace, A Country-Justice* (d.p.)
HUMPHREY: *Humphry* (s.d.s and s.p.s); *Humphry, The Justice's Man* (d.p.)
TAPSTER: *Tapster* (s.p.s)
ALEWIFE: *Alewife* (s.p.s)
DRAWER: *Drawer* (s.p.s)
WIN-ALL: *Win-all, the Host* (s.d.s); *Win-all* (s.d.s and s.p.s); *Win-All, A Host of an Ordinary* (d.p.)
APOLLO: *Apollo* (s.d.s, s.p.s, and d.p.)
TERRA: *Terra* (s.d.s, s.p.s, and d.p.)
VER: *Ver* (s.d.s, s.p.s, and d.p.)
AESTAS: *Aestas* (s.d.s and d.p.); *Summer* (s.p.s)
AUTUMNUS: *Autumnus* (s.d.s and d.p.); *Autumn* (s.p.s)
HIEMS: *Hiems* (s.d.s and d.p.); *Winter* (s.p.s)
SHAB-QUACK: *Shab quack* (s.d.s); *Shab-Quack* (s.p.s); *Shab-Quack, A poor Surgeon* (d.p.)
SERGEANTS: *two Sergeants* (s.d.s)
EPILOGUE: *The Epilogue* (heading)

> B-Text
> PROLOGUE: *The Prologue* (heading)
> COMASTES: *Comastes* (s.d.s); *Comast<es>* (s.p.s); *Comastes A Jovial Soldier* (d.p.)
> ADRASTA: *Adrasta* (s.d.s); *Adrast<a>* (s.p.s); *Adrasta* [Ptocho-chirurgus'] *apprentice* (d.p.)
> POLYASTER: *Polyaster* (s.d.s); *Polyast<er>* (s.p.s); *Polyaster An Astronomer,* [Dicastes'] *son* (d.p.)
> MYSEDONUS: *Misedonus | Mysedonus* (s.d.s);

> *Misedon<us>* (s.p.s); *Mysedonus The Hermit* (d.p.)
> DICASTES: *Dicastes* (s.d.s); *Dicast<es>* (s.p.s); *Dicastes A Justice of peace* (d.p.)
> CALINOUS: *Calinous* (s.d.s); *Calin<ous>* (s.p.s); *Calinous The Justice man* (d.p.)
> MINNALL: *Minnall The Host of the Ordinary* (d.p.)
> PTOCHO-CHIRURGUS: *Ptocho-chyrurgus A poor Chirurgeon* (d.p.)

OTHER CHARACTERS
A citizen wittol who taught Drink-Fight the art of cheating (sc.1)
The wittol's wife, whose adultery made him rich (sc.1)
Win-All's wife (sc.6; but she may be the alewife in sc.5)
Win-All's maid, who gave the drinkers her sexual favours four times (sc.6)

SETTING
Period: contemporary; the entire action takes place at Christmas, from Christmas Day to Twelfth Night
Place: 'Ubivis' ('where you wish'; but evidently Oxford)

Geography
[London]: the Guildhall; Bedlam
England: Banbury
Wales
Germany: Heidelberg
Europe: France; the Low Countries; Spain; Greece; Rome; Hungary; Slavonia; Russia; Batavia
The Mediterranean Sea
Barbary
The Arctic Pole
Greenland
The Antipodes
The Antarctic Pole

SOURCES
Verbal: Bible: Genesis 28.12 (sc.3); Martial, *Epigrams* 6.24 (t.p. motto)
Works Mentioned: Aesop, *Fables* (prol.); Pliny, *Natural History* (sc.7); Apuleius, *The Golden Ass* (sc.5); Juvenal, *Satires* 1 (preface)

The Martial epigram is wrongly cited as 6.22 in Q; it is correctly identified in MS.

LANGUAGE
English
Latin: 32 words (sc.2, 5–7; Astrophil, Drink-Fight, Austin, Win-All, Humphrey)
Greek: 1 word (sc.5; Austin)

FORM
Metre: prose and pentameter
Rhyme: couplets; one passage of ABAB
Prologue: 24 lines, in couplets
Epilogue: 12 lines, in couplets

Lines (Spoken): 712 (246 verse, 466 prose)
Lines (Written): 765

B-Text
Lines (Written): 216

STAGING
Doors: two characters enter at different doors (sc.1, s.d.)
Discovery Space: Makepeace enters 'in his chair', which probably means a discovery (sc.10, s.d.; no attendants are indicated and the only other alternative would be ludicrous)
Within: sound effects (sc.8, s.d.)

MUSIC AND SOUND
Sound Effects: sounds of assault within (sc.8, s.d.)
Songs:
1: 'Beer leave to the barrel', sc.5, Tapster, Alewife, Drawer, in parts, and Drink-Fight, Austin, Roger, and Astrophil collectively, 45 lines;
2: 'This pipe's my pillar of clouds', sc.9, Astrophil, 10 lines. (This may not in fact be a song at all but a poem.)

PROPS
Clothing: the drinkers' clothes (sc.10, s.d.)
Money: an unspecified amount (sc.10, s.d.)
Food and Drink: a pot of wine (sc.5, s.d.; drunk on stage); four cups (sc.5, s.d.); tobacco (sc.7, 9, implicit); four tobacco-pipes (sc.7, s.d.; sc.9, dialogue)
Small Portable Objects: a celestial globe (sc.2, s.d.); a bill (sc.6, s.d.)
Large Portable Objects: a chair (sc.10, s.d.)

COSTUMES
DRINK-FIGHT: breeches (sc.1, dialogue); a doublet (sc.1, 3, 5, 7); no doublet (sc.9, s.d.; sc.10, implicit)
ROGER: a doublet (sc.1, 3, 5, 7); no doublet (sc.9, s.d.; sc.10, implicit)
ASTROPHIL: a doublet (sc.2, 3, 5, 7); no doublet (sc.9, s.d.; sc.10, implicit)
HUMPHREY: disguised as a traveller (sc.7, s.d.)

EARLY STAGE HISTORY
Performed at Trinity College, Oxford, by no later than c. 1677 (and probably in the mid-1630s).

EARLY TEXTUAL HISTORY
Before 1642 (?): transcribed in MS (untraced since 1948); author's initials given as H. B.

1659–60: a MS (not now known to exist) probably came into the possession of William Richards at Trinity College, Oxford.

1660: entered to Humphrey Moseley in the Stationers' Register on Friday 29 June; individually named as part of a group entry of eleven plays, and ascribed to Trinity College, Oxford.

c. 1677: partially transcribed into a MS commonplace book which belonged to Richard Enock; 12 pages on 7 leaves; author's initials given as H. B.; refers to performance; Latin epigraph; list of roles; argument.

1682: Q printed for James Courtney; collation A–D⁴, 16 leaves; Latin title-page motto; title page refers vaguely to performance and ascribes the play to W. R.; preface dated Wednesday 18 October at Helmdon, signed by W. R. (i.e. William Richards); list of roles; argument.

The extant MS bears the date 1677 beside the name of its owner, Enock. The text of the play is preceded in the MS by, among other items, the prologue and epilogue to Etherege's *The Man of Mode* (1676), a letter dated 1674, and Rochester's 'Satire Against Reason and Mankind'; this all seems to confirm a transcription date no earlier than the late 1670s.

REFERENCES
Annals 1660; Bentley, v. 1306–8; Eyre & Rivington, ii. 271; Greg Θ184; Hazlitt, 40; *PBSA* 50 (1956), 184–90; REED: Lancashire, cii; *RES* NS 58 (2007), 657–68.

1636

2524. Masque of Ladies

TEXT
Fragment printed in 1637 (STC 13358).

GENRE
masque
Contemporary: masque (heading)

TITLE
Contemporary: *A Masque Presented at Hunsdon House*
Later Assigned: *The Masque at Hunsdon*

AUTHOR
Thomas Heywood

DATE
Limits: 1635–7
Best Guess: 1 January 1636

Bergeron, Butler, and McGee-Meagher all date the masque 1 January 1637, on the assumption that the heading's reference to its performance 'the last New Year's night' refers to the New Year before Q was printed. This may be so, but it is more likely that it was the New Year before the copy was prepared, which could have been up to two years earlier. The book as a whole was entered in the Stationers' Register in August 1635, without a listing of its specific contents. The fragment appears in the 'prologues and epilogues' section, which is not presented in strict chronological order: material for *Love's Mistress* (**2451**; November 1634) is immediately followed by items for an unspecified New Year's Day, Christmas, Candlemas, and then this New Year's Day masque; after a couple of other undatable prologues, the last two items in the section are both datable to November 1635, one of them being a prologue and epilogue performed on the King's 'last birth-night', his 35th (19 November 1635). This indicates that the copy for the section was prepared at some time before November 1636, and after the collection was registered and licensed for publication. The interpretation of the heading's reference to 'the last New Year's night' thus turns on whether the copy was prepared in December 1635 or at some time between January and early November 1636; but in the former case, Heywood might well have avoided supplying copy that was about to go out of date.

It is striking that at this time Heywood seems to have returned frequently to the three goddesses of the Judgement of Paris story, as translated in **2507** and appropriated for civic use in **2517**.

ORIGINAL PRODUCTION
Earl of Dover's household at Hunsdon House, Hertfordshire

PLOT
A story is told of how a swan asked a cock why it sits so high. The cock told the swan that it crows most in December because cocks are the heralds of the incarnation of Christ. The swan joined in, and the noise summoned all estates to the hospitable gates of Hunsdon House. These people are now the audience for the masque which is to be performed. Truth presents the nine masquers, three groups of graces, goddesses, and virtues, and presumably dancing ensues.

ROLES
A SPEAKER
TRUTH
The three GRACES or Charities; daughters of Jove, handmaidens of Venus; masquers (*non-speaking*)
JUNO, a goddess and masquer (*non-speaking*)
MINERVA, a goddess and masquer (*non-speaking*)
VENUS, a goddess and masquer (*non-speaking*)
FAITH, a theological virtue; a female masquer (*non-speaking*)
HOPE, a theological virtue; a female masquer (*non-speaking*)
LOVE, a theological virtue; a female masquer (*non-speaking*)

Speaking Parts: 2
Allegorical Roles: 4

Stage Directions
TRUTH: *Truth* (s.d.s)

OTHER CHARACTERS
Jove, the Graces' fathers
Paris, a Trojan shepherd

SETTING
Geography
[*England*]: River Thames; York
[*Italy*]: River Po
[*Greece*]: Mount Parnassus
[*Asia Minor*]: River Meander; Mount Ida; Troy; River Caister

SOURCES
Verbal: Bible: 1 Corinthians 13.13 (Bishops' or Geneva translations, not the King James Version)

LANGUAGE
English

FORM
Metre: pentameter and tetrameter
Rhyme: couplets
Lines (Spoken): 68
Lines (Written): 69

STAGING
Audience: the principal members are addressed as 'great lord and lady'

MUSIC
Dance: The masquers presumably dance.

PROPS
Lighting: tapers (dialogue)
Scenery: a bower of white roses (dialogue)

EARLY STAGE HISTORY
Performed at Hunsdon House, Hertfordshire, on 1 January (which was a Friday in 1636, and a Thursday in 1635). The audience included: Henry Carey, 1st Earl of Dover; Mary Carey, Countess of Dover.

EARLY TEXTUAL HISTORY
1635: *Pleasant Dialogues and Dramas* entered in the Stationers' Register to Richard Hearne on Saturday 29 August; entry names author. Thomas Wykes had licensed the book for publication.

1637: included in Thomas Heywood's *Pleasant Dialogues and Dramas* (**O**), sigs. R3^r–R4^r, 3 pages on 2 leaves; printed by Richard Oulton for Richard Hearne, and to be sold by Thomas Slater.

1684: Nicholas Cox (Manciple of St Edmund Hall, Oxford) had a copy of O in his bookshop. It had probably been previously owned by Gerard Langbaine, and appears on a list compiled by Anthony Wood on Saturday 13 December.

EDITIONS
W. Bang, in Thomas Heywood, *Pleasant Dialogues and Dramas*, Materialien 1.3 (Louvain, 1903), 245–7.

David M. Bergeron, in *Thomas Heywood's Pageants*, The Renaissance Imagination 16 (New York, 1986), 143–7.

REFERENCES
Annals 1635; Bodleian, MS Wood E. 4, art. 1, p. 31; Butler, 375; McGee-Meagher 1634–42, 56.

2525. The Wasp

TEXT
MS (Alnwick Castle, MS 507); authorial copy annotated by one or two other hands in preparation of a prompt-book, with cuts marked in six scenes (2.2–3, 3.1–2, 5.1–2); one or more leaves are missing from the end. Some or most of the entrance warnings were marked up before the cuts were made; in one case, a new warning was substituted afterwards.

GENRE
tragicomedy

TITLE
MS: *The Wasp, or Subject's Precedent*

DATE
Limits: 1630–6
Best Guess: 1636

The actors named in the MS identify the play as belonging to the 1630s King's Revels Company. The prompt markings are similar to those in the prompt-book of *The Lady Mother* (**2516**; another King's Revels play), notably the moving of act-divisions and the way in which warnings are marked; the latter appears to be a company-specific (or perhaps bookkeeper-specific) practice. The level of stage technology required (notably the bed and discovery space) suggests that the play was designed for performance in a London theatre rather than on tour.

ORIGINAL PRODUCTION
King's Revels Company, presumably at either Salisbury Court (1630–2, 1634–6) or the Fortune (1632–4)

PLOT
Britain suffers under the oppressive rule of the Roman Prorex Marianus, who has recently deprived Gilbert of his office as High Champion and bestowed it on his unworthy favourite, Varletti. Gilbert takes to his bed, makes his will, and appears to die. His passing incites the barons to rebellion. The plain-spoken Archibald gives Marianus a list of the rebels and advises him to banish Varletti. Instead, Marianus provocatively places Varletti on the throne, wearing his crown, during a meeting with the dissident barons. No compromise is possible, and the rebels prepare for war against the Prorex.

In fact, Gilbert is not dead: with the collusion of Owlet, his man, he faked his death in order to see whether his wife and his son Geraldine will behave appropriately afterwards. One of his legacies is to Owlet: his farm, the Ivybush. In case Geraldine should dispute this, he also gives Owlet a box of jewels, to be sold if he should lose the farm or returned to the estate if not. Geraldine is appalled by the division of the estate between him and his mother; but she goes into a nunnery and gives him her share. He also tries to repossess the Ivybush, and suspects Owlet of stealing the jewels.

To test his wife, Gilbert assumes the identity of Wasp. She has left the nunnery, only to be pestered by numerous persistent suitors. 'Wasp' proposes getting rid of them by pretending that she is already married to him; but once this is put into effect, he begins to treat her property as if it is his own, including felling her oak trees. After a failed attempt to settle the matter by local arbitration (which 'Wasp' sabotages by substituting Owlet for the judge), the Countess takes it to court. Marianus upholds her case, but 'Wasp' wins the argument by revealing his true identity.

Varletti asks to marry Marianus' sister, even though he has a wife already. To avoid a civil war, Archibald delivers the rebel barons to Marianus, trusting to his mercy, and he makes them sign a paper which Varletti believes is a form of consent to his marriage; in fact it ratifies his banishment. Archibald too is banished for contempt. Marianus orders him to entrap Varletti into a treason charge, pardoning him in advance for any treasonous words spoken in the process. But Varletti's wife Katherine turns the tables, convinces Geraldine that his father was poisoned by Marianus, and gets his signature on an agreement to assassinate Marianus and seize power himself. Katherine further persuades Geraldine that he will need the support of her banished Uncle Percy. Varletti and Geraldine attempt to ambush and assassinate Marianus as he hunts, but Archibald, disguised as a woodman, rescues the Prorex. Varletti sends a letter, calculated to arrive after the attack, which implicates Archibald. Marianus has Archibald arrested and his family put to servants' work. The other barons are deprived of their offices and replaced with Varletti and Geraldine—lightweights who will be less likely to oppose him. Marianus tests Archibald's loyalty by sending Geraldine to him disguised as a hangman, but even the threat of execution cannot make him say anything seditious; on the contrary, when his son flouts the Prorex's orders and gives him better food, he refuses to plead for the boy's pardon.

Archibald is released from prison by a kinsman posing as a keeper, and he assumes the identity of 'Uncle Percy'; Geraldine agrees to submit himself absolutely to the old man's command. The rebels break into court, depose Marianus, and crown Geraldine; but when he orders a banquet, the appetizing food is magically transformed into poisonous reptiles. Varletti attempts to kill Marianus, but the barons save his life, and 'Percy' orders Geraldine to give up the throne. Once Marianus is reinvested in the throne, the wholesome banquet reappears, and Archibald explains that the creepy-crawlies only present themselves to usurpers. [*The end of the play is lost.*]

SCENE DESIGNATION
1.1–2, 2.1–3, 3.1–2, 4.1–3, 5.1–2 (act-division MS, scene-division Malone)

In revision, 2.3 was omitted and two act-divisions moved, so that 3.1 becomes 2.3, 3.2 becomes 3.1, 4.1 becomes 3.2, and 4.2–3 become 4.1–2. The reviser also considered moving the start of Act 5, but changed his mind.

ROLES
The Earl of CONON, a baron, Archibald's kinsman; poses as a keeper
ELIDURE, a baron
The Lord of DEVON, a baron
Tom ARCHIBALD, a baron, 60 years old; a married man and a father; Conon's kinsman; also called Master Archibald; poses as Percy, Katherine's uncle (also called Old Jack)
COUNTESS Clarydon, Gilbert's wife, a young woman; Geraldine's mother (or stepmother?)
GILBERT, Baron Clarydon, the Countess's husband, Geraldine's father; formerly High Champion of Britain; also called Gil, Earl Clarydon and the Earl of Clare; assumes the alias Master Wasp
OWLET, Gilbert's man, of Cumberland birth; poses first as a sheriff's man, then as Master Falbridge, the Constable of Walthamstow, then as Justice Bindover (also called Master Bindover)
MARIANUS, Roman Prorex of Britain; also called the King; a young man
Signor VARLETTI, a German musician, Marianus' favourite, High Champion of Britain, Katherine's husband; later created Marshal, General of the Roman garrison, High Admiral of the Royal Navy, and Lord of Devon
LORDS attending Marianus (1.2, *non-speaking*)
FLAMENS at Gilbert's funeral (2.1, *non-speaking*)
Two HERALDS at Gilbert's funeral (2.1, *non-speaking*)
GERALDINE, son of Gilbert and the Countess; also called Gerard; later created High Champion of Britain, Earl of Conon, Master of the Horse, and Captain of the Guards, Pensioners, and Switzers
GENTLEMEN at Gilbert's funeral (2.1, *non-speaking*)
SERVANTS at Gilbert's funeral (2.1, *non-speaking*)
A CAPTAIN (2.2)
Master GRIG Brandell, an alehouse keeper; formerly a hangman; *omitted* in revision
Master DAMPIT, a usurer, broker, and thieves' fence; *omitted* in revision
HUNTIT, a cheating lawyer and informer; *omitted* in revision
KENWELL, a dicer, cheat, and cutpurse; *omitted* in revision
KATHERINE, Varletti's wife; also called Kate
A SERVANT in Varletti's household (3.1)
LUCE, the Countess's servant
A SERVANT in Grig's alehouse (3.2); *omitted* in revision
Two OFFICERS accompanying Owlet (3.2, *non-speaking*); *omitted* in revision
ATTENDANTS on the barons (4.1, *non-speaking*)
Archibald's WIFE
Archibald's SON, a boy
A MESSENGER, who delivers Varletti's letter (4.1)
Two GUARDS, who arrest Archibald's wife and son (4.1)
DASH, who poses as Justice Bindover's clerk
A PERSON seeking Bindover (4.2)
Two LORDS attending Marianus (5.2)
Two LADIES at court (5.2)
A FURY (5.2, *non-speaking*; may alternatively be represented by a piece of scenery)

Speaking Parts:
COMPLETE TEXT: 30
ABRIDGED STAGE VERSION: 25

Doubling
The following roles were doubled:
   1: Captain (2.2), Lord (5.2);
   2: Servant (3.1), Person (4.2).

Stage Directions and Speech Prefixes
CONON: *Conon* (s.d.s and s.p.s); [one of the] *Barons* (s.d.s); *Keeper* (s.d.s)
ELIDURE: *Elidure* | [one of the] *Barons* (s.d.s); *Elyd<ure>* (s.d.s and s.p.s); *Elid<ure>* (s.p.s)
DEVON: *Devon* (s.d.s and s.p.s); [one of the] *Barons* (s.d.s)
ARCHIBALD: *Archibald* | *Archiballd* (s.d.s); *Archib<ald>* (s.p.s)
COUNTESS: *Countess Clarydon* | *The countess* (s.d.s); *Countess* (s.d.s and s.p.s)
GILBERT: *Gilbert* | *Clarydon* | *Waspe* (s.d.s); *Gilb<ert>* | *Gylbert* (s.p.s)
OWLET: *Howlet* (s.d.s); *Howl<et>* | *Houl<et>* (s.p.s)
MARIANUS: *Maryanus* (s.d.s); *Prorex* (s.d.s and s.p.s)
VARLETTI: *Varletti* (s.d.s); *Varl<etti>* (s.p.s)
LORDS: *Lords* (s.d.s)
FLAMENS: *Flamens* (s.d.s)
HERALDS: *2 Heralds* | *Heralds* (s.d.s)
GERALDINE: *young Gerard* | *Geraldine* | *Gerald* (s.d.s); *Gerard* | *Ger<aldine>* (s.p.s)
GENTLEMEN: *Gentlemen* (s.d.s)
SERVANTS: *servants* (s.d.s)
CAPTAIN: *Captain* (s.d.s and s.p.s)
GRIG: *grig* (s.d.s and s.p.s); [one of] *4 Suitors* (s.d.s)
DAMPIT: *dampit* | [one of] *4 Suitors* (s.d.s); *Damp<i>t* (s.p.s)
HUNTIT: *Huntit* | [one of] *4 Suitors* (s.d.s); *Hunt<it>* (s.p.s)
KENWELL: *Kenwell* | [one of] *4 Suitors* (s.d.s); *Kenw<ell>* (s.p.s)
KATHERINE: *Katherine* | *Kathrine* (s.d.s); *Kath<erine>* (s.p.s)
SERVANT: *servant* (s.d.s)
LUCE: *Luce* (s.d.s and s.p.s)
SERVANT: *servant* (s.d.s and s.p.s)
OFFICERS: *officers* (s.d.s)
ATTENDANTS: *other* (s.d.s)
WIFE: *Uxor* (s.d.s and s.p.s)
SON: *filius* (s.d.s and s.p.s)
MESSENGER: *messenger* (s.d.s and s.p.s)
GUARDS: *1 guard* | *2 guard* (s.p.s)
DASH: *dashe* (s.d.s); *Dash* (s.d.s and s.p.s)
PERSON: *One* (s.d.s and s.p.s)
LORDS: *Lords* (s.d.s); *1 Lord* | *2 Lord* (s.p.s)
LADIES: *Ladies* (s.d.s); *Lady* | *2 lady* (s.p.s)
FURY: *fury* (s.d.s)

OTHER CHARACTERS
A poet whom Owlet commissioned to write Gilbert's epitaph (1.1)
Owlet's ancestors (1.1)
Gilbert's servants, Owlet's colleagues (1.1, 3.2)
Caesar, ruler of Rome (1.2, 2.2, 4.3, 5.2)
Archibald's workmen and tenants (1.2)
The common people of Britain (1.2, 2.2, 3.1)
Honoria, Marianus' sister (2.2)
Turnover, the foreman of the jury, a freeholder and an intimate of Grig (2.3)
A map-maker in Kent Street (2.3)
A yeoman with whom Grig eats swan pie from time to time (2.3)
Trillebub, a fat sergeant (2.3)
James, Grig's benefactor, whose thumb-ring he wears (2.3; but this may refer to St James)
A rich widow of Walthamstow courted by Kenwell (2.3)
The Roman garrison in Britain (3.1, 4.3, 5.1)
Percy, Katherine's uncle, banished by Marianus, impersonated by Archibald (3.1, 5.1–2)
Geraldine's servants: a coachman, two footmen, and a page (3.2)
The vestal virgins (3.2)
The Countess's suitors (3.2)
Justice Bindover, impersonated by Owlet (3.2, 4.2)
A thief whom Grig branded with a cold iron (3.2)
A rascal who laid information against Dampit (3.2)
Vintners and victuallers who broke fasting regulations, and bribed Huntit to turn a blind eye (3.2)
A colleague of Huntit's, who prosecuted the vintners and victuallers (3.2)
The Countess's tenants (3.2, 4.2)
The Countess's household servants (3.2, 4.2)
A tired gentleman who gave the messenger Varletti's letter (4.1; but he may have been Varletti himself)
A company of sailors and merchants from Brazil (4.2)
The cook who gave Archibald mouldy bread (4.3)
Archibald's keeper, bribed by Conon (4.3)
Owlet's father and mother, who allegedly practised buggery (5.2)

SETTING
Period: late antiquity; the action takes place during the Roman occupation of Britain (AD 43–410)
Time-Scheme: 2.1 takes place the Friday after 1.2; 3.2 takes place before dinner; 4.1 takes place the day after 3.1
Place: Britain

Geography
[*London*]: Newgate; Kent Street; Hazard's Bridge; St Martin's Church; Gunpowder Alley; Knave's Acre
[*Middlesex*]: Paddington; Wapping; Walthamstow
[*Surrey*]: Croydon; Kingston
Great Britain: Conon [?= Conon Bridge in Scotland]; Devon; Mount Clarydon (unidentified); Cumberland; Hampshire; Flintshire; Brecknockshire; Maidstone; Kent; Brecknock; Clare
Ireland
Italy: Rome; Naples; Lombardy; Mount Etna; River Tiber
France: Boulogne
[*Europe*]: Germany; Spain; Switzerland; the Alps; Russia; Holland
Barbary
The Holy Land
Arabia

India
America: Brazil
The Antipodes

SOURCES
Narrative: Christopher Marlowe, *Edward II* (**927**; 1.2); William Shakespeare, *Richard II* (**1002**; 4.3); *The Tempest* (**1652**; 5.2); Ben Jonson, *Sejanus' Fall* (**1412**; 2.2)
Verbal: Virgil, *Aeneid* 2 (2.1), 6 (3.1); Ovid, *Heroides* 2 (2.2); St Augustine, *Epistles* 151 (3.2); Thomas Wilson, *The Art of Rhetoric* (1553, repr. 1585; 4.3); William Shakespeare, *Julius Caesar* (**1198**; 2.1); Thomas Middleton, *A Trick to Catch the Old One* (**1467**; the name Dampit); Robert Armin, *A Nest of Ninnies* (1608; 3.2)
Works Mentioned: Tertullian, unidentified work (2.1)

Varletti in 1.2 is partly based on Gaveston in *Edward II*: Marianus' provocative act of putting him on the throne and Varletti's own *'Tanti!'* are particular points of contact. In 2.2, his wish to marry into Marianus' family derives from *Sejanus*. In 4.3, Archibald's loyal readiness to have his rebel son executed is based on York in *Richard II*, while the magically transformed banquet and its ethical explanation combine elements from different parts of *The Tempest*.

LANGUAGE
English
Latin: 94 words (1.1–2, 2.1–3, 3.1–2, 4.1–3, 5.2; Archibald, Marianus, Geraldine, Varletti, Conon, Grig, Owlet, Kenwell, Gilbert, Archibald's Son, 1 Lord)
Italian: 2 words (1.2, 4.3; Varletti, Archibald's Son)
French: 3 words (5.2; Archibald's Son)

FORM
Metre: prose and pentameter; some alexandrines
Rhyme: blank verse; some couplets
Act-Division: 5 acts
Lines (Spoken):
  COMPLETE TEXT: 2,255 (684 verse, 1,571 prose)
  ABRIDGED STAGE VERSION: 1,767 (650 verse, 1,117 prose)
Lines (Written): 2,342

STAGING
Discovery Space: a bed is discovered (1.1, s.d.)
Within: noise (5.2, s.d.)
Above: a sword hangs down by a thread over Geraldine's head, with a Fury ready to cut it (5.2, s.d.)

MUSIC AND SOUND
Sound Effects: knocking (3.2, s.d.)
Music: flourish (1.2, 2.2, s.d.); solemn music of recorders (2.1, s.d.); horn (4.1, s.d.); soft music (5.2, s.d.)
On-Stage Music: Marianus winds his horn (4.1, s.d.)

PROPS
Weapons: a sword (2.1, s.d.); three or four halters (2.2, s.d.); a sword hanging by a thread (5.2, s.d.); possibly a cutting tool (5.2, implicit; used by the Fury in threatening to cut the thread)
Musical Instruments: a horn (4.1, s.d.)
Clothing: gilt spurs (2.1, s.d.); a gauntlet, possibly gilt (2.1, s.d.); armour (2.1, s.d.); a plumed helmet (2.1, s.d.); a scarf (2.3, dialogue); a gauntlet (3.2, dialogue); a signet ring (4.3, s.d.)
Animals: snakes, newts, and toads (5.2, s.d.; must be affixed to the alternative table-top)
Food and Drink: cans of liquor (2.3, dialogue); a bottle of sack (4.2, dialogue; drunk on stage); a cup (4.2, dialogue); mouldy bread (4.3, dialogue); water (4.3, dialogue); a capon (4.3, s.d.); a bottle of wine (4.3, s.d.); a banquet (5.2, dialogue; must be affixed to the table-top); wine (5.2, s.d.; drunk on stage)
Small Portable Objects: a paper (1.1, s.d.; 1.2, implicit); a will (1.1, dialogue); a box of jewels (1.1, dialogue); pen and ink (2.2, 3.1, dialogue); two papers (2.2, dialogue; one is signed on stage); a pardon (3.1, dialogue); a paper (3.1, implicit; signed on stage); a letter (4.1, implicit); a pen (4.2, dialogue); ink and paper (4.2, implicit); a book (4.2, dialogue); a paper (4.3, s.d.); a key (4.2, dialogue); a letter (4.3, dialogue); a paper (5.2, s.d.); an orb (5.2, s.d.); a casket (5.2, dialogue)
Large Portable Objects: a pillow (1.1, dialogue); a table (2.3, s.d.); two staffs of office (4.3, 5.1, s.d.); one further staff of office (4.3, s.d.); a chair and cushion (5.1, dialogue); a trick table (5.2, s.d., turns to replace the banquet with the reptiles); a chair of state (5.2, dialogue)
Scenery: a bed (1.1, s.d.); a throne (1.2, dialogue); a rich hearse with five pendants (2.1, s.d.); possibly a Fury (5.2, s.d.; may alternatively be represented by an actor)
Miscellaneous: blood (4.1, s.d.)

COSTUMES
CONON: a hat (1.2, dialogue); a shirt and nightcap (2.2, s.d.); disguised as a keeper (4.3, dialogue)
ELIDURE and DEVON: hats (1.2, dialogue); shirts and nightcaps (2.2, s.d.)
ARCHIBALD: a hat (1.2, dialogue); a shirt and nightcap (2.2, s.d.); dressed as a woodman (4.1, implicit); disguised as Percy, possibly with an eye-patch (5.1–2, implicit)
GILBERT: a cloak (3.2, s.d.; removed on stage); disguised as Wasp (3.2, s.d.), in a 'fantastic and ridiculous habit' (dialogue)
OWLET: 'some odd disguise' (2.3, s.d.); disguised as a constable (3.2, implicit); disguised as a judge (4.2, s.d.)
MARIANUS: a robe of state (1.2, dialogue; removed on stage); a golden imperial crown (1.2, dialogue; 5.2, implicit; removed on stage); Varletti's cloak (1.2, dialogue; put on on stage); a gorget (2.2, s.d.)
VARLETTI: a cloak (1.2, dialogue; removed on stage); Marianus' robe and crown (1.2, dialogue; put on on stage); a vizard (4.1, s.d.); gallantly dressed (5.1, s.d.)

GERALDINE: a vizard (4.1, s.d.); disguised as a hangman (4.3, s.d.); gallantly dressed (5.1, s.d.); Marianus' crown (5.2, implicit; put on and removed on stage)
DASH: disguised (4.2, s.d.)

EARLY STAGE HISTORY
1630s: performed by the King's Revels Company. The cast included: John Barrett (Servant in 3.1, Person in 4.2); Ellis Bedowe (Lord in 5.2); Thomas Jordan (Captain, Lord in 5.2); Ambrose [Matchit?] (Archibald's Son); Mathias Morris (Officer); Noble (Officer). However, some of these roles appear only in sequences marked for omission.

EARLY TEXTUAL HISTORY
c. 1636: transcribed in **MS**, 22 surviving leaves.

EDITION
J. W. Lever, Malone Society Reprints 135 (Oxford, 1976 for 1974).

REFERENCES
Annals 1630; Bentley, v. 1433–4.

2526. The Duke's Mistress

TEXT
Printed in 1638 (STC 22441), from authorial copy. This omits the text of the songs and the 18-line poem read out in 3.2, but the poem was printed separately in 1646 (Wing S3480).

GENRE
tragicomedy
Contemporary: play (prol., S.R.)

TITLE
Performed/Printed: *The Duke's Mistress*

AUTHOR
James Shirley

DATE
January 1636

ORIGINAL PRODUCTION
Queen Henrietta's Men at the Cockpit

PLOT
The Duke of Pavia has transferred his affections from his duchess, Euphemia, to a mistress, Ardelia. Euphemia is now neglected and disregarded at court. The Duke's heir Leontio loves the Duchess and hopes her poor treatment will encourage her to love him back. A conversation between them is reported to the Duke. Euphemia asks her husband to put her out of her misery by beheading her, but withdraws the request when Ardelia seems keen on the idea. The Duke uses her bitter words to Ardelia as a pretext for imprisoning her, but, in accordance with the dignity of her office, she is committed not to jail but to the custody of a senior courtier. The Duke gives the job to Leontio, intending to give them a chance to commit adultery and thereby create an excuse to execute the Duchess so that he can marry Ardelia.

Ardelia's fiancé Bentivolio comes to court: the couple were secretly betrothed against the wishes of his father, who is now dead. They meet in a garden through the good offices of the courtier Valerio, but Bentivolio hides when the Duke comes. He overhears Ardelia's conversation with the Duke, which establishes that she is not venally exploiting the Duke's illicit passions, and has so far remained chaste.

Puzzled at the way his wooing has foundered since Bentivolio's arrival, the Duke asks Valerio to investigate. Valerio attempts to seduce Ardelia and, when that fails, seeks to extort her sexual favours by blackmail. Meanwhile, Leontio declares his love for Euphemia, but she will not wrong her husband. He asks Pallante, an unemployed soldier to whom he has given patronage, to kill the Duke. Valerio overhears Leontio talking about the plot, and joins in: each of them wants one of the Duke's women, and can only have her if the Duke himself is dead. At Valerio's suggestion, they induce Bentivolio to attempt the murder. Valerio visits Ardelia, intending to rape her, but hides behind the arras when Bentivolio comes. Ardelia tells him the person hiding is the Duke, so Bentivolio kills him. He confesses to the murder, but in the meantime Pallante has also reported his mission complete. Leontio assumes the dukedom and has both arrested, but promises each that the other will be allowed to take the blame. But, in fact, the Duke is still alive, spared by Pallante after showing genuine regret for his misdeeds, and he visits Euphemia in disguise to beg her pardon. When Leontio also comes to Euphemia's room, the Duke orders his arrest. Leontio is killed in the struggle. Bentivolio is pardoned for Valerio's death and allowed to marry Ardelia.

In the sub-plot, Valerio helps with the love-life of his friend Horatio, who is interested only in plain women, declaring his love to be Platonic. Valerio introduces him to three court ladies, and he offends the two beautiful ones by preferring the ugly Fiametta. Valerio then introduces the even more hideous Scolopendra as a rival for Fiametta, and Horatio realizes that ugly women are just as prone to petty jealousy as pretty ones.

SCENE DESIGNATION
prol., 1.1, 2.1–2, 3.1–3, 4.1, 5.1–4, ep. (Q has act-division only)

ROLES
PROLOGUE

SILVIO, a courtier
Signor VALERIO, an unmarried courtier
LEONTIO, a young lord, the Duke's favourite, kinsman, and heir apparent; alternatively written as Leonato
ASCANIO, a courtier
EUPHEMIA, Duchess of Pavia, the Duke's wife
MACRINA, a beautiful court lady, Euphemia's waiting-woman
COURTIERS, who ignore the Duchess (1.1, non-speaking)
STROZZI, a courtier and spy
PALLANTE, a military captain
Dionisio, DUKE of Pavia, the Duchess's husband; alternatively written as Farnese, Duke of Parma
SINGERS, at least two in number (2.2)
ARDELIA, the Duke's mistress, Bentivolio's fiancée
Signor BENTIVOLIO, a gentleman, Ardelia's fiancé
Signor HORATIO, Bentivolio's friend, a foreign-born gentleman
FIAMETTA, Ardelia's waiting-woman, an ugly, long-nosed, wall-eyed, squinting lady
LADIES attending the Duke (2.2, non-speaking)
A SERVANT, who announces the Duke's arrival (3.1)
Lady AURELIA, a beautiful court lady
A SERVANT, who announces Aurelia and Macrina (4.1)
SCOLOPENDRA, an ugly woman, formerly a cook-maid
A SERVANT, who announces the Duke (4.1)
VOICES (5.2, within)
OFFICERS (5.2-4; up to three speak individually)

Speaking Parts: 20-4

Stage Directions and Speech Prefixes
PROLOGUE: *The Prologue* (heading)
SILVIO: *Silvio* (s.d.s); *Sil<vio>* (s.p.s)
VALERIO: *Valerio* (s.d.s); *Val<erio>* (s.p.s)
LEONTIO: *Leontio | Leonato* (s.d.s); *Leo<ntio>* (s.p.s)
ASCANIO: *Ascanio* (s.d.s); *Asc<anio>* (s.p.s)
EUPHEMIA: *Euphemia* (s.d.s); *Eup<hemia>* (s.p.s)
MACRINA: *Macrina* (s.d.s); *Lady | Mac<rina>* (s.p.s)
COURTIERS: *Courtiers* (s.d.s)
STROZZI: *Strozzi* (s.d.s); *Str<ozzi>* (s.p.s)
PALLANTE: *Pallante* (s.d.s); *Pall<ante>* (s.p.s)
DUKE: *the Duke* (s.d.s); *Duke* (s.d.s and s.p.s)
ARDELIA: *Ardelia* (s.d.s); *Ard<elia>* (s.p.s)
BENTIVOLIO: *Bentivolio* (s.d.s); *Ben<tivolio>* (s.p.s)
HORATIO: *Horatio* (s.d.s); *Hor<atio>* (s.p.s)
FIAMETTA: *Fiametta* (s.d.s); *Fia<metta>* (s.p.s)
LADIES: *Ladies* (s.d.s)
SERVANT: *a Servant* (s.d.s); *Servant* (s.p.s)
AURELIA: *Aurelia* (s.d.s); *Aur<elia>* (s.p.s)
SERVANT: *Servant* (s.d.s and s.p.s)
SCOLOPENDRA: *Scolopendra* (s.d.s); *Sco<lopendra>* (s.p.s)
SERVANT: *a servant* (s.d.s); *Servant* (s.p.s)
VOICES: *Some* (s.d.s)
OFFICERS: *officers | a guard* (s.d.s); *Within | Officer | 1* (s.p.s)

OTHER CHARACTERS
The people of Pavia (1.1)
The soldiers of Pavia (1.1)
Valerio's hundred former mistresses (1.1)
Bentivolio's dead father (2.1, 3.1)

SETTING
Period: sixteenth or seventeenth century
Place: Pavia (or, later, Parma)

Geography
Italy
[*Europe*]: Lapland; Crete
Africa
[*Asia*]: Turkey; Scythia; Arabia
The East Indies
The West Indies

The location is specified as Pavia in 2.1 and 3.1, but an oblique reference to Parma in 5.2 suggests that Shirley changed his mind during composition. An alternative explanation is that 'Parma' might be a misreading of 'Pauia' in copy; but since there are other inconsistencies of proper names, this seems less likely.

SOURCES
Narrative: William Shakespeare, *Hamlet* (**1259**; 5.1); Thomas Middleton, *The Revenger's Tragedy* (**1520**; 5.4)
Verbal: possibly Bible: Mark 5.9 (3.1)

Forsythe's claims for similarities with *A Wife for a Month* (**2096**) seem very overstated.

LANGUAGE
English
French: 3 words (4.1; Valerio)
Latin: 1 word (4.1; Valerio)

FORM
Metre: pentameter; some prose
Rhyme: blank verse
Prologue: 24 lines, in couplets
Act-Division: 5 acts
Epilogue: 13 lines (2 verse, 11 prose), spoken by Horatio
Lines (Spoken): 2,236 (2,144 verse, 92 prose)

This includes the text of the poem from 3.2, which does not appear in Q.

Lines (Written): 2,700

STAGING
Doors: mentioned (5.1, 5.4, s.d.)
Stage: mentioned (5.1, s.d.)
Within: speech (5.2, s.d.); noise (5.3, s.d.)
Audience: ladies are directly addressed by Horatio (5.3, implicit); addressed as 'gentlemen and ladies' (ep.)
Miscellaneous: The performance is said to last two hours (prol.). No provision is made to remove Valerio's

dead body at the end of 5.1 (and it is explicitly said to fall from behind the hangings onto the stage, so it cannot be curtained off).

MUSIC
Music: lutes (1.1, dialogue)
Songs:
  1: 1.1;
  2: 2.2, in dialogue;
  3: 4.1.
Dance: Duke and Ardelia dance (2.2, s.d.); Horatio and Fiametta dance a coranto (4.1, s.d.).

PROPS
Weapons: a pistol (5.1, s.d.); Bentivolio's sword (5.1–2, implicit); Leontio's sword (5.4, dialogue)
Clothing: a ring (5.1, dialogue; 5.3, implicit)
Money: an unspecified amount (1.1, dialogue)
Small Portable Objects: a document (3.2, implicit); a key (5.1, dialogue); another key (5.4, dialogue)
Large Portable Objects: seating for one or two characters (4.1, implicit)
Scenery: a hedge (3.1, dialogue; possibly merely imagined); arras hangings (5.1, s.d.; ep., dialogue)
Miscellaneous: blood (5.1–2, dialogue)

COSTUMES AND MAKE-UP
EUPHEMIA: black clothes (1.1, dialogue)
MACRINA: curly hair (dialogue; a veil (3.2, s.d.); taffeta patches on her face (3.3, dialogue)
PALLANTE: mean, buff-coloured clothes (1.1, dialogue)
DUKE: disguised (5.4, s.d.; removed on stage)
ARDELIA: pinioned (5.3, dialogue)
FIAMETTA: a long nose with pimples or moles on it (dialogue); a periwig (3.2, dialogue)
AURELIA: curly hair (dialogue); possibly a veil (3.2, s.d.); taffeta patches on her face (3.3, dialogue)
SCOLOPENDRA: a big nose, a hairy eyebrow (or 'monobrow') meeting above her nose, spots and yellow warts on her forehead, red cheeks, sallow lips, and a white cataract in her eye (dialogue)

EARLY STAGE HISTORY
1636: presumably performed, as licensed, no doubt by Queen Henrietta's Men at the Cockpit, to whom it was attributed in 1638.

1636: performed at St James's Palace on Monday 22 February (or possibly Thursday 25 February). The audience presumably included King Charles I and/or some other royal personage. Christopher Beeston was later paid £150 covering this, eight other Queen Henrietta's Men performances, and two performances by Beeston's Boys, by a warrant dated Wednesday 10 May 1637.

EARLY TEXTUAL HISTORY
1636: On Monday 18 January, Sir Henry Herbert licensed the text for performance.

1636–40: an extract (from 3.2) was set to music by William Lawes.

1638: entered in the Stationers' Register to Andrew Crooke and William Cooke on Tuesday 13 March; entry names author. Thomas Wykes had licensed the book for publication.

1638: Q printed by John Norton for Andrew Crooke and William Cooke; collation A², B–K⁴, 38 leaves; title page names author, acting company, and playhouse.

c. 1630s–40s: a copy of Q was in the possession of John Horne (Vicar of Headington, Oxfordshire). After his death, his entire collection of play-books passed into the possession of John Houghton of Brasenose College, Oxford (c. 1608–77), then to James Herne (died 1685), and then to the library of Ralph Sheldon (1623–84) at Weston, where it was catalogued by Anthony Wood, probably in the late 1670s. By then the copy had been bound into a single volume with 21 other plays by Shirley (and, presumably in error, with Henry Shirley's *The Martyred Soldier*, **2030**).

c. 1640: extract (from 3.2) included, with Lawes's musical setting, in a MS songbook (New York Public Library, MS Drexel 4041, fos. 88ᵛ–89ʳ).

c. 1640–1: Humphrey Moseley was selling copies of Q at 6d each.

1646: rights to James Shirley's *Poems &c.* transferred in the Stationers' Register from Francis Constable to Humphrey Moseley on Saturday 31 October.

1646: extract (from 3.2) included in Shirley's *Poems &c.*, sig. D1ʳ⁻ᵛ; printed for Humphrey Moseley.

1655: *The English Treasury of Wit and Language* entered in the Stationers' Register to Humphrey Moseley on Tuesday 16 January.

1655: two extracts (from 4.1, 5.4) included in John Cotgrave's *The English Treasury of Wit and Language*, sigs. I6ᵛ, M8ᵛ; printed for Humphrey Moseley.

1657: advertised as for sale by the Newcastle-upon-Tyne bookseller William London.

c. 1659: extract (from 3.2), with the Lawes musical setting, included in a MS music book (New York Public Library, MS Drexel 4257, no. 24, fo. 21) owned and partly compiled by John Gamble.

1684: Nicholas Cox (Manciple of St Edmund Hall, Oxford) had a copy of Q in his bookshop. It had probably been previously owned by Gerard Langbaine, and appears on a list compiled by Anthony Wood on Saturday 13 December.

EDITIONS
William Gifford, in *The Dramatic Works and Poems of James Shirley* (London, 1833), iv. 189–274.
James Shirley, *The Complete Works*, gen. eds. Eugene Giddens, Teresa Grant, and Barbara Ravelhofer (Oxford, forthcoming).

REFERENCES
Annals 1636; Bawcutt, 337, 342; Beal 2 ShJ 56–7; Bentley, v. 1107–8; Bodleian, MS Wood E. 4, art. 1, p. 2; Eyre & Rivington, i. 250, 463; Robert Stanley

Forsythe, *The Relations of Shirley's Plays to the Elizabethan Drama* (New York, 1914), 199–205; Greg 536; Hazlitt, 68; William London, *A Catalogue of the Most Vendible Books in England* (London, 1657), sig. 2F1ᵛ; *MLR* 13 (1918), 401–11; MSC 2.3, 383; *Oxford Bibliographical Society Proceedings and Papers* 2.2 (1929), 132–3; *SP* 40 (1943), 186–203; Steele, 255.

2527. Masque at Skipton Castle

EVIDENCE
Household accounts of the Earl of Cumberland (Chatsworth: Bolton MS 175, fo. 181ʳ, 183ʳ), and of the Ingram family (Leeds: West Yorkshire Archive Service, Ingram MS, TN/EA/13/23, fo. 14ᵛ).

GENRE
masque
Contemporary: masque

TITLE
Later Assigned: *First Skipton Castle Masque*

DATE
January or February 1636

ORIGINAL PRODUCTION
Earl of Cumberland's household at Skipton Castle, Yorkshire

ROLES
Six MASQUERS

MUSIC
Music: probably a drum

COSTUMES
MASQUERS: gloves; pumps

EARLY STAGE HISTORY
Preparation: Paul went to York to fetch things for the masque, and was paid 4s.6d.
Performance: at Skipton Castle, Yorkshire, the household of Francis Clifford, 4th Earl of Cumberland, in late January or early February 1636. Sir Arthur Ingram the younger was present, having travelled from Temple Newsam for the occasion.

Production Expenses
Cumberland Household: The total recorded expenses amount to £3.5s.6d (but are incomplete). The following payments were made: six pairs of gloves (8s); 36 ribbons (9s); other ribbon (14s.6d); flax and pasteboard (1s); repairs to a drum (1s); tape, nails, etc. (amount unspecified); pumps (3s; a part-payment only); gloves, ribbon, and other items supplied by Montgomery's wife (£1.4s.6d; apparently a late payment).

Private: Sir Arthur Ingram's attendance entailed expenditure of 9s.8d on a new hat and black stockings, supplied by Mr Calbert.

REFERENCES
McGee-Meagher 1634–42, 42; *MRDE* 7 (1995), 340; *RenD* 17 (1986), 154, 156; Walter Woodfill, *Musicians in English Society from Elizabeth to Charles I* (New York, 1969), 259.

2528. The Fancies

TEXT
Printed in 1638 (STC 11159), from authorial fair copy or a transcript thereof.

GENRE
comedy
Contemporary: play (prol., S.R.); poem (ded.)

TITLE
Performed: *The Fancies*
Printed: *The Fancies, Chaste and Noble*
Contemporary: possibly [*The*] *Bower of Fancies*

AUTHOR
John Ford

DATE
Limits: 1635–6
Best Guess: 1636

ORIGINAL PRODUCTION
Queen Henrietta's Men at the Cockpit

PLOT
Before the start of the action, Lord Julio was advised by his physicians that his malady could be cured by marriage to a particular woman, Flavia. He duly arranged to purchase her from her husband, Fabricio, who procured a divorce by pretending a pre-contract. Flavia's brother Romanello is outraged and refuses to see her. Flavia herself feels ashamed of the arrangement and, at her request, Julio pensions off Fabricio and sends him into exile; he goes to Bologna and becomes a Capuchin monk. The gallants Camillo and Vespucci pursue Flavia, hoping that her track record indicates a propensity to adultery, but later see the error of their ways.
Troilo Savelli procures a place at court for his friend Livio; but the price is that he must bring his sister Castamela to join the Bower of Fancies, a group of chaste young women visited by the Marquess Octavio for recreational purposes, and debarred most other company. Livio complies, breaking off Castamela's liaison with Romanello. The situation is not what it may seem, however: Octavio is impotent. Romanello

comes to court disguised as a mountebank and manages to see the Fancies. Left alone with Castamela while the Fancies have a singing lesson, Octavio asks for her love, but she refuses, and later vents her annoyance on her brother for bringing her to court. Livio decides after all to give his blessing to her marriage to Romanello.

Octavio is annoyed that scandalous rumours are in circulation concerning his relationship with the Fancies. He invites the principal characters to supper and the truth emerges: the Fancies are his nieces, and he was charged by their dead mother to supervise their education. Now that this is complete, he allows the courtiers to woo them. Romanello renounces his claim on Castamela, and she accepts Troilo's offer of marriage.

In the sub-plot, Secco the young barber, whom Octavio has married to the Fancies' ancient guardian Morosa, is persuaded by the eunuch Spadone that he has been cuckolded by Octavio's page Nitido. Troilo saves the boy from a thrashing, and Secco takes his revenge by trapping Spadone in his barber's chair. Spadone confesses that he is only pretending to be a eunuch, and that he is the one who cuckolded Secco.

SCENE DESIGNATION
prol., 1.1–3, 2.1–2, 3.1–3, 4.1–2, 5.1–3, ep. (Q has act-divisions only)

ROLES
PROLOGUE
Signor TROILO Savelli, a gentleman, Octavio's nephew and heir, cousin of Floria, Clarella, and Silvia; ultimately Castamela's fiancé
LIVIO, a young gentleman, Castamela's brother, Troilo's friend; later appointed Octavio's Chief Provisor of the Horse
OCTAVIO, Marquess of Siena, an old bachelor, uncle of Troilo and the Fancies, Floria, Carella, and Silvia; vice-gerent of the Great Duke of Florence
NITIDO, Octavio's page; said to be little
SECCO, a barber; 18 years old; later Morosa's husband
SPADONE, supposed a eunuch
ROMANELLO, a young gentleman gallant, Flavia's only brother; poses as Signor Prugniolo, a mountebank
CASTAMELA, Livio's sister; later Troilo's wife
FLORIA, a young woman, one of the Fancies; sister of Clarella and Silvia, Octavio's niece, Troilo's cousin; ultimately Troilo's fiancée
CLARELLA, a young woman, one of the Fancies; sister of Floria and Silvia, Octavio's niece, Troilo's cousin
SILVIA, a young woman, one of the Fancies; sister of Clarella and Floria, Octavio's niece, Troilo's cousin
FLAVIA, Julio's wife and Countess, Romanello's sister; formerly Fabricio's wife
CAMILLO, a gallant
VESPUCCI, a gallant
FABRICIO, a merchant and former scholar, Flavia's first husband

Lord JULIO de Varana, Count of Camerino, Flavia's second husband; also said to be an earl, and called Count Julio and Lord of Camerine
Madam MOROSA, the Mother of the Fancies (the title of her office as guardian; there is no biological affinity); over 60 years old; later Secco's wife
Romanello's SERVANT (4.2)
Six DANCERS, representing a soldier, a gentleman, a fool, a scholar, a merchant, and a clown (5.3, non-speaking)

Speaking Parts: 19

Stage Directions and Speech Prefixes
PROLOGUE: *Prologue* (heading)
TROILO: *Troylo* (s.d.s and s.p.s); *Troylo Savelli* (s.d.s)
LIVIO: *Livio* (s.d.s and s.p.s)
OCTAVIO: *Octavo | Octavio* (s.d.s); *Octa<vio>* (s.p.s)
NITIDO: *Nitido | Page* (s.d.s); *Nit<ido>* (s.p.s)
SECCO: *Secco* (s.d.s and s.p.s)
SPADONE: *Spadone* (s.d.s and s.p.s)
ROMANELLO: *Romanello* (s.d.s); *Rom<anello>* (s.p.s)
CASTAMELA: *Castamela* (s.d.s); *Chast<amela> | Cast<amela>* (s.p.s)
FLORIA: *Floria* (s.d.s); *Flo<ria>* (s.p.s)
CLARELLA: *Clarelia | Clarella* (s.d.s); *Clar<ella>* (s.p.s)
SILVIA: *Silvia* (s.d.s); *Sil<via>* (s.p.s)
FLAVIA: *Flavia* (s.d.s and s.p.s; also misprinted *Flavio*)
CAMILLO: *Camillo* (s.d.s); *Cam<illo>* (s.p.s)
VESPUCCI: *Vespuci* (s.d.s); *Vesp<uci>* (s.p.s)
FABRICIO: *Fabricio | Fabritio* (s.d.s); *Fab<ricio>* (s.p.s)
JULIO: *Julio* (s.d.s and s.p.s)
MOROSA: *Morosa* (s.d.s); *Mor<osa>* (s.p.s)
SERVANT: *a Servant* (s.d.s); *Servant* (s.p.s)

OTHER CHARACTERS
The Great Duke of Florence, overlord of Siena (1.1, 3.1, 4.2)
The Great Duke's favourites (1.1)
A man who gained a place at court by allowing the Great Duke to sleep with his wife, and who was rewarded with the supervision of the galleys and the collection of customs at Leghorn (1.1)
A man who won a place at court by panderism (1.1)
The pander's brother (1.1)
The pander's niece, a married woman (1.1)
Mont-Argentorato, a lord who slept with the niece (1.1)
The Lord of Talamone, husband of the niece (1.1)
Julio's physicians (1.1)
Livio's tailor (1.3)
Female courtiers who condescended to visit the city wives on the city's play day (2.1)
The fiddlers who play for the Fancies (2.2)
Signor Prugniolo, a mountebank impersonated by Romanello; also called Signor Mushrumpo (3.1, 5.3)
The father of Livio and Castamela (4.1, 5.1)
Romanello's mother (4.2)
Troilo's father, Octavio's brother (5.1)

Troilo's mother (5.1)
The mother of Livio and Castamela (5.1)
Octavio's dead sister, mother of the Fancies (5.2–3)
An old man, aged 112, who did penance for getting a 15-year-old wench with child (5.2; barber's news, so perhaps imaginary—though the allusion is to the ancient Englishman Old Parr)
The Capuchins of Bologna (5.3)
Spadone's mother, Troilo's wet-nurse (5.3)

SETTING
Period: sixteenth century (?); the ruler of Florence is styled the Great Duke (1569 onwards), and the play is very loosely based on events from the life of Troilo Savelli (died 1592)
Time-Scheme: 3.2 may take place at around 10.45; 5.3 takes place the night ensuing 5.1
Place: Siena

Geography
Italy: Florence; Leghorn; Talamone; Camerino; Rome; Venice; Bologna
France
Spain
The Indies
[*Asia*]: Turkey; Persia

SOURCES
Narrative: Giuseppe Biondi, *A Relation of the Most Illustrious Lord, Troilo Savelli*, tr. Tobie Matthew (1620); Terence, *Eunuchus* (Spadone); possibly James Shirley, *The Beauties* (**2396**; the Fancies)

There are also touches of specific Jacobean tragedies in the underlying scenario: Livio's provisorship of the horse draws on Bosola's elevation to the same office in *The Duchess of Malfi* (**1726**), and the link between places at court and procuring sexual irregularity recalls the plot of *Women, Beware Women* (**1981**). If identified, these hints would help to misdirect the audience about the more innocent situation in this play; but they are perhaps too numinous to warrant naming the earlier plays as sources. There does not seem to me to be any significant link between the dance in 5.3 and the second antimasque in *The Triumphs of the Prince D'Amour* (**2532**).

Verbal: *Crabbed Age* (ballad, before 1599; 4.1); 'Whoop, Do Me No Harm' (song, before 1610; 3.3); John Fletcher, *Wit without Money* (**1758**; 4.1); John Ford, *The Broken Heart* (**2281**; 2.2)

LANGUAGE
English
Latin: 6 words (3.3, 5.2; Romanello, Secco, Nitido)
Italian: 3 words (1.2, 3.1; Spadone, Nitido)

FORM
Metre: pentameter; some alexandrines
Rhyme: blank verse
Prologue: 16 lines, in couplets
Act-Division: 5 acts

Epilogue: 8 lines, in couplets, spoken in parts by Morosa, Clarella, Castamela, and Flavia
Lines (Spoken): 2,186 (1,696 verse, 490 prose)
Lines (Written): 2,633

STAGING
Doors: characters exit severally (2.2, s.d.)
Within: song and music (2.2, implicit); speech (3.3, s.d.)
Audience: addressed as 'gentlemen' (ep.)

MUSIC
Music: fiddles within (2.2, implicit); dance music (2.2, implicit); unspecified music (3.3, s.d.); masque music (5.3, implicit)
Song: 2.2, Fancies within
Other Singing: Nitido sings a line (1.2, s.d.)
Dance: Floria, Clarella, Silvia, Morosa, Secco, Spadone, Troilo, and Livio dance (2.2, s.d.); masque dance (5.3, s.d.)

PROPS
Weapons: a rod (4.1, s.d.)
Money: two ducats (1.2, dialogue); ducats (2.1, dialogue); a purse of twenty ducats (3.1, dialogue); an unspecified sum (3.1, implicit)
Food and Drink: probably a bride-cake (2.2, dialogue)
Small Portable Objects: a casting-bottle (1.2, s.d.); a letter (1.2, dialogue); a petition (2.1, dialogue); a watch (3.2, dialogue); a handkerchief (3.2, dialogue); scissors (5.2, s.d.); a comb (5.2, s.d.); a razor (5.2, s.d.); a ball of shaving soap (5.2, dialogue)
Large Portable Objects: a basin of water (5.2, s.d.); towels (5.2, s.d.); a chair (5.2, dialogue)

COSTUMES
LIVIO: fine new clothes (1.3, s.d.)
NITIDO: a garter round his neck (4.1, s.d.)
SECCO: a hat (1.2, s.d.); a girdle with a little mirror hanging from it (1.2, s.d.); an apron (5.2, s.d.)
ROMANELLO: disguised as 'a courtly mountebank' (3.3, s.d.)
JULIO: a brimmed hat (3.2, dialogue)

EARLY STAGE HISTORY
Performed by Queen Henrietta's Men at the Cockpit by 1638 (and presumably by May 1636).

EARLY TEXTUAL HISTORY
1638: entered (as *The Fancies*) to Henry Seile in the Stationers' Register on Saturday 3 February; entry names author. Thomas Wykes had licensed the book for publication.
 1638: **Q** printed by Elizabeth Purslowe for Henry Seile; collation A⁴ (A1 + a²) B–K⁴, 42 leaves; title page names playhouse and acting company, and carries author's anagrammatic Latin motto ('Fide Honor'); authorial dedication to Randal MacDonnell, 2nd Earl of Antrim; commendatory verses by Edward Greenfield.

1652: a copy of Q was bound with six other Ford quartos, with a specially printed title page: *Comedies, tragi-comedies; & tragaedies*; the book was owned by Walter Chetwynd of Ingestre, Staffordshire. The other plays were *The Lover's Melancholy* (**2259**), *The Broken Heart* (**2281**), *'Tis Pity She's a Whore* (**2329**), *Love's Sacrifice* (**2360**), *Perkin Warbeck* (**2399**), and *The Lady's Trial* (**2617**).

1655: *The English Treasury of Wit and Language* entered in the Stationers' Register to Humphrey Moseley on Tuesday 16 January.

1655: extract (from 1.3) included in John Cotgrave's *The English Treasury of Wit and Language*, sig. S3^r; printed for Humphrey Moseley.

Late seventeenth century (before 1693): six extracts (from 1.1, 1.3, 2.2, 5.1) copied into a MS miscellany (Oxford: Bodleian, MS Sancroft 29, pp. 1, 23–4, 55) compiled by William Sancroft.

1684: Nicholas Cox (Manciple of St Edmund Hall, Oxford) had a copy of Q in his bookshop. It had probably been previously owned by Gerard Langbaine, and appears on a list compiled by Anthony Wood on Saturday 13 December.

EDITION
Dominick J. Hart, The Renaissance Imagination 12 (New York and London, 1985).
Lisa Hopkins, in *The Collected Works of John Ford*, gen. ed. Brian Vickers (Oxford, 2012–), vol. v.

REFERENCES
Annals 1635; Bentley, iii. 442–4; Bodleian, MS Wood E. 4, art. 1, p. 4; Eyre & Rivington, i. 463; Greg 532; Hazlitt, 82; *SP* 40 (1943), 186–203.

2529. Claracilla

TEXT
Three early witnesses:
- **D:** printed in 1641 (Wing K452);
- **F:** printed in 1663–4 (Wing K450); a post-Catalogue revision (not described here);
- **MS:** Cambridge, Mass.: Harvard, Houghton Library, MS Thr 7; scribal copy.

GENRE
tragicomedy
Contemporary: play (S.R., 1641 comm. verses); tragicomedy (t.p.); tragic comedy (MS t.p.)

TITLE
Performed/Printed/MS: *Claracilla*
Alternative Modernizations: *Clarasilla*; *Claricilla*

AUTHOR
Thomas Killigrew

DATE
Limits: 1636–9
Best Guess: 1636

The central dating problem is that all of the direct evidence contra-indicates: the 1663–4 edition says the play was written in Rome, which is usually taken to mean during Killigrew's visit to Italy in 1636; but the licence for performance was issued in 1639, the same year the surviving MS was copied; and the title-page attribution to Queen Henrietta's Men at the Cockpit would require us to infer that it was performed before the company left that theatre at the time of the plague closure in 1636, which would mean in turn that Killigrew must have written it before he left for Italy on 15 October 1635 (or else sent it back from Rome ahead of his own return). It may also be worth registering that Killigrew based the play on the same French source he used for his other two plays of this period, *The Prisoners* (**2487**) and *The Princess* (**2538**).

The 1639 licence as good as rules out the possibility of earlier performances, though not necessarily earlier composition. Since the play was printed with *The Prisoners*, which has the same company and playhouse ascription, the information might simply have been carried over to *Claracilla* in error, especially in view of the fact that the ascriptions were printed from the same setting of type. (However, the book's general title page, set separately and printed in the same quire as the individual title page for *The Prisoners*, also makes the ascription and explicitly applies it to both plays.)

The issue is, therefore, whether the play was performed by Queen Henrietta's Men at Salisbury Court or by Beeston's Boys at the Cockpit: one or other element of the title-page ascription must be mistaken. It may be relevant that *Claracilla* does not appear in the 10 August 1639 list of the Cockpit repertory, but this could bear any of three interpretations: that the play did not belong to the Cockpit at all; that it was acquired and licensed after the compilation of the repertory list; or that there was no reason to suppose that it might be in another company's hands, and was therefore in no need of protection (or, consequently, inclusion on the list). It may also be relevant that *Claracilla*'s cast size is markedly smaller than those of *The Prisoners* or *The Princess*, and in line with what seems to have been the norm for Beeston's Boys; but any inference drawn from that would be incompatible with dating the play, or at least its earliest known version, before the company's formation in 1637.

There are two ways of reconciling the remaining evidence. The 1663–4 statement of the place of composition could refer not to the play's original writing but to the revision printed in that edition; Killigrew could have undertaken this when he was in Italy in 1647–8 or, less probably, in 1649–52 (a period he spent mainly in Venice rather than Rome). Alternatively, he might indeed have written the play in Rome in the early months of 1636, but, since in the first instance it would have been written to pass the time rather than with a view to production, he may not have released it for public performance until 1639. This would be consistent with the usual interpretation of the composition of *The Princess*. The long interim is easily, albeit only hypothetically, explained: upon his return to England, he married Cecilia Crofts, and perhaps only felt inclined to revisit his bachelor writings in the aftermath of her death on New Year's Day 1638.

ORIGINAL PRODUCTION
Queen Henrietta's Men, presumably at Salisbury Court (?), or perhaps the King and Queen's Young Company (Beeston's Boys; presumably) at the Cockpit

PLOT

Everybody loves Claracilla, the Princess, including the King's two nephews, Melintus and Philemon. Before the start of the action, Philemon was lost in battle and presumed killed, but in fact was captured by slave-trading pirates. Silvander deposed the King, Claracilla's father, and attempted to force Claracilla into a marriage; but the King mustered an army, and promised Claracilla's hand to Prince Appius in return for his help.

The action begins as the King's forces attack Silvander's house. The first to reach Claracilla is Melintus, serving in the army incognito. He kills Silvander and identifies himself to her. After the victory, Seleucus the King's favourite decides to secure a claim on the throne by wooing Claracilla, even though she rejects him when he broaches his suit. The maid Olinda reports to him that he has a secret rival, so he challenges Melintus to a duel; at Claracilla's request, Melintus refuses to fight.

Claracilla tells Appius that she loves Melintus, and he withdraws with good grace. She further asks him to arrange a night-time assignation with Melintus, and to let her father know of Seleucus' misbehaviour. Seleucus learns of these plans, fails to reach the King first, but justifies himself with a counter-accusation against Melintus. The King acts in time to prevent Claracilla eloping with Melintus, and banishes him. Melintus fights Seleucus, and seriously wounds him; but, despite the loss of blood, Seleucus' life is saved by a surgeon.

Philemon's captor, the pirate Manlius, had helped Silvander to abduct Claracilla, but then had a change of heart and made an abortive attempt to help her escape. On hearing of the King's restoration, he decides to return to Sicily in the hope of favour. He brings with him Philemon, who is evidently no ordinary slave but who has sworn not to reveal his identity until he is at liberty. On arrival, Philemon meets Melintus, who forces the pirates to free him.

Melintus sends Manlius to deliver a letter to Claracilla, proposing an elopement. Manlius shows it not only to the Princess but also her father, in order to precipitate action; as a result, Claracilla learns that Olinda is betraying her, and she and Manlius use the maid to feed the King and Seleucus information about her escape plans. Melintus arrives to take her away, but the King catches them in the act. Seleucus has other plans, however: he intends to assassinate the King, marry Claracilla, and seize power. Melintus exposes his treachery, and he kills himself. The King agrees that Melintus may marry Claracilla after all.

Most previous scholarly accounts of the narrative follow F's revised version, in which Killigrew made some much-needed clarifications; some of these, however, seem to have been alterations from the original conception, opaque though that was.

SCENE DESIGNATION

1.1–4, 2.1–6, 3.1–7, 4.1, 5.1–13 (D has act-division only)

ROLES

The KING of Rhodes, Claracilla's father, uncle of Melintus and Philemon
Prince APPIUS, Claracilla's suitor
Lord SELEUCUS, the King's favourite
ATTENDANTS on the King (1.1, 1.4, 3.3, 3.5, 3.7; two speak in 3.7)
MELINTUS, a young prince, the King's nephew, cousin of Philemon and Claracilla
TIMILLUS, Melintus' friend
JACOMO, Melintus' servant
CLARACILLA, the Princess, the King's daughter, cousin of Melintus and Philemon
OLINDA, Claracilla's maid
SILVANDER, a usurper
TITIUS, Silvander's servant
MANLIUS, a pirate, formerly Silvander's ally, then Claracilla's
TULLIUS, a pirate
DION, presumably a pirate (*non-speaking*)
PHILEMON, a young prince, the King's nephew, cousin of Melintus and Claracilla
CARILLUS, Seleucus' friend
The GUARD (3.3, *non-speaking*)
Manlius' SERVANT (4.1, *non-speaking*)
A SOLDIER pursued by Melintus (4.1)
RAVACK, a slave
A SURGEON (5.4)
ATTENDANTS on Seleucus (5.4, *non-speaking*)
A SERVANT, who keeps the door (5.4)
A PRIEST (5.13, *non-speaking*)

Speaking Parts: 20

Stage Directions and Speech Prefixes

KING: *King* (s.d.s and s.p.s); *the King* (s.d.s and d.p.)
APPIUS: *Appius* (s.d.s); *Ap<pius>* (s.p.s); *Appius a Prince* (d.p.)
SELEUCUS: *Selucus* (s.d.s); *Sel<ucus>* (s.p.s); *Seleucus, A Lord, and favourite to the King, in love with Claracilla* (d.p.)
ATTENDANTS: *Attendants* (s.d.s); *1 Attendant | 2 Attendant* (s.p.s)
MELINTUS: *Melintus | [one of] the slaves* (s.d.s); *Mel<intus>* (s.p.s); *Melintus, Lover of Claracilla [one of the] Sons to the King's brothers* (d.p.)
TIMILLUS: *Timillus* (s.d.s); *Tim<illus>* (s.p.s); *Timillus, Friend to Melintus* (d.p.)
JACOMO: *Jacomo* (s.d.s); *Ja<como>* (s.p.s)
CLARACILLA: *Claracilla* (s.d.s); *Cla<racilla>* (s.p.s); *Claracilla, The Princess* (d.p.)
OLINDA: *Olinda* (s.d.s); *Olin<da>* (s.p.s); *Olinda, A Maid* (d.p.)
SILVANDER: *Silvander* (s.d.s); *Sil<vander>* (s.p.s); *Silvander, a usurper, in love with Claracilla* (d.p.)
TITIUS: *Titius* (s.d.s); *Tit<ius>* (s.p.s)
MANLIUS: *Manlius* (s.d.s); *Man<lius>* (s.p.s); *Manlius [one of] Two Pirates disguised on Silvander's Party* (d.p.)

TULLIUS: *Tullius* (s.d.s); *Tull<ius>* (s.p.s); *Tullius* [one of] *Two Pirates disguised on Silvander's Party* (d.p.)
DION: *Dion* (s.d.s)
PHILEMON: *Philemon* | [one of] *the slaves* (s.d.s); *Phil<emon>* (s.p.s); *Philemon, Friend to Melintus* [one of the] *Sons to the King's brothers* (d.p.)
CARILLUS: *Carillus* (s.d.s); *Car<illus>* (s.p.s)
GUARD: *The Guard* (s.d.s)
SERVANT: *one* (s.d.s)
SOLDIER: *a Soldier* (s.d.s)
RAVACK: *Ravack* | [one of] *the slaves* | *Ravak* (s.d.s); *Ra<vack>* (s.p.s); *Ravack A Slave* (d.p.)
SURGEON: *Surgeon* (s.d.s and s.p.s)
ATTENDANTS: *attendants* (s.d.s)
SERVANT: *Servant* (s.d.s and s.p.s)
PRIEST: *a Priest* (s.d.s)

Based on D.

OTHER CHARACTERS
Troops of horsemen under Silvander's command (1.1)
The King's army (1.1)
Melintus' father, [the King's brother], who was apparently murdered by Silvander (1.3, 3.5)
Slaves taken by Manlius (2.1)
Thisander, killed in Silvander's coup (2.1)
A guard who arrested Manlius (2.1)
Pirates killed in battle (2.1)
Pelius, apparently the ruler of Messina (3.5)
Seleucus' servant, whom he sends to Olinda (5.4)

SETTING
Time-Scheme: 2.3–4 take place in the morning, and 3.3 on the same day; a day passes between 1.4 and 3.1; 3.5–7 take place the night after 3.1; 5.8–12 take place the night following 5.5–6
Place: Sicily

Geography
Sicily: Messina
Rhodes

SOURCES
Narrative: Jean Desmarets de Saint-Sorlin, *Ariane* (1632; English tr. 1636)
Verbal: William Shakespeare, *1 Henry IV* (**1059**; 1.4)

Killigrew probably used the French version of *Ariane*, as he had previously done for *The Prisoners* (**2487**) before the English translation was available.

LANGUAGE
English

FORM
Metre: irregular pentameter; some prose
Rhyme: blank verse
Act-Division: 5 acts
Lines (Spoken): 2,300 (2,053 verse, 247 prose)
Lines (Written): 2,557

STAGING
Doors: characters enter severally (3.7, s.d.)
Discovery Space: Philemon is probably discovered asleep (3.4, implicit)
Stage: mentioned (3.4, 5.13, s.d.)
Within: speech (1.3, 3.3, 3.7, s.d.); sound effects (4.1, s.d.)
Above: characters appear above (5.10, 5.12–13, s.d.; the maximum number to be accommodated at once is two)
Stage Posts: possibly used to represent a tree (3.5, implicit)
Miscellaneous: No provision is made to remove Silvander's dead body at the end of 1.3. Manlius and Claracilla exit at the end of 5.10 (he from the main stage and she from above), then immediately re-enter on the main stage at the start of 5.11.

MUSIC AND SOUND
Sound Effects: noise within (4.1, s.d.); knocking (5.4, s.d.)
Music: a charge (1.1–2, s.d.)
On-Stage Music: Manlius whistles (5.9, s.d.)
Singing: characters exit singing (5.13, s.d.)

PROPS
Weapons: Silvander's sword (1.3, s.d.); Melintus' sword (1.3, implicit; 1.4, 2.4, 3.7, dialogue; 4.1, s.d.); Seleucus' sword (2.4, 3.7, implicit; Seleucus' dagger (3.3, implicit; 5.13, s.d.); Tullius' sword (4.1, s.d.); Manlius' sword (4.1, implicit); a dagger (4.1, s.d.); Philemon's sword (5.13, s.d.); Ravack's sword (5.13, implicit); Appius' sword (5.13, implicit); a dagger (5.13, s.d.)
Small Portable Objects: a letter (5.3–4, s.d.)
Large Portable Objects: a rope (5.13, s.d.)
Scenery: possibly a tree (3.5, dialogue; alternatively represented by a stage post)

COSTUMES AND MAKE-UP
APPIUS: a scabbard (5.13, implicit)
MELINTUS: fair hair (dialogue); wounded and bloody (1.3, s.d.; 1.4, dialogue); a patch over his eye (1.3, implicit; 1.4, s.d.; removed and replaced on stage); a scabbard (2.3, implicit); a slave's habit (5.2, s.d.; 5.6, 5.8–9, 5.11, 5.13, implicit); a false beard (5.2, 5.6, 5.8–9, 5.11, implicit; 5.13, s.d.; removed on stage)
TIMILLUS: visibly wounded (1.4, dialogue)
SILVANDER: a scabbard (1.3, implicit)
MANLIUS and TULLIUS: scabbards (4.1, implicit)
PHILEMON: chains (2.1, dialogue; 4.1, s.d.; removed on stage); a slave's habit (5.2, s.d.; 5.6, 5.8–9, 5.11, 5.13, implicit); a scabbard (5.13, implicit)
RAVACK: a slave's habit (5.2, s.d.; 5.6, 5.8–9, 5.11, 5.13, implicit); a scabbard (5.13, implicit)

EARLY STAGE HISTORY
1639: presumably performed as licensed. The 1641 title page claims it was performed by Queen Henrietta's

Men at the Cockpit, but by 1639 they were performing at Salisbury Court. (The Cockpit company at the time was Beeston's Boys.)

EARLY TEXTUAL HISTORY

1636 (?): the play was reportedly written in Rome.

1639: Sir Henry Herbert licensed the text for performance.

1639: transcribed in **MS** in June; 41 leaves; list of roles. Thomas Killigrew wrote the title page in his own hand, dating the copy and naming himself as the author.

1640: licensed for publication, presumably by Thomas Wykes, on an unknown date before Thursday 16 July, and entered to Andrew Crooke in the Stationers' Register on Tuesday 4 August; entry names author.

1641: included in Killigrew's *Two Tragicomedies* (**¹D**), sigs. C12ʳ-F12ᵛ, 37 leaves; printed by Thomas Cotes for Andrew Crooke; list of roles. The play's individual title page names the author, acting company, and playhouse (but at least one of the latter must be wrong). The other play in the collection was *The Prisoners* (**2487**). The volume also contains commendatory verses, pertaining to both plays, by Henry Bennet, the author's nephew-in-law (in English), Robert Waring (in Latin), and William Cartwright (in Latin and English).

c. 1640s: a copy of D was in the possession of John Horne (Vicar of Headington, Oxfordshire). After his death, his entire collection of play-books passed into the possession of John Houghton of Brasenose College, Oxford (c. 1608–77), then to James Herne (died 1685), and then to the library of Ralph Sheldon (1623–84) at Weston, where it was catalogued by Anthony Wood, probably in the late 1670s.

1655: *The English Treasury of Wit and Language* entered in the Stationers' Register to Humphrey Moseley on Tuesday 16 January.

1655: four extracts (from 2.4, 3.2, 3.4, 5.8) included in John Cotgrave's *The English Treasury of Wit and Language*, sigs. B6ᵛ, L2ᵛ, L3ʳ⁻ᵛ, R6ʳ⁻ᵛ; printed for Humphrey Moseley.

1663: Killigrew's *Comedies and Tragedies* entered in the Stationers' Register to Henry Herringman on Saturday 24 October. Sir John Berkenhead had licensed the book for publication.

1663-4: included in Killigrew's *Comedies and Tragedies* (**²F**), sigs. a3ʳ-f3ᵛ, 23 leaves; printed (by Thursday 28 January 1664) by John Macock for Henry Herringman; the play has an individual title page with a dedication to Elizabeth Boyle, Viscountess Shannon, the author's sister; list of roles. The book was issued in January 1664.

1664: F reissued, probably in May, with a cancel title page.

1665: an O edition of *The Prisoners* (**2487**) and *Claracilla* was advertised as printed by John Playfere.

c. 1664-8: Killigrew marked corrections in his copy of F (now in the library of Worcester College, Oxford).

1684: Nicholas Cox (Manciple of St Edmund Hall, Oxford) had a copy of F in his bookshop. It had probably been previously owned by Gerard Langbaine, and appears on a list compiled by Anthony Wood on Saturday 13 December.

EDITION

William T. Reich, Garland Renaissance Drama (New York, 1980).

REFERENCES

Annals 1636; Bawcutt 389; Beal Online KiT 5-6; Bentley, iv. 698-700; Bodleian, MS Wood E. 4, art. 1, p. 81; Eyre & Rivington, i. 463; Greg 620; Hazlitt, 43; *MLR* 13 (1918), 401-11; *PBSA* 107 (2013), 45-6; *PMLA* 51 (1936), 129; *SP* 40 (1943), 186-203; *TLS* 2198 (18 March 1944), 144.

2530. 1 Arviragus and Philicia

TEXT

Three early witnesses:
- **B**: MS (Oxford: Bodleian, MS Eng. misc. d. 11, fos. 4ʳ-5ʳ, 39ʳ-89ʳ); presentation copy;
- **D**: printed in 1639 (STC 4627);
- **P**: MS (Petworth House, Sussex); amateur transcript.

GENRE

romance

Contemporary: play (prol., ep., S.R.)

TITLE

Performed/MS: *The First Part of Arviragus and Philicia*
Printed: *Arviragus and Philicia, The First Part*
Contemporary: *Arviragus and Philicia*; *The First Part of Arviragus*

AUTHOR

Lodowick Carlell

DATE

Limits: 1635-6
Best Guess: 1636

ORIGINAL PRODUCTION

King's Men at the Blackfriars (and perhaps also the Globe)

PLOT

Years ago, the Saxon King of Britain annexed Pictland, and agreed, as a sop to the Pictish nobility, to bring up the dispossessed Prince Arviragus as a member of his own family. Initially there was friendship between him and Prince Guimantes, but this has since been supplanted by bitter jealousy on Guimantes' part, exacerbated by the King's appointment of Arviragus to replace the incompetent Adrastus as general of the British army. Arviragus goes to war against the Danes, with the promise that his kingdom will be restored if he returns victorious. He does, but the King never meant to honour the promise. The King manipulates Guimantes' hatred by granting Arviragus a triumphal entry to the city, and asks Adrastus to arrange his assassination.

Arviragus loves the King's daughter, Philicia, but a nocturnal assignation in the royal garden does not go according to plan: while Arviragus is awaiting Philicia, Adrastus' servants attempt to murder him, and then, before the lovers have got very far, the King comes looking for his daughter, causing Arviragus to make a swift exit. When the King refuses to restore Pictland, Arviragus realizes he has no option but to raise rebellion, but is reluctant to leave the court and Philicia. At a second meeting in the garden, she avers that she loves him, but will not dishonour herself with a secret marriage. Arviragus tells her he must go into exile, but cannot bring himself to admit that he plans to lead an army against her father, so he gives her a letter to that effect.

The King appoints Guimantes to lead the army against Arviragus, but the British are beaten in battle: the soldiers are still too respectful of their former general to fight against him effectively. However, Arviragus is betrayed by his allies, Eugenius and his son Guiderius: the King offers them a marriage alliance that will place Guiderius on the Pictish throne, and appoints Eugenius general of the British army. Neither of the prospective brides is happy with the arrangement: Philicia is appalled at Guiderius' betrayal of his friend, and brings out his finer feelings with her censure; and Eugenius' daughter, Artemia, is indifferent to Guimantes and insists on a trial period as his mistress, without obligation to marry him at the end.

Eugenius leads the British army to another defeat at Arviragus' hands, and the King decides to take charge of the war himself. No longer fearing reprisals after Eugenius' disgrace, Guimantes attempts to rape Artemia, but she dissuades him with a knife. Arviragus besieges the King in his own capital city. The King sends Adrastus to consult a witch, who foretells that the British army will win the coming battle, but that the King will be murdered by Adrastus himself. At a parley, the King offers Arviragus a deal: to marry Philicia, and receive the Pictish throne as her dowry. Arviragus is tempted, but honour trumps love: he cannot accept as a dowry what is already his by right. He counter-proposes that he should marry Philicia and give back the parts of Britain that he has conquered, but the King cannot be seen to offer his daughter as the price of peace. At Philicia's suggestion, they agree on a three-day truce to think it over. Adrastus realizes that the witch's prophecy puts him under permanent suspicion, which he can only escape by fulfilling it, so he assassinates the King and contrives to put the blame on Eugenius and Arviragus' friends. Guimantes, who has been waiting impatiently for power, assumes the throne and declares that he is not bound by his father's truce: he will take revenge by attacking Arviragus.

SCENE DESIGNATION
prol., 1.1-6, 2.1-3, 3.1-6, 4.1-3, 5.1-9, ep. (D has act-division only)

ROLES
PROLOGUE
SINATUS, an old lord, Arviragus' foster-father
ADRASTUS, a lord, Cratus' brother; formerly the general of the British army
The KING of Britain; a Saxon; an old man; father of Guimantes and Philicia
Prince GUIMANTES of Britain, a young man; the King's son, Philicia's brother; later general of the British army
ATTENDANTS on the King (1.1, 1.4, 1.6, 2.1, 4.1, 5.3, 5.9; one speaks in 1.6)
Lord EUGENIUS, a married man (or widower), father of Guiderius and Artemia, Arviragus' kinsman; later general of the British army
A LORD at court (1.2)
GUIDERIUS, a young man, Eugenius' son, Artemia's brother, Arviragus' kinsman; later given the title Prince Guiderius
Prince ARVIRAGUS of Pictland, general of the British army, a young man; kinsman of Eugenius, Guiderius, and Artemia
BRITISH SOLDIERS at the triumph (1.4, *non-speaking*)
The GENERAL of the defeated Danes (1.4, *non-speaking*)
Danish PRISONERS (1.4, *non-speaking*)
PHILICIA, the Princess, the King's daughter, Guimantes' sister
Two MURDERERS, Adrastus' servants (1.5-6)
SERVANTS (1.6; one speaks)
A MESSENGER, who brings news of the Pictish rebellion (3.1)
Four or more CAPTAINS in the Pictish army under Arviragus (3.2, 3.4, 3.6, *non-speaking*)
CAPTAINS in the British army under Guimantes (3.3, 3.5; two or three speak)
SOLDIERS in the British army under Guimantes (3.3, 3.5; one or two speak)
CLEANTHUS, Arviragus' ally
A MESSENGER from Pictland (3.6)
CAPTAINS appointed by the King to follow Eugenius (4.1; one speaks)
ARTEMIA, Eugenius' daughter, Guiderius' sister, Arviragus' kinswoman
A LADY attending Philicia (4.2)
A CAPTAIN, a messenger from the British army (4.3)
A LORD, Sinatus' kinsman (5.1)
CRATUS, Adrastus' brother
A LORD, who announces Eugenius' arrival (5.3)
A LORD at court (5.3)

Three PEOPLE, who mock Eugenius, including one who claims to be a pageant-maker (5.3)
A WITCH, an old prophetess (5.4)
Two CAPTAINS, one British, the other Pictish (5.5)
A LORD at court (5.8)
ATTENDANTS on Guimantes (5.9, *non-speaking*)
LORDS at court (5.9; two or three speak)
A GUARD, who arrest Eugenius and Sinatus (5.9, *non-speaking*)
EPILOGUE

Speaking Parts: 32–41

Stage Directions and Speech Prefixes
PROLOGUE: *The Prologue* (heading)
SINATUS: *Sinatus* (D & B s.d.s, D s.p.s); *Sinat\<us\>* (B s.p.s); *Sinatus,* [one of the] *Lords, & friends to Arviragus* (D d.p.)
ADRASTUS: *Adrastus* (D & B s.d.s, D s.p.s); *Adrast\<us\>* (B s.p.s); *Adrastus, a Lord, an enemy to Arviragus* (D d.p.)
KING: *the King* (D & B s.d.s); *King* (D & B s.d.s and s.p.s); *The King, an enemy to Arviragus* (D d.p.)
GUIMANTES: *Prince* | *Guimantes* | *the Prince* (D s.d.s); *Guimanthes* (B s.d.s); *Guimanth\<es\>* (B s.p.s); *Gui\<mantes\>* (D s.p.s); *Guimantes, the Prince* (D d.p.)
ATTENDANTS: *others* | *one other* | *attendants* (D s.d.s); *&c.* (B s.d.s); *1* (D s.p.s)
EUGENIUS: *Eugenius* (D & B s.d.s, D s.p.s); *Eugen\<ius\>* (B s.p.s); *Eugenius, Cousin to Arviragus* (D d.p.)
LORD: *Lord* (D s.p.s); *Courtiers* (D d.p.)
GUIDERIUS: *Guiderius* (D & B s.d.s); *Guid\<erius\>* (D s.p.s); *Guider\<ius\>* (B s.p.s); *Guiderius, son to Eugenius* (D d.p.)
ARVIRAGUS: *Arviragus* (D & B s.d.s); *Arvi\<ragus\>* (D s.p.s); *Arvirag\<us\>* (B s.p.s); *Arviragus, in love with Philicia* (D d.p.)
BRITISH SOLDIERS: *others* (D & B s.d.s)
GENERAL: *the General* (D s.d.s); *A General* (B s.d.s)
PRISONERS: *other Captives, and Prisoners* (D s.d.s); *other captives* (B s.d.s)
PHILICIA: *Philicia* | *the Princess* (D & B s.d.s); *Philitia* (B s.d.s); *Philic\<ia\>* (B s.p.s); *Phi\<licia\>* (D s.p.s); *Philicia, daughter to the King, and in love with Arviragus* (D d.p.)
MURDERERS: *2 Murderers* (D & B s.d.s); *1 Murderer* (B s.d.s and s.p.s); *1* | *2* (D & B s.p.s); *Murderers* (D d.p.)
SERVANTS: *servants* (D s.d.s); *1* (D s.p.s); *1 Servant* (B s.p.s)
MESSENGER: *one* (D s.d.s); *a Messenger* (B s.d.s); *Messenger* (B s.p.s); *1* (D s.p.s); *Messengers* (D d.p.)
CAPTAINS: *other Captains* | *four Captains* | *others* (D s.d.s); *4 Captains* (B s.d.s); *Captains* (D d.p.)
CAPTAINS: *Captains* (D & B s.d.s and D d.p.s); *the Captain* | *a Captain* (D & B s.d.s); *one of the Prince's Captains* (D s.d.s); *Captain* (D & B s.p.s)
SOLDIERS: *Soldiers* (D & B s.d.s and D d.p.); *a Soldier* (B s.d.s); *Soldier* (D s.d.s and B s.p.s); *1 Soldier* (D s.p.s)
CLEANTHUS: *Cleantes* | *Cleanthus* (D s.d.s); *Cleanthes* (B s.d.s); *Clean\<thes\>* (B s.p.s); *Clea\<nthus\>* (D s.p.s); *Cleanthes,* [one of the] *Lords, & friends to Arviragus* (D d.p.)
MESSENGER: *a Messenger* (D & B s.d.s); *Messenger* (D & B s.p.s); *Messengers* (D d.p.)
CAPTAINS: *others* (D & B s.d.s); *Captain* (D & B s.p.s); *Captains* (D d.p.)
ARTEMIA: *Artemia* (D & B s.d.s); *Arte\<mia\>* (D & B s.p.s); *Artemia, daughter to Eugenius, in love with Guimantes* (D d.p.)
LADY: *Lady* (D & B s.d.s and s.p.s); *a lady* (B s.d.s); *Ladies* (D d.p.)
CAPTAIN: *a Captain* (D s.d.s); *Captain* (D s.p.s); *Captains* (D d.p.)
LORD: *a Lord* (D & B s.d.s); *Lord* (D & B s.p.s); *Courtiers* (D d.p.)
CRATUS: *Cratus* (D & B s.d.s); *Cra\<tus\>* (D s.p.s); *Crat\<us\>* (B s.p.s); *Cratus, Brother to Adrastus* (D d.p.)
LORD: *a Lord* (D & B s.d.s); *Lord* (D & B s.p.s); *Courtiers* (D d.p.)
LORD: *2 Lord* (D s.p.s); *Courtiers* (D d.p.)
PEOPLE: *one* | *two* (D s.d.s); *1* | *2* (B s.d.s, D & B s.p.s)
WITCH: *Witch* (D & B s.d.s and s.p.s, D d.p.)
CAPTAINS: *two Captains* (D s.d.s); *2 Captains* (B s.d.s); *1* | *2* (B s.p.s); *1 Captain* | *2 Captain* (D s.p.s); *Captains* (B s.d.s and D d.p.)
LORD: *a Lord* (D s.d.s); *Lord* (B s.d.s and D s.p.s); *Courtiers* (D d.p.)
ATTENDANTS: *others* (D s.d.s)
LORDS: *Lords* (D s.d.s); *a Lord* (D & B s.d.s); *Lord* (B s.d.s & s.p.s); *1* | *1 Lord* | *2 Lord* (D s.p.s); *1 Lord* (D & B s.p.s); *2* (B s.p.s); *Courtiers* (D d.p.)
GUARD: *a guard* (s.d.s); *Guard* (B s.d.s)
EPILOGUE: *Epilogue* (heading)

OTHER CHARACTERS
Soldiers in the British army under Adrastus, some of whom deserted, and others mutinied (1.1)
The people of Britain, the King's subjects (1.1–2, 1.4, 3.1, 5.3)
The deposed King of Pictland, Arviragus' father (1.1, 2.1, 3.1, 4.2)
The Lords of Pictland, whom the King kept docile by agreeing to bring up Arviragus as a member of his own family (1.2)
Philicia's maids and women (1.6, 2.1–2)
The Picts (2.1, 2.3)
One or two friends of Guiderius, who await Arviragus with a horse (2.3)
Pictish rebels, initially numbering 1,000 men, later 3,000 (3.1–2)
Eugenius' wife, Guiderius' mother, and presumably Artemia's (3.2, 4.1)
Pictish soldiers following Cleanthes (3.4)

Sinatus' servants (3.6)
The Pictish army under Arviragus (5.1–3, 5.6, 5.8)
Soldiers in the British army under Eugenius, many of whom were killed in battle (5.1–3)
A herald sent from the King to Arviragus (5.3)
The King's three elder brothers, presumably dead (5.4)
The British army under the King, significantly larger than the Pictish army (5.4, 5.6, 5.9)

SETTING
Period: the dark ages
Time-Scheme: a night passes between 1.4 and 1.5; 1.5–6 take place at night, and 2.1 the following day; 2.2–3 take place at night, ending near dawn; 3.6 takes place in the evening; 5.3 probably takes place the evening after 5.1
Place: Britain

Geography
Britain: Stamford; 'the chief city'; 'the second city'
Pictland
Denmark

SOURCES
Narrative: William Shakespeare, *Cymbeline* (**1623**; 2.3)
Verbal: William Shakespeare, *Cymbeline* (**1623**; the names Arviragus and Guiderius)

LANGUAGE
English

FORM
Metre: prose; some pentameter, a few alexandrines and long lines
Rhyme: couplets
Prologue: 28 lines, in couplets
Act-Division: 5 acts
Epilogue: 16 lines, in couplets
Lines (Spoken): 2,507 (78 verse, 2,429 prose)

D sets some of the prose as verse.

Lines (Written): 3,313

STAGING
Doors: characters enter at two doors (1.4, 5.6, s.d.); mentioned (1.6, s.d.); characters exit at several doors (4.1, s.d.)
Discovery Space: represents a cave (5.4, s.d.)
Stage: characters 'march half the stage' (1.4, s.d.)
Within: shout (1.4, s.d.); sound effect (1.5, s.d.)
Audience: addressed as 'gentlemen' (prol. as it appears in B); said to include women (ep.)

MUSIC AND SOUND
Sound Effects: pistol shot within (1.5, s.d.); owl shrieks (2.3, s.d.); a hideous noise (5.4, s.d.)
Music: horn (4.3, s.d.); trumpet (5.5, implicit)

PROPS
Lighting: lights (1.6, s.d.)
Pyrotechnics: fire flashes out of the cave (5.4, s.d.)
Weapons: Guimantes' sword (1.4, 3.1, dialogue; 2.1, 3.3, implicit); a pistol (1.5, dialogue; the Second Murderer's sword (1.5, dialogue); Arviragus' weapon (1.6, implicit); Guiderius' sword (1.6, dialogue); swords (2.1, implicit); Eugenius' sword (4.1, dialogue); a knife (5.3, dialogue); Cratus' sword (5.9, s.d.); Adrastus' sword (5.9, implicit)
Clothing: a bracelet (2.3, dialogue); a seal-ring (2.3, dialogue); another ring (3.1, dialogue)
Small Portable Objects: letters (1.1, s.d.); a letter (1.3, dialogue); a key (1.6, dialogue); a letter (2.3, s.d.); letters (3.6, dialogue)
Miscellaneous: blood (1.6, 2.3, 5.9, dialogue)

COSTUMES AND MAKE-UP
SINATUS: a wound (3.6, dialogue); bound (5.9, s.d.)
ADRASTUS: gets blood on his clothes when he kills the King on stage (5.9, dialogue)
KING: grey hair (dialogue)
GUIMANTES and ATTENDANTS: scabbards (2.1, implicit)
EUGENIUS: wounds (5.3, dialogue); bound (5.9, s.d.)
GUIDERIUS: a wounded hand (1.6, dialogue)
ARVIRAGUS: a garland (1.4, s.d.; put on on stage)
ARTEMIA: 'in disorder' (5.3, s.d.)
CRATUS: a scabbard (5.9, implicit)

EARLY STAGE HISTORY
1636: presumably performed at court at some time before Tuesday 16 February (on which date the second part, **2531**, was performed).

1636: performed by the King's Men at the Cockpit in Court on Monday 18 April (Easter Monday). The audience included: King Charles I; Queen Henrietta Maria; Prince Charles; Charles Louis, Elector Palatine.

1636: performed by the King's Men at Hampton Court on Monday 26 December. The performance took place in the afternoon. The audience included: King Charles I; Queen Henrietta Maria. John Lowin and Joseph Taylor were later paid £210 for the two court performances, and nineteen others, by a warrant dated either Sunday 12 or Wednesday 15 March 1637.

Reported (in 1669) as having been in the repertory of the King's Men at the Blackfriars before 1642.

EARLY TEXTUAL HISTORY
c. 1636: transcribed in MS (**B**), 54 leaves; the prologue and epilogue were transcribed before, but the text after, the text of 2 Arviragus and Philicia (**2531**); the epilogue appears again at the end of the text.

1638: On Wednesday 26 October, Matthew Clay licensed the play (with 2 *Arviragus and Philicia*, **2531**) for publication. On the same day, the two plays were entered in the Stationers' Register to John Crooke and Richard Sergier.

1639: printed (with *2 Arviragus and Philicia*, **2531**) in **D**, sigs. A3ʳ–ˣE4ʳ, 99 pages on 54 leaves; printed by John Norton for John Crooke and Richard Sergier; list of roles (covering both parts, and printed between the two, on sig. ˣE5ʳ). The volume's overall title page names the acting company and playhouse. The compositor significantly overran his allotted space, forcing the insertion of an additional half-sheet E before the second play.

c. 1630s–40s: a copy of D was in the possession of John Horne (Vicar of Headington, Oxfordshire). After his death, his entire collection of play-books passed into the possession of John Houghton of Brasenose College, Oxford (*c.* 1608–77), then to James Herne (died 1685), and then to the library of Ralph Sheldon (1623–84) at Weston, where it was catalogued by Anthony Wood, probably in the late 1670s.

c. 1643–60 (?): transcribed (with *2 Arviragus and Philicia*, **2531**) in MS (**P**); names author. The MS may have been a gift from Lodowick Carlell to Lucy Hay, Countess of Carlisle.

1655: *The English Treasury of Wit and Language* entered in the Stationers' Register to Humphrey Moseley on Tuesday 16 January.

1655: six extracts (from 1.1–2, 3.6, 4.3, 5.3) included in John Cotgrave's *The English Treasury of Wit and Language*, sigs. G6ᵛ, H2ᵛ, L5ʳ, P2ʳ⁻ᵛ, P4ᵛ, S2ᵛ; printed for Humphrey Moseley.

1684: Nicholas Cox (Manciple of St Edmund Hall, Oxford) had a copy of D in his bookshop. It had probably been previously owned by Gerard Langbaine, and appears on a list compiled by Anthony Wood on Saturday 13 December.

REFERENCES
Adams, 75–6; *Annals* 1636; Bawcutt, 347, 353; Bentley, iii. 113–15; Bodleian, MS Wood E. 4, art. 1, p. 113b; Eyre & Rivington, i. 463; Greg 551; Hazlitt, 19; *MLR* 13 (1918), 401–11; MSC 2.3, 382; *N&Q* 200 (1955), 21–2, 204; Allardyce Nicoll, *A History of English Drama*, 4th edn (Cambridge, 1952–9), i. 354; *SP* 40 (1943), 186–203; Steele, 258, 264.

2531. *2 Arviragus and Philicia*

TEXT
Three early witnesses:
- **B**: MS (Oxford: Bodleian, MS Eng. misc. d. 11, fos. 6ʳ–38ʳ); presentation copy; includes the prologue;
- **D**: printed in 1639 (STC 4627); omits the prologue;
- **P**: MS (Petworth House, Sussex); amateur transcript.

GENRE
romance
Contemporary: romance (prol.); play (prol., S.R.)

TITLE
Performed/MS/Printed: *The Second Part of Arviragus and Philicia*
Contemporary: *The Second Part of Arviragus*

AUTHOR
Lodowick Carlell

DATE
Limits: 1635–6
Best Guess: 1636

ORIGINAL PRODUCTION
King's Men at the Blackfriars (and perhaps also the Globe)

PLOT
After his succession to the throne, Guimantes broke his father's truce with Arviragus and defeated the Picts in battle; but the victory has left his forces so depleted that he is unable to resist the Danes when they invade Britain under their Queen, Cartandes. She has vowed to make a human sacrifice of the first prisoner taken on British soil, but the matter is complicated when two are taken simultaneously: Arviragus (whom the Danes do not recognize, thinking he has been killed in battle) and Guiderius (whom Arviragus still thinks a traitor). Each nobly wants to be the one sacrificed, and Guiderius persuades Arviragus that his treachery was a temporary aberration. Eavesdropping on the discussion, Cartandes admires their courage but chooses Arviragus for slaughter—until she realizes his identity. She explains that she fell in love with him in Denmark from the report of his deeds. He accepts command of the Danish forces, on condition that he leads them as a liberator and not a conqueror, but he is not responsive to her proffered love. Suspecting that his affections are otherwise engaged, Cartandes consults Guiderius, who has fallen in love with her but will not betray his friend's confidences. Cartandes' kinsman, Oswald, worries about the possibility of her marrying Arviragus, giving him control of the kingdom.

Under pressure from Philicia and Artemia, Guimantes considers releasing Eugenius and Sinatus, held for his father's murder. Concerned that their vindication could lead the crime to be correctly attributed, Adrastus consults the witch again, but she refuses to tell his fortune. He is arrested and beheaded, and Guimantes sends Arviragus his head in an attempt to persuade him to defect from the Danes. Philicia goes to the Danish camp in male disguise and warns him not to accept: her brother cannot be trusted. They spend the night in the same room, with Arviragus chastely on the floor while Philicia has the bed, but Cartandes, annoyed by his rejection, finds them there and arrests them. Arviragus tries to convince her that Philicia is a young man, but she is not taken in and offers Philicia poison, claiming that Arviragus has asked her to drink it; Philicia refuses, and stops Cartandes from drinking it either.

Oswald, who loves Cartandes, challenges Arviragus to a duel. Cartandes sends Guiderius in Oswald's place, and they fight until Guiderius recognizes Arviragus and realizes the Queen's treachery. Cartandes, however, says it has all been a test of their love for Arviragus; so she gives her blessing to Arviragus' marriage to Philicia, and decides that, for her, the next best thing is to marry his friend, Guiderius. Meanwhile, Eugenius and Artemia escape from the besieged city and rendezvous with the Danes. Guimantes follows them in disguise, but only to ask for Artemia's hand in marriage; she softens towards him and accepts. Peace ensues.

SCENE DESIGNATION
prol., 1.1–6, 2.1–6, 3.1–5, 4.1–3, 5.1–5, ep. (D has act-division only)

ROLES
PROLOGUE
GUIMANTES, the Saxon King of Britain, Philicia's brother
ADRASTUS, a British lord
PHILICIA, the Princess, Guimantes' sister; poses as a Pictish youth, and as Agenor, Prince of Scotland
ARTEMIA, Eugenius' daughter, Guiderius' sister, Arviragus' kinswoman
OSWALD, Cartandes' kinsman
A DANISH CAPTAIN meeting Oswald (1.3)
Queen CARTANDES of Denmark, Oswald's kinswoman
LADIES and LORDS attending Cartandes; their total number is specified as two or three, but both nouns are plural (1.3; only speak collectively)
Prince ARVIRAGUS, a Pict, kinsman of Eugenius, Guiderius, and Artemia
GUIDERIUS, Eugenius' son, Artemia's brother, Arviragus' kinsman; a young man
A DANISH CAPTAIN, who captured Arviragus
ALDRED, a Danish captain
DANISH SOLDIERS (1.3; speak collectively)
ATTENDANTS on Guimantes (1.4, 4.2, 5.5, non-speaking)
A DANISH CAPTAIN (1.5–6)
A DANISH CAPTAIN, Guiderius' escort (1.6; may be the same captain who appears earlier in the scene)
A WITCH, an old prophetess (2.1)
EGLON, a devil
SPIRITS, who dance a masque (2.1, non-speaking)
Two BRITISH SOLDIERS, addressed as captains (2.1; one may be non-speaking)
A MESSENGER, Guiderius' kinsman, who brings news of Arviragus' capture (2.2)
DANISH SOLDIERS at the sacrifice (2.3; only speak collectively)
DANISH CAPTAINS at the sacrifice (2.3; one or two speak)
LIRIANA, Philicia's companion
Two DANES, Cartandes' whifflers (2.5; only one speaks)
CLEANTHUS, Arviragus' ally
EUGENIUS, a Pictish lord, father of Guiderius and Artemia, Arviragus' kinsman; later appointed Guimantes' deputy
SINATUS, a British lord and councillor; later appointed Guimantes' ambassador to Arviragus
ATTENDANTS on Cartandes (3.3, non-speaking)
A DANISH CAPTAIN (3.4)
Two COURTIERS, who mocked Eugenius in the previous play, and now flatter him (4.2)
DANISH LORDS (4.3, non-speaking)
A BRITISH LORD and captain, keeper of the west gate of the city (5.3)
EPILOGUE

Speaking Parts: 25–31

Stage Directions and Speech Prefixes
PROLOGUE: *Prologue* (B heading)
GUIMANTES: *Guimantes | the King* (D s.d.s); *Guimanthes* (D & B s.d.s); *King* (D & B s.d.s and s.p.s); *Gui<mantes>* (D s.p.s); *Guimantes, the Prince* (D d.p.)
ADRASTUS: *Adrastus* (D & B s.d.s); *Adr<astus>* (D s.p.s); *Adrast<us>* (B s.p.s); *Adrastus, a Lord, an enemy to Arviragus* (D d.p.)
PHILICIA: *Philicia | Philitia* (D & B s.d.s); *Phillicia* (B s.d.s); *Phi<licia>* (D s.p.s); *Phili<cia>* (B s.p.s); *Philicia, daughter to the King, and in love with Arviragus* (D d.p.)
ARTEMIA: *Artemia* (D & B s.d.s); *Arte<mia>* (D s.p.s); *Artem<ia>* (B s.p.s); *Artemia, daughter to Eugenius, in love with Guimantes* (D d.p.)
OSWALD: *Oswald* (D & B s.d.s); *Os<wald>* (D s.p.s); *Osw<ald>* (B s.p.s); *Oswald, a Captain, Cousin to Cartandes, in love with Cartandes* (D d.p.)
DANISH CAPTAIN: *a Danish Captain* (D & B s.d.s); *Captain* (D & B s.p.s); [one of the] *Captains* (D d.p.)
CARTANDES: *Cartandes | the Queen* (D & B s.d.s); *Cartandus* (D s.d.s); *Cartendes* (B s.d.s); *Car<tandes>* (D s.p.s); *Cart<andes>* (B s.p.s); *Cartandes, Queen of the Danes, in love with Arviragus* (D d.p.)
LADIES and LORDS: *two or three Ladies and Lords* (D s.d.s); *2 or 3 Ladies | Lords* (B s.d.s); *Ladies | Courtiers* (D d.p.)
ARVIRAGUS: *Arviragus* (D & B s.d.s); *Arvi<ragus>* (D s.p.s); *Arv<iragus>* (B s.p.s); *Arviragus, in love with Philicia* (D d.p.)
GUIDERIUS: *Guiderius* (D & B s.d.s); *Guid<erius>* (D & B s.p.s); *Guiderius, son to Eugenius* (D d.p.)
DANISH CAPTAIN: [one of] *two Captains* (D s.d.s); [one of] *2 Captains* (B s.d.s); *1 Captain* (D & B s.p.s); *Captain* (D s.p.s); [one of the] *Captains* (D d.p.)
ALDRED: [one of] *two Captains* (D s.d.s); *Aldred* (D & B s.d.s); [one of] *2 Captains* (B s.d.s); *Aldr<ed> | All<dred>* (D s.p.s); *Ald<red>* (B s.p.s); *Aldred, a Danish Captain* (D d.p.)
DANISH SOLDIERS: *Soldiers* (D & B s.d.s and D d.p.)

ATTENDANTS: *a Train* (D & B s.d.s); *others | two* (D s.d.s)
DANISH CAPTAIN: *a Captain | the same Captain* (D & B s.d.s); *Captain* (D & B s.p.s); *1 Captain* (B s.p.s); [one of the] *Captains* (D d.p.)
DANISH CAPTAIN: *a Captain* (D & B s.d.s); *Captain* (D & B s.p.s); [one of the] *Captains* (D d.p.)
WITCH: *the Witch* (D & B s.d.s); *Witch* (D & B s.p.s and D d.p.)
EGLON: *Eglon* (D & B s.d.s and D s.p.s); *Eglo<n>* (B s.p.s); *Spirits* (D d.p.)
SPIRITS: *Spirits* (D d.p.)
BRITISH SOLDIERS: *two Soldiers* (D s.d.s); *2 soldiers* (B s.d.s); *1 Soldier | Soldier* (D & B s.p.s); *Soldiers* (D d.p.)
MESSENGER: *1* (D & B s.d.s and s.p.s); *Messenger* (D d.p.)
DANISH SOLDIERS: *Soldiers* (D d.p.)
DANISH CAPTAINS: *Captains* (D d.p.)
LIRIANA: *Liriana* (D & B s.d.s); *Li<riana>* (D s.p.s); *Lir<iana>* (B s.p.s)
DANES: *two Danes* (D s.d.s); *2 Danes* (B s.d.s); *1* (D & B s.p.s)
CLEANTHUS: *Cleantes | Cleanthus* (D s.d.s); *Cleanthes* (D & B s.d.s); *Clean<thes>* (D & B s.p.s); *Cleanthes,* [one of the] *Lords, & friends to Arviragus* (D d.p.)
EUGENIUS: *Eugenius* (D s.d.s); *Ewgenius* (B s.d.s); *Ew<genius>* (B s.p.s); *Eug<enius>* (D s.p.s); *Eugenius, Cousin to Arviragus* (D d.p.)
SINATUS: *Sinatus* (D & B s.d.s); *Sinattus* (B s.d.s); *Sin<atus>* (D & B s.p.s); *Sinatus,* [one of the] *Lords, & friends to Arviragus* (D d.p.)
ATTENDANTS: *others* (D & B s.d.s)
DANISH CAPTAIN: *a Captain* (D & B s.d.s); *Captain* (D & B s.p.s); [one of the] *Captains* (D d.p.)
COURTIERS: *the two that mocked* [Eugenius] *in his disgrace* (D s.d.s); *the 2 that mock* [Eugenius] *in his disgrace* (B s.d.s); *1 | 2* (D & B s.p.s); [two of the] *Courtiers* (D d.p.)
DANISH LORDS: *Lords* (D & B s.d.s); *Courtiers* (D d.p.)
BRITISH LORD: *a Lord* (D & B s.d.s); *Lord* (D & B s.p.s); [one of the] *Courtiers* (D d.p.)
EPILOGUE: *Epilogue* (D & B heading)

OTHER CHARACTERS
The Scots and Welsh, who join Guimantes to fight the Danes (1.1)
The King of Scotland, Agenor's father (1.1, 3.5, 4.3)
The Prince of Wales (1.1, 3.5)
The former British army in the war against Arviragus (1.2, 1.4)
The dead King of Denmark, Cartandes' brother (1.3, 2.3, 2.6)
A Danish priest (1.3)
The dead King of Britain, father of Guimantes and Philicia, murdered by Adrastus (1.4, 1.6, 2.1–2, 3.1, 4.2–3, 5.1)
The Danish cavalry (1.6)
Lucifer, the Prince of devils (2.1)

A Danish sentinel taken prisoner (2.2)
The former Danish army, defeated by Arviragus (2.6)
A herald from Guimantes to Cartandes, asking safe conduct for his ambassadors (3.3)
Cartandes' council (4.1)
Agenor, Prince of Scots, impersonated by Philicia (4.3, 5.2)

SETTING
Period: the dark ages
Time-Scheme: 4.3 starts at midnight
Place: Britain

Geography
Britain: Scotland; Wales; Pictland
Denmark

SOURCES
Narrative: The play is a sequel to (or, more accurately, the second half of) *1 Arviragus and Philicia* (**2530**).
Verbal: William Shakespeare, *Cymbeline* (**1623**; the names Arviragus and Guiderius)

LANGUAGE
English

FORM
Metre: prose; some pentameter
Rhyme: couplets; a few unrhymed lines; one ABBACC stanza
Prologue: 28 lines, in couplets
Act-Division: 5 acts
Epilogue: 6 lines, in couplets
Lines (Spoken): 2,361 (92 verse, 2,269 prose)
Lines (Written): 2,405

The lengths are calculated from D, but including the prologue from B. D sets some of the prose as verse.

STAGING
Discovery Space: set with a bed (4.3, implicit)
Within: noise (5.5, s.d.)
Beneath: an altar is raised (2.3, s.d.; possibly from under the stage)
Miscellaneous: a Danish Captain exits at the end of 1.5 and immediately re-enters at the start of 1.6

MUSIC AND SOUND
Sound Effects: noise within (5.5, s.d.)
Music: loud music (1.3, s.d.); unspecified dance music (2.1, dialogue)
Dance: spirits dance a masque (2.1, s.d.)

PROPS
Lighting: a light (4.3, dialogue)
Weapons: Adrastus' weapon (2.1, implicit); a sword (2.1, dialogue; described as a warrant); a sacrificial knife (2.3, dialogue); a sword (2.3, dialogue); a dagger (5.2, s.d.); Guiderius' sword (5.5, dialogue); Arviragus' sword (5.5, implicit)

Money: a bribe (2.1, dialogue; not necessarily cash)
Food and Drink: a cup of poison (5.2, s.d.)
Small Portable Objects: a miniature picture (2.6, s.d.); two letters (3.2, s.d.; one is torn up on stage); Adrastus' severed head (3.5, s.d.)
Large Portable Objects: a seat (2.1, implicit)
Scenery: an altar (2.3, s.d.); a bed (4.3, dialogue)

COSTUMES AND MAKE-UP
GUIMANTES: disguised (5.5, implicit; removed on stage)
PHILICIA: mourning clothes (2.2, s.d.); cross-dressed as a man (2.5, s.d.; 3.5, 5.2, implicit)
ARTEMIA: mourning clothes (2.2, s.d.)
ARVIRAGUS: a wound on his head (1.3, implicit; 1.6, dialogue); bound (2.3, dialogue; unbound on stage)
GUIDERIUS: armour (5.4, implicit; 5.5, dialogue)

EARLY STAGE HISTORY
1635–6: performed by the King's Men at Blackfriars; reportedly the play was 'hugely liked of everyone'. On an unknown date between November 1635 and May 1636, the audience included Queen Henrietta Maria.

1636: performed by the King's Men at court, presumably at Whitehall Palace, on Tuesday 16 February 1636. The audience included King Charles I and Queen Henrietta Maria, who both liked it.

1636: performed by the King's Men at the Cockpit in Court on Tuesday 19 April. The audience included: King Charles I; Queen Henrietta Maria; Prince Charles; Charles Louis, Elector Palatine.

1636: performed by the King's Men at Hampton Court on Tuesday 27 December. The audience included: King Charles I; Queen Henrietta Maria. John Lowin and Joseph Taylor were later paid £210 for the April and December court performances, and nineteen others, by a warrant dated either Sunday 12 or Wednesday 15 March 1637.

The Blackfriars performance seen by the Queen was more likely to have been in 1636 than the last months of 1635, since she was then pregnant with Princess Elizabeth, though admittedly she did see a play and masque (**2522**) at Whitehall on 21 December. The child was born on 28 December, and the lying-in period would have occupied at least part of January; she was apparently out and about again by the middle of the month, since it was envisaged that she might attend the performance of **2532** scheduled for then (but eventually postponed until late February). The performance took place on the same day as the King was sitting for a portrait by van Dyck, but I have not been able to pin down the date of the sitting, nor indeed identify it among the several van Dyck portraits of Charles I executed at about this time.

EARLY TEXTUAL HISTORY
c. 1636: transcribed in MS (**B**), 33 leaves. This play was transcribed after the prologue and epilogue to, but before the text of, 1 Arviragus and Philicia (**2530**).

1638: On Wednesday 26 October, Matthew Clay licensed the play (with 1 Arviragus and Philicia, **2530**) for publication. On the same day, the two plays were entered in the Stationers' Register to John Crooke and Richard Sergier.

1639: printed (with 1 Arviragus and Philicia, **2530**) in **D**, sigs. E1^r–G12^r, 36 leaves; printed by John Norton for John Crooke and Richard Sergier; list of roles (covering both parts, and printed between the two, on sig. ^{x}E5^r). The volume's overall title page names the acting company and playhouse.

c. 1630s–40s: a copy of D was in the possession of John Horne (Vicar of Headington, Oxfordshire). After his death, his entire collection of play-books passed into the possession of John Houghton of Brasenose College, Oxford (c. 1608–77), then to James Herne (died 1685), and then to the library of Ralph Sheldon (1623–84) at Weston, where it was catalogued by Anthony Wood, probably in the late 1670s.

c. 1643–60 (?): transcribed (with 1 Arviragus and Philicia, **2530**) in MS (**P**); MS names author. The MS may have been a gift from Lodowick Carlell to Lucy Hay, Countess of Carlisle.

1655: *The English Treasury of Wit and Language* entered in the Stationers' Register to Humphrey Moseley on Tuesday 16 January.

1655: three extracts (from 1.6, 3.6) included in John Cotgrave's *The English Treasury of Wit and Language*, sigs. B1^v, H3^r, I1^r; printed for Humphrey Moseley.

1656: *The English Parnassus* entered to Evan Tyler, Thomas Johnson, and Thomas Davies in the Stationers' Register on Wednesday 24 December.

1657: extract (from 4.2) included in Joshua Poole's *The English Parnassus*, sig. 2A6^r; printed for Thomas Johnson.

1677: *The English Parnassus* reprinted by Henry Brome for Thomas Bassett and John Wright; the extract now appears on sig. 2A2^r.

1684: Nicholas Cox (Maniciple of St Edmund Hall, Oxford) had a copy of D in his bookshop. It had probably been previously owned by Gerard Langbaine, and appears on a list compiled by Anthony Wood on Saturday 13 December.

REFERENCES
Adams, 75–6; *Annals* 1636; Bawcutt, 338, 347, 354; Bentley, iii. 113–15; Bodleian, MS Wood E. 4, art. 1, p. 113b; Eyre & Rivington, i. 463, ii. 103; Greg 552; Hazlitt, 19; HMC 3, 118; *MLR* 13 (1918), 401–11; MSC 2.3, 382; *SP* 40 (1943), 186–203; Steele, 255, 258, 264.

2532. *Les Triomphes du Prince D'Amour* [The Triumphs of the Prince of Love]

TEXT
Printed in 1636 (STC 6308).

1636

2532. Les Triomphes du Prince D'Amour

GENRE
masque
Contemporary: triumphs (title); masque (t.p.); entertainment (epistle); 'mock show of royalty' (Gervase Holles)

TITLE
Performed: *Les Triomphes du Prince D'Amour*
Printed: *The Triumphs of the Prince D'Amour*

AUTHOR
William Davenant

DATE
24 February 1636

ORIGINAL PRODUCTION
Middle Temple

PLOT
The Knights of Mars have won a famous victory. Cupid declares that, no matter how strong their armour, it will not be proof against his arrows. He shoots them, and they are transformed into lovers, Knights of Venus.

The Priests of Apollo report that their deity proposes to unite himself with the forces of war and love, and call wild men out of the trees, who serve the audience a banquet. The three gods bless the Prince D'Amour with military glory, amorous passion, and prophetic wisdom.

SCENE DESIGNATION
The masque is here divided as follows:
  sc.1: first antimasque (soldiers);
  sc.2: Temple of Mars;
  sc.3: second antimasque (lovers);
  sc.4: Temple of Venus;
  sc.5: Temple of Apollo;
  sc.6: Valediction.

ROLES
INDIAN BOYS (sc.1, *non-speaking*)
Two SOLDIERS, swaggering, cowardly roarers, antimasquers (sc.1, *non-speaking*)
Two DUTCH SEA OFFICERS, a gunner and a boatswain, antimasquers (sc.1, *non-speaking*)
A CAVALIER, overgrown and debauched, an antimasquer (sc.1, *non-speaking*)
A BEGGING SOLDIER, an antimasquer (sc.1, *non-speaking*)
A SUTLER'S WIFE, an antimasquer (sc.1, *non-speaking*)
The PRIESTS OF MARS (sc.2, 5–6; sing collectively)
Eleven KNIGHTS of Mars, the masquers; later Knights of Venus (*non-speaking*)
CUPID, god of love
A SPANISH LOVER, an antimasquer (sc.3, *non-speaking*)
An ITALIAN LOVER, an antimasquer (sc.3, *non-speaking*)
A FRENCH LOVER, an antimasquer (sc.3, *non-speaking*)
A DUTCH LOVER, an antimasquer (sc.3, *non-speaking*)
An ENGLISH LOVER, an antimasquer (sc.3, *non-speaking*)
The PRIESTS OF VENUS (sc.4–6; sing collectively)
The PRIESTS OF APOLLO (sc.5–6; sing collectively)
Twelve WILD MEN (sc.5, *non-speaking*)

The five lovers in the second antimasque all address paramours, but these women are not required to move or speak, and appear to be painted in the scenery rather than embodied by performers.

Speaking Parts: 1, plus singing Priests

Doubling
One actor, Edward Smyth, appeared in both the first antimasque (sc.1) and as one of the masquers (from sc.2); he therefore had to change costume during the time taken to change the scene and perform Songs 1 and 2. (The description suggests that the pace of the action was markedly slow during this section of the performance.)

Stage Directions and Speech Prefixes
INDIAN BOYS: *Indian Boys* (s.d.s)
SOLDIERS: *swaggering Soldiers* (s.d.s)
DUTCH SEA OFFICERS: *Two Dutch Sea Officers, a Gunner and a Boatswain* (s.d.s)
CAVALIER: *An old overgrown debauched Cavalier* (s.d.s)
BEGGING SOLDIER: *A Begging Soldier* (s.d.s)
SUTLER'S WIFE: *A Sutler's wife* (s.d.s)
PRIESTS OF MARS: *the Priests of Mars | the Priests* (s.d.s); *Priests of Mars* (s.p.s)
KNIGHTS: *The Masquers* (s.d.s)
CUPID: *Cupid* (s.d.s)
SPANISH LOVER: *A grave formal Spanish Lover* (s.d.s)
ITALIAN LOVER: *A jealous Italian Lover* (s.d.s)
FRENCH LOVER: *A giddy Fantastic French Lover* (s.d.s)
DUTCH LOVER: *A dull Dutch Lover* (s.d.s)
ENGLISH LOVER: *A furious debauched English Lover* (s.d.s)
PRIESTS OF VENUS: *the Priests of Venus | the Priests* (s.d.s); *Priests of Venus* (s.p.s)
PRIESTS OF APOLLO: *The Priests of Apollo | the Priests* (s.d.s); *Priests of Apollo* (s.p.s)
WILD MEN: *twelve men* (s.d.s)

OTHER CHARACTERS
Mars, god of war (sc.2, 6)
The foe vanquished by the Knights of Mars (sc.2)
Venus, Cupid's mother (sc.2, 4)
Apollo, the prophetic sun god (sc.5)

SETTING
Geography
England
The Low Countries: Utrecht

Italy: Venice; Sicily
[*Greece*]: Delphos [i.e. Delphi]
[*Europe*]: Spain; France
The Indies

LANGUAGE
English

FORM
Lines (Spoken): 120
Lines (Written): 390

Q includes a 30-line speech by the Prince D'Amour's Master of Ceremonies to his principal guest, the Elector Palatine. Though printed as part of the text and no doubt also written by Davenant, it is not strictly speaking part of the masque proper, and is omitted from the spoken length (but is included in the written length).

STAGING
Stage: mentioned (desc.).
Above: Cupid descends in a cloud (sc.2, desc.).
Other Openings: the masquers enter from different tents (sc.2, desc.); Priests of Apollo enter from different parts of the temple (sc.5, desc.).
Audience: the Prince D'Amour in the audience is presented with a banquet (sc.5, desc.).

MUSIC
On-Stage Music: Priests of Mars play their instruments (sc.2, desc.); Priests of Venus play on their instruments (sc.4, desc.).
Songs:
  1: 'Come, shut our temple and away', sc.2, Priests of Mars, 12 lines;
  2: 'Hark, hark, the trouble of the day draws near', sc.2, Priests of Mars, 30 lines;
  3: 'Whither so gladly and so fast', sc.2, Cupid, 18 lines; *musical setting survives*;
  4: 'Unarm, unarm, no more your fights', sc.4, Priests of Venus, 20 lines;
  5: 'Make room for our god too', sc.5, Priests of Apollo, 12 lines;
  6: 'Behold how this conjunction thrives', sc.5, Priests of Apollo, 12 lines; *musical setting survives*;
  7: 'The furious steed, the fife and drum', sc.6, Priests of Mars, Venus, and Apollo, in parts, 16 lines; *musical setting survives*.
Dance: masquers dance a first entry dance (sc.2, desc.); antimasque lovers dance an entry dance (3, desc.); masquers dance a second entry dance (sc.4, desc.); *some of the dance music survives*

PROPS
Weapons: Cupid's darts (sc.2, desc.); English lover's sword (sc.3, desc.).
Musical Instruments: unspecified instruments (sc.2, 4, desc.).
Food and Drink: liquor (sc.1, desc.; drunk on stage); a charger of fruit (sc.5, desc.); a banquet (sc.5, desc.).
Small Portable Objects: a handkerchief (sc.3, desc.); twigs and flowers (sc.5, desc.; covering the fruit).
Large Portable Objects: a knapsack (sc.1, desc.); a square frame made of green boughs (sc.5, desc.); a table (sc.5, desc.).
Scenery: a proscenium with pilasters, and an oval compartment in the corniche bearing the title of the masque (desc.); a curtain (desc.); a village with red-latticed alehouses and tobacco shops, with globes and pipes for shop signs (sc.1, desc.); logs and trunks of hollow trees (sc.1, desc.); a camp of different coloured tents (sc.2, desc.; probably eleven tents); the temple of Mars, square with Doric pillars and trophies of arms on the front (sc.2, desc.); a copper statue of Mars on a pedestal (sc.2, desc.); a bright cloud (sc.2, desc.; descends with Cupid on board); a square piazza, with palaces, and courtesans in Italian and Turkish clothes looking out of windows and balconies (sc.3, desc.); a grove of cypress and myrtle trees (sc.4, desc.); the Temple of Venus, 'an eight square' with Corinthian columns (sc.4, desc.); a silver statue of Venus standing in a niche and giving an arrow to Cupid, with silvered pilasters and ornaments (sc.4, desc.); a grove of laurel trees (sc.5, desc.); the Temple of Apollo, round and transparent, with gilt columns of the order of Composita, and gilt ornaments (sc.5, desc.); a golden statue of Apollo on a round pedestal (sc.5, desc.); a prospect of landscape between the temple columns (sc.5, desc.).

COSTUMES AND MAKE-UP
INDIAN BOYS: black skin (desc.).
SOLDIERS: misshapen beards, with long whiskers 'of the stiletto cut' (desc.).
CAVALIER: is fat (desc.).
SUTLER'S WIFE: 'dress of the camp', and her head 'bound with the saddle girth instead of filleting' (sc.1, desc.).
PRIESTS OF MARS: antique crimson robes, girt at the waist and tucked up; mitres shaped like helmets, topped with poniards (2, desc.).
KNIGHTS: richly embroidered martial habits; plumed helmets with beavers (sc.2, desc.); courtlier vests than before, with adornments suggestive of lovers (sc.4, desc.).
FRENCH LOVER: 'divers notes of levity in his habit', including a fan tied to his ear with a ribbon (sc.3, desc.).
ENGLISH LOVER: a muff hung in his right ear and a lady's shoe in his left (sc.3, desc.); hangers (sc.3, implicit).
PRIESTS OF VENUS: loose white robes; coronets of flowers (sc.4, desc.).
PRIESTS OF APOLLO: carnation robes; laurel wreaths (sc.5, desc.).
WILD MEN: flesh-coloured waistcoats which make them appear naked to the waist; green leaves

covering their heads; fringed green knee-length bases (sc.5, desc.).

EARLY STAGE HISTORY
Postponement: The masque was scheduled for performance in December 1635, but postponed in order to enable the Queen to attend: she gave birth to Princess Elizabeth on Monday 28 December. On Friday 15 January, it was reported that the performance might take place the following week, if the Elector Palatine was well enough to attend.
Preparation: By Friday 19 February, the Prince D'Amour had formally invited the Elector Palatine to the masque. At that stage the performance was understood to be scheduled for the following Tuesday, 23 February.
Performance: at the Middle Temple on Wednesday 24 February 1636. The performance was originally to have taken place after supper, but the Middle Temple was persuaded by Sir John Finet (Master of Ceremonies) that, since only one room was available, it would be more convenient to serve a banquet during the masque. The stage was six feet high. The cast included: John Bramston, John Freeman, William Lisle, Philip Morgan, John Norden, Clement Spelman (Military Antimasquers); Edward Smyth (Military Antimasquer/Masquer); Thomas Bourke, Michael Hutchinson, Sir Laurence Hyde, Thomas Mansell, William Morgan, George Probert, Thomas Trenchard, Edward Turner, Thomas Way, William Wheeler (Masquers); Charles Adderly, Giles Hungerford, Richard May, John Ratcliffe, John Stepkin (Amorous Antimasquers). The music was composed by William Lawes and Henry Lawes. (Some antimasque music by John Jenkins has also been uncertainly attributed to this masque.) The scenery was made by James Corsellis. The audience included: Richard Vivian (the Prince D'Amour); Charles Louis, Elector Palatine; Prince Rupert; King Charles I; Queen Henrietta Maria; Henry Rich, 1st Earl of Holland; Lord George Goring; Mary Hamilton, Marchioness of Hamilton; Susan Feilding, Countess of Denbigh; Isabel Rich, Countess of Holland; Lady Elizabeth Feilding; Henry Jermyn; Henry Percy; Mrs Bassett (a lace-woman). Elias Ashmole was present, though it is not known whether in the cast or the audience. The English royal party were disguised as commoners.
Reportedly there were two other performances of the masque, one before and the other after the royal visit of 24 February.

Financial Aftermath
Expenditure was estimated, long after the event, at £20,000, but this is probably a great exaggeration. The Middle Temple remained out of pocket for several years as a result of the masque. Between Trinity Term 1638 and Trinity Term 1639, £2 was collected (£1 each from Gervase Holles and John Mitchell), but the account was reported to be still £12.8s in arrears (in money owing to the steward alone) on Friday 24 May 1639. A further £11 was collected in 1640–1, and £2 in 1641–2. Some of these sums may pertain to the costs of *The Triumph of Peace* (**2423**), or indeed to both masques.

EARLY TEXTUAL HISTORY
1635: The masque was reportedly written in three days.
1636: entered to Richard Meighen in the Stationers' Register on Friday 19 February; entry gives author's initials. Thomas Mansell had licensed the text for publication in his capacity as the Prince D'Amour's Master of the Revels.
1636: ¹Q printed (before Friday 25 March) by Marmaduke Parsons for Richard Meighen; collation A–C⁴, 12 leaves; title page refers to performance; mock-imprimatur, dated February, by Thomas Mansell; authorial epistle to the reader.
1636–45: Songs 6 and 7, with William Lawes's musical setting, included in Lawes's autograph songbook (Oxford: Bodleian, MS Mus. Sch. b. 2, fos. 41^{r-v}, 43^{r-v}).
1640–1: this was probably the 'Prince's Masque', copies of which were being sold by Humphrey Moseley for 6d each.
1646: Meighen's rights transferred in the Stationers' Register from his widow, Mercy Meighen, to herself and Gabriel Bedell on Saturday 7 November, by order of a court held on Wednesday 21 October; masque and author individually named as part of a group transfer of nineteen titles.
Mid-seventeenth century (c. 1637–62): Song 3 (headed 'Cupid, to the Knights Templars in a Masque at the Middle Temple') included with Henry Lawes's musical setting in his autograph MS songbook (London: British Library, Add. MS 53723, fo. 42^r).
Seventeenth century: dance music by William Lawes included, in a three-part setting, in a set of MS musical part-books (Oxford: Christ Church, MS 379–81, no. 28).
c. 1650s: Song 6 included, with William Lawes's musical setting, in a set of MS songbooks compiled by Edward Lowe, of which two, both for treble parts, survive (Oxford: Bodleian, MS Mus. d. 238, pp. 189–8; Edinburgh University Library MS Dc. 1 69, fos. 105–104^v).
1653–6: advertised as for sale by Mercy Meighen, Gabriel Bedell, and Thomas Collins.
1655: William Lawes's dance music (headed 'Temple Masque') included in John Playford's *Court Airs*, sig. D1^r (item 67); printed for John Playford.
1657: advertised as for sale by the Newcastle-upon-Tyne bookseller William London.
1662: William Lawes's dance music (headed 'Temple Masque') included in John Playford's *Courtly Masquing Airs*, sig. G3^r (item 19); printed by William Godbid for John Playford.

c. 1665: Song 3 included, with a musical setting by John Wilson, in a MS songbook compiled by John Playford (Paris: Bibliothèque Nationale, Conservatoire MS Réserve 2489, fo. 21).

1669: Song 3 (entitled 'Cupid's Alarm') included, with Henry Lawes's setting, in John Playford's *Select Airs and Dialogues*, sig. L2^r; printed by William Godbid for John Playford.

1672: William Davenant's *Works* entered to Henry Herringman in the Stationers' Register on Thursday 31 October. Roger L'Estrange had licensed the book for the press. On Monday 18 November, it was advertised for sale by Henry Herringman, John Martin, John Starkey, and Robert Horne; however, it was apparently not issued until the following year.

1673: included in William Davenant's *Works* (^{2}F), sigs. 3D3^r–3E2^v; 4 leaves; printed by Thomas Newcomb for Henry Herringman.

1675: Davenant's *Works* advertised as for sale by John Starkey.

Late seventeenth century (before 1695): a copy of Q was owned by the antiquarian Anthony Wood.

EDITIONS

Murray Lefkowitz, in *Trois Masques a la Cour de Charles Ier D'Angleterre* (Paris, 1970), 111–69.

Sabol, nos. 45–7, 234, 416; see also 230, 235 (songs and music only).

Alan H. Nelson and John R. Elliott, jun., in REED: Inns of Court (Cambridge, 2010), 613–23.

REFERENCES

Annals 1636; Bawcutt 340; Beal DaW 111–16; Bentley, iii. 218–20; Butler, 321–6, 374; *ELR* 13 (1983), 326–32; Greg 502; Hazlitt, 237; HMC Various, vii. 411; C. H. Josten (ed.), *Elias Ashmole* (Oxford, 1966), ii. 318; Nicolas K. Kiessling, *The Library of Anthony Wood* (Oxford, 2002) 2171; William London, *A Catalogue of the Most Vendible Books in England* (London, 1657), sig. 2F1^v; Loomie, 196–7; McGee-Meagher 1634–42, 43–9; *MLR*, 20 (1925), 205; *MRDE* 7 (1995), 344–6; MSC 15, 186–8; *Oxford Bibliographical Society Proceedings and Papers* 2.2 (1929), 132–3; REED: Inns of Court, 342–3, 353, 355, 360, 362, 707–12, 740; REED: Lincolnshire, 364; Reyher, 531; Steele, 256; *Theatre Survey* 20 (1979), 22.

2533. *Corona Minervae* [The Crown of Minerva]

TEXT
Printed in 1636 (STC 15100 and 16781); there appears to be a brief lacuna before the song.

GENRE
entertainment

Contemporary: masque (t.p.)

TITLE
Performed: *Corona Minervae*
Printed: *Corona Minervae, or A Masque presented before Prince Charles, His Highness the Duke of York his Brother, and the Lady Mary his Sister*

AUTHOR
The entertainment is usually ascribed to Francis Kynaston, the founder and Regent of the Museum Minervae. I have seen no evidence that he actually wrote it, though he was obviously the person with ultimate responsibility for the event; such people typically, though not invariably, hired authors to do their writing for them.

DATE
27 February 1636

ORIGINAL PRODUCTION
Museum Minervae, Covent Garden

PLOT
The royal children are visiting the Temple of Minerva. On arrival, they are greeted by Minerva herself, who is pleased to see them because she rarely encounters even metaphorical treasure. Time assures her that the current climate is better than it has ever been, and introduces the seasons, who are also keen to see the visitors. But they are also quarrelsome, and dispute their precedence: Spring insists that she is the beginning of all things, Summer that he sees them ripened and perfected, Autumn that he gathers the fruits of the process; Winter argues that they only take from the earth, wearing it out, whereas he undertakes the essential task of regeneration. At Time's request, they all send representatives to dance, then present the children with gifts of fruit and flowers.

Minerva presents Prince Charles with the crown of learning, and Time describes its history from its origins in ancient Athens onwards. After a dance of the four nations subject to the British crown, the children are taken into the Chamber of Arts, where a library and a banquet awaits them. Each book contains food: there are sweetmeats in Suetonius, apples in Apuleius, oranges in Origen, jellies in Aulus Gellius, and so on. Finally, Minerva tells the Prince she is sorry he is leaving, and asks him to bestow a smile.

SCENE DESIGNATION
sc.1–4 (Q undivided), as follows:
  sc.1: Minerva, Time;
  sc.2: Time, Seasons;
  sc.3: Temple of Minerva;
  sc.4: banquet.

ROLES
MINERVA, maiden goddess of wisdom; also called Pallas

1636

TIME, an old man
WINTER, an old man
SPRING, a girl
SUMMER, a male figure
AUTUMN, a male figure; also called Autumnus
A dancing FROG, Spring's attendant (sc.2, *non-speaking*)
A dancing FISHERMAN, Spring's attendant (sc.2, *non-speaking*)
A dancing SHEEP-SHEARER, Summer's attendant (sc.2, *non-speaking*)
A dancing RAM, Summer's attendant (sc.2, *non-speaking*)
A dancing though DRUNKEN BUTCHER, Autumn's attendant (sc.2, *non-speaking*)
A dancing PIG, Autumn's attendant (sc.2, *non-speaking*)
A dancing CHIMNEY-SWEEPER, Winter's attendant (sc.2, *non-speaking*)
A dancing CAT, Winter's attendant (sc.2, *non-speaking*)
A CUPID, who presents the crown (sc.3, *non-speaking*)
DANCERS, representing the nations of England, Scotland, France, and Ireland (sc.3, *non-speaking*)

Speaking Parts: 6
Allegorical Roles: 5

Stage Directions and Speech Prefixes
MINERVA: *Minerva* (s.d.s and s.p.s)
TIME: *Time* (s.d.s and s.p.s)
WINTER: *Winter* (s.d.s and s.p.s)
SPRING: *Spring* (s.d.s and s.p.s)
SUMMER: *Summer* (s.d.s and s.p.s)
AUTUMN: *Autumn* (s.d.s and s.p.s)
FROG: *a Frog* (s.d.s)
FISHERMAN: *a Fisherman* (s.d.s)
SHEEP-SHEARER: *a Sheep-shearer* (s.d.s)
RAM: *a Ram* (s.d.s)
DRUNKEN BUTCHER: *a Drunken Butcher* (s.d.s)
PIG: *a Pig* (s.d.s)
CHIMNEY-SWEEPER: *a Chimney-sweeper* (s.d.s)
CAT: *a Cat* (s.d.s)
CUPID: *a Cupid* (s.d.s)
DANCERS: *the Dancers* (s.d.s)

OTHER CHARACTERS
Jove, Minerva's father (sc.1)
Truth, Time's daughter (sc.1)
The nine Muses—of whom Clio, Urania, Thalia, Erato, Euterpe, and Melpomene are named—who send gifts of wine from their various Greek springs (sc.4)
Bacchus, Minerva's bottle-man, who brings the wine (sc.4)

SETTING
Geography
Britain: England; Scotland; Ireland
Greece: Candy; Athens; Helicon; Eridanus [apparently not here the Po in Italy]; Ionia; Thespis; Hippocrene; Aganippe
[Europe]: Florence; France; Rotterdam

Panchaia
India

SOURCES
Verbal: Hippocrates, *Epistles* 2 (notes; letter from Paetus to Artaxerxes)
Works Mentioned: Plato, unspecified work (sc.4); Quintus Curtius Rufus, *Historiae Alexandri Magni* (sc.4); Suetonius, *Twelve Caesars* (sc.4); Florus, *Epitome* (sc.4); Apuleius, *The Golden Ass* (sc.4); Aulus Gellius, *Attic Nights* (sc.4); *Disticha Catonis* (sc.4); Origen, unspecified work (sc.4); Joannes Damascenus, unspecified medical work (eighth century; sc.4); Roger Bacon, *Works* (thirteenth century; sc.4); Hermolaus Barbarus, unspecified work (fifteenth century; sc.4); Sir Thomas Littleton, *Les Tenures* (1481; sc.4); Desiderius Erasmus, unspecified work (sixteenth century; sc.4); Hieronymus Cardanus, *Works* (sixteenth century; sc.4); Levinus Lemnius, *De occultis naturae miraculis* (1559; sc.4); Sir Edward Coke, *Institutes* (1628; sc.4)

LANGUAGE
English
Latin: 4 words (sc.2, 4; Winter, Minerva)

FORM
Metre: pentameter
Rhyme: couplets
Lines (Spoken): 456
Lines (Written): 684

The verses in the frontispieces of the books in sc.4 are not written to be spoken aloud (which is not to say that the recipients did not read them out); they amount to 58 lines.

STAGING
Above: a Cupid descends (sc.3, desc.).
Audience: the royal children are directly addressed (sc.1), and receive food (sc.4); the Prince is directly addressed (sc.3–4), and receives a crown (sc.4)

MUSIC AND SOUND
Sound Effects: differentiated birdsong and noise of animals (sc.2, desc.), including wren, robin, nightingale, cuckoo, owl, lamb, crow, fawn, swallow, thrush, boar-pig, and cow (dialogue)
Music: dance music (sc.2–3, desc.)
Song: 'Those flowers your infancy did crown', sc.2, Spring, Summer, Autumn, Winter, in parts, 94 lines
Dance: the Seasons' eight attendants dance (sc.2, desc.); dance of the four nations (sc.3, desc.)

PROPS
Lighting: a light (sc.3, desc.); candles in candle-holders resembling little angels (sc.4, desc.; designed to hang in the air without discernible support)
Weapons: a pruning knife (sc.2, desc.)
Clothing: a crown (sc.3, desc.)

Food and Drink: mulberries, raspberries, apricots, pears, damsons, figs, peaches, a gourd, melocotons, and nectarines (sc.2, dialogue); nine glass amphoras, each containing a different type of wine (sc.4, desc.); a banquet, including sweetmeats, jellies, collops of fried bacon, biscuit cakes, sugar plates, raspberries, damsons, candied lemons, quinces, apples, oranges, flowers de luce, served in at least sixteen artificial books (sc.4, desc.).

Large Portable Objects: Spring's basket (sc.2, desc.), containing primroses, eglantines, pinks, violets, cherries, dew-berries, grass, musk-roses, and fennel (dialogue); Summer's basket (sc.2, desc.), containing elm, sycamore, bay, lilies, damask roses, jessamine, rosemary, thistledown, and lavender (dialogue); Autumn's basket (sc.2, desc.), containing hyacinth, narcissus, and various fruits (dialogue; see also under **Food and Drink**); Winter's basket (sc.2, desc.), containing myrtle, savory, sage, sempervive, laurel, arbutus, palms, and olives (dialogue).

Scenery: a curtain (sc.1, desc.; drawn to reveal the first scene); a frontispiece with two Corinthian niches containing brass statues of Mars and Mercury, supporting two returns of a broken arch and a stone in between with an image of Minerva sitting on it, and underneath a prospective of a paved gallery with Doric columns on either side (sc.1, desc.; this appears to be a flat which 'flies away'); a square title board (sc.1, desc.); the Temple of Minerva, with a gate, supported with Doric columns, standing in an arbour (sc.3, desc.); a Greek altar (sc.3, desc.).

Since the performance took place in February, the various out-of-season fruits (being edible) must have been preserved, or else simulacra modelled in sugar or some other comestible substance.

COSTUMES

TIME: a parti-coloured robe, half white and half black, fringed with silver; one swan's wing and one bat's wing (sc.1–4, desc.).
WINTER: a long frieze gown; hair and beard made of icicles; a garland of holly and ivy (sc.2, desc.).
SPRING: a green taffeta habit fringed with silver and figured with flowers; a chaplet of different flowers (sc.2, desc.).
SUMMER: a straw-coloured taffeta robe; a garland of cornflowers and blue bottles (sc.2, desc.; alternatively, bluebottles).
AUTUMN: a puke-coloured [i.e. dark brown] garment; a chaplet of grapes and damsons (sc.2, desc.).
PIG: a tail (sc.2, desc.; long enough for the butcher to hold him by it).

EARLY STAGE HISTORY
1636: performed at the Museum Minervae, Bedford Street, Covent Garden, on Saturday 27 February. The audience included: Prince Charles; Prince James, Duke of York; Princess Mary.

EARLY TEXTUAL HISTORY
1636: Q printed (before Friday 25 March) for William Sheares; collation A–C⁴ D², 14 leaves; title page refers to performance occasion.
1636: Q reissued with an additional leaf, containing an address to the reader, inserted after A1, making a 15-leaf book.
1636 (?): An apparently authorial hand made MS corrections in a copy of the reissued Q (now in the Victoria and Albert Museum, Dyce Collection).

REFERENCES
Annals 1636; Bentley, iv. 717; Butler, 375; Greg 503; Hazlitt, 50; McGee-Meagher 1634–42, 49–51; Steele, 257.

2534. Play of a Jealous Lover

TEXT
Only fragments survive, in ten substantive early exemplars:
B: MS (London: British Library, MS Sloane 739, fos. 100ᵛ–101ʳ); the 'Berengarius MS'; Songs 1–2;
C: MS (London: British Library, MS Harley 6917, fos. 21ᵛ–24ʳ); the 'Calfe MS'; songs;
D: MS (London: Victoria and Albert Museum, Dyce Collection, Cat. No. 4; pressmark 25.F.37, pp. 441–5); Songs C1–4;
F: MS (Washington: Folger, MS V. b. 209, pp. 50–1); Song C1;
H: MS (Nottingham: Nottinghamshire Record Office, HU/3, pp. 231–235 rev.); Songs C1–4;
M: MS (Oxford: Bodleian, MS Malone 13, pp. 67–70); Songs C1–4;
O: printed in 1640 (STC 4620); songs;
R: MS (Philadelphia: Rosenbach Foundation, MS 1083/17, fos. 81–84); the 'Carey MS'; songs;
V: MS (Vienna: Österreich Nationalbibliotek, MS 14090, fos. 232–234ᵛ); Songs C1–4;
W: MS (Oxford: Bodleian, MS Don. b. 9, fos. 4–6, 26ᵛ, 31ᵛ–32ᵛ); the 'Wyburd MS'; prologue, songs, and epilogue.

GENRE
Contemporary: play (O)

AUTHOR
Thomas Carew

DATE
Limits: 1630–8
Best Guess: 1636

The only firm evidence about the play's date is Thomas Killigrew's 1651 statement, explaining his appropriation of Song 1 in *Cicilia and Clorinda* (1649–50), that it was written by Carew at his request in response to a quarrel with his future wife, Cecilia

Crofts, at which Carew was present; this implies that it was originally a separate, independent poem which was later incorporated into a larger work, which he says was a masque performed at Whitehall in 1633. The original writing of the song must therefore have antedated Killigrew's marriage in 1636, and probably also antedated 1633. It is likely, moreover, that the originating incident postdated not only Carew's appointment at court in 1628 but also Killigrew's (probably some time in the early 1630s, and certainly by July 1632); this is marginally less secure, in that Carew already had links with the Crofts family before he came to court, so we cannot entirely rule out the possibility that there was an adolescent spat between Thomas and Cecilia in the third quarter of the 1620s. However, the poem does not appear in, and may therefore be later than, the 'Gower MS' collection of Carew's poems, which seems to date from c. 1631. In any event, Killigrew evidently believed that the dramatic work in which Carew reused the song was performed at court in 1633.

However, it probably wasn't. Killigrew is certainly mistaken on one point: the larger work was a play, not a masque. The old-style year Killigrew gave did indeed see the performance of a court masque by Carew, *Coelum Britannicum* (**2428**); the year therefore has no necessary relevance to the play in question. Moreover, attractive as it might be to suppose that Carew got the masque commission on the back of a successful private performance, 1633 is an implausible best guess for an otherwise unknown court play seen by both the Queen and the King: court theatre in the early months of the year was dominated by the Queen's productions (**2395** and **2398**), the King left for Edinburgh in May, and the Queen's pregnancy cut her out of playgoing until November, after which Sir Henry Herbert's office-book supplies an uncommonly full list of what plays the royal couple saw that winter, with none of them being Carew's.

What we can say is that, although Killigrew's information is wrong, it must have been plausible in the light of everything else he knew (and we do not) about his life; it follows that the quarrel and the writing of the song was during an early phase of his courtship of Cecilia, before 1633. However, the writing and performance of the play, a matter of less personal significance to Killigrew, might have taken place at any subsequent time before Carew's death, including the periods Killigrew was away from court on his Continental travels.

There are various ways of possibly narrowing this down, none of them conclusive, using what we know of the author's life and the circumstances of the performance. If Carew had written a play by 1630, one might expect the fact to have been mentioned in the course of his controversy with Philip Massinger over popular taste in plays; it also seems likelier that he would have done so during the 1630s heyday of courtier drama. At the other end, he more probably wrote the play before he contracted syphilis in 1638, rather than in the final, penitential phase of his life. This leaves us with marginally narrower limits of 1630–8 rather than 1628–40, along with a preference for a date in or after 1632 but not in 1633.

According to the MS heading, the performance took place in the hall at Whitehall, as part of an entertainment laid on by the Lord Chamberlain, the Earl of Pembroke. No evidence of such an occasion has come to light, though there is a comparable example, also under Pembroke's auspices, in the 1640 court premiere of *Cleodora, Queen of Aragon* (**2738**). The Chamber Account's apparelling records give no instances of the preparation of the hall for such an event in the period 1632–6; the records are not extant for 1636–42. Performance at Whitehall tends to suggest a time other than the plague period of 1636–7. The private entertainment of the court by a senior courtier might support assignment to the winter of 1635–6, when there was no masque, but when there may have been a stage set up in the hall, left over from the performance of *Florimène* and the ensuing masque (**2522**) on 21 December. At that time, Killigrew was out of England; hearsay might, indeed, account for his error in attributing the song to a masque. However, the Queen's pregnancy and subsequent lying-in would probably rule out any performance at or soon after that Christmas; she was playgoing again by 16 February 1636, when she saw 2 *Arviragus and Philicia* (**2531**).

ORIGINAL PRODUCTION
Earl of Pembroke's household at Whitehall Palace

PLOT
Early in the action, a man becomes irrationally jealous of a woman whom he loves. She is innocent of any wrongdoing, and maintains her virtue in spite of his vindictive malice. In the middle section, the lovers are separated, but it becomes clear that their love cannot be transferred to anyone else.

The other surviving songs relate to two particular incidents in the play. In one, a lover, cross-dressed as an Amazon, encounters his mistress, but is disconcerted to find that she is sexually attracted to his feminine alter-ego; thus, he has both the physical pleasures of love and the pains of jealousy, exacerbated by the knowledge that he is his own rival. In the other incident, a lady is rescued from death by a knight, and falls in love with him; but he immediately leaves her.

ROLES
PROLOGUE
A LOVER; disguises himself as an Amazon
The lover's MISTRESS
A LADY, perhaps a princess
A KNIGHT, a young man
CHORUS, in some cases two voices in dialogue
EPILOGUE

Speaking Parts: at least 6

Stage Directions and Speech Prefixes
PROLOGUE: *The prologue* (heading)
LOVER: *A Lover* (heading)
MISTRESS: [the Lover's] *Mistress* (heading)
LADY: *A Lady* (heading)
KNIGHT: *a Knight* (heading)
CHORUS: *Question | Answer* (s.p.s)
EPILOGUE: *The Epilogue* (heading)

SOURCES
Narrative: perhaps Sir Philip Sidney, *Arcadia* (written c. 1580, printed 1590, repr. 1633; Amazon incident)

LANGUAGE
English

FORM
Prologue: 22 lines, in couplets

Chorus: four songs, presumably separating the acts
Act-Division: 5 acts (presumably)
Epilogue: 36 lines, in couplets
Lines (Spoken): 205
Lines (Written): 162 (O, which lacks the prologue and epilogue)

MUSIC
Songs:
  C1: 'From whence was first this Fury hurled', Cho.1, two voices in parts, 42 lines;
  C2: 'In what esteem did the gods hold', Cho.2, 24 lines;
  C3: 'Stop the chafèd boar, or play', Cho.3, 24 lines;
  C4: 'By what power was love confined', Cho.4, two voices in parts, 21 lines;
  1: 'Cease, thou afflicted soul, to mourn', Lover, 18 lines;
  2: 'O whither is my fair sun fled', Lady, 18 lines.

It is not possible to number the six songs sequentially in their original order in the play. Here they are assigned two separate numerical sequences, corresponding with the order of their appearance in O, and differentiating the choric songs from the narrative ones by assigning the former the letter C.

COSTUMES
LOVER: cross-dressed as an Amazon

EARLY STAGE HISTORY
1630s: performed in the great hall at Whitehall Palace. The occasion was an entertainment laid on by Philip Herbert, 4th Earl of Pembroke and 1st Earl of Montgomery (Lord Chamberlain). The audience included: King Charles I; Queen Henrietta Maria.

EARLY TEXTUAL HISTORY
c. 1638–42: songs transcribed into a MS verse miscellany (**R**). The MS was owned in c. 1642 by Horatio Carey; later owners, not necessarily all in the seventeenth century, seem to have included Thomas Arding (or Arden), William Harrington, Thomas John, John Anthehope, and Clement Poxall.
  c. late 1630s: Songs C1–4 transcribed in a MS verse miscellany (**M**).
  1640: rights to Thomas Carew's works, including poems and masques, entered to Thomas Walkley in the Stationers' Register on Monday 23 March; general entry, naming no individual work. (This was the same day as Carew's funeral.) Matthew Clay had licensed the book for publication; he reissued the imprimatur on Wednesday 29 April.
  1640: songs included in Carew's *Poems* ($^1O_1$), sigs. H2^v–H6^r; printed by John Dawson for Thomas Walkley. C1 is headed 'Of Jealousy'; C2, 'Feminine Honour'; C3, 'Separation of Lovers'; C4, 'Incommunicability of Love'. The headings of Songs 1–2 describe the dramatic situations to which they applied.
  c. 1641: songs transcribed by Peter Calfe in a MS verse miscellany (**C**).

1642: songs included in Carew's *Poems* ($^2O_2$), sigs. G4^v–G8^r; printed by John Dawson for Thomas Walkley. The copy was O$_1$.
  c. 1640s: prologue, songs, and epilogue included in a MS miscellany collection of Carew's verse (**W**); Song 1 is headed 'The Amazon's Song' and Song 2, 'The Princess Song'.
  c. 1649: Songs 1–2 (respectively headed 'A Lover in Disguise' and 'A Lady Resolved') transcribed in a MS miscellany (**B**).
  1650: Walkley's rights to Carew's *Poems* transferred in the Stationers' Register to Humphrey Moseley on Saturday 8 June; general entry, naming no individual work.
  1650–60: Carew's *Poems* advertised as for sale by Humphrey Moseley.
  1651: songs included in Carew's *Poems* ($^3O_3$), sigs. E8^v–F4^r; printed for Humphrey Moseley.
  1651: O$_3$ reissued (probably in early May) with a cancel title page naming John Martin as the bookseller.
  c. 1651: Thomas Killigrew transcribed Song C1 at the end of his MS play, *Cicilia and Clorinda* (**F**).
  1650s: Songs C1–4 transcribed into a verse miscellany by Lucy Hutchinson (**H**).
  1660: Song C1 (headed 'Of Jealousy') included in a collection of the *Poems* of William Herbert, 3rd Earl of Pembroke, and Sir Benjamin Rudyerd, sig. F3^{r-v}; printed by Matthew Inman for sale by James Magnes. The song is one of a minority of poems in the book not ascribed to either Pembroke or Rudyerd. The collection was compiled by John Donne, jun., who was supplied with most of the contents by Henry Lawes and Nicholas Lanier (who was in Germany at the time).
  1664: Song C1 included in Thomas Killigrew's *Comedies and Tragedies*, sigs. 2Q2^v–2Q3^r; printed by John Macock for Henry Herringman.
  1667: Moseley's rights to Carew's *Poems* transferred in the Stationers' Register by his widow, Ann, to Henry Herringman on Monday 19 August; group transfer of nine titles, the *Works* being one.
  c. 1667–8: Song C3 included in a MS miscellany ('Frendraught MS', pp. 4–5; privately owned in New York) owned by James Crichton, 2nd Viscount Frendraught.
  1668: O$_3$ advertised as for sale by Henry Herringman.
  1670: songs included in Carew's *Poems, Songs, and Sonnets* ($^4O_4$), sigs. F2^v–F6^r; printed for Henry Herringman. The copy was O$_3$.
  1671: O$_4$ reissued with a cancel title page naming Hobart Kemp as the bookseller.
  1679–86: O$_4$ advertised as for sale by Henry Herringman.
  c. 1690s: Songs C1–4 transcribed into a MS verse miscellany (**D**).
  c. 1690s: Songs C1–4 transcribed into a MS verse miscellany (**V**).

EDITION
Rhodes Dunlap, in *The Poems of Thomas Carew* (Oxford, 1949), 53–64, 127–8.

REFERENCES
Arber, iv. 504; Beal 2 CwT 11–14, 198, 305–7, 309–13, 436–9, 594; Beal Online CwT 313.5; Bentley, iii. 110–11; Eyre & Rivington, i. 344, ii. 380.

2535. One or Two Masques

EVIDENCE
Letter from George Garrard to Thomas, Viscount Wentworth, dated 8 January 1636; letter from Anthony Mingay to Framlingham Gawdy dated 8 March 1636.

It is sometimes suggested that Aurelian Townshend's song, 'Let soldiers fight for pay or praise', might be a surviving fragment of this masque. The only reason to suppose that is its heading identifying it as 'a bacchanal song in a masque before their majesties'; but *masque* was a fluid generic term in the 1630s, also used of *The Shepherds' Paradise* (**2395**) and *Love's Mistress* (**2451**), which were plays that received royal performances. The song is more plausibly identified as one added for the Hampton Court performance of *The Royal Slave* (**2552**), and is listed as Song α in the entry on that play.

GENRE
masque
Contemporary: masque (Garrard); 'brave masque' (Mingay)

TITLE
Later Assigned: *Lady Hatton's Masque*; *The Palatine Prince's Masques*

AUTHOR
Martin Butler (in *ELR*) proposes Henry Glapthorne as a likely librettist.

DATE
Limits: 1635–6
Best Guess: 1 March 1636

ORIGINAL PRODUCTION
Lady Elizabeth Hatton's household at Hatton House (a.k.a. Ely House), Holborn

EARLY STAGE HISTORY
Inception: Lady Elizabeth Hatton planned to entertain the King, Queen, and Palatine princes at her house on Tuesday 29 December 1635; she intended to mount two masques as part of the entertainment. However, on Monday 28 December, the Queen went into labour and the event was postponed.
  Performance: possibly at Hatton House, Holborn, on Tuesday 1 March 1636 (Shrove Tuesday). The event took place in the evening. The audience included: King Charles I; Queen Henrietta Maria; Charles Louis, Elector Palatine, and his brother, Prince Rupert; Lady Elizabeth Hatton (hostess).

There is no positive evidence that the masques planned in December were the same as the one performed at Shrovetide, but since the December visit was called off at only one day's notice, they must have already been written; so, the only reason not to show them (or at least one of them) when the royal visit did eventually take place would be if their content was season-specific.

REFERENCES
Butler, 375; *ELR* 13 (1983), 332–3; Willa McLung Evans, *Henry Lawes* (New York, 1941), 120 HMC Gawdy, 157; McGee-Meagher 1634–42, 51–2; *MRDE* 7 (1995), 345; Steele, 257; *Theatre Survey* 20 (1979), 22–3.

2536. Love's Trial

TEXT
Printed in 1640 (STC 11909).

GENRE
comedy
Contemporary: play (Herbert, ded.); comedy (S.R., t.p.)

TITLE
Performed: *Love's Trial, or The Hollander*
Printed: *The Hollander*

AUTHOR
Henry Glapthorne

DATE
March 1636

ORIGINAL PRODUCTION
Queen Henrietta's Men at the Cockpit

PLOT
Dr Artless has grown rich by taking in resident lady patients, and is concerned that his house should keep its good name. One of his current guests has a jealous husband, Sir Martin Yellow, who believes the house is really a place of assignation, and sends his nephew Popinjay there in search of evidence. Popinjay meets Artless's daughter, Dalinea, and falls in love. Meanwhile, the apothecary Mixum has sent Artless a young man, Sconce, as a potential son-in-law; Artless is unconcerned that he is a fool because he is also rich. Sconce's main preoccupation is with Mixum's weapon-salve which will cure any wound if applied to the weapon that made it. When Sir Martin wounds him in

a jealous rage, he takes away Sir Martin's sword but finds the salve ineffectual and concludes that there must be something wrong with his blood.

Another visitor to Artless's house is Freewit, a suitor to Mistress Know-worth, but she breaks up with him, having heard from Lovering, her servant, that he has slept with the servant-girl Martha and got her pregnant. When he proves reluctant to marry Martha, Mistress Know-worth gives him an alternative: she will consider his suit if he can persuade Martha to release him from his prior obligation.

Artless's servant Urinal offers to prove to Sir Martin that Lady Yellow is chaste: he is to visit his wife in her bedroom, incognito, while the rest of the household is out at Dalinea's wedding. The problem is that Dalinea doesn't want to marry Sconce, to her parents' annoyance. Sconce is interested in the order of the Knights of the Twibill, which allows its members to marry but will not admit anyone who is already married; he is duly determined to be inducted before his marriage. The ceremony requires him to drink heavily and remove his clothes; but the arrival of a constable causes the Twibills to break it off before it is finished, and Sconce is left without his clothes.

Dalinea appears to change her mind about Sconce and goes off to marry him alongside another couple. When they return, however, it emerges that there has been some confusion of identity: Dalinea has married Popinjay, dressed in Sconce's clothes (acquired by Urinal from the Twibills), while the other couple turn out to be Lovering and the drunken Sconce, cross-dressed as a woman. Lovering, moreover, is really Martha (so the marriage to Sconce is valid after all), inveigled into Mistress Know-worth's service to test her loyalty to Freewit by giving him the undeserved reputation of a philanderer; Mistress Know-worth duly asks his forgiveness. Sir Martin's plan to test his wife goes less well: instead of his own wife, he approached Mistress Mixum, giving Lady Yellow a hold over him. She agrees to forgive him his apparent adultery on condition that he promises to renounce jealousy forever.

SCENE DESIGNATION
1.1, 2.1, 3.1, 4.1–2, 5.1 (Q has act-division only)

ROLES
Doctor ARTLESS, a physician, Mistress Artless's husband, Dalinea's father; formerly a country apothecary
MISTRESS ARTLESS, Dr Artless's wife, Dalinea's mother
URINAL, Artless's servant, a young man; in reality, Tristram, Freewit's servant, Martha's brother
Master Harry POPINJAY, a gentleman, nephew of Sir Martin and Lady Yellow; poses as Sir Martin's niece; later Dalinea's husband
SIR MARTIN Yellow, a knight, Lady Yellow's jealous husband, Popinjay's uncle; poses as Popinjay's servant
LADY YELLOW, a young gentlewoman, Sir Martin's wife, Mistress Know-worth's sister, Popinjay's aunt
DALINEA, daughter of Doctor and Mistress Artless; also called Mistress Dal; later Popinjay's wife
Master Jeremy SCONCE, a wealthy, naturalized Dutchman, perhaps Fortress's kinsman; also called Signor Jeremias Sconce; later Martha's husband
Master FREEWIT, a young gentleman
Mistress KNOW-WORTH, an unmarried gentlewoman, Lady Yellow's sister
Master LOVERING, a gentleman, Mistress Know-worth's attendant; in reality, Martha, a chambermaid, Tristram's sister; later Sconce's wife
Master Thomas MIXUM, an apothecary, Mistress Mixum's husband; also called Tom
MISTRESS MIXUM, Mixum's wife
Captain Furibundo FORTRESS, general of the Twibill Knights; perhaps Sconce's kinsman
Captain PERK, Fortress's associate; also called Signor Perk; said to be little
Sir Holofernes MAKESHIFT, a knight of the Twibill
Sir Pythagoras PIG, a young knight of the Twibill
Rosiran KNOCKDOWN, a knight of the Twibill and the order's wardrobe keeper
Sir Barabbas MARK, a knight of the Twibill

Speaking Parts: 19

Stage Directions and Speech Prefixes
ARTLESS: *Doctor* (s.d.s and s.p.s); *Artlesse, a Doctor of Physic* (d.p.)
MISTRESS ARTLESS: [*Doctor's*] *Wife* (s.d.s and s.p.s); *Mistress | Mistress Artlesse* (s.d.s and s.p.s); *Mrs Art<lesse> | Mistress Art<lesse>* (s.p.s)
URINAL: *Urinall* (s.d.s); *Urin<all>* (s.p.s); *Urinal, [Artless's] man* (d.p.)
POPINJAY: *Popingaie | Popingay | Popingaies* (s.d.s); *Pop<ingay>* (s.p.s); *Popingay, [Sir Martin's] Nephew* (d.p.)
SIR MARTIN: *Sir Martine Yellow | Sir Martine* (s.d.s); *Sir Mart<ine> | Mart<ine>* (s.p.s); *Sir Martin Yellow, a jealous Knight* (d.p.)
LADY YELLOW: *Lady Yellow* (s.d.s and d.p.); [*one of*] *the Ladies | the Lady* (s.d.s); *Lady* (s.d.s and s.p.s)
DALINEA: *Dalinea* (s.d.s); *Dal<inea>* (s.p.s); *Dalinea, the Doctor's daughter* (d.p.)
SCONCE: *Sconce* (s.d.s); *Scon<ce>* (s.p.s); *Sconce, a Gallant naturalized Dutchman* (d.p.)
FREEWIT: *Freewit* (s.d.s); *Free<wit>* (s.p.s); *Freewit, a young Gentleman, and a Suitor to the Lady Know-worth* (d.p.)
KNOW-WORTH: *Mistress Know-worth | Mistress knoworth | Knoworth |* [*one of*] *the Ladies* (s.d.s); *Know<-worth>* (s.p.s); *Mistress Know-worth,* [Lady Yellow's] *sister* (d.p.)
LOVERING: *Martha, as Mr Lovering | Lovring | Lovering | Martha* (s.d.s); *Love<ring>* (s.p.s); *Lovering, a Chambermaid disguised* (d.p.)

MIXUM: *Mixum* | *Tom Mixum* (s.d.s); *Mix<um>* (s.p.s); *Mixum*, [Artless's] *Apothecary* (d.p.)
MISTRESS MIXUM: [Mixum's] *wife* | *Mrs Mixum* (s.d.s); *Mistress Mixum* (s.d.s and d.p.); *Mrs Mix<um>* (s.p.s)
FORTRESS: *Fortresse* | [one of] *the Twibill Knights* (s.d.s); *Fort<resse>* (s.p.s); *Fortresse, a Knight of the Twibill* (d.p.)
PERK: *Pirke* | *Pirk* (s.d.s and s.p.s); [one of the] *Knights* | [one of] *the Twibill Knights* (s.d.s); *Captain Picke* (d.p.; sic)
MAKESHIFT: [one of the] *Knights* | [one of] *the Twibill Knights* (s.d.s); *Make<shift>* (s.p.s)
PIG: [one of the] *Knights* | [one of] *the Twibill Knights* (s.d.s); *Pig* (s.p.s)
KNOCKDOWN: [one of the] *Knights* | [one of] *the Twibill Knights* (s.d.s); *Knocke<downe>* (s.p.s)
MARK: [one of the] *Knights* | [one of] *the Twibill Knights* (s.d.s); *Mark* (s.p.s)

OTHER CHARACTERS
Urinal's father, said to be an apothecary (1.1)
Urinal's mother (1.1)
Artless's patients, including city wives, country wives, and sailors' wives (1.1)
The local beadles (1.1)
The local justice (1.1, 5.1)
The justice's man (1.1)
Sconce's father, a Dutchman who fled to England after political difficulties at home (1.1)
Barnevelt, hanged for a conspiracy which also involved Sconce's father (1.1)
Vintners and gallants who scuppered Sconce's father's scheme to acquire a tobacco monopoly (1.1)
The Kickinpot family, Sconce's ancestors (1.1, 4.2)
Sconce's cousin-german, perhaps named Skinks Sconce (1.1; but the reference may be to the taking of Schenck's Sconce)
The enemy, who captured Schenck's Sconce (1.1)
Freewit's mother, Martha's mistress (1.1)
A Welsh doctor in London, reputedly a skilled maker of the weapon-salve (2.1, 3.1)
A city captain who reportedly possesses the weapon-salve (2.1)
An alderman's daughter who was reportedly cured of an arrow-wound (or pregnancy) by the weapon-salve (2.1)
The gentleman responsible for the daughter's condition, possibly through careless archery (2.1)
A Puritan who tried to hang himself on a church bell-rope after seeing a surplice, but was reportedly saved with the weapon-salve (2.1; probably imaginary)
Alewives whose pies and custards were spoiled by the vibrations of gunfire (2.1)
Sixty or more people who were blown up at a city muster, thirty of whom were reportedly saved by the weapon-salve (2.1; probably imaginary)
Two sergeants and their yeomen, who were reportedly saved by the weapon-salve (2.1, 3.1; probably imaginary)

The Mixums' neighbour, who has lived in Spain (2.1)
Lady Popinjay, Sir Martin's sister, Harry Popinjay's mother (2.1)
Sir Martin's other sister or sisters (2.1)
Jack Shirk, Fortress's beadle (3.1)
26 knights of the Twibill (3.1; but perhaps including Pig and Mark, who appear on stage; others may do too, but not all of them)
Donna Jesabella Garretta, a Lambeth bawd (3.1)
A bawd at the Three Squirrels (3.1)
A female ballad-singer (3.1)
The musicians attending the Twibill ceremony (4.2)
The broker who has the Twibill robes in his possession (4.2)
Fortress's father (4.2)
Constables who have come to arrest Fortress (4.2)
Artless's neighbours (5.1)

SETTING
Period: contemporary; the action takes place early in the month (3.1 on the 3rd)
Time-Scheme: 1.1 takes place in the morning; 2.1 takes place the day after 1.1; 4.1–5.1 take place the day after 3.1 (4.2 in the evening and 5.1 starting around 9 p.m.)
Place: London

Geography
London: the Bear Garden; Holland's Leaguer; Lambeth Marsh; the Three Squirrels; the New Exchange; Bridewell; Tyburn; Turnbull Street; Rotten Row; the Garden Alleys; Gun Alley; Rosemary Lane; Fleet Street Conduit; the Pinner of Wakefield tavern
[*Middlesex*]: Islington; Finsbury; Holborn; St Pancras Church; Bloomsbury
England: the Fens; Crowland; York
Britain: Wales
The Low Countries: Holland; Amsterdam; Schenck's Sconce [= Schenckenschans]; Dunkirk; Rotterdam; Friesland; Tirlemont
[*Italy*]: Naples; Rome
[*Europe*]: France; Westphalia; Lapland; Spain
Malta
[*Asia*]: Turkey; Cimmeria; Sarmatia
Africa
The Indies
The Arctic Pole

SOURCES
Narrative: Ben Jonson, *The Alchemist* (**1621**; 3.1); Shackerley Marmion, *A Fine Companion* (**2378**; the Twibills); Richard Brome, *The Weeding of the Covent Garden* (**2401**; the Twibills)
Verbal: Aesop, *Fables* (5.1); W. A., dedication appended to James Shirley's *Love's Cruelty* (**2349**; ded.); *Time's Alteration* (ballad, 1628–9; 4.2)
Works Mentioned: Bible: Luke 15.11–32 (prodigal son; 4.2); Francisco Vazquez, *Palmerin de Oliva* (1511; English tr. by Anthony Munday, 1588; 3.1); François

Rabelais, *Gargantua* (1534; 4.2); *Mercurius Gallo-Belgicus* (newsbook; from 1588; 3.1); Statute of Bigamy (1603; 1 James I c. 11; 5.1); *Tom Thumb* (1621; 3.1)

LANGUAGE
English
Latin: 29 words (1.1, 2.1, 3.1, 4.1–2; Mistress Artless, Urinal, Artless, Sconce, Mixum, Fortress)
French: 184 words (1.1, 2.1, 3.1, 4.1–2; Sconce, Lady Yellow, Fortress, Mark)
Italian: 1 word (4.1; Sconce)
Dutch: 5 words (2.1, 4.1, 5.1; Sconce, Artless)
Welsh: 3 words (2.1; Urinal)
Dialect: Sconce speaks intermittently in 'Dutch' accented English.

FORM
Metre: prose and pentameter
Rhyme: blank verse
Act-Division: 5 acts
Lines (Spoken): 2,362 (1,038 verse, 1,324 prose)
Lines (Written): 2,431

STAGING
Doors: one is mentioned (4.2, dialogue)

MUSIC
Music: dance music (4.2, dialogue); wind instrument sounds (4.2, s.d.)
Song: 4.2, Perk
Dance: the Twibill knights dance (4.2, s.d.)

PROPS
Lighting: a torch (5.1, s.d.)
Weapons: Sir Martin's sword (2.1, 5.1, implicit; 3.1, s.d.); Sconce's sword (2.1, dialogue)
Money: gold (1.1, dialogue; two separate sums); unspecified sums (1.1, dialogue; 2.1, implicit); a purse containing one hundred pieces (4.2, 5.1, dialogue)
Food and Drink: a cup of wine (4.2, dialogue; drunk on stage); a bowl of sack (4.2, dialogue; drunk on stage)
Small Portable Objects: a box of salve (2.1, s.d.; 3.1, dialogue); a document (3.1, implicit); a watch (4.2, implicit; 5.1, dialogue); a willow branch (5.1, dialogue); a key (5.1, dialogue)
Large Portable Objects: a rattan staff of office (3.1, dialogue)

COSTUMES
ARTLESS: satin and plush clothes (1.1, dialogue)
POPINJAY: a beard (1.1, dialogue; presumably shaved off by 4.1); disguised as a woman (4.1–2, s.d.); Sconce's doublet, beaver hat, and linen band (5.1, s.d.)
LADY YELLOW: satin and plush clothes (2.1, dialogue)
SCONCE: hangers (2.1, dialogue; removed on stage); his arm in a sling (3.1, dialogue); a beaver hat (4.2, dialogue; removed on stage); a Dutch felt cap (4.2, dialogue; put on on stage); a linen band (4.2, dialogue; removed on stage); a doublet (4.2, dialogue; removed on stage); a ragged military cassock (4.2, dialogue; put on on stage); breeches (4.2, dialogue); a blindfold (4.2, implicit; put on and removed on stage; unless the Dutch cap can be pulled down over his eyes); cross-dressed in Popinjay's women's clothes (5.1, s.d.)
FREEWIT: a wreath of flowers and laurel (5.1, dialogue)
KNOW-WORTH: satin and plush clothes (2.1, dialogue)
LOVERING/MARTHA: cross-dressed as a man (2.1, s.d.; 5.1, implicit); women's clothes (4.2, s.d.); a periwig (5.1, s.d.; removed on stage)
PIG: a coat (4.2, dialogue)
KNOCKDOWN: a buff jerkin (4.2, dialogue)

EARLY STAGE HISTORY
1636: presumably performed, as licensed, by Queen Henrietta's Men.
Performed at court by 1640. The audience included: King Charles I; Queen Henrietta Maria.
1637–40: performed at the Cockpit by the King's and Queen's Young Company (Beeston's Boys).

EARLY TEXTUAL HISTORY
1636: On Saturday 12 March, Sir Henry Herbert licensed the text for performance by Queen Henrietta's Men; the licensing fee was £2.
1640: entered in the Stationers' Register to Anne Wilson on Friday 22 May; entry names author. Matthew Clay had licensed the book for publication.
1640: Q printed by John Okes for Anne Wilson; collation A–I⁴, 36 leaves; title page names author, current acting company, and playhouse, and gives date of composition; list of roles; authorial dedication to Sir Thomas Fisher.
c. 1640s: a copy of Q was in the possession of John Horne (Vicar of Headington, Oxfordshire). After his death, his entire collection of play-books passed into the possession of John Houghton of Brasenose College, Oxford (c. 1608–77), then to James Herne (died 1685), and then to the library of Ralph Sheldon (1623–84) at Weston, where it was catalogued by Anthony Wood, probably in the late 1670s.
1652–60: advertised as for sale by William Leake.
1655: *The English Treasury of Wit and Language* entered in the Stationers' Register to Humphrey Moseley on Tuesday 16 January.
1655: two extracts (from 4.1, 5.1) included in John Cotgrave's *The English Treasury of Wit and Language*, sigs. M2ʳ, S7ʳ; printed for Humphrey Moseley.
1655: *Wit's Interpreter* entered to Nathaniel Brooke in the Stationers' Register on Wednesday 14 March.
1655: five extracts (from 1.1, 2.1, 4.1, 5.1) included in John Cotgrave's *Wit's Interpreter*, sigs. D7ʳ–D8ᵛ, E1ʳ; printed for Nathaniel Brooke. The extracts were omitted from subsequent editions.
1684: Nicholas Cox (Manciple of St Edmund Hall, Oxford) had a copy of Q in his bookshop, as part of a bound collection of Henry Glapthorne's plays; the

other plays in the volume were *Argalus and Parthenia* (**2579**), *The Ladies' Privilege* (**2593**), *Wallenstein, Duke of Friedland* (**2702**), and *Wit in a Constable* (**2730**). It had probably been previously owned by Gerard Langbaine, and appears on a list compiled by Anthony Wood on Saturday 13 December.

1691–4: advertised as printed for (and so for sale by) Richard Bentley.

EDITION
R. H. Shepherd, in *The Plays and Poems of Henry Glapthorne* (London, 1874), i. 67–157.

REFERENCES
Annals 1636; Bawcutt 346; Bentley, iv. 482–3; Bodleian, MS Wood E. 4, art. 1, p. 45; Eyre & Rivington, i. 463, 467; Greg 594; Hazlitt, 108; *MLR* 13 (1918), 401–11; *RES* NS 54 (2003), 601–14; *SP* 40 (1943), 186–203; Steele, 279–80.

2537. Masque of Mariners

TEXT
MS (Aberystwyth: National Library of Wales, MS 5308E, fo. 12^{r-v}); transcript of the songs only.

GENRE
masque
Contemporary: masque (MS)

AUTHOR
Aurelian Townshend

DATE
Limits: 1631–7
Best Guess: 16 March 1636

Annotation on the MS indicates that the performance may have taken place on 16 March (which would have been during Lent in any year). The limits are the period of Townshend's known involvement with court masques. In practice, the King was not in London in mid-March of the years 1632–5, and 1637 was a plague year, so the likeliest options are 1631 or 1636. The former might recommend itself circumstantially in the light of Townshend's selection as the librettist for the two major court masques of 1632 (**2353** and **2359**), but matters nautical were exceptionally topical in March 1636 (*Cal. Ven. 1632–6*, 533, 535). This was also a time when the court was going out to other people's masques strikingly often (see **2532–3**, **2535**, and, arguably, **2539**), having had none of its own that Christmas. The immediately preceding court masque (**2522**) had been by Townshend.

PLOT
A group of dancing mariners bring ashore a ship's precious cargo. A sea-captain sings of trade and disavows suggestions that merchants make excessive profits.

ROLES
MARINERS, perhaps the antimasquers
A SEA-CAPTAIN
MASQUERS

Speaking Parts: 1 (?)

SETTING
Geography
Asia: Colchis; Arabia

LANGUAGE
English

FORM
Lines (Spoken): 41
Lines (Written): 46

STAGING
Audience: the King is referred to as 'the merchant royal'

MUSIC
Music: kettle drums (dialogue)
Songs:
   1: 'After this rabble whom the sea hath taught', Sea-Captain, 20 lines;
   2: 'Fair sureties of my truth, appear', Sea-Captain, 15 lines;
   3: 'Rise, rise, ye cold spectators, rise', Sea-Captain, 6 lines.
Dance: the Mariners dance lavoltas and a reel (dialogue)

PROPS
Musical Instruments: mariners' whistles (dialogue)
Large Portable Objects: a cargo of gold, diamonds, cochineal, raw silk, and sugar (dialogue)

COSTUMES
MASQUERS: masks (implicit; removed on stage)

EARLY STAGE HISTORY
Performed, probably on 16 March (which was a Wednesday in 1636). The audience probably included King Charles I.

EARLY TEXTUAL HISTORY
Seventeenth century (before 1673): Sir Henry Herbert transcribed the songs in **MS**; 1 leaf (of a bifolium).

EDITION
Peter Beal, *MRDE* 15 (2003), 243–60.

REFERENCES
Beal Online ToA 95–7; Karen Britland, *Drama at the Courts of Queen Henrietta Maria* (Cambridge, 2006), 225–8.

2538. The Princess

TEXT
Printed in 1663–4 (Wing K450). The extant prose text may have been revised from an original written in Killigrew's usually unmetrical verse; the revision may have included the insertion of a new scene (either 1.5 or, more probably, 2.1, both headed 2.1 in F).

GENRE
tragicomedy
Contemporary: tragicomedy (t.p.)

TITLE
Printed: *The Princess, or Love at First Sight*

AUTHOR
Thomas Killigrew

DATE
Limits: 1636–7
Best Guess: Spring 1636

It is generally accepted that Killigrew wrote the play while he was in Naples during his Continental tour of 1635–6; he had reached Vercelli in northern Italy by mid-January, continued south to Rome and Naples, and was back in England in time to marry, on 29 June, Cecilia Crofts (after whom he probably named one of this play's two princesses). It is unlikely that the play can have been staged immediately upon his return; even if he was back before plague closed the playhouses on 12 May, there would not have been the time to get it accepted by an acting company and into production, so the play may not have opened until 1637. The other play written during his time in Italy, *Claracilla* (**2529**), had to wait until 1639 to be staged in London.

ORIGINAL PRODUCTION
King's Men at the Blackfriars (?; and if so, perhaps also the Globe)

The 1646 group Stationers' Register entry consists substantially or entirely of plays belonging to, and presumably acquired from, the King's Men.

PLOT
An expansionist Rome has conquered Sicily: the King has been killed in battle and his son, Facertes, taken to Rome in triumph. He would have been executed but for the intercession of the Emperor's children, Virgilius and Sophia: Virgilius hopes for a dynastic, peace-making marriage with Facertes' sister Cicilia, and Sophia has fallen in love with Facertes himself. Virgilius is sent to take command of the legions in Gallia, while Sophia goes to Sicily. There she is taken prisoner by an enclave of Sicilian soldiers who are still resisting the Romans, and have formed themselves into a pirate band; one of them, Cilius, falls in love with her. Unaware of this, Virgilius abandons his command, sets Facertes free, and goes with him to Sicily.

Cicilia, posing as a Greek, is being taken to Rome by the Viceroy of Sicily as a gift to the Emperor. The party is ambushed, the Viceroy killed, and Cicilia captured by Sicilian soldiers; like all prisoners of war, she is to be sold into slavery. Virgilius sees her in the Neapolitan slave-market and falls in love with her not knowing her identity. He tries to buy her, but his servant is slow to fetch the money and she goes to another buyer, Bragadine. He tries forcibly to release her. The courtesan Paulina, watching from a window, falls in love with him and, realizing her love is hopeless, offers to help him win Cicilia; to this end, she borrows the new slave from Bragadine. Facertes recognizes her as his sister, visits her, and tries to pave the way for Virgilius to woo her, but Cicilia will not admit the possibility that the Roman can be anything but their enemy. Nevertheless Facertes sets up a meeting for them, preparatory to effecting Cicilia's escape overnight. Paulina's servant Olympia, whom Virgilius has offended, tells Bragadine about the scheme, and he ambushes them as they are going; Virgilius is wounded, but Bragadine is killed, and the lovers must now leave Naples to escape justice. Facertes plans to make for Sicily: with the Viceroy dead, he can assert his authority in his own kingdom.

Cilius tries to have Sophia released, but his commander, Teresius, insists that she must be sold as a slave. Cilius then plans to arrange her escape by fomenting a slave mutiny aboard the galley taking her to the slave-market. Meanwhile, Teresius learns of Cicilia's enslavement and plans to rush to Naples to rescue her. In the event, the galley does not set sail: they encounter Virgilius and his friends, who were caught in a storm and have taken shelter on the coast near the Sicilians' hideout. A battle ensues in which Cilius' fellow conspirator is killed and the galley burned. Facertes and Cicilia are captured and imprisoned with the other slaves-to-be. Sophia recognizes Facertes, and Teresius submits to his authority. It turns out that Cilius, who is looking for revenge on Virgilius, is really Facertes' missing brother, Lucius. Teresius rushes to forestall Cicilia losing either brother or lover, and intervenes in the fight in time to prevent a fatality. The war between Rome and Sicily effectively ends with a pair of restored and intermarried ruling families.

In the sub-plot, Teresius expects not to be re-elected captain: Cilius will be chosen instead. Whoever is captain will be heir to the sickly Tullius, so the Sicilian soldiers try to persuade him to die before Teresius has to give up his command. They are not successful.

SCENE DESIGNATION
1.1–5, 2.1–4, 3.1–6, 4.1–10, 5.1–8 (F, corrected)

F marks two scenes 2.1. One of them may have been inserted in revision; if so, it is more likely to have been the second, since the first seems the more narratively indispensable of the two. The intention may have been to move the first (and original?) 2.1 back into the first Act, obviating the need for Crabb to exit at the end of one scene and immediately re-enter at the start of the next; accordingly, the scene is here treated as 1.5. The effect is to shorten an already very short Act 2; but, in any event, there is an imbalance in the play's act-lengths: Acts 2 and 3 are short and Acts 4 and 5 are extremely long. An alternative interpretation of the evidence would have Acts 1–2 structured as 1.1–4 and 2.1–5, with F's second 2.1 numbered 2.2 and 2.2–4 as 2.3–5.

The stage is not clear at the following act-divisions: 1.1–2, 2.2–3 (above space only). The stage is briefly clear during 2.1, 4.5, 4.7, 4.8, 4.10, 5.4, and 5.5.

ROLES

Four or more SICILIAN SOLDIERS (two speak in 1.1, one in 1.2, one in 1.4, three in 1.5, one in 2.1, three in 2.2–4, one in 3.3 and 4.4, three in 5.2 and 5.4, possibly one other in 5.4, one in 5.6, and one in 5.8)
CRABB, a Sicilian soldier
TORRAFUCO, the Sicilian lieutenant, an older man; poses as the god Bacchus
Princess SOPHIA, a Roman, Virgilius' sister
TERESIUS, the Sicilian captain
ROMAN SOLDIERS captured by the Sicilians (one speaks in 1.2, one in 2.2, two in 5.3, and one in 5.6)
CILIUS, a young Sicilian soldier; in reality, Prince Lucius, brother of Facertes and Cicilia
Prince VIRGILIUS of Rome, Sophia's brother; a young man
Prince FACERTES of Sicily, brother of Cicilia and Lucius; a young man, the rightful King
NIGRO, the old foster-father of Cicilia and Facertes
Princess CICILIA, sister of Facertes and Lucius; poses as a Greek
The VICEROY of Sicily (1.5, *non-speaking*)
A PIMP in Naples (2.2)
OLYMPIA, an old she-bawd, Paulina's servant
Prince BRAGADINE, son of the Governor of Naples
Bragadine's SERVANT (2.2)
MINETES, Virgilius' servant
PAULINA, a Neapolitan courtesan
TULLIUS, a sickly Sicilian, old and rich
ATTENDANTS on Bragadine (3.6, *non-speaking*)
ENNIUS, a bravo abetting Bragadine
A BRAVO abetting Bragadine (4.8, 4.10)

Speaking Parts: 23–41

Stage Directions and Speech Prefixes

SICILIAN SOLDIERS: *two Soldiers* | *[two of] three others* | *the two Soldiers* | *Soldiers* | *a Soldier* | *the Soldiers* | *The Soldier* (s.d.s); *1 Soldier* | *2 Soldier* | *Soldier* | *3 Soldier* | *1* | *2* | *3* (s.p.s); *Other Soldiers of [Teresius' and the Lieutenant's] gang* (d.p.)
CRABB: *[one of] three others* (s.d.s); *Crabb* (s.d.s and s.p.s); *Soldier* (s.p.s); *Crabb, a Soldier of [Teresius and the Lieutenant]* (d.p.)
TORRAFUCO: *the Lieutenant* (s.d.s); *Lieutenant* (s.d.s and s.p.s); *Bacchus* (s.p.s); *Lieutenant, [Teresius'] Associate* (d.p.)
SOPHIA: *Sophia* (s.d.s and s.p.s); *Sophia, Sister to Virgilius* (d.p.)

TERESIUS: *the Captain* (s.d.s); *Captain* (s.d.s and s.p.s); *Terresius, a Sicilian Commander, turned Pirate* (d.p.)
ROMAN SOLDIERS: *the Romans* | *the rest of the Prisoners* | *the slaves* | *Romans* (s.d.s); *Prisoners* (s.d.s and d.p.); *1 Roman* | *2 Roman* | *Slave* (s.p.s); *Roman Soldiers* (d.p.)
CILIUS: *Cilius* (s.d.s and s.p.s); *Lucius (under the name of Cilius) Brother to Facertes* (d.p.)
VIRGILIUS: *Virgilius* (s.d.s); *Virgil<ius>* (s.p.s); *Virgilius, Son to Julius Caesar* (d.p.)
FACERTES: *Facertes* (s.d.s and s.p.s); *Facertes, late Prince, now King of Sicily* (d.p.)
NIGRO: *Nigro* (s.d.s and s.p.s); *Nigro, Foster-father to Facertes* (d.p.)
CICILIA: *Cicilia* (s.d.s and s.p.s); *[Facertes'] Sister* (s.d.s); *Cicilia, Sister to Facertes and Lucius* (d.p.)
VICEROY: *the Viceroy* (s.d.s); *Viceroy of Sicily for Facertes* (d.p.)
PIMP: *a Pimp* (s.d.s); *Pimp* (s.p.s); *Pimp . . . of Naples* (d.p.)
OLYMPIA: *a she Bawd* | *the Bawd* | *the Bawd, Olympia* (s.d.s); *Bawd* (s.d.s and s.p.s); *Bawd of Naples (Bawd's name Olympia)* (d.p.)
BRAGADINE: *Bragadine* (s.d.s); *Bragad<ine>* (s.p.s); *Bragadine, Son to the Governor of Naples* (d.p.)
SERVANT: *a servant* | *The Prince's Servant* (s.d.s); *Servant* (s.p.s); *Servants* (d.p.)
MINETES: *[Virgilius'] man* | *Virgilius' Servant* | *Minetes* (s.d.s); *Servant* (s.d.s and s.p.s); *Minetes, [Virgilius'] Servant* (d.p.)
PAULINA: *Paulina* (s.d.s and s.p.s); *Paulina, a Neapolitan Lady* (d.p.)
TULLIUS: *Tullius* (s.d.s); *Tull<ius>* (s.p.s); *Tullius, a humorous Companion of [Teresius and the Lieutenant]* (d.p.)
ATTENDANTS: *others* (s.d.s); *Servants* (d.p.)
ENNIUS: *[one of the] Bravos* (s.d.s and d.p.); *Bravo* | *Ennius* (s.d.s and s.p.s); *1 Bravo* (s.p.s)
BRAVO: *[one of the] Bravos* (s.d.s and d.p.); *2 Bravo* (s.p.s)

OTHER CHARACTERS
Doll, Crabb's old lover (1.1)
Boys, prisoners of war captured while swimming, who are to be sold into slavery (1.2, 4.1)
A Moor, a former captain of the Sicilian army (1.2)
The people of Sicily (1.2)
Sicilian soldiers wounded or killed in the last battle (1.2)
Julius Caesar, the Emperor, father of Sophia and Virgilius (1.2–3, 4.1, 4.6–7; apparently not to be identified with 'the first Julius')
The dead King of Sicily, father of Facertes, Cicilia, and Lucius (1.2, 4.2, 4.5–7, 5.3, 5.6)
The Roman legions in Gallia (1.3)
A married man who refused to drink Teresius' health (2.1)

An old woman, the non-drinker's wife, whom Torrafuco met at Teresius' quarters (2.1)
The Governor of Naples, Bragadine's father; also called the Viceroy (2.2, 4.10)
Sailors who brought Cicilia to Bragadine's house (2.4)
Tullius' physician (3.3, 4.4)
Roman soldiers, one of them old, who were escorting Cicilia and the Viceroy of Sicily to Rome (4.1)
Women prisoners of war to be sold as slaves (4.1)
Galley-slaves aboard the slave-ship bound for Naples (4.3, 5.1)
Gorgianus, a Briton loved by Olympia (4.7)
Facertes' dead mother (4.7)
Two people whom Ennius killed for Olympia (4.8)
Virgilius' friends (4.10)
Cilius' friends (5.1)
Torrafuco's wench (5.2, 5.5)
A corporal killed by Virgilius (5.4)
Celia, a friend of Tullius (5.5)
A dying soldier who told Virgilius where to find Cilius (5.7)

SETTING
Period: antiquity
Time-Scheme: 3.2–4 take place in the morning, 4.5 later the same day, and 4.8–10 the ensuing night; two days pass between 1.2 and 5.1; 5.3 takes place in the morning
Place: Sicily, Naples, and Calabria

Geography
Sicily: Syracuse
Naples: the Mole
Italy: Rome; Baia
[*Europe*]: Gallia; Greece; Britain

SOURCES
Narrative: Armand Desmarets de Saint-Sorlin, *Ariane* (1632; English tr. 1636)

LANGUAGE
English
Latin: 3 words (2.1, 5.1; Torrafuco)
French: 2 words (5.1; Torrafuco)

FORM
Metre: prose; some rough pentameter
Rhyme: a few couplets
Act-Division: 5 acts
Lines (Spoken): 2,814 (51 verse, 2,763 prose)
Lines (Written): 2,923

STAGING
Doors: characters enter at two doors (2.2, s.d.); mentioned (3.1, 4.6, dialogue; 4.4, 4.7, s.d.); knocked at (3.3, implicit)
Discovery Space: Tullius enters 'on his bed' (3.3, 4.4, s.d.)

Stage: mentioned (5.2, 5.4–5, s.d.)
Within: sound effects (1.5, 5.5, 5.8, s.d.; 4.3–5, implicit); speech (3.3, 4.10, 5.8, s.d.)
Above: characters appear above 'in the window' (2.2–3, s.d.), or just 'above' (3.1, 4.10, s.d.; up to two at a time; it take no more then 5 lines to get down to the main stage)
Beneath: bottles are thrown into 'a hole upon the stage' (5.2, s.d.)
Audience: referred to as the actors' 'judges' (5.8, implicit)
Miscellaneous: Virgilius is shot in the face on stage; the effect is simulated by the actor's applying a bloody sponge as the pistol is fired (4.10, s.d.); Torrafuco exits at the end of 5.1 and immediately re-enters at the start of 5.2

MUSIC AND SOUND
Sound Effects: noise of fighting within (1.5, s.d.); noise within (1.5, 5.5, 5.8, s.d.); knocking within (4.3–5, s.d.)
Music: drums (4.4, s.d.)
On-Stage Music: Torrafuco winds a horn (5.4, s.d.)
Song: 'To Bacchus bow, to Bacchus sing', 5.2, a catch, three Sicilian Soldiers and Torrafuco (posing as Bacchus), in parts, 51 lines; *musical setting survives*
Other Singing: Tullius sings (4.4, s.d.); Sicilian Soldiers and Tullius exit singing (5.2, s.d.); Torrafuco and Sicilian Soldiers enter singing the catch from 5.2 (5.4, s.d.)

PROPS
Weapons: Crabb's sword (1.1, s.d.); four Sicilian Soldiers' swords (1.1, s.d./dialogue); Cilius' sword (1.2, 5.1, dialogue; 1.4, 5.8, s.d.); Facertes' sword (1.3, 4.10, s.d.; 2.3, 5.4, implicit; 3.1, dialogue); Virgilius' sword (1.3, 5.8, dialogue; 2.2, 5.4, implicit; 4.10, s.d.); Torrafuco's sword (2.1, s.d.; 4.4, 5.2, 5.4, implicit; 5.5, dialogue); Sicilian Soldiers' swords (2.2, 5.4, 5.8, implicit); Bragadine's sword (2.2, implicit; 4.10, dialogue); a knife (4.4, dialogue); Torrafuco's dagger (4.4, dialogue); a pistol (4.8, dialogue; 4.10, implicit; discharged on stage); Ennius' sword (4.10, dialogue); Tullius' dagger (5.5, s.d.)
Musical Instruments: a horn (5.4, s.d.)
Clothing: Crabb's hat (2.1, s.d.); a ring (4.6, s.d.)
Money: a purse of coins (1.1, s.d.); unspecified amounts (2.1, 3.1, 4.7, s.d.; 2.2, dialogue)
Food and Drink: a little bottle (2.1, s.d.; 5.5, dialogue); a large bottle of wine or sack (4.4, s.d.; drunk on stage); a gammon of bacon (4.4, s.d.; cut and eaten on stage); bread (4.4, s.d.); bottles of liquor (5.2, s.d.; drunk on stage)
Small Portable Objects: a letter (1.3, s.d.); a piece of dirty paper (2.1, s.d.); a tobacco-box (2.1, dialogue); three or more cups or bowls (4.4, s.d./dialogue); a napkin (4.4, s.d.)
Large Portable Objects: seating for at least two characters (4.4, implicit)

Scenery: curtains (2.1, s.d.); hangings (3.2, s.d.); a bed (3.3, 4.4, s.d.)
Miscellaneous: blood in a sponge (4.10, s.d.; the sponge is unseen, used covertly to apply the blood to Virgilius' face); blood (5.5, implicit)

COSTUMES AND MAKE-UP
SICILIAN SOLDIERS: sheaths (1.1, 2.2, 5.4, 5.8, implicit); chains (5.2, s.d.)
CRABB: a sheath (1.1, implicit)
TORRAFUCO: a doublet (1.1–2, 5.5, dialogue; removed on stage); a sheath (2.1, 4.4, 5.5, implicit); breeches (2.1, 5.5, dialogue; removed on stage), with a pocket (s.d.); a slashed buff coat and a hat with a feather (5.5, dialogue; removed on stage); wounded (5.5, s.d.)
SOPHIA: chains (4.3, dialogue)
TERESIUS: a hat (4.4, dialogue); wounded (5.4, s.d.)
ROMAN SOLDIERS: bound (1.2, s.d.; 5.3, dialogue); prices written on their backs (2.2, implicit)
CILIUS: a sheath (1.4, implicit)
VIRGILIUS: brown hair (dialogue); a sheath (1.3, 4.10, implicit); wounded (5.5, s.d.)
FACERTES: a sheath (1.3, 2.3, 3.1, 4.10, implicit); an eye-patch (4.6, s.d.; removed on stage)
NIGRO: silver hair (dialogue); wounded (1.5, s.d.; 3.2, dialogue)
CICILIA: chains (2.2, s.d.; removed on stage)
BRAGADINE: a sheath (2.2, 4.10, implicit)
TULLIUS: wounded (5.5, s.d.); a dagger sheath (5.5, implicit)
ENNIUS: a sheath (4.10, implicit)

EARLY STAGE HISTORY
Said (in 1661) to have been acted before 1642.

EARLY TEXTUAL HISTORY
1636 (?): said to have been written in Naples, probably in the late winter or early spring.
1646: entered to Humphrey Robinson and Humphrey Moseley in the Stationers' Register between Friday 4 and Tuesday 15 September; play and author individually named as a late addition to a group entry of 47 plays. John Langley had licensed the book for publication.
1652: Song included, with a musical setting by Charles Coleman, in John Playford's *Select Musical Airs and Dialogues*, sigs. M1ᵛ–M2ʳ; printed for John Playford. (The song was omitted from the second edition of 1653.)
1659: Song included, with Coleman's setting, in John Playford's *Select Airs and Dialogues*, sigs. Y1ᵛ–Y2ʳ; printed by William Godbid for John Playford.
1663: entered to Henry Herringman in the Stationers' Register on Saturday 24 October; individually named as part of a group entry of nine titles in a collection of Thomas Killigrew's plays. Sir John Berkenhead had licensed the book for publication.
1663–4: included in Killigrew's *Comedies and Tragedies* (F), sigs. A1ʳ–I2ʳ, 67 pages on 34 leaves; printed (by Thursday 28 January 1664) by John Macock for Henry Herringman; the play has an individual title page with a dedication to Lady Anne Wentworth (niece of the author's first wife); list of roles. The book was issued in January 1664.
1664: F reissued, probably in May, with a cancel title page.
1669: *Select Airs and Dialogues* reissued as *The Treasury of Music*.
1673: Robinson's rights transferred in the Stationers' Register by his executor (also named Humphrey Robinson) to John Martin and Henry Herringman on Thursday 30 January, as part of a list of 105 titles, by assignment of Saturday 13 May 1671.
1683: Martin's rights transferred in the Stationers' Register from his widow, Sarah, to Robert Scott, on Tuesday 21 August, by assignment of Tuesday 14 June 1681 and order of a court of Monday 7 November 1681; individually named as part of a group transfer of 360 titles.
1684: Nicholas Cox (Manciple of St Edmund Hall, Oxford) had a copy of F in his bookshop. It had probably been previously owned by Gerard Langbaine, and appears on a list compiled by Anthony Wood on Saturday 13 December.
c. 1690s: Song included in a MS commonplace book (Austin: University of Texas at Austin, MS (Killigrew, T) Works B Commonplace book, fo. 61ʳ⁻ᵛ).

REFERENCES
Annals 1636; Beal Online KiT 9; Bentley, iv. 706–8; Bodleian, MS Wood E. 4, art. 1, p. 81; Greg 828; Hazlitt, 185; *PBSA* 107 (2013), 45–6; *PMLA* 51 (1936), 129.

2539. Entertainment for the Elector Palatine ◆

TEXT
Printed in 1639 (STC 11911).

GENRE
entertainment
Contemporary: entertainment

TITLE
Printed: *Entertainment to the Prince Elector at Mr Osbaldeston's*
Alternative Modernization: *Entertainment to the Prince Elector at Mr Osbalston's*

AUTHOR
Henry Glapthorne

DATE
Limits: 1635–7

2540. A Fiddler and a Poet

Best Guess: 1636

The Elector Palatine arrived in England on Saturday 21 November 1635 and left on Sunday 25 June 1637. No full record of his English itinerary is available, but if the performance was in London, as seems likely from the fact that Osbaldeston was the headmaster of Westminster School, it more probably took place at the end of 1635 or the first nineteen weeks of 1636: London during plague-time was not a place to linger, nor to pay social visits. The Elector was also out of London in early February, when he visited Bishop's Stortford, but had returned in time to see **2532** on Wednesday 24 February; he is again found in London in mid-April, when he saw *Arviragus and Philicia* (**2530–1**) at court. The entertainment is cognate with other instances of court visiting around London, with dramatic presentations, in the spring of 1636 (see **2537**)

ORIGINAL PRODUCTION
Lambert Osbaldeston's house

PLOT
Inspired by the presence of the Elector Palatine, a prophet predicts that Delight and the Graces will leave Tempe and set up home in England, making a perpetual summer.

ROLES
A PROPHET

Speaking Parts: 1

OTHER CHARACTERS
Delight, who lives in the vale of Tempe
The Graces, who live in Tempe
Mirth, who will be the architect of the Graces' new palace in England
The Genius of the place of the performance

SETTING
Geography
[Greece]: Tempe
Arabia
England

LANGUAGE
English

FORM
Metre: pentameter
Rhyme: couplets
Lines (Spoken): 30
Lines (Written): 30

EARLY STAGE HISTORY
1635–7: performed at the house of Lambert Osbaldeston. The audience included Charles Louis, Elector Palatine.

EARLY TEXTUAL HISTORY
1639: Henry Glapthorne's *Poems* entered to Daniel Pakeman in the Stationers' Register on Friday 11 January.

1639: included in Glapthorne's *Poems* (Q), sigs. B1ᵛ–B2ʳ; 2 pages on 2 leaves; printed by Richard Bishop for Daniel Pakeman.

EDITION
R. H. Shepherd, in *The Plays and Poems of Henry Glapthorne* (London, 1874), ii. 169–70.

REFERENCES
Arber, iv. 450; *ELR* 13 (1983), 333.

2540. A Fiddler and a Poet

TEXT
MS (London: British Library, Add. MS 30982, fos. 90ʳ–95ᵛ).

GENRE
entertainment (probably academic)
Contemporary: show (MS)

TITLE
MS: *A Fiddler and a Poet*

The title is added in a different, but seventeenth-century, hand using a darker ink.

DATE
Limits: 1610–40 (?)
Best Guess: 1636

Spenser is presumed to be dead and Jonson apparently, but not certainly, alive. Although the miscellany is not certainly chronological in its arrangement, it is noticeable that the datable and Jacobean pieces appear in the earlier part and the datable and Caroline ones later on. The playlet appears in the later part, not long before a couple of poems about the Short Parliament.

PLOT
A poet tries to collect money which a fiddler owes him for writing songs. They argue about the relative merits of music and poetry, with regard to profitability, origins, and claim to divine favour. They fight, but agree to accept a third party's arbitration. After the fiddler rejects a Puritan, a tailor, and a physician as suitable judges, they agree to put the matter to the audience. A boy sings about the passing of the seasons and the poet commends his song to the audience.

ROLES
ALPHONSO, a fiddler
A POET, possibly named Skelton
A BOY, who sings
MUSICIANS (*non-speaking*)

Speaking Parts: 3

1636

Stage Directions and Speech Prefixes
ALPHONSO: *the fiddler* (s.d.s); *Fiddler* (s.p.s)
POET: *the Poet* (s.d.s); *Poet* (s.p.s)
BOY: *the Boy* (s.d.s)
MUSICIANS: *the rest of the company* (s.d.s)

OTHER CHARACTERS
Pake, probably an alehouse keeper
Farlow, probably a vendor of liquor
Hewson, probably a vendor of cake and liquor
Members of an audience for the Poet's songs, who applauded but paid nothing

SETTING
Period: contemporary

Geography
Britain: Oxford; Wales; the Welsh mountains
Barbary
The Equator
The Pole [it is unclear which one]

SOURCES
Verbal: Ovid, *Tristia* 4.10 (probably quoted via the 1595 edn of Sir Philip Sidney, *An Apology for Poetry*); *Fortune, My Foe* (ballad, before 1590)
Works Mentioned: Pindar, *Odes*; Ovid, *Metamorphoses*; Ravisius Textor, *Officina* (*c*. 1522); Ben Jonson, *The Alchemist* (**1621**); there are also general references to Homer, Ennius, Ovid, Persius, Lucan, Martial, Claudian, Edmund Spenser, Richard Tarlton, and probably John Skelton

LANGUAGE
English
Latin: 5 words (Poet)

FORM
Metre: pentameter; two fourteeners
Rhyme: couplets
Lines (Spoken): 307 (303 verse, 4 prose)
Lines (Written): 315

STAGING
Audience: addressed as 'gentlemen' (implicit); co-opted as judges and referred to as 'the audience' (dialogue)

MUSIC
On-Stage Music: the Fiddler tunes his fiddle (s.d.); Musicians play to accompany the song (s.d.)
Song: 'Let Niobe, that doleful dame', Boy, 64 lines, with musical accompaniment

PROPS
Weapons: the Poet's sword (implicit)
Musical Instruments: a fiddle (s.d.; also used as a weapon; later a string breaks as it is about to be played); unspecified instruments (implicit)

COSTUMES
ALPHONSO: a garment with a sleeve (s.d.); a hat (implicit)
POET: possibly a laurel wreath (dialogue); a scabbard (implicit)

EARLY TEXTUAL HISTORY
c. 1630s–40: transcribed into a **MS** verse miscellany associated with the University of Oxford; at different times the MS belonged to Daniel Leare and (apparently later) Alexander Croke and Anthony Evans.

2541. The Governor

EVIDENCE
King's Men bill for the 1637 performance; Sir Henry Herbert's records; Stationers' Register; list of MS plays said to have been in the possession of John Warburton (1682–1759), and destroyed by his cook (London: British Library, MS Lansdowne 807, fo. 1).

The first issue is whether the different pieces of evidence all pertain to the same play. The records of the court performance by the King's Men sit neatly enough with Moseley's 1653 Stationers' Register entry, since many of the plays he entered then had been acquired from the King's Men. This establishes the author and, by extension, the play's likely date.

What complicates matters is the existence of a MS play entitled *The Governor* (London: British Library, Add. MS 10419). It is a tragicomedy set in Barcelona, and in 1924 Percy Simpson identified it as the play the King's Men performed at court in 1637. This proposal needs to be taken seriously, but one obstacle to it, *prima facie*, is that the MS has the date 1656 prominently written after the title. This could be the date of composition or, less probably, of transcription; just possibly, it might also be a scribal error for 1636—but in any event such an error would hardly have been committed before the year 1656, so the post-1642 provenance of the MS is not in doubt. The scribe was indeed noticeably careless, to the extent that another hand made corrections throughout the text, and finally wrote, with evident irritation, the word 'senseless' at the head of the epilogue (which contains some exceptionally garbled passages). The problem is that this hand appears to be that of the author: its corrections include the insertion of three substantive lines in the first act and, intermittently, of vocative uses of character names in dialogue. If these amendments were indeed authorial, then the extant text cannot be the play performed in 1637, whose author died in 1638.

It is worth adding that the surviving play's prologue and epilogue contain no insinuation whatever of a court performance, but rather assume a commercial performance, without specific indication of company. (Of course, this could be nothing more than an Interregnum fantasy.) The epilogue's parting shot seems especially ill-tailored to the prissy tastes of Charles I: the author threatens, if the play is poorly received, to write another equally bad, thinking it 'no mishap' because 'He'd rather be twice hissed than have one clap'.

GENRE
tragedy

2542. The Faithless Relict

TITLE
Contemporary: *The Governor*

AUTHOR
Sir Cornelius Fermedo

DATE
Limits: 1628–36
Best Guess: 1636

The MS in Moseley's possession presumably bore the author's name; the form in which it appears in the Stationers' Register therefore implies a date after he was knighted (on 25 September 1628).

ORIGINAL PRODUCTION
King's Men, presumably at the Blackfriars and/or Globe

ROLES
A GOVERNOR

EARLY STAGE HISTORY
1637: performed at St James's Palace by the King's Men on either Thursday 16 or Friday 17 February. The audience included: King Charles I; Queen Henrietta Maria. John Lowin and Joseph Taylor were later paid £210 for this and twenty other court performances, by a warrant dated either Sunday 12 or Wednesday 15 March.

EARLY TEXTUAL HISTORY
1653: entered to Humphrey Moseley in the Stationers' Register on Friday 9 September; group entry of 41 (or 55) plays; entry names author.

REFERENCES
Adams, 76; *Annals* 1637; Bawcutt 364; Bentley, iii. 465–8; Greg Θ65; *The Library*, 3rd ser., 2 (1911), 225–59; MSC 2.3, 382; Steele, 258, 267.

2542. The Faithless Relict

TEXT
MS (London: British Library, MS Sloane 3709); scribal copy with corrections, which may be authorial (though the correcter does not intervene to complete several lines which are partly transcribed as dashes).

GENRE
comedy
Contemporary: play (prol.1, ep.)

TITLE
MS: *The Faithless Relict, or The Cyprian Conqueror*
Contemporary: *The Cyprian Conqueror, or The Faithless Relict*

The play is usually known as *The Cyprian Conqueror*, but this title has priority over *The Faithless Relict* only at the head of the list of roles; at the head of the text itself, the order is reversed.

AUTHOR
said to be a countryman

DATE
Limits: 1634–42
Best Guess: 1636

The MS appears to be of mid-seventeenth-century origin. The preface's quotation from Nicolas Caussin establishes the upper limit, while the lower is determined by its assumption that the theatres are still open. The engagement with the antitheatrical controversy and the allusion to William Prynne suggests an earlier date, and Aeneas' plans to dress Dido '*a la mode*' in black bag headgear refers to a style that was apparently new in c. 1636.

PLOT
Philander asks his wife Petronia not to remarry after his death. She takes up residence in his tomb and lives in seclusion with her servant Dido. Cupid comes from Cyprus to Ephesus, and intends to demonstrate his superiority over the local deity, Diana, by making the inhabitants fall in love; Venus enlists the help of other gods, including Somnus and Boreas. Somnus anoints Petronia to help her sleep, and she dreams that Philander has given her permission to remarry. Boreas whips up a storm which drives Martiatus away from his post guarding the body of a hanged rapist. He takes shelter in Philander's tomb, and falls in love with Petronia. She resists his advances, but then remembers her dream and capitulates.

While Martiatus is with Petronia, the body he was guarding is stolen, which means he will be punished for dereliction of duty. Petronia offers Philander's body as a replacement, and mutilates it to deter recognition. Offended by Cupid's activities, Diana sends Alecto to poison the lovers, and a murderous quarrel erupts. Cupid intervenes to prevent Martiatus from killing Petronia, and they agree to marry.

In the sub-plot, Calista feels obliged after Philander's death to become a votaress of Diana, despite her hopes of marrying Philanthes. Philanthes accepts the situation and goes into exile, but suggests that his sister Divina, who looks uncannily like him, should join Calista in the convent. In fact, 'Divina' is just Philanthes himself, cross-dressed. The two novices are accepted, but must serve a year's probation before being accepted as full nuns. They find that the convent is not quite what they expected: Phaleria the matron is a bawd, and Ignatus the confessor, a lecher. Philanthes reveals himself to Calista, and they take comfort in one another. When Phaleria confronts Calista with an accusation of unchastity, she maintains the pretence that 'Divina' is a woman, and makes a counter-accusation about Phaleria's own conduct. Philanthes persuades Calista to withdraw from the convent and marry him, and they join Martiatus and Petronia in celebration. Cupid is triumphant: the Cyprian conqueror.

SCENE DESIGNATION
prol.1–2, 1.1–3, 2.1–8, 3.1–5, 4.1–3, 5.1–4, ep. (MS, corrected)

MS has partial numbered scene-division, but in several scenes during the first three acts the stage is clear and a new scene starts without a heading, while the numbering continues almost consistently whenever there is a heading (except that between 2.2 and 2.4 there are two scene headings without scene numbers). The scene-division used here maps onto that in the MS as follows: 1.1–2 = MS 1.1b; 1.3 = MS 1.2; 2.3 = MS 2.2b; 2.4 = MS 2.3 (first unnumbered); 2.5 = MS 2.3a (second unnumbered); 2.6 = MS 2.3b (second unnumbered); 2.7 = MS 2.4; 2.8 = MS 2.5; 3.4 = MS 3.3b; 3.5 = MS 3.3c.

Venus' entry for the start of 5.4 overlaps the dancing exit at the end of 5.3.

ROLES
PROLOGUE
An ATTORNEY (prol.2, *non-speaking*)
An ARRESTED MAN, who speaks the second prologue
PHILANDER, a civil lawyer, Petronia's husband; also appears as a dead body
PETRONIA, Philander's wife of seven years, and later his widow; Calista's sister
DEATH, a male figure
CUPID of Cyprus, boy god of love, Venus' son
DIDO, Petronia's maidservant
CALISTA, Petronia's sister, a young virgin
PHILANTHES, a senator's son; a young man; poses as his own sister, Divina
MOURNERS at Philander's funeral, including senators (1.3, *non-speaking*)
IGNATUS, a priest
PHALERIA, a votaress of Diana and matron of the nunnery, an old woman
VENUS, goddess of love, Cupid's mother; also called Cytherea
CASTELLA, Phaleria's maid
SOMNUS, god of sleep
BOREAS, god of the north wind
MARTIATUS, a Thracian colonel, a widower and former father
Silvius AENEAS, Martiatus' follower; formerly his corporal
DIANA of Ephesus, goddess of chastity; also called Cynthia and Dame Dian
ALECTO, a Fury

Speaking Parts: 19
Allegorical Roles: 1

Stage Directions and Speech Prefixes
PROLOGUE: *The Prologue* (heading)
ATTORNEY: *one* (s.d.s)
ARRESTED MAN: *another* (s.d.s)

PHILANDER: *Philander* (s.d.s); *Phil<ander>* (s.p.s); *Philander* [Petronia's] *husband* (d.p.)
PETRONIA: *Petronia* (s.d.s); *Petro<nia>* (s.p.s); *Petronia the faithless relict* (d.p.)
DEATH: *Death* (s.d.s, s.p.s, and d.p.)
CUPID: *Cupit* | *Cupid* (s.d.s); *Cup<id>* (s.p.s); *Cupid the Cyprian conqueror* (d.p.)
DIDO: *Dido* (s.d.s and s.p.s); *Dido Petronia's maid a grass widow* (d.p.)
CALISTA: *Calistae* | *Calista* | *Calesta* (s.d.s); *Cal<ista>* (s.p.s); *Calista sister to Petronia* (d.p.)
PHILANTHES: *Philanthes* | *Divina* (s.d.s); *Phil<anthes>* (s.p.s); *Philanthes in love with Calista* (d.p.)
MOURNERS: *others* (s.d.s); *mourners* (d.p.)
IGNATUS: *Ignatus* (s.d.s); *Ign<atus>* (s.p.s); *Ignatus Phaleria's confessor* (d.p.)
PHALERIA: *Phaleria* (s.d.s and d.p.); *Phel<aria>* | *Phal<eria>* (s.p.s)
VENUS: *Venus* (s.d.s and d.p.); *Ven<us>* (s.p.s)
CASTELLA: *Castella* (s.d.s); *Cast<ella>* (s.p.s); *Castella Phaleria's maid* (d.p.)
SOMNUS: *Somnus* (s.d.s); *Som<nus>* (s.p.s); *Somnus God of sleep* (d.p.)
BOREAS: *Boreas* (s.d.s); *Bore<as>* (s.p.s); *Boreas God of the northern winds* (d.p.)
MARTIATUS: *Martiatus* (s.d.s); *Marti<atus>* (s.p.s); *Martiatus second husband to Petronia* (d.p.)
AENEAS: *Eneas* (s.d.s); *En<eas>* (s.p.s)
DIANA: *Dian<a>* (s.p.s); *Diana* (d.p.)
ALECTO: *Alecto* (s.d.s and s.p.s); *Alecto a fury* (d.p.)
D.p. also lists: *Senators*

OTHER CHARACTERS
Philanthes' uncle, a priest of Apollo (2.1; possibly imaginary)
Divina, Philanthes' sister (2.1; impersonated by Philanthes, but possibly imaginary)
Ephesians upon whom Cupid has inflicted an epidemic of lasciviousness (3.1)
Petronia's mother (3.2)
A hanged rapist (3.3–4, 4.1, 4.3, 5.2)
Zephyr's maid, whom Venus promises to Boreas in return for his help (3.4)
Martiatus' wife and children, who died in the plague (4.1)
The senators of Ephesus (4.1, 4.3, 5.2)
Adonis, Venus' former love, killed by a boar (5.4)
A swain whom Cupid has induced to fall in love with Venus after seeing her out hunting (5.4)

SETTING
Period: antiquity
Time-Scheme: 2.8 takes place at midnight; 3.2 takes place after midnight; 3.5–4.1 take place at night
Place: Ephesus

Geography
Ephesus: the Temple of Diana

Cyprus: Paphos
Thrace
Greece: Helicon; Pharsalus; Delphos (i.e. Delphi)
Crete
[*Asia*]: Tyre; Arabia; Assyria
Egypt
The Underworld: River Lethe; River Acheron

SOURCES
Narrative: Petronius, *Satyricon* (main plot); Giovanni Boccaccio, *Decameron* 9.2 (1348–53; sub-plot); possibly George Chapman, *The Widow's Tears* (**1456**)
Verbal: Plato, *Symposium* (preface; Latin version cited as *Convivium de amore*); Cicero, *De oratore* (preface; cited); Horace, *Odes* 3.6 (preface), 3.16 (preface); Ovid, *Remedia amoris* (preface), *Heroides* 1 (preface), *Metamorphoses* 1 (1.1; cited); Seneca the Elder, *Controversiae* 3 (preface; cited); Julius Pollux, *Onomasticon* (the author used the 1608 Balthasar Gualtherus edn; preface); *The Wandering Prince of Troy* (ballad, before 1620; 4.3, 5.3); Nicolas Caussin, *De eloquentia sacra et humana* (1634; preface)
Works Mentioned: Ausonius, *Epigrams* 26 (preface); George Ruggle, *Ignoramus* (**1768**; prol.2); William Prynne, *Histriomastix* (1633; preface, oblique allusion)

LANGUAGE
English
Latin: 2 words (prol.2; Arrested Man)
French: 3 words (4.3; Aeneas)

FORM
Metre: iambic pentameter, trochaic tetrameter, and prose
Rhyme: couplets
Prologue:
 1: 20 lines, in couplets;
 2: 19 lines, in couplets and a triplet, spoken by the Arrested Man.
Act-Division: 5 acts
Epilogue: 14 lines, in couplets, spoken by Aeneas
Lines (Spoken): 1,615 (1,551 verse, 64 prose)
Lines (Written): 1,791

STAGING
Doors: knocked at (2.8, s.d.); mentioned (2.8, s.d.); there are presumably two doors representing Phaleria's and Calista's chambers, and the former has an aperture Phaleria can look out of (2.8, s.d.)
Discovery Space: perhaps set with a bed (2.8, implicit); probably represents a tomb (3.2, 4.1, implicit; there is a door, but it is wide enough to show a bier inside)
Stage: mentioned (4.1, s.d.)
Within: speech (2.8, 4.1, implicit)
Above: Phaleria's chamber seems originally to have been intended to be above, but the direction to 'come down' from it is deleted (2.8, s.d.; this may be because descent to the main stage would have to be instantaneous); Cupid descends (5.2, s.d.)

Audience: assumed to be seated (prol.1, dialogue); addressed as 'kind judges' (prol.2)
Miscellaneous: Calista and Philanthes exit at the end of 2.3 and immediately re-enter at the start of 2.4; Castella does likewise at 2.7–8, as do Cupid at 3.3–4 and Boreas at 3.4–5. The location appears to change during 2.8 and 4.1: characters open the door to others outside, who go in, and the action then continues uninterrupted inside. In 4.1, the stage seems to be further subdivided: Dido and Petronia exit and immediately re-enter 'aside the stage', then cross back to where Martiatus is sitting (4.1, s.d.).

MUSIC AND SOUND
Sound Effects: a great storm (3.5, 4.1, s.d.)
Music: soft music (5.2, s.d.; accompanying Song 10)
Songs:
 1: 'O the disdain', 1.2, Philanthes and Calista, 12 lines;
 2: 'Pale death doth what he will', 1.3, 8 lines;
 3: 'Welcome, welcome unto this cell', 2.4, Phaleria, 13 lines;
 4: 'In this blest shade I'll mourn and dwell', 3.2, Dido, 12 lines;
 5: 'Drop, gentle slumber, sweetly down', 3.2, Dido, 12 lines;
 6: 'Whilst my cups I off drink', 4.3, Aeneas, 16 lines;
 7: 'When Troy town for ten years' wars withstood the Greeks in manful wise', 4.3, Aeneas, 6 lines (?); *musical setting survives*;
 8: 'And reason is treason', 4.3, Dido, 15 lines;
 9: ' 'Tis wine that raises the spirits', 4.3, Aeneas, 10 lines;
 10: 'Stay, stay awhile, O stay', 5.2, 12 lines, with musical accompaniment;
 11: 'There is no trust', 5.3, Dido, 16 lines.
Other Singing: Aeneas sings two lines from Song 7 (5.3, s.d.)
Dance: Philanthes, Calista, Martiatus, Petronia, Aeneas, and Dido dance (5.3, s.d.)

Song 7 is a pre-existent ballad, *The Wandering Prince of Troy*, also known as *Queen Dido* (which is why the play's Aeneas sings it to his Dido). It is first mentioned in Richard Johnson's *The Golden Garland of Princely Pleasures* (1620); its full text was printed in 1648 (Wing P3666B), and a musical setting by John Wilson was printed in John Playford's *Select Airs and Dialogues* (1659). The MS gives only the incipit, and Aeneas says that he will sing 'only the first part'; the full text runs to 138 lines, and is not formally divided into parts; I assume, therefore, that he sings the first stanza, a hypothesis reinforced by the fact that he reprises the last two lines of the stanza in 5.3.

PROPS
Lighting: a light (4.1, s.d.)
Pyrotechnics: a fire (4.1, s.d.)
Weapons: Death's javelin (1.1, s.d.); Cupid's javelin (2.5, dialogue); Martiatus' sword (5.2, s.d.)

Money: an unspecified amount (4.1, s.d.)
Food and Drink: wine (4.1, 4.3, s.d.; drunk on stage); a bottle of liquor (4.3, s.d.; the entire contents are drunk on stage, so that it is obviously empty at the end of the scene)
Small Portable Objects: a green bag (prol.2, s.d.); a sealed parchment (prol.2, s.d.); a will (1.1, s.d.); a letter (2.3, s.d.); a severed nose (4.3, s.d.); two severed hands (4.3, s.d.); two severed ears (4.3, s.d.)
Large Portable Objects: a human corpse (3.5, s.d.); a seat (4.1, implicit)
Scenery: a bed (2.8, s.d.); a bier (3.2, s.d.); a gibbet (3.5, dialogue)
Miscellaneous: an ointment (3.2, implicit)

COSTUMES
ATTORNEY: a great beard, a gown, a cap (prol.2, s.d.)
PETRONIA, DIDO, and CALISTA: mourning clothes (1.2, s.d.)
PHILANTHES: cross-dressed as a woman (2.3, s.d.; 2.4, 2.6, 2.8, implicit; partially removed on stage)
IGNATUS: probably a hood (2.2, implicit)
PHALERIA: Ignatius' hood (2.8, s.d.; removed on stage)
MARTIATUS: armour (4.1, dialogue)

EARLY TEXTUAL HISTORY
1634–42 (?): transcribed in **MS**; 51 leaves; list of roles; preface.

EDITION
Karen Murray Yolton, unpublished M.A. dissertation (Virginia Polytechnic Institute, 1977).

REFERENCES
Annals 1640; Bentley, v. 1316–17; Hazlitt, 57; *MLN* 23 (1908), 65–7.

2543. *Microcosmus*

TEXT
Printed in 1637 (STC 18342); lacks the epilogue.

GENRE
masque
Contemporary: moral masque (t.p.); work (comm. verses)

TITLE
Printed: *Microcosmus*
Contemporary: *A Moral Masque*

AUTHOR
Thomas Nabbes

DATE
Limits: 1629–37
Best Guess: Spring 1636

Plague closed the London theatres in May 1636, three months before the text was entered in the Stationers' Register. Richard Brome's commendatory verses mention the closure and say that people will 'fetch new shares of profit and delight' from the masque when the inhibition is eventually lifted. Bentley takes this to mean that, despite the title page's clear statement to the contrary, no performance had yet taken place. There are at least two other possible interpretations which do not entail disregarding the title-page evidence. First, Brome's verses could have been written before, but the title page set after, the theatres reopened in October 1637, and that the masque had by then been performed; this would require us to suppose, not at all impossibly, that the publisher waited at least fourteen months after registering the copy before having the book printed. Alternatively, the masque may have been performed before the closure, perhaps for a very limited or curtailed run, and Brome was anticipating that it would be revived once the plague had abated. This makes good sense of Brome's final statement that he hopes for the reopening 'In part for mine own sake as well as thine': he was effectively in the same boat as Nabbes in respect of the curtailed run of *The New Academy* (**2544**) at the same playhouse.

ORIGINAL PRODUCTION
King's Revels Company (presumably) at Salisbury Court

PLOT
The four elements, children of Nature and Janus, fight with one another. Janus' attempts to discipline them prove ineffectual, so Nature tries to persuade them to procreate. She invokes the help of Love, who creates concord between the elements through the music of the spheres. Earth gives birth to Physander, the perfect being. The four humours become his servants, and Love brings him Bellanima to be his wife. But Bellanima brings with her a good and bad genius, who can each influence Physander's moral actions. He succumbs to temptation, dismisses the good genius, and seeks out the whore Sensuality. The four humours suggest ways of wooing her: Choler proposes violence, Blood, dance, Phlegm, language, and Melancholy, pathos. The five senses, Sensuality's servants, conduct him to her, and she seduces him with the promise of luxury. Bellanima attempts to reclaim him, but he refuses her.

After sleeping with Sensuality, Physander falls ill. The humours drunkenly attack him, and Sensuality disowns him. He feels ashamed at having left his wife for a whore. Bellanima summons Temperance to cure his wounds; she prescribes a simple life and frugal diet, and he is cured. The evil genius still maliciously seeks his destruction, and plans to drive him to suicide through remorse. He is tormented by Furies and accused before the court of Conscience; Despair prosecutes, and Hope speaks for the defence. Physander admits his marital crimes, but his penitence and commitment to future fidelity save him from punishment. With no further power over him, the evil genius can only torment herself; Sensuality, reduced to beggary, joins her on the road to Hell. Love accepts Physander and Bellanima into Elysium, and they are crowned with stars.

SCENE DESIGNATION
1.1–2, 2.1–3, 3.1–2, 4.1–2, 5.1–2, ep. (Q has act-division only)

The stage is never clear within the acts, but in each case the action builds up to the display of a 'scene' (i.e. a piece of pictorial background scenery); in the second act, the action also continues after the scene has been covered again. The scene-division is assigned in accordance with the appearance and disappearance of each act's 'scene'.

ROLES

NATURE, a beautiful woman, Janus' wife, mother of Fire, Air, Water, and Earth
JANUS, Nature's husband, father of Fire, Air, Water, and Earth; representing providence
FIRE, an element; a young man, son of Nature and Janus, quad brother of Air, Water, and Earth; father of Choler
A VULCAN attending Fire (1.1, *non-speaking*)
AIR, an element; a young man, son of Nature and Janus, quad brother of Fire, Water, and Earth; father of Blood
A GIANT or Sylvan attending Air (1.1, *non-speaking*)
WATER, an element; daughter of Nature and Janus, quad sister of Air, Fire, and Earth; mother of Phlegm
A SIREN attending Water (1.1, *non-speaking*)
EARTH, an element; daughter of Nature and Janus, quad sister of Air, Water, and Fire; mother of Physander and Melancholy
A PYGMY attending Earth (1.1, *non-speaking*)
LOVE, a god, Bellanima's father
PHYSANDER, Lord of Microcosmus, son of Earth; later Bellanima's husband
CHOLER, a complexion; a fencer, son of Fire
BLOOD, a complexion; a dancer, son of Air
PHLEGM, a complexion; an old physician, son of Water
MELANCHOLY, a complexion; a musician, son of Earth
BELLANIMA, Love's daughter, Physander's wife; representing the soul
BONUS GENIUS, an angel
MALUS GENIUS, a devil; a female figure
SEEING, a sense; Sensuality's chambermaid
HEARING, a sense; Sensuality's usher of the hall; a married man
SMELLING, a sense; Sensuality's huntsman and gardener
TASTING, a sense; Sensuality's cook
TOUCHING, a sense; Sensuality's gentleman usher
SENSUALITY, a whore
TEMPERANCE, a lady physician, one of the virtues
A PHILOSOPHER, Temperance's companion (4.2, *non-speaking*)
A HERMIT, Temperance's companion (4.2, *non-speaking*)
A PLOUGHMAN, Temperance's companion (4.2, *non-speaking*)
A SHEPHERD, Temperance's companion (4.2, *non-speaking*)
Three FURIES, agents of Malus Genius; also called Erinnyes
FEAR, an officer of the court; a male character
Lord CONSCIENCE, a judge
HOPE, an advocate; a male figure
DESPAIR, a lawyer
JUSTICE, a virtue (5.2, *non-speaking*)
PRUDENCE, a virtue (5.2, *non-speaking*)
FORTITUDE, a virtue (5.2, *non-speaking*)
The HEROES in Elysium (5.2, *non-speaking*)

Speaking Parts: 29
Allegorical Roles: 25

Stage Directions and Speech Prefixes
NATURE: *Nature* (s.d.s, s.p.s, and d.p.)
JANUS: *Janus* (s.d.s, s.p.s, and d.p.)
FIRE: [one of] *the four Elements* (s.d.s); *Fire* (s.p.s and d.p.)
VULCAN: [one of the four elements'] *several anthropoi phanatikoi* | [one of the four Elements'] *creatures* (s.d.s); *A Vulcan* (d.p.)
AIR: [one of] *the four Elements* (s.d.s); *Air* (s.p.s and d.p.)
GIANT: [one of the four elements'] *several anthropoi phanatikoi* | [one of the four Elements'] *creatures* (s.d.s); *A Giant or Sylvan* (d.p.)
WATER: [one of] *the four Elements* (s.d.s); *Water* (s.p.s and d.p.)
SIREN: [one of the four elements'] *several anthropoi phanatikoi* | [one of the four Elements'] *creatures* (s.d.s); *A Siren* (d.p.)
EARTH: [one of] *the four Elements* (s.d.s); *Earth* (s.p.s and d.p.)
PYGMY: [one of the four elements'] *several anthropoi phanatikoi* | [one of the four Elements'] *creatures* (s.d.s); *A Pygmy* (d.p.)
LOVE: *Love* (s.d.s, s.p.s, and d.p.)
PHYSANDER: *Physander* (s.d.s and d.p.); *Phys<ander>* (s.p.s)
CHOLER: [one of] *the 4 Complexions* (s.d.s); *Choler* (s.d.s, s.p.s, and d.p.)
BLOOD: [one of] *the 4 Complexions* (s.d.s); *Blood* (s.d.s, s.p.s, and d.p.)
PHLEGM: [one of] *the 4 Complexions* (s.d.s); *Phlegm* (s.p.s and d.p.)
MELANCHOLY: [one of] *the 4 Complexions* (s.d.s); *Melancholy* (s.p.s and d.p.)
BELLANIMA: *Bellanima* (s.d.s and s.p.); *Bellanima* (s.d.s); *Bella<nima>* (s.p.s)
BONUS GENIUS: *the Bonus . . . Genius* | [one of] *the two Genii* (s.d.s); *Bonus Genius* (s.d.s, s.p.s, and d.p.)
MALUS GENIUS: *Malus Genius* (s.d.s, s.p.s, and d.p.); [one of] *the two Genii* | *the Malus Genius* (s.d.s)

SEEING: [one of] *the 5 Senses* (s.d.s and d.p.); *Seeing* (s.p.s); *Seeing a Chambermaid* (d.p.)
HEARING: [one of] *the 5 Senses* (s.d.s and d.p.); *Hearing* (s.p.s); *Hearing the usher of the Hall* (d.p.)
SMELLING: [one of] *the 5 Senses* (s.d.s and d.p.); *Smell* (s.p.s); *Smelling a Huntsman or Gardener* (d.p.)
TASTING: [one of] *the 5 Senses* (s.d.s and d.p.); *Tasting* (s.d.s); *Taste* (s.p.s); *Tasting a Cook* (d.p.)
TOUCHING: [one of] *the 5 Senses* (s.d.s and d.p.); *Touch* (s.p.s); *Touching a Gentleman-usher* (d.p.)
SENSUALITY: *Sensuality* (s.d.s, s.p.s, and d.p.)
TEMPERANCE: *Temperance* (s.d.s, s.p.s, and d.p.); [one of] *the Virtues* (s.d.s)
PHILOSOPHER: *a Philosopher* (s.d.s and d.p.)
HERMIT: *a Hermit* (s.d.s); *An Eremite* (d.p.)
PLOUGHMAN: *a Ploughman* (s.d.s and d.p.)
SHEPHERD: *a Shepherd* (s.d.s and d.p.)
FURIES: *three Furies* (s.d.s and d.p.); *1 Fury* | *2 Fury* | *3 Fury* (s.p.s)
FEAR: *Fear* (s.d.s, s.p.s, and d.p.)
CONSCIENCE: *Conscience* (s.d.s, s.p.s, and d.p.)
HOPE: *Hope* (s.d.s, s.p.s, and d.p.)
DESPAIR: *Despair* (s.d.s, s.p.s, and d.p.)
JUSTICE: *Justice* | [one of] *the Virtues* (s.d.s); [one of] *the other 3 virtues* (d.p.)
PRUDENCE: *Prudence* | [one of] *the Virtues* (s.d.s); [one of] *the other 3 virtues* (d.p.)
FORTITUDE: *Fortitude* | [one of] *the Virtues* (s.d.s); [one of] *the other 3 virtues* (d.p.)
HEROES: *divers* (s.d.s); *The Heroes* (d.p.)

OTHER CHARACTERS
Nature's cook-maid, Choler's mother (2.1)
A lean butter-wife, who nursed Choler (2.1)
Mars, a fencing-master who trained Choler (2.1)
A prostitute, Blood's mother (2.1)
Apollo, a musical god (2.1, 4.1)
Apollo's herb-wife, who nursed Phlegm (2.1)
Venus, who employs Phlegm as a midwife (2.1)
Phlegm's apothecary (2.1)
A glass-maker, Seeing's parent (3.1)
Hearing's wife (3.1)
Mistress Cloaca, who had bad breath (3.1)
Misackmos, who cured Cloaca's malodorous breath (3.1)
Sensuality's waiting-woman (3.2)
Night and Acheron, the Furies' parents (5.1)
Sensuality's clients, including initially lords, but latterly persons of lower rank, including a constable and watchmen (5.1)
Butchers and poulterers' wives cheated by Tasting (5.1)

SETTING
Place: Microcosmus

Geography
[*Italy*]: Lake Benacus; Lucrine Lake; Falernum; Calabria; Crotona; the Acherusian Marsh
[*Spain*]: Tartessus; River Turia
[*Greece*]: Arcadia; Mount Parthenium; Eleusis; River Peneus; Tempe
[*Mediterranean*]: Samos
[*Europe*]: France; Ambracia; Flanders; Carpathian Mountains
[*Asia*]: Arabia; Hyrcania; Saba; Assyria; Persia; River Caister; Pontus; Tyre; Idumaea
India
[*Africa*]: Numidia
[*The Atlantic Ocean*]
The North Pole

SOURCES
Narrative: Paracelsus, *De nymphis, sylphis, pygmaeis, et salamandris et de caeteris spiritibus* (c. 1515; 1.1, cited)
Verbal: Virgil, *Aeneid* 1 (5.1); Horace, *Ars poetica* (t.p. motto, Brome comm. verses)
Works Mentioned: John Dowland, *The Second Book of Songs or Airs* 2: Lachrymae (1600; 3.1)

LANGUAGE
English
Latin: 11 words (2.1, 3.1, 5.1; Blood, Phlegm, Melancholy, Conscience, Touching)
French: 3 words (2.1; Blood)
Italian: 11 words (2.1; Choler)
Greek: 1 word (5.1; Conscience)

FORM
Metre: pentameter and prose; Love speaks mainly in tetrameter
Rhyme: blank verse
Act-Division: 5 acts
Epilogue: spoken by Love; missing from the surviving text
Lines (Spoken): 1,385 (1,003 verse, 382 prose)
Lines (Written): 1,560

STAGING
Doors: characters exit (3.2, s.d.) and enter severally (4.1, s.d.)
Discovery Space: probably used, with a proscenium, to effect the discovery of the scenery

MUSIC AND SOUND
Sound Effects: 'a confused noise' (1.1, s.d.)
Music: out-of-tune music (1.1, s.d.); recorders (2.1, s.d.); unspecified music (3.1, s.d.); lively music (3.2, dialogue)
On-Stage Music: the four elements play antique instruments out of tune (1.1, s.d.)
Songs:
  1: 'Hence, confusion and dissension', 1.1–2, 11 lines;
  2: 'Descend, thou fairest of all creatures', 2.2, 16 lines;
  3: 'Flow, flow delight', 3.1–2, 11 lines;

4: 'Welcome, welcome, happy pair', 5.2, 10 lines.
Dance: the four elements and their creatures dance (1.1, s.d.); Love and the elements dance (1.2, s.d.); the humours and genii dance (2.3, s.d.); a country dance (3.2, s.d.); Temperance's companions dance (4.2, s.d.); the Heroes dance (5.2, s.d.).

PROPS
Weapons: Love's bow and quiver (d.p.; 1.1–2, 2.2, implicit)
Musical Instruments: antique instruments (1.1, s.d.); Melancholy's lute (d.p.; 2.1–3, 3.1–2, 4.1, implicit)
Animals: three sets of knotted snakes (5.1, dialogue)
Food and Drink: five bottles of wine (4.1, s.d.)
Small Portable Objects: two books (5.1, s.d.); an indictment (5.1, dialogue)
Large Portable Objects: a tipstaff (d.p.; 5.1, implicit); a judicial bench (5.1, implicit); cushions (5.1, dialogue)
Scenery: a 'front' decorated with brass figures of angels and devils, and with four Latin inscriptions; the title appears in an escutcheon supported by an angel and a devil (d.p.); a curtain showing a perspective of ruins (1.1, 2.1, 2.3, 3.1, 4.1, 5.1, d.p.; drawn to reveal the other scenery); a sphere, with seating for four (1.2, s.d.); a perspective of clouds, with seating for five (2.2, s.d.); a pleasant arbour with a building behind it, and seating for one (3.2, s.d.); a rock with a spring of water issuing from it and a cave at the foot, with a landscape behind, and seating for five (4.2, s.d.); a glorious throne with degrees, seating five at the top and others beneath (5.2, s.d.)
Miscellaneous: blood (4.1–2, dialogue); balsam (4.2, dialogue)

COSTUMES AND MAKE-UP
NATURE: a white robe embroidered with birds, animals, fruit, flowers, clouds, and stars; a wreath of flowers interwoven with stars (d.p.; 1.1–2, 2.2, implicit)
JANUS: two faces; a yellow robe embroidered with snakes; a crown (d.p.; 1.1, 2.1, implicit)
FIRE: red hair; a flame-coloured robe embroidered with 'gleams of fire'; a crown of flames (d.p.; 1.1–2, implicit)
AIR: blue hair; a blue robe embroidered with multi-coloured clouds; a wreath of clouds (d.p.; 1.1–2, implicit)
WATER: sea-green hair; a sea-green robe embroidered with waves; a wreath of sedges bound with waves (d.p.; 1.1–2, implicit)
EARTH: black hair; a grass-green robe embroidered with fruit and flowers; a chaplet of flowers (d.p.; 1.1–2, implicit)
LOVE: dressed as a Cupid, in a flame-coloured habit; a crown of flaming hearts (d.p.; 1.1–2, 2.2, implicit)
PHYSANDER: a long white robe; a garland of white lilies and roses (d.p.; 2.1–3, implicit; 5.1, s.d.); 'richly habited' (3.1–2, s.d.; 4.1–2, implicit); a crown of stars (5.2, dialogue; put on on stage)

CHOLER: red clothes (d.p.; 2.1–3, 3.1–2, 4.1, 5.1, implicit)
BLOOD: a watchet-coloured suit (d.p.; 2.1–3, 3.1–2, 4.1, 5.1, implicit)
PHLEGM: a black and white doublet; trunk hose (d.p.; 2.1–3, 3.1–2, 4.1, 5.1, implicit)
MELANCHOLY: black complexion, hair, and clothes (d.p.; 2.1–3, 3.1–2, 4.1, 5.1, implicit)
BELLANIMA: a long white robe (d.p.; 2.2–3, dialogue; 5.1–2, s.d.); a wreath of white flowers (d.p.; 2.2–3, 5.1–2, implicit); mourning clothes (3.2, s.d.; 4.1–2, implicit); a crown of stars (5.2, dialogue; put on on stage)
BONUS GENIUS: a long white robe; wings; a wreath (d.p.; 2.2–3, 3.2, 4.1–2, 5.1, implicit)
MALUS GENIUS: a black robe; wings; a wreath (d.p.; 2.2–3, dialogue; 3.1, 4.1, 5.1, implicit)
SEEING, HEARING, and SMELLING: torn and beggar-like habits (5.1, s.d.)
TASTING: a coat (4.1, dialogue); a torn and beggar-like habit (5.1, s.d.)
TOUCHING: a torn and beggar-like habit (5.1, s.d.)
SENSUALITY: richly but lasciviously dressed (d.p.; 3.2, 4.1, implicit); a torn and beggar-like habit (5.1, s.d.)
TEMPERANCE: plain, decent garments (d.p.; 5.2, implicit)
HEROES: bright antique habits (d.p.; 5.2, implicit)

EARLY STAGE HISTORY
Performed at Salisbury Court by 1637 (presumably before 10 May 1636, and presumably by the King's Revels Company); said to have been received 'with general liking'.

EARLY TEXTUAL HISTORY
1636: entered (as *A Moral Masque*) in the Stationers' Register to Charles Greene on Saturday 6 August; entry names author. William Blagrave, Sir Henry Herbert's deputy, had licensed the book for publication.
1637: Q printed by Richard Oulton for Charles Greene; collation A–G⁴, 28 leaves; title page names author and playhouse; Latin title-page motto; dedication to 'all truly noble, generous, and honest spirits'; commendatory verses by Richard Brome and William Cuffaud; list of roles.
c. 1630s–40s: a copy of Q was in the possession of John Horne (Vicar of Headington, Oxfordshire). After his death, his entire collection of play-books passed into the possession of John Houghton of Brasenose College, Oxford (c. 1608–77), then to James Herne (died 1685), and then to the library of Ralph Sheldon (1623–84) at Weston, where it was catalogued by Anthony Wood, probably in the late 1670s.
1640 or later: copies of Q were bound with six other Nabbes quartos to create a collection of Nabbes's *Poems, Masques, &c.* (with a title page dated 1639); possibly sold by Nicholas Fussell. The other plays were *Tottenham Court* (**2405**), *Covent Garden* (**2424**), *Hannibal and Scipio* (**2480**), *The Spring's Glory* (**2597**),

an edition which also included the text of his Masque of Time and the Almanac-Makers (**2635**), *The Bride* (**2645**), and *The Unfortunate Mother* (**2713**).

1640–1: Humphrey Moseley was selling copies of Q for 6d each.

1655: *The English Treasury of Wit and Language* entered in the Stationers' Register to Humphrey Moseley on Tuesday 16 January.

1655: thirteen extracts (from 4.1–2, 5.1) included in John Cotgrave's *The English Treasury of Wit and Language*, sigs. E2^v, F2^r, K2^v, K4^v, O2^r, P4^v–P3^r, Q2^r, R1^v–R2^r, R3^r, T1^r, T5^v–T6^r; printed for Humphrey Moseley.

1684: Nicholas Cox (Manciple of St Edmund Hall, Oxford) had a copy of Q in his bookshop. It had probably been previously owned by Gerard Langbaine, and appears on a list compiled by Anthony Wood on Saturday 13 December.

EDITION
A. H. Bullen, in *The Works of Thomas Nabbes* (London, 1887), ii. 159–218.

REFERENCES
Annals 1637; Bawcutt C93; Bentley, iv. 936–8; Bodleian, MS Wood E. 4, art. 1, p. 16; Eyre & Rivington, i. 463; Greg 514; Hazlitt, 156; *MLR* 13 (1918), 401–11; *Oxford Bibliographical Society Proceedings and Papers* 2.2 (1929), 132–3; *SP* 40 (1943), 186–203.

2544. The New Academy

TEXT
Printed in 1658–9 (Wing B4872), probably from authorial papers.

The authorial origins of the copy are suggested by the speech prefixes for Papillon and Galliard, which in 3.2 momentarily become *Phil.* and *Fran.*, even though it will be a long time before these characters are revealed to be aliases for Philip and François.

GENRE
comedy
Contemporary: play (S.R.)

TITLE
Printed: *The New Academy, or The New Exchange*
Contemporary: *A New Academy or Exchange*

AUTHOR
Richard Brome

DATE
May 1636

ORIGINAL PRODUCTION
King's Revels Company at Salisbury Court

PLOT
Years ago, Matchill of London and Lafoy of Paris swapped offspring: Matchill's son Philip went to be brought up in Lafoy's household, and Matchill likewise took in Lafoy's daughter Gabriella. Now news arrives that Philip has been killed in a duel. This makes Joyce, Matchill's surviving daughter, his heir and highly desirable in marriage; his cadging half-brother Strygood encourages him to bestow her on his nephew, the foolish Nehemiah, and so keep the estate in the family. Blaming Lafoy, Matchill plans to go to France to avenge his son, puts his affairs in order, and throws Gabriella out of the house. When Joyce speaks in her foster-sister's defence, he disowns her and decides to marry again, choosing his maid Rachel in the naive expectation that, unlike his first wife, she knows how to be obedient. He soon learns better.

Lady Nestlecock takes in Joyce and Gabriella, but Strygood steals them away and lodges them in the house of a city shopkeeper, Chameleon, posing as a dancing-master and claiming them to be his daughters. When two French gallants also move in, Chameleon takes advantage of the various assembled skills to set up a new academy teaching good manners, dancing, and French. Strygood proposes to sell the two young women's chastity to the gallants.

Lady Nestlecock is trying to marry Nehemiah to Sir Swithin Whimlby's niece Blithe. She also intends to marry Sir Swithin himself, which frustrates her servant Ephraim: he has ambitions of his own in that direction. When they meet, however, Blithe and Nehemiah cannot stand each other: she breaks his toys and spits in his mouth when they kiss. Nehemiah tries to grow up by getting rid of his playthings and developing a taste for books rather than ballads. His mother and Blithe's uncle take them both for a lesson in manners and courtship at Chameleon's academy. Chameleon arranges a clandestine marriage for Blithe and another young man. Lady Nestlecock has a row with Rachel, but the academy does its work and they end up courteous and reconciled to one another; Rachel submits herself to her husband.

Lafoy comes to London in search of his son, François, who has disappeared. It emerges that the letter telling of Philip's death was forged by Strygood, but that he too is now missing. The two French gallants at the academy turn out to be Philip and François, and for a moment it appears that each has married his own sister; but in fact they are only shamming, to get their own back on Strygood. The marriages have not yet been solemnized, and the problem is solved with an exchange of partners.

In the sub-plot, Valentine claims to have been bilked of his dead mother's estates by his stepfather, Hardyman. Now he lives on handouts from Chameleon's wife Hannah, who successfully resists his attempts at seduction. Chameleon himself is so uxorious that he refuses to be jealous in spite of the resultant gossip; but eventually he learns of the payments and assumes the worst. The truth, however, is that Hannah is Valentine's stepsister, and has been acting on Hardyman's instructions, to ensure that the prodigal stepson gets the money which he is too proud to take from his stepfather.

SCENE DESIGNATION
1.1, 2.1–2, 3.1–2, 4.1–2, 5.1–2 (O)

ROLES

VALENTINE Askall, a young gentleman, Hardyman's stepson; turns out to be Hannah's half-brother; also called Val

Master ERASMUS, a young gentleman, Valentine's friend; later Blithe's husband; also called Mus

Master CASH, Matchill's young apprentice; poses as Master Outlash

Master STRYGOOD, the illegitimate elder half-brother of Matchill and Lady Nestlecock, uncle of Philip, Joyce, and Nehemiah, reputed to be a Catholic; also called Monsieur Strygood; poses as Master Lightfoot, a dancing-master

Lady NESTLECOCK, a widow; Matchill's sister, Strygood's half-sister, Nehemiah's mother, aunt of Philip and Joyce; 55 years old; also called Madam Nestlecock

EPHRAIM, Lady Nestlecock's servant and Nehemiah's governor

Master MATCHILL, a merchant; a widower, Lady Nestlecock's brother, Strygood's half-brother, father of Joyce and Philip, Nehemiah's uncle; later Rachel's husband

Mistress JOYCE, Matchill's daughter, Philip's sister, niece of Strygood and Lady Nestlecock, Nehemiah's cousin; given the alias Jane, Lightfoot's daughter

Madam GABRIELLA, a young French gentlewoman, Lafoy's daughter, François's sister; given the alias Frances, Lightfoot's daughter

RACHEL Maudlin, Matchill's maid; later his wife, Mistress Matchill; also called Rach

Rafe CHAMELEON, a citizen shopkeeper, Hannah's husband

Mistress HANNAH Chameleon, Hardyman's daughter, Chameleon's wife; turns out to be Valentine's half-sister; also called Nan, Nanny, Nancy, and Cock

A FOOT-POST, who brings a letter for Hannah (2.1)

Master NEHEMIAH Nestlecock, a foolish gentleman; Lady Nestlecock's youngest and only surviving son, nephew of Strygood and Matchill, cousin of Joyce and Philip; 18 years old; also called Neh

Sir Swithin WHIMLBY, an old knight and widower, Blithe's uncle; 60 years old; also called Sir Whimlby, Powell, and Knight Whimlby

Mistress BLITHE Tripshort, Whimlby's young niece; later Erasmus' wife

Matchill's SERVANT (3.1, 5.1)

Monsieur PAPILLON, a Frenchman who speaks good English; in reality, Philip Matchill, Matchill's son, Joyce's brother, nephew of Strygood and Lady Nestlecock, Nehemiah's cousin

Monsieur GALLIARD, a Frenchman who speaks bad English; in reality, François Lafoy, Lafoy's son, Gabriella's brother

Monsieur LAFOY, a Parisian gentleman, father of François and Gabriella

Captain HARDYMAN, Hannah's father, Valentine's stepfather; also called Master Hardyman

Speaking Parts: 21

Stage Directions and Speech Prefixes

VALENTINE: *Valentine* (s.d.s); *Val<entine>* (s.p.s); *Valentine Askal, son-in-law to Hardyman. Hannah's half-brother* (d.p.)

ERASMUS: *Erasmus* (s.d.s); *Eras<mus>* (s.p.s); *Erasmus a young Gentleman, [Valentine's] Companion and Friend* (d.p.)

CASH: *Cash* (s.d.s and s.p.s); *Cash, Matchil's Prentice* (d.p.)

STRYGOOD: *Strigood* (s.d.s and s.p.s); *Strigood, half brother to Matchil* (d.p.)

NESTLECOCK: *Lady Nestlecock* (s.d.s); *Lady* (s.d.s and s.p.s); *Lady Nestlecock, a fond Mother* (d.p.)

EPHRAIM: *Ephraim* (s.d.s); *Eph<raim>* (s.p.s); *Ephraim, the Lady Nestlecock's Servant* (d.p.)

MATCHILL: *Matchil* (s.d.s); *Mat<chil>* (s.p.s); *Old Matchil, a Merchant that married his Maid. Gabrialla's Guardian* (d.p.; *sic*)

JOYCE: *Joyce* | [one of the] *maids* (s.d.s); *Joy<ce>* (s.p.s); *Joyce, Matchil's Daughter* [one of two] *Foster Sisters* (d.p.)

GABRIELLA: *Gabriella* | [one of the] *maids* (s.d.s); *Gab<riella>* (s.p.s); *Gabriella, Lafoy's Daughter* [one of two] *Foster Sisters* (d.p.)

RACHEL: *Rachel* (s.d.s); *Rach<el>* (s.p.s); *Maudlin, Matchil's Maid and Wife* (d.p.)

CHAMELEON: *Camelion* (s.d.s); *Cam<elion>* (s.p.s); *Rafe Camelion an uxorious Citizen* (d.p.)

HANNAH: *Hannah* (s.d.s); *Han<nah>* (s.p.s); *Hannah, Camelion's wife, Captain Hardiman's daughter* (d.p.)

FOOT-POST: *Foot-post* (s.d.s); *Post* (s.p.s); *A Footpost* (d.p.)

NEHEMIAH: *Nehemiah* (s.d.s); *Neh<emiah>* (s.p.s); *Nehemiah Nestlecock, a foolish Gentleman, the Lady's son* (d.p.)

WHIMLBY: *Whimlby* | *Whimlbie* (s.d.s); *Whim<lby>* (s.p.s); *Sir Swithin Whimlby, a melancholy Widower. Suitor to the Lady Nestlecock* (d.p.)

BLITHE: *Blith* | *Blithe* (s.d.s); *Bli<the>* (s.p.s); *Mrs Blithe Tripshort, Sir Swithin Whimlbie's Niece* (d.p.)

SERVANT: *Servant* (s.d.s and s.p.s)

PAPILLON: *Papillon* | [one of] *the young men* | [one of the] *two sons* (s.d.s); *Pap<illion>* | *Phil<ip>* | *Mat<chil> Junior* (s.p.s); *Young Matchil* [Old Matchill's] *son* | *Papillion* [one of] *Two Monsieurs, alias Philip Matchil's son* (d.p.)

GALLIARD: *Galliard* | [one of] *the young men* | [one of the] *two sons* (s.d.s); *Gali<ard>* | *Fran<ces>* | *Gall<iard>* | *Laf<oy> Junior* (s.p.s); *Young F<rances>*

Lafoy [Old Lafoy's] son | Galliard [one of] Two Monsieurs, alias Frances Lafoy's son (d.p.)
LAFOY: *Lafoy* (s.d.s); *Laf<oy>* (s.p.s); Old Lafoy, a French Gentleman, Guardian to young Matchil (d.p.)
HARDYMAN: *Hardy<man>* (s.d.s); *Hard<yman>* (s.p.s); Mr Hardyman, Captain Valentine's Father-in-law. Hannah's father (d.p.)

OTHER CHARACTERS
The mother of Strygood, Matchill, and Lady Nestlecock (1.1)
Strygood's father (1.1)
The father of Matchill [and Lady Nestlecock] (1.1)
Knights and gallants with whom Cash was seen gambling at an ordinary (1.1)
Nestlecock, a justice, Lady Nestlecock's dead husband (1.1)
A fire-eater whose performance frightened Nehemiah two years ago (1.1)
Matchill's shrewish first wife, who died six years ago (1.1, 2.1–2)
A porter, who carried away money for Cash (1.1)
A young gentleman, a customer in Chameleon's shop, who encountered Valentine there (2.1)
Valentine's dead mother (2.1, 5.2)
A one-handed boy whom Nehemiah beat (2.2)
Grissil, Whimlby's dead wife (2.2, 3.1, 4.2)
Blithe's dead mother (2.2, 4.1)
Lady Nestlecock's six dead sons, Nehemiah's elder brothers (2.2)
Whimlby's mother (2.2)
Rachel's aunt, an apple-woman (3.1)
A Jesuit, by whose example Strygood learned to disguise himself (3.2)
Gamesters with whom Valentine gambles (5.2)
A curate procured by Chameleon to marry Blithe to Erasmus (5.2)

SETTING
Period: contemporary
Time-Scheme: 1.1 takes place at dinner-time; at least three days pass between 1.1 and 2.2; 3.2 takes place at dinner-time; 4.2 takes place in the afternoon
Place: London

Geography
London: Bedlam; Newgate prison; Knightsbridge; the Exchange; the New Exhange; Turnbull Street; Hyde Park; Billingsgate
[*Middlesex*]: Tottenham; Kennington; Paddington; Hockley Hole; Islington; Hoxton
England: the Isle of Wight; Salisbury Plain
France: Paris
The Low Countries: Holland
Italy
The Red Sea

SOURCES
Verbal: Virgil, *Aeneid* 1 (Latin motto at foot of text); *The Book of Common Prayer*: Marriage service (1549, rev. 1552; 3.1); *Dainty, Come Thou To Me* (ballad, before 1599; 2.1, 3.2); A. S., *The Book of Bulls* (1636; 4.1, cited)

LANGUAGE
English
Latin: 9 words (1.1, 4.1–2, 5.2; Strygood, Ephraim, Valentine, Nehemiah)
French: 127 words (1.1, 2.1, 3.2, 4.2, 5.1–2; Strygood, Chameleon, Papillon, Galliard, Servant, Valentine)
Dutch: 1 word (2.1; Valentine)
Dialect: Galliard usually speaks 'French' accented English, which Hannah imitates in 3.2.

Nehemiah's recurring oath, 'Amardla', is also said by Blithe to be French, and may be worn down from '*A mort Dieu*'.

FORM
Metre: pentameter and prose; a little tetrameter; Whimlby often uses trimeter and skeltonics
Rhyme: blank verse; Whimlby frequently speaks in couplets
Act-Division: 5 acts
Lines (Spoken): 3,147 (2,211 verse, 936 prose)
Lines (Written): 3,796

STAGING
Within: speech (4.1, 5.2, s.d.); song (4.2, implicit)

MUSIC
Music: dance music (3.2, s.d.)
Song: 4.2, Joyce and Gabriella within
Dance: Galliard and Papillon dance (3.2, s.d.); unspecified characters dance (4.2, s.d.); Nehemiah dances (5.2, s.d.)

PROPS
Weapons: Nehemiah's sword (4.1, dialogue)
Money: ten pieces (1.1, dialogue); an unspecified sum (2.1, implicit); ten pieces (2.1, dialogue); fifty pieces (5.2, dialogue)
Animals: a toy dancing frog (4.1, dialogue; said to be very lifelike)
Food and Drink: a silver can of sack (1.1, s.d.; drunk on stage); sugar plums (2.2, dialogue; eaten on stage); a powder (4.2, dialogue)
Small Portable Objects: an open letter (1.1, s.d.); a napkin (1.1, s.d.); a letter (2.1, dialogue); a pen (2.1, dialogue); ink (2.1, implicit); a watch (3.1, s.d.); a book (4.1, dialogue); two ballads (4.1, dialogue); two documents (4.1, dialogue); a key (5.2, dialogue); a letter (5.2, dialogue)

COSTUMES
CASH: 'disguised in bravery' (3.2, s.d.; 5.1–2, implicit)
STRYGOOD: grey hair and a beard (1.1, dialogue); disguised, with a peruke and no beard (3.2, dialogue; 4.2, 5.2, implicit)
JOYCE and GABRIELLA: masks (4.2, s.d.; put on on stage)
NEHEMIAH: a hat (4.2, dialogue)

2545. The Bashful Lover

EARLY STAGE HISTORY
1636: The play was probably performed by the King's Revels Company at Salisbury Court in early May. It received very few performances before plague closed the theatres on Thursday 12 May; the customary author's benefit performance did not take place, and Richard Brome later estimated that, had it done, he would have received an amount in excess of £5.

EARLY TEXTUAL HISTORY
1636: Richard Brome delivered the script to the acting company no later than April.
1640: entered (as *A New Academy or Exchange*) to Andrew Crooke in the Stationers' Register on Tuesday 4 August; play and author individually named as part of a group entry of six Brome plays. Thomas Wykes had licensed the book for publication.
1658–9: included as the fourth of Richard Brome's *Five New Plays* (O), sigs. h3^r–O7^v, 57 leaves; printed for Andrew Crooke and Henry Brome; list of roles; Latin motto at foot of text.
1659: George Thomason acquired a copy of O in January. In *c*. 1678, some years after his death, his entire collection of books and tracts was acquired by the bookbinder Samuel Mearne, acting as agent for King Charles II; the King never paid him, and the books remained in Mearne's family until 1761.
1659: O reissued.
1664: O advertised (with the title mistakenly given as *Four New Plays*) as for sale by Henry Brome.
1684: Nicholas Cox (Manciple of St Edmund Hall, Oxford) had a copy of O in his bookshop. It had probably been previously owned by Gerard Langbaine, and appears on a list compiled by Anthony Wood on Saturday 13 December.

EDITION
Michael Leslie, Richard Brome Online (internet, 2010).

REFERENCES
Annals 1635; *Ben Jonson Journal* 13 (2006), 125–38; Bentley, iii. 81; Bodleian, MS Wood E. 4, art. 1, p. 55; Greg 809; Hazlitt, 165.

2545. The Bashful Lover

TEXT
Printed in 1655 (Wing M1050), probably from a scribal transcript of authorial papers (by the same scribe who prepared copy for *The Guardian*, **2417**).

GENRE
tragicomedy
Contemporary: poem (prol.); play (ep.); tragicomedy (t.p.)

TITLE
Performed/Printed: *The Bashful Lover*
Later Assigned: *The Bashful Lovers*

AUTHOR
Philip Massinger

DATE
May 1636

ORIGINAL PRODUCTION
King's Men at the Blackfriars (and perhaps also the Globe)

PLOT
Hortensio is living incognito in Mantua, paying the page Ascanio for information about Princess Matilda's movements and admiring her at a distance, never daring to go up and speak to her. She takes the initiative, and encourages him to make his love for her an inspiration for deeds of chivalry. Her marital destiny, however, will be determined by the necessity of state. Her father Gonzaga favours a marriage with Prince Uberti, but Lorenzo, the Duke of Florence, also claims to covet her and demands her hand as the price of peace; nevertheless, Gonzaga refuses and places Mantua on a war footing.

Ascanio faints upon seeing the Florentine ambassador, Alonzo, and then disappears from the heavily fortified city, to join Hortensio in the army. He asks Hortensio to help him get revenge on Alonzo. In the battle, Hortensio fights Alonzo, but spares him at Ascanio's entreaty, then saves Uberti's life. The Mantuan forces otherwise get the worst of it, and Lorenzo orders a forest fire to deprive the defeated fugitives of a refuge. Farnese plans to escape dressed as a Florentine soldier, but gives up his disguise to Uberti, and is captured; Uberti then rescues him by a ruse. Meanwhile, Gonzaga flees the field disguised as a shepherd and takes refuge in the fort at Mantua.

Ascanio is weak for lack of food, so Hortensio brings him to the nearest community. They are found and succoured by the former courtier Octavio, now living in exile disguised as a country friar. He identifies Ascanio as his daughter, Maria: she went missing after Alonzo enticed her into sex on a promise of marriage which he then broke.

On her father's orders, Matilda is taken from the city, but in the countryside she meets Alonzo and a friend, who attempt to gang-rape her, only to be fought off by Hortensio. Their injured bodies are found and identified by Maria and Octavio, who proposes taking revenge on Alonzo by keeping him alive and in agony by pharmaceutical means; Maria declines the offer, preferring to have her honour restored in marriage, whereupon Octavio admits that he was only testing her. Alonzo is nursed back to health, and agrees to marry Maria.

Lorenzo's army occupies Mantua. He admits that his demand for Matilda was only a pretext for a war serving his territorial ambitions, but changes his mind when Matilda is brought before him as a captive, and offers to restore the city to Gonzaga. When Uberti and Hortensio press their competing claims on Matilda, Lorenzo agrees to submit with them on equal terms to Matilda's judgement in a court of love, and refuses his doctor's attempts to make him seem younger and more attractive. Matilda rebukes him for warmongering and makes it clear that her preferred suitor is now Hortensio; but Mantuan law requires the duchy's heir to marry primarily for the state's advantage. News arrives that Hortensio is in fact a nobleman, Galeazzo, and that his brother's death has made him Lord of Milan, and therefore an eligible husband after all. Octavio returns to court with Alonzo and his new wife, Maria.

SCENE DESIGNATION

prol., 1.1–2, 2.1–8, 3.1–4, 4.1–3, 5.1–3, ep. (O has act-division only)

Gibson neglects to mark a scene-change when the stage is clear in Act 3; thus his 3.2 is here 3.2–3, and his 3.3 is here 3.4.

ROLES
PROLOGUE
HORTENSIO, a young gentleman of Milan; in reality, Galeazzo, ultimately Lord of Milan
JULIO, Hortensio's servant
BEATRIX, Matilda's waiting-gentlewoman
ASCANIO, Matilda's page; said to be little; in reality, Maria, Octavio's daughter and only child; later Alonzo's wife
Princess MATILDA, Gonzaga's daughter and heiress, Farnese's kinswoman; a young woman
Two WAITING-WOMEN attending Matilda
Lord FARNESE, kinsman of Gonzaga and Matilda
Prince UBERTI of Parma, General of the Mantuan army; the same height as Alonzo
Duke GONZAGA of Mantua, Matilda's father, Farnese's kinsman
Lord MANFROY, a nobleman
ATTENDANTS on Gonzaga (1.2, non-speaking)
Lord ALONZO, Lorenzo's nephew; the same height as Uberti; later Maria's husband
ATTENDANTS on Alonzo (1.2, non-speaking)
LORENZO, Great Duke of Florence, Alonzo's uncle; an older man; also called Duke of Tuscany
PISANO, a Florentine commander and lord
MARTINO, a Florentine captain, later a colonel
Two Florentine CAPTAINS, one of whom is later appointed Governor of Mantua (2.6, 2.8, 4.1, 4.3)
Florentine SOLDIERS (2.6, 2.8, 4.3; only speak collectively)
Lord OCTAVIO, an old, exiled courtier, Maria's father; poses as a friar
GOTHRIO, Octavio's servant, an under-shepherd; a thin man

A GUARD (4.1, non-speaking)
VOICES (4.3, within)
A DOCTOR attending Lorenzo (5.1)
A GENTLEMAN attending Lorenzo (5.1–2, non-speaking)
A PAGE attending Lorenzo (5.1–2, non-speaking)
An AMBASSADOR from Milan (5.3)
EPILOGUE

Speaking Parts: 23

Stage Directions and Speech Prefixes
PROLOGUE: *Prologue* (heading)
HORTENSIO: *Galeazzo* | *Galeazo* (s.d.s); *Galeaz<zo>* (s.p.s); *Galeazzo, a Nobleman disguised* (d.p.)
JULIO: *Julio* (s.d.s); *Jul<io>* (s.p.s); *Julio, [Galeazzo's] Man* (d.p.)
BEATRIX: *Beatrix* (s.d.s); *Beat<rix>* (s.p.s); *Beatrice, [Matilda's] waiting Gentlewoman* (d.p.)
ASCANIO: *Ascanio* | *Maria* (s.d.s); *Asca<nio>* (s.p.s)
MATILDA: *Matilda* (s.d.s); *Mat<ilda>* (s.p.s); *Matilda, Daughter to Gonzaga* (d.p.)
WAITING-WOMEN: *Two Women* (s.d.s and d.p.); *Waiting-women* | *two Waiting-women* (s.d.s); *1 Woman* | *2 Woman* (s.p.s)
FARNESE: *Farneze* (s.d.s); *Far<neze>* (s.p.s); *Farneze, Cousin to Gonzaga* (d.p.)
UBERTI: *Uberti* (s.d.s); *Uber<ti>* (s.p.s); *Uberti, Prince of Parma* (d.p.)
GONZAGA: *Gonzaga* (s.d.s); *Gonza<ga>* (s.p.s); *Gonzaga, Duke of Mantua* (d.p.)
MANFROY: *Manfroy* (s.d.s); *Manf<roy>* (s.p.s); *Manfroy, a Lord of Mantua* (d.p.)
ATTENDANTS: *Attendants* (s.d.s)
ALONZO: *Alonzo* (s.d.s); *Alonz<o>* (s.p.s); *Alonso, Cousin to Lorrenzo* (d.p.)
ATTENDANTS: *Attendants* (s.d.s)
LORENZO: *Lorenzo* (s.d.s); *Loren<zo>* (s.p.s); *Lorrenzo, Duke of Tuscany* (d.p.)
PISANO: *Pisano* (s.d.s); *Pisa<no>* (s.p.s); *Pisano, a Tuscan Lord* (d.p.)
MARTINO: *Martino* (s.d.s); *Mart<ino>* (s.p.s); *Martinio, a Captain* (d.p.; sic)
CAPTAINS: *Captains* | *two Captains* (s.d.s); *1 Captain* | *2 Captain* (s.p.s); *Two Captains more* (d.p.)
SOLDIERS: *Soldiers* (s.d.s, s.p.s, and d.p.); *the Soldiers* (s.d.s)
OCTAVIO: *Octavio* (s.d.s); *Oct<avio>* (s.p.s); *Octavio, General once to Gonzaga, now exiled* (d.p.)
GOTHRIO: *Gothrio* (s.d.s); *Goth<rio>* (s.p.s); *Gothrio, [Octavio's] Servant* (d.p.)
GUARD: *Guard* (s.d.s)
DOCTOR: *Doctor* (s.d.s and s.p.s)
GENTLEMAN: *Gentleman* | [one of the] *Attendants* (s.d.s)
PAGE: *Page* | [one of the] *Attendants* (s.d.s)
AMBASSADOR: *Ambassador* (s.d.s and s.p.s); *Ambassadors* (d.p.)
EPILOGUE: *Epilogue* (heading)

OTHER CHARACTERS
Galeazzo's noble friends (1.1)
John Galeas, Lord of Milan, Galeazzo's brother (1.1, 5.3)
A playwright, author of a comedy to be performed at court (1.1)
Amorous and learned court ladies, who intend to attend the performance (1.1)
The Second Waiting-Woman's tailor (1.1)
The Second Waiting-Woman's shoemaker (1.1)
The city guard (2.1)
The Mantuan army, many of them killed in battle (2.2, 2.5, 2.7–8, 4.3)
The Florentine army (2.2, 2.5, 3.2, 4.3, 5.1, 5.3)
A troop of Florentine cavalry, who attacked Farnese and Uberti (2.7)
A dying Florentine soldier, whose coat Farnese took (2.7)
The Catholic King [of Spain] (4.1)
The Turk [i.e. the Turkish Emperor], to whom Martino considers selling Matilda for the seraglio (4.1)
Lorenzo's father, a prince (4.1)
Lorenzo's mother (4.1)
The painter of a portrait of Matilda seen by Lorenzo (4.1)
The people of Mantua (4.1)
Lorenzo's messenger to Gonzaga (4.3)
Lorenzo's barber (5.1)
The Turks, who have attacked Italy (5.3)

SETTING
Period: fifteenth century: the action takes place at the time of the death of Gian Galeazzo Visconti, Duke of Milan (1402); however, Florence is part of the Grand Duchy of Tuscany (founded 1569)
Time-Scheme: 2.6–8 take place at night; 4.1 takes place two hours after dawn
Place: Mantua

Geography
Mantua: St Leo's Fort
Italy: Florence; Parma; Tuscany; Milan; Rome
[*Europe*: Spain]
Africa: River Nile
[*Asia*]: Saba; Tartary; Hyrcania; Turkey
The East Indies
The West Indies

SOURCES
Narrative: Sir Philip Sidney, *Arcadia* (written c. 1580, printed 1590, repr. 1633; Matilda plot); William Shakespeare, *As You Like It* (**1237**; 3.1), *Twelfth Night* (**1297**; 2.1), *The Tempest* (**1652**; Octavio); John Fletcher, *The Mad Lover* (**1809**; 1.1); André Favyn, *Le théâtre d'honneur et de chevalerie* (1620, English tr. attributed to 'I. W.', but possibly by Anthony Munday, 1623; Italian setting)
Verbal: Bible: Proverbs 16.31 (5.1; cited); Luke 15.16 (5.1); Horace, *Odes* 3.24 (1.2); Pliny, *Natural History* (2.8); Juvenal, *Satires* 10 (3.1); William Shakespeare, *Romeo and Juliet* (**987**; 3.1), *Much Ado About Nothing* (**1148**; 3.1), *As You Like It* (**1237**; 1.1), *The Moor of Venice* (**1437**; 4.2); Ben Jonson, *Sejanus' Fall* (**1412**; 1.1)
Works Mentioned: Ovid, poetry (general reference; 4.1)

Gibson allows the proposed link between Gothrio and Caliban to stand alone, and consequently does not find it very compelling. But this part of the plot also centres on a once-powerful man living in exile from the court, who has become a master of pharmacology. The parallel with Prospero and his magic is clear enough.

LANGUAGE
English
Latin: 3 words (1.1, 5.3; 1 Waiting-Woman, Lorenzo)
French: 1 word (1.1; Beatrix)
Italian: 2 words (4.1; Martino)

FORM
Metre: pentameter
Rhyme: blank verse
Prologue: 22 lines, in couplets
Act-Division: 5 acts
Epilogue: 14 lines, in couplets
Lines (Spoken): 2,359 (2,358 verse, 1 prose)
Lines (Written): 2,951

STAGING
Doors: characters enter at two doors (1.2, s.d.)
Within: speech (3.1, 4.3, s.d.); shouts (4.3, s.d.)
Above: five characters appear above (5.3, s.d.; it takes ten lines for some of them to descend to the main stage)
Stage Posts: one serves as the tree to which Matilda is bound (3.4, implicit)
Audience: mentioned (prol.); addressed as 'gentlemen' and said to be seated (ep.)
Miscellaneous: The action is organized to avoid bringing horses on stage (2.5, 3.3).

MUSIC
Music: alarum (2.2, dialogue; 2.5, implicit)

PROPS
Lighting: torches (2.8, s.d.)
Weapons: Uberti's sword (1.1, dialogue); Hortensio's sword (2.4, dialogue); Alonzo's sword (2.4, implicit; 2.8, 3.4, dialogue); Farnese's sword (2.8, s.d.); Pisano's sword (2.8, dialogue; 3.4, s.d.)
Clothing: a ring (2.2, s.d.); a shepherd's garment (2.5, dialogue); a Florentine soldier's coat (2.7, s.d.; later worn by Uberti); a diamond ring (3.4, s.d.; 4.2, dialogue)
Money: gold (1.1, 3.4, s.d.; 4.2, dialogue); an unspecified amount (1.1, implicit); a purse (3.4, 5.1, s.d.; 4.2, dialogue)
Food and Drink: two bottles (3.1, s.d.); medicines (3.4, dialogue); other medicines (5.1, dialogue)

Small Portable Objects: a letter (2.1, s.d.); a book (3.1, s.d.); a shepherd's tar-box (3.1, dialogue); a wooden dish of water (3.4, s.d.); binding cords (3.4, implicit); a document (4.3, dialogue); a looking-glass (5.1, dialogue); a letter (5.3, dialogue)
Large Portable Objects: a chair (1.1, dialogue); a scrip (3.1, s.d.); a sheep-hook (3.1, 3.4, dialogue); olive branches (4.3, s.d.)
Scenery: a chariot (4.3, s.d.)
Miscellaneous: blood (3.4, dialogue)

COSTUMES AND MAKE-UP
HORTENSIO: a beard (dialogue); dressed as a shepherd (3.4, dialogue)
ASCANIO/MARIA: cross-dressed as a boy (1.1–2, 2.2, 2.4, 3.1, implicit)
MATILDA: disguised (3.2, s.d.; 3.4, implicit); a veil (4.1, implicit); a laurel wreath (4.3, s.d.)
FARNESE: wounded (2.5, s.d.); bound (2.8, s.d.; untied on stage)
UBERTI: disguised as a Florentine soldier (2.8, s.d.; see also PROPS)
GONZAGA: an outer garment, perhaps purple (2.5, dialogue; removed on stage)
ALONZO: a sheath (3.4, implicit); a bloody head-wound (3.4, dialogue; the wound itself is sustained and the blood later wiped off, both on stage)
LORENZO: grey hair and beard (dialogue); armour (2.6, 2.8, 4.1, 4.3, dialogue); silken, embroidered clothes, with jewels and probably the badge of an order of chivalry (5.1, dialogue)
PISANO: a doublet (3.4, dialogue); a garment with at least two pockets, one of them little (3.4, s.d.); a sheath (3.4, implicit)
OCTAVIO: a friar's habit (3.1, 3.4, implicit; 4.1, dialogue)
GOTHRIO: a beard (dialogue); a coat (3.1, dialogue); clouted shoes (5.1, dialogue)

EARLY STAGE HISTORY
1636 or 1637: presumably performed by the King's Men as licensed, either between Monday 9 and Thursday 12 May 1636 (when plague closed the theatres), shortly after Friday 24 February 1637, or at any time after Monday 2 October 1637.
1641: The play was in the repertory of the King's Men. It was later reported (in 1669) as having been performed by them at the Blackfriars before 1642; the 1655 title page said it had been 'often acted ... with great applause' by them there.

EARLY TEXTUAL HISTORY
1636: On Monday 9 May, Sir Henry Herbert licensed the text for performance by the King's Men.
1641: On Saturday 7 August, Robert Devereux, 3rd Earl of Essex (Lord Chamberlain) issued a warrant prohibiting the printing of this and sixty other plays without the consent of the King's Men. On Saturday 14 August, the order was read to the Stationers' Company and instructions issued for its observance.

1653: entered (as a double title with *Alexius*, **2708**) to Humphrey Moseley in the Stationers' Register on Friday 9 September; play and author individually named as part of a group entry of 41 (or 55) plays.
1655: included as the first of Philip Massinger's *Three New Plays* (**O**), sigs. A1ʳ–G4ʳ, 101 pages on 52 leaves; printed by Thomas Newcomb for Humphrey Moseley; the play's individual title page names author, acting company, and playhouse; list of roles.
1655: George Thomason acquired a copy of O on Thursday 14 June. In *c.* 1678, some years after his death, his entire collection of books and tracts was acquired by the bookbinder Samuel Mearne, acting as agent for King Charles II; the King never paid him, and the books remained in Mearne's family until 1761.
1657: O advertised as for sale by the Newcastle-upon-Tyne bookseller William London; the author's name is given as John Fletcher.
1660: entered (as *The Bashful Lovers*) to Humphrey Moseley in the Stationers' Register on Friday 29 June; play and author individually named as part of a group entry of 26 plays.
1680: extract (from 3.4, with characters renamed and combined with material from *A Very Woman*, **2043**, and *The Guardian*, **2417**) appear as the droll, *Love Lost in the Dark, or The Drunken Couple*, included in *The Muse of Newmarket*, sig. E3ʳ; printed for Daniel Browne, Daniel Major, and James Vade.
1684: Nicholas Cox (Manciple of St Edmund Hall, Oxford) had a copy of O in his bookshop. It had probably been previously owned by Gerard Langbaine, and appears on a list compiled by Anthony Wood on Saturday 13 December.

EDITION
Colin Gibson, in *The Plays and Poems of Philip Massinger*, ed. Philip Edwards and Colin Gibson (Oxford, 1976), iv. 291–385, v. 256–62.

REFERENCES
Annals 1636; Bawcutt 348; Bentley, iv. 760–2; Bodleian, MS Wood E. 4, art. 1, p. 47; David L. Frost, *The School of Shakespeare* (Cambridge, 1968), 85, 103–5; Greg 758; Hazlitt, 22; William London, *A Catalogue of the Most Vendible Books in England* (London, 1657), sig. 2F1ᵛ; MSC 1.4–5, 364–9; Allardyce Nicoll, *A History of English Drama*, 4th edn (Cambridge, 1952–9), i. 354; *PBSA* 107 (2013), 30.

2546. The Merchant of Dublin
[possibly post-Catalogue]

EVIDENCE
John Aubrey, *Brief Lives* (Oxford: Bodleian, MS Aubr. 8, fo. 47ᵛ).

2547. Andronicus Comnenus

GENRE
Contemporary: play

TITLE
Contemporary: *The Merchant of Dublin*

AUTHOR
John Ogilby

DATE
Limits: 1633–44, 1662–6

ORIGINAL PRODUCTION
John Ogilby's company at the Werburgh Street theatre, Dublin (?)

Aubrey says only that Ogilby wrote the play while he was in Dublin, which defines the date limits. The problem is that he was in Dublin for two extended periods of his life, during both of which he founded a theatre, respectively in Werburgh Street and Smock Alley. As Bentley rightly says, the play could have been written and produced during either period; the inclusion of this entry in the main Catalogue sequence, rather than in Appendix 1, reflects a judgement that, on balance, it more probably belongs to the earlier period, but it is impossible altogether to rule out the claims of the later. It is also conceivable that he might have written it as a literary exercise before or after the years when the Werburgh Street Theatre was in operation (1635–41), without any immediate expectation that it would be produced.

Establishing Dublin's first commercial theatre entailed creating and maintaining a repertory, to which end Ogilby eventually, in late 1636, recruited James Shirley from London; prior to that he may have had assistance from John Clavell, though probably not on a full-time basis since Clavell's main work at this time was as a barrister and physician. Some of the plays performed at Werburgh Street were imports of London successes from two decades earlier (including **1621**, **1644**, **1649**, and **1799**), but there were also new scripts by Shirley and others, among them the local playwright Henry Burnell. The theatre, which seems to have opened in 1635–6, would have needed a turnover of scripts throughout its life, but the early months before Shirley's arrival would have been especially demanding. At the time, Ogilby was a man in his 30s who (according to Aubrey) had only recently first turned his hand to poetry; it is plausible that he might have offered his own work, as English courtiers were doing to the London commercial theatre. The title indicates a play tailored to local interest, comparable with others in the repertory (especially **2644**). Finally, we may reasonably suppose that, by 1661, Ogilby already had enough of a track record as a dramatic writer, rather than just as a literary translator and theatrical impresario, to make him an appropriate person to be awarded the commission to script Charles II's coronation entry into London. (The last time the city had engaged a pageant-writer who was not also an established playwright was in 1620.)

ROLES
A MERCHANT

SETTING
Place: Dublin

EARLY TEXTUAL HISTORY
The play was never printed.

REFERENCES
Annals 1662; John Aubrey, *Brief Lives*, ed. Andrew Clark (Oxford, 1898), ii. 102; Bentley, iv. 950–1; Fletcher, 487; Alan J. Fletcher, *Drama, Performance, and Polity in Pre-Cromwellian Ireland* (Toronto and Cork, 2000), 261–4.

2547. Andronicus Comnenus

TEXT
MS (London: British Library, MS Sloane 1767, fos. 18–66); holograph working draft, heavily corrected.

This play should not be confused with the lost play (**1856**), perhaps on the same theme, written by Samuel Bernard for performance at Oxford. (Klause mistakenly makes this identification.)

GENRE
tragedy
Contemporary: *tragoedia*

TITLE
MS: *Andronicus Comnenus*
Later Assigned: *Alexius Imperator*

AUTHOR
The dramatist was also the copyist, and possibly the author, of *Icon ecclesiastici* (**2482**), which appears earlier in the same MS; the hand appears to be the same throughout.

DATE
c. 1636

ORIGINAL PRODUCTION
English College, Douai (?)

The authors of verses found elsewhere in the MS were connected with the College. The play is not compliant with the Jesuit *Ratio studiorum*, which prohibited the representation of female characters on stage, but Douai plays generally ignored these rules anyway.

PLOT
Seeking revenge on the Emperor Manuel, Andronicus releases Salmanazar, a Moorish prisoner of war, and makes a blood-pact with him. Manuel's grip on the empire has weakened after his failure to resist the territorial designs of the Sultan; now he dies, and his young son Alexius succeeds to the throne, with Protosebastus as Protector. Protosebastus takes Salmanazar into his service. Learning that he is the subject of dangerous gossip, Andronicus decides that he will be safest in prison while incubating his plots, and arranges to have himself and his sons arrested. The imprisonment appals young Alexius. Protosebastus attempts to blind Andronicus, but Salmanazar,

dedicated to evil for its own sake, double-crosses him: Protosebastus himself ends up blinded and imprisoned.

Fearful of the prospective tyranny of Protosebastus, the Patriarch Theodosius decides that Andronicus is likely to be the lesser evil, and resolves to help him seize power. A rebellion breaks out in Andronicus' favour, and Alexius is induced to order Andronicus' release and the execution of the missing Protosebastus. When he goes to the prison to see his instructions carried out, he finds Protosebastus, hears how Andronicus and Salmanazar tortured him, and changes his mind. His private decision to bring the miscreants to trial is overheard and leaked to Andronicus, who murders Protosebastus and has Salmanazar dispose of the body. Popular support for Andronicus continues unabated, and Alexius is forced to release him. However, he is too old to fight, so Isaac is appointed general when the Sultan lays siege to Byzantium.

Reaffirming their plot against the imperial family, Andronicus and Salmanazar overhear two courtiers conspiring against them. Salmanazar blinds Lapardus and Andronicus blinds Comnenus; each then persuades the other's victim to avenge himself, and offers to guide him to his assailant, and the upshot is that the two blind men are misled into stabbing one another to death. Alexius finds the blood, but Salmanazar reassures him that it results from nothing more alarming than a nosebleed; then he murders the Emperor and his sister. Theodosius finds the bodies, but is persuaded of Andronicus' innocence, and confirms him as the new Emperor. The Patriarch is visited by the victims' ghosts, who affirm Andronicus' guilt; Alexius expresses a wish that Isaac should be the next Emperor.

Isaac returns in triumph, but finds the gates of Byzantium barred against him. Salmanazar treacherously abducts Andronicus' sons and offers them to Isaac as hostages. Isaac tries the scheme, but arrests Salmanazar on learning of his part in the murders. Andronicus will not yield, so Isaac blinds the youths, shaming their father. After a battle, Andronicus is captured and mutilated, then killed along with Salmanazar and denied Christian burial. Isaac becomes Emperor.

SCENE DESIGNATION
prol., 1.1–15, 2.1–11, 3.1–14, 4.1–19, 5.1–19, ep. (MS, corrected)

The stage is not clear at the following scene-divisions: 1.1–5, 1.6–12, 1.13–15, 2.1–7, 2.8–11, 3.1–14, 4.1–3, 4.4–5, 4.6–7, 4.8–12, 4.13–16, 4.17–19, 5.3–9, 5.10–11, 5.13–16, 5.17–19. Verse lines are split across the following scene-divisions: 1.1–2, 1.2–3, 1.3–4, 1.4–5, 1.7–8, 1.8–9, 1.9–10, 1.11–12, 1.13–14, 1.14–15, 2.1–2, 2.5–6, 2.6–7, 2.9–10, 3.2–3, 3.5–6, 3.6–7, 3.8–9, 3.9–10, 3.12–13, 4.1–2, 4.2–3, 4.3–4, 4.9–10, 4.14–15, 4.15–16, 4.17–18, 5.2–3, 5.3–4, 5.4–5, 5.5–6, 5.10–11, 5.11–12, 5.13–14, 5.14–15, 5.15–16, 5.16–17, 5.18–19.

ROLES
PROLOGUE
ANDRONICUS Comnenus, father of Manuel and John; 70 years old
SALMANAZAR, a Moor
THEODOSIUS, the Patriarch
PALL-BEARERS (1.3, *non-speaking*)
ALEXIUS Comnenus, Emperor of Byzantium, Maria's younger brother; 13 years old; also appears as a ghost
MARIA Caesarissa, Alexius' elder sister; also appears as a ghost
Alexius PROTOSEBASTUS, the Protector
ISAAC Angelus, a courtier; later the Byzantine General; later still Emperor of Byzantium
LAPARDUS, a nobleman of the imperial family; also appears as a ghost
COMNENUS, a nobleman of the imperial family; also appears as a ghost
MANUEL, Andronicus' son, John's brother; also called Emmanuel
JOHN, Andronicus' son, Manuel's brother
GUARDS (1.4, 5.15, *non-speaking*)
VOICES of the rebellious people of Byzantium (2.11, *within*)
EPILOGUE

At an early stage of composition, the dramatist included one further character, who was later abandoned:

XENE, the dowager Empress

Speaking Parts: 13 (plus the off-stage voices)

Stage Directions and Speech Prefixes
PROLOGUE: *Prologus* (heading)
ANDRONICUS: *Andronicus* (s.d.s); *Andronic<us>* (s.p.s); *Andronicus Commenus Imperator* (d.p.)
SALMANAZAR: *Salmanazar* (s.d.s); *Salmanaz<ar>* (s.p.s); *Salmanazar Maurus* (d.p.)
THEODOSIUS: *Theodosius* (s.d.s); *Theodos<ius>* (s.p.s); *Theodosius Patriarcha* (d.p.)
ALEXIUS: *Alexius Imperator | Alexius* (s.d.s); *Alex<ius> Com<nenus> | Alex<ius> Imperator* (s.p.s); *Alexius Commenus Imperator* (d.p.)
MARIA: *Maria soror | Maria* (s.d.s); *Mar<ia>* (s.p.s); *Maria Caesarissa, soror Alexii Comm<odi>* (d.p.)
PROTOSEBASTUS: *Alexius Protosebastus* (s.d.s and d.p.); *Alexi<us> | Alex<ius> Pr<otosebastus> | Protoseb<astus>* (s.p.s)
ISAAC: *Isaacius Angelus | Isaacius* (s.d.s); *Isaaci<us>* (s.p.s); *Isaacius Angelus Imperator* (d.p.)
LAPARDUS: *Lapardus* (s.d.s); *Lapard<us>* (s.p.s); *Lapardus* [one of the] *nobiles ex familiae imperatoria* (d.p.)
COMNENUS: *Commenus | Commenus* (s.d.s); *Comn<enus>* (s.p.s); *Commenus* [one of the] *nobiles ex familiae imperatoria* (d.p.)
MANUEL: *Manuelis | Manuell* (s.d.s); *Man<uelis> | Eman<uell>* (s.p.s); *Manuell* [one of the] *filii Andronici* (d.p.)
JOHN: *Johannes* (s.d.s); *Johann<es>* (s.p.s); *Johannes* [one of the] *filii Andronici* (d.p.)

GUARDS: *Satellites* (s.d.s and d.p.)
VOICES: *Intus* (s.p.s)
EPILOGUE: *Epilogus* (heading)
XENE: *Xene* (s.d.s and s.p.s)

OTHER CHARACTERS
Manuel, the Emperor, Alexius' father, who dies during the opening scenes (1.1–3, 1.6, 1.9, 1.14, 2.11, 3.11)
The Sultan Masut (1.2, 2.9, 3.12, 3.14, 5.13)
Jagupasan, Masut's son (1.2)
Chirashlan, Masut's son (1.2)
Baldwin of Lorraine (1.2, 2.11)
Naphthalim, King of Morocco and Fez, Salmanazar's father (1.5, 2.1)

SETTING
Period: twelfth century; the play dramatizes events which took place between 1180 and 1185
Time-Scheme: 2.1–7 take place at night, with cock-crow in 2.5; 4.1–19 also take place at night, 4.18 at around 4 a.m.
Place: Byzantium

Geography
Byzantium: Sancta Sophia
Asia: Arabia; Armenia; Jerusalem; Persia; Bactria; Phrygia; Turkey; Scythia; Tartary
The Bosphorus
[*Europe*]: Lorraine
[*Africa*]: Syrtis; Memphis; Morocco; Fez

SOURCES
Narrative: Nicetas Choniates, *Historia* (thirteenth century; the dramatist used the 1557 edn, which included a Latin tr. by Hieronymus Wolf); William Shakespeare, *Titus Andronicus* (**928**; Salmanazar, 5.18–19)
Works Mentioned: the Apostles' Creed (5.14)

LANGUAGE
Latin

FORM
Metre: iambic senarius
Prologue: 19 lines
Act-Division: 5 acts
Epilogue: 7 lines
Lines (Spoken): 2,326
Lines (Written): 3,284

STAGING
Doors: characters enter at two doors (2.11, 4.1, s.d.), and exit severally (4.5, s.d.)
Within: speech (1.4, 2.11, s.d.; 2.7, implicit); cry (2.9, implicit)
Above: characters appear above (5.16, 5.18, s.d.)
Beneath: characters enter from the prison beneath the stage (1.2, 3.7, s.d.; 2.2, implicit; 2.3, 3.3, dialogue); characters exit to the same prison (1.5, 2.5, dialogue; 3.3, s.d.); groans from beneath (3.2, 3.5, 3.10, implicit)
Miscellaneous: Andronicus cuts his arm on stage and it bleeds (1.2, dialogue); Andronicus' hand is cut off on stage (5.18, dialogue)

MUSIC
Music: drum (1.3, 2.9, 5.9, 5.15, s.d.); unspecified music (4.6, 4.9, 4.19, 5.8, s.d.)

PROPS
Lighting: a lighted torch (2.1–7, s.d.); a torch (2.5, s.d.); a candle (4.4–5, s.d.)
Pyrotechnics: a fire (2.5, s.d.)
Weapons: Andronicus' sword (1.2, 3.5, dialogue); hot irons (2.1–7, s.d.); Isaac's sword (3.6–7, 5.17–19, implicit); Lapardus' sword (3.6–7, 4.13–15, implicit); Comnenus' sword (3.6–7, 4.14–15, implicit); a blade or iron used to blind characters (4.7, dialogue; 4.9, 5.16, 5.18, implicit; may all be different tools); a halter (4.19, dialogue); Salmanazar's blade weapon (5.19, implicit)
Food and Drink: a cup of blood (1.2–3, dialogue; drunk on stage); a cup of poison (4.19, dialogue; drunk on stage)
Small Portable Objects: a pan of coals (2.1–7, s.d.); a clock (4.18, dialogue); binding cords (4.7, dialogue; 4.9, 5.15–16, implicit)
Large Portable Objects: chains (1.2–5, dialogue); a bier (1.3, s.d.); a rope (2.5, s.d.)
Miscellaneous: blood (3.5, 5.18–19, dialogue)

COSTUMES AND MAKE-UP
SALMANAZAR: black skin (dialogue)
ALEXIUS: a nightcap (2.9–11, s.d.)
MARIA: a nightgown (2.8–11, s.d.)

EARLY TEXTUAL HISTORY
c. 1636: drafted in MS, part of a literary miscellany connected with the English College, Douai; 49 leaves; list of roles; argument. The collection also includes *Icon ecclesiastici* (**2482**).

EDITION
John Klause, Renaissance Latin Drama in England 1.6 (Hildesheim and New York, 1986).

REFERENCES
Annals 1636; Bentley, iii. 26–7; Churchill-Keller, 256; REED: Oxford, 839; *Shakespeare Jahrbuch* 47 (1911), 78–9.

2548. A Dialogue betwixt a Citizen and a Poor Countryman and his Wife

TEXT
Printed in 1636 (STC 3717.5).

The citizen's last 36-line speech shifts from dialogue to past-tense narrative, but refers to the country people as if they are present.

GENRE
dialogue
Contemporary: dialogue

TITLE
Printed: *A Dialogue betwixt a Citizen and a Poor Countryman and his Wife*
Contemporary: *A Dialogue betwixt a Citizen and a Countryman*

AUTHOR
STC ascribes the dialogue to Thomas Brewer; bibliographies and catalogues often list the book under the initials T. B., even though those initials appear nowhere in it. Brewer had a long-standing connection with Henry Gosson, and was the author of a non-dramatic plague pamphlet published by Gosson in July 1636 (Arber, iv. 367; STC 3719.5), a copy of which was bound together with this one in Richard Heber's library; in consequence, both were catalogued under Brewer's name in the 1836 *Bibliotheca Heberiana* (Part 8, no. 234; p. 12). The ascription to Brewer seems, therefore, to rest on tradition and hearsay rather than evidence; that does not, of course, mean that it might not even so be right.

DATE
1636

PLOT
A Londoner arrives in the country, but one of the locals advises him that it will impossible for him to find any hospitality: everyone in the country is afraid of the plague which is ravaging the capital, and the local authority has issued orders prohibiting anyone from taking in travellers. The countryman is willing to give the citizen food, but not shelter: if any living thing should then die in his home, it will be shut up as a plague-house with him and his family inside. However, the countryman is disposed to be as kind as he can, and the Londoner's offer of handsome payment makes all the difference: he is given lodgings, but will be obliged to conceal his identity.

ROLES
A CITIZEN of London; he is given the alias Master Squire
A COUNTRYMAN, Madge's husband
MADGE, the Countryman's wife, a mother

Speaking Parts: 3

Speech Prefixes
CITIZEN: *Citizen* (s.p.s)
COUNTRYMAN: *Countryman* (s.p.s)
MADGE: *Wife* (s.p.s)

OTHER CHARACTERS
An old man who came to the country and died
A poor countryman who gave the old traveller lodgings, and took his purse when he died
The poor man's wife and children, who died of the plague
The local Justices of Peace, who have given orders not to take in lodgers during plague-time
The Countryman's neighbours
The local Constable
Joan, a neighbour who recently died
Joan's lame sons, who died
Jug, Madge's daughter
Dick, a son or servant in the Countryman's household
The Countryman's father
The bailiff
The Countryman's landlord
Cis, Madge's daughter
The local parson
Travellers who died on the road for lack of food and shelter

SETTING
Period: contemporary
Place: England, in the country

Geography
London

LANGUAGE
English
Dialect: The Countryman and Madge speak in heavy rustic accents.

FORM
Metre: pentameter
Rhyme: ABAB
Lines (Spoken): 310
Lines (Written): 312

PROPS
Money: forty shillings in gold and silver (dialogue)
Large Portable Objects: a piece of wood (dialogue)

EARLY TEXTUAL HISTORY
1636: Q printed by Richard Oulton for Henry Gosson; collation A–C⁴, 12 leaves; title-page woodcut, which also appears on the verso of the title page; the book also contains the prose text 'London Trumpet' and the poem 'Have With You into the Country' (the dialogue appears on the first 6 leaves, sigs. A1ʳ–B2ᵛ).
1636: Q reissued.

2549. Royal Entertainment at Enstone ⌒

TEXT
Two components:
  Q: Bushell's material, printed in 1636 (STC 4187.5);

O: Jordan's contribution (Calliope), printed after 1653 (Wing J1072).

GENRE
royal entertainment

TITLE
Printed: *The Several Speeches and Songs at the Presentment of Mr Bushell's Rock to the Queen's Most Excellent Majesty*
Later Assigned: *The Presentment of Bushell's Rock*

AUTHOR
possibly Thomas Bushell; *partly* Thomas Jordan

DATE
23 August 1636

ORIGINAL PRODUCTION
Thomas Bushell's household at Enstone, Oxfordshire

PLOT
As he enters a grotto on Thomas Bushell's estate in Enstone, the King is greeted by a hermit who mistakes him for Christ come again to judge the world. He tells of how a reformed prodigal, keen to redeem the time he has wasted on hedonism, dug up a marvellous rock, and with it unearthed the cave in which the hermit has lived since the great flood. He asks that the King allow him to continue living there in peace and solitude, and grant the prodigal the right to enhance the landscape.

The King is shown the rock, given a meal, and entertained with a song. Bushell asks an echo if his royal guest has enjoyed himself, and is answered in the affirmative; the echo also tells him to show the Queen the rock. A song asks the royal couple to indicate their pleasure in the entertainment.

At some point during the proceedings, Calliope arrives: she has heard rumours of a strange rock found underground, and of a great king and queen who have deigned to visit it; so she jumped straight onto Pegasus and flew there to see for herself. She remarks that the Muses would like to leave their usual dwellings and take up residence at the rock, where they will praise the King.

SCENE DESIGNATION
It is impossible to assign a secure numerical scene designation because there is no way of knowing at what point Jordan's contribution to the entertainment took place. This entry uses a variant of the division into sections proposed by McGee:
  1: Hermit;
  2: Bushell;
  3: Song 1;
  4: Bushell, Echo, Song 2;
  5: Song 3;
  J: Calliope.

ROLES
A HERMIT, apparently immensely old (or perhaps a ghost); also calls himself the Genius of the cave
A SPEAKER, either representing or played by Thomas Bushell (may be the Hermit)
One or more SINGERS
An ECHO
CALLIOPE, principal of the nine Muses

McGee proposes that the second speech was spoken by Bushell in his own person, since the 1636 printing heads it 'Mr Bushell's Contemplation on the Rock'; if so, it would not strictly be a part of the dramatic entertainment. In the 1660 printing, however, it is headed 'The Hermit's Contemplation on the Rock'. A hypothesis that would account for all the evidence is that Bushell himself played the Hermit.

Speaking Parts: 3–4 (excluding singers)

Stage Directions and Speech Prefixes
HERMIT: *The Hermit* (s.d.)
SPEAKER: *Mr Bushell* (heading)
ECHO: *an Echo* | *The Echo* (s.d.s); *Echo* (s.p.s)
CALLIOPE: *Caliope* (heading)

OTHER CHARACTERS
The other eight Muses, including Urania (J)

SETTING
Geography
Britain
[*Greece*]: Mount Parnassus; the plain of Thessaly
[*Asia Minor*]: Mount Ida
The Indies

SOURCES
Narrative: possibly Francis Bacon, *New Atlantis* (written *c.* 1625, printed 1627) or *A Dialogue between a Melancholy Dreaming Hermit, a Mutinous Brainsick Soldier, and a Busy Tedious Secretary* (**1019**; Hermit)

LANGUAGE
English

FORM
Metre: pentameter
Rhyme: couplets and blank verse
Lines (Spoken): 315 (**BUSHELL:** 245; **JORDAN:** 70)
Lines (Written): 335 (**Q:** 265; **O:** 70)

STAGING
Beneath: the Hermit ascends out of the ground (1, s.d.)
Audience: the King is directly addressed (1–2, J)
Miscellaneous: the singer is 'within the pillar of the table at the banquet' (3, s.d.)

MUSIC
Music: unspecified music accompanying the songs (s.d.)

Songs:
1: 'Come away, blest souls, no more', 3, 24 lines;
2: 'I charge thee, answer me to what I ask', 4, Bushell and Echo, 32 lines;
3: 'Hark, hark how the stones in the rock', 5, 48 lines.

PROPS
Animals: a serpent (1, s.d.)

EARLY STAGE HISTORY
1636: performed on Tuesday 23 August at Enstone, Oxfordshire. The host was Thomas Bushell. The cast included: Thomas Jordan (Calliope); possibly Thomas Bushell (Hermit); possibly a Student (i.e. College Fellow) of Christ Church, Oxford (Singer). The audience included: King Charles I; Queen Henrietta Maria. The music was composed by Simon Ives; some other music may have been contributed by Stephen Goodall, Chaplain of Christ Church.

EARLY TEXTUAL HISTORY
1636: $^1Q_{B_1}$ printed at Oxford by Leonard Lichfield; collation A^4 B^2, 6 leaves; title page refers to performance
1636: Q_{B_1} reissued with variant title page naming Thomas Allam as bookseller.
Before 1660: Jack Sydenham, Thomas Bushell's servant, gave Isaac Lyte a 'book' associated with the entertainment. This probably contained the speeches; it was later described as a 'little pamphlet' of one sheet; it was probably a copy of Q_{B_1} (which is actually a sheet and a half), but may have been a MS.
1659: extract (1–2) included in Thomas Bushell's *Abridgement of the Lord Chancellor Bacon's Philosophical Theory in Mineral Prosecutions*, pp. 24–7 (unsigned); printed by Thomas Newcomb.
1660: Bushell's text included in his *An Extract* ($^2Q_{B_2}$), sigs. I3^r–K2^v, 4 leaves; printed by Thomas Leach.
Mid-seventeenth century (after 1653, possibly 1665): extract included in Thomas Jordan's *Wit in a Wilderness of Promiscuous Poesy* (^3O_J), sigs *5^v–*6^v; printed by R. A.; heading refers to performance but erroneously dates it 1638.
After 1677: Lyte's book of the entertainment was in the possession of his grandson, John Aubrey.
1683: *The Complete Courtier* entered in the Stationers' Register to William Thackeray on Wednesday 21 February.
1683: Song 1 included in J. S.'s *The Complete Courtier*, sig. D9^v; printed for William Thackeray and to be sold by Joshua Conyers.
1694: Some years earlier, Aubrey had given his copy of the book to Anthony Wood. On Sunday 2 September he wrote to Wood asking for it back; but on Saturday 15 September Wood replied, refusing to return it, and stating his intention to give it to the University Museum. (This may have been the Bodleian Library's copy of Q_{B_1}.)

Two distinct format sequences are identified here, differentiating the editions containing the text contributed respectively by Bushell ($Q_{B_{1-2}}$) and by Jordan (O_J).

EDITION
C. E. McGee, *MRDE* 16 (2003), 39–80.

REFERENCES
Annals 1636; John Aubrey, *Brief Lives*, ed. Andrew Clark (Oxford, 1898), i. 133; Eyre & Rivington, iii. 129; Greg 511; Nicolas K. Kiessling, *The Library of Anthony Wood* (Oxford, 2002) 1229; McGee-Meagher 1634–42, 52–3; Anthony Powell, *John Aubrey and His Friends*, rev. edn (London, 1963), 233, 236.

2550. Passions Calmed

TEXT
Printed in 1655 (Wing S5983); may include at least one later interpolation (in 3.2). Additional information derives from Anthony Wood's account of the performance (Oxford: Bodleian, MS Wood F.1, pp. 861–2).

GENRE
allegory
Contemporary: play (prol.); comedy (Heylyn); tragicomedy (t.p.); poem (epistle); *comoedia* (comm. verses)

TITLE
Performed: *Passions Calmed, or The Settling of the Floating Island*
Printed: *The Floating Island*
Contemporary: *The Passions*; *Prudentius, with Intellectus Agens and the Rebellious Passions*; *The Passions Calmed*

AUTHOR
William Strode

DATE
August 1636

ORIGINAL PRODUCTION
Christ Church, Oxford

PLOT
Prudentius rules his floating island firmly, restraining the liberties of the passions, his subjects; he has recently banished Concupiscence. Sir Amorous, her father, and the other aggressive passions agree to depose or assassinate Prudentius and install Lady Fancy on the throne instead. They identify the former soldier Desperato as a suitable man for the job; but when the King arrives, his royal magnificence renders the conspirators unable to strike. Their plans are overheard

by Liveby Hope, who reports them to Prudentius. When they attempt a nocturnal coup, they find Prudentius has gone, leaving the crown behind. They offer it to Fancy, who accepts power but prefers a more diverse and imaginative range of headgear.

Under Fancy's capricious rule, the passions begin to annoy one another. Sir Amorous causes offence by representing six of them as characters in a court masque. Fancy feels like having some incest at court, and grants Hilario a dispensation to marry his sister, the recalled Concupiscence; in order to avoid having to do so, Hilario inveigles Melancholico into marrying her. Sir Timorous gets a kicking from Irato, but is unable to sue him because the law allows everyone to follow their own humour: Irato, being anger, is prone to assault people.

In order to avoid a duel with Captain Audax, Sir Timorous agrees to cross-dress and become one of Fancy's lady attendants; this will give him easier access to Fuga, his reluctant beloved. Concupiscence engages Audax to rape Fuga, but he mistakenly tries to rape Sir Timorous instead. Sir Timorous tries to persuade Fuga that he has saved her honour, but the incident only confirms her in her mistrust of men. Seeking revenge on Audax, her father, Malevolo, procures his involvement in a murder attempt: Audax and Irato both covet the generalship (even though no army has yet been levied), but Malevolo encourages them to think that Liveby Hope will get the job, and that both their chances will be improved if they kill him. The attack is witnessed by Morphe, Sir Amorous's beloved, who faints in distress; Liveby Hope is left for dead, and taken away by Intellectus Agens. Fancy is appalled, and refuses to appoint either of the murderers to the command. Sir Amorous sends for the physician Desperato to cure Morphe, but he is still offended because of the masque, and poisons her instead.

Determined to spread misery as widely as possible, Desperato hosts a banquet at which the guests are served weapons for suicidal use. Intellectus Agens, sent by Prudentius, has saved the lives of Morphe and Liveby Hope. The passions agree that things have gone badly of late, and recall Prudentius. He offers each of them the crown, but they all refuse, and restore him to the throne.

SCENE DESIGNATION
prol., 1.1–7, 2.1–6, 3.1–8, 4.1–16, 5.1–11, ep. (Q)

The stage is briefly clear during 4.12, but is not clear at the following scene-divisions: 1.1–7, 2.1–6, 3.1–4, 3.5–8, 4.1–16, 5.1–8, 5.9–11. Verse lines are split across the following scene-divisions: 1.1–2, 2.4–5, 4.1–2, 4.7–8, 4.11–12, 4.12–13, 4.14–15, 5.2–3, 5.3–4, 5.6–7, 5.9–10.

ROLES
PROLOGUE
SIR AMOROUS, a knight and a passion, father of Hilario and Concupiscence; later appointed Queen Fancy's Master of Ceremonies

MORPHE, Sir Amorous's beloved
Lord IRATO, an angry passion; later appointed Queen Fancy's Lord Comptroller
MALEVOLO, a malign passion, Fuga's father; later appointed Queen Fancy's chief counsellor; representing William Prynne
Captain AUDAX, a brave passion; also called Captain Martial Law
HILARIO, a young gentleman, Sir Amorous's son, Concupiscence's brother
King PRUDENTIUS, ruler of the floating island
INTELLECTUS AGENS, Prudentius' counsellor
LIVEBY HOPE, Prudentius' favourite; a male character; also called Hope and Live-by; later appointed Queen Fancy's Master of Requests
ATTENDANTS on Prudentius (1.4, non-speaking)
MELANCHOLICO, a malcontented Puritan passion; later Concupiscence's husband; also called Melancholy; Irato addresses him as 'brother'; representing Henry Burton
DESPERATO, a passion; formerly a soldier, later a physician; also called Despair; representing John Bastwick
SIR TIMOROUS Fear-all, a cowardly knight; also called Sir Tim; adopts the alias Madam Timida (also called Lady Timida)
A GROOM of the Chamber (1.6)
CONCUPISCENCE, a passion; Sir Amorous's daughter, Hilario's sister; later Queen Fancy's lady attendant, and later still Melancholico's wife; a mother of many daughters; also called Carnality; assumes the alias Temperance, said to be a widow
Madam FUGA, Malevolo's daughter; later Queen Fancy's lady attendant; also called Madam Simpers
Hilario's BOY, who sings
Lady FANCY, later Queen Fancy; also called Queen Fan
Recorder MEMOR, a lawyer; possibly representing John Selden
OVIDIAN, a poet; later appointed Queen Fancy's secretary
MODEL, Fancy's tireman
A PAINTER at Fancy's court
A MUSICIAN at Fancy's court
MORPHEUS, a god, King of dreams; a character in the masque
Six MASQUERS, representing Memor, Malevolo, Irato, Sir Timorous, Hilario, and Desperato (3.4, non-speaking)
Two SEDAN-BEARERS (5.6, non-speaking)
ATTENDANTS at Desperato's house, who serve a banquet (5.7; one sings bass)
EPILOGUE

Speaking Parts: 26
Allegorical Roles: 13

Stage Directions and Speech Prefixes
PROLOGUE: the Prologue (s.d.s)

SIR AMOROUS: *Sir Amorous | Amorous* (s.d.s); *Am<orous>* (s.p.s); *Sir Amorous a Courtly Knight* (d.p.)
MORPHE: *Morphe* (s.d.s); *Mor<phe>* (s.p.s); *Morphe the beauteous Mistress of Amorous* (d.p.)
IRATO: *Irato | [one of the] Passions* (s.d.s); *Ir<ato>* (s.p.s); *Irato an Angry Lord* (d.p.)
MALEVOLO: *Malevolo | [one of the] Passions* (s.d.s); *Mal<evolo>* (s.p.s); *Malevolo a Malicious contriver* (d.p.)
AUDAX: *Audax | [one of the] Passions* (s.d.s); *Au<dax>* (s.p.s); *Audax a bold Captain* (d.p.)
HILARIO: *Hilario* (s.d.s); *Hil<ario>* (s.p.s); *Hilario [Sir Amorous's] Son a merry jovial Gentleman* (d.p.)
PRUDENTIUS: *Prudentius* (s.d.s); *Pru<dentius>* (s.p.s); *Prudentius the King deposed* (d.p.)
INTELLECTUS AGENS: *Intellectus Agens | Intellectus* (s.d.s); *Int<ellectus>* (s.p.s); *Intellectus Agens [Prudentius'] Counsellor* (d.p.)
LIVEBY HOPE: *Liveby Hope | Livebyhope | Liveby* (s.d.s); *Liv<eby>* (s.p.s); *Livebyhope a Favourite* (d.p.)
ATTENDANTS: *Attendants* (s.d.s and d.p.)
MELANCHOLICO: *Melancholico | [one of the] Passions | Melancolico* (s.d.s); *Mel<ancholico>* (s.p.s); *Melancholico a Malcontent turned Puritan* (d.p.)
DESPERATO: *Desperato | [one of the] Passions* (s.d.s); *Desp<erato>* (s.p.s); *Desperato a desperate Soldier turned Physician* (d.p.)
SIR TIMOROUS: *Sir Timerous | [one of the] Passions | Timerous* (s.d.s); *Tim<erous>* (s.p.s); *Sir Timerous-Fearall a Cowardly Knight* (d.p.)
GROOM: *Groom of the Chamber* (s.d.s and d.p.); *Groom* (s.d.s and s.p.s)
CONCUPISCENCE: *Concupiscence | [one of Fancy's] women* (s.d.s); *Conc<upicence>* (s.p.s); *Concupiscence the lustful daughter of Amorous* (d.p.)
FUGA: *Fuga | [one of Fancy's] women* (s.d.s); *Fug<a>* (s.p.s); *Fuga the coy daughter of Malevolo* (d.p.)
BOY: *Hilario's Boy* (s.d.s and d.p.); *Boy* (s.p.s)
FANCY: *Fancie* (s.d.s); *Fan<cie>* (s.p.s); *Phancy the new initiated Queen* (d.p.)
MEMOR: *Memor* (s.d.s); *Mem<or>* (s.p.s); *Memor a Lawyer and Recorder* (d.p.)
OVIDIAN: *Poet Ovidian* (s.d.s); *Ovid<ian>* (s.p.s); *Ovidian a Poet* (d.p.)
MODEL: *Model [Fancy's] Tireman | Tireman | Model | the Tireman* (s.d.s); *Mod<el>* (s.p.s); *Model a Tireman* (d.p.)
PAINTER: *Painter* (s.d.s, s.p.s, and d.p.)
MUSICIAN: *Musician* (s.d.s and d.p.)
MORPHEUS: *Morpheus* (s.d.s); *Morp<heus>* (s.p.s); *Morpheus the God of Dreams* (d.p.)
MASQUERS: *six sleeping Persons | Masquers* (s.d.s); *6 Dreaming Masquers* (d.p.)
ATTENDANT: *An Attendant* (s.d.s); *Attendants* (d.p.)
EPILOGUE: *the Epilogue* (s.d.s)

OTHER CHARACTERS
Desperato's man (1.2)
Quarrelsome peers whom Prudentius has beheaded (1.2)
Valiant captains whom Prudentius has imprisoned and executed (1.2)
Sir Amorous's sisters, whipped on Prudentius' orders (1.2)
Sir Amorous's aunts, carted on Prudentius' orders (1.2)
People whom Irato has killed (1.3)
Common Sense, a judge (1.5)
Concupiscence's numerous, sinful daughters, the female passions (3.3)
Pride, Concupiscence's eldest daughter (3.3)
Afterwit, Prudentius' brother; also called Epimetheus (5.11)

SETTING
Time-Scheme: 1.7 takes place at night, 2.1 at dawn, and 4.11 in the evening
Place: a floating island

Geography
[Europe]: the Alps; Henneberg; Spain; Rome; Venice; the Low Countries
[Mediterranean]: Paphos
[Asia]: Persia; Turkey; River Araxes
New England

SOURCES
Narrative: Phineas Fletcher, *The Purple Island* (1633)
Verbal: Virgil, *Aeneid* 9 (4.9); Ben Jonson, *The Alchemist* (**1621**; 3.3); Francis Beaumont and John Fletcher, *A King and No King* (**1636**; 5.11)
Works Mentioned: Petronius, *Satyricon* (3.3); William Prynne, *The Unloveliness of Love-Locks* (1628; oblique allusion; 1.2), *Histriomastix* (1633; oblique allusion; 3.8)

LANGUAGE
English
Latin: 10 words (1.5–6, 2.4; Sir Amorous, Prudentius, Ovidian)

FORM
Metre: pentameter and prose; occasional alexandrines
Rhyme: blank verse
Prologue:
    ROYAL: 12 lines, in couplets
    UNIVERSITY: 20 lines, in couplets
Act-Division: 5 acts
Epilogue:
    ROYAL: 14 lines, in couplets
    UNIVERSITY: 6 lines, in couplets
Lines (Spoken): 2,213 (1,967 verse, 246 prose)
Lines (Written): 3,785

STAGING
Doors: characters enter from two ways (1.1, 3.4, 5.9, s.d.); one point of entry signifies the bedchamber (1.6, s.d.)

Stage: Hilario drives Fuga 'to the brink of the stage' (2.3, s.d.).
Within: speech (2.4, s.d.); sound effects (4.10, implicit); music (5.9, implicit)
Above: characters appear above (4.10, 4.12, s.d.; in 4.10, three lines are allowed for Morphe to descend to the main stage, but in 4.12, Sir Amorous has to do so in mid-speech)
Other Openings: the Prologue enters 'as coming out of the sea' (prol., s.d.); characters enter from a black cell and a black cave (3.4, s.d.)
Audience: the King and Queen in the audience are addressed as 'great monarch and bright Queen' (royal prol.); the royal epilogue identifies Prudentius with the King in the audience
Miscellaneous: The sedan in 5.6 is explicitly assigned two passengers and only two bearers, one at the front and one behind. Malevolo exits at the end of 5.8 and re-enters at the start of 5.9 (but the stage direction specifies that he does so 'soon after').

MUSIC AND SOUND

Sound Effects: clash of weapons within (4.10, dialogue)
Music: soft music (1.7, s.d.); drum within (5.9, s.d.); unspecified music at the end of the action, before the epilogue (5.11, s.d.)
Songs: *all have surviving musical settings*:
1: 'My limbs I will fling', 1.3, Hilario, 12 lines;
2: 'Hail, thou great queen of various humours', 2.4, Hilario's Boy, 7 lines;
3: 'Sweet Morphe, lend a feeling ear', 4.10, Musician, 9 lines;
4: 'Once Venus' cheeks that shamed the morn', 4.14, Musician, 9 lines; *two settings survive*;
5: 'Come, heavy souls, oppressed with the weight', 5.7, Attendant, 11 lines.
Other Singing: Hilario sings (2.3, s.d.)
Dance: Hilario dances (1.3, 2.3, s.d.); the masquers dance (3.4, s.d.)

PROPS

Lighting: a torch (1.7, s.d.).
Weapons: Irato's sword (1.2–7, s.d.; 3.8, 4.9, 4.11, 4.14, dialogue); Audax's sword (1.2–7, s.d.; 4.9, implicit; 4.11, 4.14, dialogue); Desperato's sword (1.5–6, implicit; 1.7, s.d.); a sword of state (2.4, 5.9–11, s.d.); Sir Timorous's sword (3.5, dialogue); weapons in the banquet dishes, including knives, bodkins, daggers (including a poniard), ropes (silken, hairy, and hempen) and halters, and little papers containing potions and poisons (5.7–8, dialogue)
Clothing: the golden crown (1.7, 2.4, 5.9–11, s.d.; also worn by Prudentius)
Food and Drink: wine (5.7–8, dialogue)
Small Portable Objects: a paper (2.2, s.d.); a watch (2.4, dialogue); an umbrella (2.4, s.d.); a sceptre (2.4, s.d.); a looking-glass (2.4, dialogue); a caduceus (3.4, s.d.); a ribbon (3.5, s.d.); a petition (4.15, s.d.); covered dishes (5.7–8, s.d.); a book (5.8, s.d.)
Large Portable Objects: a picture of Fancy crowned with gold (2.5, s.d.); a table (5.1–8, s.d.); a chair (5.7, s.d.; Wood's account refers to a chair, probably this one, gliding onto the stage without any visible help from stage hands)
Scenery: a shutter with two leaves, showing an animated seascape and a floating island in it (prol., ep., s.d./Wood; the island moves, and the leaves open of their own accord to reveal the scene); the court of Prudentius (1.1–7, 5.9–11, s.d.); Fancy's court (2.1–3.4, s.d.); a black cell (3.4, s.d.); a black cave (3.4, s.d.); fields, walks, and scattered houses (3.5–4.16, s.d.); the house of Despair (5.1–8, s.d.); a sedan chair (5.6, s.d.; seats two)

Leaving aside the prologue's sea and island, which are apparently mounted on an outer shutter, there are four changes of scene, the last of which restores the scenery from the start of the play, Prudentius' court. Scene changes are described in terms of the scene 'turning', which might be just a figure of speech, or might imply that the scenes were mounted on square periaktoi. Periaktoi were certainly used for the plays performed during the royal visit in 1605 (**1475–8**). However, it is not certain that this technique would have been feasible to effect the scene changes required in *The Royal Slave* (**2552**), the other play performed at Christ Church for the 1636 visit.

COSTUMES AND MAKE-UP

MALEVOLO: long hair covering his cropped ears (dialogue)
PRUDENTIUS: the crown (1.6, 5.11, s.d.; put on on stage)
DESPERATO: hangers (1.5–6, implicit); a physician's habit (4.1–2, s.d.; 4.13, implicit)
SIR TIMOROUS: spurs (2.2–5, implicit); a cap (3.5, s.d.; put on on stage); cross-dressed as a woman, in clothes matching Fuga's (4.5, s.d.); men's clothes (4.15, s.d.)
CONCUPISCENCE: a citizen's habit (3.6–8, s.d.)
FUGA: clothes matching Sir Timothy's in the same scene (4.5–8, s.d.)
FANCY: a ruff (2.4–5, dialogue); a laurel crown (2.4, s.d.; put on and removed on stage); a turban (2.4, 4.13–16, s.d.; put on and removed on stage); a cydaris (2.4, 3.3, s.d.; put on and removed on stage); a crown of coloured feathers with a circle of pearls at the bottom (2.4, s.d.; put on and removed on stage); a black wire coronet set with black and silver spangles (2.4, 5.5–8, s.d.; put on and removed on stage); dishevelled hair (5.5–8, s.d.); a black and silver habit (5.5–8, s.d.)
MORPHEUS: a cloud-coloured cassock and a wreath of poppies (3.4, s.d.)
MASQUERS: nightcaps half down their faces, waistcoats, and lower garments identifying them severally as Memor, Malevolo, Irato, Sir Timorous, Hilario, and Desperato (3.4, s.d.)

EARLY STAGE HISTORY
Preparation: By mid-July 1636, it had been decided that the University would present plays during the royal visit to Oxford. On Tuesday 16 August, Congregation decided that admission to the performances would be only by tickets to be issued by the Lord Chamberlain (Philip Herbert, 4th Earl of Pembroke and 1st Earl of Montgomery).

Preparation of Venue: Lighting branches were supplied by the court, and soldered into place in Christ Church hall.

Rehearsal: A rehearsal took place on Friday 26 August, and was attended by Gregorio Panzani.

Performance: performed in the hall at Christ Church, Oxford, on Monday 29 August 1636. The performance took place in the evening, beginning at about 7 p.m. and lasting until 9 or 10. Music was composed by Henry Lawes (who set the songs) and William Lawes; the choreography was by William Stokes. The cast included: Mr Cary; Thomas Holmes; [William and/or Henry] Lawes; probably William Stokes; boys of the Chapel Royal. The musicians included Simon Coleman, Stephen Goodall, Peter Jones, Edward Lowe, and Davis Mell. The audience included: King Charles I; Queen Henrietta Maria; Charles Louis, Elector Palatine; Prince Rupert; William Laud (Chancellor of the University); Robert Dormer, 1st Earl of Carnarvon (who thought it one of the worst plays he had ever seen, with the exception of one at Cambridge, presumably *The Rival Friends*, **2364**); Philip Herbert, 4th Earl of Pembroke; Edward Sackville, 4th Earl of Dorset; Gregorio Panzani; George Con. Pembroke and Dorset both invited Con to sit with them, but he declined. The general opinion was that the play was 'fitter for scholars than a court'; it was further suggested that the courtiers found it too grave, and simply didn't understand it.

Repeat Performance: a second performance, at Oxford in Christ Church hall on the afternoon of Saturday 3 September, was ordered by William Laud, for members of the University and guests. A different prologue and epilogue was substituted for the one addressed to the royal audience.

William Stokes was paid for 'composing and performing three dances', which could mean that he performed them in the play itself. In all, there are three dances in this play and two in *The Royal Slave* (**2552**), to which the accounts also pertain, but one of those in *The Royal Slave* is for ladies only. Stokes would have performed three dances in *Passions Calmed* if he played both Hilario and also the masquer who impersonates him.

Production Finance
In July, Christ Church complained to William Laud that the other colleges were unwilling to contribute to the cost of the plays for the royal visit. On Monday 25 July, Congregation decided that the University itself would contribute only £200 to the total cost of the visit (including, but not limited to, the cost of the plays), and that the rest should be levied from the colleges and from individual members of the University.

The colleges were assessed for contributions, but St John's and Christ Church were exempted. The others' contributions were set at 5% of their wealth, as assessed at the time of the royal visit in 1592: All Souls (£500); Balliol (£100); Brasenose (£300); Corpus Christi (£500); Exeter (£200); Lincoln (£130); Magdalen (£1,200); Merton (£400); New (£1,000); Oriel (£200); Queen's (£260); Trinity (£200); University (£100). The President of Corpus Christi College, Thomas Jackson, was absent from the assessment meeting and subsequently protested at the amount demanded and, in particular, that his college had been assessed at a higher rate than Merton; but he duly sent in his college's contribution of £25.

Three colleges had not previously been assessed, in two cases because they had not yet been founded at the time of the previous royal visits of 1592 and 1605; in the case of Jesus College, founded in 1571, the oversight may have been because the 1592 arrangements were based on those for the royal visit of 1566. The three colleges' wealth was assessed as follows: Jesus (£200); Pembroke (£200); Wadham (£200). The assessment was made in the presence of the three heads of house (respectively Francis Mansell, Thomas Clayton, and Daniel Estcott).

Individual members of the University were required to contribute at the following rates: earl's sons (£1.13s.4d); barons' sons (£1); fellow commoners and upper commoners (10s); M.A.s and ordinary commoners (5s); batlers (3s.4d). Poor scholars were exempted.

The Vice-Chancellor, Richard Baylie, recorded receipts of £718.9s.4d. Surviving accounts of individual colleges record the following payments: All Souls (£25); Jesus (£5, half the sum due); Merton (£20); New (£50); Oriel (£10); Trinity (£10). Expenses exceeded receipts, which probably explains why some college accounts for the academic year 1636-7 show them paying second instalments of a quarter as much again: All Souls (£6.5s); Jesus (£2.10s); New (£12.10s).

Production Expenses
The production costs of both this play and *The Royal Slave* (**2552**)—the two produced by Christ Church—reportedly amounted to £843.15s.6d, but this is less than the sum of the individual items in the extant account, which adds up to £845.11s.2d, plus the cost of the tallow candles (for lighting the backstage area), the sum of which has worn away. The University appointed Samuel Fell, Daniel Estcott, and John Saunders as delegates to oversee expenditure.

Staging: The total recorded expenditure for both plays, including for lighting, was £48.19s.4d, as follows: wax candles (£21.3s); 34 torches (£1.8s.4d); twelve candlesticks and loan of six flagons (9s); workmen for watching six days and nights and dismantling the stage afterwards (£5); fuel for tiring room and music room (£1); lighting branches (£19.19s).

Scenery: The cost for both plays amounted to £260.

Costumes: The total expenditure for the two plays was £384.15s.6d, as follows: costumes supplied by 'the property men' (£318); apparel for Lawes, Holmes, and Day's boys (£12.12s.8d); Mrs Morgan the tirewoman for wigs, apparel, and expenses (£29.15s); boots, shoes, and spurs (£3.16s.6d); Mr Cary's suit (£2.14s.8d); alterations and maintenance of costumes (£1); a barber's services (£1.10s); Mr Taylor's expenses for a journey undertaken in connection with the loan of costumes (£15.6s.8d).

Music: The total expenditure for the two plays was recorded as £122.12s.8d, but the total amount paid was in fact 2d more. This included fees to: William and Henry Lawes (£45); Thomas Day and his boys (£20); Thomas Holmes (£13.6s.8d); Davis Mell (£12); Peter Jones (£10); Edward Lowe (£6.13s.4d); Stephen Goodall (£3); Simon Coleman (£1). The musicians' food cost £10.12s.10d, and the college also laid out £1 to pay for a book for David Jones. Not included in the total were payments for university music (£2), to William Stokes the dancing-master for choreography, performance, pumps, and some costumes (£22), and the loan of linen for musicians (5s). Total expenditure on music was thus £146.17s.10d.

Props: Items supplied for this play cost a total of £3.6s, as follows: buckram and curtains for the sedan, with a curtain for the music room (£1.4s.6d); manufacture of the sedan, including the cost of the boards (11s.6d); Fancy's picture (£1.10s).

Sundry: paid to Mr Stutvile for binding of books presented as gifts to the royal party (£1.12s.6d).

The books given to the visitors upon their arrival in Oxford were a Bible for the King, William Camden's *Annals* (1624–9) for the Queen, and Richard Hooker's *Laws of Ecclesiastical Polity* (1593) for the Elector Palatine. It is unclear why the binding costs should have been bundled into an account pertaining specifically to the plays, and it is not inconceivable that the binding in question may have been for copies of the plays, unrelated to the University's greeting gifts.

EARLY TEXTUAL HISTORY

1636: William Strode (Public Orator of Oxford University) wrote the play 'at the instance of those who might command him', presumably the University authorities.

1636: A copy of the text may have been presented to King Charles I and Queen Henrietta Maria; Christ Church paid Mr Stutvile £1.12s.6d for binding whatever the books were.

1636: extract (from 5.11) quoted by George Leyburn in a letter (London: Archives of the Archdiocese of Westminster, A XXVIII, no. 157, p. 524) to Edward Bennett dated Saturday 3 September.

c. 1636: university prologue transcribed on a MS leaf, which was later included in a composite MS volume (Oxford: Bodleian, MS Rawlinson poet. 172, fo. 29^r).

c. 1636: Song 5 (headed 'The Passions Met at Desperato's Banquet' and ascribed to Strode) transcribed on a folio leaf and later included in a composite MS volume (Oxford: Bodleian, MS Rawlinson poet. 172, fo. 30^r). The leaf also includes Song 2 of *The Royal Slave* (**2552**).

Late 1630s (?): transcribed in a folio MS (as *The Passions Calmed*); the MS, said to be 'very neatly written', was offered for sale in 1838–43, but is now untraced.

Mid-seventeenth century (*c.* 1637–62): Songs 3–5 (the last headed 'Despair's Banquet'), included, with Henry Lawes's musical settings, in his MS songbook (London: British Library, Add. MS 53723, fos. 41^r, 61^v–62^r); Lawes gives the title of the play as *The Passions*, names Strode as the author, and refers to the occasion of the performance.

c. 1641–9: Song 4 included in a MS verse miscellany (London: British Library, MS Harley 6917, fo. 49^v), compiled by Peter Calfe.

1653: Song 5 included, with Lawes's musical setting, in his *Airs and Dialogues*, sig. H2^v; printed by Thomas Harper for John Playford.

1655: Q printed by T. C. (perhaps Thomas Child) for Henry Twyford, Nathaniel Brooke, and John Place; collation A–F^4, 24 leaves; title page names author and composer, and refers to performance; epistle to the reader; authorial verse dedication to Sir John Hele; Latin commendatory verses by J. D.; list of roles. The text is printed in double columns.

1655: George Thomason acquired a copy of O on Friday 22 June. In *c.* 1678, some years after his death, his entire collection of books and tracts was acquired by the bookbinder Samuel Mearne, acting as agent for King Charles II; the King never paid him, and the books remained in Mearne's family until 1761.

1654–70s: Songs 1 and 2, with Lawes's musical settings, transcribed by Edward Lowe in a MS songbook (London: British Library, Add. MS 29396, fos. 15^v, 27^r); Song 1 is ascribed to the character who sings it, Hilario, and Song 2 to 'Dr Strode's Play before the King'.

1657: advertised as for sale by the Newcastle-upon-Tyne bookseller William London.

1657–8: Song 4 included, with a different musical setting, in Henry Lawes's *Airs and Dialogues*, sigs. L1^v–L2^r; printed by William Godbid for John Playford.

1658–62: Q advertised as for sale by Nathaniel Brooke.

1669: *Airs and Dialogues* reissued as *Select Airs and Dialogues*.

1684: Nicholas Cox (Manciple of St Edmund Hall, Oxford) had a copy, presumably of Q, in his bookshop. It had probably been previously owned by Gerard Langbaine, and appears on a list compiled by Anthony Wood on Saturday 13 December.

EDITION

Bertram Dobell, in *The Poetical Works of William Strode* (London, 1907), 137–240.

REFERENCES
Annals 1636; Beal 2 StW 1477–83; Beal Online StW 1476.5; Bentley, v. 1189–95; Bodleian, MS Wood E. 4, art. 1, p. 4; *Cal. Dom.* 1636–7, 114; Greg 746; Hazlitt, 86; William London, *A Catalogue of the Most Vendible Books in England* (London, 1657), sig. 2F1ᵛ; Orgel and Strong, ii. 827–8; Michael C. Questier (ed.), *Newsletters from the Caroline Court, 1631–1638* (Cambridge, 2005), 288–90; REED: Cambridge, 857; REED: Oxford, 519–25, 528, 533, 535–7, 540, 543–4, 546, 554–6, 559–60, 810, 889–90; *The Seventeenth Century* 27 (2012), 129–56; Steele, 259–60; Stratman, 51–6, 310–11; *Theatre Notebook* 39 (1985) 7–13.

2551. The Hospital of Lovers

TEXT
Three MS witnesses:
- B: London: British Library, Add. MS 14047, fos. 7ʳ⁻ᵛ, 9ʳ–39ʳ; scribal transcript; lacks prologue and epilogue;
- R: Bodleian, MS Rawlinson poet. 172, fo. 27ʳ⁻ᵛ; prologue and epilogue for the royal performance only;
- W: Washington: Folger, MS 1487.2; fragment, containing 1.1 and the opening line of 1.2; possibly from a presentation volume transcribed from an authorial first draft.

GENRE
comedy
Contemporary: play (Laud); comedy (Crosfield)

TITLE
Performed: *The Hospital of Lovers*
MS: *Love's Hospital*
Contemporary: *Love's Hospitals*; *Lovers' Hospital*

AUTHOR
George Wilde

DATE
August 1636

ORIGINAL PRODUCTION
St John's College, Oxford

PLOT
Lepidus wants to discourage his daughter Facetia from taking an interest in the opposite sex, so he introduces her to a series of inappropriate, undesirable suitors: the dumb Piscinus, who woos through an interpreter; the deaf Surdato, whose servant communicates with him in sign language whilst audibly insulting him; and the lame Aegidius. The only suitor banned from the house is the man she loves, Comastes. He brings his own problems to the match: his father Caecilius will only sanction his marriage to Facetia if he can see the girl for himself—and he is blind. In any event, Caecilius has decided to marry again, and has been so impressed by Comastes' description of Facetia that he wants her for himself; Comastes is to disguise himself as a rustic and woo her on his father's behalf. Lepidus encourages the blind man's suit.

After jilting Comastes' sister Olympa, to whom he was betrothed, Lysander has given up earning his living and has become a parasitical member of Lepidus' household. Olympa has faked her own death, disguised herself as Nigella, a blackamoor servant, and had herself given to Facetia by Surdato, so that she can still at least see her ex-fiancé. Lysander's objective is to win Facetia for himself, and he frustrates his rivals: both Piscinus and Aegidius give him money to deliver as gifts, and he persuades Lepidus that it would be a good joke to send Caecilius off to wed Nigella, thinking her Facetia. Comastes intervenes to prevent his father marrying a Moor, but Caecilius misunderstands and disinherits him. Set on by Facetia, Surdato takes possession of Nigella and returns her to Facetia.

Lepidus starts to think seriously about who should marry his daughter, and decides on Lysander; they now have to put off the other suitors. With all the suitors gathered together, along with Comastes in his rustic guise, Lepidus grants Facetia her own choice of husband. She sets them all a task, and most of them rush off to be the first to comply. Lysander plans to marry her while they are away, but Nigella intervenes: he is already betrothed to Olympa. Lysander insists that Olympa is dead, and sends Facetia to church, escorted by the rustic, while he deals with this unexpected turn of events. Olympa removes her black make-up, and Facetia and Comastes return, married to one another. Caecilius is annoyed, but forgives both Comastes and Lysander. Hymen presents a wedding masque.

SCENE DESIGNATION
1.1–6, 2.1–8, 3.1–7, 4.1–6, 5.1–8 (MS)

The stage is not clear at the following scene-divisions: 1.1–3, 2.2–3, 2.5–6, 2.7–8, 3.1–2, 3.3–7, 4.1–3, 5.1–3, 5.4–8.

ROLES
COMASTES, Caecilius' heir and only son, Olympa's brother, a young man; later Facetia's husband; poses as a rustic, perhaps named Villanus, Caecilius' tenant, who is a married man and a father
NIGELLA, a Moor, Facetia's servant, a young woman; also called Dame Ugly; in reality, Olympa, Caecilius' daughter, Comastes' sister, Lysander's fiancée
Lady FACETIA, Lepidus' daughter; later Comastes' wife
Lord LEPIDUS, an old man, Facetia's father
Master PISCINUS, a dumb man; a landowner (speaks incoherent, non-verbal scripted utterances)
LYSANDER, Aegidius' nephew, Olympa's fiancé, Lepidus' parasite

2551. The Hospital of Lovers

AEGIDIUS, an old, lame usurer, Lysander's uncleSir
CAECILIUS, an old, blind knight, father of Comastes and Olympa, a wealthy landowner of a great family
Señor Aurelio SURDATO, a deaf Spaniard; also called Señor Don Fogo
MACILENTO, Surdato's servant of four or five years' standing; a young man
COLUMELLA, Piscinus' interpreter
Two SERGEANTS (4.4–5)
A BOY attending Caecilius (5.1)
HYMEN, god of marrage, presenter of the masque
A HARE in the antimasque (5.6, *non-speaking*)
A WOLF in the antimasque (5.6, *non-speaking*)
An ASS in the antimasque (5.6, *non-speaking*)
A LION in the antimasque (5.6, *non-speaking*)
Four SATYRS in the antimasque (5.6, *non-speaking*)
Four WOOD-NYMPHS in the antimasque, portrayed by little boys; also said to be Dryads (5.6, *non-speaking*)
MASQUERS, servants of Cupid, played by young gentlemen of Naples (5.8, *non-speaking*)

Speaking Parts: 15

Royal Performance
CUPID, god of love; speaks the prologue and epilogue; *additional role*

Speaking Parts: 16

Stage Directions and Speech Prefixes
COMASTES: *Comastes* (s.d.s and s.p.s); *Comastes son to Caecilius & lover of Facetia* (d.p.)
NIGELLA: *Olimpa | Olympa* (s.d.s and s.p.s); *Nigella* (s.d.s); *Olympa daughter to Caecilius disguised like A blackamoor called Nigella* (d.p.)
FACETIA: *Facetia* (s.d.s and s.p.s); *Facetia daughter to Lepidus* (d.p.)
LEPIDUS: *Lepidus* (s.d.s and s.p.s); [Facetia's] *father* (s.d.s); *Lepidus A merry humorous old Lord, father to Facetia* (d.p.)
PISCINUS: *Piscinus* (s.d.s and s.p.s); *Piscinus, A dumb Gentleman* [one of the] *Suitors to Facetia* (d.p.)
LYSANDER: *Lysander* (s.d.s and s.p.s); *Lysander A Gentleman nephew to Aegidius & married to Olimpa* (d.p.)
AEGIDIUS: *Aegidius* (s.d.s and s.p.s); *Aegidius A Rich lame usurer* [one of the] *Suitors to Facetia* (d.p.)
CAECILIUS: *Caecilius* (s.d.s and s.p.s); *Caecilius A rich blind Gentleman father to Olimpa & Comastes* (d.p.)
SURDATO: *Surdato* (s.d.s and s.p.s); *Surdato A deaf Spaniard* [one of the] *Suitors to Facetia* (d.p.)
MACILENTO: *Macilento* [Surdato's] *man* (s.d.s); *Macilento* (s.d.s and s.p.s); *Macilento Servant to Surdato* (d.p.)
COLUMELLA: *Columella* (s.d.s and s.p.s); *Collumella* (s.d.s); *Collum<ella>* (s.p.s); *Columella Friend and interpreter to Piscinus* (d.p.)

SERGEANTS: 2 *Sergeants* (s.d.s); *1 Sergeant | 2 Sergeant* (s.p.s); *Sergeants 2* (d.p.)
BOY: *Boy* (s.d.s, s.p.s, and d.p.)
HYMEN: *Hymen* (s.d.s and s.p.s); *Hymen the presenter of the Antimasque and masque* (d.p.)
HARE: [one of] 4 *Beasts | A Hare |* [one of] *The 4 Beasts* (s.d.s)
WOLF: [one of] 4 *Beasts | A wolf |* [one of] *The 4 Beasts* (s.d.s)
ASS: [one of] 4 *Beasts | An Ass |* [one of] *The 4 Beasts* (s.d.s)
LION: [one of] 4 *Beasts | A Lion |* [one of] *The 4 Beasts* (s.d.s)
SATYRS: 4 *Satyrs* (s.d.s)
WOOD-NYMPHS: 4 *little boys* (s.d.s)
MASQUERS: *masquers* (s.d.s)

Royal Performance
CUPID: *Cupido	Cupid* (s.d.s); *Cup<id>* (s.p.s)

OTHER CHARACTERS
Lepidus' grooms (1.1)
Facetia's dead mother (1.2, 5.4)
Caecilius' tenants (1.5)
The Viceroy of Naples (4.2, 4.5)
A yeoman, the Sergeants' associate (4.4)
The Major, whose wine the Second Sergeant drank (4.4)
Surdato's butcher (4.5; possibly imaginary)
The Neapolitan magnificos' servants, whose table-leavings go to feed the inmates of the prison (4.5)
The Venetian Ambassador (4.5)
A preacher of the order of the Friars of Mount Olivet, who told Facetia about some statues that women are not allowed to see (5.5)

SETTING
Period: sixteenth or seventeenth century, after 1504: Naples is ruled by a Spanish Viceroy
Time-Scheme: 1.1 and 2.5–6 take place in the morning
Place: Naples

Geography
Naples: St Clara's temple; St Vincent's Lane; 'the broad street' (actually in Oxford); St Domenico's temple
Italy: Venice
Europe: [Spain]; Westphalia
[*Jerusalem*]: Mount Olivet

SOURCES
Verbal: William Lily, Latin Grammar (1.3); Aurelian Townshend, *Albion's Triumph* (**2353**) or John Ford, *Love's Sacrifice* (**2360**; 1.1).
Works Mentioned: Matteo Maria Boiardo, *Orlando inamorato* (1487; 2.4); possibly Edmund Spenser, *The Shepherd's Calendar* (1579; 3.2); John Taylor, water-poetry (general reference; 3.4)

LANGUAGE
English
Latin: 10 words (1.1, 2.2, 2.6, 3.4–5, 4.6; Facetia, Aegidius, Lysander, Lepidus, Caecilius)
Italian: 4 words (1.6, 4.3; Surdato)
Spanish: 6 words (2.4, 2.6, 4.3; Macilento, Surdato)
Dialect: In disguise, Comastes affects a rustic accent (3.1–2, 5.5).

FORM
Metre: prose and pentameter
Rhyme: blank verse; some couplets
Act-Division: 5 acts
Lines (Spoken): 1,759 (415 verse, 1,344 prose)
Lines (Written): 1,922

It is difficult to tell verse from prose in this play. Comparison of the fragmentary MS W with the later, complete B indicates that B often transcribes prose as verse; yet there are occasions when a perfect pentameter line emerges in an otherwise prosy speech.

> **Royal Performance**
> **Prologue:** 28 lines, in pentameter blank verse (and one couplet), spoken by Cupid
> **Epilogue:** 10 lines, in pentameter blank verse, spoken by Cupid
> **Lines (Spoken):** 1,797 (453 verse, 1,344 prose)
> **Lines (Written):** 45 (R)

STAGING
Doors: one is knocked at (5.1, implicit); characters exit severally (5.2, s.d.)
Stage: Lepidus 'comes to the forepart of the stage' (2.2, s.d.)
Stage Posts: positioned near the hangings (2.5, s.d.; probably therefore at the back of the stage); Columella stands upright against a stage pillar, imitating a statue (2.5–6, s.d.)
Miscellaneous: characters exit at the end of one scene and immediately re-enter at the start of the next (2.6–7, 4.4–5)

> **Royal Performance**
> **Above:** Cupid first appears 'ab excelsis', which may mean he is above or descends (prol., s.d.)
> **Audience:** the King is addressed as 'dread majesty' and mentioned by name; the Queen is addressed as 'my happy Queen' (prol.); the King and Queen are addressed as 'best majesties' (ep.)

MUSIC
Singing: Macilento sings (1.6, s.d.)
Dance: Macilento dances (1.6, s.d.); antimasquers dance (5.6, s.d.); masquers dance (5.8, s.d.); *some of the masque music may be extant*

PROPS
Weapons: Comastes' sword (1.1, 4.2, dialogue); Lysander's sword (4.1–2, implicit)
Clothing: a chain of pearl (1.3, s.d.)
Money: a leather bag of money (2.7–8, 3.3, 5.7, s.d.); a second leather bag of money (3.3, s.d.); two unspecified sums (4.4, s.d.)
Small Portable Objects: an unspecified gift (1.3, s.d.); a parchment (2.6, s.d.); a letter (5.5, s.d.)
Large Portable Objects: a staff (1.4, 2.8, 5.5, implicit; 2.2, dialogue)
Scenery: arras hangings (2.1, 2.5, s.d.; 2.6, dialogue)

> **Royal Performance**
> **Scenery:** the new building at St John's College (ep., s.d.)

COSTUMES AND MAKE-UP
COMASTES: disguised as a rustic (3.1–2, 5.5, s.d.), including large, baggy breeches and manure on his face (dialogue); hangers (4.2, implicit)
NIGELLA/OLYMPA: black facial make-up (1.1, 2.1, 3.6, 4.1–3, 4.5, 5.3, dialogue; 1.3, 5.5, implicit; the make-up is removed off-stage during 5.6, with a maximum of 44 lines plus the antimasque dances to scrub her white)
FACETIA: golden hair (dialogue)
LEPIDUS: a sleeved garment (1.1–2, s.d.)
LYSANDER: hangers (4.1–2, implicit)
SURDATO: no socks (1.6, dialogue); a ruff and a doublet (4.5, dialogue)
SECOND SERGEANT: a beard (dialogue)
SATYRS: horns (5.6, dialogue)
WOOD-NYMPHS: yellow suits (5.6, s.d.)
MASQUERS: 'masked in princely guise' (5.8, dialogue)

> **Royal Performance**
> CUPID: wings (dialogue)

EARLY STAGE HISTORY
Preparation: In a letter of Friday 15 July 1636 concerning preparations for the royal visit, Archbishop Laud (Chancellor of the University) wrote that he intended the play to be performed at his own college, St John's, at his own expense.

Preparation of Venue: The stage may have been erected on Saturday 27 August; reportedly the carpenter was not finished that night, continued work on the Sunday morning, fell off the stage, and broke his neck.

Royal Performance: in the hall of St John's College, Oxford, on Tuesday 30 August 1636. The cast, primarily drawn from members of the College, included: Humphrey Brook; Edmund Gayton; John Goad; John Hyfield; George Wilde, the author (Comastes?); Abraham Wright. The wood-nymphs in the antimasque may have been played by boys from the Chapel Royal. Music was probably contributed by Henry Lawes. The performance took place in the afternoon, and lasted until 7 p.m.; a banquet was served 'in the middle of the play'. The hall was darkened and lit by candles. The audience included: King Charles

I; Queen Henrietta Maria; Charles Louis, Elector Palatine; Prince Rupert; Archbishop William Laud; Thomas Browne (Senior Proctor); John Good (Junior Proctor); Richard Baylie (Vice-Chancellor and College President); noblemen and ladies. George Con decided not to attend in order not to appear too solicitous of royal favour, but the King noticed his absence and sent a gentleman to ask where he was. The performance was thought to be too long.

Repeat Performance: a second performance was planned to take place the evening of Thursday 1 September 1636, for members of the University and visitors, but was postponed when unruly undergraduates took the places reserved for visitors. The disappointed students then made their way to Christ Church and demanded to see *The Royal Slave* (**2552**), but were disappointed again. The performance eventually took place on Monday 5 September.

Production Expenses
William Laud bore the entire cost of the royal visit to the college, which amounted to £2,666.1s.7d, excluding donated provisions. Expenses specific to the play included: the setting up of the stage and general production expenses (£394.13s); fee paid to Thomas Day and his boys (10s).

EARLY TEXTUAL HISTORY
c. 1636: transcribed in MS (**W**), possibly as a presentation copy; only 4 leaves survive.

c. 1636: prologue and epilogue transcribed in MS (**R**); the MS was later incorporated into a composite volume.

c. 1650s: music ascribed to 'H. L.' and 'St John's play' survives in a set of MS music-books (Oxford: Bodleian, MS Mus. Sch. d. 233–4, 236, fos. 32, 43, 27), transcribed by Edward Lowe; this may be music for the masque scene.

1655: entered (as *Lovers' Hospital*) in the Stationers' Register to John Grismand on Saturday 17 November; entry refers to performance occasion.

After 1660 (?): included in a MS collection of plays and poems (**B**); 32 leaves; title page names author and refers to performance (which it dates wrongly); list of roles. The scribe may possibly have had the initials W. B. The other plays in the volume are *Eumorphus* (**2463**) and *The Converted Robber* (**2475**).

EDITION
Jay Louis Funston, Salzburg Studies in English Literature: Jacobean Drama Studies 13 (Salzburg, 1973).

REFERENCES
Annals 1636; Bentley, v. 1260–4; *Cal. Dom.* 1636–7, 114; Eyre & Rivington, ii. 19; Hazlitt, 141; Michael C. Questier (ed.), *Newsletters from the Caroline Court, 1631–1638* (Cambridge, 2005), 289–90; REED: Oxford, 531, 533–4, 538–41, 543–4, 546, 558, 812–13, 890–4; Steele, 260–1; Stratman, 56.

2552. The Royal Slave

TEXT
Six substantive witnesses:
- **B**: MS (Woburn Abbey, HMC MS no. 295);
- **C**: MS (privately owned in Britain); incomplete;
- **F**: MS (Washington: Folger, MS V. b. 212);
- **P**: MS (London: British Library, Add. MS 41616); incomplete, lacking the start of 5.7;
- **Q**: printed in 1639 (STC 4717);
- **S**: MS (Oxford: Bodleian, MS Arch. Selden B 26, fos. 103–35).

Another MS (**H**: Heber MS 1043) was in the possession of Richard Heber (1773–1833), but is now untraced.

Changes of prologue and epilogue mean that there were slightly different texts in the three original performances (here designated royal, university, and Hampton Court); an additional song may also have been inserted for the Hampton Court performance.

GENRE
tragicomedy
Contemporary: play (university prol.); tragicomedy (Q t.p.); comedy (Crosfield, Heylyn)

TITLE
Performed/MS/Printed: *The Royal Slave*
Contemporary: *The Persian Slave*

AUTHOR
William Cartwright

DATE
August 1636

ORIGINAL PRODUCTION
Christ Church, Oxford

PLOT
Five Greeks are taken prisoner by the Persians after a war with Ephesus. According to a local custom, one of these slaves must be given royal power for three days, but then killed as an offering to the sun god. Cratander, who denies the efficacy of human sacrifice, is selected, and has his fellow captives released to serve him at court.

Cratander takes his royal responsibilities seriously. The lords fear that he will use his power to harm the state, and offer him the sensual pleasures of kingship, but he refuses to be distracted. Atossa, the Queen, is impressed by his self-control, and gives him a chain, exciting the jealousy of her husband, King Arsamnes. The other Greeks, however, enjoy a bibulous, lascivious good time, and are only prevented from raping Atossa's women by the chance arrival of Cratander. Fearing further attempts, the women of Sardis take refuge in the castle.

Two members of the Ephesian army who are still at liberty take the risk of coming to see Cratander at the palace. They ask him to use his power to send the Persian army back to war, with the intention that they will be massacred by the forewarned Ephesians. Cratander conscientiously refuses, but asks the Ephesian army to rendezvous with him at the castle. His plan is to allow them to be defeated in battle, but have Atossa intervene with her husband to spare them and free Ephesus.

The other Greeks plan to ambush Cratander in the woods, disguised as beggars; but he recognizes them and sends them back to prison. He then joins the women in the castle. Arsamnes engages the Ephesians in battle, defeats them, and then demands that Atossa give up Cratander for sacrifice. Cratander accepts the rule of law. Reconciled with Atossa, Arsamnes attempts to pardon Cratander, but the priests are insistent that he must die. At the ceremony, however, the sun is eclipsed and a shower of rain puts out the fire: recognizing Cratander's virtue, the sun god has refused to accept the sacrifice. Cratander accepts Arsamnes' offer to allow him to retain his royal power, and agrees to divide his time and abilities between the affairs of Persia and Ephesus.

SCENE DESIGNATION
prol., 1.1–5, 2.1–6, 3.1–5, 4.1–5, 5.1–7, ep. (Q)

The stage is not clear at the following scene-divisions: 1.1–5, 2.1–6, 3.1–3, 3.4–5, 4.3–4, 5.1–3, 5.5–6. Verse lines are split across the following scene-divisions: 1.2–3, 1.3–4, 2.4–5.

ROLES
A PERSIAN MAGUS, a priest of the sun who speaks the prologue (replaced by an anonymous prologue in the Hampton Court performance)
MOLOPS, a jailer, a married man
PHILOTAS, an Ephesian prisoner of war and slave
STRATOCLES, an Ephesian prisoner of war and slave
LEOCRATES, an Ephesian prisoner of war and slave
ARCHIPPUS, an Ephesian prisoner of war and slave
ARSAMNES, King of Persia, Atossa's husband
Lord PRAXASPES, a nobleman
HYDARNES, a lord
MASISTES, a lord
ORONTES, a lord
Four or more PRIESTS of the sun (two or three speak individually, the rest collectively)
CRATANDER, an Ephesian prisoner of war and slave, temporarily created a king
ATOSSA, Queen of Persia, Arsamnes' wife
MANDANE, Atossa's lady-in-waiting
ARIENE, Atossa's lady-in-waiting
Two WHORES, old women (2.3, 5.5, *non-speaking*)
A BOY, who sings (2.3)
HIPPIAS, an Ephesian
PHOCION, an Ephesian
FIDDLERS (3.1; two sing)
Six LADIES of Sardis; at least some are wives (4.1, 5.5, 5.7; speak collectively)
WOMEN of Sardis; at least some are wives (4.1; speak collectively)
Cratander's SERVANTS, two of them named Sisarmes and Artobazes (4.4; one speaks)
A MESSENGER (4.5)
SOLDIERS following Arsamnes (5.2, *non-speaking*)
A SOLDIER (5.2, *within*)
EPILOGUE (Hampton Court performance only)

Speaking Parts: 24–7 (HAMPTON COURT: 25–8)

Stage Directions and Speech Prefixes
PERSIAN MAGUS: *one of the Persian Magi | A Priest* (s.d.s)
MOLOPS: *Molops* (s.d.s); *Mol<ops>* (s.p.s); *Molops, A Jailer* (d.p.)
PHILOTAS: *Philotas | [one of] The Slaves | [one of the] Slaves | [one of the] 4 Slaves | [one of] The four Slaves | [one of] The 4 Slaves* (s.d.s); *Phil<otas>* (s.p.s); *Philotas, [one of] 4 other Ephesian Captives* (d.p.)
STRATOCLES: *Stratocles | [one of] The Slaves | [one of the] Slaves | [one of the] 4 Slaves | [one of] The four Slaves | [one of] The 4 Slaves* (s.d.s); *Strat<ocles>* (s.p.s); *Stratocles, [one of] 4 other Ephesian Captives* (d.p.)
LEOCRATES: *Leocrates | [one of] The Slaves | [one of the] Slaves | [one of the] 4 Slaves | [one of] The four Slaves | [one of] The 4 Slaves* (s.d.s); *Leocr<ates>* (s.p.s); *Leocrates, [one of] 4 other Ephesian Captives* (d.p.)
ARCHIPPUS: *Archippus | [one of] The Slaves | [one of the] Slaves | [one of the] 4 Slaves | [one of] The four Slaves | [one of] The 4 Slaves* (s.d.s); *Archip<pus>* (s.p.s); *Archippus, [one of] 4 other Ephesian Captives* (d.p.)
ARSAMNES: *Arsamnes | the King* (s.d.s); *Arsam<nes>* (s.p.s); *Arsamnes, King of Persia* (d.p.)
PRAXASPES: *Praxaspes | [one of] Lords | [one of] The 4 Lords* (s.d.s); *Prax<aspes>* (s.p.s); *Praxaspes, [one of Arsamnes'] Lords* (d.p.)
HYDARNES: *Hydarnes | [one of] Lords | [one of] The 4 Lords* (s.d.s); *Hyd<arnes>* (s.p.s); *Hydarnes, [one of Arsamnes'] Lords* (d.p.)
MASISTES: *Masistes | [one of the] Lords | [one of] The 4 Lords* (s.d.s); *Masist<es>* (s.p.s); *Masistes, [one of Arsamnes'] Lords* (d.p.)
ORONTES: *Orontes | [one of the] Lords | [one of] The 4 Lords* (s.d.s); *Oron<tes>* (s.p.s); *Orontes, [one of Arsamnes'] Lords* (d.p.)
PRIESTS: *Priests | The Priest | 4 Priests | a Priest | another Priest* (s.d.s); *1 Priest* (s.d.s and s.p.s); *2 Priest* (s.p.s); *3 Magi, or Persian Priests* (d.p.)
CRATANDER: *Cratander* (s.d.s); *Crat<ander>* (s.p.s); *Cratander, the Royal Slave* (d.p.)
ATOSSA: *Atossa | Queen* (s.d.s); *Atos<sa>* (s.p.s); *Atossa, Queen to Arsamnes* (d.p.)
MANDANE: *Mandane | [one of] the Ladies* (s.d.s); *Mand<ane>* (s.p.s); *Mandane, [one of Atossa's] Ladies* (d.p.)

ARIENE: *Ariene* | [one of] *the Ladies* (s.d.s); *Arie<ne>* (s.p.s); *Ariene,* [one of Atossa's] *Ladies* (d.p.)
WHORES: *Two women* | *the two women* | *the two whores* (s.d.s); *2 Strumpets* (d.p.)
BOY: *A boy* | *Boy* (s.d.s); [one of the] *Musicians* (d.p.)
HIPPIAS: *Hippias* (s.d.s); *Hip<pias>* (s.p.s); *Hippias,* [one of] *2 Citizens of Ephesus disguised* (d.p.)
PHOCION: *Phocion* (s.d.s); *Pho<cion>* (s.p.s); *Phocion,* [one of] *2 Citizens of Ephesus disguised* (d.p.)
FIDDLERS: [some of the] *Musicians* (d.p.)
LADIES: *other Ladies* | *Ladies* | *The Ladies* | *the Masquers* (s.d.s); *Masquers, 6 Ladies* (d.p.)
WOMEN: *Women of divers sorts* | *divers other women* (s.d.s)
SERVANTS: *Servants* (s.d.s and d.p.); *Servant* (s.p.s)
MESSENGER: *a Messenger* (s.d.s); *Messenger* (s.p.s)
SOLDIERS: *others* (s.d.s)
SOLDIER: *Soldier* (s.p.s)
EPILOGUE: *The Epilogue* (heading)

OTHER CHARACTERS
Molops's wife (1.1, 3.1)
The people of Sardis (2.5, 5.1, 5.6)
Molops's prisoners (3.1)
The husbands of Sardis (4.1, 5.3)
The Ephesian army, some of whom are killed in the battle (4.2, 4.5, 5.3)
The palace eunuchs (4.5)
Archippus' father (5.4)

SETTING
Period: antiquity; after the time of Socrates (died 399 BC) and Plato (died 347 BC)
Time-Scheme: 1.1 takes place in the morning and 3.1 at night; three days pass between 1.2 and 5.6
Place: Sardis

Geography
Persia
[*Asia Minor*]: Ephesus; Claros; Colophon; Magnesia
[*Aegean Sea*]: Lesbos
Greece: Sparta

SOURCES
Narrative: Dio Chrysostom, *De regno*; Theodorus Prodromus, *Rhodanthes et Dosiclis amorum*, tr. Gilbertus Gaulminus (1625); Barnabé Brisson, *De regio Persarum Principatu* (1590); John Fletcher and Philip Massinger, *Beggars' Bush* (**1799**; 4.3); possibly Philip Massinger, *The Bondman* (**2074**; 5.2–3)
Verbal: Catullus, *Carmina* 5 (5.7); Seneca, *Hercules furens* (3.3); Claudian, *De sexto consulatu Honorii Augusti* (5.5)
Works Mentioned: Socrates, unspecified philosophical work (3.2); Plato, unspecified philosophical work (2.5); William Prynne, *Histriomastix* (1633; oblique allusion; university prol.)

LANGUAGE
English
Latin: 3 words (2.4–5; Mandane, Leocrates)

FORM
Metre: pentameter and prose
Rhyme: blank verse
Prologue:
  ROYAL: 12 lines, in couplets, spoken by a Persian Magus
  UNIVERSITY: 38 lines, in couplets, spoken by a Persian Magus
  HAMPTON COURT: 25 lines, mainly in couplets (22 verse, 3 prose)
Act-Division: 5 acts
Epilogue:
  ROYAL: 24 lines, in couplets, spoken by Cratander
  UNIVERSITY: 22 lines, in couplets, spoken by Arsamnes
  HAMPTON COURT: 24 lines, in couplets
Lines (Spoken):
  ROYAL: 1,627 (1,313 verse, 314 prose)
  UNIVERSITY: 1,653 (1,339 verse, 314 prose)
  HAMPTON COURT: 1,640 (1,323 verse, 317 prose)
Lines (Written): 2,070

STAGING
Doors: mentioned (1.1, s.d.)
Stage: mentioned (university prol., dialogue; 5.7, s.d.)
Discovery Space: characters are discovered (prol., 3.3, 4.3, s.d.), and also discovered above (5.1, s.d.)
Within: speech (1.1, 5.2, s.d.); song (1.1, s.d.)
Above: characters appear above (2.3–5, 5.1–3, s.d.; there is space for at least six, and it takes four lines to get down to the main stage); an object is thrown down from above to the main stage (2.5, s.d.)
Other Openings: two characters peep out of the scenery in several places (4.3, s.d.)
Audience: the Queen in the audience is mentioned, and the King addressed as 'great sir' (royal ep.); in the Hampton Court version, they are addressed as 'most mighty King and most gracious Queen' (prol.)

MUSIC
On-Stage Music: fiddles (3.1, dialogue)
Songs: *all have surviving musical settings*:
  1: 'A pox on our jailer', 1.1, Philotas, Stratocles, Leocrates, and Archippus within, 6 lines;
  2: 'Come from the dungeon to the throne', 1.2, Priest, 14 lines;
  3: 'Come, my sweet, whiles every strain', 2.3, Boy, 27 lines;
  4: 'Now, now the sun is fled', 3.1, two Fiddlers, in parts, 26 lines;
  5: 'Thou, O bright sun, who seest all', 5.7, two Priests, in parts, 12 lines;

α: 'Bacchus, Iacchus, fill our brains', 48 lines; probably added in the Hampton Court performance.
Dance: Greek slaves and whores dance (5.5, s.d.); ladies dance (5.5, s.d.)

PROPS
Pyrotechnics: fire (5.7, s.d.; extinguished on stage)
Weapons: a halter (1.1, s.d.); Arsamnes' sword (5.5–6, dialogue); a sagar (5.7, s.d.; i.e. an axe)
Musical Instruments: fiddles (3.1, dialogue)
Clothing: a gold chain (2.5–6, s.d.)
Food and Drink: five pots of frothy liquor (3.1–3, s.d.; drunk on stage, and some is poured on the ground)
Small Portable Objects: a book (1.2, implicit); a sceptre (1.2, s.d.); five cups (3.1–3, s.d.)
Large Portable Objects: crutches (4.3–4, dialogue); a seat (5.1–4, implicit)
Scenery: a temple of the sun (prol., 5.7, s.d.); an altar (royal prol., 5.7, s.d.); a city with a prison at the side (1.1–5, s.d.); a stately palace (2.1–4.2, 5.5–6, s.d.); a wood (4.3–5, s.d.); a castle (5.1–4, s.d.); the sun (5.7, s.d.; animated to show an eclipse)
Miscellaneous: a shower of rain (5.7, s.d.)

COSTUMES
MOLOPS: a chaplet of red roses (3.1–2, s.d.)
PHILOTAS, STRATOCLES, LEOCRATES, and ARCHIPPUS: fetters (1.1–2, dialogue); rich Persian habits (2.4–5, s.d.); chaplets of red roses (3.1–3, s.d.); disguised in beggar's habits (4.3–4, s.d.; 5.4–5, implicit); Leocrates has his arm in a sling, Archippus has tattered clothes and a 'raw arm', and Stratocles has a false wooden leg and his real leg tied (4.3–4, s.d.; 5.4–5, implicit)
ARSAMNES, PRAXASPES, HYDARNES, MASISTES, and ORONTES: warlike habits (5.2, s.d.)
CRATANDER: royal robes (1.2, s.d.; put on on stage)
ATOSSA, MANDANE, and ARIENE: warlike habits (5.1–3, s.d.)
HIPPIAS and PHOCION: disguised (2.6, dialogue; 4.2, implicit)
LADIES: warlike habits (5.1–3, 5.5, s.d.)
SOLDIERS: warlike habits (5.2, s.d.)
Miscellaneous: the habits are (all?) Persian (d.p.); it is implied that all the adult Persian males, except for eunuchs, are bearded (dialogue)

EARLY STAGE HISTORY
1636: performed in the hall at Christ Church, Oxford, on Tuesday 30 August. The performance took place in the evening after supper, beginning at about 8 p.m.; the court had already seen another play, *The Hospital of Lovers* (**2551**) at St John's College that afternoon. Music was contributed by Henry Lawes, and possibly also by William Lawes. The cast reportedly included Richard Busby (Cratander). The audience included: King Charles I; Queen Henrietta Maria; Charles Louis, Elector Palatine; Prince Rupert; Philip Herbert, 4th Earl of Pembroke and 1st Earl of Montgomery (Lord Chamberlain). The King was seated on a throne. Pembroke declared it to be the best play he had ever seen; the court was particularly impressed by the costumes.

On Thursday 1 September, a group of unruly undergraduates, balked of their intention to see the planned but cancelled repeat performance of *The Hospital of Lovers* (**2551**), went to Christ Church intending to demand a repeat performance of *The Royal Slave*. The student actors were willing to perform, but a shortage of candles made it impossible.

A second performance was ordered by William Laud (Chancellor of the University), for members of the University and guests. It took place in Christ Church hall on the afternoon of Friday 2 September; a different prologue and epilogue was substituted for the one addressed to the royal audience.

Aftermath: On Tuesday 6 December 1636, the Queen wrote to the University asking to borrow the costumes and scenery for a revival by Queen Henrietta's Men; they were duly sent to Hampton Court. (Edgarly the carrier brought them in his wagon.) The university asked that care be taken to ensure that the costumes and script did not fall into the hands of common players. The Queen's intention was reportedly to see whether professional actors would perform the play as well as the university men. At this time, however, Queen Henrietta's Men were in difficulties; their relationship with Christopher Beeston, the impresario and owner of their usual theatre, the Cockpit, was coming to an end (the following February, he was patented to manage a new company there), which may explain why in the event the court performance was given instead by the King's Men.

1637: performed by the King's Men at Hampton Court on Thursday 12 January. The audience included: King Charles I; Queen Henrietta Maria; William Cartwright; possibly Jasper Mayne. The King gave Cartwright a gratuity of £40. A song (α) by Aurelian Townshend, set by Henry Lawes, was probably added for this revival. The King's Men were paid a treble fee of £30 for their trouble in learning the play, part of a £240 payment (for this and 21 other performances) to John Lowin and Joseph Taylor by a warrant dated either Sunday 12 or Wednesday 15 March 1637.

Reported (in 1669) as having been in the repertory of the King's Men at the Blackfriars before 1642.

A letter from Edward Rossingham to Sir Thomas Puckering, dated 11 January 1637, the day before the Hampton Court performance, claims that it had already taken place on Friday 6 January. The likeliest explanation of the anomaly is that the Twelfth Night play was the other one from Oxford, *The City Match* (**2553**). It is also possible that 6 January was the date originally planned for *The Royal Slave*, but that it was postponed for six days, perhaps to give the company more time to prepare it.

Production Expenses
Christ Church Performances: The production cost of both this play and *Passions Calmed* (**2550**) reportedly amounted to £843.15s.6d (but this total is slightly lower than the sum of the extant account; see **2550**).

Hampton Court Performance: The total cost, including payments for alterations to the scenery, props, and costumes, and payments to dancers and composers, came to £154. On Tuesday 4 April, the Lord Chamberlain instructed the Great Wardrobe to draw up a bill authorizing payments to the following: Peter le Huc, a property maker (£50); George Portman, a painter (£50); Stephen de Nau and Sebastian la Pierre, for themselves and twenty dancers (£54).

EARLY TEXTUAL HISTORY
1636: A copy of the text may have been presented to King Charles I and Queen Henrietta Maria; Christ Church paid Mr Stutvile £1.12s.6d for binding whatever the books were.

c. 1636: transcribed in MS (**F**); 26 leaves; list of roles; a second hand later annotated the text with descriptions of the scenery.

c. 1636: transcribed in MS (**C**); 40 pages. The MS was later used as wrapping paper.

c. 1636: Song 2 (ascribed to 'Mr Cartwright's comedy') transcribed on a MS leaf (Oxford: Bodleian, MS Rawlinson poet. 172, fo. 30^r). The leaf, which also contains Song 5 of *Passions Calmed* (**2550**), was later incorporated into a composite MS volume.

c. 1636: royal prologue and both epilogues transcribed onto the first leaf of a MS bifolium (Oxford: Bodleian, MS Rawlinson poet. 172, fos. 25^r–26^r). The pages were later incorporated into a composite MS volume.

c. 1636 (?): transcribed in MS (**H**); list of roles and actors.

c. 1637: Hampton Court prologue transcribed onto a MS leaf (Oxford: Bodleian, MS Rawlinson poet. 172, fo. 28^{r-v}). The leaf was later incorporated into a composite MS volume.

c. 1636–8: transcribed in MS (**S**); 33 leaves; list of roles. The MS was later incorporated into a composite volume.

c. 1636–8: transcribed in MS (**B**); 35 leaves; list of roles.

c. 1636–8: transcribed in MS (**P**); 24 leaves; list of roles; possibly a presentation copy. The MS was owned by a member of the Percy family.

c. 1630s: Song α transcribed, with music, in a MS notebook (Oxford: Bodleian, MS Eng. poet. f. 10, fo. 98^r) owned by Simon Sloper.

Late 1630s: Song α included in a MS verse miscellany (New Haven: Yale, Osborn MS b 356, pp. 281–3) owned by Robert Lord, and later by William Jacob.

1639: $^1Q_1$ printed at Oxford by William Turner for Thomas Robinson; collation A–H^4 I^2, 34 leaves; title page refers to royal performances; list of roles.

Corrected proof sheets survive for sheets A, G outer, and I (in two copies which are now in the Bodleian Library); one was subsequently used by Nicholas Swanne to write a note challenging Robert Milles to a duel.

After 1639: a copy of Q$_1$ was owned by Richard Busby (Headmaster of Westminster School), who had probably played Cratander in the 1636 production.

1640: $^2Q_2$ printed at Oxford by William Turner for Thomas Robinson; collation A–H^4, 32 leaves; the copy was Q$_1$. Corrected proof pages exist for sigs. B1^v and B4^r (in a copy now in the Bodleian Library).

1640–1: Humphrey Moseley was selling copies of Q$_1$ for 6d each.

c. 1641: Songs 2, 4, and 5 included, with Henry Lawes's musical settings, in a MS songbook (New York Public Library, MS Drexel 4041, fos. 89^v–92^v).

1640s: Song 2 (headed 'The Priest's Song') included in a MS commonplace book (London: British Library, Add. MS 47111, fo. 44^v) compiled by John Percival.

1648: William Cartwright's *Poems and Plays* entered to Humphrey Moseley in the Stationers' Register on Thursday 4 May; the other three plays in the volume were named, but not *The Royal Slave*. Sir Nathaniel Brent had licensed the book for publication.

Mid-seventeenth century (*c.* 1637–62): Songs 2, 3, and α (the last headed 'A Bacchanal Song in a Masque before their Majesties, 1636') included, with musical settings by Henry Lawes, in his autograph MS songbook (London: British Library, Add. MS 53723, fos. 40^{r-v}, 42^v).

c. 1640s: a copy of Q$_2$ was in the possession of John Horne (Vicar of Headington, Oxfordshire). After his death, his entire collection of play-books passed into the possession of John Houghton of Brasenose College, Oxford (*c.* 1608–77), then to James Herne (died 1685), and then to the library of Ralph Sheldon (1623–84) at Weston, where it was catalogued by Anthony Wood, probably in the late 1670s.

c. 1650: Songs 1–4 and the royal, university, and Hampton Court prologues and epilogues included in a MS verse miscellany (New Haven: Yale, Osborn MS b 200, pp. 150–8), probably compiled by members of the University of Oxford.

Mid-seventeenth century: extracts (royal and university prologues and epilogues, and parts of Songs 2 and α) transcribed in MS and later included in a composite miscellany (London: British Library, MS Egerton 2725, fos. 115^r–117^r). The MS was later owned by Thomas Meres of Kirton, Lincolnshire.

1651: included in Cartwright's *Comedies, Tragicomedies, with Other Poems* (^{3}O), sigs. g1^r–k8^v, with an independent title page naming the author; 32 leaves; printed for Humphrey Moseley; the copy was Q$_2$. The independent title page also gives Thomas Robinson's initials as bookseller.

1651: George Thomason acquired a copy of O on Monday 23 June. In *c.* 1678, some years after his death, his entire collection of books and tracts was acquired

1636 by the bookbinder Samuel Mearne, acting as agent for King Charles II; the King never paid him, and the books remained in Mearne's family until 1761.

1652: Song 1 included, with a musical setting by William Lawes, in John Hilton's *Catch that Catch Can*, sig. D3^r; printed for John Benson and John Playford.

1653: *Catch that Catch Can* entered in the Stationers' Register to John Benson and John Playford on Tuesday 3 May.

1653: Songs 3 (headed 'Love and Music') and α (headed 'A Bacchanal') included, with Henry Lawes's musical settings (Song α as a duet), in his *The First Book of Airs and Dialogues*, sigs. H2^v, 2C1^r; printed by Thomas Harper for John Playford.

1653: *The Marrow of Compliments* entered to Humphrey Moseley in the Stationers' Register on Tuesday 20 December.

1654: Songs 3–4 and an extract from 3.4 included in Samuel Sheppard's *The Marrow of Compliments*, sigs. C4^v–C6^v, C12^{r-v}; printed (before Sunday 15 July) for Humphrey Moseley.

1654–70s: Song 2 included, with Lawes's musical setting, in a MS songbook (London: British Library, Add. MS 29396, fos. 14^v–15^r) partly compiled by Edward Lowe.

1655: *Wit's Interpreter* entered to Nathaniel Brooke in the Stationers' Register on Wednesday 14 March.

1655: Songs 3 and α (the latter headed 'A Bacchanal') included in John Cotgrave's *Wit's Interpreter*, sigs. X1^r, X2^v–X3^r; printed for Nathaniel Brooke.

c. 1655: extracts transcribed by John Evans in a miscellany, *Hesperides*, intended for publication and entered to Humphrey Moseley in the Stationers' Register on Thursday 16 August 1655. The book remained unpublished in 1660, and Evans continued adding to the collection until at least 1666. Two MS exemplars are known; one was cut up by J. O. Halliwell-Phillipps in the nineteenth century; the other survives (Washington: Folger, MS V. b. 93).

1656: *The English Parnassus* entered to Evan Tyler, Thomas Johnson, and Thomas Davies in the Stationers' Register on Wednesday 24 December.

1657: nine extracts (from 1.2, 2.3–4, 2.6, 3.1, 3.4–5, 5.6) included in Joshua Poole's *The English Parnassus*, sigs. V1^v, V5^v, V7^r, X3^r, 2F3^v, 2L6^r, 2Q8^r, 2R6^r, 2S4^v; printed for Thomas Johnson.

1657: O and Q$_1$ or Q$_2$ both advertised as for sale by the Newcastle-upon-Tyne bookseller William London.

1658: *Catch that Catch Can* reprinted by William Godbid for John Benson and John Playford. The song now appears on sig. C6^v.

Late **1650s**: Songs 2 and α included in a MS verse miscellany (London: University College, MS Ogden 42, pp. 56, 244–5).

c. 1659: Song α included, with Lawes's musical setting, in a MS music book (New York Public Library, MS Drexel 4257, no. 69) owned and partly compiled by John Gamble.

1659: Songs 2 and 3 included, with Lawes's musical settings and headed 'Two Songs in the Play of *The Royal Slave*' and 'Love and Music', in John Playford's *Select Airs and Dialogues*, sig. H1^v; printed by William Godbid for John Playford.

After 1660: extracts included in a MS miscellany (Oxford: Bodleian, MS Rawlinson D. 951, fo. 63^{r-v}), probably compiled by a member of the University of Cambridge.

Mid- to late seventeenth century (before 1689): a copy of Q$_1$ was owned by Elizabeth Puckering.

1661: Song α included (as 'A Glee in Praise of Wine') in N. D.'s *An Antidote Against Melancholy*, sig. F4^r; printed by 'Mercurius Melancholicus'.

1661: Song α included (as 'The Virtue of Wine') in *Merry Drollery*, sig. C8^{r-v}; printed by J. W. for P. H.

1662: *Wit's Interpreter* reprinted (before Thursday 8 June) for Nathaniel Brooke; the songs (Song 3 now headed 'The Kiss') now appear on sigs. Q6^v, Q8^{r-v}.

1663: *Catch that Catch Can* reprinted by William Godbid for John Playford and Zachariah Watkins.

1660s: Song 2 included, in Lawes's musical setting for three voices, in a MS songbook (Krakow: Biblioteka Jagiellonska, Mus. ant. pract. P.970, B, pp. 40–1) compiled by John Patrick.

c. 1665: Songs 2–5 included, with Lawes's musical settings, in a MS songbook (Paris: Bibliothèque Nationale, Conservatoire MS Réserve 2489, pp. 254–5, 284–5, 320–2) compiled by John Playford; the setting for Song 4 is attributed to William Lawes.

1667: Songs 1 and 2 included, with the Lawes settings, in the fourth edition of *Catch that Catch Can*, sigs. L1^v, Y3^v–Y4^r; printed by William Godbid for John Playford.

1668: *The New Academy of Compliments* entered to Samuel Speed in the Stationers' Register on Saturday 2 May.

1669: *An Antidote against Melancholy* entered to John Playford in the Stationers' Register on Friday 1 January.

1669: *An Antidote Against Melancholy* reprinted for John Playford; the song is now headed 'A Glee to Bacchus', and appears on sig. K4^v.

1669: *Select Airs and Dialogues* reissued.

1669: Song 1 included in *The New Academy of Compliments*, sigs. G1^v; printed for Samuel Speed.

1669: Songs 2 and 3 included, with Lawes's musical settings, in John Playford's *Treasury of Music*, sig. H1^v; printed by William Godbid for John Playford.

1669: *Merry Drollery* entered to Simon Miller in the Stationers' Register on Monday 10 May.

1670: Songs 1 and α included in the second edition of *Merry Drollery*, sigs. O5^v–O6^r, T1^r; printed for Simon Miller.

1671: *The New Academy of Compliments* reprinted for Thomas Rookes.

1671: *Wit's Interpreter* reprinted for Nathaniel Brooke and Obadiah Blagrave.

1671: Songs 2 and α included in *Windsor Drollery*, sigs. I5ᵛ–I6ʳ, I11ʳ⁻ᵛ; printed for John Macock.

1671: *The Musical Companion* entered to John Playford in the Stationers' Register on Saturday 23 September.

1672: *Windsor Drollery* reprinted for John Macock; the songs now appear on sigs. B8ᵛ and B12ᵛ–C1ʳ.

1672–3: Songs 1–2, α, and part of Song 5 included, with Lawes's musical settings, in John Playford's *The Musical Companion*, sigs. H3ʳ, K4ᵛ, P5ᵛ–P6ʳ; printed by William Godbid for John Playford.

1673: *The Musical Companion* reissued three times.

1675: Moseley's rights to *The Marrow of Compliments* transferred from his widow, Ann, to Peter Parker in the Stationers' Register on Wednesday 8 September, by order of a court held on Monday 22 February, and by an assignment dated Thursday 26 September 1672.

c. 1670s–80s: Song 1 included in a MS commonplace book (Stafford: Staffordshire Record Office, D641/4, no. 48) compiled by Hugh Davis.

1677: *The English Parnassus* reprinted by Henry Brome for Thomas Bassett and John Wright; the extracts now appear on sigs. T5ᵛ, V1ᵛ, V3ʳ, V7ʳ, 2E7ᵛ, 2L2ʳ, 2Q4ʳ, 2R2ʳ, 2R8ᵛ.

c. 1676–93: three extracts (from all three prologues) copied into a MS miscellany (Oxford: Bodleian, MS Sancroft 29, p. 68) compiled by William Sancroft.

1680: rights to *The New Academy of Compliments* transferred in the Stationers' Register from Mary Rookes, widow and executrix of Thomas Rookes, to George Sawbridge on Wednesday 22 September.

1681: *The New Academy of Compliments* reprinted for George Sawbridge.

1682: Songs 1 and α (the latter as 'A Glee to Bacchus' and ascribed to Ben Jonson) included in *Wit and Mirth*, sigs. I2ᵛ–I3ʳ, K5ʳ; printed by Ann Godbid and John Playford, jun., for Henry Playford.

1684: *Wit and Mirth* reprinted by John Playford, jun., for Henry Playford.

Late seventeenth century (before 1695): a copy of Q₂ was owned by the antiquarian Anthony Wood.

c. 1690s: Songs 1–2 included (Song 2 twice) in a MS commonplace book (Austin: University of Texas at Austin, MS (Killigrew, T) Works B Commonplace book, p. 9, fos. 67ʳ, 68ʳ).

1691: *Merry Drollery* reprinted for William Miller.

1694: *The New Academy of Compliments* reprinted by Ichabod Dawks for Awnsham Churchill and John Churchill.

1698: *The New Academy of Compliments* reprinted by Ichabod Dawks for Awnsham Churchill and John Churchill.

EDITIONS

G. Blakemore Evans, in *The Plays and Poems of William Cartwright* (Madison, 1951), 163–253.

Ian Spink, *English Songs, 1625–1660*, 2nd edn (London, 1977), nos. 43–6 (Songs 2–4 and music only).

REFERENCES

Adams, 76; *Annals* 1636; Ashbee, v. 13; Bawcutt 358; Beal Online CaW 80–8, 90–124, ToA 90–4; Bentley, iii. 134–41; *Cal. Dom. 1636-7*, 114; *EMS* 8 (2000), 233, 261–2; Eyre & Rivington, i. 417, 463, 467, ii. 8, 103, 386, 394, 400, 430, iii. 3, 95; Greg 570; Hazlitt, 200; HMC 2, 4; Nicolas K. Kiessling, *The Library of Anthony Wood* (Oxford, 2002) 1420; *The Library* 5th ser., 25 (1970), 151–4; *The Library*, 5th ser., 28 (1973), 294–308; *The Library*, 7th ser., 1 (2000), 377; *The Library*, 7th ser., 10 (2009), 372–404; William London, *A Catalogue of the Most Vendible Books in England* (London, 1657), sigs. 2E4ᵛ, 2F1ᵛ; *MLN* 45 (1930), 515–18; *MLR* 13 (1918), 401–11; MSC 2.3, 382–3; Allardyce Nicoll, *A History of English Drama*, 4th edn (Cambridge, 1952–9), i. 354; Orgel and Strong, ii. 828–9; *Oxford Bibliographical Society Proceedings and Papers* 2.2 (1929), 132–3; Michael C. Questier (ed.), *Newsletters from the Caroline Court, 1631–1638* (Cambridge, 2005), 288–9; REED: Oxford, 519–21, 529, 534, 538, 541, 543–7, 556–7, 791, 821–2, 891; *RMA Research Chronicle* 32 (1999), 83; Steele, 258, 261–2, 265–6; Stratman, 57–63, 365–7; *Theatre Notebook* 39 (1985), 7–13; Aurelian Townshend, *The Poems and Masques*, ed. Cedric C. Brown (Reading, 1983), 115–17.

2553. *The City Match*

TEXT
Printed in 1639 (STC 17750), from authorial copy.

GENRE
comedy
Contemporary: comedy (prol., ep., t.p.); play (prol., ep., epistle), poem (epistle)

TITLE
Printed: *The City Match*

AUTHOR
Jasper Mayne

DATE
September 1636

ORIGINAL PRODUCTION
Christ Church, Oxford, (presumably) at Hampton Court

PLOT
After his father's bankruptcy, Plotwell has been forced to give up his riotous, hedonistic life as a law student and now lives soberly in the household of his uncle, Warehouse. He and his sister Penelope have also given up their plans to marry Susan and Timothy, the son and daughter of the merchant Seathrift. Now Penelope

has absconded from her duties as a seamstress. Suspecting that his nephew's reformation may be only an act, Warehouse pretends to go on a long voyage abroad in the company of Seathrift, who has similar doubts about Timothy: in their absence, the two heirs will reveal their true character, observed by the old men's spies. No sooner has Warehouse gone than Plotwell meets up with two friends from the Inns of Court and arranges to visit a newly arrived lady, Aurelia, who is actually Penelope in disguise. Plotwell plans to revive her proposed marriage to Timothy; she in turn plans to get him married to Susan, who has disguised herself as Aurelia's Puritan waiting-woman.

London flocks to see a display of a strange fish caught in the New World. It turns out that some tricksters have dressed up the drunken Timothy as a sea creature, and when he wakes there is speculation about how the 'fish' can speak. (He learned human language from years of being on display, the tricksters explain.) Plotwell and Timothy learn that Warehouse and Seathrift have drowned. Noting that their heirs are insufficiently upset by the news, the merchants reveal themselves and disinherit the young men. Warehouse sends for the match-maker Bannswright to find him a wife so that he can beget a new son and heir with immediate effect. Bannswright proposes Aurelia as a suitable candidate, but helps Plotwell to circumvent the marriage. Timothy is sent in, posing as a knight, to woo and marry Aurelia, and Warehouse is offered Dorcas as a substitute. They are married by a French priest who is really one of the tricksters in disguise, using a text from Rabelais instead of a genuine marriage service.

After Warehouse settles a portion of his estate on her, Dorcas refuses to sleep with her new husband or share his company, and insists on separate living arrangements within his house. Plotwell tells his uncle that she is a notorious whore who sleeps around and enjoys looking at pictures of men; he further arranges for the arrival of false news that Warehouse's ships have been wrecked. The plan is that he will be the one who proves the marriage unsound and the ships safe, thereby restoring himself to favour. With Bannswright's connivance, he marries Dorcas in earnest, knowing her really to be Susan and trusting that his uncle will be unable to renege on the grant of property. Bannswright reveals that he is really Plotwell's missing father, and that his own ship has also come in, resolving his financial difficulties.

SCENE DESIGNATION
prol., 1.1–5, 2.1–7, 3.1–4, 4.1–8, 5.1–9, ep. (F)

The stage is not clear at the following scene-divisions: 1.1–5, 2.1–4, 2.5–6, 3.1–4, 4.2–3, 4.4–5, 4.6–8, 5.2–9.

ROLES
PROLOGUE
Master WAREHOUSE, a merchant, Old Plotwell's brother, uncle of Francis Plotwell and Penelope, said to be about 70 years old

Master SEATHRIFT, a rich merchant, Mistress Seathrift's husband, father of Timothy and Susan
CYPHER, Warehouse's factor; poses as a waterman, and later a sailor
Master Francis PLOTWELL, a young man, Old Plotwell's son, Warehouse's nephew and heir, Penelope's brother; also called Frank; later Susan's husband
BRIGHT, a gentleman of the Inns of Court, Plotwell's friend
NEWCUT, a gentleman heir of the Inns of Court, Plotwell's friend
Master TIMOTHY Seathrift, son and heir of Seathrift and his wife, Susan's elder brother; formerly a university student; later Penelope's husband; also called Tim; poses as a knight
Madam AURELIA, a high-born lady; in reality, Penelope Plotwell, an apprentice seamstress, Old Plotwell's daughter, Warehouse's niece, Plotwell's sister; later Timothy's wife; also called Pen
Mistress DORCAS, Aurelia's waiting-woman, a Puritan; also called Goody Hoffman; in reality, Susan Seathrift, daughter of Seathrift and his wife, Timothy's younger sister; also called Mistress Sue; later Plotwell's wife
Master BANNSWRIGHT, a match-maker; in reality, Old Plotwell, Warehouse's brother, father of Plotwell and Penelope
Aurelia's FOOTMAN (2.3, 5.1, 5.7)
Captain QUARTFIELD, a soldier
ROSECLAP, an ordinary-keeper, Millicent's husband
Master SALEWIT, a poet
MILLICENT, Roseclap's wife; also called Mill
A PRENTICE (3.2, non-speaking)
MISTRESS SEATHRIFT, Seathrift's wife, mother of Timothy and Susan
Mistress HOLLAND, a seamstress; a married woman
Roseclap's BOY, who sings (3.2)
Mistress SCRUPLE, Susan's Puritan schoolmistress; a married woman and a mother
A FOOTMAN attending Timothy (4.2–3, 4.6, 5.1, 5.7)
EPILOGUE

Speaking Parts: 22

Stage Directions and Speech Prefixes
PROLOGUE: *The Prologue* (heading)
WAREHOUSE: *Ware-house* | *Warehouse* (s.d.s); *Wareh<ouse>* | *Wareh<ouse>* (s.p.s); *Warehouse An old Merchant* (d.p.)
SEATHRIFT: *Seathrift* | *Sea-thrift* (s.d.s); *Seath<rift>* (s.p.s); *Seathrift A Merchant* (d.p.)
CYPHER: *Cypher* (s.d.s); *Cypher* (s.p.s); *Cypher* [Warehouse's] *Factor* (d.p.)
PLOTWELL: *Plotwell* (s.d.s); *Plotw<ell>* (s.p.s); *Frank Plotwell* [Warehouse's] *Nephew* (d.p.)
BRIGHT: *Bright* (s.d.s); *Br<ight>* (s.p.s); *Bright* [one of] *Two Templars* (d.p.)

NEWCUT: *Newcut* (s.d.s); *Newc<ut>* (s.p.s); *Newcut* [one of] *Two Templars* (d.p.)
TIMOTHY: *Timothy* (s.d.s); *Tim<othy>* (s.p.s); *Timothy* [Seathrift's] *Son* (d.p.)
AURELIA: *Aurelia* (s.d.s); *Aur<elia>* (s.p.s); *Madam Aurelia Penelope Plotwell's daughter* (d.p.)
DORCAS: *Dorcas* (s.d.s); *Dor<cas>* (s.p.s); *Dorcas Susan Seathrift's daughter* (d.p.)
BANNSWRIGHT: *Banesright* (s.d.s); *Banesw<right>* (s.p.s); *Banesright Old Plotwell disguised* (d.p.)
FOOTMAN: *a Footman* (s.d.s); [one of] *Two Footmen* (s.d.s and d.p.); *Footman* | 1 *Footman* (s.p.s)
QUARTFIELD: *Captain Quart-field* | *Quartfield* (s.d.s); *Quartf<ield>* (s.p.s); *Quartfield A Captain* (d.p.)
ROSECLAP: *Roseclap* | *Rosclap* (s.d.s); *Ros<eclap>* (s.p.s); *Roseclappe One that keeps an Ordinary* (d.p.)
SALEWIT: *Sale-wit* | *Salewit* | *Salw<it>* (s.d.s); *Salew<it>* (s.p.s); *Salewit A Poet* (d.p.)
MILLICENT: *Millicent* (s.d.s); *Mill<icent>* (s.p.s); *Mill* [Roseclap's] *wife* (d.p.)
PRENTICE: *a Prentice* (s.d.s); *Prentice* (s.d.s and d.p.)
MISTRESS SEATHRIFT: *Mrs Seathrift* | *Mrs Sea-thrift* (s.d.s); *Mrs Seath<rift>* (s.p.s); *Mrs Seathrift* [Seathrift's] *Wife* (d.p.)
HOLLAND: *Mrs Holland* (s.d.s); *Mrs Holl<and>* (s.p.s); *Mrs Holland A Seamster on the Exchange* (d.p.)
BOY: *Boy that sings* (d.p.)
SCRUPLE: *Mrs Scruple* (s.d.s); *Mrs Scru<ple>* (s.p.s); *Mrs Scruple A Puritan Schoolmistress* (d.p.)
FOOTMAN: *a Footman* (s.d.s); [one of] *Two Footmen* (s.d.s and d.p.); *Footman* (s.d.s and s.p.s); 2 *Footman* (s.p.s)
EPILOGUE: *The Epilogue* (heading)

OTHER CHARACTERS
Plotwell's mistresses in former days (1.1)
Vintners who sent Timothy's wine bills to his father for payment (1.1)
A footman who brought Plotwell a letter (1.2)
A lady in financial difficulties, who wrote to Plotwell for help (1.2)
The King (1.4, 3.2)
Bright's mercer, a resident of Cheapside (1.4)
Aurelia's coachman (1.4)
Aurelia's footboy (1.4; may be one of the footmen who appears on stage)
Master Scruple, a Puritan, Mistress Scruple's husband, Susan's schoolmaster (2.1, 4.1, 5.5–6)
A lady whose parrot was converted to Puritanism by Dorcas (2.2; possibly imaginary)
A choleric lady given to dismissing her servants for their poor corn-cutting (2.2)
Three women servants sacked by the angry, footsore lady (2.2)
A fourth woman servant due for dismissal by the lady (2.2)
An alderman, Seathrift's friend (2.3)
Aurelia's neighbours (2.4)
The Sheriffs of London (2.5, 3.2, 5.9)
A fortune-teller who foretold that Timothy would marry a lady (2.6)
A drunkard from whom Quartfield made £20 by exhibiting him as an exotic fish (3.1)
The Queen, whom Mistress Holland claims as a customer (3.2)
Emlin, Mistress Scruple's daughter (4.1)
Mistress Scruple's pupils (4.1)
Three tiremen and two barbers whom Plotwell engaged to work on Timothy's appearance (4.2)
A boring priest procured by Plotwell to marry Timothy and Penelope; possibly named Sir John (4.2–3, 4.6)
Ladies who wanted Timothy to touch them, or so he says (4.3)
Warehouse's lawyer (4.5, 4.8)
The priest of the French church in London, impersonated by Salewit (4.5, 4.8, 5.1, 5.6, 5.9)
The benchers of Bright's and Newcut's Inn of Court, one of whom is a reader (4.7)
A christening party at the French church in London (5.1)
The city Marshal (5.3, 5.8)
Mistress Holland's husband (5.5)
A sailor from whom Cypher hired a seafaring suit (5.9)
The Sheriffs' wives (5.9)

SETTING
Period: contemporary; the action takes place during the long vacation
Time-Scheme: the action takes place during a single day, 1.1–2.4 in the morning, 2.6 at dinner-time, and 4.3 before 3 p.m.
Place: London

Geography
London: the [Inner or Middle] Temple; the Exchange; Westminster Hall; the Cross; Fleet Street; the Strand; Ludgate; Fleet Bridge; Cheapside; Spring Garden; the Guildhall; St Antholin's Church; Broad Street; Cheapside Conduit; Moorfields; Old Fish Street; New Fish Street; King Street; River Thames; St Paul's Cathedral; the Mermaid tavern; the Counter prison; Park Corner; Westminster; the French church; Hyde Park; Blackwall
Middlesex: Pimlico; Brentford
[*Surrey*]: Mortlake
Kent: Greenwich; Shooter's Hill; Dover
England: Northamptonshire; Ipswich; [Oxford or Cambridge]; Cheshire; Windsor Castle; Norfolk; Bristol
Scotland
Ireland
The Low Countries: Holland
Europe: France; Italy; Spain; Germany; Sweden; Geneva
[*Asia*]: Aleppo; Turkey; Arabia; China; Hormuz
Africa: River Nile; the Canaries
The Indies
The New World: Mexico; New England; Peru; Rio de la Plata

SOURCES
Narrative: possibly William Shakespeare, *The Tempest* (**1652**; 3.2); Ben Jonson, *The Silent Woman* (**1603**; Warehouse/Dorcas marriage); Philip Massinger, *The City Madam* (**2373**; 5.7)
Verbal: Horace, *Ars poetica* (t.p. motto); Ben Jonson, *Volpone* (**1493**; 3.2); John Ford, *'Tis Pity She's a Whore* (**2329**; 5.2); Philip Massinger, *The City Madam* (**2373**; 5.2); William Cartwright, *The Ordinary* (**2468**; 1.3, 2.5)
Works Mentioned: Sophocles, tragedies (general reference; 3.3); Aristotle, unspecified work (4.2); Euclid, *Elements* (2.5); Ovid, *Metamorphoses* (1.4); Tacitus, unspecified work (4.2); Pietro Aretino, *Postures* (1524; 5.7); François Rabelais, unspecified work (4.2, 5.1, 5.9); John Knox, unspecified works (2.2); John Foxe, *Acts and Monuments* (1563; 2.2); Diego Ortuñez de Calahorra, Pedro de la Sierra, and Marcos Martínez, *Espejo de principes y caballeros* (1555–87; English tr., *The Mirror of Princely Deeds and Knighthood*, by Margaret Tyler, R. P., and L. A., 1578–99; 4.2); Hugo Grotius, *Mare liberum* (1609; 3.2); William Prynne, *The Unloveliness of Love-Locks* (1628; 2.1), *Histriomastix* (1633; 2.2); James Shirley, *The Triumph of Peace* (**2423**; 1.5, oblique allusion); also a general reference to Galen (4.7)

The debt to *Volpone* is the fantastical discourse about the possible political uses of the fish.

LANGUAGE
English
Latin: 2 words (3.2; Plotwell)
Spanish: 1 word (4.3; Timothy)
Dialect: Salewit speaks in 'French' accented English (5.6)

FORM
Metre: pentameter
Rhyme: couplets
Prologue: 22 lines, in couplets (two versions, one for court and one for Blackfriars)
Act-Division: 5 acts
Epilogue: two versions, both in couplets: 26 lines for court, 20 lines for Blackfriars
Lines (Spoken):
    COURT: 2,344 (2,343 verse, 1 prose)
    BLACKFRIARS: 2,338 (2,337 verse, 1 prose)
Lines (Written): 2,497

STAGING
Doors: two characters exit severally (2.4, s.d.); mentioned (3.2, s.d.)
Discovery Space: curtained (3.2, s.d.); Timothy is discovered asleep (3.2, s.d.); Bright and Newcut are discovered (5.7, s.d.)
Audience: the King in the audience is directly addressed as 'royal sir' (court prol.) and 'great sir' (court ep.); possibly referred to as 'gentles' (2.5, implicit); assumed to be seated (Blackfriars ep.); the price of admission is said to be two shillings (Blackfriars ep.)
Miscellaneous: the stage needs somewhere to 'hang out' a picture (3.1, s.d.)

MUSIC AND SOUND
Sound Effects: knocking (3.2, s.d.)
Song: 'We show no monstrous crocodile', 3.2, Roseclap's Boy, 14 lines; *musical setting survives*

PROPS
Weapons: Quartfield's blade weapon (3.4, implicit)
Musical Instruments: two trumpets (3.2–4, implicit)
Money: a purse (2.4, s.d.); three shillings (3.2, dialogue); two shillings (3.2, implicit); an unspecified amount (3.3, s.d.)
Food and Drink: sack (3.2, dialogue)
Small Portable Objects: a key (1.3, 4.7, dialogue); two parchment documents (5.9, dialogue); pen and ink (5.9, implicit); a seal and sealing-wax (5.9, implicit)
Large Portable Objects: a large picture frame (5.7, s.d.)
Scenery: a picture of a strange fish (3.1–4, s.d.); a curtain (3.2, 5.7, s.d.)

COSTUMES
WAREHOUSE: white or grey hair (implicit); disguised (3.2–3, s.d.; removed on stage)
SEATHRIFT: disguised (3.2–3, s.d.; removed on stage)
CYPHER: disguised as a waterman (3.2–3, s.d.); disguised as a sailor (5.4, s.d.; 5.9, implicit; removed on stage)
PLOTWELL: kersey hose (1.3–5, dialogue); shiny shoes (1.3–5, dialogue); an old velvet jacket (1.3–4, s.d.; removed and torn to pieces on stage); dimity breeches (1.3–5, dialogue); a threadbare beaver hat (1.3–5, dialogue); silk clothes (2.3–4, 3.2–4, implicit; 2.6, dialogue)
BRIGHT: silk clothes (1.4–5, dialogue)
TIMOTHY: an expensive-looking suit (1.5, dialogue); dressed as a strange fish (3.2–4, s.d.), including fins, scales, claws on his hands, and flounders on his feet (dialogue); fantastically dressed (4.3, s.d.); a garment fastened with buttons (4.6, s.d.; unbuttoned on stage); stockings (4.6, dialogue)
DORCAS: Puritan clothes (2.1–2, implicit), including a little ruff and a [rebato] wire (dialogue); a different, fashionable costume (4.3, s.d.; 5.8–9, dialogue; 'out of her Puritan dress')
BANNSWRIGHT: disguised (5.9, s.d.; removed on stage)
QUARTFIELD: buff-coloured clothes (2.5–6, dialogue); dressed as a trumpeter (3.2–4, s.d.); disguised (5.9, s.d.; removed on stage)
SALEWIT: dressed as a trumpeter (3.2–4, s.d.); disguised as a curate (5.1, s.d.; 5.6, 5.9, implicit; removed on stage), in black (dialogue)

EARLY STAGE HISTORY

1636: a performance at Christ Church, Oxford, in September, during the royal visit, was planned but did not take place.

1636-7: performed at Hampton Court around Christmas, probably by members of Christ Church, Oxford, and probably on Friday 6 January (Twelfth Night). Music was probably composed by William Lawes. The performance took place in the evening, and was considered a success. The audience included: King Charles I; Queen Henrietta Maria; Jasper Mayne; possibly William Cartwright. (Alternative possible dates for the performance are Wednesday 28 to Saturday 31 December or Monday 2 to Wednesday 4 January, inclusive.)

Possibly performed at Whitehall Palace by 1639. The audience included: King Charles I; Queen Henrietta Maria.

c. 1637-9: performed by the King's Men at the Blackfriars.

Bentley believes that the Hampton Court performance cannot have taken place at Christmas 1636-7, but there are several reasons to believe that it did. One seventeenth-century account of the royal visit to Oxford (Bodleian, MS Twyne 17, p. 199) is precise in saying that, during the Christmas week after the visit, both William Cartwright and Jasper Mayne were summoned to Hampton Court to see their plays staged before the King and Queen. This is not information that could have been inferred from F's title page (which refers only to a performance at Whitehall), and the court was indeed at Hampton Court that Christmas; it seems, in fact, to have been the last Christmas season Charles I's court spent there.

The reason for Bentley's scepticism is that *The City Match* is not included in the King's Men's extant bill for that season, nor is the performance mentioned by Sir Henry Herbert. The King's Men did indeed perform one of the Oxford plays, *The Royal Slave* (**2552**), but the cases were slightly different. The student actors had already had the chance to perform *The Royal Slave* for the King and Queen, whereas the intended Oxford performance of *The City Match* had not taken place; they may therefore have been given their chance at Christmas rather than having their play handed over to commercial players like *The Royal Slave*. This would also explain why the performance goes unmentioned by Herbert, who only lists appearances by professional acting companies.

If we accept that the performance was not given by the King's Men, then the possible performance dates are presumably those on which the King's Men did not appear. A letter from Edward Rossingham to Sir Thomas Puckering, dated 11 January 1637, seems to indicate that there was a court performance of an Oxford play on Twelfth Night; Rossingham claims that it was *The Royal Slave*, but in fact *The Royal Slave*'s performance did not take place until the day after he wrote the letter. He may simply have mistaken one Oxford play for the other, an easy error given that by now *The Royal Slave* was famous. A performance by amateur actors might, moreover, have been perceived as an alternative to the usual Twelfth Night masque, comparable with the amateur performance of *The Shepherds' Paradise* (**2395**) four years earlier.

The Whitehall Palace performance may have been a repeat, occasioned by the success of the play's first outing at Hampton Court. However, F assigns the court prologue and epilogue to Whitehall, even though they were evidently written for the first performance; it is possible, therefore, that Whitehall is mentioned in error for Hampton Court, and that the second court performance is a ghost.

EARLY TEXTUAL HISTORY

1639 or earlier: Jasper Mayne heard that a corrupt copy of the text had come into the possession of a London publisher, who intended to issue an unauthorized edition. This overcame his reluctance to publish the play.

1639: ¹F printed at Oxford by Leonard Lichfield; collation A–S², 36 leaves; title page refers to court performance and names acting company and playhouse; Latin title-page motto; epistle; list of roles.

c. 1630s–40s: a copy of F was in the possession of John Horne (Vicar of Headington, Oxfordshire). After his death, his entire collection of play-books passed into the possession of John Houghton of Brasenose College, Oxford (c. 1608–77), then to James Herne (died 1685), and then to the library of Ralph Sheldon (1623–84) at Weston, where it was catalogued by the antiquarian Anthony Wood, probably in the late 1670s.

c. 1641: Song, with a musical setting by William Lawes, was included in a MS songbook (New York Public Library, MS Drexel 4041, no. 7).

1640-1: Humphrey Moseley was selling copies of F for 1s.6d each.

1655: *The English Treasury of Wit and Language* entered in the Stationers' Register to Humphrey Moseley on 16 January.

1655: four extracts (from 4.5, 5.3, 5.5, 5.7) included in John Cotgrave's *The English Treasury of Wit and Language*, sigs. D5^r, I6^r, N2^v, V6^v; printed for Humphrey Moseley.

1658: included as a bibliographically independent item, but with no title page, in Mayne's *Two Plays* (²Q); collation A–I⁴ K1, 37 leaves; printed at Oxford by Henry Hall for Richard Davis. The copy was F. The other play in the collection was *The Amorous War* (**2595**).

1659: ³O printed at Oxford by Henry Hall for Richard Davis, using mainly the same setting of type as for Q, adding a title page printed mainly from F, but now with the author's initials; collation π1 A–D⁸ E⁸ (–E8), 40 leaves.

c. 1670s: six extracts (from 1.4-5, 4.3, 4.7, 5.2) included in MS annotations in an interleaved copy of John Cotgrave's *The English Treasury of Wit and Language*, pp. 28a^r, 70a^r, 164a^v, 312b^r, 312e^r, 294a^r. (The copy is now at the British Library, pressmark G.16385.)

1684: Nicholas Cox (Manciple of St Edmund Hall, Oxford) had a copy of Q in his bookshop. It had probably been previously owned by Gerard Langbaine, and appears on a list compiled by Anthony Wood on Saturday 13 December.

Late seventeenth century (before 1695): a copy of F was owned by Anthony Wood.

EDITION

W. Carew Hazlitt, in *A Select Collection of Old English Plays* (London, 1874-6), xiii. 199–320.

REFERENCES
Annals 1637; Bentley, iv. 847–50; Bodleian, MS Wood E. 4, art. 1, p. 78; Eyre & Rivington, i. 463; Greg 568; Hazlitt, 42; Nicolas K. Kiessling, *The Library of Anthony Wood* (Oxford, 2002) 4426; *MLR* 13 (1918), 401–11; *Oxford Bibliographical Society Proceedings and Papers* 2.2 (1929), 132; REED: Oxford, 544–5, 556–7, 892; *SP* 40 (1943), 186–203; Steele, 263, 274.

2554. Comedy

EVIDENCE
Letter from Thomas Reade to Sir Francis Windebank, dated 8 September 1636.

It has alternatively been suggested that Reade was collecting, piecemeal, the text of *The Royal Slave* (**2552**) for Windebank. This seems unlikely: Reade writes about the play in proprietorial tones suggestive of an author.

GENRE
comedy
Contemporary: *comoedia*

AUTHOR
Thomas Reade

DATE
September 1636

FORM
Prologue: probably
Epilogue: probably

Reade describes the final elements ('extremas ... partes') added to the comedy as its 'proram ... et puppim' (prow and stern); this suggests that he first wrote the body of the play and then finished it off with discrete, separable elements at both ends. This is most likely to have been a prologue and epilogue, though the possibility of an induction cannot be ruled out.

EARLY TEXTUAL HISTORY
1636: By Thursday 8 September, Thomas Reade had finished the play, and sent a final instalment to his uncle, Sir Francis Windebank. He had apparently already sent the bulk of it.

REFERENCES
REED: Oxford, 534.

2555. Royal Entertainment at Richmond Palace

TEXT
Printed in 1636 (STC 5026).

GENRE
masque
Contemporary: entertainment, masque (t.p.)

TITLE
Printed: *The King and Queen's Entertainment at Richmond*
Contemporary: *Expeditio Britomartis*
Later Assigned: *The Entertainment at Richmond*

AUTHOR
said to be male

DATE
12 September 1636

ORIGINAL PRODUCTION
English Court at Richmond Palace

PLOT
Wiltshire Tom bursts into the royal presence looking for the Queen: he wants to give her a melon, a present from his master. He and his friends present a country dance, during which Richard tries to kiss Tom's girlfriend Madge; strife is averted when Madge makes it clear that she prefers Tom.

Moll wants to marry Wilkin the shepherd, but her mother has forbidden the liaison because Wilkin is too poor. She elopes with him, and they sing about how money can't buy true love.

Prince Britomart's army of ancient Britons invades modern Britain, but a druid advises against an aggressive military enterprise. The soldiers are pacified by the Queen's presence and lay their arms at her feet. A post seeks safe conduct for Britomart and his knights, who arrive on a triumphal arch. Dancing ensues.

SCENE DESIGNATION
sc.1–4 (Q)

ROLES
A GENTLEMAN USHER at court
TOM, a Wiltshire yokel; also called Thomas; he is literate
Master Edward SACKVILLE, a member of the audience; also called Yedward
A MUSICIAN (sc.1, *non-speaking*)
MADGE, Tom's girlfriend, a country wench
RICHARD, a country fellow; also called Ruchard
GERVASE, a country fellow (*non-speaking*)
DOLL, a country wench; also called Dorothy
JUG, a country wench (*non-speaking*)
WILKIN, a shepherd
MOLL, a shepherdess; also called Maull and Lucinda
A CAPTAIN in Britomart's army
A DRUID, an ancient British priest
PRIESTS of Apollo (sing collectively)
Five SOLDIERS in Britomart's army (sc.2, *non-speaking*)

A POST
A SPANIARD (sc.2, *non-speaking*)
Prince BRITOMART, a Romano-British prince; one of the masquers (*non-speaking*)
Five KNIGHTS ADVENTURERS, Britomart's companions, masquers (*non-speaking*)
Six DWARFS, squires to Britomart and his knights (*non-speaking*)

Speaking Parts: 11 (excluding the priests)

Doubling
In the original production, Edward Sackville played both himself and a knight; Lord Buckhurst (who played a knight) may also have taken one of the speaking parts.

However, see under EARLY STAGE HISTORY.

Stage Directions and Speech Prefixes
GENTLEMAN USHER: *a Gentleman-usher | the Gentleman-usher* (s.d.s); *Usher* (s.p.s)
TOM: *Tom* (s.d.s and s.p.s); *Tho<mas>* (s.p.s)
SACKVILLE: *M. Edward Sackvile* (s.d.s); *M. Sa<ckvile>*(s.p.s)
MADGE: *Madge* (s.d.s); *Ma<dge>* (s.p.s)
RICHARD: *Richard* (s.d.s); *Ruc<hard> | Ric<hard>* (s.p.s)
DOLL: *Doll* (s.p.s)
WILKIN: *a shepherd | The Shepherd* (s.d.s); *Shepherd* (s.d.s and s.p.s)
MOLL: *a shepherdess | Lucinda* (s.d.s); *Lu<cinda>* (s.p.s)
CAPTAIN: *a Captain | The Captain* (s.d.s); *Captain* (s.p.s)
DRUID: *a Druid | the Druid* (s.d.s); *Druid* (s.p.s)
PRIESTS: *the Priests of Apollo | The Priests | the Chorus of Priests* (s.d.s)
SOLDIERS: *the Soldiers | five tottered Soldiers* (s.d.s)
POST: *a Post* (s.d.s)
SPANIARD: *one | a Spaniard | The Spaniard* (s.d.s)
BRITOMART: *Prince Britomart* (s.d.s)
KNIGHTS ADVENTURERS: [Britomart's] *Knights | five Knights Adventurers | the Knights | the Adventurers* (s.d.s)
DWARFS: *six Squires or Dwarfs* (s.d.s)

OTHER CHARACTERS
Tom's master (sc.1)
The headborough of Tom's town (sc.1)
The High Constable [of Wiltshire], a man of insecure literacy (sc.1)
Madge's mistress, a fierce woman, and her goodman (sc.1)
The tailor of Amesbury (sc.1)
Moll's mother (sc.1)
The people of Moll's parish (sc.1)
Britomart's army (sc.2)
The King of Britain (sc.2; i.e. King Charles I, in the audience)

SETTING
Period: simultaneously generic ancient British times and contemporary
Place: Britain

Geography
Wiltshire: Amesbury
Britain: Wales
[*Europe*]: Rome; France; the Low Countries; Spain

SOURCES
Verbal: Cicero, *Pro Murena* (sc.3); Edmund Spenser, *The Faerie Queene* 1 (1590, repr. 1617; the name Britomart). Song 1 may have been an already extant work incorporated into the masque.

Bentley reports a suggestion that there are similarities with the antimasques in *The Triumph of Peace* (**2423**), but I see nothing compelling.

LANGUAGE
English
Welsh: 4 words extant (sc.2; Post; he also has another, unscripted Welsh speech)
French: 13 words (sc.2; Post)
Dialect: the Gentleman Usher speaks in a rustic accent, and Tom, Madge, Richard, and Doll in a heavy Wiltshire dialect.

FORM
Metre: prose and pentameter
Rhyme: blank verse
Lines (Spoken): 428 (172 verse 256 prose)
Lines (Written): 626

STAGING
Within: speech (sc.1, s.d.)
Openings: the Gentleman Usher stands 'at the entrance of the scene' (sc.1, s.d.)
Audience: Tom enters in search of the Queen, and mistakes a gaily-dressed woman in the audience for her (sc.1); a member of the audience (Sackville) has scripted dialogue (sc.1), and later appears as one of the masquers; the Queen in the audience is directly addressed (sc.1–2, 4); the Queen's presence is said to pacify the soldiers (sc.2); weapons are laid at the Queen's feet (sc.2, s.d.); the King and ladies in the audience are directly addressed (sc.2); attention is called to the fact that members of the audience will not dance with the masquers as usual (sc.2); scutcheons are laid at the Queen's feet (sc.3)

MUSIC
Music: post-horn (sc.2, s.d.); violin plays a pavan and a saraband (sc.2, s.d.)
On-Stage Music: Musician plays the violin (sc.1, s.d.); Musician plays country dance music, presumably on the violin (sc.1, dialogue); Wilkin plays the theorbo (sc.1, s.d.; accompanying Song 1); Priests play the lute (sc.2, dialogue; accompanying Song 2)

Songs:
1: 'Did not you once, Lucinda, vow', sc.1, Wilkin and Moll, in parts, 24 lines; with musical accompaniment; *musical setting survives*;
2: 'Behold how sweet a majesty', sc.2, Priests, 14 lines, with musical accompaniment;
3: 'The springing hopes of arms and arts', sc.2, Priests, 4 lines;
4: 'Why stay you there, brave knights? Descend!', sc.3, Priests, 8 lines;
5: 'What the sad heavens, the sun once gone', sc.4, Priests, 18 lines.

Dance: country dance by the six yokels, with musical accompaniment (sc.1, s.d.); wild dance by the Soldiers (sc.2, s.d.); the Spaniard dances (sc.2, s.d.); Britomart and Knights dance two dances (sc.3, s.d.); the Dwarfs dance a leaping dance (sc.3, s.d.).

PROPS
Weapons: five unspecified weapons (sc.2, s.d.); the Spaniard's rapier (sc.2, s.d.); six gilded scutcheons, each with a different impresa (sc.3, s.d.).
Musical Instruments: a violin (sc.1, s.d.); a theorbo (sc.1, s.d.); lutes (sc.2, dialogue)
Food and Drink: a melon (sc.1, dialogue)
Small Portable Objects: a paper (sc.2, s.d.)
Large Portable Objects: a staff (sc.1, s.d.); two sheep-hooks (sc.1, s.d.)
Scenery: four scenes: country fields (sc.1, desc.); a military camp, with tents, carriage, and munitions, surrounded by a trench, and a compartment with the scene-title 'Expeditio Britomartis' (sc.2, desc.); a triumphal arch (sc.3, desc.; seats six characters on at least two levels, and they are able to descend with ease); a temple (sc.4, desc.); a curtain (sc.4, desc.).

COSTUMES
USHER: a black beard (desc.); a black calot hat (sc.1, desc.)
MUSICIAN: whiskers (dialogue)
WILKIN and MOLL: broad hats; frieze coats (sc.1, s.d.)
CAPTAIN: a knee-length coat of scales; a petasus; buskins (sc.2, desc.)
DRUID: a crimson taffeta robe; a garland on his head (sc.2, desc.)
PRIESTS: long taffeta robes, in various colours (sc.2, s.d.)
SOLDIERS: tattered clothes (sc.2, s.d.)
SPANIARD: 'formal garb and habit', including a cloak (sc.2, s.d.; removed on stage); hangers (sc.2, implicit; removed on stage)
BRITOMART and KNIGHTS: plumed petasus caps; watchet and crimson taffeta clothes cut upon silver in scallops, with matching bases and buskins (sc.3–4, desc.)
DWARFS: short taffeta coats; taffeta bonnets with feathers around them (sc.3, s.d.).

EARLY STAGE HISTORY
Inception: The Queen indicated that she wished to see her son, Prince Charles, in a dance. The masque was developed to give a framework to the dance.
Preparation: Theobald Pierce (Keeper of the Standing Wardrobe at Richmond) prepared the venue.
Performance: at Richmond Palace on Monday 12 September 1636. Most or all of the cast were children, including: Prince Charles (Britomart); Thomas Chefinch (Yokel); John Foxe (Yokel); *either* Charles Ker *or* Henry, Lord Ker (Knight); John Quinne (Yokel); Edward Sackville (himself and Knight); Richard Sackville, Lord Buckhurst (Knight and a speaking part); Thomas Steeling (Yokel); Lord Francis Villiers (Knight); George Villiers, 2nd Duke of Buckingham (Knight). Some of the choreography was by Simon Hopper, and the music was composed by Charles Coleman. Some props were made and scenery painted by Edward Pearce. The audience included: King Charles I; Queen Henrietta Maria; probably Edward Sackville, 4th Earl of Dorset.
Aftermath: Theobald Pierce cleaned the props and costumes.

Bentley argues persuasively that 'Master Edward', the character in sc.1, is Edward Sackville junior rather than his father, the Earl of Dorset and the Queen's Lord Chamberlain. This depends on the reasonable assumption that Edward junior would be the one more properly addressed as 'Master Edward'. It is alternatively possible that Tom might commit the rustic solecism of addressing an earl as 'Master Edward', but even plucked from the audience, Dorset would arguably be out of place among a cast of children, and the concluding remarks seem to indicate that both Edward junior and Lord Buckhurst took speaking as well as dancing parts.

Production Expenses
Edward Pearce's fee for painting a scene and making, painting, and gilding six scutcheons (£10.2s); Theobald Pierce's fee (£17.4s; includes money for general wardrobe maintenance during five months that year).

EARLY TEXTUAL HISTORY
1636: Q printed at Oxford by Leonard Lichfield; collation A–D^4, 16 leaves; title page refers to performance; Latin title-page motto; verse dedication to Queen Henrietta Maria.
1652: Song 1 included, with a musical setting by Charles Coleman, in John Playford's *Select Musical Airs and Dialogues*, sigs. 2B2^v–2C1^r; printed by Thomas Harper for John Playford. The book had been advertised for sale on Monday 24 November 1651, presumably in advance of its printing.
1653: *Select Musical Airs and Dialogues* entered in the Stationers' Register to John Playford on Thursday 22 December.
1653: *Select Musical Airs and Dialogues* reprinted (in an expanded edition) by Thomas Harper for John Playford, probably in December; the song now appears on sigs. 2C1^v–2C2^r.

c. 1650s: Song 1 included in a MS miscellany (London: British Library, Add. MS 22582, fo. 15) possibly owned by Bryan Fairfax.

1659: Song 1 included (as 'A Dialogue between a Shepherd and Lucinda'), with Coleman's musical setting, in John Playford's *Select Airs and Dialogues*, sigs. T1^v–T2^r; printed by William Godbid for John Playford.

1669: *Select Airs and Dialogues* reprinted as *The Treasury of Music* by William Godbid for John Playford.

1673: an extract (from sc.1) appears as the droll *Wiltshire Tom* in *The Wits, Part 2*, sigs. B5^v–B8^v; printed by Edward Crouch for Francis Kirkman. The copy was Q.

1684: Nicholas Cox (Manciple of St Edmund Hall, Oxford) had a copy of Q in his bookshop. It had probably been previously owned by Gerard Langbaine, and appears on a list compiled by Anthony Wood on Saturday 13 December.

1686: *The Loyal Garland* licensed for publication on Wednesday 18 August.

1686: Song 1 included in *The Loyal Garland*, sigs. F6^v–F7^r; printed by John Richardson for Thomas Passinger; black letter.

EDITIONS

W. Bang and R. Brotanek, Materialien 1.2 (Louvain and Leipzig, 1903).

Ian Spink, *English Songs, 1625–1660*, 2nd edn (London, 1977), no. 74 (Song 1 and music only).

Sabol, no. 48 (Song 1 and music only).

REFERENCES

Annals 1636; Ashbee, iii. 152; Bentley, v. 1357–60; Bodleian, MS Wood E. 4, art. 1, p. 104; Butler, 327–9, 375; Eyre & Rivington, i. 438; Greg 512; Hazlitt, 125; McGee-Meagher 1634–42, 54–6; *MLQ* 6 (1903), 74; MSC 6, 123; MSC 10, 48; *REED Newsletter* 12.1 (1987), 12–18; Reyher, 531; Steele, 263.

2556. *Love in Its Ecstasy*

TEXT
Printed in 1649 (Wing P967).

GENRE
tragicomedy
Contemporary: 'a kind of royal pastoral' (t.p.); interlude, dramatic poem (epistle)

TITLE
Printed: *Love in Its Ecstasy, or The Large Prerogative*

AUTHOR
[William?] Peaps *or* Pepys (*ascription*)

DATE
Limits: 1633–42
Best Guess: 1636

The title page says that the author was a student at Eton, and the publisher's preface avers that the play was written in 'milky days' (i.e. before the Civil War) and was 'long since the early recreation of a gentleman not fully seventeen'. He is given the name Peaps in Francis Kirkman's 1661 play-list; the forename William was assigned by W. R. Chetwood in 1750. Bentley found a record of one Pepys on a list of the commensals at Eton in 1634, and this is the basis for the usually assigned date. Birley later discovered the existence of a teenage William Pepys in the 1630s, a member of a Norfolk landowning family who was not yet 24 in April 1639 (though this would probably have made him nearly 17 in 1632, which discourages his identification as the dramatist). The central problem is that, although we can place a Pepys at Eton in 1634, we don't know anything else about him, including how old he was then and whether his absence from the school's commensal records from other years was because he had left or because his status had changed to oppidan or scholar. There are, accordingly, no grounds for treating 1634 as anything more than a preliminary dating guideline.

The play's genre offers another angle of approach, albeit one just as uncertain. 1634 seems a little too early for this very elaborated and somewhat masculine kind of pastoral, full of adventure and political intrigue. It is very unlike the sort of thing that courtly faddists were writing in the immediate aftermath of *The Shepherds' Paradise* (**2395**), but rather in the mode of recent French romance, comparable with plays by Lodowick Carlell and, in particular, Thomas Killigrew that were written a few years later in the decade. It is reasonable to suppose that a private, recreational, unpublished work of art like *Love in its Ecstasy* will be later than, and in some way influenced by, public works in the same vein, rather than vice versa; it is, moreover, just as unlikely that young Pepys arrived at this mode independently. A date of 1636, still just a guess, at least keeps the play comfortably before the troubles leading up to the war, and gives the author the chance to have encountered some of the plays that seem to have been his generic models.

PLOT
Sicily is divided into three kingdoms. Charastus, the King of Lilybaeus, loves Flavanda, but her price is that he give up his crown and install her unpopular brother Bermudo as King in his place; this will make her his equal. He agrees, on condition that Bermudo never falls in love: should he do so, he must restore Charastus to power. Flavanda intended the abdication as a love-test and a means of rectifying their inequality of status; but Bermudo, whose idea it was in the first place, has a political agenda of his own. He had promised Flavanda that he would give back the crown immediately after the wedding, but once in power he reneges on this and passes a law making love illegal. It is reported that Charastus' sister Desdonella, who loves Bermudo unrequitedly, drowned herself when she heard the proclamation.

Charastus leaves court to live a simple life in the woods. There he encounters two newcomers who turn out to be the princes of the other two Sicilian kingdoms; they agree to work together as a team. Their history is entwined with each other: Fidelio was betrothed to Virtusus' sister Constantina, until an oracle told her father that she was destined to depose her brother. The engagement was broken off and she was to be put away in a nunnery, but got away just in time. Suspected as an accomplice in the escape, Virtusus was banished, and left with a mocking injunction from Thesbia, Fidelio's sister, to find both his sister and her brother. Fidelio initially has a grudge against Virtusus, but a letter from Thesbia resolves it.

Aware that his new law will cause an epidemic of emigration, Bermudo closes the borders. The two other Sicilian kings, looking for their missing offspring, are driven to harbour by a storm, arrested as spies, and sentenced to death. Their sons visit them in prison disguised as priests and effect their escape by an exchange of clothes; Charastus then sets fire to the prison so that they too can leave, but they are caught trying to get away. To save Fidelio from torture, Virtusus admits sole responsibility for the arson. Thesbia arrives at court, disguised as a young man, Anthrogonus; she impresses Bermudo, and is appointed jailer in place of the man who lost the prisoners. She discovers Virtusus' identity and successfully begs his release.

Fidelio disapproves of Flavanda and warns Charastus that she may be inconstant, so Charastus asks him to prove it by tempting her. Flavanda rejects his advances and sends her companion to warn Charastus what a false friend he has. Charastus falls in love with the messenger, who is in fact Constantina, and tries to find a way of breaking off his commitment to Flavanda. Believing Fidelio to have been wooing Flavanda in earnest, Constantina tells him that his missing fiancée has married someone else. He denounces her for unchastity, and she is condemned to death.

While out hunting, Bermudo encounters what he takes to be the goddess Diana, who appears to him in the shape of Desdonella lest her divine refulgence should blind his mortal eyes. He falls in love, breaking his own law. In reality, Desdonella did not drown herself, but went into hiding in the woods with the assistance of the old courtier Halisdus. Charastus shows Bermudo that 'Anthrogonus' and 'his' prisoner Constantina have a closer than appropriate relationship. Bermudo infers that they are lovers and insists on a human sacrifice to Diana, in accordance with his new law. Constantina and Thesbia both pre-empt the ceremony by taking poison: a dead body cannot be sacrificed. In fact, the poison was only a sleeping draught. When they wake, they pose as ghosts and scare Bermudo into admitting that he is in love, thereby triggering Charastus' restoration to the throne. Desdonella reveals herself, and Charastus offers to abdicate in her favour, on condition that she marries Bermudo and that he learns how to govern justly. It then emerges that he is not the rightful King in any case: the real heir accidentally died in infancy, and was replaced with the baby Prince of Pachynus, stolen by Halisdus, who now reveals the truth to forestall the possibility of an incestuous liaison between Charastus and his sister Constantina. Thus, the oracle is fulfilled: Constantina has caused her brother's deposition. The four couples pair off, and the outcome is the unification of Sicily.

SCENE DESIGNATION
1.1–4, 2.1–4, 3.1–5, 4.1–6, 5.1–3 (Q, corrected)

The stage is not clear at 1.1–2.

ROLES
ARONTAS, Captain of the Citadel
SPADATUS, a courtier of foreign birth
Prince CHARASTUS, King of Lilybaeus, supposed Desdonella's brother; in reality, Lunaster, son of Brabantas, brother of Virtusus and Constantina
FLAVANDA, Bermudo's sister
BERMUDO, a nobleman, Flavanda's brother; later appointed King of Lilybaeus
HALISDUS, an old commander; a married man
ATTENDANTS at court (1.2, 5.2–3; only speak collectively, if at all)
Prince VIRTUSUS of Pachynus, Brabantas's son, brother of Constantina and Lunaster
FIDELIO of Pelorus, Sperazus' son, Thesbia's brother, Constantina's fiancé; poses as a shepherd
A MESSENGER (2.1)
BRABANTAS, King of Pachynus, father of Virtusus and Constantina (and, it turns out, of Lunaster)
King SPERAZUS of Pelorus, father of Fidelio and Thesbia
A JAILER (2.3–4)
A RABBLE (2.3; only speak collectively)
The GUARD at court (2.4, 4.3, 4.6, 5.2–3; only speak collectively, if at all)
THESBIA, Sperazus' daughter, Fidelio's sister; poses as Anthrogonus, a youth
CONSTANTINA, Brabantas' daughter, sister of Virtusus and Lunaster, Fidelio's fiancée
An ECHO (3.4)
DESDONELLA, Princess of Lilybaeus, supposed Charastus' sister

Speaking Parts: 16

Stage Directions and Speech Prefixes
ARONTAS: *Arontas* (s.d.s); *Aron<tas>* (s.p.s); *Arontas, The Captain of the Citadel* (d.p.)
SPADATUS: *Spadatus* (s.d.s); *Spa<datus>* (s.p.s; also misprinted *Sapd.*); *Spadatus, A Courtier* (d.p.)
CHARASTUS: *Charastus* (s.d.s); *Char<astus>* (s.p.s); *Charastus, King of Lelybaeus* (d.p.)
FLAVANDA: *Flavanda* (s.d.s); *Fla<vanda>* (s.p.s); *Flavanda, Sister to Bermudo* (d.p.)
BERMUDO: *Bermudo* (s.d.s); *Ber<mudo>* (s.p.s); *Bermudo, a nobleman of Lelybaeus* (d.p.)
HALISDUS: *Halisdus* (s.d.s); *Hall<isdus>* (s.p.s); *Halisdus, an old commander* (d.p.)

ATTENDANTS: *Attendants* (s.d.s and d.p.); *others* (s.d.s)
VIRTUSUS: *Virtusus* (s.d.s); *Vir<tusus>* (s.p.s); *Virtusus, Son to Brabantas enamoured of Thesbia* (d.p.)
FIDELIO: *Fidelio* (s.d.s); *Fid<elio>* (s.p.s); *Fidelio, Son to Sperazus betrothed to Constantina* (d.p.)
MESSENGER: *a Messenger* (s.d.s); *Messenger* (s.p.s and d.p.)
BRABANTAS: *Brabantas* (s.d.s); *Bra<bantas>* (s.p.s); *Brabantas, King of Pachynus* (d.p.)
SPERAZUS: *Sperazus* (s.d.s); *Spe<razus>* (s.p.s); *Sperazus, King of Pelorus* (d.p.)
JAILER: *Jailer* (s.d.s, s.p.s, and d.p.)
RABBLE: *A confused company* (s.d.s)
GUARD: *Guard* (s.d.s and d.p.); *the Guard* (s.d.s)
THESBIA: *Thesbia* (s.d.s); *Thes<bia>* (s.p.s); *Thesbia, Sister to Fidelio* (d.p.)
CONSTANTINA: *Constantina* (s.d.s); *Con<stantina>* (s.p.s); *Constantina, Sister to Virtusus* (d.p.)
ECHO: *Echo* (s.p.s and d.p.)
DESDONELLA: *Desdonella* (s.d.s); *Des<donella>* (s.p.s); *Desdonella, Sister to Charastus* (d.p.)

OTHER CHARACTERS
The people of Lilybaeus (1.2, 2.2, 2.4, 4.3)
The crew of the ships which brought Brabantas and Sperazus to Lilybaeus (1.4)
The Duke of Florence (4.2–3)
Lunaster's nurse (5.3)
Halisdus' wife (5.3)
Charastus, the true Prince of Lilybaeus, who was killed when Halisdus' wife dropped him as a baby (5.3)

SETTING
Period: apparently post-classical: Caesar and Pompey are in the past, and Florence is a duchy (which it became in 1532)
Time-Scheme: 1.2 takes place in the morning; 3.2 takes place at noon; 3.4 takes place the day after 2.4
Place: Lilybaeus, Sicily

Geography
Sicily: Mount Etna; Pachynus; Pelorus; Hybla
[*Italy*]: Florence
[*Greece*]: Delphos (i.e. Delphi); Mount Pelion; Mount Ossa; Mount Olympus
[*Turkey*]: River Caister
Ethiopia
The Arctic Pole
The Antarctic Pole

SOURCES
Narrative: Francis Beaumont and John Fletcher, *A King and No King* (**1636**; 5.3).
Verbal: Thomas Kyd, *The Spanish Tragedy* (**783**; 2.3); Tycho Brahe, *De nova stella* (1573, repr. 1610; English tr. by W. S., 1632, but Pepys probably used the 1610 edition; 5.2)
Works Mentioned: Plato, *Timaeus* (4.1)

LANGUAGE
English

FORM
Metre: irregular verse, including pentameter, tetrameter, trimeter, and alexandrines; a little prose
Rhyme: blank verse
Act-Division: 5 acts
Lines (Spoken): 3,556 (3,450 verse, 106 prose)
Lines (Written): 5,198

STAGING
Doors: broken open (4.6, s.d.); characters enter severally (5.3, s.d.)
Discovery Space: set with an altar (5.2, s.d.)
Stage: characters pass over the stage (2.3, s.d.)
Within: music (1.2, 3.4, s.d.); shouts (1.2, 2.3–4, s.d.); groan (5.3, s.d.)
Above: two characters appear above (4.6, s.d.; it takes no more than 9 lines to get down to the main stage)
Beneath: music 'below ground' (3.4, s.d.); song (3.4, implicit); Desdonella enters from and exits into 'the cave' (3.4, s.d.; this seems to be situated under the stage rather than in the discovery space)

MUSIC AND SOUND
Sound Effects: knocking (3.3, 5.1, s.d.)
Music: loud music (1.2, 5.2, s.d.); trumpet within (1.2, s.d.); horns within (3.4, s.d.); lute music 'below ground' (3.4, s.d.); solemn music (5.2, s.d.)
Songs:
  1: 'Let amorous lovers take delight', 3.4, Desdonella beneath, 10 lines;
  2: 'Swell, swell, my thoughts and let my breast', 5.1, Constantina, 23 lines.

PROPS
Weapons: two rapiers (2.1, s.d.); a sword (5.2, s.d.; 5.3, dialogue)
Musical Instruments: a lute (3.4, implicit)
Food and Drink: a vial of liquid (4.4, s.d.; 5.1, implicit; drunk on stage)
Small Portable Objects: a sceptre (1.2, dialogue); a document (1.2, implicit); a paper (1.3, s.d.); a letter (2.1, s.d.); a second letter, with a seal (2.1, dialogue; 3.2, s.d.; enclosed within the first); a letter (4.2–3, s.d.)
Scenery: a throne (1.2, dialogue); an altar (5.2, s.d.)

COSTUMES AND MAKE-UP
CHARASTUS: a half-moon-shaped birthmark on his left wrist (dialogue); a crown (1.2, dialogue; removed on stage)
FLAVANDA: Charastus' crown (1.2, s.d.; put on on stage); dressed as a shepherdess (3.3, s.d.)
VIRTUSUS: disguised in a priest's robe (2.3, s.d.; removed on stage); dressed as a shepherd (2.3–4, 3.2, implicit)
FIDELIO: dressed as a shepherd (1.3, s.d.); disguised in a priest's robe (2.3, s.d.; removed on stage)

BRABANTAS: Virtusus' ecclesiastical robe (2.3, dialogue; put on on stage)
SPERAZUS: Fidelio's ecclesiastical robe (2.3, dialogue; 4.4, 5.2, implicit; put on on stage)
THESBIA: cross-dressed as a youth (2.4, s.d.; 3.2, 4.3, 4.6, 5.1–3, implicit); a veil (5.2, s.d.; removed on stage)
CONSTANTINA: dressed as a shepherdess (3.3, s.d.); a veil (5.2, s.d.; removed on stage)
DESDONELLA: 'attired like a sylvan goddess' (3.4, s.d.)

EARLY TEXTUAL HISTORY
1649: Q printed by William Wilson for Mercy Meighen, Gabriel Bedell, and Thomas Collins; collation A–G⁴, 28 leaves; Latin title-page motto; address to the reader; list of roles. The text is printed in double columns.

1649: George Thomason acquired a copy of O on Monday 17 September. In c. 1678, some years after his death, his entire collection of books and tracts was acquired by the bookbinder Samuel Mearne, acting as agent for King Charles II; the King never paid him, and the books remained in Mearne's family until 1761.

c. 1649–50: extracts included in a MS miscellany (London: British Library, Add. MS 22608, fos. 114ʳ–115ʳ) compiled by Abraham Wright. The MS later passed to Wright's son, the antiquarian James Wright (c. 1644–c. 1717).

1656: *The English Parnassus* entered to Evan Tyler, Thomas Johnson, and Thomas Davies in the Stationers' Register on Wednesday 24 December.

1657: extract (from 5.3) included in Joshua Poole's *The English Parnassus*, sig. 2A6ʳ; printed for Thomas Johnson.

1677: *The English Parnassus* reprinted by Henry Brome for Thomas Bassett and John Wright; the extract now appears on sig. 2A2ʳ.

1684: Nicholas Cox (Manciple of St Edmund Hall, Oxford) had a copy of Q in his bookshop. It had probably been previously owned by Gerard Langbaine, and appears on a list compiled by Anthony Wood on Saturday 13 December.

EDITION
Robert Birley, Roxburghe Club (Ilkley, 1981).

REFERENCES
Annals 1634; Bentley, iv. 952; Bodleian, MS Wood E. 4, art. 1, p. 97; Eyre & Rivington, ii. 103; Greg 685; Hazlitt, 139.

2557. Masque of Moors

TEXT
MS (Oxford: Bodleian, MS Ashmole 47, fos. 122ᵛ–126); transcript incorporating all the elements of the text, including the variant epilogue for the second performance and the variant prologue for the third.

GENRE
masque

TITLE
MS: *Mr Moore's Revels*
Later Assigned: *More's Masque*; *The Moor's Masque*
Alternative Modernizations: *Mr More's Revels*; *The Moors' Masque*

AUTHOR
Thomas Moore (*attribution*)

DATE
1636

ORIGINAL PRODUCTION
Oxford

Elliott suggests that this was a Christmas revel but not a college performance; however, he also identifies the author as possibly Thomas Moore of Merton College, which would be consistent with a performance near the East Gate. (Other possible colleges in the vicinity might be Magdalen or University.)

PLOT
Six Moors present their spears to the audience and dance. The audience's approbation is to transform them from black to white, so they take off their black coats as they leave the stage. Apes steal some of the coats and ink their faces to imitate the Moors. The Moors return, now no longer black, and dancing ensues.

SCENE DESIGNATION
prol., sc.1–3, ep. (MS undivided); the antimasque takes place during sc.1, the main masque in sc.3

ROLES
The PRESENTER of the revels
Six MOORS, the antimasque, and later the masquers (sc.1, 3; only one speaks)
Four APES (sc.2, *non-speaking*)

The masque is said to be 'for eight', which may mean that the six blanched Moors are joined by two who were never black to begin with.

Speaking Parts: 2

Stage Directions
PRESENTER: *The Prologue* (heading)
MOORS: *six moors | The six moors | the moors | eight* (s.d.s)
APES: *four little boys dressed for apes | the Apes* (s.d.s)

SETTING
Geography
Ethiopia
India

SOURCES
Narrative: possibly Ben Jonson, Masque of Blackness (**1453**), *The Gypsies Metamorphosed* (**1987**)
Verbal: possibly William Shakespeare, *Romeo and Juliet* (**987**; Night 3 prol.)

The earlier Jonson masque may have suggested the conceit of the Moors bleached by the effulgence of the audience; the later masque is probably the source of the conceit that this process turns them from antimasquers to masquers.

LANGUAGE
English

FORM
Metre: pentameter
Rhyme: couplets
Prologue: 12 lines (Nights 1 and 2) or 14 lines (Night 3), spoken by the presenter
Chorus: an uncharacterized presenter
Epilogue: 16 lines (Nights 1 and 3) or 18 lines (Night 2), spoken by one of the Moors
Lines (Spoken):
   NIGHT 1:   109 (108 verse, 1 prose)
   NIGHTS 2–3: 111 (110 verse, 1 prose)
Lines (Written): 176

STAGING
Stage: mentioned (sc.1, s.d.)
Audience: the entire spoken text is addressed to the audience; the Moors lay their javelins at the audience's feet (sc.1, dialogue); the audience on Night 3 is addressed as 'fair ones' (prol.)

MUSIC
Dance: the Moors dance (sc.1, s.d.); the Moors dance a country dance (sc.1, s.d.); the Apes dance, possibly doing handstands (sc.2, s.d.); 'grand masque' and 'single masque' dances (sc.3, s.d.); French dances (sc.3, s.d.); a country dance (sc.3, s.d.)

PROPS
Weapons: six javelins (sc.1, s.d.)
Small Portable Objects: four inkhorns containing black ink (sc.2, s.d.); a looking-glass (sc.2, s.d.)

COSTUMES AND MAKE-UP
MOORS: black faces (sc.1, dialogue); black buckram coats laced with yellow straw (sc.1, s.d.; removed on stage); white faces (sc.3, implicit)
APES: probably the Moors' coats (sc.2, implicit; put on on stage); inked faces (sc.2, s.d.; the ink is applied on stage)

EARLY STAGE HISTORY
1636: performed near the East Gate of Oxford. The performances took place in the evenings. The cast, who seem to be identified as scholars in the spoken text, included: Mr [Thomas?] Moore (a Moor); little boys (Apes). There were three performances: the first two nights were public, the third a private performance for gentlewomen. A different epilogue was performed on the second night, and a different prologue on the third.

EARLY TEXTUAL HISTORY
c. 1640: included in a **MS** miscellany; 9 pages on 5 leaves.
   Late seventeenth century: The MS was in the possession of Elias Ashmole. After his death in 1692, it passed to the Ashmolean Museum, Oxford.

EDITIONS
John R. Elliott, jun., *Renaissance Quarterly* 37 (1984), 411–20.
John R. Elliott, jun., in REED: Oxford (London and Toronto), 560–4.

REFERENCES
Annals 1636; Bentley, v. 1375; Butler, 374; McGee-Meagher 1634–42, 53–4; REED: Oxford, 815, 1141.

2558. Masque for the Dowager Countess of Devonshire

EVIDENCE
Countess of Devonshire's household accounts (Chatsworth, Hardwick MS 30A).

GENRE
masque

DATE
December 1636

ORIGINAL PRODUCTION
Countess of Devonshire's household, possibly at Byfleet House or Ampthill

PROPS
Scenery: possibly made of pasteboard

EARLY STAGE HISTORY
1636: performed in December in the household of Christian Cavendish, Dowager Countess of Devonshire, perhaps at Byfleet House, Surrey, or Ampthill, Bedfordshire.

Production Expenses
Payments were made in December 1636 and January 1637 for a carpenter and pasteboard.

REFERENCES
Butler, 375; *EMS* 8 (2000), 129 n. 145; Lynn Mary Hulse, 'The Musical Patronage of the English Aristocracy, *c.* 1590–1640', unpublished Ph.D. thesis (London, 1992), 346.

2559. Play with Cutpurses

TEXT
MS (Nottingham: University of Nottingham, Portland Collection, MS Pw V 26, fo. 151); holograph fragment.

See **2587** for further fragments which might belong to this play.

TITLE
MS: 'The Cutpurses' Scene'
Later Assigned: *The Cutpurse*
Alternative Modernization: 'The Cutpurse's Scene'

The MS is endorsed 'The Cutpurse' in a seventeenth-century hand. Hulse takes this to be the title of the play, but there is no evidence to support this assumption: it could as well derive from the MS heading (which should probably modernize in the plural since the scene features four cutpurses, none of whom is obviously a dominant titular character). If this is 'The Cutpurses' Scene', moreover, presumably the cutpurses did not feature significantly in the rest of the play.

AUTHOR
William Cavendish, Earl of Newcastle

DATE
Limits: 1625–44

PLOT
[*The start of the play is lost, or unwritten.*] Four cutpurses prepare for a robbery: they discuss conscience and confidence, and listen to a song. Hearing their victims coming, they steel themselves. [*The rest of the play is lost, or unwritten.*]

ROLES
Four CURPURSES, one of whom is inexperienced; all are male; one may be named Dick
The cutpurses' VICTIMS, possibly aldermen (*about to appear as the fragment ends*)

Speaking Parts: 4

Speech Prefixes
CURPURSES: 1 | 2 | 3 | 4 (s.p.s)

SOURCES
Verbal: *The Book of Common Prayer*: Catechism (1549, rev. 1552)

LANGUAGE
English

FORM
Metre: prose
Lines (Spoken): 46
Lines (Written): 47

MUSIC
Song: sung by Dick?

EARLY TEXTUAL HISTORY
William Cavendish, Earl of Newcastle, wrote the scene in **MS**; 1 leaf.

EDITION
Lynne Hulse, in William Cavendish, *Dramatic Works*, Malone Society Reprints 158 (Oxford, 1996), 6–8.

2560. Masque for the Earl of Newcastle

EVIDENCE
Mentioned in a prologue (University of Nottingham, Portland Collection, MS Pw V 26, fo. 154ʳ) written by William Cavendish, Earl of Newcastle, for a new (but unidentified) play performed on the same occasion.

This could be identified as **2457**. The play might be identified as **2559** or **2587** (if they were not one and the same), but is less likely to be *Wit's Triumvirate* (**2521**), which has its own (different) prologue.

GENRE
masque
Contemporary: masque

DATE
Limits: 1625–44

EARLY STAGE HISTORY
The masque was performed (or planned for performance) on the same occasion as a new play (for which William Cavendish, Earl of Newcastle, wrote a prologue and epilogue). The anticipated audience included gentlemen.

REFERENCES
William Cavendish, *Dramatic Works*, ed. Lynn Hulse (Oxford, 1996), 9.

INDEX OF PERSONS

This index covers real people referred to in the Catalogue: playwrights, actors, audience members, authors of works used as sources, printers and publishers, owners of manuscripts, and so on. It does not include characters in plays, even when they are based on real personages: an index entry for King Henry VIII will point to records of his doings and writings, but not to the Rowley or Shakespeare plays in which he appears as a principal character. It also does not include patrons of acting companies when the reference is solely to the company rather than the patron: mention of the King's Men does not generate an index entry for the King. The listing is by entry number rather than page number.

A., L. (translator) 2361, 2376, 2389, 2396, 2410, 2417–18, 2457, 2484, 2553
A., R. (printer) 2549
A., W. (commendator) 2536
Abbot, John, *see* Rivers
Abbott, Mr (saddler) 2423
Abbott, Sir Maurice 2423
Abdy, Anthony 2423
Abercorn, Earl of, *see* Hamilton
Abercrombie, Abraham 2353, 2398
Abernethy, Alexander, 9th Baron Saltoun 2428
Abernethy, John 2408
Acheson, Robert 2408
Acton, Sir William 2423
Adamson, John 2408
Adderly, Charles 2423, 2532
Adderly, Mrs 2423
Adson, John 2423, 2441
Aeschylus 2445, 2519
Aesop 2383, 2413, 2430, 2434, 2441, 2467, 2488, 2521, 2523, 2536
Africanus, Joannes Leo 2521
Ager, John 2359
Agostini, Ipolito 2398
Agrippa, Henry Cornelius 2378, 2421
Aiskoughe, James 2423
Akenhead, David 2408
Akominatos, *see* Nicetas
Albani, Francesco 2428
Albertus Magnus 2364, 2429
Aldworth, Richard 2398

Alexander, Mr (clothworker) 2416
Alexander, Sir William 2483
Alison, Richard 2518
Allam, Thomas (bookseller) 2549
Allam, Thomas (clothworker) 2416
Allen, Robert 2362
Allen, Thomas 2362
Allen, William 2480
Allestree, Richard 2385, 2428, 2521
Allnut, Richard 2517
Allot, Robert (stationer) 2353, 2359
Alpert, Joseph 2423
Alsop, Bernard 2396
Alworth, Richard 2398
Amy, Sir John 2423
Anastasius Bibliothecarius 2477
Andrewes, John (author) 2521
Andrews, Henry 2387
Andrews, John (stationer) 2355, 2402–3, 2512
Angennes, Jacques d', Marquis of Pougny 2448
Angus, Earl of, *see* Douglas
Annandale, Earl of, *see* Murray
Anott, Henry 2423
Anott, Thomas 2423
Anthehope, John 2534
Antoninus, St 2477
Antrim, Earl of, *see* MacDonnell
Apuleius, Lucius 2451, 2523, 2533

Aquinas, St Thomas 2477
Archimedes 2519
Arden, Goditha 2395
Arden, Thomas, *see* Arding
Arding, Thomas 2534
Aretino, Pietro 2428–9, 2453, 2488, 2553
Ariosto, Ludovico 2413, 2513
Aristophanes 2429, 2468
Aristotle 2355, 2364, 2385, 2389, 2416, 2439, 2467, 2519, 2521, 2553
Armin, Robert 2525
Arnaldus de Villanova 2429
Arundel, Earl and Countess of, *see* Howard
Ashe, Walter 2423
Ashley, Sir Francis 2423
Ashmole, Elias 2355, 2480, 2532, 2557
Athanasius of Alexandria 2444
Athenaeus 2511
Atkinson, Joseph 2398, 2428
Aubrey, John 2452, 2546, 2549
Auckland, William 2423
Audley, Hugh 2423
Audley, William 2423
Augustine of Hippo, St 2477, 2492, 2525
Ausonius, Decimus Magnus 2391, 2421, 2428, 2542
Austen, Robert 2428
Austen, Thomas 2448
Axen, Robert 2480
Ayala, *see* López

B., A. (musical miscellanist) 2371
B., E. (commendator) 2413
B., T. (dramatist) 2381
B., W. (scribe?) 2463, 2475, 2551
Backhouse, Rowland 2423
Bacon, Sir Francis, Lord Verulam 2382, 2399, 2468, 2549
Bacon, Roger 2533
Badger, Thomas 2355, 2367, 2396, 2437
Baillie, George 2408
Baker, Arthur 2423
Baker, George 2359
Baker, Thomas 2423
Baldock, Edward (flambeau-bearer) 2423
Baldock, Thomas (torchbearer) 2423
Balfour, Sir James 2408
Balfour of Burleigh, Robert, 2nd Lord 2408
Balle, Henry 2453
Banister, John 2423, 2452–3
Banks, Sir John 2423
Bannatyne, William 2408
Barbarus, Hermolaus (Ermolao Barbaro) 2533
Barberini, Francesco 2469
Barclay, John 2388
Barker, John 2423
Barker, Thomas 2423
Barkham, Sir Edward 2423
Barksted, William 2472
Barlow, William 2385
Barrett, John 2472, 2525
Barrett of Newburgh, Edward, Lord 2387
Barringer, Richard 2423
Barry, Alice, Countess of Barrymore 2393
Barry, David, 1st Earl of Barrymore 2393
Barrymore, Earl and Countess of, *see* Barry
Bartholameo, Mr (Roman workman) 2397
Barton, John (carpenter) 2423
Barton, John, sen., of the Middle Temple 2423
Bassano, Anthony 2423
Bassano, Henry 2423
Basse, Mr (mercer) 2423
Bassett, Mrs (lace-woman) 2532
Bassett, Thomas (musician) 2423

Bassett, Thomas (stationer) 2360, 2365, 2374, 2385, 2403–4, 2428, 2439, 2452, 2517, 2531, 2552, 2556
Bastable, Peter 2423
Bastwick, John 2550
Baxter, Alexander 2408
Baylie, Elizabeth 2475
Baylie, Richard 2475, 2550–1
Baylie, Toby 2395
Bayliffe, John 2423
Bayly, Lewis 2385, 2521
Beale, Edward 2362
Beale, John 2360
Beaujoyeulx, Baltazar de 2359
Beaumont, Elizabeth 2395
Beaumont, Francis 2371, 2378, 2389, 2461, 2464, 2479, 2513, 2521, 2550, 2556
Beaumont, Ursula (née Isley) 2395
Beckett, James 2432, 2434
Bedell, Gabriel 2378, 2421, 2519, 2532, 2556
Bedowe, Ellis 2525
Bedowes, Thomas 2423
Beeland, Ambrose 2423
Beeston, Christopher 2389, 2402–3, 2410, 2418, 2451, 2526, 2552
Beeston, Hugh 2360, 2399
Beeston, William 2411, 2446
Bell, Jane 2373
Bell, Moses 2355, 2364, 2367, 2396, 2437
Bellenden, Adam 2408
Bencroft, James 2423
Benfield, Richard 2365
Benlowes, Edward 2413
Bennen, John 2423
Bennet, Henry 2487, 2529
Bennett, Edward (alias Farrington and Hope) 2550
Bennett, Joseph 2412
Bennett, Thomas 2371
Benson, John 2371, 2385, 2402–4, 2439, 2552
Bentley, Richard 2371, 2512, 2536
Bentley, Robert 2423
Bercheure, Pierre, *see* Bersuire
Bergame, Nicolas de, *see* Pergamenus
Berkeley, George, 12th Lord 2410
Berkeley, Sir Robert 2423

Berkenhead, Sir John 2487, 2529, 2538
Berkshire, Countess of, *see* Howard
Bernard, Samuel 2547
Berners, Lord, *see* Bourchier
Berry, Edward 2445
Berry, William 2423
Bersuire, Pierre 2517
Bertie, Robert, 1st Earl of Lindsay 2387
Best, Richard 2374
Best, William 2423
Bèze, Theodore de (Theodore Beza) 2493
Bingham, John 2423
Binning, Lord, *see* Hamilton
Biondi, Giuseppe 2528
Bird, Epiphaneus 2423
Bird, Theophilus 2480
Birkhead, Henry 2523
Bishop, Henry 2423
Bishop, Richard 2539
Black, Patrick 2428
Blackburn, Peter 2408
Blage, William 2423
Blagrave, Obadiah 2355, 2367, 2376, 2383, 2389, 2402, 2413, 2437, 2451, 2468, 2512, 2519, 2552
Blagrave, William 2441, 2451, 2480, 2516, 2543
Blount, Ann, Countess of Newport 2359, 2469
Blount, Mountjoy, 1st Earl of Newport 2353, 2428, 2469
Bobarre, Monsieur (audience member) 2423
Boccaccio, Giovanni 2421, 2488, 2542
Bocchi, Achille (Achilles Bocchius) 2408
Bodin, Jean 2441, 2444
Boethius, Anicius Manlius Severinus 2461, 2468, 2491
Boguet, Henri 2441
Boiardo, Matteo Maria 2551
Boisrobert, Sieur de, *see* Metel
Bonport, Bouvier de 2384
Booker, John 2405, 2428, 2521
Boothby, Robert 2423
Bourchier, John, Lord Berners 2401
Bourke, Thomas 2532
Bowman, Francis 2365
Bowman, Thomas 2365

Index of Persons | 511

Bowy, James 2398
Bowyer, Michael 2480
Box, Henry 2423
Boyce, Mr (actor) 2398
Boyle, Elizabeth, Viscountess Shannon 2529
Boyle, Richard, 1st Earl of Cork 2428
Boyle, Richard, Viscount Dungarvan 2428
Bracciolini, Francesco 2477
Brackley, Viscount, *see* Egerton
Bradborne, Humphrey 2359, 2469
Bradford, John 2412
Bradley, Peter 2362
Bradshaw, John 2517
Bradwell, Stephen 2472
Brahe, Tycho 2511, 2521, 2556
Bramhall, John 2438
Bramston, John 2423, 2532
Brandt, Sebastian 2421, 2511
Brassert, Gouvert 2416
Brathwaite, Richard 2429
Brent, Sir Nathaniel 2385, 2403–4, 2433, 2439, 2445, 2468, 2552
Brereton, Peter 2423
Brewer, Thomas 2548
Brewster, Edward 2385, 2403–4, 2439
Brice, Ralph 2353, 2359, 2423
Brickenden, Mr, of Gray's Inn 2423
Bridgewater, Earl and Countess of, *see* Egerton
Bridle (tailor) 2423
Brightman, Thomas 2521
Bril, Paul 2395
Brisson, Barnabé 2552
Bristowe, Francis (glazier) 2477
Bristowe, Francis (translator) 2477
Bristowe, Francis, of Christ Church, Oxford 2477
Bristowe, Nicholas 2477
Brograve, John 2399
Brome, Alexander 2411
Brome, Henry 2360, 2365, 2374, 2401, 2423, 2428, 2449, 2452–3, 2517–18, 2531, 2544, 2552, 2556
Brome, Richard 2360, 2378, 2381, 2383, 2401, 2411, 2419, 2424, 2434, 2436, 2441, 2449, 2462, 2473,
2479, 2488, 2518, 2521, 2536, 2543–4
Bromfield, Edward 2423
Brook, Humphrey 2551
Brooke, Nathaniel 2355, 2367, 2383, 2389, 2402, 2411, 2413, 2437, 2468, 2472, 2484, 2512, 2519, 2536, 2550, 2552
Brooke, Sir William 2353
Brown, Blanche 2359, 2369
Brown, David 2408
Brown, William 2369
Browne, Mr (clothworker) 2448
Browne, Daniel 2405, 2417, 2545
Browne, Francis 2423
Browne, Thomas (Oxford proctor) 2551
Brownlowe, Richard 2423
Bruce, Thomas, 1st Earl of Elgin 2428
Bruce of Kinloss, Thomas, 3rd Lord 2353
Bruno, Giordano 2428
Bryan, Joseph 2423
Bryan, Oliver 2362
Bryan, Richard 2362, 2364
Bryan, William 2423
Brydges, George, 6th Baron Chandos 2428, 2469
Buchan, Earl of, *see* Erskine
Buck, John 2365
Buck, Thomas 2365
Buckett, Rowland 2423
Buckhurst, Lord, *see* Sackville
Buckingham, Duke and Dowager Duchess of, *see* Villiers
Buckner, John 2359, 2395, 2398
Bulstrode, Edward 2423
Buontalenti, Bernardo 2353
Burden, William 2374
Burnell, Mr (clothworker) 2416
Burnell, Henry 2546
Burroughs, Sir John 2408
Burton, Henry 2385, 2450, 2550
Burton, Robert 2355, 2364, 2396, 2434, 2441, 2515
Busby, Richard 2552
Bush, Edwin 2479
Bushell, Thomas 2549
Butter, Nathaniel 2385
Butterfield, John 2423
Butts, Henry 2364–5
Byres, John 2408
Bysshe, Edward 2459, 2515

Bysshe, Margaret (née Greene) 2459, 2515

C., J. (printer) 2405
C., T. (MS compiler) 2364
C., T. (printer) 2550
Caccini, Giulio 2353
Cademan, William 2373, 2412
Caesar, Caius Julius 2511
Caesar, Robert 2423
Caesar, Thomas 2423
Caesar, William, *see* Smegergill
Calahorra, *see* Ortúñez
Calbert, Mr (haberdasher?) 2527
Calfe, Peter 2534, 2550
Callot, Jacques 2353, 2359, 2395, 2423
Calvisius, Sethus (Seth Kalwitz) 2492
Camden, William 2550
Campanello, Tommaso 2521
Campbell, Sir James 2423
Campbell, Robert 2423
Campion, Thomas 2518
Cantrell, Thomas 2362, 2364
Capell, Arthur 2468
Cardanus, Hieronymus (Girolamo Cardano) 2408, 2511, 2533
Cardonius, Camillus, *see* Cerdagni
Carew, Edmund 2423
Carew, Sophia 2359, 2395, 2398
Carew, Thomas 2421, 2428, 2445, 2534
Carew, William 2423
Carey, Henry, 1st Earl of Dover 2420, 2524
Carey, Horatio 2534
Carey, John, Viscount Rochford 2472
Carey, Mary, Countess of Dover 2420, 2524
Carlell, Lodowick 2386, 2395, 2431, 2530–1, 2556
Carlisle, Earl and Countess of, *see* Hay
Carlisle, Thomas 2362, 2364
Carnarvon, Earl and Countess of, *see* Dormer
Carnegie, Robert 2408
Carnegie, William 2408
Carolides, Georg 2472
Carr, Lady Ann 2469
Carr, Robert, Earl of Somerset 2382

512 | Index of Persons

Carranza, Jerónimo de 2417
Cartari, Vincenzo 2439
Cartwright, William, sen. (actor; d. 1636) 2472
Cartwright, William, jun. (actor; 1606–86) 2360, 2409, 2483, 2516
Cartwright, William (playwright; 1611–43) 2452, 2468, 2487, 2529, 2552–3
Carvagnion, Henry 2423
Cary, Mr (actor) 2550
Cary, Henry, 1st Viscount Falkland 2387
Cary, Lucius, 2nd Viscount Falkland 2395, 2459
Cary, Victoria 2359, 2395, 2398, 2469
Caryll, Sir John 2394
Casaubon, Isaac 2382
Cassilis, Earl of, *see* Kennedy
Cassius Dio 2491, 2517
Catlyn (torchbearer) 2423
Cato, Dionysius 2461
Catullus, Gaius Valerius 2403, 2429, 2511, 2515, 2552
Caussin, Nicolas 2542
Cavalieri, Giovanni Battista 2353
Cavendish, Lady Anne 2359
Cavendish, Charles 2359, 2428
Cavendish, Christian, Dowager Countess of Devonshire 2558
Cavendish, Elizabeth (1627–63) 2457
Cavendish, Elizabeth, Countess of Newcastle 2457
Cavendish, Jane 2457
Cavendish, William, 3rd Earl of Devonshire 2428
Cavendish, William, Earl of Newcastle 2399, 2404, 2435, 2439, 2457, 2479, 2521, 2559–60
Cecil, Charles, Viscount Cranborne 2428
Cecil, Lady Diana 2359
Cecil, Edward, Viscount Wimbledon 2387
Cecil, Lady Elizabeth 2359
Cecil, William, 2nd Earl of Exeter 2387
Cecil, William, 2nd Earl of Salisbury 2359, 2387
Cerdagni, Camillo (Camillus Cardonius) 2445

Cervantes, Miguel de 2376, 2409, 2423, 2457
Chacón, Alfonso 2469
Chafin, Francis 2423
Chamberlain, Robert 2413, 2512
Chambers, Humphrey 2423
Chandler, Daniel 2364
Chandos, Baron, *see* Brydges
Chapman, George 2361, 2373, 2389, 2401, 2423–4, 2436, 2463, 2542
Chapman, Laurence 2429
Chapman, Livewell 2423
Chapman, Thomas (flambeau-bearer) 2423
Chapman, Thomas (lace-maker) 2423
Charles I, King of England and of Scots 2353, 2359–60, 2362, 2364–5, 2378, 2382, 2385, 2395, 2398, 2402–4, 2408, 2410, 2417–18, 2421–3, 2428, 2439, 2451, 2453–4, 2459, 2468–9, 2521–2, 2524, 2526, 2530–2, 2534–7, 2541, 2549–53, 2555
Charles, Prince of Wales (later King Charles II) 2383, 2388, 2395, 2401, 2417, 2419, 2433, 2445, 2449, 2468, 2518, 2522, 2530–1, 2533, 2544–6, 2550, 2552, 2555–6
Charles Louis, Elector Palatine 2429, 2474, 2522, 2530–2, 2535, 2539, 2550–2
Charteris, Thomas 2408
Chaucer, Geoffrey 2385, 2439, 2458, 2468, 2521
Chefinch, Thomas 2555
Cheke, Henry 2477
Cherrington, William 2361
Chettle, Henry 2451
Chetwynd, Walter 2360, 2399, 2528
Child, Thomas 2355, 2364, 2367, 2396, 2437, 2550
Chiswell, Richard 2385, 2403–4, 2439
Choniates, *see* Nicetas
Christmas, Gerard 2387, 2416
Christmas, John 2517
Christmas, Mathias 2517
Chrysostom, Dio 2491, 2552
Chrysostom, St John 2416

Church, Thomas 2428
Churchill, Awnsham 2413, 2419, 2468, 2552
Churchill, John 2413, 2419, 2468, 2552
Cicero, Marcus Tullius 2385, 2416, 2419, 2429–30, 2444–5, 2458, 2463, 2474, 2480, 2511, 2517–18, 2521, 2542, 2555
Cicognini, Giacomo 2469
Clare, Stafford 2423
Clark, Alexander 2408
Clark, Andrew 2423, 2452–3
Clark, Hugh 2480
Clark, Mary 2423, 2452–3
Clarke, Sir Edward 2423
Clarke, Richard 2423
Claudian (Claudius Claudianus) 2385, 2518, 2540, 2552
Clavell, John 2393, 2546
Clavius, Christopher 2467
Claxton, Edward 2448
Clay, Matthew 2405, 2421, 2424, 2428, 2453, 2484, 2530–1, 2534, 2536
Clayton, Thomas 2550
Clement, Nicholas 2423
Clifford, Francis, 4th Earl of Cumberland 2354, 2372, 2527
Clifton, Sir Gervase 2471
Clitherow, Christopher 2423, 2517
Cocci, Marco, *see* Sabellicus
Cochrane, James 2408
Cochrane, William, of Cowdown 2408
Cockburn, Laurence 2408
Coignet, Elizabeth 2359
Cokayne, Aston 2376, 2407
Cokayne, Sir William 2420
Coke, Sir Edward 2382, 2444, 2521, 2533
Coke, Lady Elizabeth, *see* Hatton
Coke, Lady Frances, *see* Villiers
Coke, Sir John 2387, 2461
Coke, Thomas 2423
Colbatch, Edward 2445
Cole, John 2423
Cole, Robert 2423
Coleman, Charles 2423, 2538, 2555
Coleman, Simon 2550
Colletet, Guillaume 2428
Collett, James 2423

Index of Persons | 513

Collins, Jeffrey 2423
Collins, Thomas 2378, 2421, 2519, 2532, 2556
Comber, Thomas 2365
Combes, Thomas 2472
Comes, Natalis (Natale Conti) 2451, 2492
Compton, Isabella, Countess of Northampton 2412
Compton, James, 3rd Earl of Northampton 2412
Con, George 2550–1
Condell, Henry 2459
Coniack, Madam (actor) 2359
Constable, Alice 2479
Constable, Frances 2479
Constable, Francis 2355, 2367, 2435, 2437, 2464, 2479, 2526
Constable, Mary 2479
Constable, Rachael 2479
Conti, Natale, *see* Comes
Conway, Edward, 2nd Viscount 2469
Conyers, George 2385, 2403–4, 2439
Conyers, Joshua 2549
Cooke, Lady 2469
Cooke, Sir Francis 2469
Cooke, William 2355, 2367, 2389, 2396, 2410, 2418, 2423, 2437, 2455, 2464, 2515, 2526
Cooper, William 2423
Copernicus, Nicolaus 2521
Corbet, Richard 2476
Cork, Earl of, *see* Boyle
Correr, Anzolo 2448, 2469, 2485, 2517
Corsellis, James 2532
Cort, Cornelis 2469
Coryate, Thomas 2376, 2383
Cotes, Thomas 2367, 2389, 2410, 2455, 2464, 2472, 2487, 2515, 2529
Cotgrave, John 2355, 2360, 2365, 2367, 2371, 2378, 2383, 2389, 2396, 2399, 2401–2, 2405, 2410–11, 2413, 2418–19, 2421, 2424, 2437, 2451, 2455, 2458–9, 2464, 2468, 2479–81, 2487–8, 2512, 2515, 2519, 2526, 2528–9, 2530–1, 2536, 2543, 2552–3
Cotterel, Charles 2364

Cottington, Francis, Lord 2353, 2387
Courtney, James 2523
Covarrubias y Orozco, Sebastián de 2387
Coventry, Thomas, 1st Baron 2387, 2423, 2428
Cowley, Abraham 2452, 2468
Cox, Nicholas 2353, 2355, 2359–61, 2364, 2367, 2373–4, 2376, 2378, 2381, 2383, 2389, 2395–6, 2399, 2401–2, 2405, 2407, 2410–11, 2413, 2417–20, 2423–4, 2432, 2434, 2437, 2441, 2445, 2449, 2451, 2455, 2458–9, 2468, 2472, 2479–81, 2487–8, 2490–2510, 2512, 2518, 2524, 2526, 2528–31, 2536, 2538, 2543–5, 2550, 2553, 2555–6
Cradock, Matthew 2423
Crafts, John 2423
Cranborne, Viscount, *see* Cecil
Cranmer, Samuel 2423
Crauford, David 2408
Crawford, Thomas 2408
Crawley, John 2423
Crespin, Jean 2477
Creswell, Robert 2452
Crichton, James, 2nd Viscount Frendraught 2534
Cripps, Edward 2423
Crofts family 2534
Crofts, Anne, *see* Wentworth
Crofts, Cecilia 2395, 2487, 2529, 2534, 2538
Crofts, Frances, *see* Crompton
Crofts, William 2362, 2398, 2423
Croke, Alexander 2540
Croke, Sir George 2423
Cromes, William 2425
Crompton, Lady Catherine 2487
Crompton, Frances (née Crofts) 2487
Crompton, Richard 2521
Crompton, Sir Robert 2487
Cromwell, Anne 2423
Cromwell, Oliver 2423
Crooke, Andrew 2367, 2385, 2389, 2401, 2403–4, 2410, 2418, 2436–7, 2439, 2455, 2459, 2464, 2487, 2515, 2518, 2526, 2529, 2544
Crooke, Edmond 2455
Crooke, John 2530–1

Crosfield, Thomas 2423, 2478, 2551–2
Crosley, John 2365, 2371
Crouch, Edward 2555
Crouch, John 2451
Crowe, Anthony 2423
Crowther, Thomas 2445
Cuffaud, William 2543
Cumberland, Earl of, *see* Clifford
Curtius Rufus, Quintus 2533

D., J. (commendator) 2550
D., N. (miscellanist) 2371, 2437, 2552
Dadly (payee) 2423
Dalkeith, Lord of, *see* Douglas
Dalton, Michael 2521
Damport, John, *see* Davenport
Danby, Earl of, *see* Danvers
Daniel, Roger 2365
Daniel, Samuel 2402
Daniell, John 2423
Danielston, James 2408
Danvers, Henry, Earl of Danby 2387
Darny, Richard 2423
Davenant, William 2356, 2379, 2386, 2395, 2421, 2428–9, 2453, 2469, 2484, 2519, 2521, 2528, 2532
Davenport (prospective masquer) 2423
Davenport, John 2353, 2359, 2395, 2423, 2522
Davenport, Robert 2413, 2438, 2472, 2512
Davies, Thomas 2360, 2365, 2374, 2428, 2452, 2517, 2531, 2552, 2556
Davis, Hugh 2371, 2552
Davis, Richard (flambeau-bearer) 2423
Davis, Richard (printer) 2553
Davis, Robert 2423
Davison, Ralph 2423
Dawks, Ichabod 2413, 2419, 2468, 2552
Dawson, John 2385, 2403–5, 2421, 2424, 2428, 2439, 2452, 2481, 2534
Day, John 2451, 2516
Day, Robert 2423
Day, Thomas 2423, 2550–1
Dayrell, Sir Thomas 2423
Deane, Sir Richard 2423
Deane, Thomas 2423

Dekker, Thomas 2411, 2413, 2451
Deloney, Thomas 2403
Demosthenes 2430
Denbigh, Countess of, *see* Feilding
Derby, Dowager Countess of, *see* Egerton
Dering, Anthony 2423
Dering, Sir Edward 2357
Desmarets de Saint-Sorlin, Armand 2487, 2529, 2538
Desmond, Earl and Countess of, *see* Feilding
Desprez, François 2423
Devereux, Robert, 3rd Earl of Essex 2357, 2373, 2383, 2417, 2453, 2484, 2545
Devonshire, Earl and Dowager Countess of, *see* Cavendish
D'Ewes, Sir Simonds 2364, 2423, 2474
Diaconus, Paulus 2477
Dick, William 2408
Dickinson, Francis 2423
Digby, Lord George 2423
Digby, Sir Kenelm 2365, 2385, 2402–4, 2439, 2452
Digby, Robert, 1st Baron 2428
Digby, Lady Venetia 2402
Dimmock, Mr (masquer) 2353
Dio Cassius 2491, 2517
Dio Chrysostom 2491, 2552
Diodorus Siculus 2519
Diogenes Laertius 2506
'Dion' (unidentified) 2491
Dionysius the Areopagite 2491
Dixon, Thomas 2423
Dodd, Thomas 2423
Doncaster, Viscount, *see* Hay
Donne, George 2399
Donne, John 2371, 2403, 2521
Donne, John, jun. 2534
Donster, John 2423
Dormer, Anne Sophia, Countess of Carnarvon 2359, 2423, 2469
Dormer, Robert, 1st Earl of Carnarvon 2364, 2550
Dorset, Earl of, *see* Sackville
Douglas, Robert, Lord of Dalkeith 2408
Douglas, William, 11th Earl of Angus 2408
Douglas, William, 7th Earl of Morton 2408

Dover, Earl and Countess of, *see* Carey
Dowland, John 2391, 2444, 2513, 2515, 2521, 2543
Drake, Robert 2453
Drew, John 2423
Dring, Oliver 2423
Dring, Thomas 2383, 2389, 2395, 2419, 2433, 2445, 2453
Drummond, John, 2nd Earl of Perth 2408
Drummond, William, of Hawthornden 2408
Ducie, Sir Robert 2423
Ducie, Robert, of Aston 2413
Dumelle, Antoinette 2395
Duncan, Thomas 2408
Dunfermline, Earl of, *see* Seton
Dungarvan, Viscount, *see* Boyle
Dunluce, Viscount, *see* MacDonnell
Dunne, Mr 2517
Dupline, Viscount, *see* Hay
Duport, James 2365
Dupper, John 2423
Durdant, Andrew 2469
Dutton, Sir Ralph 2378
Duvall, Anthony 2395
Duvall, Clement 2395
Duvall, Nicholas 2423
Dyer, Sir James 2401, 2444
Dymoke, Mr (masquer) 2353

Earl, John 2458
East, Thomas 2423
Eck, Johann 2477
Eden, Thomas 2364
Edgarly (carrier) 2552
Edmondes, Sir Thomas 2387, 2522
Edwin, Jonathan 2435
Egerton, Alice, Dowager Countess of Derby 2433
Egerton, Lady Alice (1619–89) 2359, 2440, 2445
Egerton, Frances, Countess of Bridgewater 2440, 2445
Egerton, John, 1st Earl of Bridgewater 2353, 2387, 2440, 2445
Egerton, John, Lord Ellesmere and 2nd Viscount Brackley 2359, 2428, 2440, 2445
Egerton, Lady Katherine 2359
Egerton, Thomas 2428, 2440, 2445
Eglesfield, Francis 2458, 2481

Eglinton, Earl of, *see* Montgomerie
Ekin, Nathaniel 2435
Elgin, Earl of, *see* Bruce
Elizabeth, Princess (1635–50) 2531–2
Ellesmere, Lord, *see* Egerton
Ellis, Patrick 2408
Emery, Jasper 2451
Empedocles 2519
Ennius, Quintus 2540
Enock, Richard 2523
Epictetus 2416
Erasmus, Desiderius 2490–1, 2517, 2533
Ercilla y Zúñiga, Alonso 2376
Erizzo, Francesco, Doge of Venice 2384, 2398, 2485
'Erra Pater' 2373, 2418, 2511
Errol, Earl of, *see* Hay
Erskine, James, 7th Earl of Buchan 2408
Erskine, Thomas, 1st Earl of Kellie 2387
Escourt, Edmund 2423
Escourt, Thomas 2423
Essex, Earl of, *see* Devereux
Estcott, Daniel 2550
Etherege, George 2523
Euclid 2467, 2519, 2521, 2553
Eure, Ralph 2399
Euripides 2491
Eutropius, Flavius 2477, 2517
Evans, Mr (clothworker) 2448
Evans, Anthony 2540
Evans, John 2355, 2365, 2385, 2396, 2403–4, 2413, 2439, 2445, 2455, 2468, 2552
Evans, Thomas (torchbearer) 2423
Evans, Thomas (another torchbearer) 2423
Evans, William 2423
Ewre, Abraham 2423
Exeter, Earl of, *see* Cecil

F., C. (miscellanist) 2435
Fabricius, Vincentius 2429
Fabyan, Robert 2403
Fairfax, Bryan 2555
Fairlie, William 2408
Falkland, Viscount, *see* Cary
Fanshawe, Thomas 2423
Fantuzzi, Antonio 2353
Farrar, William 2423
Farrington, Edward, *see* Bennett

Index of Persons | 515

Farwell, John 2423
Fausse, John 2398, 2469
Favyn, André 2545
Fawcet, Thomas 2396
Feilding, Lady Anne 2359, 2395
Feilding, Basil, Baron 2428
Feilding, Bridget, Countess of Desmond 2398
Feilding, Lady Elizabeth 2359, 2469, 2532
Feilding, George, 1st Earl of Desmond 2469
Feilding, Susan, Countess of Denbigh 2359, 2532
Fell, Samuel 2550
Fenn, Ezekiel 2480
Fenn, Richard see Venn
Fennor, William 2401
Ferin, Jean Baptiste 2395
Fermedo, Sir Cornelius 2541
Ferrabosco, Alfonso 2423
Ferrabosco, Henry 2423
Ferrers, Mr (clothworker) 2416
Fettiplace, Edward 2423
Fialetti, Odoardo 2423
Fiddler, John (torchbearer) 2423
Fidler, John (musician) 2423
Field, Henry 2423
Field, Nathan 2381, 2511
Finch, Lady Elizabeth 2385
Finch, Lady Frances 2385
Finch, Sir Heneage 2355, 2385
Finch, Sir John 2423
Finch, John, of the Inner Temple 2423
Finet, Sir John 2359, 2423, 2442, 2448, 2532
Fiorentino, Ser Giovanni 2411
Fisher, Benjamin 2441
Fisher, Sir Thomas (dedicatee) 2536
Fisher, Thomas (flambeau-bearer) 2423
Fisher, William 2423
Fitzherbert, Sir Anthony 2401, 2521
Flaccus, Statilius 2421
Flelle, Jean de la 2423, 2469
Fleming, John 2408
Fleming, John, 2nd Earl of Wigtown 2408
Fleming, John, Lord 2408
Flesher, Miles 2441, 2488
Fletcher, James 2383, 2419
Fletcher, John 2360, 2371, 2373, 2378, 2389, 2396, 2414, 2417–18, 2429, 2432, 2445, 2464, 2468, 2511, 2513, 2518, 2521, 2528, 2545, 2550, 2552, 2556
Fletcher, Phineas 2550
Florus, Lucius Annaeus 2533
Flout, John 2362
Flower, John 2398
Fontenay-Mareuil, Marquis of, see Val
Fookes, Gerard 2428
Forbes, Walter 2408
Forcett, Edward 2463, 2474
Ford, John 2360, 2371, 2381, 2385, 2396, 2399, 2411, 2427, 2430, 2461, 2466, 2470, 2513, 2528, 2551, 2553
Ford, John, of Gray's Inn 2360, 2399
Forde, Emanuel 2376
Foster, Reginald 2423
Foster, Stephen 2453
Fotherbie, Charles 2365
Fougasses, Thomas 2429
Fountain, George, see Leyburn
Fox, Matthew 2423
Foxe, John (actor) 2555
Foxe, John (martyrologist) 2468, 2521, 2553
Francini, Alessandro 2423
Francis, Edward 2365
Francis, John 2423
Francis Hyacinth, Prince of Savoy 2384
Franklin, James 2423
Fraunce, Abraham 2402
Freake, Thomas 2373
Frear, Michael 2362, 2364
Frederick V, Elector Palatine 2395
Freeman, John 2532
Freeman, Ralph (Lord Mayor) 2416, 2423
Frendraught, Viscount, see Crichton
Frere, Daniel 2413, 2472
Frost, John 2423
Fussell, Nicholas 2405, 2424, 2480, 2543

G., B. (printer) 2371
G., C. (commendator) 2413, 2479
Gainsford, Thomas 2399
Gale, Thomas 2429
Galen (Claudius Galenus) 2405, 2429, 2484, 2553
Galilei, Galileo 2521
Galloway, Sir James 2408
Gallus, Gaius Cornelius 2376
Gamble, John 2435, 2452, 2468, 2526, 2552
Gammon, Richard 2412
Gardiner, Thomas 2423
Garrard, George 2423, 2535
Garraway, Henry 2423
Garrett (attendant) 2423
Gaulminus, Gilbertus (Gilbert Gaulmin) 2552
Gaultier, Jacques 2423
Gawdy, Framlingham 2423, 2535
Gawdy, William 2423
Gawen, Thomas 2423
Gayton, Edmund 2465, 2489, 2551
Geeres, William 2395, 2442
Gellin, George 2359, 2395, 2398
Gellius, Aulus 2387, 2492, 2533
Gentile, Charles 2359, 2395, 2398, 2469, 2485
George, William 2353
Gerard, John 2429
Gerrard, William 2423
Gerson, Jean de 2490
Gessner, Conrad 2387
Gesualdo, Carlo 2360
Gewen, Christopher 2413, 2479
Ghisi, Diana 2469
Gibbon, Anne 2404, 2423, 2453
Gibbon, Richard 2404, 2423, 2453
Gibbs, Richard 2423
Gil, Alexander 2385
Gilbert, William 2468
Gillett, Thomas 2423
Giovanni, Ser, see Fiorentino
Glapthorne, Henry 2436, 2483, 2516, 2521, 2535–6, 2539
Glinne, William 2423
Goad, Christopher 2472
Goad, John 2551
Godbid, Ann 2552
Godbid, William 2371, 2376, 2396, 2407, 2421, 2435, 2468, 2532, 2538, 2550, 2552, 2555
Godbold, John 2423
Goffe, John 2512
Goffe, Thomas 2436
Golding, Richard 2423

Index of Persons

Good, John 2551
Goodall, Stephen 2549–50
Goodhart, Robert 2423
Goodman, Nicholas 2381
Gore, Sir John 2423
Gorges, Sir Arthur 2364–5
Gorgias 2519
Goring, George, Baron Goring of Hurstpierpoint (1585–1663) 2356, 2532
Goring, George (1608–57) 2353, 2469
Gosson, Henry 2448, 2548
Gough, J. (playwright) 2413, 2512
Graham, George 2408
Graham, William 2423
Graham, William, 7th Earl of Menteith and 1st Earl of Strathearn 2387, 2408
Grandison, Viscount, see Villiers
Gray, William 2408
Greene, Charles 2405, 2424, 2480, 2543
Greene, John, sen. (1578–1653) 2423
Greene, John, jun. (1616–59) 2446, 2456, 2459, 2469, 2515
Greene, Leonard 2423
Greene, Margaret, see Bysshe
Greene, Robert (dramatist) 2360, 2367, 2403, 2419, 2483, 2518
Greene, Robert (torchbearer) 2423
Greenfield, Edward 2528
Greenhawe, William 2423
Gretton, Sara 2469
Greuter, Matthias 2359
Grey, Lady Elizabeth (of Stamford) 2359, 2369
Grey, Henry, 1st Earl of Stamford 2442
Grey of Groby, Thomas, Lord 2359
Griffin, Edward 2512
Griffith, Edmund 2423
Griffith, Richard 2423
Grimes, Sir George 2399
Grimestone, Edward 2412, 2447
Grinder, Ralph 2395, 2398
Grismand, John 2551
Grotius, Hugo (Huig de Groot) 2553
Grys, Sir Robert Le 2388, 2419

Gualtherus (Walther), Balthasar 2542
Guicciardini, Francesco 2376, 2521
Guillan, Mr (actor) 2398
Gulston, Joseph 2423
Gumbleton, William 2423
Gunnell, Richard 2370
Gunter (torchbearer) 2423
Gurlyn, Nathaniel 2423
Gussoni, Vicenzo 2359, 2384, 2387, 2398, 2416, 2423
Guthrie, Alexander 2408
Guy, John 2423
Guy, Thomas 2423

H., I. or J. (pamphleteer) 2488
H., P. (stationer) 2552
Haddington, Earl of, see Hamilton
Hadrian (Publius Aelius Hadrianus) 2511
Hakewill, William 2423
Hakluyt, Richard 2521
Hales, Matthew 2423
Hall, Henry 2365, 2553
Hall, William 2472
Halle, John 2385
Ham, Nicholas 2423
Hamersley, Sir Hugh 2423
Hamilton, James, 2nd Earl of Abercorn 2408
Hamilton, James, 3rd Marquess of Hamilton 2408
Hamilton, John, Lord Binning 2408
Hamilton, Mary, Marchioness of Hamilton 2395, 2398, 2469, 2522, 2532
Hamilton, Thomas, 1st Earl of Haddington 2408
Hansley, John 2374
Hardesty, John 2459
Harding, Mrs 2395
Hards, Peter 2364
Harflet, Charles 2362, 2364
Hargrave, James 2423
Harley, Sir Robert 2445
Harling, Roger 2472
Harmar, John 2405
Harper, Charles 2452
Harper, Thomas 2371, 2423, 2429, 2441, 2550, 2552, 2555
Harrington, William 2534
Harrison, Edmund 2428

Harrison, Thomas 2423
Harry (actor) 2516
Harsnett, Thomas 2423
Hartley, Richard 2423
Harvey, Martyn 2423
Hatch, Thomas 2423
Hathway, Richard 2370, 2480
Hatton, Sir Christopher (1605–70) 2365
Hatton, Lady Elizabeth 2423, 2535
Hausted, Peter 2364–5, 2463, 2474, 2511
Hausted, William 2364
Haviland, John 2453, 2484
Hawkins, John 2423
Hay, George, 1st Earl of Kinnoull and Viscount Dupline 2408
Hay, James, 1st Earl of Carlisle 2387
Hay, James, 2nd Viscount Doncaster 2353, 2469
Hay, Sir John 2408
Hay, Lucy, Countess of Carlisle 2359, 2469, 2530–1
Hay, William, 10th Earl of Errol 2408
Hay of Yester, John, 8th Lord 2408
Hayward, Thomas 2423
Hearne, Richard 2420, 2451, 2490–2510, 2524
Heath, Mr (clothworker) 2448
Heilen, John 2423
Hele, Sir John 2550
Hele, Lewis 2423
Heliodorus 2487, 2512
Helveticus, Christophorus (Christoph Helvig) 2492–3
Heminges, John 2459
Heminges, William 2400, 2412
Hemson (actor) 2362
Henley, Robert 2423
Henrietta Maria, Queen of England 2353, 2356, 2359–60, 2362, 2364–5, 2368–9, 2378, 2384, 2395, 2398, 2402–3, 2410, 2417, 2421–3, 2428, 2431, 2439, 2442, 2451, 2453–4, 2459, 2469, 2485–6, 2521–2, 2530–2, 2534–6, 2541, 2549–53, 2555
Henshawe, Anna 2359, 2395
Henslowe, Mr (steward) 2394

Index of Persons | 517

Henslowe, Philip 2508
Herbert, Lord Charles 2359, 2459, 2469
Herbert, Sir Edward 2423
Herbert, Sir Henry 2355, 2357, 2360, 2363–4, 2367–8, 2370, 2373, 2378, 2385, 2389–90, 2396, 2399–400, 2402–3, 2409–10, 2415, 2417–18, 2421–2, 2425, 2428, 2431, 2434, 2437, 2441, 2451, 2453–5, 2460, 2464, 2468, 2480, 2484, 2515, 2519, 2526, 2529, 2534, 2536–7, 2541, 2543, 2545, 2553
Herbert, Lady Mary 2469
Herbert, Lady Mary, of Shurland, *see* Villiers
Herbert, Philip, 4th Earl of Pembroke, and 1st Earl of Montgomery 2360, 2367, 2387, 2395, 2403, 2410–11, 2423, 2428, 2437, 2451, 2455, 2464, 2515, 2534, 2550, 2552
Herbert, Philip (1621–69) 2359
Herbert, Richard 2469
Herbert, Thomas 2367, 2410, 2515
Herbert, William 2428
Herbert, William, 3rd Earl of Pembroke 2534
Herbert of Cherbury, Edward, Lord 2414
Herne, Edward 2423
Herne, James 2355, 2364–5, 2367, 2378, 2389, 2396, 2399, 2402, 2405, 2410, 2413, 2418, 2421, 2424, 2432, 2434, 2437, 2441, 2445, 2451–2, 2455, 2458–9, 2479–81, 2487–8, 2512, 2515, 2519, 2526, 2529–31, 2536, 2543, 2552–3
Herne, John 2423
Herodotus 2387
Herringman, Henry 2357, 2364, 2371, 2385, 2403–4, 2421, 2428, 2431, 2439, 2453, 2464, 2469, 2484, 2487, 2519, 2529, 2532, 2534, 2538
Hesiod 2451, 2477, 2492, 2511
Heton, Richard 2454

Heydon, John 2423
Heylyn, Peter 2376, 2550, 2552
Heywood, John 2403
Heywood, Thomas 2361, 2377, 2379, 2381, 2387, 2396, 2411, 2416, 2420, 2434, 2441, 2448–9, 2451, 2458, 2462, 2473, 2490–511, 2517, 2522, 2524
Hickes, William 2371
Hill, Abraham 2434, 2436
Hills, Heigham 2364
Hills, John 2364
Hills, Ralph 2364
Hillyard, John 2423
Hilton, John 2364, 2371, 2396, 2552
Hippocrates 2429, 2533
Hitche, Bartholomew 2423
Hobbes, Thomas 2404
Hocus Pocus, *see* Vincent, William
Hodges, Mr (clothworker) 2448
Hodgkin, Thomas 2385, 2403–4, 2439
Hog, William 2445
Hohenheim, Theophrastus Bombastus von, *see* Paracelsus
Holinshed, Raphael 2367, 2376, 2399, 2403
Holland, Earl and Countess of, *see* Rich
Holland, Philemon 2382
Holles, Gervase 2423, 2532
Holmes, Mr (clothworker) 2448
Holmes, Richard 2423
Holmes, Thomas 2364, 2423, 2550
Holmes, William, sen. 2423
Homer 2376, 2385, 2404, 2430, 2451, 2479, 2483, 2491, 2493, 2503, 2505–6, 2512, 2516, 2540
Hooker, Richard 2550
Hooker, William 2423
Hope, Edward, *see* Bennett
Hopkins, John 2468
Hopper, Edward 2423
Hopper, John 2423
Hopper, Simon 2423, 2555
Horace (Quintus Horatius Flaccus) 2365, 2378, 2382, 2385, 2391, 2401, 2410, 2413, 2416, 2419, 2424, 2429–30, 2434, 2441, 2445,

2449, 2451, 2458, 2463, 2474, 2479, 2488, 2511, 2542–3, 2545, 2553
Horne, Gustavus 2398
Horne, John 2355, 2364–5, 2367, 2378, 2389, 2396, 2399, 2402, 2405, 2410, 2413, 2418, 2421, 2424, 2432, 2434, 2437, 2441, 2445, 2451–2, 2455, 2458–9, 2479–81, 2487–8, 2512, 2515, 2519, 2526, 2529–31, 2536, 2543, 2552–3
Horne, Robert 2421, 2428, 2453, 2469, 2484, 2519, 2532
Hoskyns, John 2423
Hough, Mr (clothworker) 2448
Houghton, John 2355, 2364–5, 2367, 2378, 2389, 2396, 2399, 2402, 2405, 2410, 2413, 2418, 2421, 2424, 2432, 2434, 2437, 2441, 2445, 2451–2, 2455, 2458–9, 2479–81, 2487–8, 2512, 2515, 2519, 2526, 2529–31, 2536, 2543, 2552–3
Houseman, John 2398
How, William 2364, 2367
Howard, Alethea, Countess of Arundel 2522
Howard, Elizabeth (*c.* 1622–1705) 2395
Howard, Elizabeth, Countess of Berkshire 2469
Howard, Lady Frances 2359
Howard, Lady Frances (of Berkshire) 2359
Howard, Henry (of Berkshire) 2359
Howard, James, 3rd Earl of Suffolk 2408
Howard, James, Lord Walden 2428
Howard, Lady Katherine 2469
Howard, Robert 2428
Howard, Theophilus, 2nd Earl of Suffolk 2387
Howard, Thomas 2428
Howard, Thomas, 14th Earl of Arundel 2387, 2423, 2428
Howell, James 2442
Hubbard, Richard 2359
Huc, Peter le 2359, 2423, 2428, 2442, 2552

Index of Persons

Hudson, Jeffery 2359, 2395, 2469, 2485–6
Hudson, Ralph 2517
Hughes, Francis 2364
Hungerford, Giles 2532
Hunt, Mr (procession organizer) 2423
Hunt, William 2408
Hunter, Thomas 2423
Hurst (torchbearer) 2423
Hurt, William 2395, 2398
Hutchinson, Christopher, *see* Beeston
Hutchinson, Lucy 2534
Hutchinson, Michael 2532
Hutchinson, William, *see* Beeston
Hutton, Sir Richard 2423
Hutton, Thomas 2423
Hyde, Edward 2365, 2423
Hyde, Sir Laurence 2423, 2532
Hyde, William 2423
Hyfield, John 2551
Hynde, George 2423

Ingram family 2527
Ingram, Sir Arthur, jun. 2527
Inman, Matthew 2534
Ireland, Richard 2365
Isidore of Seville 2477
Isles, William 2423
Isley, Ursula, *see* Beaumont
Islip, Susan 2435
Ives, Simon 2423, 2549

Jackson, Thomas 2550
Jacob, Peter 2423
Jacob, William 2552
James I, King of England and of Scots 2382, 2408, 2521
James, Prince, Duke of York 2423, 2533
Jameson, George 2408
Jarman, Anthony 2423
Jarman, Sir Thomas 2428
Jay, Henry 2398
Jay, Stephen 2423
Jeffreys, George 2364
Jenkins, John 2423, 2532
Jermyn, Henry 2469, 2519, 2532
Jermyn, Sir Thomas 2387
Joachimi, Albert 2416, 2448
Joannes Damascenus 2533
Jocelin, Simon 2362
John, Thomas 2534

John of Damascus, *see* Joannes Damascenus
Johnson, John 2423
Johnson, Richard (actor) 2472
Johnson, Richard (author) 2432, 2542
Johnson, Thomas 2360, 2365, 2374, 2428, 2451–2, 2517–18, 2531, 2552, 2556
Johnson, William 2362
Johnston, James 2423
Jolley, John 2423
Jones, Mr (attorney) 2423
Jones, David (horse-handler) 2423
Jones, David, of Oxford 2550
Jones, Edward 2423
Jones, Emanuel 2423
Jones, Inigo 2353, 2359, 2382, 2385, 2395, 2398, 2403, 2423, 2428, 2439, 2451, 2469, 2522
Jones, John 2488
Jones, Peter 2550
Jones, Robert (feather-maker) 2428
Jones, Robert (torchbearer) 2423
Jones, Thomas 2517
Jones, Sir William 2423
Jonson, Ben 2361, 2364–5, 2371, 2373, 2376, 2378, 2382, 2383, 2385, 2389, 2392, 2396, 2401–5, 2408, 2410, 2419, 2423, 2426, 2429, 2433, 2437, 2439, 2445, 2455, 2457–9, 2468, 2472, 2479, 2484, 2521, 2525, 2536, 2540, 2545, 2550, 2552–3, 2557
Jordan, Thomas 2361, 2413, 2472, 2512, 2525, 2549
Joy, Henry 2423
Jumper, Matthew 2469
Juvenal (Flavius Junius Juvenalis) 2373, 2382, 2385, 2391, 2396, 2409, 2440, 2451, 2458, 2463, 2472, 2488, 2511, 2518, 2523, 2545

Kalwitz, Seth, *see* Calvisius
Kaye, Sir John (d. 1641) 2438
Kaye, Sir John (1616–62) 2438
Keith, Robert 2423
Keith, William, 6th Earl Marischal 2408

Kellaway, John 2423
Kellie, Earl of, *see* Erskine
Kelly, John 2423, 2428
Kelly, Theodore 2364–5
Kemp, Edward 2362, 2364
Kemp, Hobart 2428, 2534
Kempis, Thomas a 2388
Kennedy, John, 6th Earl of Cassilis 2408
Kentsey, William 2423
Kepler, Johannes 2521
Ker, Charles 2555
Ker, Henry, Lord 2555
Ker, Robert, 1st Earl of Roxburgh 2408
Kerr, William, 1st Earl of Lothian 2408
Keyser, Hendrik de 2354
Kidby, John 2364
Kifford, Thomas 2423
Killigrew, Cecilia, *see* Crofts
Killigrew, Charlotte 2487
Killigrew, Elizabeth, *see* Boyle
Killigrew, Henry 2459
Killigrew, Thomas 2359, 2395, 2487, 2529, 2534, 2538, 2556
Kindersley, Robert 2423
King, John 2395, 2423, 2428
Kinghorne, Earl of, *see* Lyon
Kingston, Felix 2458
Kinnersley, Clement 2469
Kinnoull, Earl of, *see* Hay
Kirke, Anne 2395
Kirke, George 2353, 2428
Kirke, John 2432
Kirkman, Francis 2361, 2376, 2407, 2451, 2455, 2555–6
Knight, Arthur 2395, 2398, 2485
Knight, Edward 2385
Knight, J. 2413
Knight, John 2428
Knight, Joseph 2371
Knite, Peter le 2423
Knolles, Richard 2376, 2383
Knox, John 2553
Knyvett, Thomas 2469
Kyd, Thomas 2355, 2396, 2403, 2413, 2455, 2472, 2521, 2556
Kynaston, Francis 2533

La Bredache, Mrs (actor) 2485
Lactantius, Lucius Caecilius Firmianus 2492, 2517
Ladman, John 2423

Index of Persons | 519

Lamb, Adam 2408
Lambarde, William 2521
Lanckvelt, Joris van, *see* Macropedius
Lane, Richard 2365
Lane, Thomas 2423
Lane, William 2423
Lanfranc of Milan (Guido Lanfranchi) 2385
Langbaine, Gerard 2353, 2355, 2359–61, 2364, 2367, 2373–4, 2376, 2378, 2381, 2383, 2389, 2395–6, 2399, 2401–2, 2405, 2407, 2410–11, 2413, 2417–20, 2423–4, 2432, 2434, 2437, 2441, 2445, 2449, 2451, 2455, 2458–9, 2468, 2472, 2479–81, 2487–8, 2490–510, 2512, 2518, 2524, 2526, 2528–31, 2536, 2538, 2543–5, 2550, 2553, 2555–6
Langer, Thomas 2423
Langham, Robert 2404
Langley, John 2357, 2385, 2403–4, 2431, 2439, 2453, 2484, 2538
Lanier, Clement 2423
Lanier, John 2423
Lanier, Nicholas 2359, 2423, 2534
Lapierre, William, *see* Pierre, Guillaume la
Laud, William 2385, 2387, 2550–2
Lauderdale, Earl of, *see* Maitland
Law, Alexander 2408
Lawes, Henry 2364, 2423, 2428, 2433, 2445, 2468, 2532, 2534, 2550–2
Lawes, John 2423
Lawes, William 2404, 2423, 2428, 2435, 2453, 2526, 2532, 2550, 2552–3
Lawrence, John 2423, 2428
Lawton, Thomas 2423
Le Neve, William 2408
Leach, Thomas 2355, 2364, 2367, 2396, 2437, 2549
Leake, John 2468
Leake, William 2512, 2536
Leare, Daniel 2540
Lee, William 2373
Leech, John 2423
Legge, Thomas 2429
Leigh, Joseph 2423

Lemnius, Levinus (Lievin Lemnes) 2533
Lennox, Duke of, *see* Stewart
Lenton, Francis 2423
Leo Africanus, Joannes (Giovannii Leone) 2521
Lermitt, Peter 2359, 2398, 2469
Leslie, James 2408
Leslie, John 2408
L'Estrange, Roger 2361, 2412, 2421, 2428, 2453, 2469, 2484, 2519, 2532
Levasher, John 2423
Lewis, Henry 2423
Leyburn, George (alias Fountain and Roberts) 2550
Lichfield, Leonard 2549, 2553, 2555
Lillicrap, Peter 2361
Lilly, William (astrologer) 2355, 2480
Lily, William (grammarian) 2403, 2434, 2441, 2451, 2479, 2518, 2521, 2551
Lin (actor) 2364
Lindsay, Earl of, *see* Bertie
Lindsay, Alexander (bishop) 2408
Lindsay, Alexander, 2nd Lord Spynie 2408
Lindsay, Sir Jerome 2408
Lindsay, John, 10th Lord 2408
Lindsay, Patrick 2408
Ling, Nicholas 2387, 2416
Linlithgow, Earl of, *see* Livingston
Lipsius, Justus (Joost Lips) 2404
Lisle, William 2532
Lister, John 2423
Littleton, Sir Thomas 2364, 2401, 2444, 2521, 2533
Livingston, Alexander, 2nd Earl of Linlithgow 2408
Livingston, George, Lord 2408
Livy (Titus Livius) 2366, 2370, 2407, 2416, 2480
Loch, James 2408
Locke, William 2423
London, William 2378, 2383, 2389, 2399, 2413, 2417–19, 2421, 2423, 2434–5, 2437, 2453, 2455, 2468, 2519, 2526, 2532, 2545, 2550, 2552
Lope de Vega, Félix 2410
López de Ayala, Pedro 2465–6

Lord, Robert 2552
Lothian, Earl of, *see* Kerr
Loveday, Elizabeth 2428
Loveday, Thomas 2361
Lovel, Thomas 2361
Lovelace, Lady Anne, *see* Wentworth (1623–97) 2538
Lovelace, John, 2nd Baron, of Hurley 2515
Lovelace, Richard, 1st Baron, of Hurley 2515
Lovell, William 2423
Low, Thomas 2423, 2452–3
Lowe, Edward 2423, 2435, 2532, 2550–2
Lowe, Nicholas 2361
Lowin, John 2385, 2417, 2421–2, 2453, 2519, 2530–1, 2541, 2552
Lucan (Marcus Annaeus Lucanus) 2387, 2408, 2477, 2540
Lucian of Samosata 2432, 2435, 2480, 2493–2507
Ludovicus, Johannes 2430
Lumley, Sir Martin 2423
Lunt, Richard 2423
Lupo, Theophilus 2423
Lupo, Thomas, jun. (1577–*c*. 1647) 2423
Lupton, Thomas 2449
Lydall, Richard 2423
Lydgate, John 2484
Lyon, John, 2nd Earl of Kinghorne 2408
Lyte, Isaac 2549

M., J. (bookseller) 2380, 2412
McCall, David 2408
MacDonnell, Randall, Viscount Dunluce and 2nd Earl of Antrim 2353, 2428, 2528
Machin, Lewis 2437, 2472
Mackall, Mungo 2408
Mackenzie, George, 2nd Earl of Seaforth 2408
MacNaught, John 2408
Macock, John 2396, 2421, 2437, 2453, 2487, 2519, 2529, 2534, 2538, 2552
Macropedius, Georgius (Joris van Lanckvelt) 2365
Maffei, Raffaello, *see* Volaterranus
Magirus, Johannes 2364
Magnes, James 2534

Maitland, John, 1st Earl of Lauderdale 2408
Major, Daniel 2371, 2405, 2417, 2545
Malory, Sir Thomas 2457
Manchester, Earl of, *see* Montagu
Mandeville, Sir John 2521
Mannering (actor) 2364
Mansell, Francis 2550
Mansell, Thomas 2532
Mantegna, Andrea 2353
Mantuanus, Baptista 2434, 2449
Mar, James 2408
Mare, Pierre de la 2423
Mari, Maturin 2423
Marischal, Earl, *see* Keith
Marjoribanks, Joseph 2408
Markham, Gervase 2437
Marlowe, Christopher 2360–1, 2373, 2376, 2389, 2403, 2410–11, 2417, 2424, 2448, 2474, 2512, 2521, 2525
Marmion, Shackerley 2378, 2381, 2390, 2401, 2458, 2516, 2536
Marriott, John 2380, 2412
Marriott, Richard 2380, 2383, 2419, 2454, 2464, 2475
Marsh, Henry 2376, 2395, 2407, 2451, 2455
Marshall, William 2429
Marston, John 2360, 2370, 2373, 2472, 2480
Martial (Marcus Valerius Martialis) 2361, 2364, 2383, 2385, 2451, 2459, 2479, 2511, 2523, 2540
Martin, John 2357, 2364, 2421, 2428, 2431, 2453, 2464, 2469, 2484, 2519, 2532, 2534, 2538
Martin, Sarah 2357, 2364, 2431, 2453, 2484, 2538
Martínez, Marcos 2361, 2376, 2389, 2396, 2410, 2417–18, 2457, 2484, 2553
Mary, Princess (1631–60) 2533
Mason, Richard 2423
Mason, Robert 2423
Massinger (actor?) 2516
Massinger, Philip 2373, 2385, 2414, 2417–18, 2426, 2434, 2449, 2458, 2460, 2468, 2471, 2520, 2534, 2545, 2552–3

Masson, James 2398
Matchit, Ambrose 2361, 2525
Mathew, Richard 2423
Matthew, Tobie 2528
Matthews, Augustine 2353, 2359, 2364, 2378
Matthysz, Paulus 2423
Maunder, Nicholas 2423
Maxey, Henry 2423
Maxwell, Sir John 2408
Maxwell, William 2408
May, John 2423
May, Richard 2532
May, Thomas 2402, 2423, 2479
May, Walter 2423
Maynard, Sir John 2353, 2398
Mayne, Jasper 2521, 2552–3
Mearne, Samuel 2383, 2395, 2401, 2417, 2419, 2433, 2445, 2449, 2468, 2518, 2544–5, 2550, 2552, 2556
Medici, Ferdinand de, Grand Duke of Tuscany 2398
Meighen, Mercy 2378, 2421, 2519, 2532, 2556
Meighen, Richard 2378, 2421, 2519, 2532
Mell, Davis 2423, 2550
Mell, Leonard 2423
Mellor, Richard (mercer), *see* Miller
Menander 2491
Menteith, Earl of, *see* Graham
Menteith, Alexander 2408
'Mercurius Melancholicus' (printer) 2371, 2437, 2552
Meres, Francis (1607–83) 2365
Meres, Thomas 2552
Meriell, Jo. 2413
Metel, François de, Sieur de Boisrobert 2522
Mico, John 2468
Middleton, Thomas 2371, 2412, 2419, 2421, 2449, 2458, 2468, 2472, 2511–12, 2525–6, 2528
Mildmay, Sir Humphrey 2418, 2421–3, 2428, 2431, 2453, 2469, 2515
Mildmay, Lady Jane 2423, 2469
Miller, John 2408
Miller, Richard (mercer) 2359, 2395, 2398, 2428, 2469
Miller, Richard (musician) 2423
Miller, Simon 2376, 2389, 2459, 2552

Miller, William 2552
Milles, Robert 2552
Mills, William 2405
Milton, John 2433, 2445, 2471
Milton, Samuel 2423
Mingay, Anthony 2535
Minsheu, John 2387
Minthorpe, Arthur 2423
Mitchell, John 2423, 2532
Monger, Mr (clothworker) 2416, 2448
Montagu, Henry, 1st Earl of Manchester 2387
Montagu, Walter 2395, 2459
Montgomerie, Alexander, 6th Earl of Eglinton 2408
Montgomery, Earl of, *see* Herbert
Montgomery, Mrs (haberdasher?) 2527
Montliard, Jean de 2451
Moore, Joseph 2378
Moore, Thomas 2557
Moraes Cabral, Francisco de 2376, 2417, 2457
More, Henry 2392
More, Sir Thomas 2521
Morette, Gilbert 2398, 2469, 2486
Morgan, Mrs (tirewoman) 2550
Morgan, Philip 2423, 2532
Morgan, William 2532
Morley, Thomas 2397
Morrell, Matthew 2423
Morris, Mathias 2472, 2525
Morse, Thomas 2423
Morton, Earl of, *see* Douglas
Morton, John 2423
Moseley, Ann 2371, 2385, 2403–5, 2421, 2428, 2439, 2453, 2468, 2469, 2484, 2534, 2552
Moseley, Humphrey 2355, 2357, 2360, 2364–5, 2367, 2371, 2378, 2383, 2385–6, 2388–9, 2396, 2399, 2402–5, 2410, 2413, 2417–19, 2421, 2423–4, 2426–8, 2431, 2433–5, 2437, 2439, 2445, 2451–3, 2455, 2458–60, 2462, 2464, 2468–73, 2479–81, 2484, 2487–8, 2512, 2515, 2519–20, 2523, 2526, 2528–9, 2530–2, 2534, 2536, 2538, 2541, 2543, 2545, 2552–3

Motteux, Peter 2461
Moulson, Thomas 2423
Mountfort, Walter 2409
Muhammad al-Wazzan al-Fasi, al-Hasan ibn, *see* Leo Africanus
Mun, Thomas 2409
Munday, Anthony 2376, 2401, 2417, 2456–7, 2517, 2536, 2545
Murray, Charles 2398
Murray, Henry 2353, 2398, 2469
Murray, James 2408
Murray, John, 1st Earl of Annandale 2408
Muskett, Andrew 2423
Myddelton, Sir Thomas (1586–1666) 2440

Nabbes, Thomas 2370, 2405, 2424, 2480, 2543
Nairn, James 2408
Naismith, James 2408
Napper, Robert 2423
Nash, Thomas, of the Inner Temple 2423
Nashe, Thomas 2472
Nau, Stephen de (a.k.a. Etienne) 2423, 2552
Nauclerus, Johannes (Johann Vergenhans) 2477
Naunton, Sir Robert 2387
Necolalde, Juan de 2359, 2387, 2448
Negri, Francesco, de Bassano 2477
Neile, Richard 2387
Nemesianus, Marcus Aurelius Olympius 2451
Neville, Sophia 2398, 2469
Newcomb, Thomas 2365, 2417, 2421, 2428, 2453, 2464, 2469, 2484, 2532, 2545, 2549
Newdigate family 2382, 2444
Newdigate, John 2353, 2359, 2382, 2402, 2422–3, 2428, 2444, 2469
Newdigate, Richard 2423
Newdigate, Susanna 2423
Newman, Mr (draper) 2423
Newman, Dorman 2371, 2412
Newman, Thomas 2371
Newport, Earl and Countess of, *see* Blount
Newton, Richard 2423

Nicetas Choniates 2547
Nicholson, John 2447
Nieulandt, Willem van 2428
Nightingale, Roger 2423
Noble (actor) 2525
Norbury, George 2423
Norden, John 2532
Norman, Robert 2448, 2514, 2517
Norreys, Francis 2453
Norris, Sir Francis 2453
North, John 2423
North, Thomas 2480
Northampton, Earl and Countess of, *see* Compton
Northumberland, Earl and Countess of, *see* Percy
Norton, Harsnett 2423
Norton, John 2374, 2418, 2423, 2437, 2459, 2526, 2530–1
Noy, William 2423, 2450

Oakes, Anne 2432
Oakes, Edward 2432
Odson, William 2423
Ogilby, John 2546
Ogle, Mrs 2395
Okes, John 2377, 2402, 2413, 2432, 2479, 2536
Okes, Nicholas 2377, 2387, 2402, 2416
Origen Adamantius 2533
Orozco, *see* Covarrubias
Orrel, Thomas 2371
Ortelius (Ortels), Abraham 2492
Ortúñez de Calahorra, Diego 2361, 2376, 2389, 2396, 2410, 2417–18, 2457, 2484, 2553
Osbaldeston, Lambert 2365, 2423, 2539
Oulton, Richard 2405, 2420, 2424, 2451, 2480, 2490–2510, 2524, 2543, 2548
Overbury, Sir Thomas 2364
Overton, Richard 2362
Ovid (Publius Ovidius Naso) 2355, 2361, 2375, 2382, 2387, 2389, 2391, 2401–3, 2412, 2416–17, 2419, 2429, 2441, 2444–5, 2449, 2451, 2458, 2463, 2468, 2472, 2474, 2477, 2483–4, 2488, 2491–2, 2508–12, 2517–18, 2525, 2540, 2542, 2545, 2553

Owen, Richard 2455
Owen, Robert 2423
Oxenstierna, Henry 2398
Oxford, Countess of, *see* Vere
Oxinden, Henry 2451

P., R. (translator) 2361, 2376, 2389, 2396, 2410, 2417–18, 2457, 2484, 2553
Page, Edward (attorney) 2423
Page, Edward (masquer) 2423
Page, John (actor) 2480
Page, John (torchbearer) 2423
Page, William 2423
Paget, Mrs (masquer) 2359
Paget, William, 5th Baron 2353, 2428
Pagitt, Justinian 2406, 2416, 2423
Pakeman, Daniel 2539
Palmer, Sir Roger 2522
Palmer, Thomas 2371
Panvinio, Onuphrio 2353
Panzani, Gregorio 2469, 2550
Paracelsus 2521, 2543
Parigi, Alfonso, jun. 2395, 2469
Parigi, Giulio 2353, 2359, 2428, 2469
Parker, Francis 2423
Parker, John 2385, 2403–4, 2439
Parker, Peter 2403–5, 2453, 2468, 2552
Parker, Robert 2423
Parkhurst, Robert 2423, 2448
Parr, Thomas 2528
Parre, Paul 2359
Parrott, Henry 2385
Parry, James 2423
Parry, Robert 2423
Parsons, Marmaduke 2421, 2519, 2532
Pasley, James 2423
Passinger, Thomas 2555
Patrick, John 2552
Patten, William 2423
Pattericke, John 2423
Paul (servant) 2527
Pawe, Adriaen 2387
Payne, Robert 2404
Peaps, William, *see* Pepys
Pearce, Edward 2555
Pearson, John 2362, 2364
Peele, George 2445, 2468
Pembroke, Earl of, *see* Herbert
Pennycuike, Andrew 2373, 2412, 2426

Penrin, William 2423, 2428, 2469
Pepys, John 2423
Pepys, Samuel 2429
Pepys, [William?] 2556
Percival, John 2552
Percy family 2552
Percy, Algernon, 10th Earl of Northumberland 2423
Percy, Anne, Countess of Northumberland 2469
Percy, Henry 2532
Percy, William 2391
Peretti, Michele 2469
Pergamenus, Nicolaus (Nicolas de Bergame) 2463
Perkins, John 2401
Perkins, Richard 2480
Perkins, William 2521
Perry, Hugh 2387, 2423
Pers, Pieter 2423
Persall, Lady Frances 2395
Persius Flaccus, Aulus 2381–2, 2409, 2451, 2458, 2518, 2540
Perth, Earl of, *see* Drummond
Pestell, Thomas, jun. 2362
Petrarch (Francesco Petrarca) 2480
Petronius Arbiter, Gaius 2458, 2542, 2550
Pettie, George 2491
Pheasant, Mr, of Gray's Inn 2423
Phelips, Sir Robert 2441–2
Philips, John (dedicatee) 2361
Philips, Philip 2423
Philips, Richard 2423
Philips, Thomas 2423
Phillips, Edward 2367
Phillips, John (miscellanist) 2484
'Philomusus' (miscellanist) 2355, 2364, 2367, 2396, 2437, 2468
Philpott (torchbearer) 2423
Philpott, John 2423
Picart, Nicholas 2423
Piccolomini, Enea Silvio 2409, 2477
Pico della Mirandola, Giovanni 2378
Pierce, Theobald 2555
Pierre, Guillaume la 2398, 2423
Pierre, Sebastian la 2423, 2552

Pighius, Stephanus Winandus 2385
Pindar 2540
Pittoni, Battista 2428
Pius II, Pope, *see* Piccolomini
Place, John 2550
Platina, Bartholomeus (Bartolomeo Sacchi) 2477
Plato 2378, 2413, 2416, 2424, 2433, 2445, 2451, 2458, 2469, 2519, 2533, 2542, 2552, 2556
Plautus, Titus Maccius 2364, 2385, 2391, 2411, 2429–30, 2463, 2474, 2511
Playfere, John 2411, 2487, 2529
Playford, Henry 2552
Playford, John, sen. 2371, 2378, 2396, 2419, 2421, 2468, 2532, 2538, 2542, 2550, 2552, 2555
Playford, John, jun. 2552
Plessis, Armand Jean du, *see* Richelieu
Pliny the Elder (Gaius Plinius Secundus) 2387, 2441, 2472, 2511, 2517, 2523, 2545
Pliny the Younger (Gaius Plinius Caecilius Secundus) 2463, 2474
Plutarch 2403, 2416, 2472, 2480
Pollard, Timothy 2423
Pollux, Julius 2542
Pontanus, Jovianus (Giovanni Pontano) 2408
Poole, Joshua 2360, 2365, 2374, 2428, 2452, 2517, 2531, 2552, 2556
Pope, Dudley 2423
Pope, George 2423
Pope, Hugh 2359
Porter, Endymion 2421
Porter, Walter 2423
Portman, George 2552
Pory (lace-maker) 2423
Pory, John 2353, 2356, 2385, 2521
Pougny, Marquis of, *see* Angennes
Powell, Roger 2423
Poxall, Clement 2534
Pratt, Henry 2423
Prevost, Mr (actor) 2398
Price, William 2423
Pridmore, Isaac 2376, 2407

Primaticcio, Francesco 2353
Probert, George 2532
Prodromus, Theodorus 2552
Prust, Edward 2423
Prynne, William 2396, 2419, 2422–3, 2434, 2461, 2521, 2542, 2550, 2552–3
Ptolemy, Claudius 2408, 2458, 2468
Publilius Syrus 2391, 2408–9, 2430
Puckering, Elizabeth 2360, 2410, 2413, 2453, 2552
Puckering, Sir Henry 2433, 2445
Puckering, Sir Thomas 2385, 2552–3
Pulton, Ferdinand 2521
Purchas, Samuel 2521
Purfoot, Thomas 2399
Purslowe, Elizabeth 2528
Purslowe, George 2355
Puteanus, Erycius, *see* Putten
Putten, Hendrik van der 2417, 2445
Puy, Henri du, *see* Putten
Pye, Lady Joan 2423
Pye, Sir John 2438
Pye, Robert 2423
Pye, Sir Walter 2423
Pye, Walter, jun. 2423

Quinne, John 2555

R., J. (printer) 2468
R., T. (dramatist) 2429
Rabel, Daniel 2469
Rabelais, François 2365, 2395, 2412, 2423, 2428, 2536, 2553
Radcliffe, Sir Alexander 2429
Rae, James 2408
Raimondi, Marcantonio 2353
Rainaldi, Girolamo 2395
Rainton, Sir Nicholas 2387, 2423
Ramsbottom, Thomas 2362, 2364
Ramsey, Robert 2395, 2442
Randolph, Robert 2365
Randolph, Thomas 2365, 2429, 2445, 2452, 2516
Rands, William 2408
Randwyck, Arnaut van 2387
Ranger, John 2423
Ranger, Thomas 2423
Rankins, William 2370, 2480
Ratcliffe, John 2532

Index of Persons | 523

Ravenscroft, Thomas 2432
Rawdon family 2365
Rawlins, James 2367
Rawlins, John 2468
Rawlins, Thomas 2413, 2472, 2512
Rawlins, William 2433, 2445
Raworth, John 2451
Raworth, Robert 2434, 2451, 2517
Raworth, Ruth 2355, 2367, 2433, 2445, 2464
Raynsford, Richard 2423
Reade, John 2423
Reade, Robert 2423
Reade, Thomas 2554
Reading, John 2404, 2423, 2453
Reinoldes, Rowland 2423
Reve, Augustine 2423
Reve, Henry 2423
Reymes, Bullen 2469
Reynolds, Henry 2373, 2402
Rhys, Philip 2423
Rich, Barnaby 2378
Rich, Henry, 1st Earl of Holland 2353, 2362, 2364–5, 2367, 2387, 2408, 2428, 2532
Rich, Isabel, Countess of Holland 2532
Rich, Robert, 2nd Earl of Warwick 2356
Rich, Sir Robert 2423
Rich of Holland, Robert, Lord 2359, 2428
Richards (actor) 2362
Richards, Nathaniel 2413, 2472, 2512
Richards, William 2523
Richardson, John 2468, 2555
Richardson, Joseph 2362, 2364
Richardson, Lambert 2362, 2364
Richelieu, Cardinal (Armand Jean du Plessis) 2382
Rickets, John 2511
Ridley, Mark 2385
Riley, Mr (musical facilitator) 2423
Ripa, Cesare 2353, 2359, 2428
Rivers, John (alias Abbot) 2461
Roberts, Anthony 2423
Roberts, George, *see* Leyburn
Roberts, Hugh 2423
Robinson, Mr (hosier) 2423
Robinson, Humphrey (executor) 2357, 2364, 2431, 2453, 2484, 2538

Robinson, Humphrey (stationer) 2357, 2364, 2431, 2445, 2453, 2484, 2538
Robinson, John 2472
Robinson, Richard 2471
Robinson, Thomas (hosier) 2428, 2486
Robinson, Thomas (musician) 2518
Robinson, Thomas (stationer) 2552
Robusti, Jacopo, *see* Tintoretto
Rochester, Earl of, *see* Wilmot
Rochford, Viscount, *see* Carey
Roe, Sir Thomas 2469
Rogers, Elizabeth 2423
Rogers, John 2362, 2364
Rogers, Samuel 2362, 2364
Rogers, William 2423
Rolfe, William 2423
Rolleston family 2444
Rolleston, John 2404, 2439, 2457, 2521
Romano, Giulio 2469
Rookes, Mary 2413, 2419, 2468, 2552
Rookes, Thomas 2413, 2419, 2468, 2552
Rookwood (torchbearer) 2423
Roper, Abel 2381
Rossingham, Edward 2552–3
Rotherham, Richard 2423
Rouse, John 2445
Rowley, Samuel 2479
Rowley, William 2389, 2411–12, 2421, 2461, 2516
Roxburgh, Earl of, *see* Ker
Roybould, William 2365
Roycroft, Thomas 2419
Royston, Richard 2365, 2488
Rudstone, Thomas 2423
Rudyerd, Sir Benjamin 2534
Ruggle, George 2424, 2429, 2542
Rumsey, Edward 2423
Rupert, Prince, of the Rhine 2532, 2535, 2550–2
Russell, Lady Anne 2359
Russell, Lady Mary 2359
Russell, William, Lord 2469
Rutter, John 2423
Rutter, Joseph 2402, 2452
Ryder, John 2488
Ryder, Richard 2395

Ryley, Thomas 2365, 2429
Rynd, John 2408

S., A. (author) 2544
S., J. (miscellanist) 2549
S., S. (miscellanist) 2405
S., W. (translator) 2556
Saavedra, *see* Cervantes
Sabellicus, Marcus Antonius Coccius 2477
Sacchi, Bartolomeo, *see* Platina
Sackville, Edward (d. 1646) 2555
Sackville, Edward, 4th Earl of Dorset 2387, 2451, 2550, 2555
Sackville, Richard, Lord Buckhurst 2555
Sadeler, Aegidius 2395
Saint-Sorlin, *see* Desmarets
Salisbury, Earl of, *see* Cecil
Sallust (Gaius Sallustius Crispus) 2429–30, 2472, 2518
Saltoun, Lord, *see* Abernethy
Salusbury, Sir Thomas 2440
Salvetti, Amerigo 2395, 2398, 2469
San Martino, Gianfrancesco 2442
Sancroft, William 2458, 2519, 2528, 2552
Sandes, Thomas 2361, 2516
Sandys, George 2445
Sappho 2468
Sarracold, Mr (ironmonger) 2517
Saunders, Francis 2371
Saunders, John 2550
Savage, Anthony 2479
Savage, Dorothy 2469
Sawbridge, George 2413, 2419, 2468, 2552
Sawbridge, Thomas 2468
Sayers, Robert 2423
Scaglia, Alessandro-Cesare di 2353, 2359
Scaliger, Joseph Justus 2492
Scamozzi, Vincenzo 2353, 2428
Scot, Reginald 2399
Scott, Andrew 2408
Scott, Robert 2357, 2364, 2431, 2453, 2484, 2538
Scribonius, Cornelius 2353
Scudamore, John, 1st Viscount 2356, 2398
Scultori, Diana, *see* Ghisi
Scutt, Richard 2395, 2398

524 | Index of Persons

Seaforth, Earl of, *see* Mackenzie
Seare, William (flambeau-bearer) 2423
Seare, William (torchbearer) 2423
Seile, Henry 2452, 2528
Selden, John 2423, 2521, 2550
Seneca the Elder (Lucius or Marcus Annaeus Seneca) 2542
Seneca, Lucius Annaeus 2378, 2382, 2387, 2404, 2408, 2430, 2458, 2472, 2511, 2518, 2552
Seneca, Pseudo- 2416
Sere, William 2423
Sergier, Richard 2530–1
Serlio, Sebastiano 2353
Serres, Jean de 2412, 2447
Seton, Charles, 2nd Earl of Dunfermline 2408
Seton, George, Lord 2408
Seton, John 2361
Seton, Robert, 2nd Earl of Winton 2408
Sewster, Edward 2415
Seymour, Dorothy 2395
Seymour, Henry 2398
Seywell, John 2423
Shakespeare, William 2360–1, 2364–5, 2367, 2371, 2373, 2381, 2383, 2389, 2391, 2395–6, 2401, 2403, 2405, 2410–13, 2418, 2429–30, 2432, 2434–7, 2441, 2444–5, 2449, 2451–2, 2455, 2457–9, 2464, 2468–9, 2472, 2474–5, 2481, 2483, 2487, 2511, 2513, 2516, 2518–19, 2521, 2525–6, 2529–31, 2545, 2547, 2553, 2557
Shannon, Viscountess, *see* Boyle
Sharpham, Edward 2367
Sheares, William 2411, 2533
Sheldon, Gilbert 2444
Sheldon, Ralph 2355, 2364–5, 2367, 2378, 2389, 2396, 2399, 2402, 2405, 2410, 2413, 2418, 2421, 2424, 2432, 2434, 2437, 2441, 2445, 2451–2, 2455, 2458–9, 2479–81, 2487–8, 2512, 2515, 2519, 2526, 2529–31, 2536, 2543, 2552–3

Shelton, Sir Richard 2423
Shelton, Richard (flambeau-bearer) 2423
Shelton, Thomas 2409, 2423, 2457
Shepherd, Mrs (actor) 2359
Sheppard, Anne 2359
Sheppard, Samuel 2403–4, 2453, 2552
Shepster, Thomas 2423
Shirley, Lady Dorothy 2355, 2395
Shirley, Henry 2355, 2367, 2382, 2396, 2410, 2418, 2437, 2455, 2481, 2515, 2526
Shirley, James 2355, 2360, 2367, 2378, 2389, 2396, 2410, 2418, 2423, 2427, 2429, 2435, 2437, 2449, 2455, 2457–8, 2461, 2464, 2468, 2479, 2481, 2483, 2489, 2515–16, 2521, 2526, 2528, 2536, 2546, 2553
Shurlock, William 2480
Sicklyn, Christopher 2423
Siculus, Diodorus 2519
Sidney, Sir Philip 2355, 2360, 2364, 2376, 2402–3, 2405, 2424, 2444, 2458, 2481, 2483, 2534, 2540, 2545
Sierra, Pedro de la 2361, 2376, 2389, 2396, 2410, 2417–18, 2457, 2484, 2553
Silius Italicus, Tiberius Catius Asconius 2480
Simpson, Andrew 2408
Sinclair, Andrew 2408
Sinclair, John 2408
Sinsbury, John 2423
Skelton, John 2403, 2540
Skene, Sir James, of Curriehill 2408
Skippe, Richard 2423
Slater, Edward 2364
Slater, Thomas 2420, 2429, 2451, 2490–2510, 2524
Slaughter, Richard 2423
Slaughter, Robert 2423
Sloper, Simon 2552
Smegergill, William (a.k.a. Caesar) 2423
Smith, Mr, of St Martin's 2423
Smith, Charles 2421, 2519
Smith, Humphrey 2423
Smith, Jacob 2423
Smith, John (adventurer) 2373

Smith, John (Edinburgh bailiff) 2408
Smith, John (Edinburgh painter) 2408
Smith, John (torchbearer) 2423
Smith, Sir Thomas 2403
Smithsby, Thomas 2423
Smyth, Edward 2532
Smythson, George 2423
Socrates 2387, 2416, 2552
Solier, François 2375
Somerset, Earl of, *see* Carr
Sophocles 2413, 2461, 2553
Soranzo, Giovanni 2353, 2359
Southampton, Earl of, *see* Wriothesley
Southcott, John 2423
Southland (two audience members) 2453
Sparke, Michael 2521
Sparrow, Thomas 2430
Spartianus, Aelius 2492
Speed, John (1552–1629) 2466, 2521
Speed, John (1595–1640) 2466, 2475
Speed, Samuel 2413, 2419, 2468, 2552
Speght, Thomas 2385, 2439
Speir, Alexander 2408
Spelman, Clement 2423, 2532
Spencer, Mr (mercer) 2423
Spencer, Henry 2428
Spenser, Edmund 2373, 2391, 2405, 2445, 2448, 2519, 2540, 2551, 2555
Spiller, John 2423
Sprint, John 2367
Spynie, Lord, *see* Lindsay
Squire, John 2423
Stafford, Anthony 2365
Stafford, Robert 2468
Stafford, John 2395
Stamford, Earl of, *see* Grey
Stanino, James 2364
Stanley, Sir Robert 2353
Stanley, Venetia, *see* Digby
Stapylton, Robert 2521
Starkey, John 2395, 2421, 2428, 2453, 2469, 2484, 2519, 2532
Statilius Flaccus 2421
Statius, Publius Papinius 2402, 2419, 2491
Steadwell, Richard 2373
Steeling, Thomas 2555

Steffkin, *see* Stoeffken
Stephens, Philip, jun. 2376, 2407
Stepkin, John 2532
Sternholt, Thomas 2468
Stevenson, Matthew 2476
Stevenson, William 2385
Steward, John 2423
Stewart, James, 4th Duke of Lennox 2408, 2428, 2469
Stirling, Earl of, *see* Alexander, Sir William
Stoeffken, Dietrich 2423
Stokes, George 2423
Stokes, William 2550
Stone, Nicholas 2428
Stories, John 2408
Stories, Thomas 2408
Strabo 2468
Strachey, Ralph 2423
Strada, Octavius de 2353
Strange, Thomas 2391
Strathearn, Earl of, *see* Graham
Streete, Humphrey 2423
Strickson, Edward 2423
Stringer, Oliver 2423
Strode, William 2379, 2476, 2550
Strong, John 2423
Stubbes, Edmund 2463, 2511
Stubbes, Philip 2468
Stutesbury, Richard 2423
Stutfield, George 2381, 2480
Stutvile, Mr (book-binder) 2550, 2552
Styles, Thomas 2423
Suckling, Sir John 2371, 2424
Suetonius Tranquillus, Gaius 2382, 2387, 2391, 2429, 2451, 2472, 2511, 2533
Suffolk, Earl of, *see* Howard
'Suidas' 2492
Sumner, John 2480
Suttie, George 2408
Swalle, Abel 2452
Swanne, Nicholas 2552
Swanson, Thomas 2423
Swanston, Eliard 2385, 2417, 2421–2
Sweeting, John 2383, 2419
Swetnam, Joseph 2409
Sydenham, Jack 2549
Syrus, Publilius 2391, 2408–9, 2430

Tacitus, Publius Cornelius 2382, 2472, 2553

Tarlton, Richard 2540
Tartareau, Raphael 2398
Tasso, Torquato 2368, 2402
Tatham, John 2374, 2413, 2512
Taverner, Edmund 2353, 2359, 2428, 2469
Taylor, Mr, of Lincoln's Inn 2423
Taylor, Mr, of Oxford 2550
Taylor, Henry 2387, 2448
Taylor, John (water-poet) 2448, 2514, 2517, 2551
Taylor, Joseph 2385, 2395, 2417, 2421–2, 2453, 2530–1, 2541, 2552
Taylor, Randolph 2412, 2449
Taylor, Samuel 2423
Taylor, Thomas 2423
Taylor, William 2423
Taylor, Zachary 2448
Téllez, Gabriel, *see* Tirso de Molina
Tempest, Richard, *see* Todkill
Tempesta, Antonio 2428, 2469
Terence (Publius Terentius Afer) 2385, 2387, 2419, 2429–30, 2444, 2458, 2463, 2468, 2474, 2483, 2511, 2518, 2528
Tertullian (Quintus Septimius Florens Tertullianus) 2525
Textor, *see* Tixier
Thackeray, William 2549
Thimbleby, Lady Elizabeth 2469
Thiry, Léonard 2353, 2359, 2423
Thomason, George 2383, 2395, 2401, 2417, 2419, 2433, 2445, 2449, 2468, 2518, 2544–5, 2550, 2552, 2556
Thomson, Samuel 2472
Thorpe, Robert 2423
Thrale, Benjamin 2479
Thrale, Dorothy 2479
Thrale, Richard 2479
Tiffin, Benjamin 2364
Tilliedaff, Stephen 2408
Tintoretto (Jacopo Robusti) 2519
Tipsley, Francis 2423, 2428
Tirso de Molina 2455
Titelmannus, Franciscus (Frans Titelmans) 2355
Titian (Tiziano Vecelli) 2519
Tixier, Jean, Sieur de Ravisi (Ravisius Textor) 2492, 2540

Tod, Archibald 2408
Todkill, Richard (alias Tempest) 2366
Tomkins, Robert 2423
Tomkins, William 2423
Tomkis, Thomas 2355
Tomkyns, Nathaniel 2441–2
Tomlins, Richard 2408
Tonson, Jacob 2371, 2433, 2445, 2452
Tooken, Mr (hosier) 2423
Tottel, Richard 2421
Townshend, Aurelian 2353, 2359–60, 2369, 2445, 2457, 2522, 2535, 2537, 2551–2
Tremyll (text recipient) 2423
Trenchard, Thomas 2532
Trevet, Nicholas 2488
Trotman, Edward 2423
Trumbull, Ralph 2441, 2478
Trumbull, Sir William 2478
Trussell, Mr (clothworker) 2416
Turner, Anthony 2367, 2412, 2480
Turner, Edward 2532
Turner, Nicholas 2423
Turner, William 2552
Turrett, Thomas 2467
Tuscany, Grand Duke of, *see* Medici
Twine, Laurence 2403
Twist, Roger 2423
Twyford, Henry 2550
Tyler, Evan 2360, 2365, 2374, 2428, 2452, 2517, 2531, 2552, 2556
Tyler, Margaret 2361, 2376, 2389, 2396, 2410, 2417–18, 2457, 2484, 2553
Tyler, Thomas 2423

Udward, Nicoll 2408
Underdown, Thomas 2512
Underhill, Nicholas 2423
Upston, Thomas 2423
Urfé, Honoré d' 2402, 2458

Vade, James 2405, 2417, 2545
Val, François du, Marquis of Fontenay-Mareuil 2353, 2359, 2387
Valerius Maximus 2385
van Dyck, Sir Anthony 2531
Vane, Sir Henry 2387, 2423
Varro, Marcus Terentius 2492, 2506

Vazquez, Francisco 2376, 2417, 2457, 2536
Vecelli, Tiziano, *see* Titian
Vecellio, Cesare 2353, 2469
Velleius Paterculus, Marcus 2388
Venice, Doge of, *see* Erizzo
Venn, Richard 2423
Venning, Robert 2423
Verdier, Antoine du 2439
Vere, Anne de, Countess of Oxford 2373
Vere, Beatrice de, Countess of Oxford 2359, 2469
Vere, Thomas 2432
Vergenhans, Johann, *see* Nauclerus
Vergil, *see* Virgil
Verulam, Lord, *see* Bacon
Vester, John 2354
Villiers, Ellenor 2395, 2398
Villiers, Frances (née Coke) 2382
Villiers, Lord Francis 2555
Villiers, George, 1st Duke of Buckingham 2382
Villiers, George, 2nd Duke of Buckingham 2555
Villiers, Sir John 2382
Villiers, Katherine, Dowager Duchess of Buckingham 2353, 2459
Villiers, Lady Mary (later Lady Mary Herbert of Shurland) 2359, 2445, 2459, 2469
Villiers, William, 2nd Viscount Grandison 2428, 2469
Vincent, Augustine 2521
Vincent, Thomas 2365
Vincent, William ('Hocus Pocus') 2432, 2478
Vinte, John 2423
Virgil (Publius Virgilius Maro) 2355, 2382, 2385, 2387, 2391, 2401–2, 2408, 2416, 2419, 2423, 2429–30, 2433, 2445, 2449, 2451, 2458–9, 2463, 2468, 2474, 2479–80, 2488, 2492, 2511, 2517–18, 2525, 2543–4, 2550
Vitruvius Pollio, Marcus 2385
Vives, Joannes Ludovicus 2419
Vivian, Richard 2532
Volaterranus, Raphael Maffei 2477

Voragine, Jacobus de 2357, 2421, 2457, 2521
Vries, Hans Vredeman de 2353

W., I. (translator?) 2545
W., J. (printer) 2552
W., R. (commendator) 2413, 2479
Waite, John 2432
Wakering, John 2423
Walden, Lord, *see* Howard
Walden, John 2423
Walden, Richard 2430
Walker, John 2398, 2423
Walker, Matthew 2423
Walkley, Thomas 2385, 2403–4, 2421, 2423, 2428, 2439, 2453, 2469, 2484, 2534
Walley, John 2428
Walther, Balthasar, *see* Gualtherus
Walton, Izaak 2517
Ward, Gilbert 2359
Ward, Margaret 2395
Ward, William 2423
Waring, Robert 2487, 2529
Warne, Titus 2423
Warner, William 2399
Warren, Thomas 2423
Warwick, Earl of, *see* Rich
Warwick, Philip 2442
Watkins, Zachariah 2371, 2552
Way, Thomas 2532
Wayte, Hersey 2423
Wayte, Thomas 2423
Weal, George 2428
Weatherhead, Richard 2423
Weaver, John 2423
Webb, William 2423, 2452
Webbe, George 2421
Webbe, Joseph 2521
Webster, John 2360, 2371, 2382, 2389, 2410–12, 2418, 2429, 2434, 2449, 2455, 2461, 2468, 2472, 2487, 2516, 2528
Weckherlin, Georg Rudolf 2478
Weekson, Richard 2423
Weir, Thomas 2408
Wells, William 2362
Wemyss of Elcho, John, Lord 2408
Wendover, Edward 2423
Wentworth, Anne (née Crofts; 1604–37) 2487

Wentworth, Lady Anne (1623–97) 2487, 2538
Wentworth, Samuel 2423
Wentworth, Thomas, Viscount 2387, 2535
Weston, Anne 2359
Weston, Richard, Lord 2353, 2387
Weston, Thomas 2469
Wharton, Philip, 4th Baron 2353, 2428
Wheeler, William 2532
White, Francis 2423
White, John 2442
White, Thomas (horse-handler) 2423
White, Thomas (of Edinburgh) 2408
Whitelocke, Bulstrode 2423
Whiteway, William 2364, 2395, 2423
Whitfield, Ralph 2423
Whitmore, Sir George 2423
Wiggan, Thomas 2423
Wightwick, Samuel 2423
Wigtown, Earl of, *see* Fleming
Wilde, George 2463, 2475, 2551
Wilkins, George 2481, 2513, 2516
Wilkins, Jeremy 2423
Wilkinson, John 2423
Willett, James 2423
Williams, John (bishop) 2430
Williams, John (purveyor) 2469
Williams, John (stationer) 2458, 2481
Williams, Rhys 2395, 2398, 2469
Williams, Walter 2361
Williams, William 2423
Williamson, Francis 2423
Williamson, Gilbert 2408
Willis, Thomas 2423
Wilmot, John, 2nd Earl of Rochester 2523
Wilson, Anne 2536
Wilson, Arthur 2357
Wilson, John 2423, 2532, 2542
Wilson, Thomas 2525
Wilson, William 2556
Wimbledon, Viscount, *see* Cecil
Windebank, Sir Francis 2554
Winstanley, William 2468
Winton, Earl of, *see* Seton
Wisdom, Robert 2468
Wisdom, William 2484

Wolf, Hieronymus 2547
Wolfreston, Frances 2360, 2453
Wood, Anthony 2353, 2355, 2359–61, 2364–5, 2367, 2373–4, 2376, 2378, 2381, 2383, 2389, 2395–6, 2399, 2401–2, 2405, 2407, 2410–11, 2413, 2417–20, 2421, 2423–4, 2432, 2434, 2437, 2441, 2445, 2449, 2451–2, 2455, 2458–9, 2468, 2472, 2475, 2479–81, 2487–8, 2490–2510, 2512, 2515, 2518–19, 2524, 2526, 2528–32, 2536, 2538, 2543–5, 2549–50, 2552–3, 2555–6
Wood, John 2423
Wood, Thomas 2423
Woodhall (actor) 2362
Woodhouse, Horatio 2362, 2364

Woodington, John 2423
Woodson, Christopher 2423
Wotton, Sir Henry 2445, 2471
Wotton, Matthew 2385, 2403–4, 2439
Wrath, John 2373
Wreittoun, John 2408
Wright, Mr, of Lincoln's Inn 2423
Wright, Abraham 2355, 2367, 2396, 2410, 2421, 2515, 2519, 2551, 2556
Wright, Edmund 2423
Wright, Edward 2423
Wright, Eusebius 2423
Wright, James 2355, 2367, 2396, 2410, 2419, 2421, 2515, 2519, 2556
Wright, John 2360, 2365, 2374, 2428, 2432, 2452, 2517, 2531, 2552, 2556

Wriothesley, 4th Earl of Southampton 2412
Wyatt, Sir Thomas 2421
Wykes, Thomas 2377, 2381, 2389, 2401, 2413, 2418, 2429, 2432, 2436–7, 2447, 2452, 2455, 2458–9, 2464, 2472, 2479, 2481, 2487, 2490–2510, 2512, 2524, 2526, 2528–9, 2544

Xenophon 2480

York, Duke of, *see* James, Prince
Young, James 2441
Young, Robert 2441
Younger, Thomas 2408

Zimara, Marcantonio 2364, 2389
Zon, Michael 2353
Zuccaro, Federigo 2428
Zúñiga, *see* Ercilla

INDEX OF PLACES

This index covers places in historical rather than fictional terms. It includes places of performance (treating London selectively), places of publication (other than London), and any other places where significant events in the external history of the plays occurred. It does not list places referred to in the plays themselves, and recorded in the SETTING section of the entries, nor does it list place names which are only part of an aristocratic title. The listing is by entry number rather than page number.

Aberdeen 2408
Ampthill 2558
Amsterdam 2423
Arbury Hall 2382, 2444

Barham 2451
Bedfordshire 2558
Bingham School 2374
Bishop's Stortford 2539
Bohemia 2428
Bolsover Castle 2439
Buckinghamshire 2355, 2445, 2471, 2556
Byfleet House 2558

Cambridge 2364–5, 2429–30, 2453, 2468, 2474, 2488, 2550, 2552
  Clare Hall 2364
  Emmanuel College 2364, 2388
  Jesus College 2511
  King's College 2364
  Queens' College 2362, 2364, 2429
  St Catharine's College 2364
  Trinity College 2362, 2364–5, 2429, 2433, 2445, 2474
  Trinity Hall 2364
Canterbury 2471
  King's School 2355
Castlelyons 2393
Chartley 2357
Chester 2435
Chirk Castle 2440
Cork, County 2393
Cornwall 2388

Denbighshire 2440
Derbyshire 2439

Dorset 2411
Douai
  English College 2366, 2482, 2547
Dublin 2455
  Smock Alley Theatre 2546
  Werburgh Street Theatre 2546

East Indies 2409
Edinburgh 2408, 2534
  Cross 2408
  East Port 2408
  Fosters Wynd 2408
  High School 2408
  King James College 2408
  Nether Bow 2408
  Salt Tron 2408
  Tollbooth 2408
  West Bow 2408
  West Port 2408
Enstone 2549
Eton College 2445, 2471, 2556

Falkland 2408
Ferrara 2469
France 2407, 2414, 2487

Geneva 2445
Germany 2428, 2465, 2534
Ghent 2392
Greenwich 2398

Hamburg 2465
Hampton Court Palace 2385, 2402, 2453, 2530–1, 2535, 2552–3
Harefield House 2433
Headington 2355, 2364–5, 2367, 2378, 2389, 2396, 2399, 2402, 2405, 2410, 2413, 2418, 2421, 2424, 2432, 2434, 2437, 2441, 2445, 2451–2, 2455, 2458–9, 2479–81, 2487–8, 2512, 2515, 2519, 2526, 2529–31, 2536, 2543, 2552–3
Helmdon 2523
Herefordshire 2477
Hertfordshire 2435, 2524, 2539
Holdenby House 2442
Hunsdon House 2524
Huntingdonshire 2423

Ingestre 2360, 2399, 2528
Ireland 2393, 2428, 2438, 2455, 2546
Italy 2384, 2397, 2407, 2445, 2459, 2467, 2469, 2529, 2538

Kent 2355, 2398, 2451, 2471
Kirton 2552

Leith 2408
Lincolnshire 2552
Londesborough House 2354, 2372
London 2376, 2387, 2411, 2416, 2423, 2429, 2434, 2438, 2441–2, 2448, 2450, 2456, 2471, 2477–8, 2489, 2514, 2517, 2539, 2543, 2546
  Aldersgate Street 2423
  Banqueting House 2353, 2359, 2423, 2428, 2469
  Bedford Street 2533
  Blackfriars playhouse 2357, 2368, 2373, 2383, 2385,

2403, 2417, 2421–3, 2426, 2431, 2434, 2449, 2453, 2459–60, 2471, 2484, 2515, 2519, 2530–1, 2538, 2541, 2545, 2552–3
Blackwell Hall 2517
Broad Street 2420
Chancery Lane 2423
Cheapside 2416, 2448
Clerkenwell 2361
Clothworkers' Hall 2448
Cockpit playhouse 2360, 2367, 2389, 2396, 2399, 2401–3, 2405, 2410–12, 2418, 2423–4, 2427, 2432, 2437, 2446, 2451–2, 2455, 2458–9, 2464, 2480–1, 2487, 2515, 2526, 2528, 2529, 2536, 2552
Cockpit in Court 2378, 2385, 2402, 2422, 2530–1
Cornhill 2416, 2423
Covent Garden 2533
Denmark House 2378, 2385, 2395, 2398, 2402, 2423, 2448, 2451
Drapers' Hall 2423
Ely House 2423, 2535
Fleet Prison 2423
Fortune playhouse 2355, 2361, 2400, 2409, 2413, 2419, 2432, 2512, 2525
Foyes' Ordinary 2448
Furnivall's Inn 2423
Globe playhouse 2357, 2368, 2373, 2383, 2385, 2417, 2421–2, 2426, 2431, 2434, 2441, 2453, 2460, 2471, 2484, 2519, 2530–1, 2538, 2541 2545
Goring House 2356
Gray's Inn 2358, 2392, 2423, 2430, 2461
Greenyard 2416, 2448, 2517
Guildhall 2448
Hatton House 2423, 2535
Holborn 2435, 2535
Hyde Park 2398
Inner Temple 2386, 2423, 2430
Lawrence Lane 2448
Leadenhall 2416, 2448, 2517
Lincoln's Inn 2423
Little Conduit 2448

Long Lane 2425
Marshalsea Prison 2425
Merchant Taylors' Hall 2423
Middle Temple 2367, 2386, 2406, 2423, 2532
Musaeum Minervae 2533
Newgate Prison 2461
Paul's Wharf 2448
Phoenix playhouse, see Cockpit
Red Bull playhouse 2363, 2432, 2449, 2455, 2512
St Dunstan's tavern 2423
St James's Palace 2410, 2454, 2526, 2541
St Martin's parish 2423
St Paul's Cathedral 2448
St Paul's Churchyard 2387, 2416, 2429, 2448
Salisbury Court playhouse 2355, 2361, 2370, 2378, 2381–2, 2405, 2406, 2409, 2411–13, 2415, 2419, 2425, 2436, 2454, 2472–3, 2479, 2512, 2516, 2518, 2525, 2529, 2543–4
Salisbury Court precinct 2423
Salisbury House 2423
Somerset House, see Denmark House
Southampton House 2423
Strand 2423
Thames, River 2387, 2416, 2448, 2517
Tiltyard, Whitehall 2423
Westminster School 2452, 2539, 2552
Whitehall 2423
Whitehall Palace 2353, 2359, 2378, 2385, 2395, 2398, 2402–3, 2417–18, 2421–3, 2428, 2469, 2522, 2530–1, 2534, 2553
York House 2395, 2459
Ludlow Castle 2445

Mantua
 Palazzo del Tè 2469
Middlesex 2385, 2402, 2433, 2453, 2530–1, 2535, 2552–3

Naples 2407, 2445, 2538
Netherlands, see Spanish Netherlands and United Provinces

Newcastle-upon-Tyne 2378, 2383, 2389, 2399, 2413, 2417–19, 2421, 2423, 2434–5, 2437, 2453, 2455, 2468, 2519, 2526, 2532, 2545, 2550, 2552
Nonsuch Palace 2384
Norfolk 2556; see also Norwich
Northamptonshire 2442, 2523
Norton Cuckney 2457
Norwich 2379, 2476
Nottinghamshire 2374, 2404, 2439, 2444, 2457

Oatlands Palace 2384, 2485–6
Oxford 2365, 2371, 2392, 2423, 2429, 2435, 2441, 2452, 2465, 2468, 2474, 2478, 2488, 2512, 2540, 2547, 2549–50, 2552–3, 2555, 2557
 All Hallows' Church 2478
 All Souls College 2550
 Ashmolean Museum 2355, 2480, 2549, 2557
 Balliol College 2550
 Bear 2478
 Blue Boar 2478
 Brasenose College 2355, 2364–5, 2367, 2378, 2389, 2396, 2399, 2402, 2405, 2410, 2413, 2418, 2421, 2424, 2432, 2434, 2437, 2441, 2445, 2451–2, 2455, 2458–9, 2479–81, 2487–8, 2512, 2515, 2519, 2526, 2529–31, 2536, 2543, 2550, 2552–3
 Christ Church 2468, 2477, 2549–53
 Corpus Christi College 2550
 Crown 2478
 East Gate 2557
 Exeter College 2550
 Flower de Luce 2478
 Jesus College 2550
 King's Arms 2478
 King's Head 2441, 2478
 Lincoln College 2550
 Magdalen College 2550, 2557
 Merton College 2550, 2557
 Moot Hall 2478
 New College 2550
 Oriel College 2550
 Pembroke College 2550

Index of Places | 531

Queen's College, the 2550
St Edmund Hall 2353, 2355, 2359–61, 2364, 2367, 2373–4, 2376, 2378, 2381, 2383, 2389, 2395–6, 2399, 2401–2, 2405, 2407, 2410–11, 2413, 2417–20, 2423–4, 2432, 2434, 2437, 2441, 2445, 2449, 2451, 2455, 2458–9, 2468, 2472, 2479–81, 2487–8, 2490–2510, 2512, 2518, 2524, 2526, 2528–31, 2536, 2538, 2543–5, 2550, 2553, 2555–6
St John's College 2463, 2465–6, 2475, 2550–2
Trinity College 2523, 2550
University College 2550, 2557
University Museum, *see* Ashmolean
Wadham College 2550
Oxfordshire 2355, 2364–5, 2367, 2378, 2389, 2396, 2399, 2402, 2405, 2410, 2413, 2418, 2421, 2424, 2432, 2434, 2437, 2441, 2445, 2451–2, 2455, 2458–9, 2479–81, 2487–8, 2512, 2515, 2519, 2526, 2529–31, 2536, 2543, 2549, 2552–3; *see also* Oxford

Paris 2407
Petworth House 2360, 2399, 2405
Prague
 Clementina 2428

Richmond Palace 2555
Rome 2407, 2529, 2538
 English College 2397, 2467

St Albans 2435
St Mawes Castle 2388
Saint-Omer
 English College 2375, 2443
Scotland 2408, 2439, 2534
Shandon, Castle of 2393
Shropshire 2445
Skipton Castle 2354, 2372, 2527
Spanish Netherlands 2366, 2375, 2392, 2443, 2482, 2547
Staffordshire 2357, 2360, 2399, 2528
Surrey 2384, 2485–6, 2555, 2558
Sussex 2360, 2394, 2399, 2405
Switzerland 2445

Temple Newsam 2527
Turin 2384

United Provinces 2423
Upwood 2423

Venice 2529

Vercelli 2538

Wales 2435, 2440
Warwickshire 2355, 2364–5, 2367, 2378, 2382, 2389, 2396, 2399, 2402, 2405, 2410, 2413, 2418, 2421, 2424, 2432, 2434, 2437, 2441, 2444–5, 2451–2, 2455, 2458–9, 2479–81, 2487–8, 2512, 2515, 2519, 2526, 2529–31, 2536, 2543, 2552–3
Watnall Hall 2444
Welbeck Abbey 2404, 2439, 2457
West Harting 2394
Weston 2355, 2364–5, 2367, 2378, 2389, 2396, 2399, 2402, 2405, 2410, 2413, 2418, 2421, 2424, 2432, 2434, 2437, 2441, 2445, 2451–2, 2455, 2458–9, 2479–81, 2487–8, 2512, 2515, 2519, 2526, 2529–31, 2536, 2543, 2552–3
Woodsome Hall 2438
Worcester 2511
 All Saints' parish 2511

York 2527
Yorkshire 2354, 2372, 2438, 2527

INDEX OF PLAYS

This list covers all substantively variant forms of titles, rather than simply the title adopted in the entry heading, enabling the reader to trace plays commonly known under one title but catalogued under another. Some specific descriptors are also included, but entirely generic ones such as 'Play' or 'Masque' have been ignored. The listing is by entry number rather than page number.

Adrasta 2488
Albion's Triumph 2353
Alexius Imperator 2547
Alfonso of Castile, Tragedy of 2466
Amazon, The 2414
Amor in labyrintho 2355
Amphrisa 2510
Amphrisa, the Forsaken Shepherdess 2510
Andronicus Comnenus 2547
Ante-Masques, The 2522
Antimasques, The 2522
Antipelargesis 2375
Antiquary, The 2458
Apollo and Daphne 2509
Apollo and Mercury, A Dialogue betwixt 2498
Apprentice's Prize, The 2462
Arcades 2433
Arcadia, The 2481
Arviragus, The First Part of 2530
Arviragus, The Second Part of 2531
Arviragus and Philicia 2530–1
Arviragus and Philicia, The First Part of 2530
Arviragus and Philicia, The Second Part of 2531
As I Told You Before 2444

Ball, The 2389
Bashful Lover, The 2545
Bashful Lovers, The 2545
Battle of Lepanto, Possible Play of the 2443
Beauties, The 2396
Bellessa the Shepherds' Queen 2395
Bird in a Cage, The 2396

Bird in the Cage, The 2396
Blame Not Our Author 2467
Bolsover, The King and Queen's Entertainment at 2439
Bolsover Castle, Royal Entertainment at 2439
Bower of Fancies, The 2528
Bushell's Rock, The Several Speeches and Songs at the Presentment of Mr 2549
Byrsa basilica 2511

Challenge for Beauty, A 2434
Changes 2355
Changes, The 2355
Charles I into Edinburgh, Royal Entry of King 2408
Charles, Duke of Bourbon 2447
Charon, Menippus, and Mercury, A Dialogue betwist 2504
Charon, Menippus, Mercury 2504
Chaste Susanna 2489
Chirk Castle, Entertainment at 2440
Chirk Castle, The Entertainment at 2440
Chirke Castle, The Entertainment at 2440
Christianetta 2436
Christmas Antimasque, The 2457
Christmas Masque 2457
Christmas Ordinary, The 2523
Christopher Clitherow, Device for 2517
Citizen and a Countryman, A Dialogue betwixt 2548
Citizen and a Poor Countryman and his Wife, A Dialogue betwixt a 2548
City Cozener, The 2468

City Find . . ., [The or A] 2456
City Honest Man, The 2426
City Madam, The 2373
City Match, The 2553
City Shuffler, The 2406, 2415
City Shuffler, The Second Part of The 2415
City Wit, The 2419
Claracilla 2529
Clarasilla 2529
Claricilla 2529
Cletherow, Device for Christopher 2517
Clitherow, Device for Christopher 2517
Clown, The 2386
Coelum Britannicum 2428
Comedy of Heads, The 2391
Comus 2445
Concertatio Divum Thomae in regiam cruce armiti cum Henrico Principe et tenebrarum principis 2482
Confessor 2430
Confessor utinam feliciter nata 2430
Conspiracy, The 2459
Converted Robber, The 2475
Cornelianum dolium 2429
Corona Minervae 2533
Coronation, The 2464
Corporal, The 2357
Country Gentleman, A 2390
Country Gentleman, The 2390
Country Girl, The 2381
Country Man, The 2386
Countryman, The 2386
Countryman or Clown, The 2386
Courage of Love, The 2453
Coursing of a Hare, The 2400

Court of Babylon, The 2489
Covent Garden 2424
Covent Garden, The 2401
Covent Garden Weeded 2401
Covent Garden Weeded, The 2401
Crates and Diogenes 2503
Cumberland, Masque for the Earl of 2354, 2372
Cunning Lovers, The 2411
Cupid and Psyche 2451
Cupido adultus 2463
Cupid's Mistress 2451
Cutpurse, The 2559
Cutpurses, Play with 2559
Cutpurses' Scene, The 2559
Cyprian Conqueror, The 2542

Deorum iudicium 2507
Deorum judicium 2507
Device for Christopher Clitherow, Ironmonger 2517
Device for Ralph Freeman, Clothworker 2416
Device for Robert Parkhurst, Clothworker 2448
Device for Sir Nicholas Rainton, Haberdasher 2387
Devonshire, Masque for the Dowager Countess of 2558
Diogenes and Crates, A Dialogue betwixt 2503
Diogenes and Mausolus 2502
Don Pedro 2465
Don Pedro the Cruel King of Castile 2465
Drunken Couple, The 2417, 2545
Duke of Florence, The 2461
Duke's Mistress, The 2526

Earth and Age, The Dialogue betwixt 2492
Eccentric Magistrate, Comedy of an 2444
Edinburgh, Royal Entry of King Charles I into 2408
Elector Palatine, Entertainment for the 2539
Emperor's Favourite, The 2382
Enstone, Royal Entertainment at 2549
Entertainment at Chirk Castle, The 2440
Entertainment at Edinburgh, The 2408
Entertainment at Richmond, The 2555

Entertainment at Welbeck, The 2404
Entertainment into Edinburgh, The 2408
Entertainment of Charles I in Edinburgh, The 2408
Entertainment of the High and Mighty Monarch, Charles, King of Great Britain, France, and Ireland, into his Ancient and Royal City of Edinburgh, The 2408
Entertainment to the Prince Elector at Mr Osbaldeston's 2539
Eumorphus 2463
Eunuch, The 2380, 2412
Example, The 2437
Expeditio Britomartis 2555

Faithless Relict, The 2542
Fancies, The 2528
Fancies, Chaste and Noble, The 2528
Fatal Contract, The 2412
Felix liberorum in parentam pietas 2375
Fiddler and a Poet, A 2540
Fine Companion, A 2378
Fine Companion, The 2378
First Skipton Castle Masque 2527
Flamen, Play with a 2425
Floating Island, The 2550
Floral Play 2476
Forsaken Shepherdess, The 2510
Four Inns of Court, The Masque of the 2423
Four Seasons, The 2440
Four Seasons, The Masque of the 2440
Freeman, Device for Ralph 2416
Freewill 2477
French Dancing-Master, The 2389

Gamester, The 2418
Gentlemen of the four Honourable Societies, or Inns of Court, The Masque of the 2423
Geometry, Comedy of 2467
Goring House, Masque at 2356
Governor, The 2541
Gray's Inn, Antimasque at 2358
Guardian, The 2417

Hannibal and Scipio 2370, 2480
Heads, The Comedy of 2391

Hog's Head, The 2363
Hogshead 2363
Holdenby, The Masque at 2442
Holdenby House, Masque at 2442
Hollander, The 2536
Hospital of Lovers, The 2551
Hospitality and Delight (aristocratic entertainment) 2420
Humorous Magistrate, The 2444
Humours Reconciled 2385
Hunsdon, The Masque at 2524
Hunsdon House, A Masque Presented at 2524
Hyde Park 2367

Icon ecclesiastici 2482
Imperial Favourite Crispinus, Tragedy of the 2382
Indamora, The Queen's Masque of 2469
Indians, The Queen's Masque of 2469
Introduction to the Sword Dance, An 2393
Italian Night Masque, The 2471
Italian Night-Piece, The 2471

Jealous Lover, Play of a 2534
Jealous Lovers, The 2365
Jupiter and Cupid 2496
Jupiter and Cupid, A Dialogue betwixt 2496
Jupiter and Ganymede 2494
Jupiter and Ganymede, A Dialogue betwixt 2494
Jupiter and Io 2508
Jupiter and Juno 2495
Jupiter and Juno, A Dialogue betwixt 2495
Jupiter and Vulcan, A Dialogue betwixt 2500

King and Queen's Entertainment at Bolsover, The 2439
King and Queen's Entertainment at Richmond, The 2555
King Charles's Entertainment at Edinburgh 2408
King Freewill 2477
King's Entertainment at Welbeck, The 2404
King's Entertainment at Welbeck in Nottinghamshire, The 2404

Index of Plays | 535

Ladies, Masque of 2524
Lady Hatton's Masque 2535
Lady Mother, The 2516
Lady of Pleasure, The 2515
Lancashire Witches, The 2441
Large Prerogative, The 2556
Late Lancashire Witches, The 2441
Launching of the Mary, The 2409
Life and Death of Sir Martin Schenck, The 2473
Londini artium et scientiarum scaturigo 2387
Londini emporia 2416
Londini scaturigo 2387
Londini sinus salutis 2517
London Merchant, The 2427
London's Emporia or Mercatura 2416
London's Fountain of Arts and Sciences 2387
London's Harbour of Health and Happiness 2517
London's Mercatura 2416
London's Scaturigo 2387
London's Sinus Salutis 2517
Lord Goring's Masque for the Queen 2356
Lost Children and Comus, Masque of 2445
Love and Honour 2453
Love at First Sight 2538
Love Changes 2355
Love Crowns the End 2374
Love in a Maze 2355
Love in Its Ecstasy 2556
Love Lost in the Dark 2417, 2545
Love Yields to Honour 2368
Lovers' Hospital 2551
Love's After-Game 2454
Love's Changelings' Change 2483
Love's Conquest 2488
Love's Hospital 2551
Love's Hospitals 2551
Love's Masterpiece 2377
Love's Mistress 2451
Love's Riddle 2452
Love's Sacrifice 2360
Love's Trial 2536
Love's Welcome 2439
Love's Welcome at Bolsover 2439
Love's Welcome at Welbeck 2404
Ludlow Castle, A Masque at 2445
Ludlow Castle, A Masque Presented at 2445
Ludlow Castle, The Masque at 2445

Madcap, The 2400
Magnetic Lady, The 2385
Maia and Mercury, A Dialogue betwixt 2499
Man-Hater, The 2493
Mariners, Masque of 2537
Marriage and Hanging Go by Destiny 2436
Marriage upon Marriage 2444
Masque, A 2445
Matchless Maids, The 2453
Mausolus and Diogenes, A Dialogue betwixt 2502
Menippus, Aeacus, Pythagoras, Empedocles, and Socrates 2505
Menippus, Aeacus, Pythagoras, Empedocles, and Socrates, A Dialogue betwixt 2505
Merchant of Dublin, The 2546
Mercury and Apollo 2498
Mercury and Maia 2499
Mercury and Neptune, A Dialogue betwixt 2501
Merry Milkmaid of Islington, The 2405
Messalina, The Tragedy of 2472
Messalina, the Insatiate Roman Empress, The Tragedy of 2472
Messalina, the Roman Empress, The Tragedy of 2472
Messallina 2472
Microcosmus 2543
Middlesex Justice of Peace, The 2401
Misanthropos 2493
Misanthropus 2493
Mr Moore's Revels 2557
Mr More's Revels 2557
Money is an Ass 2361
Money's an Ass 2361
Moors, Masque of 2557
Moor's Masque, The 2557
Moral Masque, A 2543
More's Masque 2557

Naiagaion 2490
Naufragium 2490
Necromantes 2391
Neptune and Mercury 2501
Nereus, Thersites, Menippus 2506
Nero 2382
Nireus, Thersites, and Menippus, A Dialogue betwixt 2506
Nireus, Thersites, Menippus 2506

New Academy, The 2544
New Academy or Exchange, A 2544
New Exchange, The 2544
New Moon, The 2397
Newcastle, Masque for the Earl of 2560
News from Plymouth 2484
News of Plymouth 2484
Nonpareils, The 2453
Nothing Impossible to Love 2388
Novella, The 2383

Oatlands Palace, Court Masque at 2486
Obstinate Lady, The 2376
Opportunity, The 2455
Orator, The 2460
Ordinary, The 2468

Palatine Prince's Masques, The 2535
Pallantus and Eudora 2459
Parkhurst, Device for Robert 2448
Partial Law, The 2513
Passions, The 2550
Passions Calmed 2550
Passions Calmed, The 2550
Pastoral, The 2422
Pastoral at Oatlands, The 2485
Pastoral Masque, A 2522
Pedro the Cruel, Tragedy of 2465
Pelopaea and Alope 2510
Perkin Warbeck 2399
Perkin Warbeck, The Chronicle History of 2399
Persian Slave, The 2552
Petrus Crudelis, A Spanish Tragedy of 2465
Philenzo and Hippolyta 2520
Philenzo and Hyppolita 2520
Philosopher, The 2521
Piety and Policy, A Plain Familiar Dialogue between 2438
Platonic Lovers, The 2519
Policy and Piety, A Dialogue between 2438
Presentment of Bushell's Rock, the 2549
President of Wales at Ludlow, A Masque performed before the 2445
Prince Alexander and Lorenzo, Tragedy of 2461

536 | Index of Plays

Prince Charles, His Highness the Duke of York his Brother, and the Lady Mary his Sister, A Masque presented before 2533
Prince Elector at Mr Osbaldeston's, Entertainment to the 2539
Prince in Conceit, A 2455
Princess, The 2538
The Prisoner 2487
The Prisoners 2487
Procus and Puella 2491
Procus et puella 2491
Projector Lately Dead, A 2450
Proxy, The 2454
Prudentius, with Intellectus Agens and the Rebellious Passions 2550

Queen and Concubine, The 2518
Queen Elizabeth, Puppet Play of 2379
Queen's Country Village Masque, The 2384
Queen's Exchange, The 2449
Queen's Galanteria, The 2442
Queen's Masque, The 2451
Queen's Masque at Shrovetide, The 2398
Queen's Masque of Indamora, The 2469
Queen's Masque of Indians, The 2469

Rainton, Device for Sir Nicholas 2387
Ralph Freeman, Device for 2416
Rambling Gallants Defeated, The 2405
Rebellion, The 2413
Regale excambium 2511
Richmond, The Entertainment at 2555
Richmond Palace, Royal Entertainment at 2555
Rival Friends, The 2364
Robert Parkhurst, Device for 2448
Royal Combat, The 2470
Royal Entry of King Charles I into Edinburgh 2408
Royal Exchange, The 2449
Royal Slave, The 2552

Sad One, The 2371
Scaturigo 2387
Seaman's Honest Wife, The 2409
Senilis amor 2474
Settling of the Floating Island, The 2550
Seven Champions of Christendom, The 2432
Several Speeches and Songs at the Presentment of Mr Bushell's Rock to the Queen's Most Excellent Majesty, The 2549
Shepherds' Holiday, The 2402
Shepherds' Paradise, The 2395
Shipwreck, The 2490
Shrovetide Masque, The 2398
Sir Martin Schenck, The Life and Death of 2473
Sir Martin Skink 2473
Sir Nicholas Rainton, Device for 2387
Skipton Castle, Masque at 2527
Soldiers, Masque of 2393
Spanish Tragedy 2465
Spanish Tragedy of Petrus Crudelis, A 2465
Sparagus Garden, The 2479
Spartan Ladies, The 2431
Spartan Lady, The 2431
Stonehenge 2475
Strange Discovery, The 2512
Strange Truth, A 2399
Subject's Precedent 2525
Susanna, The History of 2489
Susanna and the Elders, Puppet Play of 2489

Tale of a Tub, A 2403
Tale of a Tub, The 2403
Tale of the Tub, The 2403
Tarquinio Superbo, Tragico-comoedia de 2366
Tarquinius Superbus 2366
Tempe restauratum 2359
Tempe Restored 2359
Temple of Love, The 2469
Templum amoris 2469
Timon Misanthropos 2493
Tottenham Court 2405
Tottenham Court Fair 2405
Trappolin 2407
Trappolin creduto principe 2407

Trappolin Supposed a Prince 2407
Triomphes du Prince D'Amour, Les 2532
Triumph of Beauty, The 2435
Triumph of Peace, The 2423
Triumphs of Fame and Honour, The 2448
Triumphs of the Prince D'Amour, The 2532
Truth's Triumph 2446
Truth's Triumphs 2446
Two Supposed Heads, The 2391

Versipellis 2362
Vices, Furies, and Witches, Masque of 2398
Virgineque magna matre saltus insolentiaeque barbarae aeternum victrice 2443
Vulcan and Apollo 2497
Vulcan and Apollo, A Dialogue betwixt 2497
Vulcan and Jupiter 2500

Wars of the Low Countries, The 2473
Wasp, The 2525
Wealth Outwitted 2361
Weeding of Covent Garden, The 2401
Weeding of the Covent Garden, The 2401
Welbeck, The Entertainment at 2404
Welbeck Abbey, Royal Entertainment at 2404
West Harting, Masque at 2394
Wiltshire Tom 2555
Witches and Devil of Lancashire, The 2441, 2478
Witches of Lancashire, The 2441, 2478
Wits, The 2421
Wit's Triumvirate 2521
Woman Wears the Breeches, The 2419
Woman's Spleen and Love's Conquest, The 2488

Young Admiral, The 2410